History of Israel

From 1948 to Present

Editor: Joseph Dayton

Title: History of Israel

Subtitle: From 1948 to Present

Editor: Joseph Dayton

Created on: 2018-10-25 06:52 (UTC)

Produced by: PediaPress GmbH, Moritz-Hilf-Str. 26, Limburg an der Lahn, Germany, http://pediapress.com/

The content within this book was generated collaboratively by volunteers. Please be advised that nothing found here has necessarily been reviewed by people with the expertise required to provide you with complete, accurate or reliable information. Some information in this book may be misleading or simply wrong. PediaPress does not guarantee the validity of the information found here. If you need specific advice (for example, medical, legal, financial, or risk management) please seek a professional who is licensed or knowledgeable in that area.

Sources, licenses and contributors of the articles and images are listed in the section entitled "References". Parts of the books may be licensed under the GNU Free Documentation License. A copy of this license is included in the section entitled "GNU Free Documentation License"

All third-party trademarks used belong to their respective owners.

Create your own custom Wikipedia-Book at http://pediapress.com

collection id: c8a55d70cebc631eb732927aea05e
pdf writer version: 0.10.4 mwlib version: 0.16.1

Contents

Articles   **1**

War of Independence   **1**
    1948 Arab–Israeli War 1

Armistice Agreements   **71**
    1949 Armistice Agreements 71

1948–1955: Ben-Gurion I; Sharett   **87**
    Austerity in Israel 87
    Reprisal operations 91
    Lavon Affair 97

Suez Crisis   **105**
    Suez Crisis 105

Six-Day War   **189**
    Six-Day War 189

1969–1974: Meir   **245**
    War of Attrition 245
    Jarring Mission 260
    Munich massacre 263
    Yom Kippur War 290

1974–1977: Rabin I   **375**

   Operation Entebbe 375

1977–1983: Begin   **395**

   Camp David Accords 395

   1978 South Lebanon conflict 412

   1982 Lebanon War 418

1983–1992: Shamir I; Peres I; Shamir II   **461**

   1983 Israel bank stock crisis 461

   South Lebanon conflict (1985–2000) 467

   First Intifada 486

1992–1996: Rabin II; Peres II   **501**

   Oslo Accords 501

   Assassination of Yitzhak Rabin 511

1996–2001: Netanyahu I; Barak   **519**

   2000 Camp David Summit 519

2001–2006: Sharon   **533**

   Second Intifada 533

   Israeli West Bank barrier 572

   Israeli disengagement from Gaza 603

2006–2009: Olmert   **633**

   2006 Gaza cross-border raid 633

2009–present: Netanyahu II   **641**

   2011 Israeli social justice protests 641

   2014 Israel–Gaza conflict 660

Appendix 717

References 717
Article Sources and Contributors 786
Image Sources, Licenses and Contributors 790

Article Licenses 799

Index 801

War of Independence

1948 Arab–Israeli War

<indicator name="pp-default"> 🔒 </indicator>

1948 Arab–Israeli War	
Part of 1947–49 Palestine war	
 Captain Avraham "Bren" Adan raising the Ink Flag at Umm Rashrash (a site now in Eilat), marking the end of the war.	
Date	15 May 1948 – 10 March 1949 (9 months, 3 weeks and 2 days) Final armistice agreement concluded on 20 July 1949
Location	Former British Mandate of Palestine, Sinai Peninsula, southern Lebanon
Result	• Israeli victory • Jordanian partial victory[3,4] • Palestinian Arab defeat • Egyptian defeat • Arab League strategic failure • 1949 Armistice Agreements
Territorial changes	Israel keeps area allotted to it by the Partition Plan and captures ~60% of area allotted to Arab state; Jordanian rule of West Bank, Egyptian occupation of the Gaza Strip
Belligerents	

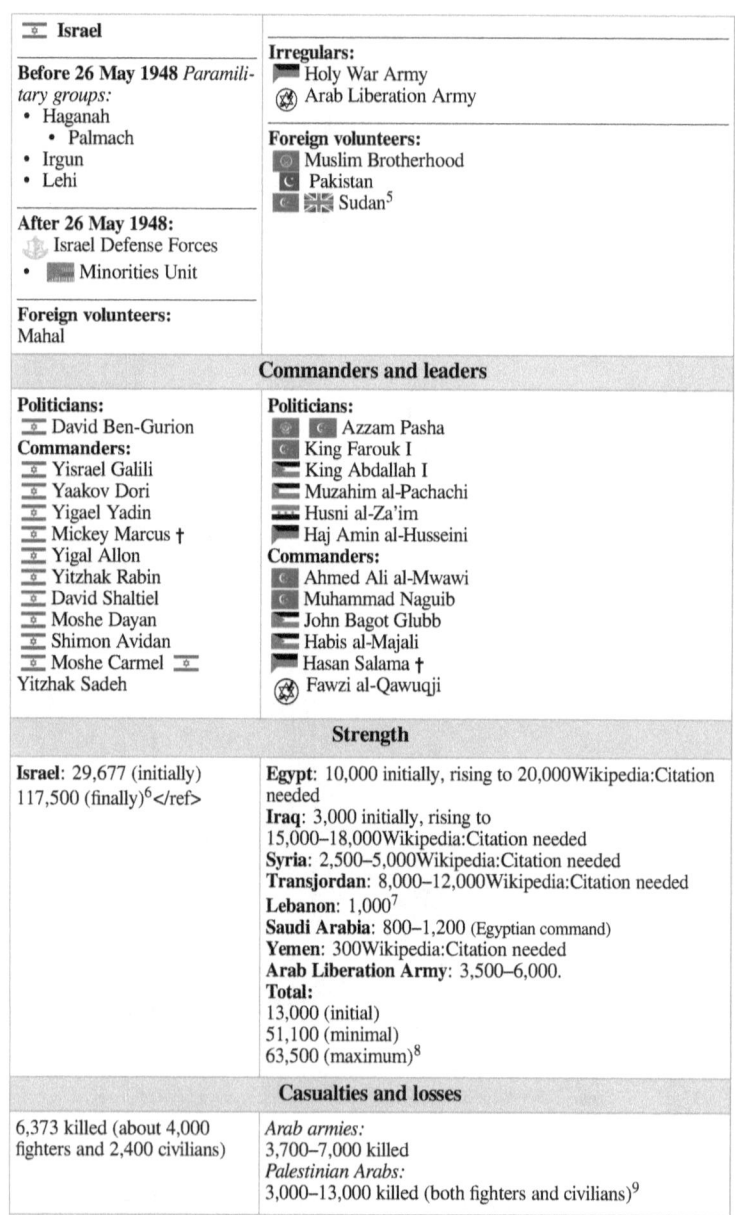

The **1948 Arab–Israeli War**, or the **Israeli War of Independence**, was fought between the newly declared State of Israel and a military coalition of Arab states over the control of former British Palestine, forming the second and final stage of the 1947–49 Palestine war.Wikipedia:No original research It is also known as the **First Arab–Israeli War**.

There had been tension and conflict between the Arabs and the Jews, and between each of them and the British forces, ever since the 1917 Balfour Declaration and the 1920 creation of the British Mandate of Palestine. British policies dissatisfied both Arabs and Jews. The Arabs' opposition developed into the 1936–1939 Arab revolt in Palestine, while the Jewish resistance developed into the Jewish insurgency in Palestine (1944–1947). In 1947 these ongoing tensions erupted into civil war, following the 29 November 1947 adoption of the United Nations Partition Plan for Palestine, which planned to divide Palestine into three areas: an Arab state, a Jewish state and the Special International Regime for the cities of Jerusalem and Bethlehem.

On 15 May 1948, the ongoing civil war transformed into an inter-state conflict between Israel and the Arab states, following the Israeli Declaration of Independence the previous day. A combined invasion by Egypt, Jordan and Syria, together with expeditionary forces from Iraq, entered Palestine – Jordan having declared privately to Yishuv emissaries on 2 May that it would abide by a decision not to attack the Jewish state.[10] The invading forces took control of the Arab areas and immediately attacked Israeli forces and several Jewish settlements.[11,12] The 10 months of fighting, interrupted by several truce periods, took place mostly on the former territory of the British Mandate and for a short time also in the Sinai Peninsula and southern Lebanon.[13]

As a result of the war, the State of Israel controlled both the area that the UN General Assembly Resolution 181 had recommended for the proposed Jewish state as well as almost 60% of the area of Arab state proposed by the 1948 Partition Plan,[14] including the Jaffa, Lydda and Ramle area, Galilee, some parts of the Negev, a wide strip along the Tel Aviv–Jerusalem road, West Jerusalem and some territories in the West Bank. Transjordan took control of the remainder of the former British mandate, which it annexed, and the Egyptian military took control of the Gaza Strip. At the Jericho Conference on 1 December 1948, 2,000 Palestinian delegates called for unification of Palestine and Transjordan as a step toward full Arab unity.[15] No state was created for the Palestinian Arabs.

The conflict triggered significant demographic change throughout the Middle East. Around 700,000 Palestinian Arabs fled or were expelled from their homes in the area that became Israel, and they became Palestinian refugees in what they refer to as Al-Nakba ("the catastrophe"). In the three years following the war, about 700,000 Jews immigrated to Israel, with many of them having been expelled from their previous countries of residence in the Middle East.[16]

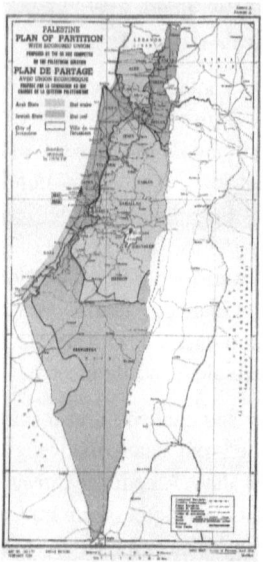

Figure 1: *Proposed separation of Palestine*

Background

Following World War II, the surrounding Arab nations were emerging from mandatory rule. Transjordan, under the Hashemite ruler Abdullah I, gained independence from Britain in 1946 and was called Jordan in 1949, but it remained under heavy British influence. Egypt gained nominal independence in 1922, but Britain continued to exert a strong influence on the country until the Anglo-Egyptian Treaty of 1936 which limited Britain's presence to a garrison of troops on the Suez Canal until 1945. Lebanon became an independent state in 1943, but French troops would not withdraw until 1946, the same year that Syria won its independence from France.

In 1945, at British prompting, Egypt, Iraq, Lebanon, Saudi Arabia, Syria, Transjordan, and Yemen formed the Arab League to coordinate policy between the Arab states. Iraq and Transjordan coordinated policies closely, signing a mutual defence treaty, while Egypt, Syria, and Saudi Arabia feared that Transjordan would annex part or all of Palestine, and use it as a steppingstone to attack or undermine Syria, Lebanon, and the Hijaz.[17]

On 29 November 1947, the United Nations General Assembly adopted a resolution recommending the adoption and implementation of a plan to partition the British Mandate of Palestine into two states, one Arab and one Jewish, and the City of Jerusalem.[18]

The General Assembly resolution on Partition was greeted with overwhelming joy in Jewish communities and widespread outrage in the Arab world. In Palestine, violence erupted almost immediately, feeding into a spiral of reprisals and counter-reprisals. The British refrained from intervening as tensions boiled over into a low-level conflict that quickly escalated into a full-scale civil war.[19,20,21,22,23,24]

From January onwards, operations became increasingly militarized, with the intervention of a number of Arab Liberation Army regiments inside Palestine, each active in a variety of distinct sectors around the different coastal towns. They consolidated their presence in Galilee and Samaria.[25] Abd al-Qadir al-Husayni came from Egypt with several hundred men of the Army of the Holy War. Having recruited a few thousand volunteers, al-Husayni organized the blockade of the 100,000 Jewish residents of Jerusalem.[26] To counter this, the Yishuv authorities tried to supply the city with convoys of up to 100 armoured vehicles, but the operation became more and more impractical as the number of casualties in the relief convoys surged. By March, Al-Hussayni's tactic had paid off. Almost all of Haganah's armoured vehicles had been destroyed, the blockade was in full operation, and hundreds of Haganah members who had tried to bring supplies into the city were killed.[27] The situation for those who dwelt in the Jewish settlements in the highly isolated Negev and North of Galilee was even more critical.

While the Jewish population had received strict orders requiring them to hold their ground everywhere at all costs,[28] the Arab population was more affected by the general conditions of insecurity to which the country was exposed. Up to 100,000 Arabs, from the urban upper and middle classes in Haifa, Jaffa and Jerusalem, or Jewish-dominated areas, evacuated abroad or to Arab centres eastwards.[29]

This situation caused the United States to withdraw its support for the Partition plan, thus encouraging the Arab League to believe that the Palestinian Arabs, reinforced by the Arab Liberation Army, could put an end to the plan for partition. The British, on the other hand, decided on 7 February 1948, to support the annexation of the Arab part of Palestine by Transjordan.[30]

Although a certain level of doubt took hold among Yishuv supporters, their apparent defeats were due more to their wait-and-see policy than to weakness. David Ben-Gurion reorganized Haganah and made conscription obligatory. Every Jewish man and woman in the country had to receive military training. Thanks to funds raised by Golda Meir from sympathisers in the United States, and Stalin's decision to support the Zionist cause, the Jewish representatives of Palestine were able to sign very important armament contracts in the East. Other Haganah agents recuperated stockpiles from the Second World War, which helped improve the army's equipment and logistics. Operation Balak

Figure 2: *Palmach M4 Sherman tank leading a convoy.*

allowed arms and other equipment to be transported for the first time by the end of March.

Ben-Gurion invested Yigael Yadin with the responsibility to come up with a plan of offense whose timing was related to the foreseeable evacuation of British forces. This strategy, called Plan Dalet, was readied by March and implemented towards the end of April.[31] A separate plan, Operation Nachshon, was devised to lift the siege of Jerusalem. 1500 men from Haganah's Givati brigade and Palmach's Harel brigade conducted sorties to free up the route to the city between 5 and 20 April. Both sides acted offensively in defiance of the Partition Plan, which foresaw Jerusalem as a corpus separatum, under neither Jewish nor Arab jurisdiction. The Arabs did not accept the Plan, while the Jews were determined to oppose the internationalization of the city, and secure it as part of the Jewish state.[32] The operation was successful, and enough foodstuffs to last two months were trucked into Jerusalem for distribution to the Jewish population.[33] The success of the operation was assisted by the death of al-Husayni in combat. During this time, and independently of Haganah or the framework of Plan Dalet, irregular fighters from Irgun and Lehi formations massacred a substantial number of Arabs at Deir Yassin, an event that, though publicly deplored and criticized by the principal Jewish authorities, had a deep impact on the morale of the Arab population and contributed to generate the exodus of the Arab population.

At the same time, the first large-scale operation of the Arab Liberation Army ended in a debacle, having been roundly defeated at Mishmar HaEmek,[34] coinciding with the loss of their Druze allies through defection.[35]

Within the framework of the establishment of Jewish territorial continuity foreseen by Plan Dalet, the forces of Haganah, Palmach and Irgun intended to conquer mixed zones. The Palestinian Arab society was shaken. Tiberias, Haifa, Safed, Beisan, Jaffa and Acre fell, resulting in the flight of more than 250,000 Palestinian Arabs.[36]

The British had, at that time, essentially withdrawn their troops. The situation pushed the leaders of the neighbouring Arab states to intervene, but their preparation was not finalized, and they could not assemble sufficient forces to turn the tide of the war. The majority of Palestinian Arab hopes lay with the Arab Legion of Transjordan's monarch, King Abdullah I, but he had no intention of creating a Palestinian Arab-run state, since he hoped to annex as much of the territory of the British Mandate for Palestine as he could. He was playing a double-game, being just as much in contact with the Jewish authorities as with the Arab League.

In preparation for the offensive, Haganah successfully launched Operations Yiftah[37] and Ben-'Ami[38] to secure the Jewish settlements of Galilee, and Operation Kilshon, which created a united front around Jerusalem. The inconclusive meeting between Golda Meir and Abdullah I, followed by the Kfar Etzion massacre on 13 May by the Arab Legion led to predictions that the battle for Jerusalem would be merciless.

On 14 May 1948, David Ben-Gurion declared the establishment of the State of Israel and the 1948 Palestine war entered its second phase with the intervention of the Arab state armies and the beginning of the 1948 Arab–Israeli War.

Armed forces

By September 1947 the Haganah had "10,489 rifles, 702 light machine-guns, 2,666 submachine guns, 186 medium machine-guns, 672 two-inch mortars and 92 three-inch (76 mm) mortars".

Importing arms

In 1946, Ben-Gurion decided that the Yishuv would probably have to defend itself against both the Palestinian Arabs and neighbouring Arab states and accordingly began a "massive, covert arms acquisition campaign in the West", and acquired many more during the first few months of hostilities.

The Yishuv managed to clandestinely amass arms and military equipment abroad for transfer to Palestine once the British blockade was lifted. In the United States, Yishuv agents purchased three Boeing B-17 Flying Fortress

Figure 3: *An Israeli Avia S-199, in June 1948*

bombers, one of which bombed Cairo in July 1948, some Curtiss C-46 Commando transport planes, and dozens of half-tracks, which were repainted and defined as "agricultural equipment". In Western Europe, Haganah agents amassed fifty 65mm French mountain guns, twelve 120mm mortars, ten H-35 light tanks, and a large number of half-tracks. By mid-May or thereabouts the Yishuv had purchased from Czechoslovakia 25 Avia S-199 fighters (an inferior version of the Messerschmitt Bf-109), 200 heavy machine guns, 5,021 light machine guns, 24,500 rifles, and 52 million rounds of ammunition, enough to equip all units, but short of heavy arms.[39] The airborne arms smuggling missions from Czechoslovakia were codenamed Operation Balak.

The airborne smuggling missions were carried out by mostly American aviators – Jews and non-Jews – led by ex-U.S. Air Transport Command flight engineer Al Schwimmer.

Schwimmer's operation also included recruiting and training fighter pilots such as Lou Lenart, commander of the first Israeli air assault against the Arabs.

Arms production

The Yishuv also had "a relatively advanced *arms producing* capacity", that between October 1947 and July 1948" produced 3 million 9 mm bullets, 150,000 Mills grenades, 16,000 submachine guns (Sten Guns) and 210 three-inch

(76 mm) mortars", along with a few "Davidka" mortars, which had been indigenously designed and produced. They were inaccurate but had a spectacularly loud explosion that demoralized the enemy. A large amount of the munitions used by the Israelis came from the Ayalon Institute, a clandestine bullet factory underneath kibbutz Ayalon, which produced about 2.5 million bullets for Sten guns. The munitions produced by the Ayalon Institute were said to have been the only supply that was not in shortage during the war. Locally produced explosives were also plentiful. After Israel's independence, these clandestine arms manufacturing operations no longer had to be concealed, and were moved above ground. All of the Haganah's weapons-manufacturing was centralized and later became Israel Military Industries.

Manpower

In November 1947, the Haganah was an underground paramilitary force that had existed as a highly organized, national force, since the Arab riots of 1920–21, and throughout the riots of 1929, Great Uprising of 1936–39,[40] and World War 2. It had a mobile force, the HISH, which had 2,000 full-time fighters (men and women) and 10,000 reservists (all aged between 18 and 25) and an elite unit, the Palmach composed of 2,100 fighters and 1,000 reservists. The reservists trained three or four days a monthWikipedia:Citation needed and went back to civilian life the rest of the time. These mobile forces could rely on a garrison force, the HIM (*Heil Mishmar*, lit. Guard Corps), composed of people aged over 25. The Yishuv's total strength was around 35,000 with 15,000 to 18,000 fighters and a garrison force of roughly 20,000.[41]

There were also several thousand men and women who had served in the British Army in World War II who did not serve in any of the underground militias but would provide valuable military experience during the war. Walid Khalidi says the Yishuv had the additional forces of the Jewish Settlement Police, numbering some 12,000, the Gadna Youth Battalions, and the armed settlers.[42] Few of the units had been trained by December 1947. On 5 December 1947, conscription was instituted for all men and women aged between 17 and 25 and by the end of March, 21,000 had been conscripted.[43] On 30 March, the call-up was extended to men and single women aged between 26 and 35. Five days later, a General Mobilization order was issued for all men under 40.[44]

Irgun

The Irgun, whose activities were considered by MI5 to be terrorism, was monitored by the British.

By March 1948, the Yishuv had a numerical superiority, with 35,780 mobilised and deployed fighters for the Haganah,[45,46] 3,000 of Stern and Irgun, and a few thousand armed settlers.[47]

Arab forces

The effective number of Arab combatants is listed at 12,000 by some historians[48] while others calculate a total Arab strength of approximately 23,500 troops, and with this being more of less or roughly equal to that of the Yishuv. However, as Israel mobilized most of its most able citizens during the war while the Arab troops were only a small percentage of its far greater population, the strength of the Yishuv grew steadily and dramatically during the war.

According to Benny Morris, by the end of 1947, the Palestinians "had a healthy and demoralising respect for the Yishuv's military power" and if it came to battle the Palestinians expected to lose.

Political objectives

Yishuv

Yishuv's aims evolved during the war.[49] Mobilization for a total war was organized.[50] Initially, the aim was "simple and modest": to survive the assaults of the Palestinian Arabs and the Arab states. "The Zionist leaders deeply, genuinely, feared a Middle Eastern reenactment of the Holocaust, which had just ended; the Arabs' public rhetoric reinforced these fears". As the war progressed, the aim of expanding the Jewish state beyond the UN partition borders appeared: first to incorporate clusters of isolated Jewish settlements and later to add more territories to the state and give it defensible borders. A third and further aim that emerged among the political and military leaders after four or five months was to "reduce the size of Israel's prospective large and hostile Arab minority, seen as a potential powerful fifth column, by belligerency and expulsion".

Plan Dalet, or Plan D, (Hebrew: תוכנית ד', Tokhnit dalet) was a plan worked out by the Haganah, a Jewish paramilitary group and the forerunner of the Israel Defense Forces, in autumn 1947 to spring 1948, which was sent to Haganah units in early March 1948. According to the academic Ilan Pappé, its purpose was to conquer as much of Palestine and to expel as many Palestinians as possible,[51] though according to Benny Morris there was no such intent. In his book *The Ethnic Cleansing of Palestine*, Pappé asserts that Plan Dalet was a "blueprint for ethnic cleansing" with the aim of reducing both rural and urban areas of Palestine.[52] According to Gelber, the plan specified that in case of resistance, the population of conquered villages was to be expelled outside the borders of the Jewish state. If no resistance was met, the residents could stay put, under military rule.[53] According to Morris, Plan D called for occupying the areas within the U.N sponsored Jewish state, several concentrations of Jewish population outside those areas (West Jerusalem and Western Galilee), and areas along the roads where the invading Arab armies were expected to attack.[54]

The intent of Plan Dalet is subject to much controversy, with historians on the one extreme asserting that it was entirely defensive, and historians on the other extreme asserting that the plan aimed at maximum conquest and expulsion of the Palestinians.

The Yishuv perceived the peril of an Arab invasion as threatening its very existence. Having no real knowledge of the Arabs' true military capabilities, the Jews took Arab propaganda literally, preparing for the worst and reacting accordingly."

The Arab League as a whole

The Arab League had unanimously rejected the UN partition plan and were bitterly opposed to the establishment of a Jewish state.

The Arab League before partition affirmed the right to the independence of Palestine, while blocking the creation of a Palestinian government.Wikipedia:Please clarify Towards the end of 1947, the League established a military committee commanded by the retired Iraqi general Isma'il Safwat whose mission was to analyse the chance of victory of the Palestinians against the Jews.[55] His conclusions were that they had no chance of victory and that an invasion of the Arab regular armies was mandatory. The political committee nevertheless rejected these conclusions and decided to support an armed opposition to the Partition Plan excluding the participation of their regular armed forces.[56]

In April with the Palestinian defeat, the refugees coming from Palestine and the pressure of their public opinion, the Arab leaders decided to invade Palestine.[57]

The Arab League gave reasons for its *invasion* in Palestine in the cablegram:

- the Arab states find themselves compelled to intervene in order to restore law and order and to check further bloodshed
- the Mandate over Palestine has come to an end, leaving no legally constituted authority
- *the only solution of the Palestine problem is the establishment of a unitary Palestinian state.*

British diplomat Alec Kirkbride wrote in his 1976 memoirs about a conversation with the Arab League's Secretary-General Azzam Pasha a week before the armies marched: "...when I asked him for his estimate of the size of the Jewish forces, [he] waved his hands and said: 'It does not matter how many there are. We will sweep them into the sea.'"[58] Approximately six months previously, according to an interview in an 11 October 1947 article of *Akhbar al-Yom*,

Figure 4: *King Abdullah outside the Church of the Holy Sepulchre, Jerusalem, 29 May 1948.*

Azzam said: "I personally wish that the Jews do not drive us to this war, as this will be a war of extermination and a momentous massacre which will be spoken of like the Mongolian massacres and the Crusades".Wikipedia:Neutral point of view#Due and undue weight

According to Yoav Gelber, the Arab countries were "drawn into the war by the collapse of the Palestinian Arabs and the Arab Liberation Army [and] the Arab governments' primary goal was preventing the Palestinian Arabs' total ruin and the flooding of their own countries by more refugees. According to their own perception, had the invasion not taken place, there was no Arab force in Palestine capable of checking the Haganah's offensive".[59]

King Abdullah I of Jordan

King Abdullah was the commander of the Arab Legion, the strongest Arab army involved in the war according to Rogan and Shlaim in 2007.[60] However, Morris wrote in 2008 that the Egyptian army was the most powerful and threatening army.[61] The Arab Legion had about 10,000 soldiers, trained and commanded by British officers.

In 1946–47, Abdullah said that he had no intention to "resist or impede the partition of Palestine and creation of a Jewish state."[62] Ideally, Abdullah would have liked to annex all of Palestine, but he was prepared to compromise. He supported the partition, intending that the West Bank area of the British Mandate allocated for the Arab state be annexed to Jordan.[63] Abdullah had secret meetings with the Jewish Agency (at which the future Israeli Prime Minister Golda Meir was among the delegates) that reached an agreement of Jewish non-interference with Jordanian annexation of the West Bank (although Abdullah failed in his goal of acquiring an outlet to the Mediterranean Sea through the Negev desert) and of Jordanian agreement not to attack the area of the Jewish state contained in the United Nations partition resolution (in which Jerusalem was given neither to the Arab nor the Jewish state, but was to be an internationally administered area). In order to keep their support to his plan of annexation of the Arab State, Abdullah promised to the British he would not attack the Jewish State.

The neighbouring Arab states pressured Abdullah into joining them in an "all-Arab military invasion" against the newly created State of Israel, that he used to restore his prestige in the Arab world, which had grown suspicious of his relatively good relationship with Western and Jewish leaders. Jordan's undertakings not to cross partition lines were not taken at face value. While repeating assurances that Jordan would only take areas allocated to a future Arab State, on the eve of war Tawfik Abu al-Huda told the British that were other Arab armies to advance against Israel, Jordan would follow suit.[64] On 23 May Abdullah told the French consul in Amman that he "was determined to fight Zionism and prevent the establishment of an Israeli state on the border of his kingdom".[65]

Abdullah's role in this war became substantial. He saw himself as the "supreme commander of the Arab forces" and "persuaded the Arab League to appoint him" to this position.[66] Through his leadership, the Arabs fought the 1948 war to meet Abdullah's political goals.

The other Arab states

King Farouk of Egypt was anxious to prevent Abdullah from being seen as the main champion of the Arab world in Palestine, which he feared might damage his own leadership aspirations of the Arab world. In addition, Farouk wished to annex all of southern Palestine to Egypt. According to Gamal Abdel Nasser the Egyptian army first communique described the Palestine operations as a merely punitive expedition against the Zionist "gangs", using a term frequent in Haganah reports of Palestinian fighters.[67]

Nuri as-Said, the strongman of Iraq, had ambitions for bringing the entire Fertile Crescent under Iraqi leadership. Both Syria and Lebanon wished to take certain areas of northern Palestine.

One result of the ambitions of the various Arab leaders was a distrust of all the Palestinian leaders who wished to set up a Palestinian state, and a mutual distrust of each other. Co-operation was to be very poor during the war between the various Palestinian factions and the Arab armies.

Arab Higher Committee of Amin al-Husayni

Following rumours that King Abdullah was re-opening the bilateral negotiations with Israel that he had previously conducted in secret with the Jewish Agency, the Arab League, led by Egypt, decided to set up the All-Palestine Government in Gaza on 8 September under the nominal leadership of the Mufti.[68] Abdullah regarded the attempt to revive al-Husayni's Holy War Army as a challenge to his authority and all armed bodies operating in the areas controlled by the Arab Legion were disbanded. Glubb Pasha carried out the order ruthlessly and efficiently.[69,70]

Initial line-up of forces

Military assessments

Though the state of Israel faced the formidable armies of neighboring Arab countries, yet due to previous battles by the middle of May the Palestinians themselves hardly existed as a military force.[71] The British Intelligence and Arab League military reached similar conclusions.[72]

The British Foreign Ministry and C.I.A believed that the Arab States would finally win in case of war.[73,74] Martin Van Creveld says that in terms of manpower, the sides were fairly evenly matched.[75]

In May, Egyptian generals told their government that the invasion will be "A parade without any risks" and Tel Aviv "in two weeks".[76] Egypt, Iraq, and Syria all possessed air forces, Egypt and Syria had tanks, and all had some modern artillery.[77] Initially, the Haganah had no heavy machine guns, artillery, armoured vehicles, anti-tank or anti-aircraft weapons, nor military aircraft or tanks. The four Arab armies that invaded on 15 May were far stronger than the Haganah formations they initially encountered.[78]

On 12 May, three days before the invasion, David Ben-Gurion was told by his chief military advisers (who over-estimated the size of the Arab armies and the numbers and efficiency of the troops who would be committed – much as the Arab generals tended to exaggerate Jewish fighters' strength) that Israel's chances of winning a war against the Arab states were only about even.

Yishuv/Israeli forces

Jewish forces at the invasion: Sources disagree about the amount of arms at the Yishuv's disposal at the end of the Mandate. According to Karsh before the arrival of arms shipments from Czechoslovakia as part of Operation Balak, there was roughly one weapon for every three fighters, and even the Palmach could arm only two out of every three of its active members. According to Collins and LaPierre, by April 1948, the Haganah had managed to accumulate only about 20,000 rifles and Sten guns for the 35,000 soldiers who existed on paper.[79] According to Walid Khalidi "the arms at the disposal of these forces were plentiful". France authorized Air France to transport cargo to Tel Aviv on 13 May.

Yishuv forces were organised in 9 brigades, and their numbers grew following Israeli independence, eventually expanding to 12 brigades. Although both sides increased their manpower over the first few months of the war, the Israeli forces grew steadily as a result of the progressive mobilization of Israeli society and the influx of an average of 10,300 immigrants each month. By the end of 1948, the Israel Defense Forces had 88,033 soldiers, including 60,000 combat soldiers.[80]

Brigade	Commander	Size[81]	Operations
Golani	Moshe Mann	4,500	Dekel, Hiram
Carmeli	Moshe Carmel	2,000	Hiram
Alexandroni	Dan Even	5,200	Latrun, Hametz
Kiryati	Michael Ben-Gal	1,400	Dani, Hametz
Givati	Shimon Avidan	5,000	Hametz, Barak, Pleshet
Etzioni	David Shaltiel		Battle of Jerusalem, Shfifon, Yevusi, Battle of Ramat Rachel
7th Armoured	Shlomo Shamir		Battles of Latrun
8th Armoured	Yitzhak Sadeh		Danny, Yoav, Horev
Oded	Avraham Yoffe		Yoav, Hiram
Harel	Yitzhak Rabin[82]	1,400	Nachshon, Danny
Yiftach	Yigal Allon	4,500 inc. some Golani	Yiftah, Danny, Yoav, Battles of Latrun
Negev	Nahum Sarig	2,400	Yoav

Figure 5: *Sherman tanks of the Israeli 8th Armoured Brigade, 1948*

After the invasion: France allowed aircraft carrying arms from Czechoslovakia to land on French territory in transit to Israel, and permitted two arms shipments to 'Nicaragua', which were actually intended for Israel.

Czechoslovakia supplied vast quantities of arms to Israel during the war, including thousands of vz. 24 rifles and MG 34 and ZB 37 machine guns, and millions of rounds of ammunition. Czechoslovakia supplied fighter aircraft, including at first ten Avia S-199 fighter planes.

The Haganah readied twelve cargo ships throughout European ports to transfer the accumulated equipment, which would set sail as soon as the British blockade was lifted with the expiration of the Mandate.[83]

Following Israeli independence, the Israelis managed to build three Sherman tanks from scrap-heap material found in abandoned British ordnance depots.[84]

The Haganah also managed to obtain stocks of British weapons due to the logistical complexity of the British withdrawal, and the corruption of a number of officials.[85]

After the first truce: By July 1948, the Israelis had established an air force, a navy, and a tank battalion.

On June 29, 1948, the day before the last British troops left Haifa, two British soldiers sympathetic to the Israelis stole two Cromwell tanks from an arms depot in the Haifa port area, smashing them through the unguarded gates, and

Figure 6: *A Cromwell tank*

joined the IDF with the tanks. These two tanks would form the basis of the Israeli Armored Corps.

After the second truce: Czechoslovakia supplied Supermarine Spitfire fighter planes, which were smuggled to Israel via an abandoned Luftwaffe runway in Yugoslavia, with the agreement of the Yugoslav government.Wikipedia:Citation needed The airborne arms smuggling missions from Czechoslovakia were codenamed Operation Balak.

Arab forces

At the invasion: In addition to the local irregular Palestinians militia groups, the five Arab states that joined the war were Egypt, Jordan (Transjordan), Syria, Lebanon and Iraq sending expeditionary forces of their regular armies. Additional contingents came from Saudi Arabia and Yemen. On the eve of the war, the available number of Arab troops likely to be committed to war was between 23,500 and 26,500 (10,000 Egyptians, 4,500 Jordanians, 3,000 Iraqis, 3,000–6,000 Syrians, 2,000 ALA volunteers, 1,000 Lebanese, and several hundred Saudis), in addition to the irregular Palestinians already present. Prior to the war, Arab forces had been trained by British and French instructors. This was particularly true of Jordan's Arab Legion under command of Lt Gen Sir John Glubb.

Figure 7: *IDF soldiers of the Samson's Foxes unit advance in a captured Egyptian Bren Gun carrier.*

Syria bought a quantity of small arms for the Arab Liberation Army from Czechoslovakia, but the shipment never arrived due to Haganah force intervention.[86]

Arab states

Jordan's Arab Legion was considered the most effective Arab force. Armed, trained and commanded by British officers, this 8,000–12,000 strong force was organised in four infantry/mechanised regiments supported by some 40 artillery pieces and 75 armoured cars. Until January 1948, it was reinforced by the 3,000-strong Transjordan Frontier Force. As many as 48 British officers served in the Arab Legion. Glubb Pasha, the commander of the Legion, organized his forces into four brigades as follows:

Military Division	Commander[87,88]	Rank	Military Zone of operations
First Brigade, includes: 1st and 3rd regiments	Desmond Goldie	Colonel	Nablus Military Zone
Second Brigade, includes: Fifth and Sixth Regiments	Sam Sidney Arthur Cooke	Brigadier	Support force
Third Brigade, includes: Second and Fourth Regiments	Teel Ashton	Colonel	Ramallah Military Zone

| Fourth Brigade | Ahmad Sudqi al-Jundi | Colonel | Support: Ramallah, Hebron, and Ramla |

The Arab Legion joined the war in May 1948, but fought only in the area that King Abdullah wanted to secure for Jordan: the West Bank, including East Jerusalem.

France prevented a large sale of arms by a Swiss company to Ethiopia, brokered by the U.K foreign office, which was actually destined for Egypt and Jordan, denied a British request at the end of April to permit the landing of a squadron of British aircraft on their way to Transjordan, and applied diplomatic pressure on Belgium to suspend arms sales to the Arab states.

The Jordanian forces were probably the best trained of all combatants. Other combatant forces lacked the ability to make strategic decisions and tactical maneuvers,[89] as evidenced by positioning the fourth regiment at Latrun, which was abandoned by ALA combatants before the arrival of the Jordanian forces and the importance of which was not fully understood by the Haganah generalstaff. In the later stages of the war, Latrun proved to be of extreme importance, and a decisive factor in Jerusalem's fate.

In 1948, **Iraq's** army had 21,000 men in 12 brigades and the Iraqi Air Force had 100 planes, mostly British. Initially the Iraqis committed around 3,000 men[90] to the war effort, including four infantry brigades, one armoured battalion and support personnel. These forces were to operate under Jordanian guidance[91] The first Iraqi forces to be deployed reached Jordan in April 1948 under the command of Gen. Nur ad-Din Mahmud.[92]

In 1948, **Egypt's** army was able to put a maximum of around 40,000 men into the field, 80% of its military-age male population being unfit for military service and its embryonic logistics system being limited in its ability to support ground forces deployed beyond its borders.Wikipedia:Citation needed Initially, an expeditionary force of 10,000 men was sent to Palestine under the command of Maj. Gen. Ahmed Ali al-Mwawi. This force consisted of five infantry battalions, one armoured battalion equipped with British Light Tank Mk VI and Matilda tanks, one battalion of sixteen 25-pounder guns, a battalion of eight 6-pounder guns and one medium-machine-gun battalion with supporting troops.Wikipedia:Citation needed

The Egyptian Air Force had over 30 Spitfires, 4 Hawker Hurricanes and 20 C47s modified into crude bombers.Wikipedia:Citation needed

Syria had 12,000 soldiers at the beginning of the 1948 War, grouped into three infantry brigades and an armoured force of approximately battalion size. The Syrian Air Force had fifty planes, the 10 newest of which were World War II–generation models.

Figure 8: *Vickers light tanks in the desert*

France suspended arms sales to Syria, notwithstanding signed contracts.

Lebanon's army was the smallest of the Arab armies, consisting of only 3,500 soldiers. According to Gelber, in June 1947, Ben-Gurion "arrived at an agreement with the Maronite religious leadership in Lebanon that cost a few thousand pounds and kept Lebanon's army out of the War of Independence and the military Arab coalition."[93] According to Rogan and Shlaim, a token force of 1,000 was committed to the invasion. It crossed into the northern Galilee and was repulsed by Israeli forces. Israel then invaded and occupied southern Lebanon until the end of the war.[94]

Arab forces after the first truce: By the time of the second truce, the **Egyptians** had 20,000 men in the field in thirteen battalions equipped with 135 tanks and 90 artillery pieces.[95]

During the first truce, the **Iraqis** increased their force to about 10,000.[96] Ultimately, the Iraqi expeditionary force numbered around 18,000 men.[97]

Saudi Arabia sent hundreds of volunteers to join the Arab forces. In February 1948, around 800 tribesmen had gathered near Aqaba so as to invade the Negev, but crossed to Egypt after Saudi rival King Abdallah officially denied them permission to pass through Jordanian territory.[98] The Saudi troops were attached to the Egyptian command throughout the war,[99] and estimates of their total strength ranged up to 1,200.[100,101] By July 1948, the Saudis comprised

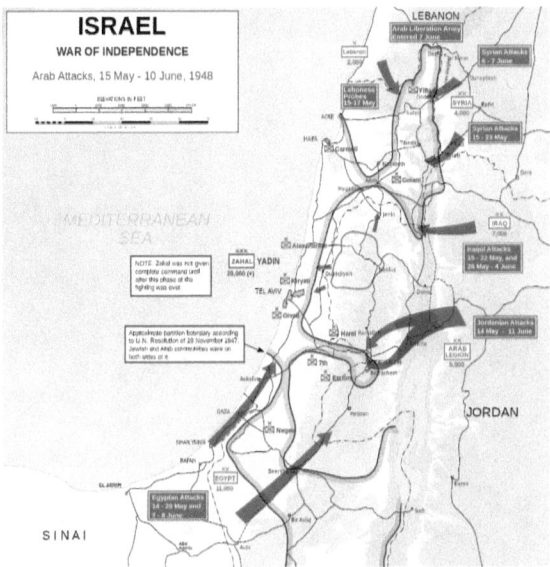

Figure 9: *Arab offensive, 15 May – 10 June 1948*

three brigades within the Egyptian expeditionary force, and were stationed as guards between Gaza city and Rafah.[102] This area came under heavy aerial bombardment during Operation Yoav in October,[103] and faced a land assault beginning in late December which culminated in the Battle of Rafah in early January of the new year. With the subsequent armistice of 24 February 1949 and evacuation of almost 4,000 Arab soldiers and civilians from Gaza, the Saudi contingent withdrew through Arish and returned to Saudi Arabia.[104]

During the first truce, **Sudan** sent six companies of regular troops to fight alongside the Egyptians.[105] **Yemen** also committed a small expeditionary force to the war effort, and contingents from **Morocco** joined the Arab armies as well.

Course of the war

At the last moment, several Arab leaders, to avert catastrophe – secretly appealed to the British to hold on in Palestine for at least another year.

First phase: 15 May – 11 June 1948

On 14 May 1948, David Ben-Gurion declared the establishment of a Jewish state in Eretz-Israel to be known as the State of Israel, a few hours before the

Figure 10: A "Butterfly" improvised armored car of the Haganah at Kibbutz Dorot in the Negev, Israel 1948. The armored car is based on CMP-15 truck. The car has brought supply to the kibbutz. The Negev Kibbutz'sWikipedia:Accuracy dispute#Disputed statement children were later evacuated by those cars from their kibbutz, before an expected Egyptian Army attack.

termination of the Mandate. At midnight on 15 May 1948, the British Mandate was officially terminated, and the State of Israel came into being. Several hours later, Iraq and the neighboring Arab states, Egypt, Jordan (Transjordan) and Syria, invaded the newborn state,[106] and immediately attacked Jewish settlements. What was now Israel had already, from 1 April down to 14 May, conducted 8 of its 13 full-scale military operations outside of the area allotted to a Jewish state by partition, and the operational commander Yigal Allon later stated that had it not been for the Arab invasion, Haganah's forces would have reached 'the natural borders of western Israel.'[107] Although the Arab invasion was denounced by the United States, the Soviet Union, and UN secretary-general Trygve Lie, it found support from the Republic of China and other UN member states.

The initial Arab plans called for Syrian and Lebanese forces to invade from north while Jordanian and Iraqi forces were to invade from east in order to meet at Nazareth and then to push forward together to Haifa. In the south, the Egyptians were to advance and take Tel Aviv.[108] At the Arab League meeting in Damascus on 11–13 May, Abdullah rejected the plan, which served Syrian

Figure 11: *Israeli soldiers in Nirim*

interests, using the fact his allies were afraid to go to war without his army. He proposed that the Iraqis attack the Jezreel valley and the Arab Legion enter Ramallah and Nablus and link with the Egyptian army at Hebron, which was more in compliance with his political objective to occupy the territory allocated to the Arab State by the partition plan and promises not to invade the territory allocated to the Jewish State by the partition plan. In addition, Lebanon decided not to take part in the war at the last minute, due to the still-influential Christians' opposition and due to Jewish bribes.

Intelligence provided by the French consulate in Jerusalem on 12 May 1948 on the Arab armies' invading forces and their revised plan to invade the new state contributed to Israel's success in withstanding the Arab invasion.

The first mission of the Jewish forces was to hold on against the Arab armies and stop them, although the Arabs had enjoyed major advantages (the initiative, vastly superior firepower).[109] As the British stopped blocking the incoming Jewish immigrants and arms supply, the Israeli forces grew steadily with large numbers of immigrants and weapons, that allowed the Haganah to transform itself from a paramilitary force into a real army. Initially, the fighting was handled mainly by the Haganah, along with the smaller Jewish militant groups Irgun and Lehi. On 26 May 1948, Israel established the Israel Defense Forces (IDF), incorporating these forces into one military under a central command.

Figure 12: *Israeli soldiers in Negba*

Southern front – Negev

The Egyptian force, the largest among the Arab armies, invaded from the south.

On 15 May 1948, the Egyptians attacked two settlements: Nirim, using artillery, armoured cars carrying cannons, and Bren carriers; and Kfar Darom using artillery, tanks and aircraft. The Egyptians attacks met fierce resistance from the few and lightly armed defenders of both settlements, and failed. On 19 May the Egyptians attacked Yad Mordechai, where an inferior force of 100 Israelis armed with nothing more than rifles, a medium machinegun and a PIAT anti-tank weapon, held up a column of 2,500 Egyptians, well-supported by armor, artillery and air units, for five days. The Egyptians took heavy losses, while the losses sustained by the defenders were comparatively light.

One of the Egyptian force's two main columns made its way northwards along the shoreline, through what is today the Gaza Strip and the other column advanced eastwards toward Beersheba.[110] To secure their flanks, the Egyptians attacked and laid siege to a number of kibbutzim in the Negev, among those Kfar Darom, Nirim, Yad Mordechai, and Negba.[111] The Israeli defenders held out fiercely for days against vastly superior forces, and managed to buy valuable time for the IDF's Givati Brigade to prepare to stop the Egyptian drive on Tel Aviv.

On 28 May the Egyptians renewed their northern advance, and stopped at a destroyed bridge north to Isdud. The Givati Brigade reported this advance but no fighters were sent to confront the Egyptians. Had the Egyptians wished to continue their advance northward, towards Tel Aviv, there would have been no Israeli force to block them.[112,113]

From 29 May to 3 June, Israeli forces stopped the Egyptian drive north in Operation Pleshet. In the first combat mission performed by Israel's fledgling air force, four Avia S-199s attacked an Egyptian armored column of 500 vehicles on its way to Isdud. The Israeli planes dropped 70 kilogram bombs and strafed the column, although their machine guns jammed quickly. Two of the planes crashed, killing a pilot. The attack caused the Egyptians to scatter, and they had lost the initiative by the time they had regrouped. Following the air attack, Israeli forces constantly bombarded Egyptian forces in Isdud with *Napoleonchik* cannons, and IDF patrols engaged in small-scale harassment of Egyptian lines. Following another air attack, the Givati Brigade launched a counterattack. Although the counterattack was repulsed, the Egyptian offensive was halted as Egypt changed its strategy from offensive to defensive, and the initiative shifted to Israel.

On 6 June, in the Battle of Nitzanim, Egyptian forces attacked the kibbutz of Nitzanim, located between Majdal (now Ashkelon) and Isdud, and the Israeli defenders surrendered after resisting for five days.

Battles of Latrun

The heaviest fighting occurred in Jerusalem and on the Jerusalem – Tel Aviv road, between Jordan's Arab Legion and Israeli forces. As part of the redeployment to deal with the Egyptian advance, the Israelis abandoned the Latrun fortress overlooking the main highway to Jerusalem, which the Arab Legion immediately seized. The Arab Legion also occupied the Latrun Monastery. From these positions, the Jordanians were able to cut off supplies to Israeli fighters and civilians in Jerusalem.

The Israelis attempted to take the Latrun fortress in a series of battles lasting from 24 May to 18 July. The Arab Legion held Latrun and managed to repulse the attacks. During the attempts to take Latrun, Israeli forces suffered some 586 casualties, among them Mickey Marcus, Israel's first general, who was killed by friendly fire. The Arab Legion also took losses, losing 90 dead and some 200 wounded up to 29 May.[114]

Building the Burma Road

A bulldozer tows a truck on the "Burma road", June 1948

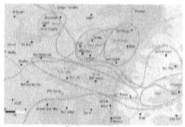
Area map

The besieged Israeli Jerusalem was only saved via the opening of the so-called "Burma Road", a makeshift bypass road built by Israeli forces that allowed Israeli supply convoys to pass into Jerusalem. Parts of the area where the road was built were cleared of Jordanian snipers in May and the road was completed on 14 June. Supplies had already begun passing through before the road was completed, with the first convoy passing through on the night of 1–2 June. The Jordanians spotted the activity and attempted to shell the road, but were ineffective, as it could not be seen. However, Jordanian sharpshooters killed several road workers, and an attack on 9 June left eight Israelis dead. On 18 July, elements of the Harel Brigade took about 10 villages to the south of Latrun to enlarge and secure the area of the Burma Road.

The Arab Legion was able to repel an Israeli attack on Latrun. The Jordanians launched two counterattacks, temporarily taking Beit Susin before being forced back, and capturing Gezer after a fierce battle, which was retaken by two Palmach squads the same evening.[115]

Jordanian artillery shelling Jerusalem in 1948

Arab Legion soldier standing in ruins of the most sacred Synagogue, the "Hurva", Old City.

Jewish residents of Jerusalem Old City fleeing during the Jordanian offensive

Battle for Jerusalem

The Jordanians in Latrun cut off supplies to western Jerusalem. Though some supplies, mostly munitions, were airdropped into the city, the shortage of food, water, fuel and medicine was acute. The Israeli forces were seriously short of food, water and ammunition.

Figure 13: *Mathematics professor Michael Fekete, the Provost of the Hebrew University of Jerusalem, with his water quota, during the siege of Jerusalem*

King Abdullah ordered Glubb Pasha, the commander of the Arab Legion, to enter Jerusalem on 17 May. The Arab Legion fired 10,000 artillery and mortar shells a day, and also attacked West Jerusalem with sniper fire.

Heavy house-to-house fighting occurred between 19 and 28 May, with the Arab Legion eventually succeeding in pushing Israeli forces from the Arab neighborhoods of Jerusalem as well as the Jewish Quarter of the Old City. The 1,500 Jewish inhabitants of the Old City's Jewish Quarter were expelled, and several hundred were detained. The Jews had to be escorted out by the Arab Legion to protect them against Palestinian Arab mobs that intended to massacre them.[116] On 22 May, Arab forces attacked kibbutz Ramat Rachel south of Jerusalem. After a fierce battle in which 31 Jordanians and 13 Israelis were killed, the defenders of Ramat Rachel withdrew, only to partially retake the kibbutz the following day. Fighting continued until 26 May, until the entire kibbutz was recaptured. Radar Hill was also taken from the Arab Legion, and held until 26 May, when the Jordanians retook it in a battle that left 19 Israelis and 2 Jordanians dead. A total of 23 attempts by the Harel Brigade to capture Radar Hill in the war failed.

The same day, Thomas C. Wasson, the US Consul-General in Jerusalem and a member of the UN Truce Commission was shot dead in West Jerusalem. It was disputed whether Wasson was killed by the Arabs or Israelis.

Figure 14: *Israeli soldiers in Afula.*

In mid to late October 1948, the Harel Brigade began its offensive in what was known as Operation Ha-Har, to secure the Jerusalem Corridor.

Northern Samaria

An Iraqi force consisting of two infantry and one armoured brigade crossed the Jordan River from northern Jordan, attacking the Israeli settlement of Gesher with little success. Following this defeat, Iraqi forces moved into the strategic triangle bounded by the Arab towns Nablus, Jenin and Tulkarm. On 25 May, they were making their way towards Netanya, when they were stopped. On 29 May, an Israeli attack against the Iraqis led to three days of heavy fighting over Jenin, but Iraqi forces managed to hold their positions. After these battles, the Iraqi forces became stationary and their involvement in the war effectively ended.

Iraqi forces failed in their attacks on Israeli settlements with the most notable battle taking place at Gesher, and instead took defensive positions around Jenin, Nablus, and Tulkarm, from where they could put pressure on the Israeli center.Wikipedia:Citation needed[117] On 25 May, Iraqi forces advanced from Tulkarm, taking Geulim and reaching Kfar Yona and Ein Vered on the Tulkarm-Netanya road. The Alexandroni Brigade then stopped the Iraqi advance and retook Geulim. On 1 June, the Carmeli and Golani Brigades captured Jenin from Iraqi forces. They were pushed out by an Iraqi counterattack, and lost 34 dead and 100 wounded.

Figure 15: *Syrian R-35 light tank destroyed at Degania Alef.*

Northern front – Lake of Galilee

On 14 May Syria invaded Palestine with the 1st Infantry Brigade supported by a battalion of armoured cars, a company of French R 35 and R 37 tanks, an artillery battalion and other units.[118] The Syrian president, Shukri al-Quwwatli instructed his troops in the front, "to destroy the Zionists". "The situation was very grave. There aren't enough rifles. There are no heavy weapons," Ben-Gurion told the Israeli Cabinet.[119,120] On 15 May, the Syrian forces turned to the eastern and southern Sea of Galilee shores, and attacked Samakh the neighboring Tegart fort and the settlements of Sha'ar HaGolan, Ein Gev, but they were bogged down by resistance. Later, they attacked Samakh using tanks and aircraft, and on 18 May they succeeded in conquering Samakh and occupied the abandoned Sha'ar HaGolan.

On 21 May, the Syrian army was stopped at kibbutz Degania Alef in the north, where local militia reinforced by elements of the Carmeli Brigade halted Syrian armored forces with Molotov cocktails, hand grenades and a single PIAT. One tank that was disabled by Molotov cocktails and hand grenades still remains at the kibbutz. The remaining Syrian forces were driven off the next day by four Napoleonchik mountain guns – Israel's first use of artillery during the war. Following the Syrian forces' defeat at the Deganias a few days later, they abandoned the Samakh village. The Syrians were forced to besiege the kibbutz

Figure 16: *Kaukji, the Arab Liberation Army commander*

rather than advance. One author claims that the main reason for the Syrian defeat was the Syrian soldiers' low regard for the Israelis who they believed would not stand and fight against the Arab army.

On 6 June, nearly two brigades of the Arab Liberation Army and the Lebanese Army took Al-Malkiyya and Qadas in what became the only intervention of the Lebanese army during the war.

On 6 June, Syrian forces attacked Mishmar HaYarden, but they were repulsed. On 10 June, the Syrians overran Mishmar HaYarden and advanced to the main road, where they were stopped by units of the Oded Brigade. Subsequently, the Syrians reverted to a defensive posture, conducting only a few minor attacks on small, exposed Israeli settlements.

Palestinian forces

In the continuity of the civil war between Jewish and Arab forces that had begun in 1947, battles between Israeli forces and Palestinian Arab militias took place, particularly in the Lydda, al-Ramla, Jerusalem, and Haifa areas. On 23 May, the Alexandroni Brigade captured Tantura, south of Haifa, from Arab forces. On 2 June, Holy War Army commander Hasan Salama was killed in a battle with Haganah at Ras al-Ein.

Figure 17: *An Egyptian Spitfire shot down over Tel Aviv on 15 May 1948*

Air operations

All Jewish aviation assets were placed under the control of the *Sherut Avir* (Air Service, known as the SA) in November 1947 and flying operations began in the following month from a small civil airport on the outskirts of Tel Aviv called Sde Dov, with the first ground support operation (in an RWD-13) taking place on 17 December. The Galilee Squadron was formed at Yavne'el in March 1948, and the Negev Squadron was formed at Nir-Am in April. By 10 May, when the SA suffered its first combat loss, there were three flying units, an air staff, maintenance facilities and logistics support. At the outbreak of the war on 15 May, the SA became the Israeli Air Force. With its fleet of light planes it was no match for Arab forces during the first few weeks of the war with their T-6s, Spitfires, C-47s, and Avro Ansons.

On 15 May, with the beginning of the war, four Royal Egyptian Air Force (REAF) Spitfires attacked Tel Aviv, bombing Sde Dov Airfield, where the bulk of Sherut Avir's aircraft were concentrated, as well as the Reading Power Station. Several aircraft were destroyed, some others were damaged, and five Israelis were killed. Throughout the following hours, additional waves of Egyptian aircraft bombed and strafed targets around Tel Aviv, although these raids had little effect. One Spitfire was shot down by anti-aircraft fire, and its pilot was taken prisoner. Throughout the next six days, the REAF would continue to attack Tel Aviv, causing civilian casualties. On 18 May, Egyptian warplanes attacked the Tel Aviv Central Bus Station, killing 42 people and wounding

Figure 18: *Volunteers evacuating a wounded man during Egyptian bombardment of Tel Aviv.*

100. In addition to their attacks on Tel Aviv, the Egyptians also bombed rural settlements and airfields, though few casualties were caused in these raids.[121]

At the outset of the war, the REAF was able to attack Israel with near impunity, due to the lack of Israeli fighter aircraft to intercept them,[122] and met only ground fire.

As more effective air defenses were transferred to Tel Aviv, the Egyptians began taking significant aircraft losses. As a result of these losses, as well as the loss of five Spitfires downed by the British when the Egyptians mistakenly attacked RAF Ramat David, the Egyptian air attacks became less frequent. By the end of May 1948, almost the entire REAF Spitfire squadron based in El Arish had been lost, including many of its best pilots.

Although lacking fighter or bomber aircraft, in the first few days of the war, Israel's embryonic air force still attacked Arab targets, with light aircraft being utilized as makeshift bombers, striking Arab encampments and columns. The raids were mostly carried out at night to avoid interception by Arab fighter aircraft. These attacks usually had little effect, except on morale.

The balance of air power soon began to swing in favor of the Israeli Air Force following the arrival of 25 Avia S-199s from Czechoslovakia, the first of which arrived in Israel on 20 May. Ironically, Israel was using the Avia S-199, an

Figure 19: *Avia S-199 Israeli 1st fighter aircraft*

Figure 20: *Israeli Spitfire F Mk*

inferior derivative of the Bf-109 designed in Nazi Germany to counter British-designed Spitfires flown by Egypt. Throughout the rest of the war, Israel would acquire more Avia fighters, as well as 62 Spitfires from Czechoslovakia. On 28 May 1948, Sherut Avir became the Israeli Air Force.

Many of the pilots who fought for the Israeli Air Force were foreign volunteers or mercenaries, including many World War II veterans.

On 3 June, Israel scored its first victory in aerial combat when Israeli pilot Modi Alon shot down a pair of Egyptian DC-3s that had just bombed Tel Aviv. Although Tel Aviv would see additional raids by fighter aircraft, there would be no more raids by bombers for the rest of the war. From then on, the Israeli Air Force began engaging the Arab air forces in air-to-air combat. The first dogfight took place on 8 June, when an Israeli fighter plane flown by Gideon Lichtman shot down an Egyptian Spitfire. By the fall of 1948, the IAF had

Figure 21: *Israeli B-17s in flight*

achieved air superiority and had superior firepower and more knowledgeable personnel, many of whom had seen action in World War II.[123] Israeli planes then began intercepting and engaging Arab aircraft on bombing missions.

Following Israeli air attacks on Egyptian and Iraqi columns, the Egyptians repeatedly bombed Ekron Airfield, where IAF fighters were based. During a 30 May raid, bombs aimed for Ekron hit central Rehovot, killing 7 civilians and wounding 30. In response to this, and probably to the Jordanian victories at Latrun, Israel began bombing targets in Arab cities. On the night of 31 May/1 June, the first Israeli raid on an Arab capital took place when three IAF planes flew to Amman and dropped several dozen 55 and 110-pound bombs, hitting the King's Palace and an adjacent British airfield. Some 12 people were killed and 30 wounded. During the attack, an RAF hangar was damaged, as were some British aircraft. The British threatened that in the event of another such attack, they would shoot down the attacking aircraft and bomb Israeli airfields, and as a result, Israeli aircraft did not attack Amman again for the rest of the war. Israel also bombed Arish, Gaza, Damascus, and Cairo. Israeli Boeing B-17 Flying Fortress bombers coming to Israel from Czechoslovakia bombed Egypt on their way to Israel.[124,125] According to Alan Dershowitz, Israeli planes focused on bombing military targets in these attacks, though Benny Morris wrote that an 11 June air raid on Damascus was indiscriminate.

Figure 22: *Northland in Greenland circa 1944 which became the Israeli INS Eilat*

Sea battles

At the outset of the war, the Israeli Navy consisted of three former Aliyah Bet ships that had been seized by the British and impounded in Haifa harbor, where they were tied up at the breakwater. Work on establishing a navy had begun shortly before Israeli independence, and the three ships were selected due to them having a military background – one, the INS *Eilat*, was an ex-US Coast Guard icebreaker, and the other two, the INS *Haganah* and INS *Wedgwood*, had been Royal Canadian Navy corvettes. The ships were put into minimum running condition by contractors dressed as stevedores and port personnel, who were able to work in the engine rooms and below deck. The work had to be clandestine to avoid arousing British suspicion. On 21 May 1948, the three ships set sail for Tel Aviv, and were made to look like ships that had been purchased by foreign owners for commercial use. In Tel Aviv, the ships were fitted with small field guns dating to the late 19th century and anti-aircraft guns. After the British left Haifa port on 30 June, Haifa became the main base of the Israeli Navy. In October 1948, a submarine chaser was purchased from the United States. The warships were manned by former merchant seamen, former crewmembers of Aliyah Bet ships, Israelis who had served in the Royal Navy during World War II, and foreign volunteers. The newly refurbished and crewed warships served on coastal patrol duties and bombarded Egyptian coastal installations in and around the Gaza area all the way to Port Said.[126]

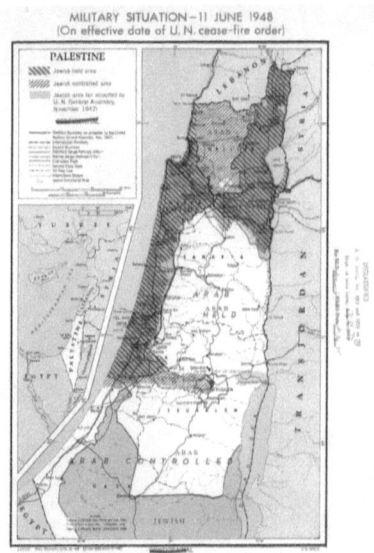

Figure 23: *Palestine Military Situation, June 11, 1948. Truman Papers*

End of the first phase

Throughout the following days, the Arabs were only able to make limited gains due to fierce Israeli resistance, and were quickly driven off their new holdings by Israeli counterattacks.

As the war progressed, the IDF managed to field more troops than the Arab forces. In July 1948, the IDF had 63,000 troops; by early spring 1949, they had 115,000. The Arab armies had an estimated 40,000 troops in July 1948, rising to 55,000 in October 1948, and slightly more by the spring of 1949.

Upon the implementation of the truce, the IDF had control over nine Arab cities and towns or mixed cities and towns: New Jerusalem, Jaffa, Haifa, Acre, Safed, Tiberias, Baysan (Beit She'an), Samakh and Yibna (Yavne). Another city, Jenin, was not occupied but its residents fled. The combined Arab forces captured 14 Jewish settlement points, but only one of them, Mishmar Ha-Yarden, was in the territory of the proposed Jewish State according to Resolution 181. Within the boundaries of the proposed Jewish state, there were twelve Arab villages which opposed Jewish control or were captured by the invading Arab armies, and in addition to them, the Lod Airport and pumping station near Antipatris, which were within the boundaries of the proposed Jewish state, were under the control of the Arabs. The IDF captured about 50 large Arab villages outside of the boundaries of the proposed Jewish State and a larger number of hamlets and Bedouin encampments. 350 square kilometers of the proposed Jewish State were under the control of the Arab forces, while 700 square kilometers of the proposed Arab State were under the control of the IDF. This figure ignores the Negev desert which wasn't under any absolute control of either side.[127]

In the period between the invasion and the first truce the Syrian army had 315 of its men killed and 400–500 injured; the Iraqi expeditionary force had 200 of its men killed and 500 injured; the Jordanian Arab Legion had 300 of its men killed and 400–500 (including irregulars and Palesinian volunteers fighting under the Jordanians); the Egyptian army had 600 of its men killed and 1,400 injured (including irregulars from the Muslim Brotherhood); the ALA, which returned to fight in early June, had 100 of its men killed or injured. 800 Jews were taken hostage by the Arabs and 1,300 Arabs were taken hostage by the Jews, mostly Palestinians.

First truce: 11 June – 8 July 1948

The UN declared a truce on 29 May, which came into effect on 11 June and lasted 28 days. The truce was designed to last 28 days and an arms embargo was declared with the intention that neither side would make any gains from the truce. Neither side respected the truce; both found ways around the restrictions placed on them. Both the Israelis and the Arabs used this time to improve their positions, a direct violation of the terms of the ceasefire.[128]

Reinforcements

Israeli Forces 1948[129]

Initial strength	29,677
4 June	40,825
17 July	63,586
7 October	88,033
28 October	92,275
2 December	106,900
23 December	107,652
30 December	108,300

At the time of the truce, the British view was that "the Jews are too weak in armament to achieve spectacular success". As the truce commenced, a British officer stationed in Haifa stated that the four-week-long truce "would certainly be exploited by the Jews to continue military training and reorganization while the Arabs would waste [them] feuding over the future divisions of the spoils".

Figure 24: *Altalena burning near Tel Aviv beach*

During the truce, the Israelis sought to bolster their forces by massive import of arms. The IDF was able to acquire weapons from Czechoslovakia as well as improve training of forces and reorganization of the army during this time. Yitzhak Rabin, an IDF commander at the time of the war and later Israel's fifth Prime Minister, stated "[w]ithout the arms from Czechoslovakia... it is very doubtful whether we would have been able to conduct the war".

The Israeli army increased its manpower from approximately 30,000–35,000 men to almost 65,000 during the truce due to mobilization and the constant immigration into Israel. It was also able to increase its arms supply to more than 25,000 rifles, 5,000 machine guns, and fifty million bullets. As well as violating the arms and personnel embargo, they also sent fresh units to the front lines, much as their Arab enemies did.

During the truce, Irgun attempted to bring in a private arms shipment aboard a ship called *Altalena*. When they refused to hand the arms to the Israeli government, Ben-Gurion ordered that the arms be confiscated by force if necessary. After meeting with armed resistance, the army was ordered by Ben-Gurion to sink the ship. Several Irgun members and IDF soldiers were killed in the fighting.

UN mediator Bernadotte

The ceasefire was overseen by UN mediator Folke Bernadotte and a team of UN Observers made up of army officers from Belgium, United States, Sweden and France. Bernadotte was voted in by the General Assembly to "assure the safety of the holy places, to safeguard the well being of the population, and to promote 'a peaceful adjustment of the future situation of Palestine'".

Folke Bernadotte reported:

> *During the period of the truce, three violations occurred ... of such a serious nature:*
>
> *1. the attempt by ...the Irgun Zvai Leumi to bring war materials and immigrants, including men of military age, into Palestine aboard the ship Altalena on 21 June...*
> *2. Another truce violation occurred through the refusal of Egyptian forces to permit the passage of relief convoys to Jewish settlements in the Negeb...*
> *3. The third violation of the truce arose as a result of the failure of the Transjordan and Iraqi forces to permit the flow of water to Jerusalem.*[130]

After the truce was in place, Bernadotte began to address the issue of achieving a political settlement. The main obstacles in his opinion were "the Arab world's continued rejection of the existence of a Jewish state, whatever its borders; Israel's new 'philosophy', based on its increasing military strength, of ignoring the partition boundaries and conquering what additional territory it could; and the emerging Palestinian Arab refugee problem".

Taking all the issues into account, Bernadotte presented a new partition plan. He proposed there be a Palestinian Arab state alongside Israel and that a "Union" "be established between the two sovereign states of Israel and Jordan (which now included the West Bank); that the Negev, or part of it, be included in the Arab state and that Western Galilee, or part of it, be included in Israel; that the whole of Jerusalem be part of the Arab state, with the Jewish areas enjoying municipal autonomy and that Lydda Airport and Haifa be 'free ports' – presumably free of Israeli or Arab sovereignty". Israel rejected the proposal, in particular the aspect of losing control of Jerusalem, but they did agree to extend the truce for another month. The Arabs rejected both the extension of the truce and the proposal.

Figure 25: *An Egyptian artillery piece captured by battalion 53 of the Givati Brigade.*

Second phase: 8–18 July 1948 ("Ten Day Battles")

On 8 July, the day before the expiration of the truce, Egyptian forces under General Muhammad Naguib renewed the war by attacking Negba.[131] The following day, Israeli air forces launched a simultaneous offensive on all three fronts, ranging from Quneitra to Arish and the Egyptian air force bombed the city of Tel Aviv.[132] During the fighting, the Israelis were able to open a lifeline to a number of besieged kibbutzim.

The fighting continued for ten days until the UN Security Council issued the Second Truce on 18 July. During those 10 days, the fighting was dominated by large-scale Israeli offensives and a defensive posture from the Arab side.

Southern front

In the south, the IDF carried out several offensives, including Operation An-Far and Operation Death to the Invader. The task of the 11th Brigades's 1st Battalion on the southern flank was to capture villages, and its operation ran smoothly, with but little resistance from local irregulars. According to Amnon Neumann, a Palmach veteran of the Southern front, hardly any Arab villages in the south fought back, due to the miserable poverty of their means and lack of weapons, and suffered expulsion.[133] What slight resistance was offered was

Figure 26: *Israeli soldiers in Lod (Lydda) or Ramle.*

quelled by an artillery barrage, followed by the storming of the village, whose residents were expelled and houses destroyed.[134]

On 12 July, the Egyptians launched an offensive action, and again attacked Negba, which they had previously failed to capture, using three infantry battalions, an armored battalion, and an artillery regiment. In the battle that followed, the Egyptians were repulsed, suffering 200–300 casualties, while the Israelis lost 5 dead and 16 wounded.[135]

After failing to take Negba, the Egyptians turned their attention to more isolated settlements and positions. On 14 July, an Egyptian attack on Gal On was driven off by a minefield and by resistance from Gal On's residents.[136]

The Egyptians then assaulted the lightly defended village of Be'erot Yitzhak. The Egyptians managed to penetrate the village perimeter, but the defenders concentrated in an inner position in the village and fought off the Egyptian advance until IDF reinforcements arrived and drove out the attackers. The Egyptians suffered an estimated 200 casualties, while the Israelis had 17 dead and 15 wounded. The battle was one of Egypt's last offensive actions during the war, and the Egyptians did not attack any Israeli villages following this battle.

Figure 27: *Israeli armored vehicles in Lydda airport after the town's capture by Israeli forces.*

Lydda and al-Ramla

On 10 July, Glubb Pasha ordered the defending Arab Legion troops to "make arrangements...for a phony war". Israeli Operation Danny was the most important Israeli offensive, aimed at securing and enlarging the corridor between Jerusalem and Tel Aviv by capturing the roadside cities Lod (Lydda) and Ramle. In a second planned stage of the operation the fortified positions of Latrun – overlooking the Tel Aviv-Jerusalem highway – and the city of Ramallah were also to be captured. Hadita, near Latrun, was captured by the Israelis at a cost of 9 dead.

The objectives of Operation Danny were to capture territory east of Tel Aviv and then to push inland and relieve the Jewish population and forces in Jerusalem. Lydda had become an important military center in the region, lending support to Arab military activities elsewhere, and Ramle was one of the main obstacles blocking Jewish transportation. Lydda was defended by a local militia of around 1,000 residents, with an Arab Legion contingent of 125–300.[137]

The IDF forces gathered to attack the city numbered around 8,000. It was the first operation where several brigades were involved. The city was attacked from the north via Majdal al-Sadiq and al-Muzayri'a, and from the east via Khulda, al-Qubab, Jimzu and Daniyal. Bombers were also used for the first time in the conflict to bombard the city. The IDF captured the city on 11 July.

Figure 28: *Arab forces surrender to the victorious Israelis in Ramla.*

Up to 450 Arabs and 9–10 Israeli soldiers were killed. The next day, Ramle fell. The civilian populations of Lydda and Ramle fled or were expelled to the Arab front lines, and following resistance in Lydda, the population there was expelled without provision of transport vehicles; some of the evictees died on the long walk under the hot July sun.

On 15–16 July, an attack on Latrun took place but did not manage to occupy the fort. A desperate second attempt occurred on 18 July by units from the Yiftach Brigade equipped with armored vehicles, including two Cromwell tanks, but that attack also failed. Despite the second truce, which began on 18 July, the Israeli efforts to conquer Latrun continued until 20 July.

Jerusalem

Operation Kedem's aim was to secure the Old City of Jerusalem, but fewer resources were allocated. The operation failed.[138] Originally the operation was to begin on 8 July, immediately after the first truce, by Irgun and Lehi forces. However, it was delayed by David Shaltiel, possibly because he did not trust their ability after their failure to capture Deir Yassin without Haganah assistance.

Irgun forces commanded by Yehuda Lapidot were to break through at the New Gate, Lehi was to break through the wall stretching from the New Gate to the Jaffa Gate, and the Beit Horon Battalion was to strike from Mount Zion.

Figure 29: *Beit Horon Battalion soldiers in the Russian Compound in Jerusalem, 1948*

The battle was planned to begin on the Shabbat, at 20:00 on 16 July, two days before the second ceasefire of the war. The plan went wrong from the beginning and was postponed first to 23:00 and then to midnight. It was not until 02:30 that the battle actually began. The Irgun managed to break through at the New Gate, but the other forces failed in their missions. At 05:45 on 17 July, Shaltiel ordered a retreat and to cease hostilities.

On 14 July 1948, Irgun occupied the Arab village of Malha after a fierce battle. Several hours later, the Arabs launched a counterattack, but Israeli reinforcements arrived, and the village was retaken at a cost of 17 dead.

Southern Galilee

The second plan was Operation Dekel, which was aimed at capturing the Lower Galilee including Nazareth. Nazareth was captured on 16 July, and by the time the second truce took effect at 19:00 18 July, the whole Lower Galilee from Haifa Bay to the Sea of Galilee was captured by Israel.

Eastern Galilee

Operation Brosh was launched in a failed attempt to dislodge Syrian forces from the Eastern Galilee and the Benot Yaakov Bridge. During the operation, 200 Syrians and 100 Israelis were killed. The Israeli Air Force also bombed Damascus for the first time.

Second truce: 18 July – 15 October 1948

At 19:00 on 18 July, the second truce of the conflict went into effect after intense diplomatic efforts by the UN.

On 16 September, Count Folke Bernadotte proposed a new partition for Palestine in which the Negev would be divided between Jordan and Egypt, and Jordan would annex Lydda and Ramla. There would be a Jewish state in the whole of Galilee, with the frontier running from Faluja northeast towards Ramla and Lydda. Jerusalem would be internationalized, with municipal autonomy for the city's Jewish and Arab inhabitants, the Port of Haifa would be a free port, and Lydda Airport would be a free airport. All Palestinian refugees would be granted the right of return, and those who chose not to return would be compensated for lost property. The UN would control and regulate Jewish immigration.

The plan was once again rejected by both sides. On the next day, 17 September, Bernadotte was assassinated in Jerusalem by the militant Zionist group Lehi. A four-man team ambushed Bernadotte's motorcade in Jerusalem, killing him and a French UN observer sitting next to him. Lehi saw Bernadotte as a British and Arab puppet, and thus a serious threat to the emerging State of Israel, and feared that the provisional Israeli government would accept the plan, which it considered disastrous. Unbeknownst to Lehi, the government had already decided to reject it and resume combat in a month. Bernadotte's deputy, American Ralph Bunche, replaced him.[139,140,141]

On 22 September 1948, the Provisional State Council of Israel passed the Area of Jurisdiction and Powers Ordnance, 5708–1948. The law officially added to Israel's size by annexing all land it had captured since the war began. It also declared that from then on, any part of Palestine captured by the Israeli army would automatically become part of Israel.

Little triangle pocket

The Arab villagers of the area known as the "Little Triangle" south of Haifa, repeatedly fired at Israeli traffic along the main road from Tel Aviv to Haifa and were supplied by the Iraqis from northern Samaria. The sniping at traffic continued during the Second Truce. The poorly planned assaults on 18 June and 8 July had failed to dislodge Arab militia from their superior positions. The Israelis launched Operation Shoter on 24 July in order to gain control of the main road to Haifa and to destroy all the enemy in the area. Israeli assaults on 24 and 25 July were beaten back by stiff resistance. The Israelis then broke the Arab defenses with an infantry and armour assault backed by heavy artillery shelling and aerial bombing. Three Arab villages surrendered, and most of the inhabitants fled before and during the attack. The Israeli soldiers and aircraft struck

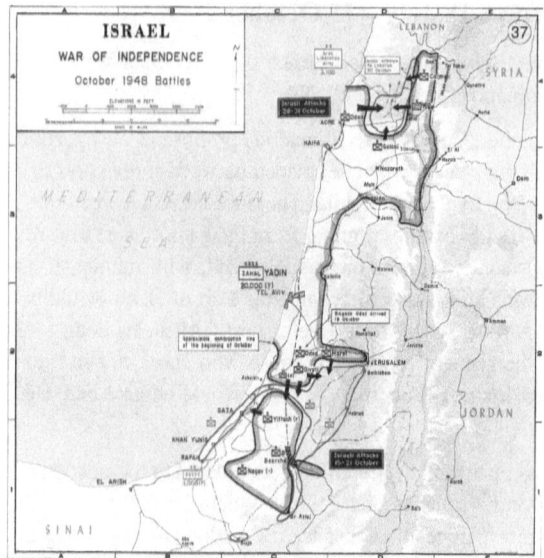

Figure 30: *October battles*

at one of the Arab retreat routes, killing 60 Arab soldiers.Wikipedia:Accuracy dispute#Disputed statement. Most of the inhabitants fled before and during the attack, reaching northern Samaria; hundreds were forcibly expelled during the following days. At least a hundred militiamen and civilians were killed.

The Arabs claimed that the Israelis had massacred Arab civilians, but the Israelis rejected the claims.Wikipedia:Accuracy dispute#Disputed statement A United Nations investigation found no evidence of a massacre. Following the operation, the Tel Aviv-Haifa road was open to Israeli military and civilian traffic, and Arab roadblocks along the route were removed. Traffic along the Haifa-Hadera coastal railway was also restored.

Third phase: 15 October 1948 – 10 March 1949

Israel launched a series of military operations to drive out the Arab armies and secure the northern and southern borders of Israel.

Northern front – Galilee

On 22 October, the third truce went into effect.[142] Irregular Arab forces refused to recognize the truce, and continued to harass Israeli forces and settlements in the north. On the same day that the truce came into effect, the Arab Liberation Army violated the truce by attacking Manara, capturing the

Figure 31: *An Israeli mortar team outside Safsaf in October 1948.*

Figure 32: *Israeli soldiers attack Sasa during Operation Hiram, October 1948.*

strongpoint of Sheikh Abed, repulsing counterattacks by local Israeli units, and ambushed Israeli forces attempting to relieve Manara. The IDF's Carmeli Brigade lost 33 dead and 40 wounded.[143] Manara and Misgav Am were totally cut off, and Israel's protests at the UN failed to change the situation.

On 24 October, the IDF launched Operation Hiram and captured the entire upper Galilee area, driving the ALA and Lebanese Army back to Lebanon, and ambushing and destroying an entire Syrian battalion. The Israeli force of four infantry brigades was commanded by Moshe Carmel. The entire operation lasted just 60 hours, during which numerous villages were captured, often after locals or Arab forces put up resistance. Arab losses were estimated at 400 dead and 550 taken prisoner, with low Israeli casualties.

Some prisoners were reportedly executed by the Israeli forces. An estimated 50,000 Palestinian refugees fled into Lebanon, some of them fleeing ahead of the advancing forces, and some expelled from villages which had resisted, while the Arab inhabitants of those villages which had remained at peace were allowed to remain and became Israeli citizens. The villagers of Iqrit and Birim were persuaded to leave their homes by Israeli authorities, who promised them that they would be allowed to return. Israel eventually decided not to allow them to return, and offered them financial compensation, which they refused to accept.

At the end of the month, the IDF had captured the whole of Galilee, driven all Lebanese forces out of Israel, and had advanced 5 miles (8.0 km) into Lebanon to the Litani River, occupying thirteen Lebanese villages. In the village of Hula, two Israeli officers killed between 35 and 58 prisoners as retaliation for the Haifa Oil Refinery massacre. Both officers were later put on trial for their actions.

Negev

Israel launched a series of military operations to drive out the Arab armies and secure the borders of Israel. However, invading the West Bank might have brought into the borders of the expanding State of Israel a massive Arab population it could not absorb. The Negev desert was an empty space for expansion, so the main war effort shifted to Negev from early October.[144] Israel decided to destroy or at least drive out the Egyptian expeditionary force since the Egyptian front lines were too vulnerable as permanent borders.

On 15 October, the IDF launched Operation Yoav in the northern Negev. Its goal was to drive a wedge between the Egyptian forces along the coast and the Beersheba-Hebron-Jerusalem road and ultimately to conquer the whole Negev. This was a special concern on the Israeli part because of a British diplomatic campaign to have the entire Negev handed over to Egypt and Jordan, and which

Figure 33: *Israeli troops occupying abandoned Egyptian trenches at Huleiqat, October 1948.*

Figure 34: *IDF forces in Beersheba during Operation Yoav.*

Figure 35: *IDF artillery unit in the Negev*

Figure 36: *IDF forces near Bayt Nattif (near Hebron) after it was captured. Oct 1948.*

thus made Ben-Gurion anxious to have Israeli forces in control of the Negev as soon as possible.

Operation Yoav was headed by the Southern Front commander Yigal Allon. Committed to Yoav were three infantry and one armoured brigades, who were given the task of breaking through the Egyptian lines. The Egyptian positions were badly weakened by the lack of a defense in depth, which meant that once the IDF had broken through the Egyptian lines, there was little to stop them. The operation was a huge success, shattering the Egyptian ranks and forcing the Egyptian Army from the northern Negev, Beersheba and Ashdod.

In the so-called "Faluja Pocket", an encircled Egyptian force was able to hold out for four months until the 1949 Armistice Agreements, when the village was peacefully transferred to Israel and the Egyptian troops left. Four warships of the Israeli Navy provided support by bombarding Egyptian shore installations in the Ashkelon area, and preventing the Egyptian Navy from evacuating retreating Egyptian troops by sea.

On 19 October, Operation Ha-Har commenced in the Jerusalem Corridor, while a naval battle also took place near Majdal (now Ashkelon), with three Israeli corvettes facing an Egyptian corvette with air support. An Israeli sailor was killed and four wounded, and two of the ships were damaged. One Egyptian plane was shot down, but the corvette escaped. Israeli naval vessels also shelled Majdal on 17 October, and Gaza on 21 October, with air support from the Israeli Air Force. The same day, the IDF captured Beersheba, and took 120 Egyptian soldiers prisoner. On 22 October, Israeli naval commandos using explosive boats sank the Egyptian flagship *Emir Farouk*, and damaged an Egyptian minesweeper.

On 9 November 1948, the IDF launched Operation Shmone to capture the Tegart fort in the village of Iraq Suwaydan. The fort's Egyptian defenders had previously repulsed eight attempts to take it, including two during Operation Yoav. Israeli forces bombarded the fort before an assault with artillery and airstrikes by B-17 bombers. After breaching the outlying fences without resistance, the Israelis blew a hole in the fort's outer wall, prompting the 180 Egyptian soldiers manning the fort to surrender without a fight. The defeat prompted the Egyptians to evacuate several nearby positions, including hills the IDF had failed to take by force. Meanwhile, IDF forces took Iraq Suwaydan itself after a fierce battle, losing 6 dead and 14 wounded.

From 5 to 7 December, the IDF conducted Operation Assaf to take control of the Western Negev. The main assaults were spearheaded by mechanized forces, while Golani Brigade infantry covered the rear. An Egyptian counterattack was repulsed. The Egyptians planned another counterattack, but it failed after Israeli aerial reconnaissance revealed Egyptian preparations,

Figure 37: *An Israeli convoy in the Negev during Operation Horev*

and the Israelis launched a preemptive strike. About 100 Egyptians were killed, and 5 tanks were destroyed, with the Israelis losing 5 killed and 30 wounded.Wikipedia:Citation needed

On 22 December, the IDF launched Operation Horev (also called Operation Ayin). The goal of the operation was to drive all remaining Egyptian forces from the Negev, destroying the Egyptian threat on Israel's southern communities and forcing the Egyptians into a ceasefire. During five days of fighting, the Israelis secured the Western Negev, expelling all Egyptian forces from the area.

Israeli forces subsequently launched raids into the Nitzana area, and entered the Sinai Peninsula on 28 December. The IDF captured Umm Katef and Abu Ageila, and advanced north towards Al Arish, with the goal of encircling the entire Egyptian expeditionary force. Israeli forces pulled out of the Sinai on 2 January 1949 following joint British-American pressure and a British threat of military action. IDF forces regrouped at the border with the Gaza Strip. Israeli forces attacked Rafah the following day, and after several days of fighting, Egyptian forces in the Gaza Strip were surrounded. The Egyptians agreed to negotiate a ceasefire on 7 January, and the IDF subsequently pulled out of Gaza. According to Morris, *"the inequitable and unfair rules of engagement: the Arabs could launch offensives with impunity, but international interventions always hampered and restrained Israel's counterattacks."*[145]

Figure 38: *The funeral of a Royal Air Force pilot killed during a clash with the Israeli Air Force.*

On 28 December, the Alexandroni Brigade failed to take the Falluja Pocket, but managed to seize Iraq el-Manshiyeh and temporarily hold it. The Egyptians counterattacked, but were mistaken for a friendly force and allowed to advance, trapping a large number of men. The Israelis lost 87 soldiers.Wikipedia:Citation needed

On 5 March, Operation Uvda was launched following nearly a month of reconnaissance, with the goal of securing the Southern Negev from Jordan. The IDF entered and secured the territory, but did not meet significant resistance along the way, as the area was already designated to be part of the Jewish state in the UN Partition Plan, and the operation meant to establish Israeli sovereignty over the territory rather than actually conquer it. The Golani, Negev, and Alexandroni brigades participated in the operation, together with some smaller units and with naval support.

On 10 March, Israeli forces secured the Southern Negev, reaching the southern tip of Palestine: Umm Rashrash on the Red Sea (where Eilat was built later) and taking it without a battle. Israeli soldiers raised a hand-made Israeli flag ("The Ink Flag") at 16:00 on 10 March, claiming Umm Rashrash for Israel. The raising of the Ink Flag is considered to be the end of the war.

Anglo-Israeli air clashes

As the fighting progressed and Israel mounted an incursion into the Sinai, the Royal Air Force began conducting almost daily reconnaissance missions over Israel and the Sinai. RAF reconnaissance aircraft took off from Egyptian airbases and sometimes flew alongside Royal Egyptian Air Force planes. High-flying British aircraft frequently flew over Haifa and Ramat David Airbase, and became known to the Israelis as the "shuftykeit."

On 20 November 1948, an unarmed RAF photo-reconnaissance De Havilland Mosquito of No. 13 Squadron RAF was shot down by an Israeli Air Force P-51 Mustang flown by American volunteer Wayne Peake as it flew over the Galilee towards Hatzor Airbase. Peake opened fire with his cannons, causing a fire to break out in the port engine. The aircraft turned to sea and lowered its altitude, then exploded and crashed off Ashdod. The pilot and navigator were both killed.[146]

Just before noon on 7 January 1949, four Spitfire FR18s from No. 208 Squadron RAF on a reconnaissance mission in the Deir al-Balah area flew over an Israeli convoy that had been attacked by five Egyptian Spitfires fifteen minutes earlier. The pilots had spotted smoking vehicles and were drawn to the scene out of curiosity. Two planes dived to below 500 feet altitude to take pictures of the convoy, while the remaining two covered them from 1,500 feet.[147]

Israeli soldiers on the ground, alerted by the sound of the approaching Spitfires and fearing another Egyptian air attack, opened fire with machine guns. One Spitfire was shot down by a tank-mounted machine gun, while the other was lightly damaged and rapidly pulled up. The remaining three Spitfires were then attacked by patrolling IAF Spitfires flown by Slick Goodlin and John McElroy, volunteers from the United States and Canada respectively. All three Spitfires were shot down, and one pilot was killed.

Two pilots were captured by Israeli soldiers and taken to Tel Aviv for interrogation, and were later released. Another was rescued by Bedouins and handed over to the Egyptian Army, which turned him over to the RAF. Later that day, four RAF Spitfires from the same squadron escorted by seven Hawker Tempests from No. 213 Squadron RAF and eight from No. 6 Squadron RAF went searching for the lost planes, and were attacked by four IAF Spitfires. The Israeli formation was led by Ezer Weizman. The remaining three were manned by Weizman's wingman Alex Jacobs and American volunteers Bill Schroeder and Caesar Dangott. The Tempests found they could not jettison their external fuel tanks, and some had non-operational guns. Schroeder shot down a British Tempest, killing pilot David Tattersfield, and Weizman severely damaged a British plane flown by Douglas Liquorish. Weizman's plane and two other British aircraft also suffered light damage during the engagement. The battle ended after the British wiggled their wings to be more clearly identified, and the Israelis eventually realized the danger of their situation and disengaged, returning to Hatzor Airbase.

Israeli Prime Minister David Ben-Gurion personally ordered the wrecks of the RAF fighters that had been shot down to be dragged into Israeli territory. Israeli troops subsequently visited the crash sites, removed various parts, and buried the other aircraft. However, the Israelis did not manage to conceal the wrecks in time to prevent British reconnaissance planes from photographing them. An RAF salvage team was deployed to recover the wrecks, entering Israeli territory during their search. Two were discovered inside Egypt, while Tattersfield's Tempest was found north of Nirim, four miles inside Israel. Interviews with local Arabs confirmed that the Israelis had visited the crash sites to remove and bury the wrecks. Tattersfield was initially buried near the wreckage, but his body was later removed and reburied at the British War Cemetery in Ramla.[148]

In response, the RAF readied all Tempests and Spitfires to attack any IAF aircraft they encountered and bomb IAF airfields. British troops in the Middle East were placed on high alert with all leave cancelled, and British citizens were advised to leave Israel. The Royal Navy was also placed on high alert. At Hatzor Airbase, the general consensus among the pilots, most of whom had flown with or alongside the RAF during World War II, was that the RAF would not allow the loss of five aircraft and two pilots to go without retaliation, and would probably attack the base at dawn the next day. That night, in anticipation of an impending British attack, some pilots decided not to offer any resistance and left the base, while others prepared their Spitfires and were strapped into the cockpits at dawn, preparing to repel a retaliatory airstrike. However, despite pressure from the squadrons involved in the incidents, British commanders refused to authorize any retaliatory strikes.[149]

The day following the incident, British pilots were issued a directive to regard any Israeli aircraft infiltrating Egyptian or Jordanian airspace as hostile and to shoot them down, but were also ordered to avoid activity close to Israel's borders. Later in January 1949, the British managed to prevent the delivery of aviation spirit and other essential fuels to Israel in retaliation for the incident. The British Foreign Office presented the Israeli government with a demand for compensation over the loss of personnel and equipment.[150]

UN Resolution 194

In December 1948, the UN General Assembly passed Resolution 194. It called to establish a UN Conciliation Commission to facilitate peace between Israel and Arab states. However, many of the resolution's articles were not fulfilled, since these were opposed by Israel, rejected by the Arab states, or were overshadowed by war as the 1948 conflict continued.

Weapons

Largely leftover World War II era weapons were used by both sides. Egypt had some British equipment; the Syrian army had some French. German, Czechoslovak and British equipment was used by Israel.

Type	Arab armies	IDF
Tanks	Matilda tanks, R-39s, FT-17s, R35s, Panzer IVs (dug in and used as stationary gun emplacements by Egypt), Fiat M13/-40, Sherman M4, M-22, Vickers MK-6.	Cromwell tanks, H39s, M4 Sherman
APCs/-IFVs	British World War II era trucks, Humber Mk III & IV, Automitrailleuses Dodge/-Bich type, improvised armored cars/-trucks, Marmon-Herrington Armoured Cars, Universal Carriers, Lloyd Towing Carriers	British World War II era trucks, improvised armored cars/trucks, White M3A1 Scout Cars, Daimler Armoured Cars, M3 Half-tracks, IHC M14 Half-tracks, M5 Half-tracks
Artillery	Mortars, 15 cm sIG33 auf Pz IIs, 25 mm anti-tank guns on Bren carriers, improvised self-propelled guns used by Syrians in 1948–49, 65 mm mountain guns on Lorraine 38L *chenillettes*, 2-pounder anti-tank guns, 6-pounder anti-tank guns	Mortars, 2-inch (51 mm) British mortars, 65 mm French howitzers (*Napoleonchiks*), 120 mm French mortars, Davidka mortars
Aircraft	Spitfires, T-6 Texans, C-47 Dakotas, Hawker Hurricanes, Avro Ansons	Spitfires, Avia S-199s, B-17 Flying Fortresses, P-51 Mustangs, C-47 Dakotas
Small Arms	Lee–Enfield rifles, Bren Guns, Sten guns, MAS 36s	Sten guns, Mills grenades, Karabiner 98k (Czech copies), Bren Guns, MG-34 Machine guns, Thompson submachine guns, Lee–Enfield rifles, Molotov cocktails, PIAT anti-tank infantry weapon

Aftermath

1949 Armistice Agreements

In 1949, Israel signed separate armistices with Egypt on 24 February, Lebanon on 23 March, Jordan on 3 April, and Syria on 20 July. The Armistice Demarcation Lines, as set by the agreements, saw the territory under Israeli control encompassing approximately three-quarters of the prior British administered Mandate as it stood after Transjordan's independence in 1946. Israel controlled territories of about one-third more than was allocated to the Jewish State under the UN partition proposal.[151] After the armistices, Israel had control over 78% of the territory comprising former Mandatory Palestine or some 8,000 square miles (21,000 km^2), including the entire Galilee and Jezreel Valley in the north, whole Negev in south, West Jerusalem and the coastal plain in the center.

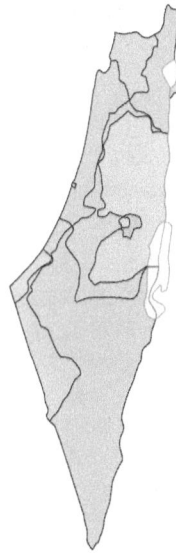

Figure 39:

Boundaries defined in the 1947 UN Partition Plan for Palestine:
Area assigned for a Jewish state
Area assigned for an Arab state
Planned Corpus separatum with the intention
that Jerusalem would be neither Jewish nor Arab

Armistice Demarcation Lines of 1949 (Green Line):
Israeli controlled territory from 1949
Egyptian and Jordanian controlled territory from 1948 until 1967

The armistice lines were known afterwards as the "Green Line". The Gaza Strip and the West Bank (including East Jerusalem) were occupied by Egypt and Jordan respectively. The United Nations Truce Supervision Organization and Mixed Armistice Commissions were set up to monitor ceasefires, supervise the armistice agreements, to prevent isolated incidents from escalating, and assist other UN peacekeeping operations in the region.

Just before the signing of the Israel-Jordan armistice agreement, general Yigal Allon proposed to conquer the West Bank up to the Jordan River as the natural, defensible border of the state. Ben-Gurion refused, although he was aware that the IDF was militarily strong enough to carry out the conquest. He feared the reaction of Western powers and wanted to maintain good relations with the

United States and not to provoke the British. More, the results of the war were already satisfactory and Israeli leaders had to build a nation.

Casualties

Israel lost 6,373 of its people, about 1% of its population at the time, in the war. About 4,000 were soldiers and the rest were civilians. Around 2,000 were Holocaust survivors.

The exact number of Arab casualties is unknown. One estimate places the Arab death toll at 7,000, including 3,000 Palestinians, 2,000 Egyptians, 1,000 Jordanians, and 1,000 Syrians. In 1958, Palestinian historian Aref al-Aref calculated that the Arab armies' combined losses amounted to 3,700, with Egypt losing 961 regular and 200 irregular soldiers and Jordan losing 362 regulars and 200 irregulars. According to Henry Laurens, the Palestinians suffered double the Jewish losses, with 13,000 dead, 1,953 of whom are known to have died in combat situations. Of the remainder, 4,004 remain nameless but the place, tally and date of their death is known, and a further 7,043, for whom only the place of death is known, not their identities nor the date of their death. According to Laurens, the largest part of Palestinian casualties consisted of non-combatants and corresponds to the successful operations of the Israelis.[152]

Demographic outcome

Palestinian Arabs

1948 Palestinian exodus

Main Articles

- 1947–48 civil war
- 1948 Arab–Israeli War
- 1948 Palestine war
- Causes of the exodus
- Nakba Day
- Palestinian refugee
- Palestine refugee camps
- Palestinian right of return
- Palestinian return to Israel
- Present absentee

- Transfer Committee
- Resolution 194

Background

- Mandatory Palestine
- Israeli Declaration of Independence
- Israeli–Palestinian conflict history
- New Historians
- Palestine · Plan Dalet
- 1947 partition plan · UNRWA

Key incidents

- Battle of Haifa
- Deir Yassin massacre
- Exodus from Lydda and Ramle

Notable writers

- Aref al-Aref · Yoav Gelber
- Efraim Karsh · Walid Khalidi
- Nur-eldeen Masalha · Benny Morris
- Ilan Pappé · Tom Segev
- Avraham Sela · Avi Shlaim

Related categories/lists

- List of depopulated villages

Related templates

- Palestinians

- v
- t
- e[153]

During the 1947–1948 Civil War in Mandatory Palestine and the 1948 Arab–Israeli War that followed, around 750,000 Palestinian Arabs fled or were expelled from their homes, out of approximately 1,200,000 Arabs living in former British Mandate of Palestine. In 1951, the UN Conciliation Commission for Palestine estimated that the number of Palestinian refugees displaced from Israel was 711,000.[154]

This number did not include displaced Palestinians inside Israeli-held territory. More than 400 Arab villages, and about ten Jewish villages and neighborhoods, were depopulated during the Arab–Israeli conflict, most of them during 1948. According to estimate based on earlier census, the total Muslim population in Palestine was 1,143,336 in 1947.[155] The causes of the 1948 Palestinian exodus are a controversial topic among historians.[156] After the war, around 156,000 Arabs remained in Israel and became Israeli citizens.

Displaced Palestinian Arabs, known as Palestinian refugees, were settled in Palestinian refugee camps throughout the Arab world. The United Nations established UNRWA as a relief and human development agency tasked with providing humanitarian assistance to Palestinian refugees. Arab nations refused to absorb Palestinian refugees, instead keeping them in refugee camps while insisting that they be allowed to return.

Refugee status was also passed on to their descendants, who were also largely denied citizenship in Arab states, except in Jordan. The Arab League instructed its members to deny Palestinians citizenship "to avoid dissolution of their identity and protect their right of return to their homeland." More than 1.4 million Palestinians still live in 58 recognized refugee camps, while more than 5 million Palestinians live outside Israel and the Palestinian territories.

The Palestinian refugee problem and debate about the Palestinian right of return are also major issues of the Arab–Israeli conflict. Palestinians and their supporters have staged annual demonstrations and commemorations on 15 May of each year, which is known to them as "Nakba Day". The popularity and number of participants in these annual Nakba demonstrations has varied over time. During the Second Intifada after the failure of the Camp David 2000 Summit, the attendance at the demonstrations against Israel increased.

Jews

Jewish exodus from Arab and Muslim countries
Communities

• Mizrahi
  • Persian
  • Baghdadi
• Sephardi

Background

• Jews under Muslim rule
  • Ottoman
  • Old Yishuv
• Antisemitism in the Arab World
  • The Holocaust in Libya
  • Farhud
• Zionism
• Arab–Israeli conflict
  • 1948 Arab–Israeli War
  • Suez Crisis
  • Six-Day War
• Algerian War

Main events
• Magic Carpet (Yemen)
• Ezra and Nehemiah (Iraq)
• Lebanese exodus
• Egyptian exodus
• Moroccan exodus   • Operation Yachin
• Pied-Noir (Algeria)
• Day of Revenge (Libya)
• Exodus of Iran's Jews
Resettlement
• Aliyah
• HIAS • Mossad LeAliyah Bet • JDC   • Mizrahi Jews in Israel
• Iranian • Iraqi • Kurdish • Moroccan

• Syrian • Turkish • Yemenite
  • Transition camps
  • Immigrant camps
  • Development towns
  • Austerity

• North African Jews in France
Advocation
• Remembrance Day
• JIMENA
• JJAC
• WOJAC
• *The Forgotten Refugees*
Related topics
• Arab Jews
• Musta'arabi
• Maghrebi Jews
• Berber Jews
• v̲
• t̲
• e̲[157]

During the 1948 War, around 10,000 Jews were forced to evacuate their homes from Arab dominated parts of former Mandatory Palestine. But in the three years from May 1948 to the end of 1951, 700,000 Jews settled in Israel, mainly along the borders and in former Arab lands, doubling the Jewish population there. Of these, upwards of 300,000 arrived from Asian and North African nations.[158,159] Among them, the largest group (over 100,000) was from Iraq. The remaining came mostly from Europe, including 136,000 from the 250,000 displaced Jews of World War II living in refugee camps and urban centers in Germany, Austria, and Italy,[160] and more than 270,000 coming from Eastern Europe,[161] mainly Romania and Poland (over 100,000 each). On the establishment of the state, a top priority was given to a policy for the "ingathering of exiles", and the Mossad LeAliyah Bet gave key assistance to the Jewish Agency to organize immigrants from Europe and the Middle East, and arrange for their transport to Israel. For Ben-Gurion, a fundamental defect of the State was that 'it lacked Jews'.[162]

Jewish immigrants from Arab and Muslim countries left for numerous reasons. The war's outcome had exacerbated Arab hostilities to local Jewish communities. News of the victory aroused messianic expectations in Libya and Yemen; Zionism had taken root in many countries; active incentives for making aliyah formed a key part of Israeli policy; and better economic prospects and security were to be expected from a Jewish state. Some Arab governments, Egypt, for example, held their Jewish communities hostage at times. Persecution, political instability, and news of a number of violent pogroms also played a role. Some 800,000–1,000,000 Jews eventually left the Arab world over the next three decades as a result of these various factors. Approximately 680,000 of them immigrated to Israel; the rest mostly settled in Europe (mainly France) or the Americas.

Israel initially relied on Jewish Agency-run tent camps known as immigrant camps to accommodate displaced Jews from Europe and Muslim nations. In the 1950s, these were transformed into transition camps ("Ma'abarot"), where living conditions were improved and tents were replaced with tin dwellings. Unlike the situation in the immigrant camps, when the Jewish Agency provided for immigrants, residents of the transition camps were required to provide for themselves. These camps began to decline in 1952, with the last one closing in 1963. The camps were largely transformed into permanent settlements known as development towns, while others were absorbed as neighborhoods of the towns they were attached to, and the residents were given permanent housing in these towns and neighborhoods.

Most development towns eventually grew into cities. Some Jewish immigrants were also given the vacant homes of Palestinian refugees. There were also attempts to settle Jewish refugees from Arab and Muslim countries in moshavim (cooperative farming villages), though these efforts were only partially successful, as they had historically been craftsmen and merchants in their home countries, and did not traditionally engage in farm work.

Historiography

After the war, Israeli and Palestinian historiographies differed on the interpretation of the events of 1948:[163] in the West the majority view was of a tiny group of vastly outnumbered and ill-equipped Jews fighting off the massed strength of the invading Arab armies; it was also widely believed that the Palestinian Arabs left their homes on the instruction of their leaders.[164]

From 1980, with the opening of the Israeli and British archives, some Israeli historians have developed a different account of the period. In particular, the role played by Abdullah I of Jordan, the British government, the Arab aims during the war, the balance of force and the events related to the Palestinian exodus have been nuanced or given new interpretations. Some of them are still hotly debated among historians and commentators of the conflict today.[165]

In popular culture

A 2015 PBS documentary, *A Wing and a Prayer*, depicts the Al Schwimmer-led airborne smuggling missions to arm Israel.

The film *Cast a Giant Shadow* tells the story of an American colonel who was instrumental in the Israeli victory.

Maps

- Operation Sinai 22 December 1948 – 7 January 1949[166]

Notes

References

<templatestyles src="Refbegin/styles.css" />

- Adrian, Nathan (2004). *Britain, Israel and Anglo-Jewry 1949–57*. Routledge
- Bickerton, Ian and Hill, Maria (2003). *Contested Spaces: The Arab-Israeli Conflict*. McGraw-Hill. <templatestyles src="Module:Citation/CS1/styles.css" />ISBN 978-0-07-471217-7
- Black, Ian (1992). *Israel's Secret Wars: A History of Israel's Intelligence Services*. Grove Press. <templatestyles src="Module:Citation/CS1/styles.css" />ISBN 978-0-8021-3286-4
- Bowyer Bell, John (1996). *Terror Out of Zion: The Fight For Israeli Independence*. Transaction Publishers. <templatestyles src="Module:Citation/CS1/styles.css" />ISBN 978-1-56000-870-5
- Bregman, Ahron (2002). *Israel's Wars: A History Since 1947*. London: Routledge. <templatestyles src="Module:Citation/CS1/styles.css" />ISBN 978-0-415-28716-6
- Brown, Judith and Louis, Roger (1999). *The Oxford History of the British Empire*. Oxford: Oxford University Press. <templatestyles src="Module:Citation/CS1/styles.css" />ISBN 978-0-19-820564-7

- Cragg, Kenneth. *Palestine. The Prize and Price of Zion*. Cassel, 1997. <templatestyles src="Module:Citation/CS1/styles.css" />ISBN 978-0-304-70075-2
- van Creveld, Martin (2004). *Moshe Dayan*. Weidenfeld & Nicolson. <templatestyles src="Module:Citation/CS1/styles.css" />ISBN 978-0-297-84669-7
- Collins, Larry and Lapierre, Dominique (1973). *O Jerusalem!",* Pan Books. *<templatestyles src="Module:Citation/CS1/styles.css" />ISBN 978-0-330-23514-3*
- El-Nawawy, Mohammed (2002), *The Israeli-Egyptian Peace Process in the Reporting of Western Journalists*, Ablex/Greenwood, <templatestyles src="Module:Citation/CS1/styles.css" />ISBN 978-1-56750-544-3
- Geddes, Charles L. (1991). *A Documentary History of the Arab-Israeli Conflict*. Praeger. <templatestyles src="Module:Citation/CS1/styles.css" />ISBN 978-0-275-93858-1
- Gelber, Yoav (1997). *Jewish-Transjordanian Relations 1921–48: Alliance of Bars Sinister*. London: Routledge. <templatestyles src="Module:Citation/CS1/styles.css" />ISBN 978-0-7146-4675-6
- Gelber, Yoav (2004). *Israeli-Jordanian Dialogue, 1948–1953: Cooperation, Conspiracy, or Collusion?*. Sussex Academic Press.
- Gelber, Yoav (2004) *"Independence Versus Nakba"*; Kinneret Zmora-Bitan Dvir Publishing, <templatestyles src="Module:Citation/CS1/styles.css" />ISBN 965-517-190-6
- Gelber, Yoav (2006). *Palestine 1948. War, Escape and the Emergence of the Palestinian Refugee Problem*. Sussex Academic Press. <templatestyles src="Module:Citation/CS1/styles.css" />ISBN 978-1-84519-075-0
- Gershoni, Haim (1989). *Israel: The Way it was*. Associated University Presses.
- Gilbert, Martin (1998). *Israel: A History*[167]. Black Swan. <templatestyles src="Module:Citation/CS1/styles.css" />ISBN 978-0-552-99545-0
- Gold, Dore (2007), *The Fight for Jerusalem: Radical Islam, the West, and the Future of the Holy City*, Regnery Publishing, <templatestyles src="Module:Citation/CS1/styles.css" />ISBN 978-1-59698-029-7
- Israel Foreign Ministry, Foreign Ministry of the Russian Federation, Israel State Archives, Russian Federal Archives, Cummings Center for Russian Studies Tel Aviv University, Oriental Institute (2000). *Documents on Israeli Soviet Relations, 1941–53*. London: Routledge. <templatestyles src="Module:Citation/CS1/styles.css" />ISBN 978-0-7146-4843-9
- Joseph, Dov. *The Faithful City – The Siege of Jerusalem, 1948*. Simon & Schuster, 1960. Congress # 60 10976
- Kaniuk, Yoram (2001). *Commander of the Exodus*. Grove Press. <templatestyles src="Module:Citation/CS1/styles.css" />ISBN 978-0-8021-

3808-8
- Karsh, Efraim (2002), *The Arab-Israeli Conflict. The Palestine War 1948*, Osprey, ISBN 978-1-84176-372-9<templatestyles src="Module:Citation/CS1/styles.css"></templatestyles>
- Fischbach, Michael R. 'Land'. In Philip Mattar (ed.) *Encyclopedia of the Palestinians,* Infobase Publishing. 2005. pp. 291–98
- Flint, Colin. *Introduction to Geopolitics,* Routledge 2012
- Heller, Joseph. *The Birth of Israel, 1945–1949: Ben-Gurion and His Critics*, University Press of Florida, 2001
- Karsh, Inari & Karsh, Efraim (1999). *Empires of the Sand: The Struggle for Mastery in the Middle East, 1789–1923.* Harvard University Press. <templatestyles src="Module:Citation/CS1/styles.css" />ISBN 978-0-674-00541-9
- Katz, Sam (1988). *Israeli Units Since 1948.* Osprey Publishing. <templatestyles src="Module:Citation/CS1/styles.css" />ISBN 978-0-85045-837-4
- Khalaf, Issa *Politics in Palestine: Arab Factionalism and Social Disintegration, 1939–1948.* SUNY Press, 1991
- Khalidi, Rashid (2001). "The Palestinians and 1948: the underlying causes of failure." In Eugene Rogan and Avi Shlaim (eds.). *The War for Palestine* (pp. 12–36). Cambridge: Cambridge University Press. <templatestyles src="Module:Citation/CS1/styles.css" />ISBN 978-0-521-79476-3
- Khalidi, Rashid (2006). *The Iron Cage:The Story of the Palestinian Struggle for Statehood.* Boston, MA:Beacon Press. <templatestyles src="Module:Citation/CS1/styles.css" />ISBN 978-0-8070-0309-1
- Khalidi, Walid (1987). *From Haven to Conquest: Readings in Zionism and the Palestine Problem Until 1948*[168]. Institute for Palestine Studies. <templatestyles src="Module:Citation/CS1/styles.css" />ISBN 978-0-88728-155-6
- Khalidi, Walid (ed.) (1992). *All that remains.* Institute for Palestine Studies. <templatestyles src="Module:Citation/CS1/styles.css" />ISBN 978-0-88728-224-9
- Krämer, Gudrun, *A History of Palestine: From the Ottoman Conquest to the Founding of the State of Israel,* Princeton UP 2011.
- Kurzman, Dan (1970), *Genesis 1948 – the first Arab-Israeli war*, New American Library, New York, Library of Congress CCN: 77-96925
- Levenberg, Haim (1993). *Military Preparations of the Arab Community in Palestine: 1945–1948.* London: Routledge. <templatestyles src="Module:Citation/CS1/styles.css" />ISBN 978-0-7146-3439-5
- Levin, Harry. *Jerusalem Embattled – A Diary of the City under Siege.* Cassels, 1997. <templatestyles src="Module:Citation/CS1/styles.css"

/>ISBN 9780304337651
- Lockman, Zachary. *Comrades and Enemies: Arab and Jewish Workers in Palestine, 1906–1948.* University of California Press, 1996
- Makdisi Saree, *Palestine Inside Out: An Everyday Occupation,* W.W. Norton & Company 2010
- Morris, Benny (1988), *The Birth of the Palestinian Refugee Problem, 1947–1949,* Cambridge Middle East Library
- Morris, Benny (1994), *1948 and after; Israel and the Palestinians*
- Morris, Benny (2001). *Righteous Victims: A History of the Zionist-Arab Conflict, 1881–2001.* Vintage Books. <templatestyles src="Module:Citation/CS1/styles.css" />ISBN 978-0-679-74475-7
- Morris, Benny (2004), *The Birth of the Palestinian Refugee Problem Revisited,* Cambridge University Press, Cambridge UK, <templatestyles src="Module:Citation/CS1/styles.css" />ISBN 978-0-521-81120-0
- Morris, Benny (2008), *1948: The First Arab-Israeli War*[169], Yale University Press, New Haven, <templatestyles src="Module:Citation/CS1/styles.css" />ISBN 978-0-300-12696-9
- Oring, Elliott (1981). *Israeli Humor – The Content: The Content and Structure of the Chizbat of the Palmah.* SUNY Press. <templatestyles src="Module:Citation/CS1/styles.css" />ISBN 978-0-87395-512-6
- Oren, Michael, *Six Days of War,* Random House Ballantine Publishing Group, (New York 2003, <templatestyles src="Module:Citation/CS1/styles.css" />ISBN 0-345-46192-4
- Pappe, Ilan (2006), *The Ethnic Cleansing of Palestine,* Oneworld Publications, Oxford, England, <templatestyles src="Module:Citation/CS1/styles.css" />ISBN 978-1-85168-467-0
- Penkower, Monty Noam (2002). *Decision on Palestine Deferred: America, Britain and Wartime Diplomacy, 1939–1945.* London: Routledge. <templatestyles src="Module:Citation/CS1/styles.css" />ISBN 978-0-7146-5268-9
- Pollack, Kenneth (2004). *Arabs at War: Military Effectiveness, 1948–1991.* University of Nebraska Press. <templatestyles src="Module:Citation/CS1/styles.css" />ISBN 978-0-8032-8783-9
- Richelson, Jeffrey T. (1997). *A Century of Spies: Intelligence in the Twentieth Century.* Oxford: Oxford University Press. <templatestyles src="Module:Citation/CS1/styles.css" />ISBN 978-0-19-511390-7
- Rogan, Eugene L. and Avi Shlaim, eds. *The War for Palestine: Rewriting the History of 1948.* Cambridge: Cambridge UP, 2001
- Rogan, Eugene L. and Avi Shlaim, eds. *The War for Palestine: Rewriting the History of 1948.* 2nd edition. Cambridge: Cambridge UP, 2007
- Rogan, Eugene L. "Jordan and 1948: the persistence of an official history." Rogan and Shlaim. *The War for Palestine.* pp. 104–24

- Sadeh, Eligar (1997). *Militarization and State Power in the Arab-Israeli Conflict: Case Study of Israel, 1948–1982.* Universal Publishers. <templatestyles src="Module:Citation/CS1/styles.css" />ISBN 978-0-9658564-6-1
- Sachar, Howard M. (1979). *A History of Israel,* New York: Knopf. <templatestyles src="Module:Citation/CS1/styles.css" />ISBN 978-0-679-76563-9
- Sayigh, Yezid (2000). *Armed Struggle and the Search for State: The Palestinian National Movement, 1949–1993.* Oxford: Oxford University Press. <templatestyles src="Module:Citation/CS1/styles.css" />ISBN 978-0-19-829643-0
- Sela, Avraham. "Abdallah Ibn Hussein." *The Continuum Political Encyclopedia of the Middle East.* Ed. Avraham Sela. New York: Continuum, 2002. pp. 13–14.
- Shapira, Anita (1992). *Land and Power: Zionist Resort to Force, 1881–1948.* Oxford University Press. <templatestyles src="Module:Citation/CS1/styles.css" />ISBN 978-0-19-506104-8
- Shlaim, Avi (2001). "Israel and the Arab Coalition." In Eugene Rogan and Avi Shlaim (eds.). *The War for Palestine* (pp. 79–103). Cambridge: Cambridge University Press. <templatestyles src="Module:Citation/CS1/styles.css" />ISBN 978-0-521-79476-3
- Sicker, Martin (1999). *Reshaping Palestine: From Muhammad Ali to the British Mandate, 1831–1922.* Praeger/Greenwood. <templatestyles src="Module:Citation/CS1/styles.css" />ISBN 978-0-275-96639-3
- Stearns, Peter N. Citation[170] from *The Encyclopedia of World History* Sixth Edition, Peter N. Stearns (general editor), 2001 Houghton Mifflin Company, at Bartleby.com.
- Tripp, Charles. "Iraq and the 1948 War: mirror of Iraq's disorder." in Rogan and Shlaim. *The War for Palestine.* pp. 125–50.

Further reading

History

- Aloni, Shlomo (2001). *Arab-Israeli Air Wars 1947–82.* Osprey Publishing. <templatestyles src="Module:Citation/CS1/styles.css" />ISBN 978-1-84176-294-4
- Beckman, Morris (1999). *The Jewish Brigade: An Army With Two Masters, 1944–45.* Sarpedon Publishers. <templatestyles src="Module:Citation/CS1/styles.css" />ISBN 978-1-86227-423-5
- Ben-Ami, Shlomo (2006). *Scars of War, Wounds of Peace: The Israeli-Arab Tragedy.* Oxford University Press. <templatestyles src="Module:Citation/CS1/styles.css" />ISBN 978-0-19-518158-6

- Benvenisti, Meron (2002). *Sacred Landscape*. University of California Press. <templatestyles src="Module:Citation/CS1/styles.css" />ISBN 978-0-520-23422-2
- Flapan, Simha (1987), *The Birth of Israel: Myths and Realities*, Pantheon Books, New York.
- Gilbert, Martin (1976). *The Arab-Israeli Conflict: Its History in Maps* Weidenfeld & Nicolson. <templatestyles src="Module:Citation/CS1/styles.css" />ISBN 978-0-297-77241-5
- Landis, Joshua. "Syria and the Palestine War: fighting King 'Abdullah's 'Greater Syria plan.'" Rogan and Shlaim. *The War for Palestine*. 178–205.
- Masalha, Nur (1992). *Expulsion of the Palestinians: The Concept of 'Transfer' in Zionist Political Thought, 1882–1948*, Institute for Palestine Studies, <templatestyles src="Module:Citation/CS1/styles.css" />ISBN 978-0-88728-235-5
- Pappe, Ilan (2006), *The Ethnic Cleansing of Palestine*, Oneworld Publications, Oxford, England, <templatestyles src="Module:Citation/CS1/styles.css" />ISBN 978-1-85168-467-0
- Reiter, Yitzhak, "National Minority, Regional Majority: Palestinian Arabs Versus Jews in Israel" (*Syracuse Studies on Peace and Conflict Resolution*), (2009) Syracuse Univ Press (Sd). <templatestyles src="Module:Citation/CS1/styles.css" />ISBN 978-0-8156-3230-6
- Sheleg, Yair (2001). "A Short History of Terror[171]" *Haaretz*.
- Zertal, Idith (2005). *Israel's Holocaust and the Politics of Nationhood*. Cambridge: Cambridge University Press. <templatestyles src="Module:Citation/CS1/styles.css" />ISBN 978-0-521-85096-4

Fiction

- *The Hope* by Herman Wouk, a historical novel that includes a fictionalized version of Israel's War of Independence.

External links

 Wikimedia Commons has media related to *1948 Arab-Israeli War*.

- One of last surviving founders of IAF recalls mission that stopped Egypt from advancing on Tel Aviv.[172]
- Pictorial History: Air Force Volunteers.[173]
- Overview of The 1948 Israeli War of Independence (documentary)[174] on YouTube
- Video footage of the Israeli Independence War[175] on YouTube

- About the War of Independence[176]
- United Nations: System on the Question of Palestine[177]
- Summary of Arab-Israeli wars[178]
- History of Palestine, Israel and the Israeli-Palestinian Conflict[179]
- Palestinian viewpoint concerning the context of the 1948 war[180] at the Library of Congress Web Archives (archived 2002-09-13)
- The BBC on the UN Partition Plan[181]
- The BBC on the Formation of Israel[182]
- Israeli War of Independence: an autobiographical account by a South African participant[183]
- Israel and the Arab Coalition in 1948[184]
- "I Have Returned"[185]. *Time Magazine*. 15 March 1948. Retrieved 31 October 2009.<templatestyles src="Module:Citation/CS1/styles.css"></templatestyles>
- "War for Jerusalem Road"[186]. *Time Magazine*. 19 April 1948. Retrieved 31 October 2009.<templatestyles src="Module:Citation/CS1/styles.css"></templatestyles>

Armistice Agreements

1949 Armistice Agreements

<indicator name="pp-default"> 🔒 </indicator>

The **1949 Armistice Agreements** are a set of armistice agreements signed during 1949 between Israel and neighboring Egypt,[187] Lebanon,[188] Jordan,[189] and Syria[190] to formally end the official hostilities of the 1948 Arab–Israeli War, and establish armistice lines between Israeli forces and Jordanian-Iraqi forces, also known as the *Green Line*.

The United Nations established supervising and reporting agencies to monitor the established armistice lines. In addition, discussions related to the armistice enforcement, led to the signing of the separate Tripartite Declaration of 1950 between the United States, Britain, and France. In it, they pledged to take action within and outside the United Nations to prevent violations of the frontiers or armistice lines. It also outlined their commitment to peace and stability in the area, their opposition to the use or threat of force, and reiterated their opposition to the development of an arms race. These lines held until the 1967 Six-Day War.

Agreements

With Egypt

On 6 January 1949, Dr. Ralph Bunche announced that Egypt had finally consented to start talks with Israel on an armistice. The talks began on the Greek island of Rhodes on 12 January. Shortly after their commencement, Israel agreed to the release of a besieged Egyptian brigade in Faluja, but soon rescinded their agreement. At the end of the month, the talks floundered. Israel demanded that Egypt withdraw all its forces from the former area of Mandate

Figure 40: *1955 United Nations map showing the Armistice Agreements, with original map reference points ("MR") on the Palestine grid referenced in the respective agreements.*

Palestine.Wikipedia:Citation needed Egypt insisted that Arab forces withdraw to the positions which they held on 14 October 1948, as per the Security Council Resolution S/1070 of 4 November 1948, and that the Israeli forces withdraw to positions north of the Majdal–Hebron road.

The deadlock culminated on 12 February 1949 with the murder of Hassan al-Banna, leader of the Islamist group Muslim Brotherhood. Israel threatened to abandon the talks, whereupon the United States appealed to the parties to bring them to a successful conclusion.

On 24 February the *Israel–Egypt Armistice Agreement* was signed in Rhodes. The main points of the armistice agreement were:

- The Armistice Demarcation Line is not to be construed in any sense as a political or territorial boundary, and is delineated without prejudice to rights, claims and positions of either Party to the Armistice as regards ultimate "settlement of the Palestine question".
- The armistice demarcation line was drawn for the most part along the 1922 international border between Egypt and Mandatory Palestine, except near the Mediterranean Sea, where Egypt remained in control of a strip of land along the coast, which became known as the Gaza Strip.

Figure 41: *The Israeli delegation to the 1949 Armistice Agreements talks. Left to right: Commanders Yehoshafat Harkabi, Aryeh Simon, Yigael Yadin, and Yitzhak Rabin (1949)*

- The Egyptian forces besieged in the *Faluja Pocket* were allowed to return to Egypt with their weapons, and the area was handed over to Israeli military control.[191]
- A zone on both sides of the border around 'Uja al-Hafeer was to be demilitarized, and became the seat of the bilateral armistice committee.

With Lebanon

The agreement with Lebanon was signed on 23 March 1949. The main points were:

- The provisions of this agreement being dictated exclusively by military considerations.
- The armistice line ("Green Line", see also Blue Line (Lebanon)) was drawn along the international boundary between Lebanon and Mandatory Palestine.[192]
- Israel withdrew its forces from 13 villages in Lebanese territory, which were occupied during the war.

With Jordan

The agreement with Jordan was signed on 3 April 1949. The main points:

- No provision of this Agreement shall in any way prejudice the rights, claims and positions of either Party hereto in the ultimate peaceful settlement of the Palestine question, the provisions of this Agreement being dictated exclusively by military considerations.
- Jordanian forces remained in most positions held by them, particularly East Jerusalem which included the Old City.
- Jordan withdrew its forces from their front posts overlooking the Plain of Sharon. In return, Israel agreed to allow Jordanian forces to take over positions previously held by Iraqi forces.
- Exchange of territorial control: Israel received control in the area known as Wadi Ara and the Little Triangle in exchange for territory in the southern hills of Hebron.

In March 1949 as the Iraqi forces withdrew from Palestine and handed over their positions to the smaller Jordanian legion, 3 Israeli brigades maneuvered into positions of advantage in Operation *Shin-Tav-Shin*. The operation allowed Israel to renegotiate the cease fire line in the Wadi Ara area in a secret agreement reached on 23 March 1949 and incorporated into the General Armistice Agreement. The Green Line was then redrawn in blue ink on the southern map to give the impression that a shift of the Green Line had been made.[193] The events that led to a change in the Green Line was an exchange of fertile land in the Bethlehem area to Israeli control and the village of Wadi Fukin being given to Jordanian control. On 15 July when the Israeli Army expelled the population of Wadi Fukin after the village had been transferred to the Israeli-occupied area under the terms of the Armistice Agreement concluded between Israel and the Jordan Kingdom the Mixed Armistice Commission decided on 31 August, by a majority vote, that Israel had violated the Armistice Agreement by expelling villagers across the demarcation line and decided that the villagers should be allowed to return to their homes. However, when the villagers returned to Wadi Fukin under the supervision of the United Nations observers on September 6, they found most of their houses destroyed and were again compelled by the Israeli Army to return to Jordanian controlled territory.[194]

The United Nations Chairman of the Mixed Commission, Colonel Garrison B. Coverdale (US), pressed for a solution of this issue to be found in the Mixed Armistice Commission, in an amicable and UN spirit. After some hesitation, this procedure was accepted and finally an agreement was reached whereby the Armistice Demarcation Line was changed to place Wadi Fukin under Jordanian authority who, in turn, agreed to transfer of some uninhabited, but fertile territory south of Bethlehem to Israel control.

- A Special Committee was to be formed to make arrangements for safe movement of traffic between Jerusalem and Mount Scopus campus of Hebrew University, along the Latrun-Jerusalem Highway, free access to the Holy Places, and other matters.

With Syria

Armistice talks with Syria started at Gesher B'not Yaacov, on the River Jordan, in April 1949,[195] after the other armistice agreements had been concluded. The agreement with Syria was signed on 20 July 1949.

Syria withdrew its forces from most of the territories it controlled west of the international border, which became demilitarized zones. The territory retained by Syria that lay west of the 1923 Palestinian Mandate border and which had been allocated to the Jewish state under the UN partition plan comprised 66 square kilometers in the Jordan Valley.[196] These territories were designated demilitarized zones (DMZs) and remained under Syrian control. It was emphasised that the armistice line was "not to be interpreted as having any relation whatsoever to ultimate territorial arrangements." (Article V)

Iraq

Iraq, whose forces took an active part in the war (although it has no common border with Israel), withdrew its forces from the region in March 1949. The front occupied by Iraqi forces was covered by the armistice agreement between Israel and Jordan, and there was no separate agreement with Iraq.

Cease-fire line vs. permanent border

The new military frontiers for Israel, as set by the agreements, encompassed about 78% of mandatory Palestine as it stood after the independence of Transjordan (now Jordan) in 1946. The Arab populated areas not controlled by Israel prior to 1967 were the Jordan ruled West Bank and the Egypt occupied Gaza Strip.

The armistice agreements were intended to serve only as interim agreements until replaced by permanent peace treaties. However, no peace treaties were actually signed until decades later.

The armistice agreements were clear (at Arab insistence) that they were not creating permanent borders. The Egyptian-Israeli agreement stated "The Armistice Demarcation Line is not to be construed in any sense as a political or territorial boundary, and is delineated without prejudice to rights, claims and positions of either Party to the Armistice as regards ultimate settlement of the Palestine question."

The Jordanian-Israeli agreement stated: "... no provision of this Agreement shall in any way prejudice the rights, claims, and positions of either Party hereto in the peaceful settlement of the Palestine questions, the provisions of this Agreement being dictated exclusively by military considerations" (Art. II.2), "The Armistice Demarcation Lines defined in articles V and VI of this Agreement are agreed upon by the Parties without prejudice to future territorial settlements or boundary lines or to claims of either Party relating thereto." (Art. VI.9)

As the Armistice Demarcation Lines were technically not borders, the Arabs considered that Israel was restricted in its rights to develop the DMZ and exploitation of the water resources. Further that as a state of war still existed with the Arab nations, the Arab League was not hindered in their right to deny Israel the freedom of navigation through the Arab League waters. Also it was argued that the Palestinians had the right of return and that the Israeli use of abandoned property was therefore not legitimate.[197]

In the Knesset then Foreign Minister and future Prime Minister Moshe Sharett called the armistice lines "provisional boundaries" and the old international borders which the armistice lines, except with Jordan, were based on, "natural boundaries".[198] Israel did not lay claim to territory beyond them and proposed them, with minor modifications except at Gaza, as the basis of permanent political frontiers at the Lausanne Conference, 1949.[199]

After the 1967 Six-Day War several Israeli leaders argued against turning the Armistice Demarcation Lines into permanent borders on the grounds of Israeli security:

- Prime Minister Golda Meir said the pre-1967 borders were so dangerous that it "would be treasonable" for an Israeli leader to accept them (*The New York Times*, December 23, 1969).
- The Foreign Minister Abba Eban said the pre-1967 borders have "a memory of Auschwitz" (*Der Spiegel*, November 5, 1969).
- Prime Minister Menachem Begin described a proposal for a retreat to the pre-1967 borders as "national suicide for Israel."

The internationally recognized border between Egypt and Israel was eventually demarcated as part of the Egypt–Israel Peace Treaty.Wikipedia:Citation needed The border between Israel and Jordan (except for Jordan's border with the post-1967 West Bank) was demarcated as part of the Israel–Jordan peace treaty. This occurred after Jordan had recognized Palestine, which had not declared its borders at the time. In its application for membership to the United Nations, Palestine declared its territory to consist of the West Bank and Gaza, implying that some of Jordan's previous border with Israel is now with Palestine.

Violations

In each case Mixed Armistice Commissions (MACs) were formed under the auspices of the United Nations Truce Supervision Organization, (UNTSO) which investigated complaints by all parties and made regular reports to the UN Security Council.

As part of its dispute with Syria over use of the Demilitarized Zone created by the Israel-Syria Armistice Agreement, Israel from 1951 refused to attend meetings of the Israel/Syria Mixed Armistice Commission. The U.N. Security Council, in its resolution of 18 May 1951, criticized Israel's refusal to participate in Mixed Armistice Commission meetings as being "inconsistent with the objectives and intent of the Armistice Agreement".[200]

The discussion of complaints by the Hashemite Kingdom of Jordan/Israel Mixed Armistice Commission during the year 1952 resulted in:

- 1. Jordan being condemned for 19 violations of the General Armistice Agreement;
- 2. Israel being condemned for 12 violations of the General Armistice Agreement;

Statistics Taken from The Official Records of The Hashemite Kingdom of Jordan/Israel Mixed Armistice Commission Period from 1 January 1953 Through 15 October 1953:

- The discussion of the 171 Israeli complaints by the Mixed Armistice Commission resulted in Jordan being condemned for 20 violations of the General Armistice Agreement.
- The discussion of the 161 Jordanian complaints by the Mixed Armistice Commission resulted in Israel being condemned for 21 violations of the General Armistice Agreement.

Specific Incidents

On 28–29 January 1953 Israeli military forces estimated at 120 to 150 men, using 2-inch (51 mm) mortars, 3-inch mortars, PIAT weapons, bangalore torpedoes, machine-guns, grenades and small arms, crossed the demarcation line and attacked the Arab villages of Falameh and Rantis. At Falameh the mukhtar was killed, seven other villagers were wounded, and three houses were demolished. The attack lasted four and a half hours. Israel was condemned for this act by the Mixed Armistice Commission.[201]

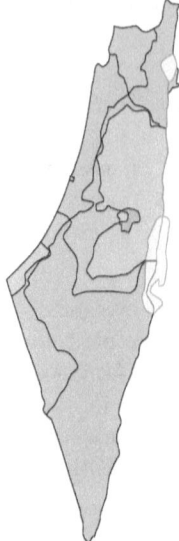

Figure 42:

Boundaries defined in the 1947 UN Partition Plan for Palestine: *Area assigned for a Jewish state* *Area assigned for an Arab state* *Planned Corpus separatum with the intention* *that Jerusalem would be neither Jewish nor Arab*
Armistice Demarcation Lines of 1949 (Green Line): *Israeli controlled territory from 1949* *Egyptian and Jordanian controlled territory from 1948 until 1967*

22 April 1953, firing broke out at sunset within Jerusalem along the demarcation line on a length of about 4 kilometres. It lasted two hours, until the cease-fire arranged by United Nations observers came into effect. On the following day, there were isolated shots in the early morning and in the afternoon. There were twenty Jordanian casualties—ten killed and ten wounded. Six Israelis were wounded. The Jerusalem incident was investigated by United Nations observers. After studying the evidence collected, General Riley, in a report to the Security Council on the violation of the cease-fire [S/3607], stated that it appeared impossible to determine who fired the first shot.

On 25, 26, and 27 May, the two parties submitted complaints alleging violation of the General Armistice Agreement by civilians and military personnel in the Al-Dawayima area. In an emergency meeting of the Mixed Armistice

Commission, both parties agreed to a mixed investigation. United Nations observers accompanied the representatives to the demarcation line to establish the facts. Despite the cease-fire which had been previously arranged, heavy firing broke out during the investigation. Israel troops had fired across the demarcation line at Jordanians in Jordan territory in response to illegal border trespassing by Jordanian farmers and Israeli soldiers were suspected to have burned crops in Jordan territory. The origin of the incident was the illegal cultivation by Jordanians of land in Israel territory. Armed Jordanians had penetrated Israel territory to harvest crops, and other Jordanians had fired across the demarcation line to protect the harvesters. The Jordanian government took no action to encourage or prevent the actions taken, though later considerations were made.

During the latter part of May 1953, incidents took place which cost the lives of three persons and in which six others were wounded. On the night of 25–26 May, an armed group from Jordan attacked two homes in Beit Arif, wounding two women. The same night, armed Jordanians attacked a home in Beit Nabala, killing a woman and wounding her husband and two children. Jordan was condemned for all three of these attacks. On the night of 9 June, armed Jordanians blew up a house in Tirat Yehuda, killing one man, and two nights later an armed band struck at a house in Kfar Hess, killing a woman and seriously wounding her husband. Jordan was again condemned by the Mixed Armistice Commission for these attacks. Both governments were greatly concerned over the happenings during this fortnight, and a great effort was made to stop the work of these groups, which seemed bent on creating tension along the border.

11 August 1953, Israel military forces using demolition mines, bangalore torpedoes, 2-inch mortars, machine-guns and small arms attacked the villages of Idna, Surif and Wadi Fukin, inflicting casualties among the inhabitants and destroying dwellings. The body of an Israel soldier in full uniform with identification tag was found in the village of Idna after the attack. The Mixed Armistice Commission condemned Israel for these attacks.

2 September 1953: Arabs, infiltrated from Jordan, reached the neighbourhood of Katamon, in the heart of Jerusalem where they threw hand grenades in all directions. Miraculously, no one was hurt.

3 September 1953: Sovereignty over the DMZ (Demarcation Zone) between Syria Israel is questioned when Israel start a creeping border attempt by using a water diversion in DMZ; USA threatens to end aid channelled to Israel by the Foreign Operations Administration. Israel moves intake out of DMZ.

In September 1953 the General Headquarters orders Unit 101 to drive Bedouins out from the Negev and push them southward to Sinai. Unit 101 soldiers act aggressively: they raid the Bedouin camp, shooting aimlessly, confiscating arms and burning tents. The Bedouins run away, leaving many wounded behind. For a few days Unit 101 pursuits the Bedouins until they are out of the Negev.

2 October 1953: The explosion of a land mine on the Israel railway north of Eyal derailed an Israel freight train. The Mixed Armistice Commission has held Jordan responsible for this act of violence which fortunately caused no loss of life and relatively little damage, as the train was made up of empty tank cars.

14 October 1953: Qibya massacre – 130 Israeli troops crossed the demarcation line into Qibya village, attacking the inhabitants by firing from automatic weapons and explosives. Forty-one dwelling houses and a school building were destroyed. Resulting in the murder of forty-two lives and the wounding of fifteen persons and the damage of a police car, and at the same time, the crossing of a part of the same group into Shuqba village, breaching article III, paragraph 2 of the General Armistice Agreement. A number of unexploded hand grenades, marked with Hebrew letters and three bags of TNT were found in and about the village.[202]

24 November 1953: Resolution 101 the Security Council is passed which "took note of the fact that there is substantial evidence of crossing of the demarcation line by unauthorized persons, ten resulting in acts of violence and requests the Government of Jordan to continue and strengthen the measures which they are already taking to prevent such crossing." The Security Council condemned Israel for the operation in Qibya.

December 1953: The Jordanian authorities carried out the following measures:-[203]

- (a) Increase of the number of Jordanian police assigned to the border area;
- (b) Increase of the number of patrols of the Jordanian border by Jordanian forces;
- (c) Replacement of village mukhtars and area commanders, where laxity of border control was suspected;
- (d) Removal from the border area of suspected infiltrators and imposing of heavy sentences on known infiltrators;

16 December 1953, two Israeli soldiers were killed while on patrol inside Israel territory (approximate M. R. 1433-1097). On 21 December, the Mixed Armistice Commission condemned Jordan for this incident.

18 December 1953, a car was ambushed on the Hebron road (approximate M.R. 1658-1221) inside Jordan and an Arab Legion medical officer was killed.

Israel was condemned by the Mixed Armistice Commission for this incident (21 December).

21 December 1953, an armed group attacked a Bedouin camp near Tarqumyia (approximate M.R. 1512-1092) wounding one man. Israel was condemned by the Mixed Armistice Commission for this incident (23 December).

21 December, an armed group, using explosives and automatic weapons, attacked a house near Hebron (approximate M.R. 1591-1066) killing one pregnant woman and two men, and wounding another man. Israel was condemned for this incident (24 December). The last three incidents were apparently reprisal attacks for the killing of the two Israeli soldiers on 16 December. Two Arabs responsible for this crime were arrested by the Jordan police a few days later.

14 February 1954, an Israeli villager on guard duty at Mahasyia, near Deiraban, (approximate M. R. 1510-1282) in the central area, was killed. No evidence was introduced to indicate that Jordanians were guilty of this crime and on 18 February the Chairman voted against the Israeli draft resolution condemning Jordan.

17 February 1954: the Israel delegation complained that five armed persons dressed in khaki crossed the demarcation line during the night and, on the morning of 16 February, stole a flock of 260 sheep belonging to an Israeli kibbutz. According to the complaint, the Israeli shepherd and his flock were taken into caves and kept there till 5.30 p.m. when the shepherd was released and the marauders returned to the Gaza Strip with the flock crossing the demarcation line at M.R. 1067-1024. The Israel delegation considered that "the above was a carefully planned action ordered by the Egyptian authorities and carried out by a well-trained military unit."

17 February 1954: the Israel delegation complained that two Arabs crossed the demarcation line into Israel at M.R. 1018-0992, on 16 February. According to the complaint, they started to escape when challenged by Israeli guards, and fire having been opened on them, one was hit and was dragged over the demarcation line by the second.

18 February, the Mixed Armistice Commission condemned Israel and Jordan for firing across the demarcation line on 14 February near Deir el Ghusun (approximate M. R. 1575-1955) in the northern area. This firing resulted in the killing, of one Jordanian.

18 February: the Israel delegation complained that on 18 February at 1 p.m. two armed Egyptian soldiers crossed the demarcation line at M.R. 10884-10486. According to the complaint, the Egyptian soldiers refused to stop, when challenged by an Israeli patrol; two warning shots were fired; one of the

Egyptian soldieries escaped, and the other was killed 15 meters inside Israel territory

18 February: the Israel delegation complained that on 18 February four armed infiltrators crossed the demarcation line into Israel and that when challenged by an Israel patrol at M.R. 1023-1123 they started to escape while firing on the patrol. During the exchange of fire one of the infiltrators was killed.

19 February: the Egyptian delegation complained that on 18 February, at M.R. 1087-1050, a patrol of two Egyptian soldiers in Egyptian territory was attacked by armed Israelis hiding in ambush. One of the Egyptian soldiers was kidnapped and killed inside Israel-controlled territory, close to the demarcation line (Cf. sub-paragraph (c) above summarizing an Israeli complaint dated 18 February).

19 February: the Egyptian delegation complained that on 19 February armed Israelis opened automatic fire across the demarcation line at an Arab working in his field at M.R. 0952-0931. The Arab was seriously injured.

24 February One Arab was reported killed and another wounded by the Egyptian delegation.

16 March 1954, Israelis of the Ein Gev colony began ploughing 130 dunums of land situated near the colony and belonging to the Arab population of demilitarised Nuqeib, in violation of the verbal agreement concluded at Samara in 1950 to the effect that the two parties should retain and work the said land until the problem was settled.

17 March 1954: Ma'ale Akrabim [Scorpion Pass].Terrorists ambushed a bus traveling from Eilat to Tel Aviv, and opened fire at short range when the bus reached the area of Maale Akrabim in the northern Negev. In the initial ambush, the terrorists killed the driver and wounded most of the passengers. The terrorists then boarded the bus, and shot each passenger, one by one. Eleven passengers were murdered. Survivors recounted how the murderers spat on the bodies and abused them. The Israeli claimed that the terrorists could clearly be traced back to the Jordanian border, some 20 km from the site of the terrorist attack. The MAC investigation found that the claim could not be substantiated and that the attack was more likely to have been by Bedu tribesman from within Israel and the Israeli complaint was not upheld.[204]

23 March 1954: The Israel Government has severed all connections with the Mixed Armistice Commission. It has also discontinued attendance at the local commanders' meetings provided for under a separate Israel-Jordan agreement. Israel communications referring to alleged violations by Jordan of the General Armistice Agreement have been addressed to the Secretary-General of the United Nations, with the request that they should be circulated to the

members of the Security Council. The Chief of Staff of the Truce Supervision Organization in Jerusalem has been informed of such alleged violations of the General Armistice Agreement only on receiving from New York a copy of the Security Council document. The non-co-operation of the Israel Government has prevented the investigation of such alleged violations in conformity with the provisions of the General Armistice Agreement.

On 29 March 1954, at 07.00 hours, local time, the Jordanian delegation presented to the Chairman of the Mixed Armistice Commission a verbal complaint dealing with an incident which had occurred on 29 March 1954 at 07.00 hours, local time, at Nahhalin village, some 35 kilometers from the demarcation line "an Israel armed force, well equipped, surrounded the village from three directions and penetrated inside the village and opened fire from different automatic weapons, threw hand-grenades and placed mines at some houses, including the mosque of the village. As a result of this brutal attack, 9 persons—8 men and 1 woman—were killed, and 14 others were injured and taken to hospital. Fire lasted for about one hour and a half, and was returned by the village guards. Then the aggressors withdrew. Mines, grenades and other warlike materials bearing Hebrew markings were found on the spot. This complaint was upheld by the Mixed Armistice Commission

30 June 1954, two Israeli armoured launchers attacked the Syrian post of El Koursi, situated on Syrian soil, with their 20-mm. and 57-mm. guns, this time with the support of Israel field artillery sited in the defensive area. This artillery continued firing for approximately one hour and 45 minutes, causing material damage to the post.

5 December 1954, at approximately 16.30 hours, a group of 8 armed Israel State policemen stationed approximately at MR 209600 233400 opened fire on two Arab farmers at approximately MR 209600 233450 in the southern demilitarised zone (Tawafiq). The fire was returned by the two Arabs. One of them was hit by a bullet and immediately taken to hospital. The MAC Decided that the presence of a regular Israel police force in the southern demilitarised zone is a flagrant violation of article V of the General Armistice Agreement and requested that the Israel authorities to pay to the wounded Arab civilian an appropriate compensation.

A list of 29 complaints of allegedof 27 October 1953 Report the Chief of Staff of the Truce Supervision Organization. See appendix I, II and II for a tabulated list of Israel and Jordanian complaints to the MAC the number of condemnations given to each country as a result of MAC investigations infractions of the agreement by Jordan was submitted on April 6, 1954.[205] These alleged infractions included alleged Jordanian attacks on an Israeli civilian bus, killing 11 people (see 17 March above), attacks on Israeli farmers and Bedouin shepherds, sniping at Israeli civilians from the Old City of Jerusalem, kidnappings, shooting at civilian aircraft, ambushing roads and laying mines. In violation of the agreements, the Jordanians denied Jewish access to the holy places in Jerusalem, prohibited visits to Rachel's Tomb and vandalized the Jewish cemetery on the Mount of Olives, using tombstones for construction of pavements and latrines.Wikipedia:Citation needed The 'Uja al-Hafeer demilitarized zone on the Israeli-Egyptian border was the site of numerous border incidents and armistice violations. In September 1955, Ariel Sharon's paratroopers entered the United Nation sector of the demilitarized zone. Benny Morris writes that Sharon "didn't realize that the UN area was off limits for his men."[206] On May 28, 1958, Israel reported a shooting incident in the demilitarized zone on Mount Scopus in which 4 Israel police officers patrolling the botanical gardens of the Hebrew University of Jerusalem, along with the United Nations observer sent to extricate them, were killed by Jordanian fire from Issawiya.[207,208] Israel sent soldiers into Jordanian territory to conduct raids in retaliation for incursions by armed persons into Israel.Wikipedia:Citation needed From their positions on the Golan Heights Syrian forces shelled Israeli settlements in the demilitarized zone, attacked fishing boats on the Kinneret and fired on agricultural workers.

Texts

The complete texts of the Armistice Agreements can be found at The Avalon Project at Yale Law School[209]

- Egyptian-Israeli General Armistice Agreement[210], February 24, 1949
- Jordanian-Israeli General Armistice Agreement[211], April 3, 1949
- Lebanese-Israeli General Armistice Agreement[212], March 23, 1949
- Israeli-Syrian General Armistice Agreement[213], July 20, 1949

A search[214] at the United Nations web site for "Mixed Armistice Commission" will reveal many of the reports made to the UN by those commissions.

Further reading

- Ben-Dror, Elad (2016). *Ralph Bunche and the Arab-Israeli Conflict: Mediation and the UN 1947–1949,*. Routledge. ISBN 978-1138789883.<templatestyles src="Module:Citation/CS1/styles.css"></templatestyles>

References

- Morris, Benny (1993) *Israel's Border Wars, 1949 - 1956. Arab Infiltration, Israeli Retaliation, and the Countdown to the Suez War*. Oxford University Press, <templatestyles src="Module:Citation/CS1/styles.css" />ISBN 0-19-827850-0
- Shlaim, Avi (2000) *The Iron Wall; Israel and the Arab World*. Penguin Books, <templatestyles src="Module:Citation/CS1/styles.css" />ISBN 0-14-028870-8

External links

- E.H. Hutchison, *Violent Truce*[215]

1948–1955: Ben-Gurion I; Sharett

Austerity in Israel

From 1949 to 1959, the state of Israel was, to a varying extent, under a regime of austerity (Hebrew: צנע, *Tzena'*), during which rationing and similar measures were enforced.

Rationale

Soon after establishment in 1948, the emerging state of Israel found itself lacking in both food and foreign currency. In just three and a half years, the Jewish population of Israel had doubled, increased by nearly 700,000 immigrants. Consequently, the Israeli government instigated measures to control and oversee distribution of necessary resources to ensure equal and ample rations for all Israeli citizens.

In addition to the problems with the provision of food, national austerity was also required because the state was lacking in foreign currency reserves. Export revenues covered less than a third of the cost of imports, and less than half of the consequent deficit was covered by the Jewish loan system known as *Magbiyot* (Hebrew: מגביות, lit. *Collections*). Most financing was obtained from foreign banks and gas companies, which, as 1951 drew to an end, refused to expand the available credit. In order to supervise austerity, the prime minister, David Ben-Gurion, ordered the establishment of the Ministry of Rationing and Supply (Hebrew: והאספקה, הקיצוב משרד *Misrad HaKitzuv Ve-HaAspaka*), headed by Dov Yosef.

Figure 43: *Tel Aviv residents standing in line to buy food rations, 1954*

Life under austerity

At first this rationing was set for staple foods alone—oil, sugar and margarine, for instance—but it was later expanded to furniture and footwear. Each month, each citizen would get food coupons worth 6 Israeli pounds, and each family was allotted a given amount of foodstuffs. The diet chosen, fashioned after that used in the United Kingdom during World War II, allowed a meager 1,600 calories a day for Israeli citizens, with additional calories for children, the elderly, and pregnant women.

The enforcement of austerity required the establishment of a bureaucracy of quite some proportions, which nonetheless proved ineffective in preventing the emergence of a black market in which rationed products—often smuggled from the countryside—were sold at higher prices. To counter this, the government established in September 1950 the *Office for Fighting the Black Market* (Hebrew: מטה השחור, בשוק למלחמה *Mate LeMilhama BaShuk HaShahor*), whose goal it was to combat the forming of such a market. Yet despite the increased supervision, and the specially summoned courts, all such attempts at suppression proved ineffective.Wikipedia:Citation needed

Austerity in Israel

Figure 44: *A Wonder Pot (right), a top-of-the-stove baking utensil invented during the austerity period to help homemakers bake cakes and casseroles without an oven.*

Figure 45: *1956 Ministry price notification poster placed inside a local grocery store in Kfar Saba.*

End of austerity

In 1952 the reparations agreement was signed with Germany, compensating the Jewish state for confiscation of Jewish property during the Holocaust. The resulting influx of foreign capital was a huge boost to the state's struggling economy, and led to the cancellation of most restrictions in 1953. In 1956, the list of rationed goods was narrowed to just fifteen goods, and it shrank to eleven in 1958. Shortly afterwards, it was abolished for all goods except jam, sugar and coffee. In 1959, rationing was abolished altogether.

Results

Economically, austerity proved a failure, mostly due to the enormous government deficit, covered by bank loans, creating an increase in the amount of money use. Throughout austerity unemployment remained high, and inflation grew as of 1951. Yet austerity did have its advantages – living standards were preserved at tolerable levels, while the resources saved were made available to feed and clothe and shelter the entire population adequately, while at the same time integrating and successfully resettling over 700,000 Jewish refugees from European, Arab, and Muslim lands.

Reprisal operations

Reprisal operations	
Part of the Palestinian Fedayeen insurgency (during Arab–Israeli conflict)	
Date	1950s–1960s
Location	Middle East
Result	Israeli victory
Belligerents	
Israel	All-Palestine • Palestinian fedayeen *Supported by:* Kingdom of Egypt Jordan Syrian Republic
Commanders and leaders	
David Ben-Gurion Moshe Sharett Levi Eshkol	Gamal Abdel Nasser Hafez al-Assad Hussein bin Talal
Strength	
Unknown	Unknown
Casualties and losses	
400–967 civilians and soldiers killed during this period by fedayeen attacks (1951–55)	2,700–5,000 Arab soldiers and Palestinians* killed by retribution operations (1951–55)[216]
• Both guerrillas and civilians	

Reprisal operations (Hebrew: חתגמול פעולות, *Pe'ulot HaTagmul*) were raids carried out by the Israel Defense Forces in the 1950s and 1960s in response to frequent fedayeen attacks during which armed Arab militants infiltrated Israel from Syria, Egypt and Jordan to carry out attacks on Israeli civilians and soldiers. Most of the reprisal operations followed raids that resulted in Israeli fatalities. The goal of these operations was to create deterrence and prevent future attacks. Two other factors behind the raids were restoring public morale and training newly formed army units.[217]

Background: 1949–1956

Reprisal operations were carried out following raids by armed infiltrators into Israel during the entire period from 1948 Arab–Israeli War until October 1956. Most of Reprisal operations followed raids that resulted in Israeli fatalities. From 1949 to 1954 the reprisal operations were directed against Jordan. In 1954 the Jordanian authorities decided to curb the infiltration due to fierce

Israeli activity, and the cross-border infiltration from Jordan substantially declined, along with the number of victims. The IDF stopped the reprisals against Jordan from September of that year.

From 1949 there were infiltrations from Gaza strip under Egyptian control, and the Egyptian authorities tried to curb them. The Egyptian republican regime told Israel during secret talks that such acts as the blockade and armed infiltration were political necessities for Egypt and Israel had to accept it. From February 1954, Egyptian soldiers opened fire against Israeli border patrols, and infiltrators from the Gaza Strip planted mines on the patrol routes, on top of the conventional infiltrations. However, Moshe Sharet, the Israeli prime minister, did not authorize reprisal attacks against Egypt. In mid 1954 a senior Egyptian military intelligence in the Gaza reported: "The main objective of the military presence along the armistice line is to prevent infiltration, but the Palestinian troops encourage the movement of infiltrators and carry out attacks along the line."

In 1955 Ben Gurion returned to the government, and a reprisal operation against an Egyptian military camp near Gaza was authorized, after a murder of an Israeli civilian in the center of Israel was committed by Egyptian intelligence agents. In the operation the IDF lost eight soldiers, and the Egyptians 38 soldiers. Later Nasser claimed that this operation motivated the Czech arms deal, although Egypt had previously signed arms contracts with Czechoslovakia (which never materialized). Nasser refused to order his army to stop firing at Israeli patrols. Moreover, this shooting was intensified after the Gaza raid. According to Israeli casualty statistics, 7 or 8 Israelis were killed by infiltrators from Gaza annually from 1951 to 1954, with a dramatic rise to 48 in 1955.

Ben Gurion continued to adhere to the status quo and followed the terms of the armistice regime, but in September 1955 Egypt tightened its blockade of the Straits of Tiran, closed the air space over the Gulf of Aqaba to Israeli aircraft, initiated fedayeen attacks against the Israeli population across the Lebanese and Jordanian borders, and announced the Czech arms deal. However, with the revelation of the Czech arms deal, Ben Gurion believed that Nasser now possessed the tools with which to put his aggressive intentions into practice. Ben Gurion therefore attempted to provoke a preemptive war with Egypt.

From December 1955 to February 1956 the Egyptians clamped down on "civilian" infiltration into Israel, yet their soldiers frequently fired across the line at Israeli patrols.

Some infiltration activities were initiated by Palestinian Arab refugees who were ostensibly looking for relatives, returning to their homes, recovering possessions, tending to their fields, collecting their crops, as well as exacting revenge. Half of Jordan's prison population at the time consisted of people arrested for attempting to return to, or illegally enter, Israeli territory, but the number of complaints filed by Israel over infiltrations from the West Bank show a considerable reduction, from 233 in the first nine months of 1952, to 172 for the same period in 1953, immediately before the Qibya attack. This marked reduction was in good part the result of increased Jordanian efficiency in patrolling. According to some Israeli sources, between June 1949 and the end of 1952, a total of 57 Israelis, mostly civilians, were killed by Palestinian infiltrators from the West Bank and Jordan. The Israeli death toll for the first nine months of 1953 was 32. During roughly the same time period (November 1950 – November 1953), the Mixed Armistice Commission condemned Israeli raids 44 times. Furthermore, during the same period, 1949–1953, Jordan maintained that it had suffered 629 killed and injured stemming from Israeli incursions and cross-border bombings. UN sources for the period, based on the documentation at General Bennike's disposal (prepared by Commander E H Hutchison USNR), lower both estimates.Wikipedia:Please clarify

Policy

Israeli prime minister David Ben-Gurion and Israeli chief of staff Moshe Dayan ordered reprisal raids as a tough response to terror attacks. The message was that any attack on Israelis would be followed by a strong Israeli response. In the words of Ben-Gurion, from his lecture "retribution operations as a means to ensure the Peace":

<templatestyles src="Template:Quote/styles.css"/>

> *We do not have power to ensure that the water pipe lines won't be exploded or that the trees won't be uprooted. We do not have the power to prevent the murders of orchard workers or families while they are asleep, but we have the power to set a high price for our blood, a price which would be too high for the Arab communities, the Arab armies and the Arab governments to bear.*[218]

This approach dominated in Israel during the 1950s and 1960s, although it was not the only one. Moshe Sharett, the Israeli prime minister during the retribution operations, objected to this policy and after the Ma'ale Akrabim massacre he wrote in his diary:

<templatestyles src="Template:Quote/styles.css"/>

> *Committing a severe responsive act to this bloodbath would only obscure its horrors, and put us in an equal level with murderers of the other party. We should rather this instance to raise political pressure on the world powers, to have them exert unprecedented pressure on Jordan.*

The head of the United Nations truce observers, Canadian Lieutenant-General E.L.M. Burns, was very critical of what he described as "constant provocation of the Israeli forces and armed kibbutzim." His conclusion was "The retaliation does not end the matter; it goes on and on ..."[219]

Major operations

April 1951 – October 1956

- **Attack on al-Hamma** (התקיפה) (באל-חמה) – Following the el-Hamma incident on 4 April 1951 in which seven Israeli soldiers were killed after attempting to enforce Israel's sovereignty in the demilitarized zone to include the el-Hamma enclave – Hamat Gader. The next day the first retribution operation since signing the cease-fire agreements was carried out. Unlike the following retribution operations, this operation was carried out by the Israeli Air Force. The operation failed when the attacking planes missed their target.
- **Beit Jala raid** – In reprisal for the rape and murder of a Jewish girl in Israeli-controlled Jerusalem, three houses in the Palestinian Arab village of Beit Jalla are blown up, and seven Arab civilians are killed. Israel formally denies involvement, but international investigators blame an IDF platoon for the raid.
- **Operation Shoshana** (מבצע) (שושנה) known as Qibya massacre – Carried out on 14 October 1953 following an attack in which an Israeli mother and her two children were killed. Commanded by Ariel Sharon, a force made up of paratroopers and members of Unit 101 made a night-time attack on the village of Qibya in the West Bank, which was controlled by Jordan at the time. Sixty-nine villagers were killed during the operation. In addition to that, forty-five houses, a school, and a mosque were destroyed.[220]
- **Operation Black Arrow** (מבצע) (חץ שחור) – Carried out in Egyptian-control Gaza between 28 February until 1 March 1955. The operation was aimed at the Egyptian army. Thirty eight Egyptian soldiers were killed during the operation with 30 injured; eight IDF soldiers were also killed and 13 were injured. According to President Gamal Abdel Nasser, this operation was the main motivation for the Egyptian-Czech arms deal later in 1955.

- **Operation Elkayam** (מבצע אלק״ים) – Carried out on 31 August 1955 against the police forces of Khan Yunis from where attacks had been carried out against Israelis. 72 Egyptian soldiers were killed during the operation. The operation was followed by a massive buildup of Egyptian troops in the Gaza Strip.
- **Operation Jonathan** (מבצע יונתן) – An attack carried out on 11–12 September 1955 by two paratroop companies on Khirbet al Rahwa police fort, on the Hebron–Beersheba road, in which over twenty Jordanian soldiers and policemen were killed. Amongst the Israeli wounded was Captain Meir Har-Zion.[221,222]
- **Operation Egged** (מבצע אגד) – Following an Egyptian border provocation in the Nitzana Demilitarized Zone, two-hundred paratroopers carried out a reprisal raid against an Egyptian military post at Kuntilla on 28–29 October 1955. Twelve Egyptian soldiers were killed and twenty-nine others were taken prisoner.
- **Operation Volcano** (מבצע הר געש) – Following the invasion of the Egyptian forces into an Israeli youth village and communal settlement Nitzana in the Demilitarized Zone, the IDF carried out an attack in that area on 2 November 1955. 81 Egyptian soldiers were killed during the operations and 55 were captured.[223] Seven IDF soldiers were killed during the operation.
- **Operation Sa'ir** (מבצע שעיר) – Carried out on 22 December 1955, the IDF forces raided Syrian outposts on the slopes of the Golan Heights.
- **Operation Olive Leaves** (מבצע עלי זית) – Carried out on 11 December 1955 at Syrian posts located on the eastern coast of the Sea of Galilee in response to constant Syrian attacks on Israeli fishermen. 54 Syrian soldiers were killed and 30 were captured. Six IDF soldiers were killed during the operation.
- **Operation Gulliver** (מבצע גוליבר) – Carried out on 13 September 1956 in Jordan.
- **Operation Lulav** (מבצע לולב) – Carried out on 25 September 1956 in the Arab village Husan, near Bethlehem. The operation was in response to the murder of participants in an archaeological conference held in Ramat Rachel and the murder of two farmers from Moshav Aminadav and Kibbutz Maoz Haim.
- **Targeted killings** – On 11 July 1956, Mustafa Hafez, the Egyptian military intelligence commander in the Gaza Strip and an organizer of fedayeen raids, was assassinated by Israeli Military Intelligence in an operation planned by Major General Yehoshafat Harkabi. The following day, Israel assassinated Salah Mustafa, the Egyptian military attache in Amman who had dispatched infiltrators into Israel via the West Bank.[224]
- **Operation Samaria** (מבצע שומרון) – Carried out on 10 October 1956

in which IDF forces attacked the Qalqilya police forces. 100 Jordanian soldiers and 17 IDF soldiers were killed during the operation. The operation was carried out in response to the constant infiltrations from the West Bank, and in response to the constant attacks from the Jordanian army aimed at Israeli soldiers and civilians.

Casualties 1949–1956

Between 1949 and 1956 cross border attacks from Israel's neighbours killed around 200 Israelis, with perhaps another 200 Israeli soldiers being killed in border clashes or IDF raids. Over the same period between 2,700 and 5,000 Arabs were killed. This figure includes many unarmed civilians who had crossed the border for economic or social reasons. Most were killed during 1949–1951. After which the average was between 300 and 500 killed a year.[225]

January 1960 – November 1966

The Sinai War of 1956 ended the first phase of the Israeli retribution operations. The retribution operations policy continued after the Sinai War, but were initiated mainly against Jordan and Syria, because at that time the majority of attacks originated over the Jordanian and Syrian borders. The main retribution operations held after the Sinai War include:

- **Operation Cricket** (מבצע) (חרגול) – Carried out on 31 January 1960, was the first Israeli retribution operation carried out after the Sinai war. The operation was carried out by Golani forces at the Syrian village of Tawfiq, in response to attacks on Israelis in Tel Katzir. Tawfiq was designated by the IDF as the center of many Syrian attacks and as a result it was decided that the destruction of the village was vital. During the operation the village was overrun and destroyed while Israeli forces were under attack by Syrian artillery. Six Syrian soldiers were killed during the operation. Three IDF soldiers were killed and seven were injured.
- **Operation Swallow** (מבצע) (סנונית) – Another operation which was carried out in retaliation for Syrian attacks on Israeli fishermen in the Sea of Galilee. During the operation (carried out on 16 March 1962), Israeli forces from the Golani Brigade raided Syrian posts in the village of Nuqayb. 30 Syrian soldiers were killed while seven IDF soldiers were killed and seven were injured during the operation.
- **Samu Incident** (פעולת) (סמוע) – Carried out on 13 November 1966, brigade strength IDF forces, accompanied by air support, attacked the village of as-Samu, south of the city of Hebron, in response to previous acts of sabotage aimed at Israeli targets. During the operation dozens of houses were bombed while 18 Jordanians were killed. One IDF soldier

was also killed – the paratroop battalion commander, Lt. Col. Yoav Shaham. In addition to the ground operation, an air battle was conducted between eight Hawker Hunter aircraft of the Royal Jordanian Air Force and four Dassault Mirage III aircraft of the Israeli Air Force.

Israeli commemoration of the retribution operations

A commemoration site called "Black Arrow" (חץ), (שחור which commemorates the various retribution operations and the heritage of the Israeli paratrooper units, is located in the Negev.

Lavon Affair

The **Lavon affair** refers to a failed Israeli covert operation, codenamed **Operation Susannah**, conducted in Egypt in the summer of 1954.Wikipedia:Vagueness As part of the false flag operation, a group of Egyptian Jews were recruited by Israeli military intelligence to plant bombs inside Egyptian-, American-, and British-owned civilian targets: cinemas, libraries and American educational centers. The bombs were timed to detonate several hours after closing time. The attacks were to be blamed on the Muslim Brotherhood, Egyptian Communists, "unspecified malcontents" or "local nationalists" with the aim of creating a climate of sufficient violence and instability to induce the British government to retain its occupying troops in Egypt's Suez Canal zone. The operation caused no casualties among the population, but cost the lives of four operatives: two cell members who committed suicide after being captured; and two operatives who were tried, convicted, and executed by the Egyptian authorities.

The operation ultimately became known as the **Lavon affair** after the Israeli defense minister Pinhas Lavon was forced to resign as a consequence of the incident. Before Lavon's resignation, the incident had been euphemistically referred to in Israel as the **"Unfortunate Affair"** or **"The Bad Business"** (Hebrew: העסק, הביש *HaEsek HaBish*). Israel publicly denied any involvement in the incident for 51 years; however, the surviving agents were officially honored in 2005, being awarded certificates of appreciation by Israeli President Moshe Katsav.

Figure 46: *Pinhas Lavon*

Operation Susannah

Aim

In the early 1950s, the United States initiated a more activist policy of support for Egyptian nationalism; this aim was often in contrast with Britain's policy of maintaining its regional hegemony. Israel feared that the US policy, which encouraged Britain to withdraw its military forces from the Suez Canal, would embolden the military ambitions towards Israel of Gamal Abdel Nasser, the President of Egypt. Israel at first sought to influence this policy through diplomatic means, but was frustrated.

In the summer of 1954, Colonel Binyamin Gibli, the chief of Israel's military intelligence directorate Aman, initiated 'Operation Susannah' in order to reverse that decision. The goal of the Operation was to carry out bombings and other acts of sabotage in Egypt, with the aim of creating an atmosphere in which the British and American opponents of British withdrawal from Egypt would be able to gain the upper hand and block the British withdrawal from Egypt.

According to historian Shabtai Teveth, who wrote one of the more detailed accounts, the assignment was "To undermine Western confidence in the existing [Egyptian] regime by generating public insecurity and actions to bring about arrests, demonstrations, and acts of revenge, while totally concealing the Israeli factor. The team was accordingly urged to avoid detection, so that suspicion would fall on the Muslim Brotherhood, the Communists, 'unspecified malcontents' or 'local nationalists'."

Secret cell

The top-secret cell, Unit 131, which was to carry out the operation, had existed since 1948 and under Aman since 1950. At the time of Operation Susannah, Unit 131 was the subject of a bitter dispute between Aman (military intelligence) and Mossad (national intelligence agency) over who should control it.

Unit 131 operatives had been recruited several years earlier, when the Israeli intelligence officer Avraham Dar arrived in Cairo under the cover of a British citizen from Gibraltar named John Darling. He had recruited several Egyptian Jews who had previously been active in illegal emigration activities and trained them for covert operations.

Operation commenced

Aman decided to activate the network in the spring of 1954. On 2 July, the cell detonated bombs at a post office in Alexandria, and on 14 July, it bombed the libraries of the U.S. Information Agency in Alexandria and Cairo, and a British-owned theater. The homemade bombs, consisting of bags containing acid placed over nitroglycerine, were inserted into books, and placed on the shelves of the libraries just before closing time. Several hours later, as the acid ate through the bags, the bombs would explode. They did little damage to the targets, and caused no injuries or deaths.

Before the group began the operation, Israeli agent Avri Elad (Avraham Seidenwerg) was sent to oversee the operations. Elad assumed the identity of Paul Frank, a former SS officer with Nazi underground connections. Avri Elad allegedly informed the Egyptians, resulting in the Egyptian intelligence agency following a suspect to his target, the Rio Theatre, where a fire engine was standing by. Egyptian authorities arrested this suspect, Philip Natanson, when his bomb accidentally ignited prematurely in his pocket. Having searched his apartment, they found incriminating evidence and names of accomplices to the operation.

Several suspects were arrested, including Egyptian Jews and undercover Israelis. Elad and Colonel Dar managed to escape. Two suspects, Yosef Carmon and Israeli Meir Max Bineth, committed suicide in prison.

Figure 47: *Meir Max Bineth*

Trials and jail

The Egyptian trial began on 11 December and lasted until 27 January 1955; two of the accused (Moshe Marzouk and Shmuel Azar) were condemned to execution by hanging, two were acquitted, and the rest received lengthy prison terms.

In 1954, on behalf of both Winston Churchill and the World Jewish Congress, Maurice Orbach went to Cairo to intercede for the lives of Jews sentenced to death. Later, he said that Egypt's President, Nasser, had agreed to spare their lives but then reneged on this, balancing their deaths with those of members of the Muslim Brotherhood.

The trial was criticised in Israel as a show trial, although strict Israeli military censorship of the press at the time meant that the Israeli public was kept in the dark about the facts of the case, and in fact were led to believe that the defendants were innocent. There were allegations that evidence had been extracted by torture.

After serving seven-year jail sentences, two of the imprisoned operatives (Meir Meyuhas and Meir Za'afran) were released in 1962. The rest were eventually freed in February 1968, in a secret addendum to a prisoner-of-war exchange.

Soon after the affair, Mossad chief Isser Harel expressed suspicion to Aman concerning the integrity of Avri Elad. Despite his concerns, Aman continued using Elad for intelligence operations until 1956, when he was caught trying to sell Israeli documents to the Egyptians. Elad was tried in Israel and sentenced to 10 years imprisonment. During his imprisonment in Ayalon Prison, the media were only able to refer to him as the "Third Man" or "X" due to government censorship. In 1976, while living in Los Angeles, Elad publicly identified himself as the "Third Man" from the Lavon Affair. In 1980, Harel publicly revealed evidence that Elad had been turned by the Egyptians even before Operation Susannah.

Political aftermath

Denial and first inquiry

In meetings with prime minister Moshe Sharett, minister of defense Pinhas Lavon denied any knowledge of the operation. When intelligence chief Gibli contradicted Lavon, Sharett commissioned a board of inquiry consisting of Israeli Supreme Court Justice Isaac Olshan and the first chief of staff of the Israel Defense Forces, Yaakov Dori that was unable to find conclusive evidence that Lavon had authorized the operation. Lavon tried to fix the blame on Shimon Peres, who was the secretary general of the defense ministry, and on Gibli for insubordination and criminal negligence.Wikipedia:Citation needed

Sharett resolved the dilemma by siding with Peres (who had, along with Moshe Dayan, testified against Lavon), after which Lavon resigned on 17 February 1955. Former prime minister David Ben-Gurion succeeded Lavon as minister of defense. On 3 November 1955, Sharett (who had not known about the operation in advance, and had therefore strongly denied Israel's involvement) resigned as Prime Minister and was replaced by Ben-Gurion.Wikipedia:Citation needed

Subsequent revelations and inquiries

In April 1960, a review of minutes from the inquiry found inconsistencies and possibly a fraudulent document in Gibli's original testimony that seemed to support Lavon's account of events. During this time it came to light that Elad (the Israeli agent running Operation Susannah in Egypt) had committed perjury during the original inquiry. Elad was also suspected of betraying the group to Egyptian authorities, though the charges were never proven. He was eventually sentenced to a jail term of 10 years for trying to sell Israeli documents to the Egyptians in an unrelated matter. Ben-Gurion scheduled closed hearings with a new board of inquiry chaired by Haim Cohn, a Supreme Court justice.Wikipedia:Citation needed

This inquiry found that the perjury indeed had been committed, and that Lavon had not authorized the operation. Sharett and Levi Eshkol tried to issue a statement that would placate both Lavon and those who had opposed him. Ben-Gurion refused to accept the compromise, and viewed it as a divisive play within the Mapai party.Wikipedia:Citation needed

Another investigative committee took up the matter and sided with the Cohn inquiry. Ben-Gurion then resigned from his post as defense minister. This led to the expulsion of Lavon from the Histadrut labor union and an early call for new elections, the results of which changed the political structure in Israel. The specifics of Operation Susannah were kept secret from the Israeli public at the time of the political upheaval.Wikipedia:Citation needed

Public debate

Due to Israel's military censorship the details of the affair could originally not be openly discussed in the media. Despite this, debate occurred but with the use of code words such as the "Senior Officer", to refer to Gibli, and the "unfortunate business" to refer to the Egyptian operation.[226]

Legacy

Operation Susannah and the Lavon Affair turned out to be disastrous for Israel in several ways:

- Israel lost significant standing and credibility in its relations with the United Kingdom and the United States, that took years to repair.
- The aftermath saw considerable political turmoil in Israel, which affected the influence of its government.

Israel publicly honored the surviving spies on March 30, 2005; President Moshe Katsav presented each with a certificate of appreciation for their efforts on behalf of the state, ending decades of official denial by Israel.

Further reading

- Aviezer Golan, Ninio Marcelle, Victor Levy, Robert Dassa and Philip Natanson (As told to Aviezer Golan) (Translated from Hebrew by Peretz Kidron) (Fwd by Golda Meir): *Operation Susannah*, Harper & Row, NYC, 1978 <templatestyles src="Module:Citation/CS1/styles.css" />ISBN 978-0-06-011555-5

- Joel Beinin: Nazis and Spies The Discourse of Operation Susannah[227], ch 4 in *The Dispersion Of Egyptian Jewry Culture, Politics, And The Formation Of A Modern Diaspora*[228] Berkeley: University of California Press, c1998. Amer Univ in Cairo Pr, 2005, <templatestyles src="Module:Citation/CS1/styles.css" />ISBN 978-977-424-890-0
- Joel Beinin: Egyptian Jewish Identities. Communitarianisms, nationalisms, nostalgias[229] Stanford Humanities Review, 1996
- Ostrovsky, Victor; Hoy, Claire (1991). *By way of deception*. St. Martin's Press. ISBN 978-0-312-92614-4.<templatestyles src="Module:Citation/CS1/styles.css"></templatestyles>

External links

- *The Lavon Affair*[230] by Doron Geller, JUICE, The Jewish Agency for Israel, Education Department
- The Lavon Affair[231] by David Hirst, Excerpts from his book: The Gun and the Olive Branch, 1977, 1984, Futura Publications
- List of books about the Lavon Affair[232]

Suez Crisis

Suez Crisis

<indicator name="pp-default"> 🔒 </indicator>

- Suez Crisis
- Tripartite Aggression
- Sinai War

Part of the Cold War and the Arab–Israeli conflict

Damaged Egyptian equipment

Date	29 October 1956 – 7 November 1956 (1 week and 2 days) (Sinai under Israeli occupation until March 1957)
Location	Gaza Strip and Egypt (Sinai and Suez Canal zone)
Result	Coalition military victory;[233] Egyptian political victory[234]<ul><li>Anglo-French withdrawal following international pressure (December 1956)</li><li>Israeli occupation of Sinai (until March 1957)</li><li>UNEF deployment in Sinai</li><li>Straits of Tiran re-opened to Israeli shipping</li><li>Resignation of Anthony Eden as British Prime Minister, end of Britain's role as a superpower[235]</li><li>Guy Mollet's position as French Prime Minister heavily damaged</li></ul>

Belligerents

• Israel • United Kingdom • France	• Egypt

Commanders and leaders	
• David Ben-Gurion • Moshe Dayan • Asaf Simhoni • Haim Bar-Lev • Avraham Yoffe • Israel Tal • Ariel Sharon • Uri Ben-Ari • Anthony Eden • Gerald Templer • Charles Keightley • Hugh Stockwell • Manley Power • René Coty • Guy Mollet • Pierre Barjot • André Beaufre • Jacques Massu	• Gamal Abdel Nasser • Abdel Hakim Amer • Saadedden Mutawally • Sami Yassa • Jaafar al-Abd • Salahedin Moguy • Raouf Mahfouz Zaki
Strength	
• 175,000 • 45,000 • 34,000	300,000[236]
Casualties and losses	

• **Israel**:
  • 172 killed[237]
  • 817 wounded
  • 1 captured
• **United Kingdom**:
  • 16 killed
  • 96 wounded
• **France**:
  • 10 killed
  • 33 wounded
	• 1,650[238],[239]–3,000 killed
	• 1,000 civilians killed
	• 4,900 wounded
	• 5,000[240]–30,000+ captured

The **Suez Crisis**, or the **Second Arab–Israeli War**, also named the **Tripartite Aggression** in the Arab world and **Operation Kadesh** or **Sinai War** in Israel,[241] was an invasion of Egypt in late 1956 by Israel, followed by the United Kingdom and France. The aims were to regain Western control of the Suez Canal and to remove Egyptian President Gamal Abdel Nasser, who had just nationalized the canal. After the fighting had started, political pressure from the United States, the Soviet Union and the United Nations led to a withdrawal by the three invaders. The episode humiliated the United Kingdom and France and strengthened Nasser.[242]

On 29 October, Israel invaded the Egyptian Sinai. Britain and France issued a joint ultimatum to cease fire, which was ignored. On 5 November, Britain and France landed paratroopers along the Suez Canal. The Egyptian forces were defeated, but they did block the canal to all shipping. It later became clear that the Israeli invasion and the subsequent Anglo-French attack had been planned beforehand by the three countries.

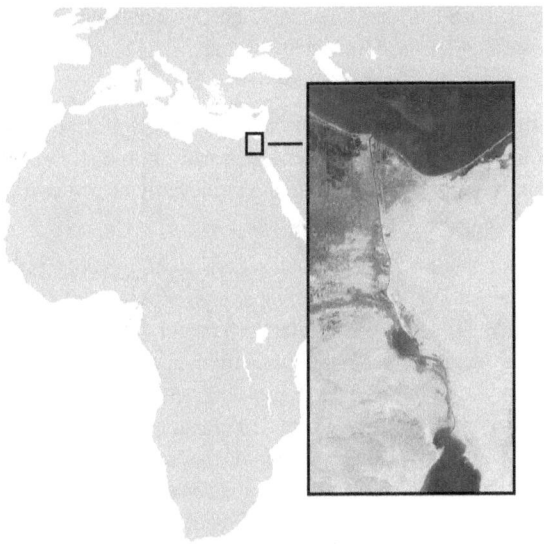

Figure 48: *The location of the Suez Canal, which connects the Mediterranean and the Indian Ocean via the Red Sea.*

The three allies had attained a number of their military objectives, but the canal was useless. Heavy political pressure from the United States and the USSR led to a withdrawal. U.S. President Dwight D. Eisenhower had strongly warned Britain not to invade; he threatened serious damage to the British financial system by selling the US government's pound sterling bonds. Historians conclude the crisis "signified the end of Great Britain's role as one of the world's major powers". The Suez Canal was closed from October 1956 until March 1957. Israel fulfilled some of its objectives, such as attaining freedom of navigation through the Straits of Tiran, which Egypt had blocked to Israeli shipping since 1950.

As a result of the conflict, the United Nations created the UNEF Peacekeepers to police the Egyptian–Israeli border, British Prime Minister Anthony Eden resigned, Canadian Minister of External Affairs Lester Pearson won the Nobel Peace Prize, and the USSR may have been emboldened to invade Hungary.

Background

History of the Suez Canal

The Suez Canal was opened in 1869, after ten years of work financed by the French and Egyptian governments.[243] The canal was operated by the Universal

Company of the Suez Maritime Canal, an Egyptian-chartered company; the area surrounding the canal remained sovereign Egyptian territory and the only land-bridge between Africa and Asia.

The canal instantly became strategically important, as it provided the shortest ocean link between the Mediterranean and the Indian Ocean. The canal eased commerce for trading nations and particularly helped European colonial powers to gain and govern their colonies.

In 1875, as a result of debt and financial crisis, the Egyptian ruler was forced to sell his shares in the canal operating company to the British government of Benjamin Disraeli. They were willing buyers and obtained a 44 percent share in the canal's operations for less than £4 million; this maintained the majority shareholdings of the mostly French private investors. With the 1882 invasion and occupation of Egypt, the United Kingdom took *de facto* control of the country as well as the canal proper, and its finances and operations. The 1888 Convention of Constantinople declared the canal a neutral zone under British protection. In ratifying it, the Ottoman Empire agreed to permit international shipping to pass freely through the canal, in time of war and peace.[244] The Convention came into force in 1904, the same year as the *Entente cordiale* between Britain and France.

Despite this convention, the strategic importance of the Suez Canal and its control were proven during the Russo-Japanese War of 1904–1905, after Japan and Britain entered into a separate bilateral agreement. Following the Japanese surprise attack on the Russian Pacific Fleet based at Port Arthur, the Russians sent reinforcements from their fleet in the Baltic Sea. The British denied the Russian fleet use of the canal and forced it to steam around Africa, giving the Japanese forces time to consolidate their position in East Asia.

The importance of the canal as a strategic intersection was again apparent during the First World War, when Britain and France closed the canal to non-Allied shipping. The attempt by German-led Ottoman forces to storm the canal in February 1915 led the British to commit 100,000 troops to the defense of Egypt for the rest of the war.[245]

Oil

The canal continued to be strategically important after the Second World War as a conduit for the shipment of oil.[246] Petroleum business historian Daniel Yergin wrote of the period: "In 1948, the canal abruptly lost its traditional rationale. ... [British] control over the canal could no longer be preserved on grounds that it was critical to the defence either of India or of an empire that was being liquidated. And yet, at exactly the same moment, the canal was gaining a new role—as the highway not of empire, but of oil. ... By 1955, petroleum accounted for half of the canal's traffic, and, in turn, two thirds of Europe's oil passed through it".[247]

At the time, Western Europe imported two million barrels per day from the Middle East, 1,200,000 by tanker through the canal, and another 800,000 via pipeline from the Persian Gulf to the Mediterranean, where tankers received it. The US imported another 300,000 barrels daily from the Middle East.[248] Though pipelines linked the oil fields of Iraq and the Persian Gulf states to the Mediterranean, these routes were prone to suffer from instability, which led British leaders to prefer to use the sea route through the Suez Canal. As it was, the rise of super-tankers for shipping Middle East oil to Europe, which were too big to use the Suez Canal meant that British policy-makers greatly overestimated the importance of the canal. By 2000, only 8 percent of the imported oil in Britain arrived via the Suez canal with the rest coming via the Cape route.

In August 1956 the Royal Institute of International Affairs published a report titled "Britain and the Suez Canal" revealing government perception of the Suez area. It reiterates several times the strategic necessity of the Suez Canal to the United Kingdom, including the need to meet military obligations under the Manila Pact in the Far East and the Baghdad Pact in Iraq, Iran, or Pakistan. The report also points out how the canal was used in past wars and could be used in future wars to transport troops from the Dominions of Australia and New Zealand in the event of war in Europe. The report also cites the amount of material and oil that passes through the canal to the United Kingdom, and the economic consequences of the canal being put out of commission, concluding:
<templatestyles src="Template:Quote/styles.css"/>

> *The possibility of the Canal being closed to troopships makes the question of the control and regime of the Canal as important to Britain today as it ever was.*[249]

After 1945

In the aftermath of the Second World War, Britain was reassessing its role in the region in light of the severe economic constraints and its colonial history. The economic potential of the Middle East, with its vast oil reserves, as well as the Suez Canal's geo-strategic importance against the background of the Cold War, prompted Britain to consolidate and strengthen its position there. The kingdoms of Egypt and Iraq were seen as vital to maintaining strong British influence in the region.

Britain's military strength was spread throughout the region, including the vast military complex at Suez with a garrison of some 80,000, making it one of the largest military installations in the world. The Suez base was considered an important part of Britain's strategic position in the Middle East; however, increasingly it became a source of growing tension in Anglo-Egyptian relations. Egypt's post-war domestic politics were experiencing a radical change, prompted in no small part by economic instability, inflation, and unemployment. Unrest began to manifest itself in the growth of radical political groups, such as the Muslim Brotherhood in Egypt, and an increasingly hostile attitude towards Britain and its presence in the country. Added to this anti-British fervour was the role Britain had played in the creation of Israel.[250] As a result, the actions of the Egyptian government began to mirror those of its populace and an anti-British policy began to permeate Egypt's relations with Britain.

In October 1951, the Egyptian government unilaterally abrogated the Anglo-Egyptian Treaty of 1936, the terms of which granted Britain a lease on the Suez base for 20 more years.[251] Britain refused to withdraw from Suez, relying upon its treaty rights, as well as the presence of the Suez garrison. The price of such a course of action was a steady escalation in increasingly violent hostility towards Britain and British troops in Egypt, which the Egyptian authorities did little to curb.

On 25 January 1952, British forces attempted to disarm a troublesome auxiliary police force barracks in Ismailia, resulting in the deaths of 41 Egyptians.[252] This in turn led to anti-Western riots in Cairo resulting in heavy damage to property and the deaths of several foreigners, including 11 British citizens. This proved to be a catalyst for the removal of the Egyptian monarchy. On 23 July 1952 a military coup by the Egyptian nationalist 'Free Officers Movement'—led by Muhammad Neguib and future Egyptian President Gamal Abdul Nasser—overthrew King Farouk and established an Egyptian republic.

Post Egyptian revolution period

In the 1950s the Middle East was dominated by four distinct but interlinked struggles. The first was the geopolitical battle for influence between the United States and the Soviet Union known as the Cold War. The second was the anti-colonial struggle of Arab nationalists against the two remaining imperial powers, Britain and France. The third was the Arab–Israeli dispute, and the fourth was the race between different Arab states for the leadership of the Arab world,[253] known as the Arab Cold War.

Egypt and Britain

Britain's desire to mend Anglo-Egyptian relations in the wake of the coup saw the country strive for rapprochement throughout 1953 and 1954. Part of this process was the agreement, in 1953, to terminate British rule in Sudan by 1956 in return for Cairo's abandoning of its claim to suzerainty over the Nile Valley region. In October 1954, Britain and Egypt concluded an agreement on the phased evacuation of British troops from the Suez base, the terms of which agreed to withdrawal of all troops within 20 months, maintenance of the base to be continued, and for Britain to hold the right to return for seven years.[254] The Suez Canal Company was not due to revert to the Egyptian government until 16 November 1968 under the terms of the treaty.

Britain's close relationship with the two Hashemite kingdoms of Iraq and Jordan were of particular concern to Nasser. In particular, Iraq's increasingly amicable relations with Britain were a threat to Nasser's desire to see Egypt as head of the Arab world. The creation of the Baghdad Pact in 1955 seemed to confirm Nasser's fears that Britain was attempting to draw the Eastern Arab World into a bloc centred upon Iraq, and sympathetic to Britain.[255] Nasser's response was a series of challenges to British influence in the region that would culminate in the Suez Crisis.

Egypt and the Arab leadership

In regard to the Arab leadership, particularly venomous was the feud between Nasser and the Prime Minister of Iraq, Nuri el-Said, for Arab leadership, with the Cairo-based Voice of the Arabs radio station regularly calling for the overthrow of the government in Baghdad. The most important factors that drove Egyptian foreign policy in this period was on the one hand, a determination to see the entire Middle East as Egypt's rightful sphere of influence, and on the other, a tendency on the part of Nasser to fortify his pan-Arabist and nationalist credibility by seeking to oppose any and all Western security initiatives in the Near East.

Despite the establishment of such an agreement with the British, Nasser's position remained tenuous. The loss of Egypt's claim to Sudan, coupled with the continued presence of Britain at Suez for a further two years, led to domestic unrest including an assassination attempt against him in October 1954. The tenuous nature of Nasser's rule caused him to believe that neither his regime, nor Egypt's independence would be safe until Egypt had established itself as head of the Arab world.[256] This would manifest itself in the challenging of British Middle Eastern interests throughout 1955.

US and a defense treaty against the Soviet threat

The United States, while attempting to erect an alliance in the form of a Middle East Defense Organization to keep the Soviet Union out of the Near East, tried to woo Nasser into this alliance.[257] The central problem for American policy in the Middle East was that this region was perceived as strategically important due to its oil, but the United States, weighed down by defense commitments in Europe and the Far East, lacked sufficient troops to resist a Soviet invasion of the Middle East.[258] In 1952, General Omar Bradley of Joint Chiefs of Staff declared at a planning session about what to do in the event of a Soviet invasion of the Near East: "Where will the staff come from? It will take a lot of stuff to do a job there".

As a consequence, American diplomats favoured the creation of a NATO-type organization in the Near East to provide the necessary military power to deter the Soviets from invading the region. The Eisenhower administration, even more than the Truman administration saw the Near East as a huge gap into which Soviet influence could be projected, and accordingly required an American-supported security system.[259] American diplomat Raymond Hare later recalled:

<templatestyles src="Template:Quote/styles.css"/>

> *It's hard to put ourselves back in this period. There was really a definite fear of hostilities, of an active Russian occupation of the Middle East physically, and you practically hear the Russian boots clumping down over the hot desert sands.*[260]

The projected Middle East Defense Organization (MEDO) was to be centered on Egypt. A National Security Council directive of March 1953 called Egypt the "key" to the Near East and advised that Washington "should develop Egypt as a point of strength".

A major dilemma for American policy was that the two strongest powers in the Near East, Britain and France, were also the nations whose influence many local nationalists most resented. From 1953 onwards, American diplomacy had attempted unsuccessfully to persuade the powers involved in the Near East, both local and imperial, to set aside their differences and unite against the Soviet Union.[261] The Americans took the view that, just as fear of the Soviet Union had helped to end the historic Franco-German enmity, so too could anti-Communism end the more recent Arab–Israeli dispute. It was a source of constant puzzlement to American officials in the 1950s that the Arab states and the Israelis had seemed to have more interest in fighting each other rather than uniting against the Soviet Union.Wikipedia:Citation needed After his visit to the Middle East in May 1953 to drum up support for MEDO, the Secretary of State, John Foster Dulles found much to his astonishment that the Arab states were "more fearful of Zionism than of the Communists".[262]

The policy of the United States was colored by considerable uncertainty as to whom to befriend in the Near East. American policy was torn between a desire to maintain good relations with NATO allies such as Britain and France who were also major colonial powers, and a desire to align Third World nationalists with the Free World camp.[263] Though it would be entirely false to describe the coup deposing King Farouk in July 1952 as a Central Intelligence Agency (CIA) coup, Nasser and his Society of Free Officers were nonetheless in close contact with CIA operatives led by Miles Copeland beforehand (Nasser maintained links with any and all potential allies from the Egyptian Communist Party on the left to the Muslim Brotherhood on the right).[264]

Nasser's friendship with certain CIA officers in Cairo led Washington to vastly overestimate its influence in Egypt.[265] That Nasser was close to CIA officers led the Americans for a time to view Nasser as a CIA "asset".[266] In turn, the British who were aware of Nasser's CIA ties deeply resented this relationship, which they viewed as an American attempt to push them out of Egypt. The principal reason for Nasser's courting of the CIA before the July Revolution of 1952 was his hope that the Americans would act as a restraining influence on the British should Britain decide on intervention to put an end to the revolution (until Egypt renounced it in 1951, the 1936 Anglo-Egyptian treaty allowed Britain the right of intervention against all foreign and domestic threats).[267] In turn, many American officials, such as Ambassador Jefferson Caffery, saw the continued British military presence in Egypt as anachronistic, and viewed the Revolutionary Command Council (as Nasser called his government after the coup) in a highly favourable light.[268]

Caffery was consistently very positive about Nasser in his reports to Washington right up until his departure from Cairo in 1955. The regime of King Farouk was viewed in Washington as weak, corrupt, unstable, and anti-American, so Free Officers' July coup was welcomed by the United States.[269] As it was, Nasser's contacts with the CIA were not necessary to prevent British intervention against the July coup as Anglo-Egyptian relations had deteriorated so badly in 1951–52 that the British viewed any Egyptian government not headed by King Farouk as a huge improvement.[270] In May 1953, during a meeting with Secretary Dulles, who asked Egypt to join an anti-Soviet alliance, Nasser responded by saying that the Soviet Union has

<templatestyles src="Template:Quote/styles.css"/>

> *never occupied our territory ... but the British have been here for seventy years. How can I go to my people and tell them I am disregarding a killer with a pistol sixty miles from me at the Suez Canal to worry about somebody who is holding a knife a thousand miles away?*

Dulles informed Nasser of his belief that the Soviet Union was seeking world conquest, that the principal danger to the Near East came from the Kremlin, and urged Nasser to set aside his differences with Britain to focus on countering the Soviet Union. In this spirit, Dulles suggested that Nasser negotiate a deal that would see Egypt assume sovereignty over the canal zone base, but then allow the British to have "technical control" in the same way that Ford auto company provided parts and training to its Egyptian dealers.

Nasser did not share Dulles's fear of the Soviet Union taking over the Middle East, and insisted quite vehemently that he wanted to see the total end of all British influence not only in Egypt, but all the Middle East. The CIA offered Nasser a $3 million bribe if he would join the proposed Middle East Defense Organization; Nasser took the money, but then refused to join.[271] At most, Nasser made it clear to the Americans that he wanted an Egyptian-dominated Arab League to be the principal defense organization in the Near East, which might be informally associated with the United States.

After he returned to Washington, Dulles advised Eisenhower that the Arab states believed "the United States will back the new state of Israel in aggressive expansion. Our basic political problem ... is to improve the Moslem states' attitudes towards Western democracies because our prestige in that area had been in constant decline ever since the war". The immediate consequence was a new policy of "even-handedness" where the United States very publicly sided with the Arab states in several disputes with Israel in 1953–54.[272] Moreover, Dulles did not share any sentimental regard for the Anglo-American "special relationship", which led the Americans to lean towards the Egyptian side in the Anglo-Egyptian disputes.[273] During the extremely difficult negotiations over the British evacuation of the Suez Canal base in 1954–55, the Americans generally supported Egypt, though at the same time trying hard to limit the extent of the damage that this might cause to Anglo-American relations.[274]

In the same report of May 1953 to Eisenhower calling for "even-handedness", Dulles stated that the Egyptians were not interested in joining the proposed MEDO; that the Arabs were more interested in their disputes with the British, the French, the Israelis and each other than in standing against the Soviets; and that the "Northern Tier" states of Turkey, Iran and Pakistan were more useful as allies at present than Egypt. Accordingly, the best American policy towards Egypt was to work towards Arab–Israeli peace and the settlement of the Anglo-Egyptian dispute over the British Suez Canal base as the best way of securing Egypt's ultimate adhesion to an American sponsored alliance centered on the "Northern Tier" states.[275]

The "Northern Tier" alliance was achieved in early 1955 with the creation of the Baghdad Pact comprising Pakistan, Iran, Turkey, Iraq and the United Kingdom.[276] The presence of the last two states was due to the British desire to continue to maintain influence in the Middle East, and Nuri Said's wish to associate his country with the West as the best way of counterbalancing the increasing aggressive Egyptian claims to regional predominance. The conclusion of the Baghdad Pact occurred almost simultaneously with a dramatic

Israeli raid on the Gaza Strip on 28 February 1955 in retaliation for *fedayeen* raids into Israel, during which the Israeli Unit 101 commanded by Ariel Sharon gave the Egyptian Army a bloody nose.

The close occurrence of the two events was mistakenly interpreted by Nasser as part of coordinated Western effort to push him into joining the Baghdad Pact.[277] The signing of the Baghdad Pact and the Gaza raid marked the beginning of the end of Nasser's once good relations with the Americans. In particular, Nasser saw Iraq's participation in the Baghdad Pact as a Western attempt to promote his archenemy Nuri al-Said as an alternative leader of the Arab world.[278]

Nasser and the Soviet bloc

Instead of siding with either superpower Nasser took the role of the spoiler and tried to play off the superpowers in order to have them compete with each other in attempts to buy his friendship.[279]

Under the new leadership of Nikita Khrushchev, the Soviet Union was making a major effort to win influence in the so-called "third world".[280] As part of the diplomatic offensive, Khrushchev had abandoned Moscow's traditional line of treating all non-communists as enemies and adopted a new tactic of befriending so-called "non-aligned" nations, which often were led by leaders who were non-Communists, but in varying ways and degrees were hostile towards the West. Khrushchev had realized that by treating non-communists as being the same thing as being anti-communist, Moscow had needlessly alienated many potential friends over the years in the third world. Under the banner of anti-imperialism, Khrushchev made it clear that the Soviet Union would provide arms to any left-wing government in the third world as a way of undercutting Western influence.[281]

The Chinese Premier Zhou Enlai met Nasser at the 1955 Bandung Conference and was impressed by him. Zhou recommended that Khrushchev treat Nasser as a potential ally. Zhou described Nasser to Khrushchev as a young nationalist, who though no Communist, could if used correctly do much damage to Western interests in the Middle East. Marshal Josip Broz Tito of Yugoslavia, who also came to know Nasser at Bandung told Khrushchev in a 1955 meeting that "Nasser was a young man without much political experience, but if we give him the benefit of the doubt, we might be able to exert a beneficial influence on him, both for the sake of the Communist movement, and ... the Egyptian people". Traditionally, most of the equipment in the Egyptian military had come from Britain, but Nasser's desire to break British influence in Egypt meant that he was desperate to find a new source of weapons to replace Britain. Nasser had first broached the subject of buying weapons from the Soviet Union in 1954.[282]

Nasser and arms purchase

Most of all, Nasser wanted the United States to supply arms on a generous scale to Egypt.[283] Nasser refused to promise that any U.S. arms he might buy would not be used against Israel, and rejected out of hand the American demand for a Military Advisory Group to be sent to Egypt as part of the price of arms sales.[284]

Nasser's first choice for buying weapons was the United States, but his frequent anti-Israeli speeches and his sponsorship for the *fedayeen* who were making raids into Israel had made it difficult for the Eisenhower administration to get the approval of Congress to sell weapons to Egypt. American public opinion was deeply hostile towards selling arms to Egypt that might be used against Israel, and moreover Eisenhower feared starting a Middle Eastern arms race. Eisenhower very much valued the Tripartite Declaration as a way of keeping peace in the Near East. In 1950, in order to limit the extent that the Arabs and the Israelis could engage in an arms race, the three nations which dominated the arms trade in the non-Communist world, namely the United States, the United Kingdom and France had signed the Tripartite Declaration, where they had committed themselves to limiting how much arms they could sell in the Near East, and also to ensuring that any arms sales to one side was matched by arms sales of equal quantity and quality to the other.[285] Eisenhower viewed the Tripartite Declaration, which sharply restricted how many arms Egypt could buy in the West, as one of the key elements in keeping the peace between Israel and the Arabs, and believed that setting off an arms race would inevitably lead to a new war.

The Egyptians made continuous attempts to purchase heavy arms from Czechoslovakia years before the 1955 deal.

Nasser had let it be known, in 1954–55, that he was considering buying weapons from the Soviet Union as a way of pressuring the Americans into selling him the arms he desired. Nasser's hope was that faced with the prospect of Egypt buying Soviet weapons, and thus coming under Soviet influence the Eisenhower administration would be forced to sell Egypt the weapons he wanted. Khrushchev who very much wanted to win the Soviet Union influence in the Middle East, was more than ready to arm Egypt if the Americans proved unwilling. During secret talks with the Soviets in 1955, Nasser's demands for weapons were more than amply satisfied as the Soviet Union had not signed the Tripartite Declaration.[286] The news in September 1955 of the Egyptian purchase of a huge quantity of Soviet arms via Czechoslovakia was greeted with shock and rage in the West, where this was seen as a major increase in Soviet influence in the Near East.[287] In Britain, the increase of Soviet influence in the Near East was seen as an ominous development that threatened to put an end to British influence in the oil-rich region.[288]

France and the Egyptian support for the Algeria rebellion

Over the same period, the French Premier Guy Mollet, was facing an increasingly serious rebellion in Algeria, where the FLN rebels were being supported by Egypt, and he also came to perceive Nasser as a major threat.[289] During a visit to London in March 1956, Mollet told Eden his country was faced with an Islamic threat to the very soul of France supported by the Soviet Union. Mollet stated: "All this is in the works of Nasser, just as Hitler's policy was written down in *Mein Kampf*. Nasser has the ambition to recreate the conquests of Islam. But his present position is largely due to the policy of the West in building up and flattering him".

In a May 1956 gathering of French veterans, Louis Mangin spoke in place of the unavailable Minister of Defence and gave a violently anti-Nasser speech, which compared the Egyptian leader to Hitler. He accused Nasser of plotting to rule the entire Middle East and of seeking to annex Algeria, whose "people live in community with France".[290] Mangin urged France to stand up to Nasser, and being a strong friend of Israel, urged an alliance with that nation against Egypt.[291]

Egypt and Israel

Since the establishment of Israel in 1948, cargo shipments to and from Israel had been subject to Egyptian authorization, search and seizure while attempting to pass through the Suez Canal. On 1 September 1951, the United Nations Security Council Resolution 95 called upon Egypt: "to terminate the restrictions on the passage of international commercial ships and goods through the Suez Canal, wherever bound, and to cease all interference with such shipping." This interference and confiscation, contrary to the laws of the canal (Article 1 of the 1888 Suez Canal Convention), increased following the coup.Wikipedia:Citation needed

In late 1954, Nasser began a policy of sponsoring raids into Israel by the *fedayeen*, who almost always attacked civilians. The raids triggered a series of Israeli reprisal operations.[292] The raids were targeted as much politically as against Israel militarily. It was Nasser's intention to win himself the laurels of the foremost anti-Zionist state as a way of establishing his leadership over the Arab world. Before 1954, the principal target of Nasser's speeches had been Britain. Only after the Anglo-Egyptian agreement on evacuating the canal zone did Israel emerge as one of Nasser's main enemies.[293]

Franco-Israeli alliance emerges

Starting in 1949 owing to shared nuclear research, France and Israel started to move towards an alliance.[294] Following the outbreak of the Algerian War in late 1954, France began to ship more and more arms to Israel.[295] In November 1954, the Director-General of Israel's Ministry of Defense Shimon Peres visited Paris, where he was received by the French Defense Minister Marie-Pierre Kœnig, who told him that France would sell Israel any weapons it wanted to buy.[296] By early 1955, France was shipping large amounts of weapons to Israel. In April 1956, following another visit to Paris by Peres, France agreed to totally disregard the Tripartite Declaration, and supply even more weapons to Israel.[297] During the same visit, Peres informed the French that Israel had decided upon war with Egypt in 1956.[298] Peres claimed that Nasser was a genocidal maniac intent upon not only destroying Israel, but also exterminating its people, and as such, Israel wanted a war before Egypt received even more Soviet weapons, and there was still a possibility of victory for the Jewish state. Peres asked for the French, who had emerged as Israel's closest ally by this point, to give Israel all the help they could give in the coming war.

Frustration of British aims

Throughout 1955 and 1956, Nasser pursued a number of policies that would frustrate British aims throughout the Middle East, and result in increasing hostility between Britain and Egypt. Nasser saw Iraq's inclusion in the Baghdad Pact as indicating that the United States and Britain had sided with his much hated archenemy Nuri as-Said's efforts to be the leader of the Arab world, and much of the motivation for Nasser's turn to an active anti-Western policy starting in 1955 was due to his displeasure with the Baghdad Pact.[299] For Nasser, attendance at such events as the Bandung conference in April 1955 served as both the means of striking a posture as a global leader, and of playing hard to get in his talks with the Americans, especially his demand that the United States sell him vast quantities of arms.[300]

Nasser "played on the widespread suspicion that any Western defence pact was merely veiled colonialism and that Arab disunity and weakness—especially in the struggle with Israel—was a consequence of British machinations." He also began to align Egypt with the kingdom of Saudi Arabia—whose rulers were hereditary enemies of the Hashemites—in an effort to frustrate British efforts to draw Syria, Jordan and Lebanon into the orbit of the Baghdad Pact. Nasser struck a further blow against Britain by negotiating an arms deal with communist Czechoslovakia in September 1955[301] thereby ending Egypt's reliance on Western arms. Later, other members of the Warsaw Pact also sold arms to Egypt and Syria. In practice, all sales from the Eastern Bloc were authorised by the Soviet Union, as an attempt to increase Soviet influence over the Middle

East. This caused tensions in the United States because Warsaw Pact nations now had a strong presence in the region.

Nasser and 1956 events

Nasser and Jordan

Nasser frustrated British attempts to draw Jordan into the pact by sponsoring demonstrations in Amman, leading King Hussein to dismiss the British commander of the Arab Legion, Sir John Bagot Glubb (known to the Arabs as Glubb Pasha) in March 1956 and throwing Britain's Middle Eastern security policy into chaos.[302] After one round of bloody rioting in December 1955 and another in March 1956 against Jordan joining the Baghdad Pact, both instigated by Cairo-based Voice of the Arabs radio station, Hussein believed his throne was in danger.[303] In private, Hussein assured the British that he was still committed to continuing the traditional Hashemite alliance with Britain, and that his sacking of Glubb Pasha and all the other British officers in the Arab Legion were just gestures to appease the rioters.

Nasser and Britain

British Prime Minister Anthony Eden was especially upset at the sacking of Glubb Pasha, and as one British politician recalled: <templatestyles src="Template:Quote/styles.css"/>

> *For Eden ... this was the last straw.... This reverse, he insisted was Nasser's doing.... Nasser was our Enemy No. 1 in the Middle East and he would not rest until he destroyed all our friends and eliminated the last vestiges of our influence.... Nasser must therefore be ... destroyed.*[304]

After the sacking of Glubb Pasha, which he saw as a grievous blow to British influence, Eden became consumed with an obsessional hatred for Nasser, and from March 1956 onwards, was in private committed to the overthrow of Nasser.[305] The American historian Donald Neff wrote that Eden's often hysterical and overwrought views towards Nasser almost certainly reflected the influence of the amphetamines to which Eden had become addicted following a botched operation in 1953 together with the related effects of sustained sleep deprivation (Eden slept on average about 5 hours per night in early 1956).[306]

Increasingly Nasser came to be viewed in British circles—and in particular by Eden—as a dictator, akin to Benito Mussolini. Ironically,Wikipedia:Manual of Style (words to watch)#Editorializing in the buildup to the crisis, it was the Labour leader Hugh Gaitskell and the left-leaning tabloid newspaper *The Mirror* that first made the comparison between Nasser and Mussolini. Anglo-Egyptian relations would continue on their downward spiral.

Britain was eager to tame Nasser and looked towards the United States for support. However, Eisenhower strongly opposed British-French military action.[307] America's closest Arab ally, Saudi Arabia, was just as fundamentally opposed to the Hashemite-dominated Baghdad Pact as Egypt, and the U.S. was keen to increase its own influence in the region.[308] The failure of the Baghdad Pact aided such a goal by reducing Britain's dominance over the region. "Great Britain would have preferred to overthrow Nasser; America, however uncomfortable with the 'Czech arms deal', thought it wiser to propitiate him."[309]

U.S and the Aswan High Dam

On 16 May 1956, Nasser officially recognised the People's Republic of China, which angered the U.S. and Secretary Dulles, a sponsor of the Republic of China. This move, coupled with the impression that the project was beyond Egypt's economic capabilities, caused Eisenhower to withdraw all American financial aid for the Aswan Dam project on 19 July.

The Eisenhower administration believed that if Nasser were able to secure Soviet economic support for the high dam, that would be beyond the capacity of the Soviet Union to support, and in turn would strain Soviet-Egyptian relations.[310] Eisenhower wrote in March 1956 that "If Egypt finds herself thus isolated from the rest of the Arab world, and with no ally in sight except Soviet Russia, she would very quickly get sick of the prospect and would join us in the search for a just and decent peace in the region". Dulles told his brother, CIA director Allen Dulles, "If they [the Soviets] do make this offer we can make a lot of use of it in propaganda within the satellite bloc. You don't get bread because you are being squeezed to build a dam".

Finally, the Eisenhower administration had become very annoyed at Nasser's efforts to play the United States off against the Soviet Union, and refused to finance the Aswan high dam. As early as September 1955, when Nasser announced the purchase of the Soviet military equipment via Czechoslovakia, Dulles had written that competing for Nasser's favour was probably going to be "an expensive process", one that Dulles wanted to avoid as much as possible.[311]

1956 American peace initiative

In January 1956, to end the incipient arms race in the Middle East set off by the Soviet Union selling Egypt arms on a scale unlimited by the Tripartite Declaration and with France doing likewise with Israel, which he saw as opening the Near East to Soviet influence, Eisenhower launched a major effort to make peace between Egypt and Israel. Eisenhower sent out his close friend Robert B. Anderson to serve as a secret envoy who would permanently end the Arab–Israeli dispute.[312] During his meetings with Nasser, Anderson offered large quantities of American aid in exchange for a peace treaty with Israel. Nasser demanded the return of Palestinian refugees to Israel, wanted to annex the southern half of Israel and rejected direct talks with Israel.[313] Given Nasser's territorial and refugee-related demands, the Israeli Prime Minister David Ben Gurion suspected that Nasser was not interested in a settlement. Still, he proposed direct negotiations with Egypt in any level.[314]

A second round of secret diplomacy by Anderson in February 1956 was equally unsuccessful.[315] Nasser sometimes suggested during his talks with Anderson that he was interested in peace with Israel if only the Americans would supply him with unlimited quantities of military and economic aid. In case of Israeli acceptance to the return of the Palestinian refugees to Israel and to Egypt annexing the southern half of Israel, Egypt would not accept a peace settlement. The United States or the United Nations would have to present the Israeli acceptance to all Arabs as a basis for peace settlements. It is not clear if Nasser was sincerely interested in peace, or just merely saying what the Americans wanted to hear in the hope of obtaining American funding for the Aswan high dam and American weapons. The truth will likely never be known as Nasser was an intensely secretive man, who managed to hide his true opinions on most issues from both contemporaries and historians.[316] However, the British historian P. J. Vatikitos noted that Nasser's determination to promote Egypt as the world's foremost anti-Zionist state as a way of reinforcing his claim to Arab leadership meant that peace was unlikely.[317]

Hasan Afif El-Hasan says that in 1955–1956 the American proposed Nasser to solve the Arab–Israeli conflict peacefully and in exchange to finance the High Dam on the Nile river, but Nasser rejected the offer because it would mean siding with the West (as opposed to remaining neutral) in the Cold War. Since the alternative to a peace agreement was a war with unpredictable consequences, Nasser's refusal to accept the proposal was irrational, according to el-Hasan.

Canal nationalization

Nasser's response was the nationalization of the Suez Canal. On 26 July, in a speech in Alexandria, Nasser gave a riposte to Dulles. During his speech he deliberately pronounced the name of Ferdinand de Lesseps, the builder of the canal, a code-word for Egyptian forces to seize control of the canal and implement its nationalization.[318] He announced that the Nationalization Law had been published, that all assets of the Suez Canal Company had been frozen, and that stockholders would be paid the price of their shares according to the day's closing price on the Paris Stock Exchange.[319] That same day, Egypt closed the canal to Israeli shipping. Egypt also closed the Straits of Tiran to Israeli shipping, and blockaded the Gulf of Aqaba, in contravention of the Constantinople

Figure 49: *Nasser announces the nationalization of the canal (Universal Newsreel, 30 July 1956).*

Figure 50: *Port Said, at the entrance to the Suez Canal from the Mediterranean.*

Convention of 1888. Many argued that this was also a violation of the 1949 Armistice Agreements.[320]

According to the Egyptian historian Abd al-Azim Ramadan, the events leading up to the nationalization of the Suez Canal Company, as well as other events during Nasser's rule, showed Nasser to be far from a rational, responsible leader. Ramadan notes Nasser's decision to nationalize the Suez Canal without political consultation as an example of his predilection for solitary decision-making.

British response

The nationalisation surprised Britain and its Commonwealth. There had been no discussion of the canal at the Commonwealth Prime Ministers' Conference in London in late June and early July.:[7–8] Egypt's action, however, threatened British economic and military interests in the region. Prime Minister Eden was under immense domestic pressure from Conservative MPs who drew direct comparisons between the events of 1956 and those of the Munich Agreement in 1938. Since the U.S. government did not support the British protests, the British government decided in favour of military intervention against Egypt to avoid the complete collapse of British prestige in the region.[321]

Eden was hosting a dinner for King Feisal II of Iraq and his Prime Minister, Nuri es-Said, when he learned the canal had been nationalised. They both unequivocally advised Eden to "hit Nasser hard, hit him soon, and hit him by yourself" – a stance shared by the vast majority of the British people in subsequent weeks. "There is a lot of humbug about Suez," Guy Millard, one of Eden's private secretaries, later recorded. "People forget that the policy at the time was extremely popular." Opposition leader Hugh Gaitskell was also at the dinner. He immediately agreed that military action might be inevitable, but warned Eden would have to keep the Americans closely informed.[322] After a session of the House of Commons expressed anger against the Egyptian action on 27 July, Eden justifiably believed that Parliament would support him; Gaitskell spoke for his party when he called the nationalisation a "high-handed and totally unjustifiable step".:[8–9] When Eden made a ministerial broadcast on the nationalization, Labour declined its right to reply.

Gaitskell's support became more cautious. On 2 August he said of Nasser's behaviour, "It is all very familiar. It is exactly the same that we encountered from Mussolini and Hitler in those years before the war". He cautioned Eden, however, that "[w]e must not, therefore, allow ourselves to get into a position where we might be denounced in the Security Council as aggressors, or where the majority of the Assembly was against us". He had earlier warned Eden that Labour might not support Britain acting alone against Egypt.:[8–9] In two letters to Eden sent on 3 and 10 August 1956, Gaitskell condemned Nasser but again warned that he would not support any action that violated the United Nations charter.[323] In his letter of 10 August, Gaitskell wrote:

> Lest there should be any doubt in your mind about my personal attitude, let me say that I could not regard an armed attack on Egypt by ourselves and the French as justified by anything which Nasser has done so far or as consistent with the Charter of the United Nations. Nor, in my opinion, would such an attack be justified in order to impose a system of international control over the Canal-desirable though this is. If, of course, the whole matter were to be taken to the United Nations and if Egypt were to be condemned by them as aggressors, then, of course, the position would be different. And if further action which amounted to obvious aggression by Egypt were taken by Nasser, then again it would be different. So far what Nasser has done amounts to a threat, a grave threat to us and to others, which certainly cannot be ignored; but it is only a threat, not in my opinion justifying retaliation by war.[324]

Two dozen Labour MPs issued a statement on 8 August stating that forcing Nasser to denationalise the canal against Egypt's wishes would violate the UN charter. Other opposition politicians were less conditional in their support. Former Labour Foreign Minister Herbert Morrison hinted that he would support unilateral action by the government.[9–10] Jo Grimond, who became Liberal Party leader that November, thought if Nasser went unchallenged the whole Middle East would go his way.

In Britain, the nationalisation was perceived as a direct threat to British interests. In a letter to the British Ambassador on 10 September 1956, Sir Ivone Kirkpatrick, the Permanent Under-Secretary at the Foreign Office wrote:

> If we sit back while Nasser consolidates his position and gradually acquires control of the oil-bearing countries, he can and is, according to our information, resolved to wreck us. If Middle Eastern oil is denied to us for a year or two, our gold reserves will disappear. If our gold reserves disappear, the sterling area disintegrates. If the sterling area disintegrates and we have no reserves, we shall not be able to maintain a force in Germany, or indeed, anywhere else. I doubt whether we shall be able to pay for the bare minimum necessary for our defence. And a country that cannot provide for its defence is finished.[325]

Direct military intervention, however, ran the risk of angering Washington and damaging Anglo-Arab relations. As a result, the British government concluded a secret military pact with France and Israel that was aimed at regaining control over the Suez Canal.

Figure 51: *1956 newsreels about Western reactions to the nationalization*

French response

The French Prime Minister Guy Mollet, outraged by Nasser's move, determined that Nasser would not get his way.[326] French public opinion very much supported Mollet, and apart from the Communists, all of the criticism of his government came from the right, who very publicly doubted that a socialist like Mollet had the guts to go to war with Nasser. During an interview with publisher Henry Luce, Mollet held up a copy of Nasser's book *The Philosophy of the Revolution* and said: "This is Nasser's *Mein Kampf*. If we're too stupid not to read it, understand it and draw the obvious conclusions, then so much the worse for us."[327]

On 29 July 1956, the French Cabinet decided upon military action against Egypt in alliance with Israel, and Admiral Nomy of the French Naval General Staff was sent to Britain to inform the leaders of that country of France's decision, and to invite them to co-operate if interested. At the same time, Mollet felt very much offended by what he considered to be the lackadaisical attitude of the Eisenhower administration to the nationalization of the Suez Canal Company.[328] This was especially the case because earlier in 1956 the Soviet Foreign Minister Vyacheslav Molotov had offered the French a deal whereby if Moscow ended its support of the FLN in Algeria, Paris would pull out of NATO and became neutral in the Cold War.

Given the way that Algeria (which the French considered an integral part of France) had become engulfed in a spiral of increasing savage violence that French leaders longed to put an end to, the Mollet administration had felt tempted by Molotov's offer, but in the end, Mollet, a firm Atlanticist, had chosen to remain faithful to NATO. In Mollet's view, his fidelity to NATO had earned him the right to expect firm American support against Egypt, and when that support proved not forthcoming, he became even more determined that if the Americans were not willing to do anything about Nasser, then France would act.

Commonwealth response

Among the "White Dominions" of the British Commonwealth, Canada had few ties with the Suez Canal and twice had refused British requests for peacetime military aid in the Middle East. It had little reaction to the seizure before military action. By 1956 the Panama Canal was much more important than Suez to Australia and New Zealand; the following year two experts would write that it "is not vital to the Australian economy". The memory, however, of the two nations fighting in two world wars to protect a canal which many still called their "lifeline" to Britain or "jugular vein", contributed to Australian Prime Minister Robert Menzies and Sidney Holland of New Zealand supporting Britain in the early weeks after the seizure. On 7 August Holland hinted to his parliament that New Zealand might send troops to assist Britain, and received support from the opposition; on 13 August Menzies, who had traveled to London from the United States after hearing of the nationalisation and became an informal member of the British Cabinet discussing the issue, spoke on the BBC in support of the Eden government's position on the canal. He called the dispute over the canal "a crisis more grave than any since the Second World War ended".:13–16,56–58,84 An elder statesman of the Commonwealth who felt that Nasser's actions threatened trading nations like Australia, he argued publicly that Western powers had built the canal but that Egypt was now seeking to exclude them from a role in its ownership or management.[329] South Africa's Johannes Strijdom stated "it is best to keep our heads out of the beehive". His government saw Nasser as an enemy but would benefit economically and geopolitically from a closed canal, and politically from not opposing a nation's right to govern its internal affairs.:16–18

The "non-white Dominions" saw Egypt's seizing of the canal as an admirable act of anti-imperialism, and Nasser's Arab nationalism as similar to Asian nationalism. Jawaharlal Nehru of India was with Nasser when he learned of the Anglo-American withdrawal of aid for the Aswan Dam. As India was a user of the canal, however, he remained publicly neutral other than warning that any use of force, or threats, could be "disastrous". Suez was also very important to Ceylon's economy, and it was renegotiating defense treaties with Britain, so its government was not as vocal in supporting Egypt as it would have been otherwise. Pakistan was also cautious about supporting Egypt given their rivalry as leading Islamic nations, but its government did state that Nasser had the right to nationalise.:18–24,79

Western diplomacy

On 1 August 1956, a tripartite meeting was opened at 10 Downing Street between British Foreign Secretary Selwyn Lloyd, U.S. Ambassador Robert D. Murphy and French Foreign Affairs Minister Christian Pineau.[330]

An alliance was soon formed between Eden and Guy Mollet, French Prime Minister, with headquarters in London. General Hugh Stockwell and Admiral Barjot were appointed as Chief of Staff. Britain sought co-operation with the United States throughout 1956 to deal with what it maintained was a threat of an Israeli attack against Egypt, but to little effect.

Between July and October 1956, unsuccessful initiatives encouraged by the United States were made to reduce the tension that would ultimately lead to war. International conferences were organised to secure agreement on Suez Canal operations but all were ultimately fruitless.

Almost immediately after the nationalisation, Eisenhower suggested to Eden a conference of maritime nations that used the canal. The British preferred to invite the most important countries, but the Americans believed that inviting as many as possible amid maximum publicity would affect world opinion. Invitations went to the eight surviving signatories of the Constantinople Convention and the 16 other largest users of the canal: Australia, Ceylon, Denmark, Egypt, Ethiopia, France, West Germany, Greece, India, Indonesia, Iran, Italy, Japan, the Netherlands, New Zealand, Norway, Pakistan, Portugal, Soviet Union, Spain, Sweden, Turkey, the United Kingdom, and the United States. All except Egypt—which sent an observer, and used India and the Soviet Union to represent its interests—and Greece accepted the invitation, and the 22 nations' representatives met in London from 16 to 23 August.:81–89

15 of the nations supported the American-British-French position of international operation of the canal; Pakistan chose its western allies over its sympathy for Egypt's anti-western position despite resulting great domestic controversy. Ceylon, Indonesia, and the Soviet Union supported India's competing proposal—which Nasser had preapproved—of international supervision only. India criticized Egypt's seizure of the canal, but insisted that its ownership and operation now not change. The majority of 18 chose five nations to negotiate with Nasser in Cairo led by Menzies, while their proposal for international operation of the canal would go to the Security Council.:81–89[331]

Figure 52: *Australian Prime Minister Robert Menzies led an international committee in negotiations with Nasser in September 1956, which sought to achieve international management of the Suez Canal. The mission was a failure.*

Menzies' 7 September official communique to Nasser presented a case for compensation for the Suez Canal Company and the "establishment of principles" for the future use of the canal that would ensure that it would "continue to be an international waterway operated free of politics or national discrimination, and with financial structure so secure and an international confidence so high that an expanding and improving future for the Canal could be guaranteed" and called for a convention to recognise Egyptian sovereignty of the canal, but for the establishment of an international body to run the canal. Nasser saw such measures as a "derogation from Egyptian sovereignty" and rejected Menzies' proposals. Menzies hinted to Nasser that Britain and France might use force to resolve the crisis, but Eisenhower openly opposed the use of force and Menzies left Egypt without success.

Instead of the 18-nation proposal, the United States proposed an association of canal users that would set rules for its operation. 14 of the other nations, not including Pakistan, agreed. Britain, in particular, believed that violation of the association rules would result in military force, but after Eden made a speech to this effect in parliament on 12 September, the US ambassador Dulles insisted "we do not intend to shoot our way through" the canal.:[89–92] The United States worked hard through diplomatic channels to resolve the crisis without resorting to conflict. "The British and French reluctantly agreed to pursue the diplomatic avenue but viewed it as merely an attempt to buy time, during which they continued their military preparations." The British, Washington's closest ally, ignored Eisenhower's pointed warning that the American people would not accept a military solution.

On 25 September 1956 the Chancellor of the Exchequer Harold Macmillan met informally with Eisenhower at the White House. Macmillan misread Eisenhower's determination to avoid war and told Eden that the Americans would not in any way oppose the attempt to topple Nasser.[332] Though Eden had known Eisenhower for years and had many direct contacts with him during the crisis, he also misread the situation. The Americans refused to support any move that could be seen as imperialism or colonialism, seeing the US as the champion of decolonisation. Eisenhower felt the crisis had to be handled peacefully; he told Eden that American public opinion would not support a military solution. Eden and other leading British officials incorrectly believed Nasser's support for Palestinian fedayeen against Israel, as well as his attempts to destabilise pro-western regimes in Iraq and other Arab states, would deter the US from intervening with the operation. Eisenhower specifically warned that the Americans, and the world, "would be outraged" unless all peaceful routes had been exhausted, and even then "the eventual price might become far too heavy".[333,334] London hoped that Nasser's engagement with communist states would persuade the Americans to accept British and French actions if they were presented as a *fait accompli*. This proved to be a critical miscalculation.

Franco-British-Israeli war plan

Objectives

Britain was anxious lest it lose efficient access to the remains of its empire. Both Britain and France were eager that the canal should remain open as an important conduit of oil.

Both the French and the British felt that Nasser should be removed from power. The French "held the Egyptian president responsible for assisting the anticolonial rebellion in Algeria". France was nervous about the growing influence that Nasser exerted on its North African colonies and protectorates.

Israel wanted to reopen the Straits of Tiran leading to the Gulf of Aqaba to Israeli shipping, and saw the opportunity to strengthen its southern border and to weaken what it saw as a dangerous and hostile state. This was particularly felt in the form of attacks injuring approximately 1,300 civilians emanating from the Egyptian-held Gaza Strip.[335]

The Israelis were also deeply troubled by Egypt's procurement of large amounts of Soviet weaponry that included 530 armored vehicles, of which 230 were tanks; 500 guns; 150 MiG 15 jet fighters; 50 Ilyushin Il-28 bombers; submarines and other naval craft. The influx of this advanced weaponry altered an already shaky balance of power.[336] Israel was alarmed by the Czech arms deal, and believed it had only a narrow window of opportunity to hit Egypt's army. Additionally, Israel believed Egypt had formed a secret alliance with Jordan and Syria.[337]

British planning

In July 1956, Eden ordered his CIGS, Field Marshal Gerald Templer to begin planning for an invasion of Egypt.[338] Eden's plan called for the Cyprus-based 16th Independent Parachute Brigade Group to seize the canal zone.[339] The Prime Minister's plan was rejected by Templer and the other service chiefs, who argued that the neglect of parachute training in the 16th Independent Parachute Brigade rendered his plan for an airborne assault unsuitable. Instead, they suggested the sea-power based Contingency Plan, which called for the Royal Marines to take Port Said, which would then be used as a base for three British divisions to overrun the canal zone.

In early August, the Contingency Plan was modified by including a strategic bombing campaign that was intended to destroy Egypt's economy, and thereby hopefully bring about Nasser's overthrow. In addition, a role was allocated to the 16th Independent Parachute Brigade, which would lead the assault on Port Said in conjunction with the Royal Marine landing.[340] The commanders of the Allied Task Force led by General Stockwell rejected the Contingency Plan, which Stockwell argued failed to destroy the Egyptian military.

Franco-Israeli planning

In July 1956, IDF chief of staff General Moshe Dayan advised Prime Minister David Ben Gurion that Israel should attack Egypt at the first chance, but Ben Gurion stated he preferred to attack Egypt with the aid of France.[341] On 7 August 1956 the French Defense Minister Maurice Bourgès-Maunoury asked Peres if Israel would attack Egypt together with France, to which he received a positive reply.[342] On 1 September 1956 the French government formally asked that France and Israel begin joint planning for a war against Egypt.[343] By 6 September 1956, Dayan's chief of operations General Meir Amit, was meeting with Admiral Pierre Barjot to discuss joint Franco-Israeli operations. On 25 September 1956 Peres reported to Ben Gurion that France wanted Israel as an ally against Egypt, and that the only problem was Britain, which was opposed to Israel taking action against Nasser.[344] In late September 1956, the French Premier Guy Mollet had embarked upon a dual policy of attacking Egypt with

Britain, and if the British backed out (as Mollet believed that they might), with Israel.[345] On 30 September 1956 secret Franco-Israeli talks on planning a war started in Paris, which were based on the assumption that Britain would not be involved.[346] The French very much wanted to use airfields in Cyprus to bomb Egypt, but being not certain about Britain's attitude, wanted to use Israeli airfields if the ones in Cyprus were not free.[347] Only on 5 October 1956 during a visit by General Maurice Challe to Britain where he met with Eden, were the British informed of the secret Franco-Israeli alliance.[348]

On 22 October 1956, during negotiations leading to the Protocol of Sevres, David Ben-Gurion, Prime Minister of Israel, gave the most detailed explanation ever to foreign dignitaries, of Israel's overall strategy for the Middle East. Shlaim called this Ben-Gurion's "grand design". His main objection to the "English plan" was that Israel would be branded as the aggressor while Britain and France would pose as peace-makers.

> *Instead he presented a comprehensive plan, which he himself called "fantastic", for the reorganization of the Middle East. Jordan, he observed, was not viable as an independent state and should therefore be divided. Iraq would get the East Bank in return for a promise to settle the Palestinian refugees there and to make peace with Israel while the West Bank would be attached to Israel as a semi-autonomous region. Lebanon suffered from having a large Muslim population which was concentrated in the south. The problem could be solved by Israel's expansion up to the Litani River, thereby helping to turn Lebanon into a more compact Christian state. ... Israel declares its intention to keep her forces for the purpose of permanent annexation of the entire area east of the El Arish-Abu Ageila, Nakhl-Sharm el-Sheikh, in order to maintain for the long term the freedom of navigation in the Straits of Eilat and in order to free herself from the scourge of the infiltrators and from the danger posed by the Egyptian army bases in Sinai. ... "I told him about the discovery of oil in southern and western Sinai, and that it would be good to tear this peninsula from Egypt because it did not belong to her, rather it was the English who stole it from the Turks when they believed that Egypt was in their pocket. I suggested laying down a pipeline from Sinai to Haifa to refine the oil."*

Protocol of Sèvres

In October 1956, Eden, after two months of pressure, finally and reluctantly agreed to French requests to include Israel in Operation ReviseWikipedia:Citing sources. The British alliances with the Hashemite kingdoms of Jordan and Iraq had made the British very reluctant to fight alongside Israel, lest the ensuing backlash in the Arab world threaten London's friends in Baghdad and Amman. The coming of winter weather in November meant

Figure 53: *Newsreels about disturbances in North Africa and Egypt leading up to the Suez Crisis*

that Eden needed a pretext to begin Revise as soon as possible, which meant that Israel had to be included. This was especially the case as many Conservative backbenchers had expected Eden to launch operations against Egypt in the summer, and were disappointed when Eden had instead chosen talks. By the fall of 1956, many Tory backbenchers were starting to grow restive about the government's seeming inability to start military action, and if Eden had continued to put off military action for the winter of 1956–57, it is possible that his government might not have survived.

Three months after Egypt's nationalization of the Suez Canal company, a secret meeting took place at Sèvres, outside Paris. Britain and France enlisted Israeli support for an alliance against Egypt. The parties agreed that Israel would invade the Sinai. Britain and France would then intervene, purportedly to separate the warring Israeli and Egyptian forces, instructing both to withdraw to a distance of 16 kilometres from either side of the canal.[349]

The British and French would then argue that Egypt's control of such an important route was too tenuous, and that it needed be placed under Anglo-French management. David Ben-Gurion did not trust the British in view of their treaty with Jordan and he was not initially in favour of the plan, since it would make Israel alone look like the aggressor; however he soon agreed to it since such a good opportunity to strike back at Egypt might never again present itself.

Under the Protocol of Sèvres, the following was agreed to:
- 29 October: Israel to invade the Sinai.
- 30 October: Anglo-French ultimatum to demand both sides withdraw from the canal zone.
- 31 October: Britain and France begin Revise.

Anglo-French Operation Musketeer

Stockwell offered up Operation Musketeer, which was to begin with a two-day air campaign that would see the British gain air superiority. In place of Port Said, Musketeer called for the capture of Alexandria. Once that city had been taken in assault from the sea, British armoured divisions would engage in a decisive battle of annihilation somewhere south of Alexandria and north of Cairo.

Musketeer would require thousands of troops, leading the British to seek out France as an ally. To destroy the 300,000-strong Egyptian Army in his planned battle of annihilation, Stockwell estimated that he needed 80,000 troops, while at most the British Army could spare was 50,000 troops; the French could supply the necessary 30,000 troops to make up the shortfall.

On 11 August 1956, General Keightley was appointed commander of Musketeer with the French Admiral Barjot as his deputy commander. The appointment of Stockwell as the Allied Task Force commander charged with leading the assault on Egypt caused considerable disappointment with the other officers of the Task Force.[350] One French officer recalled that Stockwell was <templatestyles src="Template:Quote/styles.css"/>

> Extremely excitable, gesticulating, keeping no part of him still, his hands, his feet, and even his head and shoulders perpetually on the go, he starts off by sweeping objects off the table with a swish of his swagger cane or in his room by using it to make golf-strokes with the flower vases and ashtrays. Those are the good moments. You will see him pass in an instant from the most cheerfully expressed optimism to a dejection that amounts to nervous depression. He is a cyclothymic. By turns courteous and brutal, refined and coarse, headstrong in some circumstances, hesitant and indecisive in others, he disconcerts by his unpredictable responses and the contradictions of which he is made up. One only of his qualities remains constant: his courage under fire.

By contrast, the majority of the officers of the Task Force, both French and British, admired Beaufre as an elegant yet tough general with a sharp analytical mind who always kept his cool. Most of the officers of the Anglo-French Task Force expressed regret that it was Beaufre who was Stockwell's deputy rather the other way around. A major problem both politically and militarily with the planning for Musketeer was the one-week interval between sending troops to the eastern Mediterranean and the beginning of the invasion.[351] Additionally, the coming of winter weather to the Mediterranean in late November would render the invasion impossible, which thus meant the invasion had to begin before then. An additional problem was Eden, who constantly interfered with the planning and was so obsessed with secrecy that he refused to tell Keightley what his political objectives were in attacking Egypt, namely was he interested in retaking the Suez Canal or toppling Nasser, or both.[352] Eden's refusal to explain to Keightley just what exactly he was hoping to accomplish by attacking Egypt exasperated Keightley to no end, and greatly complicated the planning process.

In late August 1956, the French Admiral Pierre Barjot suggested that Port Said once again be made the main target, which lessened the number of troops needed and thus reduced the interval between sending forces to the eastern Mediterranean and the invasion.[353] Beaufre was strongly opposed to the change, warning that Barjot's modification of merely capturing the canal zone made for an ambiguous goal, and that the lack of a clear goal was dangerous.

In early September, Keightley embraced Barjot's idea of seizing Port Said, and presented Revise.

Anglo-French Operation Revise

Operation Revise called for the following:

- Phase I: Anglo-French air forces to gain air supremacy over Egypt's skies.
- Phase II: Anglo-French air forces were to launch a 10-day "aero-psychological" campaign that would destroy the Egyptian economy.
- Phase III: Air- and sea-borne landings to capture the canal zone.

On 8 September 1956 Revise was approved by the British and French cabinets.

Both Stockwell and Beaufre were opposed to Revise as an open-ended plan with no clear goal beyond seizing the canal zone, but was embraced by Eden and Mollet as offering greater political flexibility and the prospect of lesser Egyptian civilian casualties.

Israeli Operation Kadesh

At the same time, Israel had been working on Operation Kadesh for the invasion of the Sinai. Dayan's plan put an emphasis on air power combined with mobile battles of encirclement. Kadesh called for the Israeli air force to win air superiority, which was to be followed up with "one continuous battle" in the Sinai. Israeli forces would in a series of swift operations encircle and then take the main Egyptian strong points in the Sinai.

Figure 54: *Universal Newsreel from 6 August about the departure of British and French ships for Egypt*

Reflecting this emphasis on encirclement was the "outside-in" approach of Kadesh, which called for Israeli paratroopers to seize distant points first, with those closer to Israel to be seized later. Thus, the 202nd Paratroop Brigade commanded by Colonel Ariel Sharon was to land in the far-western part of the Sinai to take the Mitla Pass, and thereby cut off the Egyptian forces in the eastern Sinai from their supply lines.

American intelligence

The American Central Intelligence Agency (CIA) was taking high-altitude photos of the allied activities, and more details came from human sources in London, Paris and Tel Aviv. CIA chief Allen Dulles said that "intelligence was well alerted as to what Israel and then Britain and France were likely to do ... In fact, United States intelligence had kept the government informed".

Forces

Britain

British troops were well-trained, experienced, and had good morale, but suffered from the economic and technological limitations imposed by post-war austerity.[354] The 16th Independent Parachute Brigade Group, which was intended to be the main British strike force against Egypt, was heavily involved in the Cyprus Emergency, which led to a neglect of paratroop training in favour of counter-insurgency operations. The Royal Navy could project formidable power through the guns of its warships and aircraft flown from its carriers, but a shortage of landing craft proved to be a serious weakness.[355]

It had just undergone a major and innovative carrier modernization program. The Royal Air Force (RAF) had just introduced two long-range bombers, the Vickers Valiant and the English Electric Canberra, but owing to their recent entry into service the RAF had not yet established proper bombing techniques for these aircraft. Despite this, General Sir Charles Keightley, the commander of the invasion force, believed that air power alone was sufficient to defeat Egypt. By contrast, General Hugh Stockwell, the Task Force's ground commander believed that methodical and systematic armored operations centered on the Centurion battle tank would be the key to victory.[356]

France

French troops were experienced and well-trained but suffered from cutbacks imposed by post-war politics of economic austerity.[357] In 1956, the French military was heavily involved in the Algerian war, which made operations against Egypt a major distraction. French paratroopers of the elite *Regiment de Parachutistes Coloniaux* (RPC) were extremely experienced, battle-hardened, and very tough soldiers, who had greatly distinguished themselves in the fighting in Indochina and in Algeria. The men of the RPC followed a "shoot first, ask questions later" policy towards civilians, first adopted in Vietnam, which was to lead to the killing of a number of Egyptian civilians. The rest of the French troops were described by the American military historian Derek Varble as "competent, but not outstanding".

The main French (and Israeli) battle tank, the AMX-13, was designed for mobile, outflanking operations, which led to a tank that was lightly armoured but very fast. General André Beaufre, who served as Stockwell's subordinate, favoured a swift campaign of movement in which the main objective was to encircle the enemy. Throughout the operation, Beaufre proved himself to be more aggressive than his British counterparts, always urging that some bold step be taken at once. The French Navy had a powerful carrier force which was excellent for projecting power inland, but, like its British counterpart, suffered from a lack of landing craft.

Figure 55: *Israeli AMX-13, shown here from the rear and side*

Israel

American military historian Derek Varble called the Israel Defense Forces (IDF) the "best" military force in the Middle East while at the same time suffering from "deficiencies" such as "immature doctrine, faulty logistics, and technical inadequacies".[358] The IDF's Chief of Staff, Major General Moshe Dayan, encouraged aggression, initiative, and ingenuity among the Israeli officer corps while ignoring logistics and armoured operations. Dayan, a firm infantry man, preferred that arm of the service at the expense of armour, which Dayan saw as clumsy, pricey, and suffering from frequent breakdowns.

At the same time, the IDF had a rather disorganized logistics arm, which was put under severe strain when the IDF invaded the Sinai. Most of the IDF weapons in 1956 came from France. The main IDF tank was the AMX-13 and the main aircraft were the Dassault Mystère IVA and the Ouragan.[359] Superior pilot training was to give the Israeli Air Force an unbeatable edge over their Egyptian opponents. The Israeli Navy consisted of two destroyers, seven frigates, eight minesweepers, several landing craft, and fourteen torpedo boats.

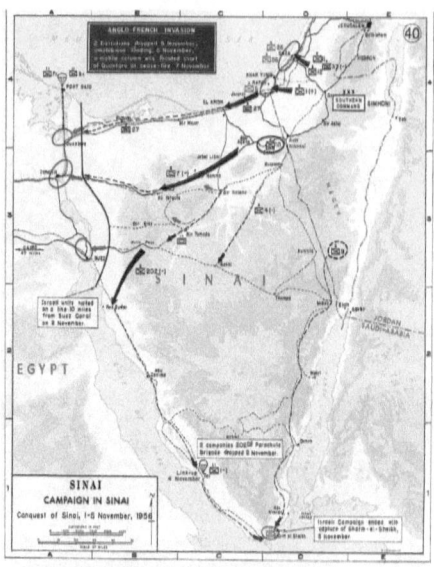

Figure 56: *Anglo-French para drops on the Suez Canal and Israeli conquest of Sinai*

Egypt

In the Egyptian Armed Forces, politics rather than military competence was the main criterion for promotion.[360] The Egyptian commander, Field Marshal Abdel Hakim Amer, was a purely political appointee who owed his position to his close friendship with Nasser. A heavy drinker, he would prove himself grossly incompetent as a general during the Crisis. In 1956, the Egyptian military was well equipped with weapons from the Soviet Union such as T-34 and IS-3 tanks, MiG-15 fighters, Ilyushin Il-28 bombers, SU-100 self-propelled guns and assault rifles.

Rigid lines between officers and men in the Egyptian Army led to a mutual "mistrust and contempt" between officers and the men who served under them.[361] Egyptian troops were excellent in defensive operations, but had little capacity for offensive operations, owing to the lack of "rapport and effective small-unit leadership".

Figure 57: *Israeli M4A4 Shermans were also used in the Sinai campaign.*

Invasion

The Israeli operation Kadesh in Sinai

Operation Kadesh received its name from ancient Kadesh, located in the northern Sinai and mentioned several times in the Hebrew Pentateuch. Israeli military planning for this operation in the Sinai hinged on four main military objectives; Sharm el-Sheikh, Arish, Abu Uwayulah (Abu Ageila), and the Gaza Strip. The Egyptian blockade of the Tiran Straits was based at Sharm el-Sheikh and, by capturing the town, Israel would have access to the Red Sea for the first time since 1953, which would allow it to restore the trade benefits of secure passage to the Indian Ocean.

The Gaza Strip was chosen as another military objective because Israel wished to remove the training grounds for Fedayeen groups, and because Israel recognised that Egypt could use the territory as a staging ground for attacks against the advancing Israeli troops. Israel advocated rapid advances, for which a potential Egyptian flanking attack would present even more of a risk. Arish and Abu Uwayulah were important hubs for soldiers, equipment, and centres of command and control of the Egyptian Army in the Sinai.[362]

Capturing them would deal a deathblow to the Egyptian's strategic operation in the entire Peninsula. The capture of these four objectives were hoped to be the means by which the entire Egyptian Army would rout and fall back into Egypt proper, which British and French forces would then be able to push up

Figure 58: *An Israeli Air Force Meteor in flight*

against an Israeli advance, and crush in a decisive encounter. On 24 October, Dayan ordered a partial mobilization. When this led to a state of confusion, Dayan ordered full mobilization, and chose to take the risk that he might alert the Egyptians. As part of an effort to maintain surprise, Dayan ordered Israeli troops that were to go to the Sinai to be ostentatiously concentrated near the border with Jordan first, which was intended to fool the Egyptians into thinking that it was Jordan that the main Israeli blow was to fall on.

On 28 October, Operation Tarnegol was effected, during which an Israeli Gloster Meteor NF.13 intercepted and destroyed an Egyptian Ilyushin Il-14 carrying Egyptian officers en route from Syria to Egypt, killing 16 Egyptian officers and journalists and two crewmen. The Ilyushin was believed to be carrying Field Marshal Abdel Hakim Amer and the Egyptian General Staff; however this was not the case.

The conflict began on 29 October 1956. At about 3:00 pm, Israeli Air Force Mustangs launched a series of attacks on Egyptian positions all over the Sinai. Because Israeli intelligence expected Jordan to enter the war on Egypt's side,[363] Israeli soldiers were stationed along the Israeli-Jordanian frontier. The Israel Border Police militarized the Israel-Jordan border, including the Green Line with the West Bank, during the first few hours of the war. Israeli-Arab villages along the Jordanian border were placed under curfew. This resulted in the killings of 48 civilians in the Arab village of Kafr Qasim in an event known as the Kafr Qasim massacre. The border policemen involved in the killings

Suez Crisis 141

Figure 59: *Israeli paratrooper near the Mitla Pass*

were later tried and imprisoned, with an Israeli court finding that the order to shoot civilians was "blatantly illegal". This event had major effects on Israeli law relating to the ethics in war and more subtle effects on the legal status of Arab citizens of Israel, who at the time were regarded as a fifth column.

Early actions in Southern Sinai

The IDF chief of staff General Moshe Dayan, first planned to block the vital Mitla Pass. Dayan planned for the Battalion 890 of the Paratroop Brigade, under the command of Lieutenant Colonel Rafael Eitan, a veteran of the 1948 Arab–Israeli War and future head of the IDF, to drop at Parker's Memorial, near one of the defiles of the pass, Jebel Heitan.[364] The rest of the brigade, under the command of Colonel Ariel Sharon would then advance to meet with the battalion, and consolidate their holdings.

On 29 October, Operation Kadesh – the invasion of the Sinai, began when an Israeli paratrooper battalion was air-dropped into the Sinai Peninsula, east of the Suez Canal near the Mitla Pass. In conjunction with the para drop, four Israeli P-51 Mustangs using their wings and propellers, cut all overhead telephone lines in the Sinai, severely disrupting Egyptian command and control.[365,366] Due to a navigation error, the Israeli DC-3 transports landed Eitan's

Figure 60: *Israeli soldiers in the Sinai wave at a passing French plane*

400 paratroopers three miles away from Parker's Memorial, their intended target.[367] Eitan marched his men towards Jebel Heitan, where they dug in while receiving supplies of weapons dropped by French aircraft.

At the same time, Colonel Sharon's 202nd Paratroop Brigade raced out towards the Mitla Pass. A major problem for Sharon was vehicle break-down. Dayan's efforts to maintain strategic surprise bore fruit when the Egyptian commander Field Marshal Abdel Hakim Amer at first treated the reports of an Israeli inclusion into the Sinai as a large raid instead of an invasion, and as such Amer did not order a general alert. By the time that Amer realized his mistake, the Israelis had made significant advances into the Sinai.

Early actions along the Gulf of Aqaba, and the central front

As the paratroopers were being dropped into the Sinai, the Israeli 9th Infantry Brigade captured Ras al-Naqb, an important staging ground for that brigade's later attack against Sharm el-Sheikh. Instead of attacking the town by a frontal attack, they enveloped the town in a night attack, and negotiated their way through some of the natural chokepoints into the rear of the town, surprising the Egyptians before they could ready themselves to defend. The Egyptians surrendered, with no Israeli casualties sustained.

The 4th Infantry Brigade, under the command of Colonel Josef Harpaz, captured al-Qusaymah, which would be used as a jumping off point for the assault

Figure 61: *Israeli paratroopers dig in near the Parker Memorial*

against Abu Uwayulah. Colonel Harpaz out-flanked al-Qusaymah with two pincers from the south-east and north-east in a night attack.[368] In a short battle lasting from 3:00 am to sunrise, the IDF stormed al-Qusaymah.

Battle of Jebel Heitan, paratroop brigade under attack

The portion of the paratroopers under Sharon's command continued to advance to meet with the 1st Brigade. En route, Sharon assaulted Themed in a dawn attack, and was able to storm the town with his armor through the Themed Gap.[369] Sharon routed the Sudanese police company, and captured the settlement. On his way to the Nakla, Sharon's men came under attack from Egyptian MIG-15s. On the 30th, Sharon linked up with Eytan near Nakla.

Dayan had no more plans for further advances beyond the passes, but Sharon decided to attack the Egyptian positions at Jebel Heitan. Sharon sent his lightly armed paratroopers against dug-in Egyptians supported by aircraft, tanks and heavy artillery. Sharon's actions were in response to reports of the arrival of the 1st and 2nd Brigades of the 4th Egyptian Armored Division in the area, which Sharon believed would annihilate his forces if he did not seize the high ground. Sharon sent two infantry companies, a mortar battery and some AMX-13 tanks under the command of Mordechai Gur into the Heitan Defile on the afternoon of 31 October 1956.

Figure 62: *Israeli AMX-13 Light tank*

The Egyptian forces occupied strong defensive positions and brought down heavy anti-tank, mortar and machine gun fire on the IDF force.[370] Gur's men were forced to retreat into the "Saucer", where they were surrounded and came under heavy fire. Hearing of this, Sharon sent in another task force while Gur's men used the cover of night to scale the walls of the Heitan Defile. During the ensuing action, the Egyptians were defeated and forced to retreat. A total of 260 Egyptian and 38 Israeli soldiers were killed in the battle.

Although the battle was an Israeli victory, the casualties sustained would surround Sharon with controversy.[371] In particular, Sharon was criticized for ordering the attack on Jebel Heitan without authorization, and not realizing that with the Israeli Air Force controlling the skies, his men were in not such danger from the Egyptian tanks as he believed. Dayan himself maintained that Sharon was correct to order the attack without orders, and that under the circumstances, Sharon made the right decision; instead he criticized Sharon for his tactics of attacking the Egyptians head-on, which Dayan claimed led to unnecessary casualties.

Air operations, first phase

From the outset, the Israeli Air Force flew paratroop drops, supply flights and medevac sorties. Israel's new French-made Dassault Mystere IV jet fighters provided air cover for the transport aircraft. In the initial phase of the conflict, the Egyptian Air Force flew attack missions against advancing Israeli ground forces. The Egyptian tactic was to use their new Soviet-made MiG-15 jets

Figure 63: *Universal Newsreel from 1 November about the attack on Egypt*

as fighter escorts, while their older British-made De Havilland Vampire and Gloster Meteor jets conducted strikes against Israeli troops and vehicles.[372]

In air combat, Israeli aircraft shot down between seven and nine Egyptian jets with the loss of one plane,[373] but Egyptian strikes against the ground forces continued through to 1 November.[374] With the attack by the British and French air forces and navies, President Nasser ordered his pilots to disengage and fly their planes to bases in Southern Egypt. The Israeli Air Force was then free to strike Egyptian ground forces at will, as Israeli forces advanced into the Western Sinai.

On 3 November, four Israeli warplanes attacked a British warship, the Black Swan class sloop HMS *Crane* as it was patrolling the approaches to the Gulf of Aqaba. According to the IDF, *Crane* had been identified as an Egyptian warship, and the Israeli General Staff authorized the attack. Three rockets penetrated the ship's hull and caused significant internal damage, including severed power mains and a ruptured oil tank. The ship also sustained some external damage from shrapnel and cannon fire, and three crewmen were wounded. *Crane* shot down one Israeli plane and damaged another during the engagement.[375,376,377]

Figure 64: *Ibrahim el Awal after its capture by the Israeli Navy*

Naval operations

On 30 October, the Egyptian Navy dispatched *Ibrahim el Awal*, an ex-British Hunt-class destroyer, to Haifa with the aim of shelling that city's coastal oil installations. On 31 October *Ibrahim el Awal* reached Haifa and began bombarding the city with its four 102 mm (4 in) guns. The French destroyer *Kersaint*, which was guarding Haifa port as part of Operation Musketeer, returned fire but failed to score any hits. *Ibrahim el Awal* disengaged and turned northwest. The Israeli destroyers INS *Eilat* and INS *Yaffo* and two Israeli Air Force Dassault Ouragans then gave chase and caught up with the Egyptian warship, and attacked it, damaging the destroyer's turbo generator, rudder and antiaircraft guns. Left without power and unable to steer, *Ibrahim el Awal* surrendered to the Israeli destroyers. During the engagement, the *Ibrahim el Awal's* crew lost 2 killed and 8 wounded. The Egyptian destroyer was subsequently incorporated into the Israeli Navy and renamed INS *Haifa*.[378]

On the night of 31 October in the northern Red Sea, the British light cruiser HMS *Newfoundland* challenged and engaged the Egyptian frigate *Domiat*, reducing it to a burning hulk in a brief gun battle. The Egyptian warship was then sunk by escorting destroyer HMS *Diana*. Of the *Domiat's* crew, 38 were killed and 69 survived and were rescued. British losses in the engagement were 1 killed and 5 wounded.[379,380] On 4 November, a squadron of Egyptian motor torpedo boats attacked a British destroyer off the northeast coast of the Nile Delta. The attack was repelled, with three torpedo boats sunk and the rest retreating.

Hedgehog-Abu Uwayulah operations

The village of Abu Uwayulah, 25 km (16 mi) inside Egyptian territory, served as the road centre for the entire Sinai, and thus was a key Israeli target. To the east of Abu Uwayulah were several ridges that formed a natural defensive zone known to the Israelis as the "Hedgehog". Holding the "Hedgehog" were 3,000 Egyptians of the 17th and 18th battalions of the 3rd Infantry Division commanded by Colonel Sami Yassa. Yassa's men held a series of well-fortified trenches. The "Hedgehog" could only be assaulted from the east flank of Umm Qataf ridge and the west flank of Ruafa ridge.

On 30 October, a probing attack by Israeli armour under Major Izhak Ben-Ari turned into an assault on the Umm Qataf ridge that ended in failure.[381] During the fighting at Umm Qataf, Colonel Yassa was badly wounded and replaced by Colonel Saadedden Mutawally.[382] To the south, another unit of the Israeli 7th Armored Brigade discovered the al-Dayyiqa gap in the Jebel Halal ridge of the "Hedgehog". The Israeli forces stormed and took the al-Dayyiqa gap. Colonel Mutawally failed to appreciate the extent of the danger to his forces posed by the IDF breakthrough at al-Dayyiqa.

Led by Colonel Avraham Adan, an IDF force entered the al-Dayyiqa and at dawn on 31 October attacked Abu Uwayulah.[383] After an hour's fighting, Abu Uwayulah fell to the IDF.[384] At the same time, another IDF battalion attacked the Ruafa ridge.

Concurrently, another attack was launched on the eastern edge of the "Hedgehog" by the IDF 10th Infantry Brigade (composed mostly of reservists) that ended in failure.[385] By noon, the Israeli Air Force had carried out a series of punishing airstrikes on the Egyptian positions, sometimes accidentally hitting IDF ground forces. Such was the tendency of the IAF to stage "friendly fire" incidents the IAF was arguably as much as danger to the Israeli troops as to the enemy.

After taking Abu Uwayulah, Adan committed all of his forces against the Ruafa ridge of the "Hedgehog".[386] Adan began a three-pronged attack with one armored force striking northeastern edge of Ruafa, a mixed infantry/armored force attacking the north edge and a feint attack from a neighbouring knoll. During the evening attack on 31 October, a chaotic battle raged on Ruafa ridge with much hand-to-hand fighting.[387] Though every IDF tank involved was destroyed, after a night's fighting, Ruafa had fallen to the IDF.[388] Another IDF assault that night, this time by the 10th Infantry Brigade on Umm Qataf was

Figure 65: *U.S. newsreel on the Sinai and Gaza invasions*

less successful with much of the attacking force getting lost in the darkness, resulting in a series of confused attacks that ended in failure. Dayan, who had grown impatient with the failure to storm the "Hedgehog", sacked the 10th Brigade's commander Colonel Shmuel Golinda and replaced him with Colonel Israel Tal.

On the morning of 1 November, Israeli and French aircraft launched frequent napalm attacks on the Egyptian troops at Umm Qataf. Joined by the 37th Armored Brigade, the 10th Brigade again assaulted Umm Qataf, and was again defeated. However, the ferocity of the IDF assault combined with rapidly dwindling stocks of water and ammunition caused Colonel Mutawally to order a general retreat from the "Hedgehog" on the evening of 1 November.

Gaza Strip operations

The city of Rafah was strategically important to Israel because control of that city would sever the Gaza Strip from the Sinai and provide a way to the main centres of the northern Sinai, al-Arish and al-Qantarah.[389] Holding the forts outside of Rafah were a mixture of Egyptian and Palestinian forces in the 5th Infantry Brigade commanded by Brigadier General Jaafar al-Abd. In Rafah itself the 87th Palestinian Infantry Brigade was stationed. Assigned to capture Rafah were 1st Infantry Brigade led by Colonel Benjamin Givli and 27th Armored Brigade commanded by Colonel Haim Bar-Lev of the IDF. To the south of Rafah were a series of mine-filled sand dunes and to the north were a series of fortified hills.

Dayan ordered the IDF forces to seize Crossroads 12 in the central Rafah area, and to focus on breaking through rather than reducing every Egyptian strongpoint. The IDF assault began with Israeli sappers and engineers clearing a path at night through the minefields that surrounded Rafah. French warships led by the cruiser *Georges Leygues* provided fire support, through Dayan had a low opinion of the French gunnery, complaining that the French only struck the Egyptian reserves.[390]

Using the two paths cleared through the southern minefields, IDF tanks entered the Rafah salient. Under Egyptian artillery fire, the IDF force raced ahead and took Crossroads 12 with the loss of 2 killed and 22 wounded. In the north, the Israeli troops fought a confused series of night actions, but were successful in storming Hills 25, 25A, 27 and 29 with the loss of six killed. In the morning of 1 November, Israeli AMX-13s encircled and took Hills 34 and 36.[391] At that point, General al-Abd ordered his forces to abandon their posts outside of Rafah and retreat into the city.[392]

With Rafah more or less cut off and Israeli forces controlling the northern and eastern roads leading into the city, Dayan ordered the AMX-13s of the 27th Armored Brigade to strike west and take al-Arish. By this point, Nasser had ordered his forces to fall back towards the Suez Canal, so at first Bar-Lev and his men met little resistance as they advanced across the northern Sinai. Hearing of the order to withdraw, General al-Abd and his men left Rafah on the morning of 1 November through a gap in the Israeli lines, and headed back towards the canal zone. Three hours later, the Israelis took Rafah. It was reported that after taking Rafah, Israeli troops killed 111 people, including 103 refugees, in Rafah's Palestinian refugee camp. The circumstances of the killings are disputed.[393,394] Not until the Jeradi Pass in the northern Sinai did the IDF run into serious opposition. A series of hooking attacks that out-flanked the Egyptian positions combined with airstrikes led to an Egyptian defeat at the Jeradi Pass. On 2 November, Bar-Lev's forces took al-Arish.[395]

Meanwhile, the IDF attacked the Egyptian defenses outside of Gaza City late on 1 November. After breaking through the Egyptian lines, the Israeli tanks headed into Gaza City. Joined by infantry, the armor attacked the al-Muntar fortress outside of Gaza City, killing or capturing 3,500 Egyptian National Guard troops. By noon of 2 November, there was no more Egyptian opposition in the Gaza City area. On 3 November, the IDF attacked Egyptian and Palestinian forces at Khan Yunis. After a fierce battle, the Israeli 37th Armored Brigade's Sherman tanks broke through the heavily fortified lines outside of Khan Yunis held by the 86th Palestinian Brigade.[396]

After some street-fighting with Egyptian soldiers and Palestinian fedayeen, Khan Yunis fell to the Israelis. There are claims that after taking Khan Yunis, the IDF committed a massacre, known as the Khan Yunis killings. Israel maintained that the Palestinians were killed in street-fighting, while the Palestinians claimed that Israeli troops started executing unarmed Palestinians after the fall of Khan Yunis.[397] The claims of a massacre were reported to the UN General Assembly on 15 December 1956 by the Director of the United Nations Relief and Works Agency, Henry Labouisse, who reported from "trustworthy sources" that 275 people were killed in the massacre of which 140 were refugees and 135 local residents.[398]

In both Gaza City and Khan Yunis, street-fighting led to the deaths of "dozens, perhaps hundreds, of non-combatants".[399] Food and medicine distribution for refugees in need of assistance was complicated when some Palestinians ransacked the warehouses belonging to the United Nations Relief and Works Agency. This was compounded by a widespread view in Israel that the responsibility for the care of the Palestinian refugees rested with the UNRWA, not Israel, which led the Israelis to be slow with providing aid.[400] By noon of 3 November, the Israelis had control of almost the entire Gaza Strip save for a few isolated strong points, which were soon attacked and taken. The UN estimated that in total 447 to 550 Palestinian civilians were killed by Israeli troops during the first weeks of Israeli occupation of the strip. The manner that these people were killed is disputed.[401]

Sharm el-Sheikh operations

By 3 November, with the IDF having successfully taken the Gaza Strip, Arish, the Hedgehog, and Mitla Pass, Sharm el-Sheikh was the last Israeli objective. The main difficulty faced by Colonel Abraham Yoffe's 9th Infantry Brigade was logistical. There were no good roads linking Ras an-Naqb to Sharm el-Sheikh. After taking the border town of Ras an-Naqb on 30 October, Dayan ordered Yoffe to wait until air superiority was ensured.[402]

To outflank Sharm el-Sheikh, Dayan ordered paratroopers to take the town of Tor in the western Sinai. The Egyptian forces at Sharm el-Sheikh had the advantage of holding one of the most strongly fortified positions in the entire Sinai, but had been subjected to heavy Israeli air attacks from the beginning of the war. Yoffe set out for Sharm el-Sheikh on 2 November, and his major obstacles were the terrain and vehicle break-down. Israeli Navy ships provided support to the 9th Division during its advance.

After numerous skirmishes on the outskirts of Sharm el-Sheikh, Yoffe ordered an attack on the port around midnight on 4 November.[403] After four hours of heavy fighting, Yoffe ordered his men to retreat. On the morning of 5 November, Israeli forces launched a massive artillery barrage and napalm

Figure 66: *A battle-damaged de Havilland Sea Venom on HMS Eagle*

strikes against Egyptian forces defending Sharm el-Sheikh. At 9:30 am on 5 November, the Egyptian commander, Colonel Raouf Mahfouz Zaki, surrendered Sharm el-Sheikh. The Israelis had lost 10 killed and 32 wounded, while the Egyptians had lost about 100 killed and 31 wounded. Another 864 Egyptian soldiers were taken prisoner.

Anglo-French Canal invasion

To support the invasion, large air forces had been deployed to Cyprus and Malta by Britain and France and many aircraft carriers were deployed. The two airbases on Cyprus were so congested that a third field which was in dubious condition had to be brought into use for French aircraft. Even RAF Luqa on Malta was extremely crowded with RAF Bomber Command aircraft.

The British deployed the aircraft carriers HMS *Eagle*, *Albion* and *Bulwark* and France had the battleship *Jean Bart* and aircraft carriers *Arromanches* and *La Fayette* on station. In addition, HMS *Ocean* and *Theseus* acted as jumping-off points for Britain's helicopter-borne assault (the world's first).

The combined fleet was shadowed and even harassed by the United States Sixth Fleet,[404,405,406] commanded by Vice Admiral Charles R. Brown. The fleet was led by the carriers USS *Coral Sea* and USS *Randolph*, later reinforced by USS *Forrestal*.[407]

Figure 67: *A Hawker Sea Hawk of 899 Naval Air Squadron, armed with rockets, about to be launched from the aircraft carrier HMS Eagle for a strike on an Egyptian airfield*

Revise: Phases I and II

In the morning of 30 October Britain and France sent ultimatums to Egypt and Israel. They initiated Operation Musketeer on 31 October, with a bombing campaign.[408] Nasser responded by sinking all 40 ships present in the canal closing it to all shipping—shipping would not move again until early 1957. Despite the risk of an invasion in the canal zone, Field Marshal Abdel Hakim Amer ordered Egyptian troops in the Sinai to stay put, as Amer confidently assured Nasser that the Egyptians could defeat the Israelis in the Sinai and then defeat the Anglo-French forces once they came ashore in the canal zone.[409]

Amer also advised Nasser to send more troops into the Sinai to inflict his promised defeat on Israel, even though the risk of their being cut off if the canal zone were seized by Anglo-French forces was enormous. Not until late on 31 October did Nasser disregard Amer's rosy assessment and ordered his forces to disengage in the Sinai and to retreat back to the canal zone to face the expected Anglo-French invasion. Eden and Mollet ordered Phase I of Operation Revise to begin 13 hours after the Anglo-French ultimatum.[410]

British bombers based in Cyprus and Malta took off to Cairo with the aim of destroying Cairo airport, only to be personally ordered back by Eden when he learned that American civilians were being evacuated at Cairo airport. Fearful of the backlash that might result if American civilians were killed in a British bombing attack, Eden sent the Valiant bombers back to Malta while the Canberra's were ordered to hit Almaza airbase outside of Cairo. British night bombing proved ineffective.

Starting on the morning of 1 November, carrier-based de Havilland Sea Venoms, Chance-Vought Corsairs and Hawker Sea Hawks began a series of daytime strikes on Egypt. By the night of 1 November the Egyptian Air Force had lost 200 planes. With the destruction of Egypt's air force, Keightley ordered the beginning of Revise Phase II.[411] As part of Revise Phase II, a wide-ranging interdiction campaign began.[412] On 3 November F4U-7 Corsairs from the 14.F and 15.F *Aéronavale* taking off from the French carriers *Arromanches* and *La Fayette*, attacked the aerodrome at Cairo.

The very aggressive French General Beaufre suggested at once that Anglo-French forces seize the canal zone with airborne landings instead of waiting the planned ten days for Revise II to be worked through, and that the risk of sending in paratroopers without the prospect of sea-borne landings for several days be taken.[413] By 3 November, Beaufre finally convinced Keightley and Stockwell of the merits of his approach, and gained the approval for Operation Telescope as Beaufre had code-named the airborne assault on the canal zone.[414]

On 2 November 1956 the First Sea Lord Admiral Mountbatten sent a letter to Eden telling him to stop the invasion before troops landed in the canal zone as the operation had already proved to be too costly politically.[415] The next day, Mountbatten made a desperate phone call to Eden asking for permission to stop the invasion before it began, only to be refused.[416] Mountbatten's views led to clash of personalities with the Chief of the Imperial General Staff, General Gerald Templer who supported the invasion.[417] In response to Mountbatten's call to cancel the invasion, Templer penned a memo, which read:

> *Some people in England today say that what we're* [sic?] *done in the Middle East will have terrible effects in the future. ... The reality is that we have checked a drift. With a bit of luck we're not only stopped a big war in the Middle East, but we're halted the march of Russia through the Middle East and on to the African continent.*[418]

Telescope modified: the paratroops land

On late 5 November, an advance element of the 3rd Battalion of the British Parachute Regiment dropped on El Gamil Airfield, a narrow strip of land, led by Brigadier M.A.H. Butler.[419] The "Red Devils" could not return Egyptian fire while landing, but once the paratroopers landed, they used their Sten guns, three-inch mortars and anti-tank weapons with great effect.[420] Having taken

Figure 68: *Smoke rises from oil tanks beside the Suez Canal hit during the initial Anglo-French assault on Port Said, 5 November 1956.*

the airfield with a dozen casualties, the remainder of the battalion flew in by helicopter. The Battalion then secured the area around the airfield.

During the ensuing street fighting, the Egyptian forces engaged in methodical tactics, fighting on the defense while inflicting maximum casualties and retreating only when overwhelming force was brought to bear. In particular, the SU-100 tank destroyers proved to be a formidable weapon in urban combat. The British forces moved up towards Port Said with air support before digging in at 13:00 to hold until the beach assault.[421] With close support from carrier-based Westland Wyverns, the British paratroopers took Port Said's sewage works and the cemetery while becoming engaged in a pitched battle for the Coast Guard barracks.

At the same time, Lieutenant Colonel Pierre Chateau-Jobert landed with a force of the 2nd RPC at Raswa. Raswa imposed the problem of a small drop zone surrounded by water, but General Jacques Massu of the 10th Parachute Division assured Beaufre that this was not an insolvable problem for his men. 500 heavily armed paratroopers of the French 2nd Colonial Parachute Regiment (*2ème RPC*), hastily redeployed from combat in Algeria, jumped over the al-Raswa bridges from Nord Noratlas 2501 transports of the *Escadrille de Transport* (ET) 1/61 and ET 3/61, together with some combat engineers of the Guards Independent Parachute Company.[422]

The paratroopers swiftly secured the western bridge at the cost of two soldiers, and F4U Corsairs of the Aéronavale 14.F and 15.F flew a series of close-air-support missions, destroying several SU-100s. F-84Fs also hit two large oil storage tanks in Port Said, which went up in flames and covered most of the city in a thick cloud of smoke for the next several days. Egyptian resistance varied, with some positions fighting back until destroyed, while others were abandoned with little resistance. The French paratroopers stormed and took Port Said's waterworks that morning, an important objective to control in a city in the desert. Chateau-Jobert followed up this success by beginning an attack on Port Fuad.[423] Derek Varble, the American military historian, later wrote "Air support and fierce French assaults transformed the fighting at Port Fuad into a rout". During the fighting in the canal zone, the French paratroopers often practiced their "no-prisoners'" code and executed Egyptian POWs.[424]

The Egyptian commander at Port Said, General Salahedin Moguy then proposed a truce. His offer was taken up, and in the ensuring meeting with General Butler, Chateau-Jobert and General Massu, was offered the terms of surrendering the city and marching his men to the Gamil airfield to be taken off to prisoner-of-war camps in Cyprus.[425] Moguy had no interest in surrendering and had only made the truce offer to buy time for his men to dig in; when fighting began again vans with loudspeakers traveled through the city encouraging resistance against the invaders, by announcing that London and Paris had been bombed by the Russians and that World War III had started. As the paratroopers alone were not enough,:173 Beaufre and British Admiral Manley Laurence Power urged that the sea-borne landings be accelerated and that Allied forces land the very next day.

Stockwell and Knightley, who wished to stick with the original plan, opposed this.[426] Stockwell was always in favour of rigidly following already agreed to plans, and was most reluctant to see any changes, whereas Beaufre was all for changing plans to match with changed circumstances.[427] The differences between Stockwell and Beaufre were summarized by the American historian Derek Varble as: "Stockwell favored existing plans; their methodical construction and underlying staff work reduced risks. Beaufre, by contrast an opportunist, saw plans merely a means to an end, without much inherent value. For him, altered circumstances or assumptions provided adequate justification to jettison part or all of the original plan".

Royal Marines come ashore at Port Said

At first light on 6 November, commandos of No. 42 and 40 Commando Royal Marines stormed the beaches, using landing craft of World War II vintage (Landing Craft Assault and Landing Vehicle Tracked).[428] The battle group

Figure 69: *Troops of the Parachute Regiment escort a captured Egyptian soldier at Port Said*

standing offshore opened fire, giving covering fire for the landings and causing considerable damage to the Egyptian batteries and gun emplacements. The town of Port Said sustained great damage and was seen to be alight.

The men of 42 Commando as much as possible chose to by-pass Egyptian positions and focused on trying to break through inland. The Royal Marines of 40 Commando had the advantage of being supported by Centurion tanks as they landed on Sierra Red beach.[429] Upon entering downtown Port Said, the Marines became engaged in fierce urban combat as the Egyptians used the Casino Palace Hotel and other strongpoints as fortresses.

Nasser proclaimed the Suez War to be a "people's war".[430] As such, Egyptian troops were ordered to don civilian clothes while guns were freely handed out to Egyptian civilians.[431] From Nasser's point of view, a "people's war" presented the British and French with an unsolvable dilemma.[432] If the Allies reacted aggressively to the "people's war", then that would result in the deaths of innocent civilians and thus bring world sympathy to his cause while weakening morale on the home front in Britain and France. If the Allies reacted cautiously to the "people's war", than that would result in Allied forces becoming bogged down by sniper attacks, who had the advantage of attacking "with near impunity by hiding among crowds of apparent non-combatants".

These tactics worked especially well against the British. British leaders, especially Eden and the First Sea Lord Admiral Sir Louis Mountbatten were afraid of being labelled "murderers and baby killers", and sincerely attempted to limit Egyptian civilian deaths. Eden frequently interfered with Revise Phase I and II bombing, striking off various targets that he felt were likely to cause excessive civilian deaths, and restricted the gun sizes that could be used at the Port Said landings, again to minimize civilian deaths.[433]

The American historian Derek Varble has commented that the paradox between Eden's concern for Egyptian civilians and the object of Revise Phase II bombing, which was intended to terrorize the Egyptian people, was never resolved.[434] Despite Eden's best efforts, British bombing still killed hundreds of Egyptian civilians during Revise II, though these deaths were due more to imprecise aiming rather than a deliberate policy of "area bombing" such as that employed against Germany in World War II.[435] At Port Said, the heavy fighting in the streets and the resulting fires destroyed much of the city, killing many civilians.[436]

In the afternoon, 522 additional French paratroopers of the 1er REP (*Régiment Étranger Parachutiste*, 1st Foreign Parachute Regiment) were dropped near Port Fouad. These were also constantly supported by the Corsairs of the French Aéronavale, which flew very intensive operations: for example, although the French carrier *La Fayette* developed catapult problems, no less than 40 combat sorties were completed. The French were aided by AMX-13 light tanks.[437] While clearing Port Fuad, the 1er *Regiment Etranger Parachutiste* killed 100 Egyptians without losing a man in return.

British commandos of No. 45 Commando assaulted by helicopter, meeting stiff resistance, with shore batteries striking several helicopters, while friendly fire from British carrier-borne aircraft caused casualties to 45 Commando and HQ.[438] The helicopter borne assault of 45 Commando was the first time helicopters were used by UK forces to lift men directly into a combat zone.[439] Lieutenant Colonel N.H. Tailyour, who was leading 45 Commando was landed by mistake in a stadium still under Egyptian control resulting in a very hasty retreat.[440] Street fighting and house clearing, with strong opposition from well-entrenched Egyptian sniper positions, caused further casualties.[441]

Especially fierce fighting took place at the Port Said's Customs House and Navy House. The Egyptians destroyed Port Said's Inner Harbour, which forced the British to improvise and use the Fishing Harbour to land their forces.[442] The 2nd Bn of the Parachute Regiment landed by ship in the harbour. Centurion tanks of the British 6th Royal Tank Regiment were landed and by 12:00 they had reached the French paratroopers. While the British were landing at Port Said, the men of the 2 RPC at Raswa fought off Egyptian counter-attacks featuring SU100 self-propelled guns.[443]

Figure 70: *A British link up between the 3rd Battalion, The Parachute Regiment, and the Commandos at the Coast Guard barracks in Port Said. The paratroopers have with them a captured SU-100 tank destroyer, and the Commandos a Buffalo amphibious assault vehicle.*

After establishing themselves in a position in downtown Port Said, 42 Commando headed down the Shari Muhammad Ali, the main north-south road to link up with the French forces at the Raswa bridge and the Inner Basin lock. While doing so, the Marines also took Port Said's gasworks.[444] Meanwhile, 40 Commando supported by the Royal Tank Regiment remained engaged in clearing the downtown of Egyptian snipers. Colonel Tailyour arranged for more reinforcements to be brought in via helicopter.

Hearing rumours that Moguy wished to surrender, both Stockwell and Beaufre left their command ship HMS *Tyne* for Port Said. Upon landing, they learned the rumours were not true. Instead of returning to the *Tyne*, both Stockwell and Beaufre spent the day in Port Said, and were thus cut off from the news. Only late in the day did Beaufre and Stockwell learn of the acceptance of the United Nations ceasefire. Rather than focusing on breaking out to take al-Qantarah, the Royal Marines became bogged down in clearing every building in Port Said of snipers. The Centurions of the Royal Tank Regiment supported by the paratroopers of 2 RPC began a slow advance down to al-Qantarah on the night of 6 November.[445]

Egyptian sniper attacks and the need to clear every building led the 3 Para to be slowed in their attempts to link up with the Royal Marines.[446] When Stockwell learned of the ceasefire to come into effect in five hours' time at 9:00 pm, he

Figure 71: *Newsreel from 12 November 1956 about the end of the invasion*

ordered Colonel Gibbon and his Centurions to race down and take al-Qantarah with all speed in order to improve the Allied bargaining position.[447] What followed was a confused series of melee actions down the road to al-Qantarah that ended with the British forces at al-Cap, a small village four miles north of al-Qantarah at 2:00 am, when the ceasefire came into effect.[448]

Casualties

British casualties stood at 16 dead and 96 wounded, while French casualties were 10 dead and 33 wounded. The Israeli losses were 172 dead and 817 wounded. The number of Egyptians killed was "never reliably established".[449] Egyptian casualties to the Israeli invasion were estimated at 1,000–3,000 dead and 4,000 wounded, while losses to the Anglo-French operation were estimated at 650 dead and 900 wounded.[450,451] 1,000 Egyptian civilians are estimated to have died.[452]

End of hostilities

Anti-war protests in Britain

Although the public believed the British government's justification of the invasion as a separation of Israeli and Egyptian forces, protests against the war occurred in Britain after it began. On the popular television talk show *Free Speech*, an especially bitter debate took place on 31 October with the leftist historian A. J. P. Taylor and the Labour journalist and future party leader Michael Foot calling their colleague on *Free Speech*, the Conservative MP Robert Boothby, a "criminal" for supporting the war.[453] One television critic spoke of *Free Speech* during the war that "the team seemed to not only on the verge of, but actually losing their tempers.... Boothby boomed, Foot fumed and Taylor trephined, with apparent real malice...."[454] The angry, passionate, much-watched debates about the Suez war on *Free Speech* mirrored the divided public response to the war. The British government pressured the BBC to support the war, and seriously considered taking over the network.

Eden's major mistake had been not to strike in July 1956 when there was widespread anger at Nasser's nationalisation of the Suez Canal Company, as by the fall of 1956 public anger had subsided, with many people in Britain having come to accept the *fait accompli*, and saw no reason for war.[455] This was especially the case as Eden's claims that the Egyptians would hopelessly mismanage the canal had proven groundless, and that by September 1956 it was clear that the change of management had not affected shipping.[456] Even more importantly, Eden's obsession with secrecy and his desire to keep the preparations for war as secret as possible meant that the Eden government did nothing in the months running up to the attack to explain to the British people why it was felt that war was necessary.[457] Many of the reservists who were called up for their National Service in the summer and fall of 1956 recalled feeling bewildered and confused as the Eden government started preparing to attack Egypt while at the same time Eden insisted in public that he wanted a peaceful resolution of the dispute, and was opposed to attacking Egypt.[458] The British author David Pryce-Jones recalled that as a young officer, that after the ultimatum was submitted to Egypt he had to explain to his troops why war with Egypt was necessary without believing a word that he was saying.[459] Only one British soldier, however, refused to fight.

Gaitskell was much offended that Eden had kept him in the dark about the planning for action against Egypt, and felt personally insulted that Eden had just assumed that he would support the war without consulting him first.[460,461] On 31 October he cited in Parliament the fact that, despite Eden's claim that the British government had consulted closely with the Commonwealth, no other member nation did; in the Security Council, not even Australia had supported the British action. He called the invasion:208–209 <templatestyles src="Template:Quote/styles.css"/>

> *an act of disastrous folly whose tragic consequences we shall regret for years. Yes, all of us will regret it, because it will have done irreparable*

harm to the prestige and reputation of our country ... we shall feel bound by every constitutional means at our disposal to oppose it

The stormy and violent debates in the House of Commons on 1 November 1956 almost degenerated into fist-fights after several Labour MPs compared Eden to Hitler.[462] Yet the Prime Minister insisted, "We [are not] at war with Egypt now.[...] There has not been a declaration of war by us. We are in an armed conflict."[463] The British historian A. N. Wilson wrote that "The letters to *The Times* caught the mood of the country, with great majority opposing military intervention...."[464] The journalist Malcolm Muggeridge and actor Robert Speaight wrote in a public letter that <templatestyles src="Template:Quote/styles.css"/>

The bitter division in public opinion provoked by the British intervention in the Middle East has already had one disastrous consequence. It has deflected popular attention from the far more important struggle in Hungary. A week ago the feelings of the British people were fused in a single flame of admiration for the courage and apparent success of the Hungarian revolt. Now, that success seems threatened by Russian treachery and brute force, and Hungary has appealed to the West.... It is the first, and perhaps will prove the only opportunity to reverse the calamitous decisions of Yalta.... The Prime Minister has told us that 50 million tons of British shipping are at stake in his dispute with President Nasser. What is at stake in Central Europe are rather more than 50 million souls. It may be objected that it is not so easy to help the Hungarians; to this excuse they are entitled to reply that it was not so easy to help themselves.[465]

Lady Violet Bonham Carter, an influential Liberal Party member, wrote in a letter to the *Times* that <templatestyles src="Template:Quote/styles.css"/>

I am one of the millions who watching the martyrdom of Hungary and listening yesterday to the transmission of her agonizing appeals of help (immediately followed by our "successful bombings" of Egyptian "targets") who have felt a humiliation, shame and anger which are beyond expression.... We cannot order Soviet Russia to obey the edict of the United Nations which we ourselves have defied, nor to withdraw her tanks and guns from Hungary while we are bombing and invading Egypt. Today we are standing in the dock with Russia.... Never in my lifetime has our name stood so low in the eyes of the world. Never have we stood so ingloriously alone.[466]

According to public opinion polls at the time, 37% of the British people supported the war while 44% were opposed.[467] *The Observer* newspaper in a leader (editorial) attacked the Eden government for its "folly and crookedness" in attacking Egypt while the *Manchester Guardian* urged its readers to write letters of protest to their MPs.[468] *The Economist* spoke of the "strange union of cynicism and hysteria" in the government and *The Spectator* stated that Eden would soon have to face "a terrible indictment". The majority of letters written to MPs from their constituents were against the Suez attack.[469] Significantly, many of the letters come from voters who identified as Conservatives.[470] The historian Keith Feiling wrote "the harm done seems to me terrifying: for my part I have resigned from the party while the present leader is there".[471] The law professor and future Conservative cabinet minister Norman St. John-Stevas wrote at the time:

> *I had wanted to stand for the party at the next election, but I cannot bring myself to vote for the party at the moment, let alone stand for it. I am thinking of joining the Labour Party and am having lunch with Frank Pakenham next week.*

The historian Hugh Trevor-Roper expressed regret that no senior minister resigned and hoped "some kind of national Tory party can be saved from the wreck". A master at Eton College in a letter to his MP declared:

> *I write to you to express my complete abhorrence of the policy which the government is pursuing.... I have voted Conservative in the last three elections, but I am quite sure my next vote will be for a Labour candidate*

The Labour Party and the Trade Union Congress organized nation-wide anti-war protests, starting on 1 November under the slogan "Law, not war!" On 4 November, at an anti-war rally in Trafalgar Square attended by 30,000 people (making it easily the biggest rally in London since 1945), the Labour MP Aneurin Bevan accused the government of "a policy of bankruptcy and despair". Bevan stated at the Trafalgar rally:

> *We are stronger than Egypt but there are other countries stronger than us. Are we prepared to accept for ourselves the logic we are applying to Egypt? If nations more powerful than ourselves accept the absence of principle, the anarchistic attitude of Eden and launch bombs on London, what answer have we got, what complaint have we got? If we are going to appeal to force, if force is to be the arbiter to which we appeal, it would at least make common sense to try to make sure beforehand that we have got it, even if you accept that abysmal logic, that decadent point of view. We are in fact in the position today of having appealed to force in the case of a small nation, where if it is appealed to against us it will result in the destruction of Great Britain, not only as a nation, but as an island containing living men and women. Therefore I say to Anthony, I say to the British government, there is no count at all upon which they can be*

defended.
They have besmirched the name of Britain. They have made us ashamed of the things of which formerly we were proud. They have offended against every principle of decency and there is only way in which they can even begin to restore their tarnished reputation and that is to get out! Get out! Get out!

Inspired by Bevan's speech, the crowd at Trafalgar Square then marched on 10 Downing Street chanting "Eden Must Go!", and attempted to storm the Prime Minister's residence.[472] The ensuing clashes between the police and the demonstrators which were captured by television cameras had a huge demoralizing effect on the Eden cabinet,[473] which was meeting there. The British historian Anthony Adamthwaite wrote in 1988 that American financial pressure was the key factor that forced Eden to accept a ceasefire, but the public protests, declining poll numbers and signs that many Conservative voters were deserting the government were important secondary factors.

Support for Eden

According to some historians, the majority of British people were on Eden's side.[474,475] On 10 and 11 November an opinion poll found 53% supported the war, with 32% opposed.[476]

The majority of Conservative constituency associations passed resolutions of support to "Sir Anthony". Gilbert Murray was among Oxford scholars who signed a statement supporting Eden; such an act by the famous advocate of internationalism amazed both sides. He explained that, if not stopped, he believed Nasserism would become a Soviet-led worldwide anti-western movement.:202–203 British historian Barry Turner wrote that <templatestyles src="Template:Quote/styles.css"/>

> *The public reaction to press comment highlighted the divisions within the country. But there was no doubt that Eden still commanded strong support from a sizable minority, maybe even a majority, of voters who thought that it was about time that the upset Arabs should be taught a lesson. The Observer and Guardian lost readers; so too did the News Chronicle, a liberal newspaper that was soon to fold as a result of falling circulation.*

A. N. Wilson wrote that <templatestyles src="Template:Quote/styles.css"/>

> *The bulk of the press, the Labour Party and that equally influential left-learning party, the London dinner party, were all against Suez together with the rent-a-mob of poets, dons, clergy and ankle-socked female graduates who deplored British action, they did not necessarily constitute the majority of unexpressed public opinion*

The economist Roy Harrod wrote at the time that the "more level-headed British, whom I believe to be in the majority though not the most vocal" were supporting the "notable act of courage and statesmanship" of the government.[477] Eden himself claimed that his mail went from eight to one against the military action immediately after its start, to four to one in support on the day before the ceasefire.[478]

The conflict exposed the division within the Labour Party between middle-class internationalist intelligentsia who opposed the conflict, and working-class voters who supported it.[479,480,481] One Conservative MP wrote: "I have lost my middle-class followers, but this has been at least balanced by backing from working-class electors who normally vote Socialist and who favour a strong line on Suez".[482] Labour MP Richard Crossman said that "when the Labour Party leadership tried to organise demonstrations in the Provinces of the kind they'd held in Trafalgar Square, there was great reluctance among the working classes, because we were at war. It was Munich in reverse. And it was very, very acute". Labour MP James Callaghan agreed: "The horny-handed sons of toil rallied to the call of the bugle. They reacted against us in the same way as they did against Chamberlain a few months after Munich".[483] He recalled that up until the fighting started "we had public opinion on our side; but as soon as we actually went to war, I could *feel* the change".[484] Labour MP Barbara Castle recalled that Labour's protest against the conflict was "drowned in a wave of public jingoism".[485]

During the Lewisham North and Warwick and Leamington by-elections held in February and March 1957, Labour instructed its activists not to emphasise their opposition to Suez because the government's action had considerable support.[486] Callaghan believed that the Conservatives increased their majority at the 1959 election in part because working-class Labour voters were still angry at the party for opposing the conflict.[487] Labour MP Stanley Evans resigned from his seat and his membership of the party due to his support for British action in Suez.[488]

International reaction

The operation,[489] aimed at taking control of the Suez Canal, Gaza, and parts of Sinai, was highly successful for the invaders from a military point of view, but was a disaster from a political point of view, resulting in international criticism and diplomatic pressure. Along with the Suez crisis, the United States was also dealing with the near-simultaneous Hungarian revolution. Vice President Richard Nixon later explained: "We couldn't on one hand, complain about the Soviets intervening in Hungary and, on the other hand, approve of the British and the French picking that particular time to intervene against Nasser". Beyond that, it was Eisenhower's belief that if the United States were seen to

Figure 72: *Eisenhower press conference about the crisis, 9 August*

acquiesce in the attack on Egypt, that the resulting backlash in the Arab world might win the Arabs over to the Soviet Union.[490]

Despite having no commercial or military interest in the area, many countries were concerned with the growing rift between Western allied nations. The Swedish ambassador to the Court of St. James, Gunnar Hägglöf wrote in a letter to the anti-war Conservative M.P. Edward Boyle, <templatestyles src="Template:Quote/styles.css"/>

> I don't think there is any part of the world where the sympathies for England are greater than in Scandinavia. But Scandinavian opinion has never been more shocked by a British government's action—not even by the British-German Naval Agreement of 1935—than by the Suez intervention.

The attack on Egypt greatly offended many in the Islamic world. In Pakistan, 300,000 people showed up in a rally in Lahore to show solidarity with Egypt while in Karachi a mob chanting anti-British slogans burned down the British High Commission.[491] In Syria, the military government blew up the Kirkuk–Baniyas pipeline that allowed Iraqi oil to reach tankers in the Mediterranean to punish Iraq for supporting the invasion, and to cut Britain off from one of its main routes for taking delivery of Iraqi oil.[492] King Saud of Saudi Arabia imposed a total oil embargo on Britain and France.[493]

Figure 73: *Presidents Eisenhower and Nasser meeting in New York, 1960*

When Israel refused to withdraw its troops from the Gaza Strip and Sharm el-Sheikh, Eisenhower declared, "We must not allow Europe to go flat on its back for the want of oil." He sought UN-backed efforts to impose economic sanctions on Israel until it fully withdrew from Egyptian territory. Senate Majority Leader Lyndon B. Johnson and minority leader William Knowland objected to American pressure on Israel. Johnson told the Secretary of State John Foster Dulles that he wanted him to oppose "with all its skill" any attempt to apply sanctions on Israel. Dulles rebuffed Johnson's request, and informed Eisenhower of the objections made by the Senate. Eisenhower was "insistent on applying economic sanctions" to the extent of cutting off private American assistance to Israel which was estimated to be over $100 million a year. Ultimately, the Democratic Party-controlled Senate would not cooperate with Eisenhower's position on Israel. Eisenhower finally told Congress he would take the issue to the American people, saying, "America has either one voice or none, and that voice is the voice of the President – whether everybody agrees with him or not." The President spoke to the nation by radio and television where he outlined Israel's refusal to withdraw, explaining his belief that the UN had "no choice but to exert pressure upon Israel".

On 30 October, the Security Council held a meeting, at the request of the United States, when it submitted a draft resolution calling upon Israel immediately to withdraw its armed forces behind the established armistice lines. It

Figure 74: *Universal Newsreel from 4 December about Dag Hammarskjöld's meeting with Nasser*

was not adopted because of British and French vetoes. A similar draft resolution sponsored by the Soviet Union was also rejected.[494] On 31 October, also as planned, France and the UK launched an air attack against targets in Egypt, which was followed shortly by a landing of their troops at the northern end of the canal zone. Later that day, considering the grave situation created by the actions against Egypt, and with lack of unanimity among the permanent members preventing it from exercising its primary responsibility to maintain international peace and security, the Security Council passed Resolution 119; it decided to call an emergency special session of the General Assembly for the first time, as provided in the 1950 "Uniting for Peace" resolution, in order to make appropriate recommendations to end the fighting.

The emergency special session was convened 1 November; the same day Nasser requested diplomatic assistance from the U.S., without requesting the same from the Soviet Union; he was at first skeptical of the efficacy of US diplomatic efforts at the UN, but later gave full credit to Eisenhower's role in stopping the war.

In the early hours of 2 November, the General Assembly adopted the United States' proposal for Resolution 997 (ES-I); the vote was 64 in favour and 5 opposed (Australia, New Zealand, Britain, France, and Israel) with 6 abstentions.[495] It called for an immediate ceasefire, the withdrawal of all forces behind the armistice lines, an arms embargo, and the reopening of the Suez Canal, which was now blocked. The Secretary-General was requested to observe and report promptly on compliance to both the Security Council and General Assembly, for further action as deemed appropriate in accordance with the UN Charter.[496] Over the next several days, the emergency special session consequently adopted a series of enabling resolutions, which established the first United Nations Emergency Force (UNEF), on 7 November by Resolution 1001.[497] This proposal of the emergency force and the resulting cease-fire was made possible primarily through the efforts of Lester B. Pearson, the Secretary of External Affairs of Canada, and Dag Hammarskjöld, the Secretary-General of the United Nations. The role of Nehru, both as Indian Prime minister and a leader of the Non Aligned Movement was significant; the Indian historian Inder Malhotra wrote that "Now Nehru—who had tried to be even-handed between the two sides—denounced Eden and co-sponsors of the aggression vigorously. He had a powerful, if relatively silent, ally in the US president Dwight Eisenhower who went to the extent of using America's clout in the IMF to make Eden and Mollet behave".

The Indian historian Inder Malhotra wrote about Nehru's role that: "So the Suez War ended in Britain's humiliation. Eden lost his job. Nehru achieved his objective of protecting Egypt's sovereignty and Nasser's honour".[498] Britain and France agreed to withdraw from Egypt within a week; Israel did not. A rare example of support for the Anglo-French actions against Egypt came from West Germany; though the Cabinet was divided, the Chancellor Konrad Adenauer was furious with the United States for its "chumminess with the Russians" as Adenauer called the U.S. refusal to intervene in Hungary and voting with the Soviet Union at the UN Security Council, and the traditionally Francophile Adenauer drew closer to Paris as a result.[499] Adenauer told his Cabinet on 7 November that Nasser was a pro-Soviet force that needed to cut down to size, and in his view the attack on Egypt was completely justified.[500] Adenauer maintained to his Cabinet that the French had every right to invade Egypt because of Nasser's support for the FLN in Algeria, but the British were partly to blame because they "inexplicably" shut down their Suez Canal base in 1954.[501] What appalled Adenauer about the crisis was that the United States had come against the attack on Egypt and voted with the Soviet Union at Security Council against Britain and France, which lead Adenauer to fear that the United States and Soviet Union would "carve up the world" according to their own interests with no thought for the interests of European states. Adenauer refused to cancel a planned visit to Paris on 5–6 November 1956 and his summit with Mollet was clearly meant to be seen as a gesture of moral support. Adenauer was especially worried by the fact that the American embassy in Bonn would not provide a clear answer as to what was the American policy in response to the Bulganin letters.[502] One of Adenauer's aides Fritz von Eckardt commented about the opening ceremony in Paris where Mollet and Adenauer stood side by side while the national anthems were played that "In the most serious hour France had experienced since the end of the war, the two governments were standing shoulder by shoulder". During the summit in Paris, Mollet commented to Adenauer that a Soviet nuclear strike could destroy Paris at any moment, which added considerably to the tension and helped to draw the French and Germans closer.

On 7 November, David Ben-Gurion addressed the Knesset and declared a great victory, saying that the 1949 armistice agreement with Egypt was dead and buried, and that the armistice lines were no longer valid and could not be restored. Under no circumstances would Israel agree to the stationing of UN forces on its territory or in any area it occupied.[503,504] He also made an oblique reference to his intention to annex the Sinai Peninsula. Isaac Alteras writes that Ben-Gurion 'was carried away by the resounding victory against Egypt' and while 'a statesman well known for his sober realism, [he] took flight in dreams of grandeur.' The speech marked the beginning of a four-month-long diplomatic struggle, culminating in withdrawal from all territory, under conditions far less palatable than those envisioned in the speech, but with conditions for sea access to Eilat and a UNEF presence on Egyptian soil. The speech immediately drew increased international pressure on Israel to withdraw. That day in New York, the emergency session passed Resolution 1002, again calling for the immediate withdrawal of Israeli troops to behind the armistice lines, and for the immediate withdrawal of British and French troops from Egyptian territory. After a long Israeli cabinet meeting late on 8 November, Ben-Gurion informed Eisenhower that Israel declared its willingness to accept withdrawal of Israeli forces from Sinai, 'when satisfactory arrangements are made with the international force that is about to enter the canal zone'.

Soviet threats

Although the Soviet Union's position in the crisis was as helpless as was the United States' regarding Hungary's uprising, Premier Nikolai Bulganin threatened to intervene on the Egyptian side, and to launch rocket attacks on Britain, France and Israel. Bulganin accused Ben-Gurion of supporting European colonialism, and Mollet of hypocrisy for leading a socialist government while pursuing a right-wing foreign policy. He did however concede in his letter to Eden that Britain had legitimate interests in Egypt.Wikipedia:Citation needed

The Soviet threat to send troops to Egypt to fight the Allies led Eisenhower to fear that this might be the beginning of World War III.[505] One of Eisenhower's aides Emmet Hughes recalled that the reaction at the White House to the Bulganin letters was "sombre" as there was fear that this was the beginning to the countdown to World War III, a war that if it occurred would kill hundreds of millions of people.⁵⁰⁶ In private, Eisenhower told Undersecretary of State Herbert Hoover Jr. of his fears that:

> *The Soviet Union might be ready for to undertake any wild adventure. They are as scared and furious as Hitler was in his last days. There's nothing more dangerous than a dictatorship in that frame of mind.*

If the Soviet Union did go to war with NATO allies Britain and France, then the United States would be unable to remain neutral, because the United States' obligations under NATO would come into effect, requiring them to go to war with the Soviet Union in defense of Britain and France. Likewise, if the Soviet Union attacked Israel, though there was no formal American commitment to defend Israel, the Eisenhower administration would come under heavy domestic pressure to intervene. From Eisenhower's viewpoint, it was better to end the war against Egypt rather than run the risk of this escalating into the Third World War, in case Khrushchev was serious about going to war in defense of Egypt as he insisted in public that he was. Eisenhower's reaction to these threats from the Soviet Union was: "If those fellows start something, we may have to hit 'em — and, if necessary, with everything in the bucket."⁵⁰⁷ Eisenhower immediately ordered the U-2s into action over Syria and Israel to search for any Soviet air forces on Syrian bases, so the British and French could destroy them. He told Hoover and CIA director Allan Dulles, "If the Soviets attack the French and British directly, we would be in a war and we would be justified in taking military action even if Congress were not in session."⁵⁰⁸ (The Americans excluded Israel from the guarantee against Soviet attack, however, alarming the Israeli government.)

Khrushchev often claimed to possess a vast arsenal of nuclear-tipped ICBMs, and while disclaiming any intention of starting a war, maintained that he would be more than happy to turn a conventional war into a nuclear one if war did come.⁵⁰⁹ The U-2 spy flights, which were intended to discover if the Soviet Union really did have the nuclear arsenal that it claimed to have, only started in July 1956, and it was not until February 1959 that it firmly established that Khrushchev had vastly exaggerated his nuclear strength.⁵¹⁰ In fact, the supposedly huge Soviet arsenal of ICBMs, with which Khrushchev would wipe out the cities of Britain, France, Israel, and if necessary the United States consisted only of four *Semyorka* missiles stationed at a swamp south of Arkhangelsk.⁵¹¹ From the viewpoint of Eisenhower, in 1956 he had no way of knowing for certain whether Khrushchev's nuclear braggadocio was for real or not. Earlier in 1956, Dulles had warned Eisenhower that Khrushchev was "the most dangerous person to lead the Soviet Union since the October Revolution" as Khrushchev was "not a coldly calculating person, but rather one who reacted emotionally. He was obviously intoxicated much of the time and could be expected to commit irrational acts."[512] Khrushchev later admitted in his memoirs that he was not seriously "thinking of going to war" in November 1956 as he claimed at the time as he lacked the necessary ICBMs to make good his threats.[513]

Financial pressure

The United States also put financial pressure on the UK to end the invasion. Because the Bank of England had lost $45 million between 30 October and 2 November, and Britain's oil supply had been restricted by the closing of the Suez Canal, the British sought immediate assistance from the IMF, but it was denied by the United States. Eisenhower in fact ordered his Secretary of the Treasury, George M. Humphrey, to prepare to sell part of the US Government's Sterling Bond holdings. The UK government considered invading Kuwait and Qatar if oil sanctions were put in place by the US.[514]

Britain's Chancellor of the Exchequer, Harold Macmillan, advised his Prime Minister, Anthony Eden, that the United States was fully prepared to carry out this threat. He also warned his Prime Minister that Britain's foreign exchange reserves simply could not sustain the devaluation of the pound that would come after the United States' actions; and that within weeks of such a move, the country would be unable to import the food and energy supplies needed to sustain the population on the islands. However, there were suspicions in the Cabinet that Macmillan had deliberately overstated the financial situation in order to force Eden out. What Treasury officials had told Macmillan was far less serious than what he told the Cabinet.[515]

In concert with U.S. actions, Saudi Arabia started an oil embargo against Britain and France. The U.S. refused to fill the gap until Britain and France agreed to a rapid withdrawal. Other NATO members refused to sell oil they received from Arab nations to Britain or France.[516]

Cease fire

The British government faced political and economic pressure. Sir Anthony Eden, the British Prime Minister, announced a cease fire on 6 November, warning neither France nor Israel beforehand. Troops were still in Port Said and on operational manoeuvres when the order came from London. Port Said had been overrun and the military assessment was that the Suez Canal could have been completely taken within 24 hours.[517] Eisenhower initially agreed to meet with Eden and Mollet to resolve their differences, but then cancelled the proposed meeting after Secretary of State Dulles advised him it risked inflaming the Middle Eastern situation further.[518]

Figure 75: *Israelis protesting against the UN order to evacuate Gaza and Sinai, 14 February 1957*

Eisenhower was not in favour of an immediate withdrawal of British, French and Israeli troops until the US ambassador to the United Nations, Henry Cabot Lodge Jr. pushed for it. Eden's predecessor Sir Winston Churchill commented on 22 November, "I cannot understand why our troops were halted. To go so far and not go on was madness."[519] Churchill further added that while he might not have dared to begin the military operation, nevertheless once having ordered it he would certainly not have dared to stop it before it had achieved its objective. Without further guarantee, the Anglo-French Task Force had to finish withdrawing by 22 December 1956, to be replaced by Danish and Colombian units of the UNEF.[520]

The Israelis refused to host any UN force on Israeli controlled territory and left the Sinai in March 1957. Before the withdrawal the Israeli forces systematically destroyed infrastructure in Sinai peninsula, such as roads, railroads and telephone lines, and all houses in the villages of Abu Ageila and El Quseima. Before the railway was destroyed, Israel Railways captured Egyptian National Railways equipment including six locomotives and a 30-ton breakdown crane.

The UNEF was formed by forces from countries that were not part of the major alliances (NATO and the Warsaw Pact—though Canadian troops participated in later years, since Canada had spearheaded the idea of a neutral force). By 24 April 1957 the canal was fully reopened to shipping.

Figure 76: *1957 newsreels about the aftermath of the crisis*

Aftermath

Egyptian sovereignty and ownership of the canal had been confirmed by the United States and the United Nations.Wikipedia:Citation needed In retirement, Anthony Eden, the British Prime Minister at the time, maintained that the military response had prevented a much larger war in the Middle East. Israel had been expecting an Egyptian invasion in either March or April 1957, as well as a Soviet invasion of Syria.[521] The crisis may also have hastened decolonization, as many of the remaining British and French colonies gained independence over the next few years. Some argued that the imposed ending to the Crisis led to over-hasty decolonization in Africa, increasing the chance of civil wars and military dictatorships in newly independent countries.[522]

The fight over the canal also laid the groundwork for the Six-Day War in 1967 due to the lack of a peace settlement following the 1956 war and rising of tensions between Egypt and Israel.[523] The failure of the Anglo-French mission was also seen as a failure for the United States, since the western alliance had been weakened and the military response had ultimately achieved nothing. Additionally, the Soviet Union was able to avoid most repercussions from its violent suppression of the rebellion in Hungary, and were able to present an image at the United Nations as a defender of small powers against imperialism.[524]

As a direct result of the Crisis and in order to prevent further Soviet expansion in the region, Eisenhower asked Congress on 5 January 1957 for authorization to use military force if requested by any Middle Eastern nation to check aggression and, secondly, to set aside $200 million to help Middle Eastern countries that desired aid from the United States. Congress granted both requests and this policy became known as the Eisenhower Doctrine.

The Soviet Union made major gains with regards to influence in the Middle East.[525] As American historian John Lewis Gaddis wrote:

> When the British-French-Israeli invasion forced them to choose, Eisenhower and Dulles came down, with instant decisiveness, on the side of the Egyptians. They preferred alignment with Arab nationalism, even if it meant alienating pro-Israeli constituencies on the eve of a presidential election in the United States, even if it meant throwing the NATO alliance into its most divisive crisis yet, even if it meant risking whatever was left of the Anglo-American 'special relationship', even if it meant voting with the Soviet Union in the United Nations Security Council at a time when the Russians, themselves, were invading Hungary and crushing—far more brutally than anything that happened in Egypt—a rebellion against their own authority there. The fact that the Eisenhower administration itself applied crushing economic pressure to the British and French to disengage from Suez, and that it subsequently forced an Israeli pull-back from the Sinai as well—all of this, one might thought, would won the United States the lasting gratitude of Nasser, the Egyptians and the Arab world. Instead, the Americans lost influence in the Middle East as a result of Suez, while the Russians gained it.

Nikita Khrushchev's much publicized threat expressed through letters written by Nikolai Bulganin to begin rocket attacks on 5 November on Britain, France, and Israel if they did not withdraw from Egypt was widely believed at the time to have forced a ceasefire. Accordingly, it enhanced the prestige of the Soviet Union in Egypt, the Arab world, and the Third World, who believed the USSR was prepared to launch a nuclear attack on Britain, France, and Israel for the sake of Egypt. Though Nasser in private admitted that it was American economic pressure that had saved him, it was Khrushchev, not Eisenhower, whom Nasser publicly thanked as Egypt's saviour and special friend. Khrushchev later boasted in his memoirs:

> Our use of international influence to halt England, France and Israel's aggression against Egypt in 1956 was a historic turning point...Previously they had apparently thought that we were bluffing, when we openly said that the Soviet Union possessed powerful rockets. But then they saw that we really had rockets. And this had its effect.

Figure 77: *Statue of Ferdinand de Lesseps (a Frenchman who built the Suez Canal) was removed following the nationalisation of the Suez Canal in 1956.*[526]

Khrushchev took the view that the Suez crisis had been a great triumph for Soviet nuclear brinksmanship, arguing publicly and privately that his threat to use nuclear weapons was what had saved Egypt.[527] Khrushchev claimed in his memoirs:

<templatestyles src="Template:Quote/styles.css"/>

The governments of England and France knew perfectly well that Eisenhower's speech condemning their aggression was just a gesture for the sake of public appearances. But when we delivered our own stern warning to the three aggressors, they knew we weren't playing games with public opinion. They took us seriously.

The conclusion that Khrushchev drew from the Suez crisis, which he saw as his own personal triumph, was that the use of nuclear blackmail was a very effective tool for achieving Soviet foreign policy goals.[528] Therefore, a long period of crises began, starting with the Berlin crisis of 1958 and culminating in the Cuban Missile Crisis of 1962.[529] U.S. Secretary of State John Foster Dulles perceived a power vacuum in the Middle East, and he thought the United States should fill it. His policies, which ultimately led to the Eisenhower Doctrine, were based on the assumption that Nasser and other Arab leaders shared America's of the Soviet Union, which was emphatically not the case.⁵³⁰ In fact, Nasser never wanted Egypt to be aligned with one single superpower, and instead preferred the Americans and Soviets vying for his friendship.

Nasser saw the Eisenhower Doctrine as a heavy-handed American attempt to dominate the Middle East (a region that Nasser believed he ought to dominate Wikipedia:Citation needed), and led him to ally Egypt with the Soviet Union as an effective counter-weight.⁵³¹ It was only with the quiet abandonment of the Eisenhower Doctrine in a National Security Council review in mid-1958 that Nasser started pulling away from the Soviet Union to resume his preferred role as an opportunist who tried to use both superpowers to his advantage, playing on their animosity.

The American conservative historian Arthur L. Herman claims that the episode ruined the usefulness of the United Nations to support American ideals: <templatestyles src="Template:Quote/styles.css"/>

> *Suez destroyed the United Nations as well. By handing it over to Dag Hammarskjöld and his feckless ilk, Eisenhower turned the organization from the stout voice of international law and order into at best a meaningless charade; at worst, a Machiavellian cesspool. Instead of teaching Nasser and his fellow dictators that breaking international law does not pay, Suez taught them that every transgression will be forgotten and forgiven, especially if oil is at stake. ... Suez destroyed the moral authority of the so-called world community. Fifty years later, we are all still living in the rubble.*

Military thought

The great military lesson that was reinforced by the Suez War was the extent that the desert favoured highly fluid, mobile operations and the power of aerial interdiction. French aircraft destroyed Egyptian forces threatening paratroopers at Raswa and Israeli air power saved the IDF several days' worth of time. To operate in the open desert without air supremacy proved to be suicidal for the Egyptian forces in the Sinai. The Royal Marine helicopter assault at Port Said "showed promise as a technique for transporting troops into small landing zones". Strategic bombing proved ineffective.⁵³²

Revise Phase II failed to achieve its aim of breaking Egyptian morale while at the same time, those civilian deaths that did occur helped to turn world opinion against the invasion and especially hurt support for the war in Britain. Egyptian urban warfare tactics at Port Said proved to be effective at slowing down the Allied advance. Finally, the war showed the importance of diplomacy. Anglo-French operations against Egypt were militarily successful, but proved to be counterproductive as opinion in both in the home front in Britain and France and the world abroad, especially in the United States, was against the operation.

Europe

In West Germany, the Chancellor Konrad Adenauer was shocked by the Soviet threat of nuclear strikes against Britain and France, and even more by the quiescent American response to the Soviet threat of nuclear annihilation against two of NATO's key members. The Bulganin letters showcased Europe's dependence upon the United States for security against Soviet nuclear threats while at the same time seeming to show that the American nuclear umbrella was not as reliable as had been advertised. As a result, the French became determined to acquire their own nuclear weapons rather than rely upon the Americans while both Germanys became even more interested in the idea of a European "Third Force" in the Cold War.[533] This helped to lead to the formation of the European Economic Community in 1957, which was intended to be the foundation of the European "Third Force".[534] The European Economic Community was the precursor to the European Union.

Egypt

Egypt ended as the winner, with UK and French troops withdrawn soon, and Israeli troops to withdraw later on, while keeping control over the Suez Canal. After the fighting ended, Abdel Hakim Amer, Egypt's Chief-of-Staff, accused Nasser of provoking an unnecessary war and then blaming the military for the result. The British historian D. R. Thorpe wrote that the imposed ending to the Crisis gave Nasser "an inflated view of his own power". In his mind, he had defeated the combined forces of the United Kingdom, France and Israel, whereas in fact the military operation had been "defeated" by pressure from the United States.[535] Despite the Egyptian defeat, Nasser emerged as a hero in the Arab world. American historian Derek Varble commented: "Although Egyptian forces fought with mediocre skill during the conflict, many Arabs saw Nasser as the conqueror of European colonialism and Zionism, simply because Britain, France and Israel left the Sinai and the northern canal zone". The Greek-American historian P. J. Vatikiotis wrote that Nasser in his speeches both in 1956 and after provided for "superficial explanations of Egypt's military collapse in Sinai, based on some extraordinary strategy" and that "Simplistic children's tales about the Egyptian air force's prowess in 1956 were linked in the myth of orderly withdrawal from Sinai. All this was necessary to construct yet another myth, that of Port Said. Inflating and magnifying odd and sporadic resistance into a Stalingrad-like tenacious defense, Port Said became the spirit of Egyptian independence and dignity."[536] During the Nasser era, the fighting at Port Said become a huge symbol of the victory that Egypt was said to have won, which in turn was linked to as part and parcel of a wider anti-colonial struggle throughout the entire world.[537] Thorpe wrote about Nasser's post Suez hubris that "The Six-Day War against Israel in 1967 was when reality kicked in—a war that would never have taken place if the Suez crisis had had a different resolution". Summarizing the arguments of the Egyptian writer Tawfiq al-Hakim about the links between the 1956 and 1967 wars Vatikiotis wrote: "Were bluffing and histrionics in the nature of Nasser? It was bluffing that led to the crushing of Egypt in 1967, because of the mass self-deception exercised by leaders and followers alike ever since the non-existent 'Stalingrad which was Port Said' in 1956."[538]

Abolishing civil liberties

Jewish exodus from Arab and Muslim countries

Communities

• Mizrahi
  • Persian
  • Baghdadi
• Sephardi

Background

• Jews under Muslim rule
  • Ottoman
  • Old Yishuv
• Antisemitism in the Arab World
  • The Holocaust in Libya
  • Farhud
• Zionism
• Arab–Israeli conflict
  • 1948 Arab–Israeli War
  • Suez Crisis
  • Six-Day War
• Algerian War

Main events
• Magic Carpet (Yemen) • Ezra and Nehemiah (Iraq) • Lebanese exodus • Egyptian exodus • Moroccan exodus   • Operation Yachin • Pied-Noir (Algeria) • Day of Revenge (Libya) • Exodus of Iran's Jews
Resettlement

• Aliyah
• HIAS • Mossad LeAliyah Bet • JDC
  • Mizrahi Jews in Israel
• Iranian • Iraqi • Kurdish • Moroccan
• Syrian • Turkish • Yemenite
  • Transition camps
  • Immigrant camps
  • Development towns
  • Austerity
• North African Jews in France

Advocation
• Remembrance Day • JIMENA • JJAC • WOJAC • *The Forgotten Refugees*
Related topics
• Arab Jews • Musta'arabi • Maghrebi Jews • Berber Jews
• v • t • e[539]

In October 1956, when the Suez Crisis erupted, Nasser brought in a set of sweeping regulations abolishing civil liberties and allowing the state to stage mass arrests without charge and strip away Egyptian citizenship from any group it desired; these measures were mostly directed against the Jews of Egypt.[540] As part of its new policy, 1,000 Jews were arrested and 500 Jewish businesses were seized by the government.[541] A statement branding the Jews as "Zionists and enemies of the state" was read out in the mosques of Cairo and Alexandria. Jewish bank accounts were confiscated and many Jews lost their jobs.[542] Lawyers, engineers, doctors and teachers were not allowed to work in their professions. Thousands of Jews were ordered to leave the country. They were allowed to take only one suitcase and a small sum of cash, and forced to sign declarations "donating" their property to the Egyptian government.[543] Some 25,000 Jews, almost half of the Jewish community left, mainly for Israel, Europe, the United States and South America. By 1957 the Jewish population of Egypt had fallen to 15,000.

Britain

The political and psychological impact of the crisis had a fundamental impact on British politics. Anthony Eden was accused of misleading parliament and resigned from office on 9 January 1957. Eden had barely been prime minister for two years when he resigned, and his unsuccessful handling of the Suez Crisis eclipsed the successes he had achieved in the previous 30 years.[544]

Eden's successor, Harold Macmillan, accelerated the process of decolonisation and sought to recapture the benevolence of the United States. He enjoyed a close friendship with Eisenhower, dating from the North African campaign in World War II, where General Eisenhower commanded allied invasion forces and Macmillan provided political liaison with Winston Churchill. Benefiting from his personal popularity and a healthy economy, Macmillan's government increased its Parliamentary majority in the 1959 general election. The Suez crisis, though a blow to British power in the Near East, did not mark its end. Britain intervened successfully in Jordan to put down riots that threatened the rule of King Hussein in 1958 and in 1961 deployed troops to Kuwait to successfully deter an Iraqi invasion; the latter deployment had been a response to the threats of the Iraqi dictator General Abd al-Karim Qasim that he would invade and annex Kuwait.[545] However, at the same time, though British influence continued in the Middle East, Suez was a blow to British prestige in the Near East from which the country never recovered.

Increasingly, British foreign policy thinking turned away from acting as a great imperial power. During the 1960s there was much speculation that Prime Minister Harold Wilson's continued refusals to send British troops to Vietnam, even as a token force, despite President Lyndon B. Johnson's persistent requests, were partially due to the Americans failing to support Britain during the Suez Crisis. Edward Heath was dismayed by the U.S. opposition to Britain during the Suez Crisis; as Prime Minister in October 1973 he refused the U.S. permission to use any of the UK's air bases to resupply during the Yom Kippur War,[546] or to allow the Americans to gather intelligence from British bases in Cyprus.

The British relationship with the United States did not suffer lasting consequences from the crisis. "The Anglo-American 'special relationship' was revitalised immediately after the Suez Crisis", writes Risse Kappen. The United States wanted to restore the prestige of its closest ally and thus "The two governments...engaged in almost ritualistic reassurances that their 'special relationship' would be restored quickly". One example came with Britain's first Hydrogen bomb test Operation Grapple which led to the 1958 U.S.–UK Mutual Defence Agreement. Six years after the crisis, the Americans amazed the British by selling them state-of-the-art missile technology at a moderate cost, which became the UK Polaris programme.

France

Franco-American ties never recovered from the Suez crisis. There were various reasons for this. Previously there had already been strains in the Franco-American relationship triggered by what Paris considered U.S. betrayal of the French war effort in Indochina at Dien Bien Phu in 1954. The incident demonstrated the weakness of the NATO alliance in its lack of planning and co-operation beyond the European stage. Mollet believed Eden should have delayed calling the Cabinet together until 7 November, taking the whole canal in the meantime, and then veto with the French any UN resolution on sanctions. From the point of view of General de Gaulle, the Suez events demonstrated to France that it could not rely on its allies; the British had initiated a ceasefire in the midst of the battle without consulting the French, while the Americans had opposed Paris politically. The damage to the ties between Paris and Washington, D.C., "culminated in President de Gaulle's 1966 decision to withdraw from the military integration of NATO". The Suez war had an immense impact on French domestic politics. Much of the French Army officer corps felt that they been "betrayed" by what they considered to be the spineless politicians in Paris when they were on the verge of victory just as they believed they had been "betrayed" in Vietnam in 1954, and accordingly become more determined to win the war in Algeria, even if it meant overthrowing the Fourth Republic to do so.[547] The Suez crisis thus help to set the stage for the military disillusionment with the Fourth Republic, which was to lead to the collapse of the republic in 1958. According to the protocol of Sèvres agreements, France secretly transmitted parts of its own atomic technology to Israel, including a detonator.[548]

Israel

The Israel Defense Forces gained confidence from the campaign-Wikipedia:Manual_of_Style/Words_to_watch#Unsupported_attributions.
The war demonstrated that Israel was capable of executing large scale military maneuvers in addition to small night-time raids and counter insurgency operations. David Ben-Gurion, reading on 16 November that 90,000 British and French troops had been involved in the Suez affair, wrote in his diary, 'If they had only appointed a commander of ours over this force, Nasser would have been destroyed in two days.'[549]

The war also had tangible benefits for Israel. The Straits of Tiran, closed by Egypt since 1950 was re-opened. Israeli shipping could henceforth move freely through the Straits of Tiran to and from Africa and Asia. The Israelis also secured the presence of UN Peacekeepers in Sinai. Operation Kadesh bought Israel an eleven-year lull on its southern border with Egypt.[550]

Israel escaped the political humiliation that befell Britain and France following their swift, forced withdrawal. In addition, its stubborn refusal to withdraw without guarantees, even in defiance of the United States and United Nations, ended all Western efforts, mainly American and British ones, to impose a political settlement in the Middle East without taking Israel's security needs into consideration.

Figure 78: *An Israeli soldier stands next to an Egyptian gun that had blocked the Tiran Straits.*

In October 1965 Eisenhower told Jewish fundraiser and Republican party supporter Max M. Fisher that he greatly regretted forcing Israel to withdraw from the Sinai peninsula; Vice-President Nixon recalled that Eisenhower expressed the same view to him on several occasions.[551]

Other parties

Lester B. Pearson, who would later become the Prime Minister of Canada, was awarded the Nobel Peace Prize in 1957 for his efforts in creating a mandate for a United Nations Peacekeeping Force, and he is considered the father of the modern concept of peacekeeping. The Suez Crisis contributed to the adoption of a new national flag of Canada in 1965, as the Egyptian government had objected to Canadian peacekeeping troops on the grounds that their flag at that time included a British ensign. As Prime Minister, Pearson would advocate the simple Maple Leaf that was eventually adopted.

After Suez, Cyprus, Aden, and Iraq became the main bases for the British in the region while the French concentrated their forces at Bizerte and Beirut. UNEF was placed in the Sinai (on Egyptian territory only) with the express purpose of maintaining the cease-fire. While it was effective in preventing the small-scale warfare that prevailed before 1956 and after 1967, budgetary cutbacks and changing needs had seen the force shrink to 3,378 by 1967.

The Soviet Union, after long peering through the keyhole of a closed door on what it considered a Western sphere of influence, now found itself invited over the threshold as a friend of the Arabs. Shortly after it reopened, the canal was traversed by the first Soviet warships since World War I. The Soviets' burgeoning influence in the Middle East, although it was not to last, included acquiring Mediterranean bases, introducing multipurpose projects, supporting the budding Palestinian liberation movement and penetrating the Arab countries.[552] Nasser claimed to be the defender of the Palestinian cause, but his anti-Israel warlike rhetoric damaged the Palestinians since it convinced a lot of the Israelis to oppose reconciliation with the Palestinians.

References

<templatestyles src="Refbegin/styles.css" />

Adamthwaite, Anthony "Suez Revisited" pages 449–464 from *International Affairs*, Volume 64, Issue #3, Summer 1988.

Arnstein, Walter L. (2001). *Britain Yesterday and Today: 1830 to the Present*. Boston: Houghton Mifflin. ISBN 978-0-618-00104-0.<templatestyles src="Module:Citation/CS1/styles.css"></templatestyles>

Alteras, Isaac. *Eisenhower and Israel: U.S.–Israeli relations, 1953–1960* (University Press of Florida, 1993)

Barnett, Michael N. (1992). *Confronting the Costs of War: Military Power, State, and Society in Egypt and Israel*. Princeton: Princeton University Press. ISBN 978-0-691-07883-0.<templatestyles src="Module:Citation/CS1/styles.css"></templatestyles>

Beaufre, André (1969). *The Suez Expedition 1956*. New York: Praeger. ISBN 0-571-08979-8.<templatestyles src="Module:Citation/CS1/styles.css"></templatestyles> (translated from French by Richard Barry)

Bregman, Ahron (2002). *Israel's Wars: A History Since 1947*. London: Routledge. ISBN 0-415-28716-2.<templatestyles src="Module:Citation/CS1/styles.css"></templatestyles>

Bromberger, Merry and Serge *Secrets of Suez* Sidgwick & Jackson London 1957 (translated from French *Les Secrets de l'Expedition d'Egypte* by James Cameron)

Burns, William J. (1985). *Economic Aid and American Policy toward Egypt, 1955–1981*. Albany: State University of New York Press. ISBN 0873958683.

Butler, L. J. (2002). *Britain and Empire: Adjusting to a Post-Imperial World*. London: I.B. Tauris. ISBN 1-86064-449-X.

Childers, Erskine B. (1962). *The Road To Suez*. MacGibbon & Kee. ASIN B000H47WG4[553].

Darwin, John (1988). *Britain and Decolonisation: The Retreat From Empire in the Post Cold War World*. Palgrave Macmillan. ISBN 0-333-29258-8.

Dietl, Ralph (April 2008), "Suez 1956: A European Intervention?", *Journal of Contemporary History*, Sage Publications, **43** (2): 259–273, doi: 10.1177/0022009408089032[554].

Doran, Michael. *Ike's Gamble*, Free Press. Oct.2016.

Gaddis, John Lewis (1998). *We Now Know: Rethinking Cold War History*. Oxford: Oxford University Press. ISBN 978-0-19-878071-7.

Hendershot, Robert M. (2008). *Family Spats: Perception, Illusion, and Sentimentality in the Anglo-American Special Relationship*. VDM Verlag. ISBN 978-3-639-09016-1.

Heikal, Mohamed (1986). *Cutting The Lion's Tail: Suez Through Egyptian eyes*. London: Deutsch. ISBN 0-233-97967-0.

Herzog, Chaim (1982). *The Arab-Israeli Wars: War and Peace in the Middle East*. New York: Random House. ISBN 0-394-50379-1.

Horne, Alistair (2008) [1988]. *Macmillan: The Official Biography* (Twentieth anniversary ed.). London: Macmillan. ISBN 978-0-230-71083-2.

Hyam, Ronald (2006). *Britain's Declining Empire: The Road to Decolonisation 1918–1969*. Cambridge University Press. ISBN 0-521-68555-9.

James, Robert Rhodes (1986). *Anthony Eden: A Biography*. McGraw Hill Book Company Inc. ASIN B0040YOVBQ[555].

Kissinger, Henry (1994). *Diplomacy*. New York, NY: Simon & Schuster. ISBN 0-671-51099-1.

Kyle, Keith (2003). *Suez: Britain's End of Empire in the Middle East*. I.B. Tauris. ISBN 1-86064-811-8.

Kunz, Diane B. (1991). *The Economic Diplomacy of the Suez Crisis*[556]. U. of North Carolina Press.

Laskier, Michael "Egyptian Jewry under the Nasser Regime, 1956–70" pp. 573–619 from *Middle Eastern Studies*, Volume 31, Issue #3, July 1995.

Leuliette, Pierre (1964). *St. Michael and the Dragon: Memoirs of a Paratrooper*. Houghton Mifflin.

Love, Kenneth (1969). *Suez The Twice Fought War*. McGraw-Hill.

Lucas, Scott (1996). *Britain and Suez: The Lion's Last Roar*[557]. Manchester University Press. pp. 118–30. ISBN 0-7190-4579-7. pp. 118–130 on historiography

Marshall, S.L.A (1958). *Sinai Victory : Command Decisions In History's Shortest War, Israel's Hundred-Hour Conquest of Egypt East of Suez, Autumn, 1956*. New York: Battery Press. ISBN 0-89839-085-0.

Neff, Donald (1981). *Warriors at Suez : Eisenhower takes America into the Middle-East*. New York: Simon and Schuster. ISBN 0-671-41010-5.

Painter, David S. (2012). "Oil and the American Century"[558] (PDF). *The Journal of American History*. **99** (1): 24–39. doi: 10.1093/jahist/jas073[559].<templatestyles src="Module:Citation/CS1/styles.css"></templatestyles>

- Pearson, Jonathan. (2002) *Sir Anthony Eden and the Suez Crisis: Reluctant Gamble* (Springer, 2002). online[560]

Reynolds, David (1991). *Brittania Overruled: British Policy and World Power in the Twentieth Century*. Longman. ISBN 0-582-38249-1.<templatestyles src="Module:Citation/CS1/styles.css"></templatestyles>

Risse-Kappen, Thomas (1997) [1995]. *Cooperation among Democracies: The European Influence on U.S. Foreign Policy* (2nd ed.). Princeton, NJ: Princeton University Press. ISBN 978-0-691-01711-2.<templatestyles src="Module:Citation/CS1/styles.css"></templatestyles>

Sayed-Ahmed, Muhammad Add al-Wahab "Relations between Egypt and the United States of America in the 1950s", pp. 89–99 from *Contemporary Egypt: Through Egyptian eyes: Essays in honour of Professor P. J. Vatikiotis* edited by Charles Tripp, Routledge: London, 1993, <templatestyles src="Module:Citation/CS1/styles.css" />ISBN 0415061032.

Sachar, Howard M. *A History of Israel from the Rise of Zionism to Our Time*. Published by Alfred A. Knopf (New York). 1976. <templatestyles src="Module:Citation/CS1/styles.css" />ISBN 978-0-394-48564-5

Sharon, Ariel (1989). *Warrior: The Autobiography Of Ariel Sharon*. New York: Simon and Schuster. ISBN 0-671-60555-0.<templatestyles src="Module:Citation/CS1/styles.css"></templatestyles>

Stewart, Dona J. (2013). *The Middle East Today: Political, Geographical and Cultural Perspectives*. Routledge. ISBN 9780415782432.<templatestyles src="Module:Citation/CS1/styles.css"></templatestyles>

Tal, David, ed. (2001). *The 1956 War*. London: Frank Cass Publishers. ISBN 0-7146-4394-7.<templatestyles src="Module:Citation/CS1/styles.css"></templatestyles>

Thornhill, Michael "Britain, the United States and the Rise of an Egyptian Leader", pp. 892–921 from *English Historical Review*, Volume CXIV, Issue #483, September 2004.

Turner, Barry (2006). *Suez 1956 The World's First War for Oil*. London: Hodder & Stoughton. ISBN 0340837683.<templatestyles src="Module:Citation/CS1/styles.css"></templatestyles>

Varble, Derek (2003). *The Suez Crisis 1956*. London: Osprey. ISBN 1841764183.<templatestyles src="Module:Citation/CS1/styles.css"></templatestyles>

Vatikiotis, Panayiotis (1978). *Nasser and His Generation*. London: Croom Helm. ISBN 0-85664-433-1.<templatestyles src="Module:Citation/CS1/styles.css"></templatestyles>

Verbeek, Bertjan (2003). *Decision-Making in Great Britain During the Suez Crisis. Small Groups and a Persistent Leader*. Aldershot: Ashgate Publishing. ISBN 978-0-7546-3253-5.<templatestyles src="Module:Citation/CS1/styles.css"></templatestyles>

Wilson, Andrew (2008). *Our Times The age of Elizabeth II*. London: Hutchinson. ISBN 0091796717.<templatestyles src="Module:Citation/CS1/styles.css"></templatestyles>

Yergin, Daniel (1991). *The Prize: The Epic Quest for Oil, Money, and Power*. New York City: Simon & Schuster. ISBN 0-671-50248-4.<templatestyles src="Module:Citation/CS1/styles.css"></templatestyles>. Chapter 24 is devoted entirely to the Suez Crisis.

External links

 Wikimedia Commons has media related to *Suez Crisis*.

- Israel's Second War of Independence[561], essay in Azure magazine.
- A Man, A Plan and A Canal[562] by Arthur L. Herman
- Sinai Campaign 1956[563]
- Canada and the Suez Crisis[564]
- July 2006, BBC, Suez 50 years on[565]
- *Suez and the high tide of Arab nationalism*[566] *International Socialism* 112 (2006)
- Detailed report on the Suez campaign by Ground Forces Chief of Staff General Beaufre, French Defense Ministry archive[567] (**French**)
- Bodleian Library Suez Crisis Fiftieth anniversary exhibition[568]
- Suez index[569] at Britains-smallwars.com – accounts by British servicemen that were present
- 26 July speech by Gamal Abdel Nasser[570] (French translation)
- Speech by Gamal Abdel Nasser[571] (Original text in Arabic)
- The short film *The Middle East (1963)*[572] is available for free download at the Internet Archive

Media links

- Newsreel film, British Prime Minister's broadcast[573] at Britishpathe.com
- *Blue Vanguard*[574] (1957), National Film Board of Canada film for the United Nations about its role in restoring peace after the Suez Crisis (60 min, Ian MacNeill, dir.)

Six-Day War

Six-Day War

<indicator name="pp-default"> 🔒 </indicator>

Six-Day War	
Part of the Arab–Israeli conflict	
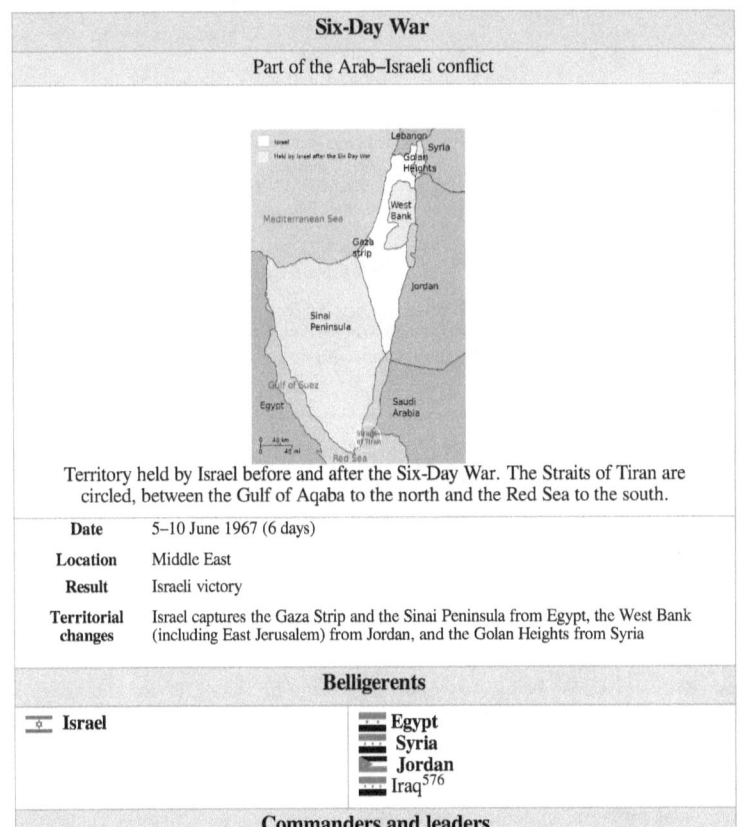 Territory held by Israel before and after the Six-Day War. The Straits of Tiran are circled, between the Gulf of Aqaba to the north and the Red Sea to the south.	
Date	5–10 June 1967 (6 days)
Location	Middle East
Result	Israeli victory
Territorial changes	Israel captures the Gaza Strip and the Sinai Peninsula from Egypt, the West Bank (including East Jerusalem) from Jordan, and the Golan Heights from Syria
Belligerents	
Israel	Egypt Syria Jordan Iraq[576]
Commanders and leaders	

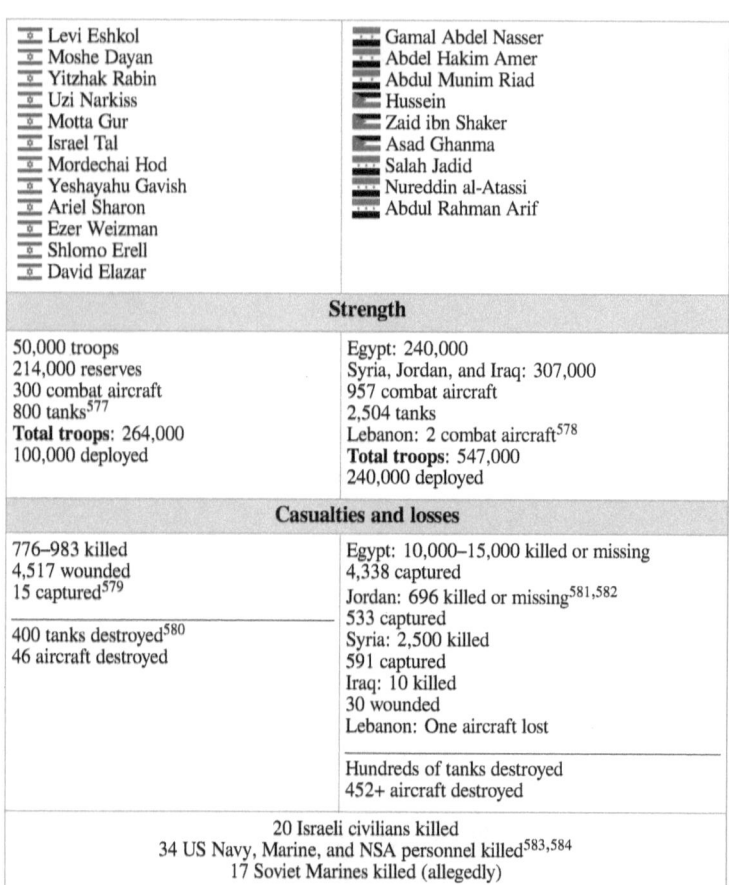

Levi Eshkol Moshe Dayan Yitzhak Rabin Uzi Narkiss Motta Gur Israel Tal Mordechai Hod Yeshayahu Gavish Ariel Sharon Ezer Weizman Shlomo Erell David Elazar	Gamal Abdel Nasser Abdel Hakim Amer Abdul Munim Riad Hussein Zaid ibn Shaker Asad Ghanma Salah Jadid Nureddin al-Atassi Abdul Rahman Arif
Strength	
50,000 troops 214,000 reserves 300 combat aircraft 800 tanks[577] **Total troops**: 264,000 100,000 deployed	Egypt: 240,000 Syria, Jordan, and Iraq: 307,000 957 combat aircraft 2,504 tanks Lebanon: 2 combat aircraft[578] **Total troops**: 547,000 240,000 deployed
Casualties and losses	
776–983 killed 4,517 wounded 15 captured[579] 400 tanks destroyed[580] 46 aircraft destroyed	Egypt: 10,000–15,000 killed or missing 4,338 captured Jordan: 696 killed or missing[581],[582] 533 captured Syria: 2,500 killed 591 captured Iraq: 10 killed 30 wounded Lebanon: One aircraft lost
	Hundreds of tanks destroyed 452+ aircraft destroyed
20 Israeli civilians killed 34 US Navy, Marine, and NSA personnel killed[583],[584] 17 Soviet Marines killed (allegedly)	

The **Six-Day War** (Hebrew: מלחמת ששת הימים, *Milhemet Sheshet Ha Yamim*; Arabic: النكسة, *an-Naksah*, "The Setback" or حرب ۱۹٦۷, *Ḥarb 1967*, "War of 1967"), also known as the **June War**, **1967 Arab–Israeli War**, or **Third Arab–Israeli War**, was fought between 5 and 10 June 1967 by Israel and the neighboring states of Egypt (known at the time as the United Arab Republic), Jordan, and Syria.

Relations between Israel and its neighbours had never fully normalised following the 1948 Arab–Israeli War. In 1956 Israel invaded the Egyptian Sinai, with one of its objectives being the reopening of the Straits of Tiran which Egypt had blocked to Israeli shipping since 1950. Israel was subsequently forced to withdraw, but won a guarantee that the Straits of Tiran would remain open. While the United Nations Emergency Force was deployed along the border, there was no demilitarisation agreement.

In the period leading up to June 1967, tensions became dangerously heightened. Israel reiterated its post-1956 position that the closure of the straits of Tiran to its shipping would be a *casus belli*. In May Egyptian President Gamal Abdel Nasser announced that the straits would be closed to Israeli vessels and then mobilised its Egyptian forces along its border with Israel. On 5 June, Israel launched what it claimed were a series of preemptive airstrikes against Egyptian airfields. Claims and counterclaims relating to this series of events are one of a number of controversies relating to the conflict.

The Egyptians were caught by surprise, and nearly the entire Egyptian air force was destroyed with few Israeli losses, giving the Israelis air supremacy. Simultaneously, the Israelis launched a ground offensive into the Gaza Strip and the Sinai, which again caught the Egyptians by surprise. After some initial resistance, Egyptian leader Gamal Abdel Nasser ordered the evacuation of the Sinai. Israeli forces rushed westward in pursuit of the Egyptians, inflicted heavy losses, and conquered the Sinai.

Nasser induced Syria and Jordan to begin attacks on Israel by using the initially confused situation to claim that Egypt had repelled the Israeli air strike. Israeli counterattacks resulted in the seizure of East Jerusalem as well as the West Bank from the Jordanians, while Israel's retaliation against Syria resulted in its occupation of the Golan Heights.

A ceasefire was signed on 11 June. In the aftermath of the war, Israel had crippled the Egyptian, Syrian and Jordanian militaries, having killed over 20,000 troops while only losing fewer than 1,000 of its own. The Israeli success was the result of a well-prepared and enacted strategy, the poor leadership of the Arab states, and their poor military leadership and strategy. Israel seized the Gaza Strip and the Sinai Peninsula from Egypt, the West Bank from Jordan and the Golan Heights from Syria. Israel's international standing greatly improved in the following years. Its victory humiliated Egypt, Jordan and Syria, leading Nasser to resign in shame; he was later reinstated after protests in Egypt against his resignation. The speed and ease of Israel's victory would later lead to a dangerous overconfidence within the ranks of the Israel Defense Forces (IDF), contributing to initial Arab successes in the subsequent 1973 Yom Kippur War, although ultimately Israeli forces were successful and defeated the Arab militaries. The displacement of civilian populations resulting from the war would have long-term consequences, as 300,000 Palestinians fled the West Bank and about 100,000 Syrians left the Golan Heights to become refugees. Across the Arab world, Jewish minority communities fled or were expelled, with refugees going mainly to Israel or Europe.

Figure 79: *On 22 May 1967, President Nasser addressed his pilots at Bir Gifgafa Airfield in Sinai: "The Jews are threatening war – we say to them ahlan wa-sahlan (welcome)!"*

Background

After the 1956 Suez Crisis, Egypt agreed to the stationing of a United Nations Emergency Force (UNEF) in the Sinai to ensure all parties would comply with the 1949 Armistice Agreements. In the following years there were numerous minor border clashes between Israel and its Arab neighbors, particularly Syria. In early November 1966, Syria signed a mutual defense agreement with Egypt.[585] Soon after this, in response to Palestine Liberation Organisation (PLO) guerilla activity,[586,587] including a mine attack that left three dead,[588] the Israeli Defence Force (IDF) attacked the village of as-Samu in the Jordanian-occupied West Bank.[589] Jordanian units that engaged the Israelis were quickly beaten back.[590] King Hussein of Jordan criticized Egyptian President Gamal Abdel Nasser for failing to come to Jordan's aid, and "hiding behind UNEF skirts".[591]

In May 1967, Nasser received false reports from the Soviet Union that Israel was massing on the Syrian border.[592] Nasser began massing his troops in two defensive lines[593] in the Sinai Peninsula on Israel's border (16 May), expelled the UNEF force from Gaza and Sinai (19 May) and took over UNEF positions at Sharm el-Sheikh, overlooking the Straits of Tiran.[594] Israel repeated declarations it had made in 1957 that any closure of the Straits would be considered an act of war, or justification for war,[595] but Nasser closed the Straits to Israeli shipping on 22–23 May. After the war, U.S. President Lyndon Johnson commented:[596]

<templatestyles src="Template:Quote/styles.css"/>

If a single act of folly was more responsible for this explosion than any other, it was the arbitrary and dangerous announced decision that the Straits of Tiran would be closed. The right of innocent, maritime passage must be preserved for all nations.

On 30 May, Jordan and Egypt signed a defense pact. The following day, at Jordan's invitation, the Iraqi army began deploying troops and armoured units in Jordan.[597] They were later reinforced by an Egyptian contingent. On 1 June, Israel formed a National Unity Government by widening its cabinet, and on 4 June the decision was made to go to war. The next morning, Israel launched Operation Focus, a large-scale surprise air strike that was the opening of the Six-Day War.

Military preparation

Before the war, Israeli pilots and ground crews had trained extensively in rapid refitting of aircraft returning from sorties, enabling a single aircraft to sortie up to four times a day (as opposed to the norm in Arab air forces of one or two sorties per day). This enabled the Israeli Air Force (IAF) to send several attack waves against Egyptian airfields on the first day of the war, overwhelming the Egyptian Air Force, and allowed it to knock out other Arab air forces on the same day. This has contributed to the Arab belief that the IAF was helped by foreign air forces (see Controversies relating to the Six-Day War). Pilots were extensively schooled about their targets, and were forced to memorize every single detail, and rehearsed the operation multiple times on dummy runways in total secrecy.

The Egyptians had constructed fortified defenses in the Sinai. These designs were based on the assumption that an attack would come along the few roads leading through the desert, rather than through the difficult desert terrain. The Israelis chose not to risk attacking the Egyptian defenses head-on, and instead surprised them from an unexpected direction.

James Reston, writing in *The New York Times* on 23 May 1967, noted, "In discipline, training, morale, equipment and general competence his [Nasser's] army and the other Arab forces, without the direct assistance of the Soviet Union, are no match for the Israelis. ... Even with 50,000 troops and the best of his generals and air force in Yemen, he has not been able to work his way in that small and primitive country, and even his effort to help the Congo rebels was a flop."

On the eve of the war, Israel believed it could win a war in 3–4 days. The United States estimated Israel would need 7–10 days to win, with British estimates supporting the U.S. view.[598]

Armies and weapons

Armies

The Israeli army had a total strength, including reservists, of 264,000, though this number could not be sustained, as the reservists were vital to civilian life.[599]

Against Jordan's forces on the West Bank, Israel deployed about 40,000 troops and 200 tanks (eight brigades).[600] Israeli Central Command forces consisted of five brigades. The first two were permanently stationed near Jerusalem and were the Jerusalem Brigade and the mechanized Harel Brigade. Mordechai Gur's 55th Paratroopers Brigade was summoned from the Sinai front. The 10th Armored Brigade was stationed north of the West Bank. The Israeli Northern Command comprised a division of three brigades led by Major General Elad Peled which was stationed in the Jezreel Valley to the north of the West Bank.

On the eve of the war, Egypt massed approximately 100,000 of its 160,000 troops in the Sinai, including all seven of its divisions (four infantry, two armoured and one mechanized), four independent infantry brigades and four independent armoured brigades. Over a third of these soldiers were veterans of Egypt's continuing intervention into the North Yemen Civil War and another third were reservists. These forces had 950 tanks, 1,100 APCs, and more than 1,000 artillery pieces.[601]

Syria's army had a total strength of 75,000 and was deployed along the border with Israel.[602]

The Jordanian Armed Forces included 11 brigades, totalling 55,000 troops.[603] Nine brigades (45,000 troops, 270 tanks, 200 artillery pieces) were deployed in the West Bank, including the elite armoured 40th, and two in the Jordan Valley. They possessed sizable numbers of M113 APCs and were equipped with some 300 modern Western tanks, 250 of which were U.S. M48 Pattons. They also had 12 battalions of artillery, six batteries of 81 mm and 120 mm mortars, a paratrooper battalion trained in the new U.S.-built school and a new battalion of mechanized infantry. The Jordanian Army, then known as the Arab Legion, was a long-term-service, professional army, relatively well-equipped and well-trained. Israeli post-war briefings said that the Jordanian staff acted professionally, but was always left "half a step" behind by the Israeli moves. The small Royal Jordanian Air Force consisted of only 24 British-made Hawker Hunter fighters, six transports, and two helicopters. According to the Israelis, the Hawker Hunter was essentially on par with the French-built Dassault Mirage III – the IAF's best plane.[604]

100 Iraqi tanks and an infantry division were readied near the Jordanian border. Two squadrons of Iraqi fighter-aircraft, Hawker Hunters and MiG 21s, were rebased adjacent to the Jordanian border.[605]

The Arab air forces were reinforced by some aircraft from Libya, Algeria, Morocco, Kuwait, and Saudi Arabia to make up for the massive losses suffered on the first day of the war. They were also aided by volunteer pilots from the Pakistan Air Force acting in an independent capacity. PAF pilots shot down several Israeli planes.

Weapons

With the exception of Jordan, the Arabs relied principally on Soviet weaponry. Jordan's army was equipped with American weaponry, and its air force was composed of British aircraft.

Egypt had by far the largest and the most modern of all the Arab air forces, consisting of about 420 combat aircraft,[606] all of them Soviet-built and with a heavy quota of top-of-the-line MiG-21s. Of particular concern to the Israelis were the 30 Tu-16 "Badger" medium bombers, capable of inflicting heavy damage on Israeli military and civilian centers.[607]

Israeli weapons were mainly of Western origin. Its air force was composed principally of French aircraft, while its armoured units were mostly of British and American design and manufacture. Some infantry weapons, including the ubiquitous Uzi, were of Israeli origin.

Type	Arab armies	IDF
AFVs	Egypt, Syria and Iraq used T-34/85, T-54, T-55, PT-76, and SU-100/152 World War II-vintage self-propelled guns. Jordan used M-47, M-48, and M-48A1 Patton tanks. Panzer IV (used by Syria)[608,609]	M50 and M51 Shermans, M48A3 Patton, Centurion, AMX-13. The Centurion was upgraded with the British 105 mm L7 gun prior to the war. The Sherman also underwent extensive modifications including a larger 105 mm medium velocity, French gun, redesigned turret, wider tracks, more armour, and upgraded engine and suspension.
APCs/-IFVs	BTR-40, BTR-152, BTR-50, BTR-60 APCs	M2, / M3 Half-track, Panhard AML
Artillery	M1937 Howitzer, BM-21, D-30 (2A18) Howitzer, M1954 field gun, M-52 105 mm self-propelled howitzer (used by Jordan)	M50 self-propelled howitzer and Makmat 160 mm self-propelled mortar, Obusier de 155 mm Modèle 50, AMX 105 mm Self-Propelled Howitzer
Aircraft	MiG-21, MiG-19, MiG-17, Su-7B, Tu-16, Il-28, Il-18, Il-14, An-12, Hawker Hunter used by Jordan and Iraq	Dassault Mirage III, Dassault Super Mystère, Sud Aviation Vautour, Mystere IV, Dassault Ouragan, Fouga Magister trainer outfitted for attack missions, Nord 2501IS military cargo plane

Heli-copters	Mi-6, Mi-4	Super Frelon, Sikorsky S-58
AAW	SA-2 Guideline, ZSU-57-2 mobile anti-aircraft cannon	MIM-23 Hawk, Bofors 40 mm
Infantry weapons	Port Said submachine gun, AK-47, RPK, RPD, DShK HMG, B-10 and B-11 recoilless rifles	Uzi, FN FAL, FN MAG, AK-47, M2 Browning, Cobra, Nord SS.10, RL-83 Blindicide anti-tank infantry weapon, Jeep-mounted 106 mm recoilless rifle

Fighting fronts

Preemptive air attack

Israel's first and most critical move was a surprise attack on the Egyptian Air Force. Initially, both Egypt and Israel announced that they had been attacked by the other country.

On 5 June at 7:45 Israeli time, as civil defense sirens sounded all over Israel, the IAF launched Operation Focus (*Moked*). All but 12 of its nearly 200 operational jets[610] launched a mass attack against Egypt's airfields.[611] The Egyptian defensive infrastructure was extremely poor, and no airfields were yet equipped with hardened aircraft shelters capable of protecting Egypt's warplanes. Most of the Israeli warplanes headed out over the Mediterranean Sea, flying low to avoid radar detection, before turning toward Egypt. Others flew over the Red Sea.[612]

Meanwhile, the Egyptians hindered their own defense by effectively shutting down their entire air defense system: they were worried that rebel Egyptian forces would shoot down the plane carrying Field Marshal Abdel Hakim Amer and Lt-Gen. Sidqi Mahmoud, who were en route from al Maza to Bir Tamada in the Sinai to meet the commanders of the troops stationed there. In any event, it did not make a great deal of difference as the Israeli pilots came in below Egyptian radar cover and well below the lowest point at which its SA-2 surface-to-air missile batteries could bring down an aircraft.[613]

Although the powerful Jordanian radar facility at Ajloun detected waves of aircraft approaching Egypt and reported the code word for "war" up the Egyptian command chain, Egyptian command and communications problems prevented the warning from reaching the targeted airfields. The Israelis employed a mixed-attack strategy: bombing and strafing runs against planes parked on the ground, and bombing to disable runways with special tarmac-shredding penetration bombs developed jointly with France, leaving surviving aircraft unable to take off. The runway at the Arish airfield was spared, as the Israelis

Figure 80: *Israeli troops examine destroyed Egyptian aircraft.*

Figure 81: *Dassault Mirage at the Israeli Air Force Museum. Operation Focus was mainly conducted using French built aircraft.*

expected to turn it into a military airport for their transports after the war. Surviving aircraft were taken out by later attack waves. The operation was more successful than expected, catching the Egyptians by surprise and destroying virtually all of the Egyptian Air Force on the ground, with few Israeli losses. Only four unarmed Egyptian training flights were in the air when the strike began.[614] A total of 338 Egyptian aircraft were destroyed and 100 pilots were killed,[615] although the number of aircraft lost by the Egyptians is disputed.[616]

Among the Egyptian planes lost were all 30 Tu-16 bombers, 27 out of 40 Il-28 bombers, 12 Su-7 fighter-bombers, over 90 MiG-21s, 20 MiG-19s, 25 MiG-17 fighters, and around 32 assorted transport planes and helicopters. In addition, Egyptian radars and SAM missiles were also attacked and destroyed. The Israelis lost 19 planes, including two destroyed in air-to-air combat and 13 downed by anti-aircraft artillery.[617] One Israeli plane, which was damaged and unable to break radio silence, was shot down by Israeli Hawk missiles after it strayed over the Negev Nuclear Research Center.[618] Another was destroyed by an exploding Egyptian bomber.[619]

The attack guaranteed Israeli air supremacy for the rest of the war. Attacks on other Arab air forces by Israel took place later in the day as hostilities broke out on other fronts.

The large numbers of Arab aircraft claimed destroyed by Israel on that day were at first regarded as "greatly exaggerated" by the Western press. However, the fact that the Egyptian Air Force, along with other Arab air forces attacked by Israel, made practically no appearance for the remaining days of the conflict proved that the numbers were most likely authentic. Throughout the war, Israeli aircraft continued strafing Arab airfield runways to prevent their return to usability. Meanwhile, Egyptian state-run radio had reported an Egyptian victory, falsely claiming that 70 Israeli planes had been downed on the first day of fighting.

Gaza Strip and Sinai Peninsula

The Egyptian forces consisted of seven divisions: four armoured, two infantry, and one mechanized infantry. Overall, Egypt had around 100,000 troops and 900–950 tanks in the Sinai, backed by 1,100 APCs and 1,000 artillery pieces.[620] This arrangement was thought to be based on the Soviet doctrine, where mobile armour units at strategic depth provide a dynamic defense while infantry units engage in defensive battles.

Israeli forces concentrated on the border with Egypt included six armoured brigades, one infantry brigade, one mechanized infantry brigade, three paratrooper brigades, giving a total of around 70,000 men and 700 tanks, who were organized in three armoured divisions. They had massed on the border

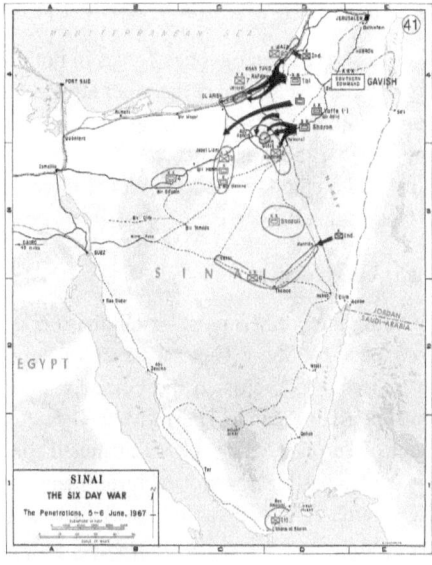

Figure 82: *Conquest of Sinai. 5–6 June 1967*

Figure 83: *People in a bomb shelter at Kfar Maimon*

the night before the war, camouflaging themselves and observing radio silence before being ordered to advance.

The Israeli plan was to surprise the Egyptian forces in both timing (the attack exactly coinciding with the IAF strike on Egyptian airfields), location (attacking via northern and central Sinai routes, as opposed to the Egyptian expectations of a repeat of the 1956 war, when the IDF attacked via the central and southern routes) and method (using a combined-force flanking approach, rather than direct tank assaults).

Northern (El Arish) Israeli division

On 5 June, at 7:50 a.m., the northernmost Israeli division, consisting of three brigades and commanded by Major General Israel Tal, one of Israel's most prominent armour commanders, crossed the border at two points, opposite Nahal Oz and south of Khan Yunis. They advanced swiftly, holding fire to prolong the element of surprise. Tal's forces assaulted the "Rafah Gap", a seven-mile stretch containing the shortest of three main routes through the Sinai towards El-Qantarah el-Sharqiyya and the Suez Canal. The Egyptians had four divisions in the area, backed by minefields, pillboxes, underground bunkers, hidden gun emplacements and trenches. The terrain on either side of the route was impassable. The Israeli plan was to hit the Egyptians at selected key points with concentrated armour.

Tal's advance was led by the 7th Armored Brigade under Colonel Shmuel Gonen. The Israeli plan called for the 7th Brigade to outflank Khan Yunis from the north and the 60th Armored Brigade under Colonel Menachem Aviram would advance from the south. The two brigades would link up and surround Khan Yunis, while the paratroopers would take Rafah. Gonen entrusted the breakthrough to a single battalion of his brigade.[621]

Initially, the advance was met with light resistance, as Egyptian intelligence had concluded that it was a diversion for the main attack. However, as Gonen's lead battalion advanced, it suddenly came under intense fire and took heavy losses. A second battalion was brought up, but was also pinned down. Meanwhile, the 60th Brigade became bogged down in the sand, while the paratroopers had trouble navigating through the dunes. The Israelis continued to press their attack, and despite heavy losses, cleared the Egyptian positions and reached the Khan Yunis railway junction in little over four hours.

Gonen's brigade then advanced nine miles to Rafah in twin columns. Rafah itself was circumvented, and the Israelis attacked Sheikh Zuweid, eight miles to the southwest, which was defended by two brigades. Though inferior in numbers and equipment, the Egyptians were deeply entrenched and camouflaged. The Israelis were pinned down by fierce Egyptian resistance, and called in air

Figure 84: *Israeli reconnaissance forces from the "Shaked" unit in Sinai during the war.*

and artillery support to enable their lead elements to advance. Many Egyptians abandoned their positions after their commander and several of his staff were killed.

The Israelis broke through with tank-led assaults. However, Aviram's forces misjudged the Egyptians' flank, and were pinned between strongholds before they were extracted after several hours. By nightfall, the Israelis had finished mopping up resistance. Israeli forces had taken significant losses, with Colonel Gonen later telling reporters that "we left many of our dead soldiers in Rafah, and many burnt-out tanks." The Egyptians suffered some 2,000 casualties and lost 40 tanks.

Advance on Arish

On 5 June, with the road open, Israeli forces continued advancing towards Arish. Already by late afternoon, elements of the 79th Armored Battalion had charged through the seven-mile long Jiradi defile, a narrow pass defended by well-emplaced troops of the Egyptian 112th Infantry Brigade. In fierce fighting, which saw the pass change hands several times, the Israelis charged through the position. The Egyptians suffered heavy casualties and tank losses, while Israeli losses stood at 66 dead, 93 wounded and 28 tanks. Emerging at the western end, Israeli forces advanced to the outskirts of Arish.[622] As it reached the outskirts of Arish, Tal's division also consolidated its hold on Rafah and Khan Yunis.

Figure 85: *Major-General Ariel Sharon during the Battle of Abu-Ageila*

The following day, 6 June, the Israeli forces on the outskirts of Arish were reinforced by the 7th Brigade, which fought its way through the Jiradi pass. After receiving supplies via an airdrop, the Israelis entered the city and captured the airport at 7:50 am. The Israelis entered the city at 8:00 am. Company commander Yossi Peled recounted that "Al-Arish was totally quiet, desolate. Suddenly, the city turned into a madhouse. Shots came at us from every alley, every corner, every window and house." An IDF record stated that "clearing the city was hard fighting. The Egyptians fired from the rooftops, from balconies and windows. They dropped grenades into our half-tracks and blocked the streets with trucks. Our men threw the grenades back and crushed the trucks with their tanks."[623] Gonen sent additional units to Arish, and the city was eventually taken.

Brigadier-General Avraham Yoffe's assignment was to penetrate Sinai south of Tal's forces and north or Sharon's. Yoffe's attack allowed Tal to complete the capture of the Jiradi defile, Khan Yunis. All of them were taken after fierce fighting. Gonen subsequently dispatched a force of tanks, infantry and engineers under Colonel Yisrael Granit to continue down the Mediterranean coast towards the Suez Canal, while a second force led by Gonen himself turned south and captured Bir Lahfan and Jabal Libni.

Figure 86: *Israeli Armor of the Six Day War: pictured here the AMX 13*

Mid-front (Abu-Ageila) Israeli division

Further south, on 6 June, the Israeli 38th Armored Division under Major-General Ariel Sharon assaulted Um-Katef, a heavily fortified area defended by the Egyptian 2nd Infantry Division under Major-General Sa'adi Nagib, and consisting of some 16,000 troops. The Egyptians also had a battalion of tank destroyers and a tank regiment, formed of Soviet World War II armour, which included 90 T-34-85 tanks, 22 SU-100 tank destroyers, and about 16,000 men. The Israelis had about 14,000 men and 150 post-World War II tanks including the AMX-13, Centurions, and M50 Super Shermans (modified M-4 Sherman tanks).

Two armoured brigades in the meantime, under Avraham Yoffe, slipped across the border through sandy wastes that Egypt had left undefended because they were considered impassable. Simultaneously, Sharon's tanks from the west were to engage Egyptian forces on Um-Katef ridge and block any reinforcements. Israeli infantry would clear the three trenches, while heliborne paratroopers would land behind Egyptian lines and silence their artillery. An armoured thrust would be made at al-Qusmaya to unnerve and isolate its garrison.

As Sharon's division advanced into the Sinai, Egyptian forces staged successful delaying actions at Tarat Umm, Umm Tarfa, and Hill 181. An Israeli jet was downed by anti-aircraft fire, and Sharon's forces came under heavy shelling as they advanced from the north and west. The Israeli advance, which had to cope with extensive minefields, took a large number of casualties. A column of Israeli tanks managed to penetrate the northern flank of Abu Ageila, and by dusk, all units were in position. The Israelis then brought up ninety 105 mm and 155 mm artillery guns for a preparatory barrage, while civilian buses brought reserve infantrymen under Colonel Yekutiel Adam and helicopters arrived to ferry the paratroopers. These movements were unobserved by the Egyptians, who were preoccupied with Israeli probes against their perimeter.[624]

As night fell, the Israeli assault troops lit flashlights, each battalion a different color, to prevent friendly fire incidents. At 10:00 pm, Israeli artillery began a barrage on Um-Katef, firing some 6,000 shells in less than twenty minutes, the most concentrated artillery barrage in Israel's history.[625,626] Israeli tanks assaulted the northernmost Egyptian defenses and were largely successful, though an entire armoured brigade was stalled by mines, and had only one mine-clearance tank. Israeli infantrymen assaulted the triple line of trenches in the east. To the west, paratroopers commanded by Colonel Danny Matt landed behind Egyptian lines, though half the helicopters got lost and never found the battlefield, while others were unable to land due to mortar fire.[627,628] Those that successfully landed on target destroyed Egyptian artillery and ammunition dumps and separated gun crews from their batteries, sowing enough confusion to significantly reduce Egyptian artillery fire. Egyptian reinforcements from Jabal Libni advanced towards Um-Katef to counterattack, but failed to reach their objective, being subjected to heavy air attacks and encountering Israeli lodgements on the roads. Egyptian commanders then called in artillery attacks on their own positions. The Israelis accomplished and sometimes exceeded their overall plan, and had largely succeeded by the following day. The Egyptians took heavy casualties, while the Israelis lost 40 dead and 140 wounded.

Yoffe's attack allowed Sharon to complete the capture of the Um-Katef, after fierce fighting. The main thrust at Um-Katef was stalled due to mines and craters. After IDF engineers had cleared a path by 4:00 pm, Israeli and Egyptian tanks engaged in fierce combat, often at ranges as close as ten yards. The battle ended in an Israeli victory, with 40 Egyptian and 19 Israeli tanks destroyed. Meanwhile, Israeli infantry finished clearing out the Egyptian trenches, with Israeli casualties standing at 14 dead and 41 wounded and Egyptian casualties at 300 dead and 100 taken prisoner.[629]

Other Israeli forces

Further south, on 5 June, the 8th Armored Brigade under Colonel Albert Mandler, initially positioned as a ruse to draw off Egyptian forces from the real invasion routes, attacked the fortified bunkers at Kuntilla, a strategically valuable position whose capture would enable Mandler to block reinforcements from reaching Um-Katef and to join Sharon's upcoming attack on Nakhl. The defending Egyptian battalion, outnumbered and outgunned, fiercely resisted the attack, hitting a number of Israeli tanks. However, most of the defenders were killed, and only three Egyptian tanks, one of them damaged, survived. By nightfall, Mendler's forces had taken Kuntilla.

With the exceptions of Rafah and Khan Yunis, Israeli forces had initially avoided entering the Gaza Strip. Israeli Defense Minister Moshe Dayan had expressly forbidden entry into the area. After Palestinian positions in Gaza opened fire on the Negev settlements of Nirim and Kissufim, IDF Chief of Staff Yitzhak Rabin overrode Dayan's instructions and ordered the 11th Mechanized Brigade under Colonel Yehuda Reshef to enter the Strip. The force was immediately met with heavy artillery fire and fierce resistance from Palestinian forces and remnants of the Egyptian forces from Rafah.

By sunset, the Israelis had taken the strategically vital Ali Muntar ridge, overlooking Gaza City, but were beaten back from the city itself. Some 70 Israelis were killed, along with Israeli journalist Ben Oyserman and American journalist Paul Schutzer. Twelve members of UNEF were also killed. On the war's second day, 6 June, the Israelis were bolstered by the 35th Paratroopers Brigade under Colonel Rafael Eitan, and took Gaza City along with the entire Strip. The fighting was fierce, and accounted for nearly half of all Israeli casualties on the southern front. However, Gaza rapidly fell to the Israelis.

Meanwhile, on 6 June, two Israeli reserve brigades under Yoffe, each equipped with 100 tanks, penetrated the Sinai south of Tal's division and north of Sharon's, capturing the road junctions of Abu Ageila, Bir Lahfan, and Arish, taking all of them before midnight. Two Egyptian armoured brigades counterattacked, and a fierce battle took place until the following morning. The Egyptians were beaten back by fierce resistance coupled with airstrikes, sustaining heavy tank losses. They fled west towards Jabal Libni.[630]

The Egyptian Army

During the ground fighting, remnants of the Egyptian Air Force attacked Israeli ground forces, but took losses from the Israeli Air Force and from Israeli anti-aircraft units. Throughout the last four days, Egyptian aircraft flew 150 sorties against Israeli units in the Sinai.

Many of the Egyptian units remained intact and could have tried to prevent the Israelis from reaching the Suez Canal, or engaged in combat in the attempt to reach the canal. However, when the Egyptian Field Marshal Abdel Hakim Amer heard about the fall of Abu-Ageila, he panicked and ordered all units in the Sinai to retreat. This order effectively meant the defeat of Egypt.

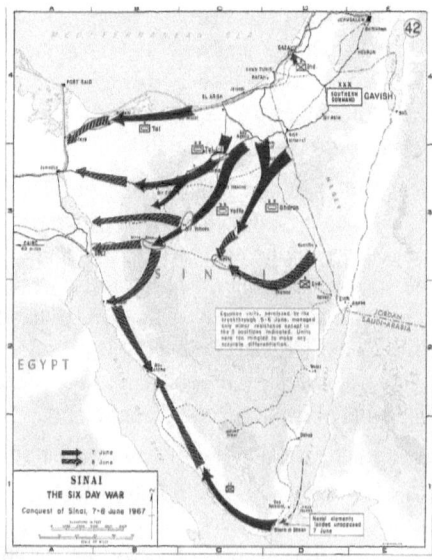

Figure 87: *Conquest of Sinai. 7–8 June 1967*

Meanwhile, President Nasser, having learned of the results of the Israeli air strikes, decided together with Field Marshal Amer to order a general retreat from the Sinai within 24 hours. No detailed instructions were given concerning the manner and sequence of withdrawal.

Next fighting days

As Egyptian columns retreated, Israeli aircraft and artillery attacked them. Israeli jets used napalm bombs during their sorties. The attacks destroyed hundreds of vehicles and caused heavy casualties. At Jabal Libni, retreating Egyptian soldiers were fired upon by their own artillery. At Bir Gafgafa, the Egyptians fiercely resisted advancing Israeli forces, knocking out three tanks and eight half-tracks, and killing 20 soldiers. Due to the Egyptians' retreat, the Israeli High Command decided not to pursue the Egyptian units but rather to bypass and destroy them in the mountainous passes of West Sinai.

Therefore, in the following two days (6 and 7 June), all three Israeli divisions (Sharon and Tal were reinforced by an armoured brigade each) rushed westwards and reached the passes. Sharon's division first went southward then westward, via An-Nakhl, to Mitla Pass with air support. It was joined there by parts of Yoffe's division, while its other units blocked the Gidi Pass. These passes became killing grounds for the Egyptians, who ran right into waiting Israeli positions and suffered heavy losses. According to Egyptian diplomat

Figure 88: *Newsreel from 6 June about the first Israeli-Egyptian fighting.*

Figure 89: *An Israeli gunboat passes through the Straits of Tiran near Sharm El Sheikh.*

Mahmoud Riad, 10,000 men were killed in one day alone, and many others died from hunger and thirst. Tal's units stopped at various points to the length of the Suez Canal.

Israel's blocking action was partially successful. Only the Gidi pass was captured before the Egyptians approached it, but at other places, Egyptian units managed to pass through and cross the canal to safety. Due to the haste of the Egyptian retreat, soldiers often abandoned weapons, military equipment, and hundreds of vehicles. Many Egyptian soldiers were cut off from their units had to walk about 200 kilometers on foot before reaching the Suez Canal with limited supplies of food and water and were exposed to intense heat. Thousands of soldiers died as a result. Many Egyptian soldiers chose instead to surrender to the Israelis. However, the Israelis eventually exceeded their capabilities to provide for prisoners. As a result, they began directing soldiers towards the Suez Canal and only taking prisoner high-ranking officers, who were expected to be exchanged for captured Israeli pilots.

According to some accounts, during the Egyptian retreat from the Sinai, a unit of Soviet Marines based on a Soviet warship in Port Said at the time came ashore and attempted to cross the Suez Canal eastward. The Soviet force was reportedly decimated by an Israeli air attack and lost 17 dead and 34 wounded. Among the wounded was the commander, Lt. Col. Victor Shevchenko.[631]

During the offensive, the Israeli Navy landed six combat divers from the Shayetet 13 naval commando unit to infiltrate Alexandria harbour. The divers sank an Egyptian minesweeper before being taken prisoner. Shayetet 13 commandos also infiltrated into Port Said harbour, but found no ships there. A planned commando raid against the Syrian Navy never materialized. Both Egyptian and Israeli warships made movements at sea to intimidate the other side throughout the war, but did not engage each other. However, Israeli warships and aircraft did hunt for Egyptian submarines throughout the war.

On 7 June, Israel began the conquest of Sharm el-Sheikh. The Israeli Navy started the operation with a probe of Egyptian naval defenses. An aerial reconnaissance flight found that the area was less defended than originally thought. At about 4:30 am, three Israeli missile boats opened fire on Egyptian shore batteries, while paratroopers and commandos boarded helicopters and Nord Noratlas transport planes for an assault on Al-Tur, as Chief of Staff Rabin was convinced it was too risky to land them directly in Sharm el-Sheikh.[632] However, the city had been largely abandoned the day before, and reports from air and naval forces finally convinced Rabin to divert the aircraft to Sharm el-Sheikh. There, the Israelis engaged in a pitched battle with the Egyptians and took the city, killing 20 Egyptian soldiers and taking 8 prisoner. At 12:15 pm, Defense Minister Dayan announced that the Straits of Tiran constituted an international waterway open to all ships without restriction.

Figure 90: *The Jordan salient, 5–7 June.*

On 8 June, Israel completed the capture of the Sinai by sending infantry units to Ras Sudar on the western coast of the peninsula.

Several tactical elements made the swift Israeli advance possible: first, the surprise attack that quickly gave the Israeli Air Force complete air superiority over the Egyptian Air Force; second, the determined implementation of an innovative battle plan; third, the lack of coordination among Egyptian troops. These factors would prove to be decisive elements on Israel's other fronts as well.

West Bank

Jordan was reluctant to enter the war. Nasser used the confusion of the first hours of the conflict to convince King Hussein that he was victorious; he claimed as evidence a radar sighting of a squadron of Israeli aircraft returning from bombing raids in Egypt, which he said was an Egyptian aircraft en route to attack Israel.[633] One of the Jordanian brigades stationed in the West Bank was sent to the Hebron area in order to link with the Egyptians. Hussein decided to attack.

The IDF's strategic plan was to remain on the defensive along the Jordanian front, to enable focus in the expected campaign against Egypt.

Intermittent machine-gun exchanges began taking place in Jerusalem at 9:30 am, and the fighting gradually escalated as the Jordanians introduced mortar and recoilless rifle fire. Under the orders from General Narkis, the Israelis responded only with small-arms fire, firing in a flat trajectory to avoid hitting civilians, holy sites or the Old City. At 10:00 am on 5 June, the Jordanian Army began shelling Israel. Two batteries of 155 mm Long Tom cannons opened fire on the suburbs of Tel Aviv and Ramat David Airbase. The commanders of these batteries were instructed to lay a two-hour barrage against military and civilian settlements in central Israel. Some shells hit the outskirts of Tel Aviv.[634]

By 10:30 am, Eshkol had sent a message via Odd Bull to King Hussein promising not to initiate any action against Jordan if it stayed out of the war. King Hussein replied that it was too late, "the die was cast". At 11:15 am, Jordanian howitzers began a 6,000-shell barrage at Israeli Jerusalem. The Jordanians initially targeted kibbutz Ramat Rachel in the south and Mount Scopus in the north, then ranged into the city center and outlying neighborhoods. Military installations, the Prime Minister's Residence, and the Knesset compound were also targeted. Israeli civilian casualties totalled 20 dead and about 1,000 wounded. Some 900 buildings were damaged, including Hadassah Ein Kerem Hospital.[635]

At 11:50 am, sixteen Jordanian Hawker Hunters attacked Netanya, Kfar Sirkin and Kfar Saba, killing one civilian, wounding seven and destroying a transport plane. Three Iraqi Hawker Hunters strafed civilian settlements in the Jezreel Valley, and an Iraqi Tupolev Tu-16 attacked Afula, and was shot down near the Megiddo airfield. The attack caused minimal material damage, hitting only a senior citizens' home and several chicken coops, but sixteen Israeli soldiers were killed, most of them when the Tupolev crashed.

Israeli cabinet meets

When the Israeli cabinet convened to decide what to do, Yigal Allon and Menahem Begin argued that this was an opportunity to take the Old City of Jerusalem, but Eshkol decided to defer any decision until Moshe Dayan and Yitzhak Rabin could be consulted.[636] Uzi Narkiss made a number of proposals for military action, including the capture of Latrun, but the cabinet turned him down. Dayan rejected multiple requests from Narkiss for permission to mount an infantry assault towards Mount Scopus. However, Dayan sanctioned a number of more limited retaliatory actions.[637]

Initial response

Shortly before 12:30 pm, the Israeli Air Force attacked Jordan's two airbases. The Hawker Hunters were refueling at the time of the attack. The Israeli aircraft attacked in two waves, the first of which cratered the runways and knocked out the control towers, and the second wave destroyed all 21 of Jordan's Hawker Hunter fighters, along with six transport aircraft and two helicopters. One Israeli jet was shot down by ground fire.

Israeli aircraft also attacked H-3, an Iraqi Air Force base in western Iraq. During the attack, 12 MiG-21s, 2 MiG-17s, 5 Hunter F6s, and 3 Il-28 bombers were destroyed or shot down. A Pakistani pilot stationed at the base shot down an Israeli fighter and a bomber during the raid. The Jordanian radar facility at Ajloun was destroyed in an Israeli airstrike. Israeli Fouga Magister jets attacked the Jordanian 40th Brigade with rockets as it moved south from the Damiya Bridge. Dozens of tanks were knocked out, and a convoy of 26 trucks carrying ammunition was destroyed. In Jerusalem, Israel responded to Jordanian shelling with a missile strike that devastated Jordanian positions. The Israelis used the L missile, a surface-to-surface missile developed jointly with France in secret.

Jordanian battalion at Government House

A Jordanian battalion advanced up Government House ridge and dug in at the perimeter of Government House, the headquarters of the United Nations observers,[638,639] and opened fire on Ramat Rachel, the Allenby Barracks and the Jewish section of Abu Tor with mortars and recoilless rifles. UN observers fiercely protested the incursion into the neutral zone, and several manhandled a Jordanian machine gun out of Government House after the crew had set it up in a second-floor window. After the Jordanians occupied Jabel Mukaber, an advance patrol was sent out and approached Ramat Rachel, where they came under fire from four civilians, including the wife of the director, who were armed with old Czech-made weapons.[640]

The immediate Israeli response was an offensive to retake Government House and its ridge. The Jerusalem Brigade's Reserve Battalion 161, under Lieutenant-Colonel Asher Dreizin, was given the task. Dreizin had two infantry companies and eight tanks under his command, several of which broke down or became stuck in the mud at Ramat Rachel, leaving three for the assault. The Jordanians mounted fierce resistance, knocking out two tanks.[641]

The Israelis broke through the compound's western gate and began clearing the building with grenades, before General Odd Bull, commander of the UN observers, compelled the Israelis to hold their fire, telling them that the Jordanians had already fled. The Israelis proceeded to take the Antenna Hill, directly behind Government House, and clear out a series of bunkers to the west and south. The fighting, often conducted hand-to-hand, continued for nearly four hours before the surviving Jordanians fell back to trenches held by the Hittin Brigade, which were steadily overwhelmed. By 6:30 pm, the Jordanians had retreated to Bethlehem, having suffered about 100 casualties. All but ten

Figure 91: *Israeli paratroopers flush out Jordanian soldiers from trenches during the Battle of Ammunition Hill.*

Figure 92: *Silhouette of Israeli paratroops advancing on Ammunition Hill.*

of Dreizin's soldiers were casualties, and Dreizin himself was wounded three times.

Israeli invasion

During the late afternoon of 5 June, the Israelis launched an offensive to encircle Jerusalem, which lasted into the following day. During the night, they were supported by intense tank, artillery and mortar fire to soften up Jordanian positions. Searchlights placed atop the Labor Federation building, then the tallest in Israeli Jerusalem, exposed and blinded the Jordanians. The Jerusalem Brigade moved south of Jerusalem, while the mechanized Harel Brigade and 55th Paratroopers Brigade under Mordechai Gur encircled it from the north.[642]

A combined force of tanks and paratroopers crossed no-man's land near the Mandelbaum Gate. One of Gur's paratroop battalions approached the fortified Police Academy. The Israelis used bangalore torpedoes to blast their way through barbed wire leading up to the position while exposed and under heavy fire. With the aid of two tanks borrowed from the Jerusalem Brigade, they captured the Police Academy. After receiving reinforcements, they moved up to attack Ammunition Hill.[643]

The Jordanian defenders, who were heavily dug-in, fiercely resisted the attack. All of the Israeli officers except for two company commanders were killed, and the fighting was mostly led by individual soldiers. The fighting was conducted at close quarters in trenches and bunkers, and was often hand-to-hand. The Israelis captured the position after four hours of heavy fighting. During the battle, 36 Israeli and 71 Jordanian soldiers were killed.

The battalion subsequently drove east, and linked up with the Israeli enclave on Mount Scopus and its Hebrew University campus. Gur's other battalions captured the other Jordanian positions around the American Colony, despite being short on men and equipment and having come under a Jordanian mortar bombardment while waiting for the signal to advance.

At the same time, the mechanized Harel Brigade attacked the fortress at Latrun, which the Jordanians had abandoned due to heavy Israeli tank fire. The brigade attacked Har Adar, but seven tanks were knocked out by mines, forcing the infantry to mount an assault without armoured cover. The Israeli soldiers advanced under heavy fire, jumping between stones to avoid mines. The fighting was conducted at close-quarters, often with knives and bayonets.

The Jordanians fell back after a battle that left two Israeli and eight Jordanian soldiers dead, and Israeli forces advanced through Beit Horon towards Ramallah, taking four fortified villages along the way. By the evening, the brigade arrived in Ramallah. Meanwhile, the 163rd Infantry Battalion secured Abu

Tor following a fierce battle, severing the Old City from Bethlehem and Hebron.

Meanwhile, 600 Egyptian commandos stationed in the West Bank moved to attack Israeli airfields. Led by Jordanian intelligence scouts, they crossed the border and began infiltrating through Israeli settlements towards Ramla and Hatzor. They were soon detected and sought shelter in nearby fields, which the Israelis set on fire. Some 450 commandos were killed, and the remainder escaped to Jordan.[644]

From the American Colony, the paratroopers moved towards the Old City. Their plan was to approach it via the lightly defended Salah al-Din Street. However, they made a wrong turn onto the heavily defended Nablus Road. The Israelis ran into fierce resistance. Their tanks fired at point-blank range down the street, while the paratroopers mounted repeated charges. Despite repelling repeated Israeli charges, the Jordanians gradually gave way to Israeli firepower and momentum. The Israelis suffered some 30 casualties – half the original force – while the Jordanians lost 45 dead and 142 wounded.[645]

Meanwhile, the Israeli 71st Battalion breached barbed wire and minefields and emerged near Wadi Joz, near the base of Mount Scopus, from where the Old City could be cut off from Jericho and East Jerusalem from Ramallah. Israeli artillery targeted the one remaining route from Jerusalem to the West Bank, and shellfire deterred the Jordanians from counterattacking from their positions at Augusta-Victoria. An Israeli detachment then captured the Rockefeller Museum after a brief skirmish.

Afterwards, the Israelis broke through to the Jerusalem-Ramallah road. At Tel al-Ful, the Israelis fought a running battle with up to thirty Jordanian tanks. The Jordanians stalled the advance and destroyed a number of half-tracks, but the Israelis launched air attacks and exploited the vulnerability of the external fuel tanks mounted on the Jordanian tanks. The Jordanians lost half their tanks, and retreated towards Jericho. Joining up with the 4th Brigade, the Israelis then descended through Shuafat and the site of what is now French Hill, through Jordanian defenses at Mivtar, emerging at Ammunition Hill.[646]

With Jordanian defenses in Jerusalem crumbling, elements of the Jordanian 60th Brigade and an infantry battalion were sent from Jericho to reinforce Jerusalem. Its original orders were to repel the Israelis from the Latrun corridor, but due to the worsening situation in Jerusalem, the brigade was ordered to proceed to Jerusalem's Arab suburbs and attack Mount Scopus. Parallel to the brigade were infantrymen from the Imam Ali Brigade, who were approaching Issawiya. The brigades were spotted by Israeli aircraft and decimated by rocket and cannon fire. Other Jordanian attempts to reinforce Jerusalem were beaten back, either by armoured ambushes or airstrikes.

Figure 93: *An Israeli airstrike near the Augusta-Victoria Hospital*

Fearing damage to holy sites and the prospect of having to fight in built-up areas, Dayan ordered his troops not to enter the Old City. He also feared that Israel would be subjected to a fierce international backlash and the outrage of Christians worldwide if it forced its way into the Old City. Privately, he told David Ben-Gurion that he was also concerned over the prospect of Israel capturing Jerusalem's holy sites, only to be forced to give them up under the threat of international sanctions.

The West Bank (7 June)

On 7 June, heavy fighting ensued. Dayan had ordered his troops not to enter the Old City; however, upon hearing that the UN was about to declare a ceasefire, he changed his mind, and without cabinet clearance, decided to capture it. Two paratroop battalions attacked Augusta-Victoria Hill, high ground overlooking the Old City from the east. One battalion attacked from Mount Scopus, and another attacked from the valley between it and the Old City. Another paratroop battalion, personally led by Gur, broke into the Old City, and was joined by the other two battalions after their missions were complete. The paratroopers met little resistance. The fighting was conducted solely by the paratroopers; the Israelis did not use armour during the battle out of fear of severe damage to the Old City.

In the north, one battalion from Peled's division was sent to check Jordanian defenses in the Jordan Valley. A brigade belonging to Peled's division captured the western part of the West Bank. One brigade attacked Jordanian artillery positions around Jenin, which were shelling Ramat David Airbase. The Jordanian 12th Armored Battalion, which outnumbered the Israelis, held off repeated attempts to capture Jenin. However, Israeli air attacks took their toll, and the Jordanian M48 Pattons, with their external fuel tanks, proved vulnerable at short distances, even to the Israeli-modified Shermans. Twelve Jordanian tanks were destroyed, and only six remained operational.

Just after dusk, Israeli reinforcements arrived. The Jordanians continued to fiercely resist, and the Israelis were unable to advance without artillery and air support. One Israeli jet attacked the Jordanian commander's tank, wounding him and killing his radio operator and intelligence officer. The surviving Jordanian forces then withdrew to Jenin, where they were reinforced by the 25th Infantry Brigade. The Jordanians were effectively surrounded in Jenin.

Jordanian infantry and their three remaining tanks managed to hold off the Israelis until 4:00 am, when three battalions arrived to reinforce them in the afternoon. The Jordanian tanks charged, and knocked out multiple Israeli vehicles, and the tide began to shift. After sunrise, Israeli jets and artillery conducted a two-hour bombardment against the Jordanians. The Jordanians lost 10 dead and 250 wounded, and had only seven tanks left, including two without gas, and sixteen APCs. The Israelis then fought their way into Jenin, and captured the city after fierce fighting.[647]

After the Old City fell, the Jerusalem Brigade reinforced the paratroopers, and continued to the south, capturing Judea and Gush Etzion. Hebron was taken without any resistance. Fearful that Israeli soldiers would exact retribution for the 1929 massacre of the city's Jewish community, Hebron's residents flew white sheets from their windows and rooftops, and voluntarily gave up their weapons. Wikipedia:Citation needed The Harel Brigade proceeded eastward, descending to the Jordan River.

On 7 June, Israeli forces seized Bethlehem, taking the city after a brief battle that left some 40 Jordanian soldiers dead, with the remainder fleeing. On the same day, one of Peled's brigades seized Nablus; then it joined one of Central Command's armoured brigades to fight the Jordanian forces; as the Jordanians held the advantage of superior equipment and were equal in numbers to the Israelis.

Again, the air superiority of the IAF proved paramount as it immobilized the Jordanians, leading to their defeat. One of Peled's brigades joined with its Central Command counterparts coming from Ramallah, and the remaining two blocked the Jordan river crossings together with the Central Command's 10th. Engineering Corps sappers blew up the Abdullah and Hussein bridges with captured Jordanian mortar shells, while elements of the Harel Brigade crossed the river and occupied positions along the east bank to cover them, but quickly pulled back due to American pressure. The Jordanians, anticipating an Israeli offensive deep into Jordan, assembled the remnants of their army and Iraqi units in Jordan to protect the western approaches to Amman and the southern slopes of the Golan Heights.

No specific decision had been made to capture any other territories controlled by Jordan. After the Old City was captured, Dayan told his troops to dig in to hold it. When an armoured brigade commander entered the West Bank on his own initiative, and stated that he could see Jericho, Dayan ordered him back. It was only after intelligence reports indicated that Hussein had withdrawn his forces across the Jordan River that Dayan ordered his troops to capture the West Bank. According to Narkis:

> *First, the Israeli government had no intention of capturing the West Bank. On the contrary, it was opposed to it. Second, there was not any provocation on the part of the IDF. Third, the rein was only loosened when a real threat to Jerusalem's security emerged. This is truly how things happened on June 5, although it is difficult to believe. The end result was something that no one had planned.*[648]

Golan Heights

In May–June 1967, the Israeli government did everything in its power to confine the confrontation to the Egyptian front. Eshkol and his colleagues took into account the possibility of some fighting on the Syrian front.

Syria's attack

False Egyptian reports of a crushing victory against the Israeli army and forecasts that Egyptian forces would soon be attacking Tel Aviv influenced Syria's decision to enter the war. Syrian artillery began shelling northern Israel, and twelve Syrian jets attacked Israeli settlements in the Galilee. Israeli fighter jets intercepted the Syrian aircraft, shooting down three and driving off the rest.[649] In addition, two Lebanese Hawker Hunter jets, two of the twelve Lebanon had, crossed into Israeli airspace and began strafing Israeli positions in the Galilee. They were intercepted by Israeli fighter jets, and one was shot down.

A minor Syrian force tried to capture the water plants at Tel Dan (the subject of a fierce escalation two years earlier), Dan, and She'ar Yashuv. These attacks were repulsed with the loss of twenty soldiers and seven tanks. An Israeli officer was also killed. But a broader Syrian offensive quickly failed.

Figure 94: *The Battle of Golan Heights, 9–10 June.*

Figure 95: *People in a bomb shelter at Kibbutz Dan*

Syrian reserve units were broken up by Israeli air attacks, and several tanks were reported to have sunk in the Jordan River.

Other problems included tanks being too wide for bridges, lack of radio communications between tanks and infantry, and units ignoring orders to advance. A post-war Syrian army report concluded:

> *Our forces did not go on the offensive either because they did not arrive or were not wholly prepared or because they could not find shelter from the enemy's planes. The reserves could not withstand the air attacks; they dispersed after their morale plummeted.*[650]

The Syrians abandoned hopes of a ground attack and began a massive bombardment of Israeli communities in the Hula Valley instead.

Israeli Air Force attacks the Syrian airfields

On the evening of 5 June, the Israeli Air Force attacked Syrian airfields. The Syrian Air Force lost some 32 MiG 21s, 23 MiG-15 and MiG-17 fighters, and two Ilyushin Il-28 bombers, two-thirds of its fighting strength. The Syrian aircraft that survived the attack retreated to distant bases and played no further role in the war. Following the attack, Syria realised that the news it had received from Egypt of the near-total destruction of the Israeli military could not have been true.

Israelis debate whether the Golan Heights should be attacked

On 7 and 8 June, the Israeli leadership debated about whether to attack the Golan Heights as well. Syria had supported pre-war raids that had helped raise tensions and had routinely shelled Israel from the Heights, so some Israeli leaders wanted to see Syria punished.[651] Military opinion was that the attack would be extremely costly, since it would entail an uphill battle against a strongly fortified enemy. The western side of the Golan Heights consists of a rock escarpment that rises 500 meters (1,700 ft) from the Sea of Galilee and the Jordan River, and then flattens to a gently sloping plateau. Dayan opposed the operation bitterly at first, believing such an undertaking would result in losses of 30,000 and might trigger Soviet intervention. Prime Minister Eshkol, on the other hand, was more open to the possibility, as was the head of the Northern Command, David Elazar, whose unbridled enthusiasm for and confidence in the operation may have eroded Dayan's reluctance.

Eventually, the situation on the Southern and Central fronts cleared up, intelligence estimated that the likelihood of Soviet intervention had been reduced, reconnaissance showed some Syrian defenses in the Golan region collapsing, and an intercepted cable revealed that Nasser was urging the President of Syria to immediately accept a cease-fire. At 3 am on 9 June, Syria announced its acceptance of the cease-fire. Despite this announcement, Dayan became more enthusiastic about the idea and four hours later at 7 am, "gave the order to go into action against Syria"[i] without consultation or government authorisation.[652]

The Syrian army consisted of about 75,000 men grouped in nine brigades, supported by an adequate amount of artillery and armour. Israeli forces used in combat consisted of two brigades (the 8th Armored Brigade and the Golani Brigade) in the northern part of the front at Givat HaEm, and another two (infantry and one of Peled's brigades summoned from Jenin) in the center. The Golan Heights' unique terrain (mountainous slopes crossed by parallel streams every several kilometers running east to west), and the general lack of roads in the area channeled both forces along east-west axes of movement and restricted the ability of units to support those on either flank. Thus the Syrians could move north-south on the plateau itself, and the Israelis could move north-south at the base of the Golan escarpment. An advantage Israel possessed was the excellent intelligence collected by Mossad operative Eli Cohen (who was captured and executed in Syria in 1965) regarding the Syrian battle positions. Syria had built extensive defensive fortifications in depths up to 15 kilometers,[653] comparable to the Maginot Line.

As opposed to all the other campaigns, IAF was only partially effective in the Golan because the fixed fortifications were so effective. However, the Syrian forces proved unable to put up effective defense largely because the officers were poor leaders and treated their soldiers badly; often officers would retreat from danger, leaving their men confused and ineffective. The Israelis also had the upper hand during close combat that took place in the numerous Syrian bunkers along the Golan Heights, as they were armed with the Uzi, a submachine gun designed for close combat, while Syrian soldiers were armed with the heavier AK-47 assault rifle, designed for combat in more open areas.

Israeli attack: first day

On the morning of 9 June, Israeli jets began carrying out dozens of sorties against Syrian positions from Mount Hermon to Tawfiq, using rockets salvaged from captured Egyptian stocks. The airstrikes knocked out artillery batteries and storehouses and forced transport columns off the roads. The Syrians suffered heavy casualties and a drop in morale, with a number of senior officers and troops deserting. The attacks also provided time as Israeli forces cleared paths through Syrian minefields. However, the airstrikes did not seriously damage the Syrians' bunkers and trench systems, and the bulk of Syrian forces on the Golan remained in their positions.[654]

Six-Day War

Figure 96: *Israeli tanks advancing on the Golan Heights. June 1967*

About two hours after the airstrikes began, the 8th Armored Brigade, led by Colonel Albert Mandler, advanced into the Golan Heights from Givat HaEm. Its advance was spearheaded by Engineering Corps sappers and eight bulldozers, which cleared away barbed wire and mines. As they advanced, the force came under fire, and five bulldozers were immediately hit. The Israeli tanks, with their maneuverability sharply reduced by the terrain, advanced slowly under fire toward the fortified village of Sir al-Dib, with their ultimate objective being the fortress at Qala. Israeli casualties steadily mounted. Part of the attacking force lost its way and emerged opposite Za'ura, a redoubt manned by Syrian reservists. With the situation critical, Colonel Mandler ordered simultaneous assaults on Za'ura and Qala. Heavy and confused fighting followed, with Israeli and Syrian tanks struggling around obstacles and firing at extremely short ranges. Mandler recalled that "the Syrians fought well and bloodied us. We beat them only by crushing them under our treads and by blasting them with our cannons at very short range, from 100 to 500 meters." The first three Israeli tanks to enter Qala were stopped by a Syrian bazooka team, and a relief column of seven Syrian tanks arrived to repel the attackers. The Israelis took heavy fire from the houses, but could not turn back, as other forces were advancing behind them, and they were on a narrow path with mines on either side. The Israelis continued pressing forward, and called for air support. A pair of Israeli jets destroyed two of the Syrian tanks, and the remainder withdrew. The surviving defenders of Qala retreated after their commander was killed. Meanwhile, Za'ura fell in an Israeli assault, and the Israelis also captured the

Figure 97: *Universal Newsreel from 9 June about the war and UN reactions.*

'Ein Fit fortress.[655]

In the central sector, the Israeli 181st Battalion captured the strongholds of Dardara and Tel Hillal after fierce fighting. Desperate fighting also broke out along the operation's northern axis, where Golani Brigade attacked thirteen Syrian positions, including the formidable Tel Fakhr position. Navigational errors placed the Israelis directly under the Syrians' guns. In the fighting that followed, both sides took heavy casualties, with the Israelis losing all nineteen of their tanks and half-tracks.[656] The Israeli battalion commander then ordered his twenty-five remaining men to dismount, divide into two groups, and charge the northern and southern flanks of Tel Fakhr. The first Israelis to reach the perimeter of the southern approach laid bodily down on the barbed wire, allowing their comrades to vault over them. From there, they assaulted the fortified Syrian positions. The fighting was waged at extremely close quarters, often hand-to-hand.

On the northern flank, the Israelis broke through within minutes and cleared out the trenches and bunkers. During the seven-hour battle, the Israelis lost 31 dead and 82 wounded, while the Syrians lost 62 dead and 20 captured. Among the dead was the Israeli battalion commander. The Golani Brigade's 51st Battalion took Tel 'Azzaziat, and Darbashiya also fell to Israeli forces.

By the evening of 9 June, the four Israeli brigades had all broken through to the plateau, where they could be reinforced and replaced. Thousands of reinforcements began reaching the front, those tanks and half-tracks that had survived the previous day's fighting were refueled and replenished with ammunition, and the wounded were evacuated. By dawn, the Israelis had eight brigades in the sector.

Syria's first line of defense had been shattered, but the defenses beyond that remained largely intact. Mount Hermon and the Banias in the north, and the entire sector between Tawfiq and Customs House Road in the south remained in Syrian hands. In a meeting early on the night of 9 June, Syrian leaders decided to reinforce those positions as quickly as possible, and to maintain a steady barrage on Israeli civilian settlements.

Israeli attack: the next day

Throughout the night, the Israelis continued their advance. Though it was slowed by fierce resistance, an anticipated Syrian counterattack never materialized. At the fortified village of Jalabina, a garrison of Syrian reservists, leveling their anti-aircraft guns, held off the Israeli 65th Paratroop Battalion for four hours before a small detachment managed to penetrate the village and knock out the heavy guns.

Meanwhile, the 8th Brigade's tanks moved south from Qala, advancing six miles to Wasit under heavy artillery and tank bombardment. At the Banias in the north, Syrian mortar batteries opened fire on advancing Israeli forces only after Golani Brigade sappers cleared a path through a minefield, killing sixteen Israeli soldiers and wounding four.

On the next day, 10 June, the central and northern groups joined in a pincer movement on the plateau, but that fell mainly on empty territory as the Syrian forces retreated. At 8:30 am, the Syrians began blowing up their own bunkers, burning documents and retreating. Several units joined by Elad Peled's troops climbed to the Golan from the south, only to find the positions mostly empty. When the 8th Brigade reached Mansura, five miles from Wasit, the Israelis met no opposition and found abandoned equipment, including tanks, in perfect working condition. In the fortified Banias village, Golani Brigade troops found only several Syrian soldiers chained to their positions.[657]

During the day, the Israeli units stopped after obtaining manoeuvre room between their positions and a line of volcanic hills to the west. In some locations, Israeli troops advanced after an agreed-upon cease-fire to occupy strategically strong positions.[658] To the east, the ground terrain is an open gently sloping plain. This position later became the cease-fire line known as the "Purple Line".

Figure 98: *Universal Newsreel from 13 June about the war*

Time magazine reported: "In an effort to pressure the United Nations into enforcing a ceasefire, Damascus Radio undercut its own army by broadcasting the fall of the city of Quneitra three hours before it actually capitulated. That premature report of the surrender of their headquarters destroyed the morale of the Syrian troops left in the Golan area."

Conclusion

<templatestyles src="Template:Quote_box/styles.css" />

A week ago, the fateful campaign began. The existence of the State of Israel hung in the balance, the hopes of generations, and the vision that was realised in our own time... During the fighting, our forces destroyed about 450 enemy planes and hundreds of tanks. The enemy forces were decisively defeated in battles. Many fled for their lives or were captured. For the first time since the establishment of the state, the threat to our security has been removed at once from the Sinai Peninsula, the Gaza Strip, Jerusalem, the West Bank and the northern border.

— Levi Eshkol, 12 June 1967 (Address to Israeli Parliament)

By 10 June, Israel had completed its final offensive in the Golan Heights, and a ceasefire was signed the day after. Israel had seized the Gaza Strip, the Sinai

Peninsula, the West Bank of the Jordan River (including East Jerusalem), and the Golan Heights. About one million Arabs were placed under Israel's direct control in the newly captured territories. Israel's strategic depth grew to at least 300 kilometers in the south, 60 kilometers in the east, and 20 kilometers of extremely rugged terrain in the north, a security asset that would prove useful in the Yom Kippur War six years later.

Speaking three weeks after the war ended, as he accepted an honorary degree from Hebrew University, Yitzhak Rabin gave his reasoning behind the success of Israel:

> Our airmen, who struck the enemies' planes so accurately that no one in the world understands how it was done and people seek technological explanations or secret weapons; our armoured troops who beat the enemy even when their equipment was inferior to his; our soldiers in all other branches ... who overcame our enemies everywhere, despite the latter's superior numbers and fortifications—all these revealed not only coolness and courage in the battle but ... an understanding that only their personal stand against the greatest dangers would achieve victory for their country and for their families, and that if victory was not theirs the alternative was annihilation.[659]

In recognition of contributions, Rabin was given the honour of naming the war for the Israelis. From the suggestions proposed, including the "War of Daring", "War of Salvation", and "War of the Sons of Light", he "chose the least ostentatious, the Six-Day War, evoking the days of creation".[660]

Dayan's final report on the war to the Israeli general staff listed several shortcomings in Israel's actions, including misinterpretation of Nasser's intentions, overdependence on the United States, and reluctance to act when Egypt closed the Straits. He also credited several factors for Israel's success: Egypt did not appreciate the advantage of striking first and their adversaries did not accurately gauge Israel's strength and its willingness to use it.

In Egypt, according to Heikal, Nasser had admitted his responsibility for the military defeat in June 1967. According to historian Abd al-Azim Ramadan, Nasser's mistaken decisions to expel the international peacekeeping force from the Sinai Peninsula and close the Straits of Tiran in 1967 led to a state of war with Israel, despite Egypt's lack of military preparedness.

After the 1973 Yom Kippur War, Egypt reviewed the causes of its loss of the 1967 war. Issues that were identified included "the individualistic bureaucratic leadership"; "promotions on the basis of loyalty, not expertise, and the army's fear of telling Nasser the truth"; lack of intelligence; and better Israeli weapons, command, organization, and will to fight.

Casualties

Between 776[661] and 983 Israelis were killed and 4,517 were wounded. Fifteen Israeli soldiers were captured. Arab casualties were far greater. Between 9,800[662] and 15,000[663] Egyptian soldiers were listed as killed or missing in action. An additional 4,338 Egyptian soldiers were captured.[664] Jordanian losses are estimated to be 700 killed in action with another 2,500 wounded. The Syrians were estimated to have sustained between 1,000[665] and 2,500 killed in action. Between 367 and 591 Syrians were captured.

Controversies

Preemptive strike v. unjustified attack

At the commencement of hostilities, both Egypt and Israel announced that they had been attacked by the other country. The Israeli government later abandoned its initial position, acknowledging Israel had struck first, claiming that it was a preemptive strike in the face of a planned invasion by Egypt. On the other hand, the Arab view was that it was unjustified to attack Egypt.[666] Many commentators consider the war as the classic case of anticipatory attack in self-defense.

Allegations of atrocities committed against Egyptian soldiers

It has been alleged that Nasser did not want Egypt to learn of the true extent of his defeat and so ordered the killing of Egyptian army stragglers making their way back to the Suez canal zone.[667] There have also been allegations from both Israeli and Egyptian sources that Israeli troops killed unarmed Egyptian prisoners.[668,669,670,671,672,673]

Allegations of military support from the US, UK and Soviet Union

There have been a number of allegations of direct military support of Israel during the war by the US and the UK, including the supply of equipment (despite an embargo) and the participation of US forces in the conflict.[674,675,676,677,678] Many of these allegations and conspiracy theories[679] have been disputed and it has been claimed that some were given currency in the Arab world to explain the Arab defeat.[680] It has also been claimed that the Soviet Union, in support of its Arab allies, used its naval strength in the Mediterranean to act as a major restraint on the US Navy.[681]

America features prominently in Arab conspiracy theories purporting to explain the June 1967 defeat. Mohamed Hassanein Heikal, a confidant of Nasser, claims that President Lyndon B. Johnson was obsessed with Nasser and that Johnson conspired with Israel to bring him down.[682] The reported Israeli troop movements seemed all the more threatening because they were perceived in the context of a US conspiracy against Egypt. Salah Bassiouny of the Foreign ministry, claims that Foreign Ministry saw the reported Israeli troop movements as credible because Israel had reached the level at which it could find strategic alliance with the United States.[683] During the war, Cairo announced that American and British planes were participating in the Israeli attack. Nasser broke off diplomatic relations following this allegation. Nasser's image of the United States was such that he might well have believed the worst. However Anwar Sadat implied that Nasser used this deliberate conspiracy in order to accuse the United States as a political cover-up for domestic consumption.[684] Lutfi Abd al-Qadir, the director of Radio Cairo during the late 1960s, who accompanied Nasser to his visits in Moscow, had his conspiracy theory that both the Soviets and the Western powers wanted to topple Nasser or to reduce his influence.[685]

USS *Liberty* incident

On 8 June 1967, USS *Liberty*, a United States Navy electronic intelligence vessel sailing 13 nautical miles (24 km) off Arish (just outside Egypt's territorial waters), was attacked by Israeli jets and torpedo boats, nearly sinking the ship, killing 34 sailors and wounding 171. Israel said the attack was a case of mistaken identity, and that the ship had been misidentified as the Egyptian vessel *El Quseir*. Israel apologized for the mistake, and paid compensation to the victims or their families, and to the United States for damage to the ship. After an investigation, the U.S. accepted the explanation that the incident was friendly fire and the issue was closed by the exchange of diplomatic notes in 1987. Others however, including the then United States Secretary of State Dean Rusk, Chief of Naval Operations at the time, Admiral Thomas Moorer, some survivors of the attack and intelligence officials familiar with transcripts of intercepted signals on the day, have rejected these conclusions as unsatisfactory and maintain that the attack was made in the knowledge that the ship was American.[686,687]

Aftermath

The political importance of the 1967 War was immense; Israel demonstrated that it was able and willing to initiate strategic strikes that could change the regional balance. Egypt and Syria learned tactical lessons and would launch an attack in 1973 in an attempt to reclaim their lost territory.[688]

After following other Arab nations in declaring war, Mauritania remained in a declared state of war with Israel until about 1999.[689] The United States imposed an embargo on new arms agreements to all Middle East countries, including Israel. The embargo remained in force until the end of the year, despite urgent Israeli requests to lift it.

Israel and Zionism

Following the war, Israel experienced a wave of national euphoria, and the press praised the military's performance for weeks afterward. New "victory coins" were minted to celebrate. In addition, the world's interest in Israel grew, and the country's economy, which had been in crisis before the war, flourished due to an influx of tourists and donations, as well as the extraction of oil from the Sinai's wells.[690] The aftermath of the war also saw a baby boom, which lasted for four years.

The aftermath of the war is also of religious significance. Under Jordanian rule, Jews were expelled from Jerusalem and were effectively barred from visiting the Western Wall, despite Article VIII of the 1949 Armistice Agreement demanded Israeli Jewish access to the Western Wall. Jewish holy sites were not maintained, and Jewish cemeteries had been desecrated. After the annexation to Israel, each religious group was granted administration over its holy sites. For the first time since 1948, Jews could visit the Old City of Jerusalem and pray at the Western Wall, the holiest site where Jews are permitted to pray, an event celebrated every year during Yom Yerushalayim. Despite the Temple Mount being the most important holy site in Jewish tradition, the al-Aqsa Mosque has been under sole administration of the Jordanian Muslim Waqf, and Jews are barred from praying on the Temple Mount, although they are allowed to visit it.[691,692] In Hebron, Jews gained access to the Cave of the Patriarchs – the second most holy site in Judaism, after the Temple Mount – for the first time since the 14th century (previously Jews were allowed to pray only at the entrance).[693] Other Jewish holy sites, such as Rachel's Tomb in Bethlehem and Joseph's Tomb in Nablus, also became accessible.

The war inspired the Jewish diaspora, which was swept up in overwhelming support for Israel. According to Michael Oren, the war enabled American Jews to "walk with their backs straight and flex their political muscle as never before. American Jewish organizations which had previously kept Israel at arms length suddenly proclaimed their Zionism."[694] Thousands of Jewish immigrants arrived from Western countries such as the United States, United Kingdom, Canada, France, and South Africa after the war. Many of them returned to their countries of origin after a few years; one survey found that 58% of American Jews who immigrated to Israel between 1961 and 1972 returned to the US. Nevertheless, this immigration to Israel of Jews from Western countries, which was previously only a trickle, was a significant force for the first time.[695] Most notably, the war stirred Zionist passions among Jews in the Soviet Union, who had by that time been forcibly assimilated. Many Soviet Jews subsequently applied for exit visas and began protesting for their right to immigrate to Israel. Following diplomatic pressure from the West, the Soviet government began granting exit visas to Jews in growing numbers. From 1970 to 1988, some 291,000 Soviet Jews were granted exit visas, of whom 165,000 immigrated to Israel and 126,000 immigrated to the United States.[696] The great rise in Jewish pride in the wake of Israel's victory also fueled the beginnings of the baal teshuva movement. The war gave impetus to a Chabad campaign in which the Lubavitcher Rebbe directed his followers to put tefillin on Jewish men around world.

Jews in Arab countries

In the Arab nations, populations of minority Jews faced persecution and expulsion following the Israeli victory. According to historian and ambassador Michael B. Oren:

> Mobs attacked Jewish neighborhoods in Egypt, Yemen, Lebanon, Tunisia, and Morocco, burning synagogues and assaulting residents. A pogrom in Tripoli, Libya, left 18 Jews dead and 25 injured; the survivors were herded into detention centers. Of Egypt's 4,000 Jews, 800 were arrested, including the chief rabbis of both Cairo and Alexandria, and their property sequestered by the government. The ancient communities of Damascus and Baghdad were placed under house arrest, their leaders imprisoned and fined. A total of 7,000 Jews were expelled, many with merely a satchel.[697]

Antisemitism against Jews in Communist countries

Following the war, a series of antisemitic purges began in Communist countries.[698] Some 11,200 Jews from Poland immigrated to Israel during the 1968 Polish political crisis and the following year.[699]

Peace and diplomacy

Following the war, Israel made an offer for peace that included the return of most of the recently captured territories. According to Chaim Herzog:

<templatestyles src="Template:Quote/styles.css"/>

> On June 19, 1967, the National Unity Government [of Israel] voted unanimously to return the Sinai to Egypt and the Golan Heights to Syria in return for peace agreements. The Golans would have to be demilitarized

and special arrangement would be negotiated for the Straits of Tiran. The government also resolved to open negotiations with King Hussein of Jordan regarding the Eastern border.[700]

The 19 June Israeli cabinet decision did not include the Gaza Strip, and left open the possibility of Israel permanently acquiring parts of the West Bank. On 25–27 June, Israel incorporated East Jerusalem together with areas of the West Bank to the north and south into Jerusalem's new municipal boundaries.

The Israeli decision was to be conveyed to the Arab nations by the United States. The U.S. was informed of the decision, but not that it was to transmit it. There is no evidence of receipt from Egypt or Syria, and some historians claim that they may never have received the offer.[701]

In September, the Khartoum Arab Summit resolved that there would be "no peace, no recognition and no negotiation with Israel". However, as Avraham Sela notes, the Khartoum conference effectively marked a shift in the perception of the conflict by the Arab states away from one centered on the question of Israel's legitimacy, toward one focusing on territories and boundaries. This was shown on 22 November when Egypt and Jordan accepted United Nations Security Council Resolution 242.[702] Nasser forestalled any movement toward direct negotiations with Israel. In dozens of speeches and statements, Nasser posited the equation that any direct peace talks with Israel were tantamount to surrender.

After the war, the entire Soviet bloc of Eastern Europe (with the exception of Romania) broke off diplomatic relations with Israel.

The 1967 War laid the foundation for future discord in the region, as the Arab states resented Israel's victory and did not want to give up territory.

On 22 November 1967, the United Nations Security Council adopted Resolution 242, the "land for peace" formula, which called for Israeli withdrawal "from territories occupied" in 1967 and "the termination of all claims or states of belligerency". Resolution 242 recognized the right of "every state in the area to live in peace within secure and recognized boundaries free from threats or acts of force." Israel returned the Sinai to Egypt in 1978, after the Camp David Accords, and disengaged from the Gaza Strip in the summer of 2005. Its army frequently re-enters Gaza for military operations and still retains control of the seaports, airports and most of the border crossings.

Captured territories and Arab displaced populations

There was extensive displacement of populations in the captured territories: of about one million Palestinians in the West Bank and Gaza, 300,000 (according to the United States Department of State) either fled, or were displaced from their homes, to Jordan, where they contributed to the growing unrest. The other 700,000 remained. In the Golan Heights, an estimated 80,000 Syrians fled. Israel allowed only the inhabitants of East Jerusalem and the Golan Heights to receive full Israeli citizenship, applying its law, administration and jurisdiction to these territories in 1967 and 1981, respectively. The vast majority of the populations in both territories declined to take citizenship. See also Israeli–Palestinian conflict and Golan Heights.

In his book *Righteous Victims* (1999), Israeli "New Historian" Benny Morris writes: <templatestyles src="Template:Quote/styles.css"/>

> *In three villages southwest of Jerusalem and at Qalqilya, houses were destroyed "not in battle, but as punishment ... and in order to chase away the inhabitants ... contrary to government ... policy," Dayan wrote in his memoirs. In Qalqilya, about a third of the homes were razed and about 12,000 inhabitants were evicted, though many then camped out in the environs. The evictees in both areas were allowed to stay and later were given cement and tools by the Israeli authorities to rebuild at least some of their dwellings.*

> *But many thousands of other Palestinians now took to the roads. Perhaps as many as seventy thousand, mostly from the Jericho area, fled during the fighting; tens of thousands more left over the following months. Altogether, about one-quarter of the population of the West Bank, about 200–250,000 people, went into exile. ... They simply walked to the Jordan River crossings and made their way on foot to the East Bank. It is unclear how many were intimidated or forced out by the Israeli troops and how many left voluntarily, in panic and fear. There is some evidence of IDF soldiers going around with loudspeakers ordering West Bankers to leave their homes and cross the Jordan. Some left because they had relatives or sources of livelihood on the East Bank and feared being permanently cut off.*

> *Thousands of Arabs were taken by bus from East Jerusalem to the Allenby Bridge, though there is no evidence of coercion. The free Israeli-organized transportation, which began on June 11, 1967, went on for about a month. At the bridge they had to sign a document stating that they were leaving of their own free will. Perhaps as many as 70,000 people emigrated from the Gaza Strip to Egypt and elsewhere in the Arab world.*

> On July 2, the Israeli government announced that it would allow the return
> of those 1967 refugees who desired to do so, but no later than August
> 10, later extended to September 13. The Jordanian authorities probably
> pressured many of the refugees, who constituted an enormous burden, to
> sign up to return. In practice only 14,000 of the 120,000 who applied were
> allowed by Israel back into the West Bank by the beginning of September.
> After that, only a trickle of "special cases" were allowed back, perhaps
> 3,000 in all. (328–29)

In addition, between 80,000 and 110,000 Syrians fled the Golan Heights,[703] of which about 20,000 were from the city of Quneitra. According to more recent research by the Israeli daily *Haaretz*, a total of 130,000 Syrian inhabitants fled or were expelled from the territory, most of them pushed out by the Israeli army.[704]

Long term

Israel made peace with Egypt following the Camp David Accords of 1978 and completed a staged withdrawal from the Sinai in 1982. However, the position of the other occupied territories has been a long-standing and bitter cause of conflict for decades between Israel and the Palestinians, and the Arab world in general. Jordan and Egypt eventually withdrew their claims to sovereignty over the West Bank and Gaza, respectively. Israel and Jordan signed a peace treaty in 1994.

After the Israeli conquest of these newly acquired territories, the Gush Emunim movement launched a large settlement effort in these areas to secure a permanent foothold. There are now hundreds of thousands of Israeli settlers in the West Bank. They are a matter of controversy within Israel, both among the general population and within different political administrations, supporting them to varying degrees. Palestinians consider them a provocation. The Israeli settlements in Gaza were evacuated in August 2005 as a part of Israel's disengagement from Gaza.

Notes

1. ^ Photograph:

   It was twenty minutes after the capture of the Western Wall that David Rubinger shot his "signature" photograph of three Israeli paratroopers gazing in wonder up at the wall [Kaniuk, Yoram. "June 10, 1967 – Israeli paratroopers reach the Western Wall"[705]. The Digital Journalist. Retrieved 2 December 2008.<templatestyles src="Module:Citation/CS1/styles.css"></templatestyles>]. As part of the terms for his access to the front lines, Rubinger handed the negatives to the Israeli government, who then distributed this image widely. Although he was displeased with the violation of his copyright, the widespread use of his photo made it famous [Silver, Eric (16 February 2006). "David Rubinger in the picture"[706]. The Jewish Chronicle. Retrieved 17 July 2010.<templatestyles src="Module:Citation/CS1/styles.css"></templatestyles>], and it is now considered a defining image of the conflict and one of the best-known in the history of Israel [Urquhart, Conal (6 May 2007). "Six days in June"[707]. *The Observer*. Retrieved 2 December 2008.<templatestyles src="Module:Citation/CS1/styles.css"></templatestyles>]

3.^ Both Egypt and Israel announced that they had been attacked by the other country.

1. Gideon Rafael [Israeli Ambassador to the UN] received a message from the Israeli foreign office: "Inform immediately the President of the Sec. Co. that Israel is now engaged in repelling Egyptian land and air forces." At 3:10 am, Rafael woke ambassador Hans Tabor, the Danish President of the Security Council for June, with the news that Egyptian forces had "moved against Israel". Bailey 1990, p. 225.
2. [At Security Council meeting of 5 June], both Israel and Egypt claimed to be repelling an invasion by the other. Bailey 1990, p. 225.
3. "Egyptian sources claimed that Israel had initiated hostilities [...] but Israeli officials – Eban and Evron – swore that Egypt had fired first" Oren 2002, p. 196.
4. "Gideon Rafael phoned Danish ambassador Hans Tabor, Security Council president for the month of June, and informed him that Israel was responding to a 'cowardly and treacherous' attack from Egypt..." Oren, p. 198.

4. ^ Lenczowski 1990, pp. 105–15, Citing Moshe Dayan, *Story of My Life*, and Nadav Safran, *From War to War: The Arab–Israeli Confrontation, 1948–1967*, p. 375

> *Israel clearly did not want the US government to know too much about its dispositions for attacking Syria, initially planned for June 8, but postponed for 24 hours. It should be pointed out that the attack on the Liberty occurred on June 8, whereas on June 9 at 3 am, Syria announced its acceptance of the cease-fire. Despite this, at 7 am, that is, four hours later, Israel's minister of defense, Moshe Dayan, "gave the order to go into action against Syria.*

References

<templatestyles src="Refbegin/styles.css" />

- al-Qusi, Abdallah Ahmad Hamid. (1999). *Al-Wisam fi at-Ta'rikh*. Cairo: Al-Mu'asasa al-'Arabiya al-Haditha. No ISBN available.
- Aloni, Shlomo (2001). *Arab–Israeli Air Wars 1947–1982*. Osprey Aviation. <templatestyles src="Module:Citation/CS1/styles.css" />ISBN 1-84176-294-6
- Alteras, Isaac. (1993). *Eisenhower and Israel: U.S.–Israeli Relations, 1953–1960*[708], University Press of Florida. <templatestyles src="Module:Citation/CS1/styles.css" />ISBN 0-8130-1205-8.
- Bailey, Sydney (1990). *Four Arab–Israeli Wars and the Peace Process*. London: The MacMillan Press. <templatestyles src="Module:Citation/CS1/styles.css" />ISBN 0-312-04649-9.
- Bar-On, Mordechai; Morris, Benny & Golani, Motti (2002). Reassessing Israel's Road to Sinai/Suez, 1956: A "Trialogue". In Gary A. Olson (Ed.). *Traditions and Transitions in Israel Studies: Books on Israel, Volume VI* (pp. 3–42). SUNY Press. <templatestyles src="Module:Citation/CS1/styles.css" />ISBN 0-7914-5585-8
- Bar-On, Mordechai (2006). *Never-Ending Conflict: Israeli Military History*, <templatestyles src="Module:Citation/CS1/styles.css" />ISBN 0-275-98158-4
- Bard, Mitchell G. (2002, 2008). *The Complete Idiot's Guide to Middle East Conflict*. NY: Alpha books. <templatestyles src="Module:Citation/CS1/styles.css" />ISBN 0-02-864410-7. 4th Edition <templatestyles src="Module:Citation/CS1/styles.css" />ISBN 1-59257-791-1. Chapter 14, "Six Days to Victory" is reproduced online as *The 1967 Six-Day War*[709]. at the Jewish Virtual Library of the American-Israeli Cooperative Enterprise.
- Ben-Gurion, David. (1999). Ben-Gurion diary: May–June 1967. *Israel Studies* 4(2), 199–220.
- Black, Ian (1992). *Israel's Secret Wars: A History of Israel's Intelligence Services*. Grove Press. <templatestyles src="Module:Citation/CS1/styles.css" />ISBN 0-8021-3286-3
- Bober, Arie (ed.) (1972). *The other Israel*. Doubleday Anchor. <templatestyles src="Module:Citation/CS1/styles.css" />ISBN 0-385-01467-8.
- Boczek, Boleslaw Adam (2005). *International Law: A Dictionary*. Scarecrow Press. <templatestyles src="Module:Citation/CS1/styles.css" />ISBN 0-8108-5078-8
- Borowiec, Andrew. (1998). *Modern Tunisia: A Democratic Apprenticeship*. Greenwood Publishing Group. <templatestyles src="Module:Citation/CS1/styles.css" />ISBN 0-275-96136-2.

- Bowen, Jeremy (2003). *Six Days: How the 1967 War Shaped the Middle East*. London: Simon & Schuster. <templatestyles src="Module:Citation/CS1/styles.css" />ISBN 0-7432-3095-7
- Brams, Steven J. & Jeffrey M. Togman. (1998). *Camp David: Was the agreement fair?* In Paul F. Diehl (Ed.), *A Road Map to War: Territorial Dimensions of International Conflict*. Nashville: Vanderbilt University Press. <templatestyles src="Module:Citation/CS1/styles.css" />ISBN 0-8265-1329-8.
- Brecher, Michael. (1996). Eban and Israeli foreign policy: Diplomacy, war and disengagement. In *A Restless Mind: Essays in Honor of Amos Perlmutter*, Benjamin Frankel (ed.), pp. 104–117. Routledge. <templatestyles src="Module:Citation/CS1/styles.css" />ISBN 0-7146-4607-5
- Bregman, Ahron. (2000). *Israel's Wars, 1947–1993*. Routledge. <templatestyles src="Module:Citation/CS1/styles.css" />ISBN 0-415-21468-8.
- Bregman, Ahron (2002). *Israel's Wars: A History Since 1947*. London: Routledge. <templatestyles src="Module:Citation/CS1/styles.css" />ISBN 0-415-28716-2
- Burrowes, Robert & Muzzio, Douglas. (1972). The Road to the Six Day War: Towards an Enumerative History of Four Arab States and Israel, 1965–67. *The Journal of Conflict Resolution*, Vol. 16, No. 2, Research Perspectives on the Arab–Israeli Conflict: A Symposium, pp. 211–26.
- Cohen, Raymond. (1988) Intercultural Communication between Israel and Egypt: Deterrence Failure before the Six-Day war. *Review of International Studies*, Vol. 14, No. 1, pp. 1–16
- Christie, Hazel (1999). *Law of the Sea*. Manchester: Manchester University Press. <templatestyles src="Module:Citation/CS1/styles.css" />ISBN 0-7190-4382-4
- Churchill, Randolph & Churchill, Winston. (1967). *The Six Day War*. Houghton Mifflin Company. <templatestyles src="Module:Citation/CS1/styles.css" />ISBN 0-395-07532-7
- Colaresi, Michael P. (2005). *Scare Tactics: The politics of international rivalry*. Syracuse University Press. <templatestyles src="Module:Citation/CS1/styles.css" />ISBN 978-0-8156-3066-1
- Eban, Abba (1977). *Abba Eban: An Autobiography*. Random House. <templatestyles src="Module:Citation/CS1/styles.css" />ISBN 0-394-49302-8
- Ehteshami, Anoushiravan and Hinnebusch, Raymond A. (1997). *Syria & Iran: Middle Powers in a Penetrated Regional System*. London: Routledge. <templatestyles src="Module:Citation/CS1/styles.css" />ISBN 0-415-15675-0
- Eshkol, Levi (1967). *Prime-Minister Levi Eshkol - His words and his writings*[710]. ISA-PMO-PrimeMinisterBureau-000d0t9. Israel

- Government Archives. Retrieved June 6, 2018.<templatestyles src="Module:Citation/CS1/styles.css"></templatestyles>
- Feron, James (13 May 1967). "Israelis Ponder Blow at Syrians; Some Leaders Decide That Force is the Only Way to Curtail Terrorism Some Israeli Leaders See Need for Force to Curb Syrians"[711]. *The New York Times*.<templatestyles src="Module:Citation/CS1/styles.css"></templatestyles>
- El-Gamasy, Mohamed Abdel Ghani. (1993). *The October War*. The American University in Cairo Press. <templatestyles src="Module:Citation/CS1/styles.css" />ISBN 977-424-316-1.
- Gawrych, George W. (2000). *The Albatross of Decisive Victory: War and Policy Between Egypt and Israel in the 1967 and 1973 Arab-Israeli Wars*. Greenwood Press. <templatestyles src="Module:Citation/CS1/styles.css" />ISBN 0-313-31302-4. Available in multiple PDF files from the Combat Studies Institute and the Combined Arms Research Library, CSI Publications in parts[712].
- Gelpi, Christopher (2002). *Power of Legitimacy: Assessing the Role of Norms in Crisis Bargaining*. Princeton University Press. <templatestyles src="Module:Citation/CS1/styles.css" />ISBN 0-691-09248-6
- Gerner, Deborah J. (1994). *One Land, Two Peoples*. Westview Press. <templatestyles src="Module:Citation/CS1/styles.css" />ISBN 0-8133-2180-8, p. 112
- Gerteiny, Alfred G. & Ziegler, Jean (2007). *The Terrorist Conjunction: The United States, the Israeli-Palestinian Conflict, and Al-Qā'ida*. Greenwood Publishing Group. <templatestyles src="Module:Citation/CS1/styles.css" />ISBN 0-275-99643-3, p. 142
- Gilbert, Martin. (2008). *Israel – A History*. McNally & Loftin Publishers. <templatestyles src="Module:Citation/CS1/styles.css" />ISBN 0-688-12363-5. Chapter available online: Chapter 21: Nasser's Challenge[713].
- Goldstein, Erik (1992). *Wars and Peace Treaties, 1816–1991*. Routledge. <templatestyles src="Module:Citation/CS1/styles.css" />ISBN 0-415-07822-9
- Green, Stephen J. (1984). *Taking Sides: America's Secret Relations With Militant Israel*. William Morrow & Co. <templatestyles src="Module:Citation/CS1/styles.css" />ISBN 978-0-688-02643-1.
- Griffin, David J. (2006). *Hawker Hunter 1951 to 2007* Lulu.com, 4 edition. <templatestyles src="Module:Citation/CS1/styles.css" />ISBN 1-4303-0593-2.
- Haddad, Yvonne. (1992). Islamists and the "Problem of Israel": The 1967 Awakening. *Middle East Journal*, Vol. 46, No. 2, pp. 266–85.
- Hajjar, Sami G. The Israel-Syria Track[714], *Middle East Policy*, Volume VI, February 1999, Number 3. Retrieved 30 September 2006.

- Hammel, Eric (1992). *Six Days in June: How Israel Won the 1967 Arab–Israeli War*. Simon & Schuster. <templatestyles src="Module:Citation/CS1/styles.css" />ISBN 0-7434-7535-6
- Hattendorf, John B. (2000). *Naval Strategy and Power in the Mediterranean: Past, Present and Future*. Taylor & Francis. ISBN 0-7146-8054-0.<templatestyles src="Module:Citation/CS1/styles.css"></templatestyles>
- Handel, Michael I. (1973). *Israel's political-military doctrine*. Center for International Affairs, Harvard University. <templatestyles src="Module:Citation/CS1/styles.css" />ISBN 0-87674-025-5
- Hart, Alan (1989) *Arafat, A political biography*. Indiana University Press <templatestyles src="Module:Citation/CS1/styles.css" />ISBN 0-253-32711-3.
- Herzog, Chaim (1982). *The Arab-Israeli Wars*. Arms & Armour Press. <templatestyles src="Module:Citation/CS1/styles.css" />ISBN 0-85368-367-0
- Herbert, Nicholas (17 May 1967). *Egyptian Forces On Full Alert: Ready to fight for Syria*. The Times, p. 1; Issue 56943; col E.
- Herzog, Chaim (1989). *Heroes of Israel: Profiles of Jewish Courage*. Little Brown and Company. <templatestyles src="Module:Citation/CS1/styles.css" />ISBN 0-316-35901-7.
- Higham, Robin. (2003). *100 Years of Air Power and Aviation*. TAMU Press. <templatestyles src="Module:Citation/CS1/styles.css" />ISBN 1-58544-241-0.
- Hinnebusch, Raymond A. (2003). *The international politics of the Middle East*. Manchester University Press. <templatestyles src="Module:Citation/CS1/styles.css" />ISBN 978-0-7190-5346-7
- Israel Ministry of Foreign Affairs (2004). *Background on Israeli POWs and MIAs*[715].
- Israel Ministry of Foreign Affairs (2008). *The Six-Day War (June 1967)*[716].
- " Israel Reportedly Killed POWs in '67 War; Historians Say Deaths of Hundreds of Egyptians Was Covered Up Israel Reportedly Killed POWs in '67 War; Historians Say Deaths of Hundreds of Egyptians Was Covered Up[717]", *The Washington Post*, 17 August 1995, p. A.30 (Fee required).
- James, Laura (2005). The Nassar And His Enemies: Foreign Policy Decision Making In Egypt On The Eve Of The Six Day War[718]. *The Middle East Review of International Affairs*. Volume 9, No. 2, Article 2.
- "Israelis Say Tape Shows Nasser Fabricated 'Plot'; Recording Said to Be of Phone Call to Hussein Gives Plan to Accuse U.S. and Britain"[719]. *The New York Times*. 9 June 1967. p. 17. Retrieved 28 June 2007.<templatestyles src="Module:Citation/CS1/styles.css"></templatestyles>

- Jia, Bing Bing. (1998). *The Regime of Straits in International Law*[720] (Oxford Monographs in International Law). Oxford University Press, USA. <templatestyles src="Module:Citation/CS1/styles.css" />ISBN 0-19-826556-5.
- Koboril, Iwao and Glantz, Michael H. (1998). *Central Eurasian Water Crisis*. United Nations University Press. <templatestyles src="Module:Citation/CS1/styles.css" />ISBN 92-808-0925-3
- Krauthammer, Charles (18 May 2007). "Prelude to the Six Days"[721]. *The Washington Post*. pp. A23. ISSN 0740-5421[722]. Retrieved 20 June 2008.<templatestyles src="Module:Citation/CS1/styles.css"></templatestyles>
- Lavoy, Peter R.; Sagan, Scott Douglas & Wirtz, James J. (Eds.) (2000). *Planning the Unthinkable: How New Powers Will Use Nuclear, Biological, and Chemical Weapons*. Cornell University Press. <templatestyles src="Module:Citation/CS1/styles.css" />ISBN 0-8014-8704-8.
- Leibler, Isi (1972). *The Case For Israel*. Australia: The Executive Council of Australian Jewry. <templatestyles src="Module:Citation/CS1/styles.css" />ISBN 0-9598984-0-9.
- Lenczowski, George. (1990). *American Presidents and the Middle East*. Duke University Press. <templatestyles src="Module:Citation/CS1/styles.css" />ISBN 0-8223-0972-6.
- Lyndon Baines Johnson Library. (1994). [[Category:All articles with dead external links[723]]Wikipedia:Link rot Transcript, Robert S. McNamara Oral History]Wikipedia:Link rot, Special Interview I, 26 March 1993, by Robert Dallek, Internet Copy, LBJ Library. Retrieved 20 July 2010.
- "McNamara: US Near War in '67"[724]. *The Boston Globe*. 16 September 1983. p. 1.<templatestyles src="Module:Citation/CS1/styles.css"></templatestyles>
- Mansour, Camille. (1994). *Beyond Alliance: Israel and US Foreign Policy*. Columbia University Press. <templatestyles src="Module:Citation/CS1/styles.css" />ISBN 0-231-08492-7.
- Maoz, Zeev (2006). *Defending the Holy Land: A Critical Analysis of Israel's Security & Foreign Policy*. The University of Michigan Press. <templatestyles src="Module:Citation/CS1/styles.css" />ISBN 978-0-472-03341-6
- Morris, Benny (2001) *Righteous Victims* New York, Vintage Books. <templatestyles src="Module:Citation/CS1/styles.css" />ISBN 978-0-679-74475-7
- Miller, Benjamin. (2007). *States, Nations, and the Great Powers: The Sources of Regional War and Peace*. Cambridge University Press. <templatestyles src="Module:Citation/CS1/styles.css" />ISBN 0-521-69161-3
- Murakami, Masahiro. (1995). *Managing Water for Peace in the Middle*

- *East: Alternative Strategies*[725]. United Nations University Press. <templatestyles src="Module:Citation/CS1/styles.css" />ISBN 92-808-0858-3.
- Mutawi, Samir A. (18 July 2002). *Jordan in the 1967 War*[726]. Cambridge University Press. ISBN 978-0-521-52858-0.<templatestyles src="Module:Citation/CS1/styles.css"></templatestyles>
- Nordeen, Lon & Nicole, David. (1996). *Phoenix over the Nile: A history of Egyptian Air Power 1932–1994*. Washington DC: Smithsonian Institution. *<templatestyles src="Module:Citation/CS1/styles.css" />ISBN 1-56098-626-3.*
- " Mediterranean Eskadra[727]". (2000). Federation of American Scientists.
- Oren, Michael (2002). *Six Days of War*. Oxford University Press. <templatestyles src="Module:Citation/CS1/styles.css" />ISBN 0-19-515174-7
- Oren, Michael. (2005). The Revelations of 1967: New Research on the Six Day War and Its Lessons for the Contemporary Middle East[728], *Israel Studies*, volume 10, number 2. (Subscription required).
- Oren, Michael. (2006). "The Six-Day War", in Bar-On, Mordechai (ed.), *Never-Ending Conflict: Israeli Military History*. Greenwood Publishing Group. <templatestyles src="Module:Citation/CS1/styles.css" />ISBN 0-275-98158-4.
- Parker, Richard B. (1996). *The Six-day War: A Retrospective*. University Press of Florida. <templatestyles src="Module:Citation/CS1/styles.css" />ISBN 0-8130-1383-6.
- Parker, Richard B. (August 1997). "USAF in the Sinai in the 1967 War: Fact or Fiction"[729] (PDF). *Journal of Palestine Studies*. XXVII (1): 67–75. doi: 10.1525/jps.1997.27.1.00p01641[730].<templatestyles src="Module:Citation/CS1/styles.css"></templatestyles>
- Phythian, Mark (2001). *The Politics of British Arms Sales Since 1964*. Manchester: Manchester University Press. <templatestyles src="Module:Citation/CS1/styles.css" />ISBN 0-7190-5907-0
- Podeh, Elie (Winter 2004). "The Lie That Won't Die: Collusion, 1967"[731]. *Middle East Quarterly*. **11** (1).<templatestyles src="Module:Citation/CS1/styles.css"></templatestyles>
- Pimlott, John. (1983). Middle East Conflicts: From 1945 to the Present. Orbis. <templatestyles src="Module:Citation/CS1/styles.css" />ISBN 0-85613-547-X.
- Pollack, Kenneth (2004). *Arabs at War: Military Effectiveness, 1948–1991*. University of Nebraska Press. <templatestyles src="Module:Citation/CS1/styles.css" />ISBN 0-8032-8783-6
- Pollack, Kenneth (2005). Air Power in the Six-Day War. *The Journal of Strategic Studies*. 28(3), 471–503.
- Prior, Michael (1999). *Zionism and the State of Israel: A Moral Inquiry*. London: Routledge. <templatestyles

src="Module:Citation/CS1/styles.css" />ISBN 0-415-20462-3
- Quandt, William B. (2005). *Peace Process: American Diplomacy and the Arab–Israeli Conflict Since 1967*. Brookings Institution Press and the University of California Press; 3 edition. <templatestyles src="Module:Citation/CS1/styles.css" />ISBN 0-520-24631-4
- Quigley, John B. (2005). *Case for Palestine: An International Law Perspective*. Duke University Press. <templatestyles src="Module:Citation/CS1/styles.css" />ISBN 0-8223-3539-5
- Quigley, John B. (1990). *Palestine and Israel: A Challenge to Justice*. Duke University Press. <templatestyles src="Module:Citation/CS1/styles.css" />ISBN 0-8223-1023-6
- Rabil, Robert G. (2003). *Embattled Neighbors: Syria, Israel, and Lebanon*. Lynne Rienner Publishers. <templatestyles src="Module:Citation/CS1/styles.css" />ISBN 1-58826-149-2
- Rabin, Yitzhak (1996). *The Rabin Memoirs*. University of California Press. <templatestyles src="Module:Citation/CS1/styles.css" />ISBN 0-520-20766-1.
- Rauschning, Dietrich; Wiesbrock, Katja & Lailach, Martin (eds.) (1997). Key Resolutions of the United Nations General Assembly 1946–1996[732]. Cambridge University Press. <templatestyles src="Module:Citation/CS1/styles.css" />ISBN 0-521-59704-8.
- Rikhye, Indar Jit (1980). *The Sinai Blunder*. London: Routledge. <templatestyles src="Module:Citation/CS1/styles.css" />ISBN 0-7146-3136-1
- Robarge, David S. (2007). *Getting It Right: CIA Analysis of the 1967 Arab-Israeli War*[733], Center for the Study of Intelligence, Vol. 49 No. 1
- Rubenberg, Cheryl A. (1989). *Israel and the American National Interest*. University of Illinois Press. <templatestyles src="Module:Citation/CS1/styles.css" />ISBN 0-252-06074-1
- Sachar, Howard M. (1976, 2007) *A History of Israel from the Rise of Zionism to Our Time*. New York: Alfred A. Knopf. <templatestyles src="Module:Citation/CS1/styles.css" />ISBN 0-394-48564-5; <templatestyles src="Module:Citation/CS1/styles.css" />ISBN 0-375-71132-5.
- Sadeh, Eligar (1997). *Militarization and State Power in the Arab–Israeli Conflict: Case Study of Israel, 1948–1982*. Universal Publishers. <templatestyles src="Module:Citation/CS1/styles.css" />ISBN 0-9658564-6-1
- Sandler, Deborah; Aldy, Emad & Al-Khoshman Mahmoud A. (1993). *Protecting the Gulf of Aqaba. – A regional environmental challenge*. Environmental Law Institute. 0911937463.
- Seale, Patrick (1988). *Asad: The Struggle for Peace in the Middle East*. University of California Press. <templatestyles src="Module:Citation/CS1/styles.css" />ISBN 0-520-06976-5
- Segev, Samuel (1967). A Red Sheet: the Six Day War.

- Segev, Tom (2005). *Israel in 1967*. Keter. ISBN 965-07-1370-0.<templatestyles src="Module:Citation/CS1/styles.css"></templatestyles>
- Segev, Tom (2007). *1967: Israel, the War, and the Year that Transformed the Middle East* Metropolitan Books. <templatestyles src="Module:Citation/CS1/styles.css" />ISBN 978-0-8050-7057-6
- Sela, Avraham (1997). *The Decline of the Arab-Israeli Conflict: Middle East Politics and the Quest for Regional Order*. SUNY Press. <templatestyles src="Module:Citation/CS1/styles.css" />ISBN 0-7914-3537-7
- Shafqat, Saeed (2004). *Islamic world and South Asia: Rise of Islamism and Terror, Causes and Consequences?*[734]. In Kaniz F. Yusuf (Ed.) *Unipolar World & The Muslim States*. Islamabad: Pakistan Forum, pp 217–246.
- Shemesh, Moshe (2008). *Arab Politics, Palestinian Nationalism and the Six Day War*. Sussex Academic Press. <templatestyles src="Module:Citation/CS1/styles.css" />ISBN 1-84519-188-9.
- Shlaim, Avi (2000). *The Iron Wall: Israel and the Arab World*. W. W. Norton & Company. ISBN 0-393-32112-6.<templatestyles src="Module:Citation/CS1/styles.css"></templatestyles> <templatestyles src="Module:Citation/CS1/styles.css" />ISBN 0-393-04816-0
- Shlaim, Avi (2007) *Lion of Jordan: The Life of King Hussein in War and Peace* Vintage Books <templatestyles src="Module:Citation/CS1/styles.css" />ISBN 978-1-4000-7828-8
- Shlaim, Avi; Louis, William Roger (13 February 2012), *The 1967 Arab–Israeli War: Origins and Consequences*[735], Cambridge University Press <templatestyles src="Module:Citation/CS1/styles.css" />ISBN 978-1-107-00236-4
- Smith, Hedrick (15 June 1967). "As the Shock Wears Off; Arab World, Appraising Its Defeat, Is Split as It Gropes for Strategy"[736]. *The New York Times*. p. 16. Retrieved 28 June 2006.<templatestyles src="Module:Citation/CS1/styles.css"></templatestyles>
- Smith, Hedrick (15 September 1967). "Envoys Say Nasser Now Concedes U.S. Didn't Help Israel". *The New York Times*. pp. Page 1, Col. 5, Page 3, Col. 1.<templatestyles src="Module:Citation/CS1/styles.css"></templatestyles>
- Stein, Janice Gross. (1991). The Arab-Israeli War of 1967: Inadvertent War Through Miscalculated Escalation, in *Avoiding War: Problems of Crisis Management*, Alexander L. George, ed. Boulder: Westview Press.
- Stephens, Robert H. (1971). *Nasser: A Political Biography*. London: Allen Lane/The Penguin Press. <templatestyles src="Module:Citation/CS1/styles.css" />ISBN 0-7139-0181-0
- Stone, David (2004). *Wars of the Cold War*. Brassey's. <templatestyles src="Module:Citation/CS1/styles.css" />ISBN 1-85753-342-9

- Tolan, Sandy (4 June 2007). "Rethinking Israel's David-and-Goliath past"[737]. Salon.com. Retrieved 29 April 2010.<templatestyles src="Module:Citation/CS1/styles.css"></templatestyles>
- Tucker, Spencer (2004). *Tanks: An Illustrated History of Their Impact*. ABC-CLIO. <templatestyles src="Module:Citation/CS1/styles.css" />ISBN 1-57607-995-3
- United Nations (967, 5 June). 1347 Security Council MEETING : June 5, 1967[738]. Provisional agenda (S/PV.1347/Rev.1). On a subpage of the website of The United Nations Information System on the Question of Palestine (UNISPAL).
- van Creveld, Martin (2004). *Defending Israel: A Controversial Plan Toward Peace*. Thomas Dunne Books. <templatestyles src="Module:Citation/CS1/styles.css" />ISBN 0-312-32866-4
- Youngs, Tim. (2001). *Developments in the Middle East Peace Process 1991–2000*[739] London: International Affairs and Defence Section, House of Commons Library. ISSN 1368-8456.
- Finkelstein, Norman (2003). *Image and Reality of the Israel–Palestine Conflict*[740]. Verso. ISBN 1-85984-442-1.<templatestyles src="Module:Citation/CS1/styles.css"></templatestyles>

Further reading

- Barzilai, Gad (1996). *Wars, Internal Conflicts, and Political Order: A Jewish Democracy in the Middle East*. New York University Press. <templatestyles src="Module:Citation/CS1/styles.css" />ISBN 978-0-7914-2944-0
- Cristol, A Jay (2002). *Liberty Incident: The 1967 Israeli Attack on the U.S. Navy Spy Ship*. Brassey's. <templatestyles src="Module:Citation/CS1/styles.css" />ISBN 1-57488-536-7
- Finkelstein, Norman (June 2017). *Analysis of the war and its aftermath, on the 50th anniversary of the June 1967 war*[741] (3 parts, each about 30 min)
- Gat, Moshe (2003). *Britain and the Conflict in the Middle East, 1964–1967: The Coming of the Six-Day War*. Praeger/Greenwood. <templatestyles src="Module:Citation/CS1/styles.css" />ISBN 0-275-97514-2
- Hammel, Eric (October 2002). "Sinai air strike: June 5, 1967". *Military Heritage*. **4** (2): 68–73.<templatestyles src="Module:Citation/CS1/styles.css"></templatestyles>
- Hopwood, Derek (1991). *Egypt: Politics and Society*. London: Routledge. <templatestyles src="Module:Citation/CS1/styles.css" />ISBN 0-415-09432-1

- Hussein of Jordan (1969). *My "War" with Israel*. London: Peter Owen. <templatestyles src="Module:Citation/CS1/styles.css" />ISBN 0-7206-0310-2
- Katz, Samuel M. (1991) *Israel's Air Force*; The Power Series. Motorbooks International Publishers & Wholesalers, Osceola, WI.
- Makiya, Kanan (1998). *Republic of Fear: The Politics of Modern Iraq*. University of California Press. <templatestyles src="Module:Citation/CS1/styles.css" />ISBN 0-520-21439-0
- Morris, Benny (1997). *Israel's Border Wars, 1949–1956*. Oxford: Oxford University Press. <templatestyles src="Module:Citation/CS1/styles.css" />ISBN 0-19-829262-7
- Pressfield, Steven (2014). *The Lion's Gate: On the Front Lines of the Six Day War*. Sentinel HC, 2014. <templatestyles src="Module:Citation/CS1/styles.css" />ISBN 1-59523-091-2
- Rezun, Miron (1990). "Iran and Afghanistan." In A. Kapur (Ed.). *Diplomatic Ideas and Practices of Asian States* (pp. 9–25). Brill Academic Publishers. <templatestyles src="Module:Citation/CS1/styles.css" />ISBN 90-04-09289-7
- Smith, Grant (2006). *Deadly Dogma*. Institute for Research: Middle Eastern Policy. <templatestyles src="Module:Citation/CS1/styles.css" />ISBN 0-9764437-4-0
- Oren, Michael (April 2002). *Six Days of War: June 1967 and the Making of the Modern Middle East*. Oxford University Press. <templatestyles src="Module:Citation/CS1/styles.css" />ISBN 978-0-19-515174-9

External links

 Wikimedia Commons has media related to *1967 Arab-Israeli War*.

- The Photograph: A Search for June 1967[742]. Retrieved 17 July 2010.
- The three soldiers – background to that photograph[743]
- Six Day War Personal recollections & Timeline[744]
- Video Clip: Sandhurst military historian analysing how King Hussein became involved in the Six Day War.[745] on YouTube
- Video Clip: Analysis of Israel's Sinai Campaign in 1967 by Sandhurst military historian.[746] on YouTube
- Video Clip: Military analysis of the attack on Jerusalem and the Jordanian defence.[746] on YouTube
- Six-Day War[747] Encyclopaedia of the Orient
- All State Department documents related to the crisis[748]

- Letters from David Ben-Gurion on the Six-Day War[749] Shapell Manuscript Foundation
- UN Resolution 242[750]. Retrieved 17 July 2010.
- The status of Jerusalem, United Nations, New York, 1997 (Prepared for, and under the guidance of, the Committee on the Exercise of the Inalienable Rights of the Palestinian People)[751]
- Status of Jerusalem: Legal Aspects[752]. Retrieved 22 July 2014.
- Legal Aspects The Six Day War – June 1967 and Its Aftermath – Professor Gerald Adler[753]
- General Uzi Narkiss[754] – A historic radio interview with General Uzi Narkiss taken on 7 June – one day after the Six-Day War, describing the battle for Jerusalem
- Liberation of the Temple Mount and Western Wall by Israel Defense Forces[755] – Historic Live Broadcast on Voice of Israel Radio, 7 June 1967
- How The USSR Planned To Destroy Israel in 1967[756] by Isabella Ginor. Published by *Middle East Review of International Affairs* (MERIA) Journal Volume 7, Number 3 (September 2003)
- Position of Arab forces May 1967[757]. Retrieved 22 July 2014.

1969–1974: Meir

War of Attrition

<indicator name="pp-default"> 🔒 </indicator>

War of Attrition
Part of the Arab–Israeli conflict and the Cold War
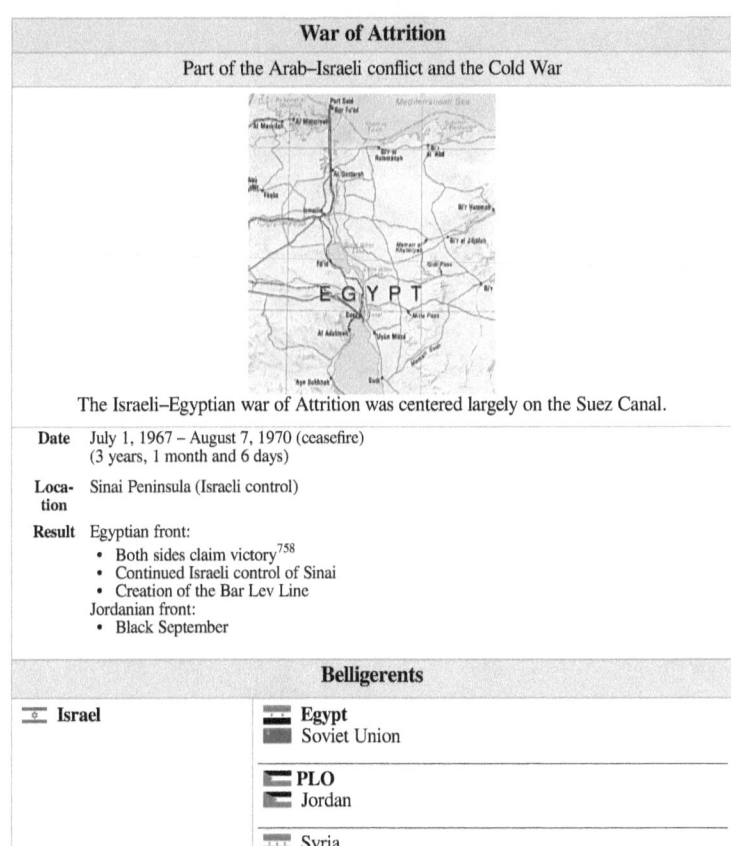 The Israeli–Egyptian war of Attrition was centered largely on the Suez Canal.
Date   July 1, 1967 – August 7, 1970 (ceasefire) (3 years, 1 month and 6 days)
Location   Sinai Peninsula (Israeli control)

Result   Egyptian front:
    • Both sides claim victory[758]
    • Continued Israeli control of Sinai
    • Creation of the Bar Lev Line
Jordanian front:
    • Black September

Belligerents

Israel	Egypt Soviet Union
	PLO Jordan
	Syria Cuba

Commanders and leaders	
Levi Eshkol Yigal Allon Zalman Shazar Haim Bar-Lev Mordechai Hod Uzi Narkiss	Gamal Abdel Nasser Ahmad Ismail Ali Anwar El Sadat Saad El Shazly Abdul Munim Riad † Nikolai Yurchenko †
Strength	
275,000 (including reserves)	Egyptian: 200,000 Soviet: 10,700–15,000[759] Jordanian: 15,000[760] PLO: 900–1,000[761,762]
Casualties and losses	
694[763]–1,424 soldiers killed 227 civilians killed 2,659 wounded, from this 999 at the Egyptian front 14[764]–30[765] aircraft	**Egypt**: 2,882[766]–10,000 soldiers and civilians killed 6,285 wounded[767] 60–114[768] aircraft lost **PLO**: 1,828 killed 2,500 captured[769] **Jordan**: 40–84 killed 108–250 wounded 4 captured 30 tanks **Soviet Union**: 58 dead[770] 4–5 aircraft **Cuba**: 180 dead 250 wounded[771] **Syria**: Hundreds of casualties

The **War of Attrition** (Arabic: حرب الاستنزاف *Ḥarb al-Istinzāf*, Hebrew: מלחמת ההתשה *Milhemet haHatashah*) involved fighting between Israel and Egypt, Jordan, PLO and their allies from 1967 to 1970.

Following the 1967 Six-Day War, no serious diplomatic efforts tried to resolve the issues at the heart of the Arab–Israeli conflict. In September 1967, the Arab states formulated the "three nos" policy, barring peace, recognition or negotiations with Israel. Egyptian President Gamal Abdel Nasser believed that only military initiative would compel Israel or the international community to facilitate a full Israeli withdrawal from Sinai, and hostilities soon resumed along the Suez Canal.

These initially took the form of limited artillery duels and small-scale incursions into Sinai, but by 1969 the Egyptian Army judged itself prepared for larger-scale operations. On March 8, 1969, Nasser proclaimed the official launch of the War of Attrition, characterized by large-scale shelling along the

Suez Canal, extensive aerial warfare and commando raids. Hostilities continued until August 1970 and ended with a ceasefire, the frontiers remaining the same as when the war began, with no real commitment to serious peace negotiations.

Egyptian front

Israel's victory in the Six-Day War left the entirety of the Egyptian Sinai Peninsula up to the eastern bank of the Suez Canal under Israeli control. Egypt was determined to regain Sinai, and also sought to mitigate the severity of its defeat. Sporadic clashes were taking place along the cease-fire line, and Egyptian missile boats sank the Israeli destroyer INS *Eilat* on October 21 of the same year.

Egypt began shelling Israeli positions along the Bar Lev Line, using heavy artillery, MiG aircraft and various other forms of Soviet assistance with the hope of forcing the Israeli government into concessions. Israel responded with aerial bombardments, airborne raids on Egyptian military positions, and aerial strikes against strategic facilities in Egypt.

The international community and both countries attempted to find a diplomatic solution to the conflict. The Jarring Mission of the United Nations was supposed to ensure that the terms of UN Security Council Resolution 242 would be observed, but by late 1970 it was clear that this mission had been a failure. Fearing the escalation of the conflict into an "East vs. West" confrontation during the tensions of the mid-Cold War, the American president, Richard Nixon, sent his Secretary of State, William Rogers, to formulate the Rogers Plan in view of obtaining a ceasefire.

In August 1970, Israel, Jordan, and Egypt agreed to an "in place" ceasefire under the terms proposed by the Rogers Plan. The plan contained restrictions on missile deployment by both sides, and required the cessation of raids as a precondition for peace. The Egyptians and their Soviet allies rekindled the conflict by violating the agreement shortly thereafter, moving their missiles near to the Suez Canal, and constructing the largest anti-aircraft system yet implemented at that point in history.

The Israelis responded with a policy which their Prime Minister, Golda Meir, dubbed "asymmetrical response", wherein Israeli retaliation was disproportionately large in comparison to any Egyptian attacks.

Following Nasser's death in September 1970, his successor, Anwar Al-Sadat, continued the ceasefire with Israel, focusing on rebuilding the Egyptian army and planning a full-scale attack on the Israeli forces controlling the eastern bank of the Suez Canal. These plans would materialize three years later in the

Yom Kippur War. Ultimately, Israel would return Sinai to Egypt after the two nations signed a peace treaty.

Various military historians have commented on the war with differing opinions. Chaim Herzog notes that Israel withstood the battle and adapted itself to a "hitherto alien type of warfare."[772] Ze'ev Schiff notes that though Israel suffered losses, she was still able to preserve her military accomplishments of 1967 and that despite increased Soviet involvement, Israel had stood firm.[773]

Simon Dunstan notes that, although Israel continued to hold the Bar Lev Line, the war's conclusion "led to a dangerous complacency within the Israeli High Command about the resolve of the Egyptian armed forces and the strength of the Bar-Lev Line." On the tactical level, Kenneth Pollack notes that Egypt's commandos performed "adequately" though they rarely ventured into risky operations on a par with the daring of Israel's commandos,[774] Egypt's artillery corps encountered difficulty in penetrating the Bar-Lev forts and eventually adopted a policy of trying to catch Israeli troops in the exterior parts of the forts.[775]

The Egyptian Air Force and Air Defense Forces performed poorly.[774] Egyptian pilots were rigid, slow to react and unwilling to improvise.[776] According to U.S. intelligence estimates, Egypt lost 109 aircraft, most in air-to-air combat, while only 16 Israeli aircraft were lost, most to anti-aircraft artillery or SAMs.[776] It took a salvo of 6 to 10 SA-2 Egyptian anti-aircraft missiles to obtain a better than fifty percent chance of a hit.[776]

Timeline

1967

July 1, 1967: An Egyptian commando force from Port Fuad moves south and takes up a position at Ras el 'Ish, located 10 miles south of Port Said on the eastern bank of the Suez Canal, an area controlled by the Israelis since the ceasefire on June 9, 1967. An Israeli armored infantry company attacks the Egyptian force. The Israeli company drives off the Egyptians but loses 1 dead and 13 wounded.[777] However, another source claims that an Israeli attack on Port Fuad was repulsed. According to Zeev Maoz, the battle was decided in favor of the Egyptians.

July 2, 1967: The Israeli Air Force bombs Egyptian artillery positions that had supported the commandos at Ras Al-'Ish.[778]

July 4, 1967: Egyptian Air Force jets strike several Israeli targets in Sinai. An Egyptian MiG-17 is shot down.

Figure 99: *Israeli naval personnel celebrate their victory after an engagement with Egyptian naval forces near Rumani.*

July 8, 1967: An Egyptian Air Force MiG-21 is shot down by Israeli air defenses while on a reconnaissance mission over el-Qanatra. Two Su-7s equipped with cameras are then sent out to carry out the mission, and manage to complete several turns over Sinai without any opposition. Two other Su-7s are sent for another reconnaissance mission hours later, but are attacked by Israeli Air Force fighter jets. One Su-7 is shot down.

July 11–12, 1967: Battle of Rumani Coast - The Israeli Navy destroyer INS *Eilat* and two torpedo boats sink two Egyptian torpedo boats off the Rumani coast. No crewmen on the Egyptian torpedo boats are known to have survived, and there were no Israeli casualties.

July 14, 1967: Artillery exchanges and aerial duels erupt near the Suez Canal. Seven Egyptian fighter aircraft are shot down.[779]

July 15, 1967: An Israeli Air Force Mirage III is shot down by an Egyptian MiG-21.[780]

October 21, 1967: Two missile boats from the Egyptian Navy sinks the Israeli destroyer INS *Eilat* with anti-ship missiles, killing forty-seven sailors.

October, 1967: In retaliation to the sinking of the *Eilat*, Israeli artillery bombards oil refineries and depots near Suez. In a series of artillery exchanges

Figure 100: *Israeli destroyer INS Eilat that was sunk by the Egyptian Navy, killing forty-seven sailors.*

throughout October, the Egyptians sustain civilian casualties. Egypt evacuates a large number of the civilian population in the canal region.[781]

1968

March 21, 1968: In response to persistent PLO raids against Israeli civilian targets, Israel attacks the town of Karameh, Jordan, the site of a major PLO camp. The goal of the invasion was to destroy Karameh camp and capture Yasser Arafat in reprisal for the attacks by the PLO against Israeli civilians, which culminated in an Israeli school bus hitting a mine in the Negev. However, plans for the two operations were prepared in 1967, one year before the bus incident. When Jordan saw the size of the raiding forces entering the battle it was led to the assumption that Israel had another goal of capturing Balqa Governorate to create a Golan Heights similar situation. Israel assumed that the Jordanian Army would ignore the invasion, but the latter fought alongside the Palestinians and opened heavy fire that inflicted losses upon the Israeli forces. This engagement marked the first known deployment of suicide bombers by Palestinian forces.[782] The Israelis were repelled at the end of a day's battle, having destroyed most of the Karameh camp and taken around 141 PLO prisoners. Both sides declared victory. On a tactical level, the battle went in Israel's favor[783] and the destruction of the Karameh camp

Figure 101: *King Hussein after checking an abandoned Israeli tank in the aftermath of the Battle of Karameh in 1968*

Figure 102: *President Nasser of Egypt (with binoculars), surveys positions at the Suez Canal in November 1968*

was achieved.[784] However, the relatively high casualties were a considerable surprise for the Israel Defense Forces and was stunning to the Israelis. Although the Palestinians were not victorious on their own, King Hussein let the Palestinians take credit.

June 1968: The war "officially" begins, with sparse Egyptian artillery bombardment of the Israeli front line on the east bank of the Suez Canal. More artillery bombardments in the following months cause Israeli casualties.

September 8, 1968: An Egyptian artillery barrage kills 10 Israeli soldiers and injures 18. Israel responds by shelling Suez and Ismaïlia.

October 30, 1968: Israeli helicopter-borne Sayeret Matkal commandos carry out Operation Helem (Shock), destroying an Egyptian electric transformer station, two dams along the Nile River and a bridge. The blackout causes Nasser to cease hostilities for a few months while fortifications around hundreds of important targets are built. Simultaneously, Israel reinforces its position on the east bank of the Suez Canal by construction of the Bar Lev Line.

November 3, 1968: Egyptian MiG-17s attack Israeli positions, and are met by Israeli interceptors. One Israeli plane is damaged.

December 1, 1968: Israeli helicopter-borne commandos destroy four bridges near Amman, Jordan.

December 3, 1968: The Israeli Air Force bombs PLO camps in Jordan. The Israeli jets are intercepted by Hawker Hunters of the Royal Jordanian Air Force, and an Israeli fighter jet is damaged during the brief air battle.

1969

March 8, 1969: Egypt strikes the Bar Lev Line with artillery fire and airstrikes, causing heavy casualties. Israel retaliates with raids deep into Egyptian territory, causing severe damage.

March 9, 1969: The Egyptian Chief of Staff, General Abdul Munim Riad, is killed in an Israeli mortar attack while visiting the front lines along the Suez Canal.

May–July 1969: Heavy fighting takes place between Israeli and Egyptian forces. Israel loses 47 dead and 157 wounded, while Egyptian casualties are far heavier.

July 18, 1969: Egyptian commandos raid Israeli military installations in Sinai.

July 19–20, 1969: Operation Bulmus 6 – Israeli Shayetet 13 and Sayeret Matkal commandos raid Green Island, resulting in the total destruction of the Egyptian facility. Six Israeli soldiers and 80 Egyptian soldiers are killed. Some Egyptian casualties are caused by their own artillery.

Figure 103: *F-4E Phantom of the Israeli Air Force. The aircraft was used to good effect as "flying artillery" during the war. Roundel markings on nose credit this aircraft with three aerial kills.*

July 20–28, 1969: Operation Boxer – Nearly the entire Israeli Air Force attacks the northern sector of the Canal, destroying anti-aircraft positions, tanks and artillery, and shooting down eight Egyptian aircraft. An estimated 300 Egyptian soldiers are killed, and Egyptian positions are seriously damaged. Israeli losses amount to two aircraft. Egyptian artillery fire is reduced somewhat. However, shelling with lighter weapons, particularly mortars, continues.

August 1969: The Israeli Air Force flies about 1,000 combat sorties against Egypt, destroying dozens of SAM sites and shooting down 21 aircraft. Three Israeli aircraft are lost.

September 9, 1969: Operation Raviv – Israeli forces raid Egypt's Red Sea coast. The raid is preceded by Operation Escort, with Shayetet 13 naval commandos sinking a pair of Egyptian torpedo boats that could have threatened the Israeli raiding party. Three commandos are killed when an explosive device detonates prematurely. Israeli troops backed up by aircraft captured Egyptian armor, and destroy 12 Egyptian outposts. The Egyptians suffer 100–200 casualties, and a Soviet general serving as a consultant to the Egyptians is also killed, while one Israeli soldier is lightly injured. An Israeli plane is shot down during the raid, and the pilot's fate is still unknown.

Figure 104: *Soviet/Egyptian S-125 anti-aircraft type missiles in the Suez Canal vicinity*

Figure 105: *Israeli troops at the Firdan Bridge by the Suez Canal, 1969*

September 11, 1969: Sixteen Egyptian aircraft carry out a strike mission. Eight MiGs are shot down by Israeli Mirages and a further three Su-7s are lost to Israeli anti-aircraft artillery and HAWK surface-to-air missiles.[774]

October 17, 1969: The United States and Soviet Union begin diplomatic talks to end the conflict.

December 9, 1969: Egyptian aircraft, with the assistance of newly delivered P-15 radars, defeats the Israelis in an aerial engagement, shooting down two Israeli Mirages. Later in the evening, an Egyptian fighter flown by Lt. Ahmed Atef shot down an Israeli F-4 Phantom II, making him the first Egyptian pilot to shoot down an F-4 in combat.[785] The same day, the Rogers Plan is publicized. It calls for Egyptian "commitment to peace" in exchange for the Israeli withdrawal from Sinai. Both parties strongly reject the plan. Nasser forestalled any movement toward direct negotiations with Israel. In dozens of speeches and statements, Nasser posited the equation that any direct peace talks with Israel were tantamount to surrender. President Nasser instead opts to plead for more sophisticated weaponry from the Soviet Union to withstand the Israeli bombings. The Soviets initially refuse to deliver the requested weapons.

December 26–27, 1969: Israel launches Operation Rooster 53, carried out by paratroopers transported by Sikorsky CH-53E and Super Frelon helicopters. The operation results in the capture of an Egyptian P-12 radar at Ras Gharib and carrying it to Israel by 2 CH-53 Sea Stallion Helicopters. The operation enabled Israeli and American learning of the latest Soviet radar technology, and caused a huge morale impact on the Egyptians.

1970

January 22, 1970: President Nasser secretly flies to Moscow to discuss the situation. His request for new SAM batteries (including the 3M9 Kub and Strela-2) is approved. Their deployment requires qualified personnel along with squadrons of aircraft to protect them. Thus, he needed Red Army personnel in large numbers, something the Kremlin did not want to provide. Nasser then threatens to resign, implying that Egypt might turn to the United States for help in the future. The Soviets had invested heavily in President Nasser's regime, and so, the Soviet leader, General-Secretary Leonid Brezhnev, finally obliged. The Soviet presence was to increase from 2,500–4,000 in January to 10,600–12,150 (plus 100–150 Soviet pilots) by June 30.

January 22, 1970: Operation Rhodes. Israeli paratroopers and naval commandos are transported by IAF Super Frelon helicopters to Shadwan Island where they kill 70 Egyptian soldiers and take 62 more prisoner at the loss of 3 dead and 7 wounded. The soldiers dismantle an Egyptian radar and other

Figure 106: *Soviet medal issued to Soviet military personnel who served in Egypt during the War of Attrition. Wikipedia: Citation needed The medal says Москва-Каир (Moscow-Cairo).*

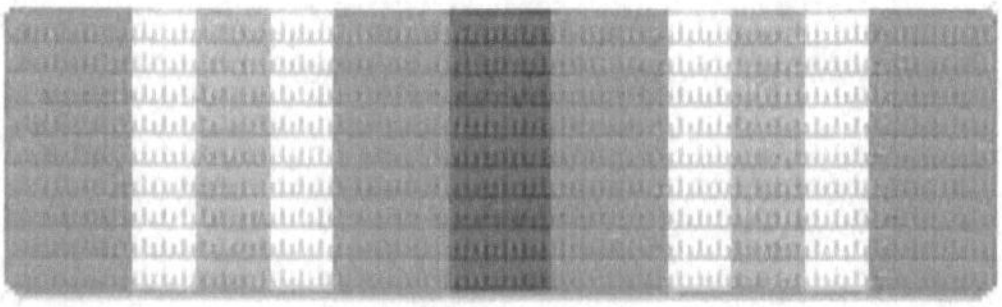

Figure 107: *Israeli war ribbon signifying participation in the War of Attrition*

military equipment for transport back to Israel. IAF aircraft sink two Egyptian P-183 torpedo boats during the operation.[786]

February, 1970: Israeli fighter jets accidentally strike an industrial plant at Abu Zaabal, killing 80 workers.

February, 1970: An Egyptian commando platoon attempts to set up an ambush in the vicinity of the Mitla Pass but is discovered. The entire unit is either killed or captured.[774]

February 5, 1970: Israeli auxiliary ships are damaged in the Port of Eilat during a raid by Egyptian frogmen.[787]

February 9, 1970: An air battle between Israeli and Egyptian warplanes takes place, with each side losing one plane.

March 15, 1970: The first fully operational Soviet SAM site in Egypt is completed. It is part of three brigades which the Soviet Union sends to Egypt. Israeli F-4 Phantom II jets repeatedly bomb Egyptian positions in Sinai.

April 8, 1970: The Israeli Air Force carries out bombing raids against targets identified as Egyptian military installations. A group of military bases about 30 kilometers from the Suez Canal is bombed. However, in what becomes known as the Bahr el-Baqar incident, Israeli F4 Phantom II fighter jets attack a single-floor school in the Egyptian town of Bahr el-Baqar, after it was mistaken for a military installation. The school is hit by five bombs and two air-to-ground missiles, killing 46 schoolchildren and injuring over 50.[788] This incident put a definite end to the campaign, and the Israelis instead then concentrate upon Canal-side installations. The respite gives the Egyptians time to reconstruct its SAM batteries closer to the canal. Soviet flown MiG fighters provide the necessary air cover. Soviet pilots also begin approaching IAF aircraft during April 1970, but Israeli pilots have orders not to engage these aircraft, and break off whenever Soviet-piloted MiGs appear.

April, 1970: the Kuwaiti Armed Forces suffered their first Kuwaiti fatality on the Egyptian front.[789]

May, 1970: During the final days of the month, the IAF launch major air raids against Port Said, believing a large amphibious force is assembling in the town. On the 16th an Israeli aircraft is shot down in air combat, probably by a MiG-21.[790]

May 3, 1970: Twenty-one Palestinian guerrillas are killed by Israeli troops in the Jordan Valley.

June 1970: An Israeli armored raid on Syrian military positions results in "hundreds of Syrian casualties."

June 25, 1970: An Israeli A-4 Skyhawk, in an attack sortie against Egyptian forces on the Canal, is attacked and pursued by a pair of Soviet MiG-21s into Sinai. According to the Soviets, the plane was shot down, while the Israelis claim that it was damaged and forced to land at a nearby airbase.

June 27, 1970: The EAF continued to launch air raids across the canal. On June 27 around eight Egyptian Su-7s and MiG-21s attack Israeli rear areas in Sinai. According to Israel, two Egyptian aircraft were shot down. An Israeli Mirage was shot down, and the pilot was captured.[791]

June, 1970: The Kuwaiti Armed Forces suffer sixteen fatalities on the Egyptian front.

July 18, 1970: An Israeli airstrike on Egypt causes casualties among Soviet military personnel.

June 30, 1970: Soviet air defenses shoot down two Israeli F-4 Phantoms. Two pilots and a navigator are captured, while a second navigator is rescued by helicopter the following night.

July 30, 1970: A large-scale dogfight occurs between Israeli and Soviet aircraft, codenamed *Rimon 20*, involving twelve to twenty-four Soviet MiG-21s (besides the initial twelve, other MiGs are "scrambled", but it is unclear if they reach the battle in time), and twelve Israeli Dassault Mirage IIIs and four F-4 Phantom II jets. The engagement takes place west of the Suez Canal. After luring their opponents into an ambush, the Israelis shoot down four of the Soviet-piloted MiGs. A fifth is possibly hit and later crashes en route back to base. Four Soviet pilots are killed, while the IAF suffers no losses except a damaged Mirage. The Soviets respond by luring Israeli fighter jets into a counter-ambush, downing two,[792] and deploying more aircraft to Egypt. Following the Soviets' direct intervention, known as "Operation Kavkaz", Washington fears an escalation and redoubles efforts toward a peaceful resolution to the conflict.

Early August, 1970: Despite their losses, the Soviets and Egyptians manage to press the air defenses closer to the canal, shooting down a number of Israeli aircraft. The SAM batteries allow the Egyptians to move in artillery which in turn threatens the Bar Lev Line.

August 7, 1970: A cease-fire agreement is reached, forbidding either side from changing "the military status quo within zones extending 50 kilometers to the east and west of the cease-fire line." Minutes after the cease-fire, Egypt begins moving SAM batteries into the zone even though the agreement explicitly forbids new military installations. By October there are approximately one-hundred SAM sites in the zone.

September 28, 1970: President Nasser dies of a heart attack, and is succeeded by Vice President Anwar Sadat.

Casualties

According to the military historian Ze'ev Schiff, some 921 Israelis, of which 694 were soldiers and the remainder civilians, were killed on all three fronts.[793] Chaim Herzog notes a slightly lower figure of just over 600 killed and some 2,000 wounded[794] while Netanel Lorch, states that 1,424 soldiers were killed in action between the period of June 15, 1967 and August 8, 1970. Between 24[795] and 26[796] Israeli aircraft were shot down. A Soviet estimate notes aircraft losses of 40. One destroyer, the INS *Eilat*, was sunk.

As with the previous Arab–Israeli wars of 1948, 1956 and 1967, Arab losses far exceeded those of Israel, but precise figures are difficult to ascertain because official figures were never disclosed. The lowest estimate comes from the former Egyptian Army Chief of Staff, Saad el Shazly, who notes Egyptian casualties of 2,882 killed and 6,285 wounded. Historian Benny Morris states that a more realistic figure is somewhere on the scale of 10,000 soldiers and civilians killed. Ze'ev Schiff notes that at the height of the war, the Egyptians were losing some 300 soldiers daily and aerial reconnaissance photos revealed at least 1,801 freshly dug graves near the Canal zone during this period. Among Egypt's war dead was the Egyptian Army Chief of Staff, Abdul Munim Riad.

Between 98 and 114 Egyptian aircraft were shot down, though a Soviet estimate notes air losses of 60.

Several Egyptian naval vessels were sunk. The Palestinian PLO suffered 1,828 killed and 2,500 were captured. Jordan's intervention on behalf of the PLO during the Battle of Karameh cost it 40-84 killed and 108-250 injured. An estimated 58 Soviet military personnel were killed and four to five Soviet-piloted MiG-21 aircraft were shot down in aerial combat. Syrian casualties are unknown but an armored raid by Israeli forces against Syrian positions in June 1970 led to "hundreds of Syrian casualties." Cuban forces, which were deployed on the Syrian front, were estimated to have lost 180 dead and 250 wounded.

Bibliography

- Pollack, Kenneth (2002). *Arabs at War: Military Effectiveness*. University of Nebraska Press.<templatestyles src="Module:Citation/CS1/styles.css"></templatestyles>
- Bar-Simon Tov, Yaacov. *The Israeli-Egyptian War of Attrition, 1969–70*. New York: Columbia University Press, 1980.
- Dunstan, Simon (2003). *Yom Kippur War 1973: The Sinai Campaign*[797]. Osprey Publishing. ISBN 978-1-84176-221-0.<templatestyles src="Module:Citation/CS1/styles.css"></templatestyles>
- Herzog, Chaim and Gazit Shlomo. *The Arab-Israeli Wars: War and Peace in the Middle East*. New York: Vintage Books, 2004.
- Morris, Benny (1999). *Righteous Victims: A History of the Zionist-Arab Conflict, 1881–1999*. Knopf. ISBN 978-0-679-42120-7.<templatestyles src="Module:Citation/CS1/styles.css"></templatestyles>
- Nicolle, David; Cooper, Tom (2004). *Arab MiG-19 and MiG-21 Units in Combat* (First ed.). Osprey Publishing. p. 96. ISBN 978-1-84176-655-3.<templatestyles src="Module:Citation/CS1/styles.css"></templatestyles>

- Rabinovitch (2004). *The Yom Kippur War: The Epic Encounter That Transformed the Middle East*. ISBN 978-0-8052-4176-1.<templatestyles src="Module:Citation/CS1/styles.css"></templatestyles>
- Schiff, Zeev, *History of the Israeli Army 1870–1974*, Straight Arrow Books (1974). <templatestyles src="Module:Citation/CS1/styles.css" />>ISBN 0-87932-077-X.
- Whetten, Lawrence L. (1974). *The Canal War: Four-Power Conflict in the Middle East*. Cambridge, Mass.: MIT Press. ISBN 978-0-262-23069-8.<templatestyles src="Module:Citation/CS1/styles.css"></templatestyles>
- Insight team of the London *Sunday Times*, *Yom Kippur War*, Doubleday & Company (1974)

External links

 Wikimedia Commons has media related to *War of Attrition*.

- War of Attrition, 1969–1970[798], ACIG, retrieved January 2, 2007
- Jewish Virtual Library[799]
- The Three Year War, General Mohamed Fawzi[800]
- 40 Years Since The War of Attrition[801]

Jarring Mission

The **Jarring Mission** refers to efforts undertaken by Gunnar Jarring to achieve a peaceful settlement of the conflict between Israel and its Arab neighbors following the Six-Day War in 1967. He was appointed on 23 November 1967 by UN Secretary-General, U Thant, as Special Envoy under the terms of UN Security Council Resolution 242 to negotiate the implementation of the resolution.

The governments of Israel, Egypt, Jordan and Lebanon recognized Jarring's appointment and agreed to participate[802] in his shuttle diplomacy, although they differed on key points of interpretation of the resolution. The government of Syria rejected Jarring's mission on grounds that total Israeli withdrawal was a prerequisite for further negotiations.[803] After denouncing it in 1967, Syria "conditionally" accepted the resolution in March 1972.

Jarring's report was presented to the public on 4 January 1971.[804] On 8 February, he submitted to the Egyptian and Israeli governments his most detailed plan for an Egyptian-Israeli peace treaty.[805] Egypt responded by stating that it

Figure 108: *US President Richard Nixon and Israeli Prime Minister Golda Meir meeting on 1 March 1973 in the Oval Office. Nixon's National Security Advisor Henry Kissinger is to the right of Nixon.*

would "only be willing to enter into a peace agreement with Israel" after Israel agreed to a set of 7 terms including the "withdrawal of the Israeli armed forces from all the territories occupied since 5 June 1967." Israel responded that it "views favourably the expression by the UAR of its readiness to enter into a peace agreement with Israel and reiterates that it is prepared for meaningful negotiations on all subjects relevant to a peace agreement between the two countries."[806] Another government statement said "As its condition for peace, Egypt would have Israel restore its past territorial vulnerability. This Israel will never do."[807] Norman Finkelstein writes that Egypt's response was "uniformly interpreted as an affirmative reply to Jarring's aide-mémoire, explicitly stating its readiness" to have a peace agreement with Israel. Israel's refusal to agree to a full withdrawal made, in Finkelstein's view, a diplomatic settlement impossible and war inevitable.

On 28 February 1973, during a visit in Washington, D.C., the then Israeli prime minister Golda Meir agreed with the then U.S. National Security Advisor Henry Kissinger's peace proposal based on "security versus sovereignty": Israel would accept Egyptian sovereignty over all Sinai, while Egypt would accept Israeli presence in some of Sinai strategic positions. The talks continued under Jarring's auspices until 1973, but bore no results. After 1973, the Jarring Mission was replaced by bilateral and multilateral peace conferences.

The impasse in Jarring's efforts appears to be related to differing interpretations of the Security Council resolution. Israel insisted that any efforts should be undertaken with the goal of direct peace negotiations between Israel and the Arab states, and that no territory concessions could be contemplated without the prospect of a lasting peace. The Arab states and the Soviet Union maintained that there would be no direct talks with Israel (in keeping with the Khartoum Resolution), and that withdrawals were a pre-condition for any further talks.

At the time of his appointment, Jarring was the Swedish ambassador to the Soviet Union and he maintained his ambassadorship during the mission. Critics since then have pointed out that Jarring had to manage a difficult conflict of interest since he had to maintain his duties as Swedish ambassador to the Soviet Union while trying to facilitate talks in which the Soviet Union had its own interests.

An unpublished study, reported in 2010, of the Jarring Mission claims that Jarring's efforts actually paved the way for the future peace talks, and thus were not as insignificant as it is common to assume.[808]

Further reading

- Finkelstein, Norman G. (2003). *Image and Reality of the Israel–Palestine Conflict (2nd edition)*. Verso. ISBN 1-85984-442-1.<templatestyles src="Module:Citation/CS1/styles.css"></templatestyles>
- Mørk, Hulda Kjeang. "The Jarring Mission: A Study of the UN Peace Effort in the Middle East, 1967-1971"[809] (pdf). Retrieved 2008-03-20.<templatestyles src="Module:Citation/CS1/styles.css"></templatestyles>Wikipedia:Link rot
- Touval, Saadia (1982). *The Peace Brokers: Mediators in the Arab-Israeli Conflict, 1948-1979*. Princeton University Press. ISBN 0-691-10138-8.<templatestyles src="Module:Citation/CS1/styles.css"></templatestyles>
- Shlaim, Avi (2007). *Lion of Jordan; The Life of King Hussein in War and Peace*. Allen Lane. ISBN 978-0-7139-9777-4.<templatestyles src="Module:Citation/CS1/styles.css"></templatestyles>
- Reuven Pedatzur, "Seeds of Peace", Haaretz[810]

Munich massacre

<indicator name="pp-default"> 🔒 </indicator>

1972 Munich Massacre	
One of the most reproduced photos taken during the siege shows a kidnapper on the balcony attached to Munich Olympic village Building 31, where members of the Israeli Olympic team and delegation were quartered.	

Location	Munich, West Germany
Coordinates	48°10′47″N 11°32′57″E[811]Coordinates: 48°10′47″N 11°32′57″E[811]
Date	5–6 September 1972 4:31 am – 12:04 am (UTC+1)
Target	Israeli Olympic team
Attack type	• Hostage-taking • Mass murder • Massacre
Deaths	17 total (including perpetrators) • 6 Israeli coaches • 5 Israeli athletes • 5 Black September members • 1 West German police officer
Perpetrators	Black September
Motive	Israeli–Palestinian conflict

The **Munich massacre** was an attack during the 1972 Summer Olympics in Munich, West Germany, in which the Palestinian terrorist group Black September took eleven Israeli Olympic team members hostage and killed them along with a West German police officer.

Shortly after the crisis began, a Black September spokesman demanded that 234 Palestinian prisoners jailed in Israel and the West German–held founders of the Red Army Faction, Andreas Baader and Ulrike Meinhof, be released. Black September called the operation *"Iqrit and Biram"*, after two Palestinian Christian villages whose inhabitants were expelled by the Israel Defense Forces (IDF) during the 1948 Arab–Israeli War. The Black September commander, Luttif Afif, was born to Jewish and Christian parents. His group was associated with secular nationalism, working for the rights of Palestinians in Israel. West German neo-Nazis gave the group logistical assistance.

Police officers killed five of the eight Black September members during a failed attempt to rescue the hostages. A West German policeman was also killed in the crossfire. The other three Palestinian hijackers were captured. The next month, however, following the hijacking of Lufthansa Flight 615, the West German government released them in a hostage exchange. Mossad responded with the 1973 Israeli raid on Lebanon and Operation Wrath of God, tracking down and killing Palestinians suspected of involvement in the Munich massacre.

Two days prior to the start of the 2016 Summer Olympics, in a ceremony led by Brazilian and Israeli officials, the International Olympic Committee honored the eleven Israelis that were killed at Munich.[812]

Prelude

At the time of the hostage-taking, the 1972 Summer Olympics were in their second week. The West German Olympic Organizing Committee had hoped to discard the military image of Germany. The Committee was wary of the image portrayed by the 1936 Summer Olympics, which Nazi dictator Adolf Hitler used for his benefit. Security personnel known as Olys were inconspicuous and prepared to deal mostly with ticket fraud and drunkenness. The documentary film *One Day in September* claims that security in the athletes' village was unfit for the Games and that athletes could come and go as they pleased. Athletes could sneak past security, and go to other countries' rooms, by going over the fencing that encompassed the village.

The absence of armed personnel had worried Israeli delegation head Shmuel Lalkin even before his team arrived in Munich. In later interviews with journalists Serge Groussard and Aaron J. Klein, Lalkin said that he had expressed concern with the relevant authorities about his team's lodgings. The team was housed in a relatively isolated part of the Olympic Village, on the ground floor of a small building close to a gate, which Lalkin felt made his team particularly vulnerable to an outside assault. The West German authorities apparently assured Lalkin that extra security would be provided to look after the Israeli team, but Lalkin doubts that any additional measures were ever taken.

Olympic organizers asked West German forensic psychologist Georg Sieber to create 26 terrorism scenarios to aid the organizers in planning security. His "Situation 21" accurately forecast armed Palestinians invading the Israeli delegation's quarters, killing and taking hostages, and demanding Israel's release of prisoners and a plane to leave West Germany. Organizers balked against preparing for Situation 21 and the other scenarios, since guarding the Games against them would have gone against the goal of "Carefree Games" without heavy security.

Accusation of German foreknowledge of the attack

The German weekly news magazine *Der Spiegel* wrote in a 2012 cover story that the West German authorities had a tip-off from a Palestinian informant in Beirut three weeks before the massacre. The informant told West Germany that Palestinians were planning an "incident" at the Olympic Games, and the Foreign Ministry in Bonn viewed the tip-off seriously enough to pass it to the secret service in Munich and urge that "all possible security measures" be taken.

But, according to *Der Spiegel*, the authorities failed to act on the tip, and have never acknowledged it in the following 40 years. The magazine said that this is only part of a 40-year cover-up by the German authorities of the mishandling of its response to the massacre.

Hostage-taking

On Monday evening, 4 September, the Israeli athletes enjoyed a night out, watching a performance of *Fiddler on the Roof* and dining with the star of the play, Israeli actor Shmuel Rodensky, before returning to the Olympic Village.[813] On the return trip in the team bus Lalkin denied his 13-year-old son — who had befriended weightlifter Yossef Romano and wrestler Eliezer Halfin — permission to spend the night in their apartment at Connollystraße 31, which probably saved the boy's life.[814]

At 4:30 am local time on 5 September, as the athletes slept, eight tracksuit-clad members of the Black September faction of the Palestine Liberation Organization, carrying duffel bags loaded with AKM assault rifles, Tokarev pistols, and grenades, scaled a 2-metre (6 $^1/_2$ ft) chain-link fence with the assistance of unsuspecting athletes who were also sneaking into the Olympic Village. The athletes were originally identified as Americans, but were claimed to be Canadians decades later.

Figure 109: *The site where the hostages were taken is almost unchanged today. The window of Apartment 1 is to the left of and below the balcony.*

Once inside, the Black September members used stolen keys to enter two apartments being used by the Israeli team at Connollystraße 31. Yossef Gutfreund, a wrestling referee, was awakened by a faint scratching noise at the door of Apartment 1, which housed the Israeli coaches and officials. When he investigated, he saw the door begin to open and masked men with guns on the other side. He shouted a warning to his sleeping roommates and threw his 135 kg (300 lb) weight against the door in a futile attempt to stop the intruders from forcing their way in. Gutfreund's actions gave his roommate, weightlifting coach Tuvia Sokolovsky, enough time to smash a window and escape. Wrestling coach Moshe Weinberg fought the intruders, who shot him through his cheek and then forced him to help them find more hostages.

Leading the intruders past Apartment 2, Weinberg lied by telling them that the residents of the apartment were not Israelis. Instead, Weinberg led them to Apartment 3; there, the gunmen corralled six wrestlers and weightlifters as additional hostages. It is possible that Weinberg had hoped that the stronger men would have a better chance of fighting off the attackers than those in Apartment 2, but they were all surprised in their sleep.

As the athletes from Apartment 3 were marched back to the coaches' apartment, the wounded Weinberg again attacked the gunmen, allowing one of his wrestlers, Gad Tsobari, to escape via the underground parking garage. Weinberg knocked unconscious one of the intruders and slashed at another with a fruit knife but failed to draw blood before being shot to death.

Weightlifter Yossef Romano, a veteran of the Six-Day War in June 1967, also attacked and wounded one of the intruders before being shot and killed. In its publication of 1 December 2015, *The New York Times* reported that Romano was castrated after he was shot.

The gunmen were left with nine hostages. They were, in addition to Gutfreund, sharpshooting coach Kehat Shorr, track and field coach Amitzur Shapira, fencing master Andre Spitzer, weightlifting judge Yakov Springer, wrestlers Eliezer Halfin and Mark Slavin, and weightlifters David Berger and Ze'ev Friedman. Berger was an expatriate American with dual citizenship; Slavin, at 18 the youngest of the hostages, had only arrived in Israel from the Soviet Union four months before the Olympic Games began. Gutfreund, physically the largest of the hostages, was bound to a chair (Groussard describes him as being tied up like a mummy); the rest were lined up four apiece on the two beds in Springer and Shapira's room, and bound at the wrists and ankles and then to each other. Romano's bullet-riddled corpse was left at his bound comrades' feet as a warning. Several of the hostages were beaten during the stand-off, with some suffering broken bones as a result.

Of the other members of Israel's team, racewalker Shaul Ladany had been jolted awake in Apartment 2 by Gutfreund's screams. He jumped from the second-story balcony of his room and fled to the American dormitory, awakening U.S. track coach Bill Bowerman and informing him of the attack. Ladany, a survivor of the Bergen-Belsen concentration camp, was the first person to spread the alert. The other four residents of Apartment 2 (sharpshooters Henry Hershkowitz and Zelig Shtroch, fencers Dan Alon and Yehuda Weisenstein), plus chef de mission Shmuel Lalkin and the two team doctors, hid and eventually fled the besieged building. The two female members of Israel's Olympic team, sprinter and hurdler Esther Shahamorov and swimmer Shlomit Nir, were housed in a separate part of the Olympic Village. Three more members of Israel's Olympic team, two sailors and their manager, were housed in Kiel, 900 kilometres (600 mi) from Munich.Wikipedia:Citation needed

The attackers were reported to be Palestinian terrorists from refugee camps in Lebanon, Syria, and Jordan. They were identified as Luttif Afif (using the codename Issa), the leader (three of Issa's brothers were also reportedly members of Black September, two of them in Israeli jails), his deputy Yusuf Nazzal ("Tony"), and junior members Afif Ahmed Hamid ("Paolo"), Khalid Jawad ("Salah"), Ahmed Chic Thaa ("Abu Halla"), Mohammed Safady ("Badran"), Adnan Al-Gashey ("Denawi"), and Al-Gashey's cousin, Jamal Al-Gashey ("Samir").

According to author Simon Reeve, Afif (the son of a Jewish mother and Christian father), Nazzal, and one of their confederates, had all worked in various capacities in the Olympic Village, and had spent a couple of weeks scouting for their potential target. A member of the Uruguayan Olympic delegation, which shared housing with the Israelis, claimed that he found Nazzal inside 31 Connollystraße less than 24 hours before the attack, but since he was recognized as a worker in the Village, nothing was thought of it at the time. The other members of the group entered Munich via train and plane in the days before the attack. All the members of the Uruguay and Hong Kong Olympic teams, which also shared the building with the Israelis, were released unharmed during the crisis.Wikipedia:Citation needed

International reaction

On 5 September, Golda Meir, then Prime Minister of Israel, appealed to other countries to "save our citizens and condemn the unspeakable criminal acts committed." She also stated, "if we [Israel] should give in, then no Israeli anywhere in the world shall feel that his life is safe ... it's blackmail of the worst kind."

King Hussein of Jordan, the only leader of an Arab country to denounce the attack publicly, called it a "savage crime against civilization ... perpetrated by sick minds."[815]

U.S. President Richard Nixon privately discussed a number of possible American responses, such as declaring a national day of mourning (favored by Secretary of State William P. Rogers), or having Nixon fly to the athletes' funerals. Nixon and Henry Kissinger decided instead to press the United Nations to take steps against international terrorism.

Negotiations

The hostage-takers demanded the release of 234 Palestinians and non-Arabs jailed in Israel, along with two West German insurgents held by the West German penitentiary system, Andreas Baader and Ulrike Meinhof, who were founders of the West German Red Army Faction. The hostage-takers threw the body of Weinberg out of the front door of the residence to demonstrate their resolve. Israel's response was immediate and absolute: there would be no negotiation. Israel's official policy at the time was to refuse to negotiate with terrorists under any circumstances, as according to the Israeli government such negotiations would give an incentive to future attacks.

It has been claimedWikipedia:Manual of Style/Words to watch#Unsupported attributions that the German authorities, under the leadership of Chancellor

Willy Brandt and Minister for the Interior Hans-Dietrich Genscher, rejected Israel's offer to send an Israeli special forces unit to West Germany.[816] The Bavarian interior minister Bruno Merk, who headed the crisis centre jointly with Genscher and Munich's police chief Manfred Schreiber, denies that such an Israeli offer ever existed.

According to journalist John K. Cooley, the hostage situation presented an extremely difficult political situation for the Germans because the hostages were Jewish. Cooley reported that the Germans offered the Palestinians an unlimited amount of money for the release of the athletes, as well as the substitution by high-ranking Germans. However, the kidnappers refused both offers.

Munich police chief Manfred Schreiber, and Bruno Merk, interior minister of Bavaria, negotiated directly with the kidnappers, repeating the offer of an unlimited amount of money. According to Cooley, the reply was that "money means nothing to us; our lives mean nothing to us." Magdi Gohary and Mohammad Khadif, both Egyptian advisers to the Arab League, and A.D. Touny, an Egyptian member of the International Olympic Committee (IOC) also helped try to win concessions from the kidnappers, but to no avail. However, the negotiators apparently were able to convince the terrorists that their demands were being considered, as "Issa" granted a total of five deadline extensions. Elsewhere in the village, athletes carried on as normal, seemingly oblivious of the events unfolding nearby. The Games continued until mounting pressure on the IOC forced a suspension some 12 hours after the first athlete had been murdered. United States marathon runner Frank Shorter, observing the unfolding events from the balcony of his nearby lodging, was quoted as saying, "Imagine those poor guys over there. Every five minutes a psycho with a machine gun says, 'Let's kill 'em now,' and someone else says, 'No, let's wait a while.' How long could you stand that?"

At 4:30 pm, a squad of 38 West German police officers was dispatched to the Olympic Village. Dressed in Olympic sweatsuits (some also wearing Stahlhelme and carrying Walther MP sub-machine guns), they were members of the German border police, although according to former Munich policeman Heinz Hohensinn they were regular Munich police officers, with no experience in combat or hostage rescue. Their plan was to crawl down from the ventilation shafts and kill the terrorists. The police took up positions awaiting the codeword "Sunshine", which upon hearing, they were to begin the assault. In the meantime, camera crews filmed the actions of the officers from the German apartments, and broadcast the images live on television. Thus, the terrorists were able to watch the police prepare to attack. Footage shows one of the kidnappers peering from the balcony door while one of the police officers stood on the roof less than 20 ft (6 m) from him. In the end, after "Issa" threatened to kill two of the hostages, the police retreated from the premises.[817]

At one point during the crisis, the negotiators demanded direct contact with the hostages to satisfy themselves the Israelis were still alive. Fencing coach Andre Spitzer, who spoke fluent German, and shooting coach Kehat Shorr, the senior member of the Israeli delegation, had a brief conversation with West German officials while standing at the second-floor window of the besieged building, with two kidnappers holding guns on them. When Spitzer attempted to answer a question, he was clubbed with the butt of an AK-47 in full view of international television cameras and pulled away from the window. A few minutes later, Hans-Dietrich Genscher and Walter Tröger, the mayor of the Olympic Village, were briefly allowed into the apartments to speak with the hostages. Tröger spoke of being very moved by the dignity with which the Israelis held themselves, and that they seemed resigned to their fate.

Tröger noticed that several of the hostages, especially Gutfreund, showed signs of having suffered physical abuse at the hands of the kidnappers, and that David Berger had been shot in his left shoulder. While being debriefed by the crisis team, Genscher and Tröger told them that they had seen "four or five" attackers inside the apartment. Fatefully, these numbers were accepted as definitive. While Genscher and Tröger were talking with the hostages, Kehat Shorr had told the West Germans that the Israelis would not object to being flown to an Arab country, provided that strict guarantees for their safety were made by the Germans and whichever nation they landed in. At 6 pm Munich time, the Palestinians issued a new dictate, demanding transportation to Cairo.Wikipedia:Citation needed

Failed rescue

Ambush plan

The authorities feigned agreement to the Cairo demandWikipedia:Please clarify (although Egyptian Prime Minister Aziz Sedki had already told the West German authorities that the Egyptians did not wish to become involved in the hostage crisis).[818]

Two Bell UH-1 military helicopters were to transport the terrorists and hostages to nearby Fürstenfeldbruck, a NATO airbase. Initially, the perpetrators' plan was to go to Riem, which was the international airport near Munich at the time, but the negotiators convinced them that Fürstenfeldbruck would be more practical. The authorities, who preceded the Black Septemberists and hostages in a third helicopter, had an ulterior motive: they planned an armed assault at the airport.Wikipedia:Citation needed

Realizing that the Palestinians and Israelis had to walk 200 metres through the underground garages to reach the helicopters, the West German police saw another opportunity to ambush the perpetrators, and placed sharpshooters there. But "Issa" insisted on checking the route first. He and some other Palestinians walked pointing their AK-47s at Schreiber, Tröger and Genscher. At that time, the police snipers were lying behind cars in the sidestreets, and when they approached the latter crawled away, making noise in the process. Thus the terrorists were immediately alerted of the dangerous presence, and they decided to use a bus instead of walking. The bus arrived at 10:00 pm and drove the contingent to the helicopters. "Issa" checked them with a flashlight before boarding in groups.[819]

Five West German policemen were deployed around the airport in sniper roles—three on the roof of the control tower, one hidden behind a service truck and one behind a small signal tower at ground level. However, none of them had any special sniper training, nor any special weapon (being equipped with the H&K G3, the ordinary battle rifle of the German Armed Forces without optics or night vision devices). The soldiersCategory:Articles contradicting other articles were selected because they shot competitively on weekends. During a subsequent German investigation, an officer identified as "Sniper No. 2" stated: "I am of the opinion that I am not a sharpshooter."

The members of the crisis team—Schreiber, Genscher, Merk and Schreiber's deputy Georg Wolf—supervised and observed the attempted rescue from the airport control tower. Cooley, Reeve and Groussard all place Mossad chief Zvi Zamir and Victor Cohen, one of Zamir's senior assistants, at the scene as well, but as observers only. Zamir has stated repeatedly in interviews over the years that he was never consulted by the Germans at any time during the rescue attempt and thought that his presence actually made the Germans uncomfortable.Wikipedia:Citation needed

A Boeing 727 jet was positioned on the tarmac with sixteen West German police inside dressed as flight crew. It was agreed that "Issa" and "Tony" would inspect the plane. The plan was that the West Germans would overpower them as they boarded, giving the snipers a chance to kill the remaining terrorists at the helicopters. These were believed to number no more than two or three, according to what Genscher and Tröger had seen inside 31 Connollystraße. However, during the transfer from the bus to the helicopters, the crisis team discovered that there were actually eight of them.Wikipedia:Citation needed

Failure

At the last minute, as the helicopters were arriving at Fürstenfeldbruck, the West German police aboard the airplane voted to abandon their mission, without consulting the central command. This left only the five sharpshooters to try to overpower a larger and more heavily armed group. At that point, Colonel Ulrich Wegener, Genscher's senior aide and later the founder of the elite German counter-terrorist unit GSG 9, said "I'm sure this will blow the whole affair!".

The helicopters landed just after 10:30 pm and the four pilots and six of the kidnappers emerged. While four of the Black September members held the pilots at gunpoint (breaking an earlier promise that they would not take any Germans hostage), Issa and Tony walked over to inspect the jet, only to find it empty. Realizing they had been lured into a trap, they sprinted back toward the helicopters. As they ran past the control tower, Sniper 3 took one last opportunity to eliminate "Issa", which would have left the group leaderless. However, due to the poor lighting, he struggled to see his target and missed, hitting "Tony" in the thigh instead. Meanwhile, the West German authorities gave the order for snipers positioned nearby to open fire, which occurred around 11:00 pm.

In the ensuing chaos, Ahmed Chic Thaa and Afif Ahmed Hamid, the two kidnappers holding the helicopter pilots, were killed while the remaining gunmen—some possibly already wounded—scrambled to safety, returning fire from behind and beneath the helicopters, out of the snipers' line of sight, shooting out many of the airport lights. A West German policeman in the control tower, Anton Fliegerbauer, was killed by the gunfire. The helicopter pilots fled; the hostages, tied up inside the craft, could not. During the gun battle, the hostages secretly worked on loosening their bonds and teethmarks were found on some of the ropes after the gunfire had ended.

Massacre

The West Germans had not arranged for armored personnel carriers ahead of time and only at this point were they called in to break the deadlock. Since the roads to the airport had not been cleared, the carriers became stuck in traffic and finally arrived around midnight. With their appearance, the kidnappers felt the shift in the status quo, and possibly panicked at the thought of the failure of their operation.

At four minutes past midnight of 6 September, one of them (likely Issa) turned on the hostages in the eastern helicopter and fired at them with a Kalashnikov assault rifle from point-blank range. Springer, Halfin and Friedman were killed instantly; Berger, shot twice in the leg, is believed to have survived the initial onslaught (as his autopsy later found that he had died of smoke inhalation). The attacker then pulled the pin on a hand grenade and tossed it into the cockpit; the ensuing explosion destroyed the helicopter and incinerated the bound Israelis inside.

Issa then dashed across the tarmac and began firing at the police, who killed him with return fire. Another, Khalid Jawad, attempted to escape and was gunned down by one of the snipers. What happened to the remaining hostages is still a matter of dispute. A German police investigation indicated that one of their snipers and a few of the hostages may have been shot inadvertently by the police. However, a *Time* magazine reconstruction of the long-suppressed Bavarian prosecutor's report indicates that a third kidnapper (Reeve identifies Adnan Al-Gashey) stood at the door of the western helicopter and raked the remaining five hostages with machine gun fire; Gutfreund, Shorr, Slavin, Spitzer and Shapira were shot an average of four times each.

Of the four hostages in the eastern helicopter, only Ze'ev Friedman's body was relatively intact; he had been blown clear of the helicopter by the explosion. In some cases, the exact cause of death for the hostages in the eastern helicopter was difficult to establish because the rest of the corpses were burned almost beyond recognition in the explosion and subsequent fire. Three of the remaining men lay on the ground, one of them feigning death, and were captured by police. Jamal Al-Gashey had been shot through his right wrist, and Mohammed Safady had sustained a flesh wound to his leg. Adnan Al-Gashey had escaped injury completely. Tony escaped the scene, but was tracked down with police dogs 40 minutes later in an airbase parking lot. Cornered and bombarded with tear gas, he was shot dead after a brief gunfight. By around 1:30 am on 6 September, the battle was over.

Outcome

Initial news reports, published all over the world, indicated that all the hostages were alive, and that all the attackers had been killed. Only later did a representative for the International Olympic Committee (IOC) suggest that "initial reports were overly optimistic." Jim McKay, who was covering the Olympics that year for the American Broadcasting Company (ABC), had taken on the job of reporting the events as Roone Arledge fed them into his earpiece. At 3:24 am, McKay received the official confirmation:

<templatestyles src="Template:Quote/styles.css"/>

> We just got the final word ... you know, when I was a kid, my father used to say "Our greatest hopes and our worst fears are seldom realized." Our worst fears have been realized tonight. They've now said that there were eleven hostages. Two were killed in their rooms yesterday morning, nine were killed at the airport tonight. They're all gone.

Several sources listed Ladany as having been killed. Ladany recalled later:

<templatestyles src="Template:Quote/styles.css"/>

> The impact did not hit me at the time, when we were in Munich. It was when we arrived back in Israel. At the airport in Lod there was a huge crowd—maybe 20,000 people—and each one of us, the survivors, stood by one of the coffins on the runway. Some friends came up to me and tried to kiss me and hug me as if I was almost a ghost that came back alive. It was then that I really grasped what had happened and the emotion hit me.

Criticism

Author Simon Reeve, among others, writes that the shootout with the well-trained Black September members showed an egregious lack of preparation on the part of the German authorities. They were not prepared to deal with this sort of situation. This costly lesson led directly to the founding, less than two months later, of police counter-terrorism branch GSG 9. German authorities made a number of mistakes. First, because of restrictions in the post-war West German constitution, the army could not participate in the attempted rescue, as the German armed forces are not allowed to operate inside Germany during peacetime. The responsibility was entirely in the hands of the Munich police and the Bavarian authorities.[820]Wikipedia:Please clarify

It was known a half-hour before the hostages and kidnappers had even arrived at Fürstenfeldbruck that the number of the latter was larger than first believed. Despite this new information, Schreiber decided to continue with the rescue operation as originally planned and the new information could not reach the snipers since they had no radios.[821]

It is a basic tenet of sniping operations that there are enough snipers (at least two for each *known* target, or in this case a minimum of ten) deployed to neutralize as many of the attackers as possible with the first volley of shots.[822] The 2006 *National Geographic* Channel's *Seconds From Disaster* profile on the massacre stated that the helicopters were supposed to land sideways and to the west of the control tower, a maneuver which would have allowed the snipers clear shots into them as the kidnappers threw open the helicopter doors. Instead, the helicopters were landed facing the control tower and at the centre of the airstrip. This not only gave them a place to hide after the gunfight began, but put Snipers 1 and 2 in the line of fire of the other three snipers on the control tower. The snipers were denied valuable shooting opportunities as a result of the positioning of the helicopters, stacking the odds against what were effectively three snipers versus eight heavily armed gunmen.Wikipedia:Citation needed

According to the same program, the crisis committee delegated to make decisions on how to deal with the incident consisted of Bruno Merk (the Bavarian interior minister), Hans-Dietrich Genscher (the West German interior minister) and Manfred Schreiber (Munich's Chief of Police); in other words, two politicians and one tactician. The program mentioned that a year before the Games, Schreiber had participated in another hostage crisis (a failed bank robbery) in which he ordered a marksman to shoot one of the perpetrators, managing only to wound the robber. As a result, the robbers shot an innocent woman dead. Schreiber was consequently charged with involuntary manslaughter. An investigation ultimately cleared him of any wrongdoing, but the program suggested that the prior incident affected his judgment in the subsequent Olympic hostage crisis.Wikipedia:Citation needed

As mentioned earlier, the five German snipers at Fürstenfeldbruck did not have radio contact with one another (nor with the German authorities conducting the rescue operation) and therefore were unable to coordinate their fire. The only contact the snipers had with the operational leadership was with Georg Wolf, who was lying next to the three snipers on the control tower giving orders directly to them.[823] The two snipers at ground level had been given vague instructions to shoot when the other snipers began shooting, and were basically left to fend for themselves.[824]

In addition, the snipers did not have the proper equipment for this hostage rescue operation. The Heckler & Koch G3 battle rifles used were considered by several experts to be inadequate for the distance at which the snipers were trying to shoot. The G3, the standard service rifle of the Bundeswehr at that time, had a 18-inch (460 mm) barrel; at the distances the snipers were required to shoot, a 27-inch (690 mm) barrel would have ensured far greater accuracy.[825] None of the rifles were equipped with telescopic or infrared sights. Additionally, none of the snipers were equipped with a steel helmet or bullet-proof vest.[826] No armored vehicles were at the scene at Fürstenfeldbruck, and were only called in after the gunfight was well underway.[827]

There were also numerous tactical errors. As mentioned earlier, "Sniper 2", who was stationed behind the signal tower, wound up directly in the line of fire of his fellow snipers on the control tower, without any protective gear and without any other police being aware of his location. Because of this, "Sniper 2" didn't fire a single shot until late in the gunfight, when hostage-taker Khalid Jawad attempted to escape on foot and ran right at the exposed sniper. "Sniper 2" killed the fleeing perpetrator but was in turn badly wounded by a fellow police officer, who was unaware that he was shooting at one of his own men. One of the helicopter pilots, Gunnar Ebel, was lying near "Sniper 2" and was also wounded by friendly fire. Both Ebel and the sniper recovered from their injuries.[828]

Many of the errors made by the Germans during the rescue attempt were ultimately detailed by Heinz Hohensinn, who had participated in Operation Sunshine earlier that day. He stated in *One Day in September* that he had been selected to pose as a crew member. He and his fellow policemen understood that it was a suicide mission, so the group unanimously voted to flee the plane. None of them were reprimanded for that desertion.[829]

Aftermath

The bodies of the five Palestinian attackers—Afif, Nazzal, Chic Thaa, Hamid and Jamal—killed during the Fürstenfeldbruck gun battle were delivered to Libya, where they received heroes' funerals and were buried with full military honours. On 8 September, Israeli planes bombed ten PLO bases in Syria and Lebanon in response to the massacre, killing scores of militants and civilians.[830]

The three surviving Black September gunmen had been arrested after the Fürstenfeldbruck gunfight, and were being held in a Munich prison for trial. On 29 October, Lufthansa Flight 615 was hijacked and threatened to be blown up if the Munich attackers were not released. Safady and the Al-Gasheys were immediately released by West Germany, receiving a tumultuous welcome when they touched down in Libya and (as seen in *One Day in September*) giving their own firsthand account of their operation at a press conference broadcast worldwide.

Further international investigations into the Lufthansa Flight 615 incident have produced theories of a secret agreement between the German government and Black September release of the surviving terrorists in exchange for assurances of no further attacks on Germany.

Effect on the Games

In the wake of the hostage-taking, competition was eventually suspended for the first time in modern Olympic history, after public criticism of the Olympic Committee's decision to continue the games. On 6 September, a memorial service attended by 80,000 spectators and 3,000 athletes was held in the Olympic Stadium. IOC President Avery Brundage made little reference to the murdered athletes during a speech praising the strength of the Olympic movement and equating the attack on the Israeli sportsmen with the recent arguments about encroaching professionalism and disallowing Rhodesia's participation in the Games, which outraged many listeners. The victims' families were represented by Andre Spitzer's widow Ankie, Moshe Weinberg's mother, and a cousin of Weinberg, Carmel Eliash. During the memorial service, Eliash collapsed and died of a heart attack.

Many of the 80,000 people who filled the Olympic Stadium for West Germany's football match with Hungary carried noisemakers and waved flags, but when several spectators unfurled a banner reading "17 dead, already forgotten?" security officers removed the sign and expelled those responsible from the grounds. During the memorial service, the Olympic Flag was flown at half-staff, along with the flags of most of the other competing nations at the request of Willy Brandt. Ten Arab nations objected to their flags being lowered to honor murdered Israelis; their flags were restored to the tops of their flagpoles almost immediately.

Willi Daume, president of the Munich organizing committee, initially sought to cancel the remainder of the Games, but in the afternoon Brundage and others who wished to continue the Games prevailed, stating that they could not let the incident halt the Games. Brundage stated "The Games must go on, and we must ... and we must continue our efforts to keep them clean, pure and honest." The decision was endorsed by the Israeli government and Israeli Olympic team chef de mission Shmuel Lalkin.

On 6 September, after the memorial service, the remaining members of the Israeli team withdrew from the Games and left Munich. All Jewish sportsmen were placed under guard. Mark Spitz, the American swimming star who had already completed his competitions, left Munich during the hostage crisis (it was feared that as a prominent Jew, Spitz might now be a kidnapping target). The Egyptian team left the Games on 7 September, stating they feared reprisals.[831] The Philippine and Algerian teams also left the Games, as did some members of the Dutch and Norwegian teams. American marathon runner Kenny Moore, who wrote about the incident for *Sports Illustrated*, quoted Dutch distance runner Jos Hermens as saying "It's quite simple. We were invited to a party, and if someone comes to the party and shoots people, how can you stay?" Many athletes, dazed by the tragedy, similarly felt that their desire to compete had been destroyed, although they stayed at the Games.Wikipedia:Citation needed

Four years later at the 1976 Summer Olympics in Montreal, the Israeli team commemorated the massacre: when they entered the stadium at the Opening Ceremony, their national flag was adorned with a black ribbon.

The families of some victims have asked the IOC to establish a permanent memorial to the athletes. The IOC has declined, saying that to introduce a specific reference to the victims could "alienate other members of the Olympic community," according to the BBC.[832] Alex Gilady, an Israeli IOC official, told the BBC: "We must consider what this could do to other members of the delegations that are hostile to Israel."

The IOC rejected an international campaign in support of a minute of silence at the Opening Ceremony of the 2012 London Olympics in honour of the Israeli victims on the 40th anniversary of the massacre. Jacques Rogge, the IOC President, said it would be "inappropriate," although the opening ceremony included a memorium for the victims of the 7 July 2005 London bombings. Speaking of the decision, Olympian Shaul Ladany, who survived the attack, commented: "I do not understand. I do not understand, and I do not accept it."

In 2014 the International Olympic Committee agreed to contribute $250,000 towards a memorial to the murdered Israeli athletes. After 44 years, the IOC commemorated the victims of the Munich massacre for the first time in the Rio 2016 Olympic Village on 4 August 2016.[833]

There is a memorial outside the Olympic stadium in Munich in the form of a stone tablet at the bridge linking the stadium to the former Olympic village. There is a memorial tablet to the slain Israelis outside the front door of their former lodging at 31 Connollystraße. On 15 October 1999 (almost a year before the Sydney 2000 Games), a memorial plaque was unveiled in one of the large light towers (Tower 14) outside the Sydney Olympic Stadium.

Israeli response

Golda Meir and the Israeli Defense Committee secretly authorized the Mossad to track down and kill those allegedly responsible for the Munich massacre.[834] The accusation that this was motivated by a desire for vengeance was disputed by Zvi Zamir, who described the mission as "putting an end to the type of terror that was perpetrated" in Europe.[835] To this end Mossad set up a number of special teams to locate and kill these fedayeen, aided by the agency's stations in Europe.[836]

In a February 2006 interview, former Mossad chief Zvi Zamir answered direct questions:

<templatestyles src="Template:Quote/styles.css"/>

> *Was there no element of vengeance in the decision to take action against the terrorists?*
>
> *No. We were not engaged in vengeance. We are accused of having been guided by a desire for vengeance. That is nonsense. What we did was to concretely prevent in the future. We acted against those who thought that they would continue to perpetrate acts of terror. I am not saying that those who were involved in Munich were not marked for death. They definitely deserved to die. But we were not dealing with the past; we concentrated on the future.*
>
> *'Did you not receive a directive from Golda Meir along the lines of 'take revenge on those responsible for Munich?*

> *Golda abhorred the necessity that was imposed on us to carry out the operations. Golda never told me to 'take revenge on those who were responsible for Munich.' No one told me that.*

The Israeli mission later became known as *Operation Wrath of God* or *Mivtza Za'am Ha'El*. Reeve quotes General Aharon Yariv—who, he writes, was the general overseer of the operation—as stating that after Munich the Israeli government felt it had no alternative but to exact justice.

<templatestyles src="Template:Quote/styles.css"/>

> *We had no choice. We had to make them stop, and there was no other way ... we are not very proud about it. But it was a question of sheer necessity. We went back to the old biblical rule of an eye for an eye ... I approach these problems not from a moral point of view, but, hard as it may sound, from a cost-benefit point of view. If I'm very hard-headed, I can say, what is the political benefit in killing this person? Will it bring us nearer to peace? Will it bring us nearer to an understanding with the Palestinians or not? In most cases I don't think it will. But in the case of Black September we had no other choice and it worked. Is it morally acceptable? One can debate that question. Is it politically vital? It was.*

Benny Morris writes that a target list was created using information from "turned" PLO personnel and friendly European intelligence services. Once completed, a wave of assassinations of suspected Black September operatives began across Europe. On 9 April 1973, Israel launched Operation "Spring of Youth", a joint Mossad–IDF operation in Beirut. The targets were Mohammad Yusuf al-Najjar (Abu Yusuf), head of Fatah's intelligence arm, which ran Black September, according to Morris; Kamal Adwan, who headed the PLO's Western Sector, which controlled PLO action inside Israel; and Kamal Nassir, the PLO spokesman. A group of Sayeret commandos were taken in nine missile boats and a small fleet of patrol boats to a deserted Lebanese beach, before driving in two cars to downtown Beirut, where they killed Najjar, Adwan and Nassir. Two further detachments of commandos blew up the PFLP's headquarters in Beirut and a Fatah explosives plant. The leader of the commando team that conducted the operations was Ehud Barak.Wikipedia:Citation needed

On 21 July 1973, in the Lillehammer affair, a team of Mossad agents mistakenly killed Ahmed Bouchiki, a Moroccan man unrelated to the Munich attack, in Lillehammer, Norway,[837] after an informant mistakenly said Bouchiki was Ali Hassan Salameh, the head of Force 17 and a Black September operative. Five Mossad agents, including two women, were captured by the Norwegian authorities, while others managed to slip away. The five were convicted of the killing and imprisoned, but were released and returned to Israel in 1975. The Mossad later found Ali Hassan Salameh in Beirut and killed him on 22 January

1979 with a remote-controlled car bomb. The attack killed four passersby and injured 18 others. According to CIA officer Duane "Dewey" Claridge, chief of operations of the CIA Near East Division from 1975 to 1978, in mid-1976, Salameh offered Americans assistance and protection with Arafat's blessings during the American embassy pull-out from Beirut during the down-spiraling chaos of the Lebanese Civil War. There was a general feeling that Americans could be trusted. However, the scene of cooperation came to an end abruptly after the assassination of Salameh. Americans were generally blamed as Israel's principal benefactors.

Simon Reeve writes that the Israeli operations continued for more than twenty years. He details the assassination in Paris in 1992 of Atef Bseiso, the PLO's head of intelligence, and says that an Israeli general confirmed there was a link back to Munich. Reeve also writes that while Israeli officials have stated *Operation Wrath of God* was intended to exact vengeance for the families of the athletes killed in Munich, "few relatives wanted such a violent reckoning with the Palestinians." Reeve states the families were instead desperate to know the truth of the events surrounding the Munich massacre. Reeve outlines what he sees as a lengthy cover-up by German authorities to hide the truth. After a lengthy court fight, in 2004 the families of the Munich victims reached a settlement of €3 million with the German government.

Alleged German cover-up

An article in 2012 in a front-page story of the German news magazine *Der Spiegel* reported that much of the information pertaining to the mishandling of the massacre was covered up by the German authorities. For twenty years, Germany refused to release any information about the attack and did not accept responsibility for the results. The magazine reported that the government had been hiding 3,808 files, which contained tens of thousands of documents. *Der Spiegel* said it obtained secret reports by authorities, embassy cables, and minutes of cabinet meetings that demonstrate the lack of professionalism of the German officials in handling the massacre. The newspaper also wrote that the German authorities were told that Palestinians were planning an "incident" at the Olympics three weeks before the massacre, but failed to take the necessary security measures, and these facts are missing from the official documentation of the German government.

In August 2012, *Der Spiegel* reported that following the massacre, Germany began secret meetings with Black September, at the behest of the West German government, due to the fear that Black September would carry out other terrorist attacks in Germany. The government proposed a clandestine meeting between German Foreign Minister Walter Scheel and a member of Black September to create a "new basis of trust." In return for an exchange of the political status of the Palestine Liberation Organization, the PLO would stop terrorist attacks on German soil. When French police arrested Abu Daoud, one of the chief organizers of the Munich massacre, and inquired about extraditing him to Germany, Bavaria's justice secretary Alfred Seidl recommended that Germany should not take any action, causing the French to release Abu Daoud and the Assad regime to shelter him until he died at a Damascus hospital in 2010.

Surviving Black September members

Two of the three surviving gunmen, Mohammed Safady and Adnan Al-Gashey, were allegedly killed by Mossad as part of *Operation Wrath of God*. Al-Gashey was allegedly located after making contact with a cousin in a Gulf State, and Safady was found by remaining in touch with family in Lebanon.[838] This account was challenged in a book by Aaron J. Klein, who claims that Al-Gashey died of heart failure in the 1970s, and that Safady was killed by Christian Phalangists in Lebanon in the early 1980s. However, in July 2005, PLO veteran Tawfiq Tirawi told Klein that Safady, whom Tirawi claimed as a close friend, was "as alive as you are."

The third surviving gunman, Jamal Al-Gashey, was known to be alive as of 1999, hiding in North Africa or in Syria, claiming to still fear retribution from Israel. He is the only one of the surviving terrorists to consent to interviews since 1972, having granted an interview in 1992 to a Palestinian newspaper, and having briefly emerged from hiding in 1999 to participate in an interview for the film *One Day in September*, during which he was disguised and his face shown only in blurry shadow.

Abu Daoud

Of those believed to have planned the massacre, only Abu Daoud, the man who claims that the attack was his idea, is known to have died of natural causes. Historical documents released to *Der Spiegel* by the German secret service show that Dortmund police had been aware of collaboration between Abu Daoud and neo-Nazi Willi Pohl (a.k.a. E. W. Pless and, since 1979, officially named Willi Voss) seven weeks before the attack.[839] In January 1977, Abu Daoud was intercepted by French police in Paris while traveling from Beirut under an assumed name. Under protest from the PLO, Iraq, and Libya, who claimed that because Abu Daoud was traveling to a PLO comrade's funeral he should receive diplomatic immunity, the French government refused a West German extradition request on grounds that forms had not been filled in properly, and put him on a plane to Algeria before Germany could submit another request. On 27 July 1981, he was shot 5 times from a distance of around two meters in a Warsaw Victoria (now Sofitel) hotel coffee shop, but survived the attack, chasing his would-be assassin down to the coffee shop's front entrance before collapsing.

Abu Daoud was allowed safe passage through Israel in 1996 so he could attend a PLO meeting convened in the Gaza Strip for the purpose of rescinding an article in its charter that called for Israel's eradication. In his autobiography, *From Jerusalem to Munich*, first published in France in 1999, and later in a written interview with *Sports Illustrated*, Abu Daoud wrote that funds for Munich were provided by Mahmoud Abbas, Chairman of the PLO since 11 November 2004 and President of the Palestinian National Authority since 15 January 2005.

<templatestyles src="Template:Quote/styles.css"/>

> Though he claims he didn't know what the money was being spent for, longtime Fatah official Mahmoud Abbas, aka Abu Mazen, was responsible for the financing of the Munich attack.[840]

Abu Daoud believed that if the Israelis knew that Mahmoud Abbas was the financier of the operation, the 1993 Oslo Accords would not have been achieved, during which Mahmoud Abbas was seen in photo ops at the White House.

Abu Daoud, who lived with his wife on a pension provided by the Palestinian Authority, said that "the Munich operation had the endorsement of Arafat," although Arafat was not involved in conceiving or implementing the attack. In his autobiography, Abu Daoud writes that Arafat saw the team off on the mission with the words "God protect you."

Ankie Spitzer, widow of fencing coach Andre, declined several offers to meet with Abu Daoud, saying that the only place she wants to meet him is in a courtroom. According to Spitzer, "He [Abu Daoud] didn't pay the price for what he did." In 2006, during the release of Steven Spielberg's film, *Munich*, *Der Spiegel* interviewed Abu Daoud regarding the Munich massacre. He was quoted as saying: "I regret nothing. You can only dream that I would apologize."

Daoud died of kidney failure aged 73 on 3 July 2010 in Damascus, Syria.

List of fatalities

Shot during the initial break-in

- Moshe Weinberg, wrestling coach
- Yossef Romano, weightlifter

Shot and killed by grenade in eastern-side helicopter D-HAQO
According to the order in which they were seated, from left to right:

- Ze'ev Friedman, weightlifter
- David Berger, weightlifter (survived grenade but died of smoke inhalation)
- Yakov Springer, weightlifting judge
- Eliezer Halfin, wrestler

Shot in western-side helicopter D-HAQU
According to the order in which they were seated, from left to right:

- Yossef Gutfreund, wrestling referee
- Kehat Shorr, shooting coach
- Mark Slavin, wrestler
- Andre Spitzer, fencing coach
- Amitzur Shapira, track coach

- Anton Fliegerbauer, West German police officer

Palestinian terrorists shot dead by West German police
- Luttif Afif ("Issa")
- Yusuf Nazzal ("Tony")
- Afif Ahmed Hamid ("Paolo")
- Khalid Jawad ("Salah")
- Ahmed Chic Thaa ("Abu Halla")

Memorials gallery

Figure 110: *Memorial plaque in front of the Israeli athletes' quarters. The inscription, in German and Hebrew, translates as: "The team of the State of Israel stayed in this building during the 20th Olympic Summer Games from 21 August to 5 September 1972. On 5 September, [list of victims] died a violent death. Honor to their memory."*

Figure 111: *Memorial panel for the victims of the attack on the site of the Munich Olympic Park*

Figure 112: *Memorial for the dead athletes in front of the airport in Fürstenfeldbruck. The names of the victims are engraved.*

Figure 113: *Place of memory in Ben Shemen forest in Israel*

Figure 114: *Graves of five victims of the Munich massacre at the Kiryat Shaul Cemetery, Tel Aviv, Israel. From left to right: André Spitzer, Mark Slavin, Eliezer Halfin, Kehat Shorr and Amitzur Schapira.*

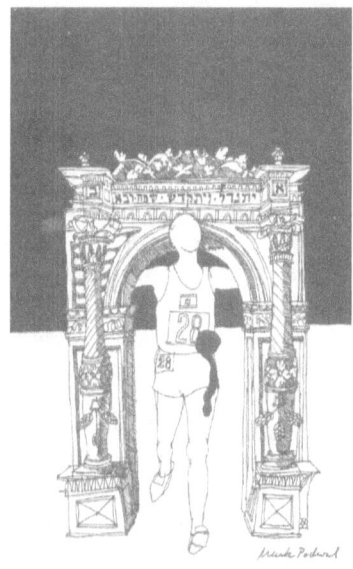

Figure 115: *Munich Massacre by Mark Podwal, published in The New York Times in 1972*

Media

- *1972*, by Sarah Morris
- *21 Hours at Munich*
- *Munich*, a 2005 American-Canadian historical drama
- *Munich: Mossad's Revenge*
- *One Day in September*, 1999 documentary by Kevin Macdonald; winner of the Academy Award for Best Documentary
- National Geographic *Seconds From Disaster* episodes
- *Sword of Gideon*
- *Visions of Eight*
- *Munich 1972 & Beyond*, 2016 documentary film by Steven Ungerleider

Further reading

- Blumenau, Bernhard (Basingstoke 2014), *The United Nations and Terrorism. Germany, Multilateralism, and Antiterrorism Efforts in the 1970s* Palgrave Macmillan, ch. 2. <templatestyles src="Module:Citation/CS1/styles.css" />ISBN 978-1-137-39196-4.

- Calahan, A. B. "The Israeli Response to the 1972 Munich Olympic Massacre and the Development of Independent Covert Action Teams"[841] (1995 thesis)
- Cooley, John K. (London 1973), *Green March Black September: The Story of the Palestinian Arabs* <templatestyles src="Module:Citation/CS1/styles.css" />ISBN 0-7146-2987-1
- Dahlke, Matthias (Munich 2006), *Der Anschlag auf Olympia '72. Die politischen Reaktionen auf den internationalen in Deutschland* Martin Meidenbauer <templatestyles src="Module:Citation/CS1/styles.css" />ISBN 3-89975-583-9 (German text)
- Daoud, Abu, (New York, 2002), *Palestine : a history of the resistance movement by the sole survivor of Black September* <templatestyles src="Module:Citation/CS1/styles.css" />ISBN 1-55970-429-2
- Groussard, Serge (New York, 1975), *The Blood of Israel: the massacre of the Israeli athletes, the Olympics, 1972* <templatestyles src="Module:Citation/CS1/styles.css" />ISBN 0-688-02910-8
- Jonas, George. (New York, 2005), *Vengeance: The True Story of an Israeli Team.*, Simon & Schuster
- Khalaf, Salah (Abu Iyad) (Tel Aviv, 1983) *Without a Homeland: Conversations with Eric Rouleau*
- Klein, A. J. (New York, 2005), *Striking Back: The 1972 Munich Olympics Massacre and Israel's Deadly Response*, Random House <templatestyles src="Module:Citation/CS1/styles.css" />ISBN 1-920769-80-3
- Large, David Clay (Lanham, MD, 2012), *Munich 1972*, Rowman & Littlefield <templatestyles src="Module:Citation/CS1/styles.css" />ISBN 978-0-7425-6739-9
- Morris, Benny. (New York, 1999 and 2001), *Righteous Victims: A History of the Zionist–Arab conflict, 1881–2000*, Vintage Books edition <templatestyles src="Module:Citation/CS1/styles.css" />ISBN 0-679-74475-4
- Reeve, Simon. (New York, 2001), *One Day in September: the full story of the 1972 Munich Olympic massacre and Israeli revenge operation "Wrath of God"* <templatestyles src="Module:Citation/CS1/styles.css" />ISBN 1-55970-547-7
- Tinnin, David B. & Dag Christensen. (1976), *The Hit Team* <templatestyles src="Module:Citation/CS1/styles.css" />ISBN 0-440-13644-X
- Yossi Melman, (17 February 2006), Interview with former Head of Mossad, Zvi Zamir ""Preventive measures""[842]. Archived from the original[843] on 1 October 2007. Retrieved 3 February 2012.<templatestyles src="Module:Citation/CS1/styles.css"></templatestyles>, Haaretz
- Mohammad Daoud Odeh (August 2008), interview with NOX magazine, "Rings Of Fire"[844]

- Kramer, Ferdinand: *Das Attentat von München*. In: Alois Schmid, Katharina Weigand: *Bayern nach Jahr und Tag. 24 Tage aus der Bayerischen Geschichte*. C. H. Beck Verlag, München 2007, <templatestyles src="Module:Citation/CS1/styles.css" />ISBN 978-3-406-56320-1. p. 400–414.
- Wolfgang Kraushaar: *"Wann endlich beginnt bei Euch der Kampf gegen die heilige Kuh Israel?" München 1970: über die antisemitischen Wurzeln des deutschen Terrorismus*. Rowohlt, Reinbek 2013, <templatestyles src="Module:Citation/CS1/styles.css" />ISBN 978-3-49803411-5, p. 496–573.

External links

Wikimedia Commons has media related to *Munich massacre*.

- The Israeli Response to the 1972 Munich Massacre[841] – Includes an extensive overview of the Munich massacre
- A Tribute to the 1972 Israeli Olympic Athletes[845] – Includes biographies and photographs for each of the 11 Israeli athletes killed
- *Time Magazine*[846], 4 December 2005
- Special Publication of Israel State Archives: The Fortieth Anniversary of the Massacre of the Israeli Athletes in Munich[847]

Yom Kippur War

<indicator name="pp-default"> 🔒 </indicator>

Yom Kippur War/October War	
Part of the Arab–Israeli conflict and Cold War	
 Egyptian forces crossing the Suez Canal on October 7	
Date	October 6–25, 1973
Location	Both banks of the Suez Canal, Golan Heights and surrounding regions
Result	Israeli military victory[848,849,850,851] </ref> • Political gains for Egypt and Israel • 1978 Camp David Accords
Territorial changes	• The Egyptian army occupied the eastern coast of the Suez Canal with the exception of the Israeli crossing point near Deversoir.[852] • The Israeli army occupied 1,600 km² (620 sq mi) of territory on the southwestern coast of the Suez Canal, within 100 km (60 mi) from Cairo, and encircled an Egyptian enclave in the east bank • The Israeli army occupied 500 km² (190 sq mi) of the Syrian Bashan, on top of the Golan Heights, which brought it within 30 km (20 mi) of Damascus.[853]
Belligerents	
Israel *Supported by*: • United States	• Egypt • Syria Expeditionary forces: • Jordan • Iraq • Saudi Arabia • Libya • Tunisia • Algeria • Morocco • Cuba[854] *Supported by*: • Soviet Union
Commanders and leaders	

- 🇮🇱 Golda Meir
- 🇮🇱 Moshe Dayan
- 🇮🇱 David Elazar
- 🇮🇱 Israel Tal
- 🇮🇱 Shmuel Gonen
- 🇮🇱 Yitzhak Hofi
- 🇮🇱 Binyamin Peled
- 🇮🇱 Haim Bar-Lev
- 🇮🇱 Albert Mandler †
- 🇮🇱 Ariel Sharon
- 🇮🇱 Benjamin Telem

- Anwar Sadat
- **Hafez al-Assad**
- Ahmad Ismail Ali
- Mustafa Tlass
- Saad El Shazly
- Yusuf Shakkour
- Abdel Ghani el-Gammasy
- Ali Aslan
- Omar Abrash †

Strength

- 375,000–415,000 troops
- 1,700 tanks[855]
- 3,000 armored carriers
- 945 artillery units[856]
- 440 combat aircraft

Egypt:
- 650,000–800,000 troops (200,000 crossed)
- 1,700 tanks (1,020 crossed)
- 2,400 armored carriers
- 1,120 artillery units
- 400 combat aircraft
- 140 helicopters[857]
- 104 Navy vessels
- 150 surface to air missile batteries (62 in the front line)[858]

Syria:
- 150,000 troops
- 1,200 tanks
  800–900 armored carriers
- 600 artillery units

Expeditionary Forces*:
- 100,000 troops
- 500–670 tanks
- 700 armored carriers

Cuba:
- 1,500–4,000[859] troops

Morocco:
- 5,500 troops
- 30 tanks
- 52 combat aircraft

Saudi-Arabia:
3,000 troops

Total:
- 914,000–1,067,500 troops
- 3,430–3,600 tanks
- 3,900–4,000 armored carriers
- 1,720 artillery units
- 452 combat aircraft
- 140 helicopters
- 104 navy vessels
- 150 surface to air missile batteries

Casualties and losses

- 2,521–2,800[860] dead
- 7,250–8,800 wounded
- 293 captured
- 1,063 tanks destroyed, damaged or captured
- 407 armored vehicles destroyed or captured
- 102–387 aircraft destroyed[861]

Egypt: 5,000–15,000 dead
- 8,372 captured

Syria:
- 3,000–3,500 dead
- 392 captured

Iraq:
- 278 dead
- 898 wounded[862]
- 13 captured

Jordan:
- 23 dead
- 77 wounded

Morocco:
- 6 captured

Total casualties:
- 8,000–18,500 dead
- 18,000–35,000[863] wounded
- 8,783 captured
- 2,250–2,300 tanks destroyed
- 341–514 aircraft destroyed
- 19 naval vessels sunk

The **Yom Kippur War**, **Ramadan War**, or **October War** (Hebrew: מלחמת יום הכיפורים, *Milḥemet Yom HaKipurim*, or מלחמת יום כיפור, *Milḥemet Yom Kipur*; Arabic: حرب أكتوبر, *Ḥarb 'Uktōbar*, or حرب تشرين, *Ḥarb Tišrīn*), also known as the **1973 Arab–Israeli War**, was a war fought from October 6 to 25, 1973, by a coalition of Arab states led by Egypt and Syria against Israel. The war took place mostly in Sinai and the Golan—occupied by Israel during the 1967 Six-Day War—with some fighting in African Egypt and northern Israel. Egypt's initial war objective was to use its military to seize a foothold on the east bank of the Suez Canal and use this to negotiate the return of the rest of Sinai.[864,865,866]

The war began when the Arab coalition launched a joint surprise attack on Israeli positions, on Yom Kippur, the holiest day in Judaism, which also occurred that year during the Muslim holy month of Ramadan. Egyptian and Syrian forces crossed ceasefire lines to enter the Sinai Peninsula and the Golan Heights, respectively. Both the United States and the Soviet Union initiated massive resupply efforts to their respective allies during the war, and this led to a near-confrontation between the two nuclear superpowers.

The war began with a massive and successful Egyptian crossing of the Suez Canal. Egyptian forces crossed the cease-fire lines, then advanced virtually unopposed into the Sinai Peninsula. After three days, Israel had mobilized most of its forces and halted the Egyptian offensive, resulting in a military stalemate. The Syrians coordinated their attack on the Golan Heights to coincide with the Egyptian offensive and initially made threatening gains into Israeli-held territory. Within three days, however, Israeli forces had pushed the Syrians back to the pre-war ceasefire lines. The Israel Defense Forces (IDF) then launched a four-day counter-offensive deep into Syria. Within a week, Israeli artillery began to shell the outskirts of Damascus, and Egyptian President Sadat began to worry about the integrity of his major ally. He believed that capturing two strategic passes located deeper in the Sinai would make his position stronger during post-war negotiations; he therefore ordered the Egyptians to go back on the offensive, but their attack was quickly repulsed. The Israelis then counter-attacked at the seam between the two Egyptian armies, crossed the Suez Canal into Egypt, and began slowly advancing southward and westward towards the city of Suez in over a week of heavy fighting that resulted in heavy casualties on both sides.[867,868]

On October 22, a United Nations-brokered ceasefire unraveled, with each side blaming the other for the breach. By October 24, the Israelis had improved their positions considerably and completed their encirclement of Egypt's Third Army and the city of Suez. This development led to tensions between the United States and the Soviet Union, and a second ceasefire was imposed co-operatively on October 25 to end the war.

The war had far-reaching implications. The Arab world had experienced humiliation in the lopsided rout of the Egyptian-Syrian-Jordanian alliance in the Six-Day War but felt psychologically vindicated by early successes in this conflict. The war led Israel to recognize that, despite impressive operational and tactical achievements on the battlefield, there was no guarantee that they would always dominate the Arab states militarily, as they had consistently through the earlier 1948 Arab-Israeli War, the Suez Crisis, and the Six-Day War. These changes paved the way for the subsequent peace process. The 1978 Camp David Accords that followed led to the return of the Sinai to Egypt and normalized relations—the first peaceful recognition of Israel by an Arab country. Egypt continued its drift away from the Soviet Union and eventually left the Soviet sphere of influence entirely.

Background

The war was part of the Arab-Israeli conflict, an ongoing dispute that included many battles and wars since 1948, when the state of Israel was formed. During the Six-Day War of 1967, Israel had captured Egypt's Sinai Peninsula, roughly half of Syria's Golan Heights, and the territories of the West Bank which had been held by Jordan since 1948.

On June 19, 1967, shortly after the Six-Day War, the Israeli government voted to return the Sinai to Egypt and the Golan Heights to Syria in exchange for a permanent peace settlement and a demilitarization of the returned territories.[869] It rejected a full return to the boundaries and the situation before the war and also insisted on direct negotiations with the Arab governments as opposed to accepting negotiation through a third party.

This decision was not made public at the time, nor was it conveyed to any Arab state. Notwithstanding Abba Eban's (Israeli Minister of Foreign Affairs in 1967) insistence that this was indeed the case, there seems to be no solid evidence to corroborate his claim. No formal peace proposal was made either directly or indirectly by Israel. The Americans, who were briefed of the Cabinet's decision by Eban, were not asked to convey it to Cairo and Damascus as official peace proposals, nor were they given indications that Israel expected a reply.

The Arab position, as it emerged in September 1967 at the Khartoum Arab Summit, was to reject any peaceful settlement with the state of Israel. The eight participating states – Egypt, Syria, Jordan, Lebanon, Iraq, Algeria, Kuwait, and Sudan – passed a resolution that would later become known as the "three no's": there would be no peace, no recognition and no negotiation with Israel. Prior to that, King Hussein of Jordan had stated that he could not rule out a possibility of a "real, permanent peace" between Israel and the Arab states.

Armed hostilities continued on a limited scale after the Six-Day War and escalated into the War of Attrition, an attempt to wear down the Israeli position through long-term pressure. A ceasefire was signed in August 1970.

President Gamal Abdel Nasser of Egypt died in September 1970. He was succeeded by Anwar Sadat. A peace initiative led by both Sadat and UN intermediary Gunnar Jarring was tabled in 1971. Sadat set forth to the Egyptian Parliament his intention of arranging an interim agreement as a step towards a settlement on 4 February 1971, which extended the terms of the ceasefire and envisaged a reopening of the Suez Canal in exchange for a partial Israeli pullback. It resembled a proposal independently made by Moshe Dayan. Sadat had signaled in an interview with the *New York Times* in December 1970 that, in return for a total withdrawal from the Sinai Peninsula, he was ready "to recognize the rights of Israel as an independent state as defined by the Security Council of the United Nations." Gunnar Jarring coincidentally proposed a similar iniative four days later, on 8 February 1971. Egypt responded by accepting much of Jarring's proposals, though differing on several issues, regarding the Gaza Strip, for example, and expressed its willingness to reach an accord if it also implemented the provisions of United Nations Security Council Resolution 242. This was the first time an Arab government had gone public declaring its readiness to sign a peace agreement with Israel.

In addition, the Egyptian response included a statement that the lasting peace could not be achieved without "withdrawal of the Israeli armed forces from all the territories occupied since 5 June 1967." Golda Meir reacted to the overture by forming a committee to examine the proposal and vet possible concessions. When the committee unanimously concluded that Israel's interests would be served by full withdrawal to the internationally recognized lines dividing Israel from Egypt and Syria, returning the Gaza Strip and, in a majority view, returning most of the West Bank and East Jerusalem, Meir was angered and shelved the document.[870] The United States was infuriated by the cool Israeli response to Egypt's proposal, and Joseph Sisco informed Yitzhak Rabin that "Israel would be regarded responsible for rejecting the best opportunity to reach peace since the establishment of the state." Israel responded to Jarring's plan also on 26 of February by outlining its readiness to make some form of withdrawal, while declaring it had no intention of returning to the pre-5 June 1967 lines. Jarring was disappointed and blamed Israel for refusing to accept a complete pullout from the Sinai peninsula.[871]

Sadat hoped that by inflicting even a limited defeat on the Israelis, the status quo could be altered. Hafez al-Assad, the leader of Syria, had a different view. He had little interest in negotiation and felt the retaking of the Golan Heights would be a purely military option. After the Six-Day War, Assad had launched a massive military buildup and hoped to make Syria the dominant military power of the Arab states. With the aid of Egypt, Assad felt that his new army could win convincingly against Israel and thus secure Syria's role in the region. Assad only saw negotiations beginning once the Golan Heights had been retaken by force, which would induce Israel to give up the West Bank and Gaza, and make other concessions.

Sadat also had important domestic concerns in wanting war. "The three years since Sadat had taken office ... were the most demoralized in Egyptian history. ... A desiccated economy added to the nation's despondency. War was a desperate option."[872] In his biography of Sadat, Raphael Israeli argued that Sadat felt the root of the problem was the great shame over the Six-Day War, and before any reforms could be introduced, he believed that that shame had to be overcome. Egypt's economy was in shambles, but Sadat knew that the deep reforms that he felt were needed would be deeply unpopular among parts of the population. A military victory would give him the popularity he needed to make changes. A portion of the Egyptian population, most prominently university students who launched wide protests, strongly desired a war to reclaim the Sinai and was highly upset that Sadat had not launched one in his first three years in office.

The other Arab states showed much more reluctance to fully commit to a new war. Jordanian King Hussein feared another major loss of territory, as had occurred in the Six-Day War, in which Jordan lost all of the West Bank, territory it had conquered and annexed in 1948–49, which had doubled its population. Sadat also backed the claim of the Palestine Liberation Organization (PLO) to the West Bank and Gaza and, in the event of a victory, promised Yasser Arafat that he would be given control of them. Hussein still saw the West Bank as part of Jordan and wanted it restored to his kingdom. Moreover, during the Black September crisis of 1970, a near civil war had broken out between the PLO and the Jordanian government. In that war, Syria had intervened militarily on the side of the PLO, estranging Hussein.

Iraq and Syria also had strained relations, and the Iraqis refused to join the initial offensive. Lebanon, which shared a border with Israel, was not expected to join the Arab war effort because of its small army and already evident instability. The months before the war saw Sadat engage in a diplomatic offensive to try to win support for the war. By the fall of 1973, he claimed the backing of more than a hundred states. These were most of the countries of the Arab League, Non-Aligned Movement, and Organization of African Unity.

Sadat had also worked to curry favour in Europe and had some success before the war. Britain and France sided with the Arab powers against Israel on the United Nations Security CouncilWikipedia:Manual of Style/Dates and numbers#Chronological items.Wikipedia:Citation needed The US considered Israel an ally in the Cold War and had been supplying the Israeli military since the 1960s. Henry Kissinger believed that the regional balance of power hinged on maintaining Israel's military dominance over Arab countries. Kissinger believed an Arab victory in the region would strengthen Soviet influence. Britain's position, on the other hand, was that war between the Arabs and Israelis could only be prevented by the implementation of United Nations Security Council Resolution 242 and a return to the pre-1967 boundaries. On October 12, nearly one week into the war, the Cypriot government announced that it would "oppose the use of British bases in Cyprus as a springboard against Arab countries", which further strained Anglo-American relations.

Events leading up to the war

Four months before the war broke out, Henry Kissinger made an offer to Ismail, Sadat's emissary. Kissinger proposed returning the Sinai Peninsula to Egyptian control and an Israeli withdrawal from all of Sinai, except for some strategic points. Ismail said he would return with Sadat's reply, but never did. Sadat was already determined to go to war. Only an American guarantee that the United States would fulfill the entire Arab program in a brief time could have dissuaded Sadat.

Sadat declared that Egypt was prepared to "sacrifice a million Egyptian soldiers" to recover its lost territory.[873] From the end of 1972, Egypt began a concentrated effort to build up its forces, receiving MiG-21 jet fighters, SA-2, SA-3, SA-6 and SA-7 antiaircraft missiles, T-55 and T-62 tanks, RPG-7 anti-tank weapons, and the AT-3 Sagger anti-tank guided missile from the Soviet

Figure 116: *Egyptian President Anwar Sadat*

Union and improving its military tactics, based on Soviet battlefield doctrines. Political generals, who had in large part been responsible for the rout in 1967, were replaced with competent ones.[874]

The role of the superpowers, too, was a major factor in the outcome of the two wars. The policy of the Soviet Union was one of the causes of Egypt's military weakness. President Nasser was only able to obtain the materiel for an anti-aircraft missile defense wall after visiting Moscow and pleading with Kremlin leaders. He said that if supplies were not given, he would have to return to Egypt and tell the Egyptian people Moscow had abandoned them, and then relinquish power to one of his peers who would be able to deal with the Americans. The Americans would then have the upper hand in the region, which Moscow could not permit.

Nasser's policy following the 1967 defeat conflicted with that of the Soviet Union. The Soviets sought to avoid a new conflagration between the Arabs and Israelis so as not to be drawn into a confrontation with the United States. The reality of the situation became apparent when the superpowers met in Oslo and agreed to maintain the status quo. This was unacceptable to Egyptian leaders, and when it was discovered that the Egyptian preparations for crossing the canal were being leaked, it became imperative to expel the Soviets from Egypt. In July 1972, Sadat expelled almost all of the 20,000 Soviet military advisers in the country and reoriented the country's foreign policy to be more favourable to the United States. The Syrians remained close to the Soviet Union.

The Soviets thought little of Sadat's chances in any war. They warned that any attempt to cross the heavily fortified Suez Canal would incur massive losses. Both the Soviets and Americans were then pursuing détente and had no interest in seeing the Middle East destabilized. In a June 1973 meeting with American President Richard Nixon, Soviet leader Leonid Brezhnev had proposed Israel pull back to its 1967 border. Brezhnev said that if Israel did not, "we will have difficulty keeping the military situation from flaring up"—an indication that the Soviet Union had been unable to restrain Sadat's plans.[875]

In an interview published in Newsweek (April 9, 1973), Sadat again threatened war with Israel. Several times during 1973, Arab forces conducted large-scale exercises that put the Israeli military on the highest level of alert, only to be recalled a few days later. The Israeli leadership already believed that if an attack took place, the Israeli Air Force (IAF) could repel it.

Almost a full year before the war, in an October 24, 1972, meeting with his Supreme Council of the Armed Forces, Sadat declared his intention to go to war with Israel even without proper Soviet support.[876] Planning had begun in 1971 and was conducted in absolute secrecy—even the upper-echelon commanders were not told of the war plans until less than a week prior to the attack, and the soldiers were not told until a few hours beforehand. The plan to attack Israel in concert with Syria was code-named Operation Badr (Arabic for "full moon"), after the Battle of Badr, in which Muslims under Muhammad defeated the Quraish tribe of Mecca.

War objectives and areas of combat

Egypt's initial war objective was to use its military to seize a limited amount of Israeli-occupied Sinai on the east bank of the Suez Canal. This would provoke a crisis which would allow it to bring American and Soviet pressure to bear on Israel to negotiate the return of the rest of Sinai, and possibly other occupied territories, from a position of relative strength.[864,865,877] Egyptian President Anwar Sadat's publicly stated position was "to recover all Arab territory occupied by Israel following the 1967 war and to achieve a just, peaceful solution to the Arab-Israeli conflict" Similarly, Syria intended to seize back some or all of the Golan and to then negotiate its retention via great power pressure.[865,878] Both Egypt and Syria expected that the use of the "oil weapon" would assist them in post-conflict negotiations, once their attacks had generated a reason for its use.[879,880]

Other than a flurry of Syrian missile attacks on Ramat David airbase and surrounding civilian settlements during the first days of the war, the fighting took place in Sinai and the Golan Heights, territories that had been occupied by Israel since the end of the Six-Day War of 1967, and in the later stages, on the west side of the Suez canal in Egypt and in areas of the Golan beyond those held by Israel prior to the outbreak of war.

Lead-up to the surprise attack

The Israel Defense Forces (IDF) Directorate of Military Intelligence's (abbreviated as "Aman") Research Department was responsible for formulating Israel's intelligence estimate. Their assessments on the likelihood of war were based on several assumptions. First, it was assumed correctly that Syria would not go to war with Israel unless Egypt did so as well. Second, the department learned from Ashraf Marwan, former President Nasser's son-in-law and also a senior Mossad agent, that Egypt wanted to regain all of the Sinai, but would not go to war until they were supplied MiG-23 fighter-bombers to neutralize the Israeli Air Force and Scud missiles to be used against Israeli cities as a deterrent against Israeli attacks on Egyptian infrastructure.

Since they had not received MiG-23s and Scud missiles had only arrived in Egypt from Bulgaria in late August and it would take four months to train the Egyptian ground crews, Aman predicted war with Egypt was not imminent. This assumption about Egypt's strategic plans, known as "the concept", strongly prejudiced the department's thinking and led it to dismiss other war warnings.

By mid-1973, Aman was almost completely aware of the Arab war plans. It knew that the Egyptian Second and Third Armies would attempt to cross the Suez Canal and advance ten kilometres into the Sinai, followed by armored divisions that would advance towards the Mitla and Gidi Passes, and that naval units and paratroopers would then attempt to capture Sharm el-Sheikh. Aman was also aware of many details of the Syrian war plan. However, Israeli analysts, following "the concept", did not believe the Arabs were serious about going to war.

The Egyptians did much to further this misconception. Both the Israelis and the Americans felt that the expulsion of the Soviet military observers had severely reduced the effectiveness of the Egyptian army. The Egyptians ensured that there was a continual stream of false information regarding maintenance problems and a lack of personnel to operate the most advanced equipment. The Egyptians made repeated misleading reports about lack of spare parts that made their way to the Israelis. Sadat had so long engaged in brinkmanship that his frequent war threats were being ignored by the world.

In April and May 1973, Israeli intelligence began picking up clear signals of Egypt's intentions for war, recognizing that it had the necessary divisions and bridging equipment to cross the Suez Canal and a missile umbrella to protect any crossing operation from air attack. However, Aman Chief Eli Zeira was still confident that the probability of war was low.

In May and August 1973, the Egyptian Army conducted military exercises near the border, and Ashraf Marwan inaccurately warned that Egypt and Syria would launch a surprise attack on May 15. The Israeli Army mobilized in response to both exercises at considerable cost. These exercises were to ensure that the Israelis would dismiss the actual war preparations right before the attack was launched as another exercise.

Egyptian and Syrian military exercises

For the week leading up to Yom Kippur, the Egyptian army staged a weeklong training exercise adjacent to the Suez Canal. Israeli intelligence, detecting large troop movements towards the canal, dismissed them as mere training exercises. Movements of Syrian troops towards the border were also detected, as were the cancellation of leaves and a call-up of reserves in the Syrian army. These activities were considered puzzling, but not a threat because, Aman believed, they would not attack without Egypt and Egypt would not attack until the weaponry they wanted arrived. Despite this belief, Israel sent reinforcements to the Golan Heights. These forces were to prove critical during the early days of the war.

On September 27 and 30, two batches of reservists were called up by the Egyptian army to participate in these exercises. Two days before the outbreak of the war, on October 4, the Egyptian command publicly announced the demobilization of part of the reservists called up during September 27 to lull Israeli suspicions. Around 20,000 troops were demobilized, and subsequently some of these men were given leave to perform the *Umrah* (pilgrimage) to Mecca.[881,882] Reports were also given instructing cadets in military colleges to resume their courses on October 9.

On October 1, an Aman researcher, Lieutenant Binyamin Siman-Tov, submitted an assessment arguing that the Egyptian deployments and exercises along the Suez Canal seemed to be a camouflage for an actual crossing of the canal. Siman-Tov sent a more comprehensive assessment on October 3. Both were ignored by his superior.

According to Egyptian General El-Gamasy, "On the initiative of the operations staff, we reviewed the situation on the ground and developed a framework for the planned offensive operation. We studied the technical characteristics of the Suez Canal, the ebb and the flow of the tides, the speed of the currents and their direction, hours of darkness and of moonlight, weather conditions, and related conditions in the Mediterranean and Red sea." He explained further by saying: "Saturday 6 October 1973 (10 Ramadan 1393) was the day chosen for the September–October option. Conditions for a crossing were good, it was a fast day in Israel, and the moon on that day, 10 Ramadan, shone from sunset until midnight." The war coincided that year with the Muslim month of Ramadan, when many Arab Muslim soldiers fast. On the other hand, the fact that the attack was launched on Yom Kippur may have *helped* Israel to more easily marshal reserves from their homes and synagogues because roads and communication lines were largely open, easing the mobilization and transportation of the military.[883]

Despite refusing to participate, King Hussein of Jordan "had met with Sadat and Assad in Alexandria two weeks before. Given the mutual suspicions prevailing among the Arab leaders, it was unlikely that he had been told any specific war plans. But it was probable that Sadat and Assad had raised the prospect of war against Israel in more general terms to feel out the likelihood of Jordan joining in."[884]

On the night of September 25, Hussein secretly flew to Tel Aviv to warn Israeli Prime Minister Golda Meir of an impending Syrian attack. "Are they going to war without the Egyptians, asked Mrs. Meir. The king said he didn't think so. 'I think they [Egypt] would cooperate.'"[885] This warning was ignored, and Aman concluded that the king had not told anything that was not already known. Throughout September, Israel received eleven warnings of war from well-placed sources. However, Mossad Director-General Zvi Zamir continued to insist that war was not an Arab option, even after Hussein's warning.[886] Zamir would later remark that "We simply didn't feel them capable [of war]."

On the day before the war, General Ariel Sharon was shown aerial photographs and other intelligence by Yehoshua Saguy, his divisional intelligence officer. General Sharon noticed that the concentration of Egyptian forces along the canal was far beyond anything observed during the training exercises, and that the Egyptians had amassed all of their crossing equipment along the canal. He then called General Shmuel Gonen, who had replaced him as head of Southern Command, and expressed his certainty that war was imminent.

On October 4–5, Zamir's concern grew, as additional signs of an impending attack were detected. Soviet advisers and their families left Egypt and Syria, transport aircraft thought to be laden with military equipment landed in Cairo and Damascus, and aerial photographs revealed that Egyptian and Syrian concentrations of tanks, infantry, and surface-to-air (SAM) missiles were at an unprecedented high. According to declassified documents from the Agranat Commission, Brigadier General Yisrael Lior, Prime Minister Golda Meir's military secretary/attaché, claimed that Mossad knew from Ashraf Marwan that an attack was going to occur under the guise of a military drill a week before it occurred, but the process of passing along the information to the Prime Minister's office failed. The information ended up with Mossad head Zvi Zamir's aide, who passed it along to Zamir at 12:30 am on 5 October. According to the claim, an unfocused and groggy Zamir thanked the aide for the information and said he would pass it along to the Prime Minister's office in the morning.[887] On the night of October 5/6, Zamir personally went to Europe to meet with Marwan at midnight. Marwan informed him that a joint Syrian-Egyptian attack was imminent. However, Marwan incorrectly told Zamir that the attack would take place at sunset.

It was this warning in particular, combined with the large number of other warnings, that finally goaded the Israeli High Command into action. Just hours before the attack began, orders went out for a partial call-up of the Israeli reserves.[888]

The attack by the Egyptian and Syrian forces caught the United States by surprise. According to future CIA Director and Defense Secretary Robert Gates, he was briefing an American arms negotiator on the improbability of armed conflict in the region when he heard the news of the outbreak of war on the radio. On the other hand, the KGB learned about the attack in advance, probably from its intelligence sources in Egypt.[889]

Lack of Israeli pre-emptive attack

The Israeli strategy was, for the most part, based on the precept that if war was imminent, Israel would launch a pre-emptive strike. It was assumed that Israel's intelligence services would give, in the worst case, about 48 hours notice prior to an Arab attack.

Prime Minister Golda Meir, Minister of Defense Moshe Dayan, and Chief of General Staff David Elazar met at 8:05 am the morning of Yom Kippur, six hours before the war began. Dayan opened the meeting by arguing that war was not a certainty. Elazar then presented his argument in favor of a pre-emptive attack against Syrian airfields at noon, Syrian missiles at 3:00 pm, and Syrian ground forces at 5:00 pm: "When the presentations were done, the prime minister hemmed uncertainly for a few moments but then came to a clear decision. There would be no preemptive strike. Israel might be needing American assistance soon and it was imperative that it would not be blamed for starting the war. 'If we strike first, we won't get help from anybody,' she said."[890] Prior to the war, Kissinger and Nixon consistently warned Meir that she must not be responsible for initiating a Middle East war. On October 6, 1973, the war opening date, Kissinger told Israel not to go for a preemptive strike, and Meir confirmed to him that Israel would not.[891]

Figure 117: *Upon learning of the impending attack, Prime Minister of Israel Golda Meir made the controversial decision not to launch a pre-emptive strike.*

Other developed nations,Wikipedia:Manual of Style/Words to watch#Unsupported attributions being more dependent on OPEC oil, took more seriously the threat of an Arab oil embargo and trade boycott, and had stopped supplying Israel with munitions. As a result, Israel was totally dependent on the United States for military resupply, and particularly sensitive to anything that might endanger that relationship. After Meir had made her decision, at 10:15 am, she met with American ambassador Kenneth Keating in order to inform the United States that Israel did not intend to preemptively start a war, and asked that American efforts be directed at preventing war. An electronic telegram with Keating's report on the meeting was sent to the United States at 16:33 GMT (6:33 pm local time).

A message arrived later from United States Secretary of State Henry Kissinger saying, "Don't preempt."[892] At the same time, Kissinger also urged the Soviets to use their influence to prevent war, contacted Egypt with Israel's message of non-preemption, and sent messages to other Arab governments to enlist their help on the side of moderation. These late efforts were futile.[893] According to Henry Kissinger, had Israel struck first, it would not have received "so much as a nail".[894]

David Elazar proposed a mobilization of the entire air force and four armored divisions, a total of 100,000 to 120,000 troops, while Dayan favored a mo-

Figure 118: *Wreckage from an Egyptian Sukhoi Su-7 shot down over the Sinai on October 6 on display at the Israeli Air Force Museum.*

bilization of the air force and two armored divisions, totaling around 70,000 troops. Meir chose Elazar's proposal.[895]

Combat operations

In the Sinai

The Sinai was once again the arena of conflict between Israel and Egypt. The Egyptians had prepared for an assault across the canal and deployed five divisions totaling 100,000 soldiers, 1,350 tanks and 2,000 guns and heavy mortars for the onslaught. Facing them were 450 soldiers of the Jerusalem Brigade, spread out in 16 forts along the length of the Canal. There were 290 Israeli tanks in all of Sinai divided into three armored brigades,[896] and only one of these was deployed near the Canal when hostilities commenced.[897]

Large bridgeheads were established on the east bank on October 6. Israeli armoured forces launched counterattacks from October 6 to 8, but they were often piecemeal and inadequately supported and were beaten back principally by Egyptians using portable anti-tank missiles. Between October 9 and October 12 the American response was a call for cease-fire in place. The Egyptian units generally would not advance beyond a shallow strip for fear of losing the protection of their surface-to-air missile (SAM) batteries, which were situated on the west bank of the canal. In the Six-Day War, the Israeli Air Force had pummeled the defenseless Arab armies. Egypt (and Syria) had heavily fortified their side of the ceasefire lines with SAM batteries provided by the Soviet Union, against which the Israeli Air Force had no time to execute a Suppression of Enemy Air Defenses (SEAD) operation due to the element of surprise. Israel, which had invested much of its defense budget building the region's strongest air force, would see the effectiveness of its air force curtailed in the initial phases of the conflict by the SAM presence.

On October 9, the IDF chose to concentrate its reserves and build up its supplies while the Egyptians remained on the strategic defensive. Nixon and Kissinger held back on a full-scale resupply of arms to Israel. Short of supplies, the Israeli government reluctantly accepted a cease-fire in place on October 12 but Sadat refused. The Soviets started an airlift of arms to Syria and Egypt. The American global interest was to prove that Soviet arms could not dictate the outcome of the fighting, by supplying Israel. With an airlift in full swing, Washington was prepared to wait until Israeli success on the battlefield might persuade the Arabs and the Soviets to bring the fighting to an end. It was decided to counterattack once Egyptian armor attempted to expand the bridgehead beyond the protective SAM umbrella. The riposte, codenamed Operation Gazelle, was launched on October 15. IDF forces spearheaded by Ariel Sharon's division broke through the Tasa corridor and crossed the Suez Canal to the north of the Great Bitter Lake.

After intense fighting, the IDF progressed towards Cairo and advanced southwards on the east bank of the Great Bitter Lake and in the southern extent of the canal right up to Port Suez. It was important for the Americans that the fighting should be ended, when all parties could still emerge from the conflict with their vital interests and self-esteem intact. Hence they indicated an acceptance of Israeli advance while violating the ceasefire, but the U.S. did not permit the destruction of the Egyptian 3rd army corps. Israeli progress towards Cairo was brought to a halt when the ceasefire was declared on October 24.

Egyptian attack

Anticipating a swift Israeli armored counterattack by three armored divisions,[898] the Egyptians had armed their assault force with large numbers of man-portable anti-tank weapons—rocket-propelled grenades and the less numerous but more advanced Sagger guided missiles, which proved devastating to the first Israeli armored counterattacks. Each of the five infantry divisions that was to cross the canal had been equipped with RPG-7 rockets and RPG-43 grenades, and reinforced with an anti-tank guided missile battalion, as they would not have any armor support for nearly 12 hours.[899]

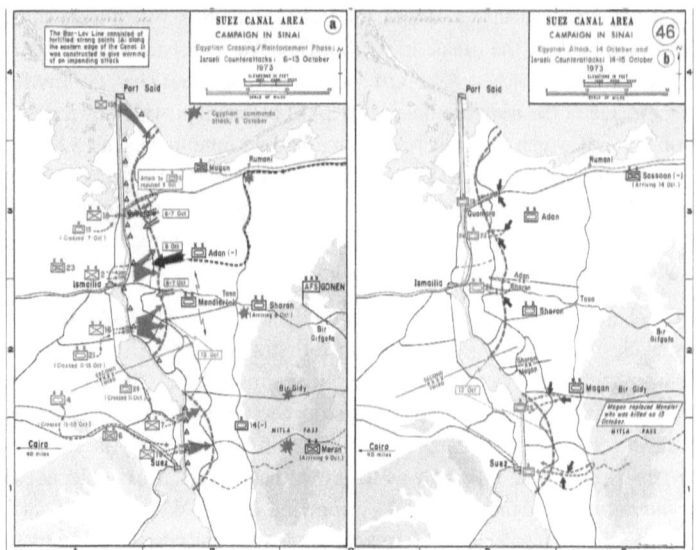

Figure 119: *The 1973 War in the Sinai, October 6–15.*

In addition, the Egyptians had built separate ramps at the crossing points, reaching as high as 21 metres (69 ft) to counter the Israeli sand wall, provide covering fire for the assaulting infantry and to counter the first Israeli armored counterattacks.[900] The scale and effectiveness of the Egyptian strategy of deploying these anti-tank weapons coupled with the Israelis' inability to disrupt their use with close air support (due to the SAM shield) greatly contributed to Israeli setbacks early in the war.

The Egyptian Army put great effort into finding a quick and effective way of breaching the Israeli defenses. The Israelis had built large 18 metre (59 foot) high sand walls with a 60 degree slope and reinforced with concrete at the water line. Egyptian engineers initially experimented with explosive charges and bulldozers to clear the obstacles, before a junior officer proposed using high pressure water cannons. The idea was tested and found to be a sound one, and several high pressure water cannons were imported from Britain and East Germany. The water cannons effectively breached the sand walls using water from the canal.[901]

At 2:00 pm on October 6, Operation Badr began with a large airstrike. More than 200 Egyptian aircraft conducted simultaneous strikes against three airbases, Hawk missile batteries, three command centers, artillery positions, and several radar installations.[902] Airfields at Refidim and Bir Tamada were temporarily put out of service, and damage was inflicted on a Hawk battery at

Figure 120: *Wreckage of an Israeli A-4 Skyhawk on display in Egypt's war museum.*

Figure 121: *Egyptian Sukhoi Su-7 fighter jets conducting air strikes over the Bar Lev Line on 6 October*

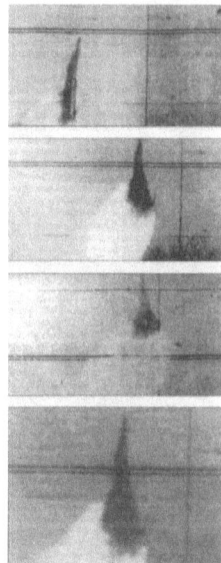

Figure 122: *An Israeli Mirage III shot down by an Egyptian MiG-21*

Ophir. The aerial assault was coupled with a barrage from more than 2,000 artillery pieces for a period of 53 minutes against the Bar Lev Line and rear area command posts and concentration bases.

Author Andrew McGregor claimed that the success of the first strike negated the need for a second planned strike.[903,904,905] Egypt acknowledged the loss of 5 aircraft during the attack. Kenneth Pollack wrote that 18 Egyptian aircraft were shot down, and that these losses prompted the cancellation of the second planned wave.[906] In one notable engagement during this period, a pair of Israeli F-4E Phantoms challenged 28 Egyptian MiGs over Sharm el-Sheikh and within half an hour, shot down seven or eight MiGs with no losses.[907,908] One of the Egyptian pilots killed was Captain Atif Sadat, President Sadat's half-brother.[909]

Simultaneously, 14 Egyptian Tupolev Tu-16 bombers attacked Israeli targets in the Sinai with Kelt missiles, while another two Egyptian Tupolevs fired two Kelt missiles at a radar station in central Israel. One missile was shot down by a patrolling Israeli Mirage fighter, and the second fell into the sea. The attack was an attempt to warn Israel that Egypt could retaliate if it bombed targets deep in Egyptian territory.[910]

Under cover of the initial artillery barrage, the Egyptian assault force of 32,000 infantry began crossing the canal in twelve waves at five separate crossing areas, from 14:05 to 17:30, in what became known as The Crossing.[911] The Egyptians prevented Israeli forces from reinforcing the Bar Lev Line and proceeded to attack the Israeli fortifications. Meanwhile, engineers crossed over to breach the sand wall.[912] The Israeli Air Force conducted air interdiction operations to try to prevent the bridges from being erected, but took losses from Egyptian SAM batteries. The air attacks were ineffective overall, as the sectional design of the bridges enabled quick repairs when hit.[913]

Despite fierce resistance, the Israeli reserve brigade garrisoning the Bar-Lev forts was overwhelmed. According to Shazly, within six hours, fifteen strongpoints had been captured as Egyptian forces advanced several kilometres into the Sinai. Shazly's account was disputed by Kenneth Pollack, who noted that for the most part, the forts only fell to repeated assaults by superior forces or prolonged sieges over many days.[914] The northernmost fortification of the Bar Lev Line, code-named 'Fort Budapest', withstood repeated assaults and remained in Israeli hands throughout the war. Once the bridges were laid, additional infantry with the remaining portable and recoilless anti-tank weapons began to cross the canal, while the first Egyptian tanks started to cross at 20:30.[915]

The Egyptians also attempted to land several heli-borne commando units in various areas in the Sinai to hamper the arrival of Israeli reserves. This attempt met with disaster as the Israelis shot down up to twenty helicopters, inflicting heavy casualties.[916,917] Israeli Major General (res.) Chaim Herzog placed Egyptian helicopter losses at fourteen.[918] Other sources claim that "several" helicopters were downed with "total loss of life" and that the few commandos that did filter through were ineffectual and presented nothing more than a "nuisance".[919] Kenneth Pollack asserted that despite their heavy losses, the Egyptian commandos fought exceptionally hard and created considerable panic, prompting the Israelis to take precautions that hindered their ability to concentrate on stopping the assault across the canal.[920]

Egyptian forces advanced approximately 4 to 5 km into the Sinai Desert with two armies (both corps-sized by western standards, included the 2nd Infantry Division in the northern Second Army). By the following morning, some 850 tanks had crossed the canal. In his account of the war, Saad El Shazly noted that by the morning of October 7, the Egyptians had lost 280 soldiers and 20 tanks, though this account is disputed.[921]

Most Israeli soldiers defending the Bar Lev Line were casualties, and some 200 were taken prisoner.[922,923,924] In the subsequent days, some defenders of the Bar Lev Line managed to break through Egyptian encirclement and return to their lines, or were extracted during Israeli counterattacks that came later on.

For the next several days, the Israeli Air Force (IAF) played a minimal role in the fighting largely because it was needed to deal with the simultaneous, and ultimately more threatening, Syrian invasion of the Golan Heights.[925]

Egyptian forces then consolidated their initial positions. On October 7, the bridgeheads were enlarged an additional 4 km, at the same time repulsing Israeli counterattacks. In the north, the Egyptian 18th Division attacked the town of El-Qantarah el-Sharqiyya, engaging Israeli forces in and around the town. The fighting there was conducted at close quarters, and was sometimes hand-to-hand. The Egyptians were forced to clear the town building by building. By evening, most of the town was in Egyptian hands. El-Qantarah was completely cleared by the next morning.[926]

Meanwhile, the Egyptian commandos airdropped on October 6 began encountering Israeli reserves the following morning. Both sides suffered heavy losses, but the commandos were at times successful in delaying the movement of Israeli reserves to the front. These special operations often led to confusion and anxiety among Israeli commanders, who commended the Egyptian commandos.[927,928] This view was contradicted by another source that stated that few commandos made it to their objectives, and were usually nothing more than a nuisance.[929] According to Abraham Rabinovich, only the commandos near Baluza and those blocking the road to Fort Budapest had measurable successes. Of the 1,700 Egyptian commandos inserted behind Israeli lines during the war, 740 were killed—many in downed helicopters—and 330 taken prisoner.[930]

Failed Israeli counter-attack

On October 7, David Elazar visited Shmuel Gonen, commander of the Israeli Southern front—who had only taken the position three months before at the retirement of Ariel Sharon—and met with Israeli commanders. The Israelis planned a cautious counterattack for the following day by Abraham Adan's 162nd Armored Division.[931] The same day, the Israeli Air Force carried out Operation Tagar, aiming to neutralize Egyptian Air Force bases and its missile defense shield.[932]

Seven Egyptian airbases were damaged with the loss of two A-4 Skyhawks and their pilots. Two more planned attacks were called off because of the increasing need for air power on the Syrian front. The IAF carried out additional air attacks against Egyptian forces on the east bank of the canal, reportedly inflicting heavy losses. Israeli jets had carried out hundreds of sorties against Egyptian targets by the following day, but the Egyptian SAM shield inflicted heavy losses. IAF aircraft losses mounted to three aircraft for every 200 sorties, an unsustainable rate. The Israelis responded by rapidly devising new tactics to thwart Egyptian air defenses.

Figure 123: *An Israeli M60 Patton tank destroyed in the Sinai.*

On October 8, after Elazar had left, Gonen changed the plans on the basis of unduly optimistic field reports. Adan's division was composed of three brigades totaling 183 tanks. One of the brigades was still en route to the area, and would participate in the attack by noon, along with a supporting mechanized infantry brigade with an additional 44 tanks.[933,934] The Israeli counterattack was in the direction of the Bar Lev strongpoints opposite the city of Ismailia, against entrenched Egyptian infantry. In a series of ill-coordinated attacks, which were met by stiff resistance, the Israelis suffered heavy losses.[935]

That afternoon, Egyptian forces advanced once more to deepen their bridgeheads, and as a result the Israelis lost several strategic positions. Further Israeli attacks to regain the lost ground proved futile. Towards nightfall, an Egyptian counterattack was repulsed with the loss of 50 Egyptian tanks by the Israeli 143rd Armored Division, which was led by General Ariel Sharon, who had been reinstated as a division commander at the outset of the war. Garwych, citing Egyptian sources, documented Egyptian tank losses up to October 13 at 240.[936]

Temporary stabilization

According to Herzog, by October 9 the front lines had stabilized. The Egyptians were unable to advance further,[937] and Egyptian armored attacks on October 9 and 10 were repulsed with heavy losses. However, this claim was

Figure 124: *An Israeli Centurion tank operating in the Sinai.*

disputed by Shazly, who claimed that the Egyptians continued to advance and improve their positions well into October 10. He pointed to one engagement, which involved elements of the 1st Infantry Brigade, attached to the 19th Division, which captured Ayoun Mousa, south of Suez.[938]

The Egyptian 1st Mechanized Brigade launched a failed attack southward along the Gulf of Suez in the direction of Ras Sudar. Leaving the safety of the SAM umbrella, the force was attacked by Israeli aircraft and suffered heavy losses.[939] Shazly cited this experience as a basis to resist pressure by Minister of War, General Ahmad Ismail Ali to attack eastward toward the Mitla and Gidi Passes.

Between October 10 and 13, both sides refrained from any large-scale actions, and the situation was relatively stable. Both sides launched small-scale attacks, and the Egyptians used helicopters to land commandos behind Israeli lines. Some Egyptian helicopters were shot down, and those commando forces that managed to land were quickly destroyed by Israeli troops In one key engagement on October 13, a particularly large Egyptian incursion was stopped and close to a hundred Egyptian commandos were killed.[940]Wikipedia:Identifying reliable sources

Yom Kippur War

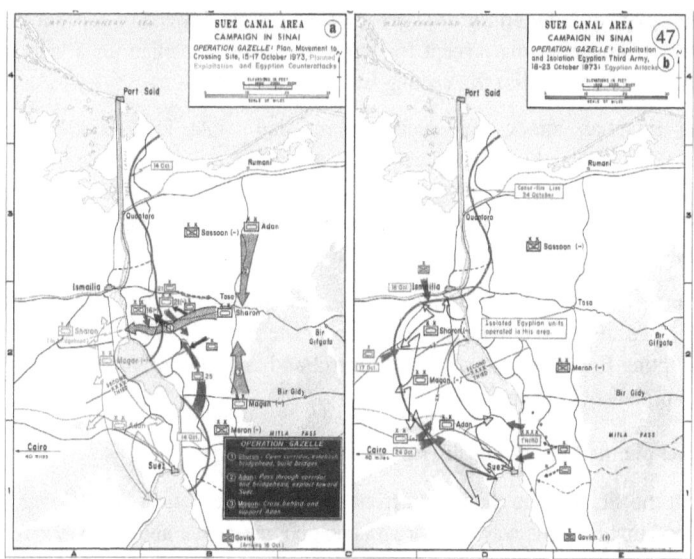

Figure 125: *The 1973 War in the Sinai, October 15–24.*

The Egyptian failed attack

General Shazly strongly opposed any eastward advance that would leave his armor without adequate air cover. He was overruled by General Ismail and Sadat, whose aims were to seize the strategic Mitla and Gidi Passes and the Israeli nerve centre at Refidim, which they hoped would relieve pressure on the Syrians (who were by now on the defensive) by forcing Israel to shift divisions from the Golan to the Sinai.[941,942]

The 2nd and 3rd Armies were ordered to attack eastward in six simultaneous thrusts over a broad front, leaving behind five infantry divisions to hold the bridgeheads. The attacking forces, consisting of 800[943]–1,000 tanks would not have SAM cover, so the Egyptian Air Force (EAF) was tasked with the defense of these forces from Israeli air attacks. Armored and mechanized units began the attack on October 14 with artillery support. They were up against 700–750 Israeli tanks.

Preparatory to the tank attack, Egyptian helicopters set down 100 commandos near the Lateral Road to disrupt the Israeli rear. An Israeli reconnaissance unit quickly subdued them, killing 60 and taking numerous prisoners. Still bruised by the extensive losses their commandos had suffered on the opening day of the war, the Egyptians were unable or unwilling to implement further commando operations that had been planned in conjunction with the armored attack.[944]

The Egyptian armored thrust suffered heavy losses. Instead of concentrating forces of maneuvering, except for the wadi thrust, Egyptian units launched head-on-attacks against the waiting Israeli defenses.[945]

The Egyptian attack was decisively repelled. At least 250 Egyptian tanks[946,947,948] and some 200 armored vehicles were destroyed. Egyptian casualties exceeded 1,000. Fewer than 40 Israeli tanks were hit and all but six of them were repaired by Israeli maintenance crews and returned to service, while Israeli casualties numbered 665.[949]

Kenneth Pollack credited a successful Israeli commando raid early on October 14 against an Egyptian signals-intercept site at Jebel Ataqah with seriously disrupting Egyptian command and control and contributing to its breakdown during the engagement.[950]

Israel planned attack considerations

With the situation on the Syrian front stabilizing, the Israeli High Command agreed that the time was ripe for an Israeli counterattack and strike across the canal.

General Sharon advocated an immediate crossing at Deversoir at the northern edge of Great Bitter Lake. On October 9, a reconnaissance force attached to Colonel Amnon Reshef's Brigade detected a gap between the Egyptian Second and Third armies in this sector. According to General Gamasy, the gap had been detected by an American SR-71 spy plane.[951] Chief of Staff Elazar and General Chaim Bar-Lev, who had by now replaced Gonen as Chief of Southern Command, agreed that this was the ideal spot for a crossing. However, given the size of the Egyptian armored reserves, the Israelis chose to wait for an opportunity that would allow them to reduce Egyptian armored strength before initiating any crossing.

The opportunity arrived on October 12, when Israeli intelligence detected signs that the Egyptians were gearing up for a major armored thrust.[952] This was precisely the moment the Israelis were waiting for. They could finally utilize their advantages in speed, maneuver and tank gunnery, areas in which they excelled. Once Egyptian armored strength was sufficiently degraded, the Israelis would commence their own canal crossing.

Israeli breakthrough – Crossing the canal

The Israelis immediately followed the Egyptian failed attack of October 14 with a multidivisional counterattack through the gap between the Egyptian 2nd and 3rd Armies. Sharon's 143rd Division, now reinforced with a paratroop brigade commanded by Colonel Danny Matt, was tasked with establishing bridgeheads on the east and west banks of the canal. The 162nd and 252nd

Figure 126: *Israeli tanks crossing the Suez Canal.*

Armored Divisions, commanded by Generals Avraham Adan and Kalman Magen respectively, would then cross through the breach to the west bank of the canal and swing southward, encircling the 3rd Army.[953] The offensive was code-named Operation Stouthearted Men or alternatively, Operation Valiant.

On the night of October 15, 750 of Colonel Matt's paratroopers crossed the canal in rubber dinghies.[954] They were soon joined by tanks ferried on motorized rafts and additional infantry. The force encountered no resistance initially and fanned out in raiding parties, attacking supply convoys, SAM sites, logistic centers and anything of military value, with priority given to the SAMs. Attacks on SAM sites punched a hole in the Egyptian anti-aircraft screen and enabled the Israeli Air Force to strike Egyptian ground targets more aggressively.[955]

On the night of October 15, 20 Israeli tanks and 7 APCs under the command of Colonel Haim Erez crossed the canal and penetrated 12 kilometres into mainland Egypt, taking the Egyptians by surprise. For the first 24 hours, Erez's force attacked SAM sites and military columns with impunity. On the morning of October 17, it was attacked by the 23rd Egyptian Armored Brigade, but managed to repulse the attack. By this time, the Syrians no longer posed a credible threat and the Israelis were able to shift their air power to the south in support of the offensive.[956] The combination of a weakened Egyptian SAM umbrella and a greater concentration of Israeli fighter-bombers meant that the IAF was capable of greatly increasing sorties against Egyptian military targets, including convoys, armor and airfields. The Egyptian bridges across the canal were damaged in Israeli air and artillery attacks.

Israeli jets began attacking Egyptian SAM sites and radars, prompting General Ismail to withdraw much of the Egyptians' air defense equipment. This in turn gave the IAF still greater freedom to operate in Egyptian airspace. Israeli jets also attacked and destroyed underground communication cables at Banha in the Nile Delta, forcing the Egyptians to transmit selective messages by radio, which could be intercepted. Aside from the cables at Banha, Israel refrained from attacking economic and strategic infrastructure following an Egyptian threat to retaliate against Israeli cities with Scud missiles. Israeli aircraft bombed Egyptian Scud batteries at Port Said several times. The Egyptian Air Force attempted to interdict IAF sorties and attack Israeli ground forces, but suffered heavy losses in dogfights and from Israeli air defenses, while inflicting light aircraft losses on the Israelis. The heaviest air battles took place over the northern Nile Delta, where the Israelis repeatedly attempted to destroy Egyptian airbases.[957]

Securing the bridgehead

Despite the success the Israelis were having on the west bank, Generals Bar-Lev and Elazar ordered Sharon to concentrate on securing the bridgehead on the east bank. He was ordered to clear the roads leading to the canal as well as a position known as the Chinese Farm, just north of Deversoir, the Israeli crossing point. Sharon objected and requested permission to expand and breakout of the bridgehead on the west bank, arguing that such a maneuver would cause the collapse of Egyptian forces on the east bank. But the Israeli high command was insistent, believing that until the east bank was secure, forces on the west bank could be cut off. Sharon was overruled by his superiors and relented.[958]

On October 16, he dispatched Amnon Reshef's Brigade to attack the Chinese Farm. Other IDF forces attacked entrenched Egyptian forces overlooking the roads to the canal. After three days of bitter and close-quarters fighting, the Israelis succeeded in dislodging the numerically superior Egyptian forces. The Israelis lost about 300 dead, 1,000 wounded, and 56 tanks. The Egyptians suffered heavier casualties, including 118 tanks destroyed and 15 captured.[959,960,961,962,963,964]

Egyptian response to the Israeli crossing

The Egyptians meanwhile failed to grasp the extent and magnitude of the Israeli crossing, nor did they appreciate its intent and purpose. This was partly due to attempts by Egyptian field commanders to obfuscate reports concerning the Israeli crossing[965] and partly due to a false assumption that the canal crossing was merely a diversion for a major IDF offensive targeting the right flank

Figure 127: *Israeli soldiers during the Battle of Ismailia. One of them has a captured Egyptian RPG-7.*

of the Second Army.[966] Consequently, on October 16, General Shazly ordered the 21st Armored Division to attack southward and the T-62-equipped 25th Independent Armored Brigade to attack northward in a pincer action to eliminate the perceived threat to the Second Army.[967]

The Egyptians failed to scout the area and were unaware that by now, Adan's 162nd Armored Division was in the vicinity. Moreover, the 21st and 25th failed to coordinate their attacks, allowing General Adan's Division to meet each force individually. Adan first concentrated his attack on the 21st Armored Division, destroying 50–60 Egyptian tanks and forcing the remainder to retreat. He then turned southward and ambushed the 25th Independent Armored Brigade, destroying 86 of its 96 tanks and all of its APCs while losing three tanks.

Egyptian artillery shelled the Israeli bridge over the canal on the morning of October 17, scoring several hits. The Egyptian Air Force launched repeated raids, some with up to twenty aircraft, to take out the bridge and rafts, damaging the bridge. The Egyptians had to shut down their SAM sites during these raids, allowing Israeli fighters to intercept the Egyptians. The Egyptians lost 16 planes and 7 helicopters, while the Israelis lost 6 planes.[968]

The bridge was damaged, and the Israeli Paratroop Headquarters, which was near the bridge, was also hit, wounding the commander and his deputy. During the night, the bridge was repaired, but only a trickle of Israeli forces crossed. According to Chaim Herzog, the Egyptians continued attacking the bridgehead until the cease-fire, using artillery and mortars to fire tens of thousands

Figure 128: *Destroyed Israeli M48 Patton tanks on the banks of the Suez Canal.*

of shells into the area of the crossing. Egyptian aircraft attempted to bomb the bridge every day, and helicopters launched suicide missions, making attempts to drop barrels of napalm on the bridge and bridgehead. The bridges were damaged multiple times, and had to be repaired at night. The attacks caused heavy casualties, and many tanks were sunk when their rafts were hit. Egyptian commandos and frogmen with armored support launched a ground attack against the bridgehead, which was repulsed with the loss of 10 tanks. Two subsequent Egyptian counterattacks were also beaten back.

After the failure of the October 17 counterattacks, the Egyptian General Staff slowly began to realize the magnitude of the Israeli offensive. Early on October 18, the Soviets showed Sadat satellite imagery of Israeli forces operating on the west bank. Alarmed, Sadat dispatched Shazly to the front to assess the situation first hand. He no longer trusted his field commanders to provide accurate reports.[969] Shazly confirmed that the Israelis had at least one division on the west bank and were widening their bridgehead. He advocated withdrawing most of Egypt's armor from the east bank to confront the growing Israeli threat on the west bank. Sadat rejected this recommendation outright and even threatened Shazly with a court martial.[970] Ahmad Ismail Ali recommended that Sadat push for a cease-fire so as to prevent the Israelis from exploiting their successes.

Israeli forces across the Suez

Israeli forces were by now pouring across the canal on two bridges, including one of indigenous design, and motorized rafts. Israeli engineers under Brigadier-General Dan Even had worked under heavy Egyptian fire to set up the bridges, and over 100 were killed and hundreds more wounded.[971] The crossing was difficult because of Egyptian artillery fire, though by 4:00 am, two of Adan's brigades were on the west bank of the canal. On the morning of October 18, Sharon's forces on the west bank launched an offensive toward Ismailia, slowly pushing back the Egyptian paratroop brigade occupying the sand rampart northward to enlarge the bridgehead. Some of his units attempted to move west, but were stopped at the crossroads in Nefalia. Adan's division rolled south toward Suez City while Magen's division pushed west toward Cairo and south toward Adabiya.[972,973] On October 19, one of Sharon's brigades continued to push the Egyptian paratroopers north towards Ismailia until the Israelis were within 8 or 10 km (5 or 6 mi) of the city. Sharon hoped to seize the city and thereby sever the logistical and supply lines for most of the Egyptian Second Army. Sharon's second brigade began to cross the canal. The brigade's forward elements moved to the Abu Sultan Camp, from where they moved north to take Orcha, an Egyptian logistics base defended by a commando battalion. Israeli infantrymen cleared the trenches and bunkers, often engaging in hand-to-hand combat, as tanks moved alongside them and fired into the trench sections to their front. The position was secured before nightfall. More than 300 Egyptians were killed and 50 taken prisoner, while the Israelis lost 18 dead. The fall of Orcha caused the collapse of the Egyptian defensive line, allowing more Israeli troops to get onto the sand rampart. There, they were able to fire in support of Israeli troops facing Missouri Ridge, an Egyptian-occupied position on the Bar-Lev Line that could pose a threat to the Israeli crossing. On the same day, Israeli paratroopers participating in Sharon's drive pushed the Egyptians back far enough for the Israeli bridges to be out of sight of Egyptian artillery observers, though the Egyptians continued shelling the area.[974]

As the Israelis pushed towards Ismailia, the Egyptians fought a delaying battle, falling into defensive positions further north as they came under increasing pressure from the Israeli ground offensive, coupled with airstrikes. On October 21, one of Sharon's brigades was occupying the city's outskirts, but facing fierce resistance from Egyptian paratroopers and commandos. The same day, Sharon's last remaining unit on the east bank attacked Missouri Ridge. Shmuel Gonen had demanded Sharon capture the position, and Sharon had reluctantly ordered the attack. The assault was preceded by an air attack that caused hundreds of Egyptian soldiers to flee and thousands of others to dig in. One battalion then attacked from the south, destroying 20 tanks and overrunning infantry positions before being halted by Sagger rockets and minefields. Another battalion attacked from southwest, and was stopped by fortified infantry. The Israelis managed to occupy one-third of Missouri Ridge. Defense Minister Moshe Dayan countermanded orders from Sharon's superiors to continue the attack.[975,976] However, the Israelis continued to expand their holdings on the east bank. According to the Israelis, the IDF bridgehead was 40 km (25 mi) wide and 32 km (20 mi) deep by the end of October 21.[977]

On October 22, Ismailia's Egyptian defenders were occupying their last line of defense, but managed to repel an Israeli attempt to get behind Ismailia and encircle the city, then push some of Sharon's forward troops back to the Sweetwater Canal. The Israeli advance on Ismailia had been stopped 10 km south of the city. Both sides had suffered heavy losses.

On the northern front, the Israelis also attacked Port Said, facing Egyptian troops and a 900-strong Tunisian unit, who fought a defensive battle.[978] The Egyptian government claimed that the city was repeatedly bombed by Israeli jets, and that hundreds of civilians were killed or wounded.[979]

Adan and Magen moved south, decisively defeating the Egyptians in a series of engagements, though they often encountered determined Egyptian resistance, and both sides suffered heavy casualties.[980] Adan advanced towards the Sweetwater Canal area, planning to break out into the surrounding desert and hit the Geneifa Hills, where many SAM sites were located. Adan's three armored brigades fanned out, with one advancing through the Geneifa Hills, another along a parallel road south of them, and the third advancing towards Mina. Adan's brigades met resistance from dug-in Egyptian forces in the Sweetwater Canal area's greenbelt. Adan's other brigades were also held by a line of Egyptian military camps and installations. Adan was also harassed by the Egyptian Air Force. The Israelis slowly advanced, bypassing Egyptian positions whenever possible. After being denied air support due to the presence of two SAM batteries that had been brought forward, Adan sent two brigades to attack them. The brigades slipped past the dug-in Egyptian infantry, moving out from the greenbelt for more than eight kilometres, and fought off multiple Egyptian counterattacks. From a distance of four kilometres, they shelled and destroyed the SAMs, allowing the IAF to provide Adan with close air support.[981] Adan's troops advanced through the greenbelt and fought their way to the Geneifa Hills, clashing with scattered Egyptian, Kuwaiti, and Palestinian troops. The Israelis clashed with an Egyptian armored unit at Mitzeneft and destroyed multiple SAM sites. Adan also captured Fayid Airport, which was subsequently prepared by Israeli crews to serve as a supply base and to fly out wounded soldiers.[982]

16 kilometres (10 mi) west of the Bitter Lake, Colonel Natke Nir's brigade overran an Egyptian artillery brigade that had been participating in the shelling

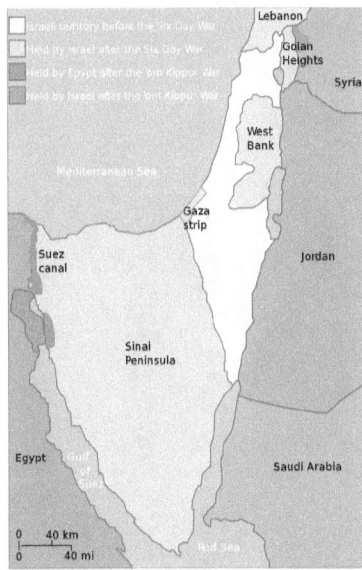

Figure 129: *When the ceasefire came into effect, Israel had lost territory on the east side of the Suez Canal to Egypt − , but gained territory west of the canal and in the Golan Heights − .*

of the Israeli bridgehead. Scores of Egyptian artillerymen were killed and many more taken prisoner. Two Israeli soldiers were also killed, including the son of General Moshe Gidron. Meanwhile, Magen's division moved west and then south, covering Adan's flank and eventually moving south of Suez City to the Gulf of Suez.[983] The Israeli advance southward reached Port Suez, on the southern boundary of the Suez Canal.

The ceasefire and further battles

The United Nations Security Council passed (14–0) Resolution 338 calling for a ceasefire, largely negotiated between the U.S. and Soviet Union, on October 22. It called upon the belligerents to immediately cease all military activity. The cease-fire was to come into effect 12 hours later at 6:52 pm Israeli time.[984] Because this was after dark, it was impossible for satellite surveillance to determine where the front lines were when the fighting was supposed to stop.[985] U.S. Secretary of State Henry Kissinger intimated to Prime Minister Meir that he would not object to offensive action during the night before the ceasefire was to come into effect.

Several minutes before the ceasefire came into effect, three Scud missiles were fired at Israeli targets by either Egyptian forces or Soviet personnel in Egypt.

Figure 130: *An Israeli soldier on the road to Ismailia.*

This was the first combat use of Scud missiles. One Scud targeted the port of Arish and two targeted the Israeli bridgehead on the Suez Canal. One hit an Israeli supply convoy and killed seven soldiers.[986] When the time for the ceasefire arrived, Sharon's division had failed to capture Ismailia and cut off the Second Army's supply lines, but Israeli forces were just a few hundred metres short of their southern goal—the last road linking Cairo and Suez.[987]

Adan's drive south had left Israeli and Egyptian units scattered throughout the battlefield, with no clear lines between them. As Egyptian and Israeli units tried to regroup, regular firefights broke out. During the night, Elazar reported that the Egyptians were attacking in an attempt to regain land at various locations, and that nine Israeli tanks had been destroyed. He asked permission from Dayan to respond to the attacks and Dayan agreed. Israel then resumed its drive south.[988]

It is unclear which side fired first[989] but Israeli field commanders used the skirmishes as justification to resume the attacks. When Sadat protested alleged Israeli truce violations, Israel said that Egyptian troops had fired first. William B. Quandt noted that regardless of who fired the first post-ceasefire shot, it was the Israeli Army that was advancing beyond the October 22 ceasefire lines.[990]

Adan resumed his attack on October 23.[991] Israeli troops finished the drive south, captured the last ancillary road south of the port of Suez, and encircled the Egyptian Third Army east of the Suez Canal.[992] The Israelis then transported enormous amounts of military equipment across the canal, which Egypt claimed was in violation of the ceasefire. Egyptian aircraft launched repeated attacks in support of the Third Army, sometimes in groups of up to 30 planes, but took severe losses.[993]

Israeli armor and paratroopers also entered Suez in an attempt to capture the city, but they were confronted by Egyptian soldiers and hastily raised local militia forces. They were surrounded, but towards night the Israeli forces managed to extricate themselves. The Israelis had lost 80 dead and 120 wounded, with an unknown number of Egyptian casualties, for no tactical gain (see Battle of Suez).[994]

The next morning, October 23, a flurry of diplomatic activity occurred. Soviet reconnaissance flights had confirmed that Israeli forces were moving south, and the Soviets accused the Israelis of treachery. Kissinger called Meir in an effort to persuade her to withdraw a few hundred metres and she indicated that Israel's tactical position on the ground had improved.

Egypt's trapped Third Army

Kissinger found out about the Third Army's encirclement shortly thereafter.[995] Kissinger considered that the situation presented the United States with a tremendous opportunity and that Egypt was dependent on the United States to prevent Israel from destroying its trapped army. The position could be parlayed later into allowing the United States to mediate the dispute and wean Egypt from Soviet influence. As a result, the United States exerted tremendous pressure on the Israelis to refrain from destroying the trapped army, even threatening to support a UN resolution demanding that the Israelis withdraw to their October 22 positions if they did not allow non-military supplies to reach the army. In a phone call with Israeli ambassador Simcha Dinitz, Kissinger told the ambassador that the destruction of the Egyptian Third Army "is an option that does not exist."[996]

Despite being surrounded, the Third Army managed to maintain its combat integrity east of the canal and keep up its defensive positions, to the surprise of many.[997] According to Trevor N. Dupuy, the Israelis, Soviets and Americans overestimated the vulnerability of the Third Army at the time. It was not on the verge of collapse, and he wrote that while a renewed Israeli offensive would probably overcome it, this was not a certainty,[998] and according to David Elazar chief of Israeli headquarter staff on December 3, 1973: "As for the third army, in spite of our encircling them they resisted and advanced to occupy in fact a wider area of land at the east. Thus, we can not say that we defeated or conquered them."

David T. Buckwalter agrees that despite the isolation of the Third Army, it was unclear if the Israelis could have protected their forces on the west bank of the canal from a determined Egyptian assault and still maintain sufficient strength along the rest of the front.[999] This assessment was challenged by Patrick Seale, who stated that the Third Army was "on the brink of collapse". Seale's position was supported by P.R. Kumaraswamy, who wrote that intense American pressure prevented the Israelis from annihilating the stranded Third Army.

Herzog noted that given the Third Army's desperate situation, in terms of being cut off from re-supply and reassertion of Israeli air superiority, the destruction of the Third Army was inevitable and could have been achieved within a very brief period.[1000] Shazly himself described the Third Army's plight as "desperate" and classified its encirclement as a "catastrophe that was too big to hide".[1001] He further noted that, "the fate of the Egyptian Third Army was in the hands of Israel. Once the Third Army was encircled by Israeli troops every bit of bread to be sent to our men was paid for by meeting Israeli demands."[1002]

Shortly before the ceasefire came into effect, an Israeli tank battalion advanced into Adabiya, and took it with support from the Israeli Navy. Some 1,500 Egyptian prisoners were taken, and about a hundred Egyptian soldiers assembled just south of Adabiya, where they held out against the Israelis. The Israelis also conducted their third and final incursion into Suez. They made some gains, but failed to break into the city center. As a result, the city was partitioned down the main street, with the Egyptians holding the city center and the Israelis controlling the outskirts, port installations and oil refinery, effectively surrounding the Egyptian defenders.

Post war battles

On the morning of October 26, the Egyptian Third Army violated the ceasefire by attempting to break through surrounding Israeli forces. The attack was repulsed by Israeli air and ground forces. The Egyptians also made minor gains in attacks against Sharon's forces in the Ismailia area. The Israelis reacted by bombing and shelling priority targets in Egypt, including command posts and water reserves.[1003] The front was quieter in the Second Army's sector in the northern canal area, where both sides generally respected the ceasefire.

Though most heavy fighting ended on October 28, the fighting never stopped until January 18, 1974. Israeli Defense Minister Moshe Dayan stated that "The cease-fire existed on paper, but the continued firing along the front was not the only characteristic of the situation between October 24, 1973 and January 18, 1974. This intermediate period also held the ever-present possibility of a renewal of full-scale war. There were three variations on how it might break out, two Egyptian and one Israeli. One Egyptian plan was to attack Israeli units west of the canal from the direction of Cairo. The other was to cut off the Israeli canal bridgehead by a link-up of the Second and Third Armies on the east bank. Both plans were based on massive artillery pounding of Israeli forces, who were not well fortified and who would suffer heavy casualties. It was therefore thought that Israel would withdraw from the west bank, since she was most sensitive on the subject of soldier's lives. Egypt, at the time had a total of 1,700 first-line tanks on both sides of the canal front, 700 on the east bank and 1,000 on the west bank. Also on the west bank, in the second line, were an additional 600 tanks for the defense of Cairo. She had some 2,000 artillery pieces, about 500 operational aircraft, and at least 130 SAM missile batteries positioned around our forces so as to deny us air support."

The IDF acknowledged the loss of 14 soldiers during this postwar period. Egyptian losses were higher, especially in the sector controlled by General Ariel Sharon, who ordered his troops to respond with massive firepower to any Egyptian provocation.[1004] Some aerial battles took place, and the Israelis also shot down several helicopters attempting to resupply the Third Army.[1005]

Final situation on the Egyptian front

By the end of the war, the Israelis had advanced to positions some 101 kilometres from Egypt's capital, Cairo, and occupied 1,600 square kilometres west of the Suez Canal.[1006] They had also cut the Cairo-Suez road and encircled the bulk of Egypt's Third Army. The Israelis had also taken many prisoners after Egyptian soldiers, including many officers, began surrendering in masses towards the end of the war.[1007] The Egyptians held a narrow strip on the east bank of the canal, occupying some 1,200 square kilometres of the Sinai. One source estimated that the Egyptians had 70,000 men, 720 tanks and 994 artillery pieces on the east bank of the canal.[1008] However, 30,000 to 45,000 of them were now encircled by the Israelis.[1009,1010]

Despite Israel's tactical successes west of the canal, the Egyptian military was reformed and organized. Consequently, according to Gamasy, the Israeli military position became "weak" for different reasons, "One, Israel now had a large force (about six or seven brigades) in a very limited area of land, surrounded from all sides either by natural or man-made barriers, or by the Egyptian forces. This put it in a weak position. Moreover, there were the difficulties in supplying this force, in evacuating it, in the lengthy communication lines, and in the daily attrition in men and equipment. Two, to protect these troops, the Israeli command had to allocate other forces (four or five brigades) to defend the entrances to the breach at the Deversoir. Three, to immobilize the Egyptian bridgeheads in Sinai the Israeli command had to allocate ten brigades to face the Second and Third army bridgeheads. In addition, it became necessary to keep the strategic reserves at their maximum state of alert. Thus, Israel

Figure 131: *President Hafez al-Assad (right) with soldiers, 1973.*

was obliged to keep its armed force-and consequently the country-mobilized for a long period, at least until the war came to an end, because the ceasefire did not signal the end of the war. There is no doubt that this in total conflict with its military theories."[1011] For those reasons and according to Dayan, "It was therefore thought that Israel would withdraw from the west bank, since she was most sensitive on the subject of soldier's lives." The Egyptian forces didn't pull to the west and held onto their positions east of the canal controlling both shores of the Suez Canal. None of the Canal's main cities were occupied by Israel; however, the city of Suez was surrounded.

Egypt wished to end the war when they realized that the IDF canal crossing offensive could result in a catastrophe.[1012] The Egyptian's besieged Third Army could not hold on without supply. The Israeli Army advanced to 100 km from Cairo, which worried Egypt. The Israeli army had open terrain and no opposition to advance further to Cairo; had they done so, Sadat's rule might have ended.

On the Golan Heights

Initial Syrian attacks

In the Golan Heights, the Syrians attacked two Israeli armored brigades, an infantry brigade, two paratrooper battalions and eleven artillery batteries with five divisions (the 7th, 9th and 5th, with the 1st and 3rd in reserve) and 188 batteries. At the onset of the battle, the Israeli brigades of some 3,000 troops,

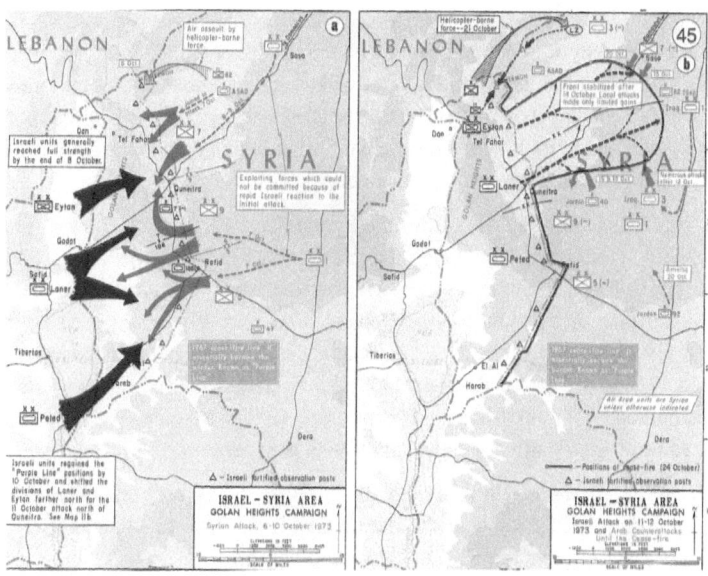

Figure 132: *A map of the fighting on the Golan Heights.*

180 tanks and 60 artillery pieces faced off against three infantry divisions with large armor components comprising 28,000 Syrian troops, 800 tanks and 600 artillery pieces. In addition, the Syrians deployed two armored divisions from the second day onwards.[1013,1014] To fight the opening phase of a possible battle, before reserves arrived, Israeli high command had conforming to the original plan allocated a single armored brigade, the 188th, accepting a disparity in tank numbers of eighteen to one.[1015] When the warning by King Hussein of an imminent Syrian attack was conveyed, Elazar at first only assigned two additional tank companies from 7th Armored Brigade: "We'll have one hundred tanks against their eight hundred. That ought to be enough".[1016] Eventually, his deputy, Israel Tal, ordered the entire 7th Armored Brigade to be brought up.[1017] Efforts had been made to improve the Israeli defensive position. The "Purple Line" ran along a series of low dormant volcanic cones, "tels", in the north and deep ravines in the south. It was covered by a continuous tank ditch, bunker complexes and dense minefields. Directly west of this line a series of tank ramps were constructed: earthen platforms on which a Centurion tank could position itself with only its upper turret and gun visible, offering a substantial advantage when duelling the fully exposed enemy tanks.[1018]

The Syrians began their attack at 14:00 with an airstrike by about a hundred aircraft and a fifty-minute artillery barrage. The two forward infantry brigades, with an organic tank battalion, of each of the three infantry divisions then crossed the cease-fire lines, bypassing United Nations observer posts. They were covered by mobile anti-aircraft batteries, and equipped with bulldozers to fill-in anti-tank ditches, bridge-layer tanks to overcome obstacles and mine-clearance vehicles. These engineering vehicles were priority targets for Israeli tank gunners and took heavy losses, but Syrian infantry at points demolished the tank ditch, allowing their armor to cross.

At 14:45, two hundred men from the Syrian 82nd Paratrooper Battalion descended on foot from Mount Hermon and around 17:00 took the Israeli observation base on the southern slope, with its advanced surveillance equipment. A small force dropped by four helicopters simultaneously placed itself on the access road south of the base.[1019] Specialised intelligence personnel were captured. Made to believe that Israel had fallen, they disclosed much sensitive information.[1020] A first Israeli attempt on 8 October to retake the base from the south was ambushed and beaten off with heavy losses.[1021]

During the afternoon 7th Armored Brigade was still kept in reserve and the 188th Armored Brigade held the frontline with only two tank battalions, the 74th in the north and the 53rd in the south.[1022] The northern battalion waged an exemplary defensive battle against the forward brigades of the Syrian 7th Infantry Division, destroying fifty-nine Syrian tanks for minimal losses.[1023] The southern battalion destroyed a similar number, but facing four Syrian tank battalions from two divisions had a dozen of its own tanks knocked out.[1024] At bunker complex 111, opposite Kudne in Syria, the defending company beat off "determined" and "bravely" pressed attacks by the Syrian 9th Infantry Division; by nightfall it was reduced to three tanks, with only sixty-nine anti-tank rounds between them.[1025] Further successful resistance by the southern battalion was contingent on reinforcements.

Direct operational command of the Golan had at first been given to the 188 AB commander, Yitzhak Ben-Shoham, who ordered the 7th AB to concentrate at Wasset.[1026] The 7th AB commander, Avigdor Ben-Gal, resented obeying an officer of equal rank and went to the Northern Command headquarters at Nafah, announcing he would place his force in the northern sector at the "Quneitra Gap", a pass south of the Hermonit peak and the main access to the Golan Heights from the east. Northern Command was in the process of moving their headquarters to Safed in Galilee and the senior staff officers were absent at this moment, having expected the Syrian attack to start at 18:00. Operations officer Lieutenant-Colonel Uri Simhoni therefore improvised an allocation of the tactical reserves, thereby largely deciding the course of the battle.[1027] The Armored School Centurion Tank Battalion (71st TB) was kept in general reserve. The 77th Tank Battalion of 7th AB was sent to Quneitra. Two companies of the 75th Mechanised Infantry Battalion, arrived in the morning, of the same brigade were sent to the southern sector. Also 82nd TB had to reinforce

Figure 133: *An Israeli Centurion tank. It was considered in many respects superior to the Soviet T-54/55.*[1031]

the south. However, Ben-Gal had split off a company of this battalion to serve as a reserve for his own brigade.[1028] Another company, soon after arriving in the south, was ambushed by an infiltrated Syrian commando force armed with Sagger missiles and almost entirely wiped out.[1029] As a result, effective reinforcement of the southern Golan sector was limited to just a single tank company.[1030]

At 16:00, Yitzhak Hofi, head Northern Command, shortly visited Nafah and split command of the Golan front: the north would be the responsibility of 7th AB, to which 53rd TB would be transferred. Command of 188th AB would be limited to the south, taking over 82nd TB.[1032] The first wave of the Syrian offensive had failed to penetrate, but at nightfall a second, larger, wave was launched. For this purpose each of the three infantry divisions, also committing their organic mechanised brigade with forty tanks, had been reinforced by an armored brigade of about ninety tanks. Two of these brigades were to attack the northern sector, four the southern sector.[1033]

Successful defense of the Quneitra Gap by the 7th Armored Brigade

Over four days of fighting, the 7th Armored Brigade in the north under Avigdor Ben-Gal managed to hold the rocky hill line defending the northern flank of their headquarters in Nafah, inflicting heavy losses on the Syrians. In the night of 6/7 October, it beat off an attack of the Syrian 78th Armoured Brigade, attached to the 7th Infantry Division.[1034] On 7 October, 7th AB had to send part of its reserves to the collapsing southern sector. Replenishment from the Nafah matériel stock became impossible. Syrian High Command, understanding that forcing the Quneitra Gap would ensure a total victory on the Golan, decided to commit its strategic armored reserves. During the night of 7/8 October, the independent 81st Armored Brigade, equipped with modern T-62's and part of the presidential guard, attacked but was beaten off.[1035] After this fight, the Israeli brigade would refer to the gap as the "Valley of Tears".[1036] Syrian Brigadier-General Omar Abrash, commander of the 7th Infantry Division, was killed on 8 October when his command tank was hit as he was preparing an attempt by 121st Mechanised Brigade to bypass the gap through a more southern route.[1037]

Having practiced on the Golan Heights numerous times, Israeli gunners made effective use of mobile artillery. During night attacks, the Syrian tanks had the advantage of active illumination infrared night vision equipment, which was not a standard Israeli equipment. The close distances during night engagements, negated the usual Israeli superiority in long-range duels. 77th Tank Battalion commander Avigdor Kahalani in the Quneitra Gap generally managed to hold a second tank ramp line.

In the afternoon of October 9, Syrian command committed the Republican Guard independent 70th Armored Brigade, equipped with T-62's and BMP-1s.[1038] To hold the gap, 7th AB could by now muster only some two dozen tanks, elements from the 77th, 74th, 82nd and 71st Tank Battalion. Israeli command had directed all reserves to the threatened southern sector, trusting that the northern sector was secure. Fighting in daylight proved to be advantageous to the Syrians: the better armored T-62's were hard to destroy at long range and their high-velocity 115 mm smoothbore guns were quite accurate at medium ranges, despite the lack of a rangefinder. Taking losses and hit by an intense artillery barrage, the Israeli Centurions withdrew from their tank ramps. The situation was restored by an ad hoc force of thirteen tanks formed by Lt. Col. Yossi Ben-Hanan from repaired vehicles and stray crews. The Syrians abandoned their last breakthrough attempt, having lost since 6 October some 260 tanks in the Quneitra Gap.[1039]

Figure 134: *Israeli tank on the Golan Heights during the Arab–Israeli War*

Syrian breakthrough in the southern Golan

In the southern sector, the Israeli Barak Armored Brigade had to defend a much flatter terrain.[1040] It also faced two-thirds of the Syrian second wave, while fielding at this time less than a third of the operational Israeli tanks. Beside these objective draw-backs, it suffered from ineffective command. Ben-Shoham initially still had his headquarters in Nafah, far from his sector. He did not realise a full war was in progress and tended to spread the 53rd TB platoons along the entire line, to stop any Syrian incursion. Also, he failed to coordinate the deployment of 82nd TB and 53rd TB.[1041] The commander of 53rd TB, Lieutenant-Colonel Oded Eres, sent the two arriving companies of 82nd TB to his right flank and centre.[1042] No further reinforcement materialising, he urgently ordered the southern company to the north again; it was ambushed on the way. His left flank at Kudne remained unreinforced, although the defending company had increased the number of operational tanks to eight. This was the main axis of the Syrian 9th Infantry Division and its commander, Colonel Hassan Tourkmani, ordered the remnants of an organic tank battalion to be sacrificed forcing the minefield belt.[1043] Subsequently, the Syrian 51st Armored Brigade bypassed bunker complex 111 after dark. It then overran the Israeli supply compound at the Hushniya cross-roads.[1044] Parts of the 75th Mechanised Infantry Battalion had been concentrated at Hushniya, but they did not consist of its two organic tank companies; they were M-113 units. Lacking modern antitank weapons, Israeli infantry was ineffective at

Figure 135: *Abandoned Syrian T-62 tanks on the Golan Heights.*

stopping Syrian armor.[1045] The 51st AB passing through the Kudne/Rafid Gap turned northwest to move along the Petroleum Road or "Tapline Road", which provided a diagonal route across the heights, running straight from Hushniya to Nafah, the Israeli Golan headquarters, in the rear of the Quneitra Gap.

Israeli command was initially slow to realise that a breakthrough had taken place. Their main concern was that the Syrians would occupy some forward bunker complex or settlement.[1046] The fact that the defending tank platoons were still intact was seen as proof that the line had not been broken. Ben-Shoham around 18:30 moved his headquarters to the south. Reports of Syrian radio traffic at Hushniya, of Israeli reserve tanks passing columns of Syrian tanks in the dark and of enemy tanks moving at the rear of the observation post on Tel Saki, were dismissed by him as misidentifications.[1047] Only when two tanks parked in the dark near his staff vehicles and were recognised for T-55s when hastily driving away upon being hailed, he understood that a large Syrian tank unit had infiltrated his lines.[1048]

As a result, no regular units were directed to block a Syrian advance to Nafah. Ben-Shoham had ordered Lieutenant Zvika Greengold, who, about to be trained as a tank company commander, had arrived at Nafah unattached to any combat unit, to gather some crews and follow him to the south with a few tanks to take command of the bunker complex 111 and 112 tank forces which had lost all officers. Three miles south of Nafah base, Greengold was warned by a truck convoy that there were Syrian tanks ahead.[1049] These belonged to the 452st Tank Battalion, hurrying north to surprise Nafah. Confronted at short range with a first group of three T-55's, Greengold's Centurion destroyed them in quick succession. He then moved parallel to the road to the south, hitting advancing Syrian tanks in the flank and destroying another ten until he approached Hushniya. From this the commander of 452st TB, Major Farouk Ismail, concluded that he had been ambushed by a strong Israeli tank unit and concentrated his remaining vehicles in a defensive position at Hushniya.[1050] Greengold decided not to reveal how precarious the Israeli situation was, in radio contact with Ben-Shoham hiding the fact that his "Force Zvika" consisted of only a single tank.[1051]

The next 9th Infantry Division unit to participate in the second wave, the 43rd Mechanised Infantry Brigade, entered the Golan at Kudne, but then sharply turned to the right advancing over the lateral "Reshet" road behind the Purple Line in the direction of Quneitra. Israeli 1st Infantry Brigade elements warned 7th Armored Brigade of the danger. Ben Gal then released the 82nd TB company he had held back, commanded by Captain Meir "Tiger" Zamir, and sent it to the south to cover his flank. Zamir ambushed the Syrian brigade; directing their fire with the xenon light projector on one of his tanks his company destroyed a dozen vehicles.[1052] At dawn he surprised the enemy column from the rear and dispersed the remnants of 43 MIB, having knocked-out all of its forty tanks.[1053]

Israeli strategic response

Around midnight, Hofi, at Safed, began to understand the magnitude of the Syrian breakthrough. He warned chief-of-staff Elazar that the entire Golan might be lost. Overhearing this message, an alarmed Dayan decided to personally visit the Northern Command headquarters.[1054] In the late night, Hofi informed Dayan that an estimated three hundred Syrian tanks had entered the southern Golan. No reserves were available to stop a Syrian incursion into Galilee. Visibly shaken by this news, the Israeli minister of defence ordered the Jordan bridges to be prepared for detonation.[1055] Next, he contacted Benjamin Peled, commander of the Israeli Air Force. He shocked Peled by announcing that the Third Temple was about to fall. The IAF had just made a successful start with Operation Tagar, a very complex plan to neutralise the Egyptian AA-missile belt. Overruling objections by Peled, Dayan ordered to immediately carry out Operation Doogman 5 instead, the destruction of the Syrian SAM-belt, to allow the IAF to halt the Syrian advance.[1056] As there was no time to obtain recent information on the location of the batteries,[1057] the attempt was a costly failure. The Israelis destroyed only one Syrian missile battery but lost six Phantom II aircraft.[1058] As a result, the IAF was unable to make a significant contribution to the defensive battle on the Golan. Over both fronts together, on 7 October only 129 bombardment sorties were flown.[1059] It also proved impossible to restart Tagar, curtailing IAF operations on the Sinai front for the duration of the war.[1060]

Less pessimistic than Dayan, Elazar was not ready yet to abandon the Golan Heights.[1061] Israeli High Command had a strategic reserve, consisting of the 146th Ugda that was earmarked for Central Command, controlling the eastern border with Jordan. In the evening of 6 October, Elazar had considered sending this division to the collapsing Sinai front in view of the initial defensive success at the Golan. The unexpected crisis led to an about-face. Priority was given to the north because of its proximity to Israeli population centers as Tiberias, Safed, Haifa and Netanya. Elazar ordered that, after mobilisation, the 146th Ugda was to reconquer the southern Golan.[1062] This division would take some time to deploy. Some smaller units could be quickly mobilised to bolster the defenses. The Syrians had expected it to take at least twenty-four hours for Israeli reserves to reach the front lines; in fact, they began to join the fight only nine hours after the war began, twelve hours after the start of the mobilisation.[1063] The Golan position had been at only 80% of its planned strength for the defensive phase of a full war with Syria.[1064] Northern Command had a headquarters reserve consisting of a unnumbered rapid deployment Centurion tank battalion. Also, the 71st Mechanised Infantry Battalion, with two organic tank companies, of the 188th AB had not yet been activated. During the night of 6/7 October, these two battalions were gradually brought up.[1065]

Around 01:00, 7 October, the 36th Ugda was activated as a divisional headquarters under Brigadier Rafael Eitan, to take direct command of the northern front.[1066] The 7th AB did not have this division as its original destination. It was an elite active General Headquarters reserve, moved from the Sinai to the Golan in reaction to the Syrian build-up. Under the original mobilisation Plan *Gir* ("Chalk"), the 36th Ugda was to be expanded by the 179th Armored Brigade. In the evening of 6 October, it was considered to send this brigade to the Sinai instead but this option was abandoned after the Syrian breakthrough. To speed up the relocation of 7th AB to the north, this brigade had left its tanks at Tasa, the main mobilisation complex of the Sinai, and used the stocked vehicles of the 179th AB to rebuild itself at Nafah. In turn, the 179th AB began to mobilise in eastern Galilee, from the mobilisation complex at the foot of the Golan Heights, using the stocked vehicles of the 164th Armoured Brigade. This latter brigade was earmarked for the 240th Ugda, a division to be held in reserve. Assuming that a sustained Syrian offensive would have led to crippling Arab tank losses, 36th Ugda and 240th Ugda were in the prewar planning intended to execute an advance in the direction of Damascus, Operation *Ze'ev Aravot* ("Desert Wolf"). All remaining stocked Centurions in the north were eventually used to rebuild 7th and 188th AB in the night of 9/10 October. The 164th AB was ultimately sent to the Sinai, to activate itself using the old 7th AB matériel.[1067] Also the 679th Armored Brigade was intended to join the 240th Ugda and ordered to mobilise at noon 6 October.[1068] Reservists of both brigades arriving at the Galilee army depots were quickly assigned to tanks and sent to the front, without waiting for the crews they trained with to arrive,[1069] machine guns to be installed, or the tank guns to be calibrated, a time-consuming process known as bore-sighting.[1070] Elements of such larger units were during 7 October fed into the battle piece-meal.[1071]

The collapse of the 188th Armored Brigade

The Syrian first and second wave had in total numbered about six hundred tanks, half of which had been lost by the morning of 7 October. By this time, the Israelis had committed about 250 tanks to battle.[1072] Of the initially arriving reserves, the 71 MIB was used to block an advance by the westernmost elements of the Syrian 9th Infantry Division towards the Bnot Yaacov Bridge, the crucial connection between Galilee and Nafah. In the late evening of 6 October, the NCTB advanced from Nafah towards Hushniya, attempting to seal the breakthrough point. The attack, running into prepared positions occupied by a superior force of T-55s, was a dismal failure, leaving all of its officers dead or wounded. Greengold incorporated the remnants of the unit into his "Force Zvika".[1073]

By the early morning of 7 October, all attempts to patch the breach in the main defensive line of the southern sector became futile because also the center and right flank of the 188th AB had started to collapse.[1074] During the night, it had largely managed to hold its ground against continuous attacks, inflicting severe losses on the Syrians with accurate cannon fire, hoping to buy time for reserve forces to reach the front lines. Some tank crews sacrificed themselves rather than voluntarily give ground. Gradually, the fighting subsided.[1075] Dawn revealed that the Syrian 5th Infantry Division under the cover of darkness had at numerous points bridged the tank ditch and cleared corridors through the minefield belt. The situation of 188th AB was rendered even more hazardous by the presence in its rear of the Syrian 9th Infantry Division. It was decided to abandon the southern Golan. In the night, many artillery and logistic units had already withdrawn, some slipping through the columns of 9th ID, others being destroyed by them. Civilian Jewish settlements had been evacuated. The same now happened with most fortifications,[1076] except bunker complex 116.[1077] Ben-Shoham with his staff outflanked the Syrian penetration via a western route and reached the north.[1078] The 82nd TB company that had reinforced the center, commanded by Eli Geva, had the previous evening destroyed about thirty Syrian tanks. It now successfully crossed the axis of 9th

ID to the north.[1079] Of the originally thirty-six tanks of 53rd TB, twelve remained. Eres hid them in the crater of Tel Faris,[1080] where a surveillance base was located. In the late evening of 7 October, he would successfully break out to the west.[1081]

The Syrian 5th ID subsequently occupied the plateau of the southern Golan. Ben-Shoham tried to maintain a foothold on the access roads by small groups of APCs manned by the 50th Paratrooper Battalion,[1082] but these were easily brushed aside. The Syrian 47th Armored Brigade advanced along the escarpment to the north, in the direction of the Bnot Yaacov Bridge. The 132nd Mechanised Infantry Brigade positioned itself east of El Al, on the road along the Jordan border, running to the south of Lake Tiberias. Israeli General Dan Lener in the late night activated the divisional headquarters of the 210th Ugda to take control over the sector between the lake and the Bnot Yaacov Bridge but he had no regular units to hold this line.[1083] For the moment, he could do little more than personally halt retreating troops and vehicles on the more southern Arik Bridge and send them over the River Jordan again. Israeli command feared that the Syrians would quickly exploit this situation by advancing into Galilee. Dayan in the morning of 7 October called Shalhevet Freier, the director-general of the Israel Atomic Energy Commission, to a meeting with Golda Meir to discuss the possible arming of nuclear weapons. Meir rejected this option.[1084] The Syrian mechanised brigades in this area did not continue the offensive but began to entrench themselves in strong defensive positions. They had been forbidden by Al-Assad to approach the River Jordan, for fear of triggering an Israeli nuclear response.[1085]

The original Syrian offensive plan *Al-Aouda* ("The Return"), devised by Major-General Adul Habeisi, had emphasized the element of tactical surprise. It was known to the Syrians that the 188th AB normally rotated its two tank battalions on the Purple Line, so that on any given moment just thirty-three tanks were guarding the tank ditch. Infiltrations by commando teams armed with Saggers were planned to quickly isolate these ten tank platoons from reinforcement by tactical reserves.[1086] Simultaneously, helicopter-borne commando attacks at the Jordan bridges, landing during conditions of dusk to avoid the IAF, would isolate the Golan Heights from strategic reinforcements. Night attacks by the three Syrian infantry divisions would then fragment the weakly-held forward Israeli defensive positions. To conclude the operation and deter any Israeli attempt to reconquer the Golan, the Syrian 1st and 3rd Armored Division would advance onto the plateau. This way, it was hoped to take the Golan within thirty hours.[1087] Coordination with Egypt forced a change of plans. The Egyptians wanted hostilities to start at noon;[1088] in the end they agreed to a compromise time of 14:00.[1089] The Syrian helicopter attacks were cancelled.[1090] Now uncertain of a successful outcome, the Syrians became

Figure 136: *An abandoned Syrian T-55 tank on the Golan Heights.*

less committed to the attack. They decided to keep one armored division as a strategic reserve, together with the two presidential guard independent armored brigades, which fielded the most modern tank matériel.[1091]

Greengold fought running battles in this area with Syrian armor for twenty hours, sometimes with his single tank and at other times as part of a larger unit, changing tanks half a dozen times as they were knocked out. Greengold suffered burn injuries, but stayed in action and repeatedly showed up at critical moments from an unexpected direction to change the course of a skirmish. For his actions, he received Israel's highest decoration, the Medal of Valor.

Brigade Commander Colonel Shoham was killed on the second day, along with his second-in-command and operations officer, as the Syrians desperately tried to advance towards the Sea of Galilee and Nafah. At this point, the Barak Brigade was no longer a cohesive force, although surviving tanks and crewmen continued fighting independently. The Syrians were close to reaching the Israeli defenders at Nafah, yet stopped the advance on Nafah's fences at 1700; the pause lasted all night, allowing Israeli forces to form a defensive line. It is surmised that the Syrians had calculated estimated advances, and the commanders in the field did not want to diverge from the plan.

Figure 137: *The aftermath of an Israeli airstrike on the Syrian General Staff headquarters in Damascus.*

Israel retakes the southern Golan

The tide in the Golan began to turn as arriving Israeli reserve forces were able to contain the Syrian advance. Beginning on October 8, the Israelis began pushing the Syrians back towards the pre-war ceasefire lines, inflicting heavy tank losses. Another Syrian attack north of Quneitra was repulsed. The tiny Golan Heights were too small to act as an effective territorial buffer, unlike the Sinai Peninsula in the south, but it proved to be a strategic geographical stronghold and was a crucial key in preventing the Syrians from bombarding the cities below. The Israelis, who had suffered heavy casualties during the first three days of fighting, also began relying more heavily on artillery to dislodge the Syrians at long-range.

On October 9, Syrian FROG-7 surface-to-surface missiles struck the Israeli Air Force base of Ramat David, killing a pilot and injuring several soldiers. Additional missiles struck civilian settlements. In retaliation, seven Israeli F-4 Phantoms flew into Syria and struck the Syrian General Staff Headquarters in Damascus. The jets struck from Lebanese airspace to avoid the heavily defended regions around the Golan Heights, attacking a Lebanese radar station along the way. The upper floors of the Syrian GHQ and the Air Force Command were badly damaged. A Soviet cultural center, a television station, and other nearby structures were also mistakenly hit. One Israeli Phantom was shot down. The strike prompted the Syrians to transfer air defense units from the Golan Heights to the home front, allowing the Israeli Air Force greater freedom of action.

On October 9, as the last Syrian units were being driven from the Golan Heights, the Syrians launched a counterattack north of Quneitra. As part of the operation, they attempted to land heli-borne troops in the vicinity of El Rom. The counterattack was repulsed, and four Syrian helicopters were shot down with total loss of life.[1092] By October 10, the last Syrian unit in the central sector was pushed back across the Purple Line, the pre-war ceasefire line. After four days of intense and incessant combat, the Israelis had succeeded in ejecting the Syrians from the entire Golan.

Israeli advance towards Damascus

A decision now had to be made—whether to stop at the post-1967 border or to continue advancing into Syrian territory. The Israeli High Command spent all of October 10 debating well into the night. Some favored disengagement, which would allow soldiers to be redeployed to the Sinai (Shmuel Gonen's defeat at Hizayon in the Sinai had taken place two days earlier). Others favored continuing the attack into Syria, towards Damascus, which would knock Syria out of the war; it would also restore Israel's image as the supreme military power in the Middle East and would give Israel a valuable bargaining chip once the war ended.[1093]

Others countered that Syria had strong defenses—antitank ditches, minefields, and strongpoints— and that it would be better to fight from defensive positions in the Golan Heights (rather than the flat terrain deeper in Syria) in the event of another war with Syria. However, Prime Minister Golda Meir realized the most crucial point of the whole debate:

> *It would take four days to shift a division to the Sinai. If the war ended during this period, the war would end with a territorial loss for Israel in the Sinai and no gain in the north—an unmitigated defeat. This was a political matter and her decision was unmitigating—to cross the purple line. ... The attack would be launched tomorrow, Thursday, October 11.*

On October 11, Israeli forces pushed into Syria and advanced towards Damascus along the Quneitra-Damascus road until October 14, encountering stiff resistance by Syrian reservists in prepared defenses. Three Israeli divisions broke the first and second defensive lines near Sasa, and conquered a further 50 square kilometres of territory in the Bashan salient. From there, they were able to shell the outskirts of Damascus, only 40 km away, using M107 heavy artillery.

Figure 138: *Israeli artillery pounds Syrian forces near the Valley of Tears.*

Figure 139: *Quneitra village after Israeli shelling, showing a church and an elevated car*

On October 12, Israeli paratroopers from the elite Sayeret Tzanhanim reconnaissance unit launched Operation Gown, infiltrating deep into Syria and destroying a bridge in the tri-border area of Syria, Iraq, and Jordan. The operation disrupted the flow of weapons and troops to Syria. During the operation, the paratroopers destroyed a number of tank transports and killed several Syrian soldiers. There were no Israeli casualties.

As the Syrian position deteriorated, Jordan sent an expeditionary force into Syria. King Hussein, who had come under intense pressure to enter the war, told Israel of his intentions through U.S. intermediaries, in the hope that Israel would accept that this was not a casus belli justifying an attack on Jordan. Israeli Defense Minister Moshe Dayan declined to offer any such assurance, but said that Israel had no intention of opening another front.[1094] Iraq also sent an expeditionary force to Syria, consisting of the 3rd and 6th Armoured Divisions, some 30,000 men, 250–500 tanks, and 700 APCs.[1095,1096] Israeli jets attacked Iraqi forces as they arrived in Syria.[1097]

The Iraqi divisions were a strategic surprise for the IDF, which had expected 24-hour-plus advance intelligence of such moves. This turned into an operational surprise, as the Iraqis attacked the exposed southern flank of the advancing Israeli armor, forcing its advance units to retreat a few kilometres in order to prevent encirclement. Combined Syrian, Iraqi and Jordanian counterattacks prevented any further Israeli gains. However, they were unable to push the Israelis back from the Bashan salient, and suffered heavy losses in their engagements with the Israelis. The most effective attack took place on October 20, though Arab forces lost 120 tanks in that engagement.

The Syrian Air Force attacked Israeli columns, but its operations were highly limited because of Israeli air superiority, and it suffered heavy losses in dogfights with Israeli jets. On October 23, a large air battle took place near Damascus during which the Israelis shot down 10 Syrian aircraft. The Syrians claimed a similar toll against Israel.[1098] The IDF also destroyed the Syrian missile defense system. The Israeli Air Force utilized its air superiority to attack strategic targets throughout Syria, including important power plants, petrol supplies, bridges and main roads. The strikes weakened the Syrian war effort, disrupted Soviet efforts to airlift military equipment into Syria, and disrupted normal life inside the country.

On October 22, the Golani Brigade and Sayeret Matkal commandos recaptured the outpost on Mount Hermon, after a hard-fought battle that involved hand-to-hand combat and Syrian sniper attacks. An unsuccessful attack two weeks prior had cost the Israelis 23 dead and 55 wounded and the Syrians 29 dead and 11 wounded, while this second attack cost Israel an additional 55 dead and 79 wounded.[1099] An unknown number of Syrians were also killed and some were taken prisoner. An IDF D9 bulldozer supported by infantry forced its way to the peak. An Israeli paratroop force, landing by helicopter took the corresponding Syrian Hermon outposts on the mountain, killing more than a dozen Syrians while losing one dead and four wounded. Seven Syrian MiGs and two Syrian helicopters carrying reinforcements were shot down as they attempted to intercede.[1100]

Northern front de-escalation

The Syrians prepared for a massive counteroffensive to drive Israeli forces out of Syria, scheduled for October 23. A total of five Syrian divisions were to take part, alongside the Iraqi and Jordanian expeditionary forces. The Soviets had replaced most of the losses Syria's tank forces had suffered during the first weeks of the war.

However, the day before the offensive was to begin, the United Nations imposed its ceasefire (following the acquiescence of both Israel and Egypt). Abraham Rabinovich claimed that "The acceptance by Egypt of the cease-fire on Monday [October 22] created a major dilemma for Assad. The cease-fire did not bind him, but its implications could not be ignored. Some on the Syrian General Staff favored going ahead with the attack, arguing that if it did so Egypt would feel obliged to continue fighting as well ... Others, however, argued that continuation of the war would legitimize Israel's efforts to destroy the Egyptian Third Army. In that case, Egypt would not come to Syria's assistance when Israel turned its full might northward, destroying Syria's infrastructure and perhaps attacking Damascus".[1101]

Ultimately, Syrian President Hafez al-Assad decided to cancel the offensive. On October 23, the day the offensive was to begin, Syria announced that it had accepted the ceasefire, and ordered its troops to cease fire, while the Iraqi government ordered its forces home.

Following the UN ceasefire, there were constant artillery exchanges and skirmishes, and Israeli forces continued to occupy positions deep within Syria. According to Syrian Foreign Minister Abdel Halim Khaddam, Syria's constant artillery attacks were "part of a deliberate war of attrition designed to paralyse the Israeli economy", and were intended to pressure Israel into yielding the occupied territory.[1102] Some aerial engagements took place, and both sides lost several aircraft. In spring 1974, the Syrians attempted to retake the summit of Mount Hermon. The fighting lasted for more than a month and saw heavy losses on both sides, but the Israelis held their positions. The situation continued until a May 1974 disengagement agreement.

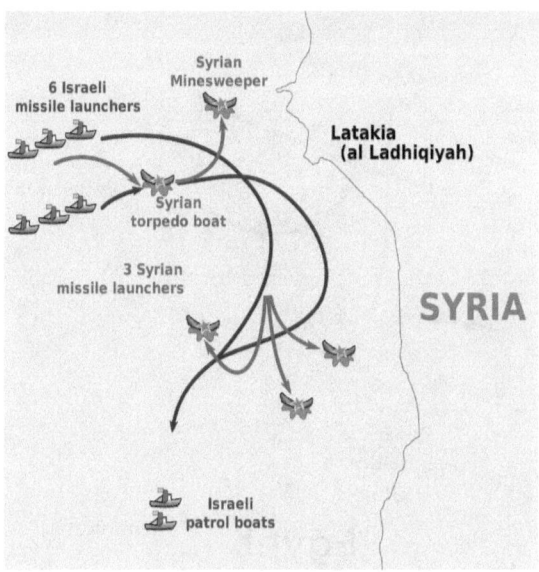

Figure 140: *Diagram of the Battle of Latakia*

Jordanian participation

The U.S. pressed King Hussein to keep Jordan out of the war. Though King Hussein of Jordan initially refrained from entering the conflict, on the night of October 12–13 Jordanian troops deployed to the Jordanian-Syrian frontier to buttress Syrian troops, and Jordanian forces joined Syrian and Iraqi assaults on Israeli positions on October 16 and October 19. Hussein sent a second brigade to the Golan front on October 21.[1103] According to historian Assaf David, declassified U.S. documents show that the Jordanian participation was only a token to preserve King Hussein's status in the Arab world. The documents reveal that Israel and Jordan had a tacit understanding that the Jordanian units would try to stay out of the fighting and Israel would try to not attack them.

Final situation on the Syrian front

The Israeli Army advanced to a 40 km distance from Damascus from where they were able to shell the outskirts of Damascus using M107 heavy artillery.

The war at sea

On the first day of the war, Egyptian missile boats bombarded the Sinai Mediterranean coast, targeting Rumana and Ras Beyron, Ras Masala and Ras

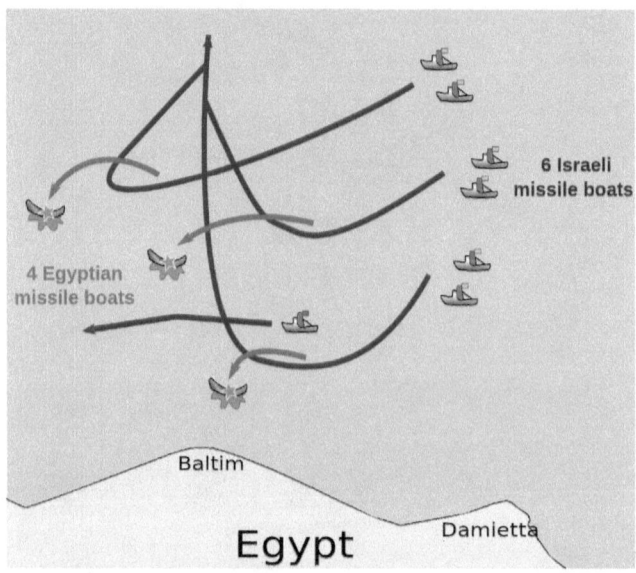

Figure 141: *Diagram of the Battle of Baltim*

Sudar on the Gulf of Suez, and Sharm el-Sheikh. Egyptian naval frogmen also raided the oil installations at Bala'eem, disabling the massive driller.[1104]

The Battle of Latakia, between the Israeli and Syrian navies, took place on October 7, the second day of the war. Five Israeli missile boats heading towards the Syrian port of Latakia, sank a Syrian torpedo boat and minesweeper before encountering five Syrian missile boats. The Israelis used electronic countermeasures and chaff to evade Syrian missiles, then sank all five Syrian missile boats. This revolutionary engagement, the first between missile boats using surface-to-surface missiles, proved the potency of small, fast missile boats equipped with advanced ECM packages. The battle also established the Israeli Navy, long derided as the "black sheep" of the Israeli military, as a formidable and effective force in its own right. The port of Latakia was the site of another engagement between October 10–11, when Israeli missile boats fired into the port, targeting two Syrian missile boats spotted maneuvering among merchant ships. Both Syrian vessels were sunk, and two merchant ships were mistakenly hit and sunk.

October 7 also witnessed the Battle of Marsa Talamat. Two Israeli Dabur class patrol boats patrolling in the Gulf of Suez encountered two Egyptian Zodiac boats loaded with Egyptian naval commandos, a patrol boat, backed up by coastal guns. The Israeli patrol boats sank both Zodiacs and the patrol boat, though both suffered damage during the battle.[1105]

The Battle of Baltim, which took place on October 8–9 off the coast of Baltim and Damietta, ended in a decisive Israeli victory. Six Israeli missile boats heading towards Port Said encountered four Egyptian missile boats coming from Alexandria. In an engagement lasting about forty minutes, the Israelis evaded Egyptian Styx missiles using electronic countermeasures and sank three of the Egyptian missile boats with Gabriel missiles and gunfire.[1106,1107,1108,1109,1110] The Battles of Latakia and Baltim "drastically changed the operational situation at sea to Israeli advantage".[1111]

Five nights after the Battle of Baltim, five Israeli patrol boats entered the Egyptian anchorage at Ras Ghareb, where over fifty Egyptian small patrol craft, including armed fishing boats mobilized for the war effort and loaded with troops, ammunition and supplies bound for the Israeli side of the Gulf, were based. In the battle that followed, 19 Egyptian boats were sunk, while others remained bottled up in port.

The Israeli Navy had control of the Gulf of Suez during the war, which made possible the continued deployment of an Israeli SAM battery near an Israeli naval base close to the southern end of the Suez Canal, depriving the Egyptian Third Army of air support and preventing it from moving southward and attempting to capture the southern Sinai.[1112]

Israeli commandos from Shayetet 13, the Israeli Navy's elite special unit, infiltrated the Egyptian port of Hurghada on the night of October 9–10 and sank a Komar-class missile boat after four previous attempts had failed. After another infiltration attempt failed, the commandos successfully infiltrated Hurghada again on the night of October 21–22 and heavily damaged a missile boat with M72 LAW rockets. During one of the raids, the commandos also blew up the port's main docking pier. On October 16, Shayetet 13 commandos infiltrated Port Said in two Hazir mini-submarines to strike Egyptian naval targets. During the raid, the commandos sank a torpedo boat, a coast guard boat, a tank landing craft, and a missile boat. Two frogmen went missing during the operation.Wikipedia:Identifying reliable sources On October 18, Israeli frogmen set off an explosion that severed two underwater communications cables off Beirut, one of which led to Alexandria and the other to Marseilles. As a result, telex and telecommunications between the West and Syria were severed, and were not restored until the cables were repaired on October 27. The cables had also been used by the Syrians and Egyptians to communicate with each other in preference to using radio, which was monitored by Israeli, U.S. and Soviet intelligence. Egypt and Syria resorted to communicating via a Jordanian radio station in Ajloun, bouncing the signals off a U.S. satellite.[1113]

On October 11, Israeli missile boats sank two Syrian missile boats in an engagement off Tartus. During the battle, a Soviet merchant ship was hit by Israeli missiles and sank.

Figure 142: *A Syrian oil terminal in Baniyas after being shelled by Israeli Sa'ar 3-class missile boats*

Having decisively beaten the Egyptian and Syrian navies, the Israeli Navy had the run of the coastlines. Israeli missile boats utilized their 76mm cannons and other armaments to strike targets along the Egyptian and Syrian coastlines, including wharves, oil tank farms, coastal batteries, radar stations, airstrips, and other targets of military value. The Israeli Navy even attacked some of Egypt's northernmost SAM batteries.[1114,1115] The Israeli Navy's attacks were carried out with minimal support from the Israeli Air Force (only one Arab naval target was destroyed from the air during the entire war).

The Egyptian Navy managed to enforce a blockade at Bab-el-Mandeb. Eighteen million tons of oil had been transported yearly from Iran to Israel through the straits of Bab-el-Mandeb. The blockade was enforced by two Egyptian destroyers and two submarines, supported by ancillary craft. Shipping destined for Israel through the Gulf of Eilat was halted by the Egyptians. The Israeli Navy had no means of lifting the blockade due to the long range involved, and the Israeli Air Force, apparently also incapable of lifting the blockade, did not challenge it. The blockade was lifted on November 1, after Israel used the surrounded Egyptian Third Army as a bargaining chip. The Egyptians unsuccessfully attempted to blockade the Israeli Mediterranean coastline, and mined the Gulf of Suez to prevent the transportation of oil from the Bala'eem and Abu Rudeis oil fields in southwestern Sinai to Eilat in southern Israel. Two oil tankers, of 48,000 ton and 2,000 ton capacity, sank after hitting mines in the

Gulf.[1116,1117] According to Admiral Ze'ev Almog, the Israeli Navy escorted tankers from the Gulf to Eilat throughout the war, and Israeli tankers sailing from Iran were directed to bypass the Red Sea. As a result of these actions and the failure of Egypt's Mediterranean blockade, the transport of oil, grain and weapons to Israeli ports was made possible throughout nearly the entire war. A post-war survey found that during the entire war period, Israel suffered no oil shortages, and even sold oil to third parties affected by the Arab oil embargo. This claim was disputed by Edgar O'Ballance, who claimed that no oil went to Israel during the blockade, and the Eilat-Ashdod pipeline was empty by the end of the war.[1118]

Israel responded with a counter-blockade of Egypt in the Gulf of Suez. The Israeli blockade was enforced by naval vessels based at Sharm el-Sheikh and the Sinai coast facing the Gulf of Suez. The Israeli blockade substantially damaged the Egyptian economy. According to historian Gammal Hammad, Egypt's principal ports, Alexandria and Port Safaga, remained open to shipping throughout the war. Throughout the war, the Israeli Navy enjoyed complete command of the seas both in the Mediterranean approaches and in the Gulf of Suez.[1119]

During the last week of the war, Egyptian frogmen carried out three or four raids on Eilat. The attacks caused minor damage, but created some alarm.

According to Israeli and Western sources, the Israelis lost no vessels in the war.[1120,1121] Israeli vessels were "targeted by as many as 52 Soviet-made anti-ship missiles", but none hit their targets.[1122] According to historian Benny Morris, the Egyptians lost seven missile boats and four torpedo boats and coastal defense craft, while the Syrians lost five missile boats, one minesweeper, and one coastal defense vessel. All together, the Israeli Navy suffered three dead or missing and seven wounded.

Atrocities against Israeli prisoners

Syrian atrocities

Syria ignored the Geneva Conventions and many Israeli prisoners of war were tortured or killed.[1123] Advancing Israeli forces, re-capturing land taken by the Syrians early in the war, came across the bodies of 28 Israeli soldiers who had been blindfolded with their hands bound and summarily executed.[1124] In a December 1973 address to the National Assembly, Syrian Defense Minister Mustafa Tlass stated that he had awarded one soldier the Medal of the Republic for killing 28 Israeli prisoners with an axe, decapitating three of them and eating the flesh of one of his victims.[1125] The Syrians employed brutal interrogation techniques utilizing electric shocks to the genitals. A number of

Israeli soldiers taken prisoner on Mount Hermon were executed. Near the village of Hushniye, the Syrians captured 11 administrative personnel from the Golan Heights Force, all of whom were later found dead, blindfolded and with their hands tied behind their backs. Within Hushniye, seven Israeli prisoners were found dead, and another three were executed at Tel Zohar. Syrian prisoners who fell into Israeli captivity confirmed that their comrades killed IDF prisoners.[1126]

Some Israeli POWs reported having their fingernails ripped out while others were described as being turned into human ashtrays as their Syrian guards burned them with lit cigarettes.[1127] A report submitted by the chief medical officer of the Israeli army notes that, "the vast majority of (Israeli) prisoners were exposed during their imprisonment to severe physical and mental torture. The usual methods of torture were beatings aimed at various parts of the body, electric shocks, wounds deliberately inflicted on the ears, burns on the legs, suspension in painful positions and other methods." Following the conclusion of hostilities, Syria would not release the names of prisoners it was holding to the International Committee of the Red Cross and in fact, did not even acknowledge holding any prisoners despite the fact they were publicly exhibited by the Syrians for television crews.[1128] The Syrians, having been thoroughly defeated by Israel, were attempting to use their captives as their sole bargaining chip in the post-war negotiations.[1129] One of the most famous Israeli POWs was Avraham Lanir, an Israeli pilot who bailed out over Syria and was taken prisoner.[1130] Lanir died under Syrian interrogation.[1131] When his body was returned in 1974, it exhibited signs of torture.

Egyptian atrocities

Israeli historian Aryeh Yitzhaki estimated that the Egyptians killed about 200 Israeli soldiers who had surrendered. Yitzhaki based his claim on army documents. In addition, dozens of Israeli prisoners were beaten and otherwise mistreated in Egyptian captivity.

Individual Israeli soldiers gave testimony of witnessing comrades killed after surrendering to the Egyptians, or seeing the bodies of Israeli soldiers found blindfolded with their hands tied behind their backs. Avi Yaffe, a radioman serving on the Bar-Lev Line, reported hearing calls from other soldiers that the Egyptians were killing anyone who tried to surrender, and also obtained recordings of soldiers who were saved from Egyptian firing squads. Photographic evidence of such executions exists, though some of it has never been made public. Photos were also found of Israeli prisoners who were photographed alive in Egyptian captivity, but were returned to Israel dead.

The order to kill Israeli prisoners came from General Shazly, who, in a pamphlet distributed to Egyptian soldiers immediately before the war, advised his troops to kill Israeli soldiers even if they surrendered.

Participation by other states

Failure of the U.S. intelligence community

The U.S. intelligence community—which includes the CIA—failed to predict in advance the Egyptian-Syrian attack on Israel. A U.S. intelligence report as late as October 4 still stated that "We continue to believe that an outbreak of major Arab–Israeli hostilities remains unlikely for the immediate future".[1132] However, one U.S. government source that was able to predict the approaching war was Roger Merrick, an analyst working for the INR (Bureau of Intelligence and Research in the State Department), but his conclusions were ignored at the time, and the report he had written to that effect was only rediscovered by U.S. government archive officials in 2013.[1133]

U.S. aid to Israel

Based on intelligence estimates at the commencement of hostilities, American leaders expected the tide of the war to quickly shift in Israel's favor, and that Arab armies would be completely defeated within 72 to 96 hours.[1134] On October 6, Secretary of State Kissinger convened the National Security Council's official crisis management group, the Washington Special Actions Group, which debated whether the U.S. should supply additional arms to Israel. High-ranking representatives of the Defense and State Departments opposed such a move. Kissinger was the sole dissenter; he said that if the U.S. refused aid, Israel would have little incentive to conform to American views in postwar diplomacy. Kissinger argued the sending of U.S. aid might cause Israel to moderate its territorial claims, but this thesis raised a protracted debate whether U.S. aid was likely to make it more accommodating or more intransigent toward the Arab world.[1135]

By October 8, Israel had encountered military difficulties on both fronts. In the Sinai, Israeli efforts to break through Egyptian lines with armor had been thwarted, and while Israel had contained and begun to turn back the Syrian advance, Syrian forces were still overlooking the Jordan River and their air defense systems were inflicting a high toll on Israeli planes.[1136] It became clear by October 9 that no quick reversal in Israel's favor would occur and that IDF losses were unexpectedly high.[1137]

During the night of October 8–9, an alarmed Dayan told Meir that "this is the end of the third temple." He was warning of Israel's impending total defeat, but

Figure 143: *An Israeli M48 Patton captured by Egyptian forces*

"Temple" was also the code word for Israel's nuclear weapons. Dayan raised the nuclear topic in a cabinet meeting, warning that the country was approaching a point of "last resort".[1138] That night Meir authorized the assembly of thirteen 20-kiloton-of-TNT (84 TJ) tactical nuclear weapons for Jericho missiles at Sdot Micha Airbase and McDonnell Douglas F-4 Phantom II aircraft at Tel Nof Airbase. They would be used if absolutely necessary to prevent total defeat, but the preparation was done in an easily detectable way, likely as a signal to the United States. Kissinger learned of the nuclear alert on the morning of October 9. That day, President Nixon ordered the commencement of Operation Nickel Grass, an American airlift to replace all of Israel's material losses.[1139] Anecdotal evidence suggests that Kissinger told Sadat that the reason for the U.S. airlift was that the Israelis were close to "going nuclear".[1140] However, subsequent interviews with Kissinger, Schlesinger, and William Quandt suggested that the nuclear aspect was not a major factor in the decision to re-supply. These officials cited the ongoing Soviet re-supply effort and Sadat's early rejection of a ceasefire as the primary motivators. European countries refused to allow U.S. airplanes carrying supplies for Israel to refuel at their bases, fearing an Arab oil embargo, with the exception of Portugal and the Netherlands. Portugal permitted the United States to use a leased base in the Azores, and the defence minister of the Netherlands, apparently acting without consulting his cabinet colleagues, secretly authorised the use of Dutch

Figure 144: *An M60 delivered during Operation Nickel Grass*

airfields.

Israel began receiving supplies via U.S. Air Force cargo airplanes on October 14,[1141] although some equipment had arrived on planes from Israel's national airline El Al before this date. By that time, the IDF had advanced deep into Syria and was mounting a largely successful invasion of the Egyptian mainland from the Sinai, but had taken severe material losses. According to Abraham Rabinovich, "while the American airlift of supplies did not immediately replace Israel's losses in equipment, it did allow Israel to expend what it did have more freely".[1142] By the end of Nickel Grass, the United States had shipped 22,395 tons of matériel to Israel. 8,755 tons of it arrived before the end of the war.[1143] American C-141 Starlifter and C-5 Galaxy aircraft flew 567 missions throughout the airlift. El Al planes flew in an additional 5,500 tons of matériel in 170 flights.[1144,1145] The airlift continued after the war until November 14. The United States delivered approximately 90,000 tons of materiel to Israel by sealift by the beginning of December, using 16 ships. 33,210 tons of it arrived by November.

By the beginning of December, Israel had received between 34 and 40 F-4 fighter-bombers, 46 A-4 attack airplanes, 12 C-130 cargo airplanes, 8 CH-53 helicopters, 40 unmanned aerial vehicles, 200 M-60/M-48A3 tanks, 250 armored personnel carriers, 226 utility vehicles, 12 MIM-72 Chaparral surface-to-air missile systems, three MIM-23 Hawk surface-to-air missile systems, 36

155 mm artillery pieces, seven 175 mm artillery pieces, and large quantities of 105 mm, 155 mm and 175 mm ammunition. State of the art equipment, such as the AGM-65 Maverick missile and the BGM-71 TOW, weapons that had only entered production one or more years prior, as well as highly advanced electronic jamming equipment, was also sent. Most of the combat airplanes arrived during the war, and many were taken directly from United States Air Force units. Most of the large equipment arrived after the ceasefire. The total cost of the equipment was approximately US$800 million (US$4.41 billion today).[1146]

On October 13 and 15, Egyptian air defense radars detected an aircraft at an altitude of 25,000 metres (82,000 ft) and a speed of Mach 3 (3,675 km/h; 2,284 mph), making it impossible to intercept either by fighter or SAM missiles. The aircraft proceeded to cross the whole of the canal zone, the naval ports of the Red Sea (Hurghada and Safaga), flew over the airbases and air defenses in the Nile delta, and finally disappeared from radar screens over the Mediterranean Sea. The speed and altitude were those of the U.S. Lockheed SR-71 Blackbird, a long-range strategic-reconnaissance aircraft. According to Egyptian commanders, the intelligence provided by the reconnaissance flights helped the Israelis prepare for the Egyptian attack on October 14 and assisted it in conducting Operation Stouthearted Men.[1147,1148,1149]

Aid to Egypt and Syria

Soviet supplies

Starting on October 9, the Soviet Union began supplying Egypt and Syria by air and by sea. The Soviets airlifted 12,500–15,000 tons of supplies, of which 6,000 tons went to Egypt, 3,750 tons went to Syria and 575 tons went to Iraq. General Shazly, the former Egyptian chief of staff, claimed that more than half of the airlifted Soviet hardware actually went to Syria. According to Ze'ev Schiff, Arab losses were so high and the attrition rate so great that equipment was taken directly from Soviet and Warsaw Pact stores to supply the airlift.[1150] Antonov An-12 and AN-22 aircraft flew over 900 missions during the airlift.[1151]

The Soviets supplied another 63,000 tons, mainly to Syria, by means of a sealift by October 30.[1152,1153] Historian Gamal Hammad asserts that 400 T-55 and T-62 tanks supplied by the sealift were directed towards replacing Syrian losses, transported from Odessa on the Black Sea to the Syrian port of Latakia. Hammad claimed that Egypt did not receive any tanks from the Soviets,[1154] a claim disputed by Schiff, who stated that Soviet freighters loaded with tanks and other weapons reached Egyptian, Algerian and Syrian ports throughout the war.Wikipedia:Citation needed The sealift may have included Soviet nuclear weapons, which were not unloaded but kept in Alexandria harbor until

Figure 145: *A Syrian BMP-1 captured by Israeli forces*

November to counter the Israeli nuclear preparations, which Soviet satellites had detected (Soviet intelligence informed Egypt that Israel had armed three nuclear weapons).[1155] American concern over possible evidence of nuclear warheads for the Soviet Scud missiles in Egypt contributed to Washington's decision to go to DEFCON 3. According to documents declassified in 2016, the move to DEFCON 3 was motivated by Central Intelligence Agency reports indicating that the Soviet Union had sent a ship to Egypt carrying nuclear weapons along with two other amphibious vessels. Soviet troops never landed, though the ship supposedly transporting nuclear weapons did arrive in Egypt. Further details are unavailable and may remain classified.

Soviet active aid

On the Golan front, Syrian forces received direct support from Soviet technicians and military personnel. At the start of the war, there were an estimated 2,000 Soviet personnel in Syria, of whom 1,000 were serving in Syrian air defense units. Soviet technicians repaired damaged tanks, SAMs and radar equipment, assembled fighter jets that arrived via the sealift, and drove tanks supplied by the sealift from ports to Damascus. On both the Golan and Sinai fronts, Soviet military personnel retrieved abandoned Israeli military equipment for shipment to Moscow.[1156] Soviet advisors were reportedly present in Syrian command posts "at every echelon, from battalion up, including supreme headquarters". Some Soviet military personnel went into battle with the Syrians, and it was estimated that 20 were killed in action and more were wounded.

Figure 146: *October 24. A UN-arranged meeting between IDF Lt. Gen. Haim Bar-Lev and Egyptian Brigadier General Bashir Sharif in Sinai.*

In July 1974, Israeli Defense Minister Shimon Peres informed the Knesset that high-ranking Soviet officers had been killed on the Syrian front during the war. There were strong rumors that a handful were taken prisoner, but this was denied. However, it was noted that certain Soviet Jews were allowed to emigrate just after the war, leading to suspicions of a covert exchange. *The Observer* wrote that seven Soviets in uniform were taken prisoner after surrendering when the Israelis overran their bunker. The Israelis reportedly took the prisoners to Ramat David Airbase for interrogation, and treated the incident with great secrecy.[1157,1158]

Israeli military intelligence reported that Soviet-piloted MiG-25 Foxbat interceptor/reconnaissance aircraft overflew the Canal Zone.

Soviet threat of intervention

On October 9, the Soviet cultural center in Damascus was damaged during an Israeli airstrike, and two days later, the Soviet merchant ship *Ilya Mechnikov* was sunk by the Israeli Navy during a battle off Syria. The Soviets condemned Israeli actions, and there were calls within the government for military retaliation. The Soviets ultimately reacted by deploying two destroyers off the Syrian coast. Soviet warships in the Mediterranean were authorized to open fire on Israeli combatants approaching Soviet convoys and transports. There were several recorded instances of Soviet ships exchanging fire with Israeli forces.

In particular, the Soviet minesweeper *Rulevoi* and the medium landing ship *SDK-137*, guarding Soviet transport ships at the Syrian port of Latakia, fired on approaching Israeli jets.

During the cease-fire, Henry Kissinger mediated a series of exchanges with the Egyptians, Israelis and the Soviets. On October 24, Sadat publicly appealed for American and Soviet contingents to oversee the ceasefire; it was quickly rejected in a White House statement. Kissinger also met with Soviet Ambassador Dobrynin to discuss convening a peace conference with Geneva as the venue. Later in the evening (9:35 pm) of October 24–25, Brezhnev sent Nixon a "very urgent" letter. In that letter, Brezhnev began by noting that Israel was continuing to violate the ceasefire and it posed a challenge to both the U.S. and USSR. He stressed the need to "implement" the ceasefire resolution and "invited" the U.S. to join the Soviets "to compel observance of the cease-fire without delay". He then threatened "I will say it straight that if you find it impossible to act jointly with us in this matter, we should be faced with the necessity urgently to consider taking appropriate steps unilaterally. We cannot allow arbitrariness on the part of Israel."[1159,1160] The Soviets were threatening to militarily intervene in the war on Egypt's side if they could not work together to enforce the ceasefire.

Kissinger immediately passed the message to White House Chief of Staff Alexander Haig, who met with Nixon for 20 minutes around 10:30 pm, and reportedly empowered Kissinger to take any necessary action. Kissinger immediately called a meeting of senior officials, including Haig, Defense Secretary James Schlesinger, and CIA Director William Colby. The Watergate scandal had reached its apex, and Nixon was so agitated and discomposed that they decided to handle the matter without him:

> When Kissinger asked Haig whether [Nixon] should be wakened, the White House chief of staff replied firmly 'No.' Haig clearly shared Kissinger's feelings that Nixon was in no shape to make weighty decisions.[1161]

The meeting produced a conciliatory response, which was sent (in Nixon's name) to Brezhnev. At the same time, it was decided to increase the Defense Condition (DEFCON) from four to three. Lastly, they approved a message to Sadat (again, in Nixon's name) asking him to drop his request for Soviet assistance, and threatening that if the Soviets were to intervene, so would the United States.

The Soviets placed seven airborne divisions on alert and airlift was marshaled to transport them to the Middle East. An airborne command post was set up in the southern Soviet Union, and several air force units were also alerted. "Reports also indicated that at least one of the divisions and a squadron of transport planes had been moved from the Soviet Union to an airbase in Yugoslavia".

Figure 147: *Plaque commemorating the supply of 8 East German Air Force MiG-21s to Syria during the war, on display at the Flugplatzmuseum Cottbus*

The Soviets also deployed seven amphibious warfare craft with some 40,000 naval infantry in the Mediterranean.

The Soviets quickly detected the increased American defense condition, and were astonished and bewildered at the response. "Who could have imagined the Americans would be so easily frightened," said Nikolai Podgorny. "It is not reasonable to become engaged in a war with the United States because of Egypt and Syria," said Premier Alexei Kosygin, while KGB chief Yuri Andropov added that "We shall not unleash the Third World War."[1162] The letter from the U.S. cabinet arrived during the meeting. Brezhnev decided that the Americans were too nervous, and that the best course of action would be to wait to reply.[1163] The next morning, the Egyptians agreed to the American suggestion, and dropped their request for assistance from the Soviets, bringing the crisis to an end.

Other countries

In total, Arab countries added up to 100,000 troops to Egypt and Syria's front-line ranks. Besides Egypt, Syria, Jordan, and Iraq, several other Arab states were also involved in this war, providing additional weapons and financing. In addition to its forces in Syria, Iraq sent a single Hawker Hunter squadron to Egypt. The squadron quickly gained a reputation amongst Egyptian field commanders for its skill in air support, particularly in anti-armor strikes.

However, nearly all Arab reinforcements came with no logistical plan or support, expecting their hosts to supply them, and in several cases causing logistical problems. On the Syrian front, a lack of coordination between Arab forces led to several instances of friendly fire.[1164]

- Algeria sent a squadron each of MiG-21s and Su-7s to Egypt, which arrived at the front between October 9 and October 11. It also sent an armored brigade of 150 tanks, the advance elements of which began to arrive on October 17, but reached the front only on October 24, too late to participate in the fighting. After the war, during the first days of November, Algeria deposited around US$200 million with the Soviet Union to finance arms purchases for Egypt and Syria. Algerian fighter jets however did participate in attacks together with Egyptians and Iraqis.[1165]
- Cuba sent approximately 4,000 troops, including tank and helicopter crews to Syria, and they reportedly engaged in combat operations against the IDF.[1166,1167]
- East German Communist Party leader Erich Honecker directed the shipment of 75,000 grenades, 30,000 mines, 62 tanks and 12 fighter jets to Syria.
- 20 North Korean pilots and 19 non-combat personnel were sent to Egypt.[1168] According to Shlomo Aloni, the last aerial engagement on the Egyptian front, which took place on December 6, saw Israeli F-4s engage North Korean-piloted MiG-21s.[1169] The Israelis shot down one MiG, and another was mistakenly shot down by Egyptian air defenses. Egyptian sources said that the North Koreans suffered no losses but claimed no aerial victories in their engagements.
- According to Chengappa, several Pakistan Air Force pilots flew combat missions in Syrian aircraft, and shot down one Israeli fighter.
- Libya, which had forces stationed in Egypt before the outbreak of the war, provided one armored brigade and two squadrons of Mirage V fighters, of which one squadron was to be piloted by the Egyptian Air Force and the other by Libyan pilots. Only Egyptian-manned squadrons participated in the war. Libyan armored brigade stationed in Egypt never took an active part in the war. Libya also sent financial aid.
- Saudi Arabia sent 3,000 soldiers to Syria, bolstered by a battalion of Panhard AML-90 armored cars. One of the Panhards was later captured by the Israelis near Golan Heights and displayed to the media as proof of Saudi involvement. The Saudi armor was deployed primarily in rearguard actions but also performed active reconnaissance for the Iraqi and Jordanian expeditionary forces between October 16 and October

19. Wikipedia:Citation needed During that time, it participated in two major engagements and the IDF claimed that most of the armoured car battalion was destroyed.Wikipedia:Citation needed The Saudis acknowledged only minor losses, including the loss of 4 AMLs.
- Kuwait dispatched 3,000 soldiers to Syria. These arrived with additional Jordanian and Iraqi reinforcements in time for a new Syrian offensive scheduled for October 23, which was later cancelled. Kuwaiti troops were also sent to Egypt.[1170]WP:NOTRS[1171] Kuwait also provided financial aid.
- Morocco sent one infantry brigade to Egypt and one armored regiment to Syria.[1172] 6 Moroccan troops were taken prisoner in the war.
- Tunisia sent 1,000–2,000 soldiers to Egypt, where they were stationed in the Nile Delta and some of them were stationed to defend Port Said.
- Lebanon sent radar units to Syria for air defense. Lebanon however did not take part in the war.[1173]
- Sudan deployed a 3,500-strong infantry brigade to Egypt. It arrived on October 28, too late to participate in the war.

Non-state participants:

- An infantry brigade composed of Palestinians was in Egypt before the outbreak of the war.[1174]

Palestinian attacks from the Lebanese border

During the course of the war, Palestinian militias from southern Lebanon launched several attacks on Israeli border communities. All of the attempts to infiltrate Israel failed and in all clashes 23 militants were killed and 4 were captured. Most of the activity was focused on Katyusha rocket and anti-tank missile fire on Israeli border communities. In the attacks some civilians were injured, mostly lightly and damage was made to property. In 10 October, after Palestinian militants fired some 40 rockets on Israeli communities, Chief of Staff David Elazar and chief of the Northern Command, Yitzhak Hofi, requested to deploy a force which will cleanse Lebanese villages from Palestinian militants, but the request was declined by Defense Minister Moshe Dayan.

Weapons

The Arab armies (with the exception of the Jordanians), were equipped with predominantly Soviet-made weapons while Israel's armaments were mostly Western-made. The Arabs' T-54/55s and T-62s were equipped with night vision equipment, which the Israeli tanks lacked, giving them an advantage in fighting at night, while Israel tanks had better armor and/or better armament.Wikipedia:Citation needed Israeli tanks also had a distinct advantage while on the ramps, in the "hull-down" position where steeper angles of depression resulted in less exposure. The main guns of Soviet tanks could only depress 4 degrees. By contrast, the 105 mm guns on Centurion and Patton tanks could depress 10 degrees.

Type	Arab armies	IDF
AFVs	Egypt, Syria, Iraq and Jordan used T-34, T-54, T-55, T-62, PT-76 and M48 Patton, as well as SU-100/152 World War II vintage self-propelled guns.	M50 and M51 Shermans with upgraded engines, M48 Patton, M60 Patton, Centurion, PT-76 and T-54/55. All tanks were upgraded with the British 105 mm L7 gun, prior to the war.
APCs/-IFVs	BTR-40, BTR-152, BTR-50, BTR-60 APC's & BMP 1 IFV's	M2 /M3 Half-track, M113
Artillery	152 mm howitzer-gun M1937 (ML-20), BM-21, D-30 (2A18) Howitzer, M1954 field gun, 152 mm towed gun-howitzer M1955 (D-20)	M109 self-propelled howitzer, M107 self-propelled gun, M110 self-propelled howitzer, M50 self-propelled howitzer and Makmat 160 mm self-propelled mortar, Obusier de 155 mm Modèle 50, Soltam M-68 and 130 mm towed field gun M1954 (M-46)
Aircraft	MiG-21, MiG-19, MiG-17, Dassault Mirage 5, Su-7B, Hawker Hunter, Tu-16, Il-28, Il-18, Il-14, An-12, Aero L-29	A-4 Skyhawk, F-4 Phantom II, Dassault Mirage III, Dassault Super Mystère, IAI Nesher
Helicopters	Mi-6, Mi-8	Super Frelon, Sea Stallion, AB-205
AAW	SA-6 Gainful, SA-3 Goa, SA-2 Guideline, ZSU-23-4, Strela 2	MIM-23 Hawk, MIM-72 Chaparral, Bofors 40 mm gun
Infantry weapons	AK-47, AKM, Hakim, Rasheed, RPK, RPD, PKM, SVD, Port Said, Browning Hi-Power, Beretta M1951, TT-33, Makarov PM, F1 grenade, RGD-5 grenade, RPG-43 anti-tank grenade, RKG-3 anti-tank grenade, DShK HMG, RPG-7, AT-3 Sagger and B-11 recoilless rifle	FN FAL, Uzi, M16, CAR-15, M14, AK-47, Karabiner 98k, Lee-Enfield, FN MAG, Browning Hi-Power, Beretta M1951, M26A2 grenade, M2HB Browning, Super Bazooka, SS.11, M72 LAW (only received during the war), BGM-71 TOW (received during the war), RL-83 Blindicide and M40 recoilless rifle
Sea to Sea Missiles	P-15 Termit	Gabriel
Air-to-Air Missiles	K-13	Shafrir 2, AIM-9 Sidewinder, AIM-7 Sparrow
Air-to-Ground Missiles		AGM-45 Shrike anti radiation missile

Home front during the war

The war created a state of emergency in the countries involved in fighting. Upon the outbreak of war, air raid sirens sounded throughout Israel. During the war, blackouts were enforced in major cities. The Egyptian government began to evacuate foreign tourists, and on October 11, 1973, the Egyptian ship *Syria* left Alexandria to Piraeus with a load of tourists wishing to exit Egypt. The U.S. Interest Section in Cairo also requested U.S. government assistance in removing U.S. tourists to Greece. On October 12, Kissinger ordered the U.S. Interest Section in Cairo to speed up preparations for the departure of U.S. tourists staying in Egypt, while notifying such actions to the IDF in order to avoid accidental military operations against them.

Casualties

Israel suffered between 2,521[1175,1176] and 2,800 killed in action.[1177] An additional 7,250[1178] to 8,800 soldiers were wounded. Some 293 Israelis were captured. Approximately 400 Israeli tanks were destroyed. Another 600 were disabled but returned to service after repairs.[1179] A major Israeli advantage, noted by many observers, was their ability to quickly return damaged tanks to combat. The Israeli Air Force lost 102 airplanes: 32 F-4s, 53 A-4s, 11 Mirages and 6 Super Mysteres. Two helicopters, a Bell 205 and a CH-53, were also lost. According to Defense Minister Moshe Dayan, nearly half of these were shot down during the first three days of the war.[1180] IAF losses per combat sortie were less than in the preceding Six-Day War of 1967.[1181]

Arab casualties were known to be much higher than Israel's, though precise figures are difficult to ascertain as Egypt and Syria never disclosed official figures. The lowest casualty estimate is 8,000 (5,000 Egyptian and 3,000 Syrian) killed and 18,000 wounded. The highest estimate is 18,500 (15,000 Egyptian and 3,500 Syrian) killed. Most estimates lie somewhere in between the two, with the Insight Team of the London *The Sunday Times* combined Egyptian and Syrian losses of 16,000 killed. and yet another source citing a figure of some 15,000 dead and 35,000 wounded.[1182] U.S. estimates placed Egyptian casualties at 13,000.[1183] Iraq lost 278 killed and 898 wounded, while Jordan suffered 23 killed and 77 wounded. Some 8,372 Egyptians, 392 Syrians, 13 Iraqis and 6 Moroccans were taken prisoner.

Arab tank losses amounted to 2,250[1184] though Garwych cites a figure of 2,300.[1185] 400 of these fell into Israeli hands in good working order and were incorporated into Israeli service. Between 341 and 514 Arab aircraft were shot down. According to Herzog, 334 of these aircraft were shot down by the Israeli Air Force in air-to-air combat for the loss of only five Israeli planes. The

Figure 148: *An Israeli Air Force Mirage IIIC. Flag markings on the nose credit this particular aircraft with 13 aerial kills.*

Figure 149: *Downed Israeli Mirage*

Figure 150: *1974 news report about warfare on the Golan prior to the May disengagement accords*

Sunday Times Insight Team notes Arab aircraft losses of 450. 19 Arab naval vessels, including 10 missile boats, were sunk for no Israeli losses.[1186]

Post-ceasefire

Kissinger pushes for peace

On October 24, the UNSC passed Resolution 339, serving as a renewed call for all parties to adhere to the ceasefire terms established in Resolution 338. Most heavy fighting on the Egyptian front ended by October 26, but clashes along the ceasefire lines and a few airstrikes on the Third Army took place. With some Israeli advances taking place, Kissinger threatened to support a UN withdrawal resolution, but before Israel could respond, Egyptian national security advisor Hafez Ismail sent Kissinger a stunning message—Egypt was willing to enter into direct talks with Israel, provided that it agree to allow non-military supplies to reach the Third Army and to a complete ceasefire.

About noon on October 25, Kissinger appeared before the press at the State Department. He described the various stages of the crisis and the evolution of U.S. policy. He reviewed the first two weeks of the crisis and the nuclear alert, reiterated opposition to U.S. and Soviet troops in the area and more strongly

Figure 151: *UN Emergency Forces at Kilometre 101*

opposed unilateral Soviet moves. He then reviewed the prospects for a peace agreement, which he termed "quite promising", and had conciliatory words for Israel, Egypt and even the USSR. Kissinger concluded his remarks by spelling out the principles of a new U.S. policy toward the Arab–Israeli conflict saying:[1187]

> Our position is that ... the conditions that produced this war were clearly intolerable to the Arab nations and that in the process of negotiations it will be necessary to make substantial concessions. The problem will be to relate the Arab concern for the sovereignty over the territories to the Israeli concern for secure boundaries. We believe that the process of negotiations between the parties is an essential component of this.

Quandt considers, "It was a brilliant performance, one of his most impressive." One hour later the United Nations Security Council adopted Resolution 340. This time the ceasefire held, and the fourth Arab–Israeli war was over.

Disengagement agreement

Disengagement talks took place on October 28, 1973, at "Kilometre 101" between Israeli Major General Aharon Yariv and Egyptian Major General Abdel Ghani el-Gamasy. Ultimately, Kissinger took the proposal to Sadat, who agreed. United Nations checkpoints were brought in to replace Israeli ones, nonmilitary supplies were allowed to pass, and prisoners-of-war were to be exchanged.

A summit conference in Geneva followed in December 1973. All parties to the war – Israel, Syria, Jordan and Egypt – were invited to a joint effort by the Soviet Union and the United States to finally usher peace between the Arabs and Israelis. This conference was recognized by UN Security Council Resolution 344 and was based on the Resolution 338, calling for a "just and durable peace". Nevertheless, the conference was forced to adjourn on January 9, 1974, as Syria refused attendance.[1188]

After the failed conference Henry Kissinger started conducting shuttle diplomacy, meeting with Israel and the Arab states directly. The first concrete result of this was the initial military disengagement agreement, signed by Israel and Egypt on January 18, 1974. The agreement commonly known as Sinai I had the official name of *Sinai Separation of Forces Agreement*. Under its terms, Israel agreed to pull back its forces from the areas West of Suez Canal, which it had occupied since the end of hostilities. Moreover, Israeli forces were also pulled back on the length of the whole front to create security zones for Egypt, UN and Israel, each roughly ten kilometres wide. Thus Israel gave up its advances reaching beyond the Suez canal, but it still held nearly all of Sinai. It became the first of many such *Land for Peace* agreements where Israel gave up territory in exchange for treaties.[1189]

On the Syrian front, skirmishes and artillery exchanges continued taking place. Shuttle diplomacy by Henry Kissinger eventually produced a disengagement agreement on May 31, 1974, based on exchange of prisoners-of-war, Israeli withdrawal to the Purple Line and the establishment of a UN buffer zone. The agreement ended the skirmishes and exchanges of artillery fire that had occurred frequently along the Israeli-Syrian ceasefire line. The UN Disengagement and Observer Force (UNDOF) was established as a peacekeeping force in the Golan.

The peace discussion at the end of the war was the first time that Arab and Israeli officials met for direct public discussions since the aftermath of the 1948 war.

Response in Israel

Though the war reinforced Israel's military deterrence, it had a stunning effect on the population in Israel. Following their victory in the Six-Day War, the Israeli military had become complacent. The shock and sudden reversals that occurred at the beginning of the war inflicted a terrible psychological blow to the Israelis, who had hitherto experienced no serious military challenges.[1190]

A protest against the Israeli government started four months after the war ended. It was led by Motti Ashkenazi, commander of Budapest, the northernmost of the Bar-Lev forts and the only one during the war not to be captured by the Egyptians.[1191] Anger against the Israeli government (and Dayan in particular) was high. Shimon Agranat, President of the Israeli Supreme Court, was asked to lead an inquiry, the Agranat Commission, into the events leading up to the war and the setbacks of the first few days.[1192]

The Agranat Commission published its preliminary findings on April 2, 1974. Six people were held particularly responsible for Israel's failings:

- Though his performance and conduct during the war was lauded,[1193] IDF Chief of Staff David Elazar was recommended for dismissal after the Commission found he bore "personal responsibility for the assessment of the situation and the preparedness of the IDF".
- Aman Chief, Aluf Eli Zeira, and his deputy, head of Research, Brigadier-General Aryeh Shalev, were recommended for dismissal.
- Lt. Colonel Bandman, head of the Aman desk for Egypt, and Lt. Colonel Gedelia, chief of intelligence for the Southern Command, were recommended for transfer away from intelligence duties.
- Shmuel Gonen, commander of the Southern front, was recommended by the initial report to be relieved of active duty.[1194] He was forced to leave the army after the publication of the Commission's final report, on January 30, 1975, which found that "he failed to fulfill his duties adequately, and bears much of the responsibility for the dangerous situation in which our troops were caught."[1195]

Rather than quieting public discontent, the report—which "had stressed that it was judging the ministers' responsibility for security failings, not their parliamentary responsibility, which fell outside its mandate"—inflamed it. Although it had absolved Meir and Dayan of all responsibility, public calls for their resignations (especially Dayan's) intensified. In the December 1973 legislative election, Meir's Alignment party lost five Knesset seats.

On April 11, 1974, Golda Meir resigned. Her cabinet followed suit, including Dayan, who had previously offered to resign twice and was turned down both times by Meir. A new government was seated in June, and Yitzhak Rabin, who had spent most of the war as an advisor to Elazar in an unofficial capacity, became Prime Minister.[1196]

In 1999, the issue was revisited by the Israeli political leadership to prevent similar shortcomings from being repeated. The Israeli National Security Council was created to improve coordination between the different security and intelligence bodies, and the political branch of government.

Response in Egypt

For the Arab states (and Egypt in particular), Arab successes during the war healed the psychological trauma of their defeat in the Six-Day War, allowing them to negotiate with the Israelis as equals. Because of the later setbacks in the war (which saw Israel gain a large salient on African soil and even more territory on the Syrian front),Wikipedia:Verifiability some believe that the war helped convince many in the Arab world that Israel could not be defeated militarily, thereby strengthening peace movements and delaying the Arab ambition of destroying Israel by force.[1197]

General Shazly had angered Sadat for advocating the withdrawal of Egyptian forces from Sinai to meet the Israeli incursion on the West Bank of the Canal. Six weeks after the war, he was relieved of command and forced out of the army, ultimately going into political exile for years. Upon his return to Egypt, he was placed under house arrest. Following his release, he advocated the formation of a "Supreme High Committee" modeled after Israel's Agranat Commission in order to "probe, examine and analyze" the performance of Egyptian forces and the command decisions made during the war, but his requests were completely ignored.[1198] He published a book, banned in Egypt, that described Egypt's military failings and the sharp disagreements he had with Ismail and Sadat in connection with the prosecution of the war.[1199]

The commanders of the Second and Third Armies, Generals Khalil and Wasel, were also dismissed from the army.[1200] The commander of the Egyptian Second Army at the start of the war, General Mamoun, suffered a heart attack, or, alternatively, a breakdown, after the Egyptian defeat during the October 14 Sinai tank battle, and was replaced by General Khalil.[1201,1202]

Response in Syria

In Syria, Colonel Rafik Halawi, the Druze commander of an infantry brigade that had collapsed during the Israeli breakthrough, was executed before the war even ended. He was given a quick hearing and sentenced to death; his execution was immediate.[1203] Military historian Zeev Schiff referred to him as Syria's "sacrificial lamb". The Syrians however offered vehement denials that Halawi was executed and expended great efforts trying to debunk the allegation. They claimed he was killed in battle with Israel and threatened severe punishment to anyone repeating the allegation of execution. Their concern stemmed from a desire to maintain Syrian Druze loyalty to Assad's regime and prevent Syrian Druze from siding with their co-religionists in Israel. On July 7, 1974, Halawi's remains were removed from a Syrian military hospital and he was interred in Damascus at the "Cemetery of the Martyrs of the October War" in the presence of many Syrian dignitaries. One analyst noted that the presence of so many high-level officials was unusual and attributed it to Syrian efforts to quell any suggestion of execution.

Response in the Soviet Union

According to Chernyaev, on 4 November 1973, Soviet leader Leonid Brezhnev said: <templatestyles src="Template:Quote/styles.css"/>

> We have offered them (the Arabs) a sensible way for so many years. But no, they wanted to fight. Fine! We gave them technology, the latest, the kind even Vietnam didn't have. They had double superiority in tanks and aircraft, triple in artillery, and in air defense and anti-tank weapons they had absolute supremacy. And what? Once again they were beaten. Once again they scrammed [sic]. Once again they screamed for us to come save them. Sadat woke me up in the middle of the night twice over the phone, "Save me!" He demanded to send Soviet troops, and immediately! No! We are not going to fight for them.

Oil embargo

In response to U.S. support of Israel, the Arab members of OPEC, led by Saudi Arabia, decided to reduce oil production by 5% per month on October 17. On October 19, President Nixon authorized a major allocation of arms supplies and $2.2 billion in appropriations for Israel. In response, Saudi Arabia declared an embargo against the United States, later joined by other oil exporters and extended against the Netherlands and other states, causing the 1973 energy crisis.[1204]

Long-term effects

Egyptian–Israeli disengagement agreement

Another Egyptian–Israeli disengagement agreement, the *Sinai Interim Agreement*, was signed in Geneva on September 4, 1975, and was commonly known as Sinai II. This agreement led Israel to withdraw from another 20–40 km with UN forces buffering the vacated area. After the agreement, Israel still held more than two thirds of Sinai, which would prove to be a valuable bargaining chip in the coming negotiations.[1205]

Figure 152: *Egyptian President Anwar Sadat and Israeli Prime Minister Menachem Begin acknowledge applause during a joint session of Congress in Washington, D.C., during which President Jimmy Carter announced the results of the Camp David Accords, September 18, 1978.*

Egyptian–Israeli Camp David Accords

The Yom Kippur War upset the status quo in the Middle East, and the war served as a direct antecedent of the 1978 Camp David Accords. The Accords resulted in the Egypt–Israel Peace Treaty, the first ever between Israel and an Arab state. According to George Friedman, the war gave the Israelis increased respect for the Egyptian military and decreased their confidence in their own, and caused the Israelis to be uncertain whether they could defeat Egypt in the event of another war. At the same time, the Egyptians recognized that despite their improvements, they were defeated in the end, and became doubtful that they could ever defeat Israel militarily. Therefore, a negotiated settlement made sense to both sides.[1206]

Rabin's government was hamstrung by a pair of scandals, and he was forced to step down in 1977. In the elections that followed, the right-wing Likud party won a majority in the Knesset, and Menachem Begin, the party's founder and leader, was appointed Prime Minister. This marked a historic change in the Israeli political landscape: for the first time since Israel's founding, a coalition not led by the Labor Party was in control of the government.

Sadat, who had entered the war in order to recover the Sinai from Israel, grew frustrated at the slow pace of the peace process. In a 1977 interview with *CBS*

News anchorman Walter Cronkite, Sadat admitted under pointed questioning that he was open to a more constructive dialog for peace, including a state visit. This seemed to open the floodgates, as in a later interview with the same reporter, the normally hard-line Begin – perhaps not wishing to be compared unfavorably to Sadat – said he too would be amenable to better relations. On November 9, 1977, Sadat stunned the world when he told parliament that he would be willing to visit Israel and address the Knesset. Shortly afterward, the Israeli government cordially invited him to address the Knesset. Thus, in November of that year, Sadat took the unprecedented step of visiting Israel, becoming the first Arab leader to do so, and so implicitly recognized Israel.

The act jump-started the peace process. United States President Jimmy Carter invited both Sadat and Begin to a summit at Camp David to negotiate a final peace. The talks took place from September 5–17, 1978. Ultimately, the talks succeeded, and Israel and Egypt signed the Egypt–Israel Peace Treaty in 1979. Israel subsequently withdrew its troops and settlers from the Sinai, in exchange for normal relations with Egypt and a lasting peace, with last Israeli troops exiting on April 26, 1982.[1207] There is still no formal peace agreement between Israel and Syria to this day.

Many in the Arab world were outraged at Egypt's peace with Israel. Sadat, in particular, became deeply unpopular both in the Arab world and in his own country. Egypt was suspended from the Arab League until 1989. Until then, Egypt had been "at the helm of the Arab world".[1208] Egypt's tensions with its Arab neighbors culminated in 1977 in the short-lived Libyan–Egyptian War.

Sadat was assassinated two years later on October 6, 1981, while attending a parade marking the eighth anniversary of the start of the war, by Islamist army members who were outraged at his negotiations with Israel.

Commemorations

October 6 is a national holiday in Egypt called Armed Forces Day. It is a national holiday in Syria as well, where it is called "Tishreen Liberation Day".[1209] Marking the 35th anniversary in 2008, Hosni Mubarak said that the conflict "breathed new life" into Egypt. He said Egypt and Syria's initial victories in the conflict eased Arab bitterness over Israel's victory in the 1967 Six-Day War and ultimately put the two nations on a path of peaceful coexistence.

In Egypt, many places were named after the date of October 6 and Ramadan 10th, which is the equivalent day in the Islamic calendar. Examples of these commemorations are 6th October Bridge in Cairo and the cities of 6th of October and 10th of Ramadan.

In addition, the Museum of the October 6 War was built in 1989 in the Heliopolis district of Cairo. The center of the museum is occupied by a rotunda

Figure 153: *A destroyed Syrian T-62 stands as part of an Israeli memorial commemorating the battle of the 'Valley of Tears', Northern Golan Heights.*

housing a panoramic painting of the struggle between Egyptian and Israeli armed forces. The panorama, the creation of which was outsourced to a group of North Korean artists and architects, is equipped with engines to rotate it 360° during a 30-minutes presentation accompanied by commentary in various languages. A similar museum, which was also built with North Korean assistance—the October War Panorama—operates in Damascus.

In Latrun, a Yom Kippur War exhibit can be found at The Armored Corps Museum at Yad La-Shiryon.

References

Notes

Bibliography

<templatestyles src="Refbegin/styles.css" />

- Asher, Jerry; Hammel, Eric (1987). *Duel for the Golan: the 100-hour battle that saved Israel*. New York: William Morrow and Company, Inc. ISBN 0-688-06911-8.<templatestyles src="Module:Citation/CS1/styles.css"></templatestyles>

- el Badri, Hassan (1979). *The Ramadan War, 1973*. Fairfax, Va: T. N. Dupuy Associates Books. ISBN 0-88244-600-2.<templatestyles src="Module:Citation/CS1/styles.css"></templatestyles>
- Bar-Joseph, Uri (2012). *The Watchman Fell Asleep: The Surprise of Yom Kippur and Its Sources*. Albany, NY: SUNY Press. ISBN 0-79148-312-6.<templatestyles src="Module:Citation/CS1/styles.css"></templatestyles>
- Bregman, Ahron (2002). *Israel's Wars: A History Since 1947*. London: Routledge. ISBN 0-415-28716-2.<templatestyles src="Module:Citation/CS1/styles.css"></templatestyles>
- Brook, Itzhak (2011). *In the Sands of Sinai: a Physician's Account of the Yom Kippur War*. Charleston: CreateSpace. ISBN 1-4663-8544-8.<templatestyles src="Module:Citation/CS1/styles.css"></templatestyles>
- Dupuy, Trevor Nevitt (1978). *Elusive victory: The Arab–Israeli Wars, 1947–1974*. San Francisco: Harper & Row. ISBN 0-06-011112-7.<templatestyles src="Module:Citation/CS1/styles.css"></templatestyles>
- Gawrych, George (2000). *The Albatross of Decisive Victory: War and Policy Between Egypt and Israel in the 1967 and 1973 Arab-Israeli Wars*. Greenwood Publishing Group. ISBN 0-313-31302-4.<templatestyles src="Module:Citation/CS1/styles.css"></templatestyles>
- Gawrych, Dr. George W. (1996). *The 1973 Arab-Israeli War: The Albatross of Decisive Victory*. Combat Studies Institute, U.S. Army Command and General Staff College.<templatestyles src="Module:Citation/CS1/styles.css"></templatestyles> **"Intro"**[1210] (PDF). Archived from the original[1211] (PDF) on June 10, 2007.<templatestyles src="Module:Citation/CS1/styles.css"></templatestyles>, **"Part I"**[1212] (PDF). Archived from the original[1213] (PDF) on May 7, 2011.<templatestyles src="Module:Citation/CS1/styles.css"></templatestyles>, **"Part II"**[1214] (PDF). Archived from the original[1215] (PDF) on May 7, 2011.<templatestyles src="Module:Citation/CS1/styles.css"></templatestyles>, **"Part III"**[1216] (PDF). Archived from the original[1217] (PDF) on May 7, 2011.<templatestyles src="Module:Citation/CS1/styles.css"></templatestyles>, **"Part IV"**[1218] (PDF). Archived from the original[1219] (PDF) on May 7, 2011.<templatestyles src="Module:Citation/CS1/styles.css"></templatestyles>, **"Part V"**[1220] (PDF). Archived from the original[1221] (PDF) on May 7, 2011.<templatestyles src="Module:Citation/CS1/styles.css"></templatestyles>, **"Part VI"**[1222] (PDF). Archived from the origi-

nal[1223] (PDF) on May 7, 2011. "**Part VII**"[1224] (PDF). Archived from the original[1225] (PDF) on May 7, 2011. "**Notes**"[1226] (PDF). Archived from the original[1227] (PDF) on March 19, 2009. Retrieved May 28, 2015.
- Haber, Eitan; Schiff, Ze'ev (2003). *Yom Kippur War Lexicon* (in Hebrew). Or-Yehuda, Israel: Zmora-Bitan-Dvir. ISBN 978-965-517-124-2.
- Hammad, Gamal (2002). *al-Ma'ārik al-ḥarbīyah 'alá al-jabhah al-Miṣrīyah: (Ḥarb Uktūbar 1973, al-'Āshir min Ramaḍān)* [*Military Battles on the Egyptian Front*] (in Arabic) (First ed.). Dār al-Shurūq.
- Heikal, Mohamed (1975). *The Road to Ramadan*. London: Collins. ISBN 0-8129-0567-9.
- Herzog, Chaim (2003) [1975]. *The War of Atonement: The Inside Story of the Yom Kippur War*. London: Greenhill Books. ISBN 978-1-85367-569-0.
- Herzog, Chaim (1982). *the Arab-Israeli Wars*. Random House. ISBN 978-0-394-50379-0.
- Herzog, Chaim (1989). *Heroes of Israel*. Boston: Little, Brown. ISBN 0-316-35901-7.
- Insight Team of the London Sunday Times (1974). *The Yom Kippur War*. Garden City: Doubleday. ISBN 978-0-385-06738-6.
- Israeli, Raphael (1985). *Man of Defiance: A Political Biography of Anwar Sadat*. London: Weidenfeld & Nicolson. ISBN 0-389-20579-6.
- Israelyan, Victor (2003) [1995]. *Inside the Kremlin During the Yom Kippur War*. University Park, PA: Pennsylvania State University Press. ISBN 0-271-01737-6.
- Karsh, Efraim (2002). *The Iran-Iraq War, 1980–1988*. Oxford: Osprey Publishing. ISBN 1-84176-371-3.

- Lanir, Zvi (2002) [1983]. *ha-Hafta'ah ha-basisit: modi'in ba-mashber [Fundamental Surprise: Intelligence in Crisis]* (in Hebrew). Tel-Aviv: Hakibbutz Hameuchad. OCLC 65842089.
- Menshawy, Mustafa. "Turning 'defeat' into 'victory': the power of discourse on the 1973 war in Egypt." *Middle Eastern Studies* 52.6 (2016): 897-916. Historiography.
- Morris, Benny (2001). *Righteous Victims*. New York: Vintage Books. ISBN 978-0-679-74475-7.
- Ma'Oz, Moshe (1995). *Syria and Israel: From War to Peacemaking*. Oxford: Clarendon Press. ISBN 0-19-828018-1.
- Neff, Donald (1988). *Warriors against Israel*. Brattleboro, Vermont: Amana Books. ISBN 978-0-915597-59-8.
- Nicolle, David; Cooper, Tom (May 25, 2004). *Arab MiG-19 and MiG-21 units in combat*. Osprey Publishing. ISBN 1-84176-655-0.
- Edgar O'Ballance. *No Victor, No Vanquished: The Yom Kippur War* (1979 ed.). Barrie & Jenkins Publishing. pp. 28–370. ISBN 978-0214206702.
- Pape, Robert A (Fall 1997). "Why Economic Sanctions Do Not Work". *International Security*. **22** (2): 90. doi: 10.2307/2539368. JSTOR 2539368. OCLC 482431341.
- Quandt, William (2005). *Peace Process: American diplomacy and the Arab–Israeli conflict since 1967*. Washington, DC: Brookings Institution / Univ. of California Press. ISBN 0-520-22374-8.
- Quandt, William B (May 1976). "Soviet Policy in the October 1973 War" (PDF). Rand Corp. R-1864-ISA. Archived from the original (PDF) on October 2, 2012.
- Rabinovich, Abraham (2005) [2004]. *The Yom Kippur War: The Epic Encounter That Transformed the Middle East*. New York, NY: Schocken Books. ISBN 0-8052-4176-0.
- Rabinovich, Abraham (2017). *The Yom Kippur War: The Epic Encounter That Transformed the Middle East. Revised and Updated Edition*. New

York, NY: Schocken Books. ISBN 9780805211245.<templatestyles src="Module:Citation/CS1/styles.css"></templatestyles>
- al Sadat, Muhammad Anwar (1978). *In Search of Identity: An Autobiography*. London: Collins. ISBN 0-00-216344-6.<templatestyles src="Module:Citation/CS1/styles.css"></templatestyles>
- Shazly, Lieutenant General Saad el (2003). *The Crossing of the Suez, Revised Edition* (Revised ed.). American Mideast Research. ISBN 0-9604562-2-8.<templatestyles src="Module:Citation/CS1/styles.css"></templatestyles>
- Shlaim, Avi (2001). *The Iron Wall: Israel and the Arab World*. W. W. Norton & Company. ISBN 0-393-32112-6.<templatestyles src="Module:Citation/CS1/styles.css"></templatestyles>
- Rodman, David (2013). "The Impact of American Arms Transfers to Israel during the 1973 Yom Kippur War"[1234] (PDF). Israel Journal of Foreign Affairs, VII:3. Archived from the original[1235] (PDF) on May 26, 2015.<templatestyles src="Module:Citation/CS1/styles.css"></templatestyles>

External links

Wikimedia Commons has media related to *Yom Kippur War*.

- CIA Symposium on the Role of Intelligence in the 1973 Arab–Israeli War, held oh January 30, 2013[1236]
- President Nixon and the Role of Intelligence in the 1973 Arab–Israeli War, collection of primary documents at the CIA website[1237]
- Hourly U.S. diplomatic reporting on the war[1238] WikiLeaks
- A second look, 40 years after the war[1239] and The downfall of the Hermon fortification[1240]. Israeli TV documentaries broadcast in October 2013 featuring original video footage filmed during the war, interviews with combatants during the war and decades later, etc. Posted on the official YouTube channel of the *Israel Broadcasting Authority*
- Israeli Air Force Wing 115 – experiences during the war, and insights 40 years later[1241]. Documentary film released in October 2013 featuring interviews with air force pilots. Posted on the official YouTube channel of the *Fisher Institute for the Strategic Study of Air and Space*

1974–1977: Rabin I

Operation Entebbe

<indicator name="pp-default"> 🔒 </indicator>

Operation Entebbe	
Part of the Arab–Israeli conflict	
Date	4 July 1976
Location	Entebbe Airport, Uganda
Result	Mission successful • 102 of 106 hostages rescued • A quarter of Uganda's air force destroyed[1242]
Belligerents	
☰ Israel	■ PFLP-EO ★ Revolutionary Cells ≡ Uganda
Commanders and leaders	
☰ Dan Shomron ☰ Yekutiel Adam ☰ Benjamin Peled ☰ Yonatan Netanyahu (KIA)	■ Wadie Haddad ★ Wilfried Böse (KIA) ≡ Idi Amin
Strength	
c.100 commandos, plus air crew and support personnel	7 hijackers 100+ Ugandan soldiers
Casualties and losses	
1 killed 5 wounded	**Hijackers**: 7 killed **Uganda**: 45 killed[1243] 11–30 aircraft destroyed[1244]
3 hostages killed 10 hostages wounded	

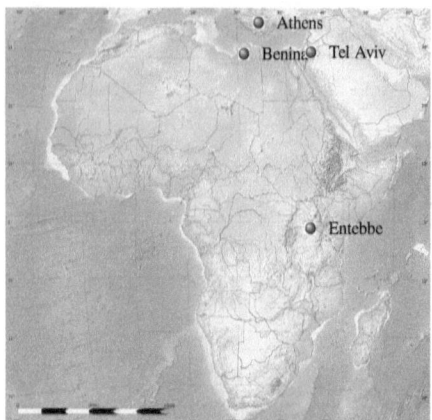

File:Africa relief location map.jpg

Sites associated with Operation Entebbe

Operation Entebbe, or **Operation Thunderbolt**, was a successful counter-terrorist hostage-rescue mission carried out by commandos of the Israel Defense Forces (IDF) at Entebbe Airport in Uganda on 4 July 1976.

A week earlier, on 27 June, an Air France plane with 248 passengers had been hijacked by two members of the Popular Front for the Liberation of Palestine – External Operations (PFLP-EO) under orders of Wadie Haddad (who had earlier broken away from the PFLP of George Habash), and two members of the German Revolutionary Cells. The hijackers had the stated objective to free 40 Palestinian and affiliated militants imprisoned in Israel and 13 prisoners in four other countries in exchange for the hostages. The flight, which had originated in Tel Aviv with the destination of Paris, was diverted after a stopover in Athens via Benghazi to Entebbe, the main airport of Uganda. The Ugandan government supported the hijackers, and dictator Idi Amin personally welcomed them. Amin had been informed of the hijacking from the beginning. After moving all hostages from the aircraft to a disused airport building, the hijackers separated all Israelis and several non-Israeli Jews from the larger group and forced them into a separate room. Over the following two days, 148 non-Israeli hostages were released and flown out to Paris. Ninety-four, mainly Israeli, passengers along with the 12-member Air France crew, remained as hostages and were threatened with death.

The IDF acted on information provided by the Israeli intelligence agency Mossad. The hijackers threatened to kill the hostages if their prisoner release demands were not met. This threat led to the planning of the rescue operation. These plans included preparation for armed resistance from Ugandan troops.

The operation took place at night. Israeli transport planes carried 100 commandos over 4,000 kilometres (2,500 mi) to Uganda for the rescue operation. The operation, which took a week of planning, lasted 90 minutes. Of the 106 remaining hostages, 102 were rescued and three were killed. The other hostage was in a hospital and was later killed. Five Israeli commandos were wounded and one, unit commander Lt. Col. Yonatan Netanyahu, was killed. All the hijackers and forty-five Ugandan soldiers were killed, and eleven Soviet-built MiG-17s and MiG-21s of Uganda's air force were destroyed. Kenyan sources supported Israel, and in the aftermath of the operation, Idi Amin issued orders to retaliate and slaughter several hundred Kenyans then present in Uganda.[1245] There were 245 Kenyans in Uganda killed and 3,000 fled.

Operation Entebbe, which had the military codename **Operation Thunderbolt**, is sometimes referred to retroactively as **Operation Jonathan** in memory of the unit's leader, Yonatan Netanyahu. He was the older brother of Benjamin Netanyahu, the current Prime Minister of Israel.

Hijacking

Air France Flight 139

The Air France Airbus A300 involved, at Charles de Gaulle Airport in 1980

Hijacking	
Date	27 June 1976
Summary	Hijacking
Site	Greek airspace
Aircraft	
Aircraft type	Airbus A300B4-203
Operator	Air France
Registration	F-BVGG
Flight origin	Ben Gurion Int'l Airport, Israel

Stopover	Athens (Ellinikon) Int'l Airport, Greece
Destination	Charles De Gaulle Int'l Airport, France
Passengers	248
Crew	12
Fatalities	4
Injuries	10
Survivors	256

On 27 June 1976, Air France Flight 139, an Airbus A300B4-203, registration F-BVGG (c/n 019), departed from Tel Aviv, Israel, carrying 246 mainly Jewish and Israeli passengers and a crew of 12. The plane flew to Athens, Greece, where it picked up an additional 58 passengers, including four hijackers.[1246] It departed for Paris at 12:30 pm. Just after takeoff, the flight was hijacked by two Palestinians from the Popular Front for the Liberation of Palestine – External Operations (PFLP-EO), and by two Germans, Wilfried Böse and Brigitte Kuhlmann, from the German Revolutionary Cells. The hijackers diverted the flight to Benghazi, Libya. There it was held on the ground for seven hours for refuelling. During that time the hijackers released British-born Israeli citizen Patricia Martell who pretended to have a miscarriage. The plane left Benghazi and at 3:15 pm on the 28th, more than 24 hours after the flight's original departure, it arrived at Entebbe Airport in Uganda.

Hostage situation at Entebbe airport

At Entebbe, the four hijackers were joined by at least four others, supported by the forces of Uganda's President, Idi Amin. The hijackers transferred the passengers to the transit hall of the disused former airport terminal where they kept them under guard for the following days. Amin came to visit the hostages almost on a daily basis, updating them on developments and promising to use his efforts to have them freed through negotiations.

On 28 June, a PFLP-EO hijacker issued a declaration and formulated their demands: In addition to a ransom of $5 million USD for the release of the airplane, they demanded the release of 53 Palestinian and Pro-Palestinian militants, 40 of whom were prisoners in Israel. They threatened that if these demands were not met, they would begin to kill hostages on 1 July 1976.

Separation of the hostages into two groups

On 29 June, after Ugandan soldiers had opened an entrance to a room next to the crowded waiting hall by destroying a separating wall, the hijackers separated the Israelis (including those holding dual citizenship) from the other hostages[1247] are in conflict with eyewitness accounts and later they were expressly disclaimed by several former hostages as a "myth" or a manipulation by "sensation-hungry journalists and film-makers." </ref> and told them to move to the adjoining room. As they did so, a Holocaust survivor showed hijacker Wilfried Böse a camp registration number tattooed on his arm. Böse protested "I'm no Nazi! ... I am an idealist".[1248] In addition, five non-Israeli hostages – two ultra-orthodox Jewish couples from the US and Belgium and a French resident of Israel – were forced to join the Israeli group. According to Monique Epstein Khalepski, the French hostage among the five, the captors had singled them out for questioning and suspected them of hiding their Israeli identities. On the other hand, according to French hostage Michel Cojot-Goldberg, the captors failed to identify at least one Israeli among the passengers who was a military officer with dual citizenship then using his non-Israeli passport and he was later freed as part of the second release of non-Israeli hostages. US citizen Janet Almog, Frenchwoman Jocelyne Monier (whose husband or boyfriend was Israeli), and French-Israeli dual citizen Jean-Jacques Mimouni, whose name had not been called up during the reading of the original passport-based list, reportedly joined the Israeli hostage group by their own choice.

Release of most non-Israeli hostages

On 30 June, the hijackers released 48 hostages. The released were picked from among the non-Israeli group – mainly elderly and sick passengers and mothers with children. Forty-seven of them were flown to Paris, and one passenger was treated in hospital for a day. On 1 July, after the Israeli government had conveyed its agreement to negotiations, the hostage-takers extended their deadline to noon on 4 July and released another group of 100 non-Israeli captives who again were flown to Paris a few hours later. Among the 106 hostages staying behind with their captors at Entebbe airport were the 12 members of the Air France crew who refused to leave,[1249] about ten young French passengers, and the Israeli group of some 84 people.

Operational planning

In the week before the raid, Israel tried using political avenues to obtain the release of the hostages. Many sources indicate that the Israeli cabinet was prepared to release Palestinian prisoners if a military solution seemed unlikely to succeed. A retired IDF officer, Baruch "Burka" Bar-Lev, had known Idi Amin for many years and was considered to have a strong personal relationship with him. At the request of the cabinet, he spoke with Amin on the phone many times, trying to gain the release of the hostages, without success.[1250,1251] The Israeli government also approached the United States government to deliver a message to Egyptian president Anwar Sadat, asking him to request that Amin release the hostages. Prime minister Yitzhak Rabin and defence minister Shimon Peres spent one week disagreeing on whether to give in to the hijackers' demands (Rabin's position) or not, to prevent more terrorism (Peres' position).

At the 1 July deadline,[1252] the Israeli cabinet offered to negotiate with the hijackers to extend the deadline to 4 July. Amin also asked them to extend the deadline until that date. This meant he could take a diplomatic trip to Port Louis, Mauritius, to officially hand over chairmanship of the Organisation of African Unity to Seewoosagur Ramgoolam.[1253] This extension of the hostage deadline proved crucial to providing Israeli forces enough time to get to Entebbe.

On 3 July, at 18:30, the Israeli cabinet approved a rescue mission, presented by Major General Yekutiel "Kuti" Adam and Brig. Gen. Dan Shomron. Shomron was appointed as the operation commander.

Attempts at a diplomatic solution

As the crisis unfolded, attempts were made to negotiate the release of the hostages. According to declassified diplomatic documents, the Egyptian government under Sadat tried to negotiate with both the PLO and the Ugandan government. PLO chairman Yasser Arafat sent his political aide Hani al-Hassan to Uganda as a special envoy to negotiate with the hostage takers and with Amin. However, the PFLP-EO hijackers refused to see him.

Raid preparation

When Israeli authorities failed to negotiate a political solution, they decided that their only option was an attack to rescue the hostages. Lt. Col. Joshua Shani, lead pilot of the operation, later said that the Israelis had initially conceived of a rescue plan that involved dropping naval commandos into Lake Victoria. The commandos would have ridden rubber boats to the airport located on the edge of the lake. They planned to kill the hijackers and after freeing the hostages, they would ask Amin for passage home. The Israelis abandoned this plan because they lacked the necessary time and also because they had received word that Lake Victoria was inhabited by the Nile crocodile.

Amnon Biran, the mission's intelligence officer, later stated that the proper layout of the airport was unknown, also the exact location of the hostages and whether the building had been prepared with explosives.

Aircraft refuelling

While planning the raid, the Israeli forces had to plan how to refuel the Lockheed C-130 Hercules aircraft they intended to use while en route to Entebbe. The Israelis lacked the logistical capacity to aerially refuel four to six aircraft so far from Israeli airspace. While several East African nations, including the logistically preferred choice Kenya, were sympathetic, none wished to incur the wrath of Amin or the Palestinians by allowing the Israelis to land their aircraft within their borders.

The raid could not proceed without assistance from at least one East African government. The Jewish owner of the Block hotels chain in Kenya, along with other members of the Jewish and Israeli community in Nairobi, may have used their political and economic influence to help persuade Kenya's President Jomo Kenyatta to help Israel. The Israeli government secured permission from Kenya for the IDF task force to cross Kenyan airspace and refuel at what is today Jomo Kenyatta International Airport.

Kenyan Minister of Agriculture Bruce MacKenzie persuaded Kenyan President Kenyatta to permit Mossad to collect intelligence prior to the operation, and to allow the Israeli Air Force access to the Nairobi airport. In retaliation, Ugandan President Idi Amin ordered Ugandan agents to assassinate MacKenzie. He was killed on 24 May 1978 when a bomb attached to his aircraft exploded. Later, Mossad Chief Director Meir Amit had a forest planted in Israel in MacKenzie's name.

Hostage intelligence

The Mossad built an accurate picture of the whereabouts of the hostages, the number of hijackers, and the involvement of Ugandan troops from the released hostages in Paris. Additionally, Israeli firms were involved in building projects in Africa during the 1960s and 1970s and while preparing the raid the Israeli army consulted with Solel Boneh, a large Israeli construction company that had built the terminal where the hostages were held. While planning the military operation the IDF erected a partial replica of the airport terminal with the assistance of civilians who had helped build the original.

Muki Betser said in a later interview that Mossad operatives extensively interviewed the hostages who had been released. He said that a French-Jewish passenger who had a military background and "a phenomenal memory" provided detailed information about the number of weapons carried by the hostage-takers.[1254] After Betzer collected intelligence and planned for several days, four Israeli Air Force C-130 Hercules transport aircraft secretly flew to Entebbe Airport at midnight without being detected by Entebbe air traffic control.

Task force

The Israeli ground task force numbered approximately 100 personnel, and comprised the following:

The ground command and control element

This small group comprised the operation and overall ground commander, Brigadier General Dan Shomron, the air force representative Col. Ami Ayalon and the communications and support personnel.

The assault element

A 29-man assault unit led by Lt. Col. Yonatan Netanyahu – this force was composed entirely of commandos from Sayeret Matkal, and was given the primary task of assaulting the old terminal and rescuing the hostages. Major Betser led one of the element's assault teams, and took command after Lt. Col. Netanyahu was killed.

The securing element

1. The Paratroopers force led by Col. Matan Vilnai – tasked with securing the civilian airport field, clearing and securing the runways, and protection and fuelling of the Israeli aircraft in Entebbe.
2. The Golani force led by Col. Uri Sagi – tasked with securing the C-130 Hercules aircraft for the hostages' evacuation, getting it as close as possible to the terminal and boarding the hostages; also with acting as general reserves.
3. The Sayeret Matkal force led by Major Shaul Mofaz – tasked with clearing the military airstrip, and destroying the squadron of MiG fighter jets on the ground, to prevent any possible interceptions by the Ugandan Air Force; also with holding off hostile ground forces from the city of Entebbe.

Raid

Attack route

Taking off from Sharm el-Sheikh, the task force flew along the international flight path over the Red Sea, mostly flying at a height of no more than 30 m (100 ft) to avoid radar detection by Egyptian, Sudanese, and Saudi Arabian forces. Near the south outlet of the Red Sea the C-130s turned south and passed south of Djibouti. From there, they went to a point northeast of Nairobi, Kenya, likely across Somalia and the Ogaden area of Ethiopia. They turned west, passing through the African Rift Valley and over Lake Victoria.

Two Boeing 707 jets followed the cargo planes. The first Boeing contained medical facilities and landed at Jomo Kenyatta International Airport in Nairobi, Kenya. The commander of the operation, General Yekutiel Adam, was on board the second Boeing, which circled over Entebbe Airport during the raid.

The Israeli forces landed at Entebbe on 3 July at 23:00 IST, with their cargo bay doors already open. Because the proper layout of the airport was not known, the first plane almost taxied into a ditch. A black Mercedes car that looked like President Idi Amin's vehicle and Land Rovers that usually accompanied Amin's Mercedes were brought along. The Israelis hoped they could use them to bypass security checkpoints. When the C-130s landed, Israeli assault team members drove the vehicles to the terminal building in the same fashion as Amin. As they approached the terminal, two Ugandan sentries, aware that Idi Amin had recently purchased a white Mercedes, ordered the vehicles to stop. Netanyahu ordered the commandos to shoot the sentries using silenced pistols, but they did not kill them. This was against the plan and against the orders. As they pulled away, an Israeli commando in one of the following Land Rovers killed them with an unsuppressed rifle. Fearing the hijackers would be alerted prematurely, the assault team quickly approached the terminal.

Hostage rescue

The Israelis left their vehicles and ran towards the terminal. The hostages were in the main hall of the airport building, directly adjacent to the runway. Entering the terminal, the commandos shouted through a megaphone, "Stay down! Stay down! We are Israeli soldiers," in both Hebrew and English. Jean-Jacques Maimoni, a 19-year-old French immigrant to Israel, stood up and was killed when Israeli company commander Muki Betzer and another soldier mistook him for a hijacker and fired at him. Another hostage, Pasco Cohen, 52, was also fatally wounded by gunfire from the commandos. In addition, a third hostage, 56-year-old Ida Borochovitch, a Russian Jew who had emigrated to Israel, was killed by a hijacker in the crossfire.

According to hostage Ilan Hartuv, Wilfried Böse was the only hijacker who, after the operation began, entered the hall housing the hostages. At first he

Figure 154: *A 1994 photograph of the old terminal with a U.S. Air Force C-130 Hercules parked in front. Bullet holes from the 1976 raid are still visible.*

pointed his Kalashnikov rifle at hostages, but "immediately came to his senses" and ordered them to find shelter in the restroom, before being killed by the commandos. According to Hartuv, Böse fired only at Israeli soldiers and not at hostages.

At one point, an Israeli commando called out in Hebrew, "Where are the rest of them?" referring to the hijackers. The hostages pointed to a connecting door of the airport's main hall, into which the commandos threw several hand grenades. Then, they entered the room and shot dead the three remaining hijackers, ending the assault. Meanwhile, the other three C-130 Hercules aeroplanes had landed and unloaded armoured personnel carriers to provide defence during the anticipated hour of refuelling. The Israelis then destroyed Ugandan MiG fighter planes to prevent them from pursuing, and conducted a sweep of the airfield to gather intelligence.

Departure

After the raid, the Israeli assault team returned to their aircraft and began loading the hostages. Ugandan soldiers shot at them in the process. The Israeli commandos returned fire with their AK47s, inflicting casualties on the Ugandans. During this brief but intense firefight, Ugandan soldiers fired from the airport control tower. At least five commandos were wounded, and

Figure 155: *Rescued passengers welcomed at Ben Gurion Airport*

the Israeli unit commander Yonatan Netanyahu was killed. Israeli commandos fired light machine guns and a rocket-propelled grenade back at the control tower, suppressing the Ugandans' fire. According to one of Idi Amin's sons, the soldier who shot Netanyahu, a cousin of the Amin family, was killed in the return fire.[1255] The Israelis finished evacuating the hostages, loaded Netanyahu's body into one of the planes, and left the airport. The entire operation lasted 53 minutes – of which the assault lasted only 30 minutes. All 7 hijackers present, and between 33 and 45 Ugandan soldiers, were killed.Wikipedia:Verifiability Eleven Soviet-built MiG-17 and MiG-21 fighter planes of the Ugandan Air Force were destroyed on the ground at Entebbe Airport. Out of the 106 hostages, 3 were killed, 1 was left in Uganda (74-year-old Dora Bloch), and approximately 10 were wounded. The 102 rescued hostages were flown to Israel via Nairobi, Kenya, shortly after the raid.

Ugandan reaction

Dora Bloch, a 74-year-old Israeli who also held British citizenship, was taken to Mulago Hospital in Kampala after choking on a chicken bone.[1256] After the raid she was murdered by officers of the Ugandan army, as were some of her doctors and nurses, apparently for trying to intervene.[1257] In April 1987, Henry Kyemba, Uganda's Attorney general and Minister of Justice at the time, told the Uganda Human Rights Commission that Bloch had been

Figure 156: *Members of family pay last respects to Dora Bloch, 75, after she was murdered by officers of the Ugandan army*

dragged from her hospital bed and killed by two army officers on Amin's orders. Bloch was shot and her body was dumped in the trunk of a car that had Ugandan intelligence services number plates. Her remains were recovered near a sugar plantation 20 miles (32 km) east of Kampala in 1979,[1258] after the Ugandan–Tanzanian War ended Amin's rule. Amin also ordered the killing of hundreds of Kenyans living in Uganda in retaliation for Kenya's assistance to Israel in the raid. There were 245 Kenyans killed as reported on 11 July, including airport staff at Entebbe, and to escape being massacred, about 3,000 Kenyans fled from Uganda as refugees.[1259]

Aftermath

The United Nations Security Council convened on 9 July 1976, to consider a complaint from the Chairman of the Organization of African Unity charging Israel with an "act of aggression". The Council allowed Israel's ambassador to the United Nations, Chaim Herzog, and Uganda's foreign minister, Juma Oris Abdalla, to participate without voting rights. UN Secretary General Kurt Waldheim told the Security Council that the raid was "a serious violation of the sovereignty of a Member State of the United Nations" though he was "fully aware that this is not the only element involved ... when the world community is now required to deal with unprecedented problems arising from international terrorism."[1260] Abdalla, the representative of Uganda, alleged that the affair was close to a peaceful resolution when Israel intervened while Herzog, the representative of Israel, accused Uganda of direct complicity in the hijacking. The US and UK sponsored a resolution which condemned hijacking and similar acts, deplored the loss of life arising from the hijacking (without condemning either Israel or Uganda), reaffirmed the need to respect the sovereignty and territorial integrity of all States, and called on the international community to enhance the safety of civil aviation.[1261] However, the resolution failed to receive the required number of affirmative votes because two voting members abstained and seven were absent.[1262] A second resolution sponsored by Benin, Libya and Tanzania, that condemned Israel, was not put to the vote.[1263]

Western nations spoke in support of the raid. West Germany called the raid "an act of self-defence". Switzerland and France praised the operation. Representatives of the United Kingdom and United States offered significant praise, calling the Entebbe raid "an impossible operation". Some in the United States noted that the hostages were freed on 4 July 1976, 200 years after the signing of the US declaration of independence. In private conversation with Israeli Ambassador Dinitz, Henry Kissinger sounded criticism for Israeli use of US equipment during the operation, but that criticism was not made public at the time. In mid-July 1976, the supercarrier USS *Ranger* (CV-61) and her escorts entered the Indian Ocean and operated off the Kenyan coast in response to a threat of military action by forces from Uganda.[1264]

Captain Bacos was awarded the Legion of Honour, and the other crew members were awarded the French Order of Merit.[1265,1266]

The Norfolk hotel in Nairobi, owned by a prominent member of the local Jewish community, was bombed on 31 December 1980. The bomb flattened the western wing of the hotel, killing 20 people,Wikipedia:Citation needed of several nationalities, and wounding 87 more. It was believed to be an act of revenge by pro-Palestinian militants for Kenya's supporting role in Operation Entebbe.

In the ensuing years, Betser and the Netanyahu brothers – Iddo and Benjamin, all Sayeret Matkal veterans – argued in increasingly public forums about who was to blame for the unexpected early firefight that caused Yonatan's death and partial loss of tactical surprise.[1267,1268]

As a result of the operation, the United States military developed rescue teams modelled on the unit employed in the Entebbe rescue.[1269] One notable attempt to imitate it was Operation Eagle Claw, a failed rescue of 53 American embassy personnel held hostage in Tehran during the Iran hostage crisis.[1270]

In a letter dated 13 July 1976, the Supreme Commander's Staff of the Imperial Iranian Armed Forces praised the Israeli commandos for the mission and extended condolences for "the loss and martyrdom" of Netanyahu.

Commemorations

In August 2012, Uganda and Israel commemorated the raid at a sombre ceremony at the base of a tower at the Old Entebbe Airport, where Yonatan Netanyahu was killed. Uganda and Israel renewed their commitment to "fight terrorism and to work towards humanity". In addition, wreaths were laid, a moment of silence was held, speeches were given, and a poem was recited. The flags of Uganda and Israel waved side by side, demonstrating the two countries' strong bilateral relations, next to a plaque bearing a history of the raid. The ceremony was attended by Ugandan State Minister for Animal Industry Bright Rwamirama and the deputy Foreign Affairs Minister of Israel Daniel Ayalon, who laid wreaths at the site. Forty years to the day after the rescue operation, Israeli Prime-Minister, Benjamin Netanyahu, and brother of the slain Israeli *Sayeret Matkal* commando, Yoni Netanyahu, visited Entebbe with an Israeli delegation, and laid the groundwork for further Israeli–sub-Saharan African bilateral relations.

Dramatisations and documentaries

Documentaries

- *Operation Thunderbolt: Entebbe*, a documentary about the hijacking and the subsequent rescue mission.
- *Rise and Fall of Idi Amin* (1980), a biopic of the Ugandan dictator which features the raid.
- Rescue at Entebbe, Episode 12 of 2005 documentary series *Against All Odds: Israel Survives* by Michael Greenspan.
- *Cohen on the Bridge* (2010), a documentary by director Andrew Wainrib, who gained access to the surviving commandos and hostages.
- *Live or Die in Entebbe* (2012) by director Eyal Boers follows Yonatan Khayat's journey to uncover the circumstances of his uncle Jean-Jacques Maimoni's death in the raid.
- "Assault on Entebbe", an episode of the National Geographic Channel documentary *Critical Situation*.
- *Operation Thunderbolt*, the fifth episode in the 2012 Military Channel documentary series *Black Ops*.

Dramatisations

- *Victory at Entebbe* (1976): with Anthony Hopkins, Burt Lancaster, Elizabeth Taylor and Richard Dreyfuss, Director: Marvin J. Chomsky.
- *Raid on Entebbe* (1977): with Peter Finch, Horst Buchholz, Charles Bronson, John Saxon, Yaphet Kotto, and James Woods, Director: Irvin Kershner, Producer: Edgar J. Scherick.
- *Operation Thunderbolt* (1977): with Yehoram Gaon played Col. Netanyahu, Sybil Danning and Klaus Kinski played the hijackers. Director: Menahem Golan.
- *The Last King of Scotland* (2006): The raid occurs as one episode in a longer story about Idi Amin.
- *Entebbe* (2018): Director: José Padilha

Films inspired by Operation Entebbe

- *The Delta Force* (1986) which featured a hostage rescue operation inspired by Operation Entebbe.
- *Zameen* (2003) is a Bollywood movie starring Ajay Devgan and Abhishekh Bachchan who draw a plan to rescue hostages of an Indian airliner hijacked by Pakistani militants on the basis of Operation Entebbe.
- *Entebbe* (2018)

Other media

- *Operation Thunderbolt,* a 1988 arcade game.
- *Tom Clancy's Rainbow Six: Rogue Spear*'s add-on "Black Thorn" (2001), included a stage which features a reenactment of the operation.
- *To Pay the Price*, a 2009 play by Peter-Adrian Cohen based in part on Yonatan Netanyahu's letters. The play, produced by North Carolina's Theatre Or opened off-off Broadway in New York in June 2009 during the Festival of Jewish Theater and Ideas.
- *Follow Me: The Yoni Netanyahu Story* (2011), a book recounting the life of the raid's commander Yonatan Netanyahu.

Gallery

Figure 157: *The old control tower as seen from the front.*

Figure 158: *Close up of the control tower.*

Figure 159: *The old terminal building as it appeared in 2009.*

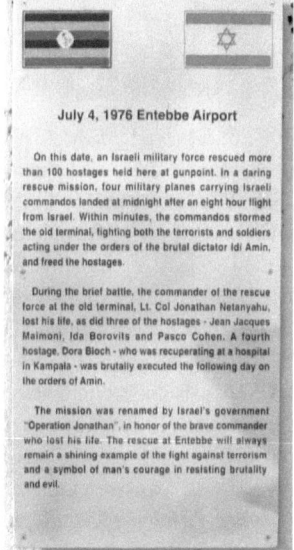

Figure 160: *Wall plaque on display at the old terminal building.*

Figure 161: *The old terminal building of the Entebbe International Airport as seen from the air.*

Further reading

<templatestyles src="Refbegin/styles.css" />

- Avner, Yehuda (2010). "26, *Entebbe: Flight 139*". *The Prime Ministers: An Intimate Narrative of Israeli Leadership*. The Toby Press. pp. 303–318. ISBN 978-1-59264-278-6.<templatestyles src="Module:Citation/CS1/styles.css"></templatestyles>
- Blumenau, Bernhard (2014). "2, *'The German silence'*: the Entebbe hijacking of 1976". *The United Nations and Terrorism. Germany, Multilateralism, and Antiterrorism Efforts in the 1970s*. Palgrave Macmillan. pp. 59–73. ISBN 978-1-137-39196-4.<templatestyles src="Module:Citation/CS1/styles.css"></templatestyles>
- Betser, Muki; Robert Rosenberg (1996). *Secret Soldier*. Sydney: Simon & Schuster. ISBN 0-671-85233-7.<templatestyles src="Module:Citation/CS1/styles.css"></templatestyles>
- David, Saul (2015). *Operation Thunderbolt: Flight 139 and the Raid on Entebbe Airport*. London: Hodder & Stoughton. ISBN 978-1-44476-251-8.<templatestyles src="Module:Citation/CS1/styles.css"></templatestyles>
- Dunstan, Simon (2009). *Israel's Lighting Strike, The raid on Entebbe 1976*. Osprey Publishing; Osprey Raid Series No. 2. ISBN 978-1-84603-397-1.<templatestyles src="Module:Citation/CS1/styles.css"></templatestyles>

- Hastings, Max. *Yoni: Hero of Entebbe*. Doubleday. ISBN 0-385-27127-1.<templatestyles src="Module:Citation/CS1/styles.css"></templatestyles>
- Netanyahu, Iddo. *Yoni's Last Battle: The Rescue at Entebbe, 1976*. Gefen Books. ISBN 965-229-283-4.<templatestyles src="Module:Citation/CS1/styles.css"></templatestyles>
- Netanyahu, Ido; Netanyahu, 'Ido; Netanyahu, Iddo; Hazony, Yoram (2003). *Entebbe: the Jonathan Netanyahu story: a defining moment in the war on terrorism*. Green Forest, AR: Balfour Books. ISBN 0-89221-553-4.<templatestyles src="Module:Citation/CS1/styles.css"></templatestyles>
- Netanyahu, Jonathan; Netanyahu, Binyamin; Netanyahu, Ido; Wouk, Herman. *Self-Portrait of a Hero: From the Letters of Jonathan Netanyahu, 1963–1976*. Warner Books Inc. ISBN 0-446-67461-3.<templatestyles src="Module:Citation/CS1/styles.css"></templatestyles>
- Netanyahu, Jonathan. *The Letters of Jonathan Netanyahu: The Commander of the Entebbe Rescue Operation*. Gefen Publishing House, Ltd. ISBN 965-229-267-2.<templatestyles src="Module:Citation/CS1/styles.css"></templatestyles>
- Stevenson, William (1976). *90 Minutes at Entebbe*. New York: Bantam Books. ISBN 0-553-10482-9.<templatestyles src="Module:Citation/CS1/styles.css"></templatestyles>

External links

 Wikimedia Commons has media related to *Operation Thunderbolt*.

- Live or Die in Entebbe[1271] Trailer
- Operation Thunderbolt[1272] on YouTube, video by National Geographic, 4 min.
- Raid on Entebbe[1273] on YouTube video and digitised re-enactment, 9 min.
- Operation Thunderbolt – part 1[1274] on YouTube video documentary – detailed, 9 min. part 2[1275] on YouTube 10 min.
- The Greatest Hostage Rescue in History: Documentary on The Entebbe Raid.[1276] on YouTube documentary – detailed, 44 min.
- Israel's raid on Entebbe was almost a disaster[1277], Daily Telegraph article by Saul David
- Entebbe: Turning Point of Terrorism[1278] in Strategy and Tactics, No. 232, January/February 2006.
- isayeret.com[1279] – The Israeli Special Forces Database

- BBC Article and Videos – 4 July 1976: Israelis rescue Entebbe hostages (BBC)[1280]
- BBC: 30th anniversary of the raid on Entebbe[1281]
- BBC Age of Terror – Episode 1: Terror International[1282]
- Operation Entebbe protocols[1283] Ynetnews 5 November 2010. transcripts of Israeli Cabinet discussions

Coordinates: 0°02′42.8784″N 32°27′13.1616″E[1284]

1977–1983: Begin

Camp David Accords

\<indicator name="pp-default"\> 🔒 \</indicator\>

Camp David Accords

Framework for Peace in the Middle East and Framework for the Conclusion of a Peace Treaty between Egypt and Israel	
 Celebrating the signing of the Camp David Accords: Menachem Begin, Jimmy Carter, Anwar Sadat	
Type	Bilateral treaty
Signed	17 September 1978
Location	Washington, DC, United States
Original signatories	• Egypt • Israel

Signatories	• Menachem Begin
	  (Prime Minister of Israel)
	• Anwar Sadat
	  (President of Egypt)
	• Jimmy Carter
	  (President of the United States)

Ratifiers	• Egypt • Israel
Language	• English • French

The **Camp David Accords** were signed by Egyptian President Anwar Sadat and Israeli Prime Minister Menachem Begin on 17 September 1978, following twelve days of secret negotiations at Camp David.[1285] The two framework agreements were signed at the White House, and were witnessed by United States President Jimmy Carter. The second of these frameworks (*A Framework for the Conclusion of a Peace Treaty between Egypt and Israel*) led directly to the 1979 Egypt–Israel Peace Treaty. Due to the agreement, Sadat and Begin received the shared 1978 Nobel Peace Prize. The first framework (*A Framework for Peace in the Middle East*), which dealt with the Palestinian territories, was written without participation of the Palestinians and was condemned by the United Nations.

Preceding diplomacy

Carter Initiative

Carter's and Secretary of State Cyrus Vance's exploratory meetings gave a basic plan for reinvigorating the peace process based on a Geneva Peace Conference and had presented three main objectives for Arab–Israeli peace: Arab recognition of Israel's right to exist in peace, Israel's withdrawal from occupied territories gained in the Six-Day War through negotiating efforts with neighboring Arab nations to ensure that Israel's security would not be threatened and securing an undivided Jerusalem.

The Camp David Accords were the result of 14 months of diplomatic efforts by Egypt, Israel, and the United States that began after Jimmy Carter became President.[1286] The efforts initially focused on a comprehensive resolution of disputes between Israel and the Arab countries, gradually evolving into a search for a bilateral agreement between Israel and Egypt.[1287]

Upon assuming office on January 20, 1977, President Carter moved to rejuvenate the Middle East peace process that had stalled throughout the 1976 presidential campaign in the United States. Following the advice of a Brookings Institution report, Carter opted to replace the incremental, bilateral peace talks which had characterized Henry Kissinger's shuttle diplomacy following the 1973 Yom Kippur War with a comprehensive, multilateral approach. The Yom Kippur War further complicated efforts to achieve the objectives written in United Nations Security Council Resolution 242.

Israel's Prime Minister Yitzhak Rabin and his successor, Menachem Begin, were both skeptical of an international conference. While Begin, who took office in May 1977, officially favored the reconvening of the conference, perhaps even more vocally than Rabin, and even accepted the Palestinian presence, in

Figure 162:
*Territory held by Israel:
before the Six-Day War
after the war*

actuality the Israelis and the Egyptians were secretly formulating a framework for bilateral talks. Even earlier, Begin had not been opposed to returning the Sinai, but a major future obstacle was his firm refusal to consider relinquishing control over the West Bank.[1288]

Participating parties

Carter visited the heads of state on whom he would have to rely to make any peace agreement feasible. By the end of his first year in office, he had already met with Anwar El Sadat of Egypt, King Hussein of Jordan, Hafez al-Assad of Syria, and Yitzhak Rabin of Israel. Despite the fact that he supported Sadat's peace initiative, King Hussein refused to take part in the peace talks; Begin offered Jordan little to gain and Hussein also feared he would isolate Jordan from the Arab world and provoke Syria and the PLO if he engaged in the peace talks as well. Hafez al-Assad, who had no particular interest in negotiating peace with Israel,[1289] also refused to come to the United States and only agreed to meet with Carter in Geneva.

Figure 163: *Menachem Begin, Jimmy Carter and Anwar Sadat at Camp David, 1978*

Begin Initiative

The key to an arrangement between Begin and Sadat took place on Sunday, 6 August 1978, as a result of a telephone call made that morning to the Israeli Prime Minister's office by a United States citizen who had an "idea for peace." The Prime Minister had not yet arrived at his office and the caller spoke to Mr. Yechiel Kadishai, a Begin staff head. Kadishai said that "no one was speaking with anyone and we expect a war in October." He also told the caller that if any high level talks were to occur the caller could be assured that they would be using his approach. Begin arrived, was informed of the plan, and contacted Sadat who agreed to the plan on that day. On the next day, Secretary of State Cyrus Vance traveled to the Middle East to obtain firsthand confirmation of the agreement between Israel and Egypt. The following day, Tuesday, 8 August, the Camp David meeting was scheduled to take place in exactly 4 weeks time; on 5 September 1978. The plan was that Israel agreed on 6 August to return the land to Egypt. Sadat's then waning popularity would be greatly enhanced as a result of such an achievement. Israel's security was insured by the specific activities to take place during the "transition period." Those activities also were included in the "idea for peace" communicated to Begin's office on 6 August.

Sadat Initiative

President Anwar El Sadat came to feel that the Geneva track peace process was more show than substance, and was not progressing, partly due to disagreements with his Arab (mainly Syria, Libya, and Iraq) and his communist allies. He also lacked confidence in the Western powers to pressure Israel after a meeting with the Western leaders. His frustration boiled over, and after clandestine preparatory meetings between Egyptian and Israeli officials, unknown even to the NATO countries, in November 1977, Sadat became the first Arab leader to visit Israel.

On 9 November 1977, President Sadat startled the world by announcing to parliament his intention to go to Jerusalem and speak before the Knesset. Shortly afterward, the Israeli government cordially invited him to address the Knesset in a message passed to Sadat via the US ambassador to Egypt. Ten days after his speech, Sadat arrived for the groundbreaking three-day visit, which launched the first peace process between Israel and an Arab state. As would be the case with later Israeli–Arab peace initiatives, Washington was taken by surprise; the White House and State Department were particularly concerned that Sadat was merely reaching out to reacquire Sinai as quickly as possible, putting aside the Palestinian problem. Considered as a man with strong political convictions who kept his eye on the main objective, Sadat had no ideological base, which made him politically inconsistent.[1290] The Sadat visit came about after he delivered a speech in Egypt stating that he would travel anywhere, "even Jerusalem," to discuss peace.[1291] That speech led the Begin government to declare that, if Israel thought that Sadat would accept an invitation, Israel would invite him. In Sadat's Knesset speech he talked about his views on peace, the status of Israel's occupied territories, and the Palestinian refugee problem. This tactic went against the intentions of both the West and the East, which were to revive the Geneva Conference.

The gesture stemmed from an eagerness to enlist the help of the NATO countries in improving the ailing Egyptian economy, a belief that Egypt should begin to focus more on its own interests than on the interests of the Arab world, and a hope that an agreement with Israel would catalyze similar agreements between Israel and her other Arab neighbors and help solve the Palestinian problem. Prime Minister Begin's response to Sadat's initiative, though not what Sadat or Carter had hoped, demonstrated a willingness to engage the Egyptian leader. Like Sadat, Begin also saw many reasons why bilateral talks would be in his country's best interests. It would afford Israel the opportunity to negotiate only with Egypt instead of with a larger Arab delegation that might try to use its size to make unwelcome or unacceptable demands. Israel felt Egypt could help protect Israel from other Arabs and Eastern communists. In addition, the commencement of direct negotiations between leaders – summit diplomacy – would distinguish Egypt from her Arab neighbors. Carter's people apparently had no inkling of the secret talks in Morocco between Dayan and Sadat's representative, Hassan Tuhami, that paved the way for Sadat's initiative. Indeed, in a sense Egypt and Israel were ganging up to push Carter off

Figure 164: *Begin and Brzezinski playing chess at Camp David*

his Geneva track. The basic message of Sadat's speech at the Knesset were the request for the implementation of Resolutions 242 and 338. Sadat's visit was the first step to negotiations such as the preliminary Cairo Conference in December 1977.

Egyptian–Israeli talks

A mechanism had yet to be created for Israel and Egypt to pursue the talks begun by Sadat and Begin in Jerusalem. The Egyptian president suggested to Begin that Israel place a secret representative in the American embassy in Cairo. With American "cover," the true identity of the Israeli, who would liaise between the Egyptian and Israeli leaders, would be known only to the American ambassador in Cairo.

Sadat's liaison initiative spoke volumes about his reasons for wanting to make peace with Israel. He wanted an alliance with the American superpower and he wanted to kill Carter's Geneva initiative. His trip to Jerusalem signaled a major reorientation of Cairo's place in the global scheme of things, from the Soviet to the American camp.[1292] Carter's acceptance of the proposed liaison scheme would have signaled American backing for Sadat's unprecedented peace initiative. But Carter said no. However, Carter could not thwart the Israeli-Egyptian peace push. Within days Israeli journalists were allowed into Cairo, breaking a symbolic barrier, and from there the peace process quickly

Figure 165: *A meeting at Camp David with (l-r) Aharon Barak, Menachem Begin, Anwar Sadat, and Ezer Weizman, 1978*

gained momentum. An Israeli-Egyptian working summit was scheduled for 25 December in Ismailiya, near the Suez Canal.

Accompanied by their capable negotiating teams and with their respective interests in mind, both leaders converged on Camp David for 13 days of tense and dramatic negotiations from 5 to 17 September 1978. By all accounts, Carter's relentless drive to achieve peace and his reluctance to allow the two men to leave without reaching an agreement are what played the decisive role in the success of the talks.Wikipedia:Citation needed

Carter's advisers insisted on the establishment of an Egyptian-Israeli agreement which would lead to an eventual solution to the Palestine issue. They believed in a short, loose, and overt linkage between the two countries amplified by the establishment of a coherent basis for a settlement. However, Carter felt they were not "aiming high enough" and was interested in the establishment of a written "land for peace" agreement with Israel returning the Sinai Peninsula and West Bank. Numerous times both the Egyptian and Israeli leaders wanted to scrap negotiations, only to be lured back into the process by personal appeals from Carter. Considered as an excellent mediator who arbitrated concessions with confidence, he played a tireless commitment to find formulas, definitions, and solutions to the many intricate variables, regardless of perceived or real political limitations, and was capable of soothing fears and anxieties, always

Figure 166: *President Carter, National Security Advisor Zbigniew Brzezinski, and Secretary of State Cyrus Vance at Camp David*

with the goal of keeping the negotiations going.Wikipedia:Citation needed He gradually understood the importance historical events had upon determining personal ideology, but he would not allow it to constrain his political options, and he did not want them to limit the options of those with whom he was negotiating.Wikipedia:Citation needed

Begin and Sadat had such mutual antipathy toward one another that they only seldom had direct contact; thus Carter had to conduct his own microcosmic form of shuttle diplomacy by holding one-on-one meetings with either Sadat or Begin in one cabin, then returning to the cabin of the third party to relay the substance of his discussions. Begin and Sadat were "literally not on speaking terms," and "claustrophobia was setting in."

A particularly difficult situation arose on the tenth stalemated day of the talks. The issues of Israeli settlement withdrawal from the Sinai and the status of the West Bank created what seemed to be an impasse. In response, Carter had the choice of trying to salvage the agreement by conceding the issue of the West Bank to Begin, while advocating Sadat's less controversial position on the removal of all settlements from the Sinai Peninsula. Or he could have refused to continue the talks, reported the reasons for their failure, and allowed Begin to bear the brunt of the blame.

Carter chose to continue and for three more days negotiated. During this time, Carter even took the two leaders to the nearby Gettysburg National Military Park in the hopes of using the American Civil War as a simile to their own struggle.Wikipedia:Citation needed

Figure 167: *Egyptian President Anwar Sadat and Israeli Prime Minister Menachem Begin acknowledge applause during a joint session of Congress in Washington, D.C., during which President Jimmy Carter announced the results of the Camp David Accords, 18 September 1978.*

Consequently, the 13 days marking the Camp David Accords were considered a success. Partly due to Carter's determination in obtaining an Israeli-Egyptian agreement, a full two-week pledge to a singular international problem. Additionally, Carter was beneficiary to a fully pledged American foreign team. Likewise, the Israeli delegation had a stable of excellent talent in Ministers Dayan and Weizman and legal experts Dr. Meir Rosenne and Aharon Barak. Furthermore, the absence of the media contributed to the Accord's successes: there were no possibilities provided to either leader to reassure his political body or be driven to conclusions by members of his opposition. An eventual scrap of negotiations by either leader would have proven disastrous, resulting in taking the blame for the summit's failure as well as a disassociation from the White House. Ultimately, neither Begin nor Sadat was willing to risk those eventualities. Both of them had invested enormous amounts of political capital and time to reach an agreement.[1293]

Partial agreements

"Remarks on the Signing of the Camp David Accords"

Jimmy Carter, seated with Egyptian President Anwar Sadat and Israeli Prime Minister Menachem Begin, makes statements at a Joint session of the United States Congress following the Camp David Accords.

Problems playing this file? See media help.

The Camp David Accords comprise two separate agreements: *"A Framework for Peace in the Middle East"* and *"A Framework for the Conclusion of a Peace Treaty between Egypt and Israel"*, the second leading towards the Egypt–Israel Peace Treaty signed in March 1979. The agreements and the peace treaty were both accompanied by "side-letters" of understanding between Egypt and the U.S. and Israel and the U.S.[1294]

Framework for Peace in the Middle East

The preamble of the *"Framework for Peace in the Middle East"* starts with the basis of a peaceful settlement of the Arab–Israeli conflict:

The agreed basis for a peaceful settlement of the conflict between Israel and its neighbors is United Nations Security Council Resolution 242, in all its parts.[1295]

The framework itself consists of 3 parts. The first part of the framework was to establish an autonomous self-governing authority in the West Bank and the Gaza strip and to fully implement Resolution 242. The Accords recognized the "legitimate rights of the Palestinian people", a process was to be implemented guaranteeing the full autonomy of the people within a period of five years. *Begin* insisted on the adjective "full" to confirm that it was the maximum political right attainable. This full autonomy was to be discussed with the participation of Israel, Egypt, Jordan and the Palestinians. The withdrawal of Israeli troops from the West Bank and Gaza was agreed to occur after an election of a self-governing authority to replace Israel's military government. The Accords did not mention the Golan Heights, Syria, or Lebanon. This was not the comprehensive peace that Kissinger, Ford, Carter, or Sadat had in mind during the previous American presidential transition.[1296] It was less clear than the agreements concerning the Sinai, and was later interpreted differently by

Israel, Egypt, and the United States. The fate of Jerusalem was deliberately excluded from this agreement.[1297]

The second part of the framework dealt with Egyptian–Israeli relations, the real content worked out in the second Egypt—Israel framework. The third part, "Associated Principles," declared principles that should apply to relations between Israel and all of its Arab neighbors.

Key points of the West Bank and Gaza section

- *Egypt, Israel, Jordan and the representatives of the Palestinian people should participate in negotiations on the resolution of the Palestinian problem in all its aspects.*
- *(1.) Egypt and Israel agree that, in order to ensure a peaceful and orderly transfer of authority, and taking into account the security concerns of all the parties, there should be transitional arrangements for the West Bank and Gaza for a period not exceeding five years. In order to provide full autonomy to the inhabitants, under these arrangements the Israeli military government and its civilian administration will be withdrawn as soon as a self-governing authority has been freely elected by the inhabitants of these areas to replace the existing military government.*
- *(2.) Egypt, Israel, and Jordan will agree on the modalities for establishing elected self-governing authority in the West Bank and Gaza. The delegations of Egypt and Jordan may include Palestinians from the West Bank and Gaza or other Palestinians as mutually agreed. The parties will negotiate an agreement which will define the powers and responsibilities of the self-governing authority to be exercised in the West Bank and Gaza. A withdrawal of Israeli armed forces will take place and there will be a redeployment of the remaining Israeli forces into specified security locations. The agreement will also include arrangements for assuring internal and external security and public order. A strong local police force will be established, which may include Jordanian citizens. In addition, Israeli and Jordanian forces will participate in joint patrols and in the manning of control posts to assure the security of the borders.*
- *(3.) When the self-governing authority (administrative council) in the West Bank and Gaza is established and inaugurated, the transitional period of five years will begin. As soon as possible, but not later than the third year after the beginning of the transitional period, negotiations will take place to determine the final status of the West Bank and Gaza and its relationship with its neighbors and to conclude a peace treaty between Israel and Jordan by the end of the transitional period. These negotiations will be conducted among Egypt, Israel, Jordan and the elected representatives of the inhabitants of the West Bank and Gaza. ... The negotiations shall be based on all the provisions and principles of UN*

Security Council Resolution 242. The negotiations will resolve, among other matters, the location of the boundaries and the nature of the security arrangements. The solution from the negotiations must also recognize the legitimate right of the Palestinian peoples and their just requirements.

The framework merely concerned autonomy of the inhabitants of West Bank and Gaza. It neither mentions the status of Jerusalem, nor the Palestinian Right of Return.

UN Rejection of the Middle East Framework

The UN General Assembly rejected the *Framework for Peace in the Middle East*, because the agreement was concluded without participation of UN and PLO and did not comply with the Palestinian right of return, of self-determination and to national independence and sovereignty. December 1978, it declared in *Resolution 33/28 A*, that agreements were only valid if they are within the framework of the United Nations and its Charter and its resolutions, include the Palestinian right of return and the right to national independence and sovereignty in Palestine, and concluded with the participation of the PLO. Also the passive attitude of the Security Council was criticised.[1298] On 6 December 1979, the UN condemned in *Resolution 34/70* all partial agreements and separate treaties that did not meet the Palestinian rights and comprehensive solutions to peace; it condemned Israel's continued occupation and demanded withdrawal from *all* occupied territories.[1299] On 12 December, in *Resolution 34/65 B*, she rejected more specific parts of the Camp David Accords and similar agreements, which were not in accordance with mentioned requirements. All such partial agreements and separate treaties were strongly condemned. The part of the Camp David accords regarding the Palestinian future and all similar ones were declared invalid.[1300]

Framework Peace Treaty Egypt and Israel

The second framework[1301] outlined a basis for the peace treaty six months later, in particular deciding the future of the Sinai peninsula. Israel agreed to withdraw its armed forces from the Sinai, evacuate its 4,500 civilian inhabitants, and restore it to Egypt in return for normal diplomatic relations with Egypt, guarantees of freedom of passage through the Suez Canal and other nearby waterways (such as the Straits of Tiran), and a restriction on the forces Egypt could place on the Sinai peninsula, especially within 20–40 km from Israel. This process would take three years to complete. Israel also agreed to limit its forces a smaller distance (3 km) from the Egyptian border, and to guarantee free passage between Egypt and Jordan. With the withdrawal, Israel also returned Egypt's Abu-Rudeis oil fields in western Sinai, which contained long term, commercially productive wells.

The agreement also resulted in the United States committing to several billion dollars worth of annual subsidies to the governments of both Israel and Egypt, subsidies which continue to this day, and are given as a mixture of grants and aid packages committed to purchasing U.S. materiel. From 1979 (the year of the peace agreement) to 1997, Egypt received military aid of US$1.3 billion annually, which also helped modernize the Egyptian military.[1302] (This is beyond economic, humanitarian, and other aid, which has totaled more than US$25 billion.) Eastern-supplied until 1979, Egypt now received American weaponry such as the M1A1 Abrams Tank, AH-64 Apache gunship and the F-16 fighter jet. In comparison, Israel has received $3 billion annually since 1985 in grants and military aid packages.[1303]

Consequences

The time that has elapsed since the Camp David Accords has left no doubt as to their enormous ramifications on Middle Eastern politics. Most notably, the perception of Egypt within the Arab world changed. With the most powerful of the Arab militaries and a history of leadership in the Arab world under Nasser, Egypt had more leverage than any of the other Arab states to advance Arab interests. Egypt was subsequently suspended from the Arab League from 1979 until 1989.

When the Camp David accords were signed, Jordan's King Hussein saw it as a slap to the face when Sadat volunteered Jordan's participation in deciding how functional autonomy would work. More specifically, Sadat effectively said that Jordan would have a role in how the West Bank would be administered. Like the Rabat Summit Resolution, the Camp David Accords circumscribed Jordan's objective to reassert its control over the West Bank. Focusing as it did on Egypt, the Carter administration accepted Sadat's claim that he could deliver Hussein. However, with Arab world opposition building against Sadat, Jordan could not risk accepting the Accords without the support from powerful Arab neighbours, like Iraq, Saudi Arabia, and Syria. Hussein consequently felt diplomatically snubbed. One of Carter's regrets was allowing Sadat to claim that he could speak for Hussein if Jordan refused to join the talks, but by then the damage was done to the Jordanians.

The Camp David Accords also prompted the disintegration of a united Arab front in opposition to Israel. Egypt's realignment created a power vacuum that Saddam Hussein of Iraq, at one time only a secondary power, hoped to fill. Because of the vague language concerning the implementation of Resolution 242, the Palestinian problem became the primary issue in the Arab–Israeli conflict immediately following the Camp David Accords (and, arguably, until today). Many of the Arab nations blamed Egypt for not putting enough pressure on

Figure 168: *United States President Jimmy Carter greeting Egyptian President Anwar Sadat at the White House shortly after the Camp David Accords went into effect, 8 April 1980.*

Israel to deal with the Palestinian problem in a way that would be satisfactory to them. Syria also informed Egypt that it would not reconcile with the nation unless it abandoned the peace agreement with Israel.

According to *The Continuum Political Encyclopedia of the Middle East*:

> The normalization of relations [between Israel and Egypt] went into effect in January 1980. Ambassadors were exchanged in February. The boycott laws were repealed by Egypt's National Assembly the same month, and some trade began to develop, albeit less than Israel had hoped for. In March 1980 regular airline flights were inaugurated. Egypt also began supplying Israel with crude oil".[1304]

According to Kenneth Stein in *Heroic Diplomacy: Sadat, Kissinger, Carter, Begin, and the Quest for Arab–Israeli Peace*:

> The Accords were another interim agreement or step, but negotiations that flowed from the Accords slowed for several reasons. These included an inability to bring the Jordanians into the discussions; the controversy over settlements; the inconclusive nature of the subsequent autonomy talks; domestic opposition sustained by both Begin and Sadat and, in Sadat's case, ostracism and anger from the Arab world; the emergence of a what became a cold peace between Egypt and Israel; and changes in foreign

policy priorities including discontinuity in personnel committed to sustaining the negotiating process[.]

Lastly, the biggest consequence of all may be in the psychology of the participants of the Arab-Israeli conflict. The success of Begin, Sadat, and Carter at Camp David demonstrated to other Arab states and entities that negotiations with Israel were possible—that progress results only from sustained efforts at communication and cooperation. Despite the disappointing conclusion of the 1993 Oslo Accords between the PLO and Israel, and even though the 1994 Israel–Jordan peace treaty has not fully normalized relations with Israel, both of these significant developments had little chance of occurring without the precedent set by Camp David.

Public support

Although most Israelis supported the Accords, the Israeli settler movement opposed them because Sadat would not agree to a treaty in which Israel had any presence in the Sinai Peninsula at all, Israel had to withdraw from the entire Sinai Peninsula.[1305] Israeli settlers tried to prevent the government from dismantling their settlements.[1306]

In Israel, there is lasting support of the Camp David Peace Accords, which have become a national consensus, supported by 85% of Israelis according to a 2001 poll taken by the Jaffee Center for Strategic Studies (Israel based).[1307] Nevertheless, a minority of Israelis believe the price Israel paid for the peace agreement was too high for its present gains, i.e. having relinquished the entire Sinai Peninsula, with its oil, tourism and land resources (Israel has no other oil wells), and the trauma of evacuating thousands of its Israeli inhabitants (many resisted, as in the settlement of Yamit and had to be forcefully evacuated, a phenomenon encountered also in the subsequent Israeli withdrawal from Gaza in 2005, known as the disengagement).Wikipedia:Citation needed

For Israel, perhaps the most evident tangible benefit of the agreement with Egypt (other than the subsequent U.S. aid, which Egypt also received) was a peaceful mutual border, enabling the Israel Defense Forces to reduce their levels of alert on Israel's southwestern frontier.

Criticism of the Accords

Although Egypt and Israel generally abided by the agreement since 1978, in the following years a common belief emerged in Israel that the peace with Egypt is a "cold peace". Others feel that the peace agreement was between the Israeli people and Egypt's charismatic President Anwar El Sadat, rather than with the Egyptian people, who were not given the opportunity to accept or reject the agreement with a free vote or a representative majority.

Assassination of Anwar Sadat

President Sadat's signing of the Camp David Accords on 17 September 1978 and his shared 1978 Nobel Peace Prize with Israeli Prime Minister Begin led to his assassination on 6 October 1981 by members of the Egyptian Islamic Jihad during the annual victory parade held in Cairo to celebrate Egypt's crossing of the Suez Canal. The president's personal protection was infiltrated by four members of this organization, who were hiding in a truck passing through the military parade with other military vehicles. As the truck approached the president, the leader of the belligerents — Lieutenant Khalid Islambouli — came out of the truck and threw three grenades towards the president; only one of the three exploded. The rest of the team opened fire with automatic assault rifles and struck President Sadat with 37 rounds. He was airlifted to a military hospital where, despite the efforts of 11 doctors and surgeons, he died just two hours after arriving.

In total, 11 were killed from collateral gunfire and 28 were injured. Among the killed were the Cuban ambassador, an Omani general, and a Coptic Orthodox bishop. Among the wounded were Egyptian Vice-President Hosni Mubarak, Irish Defence Minister James Tully, and four U.S. military liaison officers. One of the assassins was killed and the other three were wounded and taken into custody. The surviving assassins were tried and found guilty of assassinating the president and killing 10 others in the process; they were sentenced to capital punishment and were executed by firing squad on 15 April 1982.

Arab–Israeli peace diplomacy and treaties

Treaties and meetings
- Paris Peace Conference, 1919
- Faisal–Weizmann Agreement (1919)
- 1949 Armistice Agreements
- Geneva Conference (1973)
- Camp David Accords (1978)
- Egypt–Israel Peace Treaty (1979)
- Madrid Conference of 1991
- Oslo Accords (1993)
- Israel–Jordan peace treaty (1994)
- Camp David 2000 Summit

General articles
- International law and the Arab–Israeli conflict
- Israeli–Palestinian peace process
- List of Middle East peace proposals
- Projects working for peace among Israelis and Arabs

Further reading

- Medad, Yisrael, ed., Hurwitz, Zvi Harry, ed. *Peace in the Making The Menachem Begin – Anwar Sadat Personal Correspondence*, Gefen Publishing House, 2011. <templatestyles src="Module:Citation/CS1/styles.css" />ISBN 978-965-229-456-2
- Avner, Yehuda, *The Prime Ministers: An Intimate Narrative of Israeli Leadership*, The Toby Press, 2010. <templatestyles src="Module:Citation/CS1/styles.css" />ISBN 978-1-59264-278-6
- Armstrong, Karen. *Jerusalem: One City, Three Faiths*. New York: Ballantine Books, 1996.
- Bregman, Ahron *Elusive Peace: How the Holy Land Defeated America*.
- Eran, Oded. *Arab–Israel Peacemaking*. Sela.
- Gold, Dore. *The Fight for Jerusalem: Radical Islam, the West, and the Future of the Holy City*. Washington, DC: Regnery Publishing, Inc., 2007.
- Hinton, Clete A. *Camp David Accords* (2004)
- Meital, Yoram. *Egypt's Struggle for Peace: Continuity and Change, 1967–1977*.
- Quandt, William B. *Camp David: Peacemaking and Politics* (1986), by leading political scientist
- "Arab-Israel Conflict." Sela.
- Sela, Avraham, ed. *The Continuum Political Encyclopedia of the Middle East*. New York: Continuum, 2002.
- Adam Curtis' 2004 documentary *The Power of Nightmares*, in its second and third part, studies the Camp David Accords from the point of view of fundamentalist Muslims.

External links

 Wikimedia Commons has media related to *Camp David Accords*.

 Wikisourcehas original text related to this article: **Camp David Accords**

- Text of the Accords, Israeli government[1308]
- Text of Accords and additional material, Carter Library[1309]
- *Israel's Self-Rule Plan*[1310]. Knesset website, 28 December 1977
- Interview with King Hussein[1311] from the Dean Peter Krogh Foreign Affairs Digital Archives[1312]

- 2006 Egyptian public poll on attitudes to Israel[1313] and other countries, *The Sun* (New York) article. Alternate link to poll results from a BBC News article[1314]
- The Menachem Begin Heritage Foundation[1315]
- Jaffe Center Poll on Israeli public Attitudes to the Peace Process[1316]
- NY Times: Anti-Semitic 'Elders of Zion' Gets New Life on Egypt TV[1317]
- "Camp David 25th Anniversary Forum" (led by President Carter)[1318]

1978 South Lebanon conflict

1978 South Lebanon conflict	
Part of the Israeli–Lebanese conflict, the Palestinian insurgency in South Lebanon and Lebanese Civil War	
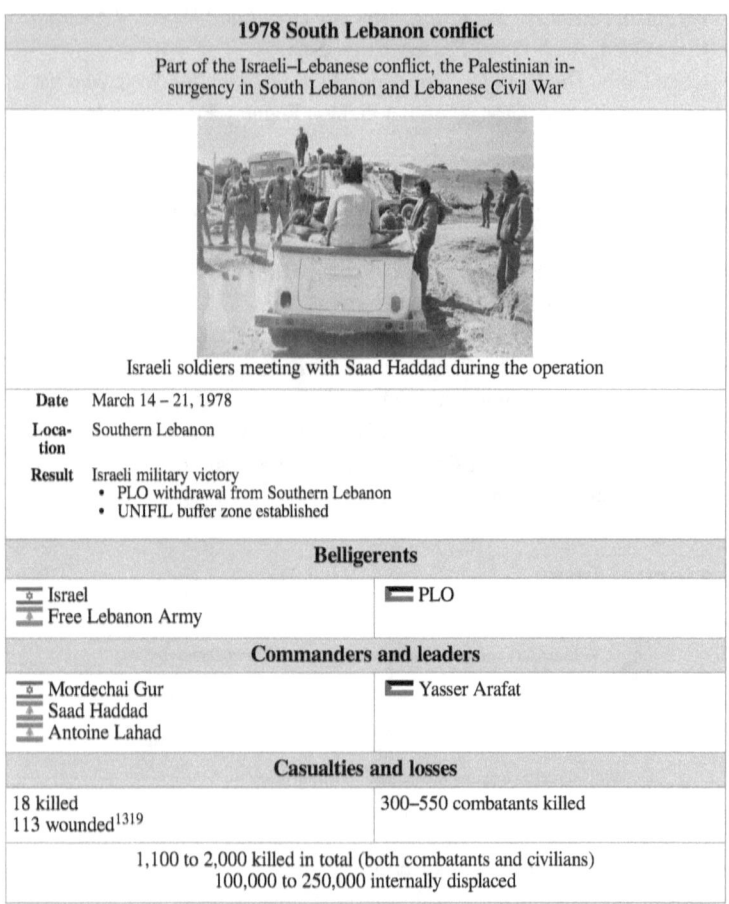 Israeli soldiers meeting with Saad Haddad during the operation	
Date	March 14 – 21, 1978
Location	Southern Lebanon
Result	Israeli military victory • PLO withdrawal from Southern Lebanon • UNIFIL buffer zone established
Belligerents	
Israel Free Lebanon Army	PLO
Commanders and leaders	
Mordechai Gur Saad Haddad Antoine Lahad	Yasser Arafat
Casualties and losses	
18 killed 113 wounded[1319]	300–550 combatants killed
1,100 to 2,000 killed in total (both combatants and civilians) 100,000 to 250,000 internally displaced	

The **1978 South Lebanon conflict** (code-named **Operation *Litani*** by Israel) was an invasion of Lebanon up to the Litani River, carried out by the Israel

Defense Forces in 1978 in response to the Coastal Road massacre. The conflict resulted in the deaths of 1,100–2,000 Lebanese and Palestinians, 20 Israelis, the internal displacement of 100,000 to 250,000 people in Lebanon, and the PLO forces retreating north of the Litani River. It led to the creation of the UNIFIL peacekeeping force and an almost complete Israeli withdrawal.

Background

Though it took the form of an Israeli military incursion into Southern Lebanon, Operation Litani was grounded in the long-running Israeli–Palestinian conflict. From 1968 on, the PLO, Popular Front for the Liberation of Palestine, and other Palestinian groups established a quasi-state in southern Lebanon, using it as a base for raids on civilian targets in northern Israel, as well as worldwide terror attacks on Israeli and other targets. This was exacerbated by an influx of 3,000 PLO militants fleeing a defeat in the Jordanian civil war and regrouping in southern Lebanon. Israel responded with damaging attacks against PLO bases.

During Israeli raids from 1968 to 1977, some of the Palestinian towns and camps in the area were totally leveled. According to estimations, by October 1977 about 300,000 refugees, mainly Shiite Muslims, fled South Lebanon. The PLO-Israeli conflict increased political tensions between Maronite Christians and Druze on the one hand and Muslims on the other, adding to the factors behind the 1975–1990 Lebanese Civil War.

In November 1977, Israel initiated an exchange of fire that led to the death of several people from both sides of the border and finally Israeli bombing of the targets in South Lebanon during which 70 people, mainly Lebanese, were killed.

On March 11, 1978, 11 Fatah members led by the 18-year-old female Dalal Mughrabi travelled from Lebanon and killed an American tourist on the beach. They then hijacked a bus on the Coastal Road near Haifa, and en route to Tel Aviv commandeered a second bus. After a lengthy chase and shootout, 38 Israeli civilians, including 13 children, were killed and 76 wounded.[1320] This massacre was the proximate cause of the Israeli invasion three days later.[1321]

Course of fighting

On March 14, 1978, Israel launched Operation Litani, after the Coastal road massacre. The operation was first called "AVI HACHOCHMA" (Father of wisdom), later changed to "Operation Litani". Its stated goals were to push Palestinian militant groups, particularly the PLO, away from the border with

Israel, and to bolster Israel's ally at the time, the South Lebanon Army, because of the attacks against Lebanese Christians and Jews and because of the relentless shelling into Northern Israel. The area south of the Litani River, excepting Tyre, was invaded and occupied in a week long offensive.

The operation began with air, artillery, and naval bombardment, after which IDF infantry and armor forces, comprising about 25,000 soldiers in total, entered south Lebanon. The Israelis first captured a belt of land approximately 10 kilometers deep, by launching a ground attack on all PLO positions along the Lebanese border with Israel. The ground forces were led by two division commanders, and attacked simultaneously along the entire front. Paratroopers landed from helicopters to capture all the bridges on the Litani River, cutting off the possibility of retreat by the PLO, and later expanded north to the Litani River.

The IDF did not succeed in engaging large numbers of PLO forces, who retreated to the north. Many Lebanese civilians were killed by heavy Israeli shelling and air strikes, which also caused extensive property damage and internal displacement. According to Augustus Richard Norton, professor of international relations at Boston University, the IDF military operation killed approximately 1,100 people, most of them Palestinian and Lebanese. According to IDF reporting and internal investigation, at least 550 of the casualties were Palestinian militants initially holding the front line and killed by the IDF ground operation. According to other sources about 2000 Lebanese and Palestinian were killed.[1322]

Estimates for the number of people displaced by the military operations range from at least 100,000 to 250,000. Syrian troops deployed inside Lebanon, some of which were within visual range of the IDF, but did not take part in the fighting. The PLO retreated north of the Litani River, continuing to fire at the Israelis. The IDF used cluster bombs provided by the United States. According to U.S. President Jimmy Carter, this use of the cluster bombs violated the legal agreement between Israel and the U.S. because the weapons had been provided for defensive purposes against an attack on Israel. Israel also transferred American weapons to Saad Haddad's Lebanese militia, a violation of American law. Carter's administration prepared to notify Congress that American weapons were being used illegally, which would have resulted in military aid to Israel being cut off. The American consul in Jerusalem informed the Israeli government of their plans and, according to Carter, Prime Minister Begin said that the operation was over.

Figure 169: *Map showing the Blue Line demarcation line between Lebanon and Israel, established by the UN after the Israeli withdrawal from southern Lebanon in 1978*

Outcome of the war

In response to the invasion, the UN Security Council passed Resolution 425 and Resolution 426 calling for the withdrawal of Israeli forces from Lebanon were both adopted on March 19, 1978. The UN Interim Force in Lebanon (UNIFIL) was created to enforce this mandate, specifically "for the purpose of confirming the withdrawal of Israeli forces, restoring international peace and security and assisting the Government of Lebanon in ensuring the return of its effective authority in the area". UNIFIL forces arrived in Lebanon on March 23, 1978, setting up headquarters in Naqoura.

Resolution 425 didn't result in an immediate end to hostilities. The Israelis continued military operations for 2 more days until they ordered a ceasefire. The PLO's initial reaction was that the resolution didn't apply to them because it didn't mention the PLO. The PLO leadership finally ordered a ceasefire on March 28, 1978, after a meeting between UNIFIL commander General Emmanual Erskine and Yasser Arafat in Beirut. Helena Cobban has described the agreement as "a turning-point in the history of the Palestinian resistance moment" because it was the first open acceptance of a ceasefire agreement with Israel that was endorsed by all official PLO bodies.

Parts of the Palestinian resistance movement opposed the agreement and tried to violate the ceasefire. In April 1978, second-level Fatah leader Mohammad Daoud Oudeh (Abu Daoud) organized cells of about 70 to 80 fighters with the intention of breaking the ceasefire. Arafat and Khalil Wazir ordered the arrest of all involved and Abu Daoud was later accused of collaborating with Fatah renegade Abu Nidal to break the ceasefire.

Israeli forces withdrew later in 1978, turning over positions inside Lebanon to their ally, the South Lebanon Army (SLA) militia under the leadership of Maj. Saad Haddad. On April 19, 1978, the SLA shelled UNIFIL headquarters, killing 8 UN soldiers. (Fisk, 138). In April 1980, three Irish UN soldiers (Privates Barrett, Smallhorne and O'Mahoney) were kidnapped and two of them murdered by Christian gunmen, Private O'Mahoney survived (being shot by sub-machine gun during the incident) in SLA territory and another Irish soldier Private S. Griffin was shot by Haddad's men, and was medvaced to Israel where he subsequently died during medical treatment. The Israeli press at the time, particularly the Jerusalem Post, accused the Irish of pro-PLO bias. (Fisk, 152–154).

Palestinian factions also attacked UNIFIL, kidnapping an Irish UNIFIL soldier in 1981 and continuing to occupy areas in southern Lebanon.[1323]

Hostilities continued, and as the Lebanese civil war escalated, the fighting intensified in the south again, with a second Israeli invasion in 1982 resulting in a 1982 flare-up that persisted over the next decade.

Resolution 425

In 2000, the UN Security Council concluded that, as of June 16, 2000, Israel had withdrawn its forces from Lebanon in accordance with Resolution 425.

Lebanon has not extended control over south Lebanon, though it was called on to do so by Resolution 1391 of 2002 and urged by Resolution 1496. Israel has lodged multiple complaints regarding Lebanon's conduct.

Lebanon's claim that Israel has not fully withdrawn (see Shebaa Farms) was explicitly rejected by the UN's Secretary-General's report which led to Resolution 1583. The Syrian occupation of Lebanon led to UN Security Council Resolution 1559 demanding the remaining 14,000 (of 50,000 originally) Syrian troop withdrawal and the dismantling of Hezbollah and Palestinian militias. On April 26, 2005, after 29 years of Syrian military presence in Lebanon, the last of the Syrian troops withdrew in accordance with the resolution.

Figure 170: *UNIFIL road block in Lebanon, 1981*

Further reading

- Bregman, Ahron (2002). *Israel's Wars: A History Since 1947.* London: Routledge. ISBN 978-0-415-28716-6.<templatestyles src="Module:Citation/CS1/styles.css"></templatestyles>
- Fisk, Robert (2002). *Pity the Nation: The Abduction of Lebanon.* Nation Books. ISBN 978-1-56025-442-3.<templatestyles src="Module:Citation/CS1/styles.css"></templatestyles>
- Shlaim, Avi (2001). *The Iron Wall: Israel and the Arab World.* W. W. Norton & Company. ISBN 978-0-393-32112-8.<templatestyles src="Module:Citation/CS1/styles.css"></templatestyles>
- Ahmad Beydoun (1992). "The South Lebanon Border Zone: A Local Perspective". *Journal of Palestine Studies.* University of California Press. **21** (3): 35–53. doi: 10.1525/jps.1992.21.3.00p01145[1324]. JSTOR 2537518[1325].<templatestyles src="Module:Citation/CS1/styles.css"></templatestyles>

External links

- Operation Litani, ALS.Miniature[1326]
- Lebanese civil war 1978 Full of Pictures and Information[1327]
- Terrorist attacks in Israel[1328], GlobalSecurity
- Conflict in Lebanon[1329], GlobalSecurity

- www.lebanon-israel.info An ongoing discussion on the Lebanon-Israel conflict[1330]

1982 Lebanon War

<indicator name="pp-default"> 🔒 </indicator>

1982 Lebanon War	
Part of Israeli-Lebanese conflict, Palestinian insurgency in South Lebanon (Israeli–Palestinian conflict) and Lebanese Civil War	
 Lebanese troops in Beirut, 1982	
Date	6 June 1982 – June 1985 (main phase June–September 1982)
Location	Southern Lebanon
Result	Israeli tactical victories but overall strategic failure.[1331],[1332],[1333] Syrian political advantage[1334] • PLO expulsion from Lebanon • Collapse of Maronite–Israeli alliance, failure to achieve Lebanese-Israeli peace[1335] • Increased Syrian influence in Lebanon • Israeli withdrawal to the Israeli security zone in Southern Lebanon • Emerging conflict between Israel & SLA vs Hezbollah over South Lebanon
Territorial changes	Self-proclaimed Free Lebanon State slowly transforms into South Lebanon Security Zone
Belligerents	
Israel Lebanese Front • Phalange • al-Tanzim Free Lebanon Army	PLO Syria Jammoul Amal
Commanders and leaders	

Israel: Menachem Begin (Prime Minister) Ariel Sharon (Ministry of Defence) Rafael Eitan (Army Chief of Staff) David Ivry (Israeli Air Force) Ze'ev Almog (Israeli Sea Corps) **Phalange:** Bachir Gemayel † Fadi Frem Elie Hobeika **Al-Tanzim:** Fawzi Mahfuz **SLA:** Saad Haddad	**PLO:** Yasser Arafat (Chairman of the PLO) **Syria:** Hafez al-Assad (President) Mustafa Tlass (Minister of Defense) **LCP:** George Hawi Elias Atallah **Hezbollah:** Abbas al-Musawi **Al-Mourabitoun:** Ibrahim Kulaylat **Amal:** Nabih Berri **ASALA:** Monte Melkonian **PKK:** Mahsum Korkmaz **Others:** Muhsin Ibrahim Abbas al-Musawi Ragheb Harb Murat Karayılan Inaam Raad Said Shaaban
Strength	
Israel: 78,000 troops 800 tanks 1,500 APCs 634 aircraft **LF:** 30,000 troops **SLA:** 5,000 troops 97 tanks	**Syria:** 22,000 troops 352 tanks 300 APCs 450 aircraft 300 artillery pieces 100 anti-aircraft guns 125 SAM batteries **PLO:** 15,000 troops 80 tanks 150 APCs 350+ artillery pieces 250+ anti-aircraft guns
Casualties and losses	

Israel:	PLO: 1,000-2,400 killed[1337]
657 dead	6,000 captured
3,887 wounded[1336]	Syria: 1,200 killed
4 missing	296 captured
8 captured	300–350 tanks lost
30 tanks lost	150 APCs lost
100 tanks damaged	~100 artillery pieces lost
175 APCs destroyed or damaged	82–86 aircraft lost
1 aircraft lost	12 helicopters lost
2 helicopters lost	29 SAM missile batteries lost[1338]
Civilians: See Casualties below.	

The **1982 Lebanon War**, dubbed **Operation Peace for Galilee** (Hebrew: מבצע שלום, הגליל or מבצע של"ג *Mivtsa Shlom HaGalil* or *Mivtsa Sheleg*) by the Israeli government, later known in Israel as the **Lebanon War** or the **First Lebanon War** (Hebrew: מלחמת לבנון, הראשונה *Milhemet Levanon Harishona*), and known in Lebanon as "the invasion" (Arabic: الاجتياح, *Al-ijtiyāḥ*), began on 6 June 1982, when the Israel Defense Forces (IDF) invaded southern Lebanon, after repeated attacks and counter-attacks between the Palestine Liberation Organization (PLO) operating in southern Lebanon and the IDF that had caused civilian casualties on both sides of the border. The military operation was launched after gunmen from Abu Nidal's organization attempted to assassinate Shlomo Argov, Israel's ambassador to the United Kingdom. Israeli Prime Minister Menachem Begin blamed Abu Nidal's enemy, the PLO, for the incident,[1339,1340] and treated the incident as a *casus belli* for the invasion.[1341,1342,1343]

After attacking the PLO – as well as Syrian, leftist, and Muslim Lebanese forces – the Israeli military, in cooperation with the Maronite allies and the self-proclaimed Free Lebanon State, occupied southern Lebanon, eventually surrounding the PLO and elements of the Syrian Army. Surrounded in West Beirut and subjected to heavy bombardment, the PLO forces and their allies negotiated passage from Lebanon with the aid of United States Special Envoy Philip Habib and the protection of international peacekeepers. The PLO, under the chairmanship of Yasser Arafat, had relocated its headquarters to Tripoli in June 1982. By expelling the PLO, removing Syrian influence over Lebanon, and installing a pro-Israeli Christian government led by President Bachir Gemayel, Israel hoped to sign a treaty which Menachem Begin promised would give Israel "forty years of peace".[1344]

Following the assassination of Gemayel in September 1982, Israel's position in Beirut became untenable and the signing of a peace treaty became increasingly unlikely. Outrage following Israel's role in the Phalangist-perpetrated Sabra and Shatila massacre, of mostly Palestinians and Lebanese Shiites, and Israeli popular disillusionment with the war would lead to a gradual withdrawal from Beirut to the areas claimed by the self-proclaimed Free Lebanon State in southern Lebanon (later to become the South Lebanon security belt), which was initiated following the 17 May Agreement and Syria's change of attitude towards the PLO. After Israeli forces withdrew from most of Lebanon, the War of the Camps broke out between Lebanese factions, the remains of the PLO and Syria, in which Syria fought its former Palestinian allies. At the same time, Shi'a militant groups began consolidating and waging a low-intensity guerrilla war over the Israeli occupation of southern Lebanon, leading to 15 years of low-scale armed conflict. The Lebanese Civil War would continue until 1990, at which point Syria had established complete dominance over Lebanon.

Background

Relocation of PLO from Jordan to South Lebanon

After the 1948 Arab-Israeli war, Lebanon became home to more than 110,000 Palestinian refugees, after their settlements in Palestine and Israel had been depopulated as a result of the war.[1345] After its founding in 1964 and the radicalization among Palestinians, which followed the Six-Day War, the PLO became a powerful force, then centred in Jordan. The large influx of Palestinians from Jordan after the Black September conflict caused an additional demographic imbalance within Lebanese society and its democratic institutions established earlier by the National Pact.[1346] By 1975, the refugees numbered more than 300,000 and the PLO in effect created an unofficial state-within-a-state, particularly in Southern Lebanon, which then played an important role in the Lebanese Civil War.

Continual violence near the Lebanese border occurred between Israel and the PLO starting from 1968; this peaked, following the relocation of PLO bases to Lebanon after the civil war in Jordan.

Lebanese Civil War

Incidents 1975–1980

The violence between Israel and the PLO peaked during Operation Litani in 1978, provoked by the Coastal Road Massacre which was carried out by Palestinian militants. The United Nations Interim Force in Lebanon (UNIFIL) was created after the incursion, following the adoption of United Nations Security Council Resolution 425 in March 1978 to confirm Israeli withdrawal from Southern Lebanon, restore international peace and security, and help the government of Lebanon restore its effective authority in the area.

As early as 1976, Israel had been assisting Lebanese Christian militias in their sporadic battles against the PLO.[1347] During Operation Litani in 1978, Israel established a security zone in southern Lebanon with mostly Christian inhabitants, in which they began to supply training and arms to Christian militias which would later form the South Lebanese Army.[1348] But Israel's main partner was to be the Maronite Phalange party, whose paramilitary was led by Bashir Gemayel, a rising figure in Lebanese politics. Gemayel's strategy during the early stages of the Lebanese Civil War was to provoke the Syrians into retaliatory attacks on Christians, such that Israel could not ignore. In 1978, Menachem Begin declared that Israel would not allow a genocide of Lebanese Christians, while refusing direct intervention.[1349] Hundreds of Lebanese militiamen began to train in Israel, at the IDF Staff and Command College. The relationship between Israel and the Maronites began to grow into a political-strategic alliance, and members of the Israeli government like Ariel Sharon began to conceive of a plan to install a pro-Israel Christian government in Lebanon, as it was known that Bashir wanted to remove the PLO and all Palestinian refugees in the country.[1350]

During the period June to December 1980 the United Nations Interim Force in Lebanon (UNIFIL) recorded an increase in activities along the border zone. No attacks by Palestinian forces on Israel were recorded, while the IDF incursions across the armistice line into Lebanon increased markedly, with minefields being laid, gun posts established, and generally involving numerous violations of Lebanese air-space and territorial waters. This was formally protested by the Lebanese government to the UN Security Council and General Assembly in several communications as violations by Israel of United Nations Security Council Resolution 425. During the same period Israel protested numerous attacks by Palestinian forces, unrelated to the Lebanese border zone.

1981 events and cease-fire

In his report for the period of 12 December 1980 to 12 June 1981 on UNIFIL activities, the Security Council Secretary General noted that infiltrations into the border zone by Palestinian armed forces had decreased relative to the previous six months. In contrast the IDF had launched various attacks on Lebanese territory often in support of the Lebanese Christian militia. In doing so Israel had violated UN Security Council resolution 425 on hundreds of occasions [paragraph 58]. Where the initiator(s) of attacks could be identified in the report, in 15 cases Palestinian militants were to blame while on 23 occasions the Militia and/or the IDF were the instigators, the latter also being responsible for the most violent confrontation of the period on 27 April [paragraph 52].

In the subsequent period 16 June to 10 December 1981, a relative quiet was reported continuing from 29 May 1981 until 10 July. This was broken when "Israeli aircraft resumed strikes against targets in southern Lebanon north of the UNIFIL area. (The Israeli strikes) led to exchanges of heavy firing between armed elements (Palestinians), on the one hand, and IDF and the de facto forces (Christian Militia) on the other. On 13 and 14 July, widespread Israeli air-strikes continued. Armed elements (Palestinians) fired into the enclave and northern Israel." Israeli-initiated attacks had led to rocket and artillery fire on northern Israel. This pattern continued in the coming days.

Israel renewed its air strikes in an attempt to trigger a war that would allow it to drive out the PLO and restore peace to the region.[1351] On 17 July, the Israel Air Force launched a massive attack on PLO buildings in downtown Beirut. "Perhaps as many as three hundred died, and eight hundred were wounded, the great majority of them civilians."[1352] The Israeli army also heavily targeted PLO positions in south Lebanon without success in suppressing Palestinian rocket launchers and guns. As a result, thousands of Israeli citizens who resided near the Lebanese border headed south. There patterns of Israeli-initiated airstrikes and Palestinian retaliations with attacks on northern Israel are in contrast with the official Israeli version "A ceasefire declared in July 1981 was broken: the terrorists continued to carry out attacks against Israeli targets in Israel and abroad, and the threat to the northern settlements became unbearable."

On 24 July 1981, United States Undersecretary of State Philip Habib brokered a ceasefire badly needed by both parties, the best achievable result from negotiations via intermediaries, aimed at complying with the decisions of UN Security Council resolution 490. The process was complicated, requiring

> shuttle diplomacy between Damascus, Jerusalem, and Beirut, United States. Philip Habib concluded a ceasefire across the Lebanon border between Israel and the PLO. Habib could not talk to the PLO directly because of Kissinger's directive, so he used a Saudi member of the royal family as mediator. The agreement was oral – nothing could be written down since Israel and the PLO did not recognize each other and refused to negotiate with each other – but they came up with a truce. ... Thus the border between Lebanon and Israel suddenly stabilized after over a decade of routine bombing.[1353]

Between July 1981 and June 1982, as a result of the Habib ceasefire, the Lebanese-Israeli border "enjoyed a state of calm unprecedented since 1968." But the 'calm' was tense. US Secretary of State, Alexander Haig filed a report with US President Ronald Reagan on Saturday 30 January 1982 that revealed Secretary Haig's fear that Israel might, at the slightest provocation, start a war against Lebanon.[1354]

The 'calm' lasted nine months. Then, on 21 April 1982, after a landmine killed an Israeli officer while he was visiting a South Lebanese Army gun emplacement in Taibe, Lebanon, the Israeli Air Force attacked the Palestinian-controlled coastal town of Damour, killing 23 people.[1355] Fisk reports further on this incident: "The Israelis did not say what the soldier was doing ... I discovered that he was visiting one of Haddad's artillery positions (Christian militia) and that the mine could have been lain [sic] as long ago as 1978, perhaps even by the Israelis themselves".

On 9 May 1982, Israeli aircraft again attacked targets in Lebanon. Later that same day, UNIFIL observed the firing of rockets from Palestinian positions in the Tyre region into northern Israel, but none of the projectiles hit Israeli towns[1356] – the gunners had been ordered to miss. Major-General Erskine (Ghana), Chief of Staff of UNTSO reported to the Secretary-General and the Security Council (S/14789, S/15194) that from August 1981 to May 1982, inclusive, there were 2096 violations of Lebanese airspace and 652 violations of Lebanese territorial waters.[1357] The freedom of movement of UNIFIL personnel and UNTSO observers within the enclave remained restricted due to the actions of Amal and the South Lebanon Army under Major Saad Haddad's leadership with the backing of Israeli military forces.

Prior to establishing ceasefire in July 1981, U.N. Secretary-General Kurt Waldheim noted: "After several weeks of relative quiet in the area, a new cycle of violence has begun and has, in the past week, steadily intensified." He further stated: "There have been heavy civilian casualties in Lebanon; there have been civilian casualties in Israel as well. I deeply deplore the extensive human suffering caused by these developments." The President of the U.N. Security Council, Ide Oumarou of Niger, expressed "deep concern at the extent of the loss of life and the scale of the destruction caused by the deplorable events that have been taking place for several days in Lebanon".[1358]

Immediate causes

From the ceasefire, established in July 1981, until the start of the war, the Israeli government reported 270 terrorist attacks by the PLO in Israel, the occupied territories, and the Jordanian and Lebanese border (in addition to 20 attacks on Israeli interests abroad).

In Ariel Sharon's biography by his son, Gilad Sharon, the author referring to the Habib ceasefire, comments: "However, the agreement was explicit only regarding preventing terror from Lebanon, which is why my father encouraged the cabinet not to accept the offer as presented by the Americans."[1359]

> *The cease-fire, as both the PLO and the Americans saw it, did not include terror attacks stemming from Lebanon and carried out against Jews in Europe and other locales. In a meeting my father had with Alexander Haig and Philip Habib on May 25, 1982, Habib repeated what he had already said many times before: 'Terrorist attacks against Israelis and Jews in Europe are not included in the cease-fire agreement.*

Arafat pressured the radical factions to maintain the ceasefire because he did not wish to provoke the Israelis into an all-out attack. The PLO acceptance of the ceasefire had led to dissension even within Fatah itself. A faction sympathetic to Abu Nidal forced a military confrontation, with accompanying arrests and executions — an event unprecedented in PLO internal disputes'. Arafat even attempted to distance himself from Palestinian unrest on the West Bank to prevent an Israeli attack. In contrast, Begin, Sharon and Eitan were searching for any excuse to neutralize their military opponents through a breach of the ceasefire. They believed that Arafat was buying time to build up his conventional forces. The Israeli interpretation of the conditions for the ceasefire placed responsibility for any act of Palestinian violence on Arafat's shoulders. It presumed that Arafat had complete control, not only over all factions within the PLO such as the rejectionist Popular Front of George Habash, but also over those outside such as Abu Nidal's Fatah Revolutionary Council and Ahmed Jibril's Popular Front — General Command. Moreover, in Begin's eyes, the ceasefire was not geographically limited to the Lebanese border. He argued that if Palestinian terrorism struck internationally, then this too would be regarded as a breach of the ceasefire. Begin thus took a stand-off in a local battle as applying to the entire war anywhere in the Middle East or any incident internationally. Eitan commented that there was no difference if a terrorist threw a grenade in Gaza or fired a shell at a Northern settlement — all such acts broke the ceasefire. Sharon similarly did not wish to draw distinctions between different Palestinian factions, since all blame had to be attached to the PLO. He dismissed attempts at more rational evaluation as masking the real issue. In a speech to a Young Herut conference in April 1982, he accused those who tried to take a more objective standpoint of erecting 'a protective wall around the PLO inside and outside Israel'.[1360]

Further support comes from George Ball, that the PLO had observed the ceasefire. Israel, he said, continued looking for the "internationally recognized provocation" that Secretary of State Alexander Haig said would be necessary to obtain American support for an Israeli invasion of Lebanon.[1361] Secretary Haig's critics have accused him of "greenlighting" the Israeli Invasion of Lebanon in June 1982. Haig denies this and says he urged restraint. In the biography of ceasefire broker Philip Habib, Alexander Haig is cited as leaving the worst impression of all in the lead up to Israel's Lebanon invasion:

> *Haig thus comes off very badly: not a team player, not able to keep the rest of the administration informed of what was going on beforehand, not willing to tell anyone in the White House why Sharon was so confident during the invasion, hoping that Reagan's special envoy would fail in his mission, and having little sense of what the national security of the United States required—which was not a confrontation between Israeli and Soviet tanks on the road from Beirut to Damascus.*[1362]

The American reaction was that they would not apply any undue pressure on Israel to quit Lebanon as the Israeli presence in Lebanon may prove to be a catalyst for the disparate groups of Lebanon to make common cause against both Syrian and Israeli forces. Haig's analysis, which Ronald Reagan agreed with, was that this uniting of Lebanese groups would allow President Elias Sarkis to reform the Lebanese central Government and give the Palestinian refugees Lebanese citizenship.[1363] Additional evidence that the United States approved the Israeli invasion comes from longtime CIA analyst Charles Cogan, who says that he was in the room during a May 1982 meeting in The Pentagon during which Sharon explained to Secretary of Defense Caspar Weinberger "in great detail how the Israelis were going to invade Lebanon ... Weinberger just sat there and said *nothing*."

According to Avi Shlaim, the real driving force behind the Israeli invasion to Lebanon was the defense minister Ariel Sharon. One of his aims was the destruction of PLO military infrastructure in Lebanon and undermining it as a political organization, in order to facilitate the absorption of the West Bank by Israel. The second aim was the establishment of the Maronite government in Lebanon, headed by Bashir Gemayel and signing the peace treaty between two countries, the third aim was the expelling of the Syrian Army from Lebanon. Also, according to Shlaim, with the completion of Israeli withdrawals from Sinai in March 1982, under the terms of the Egyptian-Israeli Peace Treaty, the Likud-led government of Israel hardened its attitude to the Arab world and became more aggressive.[1364]

According to Zeev Maoz in *Defending the Holy Land: A Critical Analysis of Israel's National Security and Foreign Policy* the goals of the war were primarily developed by then Minister of Defense Ariel Sharon and were fourfold: 1) "Destroy the PLO infrastructure in Lebanon, including the PLO headquarters in Beirut." 2) "Drive Syrian forces out of Lebanon." 3) "Install a Christian-dominated government in Lebanon, with Bashir Gemayel as President." 4) "Sign a peace treaty with the Lebanese government that would solidify the informal Israeli-Christian alliance and convert it into a binding agreement."[1365] George Ball testified before the U.S: Senate's Foreign Affairs Committee that Sharon's long-term strategy, as revealed in conversations, was one of "squeezing the Palestinians out of the West Bank . .allowing only enough of them to remain for work."[1366]

The military plan with the code name "Big Pines", prepared by IDF, envisaged invasion to Lebanon up to the highway Damascus-Beirut and linking with Maronite forces. It was first presented to Israeli cabinet on 20 December 1981 by Begin, but rejected by the majority of ministers. According to Avi Shlaim, Sharon and chief of staff Rafael Eitan, realizing that there was no chance in persuading the cabinet to approve a large-scale operation in Lebanon, adopted a different tactic and intended to implement "Operation Big Pines" in stages by manipulating enemy provocations and Israeli responses.[1367]

On 3 June 1982 Israel's ambassador to the United Kingdom, Shlomo Argov was shot and seriously wounded in London by terrorists belonging to the Iraqi-backed Abu Nidal terrorist organization. The attack was ordered by the Iraqi Intelligence Service. Following the attack, the assassins drove to the Iraqi embassy in London, where they deposited the weapon. In his memoirs, Sharon stated that the attack was "merely the spark that lit the fuse". Israeli prime Minister Begin used this as the "internationally recognized provocation" necessary to invade Lebanon. The fact that the Abu Nidal organization was the longtime rival of PLO, that its head was condemned to death by the PLO court, and that the British police reported that PLO leaders were on the "hit list" of the attackers did not deter Begin. Iraq's motives for the assassination attempt may have been to punish Israel for its destruction of Iraq's nuclear reactor in June 1981, and to provoke a war in Lebanon that Iraqi leaders calculated would be detrimental to the rival Ba'ath regime in Syria—whether Syria intervened to help the PLO or not![1368]

At the Israeli Cabinet meeting the following day, both Begin and Eitan belittled intelligence reports that the likely culprit was the Abu Nidal group. Begin cut short his own advisor on terrorism, arguing that all Palestinian terrorists were members of the PLO, while Eitan ridiculed the intelligence staff for splitting hairs and demanded to strike at the PLO. Yet Abu Nidal had broken with Arafat and PLO in 1974 over a fundamental principle: namely, that the Palestinian national movement would adopt a phased piecemeal approach to secure a Palestinian state and embark on a political path. The lack of understanding of the difference between Palestinian groups and the total ignorance of Palestinian politics on the part an overwhelming majority of Israelis and Jews played into the hands of those who did not wish to distinguish between the PLO and the Abu Nidal group. Thus, instead of an initiative to locate the Abu Nidal group in Damascus or Baghdad, the plan to invade Lebanon was activated.:119–120

The PLO denied complicity in the attack, but Israel retaliated with punishing air and artillery strikes against Palestinian targets in Lebanon, including the PLO camps. Sabra and the Shatila refugee camp were bombed for four hours and the local "Gaza" hospital was hit there. About 200 people were killed during these attacks.[1369] The PLO hit back firing rockets at northern Israel causing considerable damage and some loss of life.Wikipedia:Citation needed According to another source, twenty villages were targeted in Galilee and 3 Israelis were wounded.[1370]

According to Shlaim, Yasser Arafat, at that time being in Saudi Arabia, told the Americans through the Saudis that he was willing to suspend cross-border

Figure 171: *Israeli troops in south Lebanon*

shelling. But that message was disregarded by the Israeli government. President Reagan also sent a message to Begin urging him not to widen the attack.

On 4 June the Israeli cabinet authorized a large scale invasion.[1371,1372] Begin referred to the operation as self-defense to "avoid another Treblinka".[1373]

Timeline

Invasion

On 6 June 1982, Israeli forces under direction of Defense Minister Ariel Sharon launched a three-pronged invasion of southern Lebanon in "Operation Peace for Galilee". Roughly 60,000 troops and more than 800 tanks, heavily supported by aircraft, attack helicopters, artillery, and missile boats, crossed the Israel–Lebanon border in three areas. Simultaneously, Israeli armor, paratroopers, and naval commandos set sail in amphibious landing ships from Ashdod towards the Lebanese coast. Israel's publicly stated objective was to push PLO forces back 40 kilometers (25 mi) to the north.

The westernmost Israeli force was to advance up the coastal road to Tyre. Its mission was to bypass Tyre and destroy three PLO camps in the area, then move up the coast towards Sidon and Damour, while Israeli forces would simultaneously conduct an amphibious landing north of Sidon to cut off the retreat of PLO forces there. In the center, two divisions were to advance both

Figure 172: *An Israeli bombardment of a PLO position on the Lebanese coast*

north and south of the high ground overlooked by Beaufort Castle, which was being used as a PLO stronghold, and take the road junction at Nabatieh, while an elite reconnaissance battalion was to take the castle itself. The two divisions were then to split, with one heading west to link up with the forces along the coast, and another towards Jezzine and from there along the right flank of Syrian forces in the Bekaa Valley. The easternmost Israeli force, the largest of the three, advanced into the Bekaa Valley. Its mission was to prevent Syrian reinforcements from being sent and to stop Syrian forces from attempting to interfere with the operation on the coastal road.[1374]

Advance on Beirut

The advance along the coastal road was preceded by heavy artillery bombardment and airstrikes, but quickly became bogged down and was soon behind schedule. The narrowness of the road forced a slow advance, and Israeli armor became stuck in a large traffic jam. Several armored vehicles were knocked out by PLO fighters with anti-tank weaponry hiding in three groves along the road. One of the lead battalions, which was supposed to bypass Tyre and establish a blocking position to the north of the city, made a wrong turn and found itself in the center of the city, where it was ambushed. At eight in the evening the force finally crossed the Litani River and headed towards Sidon. In the central sector, the mission went as planned. The two Israeli divisions bypassed Beaufort Castle on both sides. Although an order to postpone the capture of Beaufort Castle was issued, it did not reach Israeli forces in time to prevent the operation, and Israeli troops of the Golani Brigade captured the castle in the fiercely-fought Battle of the Beaufort. The road junction at Nabatieh was also secured by the end of the first day. Meanwhile, the easternmost force penetrated into the Bekaa Valley and bore down on the Syrian positions. One division bypassed Mount Hermon via a road bulldozed by Israeli military engineers and cleared the town of Hasbaiya before swinging right and advancing towards Rachaiya. Though Israeli forces halted in the floor of the valley, they were flanking Syrian forces from the east and west. The Syrians put up minimal resistance and conducted some harassing artillery fire. By the end of the first day, the operation had gone almost entirely according to plan, though the advance along the coastal road was behind schedule.

Despite the delays, the Israeli advance along the coastal road continued steadily. This advance was supported by heavy air attacks against PLO positions that included the use of cluster bombs. Israeli missile boats also employed 76mm cannons to destroy targets along the coast, firing 3,500 shells during ten days of fighting. Israeli armor continued to advance towards Sidon, while other Israeli infantry attacked the three Palestinian refugee camps in the area that were used as PLO bases: Rashidiya, Burj ash-Shamali, and al-Bass. The camps were all crisscrossed with networks of bunkers, trenches, and firing positions. The Israelis took each camp section by section using the same method: warnings were blared by loudspeaker urging civilians to leave, before air and artillery bombardment commenced, followed by an infantry assault. Israeli infantry had to engage in fierce urban combat in narrow streets. The PLO defenders put up strong resistance and sometimes used civilians as human shields. It took four days of combat to secure Rashidiya and three days to secure the other three camps. At the same time, an Israeli amphibious operation was conducted north of Sidon, beginning with a diversionary bombardment of targets away from the landing zone by missile boats and aircraft. Two groups of commandos from the Shayetet 13 naval commando unit then came ashore to probe enemy defenses and secure the landing site, one of which swam to the mouth of the Awali River and another which came ashore on the landing beach in rubber dinghies. After a brief gunbattle with armed Palestinians, the main landings began, with paratroopers coming ashore in rubber dinghies to establish a beachhead followed by three landing craft that unloaded troops and armor. Over the following days, the three landing ships would run between Israel and Lebanon, shuttling more troops and armor onto the beachhead. The PLO response was limited to ineffective mortar fire, while Israeli missile boats and aircraft attacked Palestinian positions in response, and in total, about 2,400 soldiers and 400 tanks and armored personnel carriers were landed. From the beach, these forces advanced on Sidon, supported by naval

Figure 173: *A Syrian tank burning on the road outside Jezzine*

gunfire from missile boats. At the same time, Israeli forces in the central sector advanced towards Jezzine while those in the eastern sector remained in place, but began setting up heavy artillery positions that put Syrian SAM units in artillery range.[1375,834]

Meanwhile, Israeli forces advancing along the coastal road reached the outskirts of Sidon, but were delayed by heavy resistance in the main streets and the Ain al-Hilweh refugee camp on the southeastern edge of the city, and after an attempt by paratroopers to capture the city center and secure the south-north route through the city failed, the city was bypassed via a detour through the hills to the east. After linking up with the forces that had landed north of Sidon, while another force of paratroopers and armor with heavy air and artillery support advanced through central Sidon and cleared a south-north route through the city in fierce fighting. Another Israeli division passed through the city to link up with the forces north of Sidon.

In the center, most Israeli forces advancing towards Jezzine bypassed the town to continue advancing towards the main highway in the area, leaving a blocking force in the area that was soon joined by an armored brigade. Fighting broke out in Jezzine between the Israelis and Syrian forces holding the town. In the Battle of Jezzine, Israeli forces consisting of two tank battalions supported by a reconnaissance company and engineering platoon took Jezzine in a fierce daylong battle against a Syrian battalion, then repulsed a fierce counterattack by dozens of Syrian commandos during the night in combat that lasted until dawn. Meanwhile, Israeli forces continued to advance along the Syrians' right flank.

Israeli forces advancing along the coast also completed the capture of Sidon. Paratroopers attacked the Kasbah while a combined force of Golani Brigade infantry and tanks attacked Ain al-Hilweh. The Kasbah was secured in three days; the paratroopers advanced cautiously and managed to take it without suffering any casualties. However, the fighting at Ain al-Hilweh was to prove some of the fiercest of the entire war. The camp was heavily fortified and defended by PLO fighters and Islamic fundamentalists. The defenders fought fiercely over every alley and house, with civilians who wanted to surrender shot by the fundamentalists. The Israeli advance was slow and was supported by massive air and artillery bombardment. The IDF employed its previous tactics of urging civilians to leave with loudspeakers before attacking an area. It took about eight days the camp to fall, with the battle culminating in a last stand by the defenders at the camp mosque, which was blown up by the IDF.[1376]

In an effort to establish air superiority and greater freedom of action, the Israeli Air Force launched Operation Mole Cricket 19 on 9 June. During the course of the operation, the Israeli Air Force scored a dramatic victory over the Syrians, shooting down 29 Syrian planes and also destroying 17 Syrian anti-aircraft missile batteries, employing electronic warfare methods to confuse and jam the Syrian radars. The Israelis' only known losses were a single UAV shot down and two fighter jets damaged. Later that night, an Israeli air attack destroyed a Syrian armored brigade moving south from Baalbek, and the IAF attacked and destroyed six more Syrian SAM batteries the following day. The easternmost Israeli force, which had been stationary, resumed its advance forward up the Bekaa Valley.

In the center, Israeli forces were ambushed by the Syrians as they approached Ain Zhalta, and were pinned down by Syrian forces firing from superior positions. The Israelis were bogged down, and an infantry battalion was sent in by helicopter to reinforce them. The town was only captured after a two-day armored and infantry battle. After Ain Zhalta fell, the Israelis advanced to the town of Ain Dara, which overlooked the Beirut-Damascus highway, and captured the heights overlooking the town. Along the road to Ain Dara, the Israelis encountered Syrian tank and commando units, and found themselves bogged down as the Syrians took advantage of the terrain. The Israelis called in air support, and Israeli attack helicopters that took advantage of ravines to fly in low beneath their targets to gain an element of surprise proved particularly effective against Syrian tanks. After a daylong battle, the Israelis had surrounded Ain Dara and were in a position to strike on the highway.

Figure 174: *A destroyed airliner at Beirut Airport, 1982.*

In the east, Israeli forces advanced along four main routes towards Joub Jannine, along both sides of the Qaraoun reservoir. The Syrians resisted fiercely. Syrian infantrymen armed with anti-tank weapons staged ambushes against Israeli tanks, and Syrian Gazelle helicopters armed with HOT missiles proved effective against Israeli armor. However, the Israelis managed to capture the valley floor, and the Syrians retreated. The Israelis captured Rachaiya, advanced through Kfar Quoq, and took the outskirts of Yanta. Joub Jannine also fell to the Israelis. The extent of Israeli advances ensured that Syrian reinforcements were blocked from deploying west of the Qaraoun reservoir. An Israeli armored battalion then probed past Joub Jannine to the town of Sultan Yacoub, and was ambushed by Syrian forces lying in wait. In the Battle of Sultan Yacoub, the Israelis fought fiercely to extricate themselves, and called in reinforcements and artillery fire to cover the withdrawal. After six hours, the Israelis managed to retreat. In addition, another major air battle erupted in which the Israeli Air Force shot down 25 Syrian jets and 4 helicopters.

To the west, as IDF troops mopped up remaining resistance in Tyre and Sidon, the Israeli advance on Beirut continued, and Syrian tank and commando units were then deployed south of Beirut to reinforce the PLO. When the Israelis reached the Beirut suburb of Kafr Sill, they met a joint Syrian-PLO force for the first time, and fought a difficult battle to take it. The IDF temporarily halted its advance in the western sector at Kafr Sill.

On 11 June, Israel and Syria announced that they had agreed to a cease-fire at noon, which would not include the PLO. The cease-fire was to come into effect at noon. Just before the cease-fire was to take effect, the Syrians moved a column of T-72 tanks so as to position it against Israeli forces in the valley. Israeli infantry teams armed with BGM-71 TOW anti-tank missiles ambushed the Syrian column, destroying 11 tanks. Another air battle also occurred, with the Israelis shooting down 18 more Syrian jets.[1377]

As the Israeli advance on Beirut pressed forward in the west, reaching Khalde on 11 June. Six miles south of Beirut, the town was the last PLO position in front of Beirut Airport. The Israelis, who stood on the outskirts of Beirut, advanced towards the airport, and engaged in frequent combat with PLO and Syrian units as Israeli warplanes continued to bomb PLO positions in Beirut. The PLO's situation gradually grew worse as the Israeli advance gained ground, threatening to trap the PLO and a Syrian brigade deployed with them in the city. With the Israelis advancing on the south and the eastern sector of Beirut held by Lebanese Christian forces, the only way out was on the Beirut-Damascus highway, and the Israelis were building up forces at Ain Dara in the eastern sector, which were in a position to strike at the highway and block any PLO attempt to escape. On 12 June, the Israeli-Syrian cease-fire was extended to the PLO. As the Israeli advance halted, the Israelis turned their attention to the zone they already occupied in southern Lebanon, and began a policy to root out any PLO remnants. Israeli troops began searches for arms caches, and suspected PLO members were systematically rounded up and screened, and taken to a detention camp on the Amoun Heights.

On 13 June, less than twelve hours after the Israeli-PLO ceasefire had gone into effect, it fell apart, and heavy fighting erupted around Khalde. As the fighting raged, an IDF armored unit struck northeast, attempting to bypass Khalde and advance on Baabda, which overlooked the airport and could be used as another staging point to cut the Beirut-Damascus highway. By 14 June, Syrian forces were being deployed to Khalde. Syrian units in Beirut and three commando battalions armed with anti-tank weaponry took up defensive positions southwest of the airport to block any Israeli attempt to capture it. The Israelis attempted to flank these defenses by moving off the road past Shuweifat, up a narrow, steep, and winding road towards Baabda, but were ambushed by a Syrian commando battalion. The Syrians attacked Israeli armor with rocket-propelled grenades and anti-tank missiles at close range. Israeli infantry dismounted and engaged the Syrians. Fierce fighting took place, with the Israelis calling in artillery at very close range to themselves. The Israelis advanced relentlessly, and after fourteen hours of fierce combat that raged up through Ain Aanoub and Souq el-Gharb, they broke through the Syrian positions and entered Baabda. The IDF then immediately sent reinforcements to the column in Baabda to enable it to carry out further operations. From Baabda, the Israeli force split into three columns, one of which struck across the highway

1982 Lebanon War

Figure 175: *IAF Roundel for the strike aircraft that attacked Syrian SAM batteries in 1982 Lebanon war.*

and entered the mountainous area to the northeast, one swung west and took up positions in the steep hills west of Beirut, and one turned toward Kahale, which was further down the highway. To the south, the IDF drove PLO forces out of Shuweifat, but no major battles occurred. The Israelis had now cut the Beirut-Damascus highway, cutting off all PLO and Syrian forces in the city.

On 15 June, Israel offered free passage to all Syrian forces in Beirut if they would withdraw from the city to the Bekaa Valley in the east, but the Syrian government refused and sent further reinforcements to its units along the highway and north of the highway near Beirut. The Israelis faced Syrian strongpoints reinforced by armor and artillery all along the highway. However, between 16 June and 22 June, the fighting was limited to artillery duels and minor firefights between Israeli and Syrian forces, as both sides reinforced their troops.

Battles of the Beirut-Damascus highway

As the two sides prepared for combat, the IDF deemed capturing the Beirut-Damascus highway to be of critical importance. With the Syrians in control of most of the highway, occupying the towns along the highway and to the north, the Israelis could not prevent Syrian and PLO forces from escaping or launch

Figure 176: *The Israeli Navy missile boat INS Romach off the coast of Lebanon, August 1982.*

further operations into Beirut without risking a Syrian flanking attack, and the Israelis also wanted a clear transit to Christian-held eastern Beirut.

On 22 June, the IDF launched an operation to capture the highway. The Israeli Air Force flew highly effective missions against Syrian positions and vehicles, with Israeli pilots reporting 130 enemy vehicles destroyed in a single air attack alone. Israeli long-range artillery targeted Syrian strongpoints to the north. Israeli armored forces with artillery support attacked Syrian positions along the highway, with the objective of driving them from the highway all the way back to the edge of the Bekaa Valley. With air and artillery support mostly limited to targets north of the highway, the fighting was fierce, especially to the south. By the end of the day, Israel accepted an American request for a cease-fire and halted its offensive, but the cease-fire collapsed the following day and the fighting resumed. As the Israelis pushed forward, and managed to trap a large Syrian force, Syrian defenses began to collapse. For the first time in the war, Syrian troops began to break and run. At Aley, which was defended by Iranian volunteers sent to fight for the PLO, the Israelis encountered fierce resistance.

The Israelis managed to push to the eastern Bekaa Valley, and on 24 June, began to shell the outskirts of Chtaura, which was at the northern mouth of the Bekaa Valley and served as headquarters of all Syrian forces there. It was also the last major obstacle before the Syrian border, as well as Syria's capital Damascus itself. The Israelis managed to reach the mountain pass near the village of Dahr el-Baidar, which was the last obstacle before Cthaura. The Syrians fought fiercely to hold the pass, and the Israeli advance halted, with the Israelis holding their ground and harassing the Syrians with artillery fire.

Figure 177: *An aerial view of the stadium used as an ammunition supply site for the PLO, after Israeli airstrikes in 1982.*

By 25 June, with the remaining Syrian positions on and north of the highway no longer tenable, the Syrians withdrew. The Israelis allowed the withdrawal to occur but conducted artillery harassment and continued to shell the outskirts of Chtaura. The Syrians attempted to deploy a SAM battery in the Bekaa Valley at midnight, but Israeli intelligence detected this, and the battery was destroyed in an Israeli air attack. By the end of the day, a cease-fire was announced. The Israelis stopped at their present positions.

Siege of Beirut

Siege of Beirut had begun on 14 June: Israeli forces had completed the encirclement of the city the previous day. The Israelis chose to keep the city under siege rather than forcibly capture it, as they were unwilling to accept the heavy casualties that the heavy street fighting required to capture the city would have resulted in. Israeli forces bombarded targets within Beirut from land, sea, and air, and attempted to assassinate Palestinian leaders through airstrikes. The siege lasted until August, when an agreement was reached in August 1982. More than 14,000 PLO combatants evacuated the country in August and September, supervised by the Multinational Force in Lebanon, an international peacekeeping force with troops from the United States, United Kingdom, France, and Italy. About 6,500 Fatah fighters relocated from Beirut to Jordan, Syria, Iraq, Sudan, both North and South Yemen, Greece, and Tunisia—the latter of which became the new PLO headquarters. Philip Habib,

Ronald Reagan's envoy to Lebanon, provided an understanding (i.e., assurance) to the PLO that the Palestinian civilians in the refugee camps would not be harmed. However, increased hostilities against the US resulted in the April 1983 United States Embassy bombing. In response, the US brokered the May 17 Agreement, in an attempt to stall hostilities between Israel and Lebanon. However, this agreement eventually failed to take shape, and hostilities continued. These attacks were attributed to Iranian-backed Islamist guerrillas. Following this incident, international peacekeeping forces were withdrawn from Lebanon.

Further conflict and Israeli withdrawal

Following the departure of the PLO and international peacekeepers, Islamist militants began launching guerrilla attacks against Israeli forces. Suicide bombings were a particularly popular tactic, the most serious being the Tyre headquarters bombings, which twice devastated IDF headquarters in Tyre, and killed 103 Israeli soldiers, border policemen, and Shin Bet agents, as well as 49–56 Lebanese. The IDF subsequently withdrew from the Shouf Mountains but continued occupying Lebanon south of the Awali River.

An increased number of Islamic militias began operating in South Lebanon, launching guerrilla attacks on Israeli positions and on pro-Israeli Lebanese militias. Israeli forces often responded with increased security measures and airstrikes on militant positions, and casualties on all sides steadily climbed. In a vacuum left with eradication of PLO, the disorganized Islamic militants in South Lebanon began to consolidate. The emerging Hezbollah, soon to become the preeminent Islamic militia, evolved during this period. However, scholars disagree as to when Hezbollah came to be regarded as a distinct entity. Over time, a number of Shi'a group members were slowly assimilated into the organization, such as Islamic Jihad members, Organization of the Oppressed on Earth, and the Revolutionary Justice Organization.

In February 1985, Israel withdrew from Sidon and turned it over to the Lebanese Army, but faced attacks: 15 Israelis were killed and 105 wounded during the withdrawal. Dozens of pro-Israeli Lebanese militiamen were also assassinated. From mid-February to mid-March, the Israelis lost 18 dead and 35 wounded. On 11 March, Israeli forces raided the town of Zrariyah, killing 40 Amal fighters and capturing a large stock of arms. On 9 April, a Shiite girl drove a car bomb into an IDF convoy, and the following day, a soldier was killed by a land mine. During that same period, Israeli forces killed 80 Lebanese guerrillas in five weeks. Another 1,800 Shi'as were taken as prisoners.

Israel withdrew from the Bekaa valley on 24 April, and from Tyre on the 29th. In June 1985, the IDF unilaterally withdrew to a security zone in southern

Figure 178: *IAF Cobra gunships on military exercise. These attack helicopters were successfully employed against Syrian AFVs during the conflict.*

Lebanon along with its principal Lebanese ally, the South Lebanon Army, officially ending the war.

Despite this being considered the end of the war, conflict would continue. Hezbollah continued to fight the IDF and SLA in the South Lebanon conflict until Israel's final withdrawal from Lebanon in 2000.

Military analysis

During the course of combat operations, the Israeli Air Force conducted successful ground attack missions against Syrian and PLO targets, with Israeli attack helicopters inflicting heavy losses on Syrian armor. Israeli jets shot down between 82[1378] and 86 Syrian aircraft in aerial combat, without losses.[1379,1380] A single Israeli A-4 Skyhawk and two helicopters were shot down by anti-aircraft fire and SAM missiles. This was the largest aerial combat battle of the jet age with over 150 fighters from both sides engaged. Syrian claims of aerial victories were met with skepticism even from their Soviet allies. The Soviets were so shaken by the staggering losses sustained by their allies that they dispatched the deputy head of their air defense force to Syria to examine how the Israelis had been so dominant. The Israeli Air Force also performed ground attacks, notably destroying the majority of Syrian anti-aircraft batteries stationed

Figure 179: *An Israeli Merkava 1 in Lebanon after being hit, 1982*

in Lebanon. AH-1 Cobra helicopter gunships were employed against Syrian armour and fortifications. IAF Cobras destroyed dozens of Syrian Armored fighting vehicles, including some of the modern Soviet T-72 main battle tanks.

The war also witnessed the Israeli Merkava MBT make its first combat debut, squaring off against Syrian T-72 tanks. During these engagements, the Israelis claimed that the Merkava proved superior to the T-72, destroying a number of them without sustaining a single loss to T-72 fire.[1381] Former IAF commander, David Ivri would later recall a meeting with a high-ranking member of the Warsaw Pact, in which he was told that the dominance of Israeli and U.S. technology and tactics during the war was one of the factors that changed Soviet mind-set, leading to Glasnost and ultimately, the fall of the Soviet Union.[1382,1383] However, defense analysts and the Syrians claimed the opposite, saying that their T-72s were highly effective and that none were lost. The T-72 tanks of the Syrian 2nd Armored Division were credited with not only halting the advance of an Israeli armored brigade on Rashaya on 10 June but pushing them back. They tallied the destruction of 33 tanks and the capture of an M60 Patton, which was sent to Damascus and thence transported to Moscow. Syrian tanks saw similar success against Israeli armor in Ain Zhalta and Sultan Yacoub in fighting on 8–10 June, stemming their advance to capture the Beirut-Damascus highway.[1384]

Final accords

On 14 September 1982, Bachir Gemayel, the newly elected President of Lebanon, was assassinated by Habib Shartouni of the Syrian Social Nationalist Party.[1385] Israeli forces occupied West Beirut the next day. At that time, the Lebanese Christian Militia, also known as the Phalangists, were allied with Israel.[1386] The Israeli command authorized the entrance of a force of approximately 150 Phalangist fighters' into Sabra and the Shatila refugee camp. Shatila had previously been one of the PLO's three main training camps for foreign militants and the main training camp for European militants; the Israelis maintained that 2,000 to 3,000 terrorists remained in the camps, but were unwilling to risk the lives of more of their soldiers after the Lebanese army repeatedly refused to "clear them out." Between 460 and 3,500 civilians, mostly Palestinians and Lebanese Shiites were massacred by the Phalangists, who themselves suffered only two casualties. The Lebanese army's chief prosecutor investigated the killings and counted 460 dead, Israeli intelligence estimated 700–800 dead, and the Palestinian Red Crescent claimed 2,000 dead. 1,200 death certificates were issued to anyone who produced three witnesses claiming a family member disappeared during the time of the massacre. Nearly all of the victims were men. Israeli troops surrounded the camps with tanks and checkpoints, monitoring entrances and exits. Further, Israeli investigation by the Kahan Commission of Inquiry found that Ariel Sharon bore "personal responsibility" for failing to prevent the massacre, and for failing to act once he learned of the massacre. The Commission recommended that he be removed as Defense Minister and that he never hold a position in any future Israeli government. Sharon initially ignored the call to resign, but after the death of an anti-war protester, resigned as Israel's Defense Minister, remaining in Begin's cabinet as a Minister without portfolio.

Opposing forces

The 1982 Lebanon War was at first a conventional war up to and including when the PLO were expelled from Beirut.[1387] The war was limited by both Israel and Syria because they were determined to isolate the fighting, not allowing it to turn into an all-out war.[1388] Israeli forces were numerically superior, allowing Israel to maintain both the initiative and an element of surprise. The Syrian Army fielded six divisions and 500 aircraft, while Israel used five divisions and two brigades, plus 600 aircraft.[1389] There were numerous other factions involved.

Figure 180: *The Israeli Merkava Mark I tank was used throughout the First Lebanon War*

Israel

IDF forces totalled 78,000 men, 1,240 tanks and 1,500 armoured personnel carriers. IDF troops were deployed in five divisions and two reinforced brigade-size units. The IDF maintained additional forces on the Golan Heights as an area reserve. IDF forces were divided into three main axis of advances called sectors:[1390]

- Coastal Sector, (from Rosh Hanikra north to Tyre, Sidon, Damour and Beirut.) – Forces included Division 91 with three brigades including the 211th and the Golani Brigade. The 35 Paratroop Brigade and the Na'hal 50th Paratroop Battalion were attached to the division as needed. The Israeli Navy provided naval interdiction, shore gunfire support and landed a mixed brigade from Division 96 at the mouth of the Awali River near Sidon. Israeli Naval commandos had landed there previously.
- Central Sector (from Beaufort Castle to Nabatiyeh) – Jezzine was the main objective and then on to Sidon to link up with the coastal forces. IDF forces included the Divisions 36 and 162.
- Eastern Sector (from Rachaiya and Hasbaiya through the Bekaa Valley around Lake Qaraoun) – IDF forces included Divisions 90 and 252, the Vardi Force and the Special Maneuver Force which was composed of two brigades of Infantry and paratroops who were trained for anti-tank

Figure 181: *Syrian anti-tank teams deployed French-made Milan ATGMs during the war in Lebanon in 1982.*

Figure 182: *Part of a Syrian SA-6 site built near the Beirut-Damascus highway, and overlooking the Bekaa Valley, in early 1982.*

operations. These forces were primarily used to contain the Syrians with orders not to initiate combat against them.

Syria

The Syrian Army deployed over 30,000 troops in Lebanon.

The largest concentration was in the Bekaa Valley where the 1st Armoured Division consisting of the 58th Mechanised and the 76th and 91st Armoured

Figure 183: *Lebanese Army APC, Beirut 1982*

Brigades. The 62nd Independent Armored Brigade and ten commando battalions were also assigned to the division. Syria deployed around 400 tanks in the Bekaa Valley. 19 surface-to-air missile batteries, including SA6's, were also deployed in the Bekaa Valley.

In Beirut and the Shouf Mountains were the 85th Infantry Brigade, the PLA, As-Sa'iqa and 20 commando battalions. Syria deployed around 200 tanks in this area. Their primary mission was to protect the Beirut-Damascus Highway, which was Syria's primary supply line in the region.

Lebanon

Armed Forces

Lebanese Army – By 1982 the Lebanese Army had largely disintegrated and what was left was a Christian-staffed force of about 10,000 men in five brigades (the 5th, 7th, 8th, 9th, and 10th) plus some smaller independent units. The Lebanese Army was officially neutral and followed the orders of the Lebanese government, but provided tacit and active support to the Lebanese Front. The Army had lost much of its heavy equipment due to defections of its units.

A Lebanese national army unit of 1,350 was under the operational control of the UNIFIL commander, HQ located at Arzun with sub-units attached to UNIFIL Battalions.[1391]

Lebanese Navy: The mostly Christian manned force operated several patrol boats and was loyal to the government. It played little or no part in the war.

Lebanese Air Force: This largely Christian force operated a force of jet fighters, helicopters and other aircraft and it too played little part in the war.

Security forces

Internal Security Forces: the national police and internal security force of Lebanon.

Palestinians

PLO

Palestinian Liberation Organization forces continued to grow in Lebanon, with full-time military personnel numbering around 15,000 fedayeen, although only 6,000 of these − including 4,500 regulars − deployed in the south. They were armed with 80 aging tanks, many of them no longer mobile, and with 100 to 200 pieces of artillery. According to Israeli analysts Schiff and Ya'ari (1984), the PLO more than quadrupled its artillery from 80 cannons and rocket launchers in July 1981 to 250 in June 1982.[1392] The same authors also refer to Israeli intelligence estimates of the number of PLO fighters in southern Lebanon of 6,000 as

> divided into three concentrations; about 1,500 south of the Litani River in the so-called Iron Triangle (between the villages of Kana, Dir Amas, and Juya), Tyre, and its surrounding refugee camps; another 2,500 of the Kastel Brigade in three districts between the Litani and a line running from Sidon to northeast of Nabatiye; and a third large concentration of about 1,500–2,000 men of the Karameh Brigade in the east, on the slopes of Mount Hermon.[1393]

PLO primary forces consisted of three conventional brigades − each of 2,000 to 2,500 men − and of seven artillery battalions. Each brigade comprised contingents of the many PLO factions. The Yarmouk Brigade was stationed along the coastal strip while the Kastel Brigade was in the south. The Karameh Brigade was stationed on the eastern slopes of Mount Hermon in the area called Fatahland.

The PLO had around 15,000 to 18,000 fighters (of whom about 5,000 to 6,000 were alleged to be foreign mercenaries (or volunteers) from such countries as Libya, Iraq, India, Sri Lanka, Chad and Mozambique) deployed as follows:

- 6,000 in the Beirut, Ba'abda and Damour area
- 1,500 in Sidon
- 1,000 between Sidon and Tyre

- 1,500 in Tyre
- 1,000 deployed from Nabatiyeh to Beaufort Castle
- 2,000 in Fatahland
- around 1,000 in the UNIFIL Zone

Heavy weapons consisted of about 60 T-34, T-54 and T-55 tanks (most of them dug in as pillboxes), up to 250 130mm and 155 mm artillery, many BM21 Katyusha multiple-rocket launchers plus heavy mortars.[1394]

Non-PLO Palestinian groups

Palestinian groups in the radical Rejectionist Front fought on the Muslim-leftist side. The alliance did nothing to improve cooperation between member factions, and internecine bloodshed continued. The following were members of the Rejectionist Front:

- Arab Liberation Front (ALF) Pro-Iraqi
- As-Sa'iqa (also known as the Vanguard for the Popular Liberation War), a Palestinian Ba'athist political and military faction created and controlled by Syria.
- Abu Nidal's Fatah-Revolutionary Council
- Democratic Front for the Liberation of Palestine (DFLP)
- Palestine Liberation Army (PLA) Includes the Popular Liberation Forces (Arabic, quwwat at-tahrir ash-sha'biyya), better known as the Yarmouk Brigade, a PLA Commando force.
- Palestinian Popular Struggle Front (PPSF)
- Popular Front for the Liberation of Palestine (PFLP)
- Popular Front for the Liberation of Palestine - General Command (PFLP-GC)

Some, such as As-Sa'iqa, the Arab Liberation Front, the Palestine Liberation Army and the Popular Front for the Liberation of Palestine-General Command (PFLP-GC) were essentially mercenary armies for foreign governments (Syria, Iraq, and Libya, respectively).

Paramilitary forces

Right wing

- South Lebanon Army, founded in 1979 the SLA fought against both the PLO and Hezbollah. The SLA was composed of Christians, Shias and Druze from the areas that it controlled but the officers were mostly Christians.

- Guardians of the Cedars, exclusively Maronite with strong anti-Syrian views, 3,000–6,000 uniformed militiamen armed with modern small-arms. They were backed by a mechanized force consisting of a single M50 Super Sherman medium tank, a few M42 Dusters and Chaimite V200 armoured cars backed by gun-trucks (Land-Rovers, Toyota Land Cruisers, GMC and Ford light pick-ups, plus US M35A2 2-1/2 ton cargo trucks) fitted with heavy machine guns (HMGs), recoilless rifles, and a few anti-aircraft autocannons.

Left wing

- The Lebanese National Resistance Front forces totalled about 30,000 fighting men and women. It was the successor of the Lebanese National Movement.
- The Druze were initially neutral but turned against the LF when the new government attempted to force their way into Druze controlled territory in the Chouf region. The People's Liberation Army – PLA (Arabic: Jayish al-Tahrir al-Sha'aby) or Armée de Libération Populaire (ALP), the militia of the Druze Progressive Socialist Party, consisted of 10,000 to 20,000 men and boys.
- The Al-Mourabitoun (Guardians or Saviours in Arabic) is a secular, non-sectarian movement, its membership has always been overwhelmingly Muslim, being perceived within Lebanon as a predominantly Sunni organization. Its militia (Mouqatin or Fighters) numbered several thousand men and were known for wearing red painted Soviet helmets with Mourabitoun painted on front in Arabic script. The Mourabitoun fought alongside the PLO in the Beirut area until the cease fire after which they acquired much cast-off PLO equipment such as tanks and rocket launchers. They were supported largely by Libya and Syria.
- The Kurdistan Workers' Party at the time had training camps in Lebanon, where they received support from the Syrians and the PLO. During the Israeli invasion all PKK units were ordered to fight the Israeli forces. A total of 11 PKK fighters died in the conflict.

Religious

Christian

The Christian Lebanese Front, was a coalition of mainly Christian parties formed in 1976, during the Lebanese Civil War. It was intended to act as a counter force to the Lebanese National Movement (LNM) of Kamal Jumblatt and others. Combined Lebanese Front forces totalled about 30,000 fighting men and women. These forces were mostly Phalangist, though there were some men from Saad Haddad's "Free Lebanon forces" and other smaller rightwing militias, including al-Tanzim.

Muslim

Muslim forces were Shiite organizations:

- Amal Movement is the militia wing of the Movement of the Disinherited, a Shi'a political movement. Initially neutral. The Shia Amal guerrillas had been ordered by their leaders not to fight and to surrender their weapons if necessary.
- Hezbollah is the other Shiite militia ostensibly formed during the invasion around Beirut and backed by Iran.
- Pasdaran – In July 1982 Iran dispatched an expeditionary force of Revolutionary Guards to Lebanon, ostensibly to fight the Israeli invaders. The approximately 650 Pasdaran established their headquarters in the city of Baalbek in the Syrian-controlled Biqa Valley where they conducted guerrilla training, disbursed military matériel and money, and disseminated propaganda.
- The political fission that characterized Lebanese politics also afflicted the Shia movement, as groups split off from Amal. Husayn al Musawi, a former Amal lieutenant, entered into an alliance with the Revolutionary Guard and established Islamic Amal.
- Other Shia groups included Jundallah (Soldiers of God), the Husayn Suicide Commandos, the Dawah (Call) Party, and the notorious Islamic Jihad Organization, reportedly headed by Imad Mughniyyah.

UNIFIL

The United Nations Interim Force in Lebanon, or UNIFIL, was created by the United Nations, with the adoption of the United Nations Security Council Resolution 425 and the United Nations Security Council Resolution 426 on 19 March 1978, to confirm Israeli withdrawal from Lebanon which Israel had invaded five days prior, restore international peace and security, and help the Government of Lebanon restore its effective authority in the area. The first UNIFIL troops were deployed in the area on 23 March 1978; these troops were reassigned from other UN peacekeeping operations in the area (namely the United Nations Emergency Force and the United Nations Disengagement Observer Force Zone). During the 1982 Lebanon War, UN positions were overrun, primarily by the South Lebanon Army forces under Saad Haddad.

Outcome of the war

Casualties

Lebanese, Palestinian, and Syrian casualties

Numbers of the casualties in the conflict vary widely.

By the end of the first week, 14 June 1982, International Red Cross and Lebanese police figures claimed that 9,583 had died and 16,608 injured. By the end of the second week, they claimed up to 14,000 people died and 20,000 were injured, mostly civilians.[1395]

During the Siege of Beirut, by late August 1982, Lebanese sources put the death toll in Beirut at 6,776. This figure included victims of the 4 June 1982, bombing, which occurred two days before the operation officially started. Lebanese police and international doctors serving in Beirut put the number of civilian casualties at about 80%. According to American military analyst Richard Gabriel, all factions in the conflicts agree that between 4,000 and 5,000 civilians died during the siege caused by military activity of all sides. He states that most of the observers that were present on the ground and other relevant sources in Lebanon agree that estimates of 8,000–10,000 are too high.

Accurate numbers of total casualties are hard to estimate, due to "[t]he chaos of warfare, the destruction of city neighborhoods and refugee camps, the haste with which bodies were buried in mass graves and the absence of impartial agencies". Many officials in Beirut, including those of the International Red Cross, claimed that the number of deaths were extremely difficult to estimate correctly. At least one official from a relief organization claimed that in the South about 80% of deaths were civilian and only 20% military.

In early September 1982, the independent Beirut newspaper *An Nahar* published an estimate of deaths from hospital and police records covering the period from 6 June to 31 August 1982. It claimed that 17,285 people were killed: 5,515 people, both military and civilian, in the Beirut area; and 2,513 civilians, as well as 9,797 military forces, including PLO and Syrians, outside of the Beirut area.

The Lebanese authorities gave a figure of 19,085 killed and 30,000 wounded with combatants accounting for 57% of the dead and civilians 43% in 1982.

They do not include the estimated 800–3,500 killed in the Sabra and Shatila massacre.

Richard Gabriel estimated that roughly 2,400 PLO fighters were killed during the war, of whom about 1,400 were killed throughout southern Lebanon and another 1,000 killed during the Siege of Beirut. Gabriel also estimated that between 5,000 and 8,000 civilians died during the war. Some later estimates have put the total figure at 18–19,000 killed and more than 30,000 wounded, most of them civilians. 80% of villages in South Lebanon were damaged, with some completely destroyed.[1396] The Israeli government maintained that about 1,000 Palestinian fighters and 800 Lebanese civilians died during the invasion, excluding the siege of Beirut. Kenneth Pollack estimated that 1,200 Syrian soldiers were killed and about 3,000 wounded during the war.

Israeli casualties

According to Israeli figures, between 6 June 1982 and June 1985, the Israel Defense Forces suffered 657 dead and 3,887 wounded. Another three Israeli soldiers who are thought to have fallen into Syrian hands remain officially missing in action to this day. According to Kenneth Pollack, Israeli losses in action against the Syrians were 195 dead and 872 wounded. From the withdrawal to the South Lebanon Security Zone in 1985 to the pullout to the international border in May 2000, the IDF lost another 559 soldiers,[1397] including 256 from combat.

Israeli civilian casualties from cross-border shelling numbered 9–10 killed and at least 248 wounded between June 1982 and 1999.[1398]

Security buffer zone and Syrian occupation

In September 1982, the PLO withdrew most of its forces from Lebanon. With U.S. assistance, Israel and Lebanon reached an accord in May 1983, that set the stage to withdraw Israeli forces from Lebanon while letting them patrol a "security zone" together with the Lebanese Army.

The instruments of ratification were never exchanged, however, and in March 1984, under pressure from Syria, Lebanon cancelled the agreement.

In January 1985, Israel started to withdraw most of its troops, leaving a small residual Israeli force and an Israeli-supported militia, the South Lebanon Army in southern Lebanon in a "security zone", which Israel considered a necessary buffer against attacks on its northern territory. The Israeli withdrawal to the security zone ended in June 1985. Israel withdrew fully from Lebanon in 2000.

The political vacuum resulting from the 1985 Israeli withdrawal would eventually lead to the *de facto* Syrian occupation of Lebanon. Syria would gain much

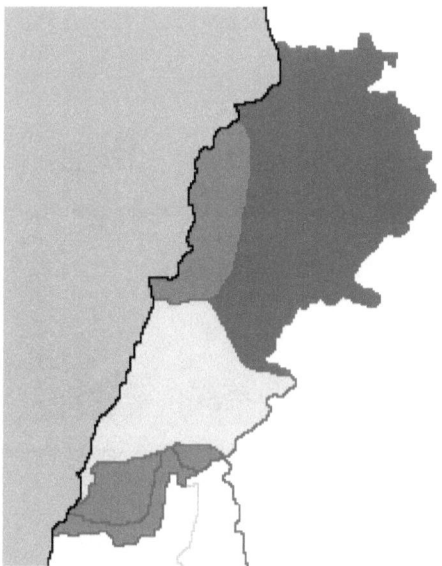

Figure 184: *Map showing power balance in Lebanon, 1983: Green – controlled by Syria, purple – controlled by Christian groups, yellow – controlled by Israel, blue – controlled by the United Nations*

Figure 185: *IDF military patrol near Ras Biada- south Lebanon (1986)*

Figure 186: *IDF military post Shakuf El-Hardun – south Lebanon (1986)*

Figure 187: *IDF military patrol above the Litani river- south Lebanon (1987)*

Figure 188: *Beaufort IDF northern military post- south Lebanon (1995)*

Figure 189: *IDF military patrol between Aaichiye to Rayhan- south Lebanon (1995)*

more power over Lebanon than what it enjoyed before 1982, but it would no longer align with the PLO. In the War of the Camps that followed the Israeli withdrawal, Syria fought their former Palestinian allies.

Relocation of PLO

Following Arafat's decision of June 1982, by September 1982, the PLO had withdrawn most of its forces from Lebanon. Syria backed the anti-Arafat PLO forces of Abu Musa in the Beka valley from May 1983. When Arafat castigated the Syrian government for blocking PLO supplies in June 1983, the Syrian government declared Arafat a *persona non-grata* on 24 June 1983.[1399]

With the withdrawal of the PLO leadership from Tripoli in December 1983 there was an Egyptian-PLO rapprochement, this was found to be encouraging by the Reagan administration but was condemned by the Israeli government.[1400]

Political results for Israel

In the voting in the Knesset on the war, only Hadash opposed the war (and even submitted a no-confidence motion against the Israeli government). Hadash Knesset member Meir Vilner said in the Knesset plenary session that: "The government is leading Israel to an abyss. It is doing something that in the course of time might lead to crying for generations". In response, they were condemned, and calls were heard, among others from the editor of Yediot Ahronoth, to prosecute them for treason. Left-wing Knesset members, including Shulamit Aloni and Yossi Sarid, were absent from the plenary for the vote. Even the Labour faction voted in support. By mid January 1983 Rabin was saying that the Israeli attempt to impose a peace agreement on Lebanon by the use of force was a "mistake" based upon an "illusion".[1401]

Heavy Israeli casualties, alleged disinformation of Israeli government leaders and the Israeli public by Israeli military, as well as political advocates of the campaign and lack of clear goals led to increasing disquiet among Israelis. This culminated in a large protest rally in Tel Aviv on 25 September 1982, organized by the Peace Now movement, following the 1982 Sabra and Shatila massacre. Organizers claimed 400,000 people participated in the rally, and it became known as the "400,000 rally". Other estimates put the figure much lower, maybe reaching 100,000 Israelis but including thousands of reserve soldiers back from Lebanon.[1402,1403]

Political outcome for Lebanon

The Israeli-Maronite alliance dissolved, and Sharon's goal of installing a pro-Israel Christian government in Beirut was not accomplished.[1404] 850,000 Christians would emigrate during the Civil War out of Lebanon, most of them permanently.

The withdrawal of the IDF from central Lebanon in the summer of 1983, was followed by one of the bloodiest phases of the Lebanese war, where the Christian Militia (the Lebanese Forces) was left alone to defend the "Mountain" area which comprised the Aley and Chouf districts against a coalition of Druze PSP, PLO remnants, Syrian Army, Lebanese Communist, and Syrian Social National Party. This heavily impacted the civilian population from both sides (more than 5,000 killed from both sides).Wikipedia:Citation needed The Mountain War ended after the Christian forces and civilians withdrew to the town of Deir el Kamar where they were besieged for 3 months before all hostilities ceased and they were transported to East Beirut.

The invasion led to the switching of sides of Amal Movement, which used to fight against the PLO prior to the invasion. The invasion is also popularly held to be the major catalyst for the creation of the Iranian and Syrian supported Hezbollah organization, which by 1991 was the sole armed militia in Lebanon not supported by Israel and by 2000 had completely replaced the vanquished PLO in Southern Lebanon.Wikipedia:Citation needed

Cold War perspective

According to Abraham Rabinovich, the complete dominance of U.S. and Israeli technology and tactics over those of the Eastern Bloc was to have been a factor that hastened the demise of the Warsaw Pact and Soviet Union.Wikipedia:Accuracy dispute#Disputed statement However, this was not the first confrontation in which Soviet weaponry had been outmatched by American weaponry. In many of the Cold War conflictsWikipedia:Avoid weasel words the Americans and their allies had superior technology. Nonetheless, the gap between the First World and Second World weaponry was more apparent in the 1980s and weighed more heavily on Second World leaders.

Long-term consequences

One of the lingering consequences of the Israeli invasion of Lebanon was the creation of Hezbollah.

In 2000, when Ehud Barak was Israeli Prime Minister, Israel finally withdrew from the security zone to behind the Blue Line. Lebanon and Hezbollah continue to claim a small area called Shebaa Farms as Lebanese territory, but

Israel insists that it is captured Syrian territory with the same status as the Golan Heights. The United Nations has not determined the final status of Shebaa Farms but has determined that Israel has complied with UNSC resolution 425. The UN Secretary-General had concluded that, as of 16 June 2000, Israel had withdrawn its forces from Lebanon in accordance with UN Security Council Resolution 425 of 1978, bringing closure to the 1982 invasion as far as the UN was concerned.[1405]

Israel's withdrawal from Lebanon led to pressure on the Syrians to withdraw their occupation forces and this pressure intensified after the assassination of the popular Lebanese Prime Minister, Rafik Hariri. On 26 April 2005 the Syrian occupation forces withdrew from Lebanon.

Other consequences

- The invasion removed PLO presence from Southern Lebanon and the Syrian military was weakened by combat losses, especially in the air. However, the removal of the PLO also paved the way for the rise of other militant groups, particularly Hezbollah.
- The failure of the larger Israeli objectives of resolving the conflict in Lebanon with a peace treaty.
- The Lebanese Council for Development and Reconstruction estimated the cost of the damage from the invasion at 7,622,774,000 Lebanese pounds, equivalent to US$2 billion at the time.
- Al-Qaeda leader Osama bin Laden said in a videotape, released on the eve of the 2004 U.S. presidential elections, that he was inspired to attack the buildings of the United States by the 1982 Israeli invasion of Lebanon, in which towers and buildings in Beirut were destroyed in the siege of the capital.[1406]

Investigation into violation of international law

On 16 December 1982, the United Nations General Assembly condemned the Sabra and Shatila massacre and declared it to be an act of genocide.[1407] The voting record[1408,1409] on section D of Resolution 37/123, which "resolves that the massacre was an act of genocide", was: yes: 123; no: 0; abstentions: 22; non-voting: 12. The abstentions were: Belgium, Denmark, France, Germany (Federal Republic), Iceland, Ireland, Italy, Luxembourg, the Netherlands, Norway, Portugal, Sweden, United Kingdom, U.S., Canada, Australia, New Zealand, Israel, Ivory Coast, Papua New Guinea, Barbados and Dominican Republic. Some delegates disputed the claim that the massacre constituted genocide.

In 1982, an international commission investigated into reported violations of International Law by Israel during its invasion of the Lebanon. Chairman was Seán MacBride, the other members were Richard Falk, Kader Asmal, Brian Bercusson, Géraud de la Pradelle, and Stefan Wild. The commission's report concluded that "the government of Israel has committed acts of aggression contrary to international law", that the government of Israel had no valid reasons under international law for its invasion of Lebanon, and that the Israeli authorities or forces were directly or indirectly responsible for the massacres and killings, which have been reported to have been carried out by Lebanese militiamen in Sabra and the Shatila refugee camp in the Beirut area between 16 and 18 September.

Following a four-month investigation, on 8 February 1983, the Kahan Commission submitted its report, which was released to the public by spokesman Bezalel Gordon simultaneously in Hebrew and English. It concluded that direct responsibility rested with the Gemayel Phalangists led by Fadi Frem, and that no Israelis were deemed directly responsible, although Israel was held to be indirectly responsible:

> The decision on the entry of the Phalangists into the refugee camps was taken without consideration of the danger – which the makers and executors of the decision were obligated to foresee as probable – the Phalangists would commit massacres and pogroms against the inhabitants of the camps, and without an examination of the means for preventing this danger.

> Similarly, it is clear from the course of events that when the reports began to arrive about the actions of the Phalangists in the camps, no proper heed was taken of these reports, the correct conclusions were not drawn from them, and no energetic and immediate action were taken to restrain the Phalangists and put a stop to their actions.

In cinema

Several films were staged, based on the events of the 1982 war:
- *Cup Final* (1991)
- *Beaufort* (2007)
- *Waltz with Bashir* (2008)
- *Lebanon* (2009)

References

- ⓘ This article incorporates public domain material from the Library of Congress Country Studies website http://lcweb2.loc.gov/frd/cs/[1410].
- Chomsky, Noam (1983). *The Fateful Triangle: the United States, Israel and the Palestinians*. South End Press. ISBN 0-89608-187-7.
- Cobban, H. (1984). *The Palestinian Liberation Organization: People, Power and Politics*. Cambridge: Cambridge University Press. ISBN 0-521-27216-5.
- Fisk, Robert (2001). *Pity the Nation: Lebanon at War*[1411]. Oxford University Press. ISBN 978-0-19-280130-2.
- Friedman, Thomas (2006). *From Beirut to Jerusalem*. New York: Anchor Books. ISBN 0-385-41372-6.
- Herzog, Chaim; Gazit, Shlomo (2005). *The Arab-Israeli Wars: War and Peace in the Middle East*. Vintage Books. p. 560. ISBN 1-4000-7963-2.
- Maoz, Zeev (2006). *Defending the Holy Land: A Critical Analysis of Israel's Security and Foreign Policy*. Ann Arbor: The University of Michigan Press. ISBN 978-0-472-115402.
- Morris, Benny (1999). *Righteous Victims*. Alfred A. Knopf, New York. p. 768. ISBN 0-679-42120-3.
- Rabinovich, Abraham (2004). *The Yom Kippur War: The Epic Encounter That Transformed the Middle East*. Schocken Books. ISBN 978-0805211245.
- Reagan, Ronald (2007). Douglas Brinkley, ed. *The Reagan Diaries*. Harper Collins. ISBN 978-0-06-087600-5.
- Sayigh, Y. (1999). *Armed Struggle and the Search for State: The Palestinian National Movement, 1949–1993*. Oxford: Oxford University Press. ISBN 0-19-829643-6.
- Schiff, Ze'ev; Ya'ari, Ehud (1984). *Israel's Lebanon War*[1412]. New York, NY: Simon & Schuster. ISBN 0-671-47991-1.

- Seale, Patrick (1989). *Asad: The Struggle for Syria*. University of California Press. ISBN 0-520-06667-7.
- Shlaim, Avi (1999). *The Iron Wall: Israel and the Arab world*. Norton. ISBN 0-393-04816-0.
- Shlaim, Avi (2007). *Lion of Jordan; The life of King Hussein in War and Peace*. Allen Lane. ISBN 978-0-7139-9777-4.
- Bryce Walker & the editors of Time-Life books (1983). *Fighting Jets: The Epic of Flight*. Time Life Books. ISBN 978-0809433629.

Further reading

- Barzilai, Gad (1996). *Wars, Internal Conflicts, and Political Order: A Jewish Democracy in the Middle East*. New York University Press. ISBN 978-0-7914-2944-0.
- Bregman, Ahron (2002). *Israel's Wars: A History Since 1947*. London: Routledge. ISBN 0-415-28716-2.
- Brzoska, M.; Pearson, F. S. (1994). *Arms and Warfare: Escalation, De-Escalation, and Negotiation*. University of South Carolina Press. ISBN 0-87249-982-0.
- Gilbert, Martin (1998). *Israel: A History*. London: Black Swan. ISBN 0-688-12362-7.
- Harkabi, Y. (1989). *Israel's Fateful Hour*. New York, NY: Harper & Row. ISBN 0-06-091613-3.
- Penslar, Derek J. (2007). *Israel in History; The Jewish state in comparative perspective*. Routledge. ISBN 0-415-40036-8.
- Sela, Avraham (editor) (2002). "Arab-Israeli Conflict". *The Continuum Political Encyclopedia of the Middle East*. New York: Continuum. ISBN 978-0-8264-1413-7.

External links

 Wikimedia Commons has media related to *1982 Lebanon War*.

- Lebanese Civil War 1982[1413]
- A detailed account of 1982 Lebanon War – From Ariel Sharon's biography[1414]
- 1978 Israel – Lebanon Conflict[1415] by Ynetnews
- Ex-spymaster: First Lebanon War was Mossad success, despite Sabra and Chatila[1416] By Nachik Navot, *Haaretz*

1983–1992: Shamir I; Peres I; Shamir II

1983 Israel bank stock crisis

The **bank stock crisis** was a financial crisis that occurred in Israel in 1983, during which the stocks of the four largest banks in Israel collapsed. In previous episodes of share price weakness, the banks bought back their own stocks, creating the appearance of constant demand for the stock, and artificially supporting their values. By October 1983, the banks no longer had the capital to buy back shares and support the prices. Bank share prices collapsed. The Tel Aviv Stock Exchange closed for eighteen days beginning October 6, 1983. As a consequence, these banks were nationalized by the state.

History

During the 1970s, Bank Hapoalim, and its dominant manager, Yaakov Levinson, began attempting to control the bank's stock price on the Tel Aviv Stock Exchange. To this end they recommended to their customers to invest in the bank's stocks by fraudulently providing guarantees that the prices of shares in the banks would rise indefinitely. These investments allowed the bank to increase its available capital for investments, loans, etc. The bank also gave out generous loans to allow the customers to continue their investments, also profiting from the interest.

Other banks joined the practice, called *adjustments*. Eventually all major banks manipulated their stock price this way, among them Bank Leumi, Discount Bank, Bank Igud, Bank HaMizrachi, and Bank Clali (*General Bank*, now U-Bank). The only prominent bank not to join the adjustments frenzy was First International Bank of Israel (FIBI).Wikipedia:Citation needed

The adjustments were performed through the use of other companies. For example, Bank Leumi used the "Holdings and Development of The Jewish Colonial Trust Company". The funding for these actions originated in loans from the bank's pension funds and similar sources. Sometimes the banks would practice mutual purchases – one bank would sell its stocks to a second bank, and buy the second bank's stocks for a similar sum.

Under the pressure of the Israeli Securities and Exchange Commission, the banks reported the adjustments in their reports, but these reports were partial, misleading, and sometimes even false. Toward their clients the bank's acted in manner later described by the Beisky Commission as based in their own interests, ignoring the clients' interests.

The adjustment were made possible, in large part, due the banks' ownership structure. Bank Hapoalim was controlled by the Histadrut labor union's Workers Company (Hevrat HaOvdim) and Bank Leumi by the "Jewish Colonial Trust". The Hapoel HaMizrachi organisation had almost none of Bank HaMizrachi's stocks, but all of its control shares. The owners' representatives were usually members of the ruling political parties (especially Alignment, and the National Religious Party, or close to them). The banks' managers ran the banks for owners who understood little of banking, and did not involve themselves in these actions. The fourth major bank to join this practice, Discount Bank, was different insofar as management and control had not been ceded to outside managers.

Also contributing to the possibility of the adjustment was the capital structure of the Israeli market. During the years following the establishment of the State of Israel, the governments used the banks as a channel for procuring capital, and instructed them on how to invest their funds. This level of control, coupled with the control of interest rates, allowed the government to effectively "print money", by getting the banks to buy government bonds. Additionally, the banks usually assumed that since their investments and loans in major players of the Israeli market, such as the Kibutzim, were according to the government's wishes, the government would guarantee these loans.

Due to these reasons, the banks believed they could act as they pleased, without fearing the consequences. The banks used the adjustments to get "easy money" by issuing more and more stocks, until, during the 1980s, the banks' stocks accounted for more than 90% of all issued stocks in the stock market. They used the capital thus gained to give out loans and invest, often without due inspection of the debtor's creditworthiness. Also, the banks grew exponentially, building hundreds of new branches and hiring thousands of new employees. The banks' managers paid themselves lavish salaries, and expended money based on the banks' nominal profits, completely unrelated to their real profits.Wikipedia:Neutral point of viewTalk:1983 Israel bank stock crisis#

The large banks got addicted to the easy capital, but this method soon became a trap. Like the government, fearing recession, the banks avoided any move to limit their expenses. They feared for the pockets and jobs of the managers, but also the fact that the first bank to make such a move would appear inferior compared to the other banks.Wikipedia:Citation needed

All of the regulatory bodies were well aware of the adjustments regime, but aside from slight warnings, easily dismissed by the banks' managers, did nothing, failing even to warn the public. The Minister of the Treasury, Yoram Aridor, even remarked on television that had he had the funds to do so, he would invest in the stock market.

The adjustments were based in the promise of a constant rise in the banks' stock prices, irrelevant of the economic situation. The artificial prices thus achieved created an Economic bubble, where everyone involved continued investing growing sums of money for lesser returns. Every new issue of bank stocks further destabilized them, since more of the capital was invested in maintaining the adjustment regime, instead of profitable loans. Also, as the bank stock market share grew, the adjustment became weaker, as every cent (agora, actually) invested by them became a smaller part of the total invested capital.

The real gain (i.e. over and above the Consumer price index) by investing in the banks' stocks diminished, from a 41% gain in 1980, to 34% in 1981, to 28% in 1982. Other investment options, especially purchasing US Dollars became more appealing, and the banks had to transfer more and more funds from their offshore tax havens to keep maintaining the illusion of safety of investing in their stocks.

Crisis

In early 1983, the Tel Aviv stock exchange suffered share price weakness across all non-financial stocks. The banks invested heavily in all issues, hoping to maintain liquidity in the market. In January through March, some regulators, among them the Minister of Treasury, Aridor, and the Governor of the Bank of Israel, Mendelbaum, approached the banks several times, trying to get them to gradually reduce their adjustments. Although some bank managers realized they could not continue this for long, they did not stop. Fearing a market collapse, Ministry of Treasury officials kept knowledge of this from the public.

Failing to stop the banks, Ministry of Treasury heads wished to execute a large devaluation of the Shekel, serving as an excuse to stop the adjustments. However, the August 8% devaluation was far too small for that end. Additionally, the supplies in the stock market grew steadily, and reached new heights in September. The public unremittingly sold bank stocks, and purchased US Dollars.

Bank stocks remained under pressure. On October 2, the first day of trade after the Sukkot holiday, the public sold more bank stocks than in the entire month of September. On October 4, the Minister of Treasury appeared on television saying "We will not let the public dictate our moves", to say the large supplies would not bring about a devaluation or change of policy.

During those years the public trust in the Minister of Treasury's promises was non-existent.Wikipedia:Citation needed Most of the public assumed the minister would lie at any time, and gave no attention to his statements.Wikipedia:Citation needed Most of all, Aridor's denial made it clear that at this point the public *was* dictating the government's moves.

Later Aridor met with the banks' managers, who demanded the government limit the public's purchases of US Dollars, and allow it only for plane tickets. They assumed that without an option to save the money themselves, due to the high inflation, the public would be forced to invest in the banks' stocks. Even if their thesis was correct, one can assume such a move would only fuel the panic, and exacerbate the current crisis.

On October 5, the stock exchange again opened with large numbers of sell offers, and on October 6, 1983, nicknamed "Black Thursday", was an onslaught of sales. It was clear a collapse was a matter of days away at most, since the banks declared that day they would be unable to absorb additional supplies without government assistance.

That night, in a meeting in Aridor's home, it was decided that the government would purchase the banks' stocks from the public, to prevent the loss of their investments. On Sunday, October 9, the stock exchange remained closed, and stayed closed till October 24. In the meantime a devaluation of 23% was executed. The stocks sold by the public were bought by the Bank of Israel (the nation's central bank) at an average loss of 17%. Eventually, 35% of the stocks' value was lost.

Results

The immediate consequences of the crisis were the loss of a third of the public's investments in them, the acquisition of the banks by the government, at a total cost of $6.9 billion (for reference, Israel's entire GDP in 1983 was about $27 billion), and the nationalization of the major banks (Leumi, Hapoalim, HaMizrachi, Discount, and Clali).

Executives of each of the banks were convicted of criminal charges. Raphael Recanati of Discount Bank and Mordechai Einhorn of Bank Leumi were both sentenced to 8-month prison terms. Recanati's sentence was suspended on appeal when one of five charges was quashed. As part of the settlement, the controlling interest in Discount Bank, as well as the other banks, was ceded to the government.

Bejski Commission

Following the scandal, in 1984, the State Comptroller issued a report on the crisis, causing the State Review Committee of the Knesset, on January 7, 1985, to decide on establishing a national commission of inquiry. Heading the commission was Judge Moshe Bejski. The commission presented its findings on April 16, 1986.

The Bejski Commission came to the conclusion that the October 1983 crisis was a direct result of the stock adjustment. The commission pointed to four criminal offenses allegedly performed during the adjustment: financing and giving loans for the purchase of bank stock by the banks themselves; fraud and deceit of the client to get them to purchase stocks; conditioning one service on another; and perjury before the commission.

The commission's report states the regulatory bodies acted negligently and irresponsibly, but there were no recommendations for actions against them. Following the commission's conclusions, and after a long struggle, the banks' managers were dismissed, but no criminal charges were brought against them initially, as there was no "public interest" in that, according to the State's Attorney. In 1990 the Supreme Court decided to bring to trial the banks' managers, and the accountants who lied to the commission.

On the administrative side, the commission concluded that investment recommendation should be separated from ownership, that is, the banks should be separated from the Pension Funds and Trust Funds. These recommendations were not executed, due to the banks' pressure, and the government's conflict of interest, as the banks' owner at the time.

The government later sold some of the banks to private investors, selling Bank Hapoalim in 1996, and HaMizrachi in 1998. The government also sold a major part of its stock in Leumi bank in 2005, and of Discount in 2006.

In the early years of the 21st century, some of the commission's recommendations were finally put into place. After all four banks were sold by the mid-2000s, the recommendations of the subsequent Bach'ar commission, which reached the same conclusions regarding separating the banks' depository and investment banking/fund management operations as the Beisky commission's were finally carried out as well. It may be argued that the timing of the crisis may have also had some additional positive effect as the implementation of the subsequent tough banking regulations and reforms, albeit somewhat belatedly, were put in place just in time to help Israeli banks avert many of the problems experienced by banks in many other Western countries during the late-2000s financial crisis – by limiting Israeli banks' exposure to risky activities. This helped ensure a stable domestic banking sector which contributed significantly to the relative resilience of the Israeli economy in face of the late-2000s recession.

References

- Blass, A.; Grossman, R. (2001). "Assessing Damages: The 1983 Israeli Bank Shares Crisis". *Contemporary Economic Policy*. **19**: 49–58. doi: 10.1111/j.1465-7287.2001.tb00049.x[1417].<templatestyles src="Module:Citation/CS1/styles.css"></templatestyles>
- Gozansky, Tamar (2004). "The Roots of Israel's Economic Crisis". In Dan Leon. *Who's Left in Israel*[1418]. Sussex Academic Press.<templatestyles src="Module:Citation/CS1/styles.css"></templatestyles>
- Blass, Asher A.; Grossman, Richard S. (April 1998). "Who needs Glass-Steagall? Evidence from Israel's Bank Shares Crisis and The Great Depression". *Contemporary Economic Policy*. **16**: 185–196. doi: 10.1111/j.1465-7287.1998.tb00511.x[1419].<templatestyles src="Module:Citation/CS1/styles.css"></templatestyles>

South Lebanon conflict (1985–2000)

<indicator name="pp-default"> 🔒 </indicator>

South Lebanon conflict
Part of the Israeli–Lebanese conflict and the Iran–Israel proxy conflict

Israeli APCs approaching an SLA outpost in South Lebanon, 1987
Date 16 February 1985 – 25 May 2000
Location Southern Lebanon
Result Hezbollah victory[1420] • The collapse and surrender of the SLA and its South Lebanon security belt administration • Israeli withdrawal from South Lebanon • Shebaa Farms conflict
Belligerents
Israel South Lebanon Army	Hezbollah Amal Jammoul
Commanders and leaders
Antoine Lahad Aql Hashem † Shimon Peres Ariel Sharon Ehud Barak Brigadier General Erez Gerstein †	Abbas al-Musawi † Hassan Nasrallah George Hawi Elias Atallah Nabih Berri
Strength
SLA: 2,500 troops **IDF:** 1,000–1,500 troops	Unknown
Casualties and losses
SLA: 621 killed (1978–2000) (SLA claim) 1,050 killed 639 wounded (1982–1999) (Hezbollah claim) **IDF:** 559 killed[1421] (256 in combat) 840 wounded 7 Israeli civilians killed by rockets[1422]	**Hezbollah:** 1,276 killed (1982–2000)[1423] ~1,000 wounded (1982–1999) 270 Lebanese civilians killed 500 Lebanese civilians wounded

Figure 190: *The Blue Line covers the Lebanese-Israeli border; an extension covers the Lebanese-Golan Heights border*

The **South Lebanon conflict (1985–2000)** or the **Security Zone conflict in Lebanon** refers to 15 years of warfare between the Lebanese Christian proxy militias SLA with military and logistic support of Israel Defense Forces against Lebanese Muslim guerrillas led by the Iranian-backed Hezbollah, within what was defined as the "Security Zone" in South Lebanon.[1424] It can also refer to the continuation of conflict in this region, beginning with the Palestine Liberation Organization (PLO) operations transfer to South Lebanon, following Black September in the Kingdom of Jordan. Historical tension between Palestinian refugees and Lebanese factions fomented the violent Lebanese internal political struggle between many different factions. In light of this, the South Lebanon conflict can be seen as a part of the Lebanese Civil War.

In earlier conflicts prior to the 1982 Israeli invasion, including Operation Litani, Israel attempted to eradicate PLO bases from Lebanon and support Christian Maronite militias. The 1982 invasion resulted in the PLO's departure from Lebanon. The creation of the Security Zone in South Lebanon benefited civilian Israelis, although at great cost to Palestinian and Lebanese civilians. Despite this Israeli success in eradicating PLO bases and its partial withdrawal in 1985, the Israeli invasion increased the severity of conflict with local Lebanese militias and resulted in the consolidation of several local Shia Muslim movements in Lebanon, including Hezbollah and Amal, from a previously unorganized guerrilla movement in the south. Over the years, military casualties of both sides grew higher, as both parties used more modern weaponry, and Hezbollah progressed in its tactics. By the early 1990s, Hezbollah, with support from Syria and Iran, emerged as the leading group and military power, monopolizing guerrilla activity in South Lebanon.

By the year 2000, following an election campaign promise, newly elected Prime Minister Ehud Barak withdrew Israeli forces from Southern Lebanon within the year,[1425] in accordance with UN Security Council Resolution 425, passed in 1978; the withdrawal consequently resulted in the immediate total collapse of the South Lebanon Army.[1426] The Lebanese government and Hezbollah still consider the withdrawal incomplete until Israel withdraws from Shebaa Farms. Following the withdrawal, Hezbollah has monopolized its military and civil control of the southern part of Lebanon.

Background

Following the 1948 Arab–Israeli War, the 1949 Armistice Agreements were signed with United Nations mediation. The Lebanese–Israeli agreement created the armistice line, which coincided exactly with the existing international boundary between Lebanon and Palestine from the Mediterranean to the Syrian tri-point on the Hasbani River. From this tri-point on the Hasbani the boundary follows the river northward to the village of Ghajar, then northeast, forming the Lebanese–Syrian border. (The southern line from the tri-point represents the Palestine–Syria border of 1923.) Israeli forces captured and occupied 13 villages in Lebanese territory during the conflict, including parts of Marjayun, Bint Jubayl, and areas near the Litani River,[1427] but withdrew following international pressure and the armistice agreement.

Although the Israel–Lebanon border remained relatively quiet, entries in the diary of Moshe Sharett point to a continued territorial interest in the area.[1428] On 16 May 1954, during a joint meeting of senior officials of the defense and foreign affairs ministries, Ben Gurion raised the issue of Lebanon due to renewed tensions between Syria and Iraq, and internal trouble in Syria. Dayan expressed his enthusiastic support for entering Lebanon, occupying the necessary territory and creating a Christian regime that would ally itself with Israel. The issue was raised again in discussions at the Protocol of Sèvres.[1429]

The Israeli victory in the 1967 Six-Day War vastly expanded their area occupied in all neighboring countries, with the exception of Lebanon, but this extended the length of the effective Lebanon–Israel border, with the occupation of the Golan Heights. Although with a stated requirement for defense, later Israeli expansion into Lebanon under very similar terms followed the 1977 elections, which for the first time, brought the Revisionist Likud to power.

Emerging conflict between Israel and Palestinian militants

Beginning with the late 1960s and especially in the 1970s, following the defeat of PLO in Black September in Jordan, displaced Palestinians, including militants affiliated with the Palestinian Liberation Organization, began to settle in South Lebanon. The unrestrained buildup of Palestinian militia, and the large autonomy they exercised, led to the popular term "Fatahland"[1430] for South Lebanon. Since the mid 1970s the tensions between the various Lebanese factions and Palestinians had exploded, resulting in Lebanese Civil War.

Following multiple attacks launched by Palestinian organizations in the 1970, which increased with the Lebanese Civil War, the Israeli government decided to take action. Desiring to break up and destroy this PLO stronghold, Israel briefly invaded Lebanon in 1978, but the results of this invasion were mixed. The PLO was pushed north of the Litani River and a buffer zone was created to keep them from returning, with the placement of the United Nations Interim Force in Lebanon (UNIFIL). In addition and despite earlier covert support, Israel established a second buffer with renegade Saad Haddad's Christian Free Lebanon Army enclave (initially based only in the towns of Marjayoun and Qlayaa); the now-public Israeli military commitment to the Christian forces was strengthened. For the first time however, Israel received substantive adverse publicity in the world press due to damage in South Lebanon, in which some 200,000 Lebanese (mostly Shia Muslims) fled the area and ended up in the southern suburbs of Beirut; this indirectly resulted in the Syrian forces in Lebanon turning against the Christians in late June and complicated the dynamics of the ongoing Lebanese Civil War.[1431]

1982 Israeli invasion

In 1982, the Israeli military began "Operation Peace for Galilee",[1432] a full scale invasion of Lebanese territory. The invasion followed the 1978 Litani Operation, which gave Israel possession of the territory near the Israeli–Lebanese border. This follow-up invasion attempted to weaken the PLO as a unified political and military force[1433] and eventually led to the withdrawal of PLO and Syrian forces from Lebanon. By the end of this operation, Israel got control over Lebanon from Beirut southward, and attempted to install a pro-Israeli government in Beirut to sign a peace accord with it. This goal had never realized, partly because of the assassination of President Bashir Gemayel in September 1982, and the refusal of the Lebanese Parliament to endorse the accord. The withdrawal of the PLO forces in 1982 forced some Lebanese nationalists to start a resistance against the Israeli army led by the Lebanese Communist Party and Amal movement. During this time, some Amal members started the formation of an Islamic group supported by Iran that was the nucleus of the future "Islamic Resistance", and eventually become Hezbollah.

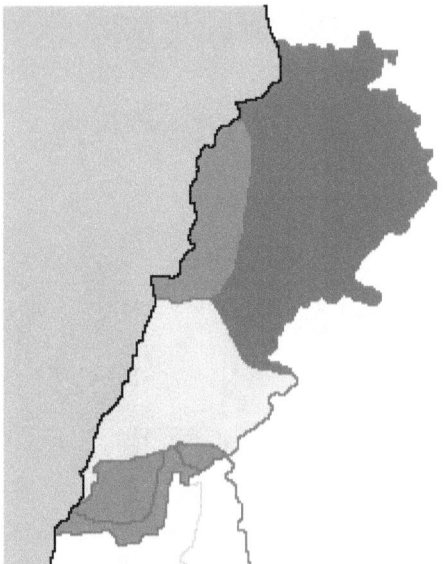

Figure 191: *Map showing power balance in Lebanon, 1983: Green – controlled by Syria, purple – controlled by Christian groups, yellow – controlled by Israel, blue – controlled by the United Nations*

Chronology

Occupation period 1982–1985 – the emergence of Hezbollah

Increased hostilities against the US resulted in the April 1983 United States Embassy bombing. In response, the US brokered the May 17 Agreement, in an attempt to stall hostilities between Israel and Lebanon. However, this agreement eventually failed to take shape, and hostilities continued. In October, the United States Marines barracks in Beirut was bombed (usually attributed to the Islamic Resistance groups). Following this incident, the United States withdrew its military forces from Lebanon.

Suicide bombings became increasingly popular at this time, and were a major concern of the Israel Defense Forces (IDF) both near Beirut and in the South. Among the most serious were the two suicide bombings against the Israeli headquarters in Tyre, which killed 103 soldiers, border policemen, and Shin Bet agents, and also killed 49–56 Lebanese. Israel believes those acts were among the first organized actions made by Shi'ite militants, later forming into Hizbullah. Subsequently, Israel withdrew from the Shouf Mountains, but continued to occupy Lebanon south of the Awali River.

Figure 192: *IDF military patrol near Ras Biada (1986)*

An increased number of Islamic militias began operating in South Lebanon, launching guerrilla attacks on Israeli and pro-Israel militia positions. Israeli forces often responded with increased security measures and airstrikes on militant positions, and casualties on all sides steadily climbed. In a vacuum left with eradication of PLO, the disorganized Islamic militants in South Lebanon began to consolidate. The emerging Hezbollah, soon to become the preeminent Islamic militia, evolved during this period. However, scholars disagree as to when Hezbollah came to be regarded as a distinct entity. Over time, a number of Shi'a group members were slowly assimilated into the organization, such as Islamic Jihad members, Organization of the Oppressed on Earth, and the Revolutionary Justice Organization.

Israeli withdrawal to Security Zone

In February 1985, Israel withdrew from Sidon and turned it over to the Lebanese Army, but faced attacks: 15 Israelis were killed and 105 wounded during the withdrawal. Dozens of SLA members were also assassinated. From mid-February to mid-March, the Israelis lost 18 dead and 35 wounded. On 11 March, Israeli forces raided the town of Zrariyah, killing 40 Amal fighters and capturing a large stock of arms. On 9 April, a Shiite girl drove a car bomb into an IDF convoy, and the following day, a soldier was killed by a land mine. During that same period, Israeli forces killed 80 Lebanese guerrillas in five

Figure 193: *IDF military patrol near Ayshiyeh Lebanon (1993)*

Figure 194: *Israeli tank position in Shamis al urqub near Aaichiye, South Lebanon (1997)*

Figure 195: *IDF military post Shakuf El-Hardun (1986)*

weeks. Another 1,800 Shi'as were taken as prisoners. Israel withdrew from the Bekaa valley on 24 April, and from Tyre on the 29th, but continued to occupy a security zone in Southern Lebanon.

Beginning of the security zone conflict

In 1985 Hezbollah released an open letter to "The Downtrodden in Lebanon and in the World", which stated that the world was divided between the oppressed and the oppressors. The oppressors were named to be mainly the United States and Israel. This letter legitimized and praised the use of violence against the enemies of Islam, mainly the West.

Israeli and SLA forces in the security zone began to come under attack. The first major incident occurred in August 1985, when Lebanese guerrillas believed to have been from Amal ambushed an Israeli convoy: two Israeli soldiers and three of the attackers were killed in the ensuing firefight.[1434]

Lebanese guerrilla attacks, mainly the work of Hezbollah, increased. Fighting the Israeli occupation included hit-and-run guerrilla attacks, suicide bombings, and the Katyusha rocket attacks on civilian targets in Northern Israel, including Kiryat Shmona. The Katyusha proved to be an effective weapon and became a mainstay of Hezbollah military capabilities in South Lebanon. The attacks resulted in both military and civilian casualties. However, a considerable number

Figure 196: *SLA outpost (1987)*

of Lebanese guerillas were killed fighting Israeli and SLA troops, and many were captured. Prisoners were often detained in Israeli military prisons, or by the SLA in the Khiam detention center, where detainees were often tortured. Lebanese prisoners in Israel were arrested and detained for participating in guerrilla movements, and many were held for long periods of time.

In 1987 Hezbollah fighters from the Islamic Resistance stormed and conquered an outpost in Bra'shit belonging to the South Lebanon Army in the security zone. A number of its defenders were killed or taken prisoner and the Hezbollah flag was raised on top of it. A Sherman tank was blown up and a M113 Armored Personal Carrier was captured and driven triumphantly all the way to Beirut.[1435]

In May 1988, Israel launched an offensive codenamed Operation Law and Order in which 1,500-2,000 Israeli soldiers raided the area around the Lebanese village of Maidun. In two days of fighting, the IDF killed 50 Hizbullah fighters while losing 3 dead and 17 wounded.[1436]

After Israel destroyed Hezbollah's headquarters in the town of Marrakeh, a Hezbollah suicide bomber destroyed an Israeli transport truck carrying soldiers on the Israel-Lebanon border. In response, Israeli forces ambushed two Hezbollah vehicles, killing eight Hezbollah fighters.[1437]

Figure 197: *IDF military patrol crossing the Khardala Bridge in south Lebanon (1988)*

On 28 July 1989, Israeli commandos captured Sheikh Abdul Karim Obeid, the leader of Hezbollah. This action led to the adoption of United Nations Security Council Resolution 638, which condemned all hostage takings by all sides.[1438]

Taif Accord

The Lebanese Civil War officially came to an end with the 1989 Ta'if Accord, but the armed combat continued at least until October 1990, and in South Lebanon until at least 1991.[1439] In fact, the continued Israeli presence in South Lebanon resulted in continued low-intensity warfare and sporadic major combat until the Israeli withdrawal in 2000.

Post Civil War conflict

Though the majority of the Lebanese civil war conflicts ended in the months following the Ta'if Accord, Israel kept maintaining a military presence in South Lebanon. Consequently, the Islamic Resistance, by now dominated by Hezbollah, continued operations in the South. On 16 February 1992, Hezbollah leader Abbas al-Musawi was killed along with his wife, son and four others when Israeli AH-64 Apache helicopter gunships fired three missiles at his motorcade. The Israeli attack came in retaliation for the killings of three Israeli soldiers two days earlier when their camp was infiltrated. Hezbollah responded with rocket fire onto the Israeli security zone, and Israel then fired back and

Figure 198: *IDF military patrol between Aaichiye to Rayhan (1995)*

Figure 199: *Beaufort IDF northern military post (1995)*

Figure 200: *Beaufort IDF northern military post (1993)*

Figure 201: *Carcom IDF military post in Lebanon (1998)*

South Lebanon conflict (1985–2000)

Figure 202: *IDF tank near Shreife IDF military post in Lebanon (1998)*

Figure 203: *Galagalit IDF military patrol south Lebanon (1999)*

sent two armored columns past the security zone to hit Hezbollah strongholds in Kafra and Yater.[1440] Musawi was succeeded by Hassan Nasrallah. One of Nasrallah's first public declarations was the "retribution" policy: If Israel hit Lebanese civilian targets, then Hezbollah would retaliate with attacks on Israeli territory. Meanwhile, Hezbollah continued attacks against IDF targets within occupied Lebanese territory. In response to the attack, Ehud Sadan, the chief of security at the Israeli Embassy in Turkey was assassinated by a car bomb.[1441]

In 1993, hostilities flared again. After a month of Hezbollah shelling on Israeli towns and attacks on its soldiers, Israel conducted a seven-day operation in July 1993 called Operation Accountability in order to hit Hezbollah. One Israeli soldier and 8–50 Hezbollah fighters were killed in the operation, along with 2 Israeli and 118 Lebanese civilians. After one week of fighting in South Lebanon, a mutual agreement mediated by the United States prohibited attacks on civilian targets by both parts.

The end of Operation Accountability saw a few days of calm before light shelling resumed. On August 17, a major artillery exchange took place, and two days later, nine Israeli soldiers were killed in two Hezbollah attacks. Israel responded with airstrikes against Hezbollah positions, killing at least two Hezbollah fighters.[1442]

Continued hostility in late 1990s

In May 1994, Israeli commandos kidnapped an Amal leader, Mustafa Dirani, and in June, an Israeli airstrike against a training camp killed 30–45 Hezbollah cadets. Hezbollah retaliated by firing four barrages of Katyusha rockets into northern Israel.[1443]

In May 1995, four Hezbollah fighters were killed in a firefight with Israeli troops while trying to infiltrate an Israeli position.[1444]

Operation Grapes of Wrath in 1996 resulted in the deaths of more than 150 civilians and refugees, most of them in the shelling of a United Nations base at Qana. Within a few days, a ceasefire was agreed between Israel and Hezbollah, committing to avoid civilian casualties; however, combat continued for at least two months. A total of 14 Hezbollah fighters, about a dozen Syrian soldiers, and 3 Israeli soldiers were killed in the fighting.Wikipedia:Citation needed

Brig. Gen. Eli Amitai, the IDF commander of the security zone, was lightly injured 14 December 1996 when an IDF convoy he was travelling in was ambushed in the eastern sector of the security zone. Less than a week later Amitai was again lightly injured when Hezbollah unleashed a mortar barrage on an SLA position near Bra'shit he was visiting together with Maj. Gen. Amiram Levine, head of the IDF's Northern Command.

In December 1996, two SLA soldiers were killed in three days of fighting, and a Hezbollah fighter was also killed by Israeli soldiers.[1445]

On 4 February 1997, two Israeli transport helicopters collided over She'ar Yashuv in Northern Israel while waiting for clearance to fly into Lebanon. A total of 73 IDF soldiers were killed in the disaster. On 28 February one Israeli soldier and four Hezbollah guerrillas were killed in a clash.

Throughout 1997, Israeli special forces, particularly the Egoz Reconnaissance Unit, hampered Hezbollah's ability to infiltrate the security zone and plant roadside bombs by staking out Hezbollah infiltration trails. Encouraged by these successes, Israeli commandos began conducting raids north of the security zone to kill Hezbollah commanders. In one particular raid, carried out on the night of August 3–4, 1997, Golani Brigade soldiers raided the village of Kfour and left behind three roadside bombs packed with ball bearings that were detonated from an Israeli Air Force UAV hours later, killing five Hezbollah members including two commanders. However, on August 28, a major friendly fire incident occurred in Wadi Saluki during a clash between IDF troops from the Golani Brigade, together with air and artillery support, and Amal militants. Although four Amal militants were killed, Israeli shelling started a fire that engulfed the area, killing four soldiers.[1446]

On 5 September 1997, a raid by 16 Israeli Shayetet 13 naval commandos failed after the troops stumbled into a Hezbollah and Amal ambush. As the force headed towards its target, it was ambushed with IEDs and subjected to withering fire that killed the commander, Lt. Col. Yossi Korakin, and caused bombs being carried by another soldier to explode, killing more of the force. The survivors radioed for help, and Israel immediately dispatched a rescue team from Unit 669 and Sayeret Matkal in two CH-53 helicopters. A rescue force of helicopters and missile boats arrived to provide support as the rescuers evacuated the dead and survivors, conducting airstrikes. Lebanese Army anti-aircraft units put up anti aircraft fire and fired illumination rounds at the helicopters, and an Israeli F-16 subsequently attacked an anti-aircraft position. Hezbollah put up mortar fire, killing a doctor with the rescue force and damaging a helicopter and Israeli missile boats fired at the source of the mortar fire. The battle ended when Israel, by means of contacting the US government and delivering a message to be passed on to Syria and from there to Hezbollah, threatened to respond with massive force if Hezbollah tried to stop the rescue mission, causing Hezbollah and Amal to cease fire while the Lebanese Army moved in. Twelve Israelis were killed, along with six Hezbollah and Amal fighters and two Lebanese soldiers. In 2010 Hassan Nasrallah claimed that Hezbollah had managed to hack into Israeli UAV:s flying over Lebanon and thus learn which route the commandos were planning to take and thus prepared the ambush accordingly.[1447] On September 13–14, IDF raids in Lebanon killed a further four Hezbollah fighters and six Lebanese soldiers.[1448]

On September 12, 1997, three Hezbollah fighters were killed in an ambush by Egoz commandos on the edge of the security zone. One of them was Hadi Nasrallah, the son of Hezbollah leader Hassan Nasrallah. On 25 May 1998 the remains of an Israeli soldiers killed in the failed commando raid were exchanged for 65 Lebanese prisoners and the bodies of 40 Hezbollah fighters and Lebanese soldiers captured by Israel. Among the bodies returned to Lebanon were the remains of Hadi Nasrallah.

During 1998, 21 Israeli soldiers were killed in southern Lebanon. Israel undertook a concerted campaign to hamper Hezbollah's capabilities, and in December 1998, the Israeli military assassinated Zahi Naim Hadr Ahmed Mahabi, a Hezbollah explosives expert, north of Baalbek.

23 February 1999 an IDF paratrooper unit on a night time patrol was ambushed in south Lebanon. Major Eitan Balahsan and two lieutenants were killed and another five soldiers were wounded.

Less than a week later (28 February) a roadside bomb exploded on the road between Kfar Ka'urkabeh and Arnoun in the Israeli-occupied security zone. Brigadier General Erez Gerstein, commander of the Golani Brigade and head of the IDF Liaison Unit in Lebanon, thus the highest ranking Israeli officer serving in Lebanon at the time, as well as two Druze Israeli soldiers and one Israeli journalist were killed in the blast.

In May 1999 Hezbollah forces simultaneously attacked 14 Israeli and SLA outposts in south Lebanon. The outpost in Beit Yahoun compound belonging to the SLA was overrun and one SLA soldier was taken prisoner. The Hizbullah fighters made off with an Armoured Personnel Carrier (APC). The area was bombed by the Israeli Air Force. The captured APC was paraded through the southern suburbs of Beirut.

In one notable battle, Hezbollah saboteurs surprised an IDF force from the Golani Brigade stationed in an old fort. Two Israeli soldiers and three Hezbollah fighters were killed.Wikipedia:Citation needed

In August 1999, Hezbollah commander Ali Hassan Deeb, better known as Abu Hassan, a leader in Hezbollah's special force, was assassinated in an Israeli military operation. Deeb was driving in Sidon when two roadside bombs were detonated by a remote signal from a UAV overhead.[1449]

Overall, in the course of 1999, several dozen Hezbollah and Amal fighters were killed. Twelve Israeli soldiers and one civilian were also killed, one of them in accident.

Figure 204: *A captured SLA Army tank, featuring a wooden portrait of the late Ayatollah Khomeini in the village of Hula*

2000: Israeli withdrawal

In July 1999, Ehud Barak became Israel's Prime Minister, promising Israel would unilaterally withdraw to the international border by July 2000. Prior to his actions, many believed that Israel would only withdraw from South Lebanon upon reaching an agreement with Syria.

In January 2000, Hezbollah assassinated the commander of the South Lebanon Army's Western Brigade, Colonel Aql Hashem, at his home in the security zone. Hashem had been responsible for day-to-day operations of the SLA and was a leading candidate to succeed General Antoine Lahad.[1450,1451] After this assassination there were doubts about the leadership of the South Lebanon Army (SLA). The pursuit and assassination of Hashim was documented step by step and the footage was broadcast on Hezbollah TV channel al-Manar. The operation and the way it was presented in media dealt a devastating blow to the morale in the SLA.[1452]

During the spring of 2000, Hezbollah operations stepped up considerably, with persistent harassment of Israeli military outposts in occupied Lebanese territory. As preparation for the major withdrawal plan, Israeli forces began abandoning several forward positions within the security zone of South Lebanon. On 24 May, Israel announced that it would withdraw all troops from South Lebanon. All Israeli forces had withdrawn from Lebanon by the end of the next day, more than six weeks before its stated deadline of 7 July.[1453]

The Israeli pullout resulted in the collapse of the SLA and the rapid advance of Hezbollah forces into the area. As the Israeli Defense Forces (IDF) withdrew, thousands of Shi'a Lebanese rushed back to the South to reclaim their properties. This withdrawal was widely considered a victory for Hezbollah and boosted its popularity in Lebanon. The completeness of the withdrawal is still disputed as Lebanese Government and Hezbollah claim Israel still holds Shebaa farms, a small piece of territory on the Lebanon-Israel-Syria border, with disputed sovereignty.

As a Syrian-backed Lebanese government refused to demarcate its border with Israel, Israel worked with UN cartographers led by regional coordinator Terje Rød-Larsen to certify Israel had withdrawn from all occupied Lebanese territory. On 16 June 2000, UN Security Council concluded that Israel had indeed withdrawn its forces from all of Lebanon, in accordance with United Nations Security Council Resolution 425 (1978).

Israel considered this move as tactical withdrawal since it always regarded the Security Zone as a buffer zone to defend Israel's citizens. By ending the occupation, Barak's cabinet assumed it would improve its worldwide image. Ehud Barak has argued that "Hezbollah would have enjoyed international legitimacy in their struggle against a foreign occupier", if the Israelis had not unilaterally withdrawn without a peace agreement.[1454]

Aftermath

Upon Israel's withdrawal, an increasing fear that Hezbollah would seek vengeance against those thought to have supported Israel became widespread among the Christian Lebanese of the Southern Lebanon. During and after the withdrawal around 10,000 Lebanese, mostly Maronites, fled into Galilee. Hezbollah later met with Lebanese Christian clerics to reassure them that the Israeli withdrawal was a victory for Lebanon as a nation, not just one sect or militia.Wikipedia:Accuracy dispute#Disputed statement

The tentative peace, resulting from the withdrawal, did not last. On 7 October 2000 Hezbollah attacked Israel. In a cross-border raid, three Israeli soldiers, who were patrolling the Lebanese border were attacked and abducted. The event escalated into a 2-month fire exchanges between Israel and Hezbollah, primarily at the Hermon ridge. The bodies of the abducted soldiers were returned to Israel in a January 2004 prisoner exchange involving 450 Lebanese prisoners held in Israeli jails. The long-time Lebanese prisoner Samir al-Quntar was excluded from the deal. The government of Israel, however, had agreed to a "further arrangement", whereby Israel would release Samir al-Quntar if it was supplied with "tangible information on the fate of captive navigator Ron Arad".

Figure 205: *An Israeli Army outpost, in 2007, as seen from the Lebanese side of the border*

According to Harel and Issacharoff the second phase of the prisoner exchange deal was only a "legal gimmick". Israel was not satisfied with the information supplied by Hezbollah and refused to release al-Quntar. "Cynics may well ask whether it was worth getting entangled in the Second Lebanon War just to keep Kuntar [...] in prison for an extra few years."

In July 2006, Hezbollah performed a cross-border raid while shelling Israeli towns and villages. During the raid Hezbollah succeeded in kidnapping two Israeli soldiers and killing eight others. In retaliation Israel began the 2006 Lebanon War to rescue the abducted soldiers and to create a bufferzone in Southern Lebanon.[1455,1456,1457,1458]

Figure 206: *IDF Bedouin memorial wall.*

First Intifada

<indicator name="pp-default"> 🔒 </indicator>

First Intifada	
Part of the Israeli–Palestinian conflict	

IDF roadblock outside Jabalya during the First Intifada, 1988	
Date	8 December 1987 – 13 September 1993 (5 years, 9 months and 5 days)
Location	• West Bank • Gaza Strip • Israel
Result	Palestinian popular uprising suppressed[1459] • Madrid Conference of 1991 and eventually Oslo I Accord: • Establishment of the Palestinian Authority • The PLO recognizes Israel[1460]

First Intifada

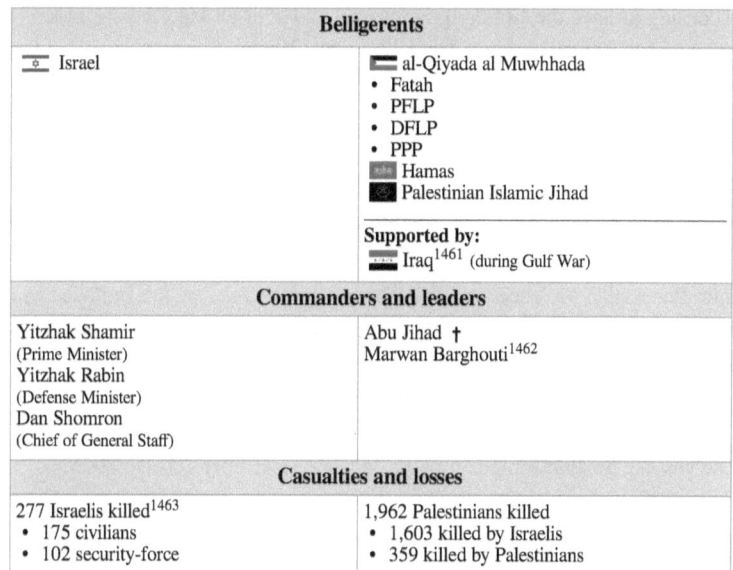

The **First Intifada** or **First Palestinian Intifada** (also known simply as **the intifada** or **intifadah**[note A]) was a Palestinian uprising against the Israeli occupation of the West Bank and Gaza.[1464] The uprising lasted from December 1987 until the Madrid Conference in 1991, though some date its conclusion to 1993, with the signing of the Oslo Accords.[1465]

The uprising began on 9 December, in the Jabalia refugee camp after an Israeli Defense Forces' (IDF) truck collided with a civilian car, killing four Palestinians.[1466,1467,1468] In the wake of the incident, a protest movement arose, involving a two-fold strategy of resistance and civil disobedience,[1469] consisting of general strikes, boycotts of Israeli Civil Administration institutions in the Gaza Strip and the West Bank, an economic boycott consisting of refusal to work in Israeli settlements on Israeli products, refusal to pay taxes, refusal to drive Palestinian cars with Israeli licenses, graffiti, barricading,[1470,1471] and widespread throwing of stones and Molotov cocktails at the IDF and its infrastructure within the West Bank and Gaza Strip.

Israel, deploying some 80,000 soldiers and initially firing live rounds, killed a large number of Palestinians. In the first 13 months, 332 Palestinians and 12 Israelis were killed. Given the high proportion of children, youths and civilians killed, it then adopted a policy of 'might, power, and beatings,' namely "breaking Palestinians' bones".[1472] The global diffusion of images of soldiers beating adolescents with clubs then led to the adoption of firing semi-lethal plastic bullets. In the intifada's first year, Israeli security forces killed 311 Palestinians, of which 53 were under the age of 17. Over the first two years, according to Save the Children, an estimated 7% of all Palestinians under 18 years of age suffered injuries from shootings, beatings, or tear gas.[1473] Over six years the IDF killed an estimated 1,162–1,204[1474] Palestinians. Between 23,600–29,900 Palestinian children required medical treatment from IDF beatings in the first 2 years.[1475]

Among Israelis, 100 civilians and 60 IDF personnel were killed[1476] often by militants outside the control of the Intifada's UNLU,[1477] and more than 1,400 Israeli civilians and 1,700 soldiers were injured.[1478]

Intra-Palestinian violence was also a prominent feature of the Intifada, with widespread executions of an estimated 822 Palestinians killed as alleged Israeli collaborators, (1988–April 1994).[1479] At the time Israel reportedly obtained information from some 18,000 Palestinians who had been compromised,[1480] although fewer than half had any proven contact with the Israeli authorities.[1481]

The ensuing Second Intifada took place from September 2000 to 2005.

General causes

According to Mubarak Awad, a Palestinian American clinical psychologist, the Intifada was a protest against Israeli repression including "beatings, shootings, killings, house demolitions, uprooting of trees, deportations, extended imprisonments, and detentions without trial".[1482] After Israel's capture of the West Bank, Jerusalem, Sinai Peninsula and Gaza Strip from Jordan and Egypt in the Six-Day War in 1967, frustration grew among Palestinians in the Israeli-occupied territories. Israel opened its labor market to Palestinians in the newly occupied territories. Palestinians were recruited mainly to do unskilled or semi-skilled labor jobs Israelis did not want. By the time of the Intifada, over 40 percent of the Palestinian work force worked in Israel daily. Additionally, Israeli confiscation of Palestinian land, high birth rates in the West Bank and Gaza Strip and the limited allocation of land for new building and agriculture created conditions marked by growing population density and rising unemployment, even for those with university degrees. At the time of the Intifada, only one in eight college-educated Palestinians could find degree-related work.[1483] Couple this with an expansion of a Palestinian university system catering to people from refugee camps, villages, and small towns generating new Palestinian elite from a lower social strata that was more activist and confrontational with Israel.[1484]

The Israeli Labor Party's Yitzhak Rabin, the then Defense Minister, added deportations in August 1985 to Israel's "Iron Fist" policy of cracking down on Palestinian nationalism.[1485] This, which led to 50 deportations in the following 4 years,[1486] was accompanied by economic integration and increasing Israeli settlements such that the Jewish settler population in the West Bank alone nearly doubled from 35,000 in 1984 to 64,000 in 1988, reaching 130,000 by the mid nineties. Referring to the developments, Israeli minister of Economics and Finance, Gad Ya'acobi, stated that "a creeping process of *de facto* annexation" contributed to a growing militancy in Palestinian society.[1487]

During the 1980s a number of mainstream Israeli politicians referred to policies of transferring the Palestinian population out of the territories leading to Palestinian fears that Israel planned to evict them. Public statements calling for transfer of the Palestinian population were made by Deputy Defense minister Michael Dekel, Cabinet Minister Mordechai Tzipori and government Minister Yosef Shapira among others. Describing the causes of the Intifada, Benny Morris refers to the "all-pervading element of humiliation", caused by the protracted occupation which he says was "always a brutal and mortifying experience for the occupied" and was "founded on brute force, repression and fear, collaboration and treachery, beatings and torture chambers, and daily intimidation, humiliation, and manipulation"

Background

While the immediate cause for the First Intifada is generally dated to a truck incident involving several Palestinian fatalities at the Erez Crossing in December 1987, Mazin Qumsiyeh argues, against Donald Neff, that it began with multiple youth demonstrations earlier in the preceding month.[1488] Some sources consider that the perceived IDF failure in late November 1987 to stop a Palestinian guerrilla operation, the Night of the Gliders, in which six Israeli soldiers were killed, helped catalyze local Palestinians to rebel.[1489]

Mass demonstrations had occurred a year earlier when, after two Gaza students at Birzeit University had been shot by Israeli soldiers on campus on 4 December 1986, the Israelis responded with harsh punitive measures, involving summary arrest, detention and systematic beatings of handcuffed Palestinian youths, ex-prisoners and activists, some 250 of whom were detained in four cells inside a converted army camp, known popularly as Ansar 11, outside Gaza city.[1490] A policy of deportation was introduced to intimidate activists in January 1987. Violence simmered as a schoolboy from Khan Yunis was shot dead by Israelis soldiers pursuing him in a Jeep. Over the summer the IDF's Lieutenant Ron Tal, who was responsible for guarding detainees at Ansar 11, was shot dead at point-blank range while stuck in a Gaza traffic jam. A curfew forbidding Gaza residents from leaving their homes was imposed for three days, during the Muslim feast of Eid al-Adha. In two incidents on 1 and 6 October 1987, respectively, the IDF ambushed and killed seven Gaza men, reportedly affiliated with Islamic Jihad, who had escaped from prison in May.[1491] Some days later, a 17-year-old schoolgirl, Intisar al-'Attar, was shot in the back while in her schoolyard in Deir al-Balah by a settler in the

Gaza Strip.[1492] The Arab summit in Amman in November 1987 focused on the Iran–Iraq War, and the Palestinian issue was shunted to the sidelines for the first time in years.[1493,1494]

Leadership and aims

The Intifada was not initiated by any single individual or organization. Local leadership came from groups and organizations affiliated with the PLO that operated within the Occupied Territories; Fatah, the Popular Front, the Democratic Front and the Palestine Communist Party.[1495] The PLO's rivals in this activity were the Islamic organizations, Hamas and Islamic Jihad as well as local leadership in cities such as Beit Sahour and Bethlehem. However, the uprising was predominantly led by community councils led by Hanan Ashrawi, Faisal Husseini and Haidar Abdel-Shafi, that promoted independent networks for education (underground schools as the regular schools were closed by the military in reprisal for the uprising), medical care, and food aid.[1496] The Unified National Leadership of the Uprising (UNLU) gained credibility where the Palestinian society complied with the issued communiques. There was a collective commitment to abstain from lethal violence, a notable departure from past practice,[1497] which, according to Shalev arose from a calculation that recourse to arms would lead to an Israeli bloodbath and undermine the support they had in Israeli liberal quarters. The PLO and its chairman Yassir Arafat had also decided on an unarmed strategy, in the expectation that negotiations at that time would lead to an agreement with Israel. Pearlman attributes the non-violent character of the uprising to the movement's internal organization and its capillary outreach to neighborhood committees that ensured that lethal revenge would not be the response even in the face of Israeli state repression.[1498] Hamas and Islamic Jihad cooperated with the leadership at the outset, and throughout the first year of the uprising conducted no armed attacks, except for the stabbing of a soldier in October 1988, and the detonation of two roadside bombs, which had no impact.[1499]

Leaflets publicizing the uprising's aims demanded the complete withdrawal of Israel from the territories it had occupied in 1967: the lifting of curfews and checkpoints; it appealed to Palestinians to join in civic resistance, while asking them not to employ arms, since military resistance would only invite devastating retaliation from Israel; it also called for the establishment of the Palestinian state on the West Bank and the Gaza Strip, abandoning the standard rhetorical calls, still current at the time, for the "liberation" of all of Palestine.[1500]

Figure 207: *An IDF soldier requesting a resident of Jabalia to erase a slogan on a wall during the first intifada.*

The Intifada

Israel's drive into the occupied territories had occasioned spontaneous acts of resistance, but the administration, pursuing an "iron fist" policy of deportations, demolition of homes, collective punishment, curfews and the suppression of political institutions, was confident that Palestinian resistance was exhausted. The assessment that the unrest would collapse proved to be mistaken.[1501]

On 8 December 1987, an Israeli army tank transporter crashed into a row of cars containing Palestinians returning from working in Israel, at the Erez checkpoint. Four Palestinians, three of them residents of the Jabalya refugee camp, the largest of the eight refugee camps in the Gaza Strip, were killed and seven others seriously injured. The traffic incident was witnessed by hundreds of Palestinian labourers returning home from work.[1502] The funerals, attended by 10,000 people from the camp that evening, quickly led to a large demonstration. Rumours swept the camp that the incident was an act of intentional retaliation for the stabbing to death of an Israeli businessman, killed while shopping in Gaza two days earlier.[1503,1504] Following the throwing of a petrol bomb at a passing patrol car in the Gaza Strip on the following day, Israeli forces, firing with live ammunition and tear gas canisters into angry crowds, shot one young Palestinian dead and wounded 16 others.[1505,1506]

Figure 208: *An Improvised tire puncturing device (slang term 'Ninja') comprising an iron nail inserted into a rubber disc (from used tire). Many of these makeshift weapons were scattered by Palestinians on main roads in the occupied territories of the West Bank during the First Intifada.*

On 9 December, several popular and professional Palestinian leaders held a press conference in West Jerusalem with the Israeli League for Human and Civil Rights in response to the deterioration of the situation. While they convened, reports came in that demonstrations at the Jabalya camp were underway and that a 17-year-old youth had been shot to death after throwing a petrol bomb at Israeli soldiers. She would later become known as the first martyr of the intifada.[1507,1508] Protests rapidly spread into the West Bank and East Jerusalem. Youths took control of neighbourhoods, closed off camps with barricades of garbage, stone and burning tires, meeting soldiers who endeavoured to break through with petrol bombs. Palestinian shopkeepers closed their businesses, and labourers refused to turn up to their work in Israel. Israel defined these activities as 'riots', and justified the repression as necessary to restore 'law and order'.[1509] Within days the occupied territories were engulfed in a wave of demonstrations and commercial strikes on an unprecedented scale. Specific elements of the occupation were targeted for attack: military vehicles, Israeli buses and Israeli banks. None of the dozen Israeli settlements were attacked and there were no Israeli fatalities from stone-throwing at cars at this early period of the outbreak.[1510] Equally unprecedented was the extent of mass participation in these disturbances: tens of thousands of civilians, including women and children. The Israeli security forces used the full panoply of crowd control measures to try and quell the disturbances: cudgels, nightsticks, tear gas, water cannons, rubber bullets, and live ammunition. But the disturbances only gathered momentum.[1511]

Soon there was widespread rock-throwing, road-blocking and tire burning throughout the territories. By 12 December, six Palestinians had died and 30 had been injured in the violence. The next day, rioters threw a gasoline bomb at the U.S. consulate in East Jerusalem though no one was hurt. The Israeli response to the Palestinian uprising was harsh. The IDF killed many Palestinians at the beginning of the Intifada, the majority killed during demonstrations and riots. Since initially a high proportion of those killed were civilians and youths, Yitzhak Rabin adopted a fallback policy of 'might, power and beatings'.[1512] Israel used mass arrests of Palestinians, engaged in collective punishments like closing down West Bank universities for most years of the uprising, and West Bank schools for a total of 12 months. Round-the-clock curfews were imposed over 1600 times in just the first year. Communities were cut off from supplies of water, electricity and fuel. At any one time, 25,000 Palestinians would be confined to their homes. Trees were uprooted on Palestinians farms, and agricultural produce blocked from being sold. In the first year over 1,000 Palestinians had their homes either demolished or blocked up. Settlers also engaged in private attacks on Palestinians. Palestinian refusals to pay taxes were met with confiscations of property and licenses, new car taxes, and heavy fines for any family whose members had been identified as stone-throwers.[1513]

Casualties

In the first year in the Gaza Strip alone, 142 Palestinians were killed, while no Israelis died. 77 were shot dead, and 37 died from tear-gas inhalation. 17 died from beatings at the hand of Israeli police or soldiers.[1514] During the whole six-year intifada, the Israeli army killed from 1,162-1,204 (or 1,284)[1515] Palestinians,241/332 being children. From 57,000 to 120,000 were arrested.[1516] 481 were deported while 2,532 had their houses razed to the ground. Between December 1987 and June 1991, 120,000 were injured, 15,000 arrested and 1,882 homes demolished.[1517] One journalistic calculation reports that in the Gaza Strip alone from 1988 to 1993, some 60,706 Palestinians suffered injuries from shootings, beatings or tear gas.[1518] In the first five weeks alone, 35 Palestinians were killed and some 1,200 wounded, a casualty rate that only energized the uprising by drawing more Palestinians into participating.[1519] B'Tselem calculated 179 Israelis killed, while official Israeli statistics place the total at 200 over the same period. 3,100 Israelis, 1,700 of them soldiers, and 1,400 civilians suffered injuries. By 1990 Ktzi'ot Prison in the Negev held approximately one out of every 50 West Bank and Gazan males older than 16 years.[1520] Gerald Kaufman remarked: "[F]riends of Israel as well as foes have been shocked and saddened by that country's response to the disturbances."[1521] In an article in the London Review of Books, John Mearsheimer and Stephen Walt asserted that IDF soldiers were given truncheons and encouraged to break the bones of Palestinian protesters. The Swedish branch of Save the Children estimated that "23,600 to 29,900 children required medical treatment for their beating injuries in the first two years of the Intifada", one third of whom were children under the age of ten years.

Israel adopted a policy of arresting key representatives of Palestinian institutions. After lawyers in Gaza went on strike to protest their inability to visit their detained clients, Israel detained the deputy head of its association without trial for six months. Dr. Zakariya al-Agha, the head of the Gaza Medical Association, was likewise arrested and held for a similar period of detention, as were several women active in Women's Work Committees. During Ramadan, many camps in Gaza were placed under curfew for weeks, impeding residents from buying food, and Al-Shati, Jabalya and Burayj were subjected to saturation bombing by tear gas. During the first year of the Intifada, the total number of casualties in the camps from such bombing totalled 16.[1522]

Intra-communal violence

Between 1988 and 1992, intra-Palestinian violence claimed the lives of nearly 1,000. By June 1990, according to Benny Morris, "[T]he Intifada seemed to have lost direction. A symptom of the PLO's frustration was the great increase in the killing of suspected collaborators."[1523] Roughly 18,000 Palestinians, compromised by Israeli intelligence, are said to have given information to the other side. Collaborators were threatened with death or ostracism unless they desisted, and if their collaboration with the Occupying Power continued, were executed by special troops such as the "Black Panthers" and "Red Eagles". An estimated 771 (according to Associated Press) to 942 (according to the IDF) Palestinians were executed on suspicion of collaboration during the span of the Intifada.[1524]

Other notable events

On 16 April 1988, a leader of the PLO, Khalil al-Wazir, *nom de guerre* Abu Jihad or 'Father of the Struggle', was assassinated in Tunis by an Israeli commando squad. Israel claimed he was the 'remote-control "main organizer" of the revolt', and perhaps believed that his death would break the back of the intifada. During the mass demonstrations and mourning in Gaza that followed, two of the main mosques of Gaza were raided by the IDF and worshippers were beaten and tear-gassed.[1525] In total between 11 and 15 Palestinians were killed during the demonstrations and riots in Gaza and West Bank that followed al-Wazir's death. In June of that year, the Arab League agreed to support the intifada financially at the 1988 Arab League summit. The Arab League reaffirmed its financial support in the 1989 summit.[1526]

Israeli defense minister Yitzhak Rabin's response was: "We will teach them there is a price for refusing the laws of Israel."[1527] When time in prison did not stop the activists, Israel crushed the boycott by imposing heavy fines and seizing and disposing of equipment, furnishings, and goods from local stores, factories and homes.[1528]

On 8 October 1990, 22 Palestinians were killed by Israeli police during the Temple Mount riots. This led the Palestinians to adopt more lethal tactics, with three Israeli civilians and one IDF soldier stabbed in Jerusalem and Gaza two weeks later. Incidents of stabbing persisted.[1529] The Israeli state apparatus carried out contradictory and conflicting policies that were seen to have injured Israel's own interests, such as the closing of educational establishments (putting more youths onto the streets) and issuing the Shin Bet list of collaborators.[1530] Suicide bombings by Palestinian militants started on 16 April 1993 with the Mehola Junction bombing, carried at the end of the Intifada.

United Nations

The large number of Palestinian casualties provoked international condemnation. In subsequent resolutions, including 607 and 608, the Security Council demanded Israel cease deportations of Palestinians. In November 1988, Israel was condemned by a large majority of the UN General Assembly for its actions against the intifada. The resolution was repeated in the following years.[1531]

Security Council

On 17 February 1989, the UN Security Council unanimously but for US condemned Israel for disregarding Security Council resolutions, as well as for not complying with the fourth Geneva Convention. The United States, put a veto on a draft resolution which would have strongly deplored it. On 9 June, the US again put a veto on a resolution. On 7 November, the US vetoed a third draft resolution, condemning alleged Israeli violations of human rights[1532]

On 14 October 1990, Israel openly declared that it would not abide Security Council Resolution 672 because it did not pay attention to attacks on Jewish worshippers at the Western Wall. Israel refused to receive a delegation of the Secretary-General, which would investigate Israeli violence. The following Resolution 673 made little impression and Israel kept on obstructing UN investigations.[1533]

Outcomes

The Intifada was recognized as an occasion where the Palestinians acted cohesively and independently of their leadership or assistance of neighbouring Arab states.[1534,1535]

The Intifada broke the image of Jerusalem as a united Israeli city. There was unprecedented international coverage, and the Israeli response was criticized in media outlets and international fora.[1536,1537]

The success of the Intifada gave Arafat and his followers the confidence they needed to moderate their political programme: At the meeting of the Palestine National Council in Algiers in mid-November 1988, Arafat won a majority for the historic decision to recognise Israel's legitimacy; to accept all the relevant UN resolutions going back to 29 November 1947; and to adopt the principle of a two-state solution.[1538]

Jordan severed its residual administrative and financial ties to the West Bank in the face of sweeping popular support for the PLO.[1539] The failure of the "Iron Fist" policy, Israel's deteriorating international image, Jordan cutting legal and administrative ties to the West Bank, and the U.S.'s recognition of the PLO as the representative of the Palestinian people forced Rabin to seek an end to the violence though negotiation and dialogue with the PLO.[1540,1541]

In the diplomatic sphere, the PLO opposed the Persian Gulf War in Iraq. Afterwards, the PLO was isolated diplomatically, with Kuwait and Saudi Arabia cutting off financial support, and 300,000-400,000 Palestinians fled or were expelled from Kuwait before and after the war. The diplomatic process led to the Madrid Conference and the Oslo Accords.[1542]

The impact on the Israeli services sector, including the important Israeli tourist industry, was notably negative.[1543]

Notes

- ^**Note A** The word *intifada* (انتفاضة) is an Arabic word meaning "uprising". Its strict Arabic transliteration is *intifāḍah*.

Bibliography

- Ackerman, Peter; DuVall, Jack (2000). *A Force More Powerful: A Century of Nonviolent Conflict*[1544]. New York: Palgrave. ISBN 978-0-312-24050-9.<templatestyles src="Module:Citation/CS1/styles.css"></templatestyles>
- Alimi, Eitan Y. (2006). *Israeli Politics and the First Palestinian Intifada*[1545] (2007 hardback ed.). Abingdon: Routledge. ISBN 978-0-415-38560-2.<templatestyles src="Module:Citation/CS1/styles.css"></templatestyles>
- Aronson, Geoffrey (1990). *Israel, Palestinians, and the Intifada: Creating Facts on the West Bank*. London: Kegan Paul International. ISBN 978-0-7103-0336-3.<templatestyles src="Module:Citation/CS1/styles.css"></templatestyles>
- Berman, Eli (2011). *Radical, Religious, and Violent: The New Economics of Terrorism*[1546]. MIT Press. p. 314. ISBN 978-0262258005.<templatestyles src="Module:Citation/CS1/styles.css"></templatestyles>
- Finkelstein, Norman (1996). *The Rise and Fall of Palestine: A Personal Account of the Intifada Years*. Minnesota: University Press. ISBN 978-0-8166-2858-2.<templatestyles src="Module:Citation/CS1/styles.css"></templatestyles>
- Hiltermann, Joost R. (1991). *Behind the Intifada: Labor and Women's Movements in the Occupied Territories*[1547] (1993 reprint ed.). Princeton, N.J: Princeton University Press. ISBN 978-0-691-07869-4.<templatestyles src="Module:Citation/CS1/styles.css"></templatestyles>
- King, Mary Elizabeth (2007). *A Quiet Revolution: The First Palestinian Intifada and Nonviolent Resistance*. New York: Nation Books. ISBN 978-1-56025-802-5.<templatestyles src="Module:Citation/CS1/styles.css"></templatestyles>
- Lockman, Zachary; Beinin, Joel, eds. (1989). *Intifada: The Palestinian Uprising Against Israeli Occupation*[1548]. Cambridge, MA: South End Press. ISBN 978-0-89608-363-9.<templatestyles src="Module:Citation/CS1/styles.css"></templatestyles>
- McDowall, David (1989). *Palestine and Israel: The Uprising and Beyond*[1549]. California: University Press. ISBN 978-0-520-06902-2.<templatestyles src="Module:Citation/CS1/styles.css"></templatestyles>
- Morris, Benny (1999). *Righteous Victims: a History of the Zionist-Arab conflict, 1881-1999*. New York:

Knopf. ISBN 978-0-679-74475-7.<templatestyles src="Module:Citation/CS1/styles.css"></templatestyles>
- Nassar, Jamal Raji; Heacock, Roger, eds. (1990). *Intifada: Palestine at the Crossroads*[1550]. New York: Praeger Publishers. ISBN 978-0-275-93411-8.<templatestyles src="Module:Citation/CS1/styles.css"></templatestyles>
- Peretz, Don (1990). *Intifada: The Palestinian Uprising*. Boulder, Colorado: Westview Press. ISBN 978-0-8133-0860-9.<templatestyles src="Module:Citation/CS1/styles.css"></templatestyles>
- Rigby, Andrew (1991). *Living the Intifada*. London: Zed Books. ISBN 978-1-85649-040-5.<templatestyles src="Module:Citation/CS1/styles.css"></templatestyles>, out-of-print, now downloadable at civilresistance.info[1551]
- Roberts, Adam; Garton Ash, Timothy, eds. (2009). *Civil Resistance and Power Politics: The Experience of Nonviolent Action from Gandhi to the Present*[1552]. Oxford: University Press. ISBN 978-0-19-955201-6.<templatestyles src="Module:Citation/CS1/styles.css"></templatestyles>
- Shay, Shaul (2005). *The Axis of Evil: Iran, Hizballah, and the Palestinian Terror*[1553]. Transaction Publishers. ISBN 978-0-7658-0255-2.<templatestyles src="Module:Citation/CS1/styles.css"></templatestyles>
- Schiff, Ze'ev; Ya'ari, Ehud (1989). *Intifada: The Palestinian Uprising: Israel's Third Front*. New York: Simon & Schuster. ISBN 978-0-671-67530-1.<templatestyles src="Module:Citation/CS1/styles.css"></templatestyles>
- Shalev, Aryeh (1991). *The Intifada: Causes and Effects*. Jerusalem: Jerusalem Post & Westview Press. ISBN 978-0-8133-8303-3.<templatestyles src="Module:Citation/CS1/styles.css"></templatestyles>
- Shlaim, Avi (2000). *The Iron Wall: Israel and the Arab World*. London: Penguin. ISBN 978-0-14-028870-4.<templatestyles src="Module:Citation/CS1/styles.css"></templatestyles>

External links

 Wikimedia Commons has media related to *First Intifada*.

- Jewish Virtual Library[1554]
- The Intifada in Palestine:Introduction[1555] (www.intifada.com)
- United Nations Security Council Resolution 605[1556]
- Palestinian Arab "collaborators"[1557] (Guardian, UK)
- The Future of a Rebellion - Palestine[1558] An analysis of the 1980s intifada revolt of Palestinian youth. on libcom.org
- U.S. Involvement with Palestine's Rebellions[1559] from the Dean Peter Krogh Foreign Affairs Digital Archives[1560]
- Israel's Post-Soviet Expansion[1561] from the Dean Peter Krogh Foreign Affairs Digital Archives[1560]

1992–1996: Rabin II; Peres II

Oslo Accords

<indicator name="pp-default"> 🔒 </indicator>

- v
- t
- e[1562]

The **Oslo Accords** are a set of agreements between the Government of Israel and the Palestine Liberation Organization (PLO): the Oslo I Accord, signed in Washington, D.C., in 1993;[1563] and the Oslo II Accord, signed in Taba,

Egypt, in 1995.[1564] The Oslo Accords marked the start of the **Oslo process**, a peace process aimed at achieving a peace treaty based on United Nations Security Council Resolutions 242 and 338, and at fulfilling the "right of the Palestinian people to self-determination." The Oslo process started after secret negotiations in Oslo, resulting in the recognition by the PLO of the State of Israel and the recognition by Israel of the PLO as the representative of the Palestinian people and as a partner in negotiations.

The Oslo Accords created a Palestinian Authority tasked with limited self-governance of parts of the West Bank and Gaza Strip; and acknowledged the PLO as Israel's partner in permanent-status negotiations about remaining questions. The most important questions relate to the borders of Israel and Palestine, Israeli settlements, the status of Jerusalem, Israel's military presence in and control over remaining territories after Israel's recognition of Palestinian autonomy, and the Palestinian right of return. The Oslo Accords, however, did not create a Palestinian state.[1565]

The Oslo process

The Oslo process is the "peace process" that started in 1993 with secret talks between Israel and the PLO. It became a cycle of negotiations, suspension, mediation, restart of negotiations and suspension again. A number of agreements were reached, until the Oslo process ended after the failure of the Camp David Summit in 2000 and the outbreak of the Second Intifada.[1566,1567]

During the *Second Intifada*, the Roadmap for Peace was introduced, which explicitly aimed at a two-state solution and the establishment of an independent Palestinian state. The Roadmap, however, soon entered a cycle similar to the Oslo process, but without producing any agreement.

Background

The Oslo Accords are based on the 1978 Camp David Accords and show therefore considerable similarity with those Accords.[1568] The Camp David's *"Framework for Peace in the Middle East"* envisioned autonomy for the local, and *only* for the local, (Palestinian) inhabitants of West Bank and Gaza. At the time, there lived some 7,400 settlers in the West Bank (excluding East Jerusalem),[1569] and 500 in Gaza,[1570] with the number in the West Bank, however, rapidly growing. As Israel regarded the PLO a terrorist organisation, it refused to talk with the sole representative of the Palestinian people. Instead, Israel preferred to negotiate with Egypt and Jordan, and *"elected representatives of the inhabitants of the West Bank and Gaza"*.

While the final goal in Camp David was a *"peace treaty between Israel and Jordan, taking into account the agreement reached in the final status of the West Bank and Gaza"*, the Oslo negotiations were directly between Israel and the PLO and aimed at a peace treaty directly between these groups. The Oslo Accords, like the 1978 Camp David Accords, merely aimed at an interim agreement that allowed first steps. This was intended to be followed by negotiation of a complete settlement within five years. When, however, an Israel–Jordan peace treaty was concluded on 26 October 1994, it was without the Palestinians.

Both plans had in common that, possibly intentionally, they did not have a "Plan B" in case a final agreement would not be reached within the set period.

Negotiation partners

Mutual recognition of sides

Only after Israel's acceptance of the PLO as negotiation partner could serious negotiations start. In their Letters of Mutual Recognition of 9 September 1993, days before the signing of the Oslo I Accord, each party agreed to accept the other as a negotiation partner.[1571] The PLO recognized the State of Israel. Israel recognized the PLO as *"the representative of the Palestinian people"*; no more, no less.

Principal participants

Palestinians

- Yasser Arafat – PLO leader during the Oslo peace process
- Ahmed Qurei (a.k.a. Abu Ala) – PLO negotiator during the Oslo peace process

Israel

- Yossi Beilin – Israeli negotiator during the Oslo peace process
- Yair Hirschfeld – Israeli negotiator during the Oslo peace process
- Shimon Peres – Israeli Foreign Minister during the Oslo peace process
- Ron Pundak – formed first Israeli negotiating team with Hirschfeld, before official Israeli involvement
- Yitzhak Rabin – Israeli Prime Minister during the Oslo peace process
- Uri Savir – former Director General of the Israeli Foreign Ministry, head of the Israeli negotiating team

Norway (facilitating)

- Jan Egeland – Norwegian Deputy Foreign Minister, provided political cover, facilities and finances for the negotiations

- Johan Jørgen Holst – Norwegian Minister of Foreign Affairs
- Terje Rød-Larsen - Norwegian facilitator during the negotiations
- Mona Juul – Norwegian facilitator during the negotiations

Outline of the peace plan

Stated goals of the Oslo Accords were among other things, Palestinian *interim* Self-Government (not the Palestinian Authority, but the Palestinian Legislative Council)[1572] and a permanent settlement of unresolved issues within five years, based on Security Council Resolutions 242 and 338. Although the agreements recognize the Palestinian "legitimate and political rights," they remain silent about their fate after the interim period. The Oslo Accords neither define the nature of the post-Oslo Palestinian self-government and its powers and responsibilities, nor do they define the borders of the territory it eventually would govern.

A core issue of the Oslo Accords was the withdrawal of the Israeli military from Palestinian territories. The plan was a withdrawal in phases and a simultaneous transfer of responsibilities to the Palestinian authorities for maintaining security. Oslo II, Article X.2 reads:

"Further redeployments of Israeli military forces to specified military locations will commence after the inauguration of the Council and will be gradually implemented commensurate with the assumption of responsibility for public order and internal security by the Palestinian Police ..."

And Article XI.2.e:

"During the further redeployment phases to be completed within 18 months from the date of the inauguration of the Council, powers and responsibilities relating to territory will be transferred gradually to Palestinian jurisdiction that will cover West Bank and Gaza Strip territory, except for the issues that will be negotiated in the permanent status negotiations."

The first phase included the withdrawal from the Areas A and B. Redeployments from Area C would follow in subsequent phases. Article XI.3 states:

""Area C" means areas of the West Bank outside Areas A and B, which, except for the issues that will be negotiated in the permanent status negotiations, will be gradually transferred to Palestinian jurisdiction in accordance with this Agreement."

The issues that will be negotiated, according to Article XVII.1, are:

"Jerusalem, settlements, specified military locations, Palestinian refugees, borders, foreign relations and Israelis; and ... powers and responsibilities not transferred to the Council."

By excluding Jerusalem and the settlements from the areas to be transferred to the Palestinians, Israeli presence, including the military to protect them, would not change without a negotiated agreement. The Accords also preserve Israel's exclusive control of the borders, the airspace and the territorial Gaza waters. Oslo II, Article XII:

"In order to guarantee public order and internal security for the Palestinians of the West Bank and the Gaza Strip, the Council shall establish a strong police force as set out in Article XIV below. Israel shall continue to carry the responsibility for defense against external threats, including the responsibility for protecting the Egyptian and Jordanian borders, and for defense against external threats from the sea and from the air, as well as the responsibility for overall security of Israelis and Settlements, for the purpose of safeguarding their internal security and public order, and will have all the powers to take the steps necessary to meet this responsibility."

The first step was a partial Israeli withdrawal from Gaza and Jericho and transfer of some powers and responsibilities on civil matters to the interim Palestinian Authority. All to agree upon within two months from October 1993 (Oslo I, Annex II).

Then, Israeli troops to withdraw from populated Palestinian areas to pave the way for Palestinian elections to establish the Council. The Council would replace the PA, and the Israeli Civil Administration in the West Bank would be dissolved (Oslo II, Article I). Further redeployments of Israeli troops would follow upon the inauguration of the Council, as detailed in the Protocol, Annex I of the Accord.[1573] Article I, 5. of Oslo II reads:

"After the inauguration of the Council, the Civil Administration in the West Bank will be dissolved, and the Israeli military government shall be withdrawn...."[1574]

Twenty years later, however, the withdrawal of Israeli troops did not take place, and the Civil Administration still has permanent military presence in more than 80% of the West Bank (Area B and C).[1575]

Permanent status negotiations about remaining issues would start not later than May 1996 (two years after the signing of the Gaza–Jericho Agreement; Oslo I, Article V) and be concluded before May 1999 (end of 5 year interim period). A peace treaty would end the Israeli–Palestinian conflict.

Palestinian Authority and Legislative Council

When the Oslo I Accord was signed in 1993, neither a government, nor a parliament existed for the Palestinian territories. The Palestinian Authority (PA or PNA) was created by the 1994 Gaza–Jericho Agreement. Article III.1 reads:

"Israel shall transfer authority as specified in this Agreement from the Israeli military government and its Civil Administration to *the Palestinian Authority, hereby established*, in accordance with Article V of this Agreement, except for the authority that Israel shall continue to exercise as specified in this Agreement."

The PA temporarily executed some powers and responsibilities until the establishment of the Council. Article I.1-2 of the Oslo II Accord read:

"1. Israel shall transfer powers and responsibilities as specified in this Agreement from the Israeli military government and its Civil Administration to the Council in accordance with this Agreement. Israel shall continue to exercise powers and responsibilities not so transferred.

2. Pending the inauguration of the Council, the powers and responsibilities transferred to the Council shall be exercised by the Palestinian Authority established in accordance with the Gaza-Jericho Agreement, which shall also have all the rights, liabilities and obligations to be assumed by the Council in this regard. Accordingly, the term 'Council' throughout this Agreement shall, pending the inauguration of the Council, be construed as meaning the Palestinian Authority."

The first elections for the Palestinian Legislative Council (PLC) were on 20 January 1996. The governments elected by the PLC retained the name "Palestinian National Authority."

Transitional Period

The Transitional Period is commonly known as the interim period (Oslo I, Article V) or interim phase.[1576] Hence the name "Interim Agreement" for the Oslo II Accord and the term "Interim Self-Government Authority" (Oslo I, Article I). The interim period was designed to bridge the period between the establishment of the Palestinian Interim Self-Government Authority and the Palestinian Legislative Council, and the end of the permanent status negotiations, "leading to a permanent settlement based on Security Council Resolutions 242 and 338" (Oslo I, Article I). The permanent settlement was not defined. The interim period ended on 4 May 1999, five years after the signing of the Gaza–Jericho Agreement.

Article V of the Declaration of Principles on Interim Self-Government Arrangements (DOP or Oslo I) reads:

Transitional Period and Permanent Status Negotiations

1. The five-year transitional period will begin upon the withdrawal from the Gaza Strip and Jericho area.

2. Permanent status negotiations will commence as soon as possible, but not later than the beginning of the third year of the interim period, between the Government of Israel and the Palestinian people's representatives.

3. It is understood that these negotiations shall cover remaining issues, including: Jerusalem, refugees, settlements, security arrangements, borders, relations and cooperation with other neighbors, and other issues of common interest.

4. The two parties agree that the outcome of the permanent status negotiations should not be prejudiced or preempted by agreements reached for the interim period.

End of the interim period

In May 1999, the five years interim period ended without reaching a comprehensive peace agreement, but elements of the Oslo Accords remained. The interim Palestinian Authority became permanent, and a dominant factor of the PLO. The West Bank remained divided into Areas A, B and C. Area C, covering some 60% of the West Bank, is under exclusive Israeli military and civilian control. Less than 1% of area C is designated for use by Palestinians, who are also unable to build in their own existing villages in area C due to Israeli restrictions. The Israeli Civil Administration, part of a larger entity known as Coordinator of Government Activities in the Territories (COGAT), which is a unit in the Defense Ministry of Israel, is still functioning in full. The Israeli–Palestinian Joint Water Committee also still exists.

At the 2000 Camp David Summit, the US tried to save the Accords by reviving the negotiations. After the failure of the Summit, the Second Intifada broke out and the "peace process" reached deadlock.

Implementation of the Israeli withdrawal

Following the Gaza–Jericho Agreement and prior to the first Palestinian Authority elections, Israel withdrew in 1994 from Jericho and from most of the Gaza Strip. In accordance with the Hebron Protocol, Israel withdrew from 80% of Hebron in January 1997. With stalled negotiations, further redeployments did not take place. By March 1998, none of the withdrawals had occurred In October 1998, the parties signed the Wye River Memorandum, promising resumption of the redeployments, but only the first stage was implemented. While Netanyahu faced opposition within his cabinet, additional withdrawals were delayed. During the Second Intifada, in 2002, the Israeli military re-occupied many of the areas previously turned over to Palestinian control.

Key agreements

Key agreements in the Oslo process were:

- *Israel–PLO letters of recognition* (1993). Mutual recognition of Israel and the PLO.
- The Oslo I Accord (1993). The *"Declaration of Principles on Interim Self-Government Arrangements"* (DOPOISGA or DOP),[1577] which declared the aim of the negotiations and set forth the framework for the interim period. Dissolution of the Israeli Civil Administration upon the inauguration of the Palestinian Legislative Council (Article VII).
- The Gaza–Jericho Agreement or Cairo Agreement (1994). Partial Israeli withdrawal within three weeks from Gaza Strip and Jericho area, being the start of the five-year transitional period (Article V of *Oslo I*). Simultaneously transfer of limited power to the Palestinian Authority (PA), which was established in the same agreement. Part of the Agreement was the Protocol on Economic Relations (Paris Protocol), which regulates the economic relationship between Israel and the Palestinian Authority, but in effect integrated the Palestinian economy into the Israeli one.[1578] This agreement was superseded by the Oslo II Accord, except for Article XX (Confidence-Building Measures). Article XX dictated the release or turn over of Palestinian detainees and prisoners by Israel. The Paris Protocol was incorporated in Article XXIV of Oslo II.
- The Oslo II Accord (1995). Division of the West Bank into Areas, in effect fragmenting it into numerous enclaves and banning the Palestinians from some 60% of the West Bank. Redeployment of Israeli troops from Area A and from other areas through "Further Re-deployments." Election of the Palestinian Legislative Council (Palestinian parliament, PLC), replacing the PA upon its inauguration. Deployment of Palestinian

Police replacing Israeli military forces in Area A. Safe passage between West Bank and Gaza. Most importantly, start of negotiations on a final settlement of remaining issues, to be concluded before 4 May 1999.

All later agreements had the purpose to implement the former three key agreements.

Additional agreements

Additional Israeli-Palestinian agreements related to the Oslo Accords are:

- *Agreement on Preparatory Transfer of Powers and Responsibilities Between Israel and the PLO (August 1994)*[1579]

    This agreement was signed on 29 August 1994 at the Erez Crossing.[1580] It is also known as *Early Empowerment Agreement*[1581] (the term is used on the Israel MFA website). Superseded by Oslo II.

- *Protocol on Further Transfer of Powers and Responsibilities (August 1995)*[1582]

    This agreement was signed on 27 August 1995 at Cairo. It is also known as *Further Transfer Protocol*. Superseded by Oslo II.

- *Protocol Concerning the Redeployment in Hebron* (January 1997)
- *Wye River Memorandum* (October 1998)
- *Sharm el-Sheikh Memorandum* (September 1999)
- *Agreement on Movement and Access* (November 2005)

Criticism

Continued settlement expansion

While Peres had limited settlement construction at the request of US Secretary of State, Madeleine Albright, Netanyahu continued construction within existing Israeli settlements, and put forward plans for the construction of a new neighborhood, Har Homa, in East Jerusalem. However, he fell far short of the Shamir government's 1991–92 level and refrained from building new settlements, although the Oslo agreements stipulated no such ban. Construction of Housing Units Before Oslo: 1991–92: 13,960, After Oslo: 1994–95: 3,840, 1996–1997: 3,570.

Norway's role

Norwegian academics, including Norway's leading authority on the negotiations, Hilde Henriksen Waage, have focused on the flawed role of Norway during the Oslo process. In 2001, the Norwegian Ministry of Foreign Affairs, who had been at the heart of the Oslo process, commissioned Waage to produce an official, comprehensive history of the Norwegian-mediated back channel negotiations. In order to do the research, she was given privileged access to all relevant, classified files in the ministry's archives. Waage was surprised to discover "not a single scrap of paper for the entire period from January to September 1993—precisely the period of the back channel talks." Involved persons kept documents privately and refused to hand them over. Waage concluded that *"there seems no doubt that the missing documents ... would have shown the extent to which the Oslo process was conducted on Israel's premises, with Norway acting as Israel's helpful errand boy."* Norway played a mediating role as a small state between vastly unequal parties and had to play by the rules of the stronger party, acting on its premises. *"Israel's red lines were the ones that counted, and if the Palestinians wanted a deal, they would have to accept them, too.... The missing documents would almost certainly show why the Oslo process probably never could have resulted in a sustainable peace. To a great extent, full documentation of the back channel would explain the disaster that followed Oslo."*[1583]

Undermining Israeli security

Israeli academic Efraim Karsh described the Accords as "the starkest strategic blunder in [Israel's] history," creating the conditions for "the bloodiest and most destructive confrontation between Israelis and Palestinians since 1948" and radicalizing "a new generation of Palestinians" living under the rule of the Palestinian National Authority and Hamas with "vile anti-Jewish (and anti-Israel) incitement unparalleled in scope and intensity since Nazi Germany." Karsh notes: "All in all, more than 1,600 Israelis have been murdered and another 9,000 wounded since the signing of the DOP [Declaration of Principles]—nearly four times the average death toll of the preceding twenty-six years."

Alternatives to the Oslo Accords

Although not an alternative to the accords themselves, a one-state solution would be an alternative to the two-state solution envisaged in the accords. This would combine Israel and the Palestinian territories into a single state with one government. An argument for this solution is that neither side can justly claim a state on all of the land.[1584] An argument against it is that it would endanger the safety of the Jewish minority.

Assassination of Yitzhak Rabin

<indicator name="pp-default"> 🔒 </indicator>

Assassination of Yitzhak Rabin	
 Site of the rally before the assassination: Kings of Israel Square (since renamed Rabin Square) with Tel Aviv's City Hall in the background during the day.	
Location	Tel Aviv, Israel
Coordinates	32°04′54.8″N 34°46′51.4″E[1585] Coordinates: 32°04′54.8″N 34°46′51.4″E[1585]
Date	November 4, 1995
Target	Yitzhak Rabin
Attack type	Shooting
Weapons	Beretta 84F semi-automatic pistol
Deaths	1 (Rabin)
Non-fatal injuries	1 (his body guard)
Perpetrator	Yigal Amir

The **assassination of Yitzhak Rabin** took place on 4 November 1995 (12th of Marcheshvan, 5756 on the Hebrew calendar) at 21:30, at the end of a rally in support of the Oslo Accords at the Kings of Israel Square in Tel Aviv. The assassin, an Israeli ultranationalist named Yigal Amir, radically opposed Rabin's peace initiative and particularly the signing of the Oslo Accords.

Prelude

The assassination of Israeli Prime Minister and Defence Minister Yitzhak Rabin was the culmination of an anti-violence rally in support of the Oslo peace process. Rabin, despite his extensive service in the Israeli military, was disparaged personally by right-wing conservatives and Likud leaders who perceived the Oslo peace process as an attempt to forfeit the occupied territories.

Figure 209: *Yitzhak Rabin's family mourn at his funeral.*

National religious conservatives and Likud party leaders believed that withdrawing from any "Jewish" land was heresy. Rallies, organized partially by Likud, became increasingly extreme in tone. Likud leader (and future Prime Minister) Benjamin Netanyahu accused Rabin's government of being "removed from Jewish tradition ... and Jewish values." Netanyahu addressed protesters of the Oslo movement at rallies where posters portrayed Rabin in a Nazi SS uniform or being the target in the cross-hairs of a sniper. Rabin accused Netanyahu of provoking violence, a charge which Netanyahu strenuously denied.[1586] Netanyahu's advisor Zalman Shoval replied that Netanyahu had in fact tried to silence the anti-Rabin chants and had not seen the SS poster.

Yigal Amir

The assassin was Yigal Amir, a 25-year-old former Hesder student and far-right law student at Bar-Ilan University. Amir had strenuously opposed Rabin's peace initiative, particularly the signing of the Oslo Accords, because he felt that an Israeli withdrawal from the West Bank would deny Jews their "biblical heritage which they had reclaimed by establishing settlements". Amir had come to believe that Rabin was a *rodef*, meaning a "pursuer" who endangered

Figure 210: *Yitzhak Rabin grave, December 1995.*

Jewish lives. The concept of *din rodef* ("law of the pursuer") is a part of traditional Jewish law. Amir believed he would be justified under *din rodef* in removing Rabin as a threat to Jews in the territories.[1587]

According to Rabbi Arthur Waskow, Amir's interpretation of *din rodef* is a gross distortion of Jewish law and tradition:

> *First of all, the law of the pursuer only applies to a spontaneous act, whereas Yigal Amir planned this assassination for two years. Secondly, the law of the pursuer is only intended to save a potential victim from imminent death. There is absolutely no proof that withdrawing from certain territories will directly lead to the death of any Jews. On the contrary, Prime Minister Rabin, over half the members of the Knesset, and over half the population of Israel believe exactly the opposite—that it will save Jewish lives. Lastly, this law does not refer to elected representatives, for if Yitzhak Rabin was really a pursuer, then so are all his followers and that would mean that Amir should have killed over half the population of Israel! In other words, even according to the law of the pursuer, this act was totally futile and senseless since the peace process will continue.*[1588]

For his radical activities, Yigal Amir had been brought under attention by the Israeli internal security service (Shin Bet), but the organization only had information on Amir's attempt on creating an anti-Arab militia, not on comments regarding assassinating Rabin, which he openly stated to a number of

Figure 211: *The monument at the site of the assassination: Solomon ibn Gabirol Street between the Tel Aviv City Hall and Gan Ha'ir (in the back). The monument is composed of broken rocks, which represent the political earthquake that the assassination represents.*

people.[1589] Another incident describing Amir's comments to a fellow student about stating the vidui prior to an earlier, aborted attempt on his life was ignored by the organization as "non-credible". The source refused to name Amir by name but instead described him as a "short Yemeni guy with curly hair".[1590]

Assassination

After the rally, Rabin walked down the city hall steps towards the open door of his car, at which time Amir fired three shots at Rabin with a Beretta 84F .380 ACP caliber semi-automatic pistol. He was immediately subdued by Rabin's bodyguards and arrested with the murder weapon. The third shot missed Rabin and slightly wounded security guard Yoram Rubin.[1591,1592]

Rabin was rushed to nearby Ichilov Hospital at the Tel Aviv Sourasky Medical Center, where he died on the operating table from blood loss and a punctured lung within 40 minutes. Rabin's bureau chief, Eitan Haber, announced outside the gates of the hospital:

Figure 212: *Yitzhak and Leah Rabin's grave on Mount Herzl.*

The government of Israel announces in consternation, in great sadness, and in deep sorrow, the death of prime minister and minister of defense Yitzhak Rabin, who was murdered by an assassin, tonight in Tel Aviv. The government shall convene in one hour for a mourning session in Tel Aviv. Blessed be his memory.

In Rabin's pocket was a blood-stained sheet of paper with the lyrics to the well-known Israeli song "Shir LaShalom" ("Song for Peace"), which was sung at the rally and dwells on the impossibility of bringing a dead person back to life and, therefore, the need for peace.

Reactions and funeral

The assassination of Rabin was a shock to the Israeli public. Rallies and memorials took place near Kings of Israel Square—later renamed Rabin Square in his honor—as well as near Rabin's home, the Knesset building, and the home of the assassin. Many other streets and public buildings around the country were named for Rabin as well.Wikipedia:Citation needed

The funeral of Rabin took place on November 6,[1593] two days after the assassination, at the Mount Herzl cemetery in Jerusalem, where Rabin was buried.

Figure 213: *US president Bill Clinton in Rabin's funeral. The final words were in Hebrew – "Shalom, Haver" (Hebrew: חבר, שלום lit. Goodbye, Friend)*

Hundreds of world leaders, including about 80 heads of state, attended the funeral.[1594] President of the United States Bill Clinton,[1595] King Hussein of Jordan,[1596] Queen Beatrix of the Netherlands,[1597] Russian Prime Minister Viktor Chernomyrdin,[1598] Spanish Prime Minister and European Council President-in-Office Felipe González[1599] Prime Minister of Canada Jean Chrétien, acting Israeli Prime Minister and Foreign Minister Shimon Peres,[1600] United Nations Secretary-General Boutros Boutros-Ghali,[1601] Rabin's granddaughter Noa Ben-Artzi Filosof,[1602] former director-general of the prime minister's office Shimon Sheves,[1603] Egyptian President Hosni Mubarak,[1604] President of the Republic of the Congo Denis Sassou Nguesso, director of the Prime Minister's Bureau Eitan Haber,[1605] and President of Israel Ezer Weizman[1606] were among those present.

Amir was sentenced to be in prison for the rest of his life.Wikipedia:Citation needed

A national memorial day for Rabin is set on the date of his death according to the Hebrew calendar.Wikipedia:Citation needed

On 28 March 1996, the Shamgar Commission issued its final report into the assassination. It was critical of Shin Bet for putting the Prime Minister at risk and ignoring threats to his life from Jewish extremists.[1607]

Further reading

- Karpin, Michael and Friedman, Ina. (1998) *Murder in the Name of God: The Plot to Kill Yitzhak Rabin*. Granta Books. <templatestyles src="Module:Citation/CS1/styles.css" />ISBN 0-8050-5749-8.
- Ephron, Dan. (2015) *Killing a King: The Assassination of Yitzhak Rabin and the Remaking of Israel*. W. W. Norton & Company. <templatestyles src="Module:Citation/CS1/styles.css" />ISBN 978-0393242096.

External links

 Wikiquote has quotations related to: *Assassination of Yitzhak Rabin*

- "Israel marks Rabin assassination"[1608], BBC, Nov 12, 2005
- "A sombre night in Rabin Square"[1609], BBC, Nov 12, 2005
- Could He Have Been Saved?[1610] An article by Ronen Bergman in *Haaretz*
- 10-minute video of Rabin's assassination[1611] hosted on Google Video
- Assassination part of the Kempler video on CNN (10 seconds)[1612]
- Koenraad Elst on Yitzhak Rabin's Assassination[1613]
- "The Night in Question"[1614]. *This American Life*. Episode 570. Chicago. October 16, 2015. Public Radio Exchange. WBEZ. Retrieved October 17, 2015.<templatestyles src="Module:Citation/CS1/styles.css"></templatestyles> Covers the assassination and its conspiracy theories, including an interview with Yigal Amir's brother and co-conspirator Hagai Amir and a new forensic examination of the shirt Rabin was wearing when he was shot.

1996–2001: Netanyahu I; Barak

2000 Camp David Summit

<indicator name="pp-default"> 🔒 </indicator>

The **2000 Camp David Summit** was a summit meeting at Camp David between United States president Bill Clinton, Israeli prime minister Ehud Barak and Palestinian Authority chairman Yasser Arafat. The summit took place between 11 and 25 July 2000 and was an effort to end the Israeli–Palestinian conflict. The summit ended without an agreement.

The summit

Part of a series on
the Israeli–Palestinian conflict
Israeli–Palestinian peace process

U.S. President Bill Clinton announced his invitation to Israeli Prime Minister Ehud Barak and Yasser Arafat on 5 July 2000, to come to Camp David, Maryland, in order to continue their negotiations on the Middle East peace process. There was a hopeful precedent in the 1978 Camp David Accords where President Jimmy Carter was able to broker a peace agreement between Egypt, represented by President Anwar Sadat, and Israel represented by Prime Minister Menachem Begin. The Oslo Accords of 1993 between the later assassinated Israeli Prime Minister Yitzhak Rabin and Palestine Liberation Organization Chairman Yasser Arafat had provided that agreement should be reached on all outstanding issues between the Palestinians and Israeli sides – the so-called final status settlement – within five years of the implementation of Palestinian autonomy. However, the interim process put in place under Oslo had fulfilled neither Israeli nor Palestinian expectations.

On 11 July, the Camp David 2000 Summit convened, although the Palestinians considered the summit premature.[1616,1617] They even saw it as a trap.[1618] The summit ended on 25 July, without an agreement being reached. At its conclusion, a Trilateral Statement was issued defining the agreed principles to guide future negotiations.

The negotiations

The negotiations were based on an all-or-nothing approach, such that "nothing was considered agreed and binding until everything was agreed." The proposals were, for the most part, verbal. As no agreement was reached and there is no official written record of the proposals, some ambiguity remains over details of the positions of the parties on specific issues.[1619]

The talks ultimately failed to reach agreement on the final status issues:

- Territory
- Jerusalem and the Temple Mount
- Refugees and Palestinian right of return
- Security arrangements
- Settlements

Figure 214: *U.S. President Bill Clinton, Israeli prime minister Ehud Barak and Palestinian leader Yasser Arafat at Camp David, July 2000*

Figure 215: *Israeli prime minister Ehud Barak and Palestinian leader Yasser Arafat shake hands at the White House in Washington.*

Territory

The Palestinian negotiators indicated they wanted full Palestinian sovereignty over the entire West Bank and the Gaza Strip, although they would consider a one-to-one land swap with Israel. Their historic position was that Palestinians had already made a territorial compromise with Israel by accepting Israel's right to 78% of "historic Palestine", and accepting their state on the remaining 22% of such land. This consensus was expressed by Faisal Husseini when he remarked:'There can be no compromise on the compromise'.[1620] They maintained that Resolution 242 calls for full Israeli withdrawal from these territories, which were captured in the Six-Day War, as part of a final peace settlement. In the 1993 Oslo Accords the Palestinian negotiators accepted the Green Line borders (1949 armistice lines) for the West Bank but the Israelis rejected this proposal and disputed the Palestinian interpretation of Resolution 242. Israel wanted to annex the numerous settlement blocks on the Palestinian side of the Green Line, and were concerned that a complete return to the 1967 borders was dangerous to Israel's security. The Palestinian and Israeli definition of the West Bank differs by approximately 5% land area as the Israeli definition does not include East Jerusalem (71 km²), the territorial waters of the Dead Sea (195 km²) and the area known as No Man's Land (50 km² near Latrun).

Based on the Israeli definition of the West Bank, Barak offered to form a Palestinian state initially on 73% of the West Bank (that is, 27% less than the Green Line borders) and 100% of the Gaza Strip. In 10–25 years, the Palestinian state would expand to a maximum of 92% of the West Bank (91 percent of the West Bank and 1 percent from a land swap). From the Palestinian perspective this equated to an offer of a Palestinian state on a maximum of 86% of the West Bank.

According to the Jewish Virtual Library, Israel would have withdrawn from 63 settlements.[1621] According to Robert Wright, Israel would only keep the settlements with large populations. Wright states that all others would be dismantled, with the exception of Kiryat Arba (adjacent to the holy city of Hebron), which would be an Israeli enclave inside the Palestinian state, and would be linked to Israel by a bypass road. The West Bank would be split in the middle by an Israeli-controlled road from Jerusalem to the Dead Sea, with free passage for Palestinians, although Israel reserved the right to close the road to passage in case of emergency. In return, Israel would allow the Palestinians to use a highway in the Negev to connect the West Bank with Gaza. Wright states that in the Israeli proposal, the West Bank and Gaza Strip would be linked by an elevated highway and an elevated railroad running through the Negev, ensuring safe and free passage for Palestinians. These would be under the sovereignty of Israel, and Israel reserved the right to close them to passage in case of emergency.

Israel would retain around 9% in the West Bank in exchange for 1% of land within the Green Line. The land that would be conceded included symbolic and cultural territories such as the Al-Aqsa Mosque, whereas the Israeli land conceded was unspecified. Additional to territorial concessions, Palestinian airspace would be controlled by Israel under Barak's offer.[1622] The Palestinians rejected the Halutza Sand region (78 km²) alongside the Gaza Strip as part of the land swap on the basis that it was of inferior quality to that which they would have to give up in the West Bank.

Additional grounds of rejection was that the Israeli proposal planned to annex areas which would lead to a cantonization of the West Bank into three blocs, which the Palestinian delegation likened to South African Bantustans, a loaded word that was disputed by the Israeli and American negotiators.[1623] Settlement blocs, bypassed roads and annexed lands would create barriers between Nablus and Jenin with Ramallah. The Ramallah bloc would in turn be divided from Bethlehem and Hebron. A separate and smaller bloc would contain Jericho. Further, the border between West Bank and Jordan would additionally be under Israeli control. The Palestinian Authority would receive pockets of East Jerusalem which would be surrounded entirely by annexed lands in the West Bank.

East Jerusalem

A particularly virulent territorial dispute revolved around the final status of Jerusalem. Leaders were ill-prepared for the central role the Jerusalem issue in general and the Temple Mount dispute in particular would play in the negotiations.[1624] Barak instructed his delegates to treat the dispute as "the central issue that will decide the destiny of the negotiations" whereas Arafat admonished his delegation to "not budge on this one thing: the Haram (the Temple Mount) is more precious to me than everything else."[1625] At the opening of Camp David, Barak warned the Americans he could not accept giving the Palestinians more than a purely symbolic sovereignty over any part of East Jerusalem.

The Palestinians demanded complete sovereignty over East Jerusalem and its holy sites, in particular, the Al-Aqsa Mosque and the Dome of the Rock, which are located on the Temple Mount (Haram al-Sharif), a site holy in both Islam and Judaism, and the dismantling of all Israeli neighborhoods built over the Green Line. The Palestinian position, according to Mahmoud Abbas, at that time Arafat's chief negotiator, was that: "All of East Jerusalem should be returned to Palestinian sovereignty. The Jewish Quarter and Western Wall should be placed under Israeli authority, not Israeli sovereignty. An open city and cooperation on municipal services."[1626]

Israel proposed that the Palestinians be granted "custodianship," though not sovereignty, on the Temple Mount (Haram al-Sharif), with Israel retaining control over the Western Wall, a remnant of the ancient wall that surrounded the Temple Mount, the most sacred site in Judaism outside of the Temple Mount itself. Israeli negotiators also proposed that the Palestinians be granted administration of, but not sovereignty over, the Muslim and Christian Quarters of the Old City, with the Jewish and Armenian Quarters remaining in Israeli hands.[1627] Palestinians would be granted administrative control over all Islamic and Christian holy sites, and would be allowed to raise the Palestinian flag over them. A passage linking northern Jerusalem to Islamic and Christian holy sites would be annexed by the Palestinian state. The Israeli team proposed annexing to Israeli Jerusalem settlements within the West Bank beyond the Green Line, such as Ma'ale Adumim, Givat Ze'ev, and Gush Etzion. Israel proposed that the Palestinians merge certain outer Arab villages and small cities that had been annexed to Jerusalem just after 1967 (such as Abu Dis, al-Eizariya, 'Anata, A-Ram, and eastern Sawahre) to create the city of Al-Quds, which would serve as the capital of Palestine. The historically important Arab neighborhoods such as Sheikh Jarrah, Silwan and at-Tur would remain under Israeli sovereignty, while Palestinians would only have civilian autonomy. The Palestinians would exercise civil and administrative autonomy in the outer Arab neighborhoods. Israeli neighborhoods within East Jerusalem would remain under Israeli sovereignty. The holy places in the Old City would enjoy independent religious administration.[1628] In total, Israel demanded that Palestine's territory in East Jerusalem be reduced to eight sections including six small enclaves according to Palestine's delegation to the summit.

Palestinians objected to the lack of sovereignty and to the right of Israel to keep Jewish neighborhoods that it built over the Green Line in East Jerusalem, which the Palestinians claimed block the contiguity of the Arab neighborhoods in East Jerusalem.

Refugees and the right of return

Due to the first Arab-Israeli war, a significant number of Palestinian Arabs fled or were expelled from their homes inside what is now Israel. These refugees numbered approximately 711,000 to 725,000 at the time. Today, they and their descendants number about four million, comprising about half the Palestinian people. Since that time, the Palestinians have demanded full implementation of the right of return, meaning that each refugee would be granted the option of returning to his or her home, with property restored, and receive compensation. Israelis asserted that allowing a right of return to Israel proper, rather than to the newly created Palestinian state, would mean an influx of Palestinians that would fundamentally alter the demographics of Israel, jeopardizing Israel's Jewish character and its existence as a whole.

At Camp David, the Palestinians maintained their traditional demand that the right of return be implemented. They demanded that Israel recognize the right of all refugees who so wished to settle in Israel, but to address Israel's demographic concerns, they promised that the right of return would be implemented via a mechanism agreed upon by both sides, which would try to channel a majority of refugees away from the option of returning to Israel.[1629] According to U.S. Secretary of State Madeleine Albright, some of the Palestinian negotiators were willing to privately discuss a limit on the number of refugees who would be allowed to return to Israel.[1630] Palestinians who chose to return to Israel would do so gradually, with Israel absorbing 150,000 refugees every year.

The Israeli negotiators denied that Israel was responsible for the refugee problem, and were concerned that any right of return would pose a threat to Israel's Jewish character. In the Israeli proposal, a maximum of 100,000 refugees would be allowed to return to Israel on the basis of humanitarian considerations or family reunification. All other people classified as Palestinian refugees would be settled in their present place of inhabitance, the Palestinian state, or third-party countries. Israel would help fund their resettlement and absorption. An international fund of $30 billion would be set up, which Israel would help contribute to, along with other countries, that would register claims for compensation of property lost by Palestinian refugees and make payments within the limits of its resources.[1631]

Security arrangements

The Israeli negotiators proposed that Israel be allowed to set up radar stations inside the Palestinian state, and be allowed to use its airspace. Israel also wanted the right to deploy troops on Palestinian territory in the event of an emergency, and the stationing of an international force in the Jordan Valley. Palestinian authorities would maintain control of border crossings under temporary Israeli observation. Israel would maintain a permanent security presence along 15% of the Palestinian-Jordanian border.[1632] Israel also demanded that the Palestinian state be demilitarized with the exception of its paramilitary security forces, that it would not make alliances without Israeli approval or allow the introduction of foreign forces west of the Jordan River, and that it dismantle terrorist groups.[1633] One of Israel's strongest demands was that Arafat declare the conflict over, and make no further demands. Israel also wanted water resources in the West Bank to be shared by both sides and remain under Israeli management.

Aftermath

In mid-October, Clinton and the parties held a summit in Sharm El Sheikh, resulting in a "Sharm memorandum" with understandings aimed at ending the violence and renewing security cooperation. From 18 to 23 December they held negotiations, followed by Clinton's presentation of his "parameters", in a last attempt to achieve peace in the Middle East before his second term ended in January 2001.[1634] Although the official statements stated that both parties had accepted the Clinton Parameters with reservations,[1635] these reservations in fact meant that the parties had rejected the parameters on certain essential points. On 2 January 2001, the Palestinians put forward their acceptance with some fundamental objections. Barak accepted the parameters with a 20-page letter of reservations.[1636] A Sharm el-Sheikh summit planned for 28 December did not take place.

Clinton's initiative led to the Taba negotiations in January 2001, where the two sides published a statement saying they had never been closer to agreement (though such issues as Jerusalem, the status of Gaza, and the Palestinian demand for compensation for refugees and their descendants remained unresolved), but Barak, facing elections, re-suspended the talks.[1637] Ehud Barak was to be defeated by Ariel Sharon in 2001.

Responsibility for failure

Accusations of Palestinian responsibility

Most of the Israeli and American criticism for the failure of the 2000 Camp David Summit was leveled at Arafat.[1638,1639] Ehud Barak portrays Arafat's behavior at Camp David as a "performance geared to exact as many Israeli concessions as possible without ever seriously intending to reach a peace settlement or sign an "end to the conflict.

Clinton blamed Arafat after the failure of the talks, stating, "I regret that in 2000 Arafat missed the opportunity to bring that nation into being and pray for the day when the dreams of the Palestinian people for a state and a better life will be realized in a just and lasting peace." The failure to come to an agreement was widely attributed to Yasser Arafat, as he walked away from the table without making a concrete counter-offer and because Arafat did little to quell the series of Palestinian riots that began shortly after the summit.[1640,1641] Arafat was also accused of scuttling the talks by Nabil Amr, a former minister in the Palestinian Authority. In *My Life*, Clinton wrote that Arafat once complimented Clinton by telling him, "You are a great man." Clinton responded, "I am not a great man. I am a failure, and you made me one."

Dennis Ross, the US Middle East envoy and a key negotiator at the summit, summarized his perspectives in his book *The Missing Peace*. During a lecture in Australia, Ross suggested that the reason for the failure was Arafat's unwillingness to sign a final deal with Israel that would close the door on any of the Palestinians' maximum demands, particularly the right of return. Ross claimed that what Arafat really wanted was "a one-state solution. Not independent, adjacent Israeli and Palestinian states, but a single Arab state encompassing all of Historic Palestine".[1642] Ross also quoted Saudi Prince Bandar as saying while negotiations were taking place: "If Arafat does not accept what is available now, it won't be a tragedy; it will be a crime."

In his book, *The Oslo Syndrome*, Harvard Medical School professor of psychiatry and historian[1643] Kenneth Levin summarized the failure of the 2000 Camp David Summit in this manner: "despite the dimensions of the Israeli offer and intense pressure from President Clinton, Arafat demurred. He apparently was indeed unwilling, no matter what the Israeli concessions, to sign an agreement that declared itself final and forswore any further Palestinian claims." Levin argues that both the Israelis and the Americans were naive in expecting that Arafat would agree to give up the idea of a literal "right of return" for all Palestinians into Israel proper no matter how many 1948 refugees or how much monetary compensation Israel offered to allow.

Alan Dershowitz, an Israel advocate and a law professor at Harvard University, said that the failure of the negotiations was due to "the refusal of the Palestinians and Arafat to give up the right of return. That was the sticking point. It wasn't Jerusalem. It wasn't borders. It was the right of return." He claimed that President Clinton told this to him "directly and personally."[1644]

Accusations of Israeli and American responsibility

In 2001 Robert Malley, present at the summit, noted three "myths" that had arisen regarding the failure of the negotiations. Those were "Camp David was an ideal test of Mr. Arafat's intentions", "Israel's offer met most if not all of the Palestinians' legitimate aspirations", and "The Palestinians made no concession of their own" and wrote that "If peace is to be achieved, the parties cannot afford to tolerate the growing acceptance of these myths as reality."[1645]

The Israeli group Gush Shalom stated that "the offer is a pretense of generosity for the benefit of the media", and included detailed maps of what the offer specifically entailed.[1646] Wikipedia:Identifying reliable sources Among Gush Shalom's concerns with Barak's offer were Barak's demand to annex large settlement blocs (9% of the West Bank), lack of trust in the commitment and/or ability of the Israeli government to evacuate the thousands of non-bloc Israeli settlers in the 15-year timeline, and limited sovereignty for Palestinians in Jerusalem.

Clayton Swisher wrote a rebuttal to Clinton and Ross's accounts about the causes for the breakdown of the Camp David Summit in his 2004 book, *The Truth About Camp David*. Swisher, the Director of Programs at the Middle East Institute, concluded that the Israelis and the Americans were at least as guilty as the Palestinians for the collapse. M.J. Rosenberg praised the book: "Clayton Swisher's 'The Truth About Camp David,' based on interviews with [US negotiators] Martin Indyk, Dennis Ross and [Aaron] Miller himself provides a comprehensive and acute account – the best we're likely to see – on the [one-sided diplomacy] Miller describes."

Shlomo Ben-Ami, then Israel's Minister of Foreign Relations who participated in the talks, stated that the Palestinians wanted the immediate withdrawal of the Israelis from the West Bank, Gaza Strip and East Jerusalem, and only subsequently the Palestinian authority would dismantle the Palestinian organizations. The Israeli response was "we can't accept the demand for a return to the borders of June 1967 as a pre-condition for the negotiation."[1647] In 2006, Shlomo Ben-Ami stated on Democracy Now! that "Camp David was not the missed opportunity for the Palestinians, and if I were a Palestinian I would have rejected Camp David, as well. This is something I put in the book. But Taba is the problem. The Clinton parameters are the problem" referring to his 2001 book *Scars of War, Wounds of Peace: The Israeli-Arab Tragedy*.[1648]

Norman Finkelstein published an article in the winter 2007 issue of *Journal of Palestine Studies*, excerpting from his longer essay called *Subordinating Palestinian Rights to Israeli "Needs"*. The abstract for the article states: "In particular, it examines the assumptions informing Ross's account of what happened during the negotiations and why, and the distortions that spring from these assumptions. Judged from the perspective of Palestinians' and Israelis' respective rights under international law, all the concessions at Camp David came from the Palestinian side, none from the Israeli side."[1649]

Berkeley political science professor Ron Hassner has argued that it was the failure of participants at the negotiations to include religious leaders in the process or even consult with religious experts prior to the negotiations, that led to the collapse of the negotiations over the subject of Jerusalem. "Both parties seem to have assumed that the religious dimensions of the dispute could be ignored. As a result, neither party had prepared seriously for the possibility that the Temple Mount issue would come to stand at the heart of the negotiations." Political Scientist Menahem Klein, who advised the Israeli government during the negotiations, confirmed that "The professional back channels did not sufficiently treat Jerusalem as a religious city... It was easier to conduct discussions about preservation of historical structures in the old city than to discuss the link between the political sanctity and the religious sanctity at the historical and religious heart of the city."[1650]

Public opinion towards the summit

The Palestinian public was supportive of Arafat's role in the negotiations. After the summit, Arafat's approval rating increased seven percentage points from 39 to 46%. Overall, 68% of the Palestinian public thought Arafat's positions on a final agreement at Camp David were just right and 14% thought Arafat compromised too much while only 6% thought Arafat had not compromised enough.

Barak did not fare as well in public opinion polls. Only 25% of the Israeli public thought his positions on Camp David were just right as opposed to 58% of the public that thought Barak compromised too much.[1651] A majority of Israelis were opposed to Barak's position on every issue discussed at Camp David except for security.[1652]

Concluding *Trilateral statement* (full text)

<templatestyles src="Template:Quote/styles.css"/>

> July 25, 2000
> President William J. Clinton
> Israeli Prime Minister Ehud Barak
> Palestinian Authority Chairman Yasser Arafat
> Between July 11 and 24, under the auspices of President Clinton, Prime Minister Barak and Chairman Arafat met at Camp David in an effort to reach an agreement on permanent status. While they were not able to bridge the gaps and reach an agreement, their negotiations were unprecedented in both scope and detail. Building on the progress achieved at Camp David, the two leaders agreed on the following principles to guide their negotiations:
>
> 1. The two sides agreed that the aim of their negotiations is to put an end to decades of conflict and achieve a just and lasting peace.
> 2. The two sides commit themselves to continue their efforts to conclude an agreement on all permanent status issues as soon as possible.
> 3. Both sides agree that negotiations based on UN Security Council Resolutions 242 and 338 are the only way to achieve such an agreement and they undertake to create an environment for negotiations free from pressure, intimidation and threats of violence.
> 4. The two sides understand the importance of avoiding unilateral actions that prejudge the outcome of negotiations and that their differences will be resolved only by good faith negotiations.
> 5. Both sides agree that the United States remains a vital partner in the search for peace and will continue to consult closely with President Clinton and Secretary Albright in the period ahead.

Bibliography

- Ehud Barak. Statement by Prime Minister Barak at Press Conference upon the Conclusion of the Camp David Summit[1653]
- Shlomo Ben-Ami. Camp David Diaries[1654]. Excerpts from a 6 April 2001 article in Ma'ariv
- Gilead Sher (2006). *The Israeli-Palestinian Peace Negotiations, 1999–2001*. Routledge. A first hand account from the chief negotiator for the Israeli team
- Mahmoud Abbas, *Reports of the Camp David Summit, 9 September 2000* Excerpts published in the Journal of Palestine Studies, vol. XXX, No. 2 (Winter 2001), pp. 168–170
- Akram Haniyah, *The Camp David Papers*, first hand account by a member of the Palestinian negotiating team, originally published in the Palestinian daily al-Ayyam. English translation in Journal of Palestine Studies, vol. XXX, No. 2 (Winter 2001), pp. 75–97
- Madeleine Albright (2003). *Madame Secretary*. New York: Hyperion (especially chapter 28)
- Bill Clinton, *My Life: The Presidential Years* (especially chapter 25)
- Dennis Ross *The Missing Peace : The Inside Story of the Fight for Middle East Peace*
- Kenneth Levin. *The Oslo Syndrome: Delusions of a People Under Siege*. Hanover: Smith and Kraus, 2005.

External links

Wikisourcehas original text related to this article:
Camp David Summit Announcement by US President Clinton

Wikisourcehas original text related to this article:
Camp David Summit Conclusion by US President Clinton

Wikisourcehas original text related to this article:
Camp David Summit Conclusion by Israeli Prime Minister Ehud Barak

General

- *Principles of Camp David's "American Plan"*[1655]. FMEP, Settlement Report, September–October 2000. American proposals, as reported in Ha'aretz and Yediot Aharanot.
- Interview with Dennis Ross about the summit[1656]
- More recent interview with Dennis Ross about the summit[1657]
- Several articles on the 2000 summit, including interviews with Clinton and Ben-Ami at the Jewish Virtual Library[1658]
- Camp David offer according to Palestinian Academic Society for the Study of International Affairs[1659]
- The Middle East Peace Summit at Camp David- July 2000[1660] Israeli Ministry of Foreign Affairs

Maps

- Camp David proposal maps (with explanations) according to MidEast-Web.[1661]
- Palestinian Maps of the Camp David 2 Proposals[1662].
- West Bank Final Status Map Presented By Israel, May 2000[1663] Foundation for Middle East Peace.
- Projection of West Bank Permanent Status Offer, Camp David, July 2000[1664] at the Wayback Machine (archived 22 February 2006) Peres Center for Peace.
- (in French) Maps: Israeli proposals, from Camp David (2000) to Taba (2001)[1665]
- Failed compromise at Camp David.[1666] December 2000 English article in *Le Monde diplomatique* refers to some of the above-linked French-language maps.
- "*East Jerusalem*"[1667]. Archived from the original on 14 May 2002. Retrieved 2013-07-09.<templatestyles src="Module:Citation/CS1/styles.css"></templatestyles> and "*Ariel and East Jerusalem*"[1668]. Archived from the original on 16 August 2001. Retrieved 2013-07-09.<templatestyles src="Module:Citation/CS1/styles.css"></templatestyles>, Orient House, 2000
- *Barak's generous offers*[1669]. Gush Shalom.

New York Review of Books series

- Robert Malley and Hussein Agha. "Camp David: The Tragedy of Errors,"[1670] New York Review of Books, 9 August 2001
- Dennis Ross, Gidi Grinstein, Hussein Agha, Robert Malley. "Camp David: An Exchange."[1671] New York Review of Books, 20 September 2001
- Camp David and After: An Exchange (1. An Interview with Ehud Barak)[1672], by Benny Morris, in response to "Camp David: The Tragedy of Errors") 13 June 2002
- Camp David and After: An Exchange (2. A Reply to Ehud Barak)[1673] By Hussein Agha, Robert Malley, 13 June 2002
- Camp David and After – Continued[1674] Benny Morris, Ehud Barak, Reply by Hussein Agha, Robert Malley, 27 June 2002

Views and Analysis

- Comparing Camp David I and II[1675], Dr. Kenneth W. Stein, Emory University
- "Was Arafat the Problem?" by Robert Wright[1676]
- "Barak: A Villa in the Jungle." Uri Avnery, July 2002[1677]
- "The Day Barak's Bubble Burst"[1678]. 15 Sept. 2001 article, by Uri Avnery, a founder of the Israeli peace group Gush Shalom. More of their articles about Camp David are here.[1679]
- Jerome M. Segal, "The Palestinian Peace Offer," originally published in Ha'aretz, 1 October 2001[1680]
- Visions in Collision: What Happened at Camp David and Taba?[1681], Dr. Jeremy Pressman, 2003.

Further reading

- Bregman, Ahron *Elusive Peace: How the Holy Land Defeated America.*

2001–2006: Sharon

Second Intifada

<indicator name="pp-default"> 🔒 </indicator>

Second Intifada
Part of the Israeli–Palestinian conflict

Israeli soldiers in Nablus, during Operation Defensive Shield
Date   28 September 2000 – 8 February 2005   (4 years, 4 months, 1 week and 4 days)
Location   Palestinian Authority, Israel
Result   Uprising suppressed   • Construction of the Israeli West Bank barrier   • Decrease of violence in the West Bank   • Israeli withdrawal from the Gaza Strip
Belligerents

Israel	Palestinian Authority

• Israel Defense Forces
• Shin Bet
• Israel Police
   • Israel Border Police
• Civil Guard
• Mishmeret Yesha
	• PLO
	• Preventive Security Force
	Palestinian National Security Forces
	• Fatah (al-Aqsa Martyrs' Brigades)
	   • PFLP
	   • DFLP
	• Hamas
	• Islamic Jihad
	• Popular Resistance Committees
	• Others
	Supported by; Iraq[1682] (until 2003)

Commanders and leaders	
Ariel Sharon Avi Dichter Ehud Barak Shaul Mofaz Moshe Ya'alon Dan Halutz Gabi Ashkenazi	**PLO leaders** Yasser Arafat Mahmoud Abbas Marwan Barghouti (POW) Abu Ali Mustafa (KIA) Ahmad Sa'adat (POW) Nayef Hawatmeh **Hamas leaders** Ahmed Yasin (KIA) Abdel Rantissi (KIA) Khaled Mashaal Ismail Haniyeh Mohammed Deif **Other leaders** Abd Al Aziz Awda Ramadan Shalah Jamal Abu Samhadana (KIA)
Casualties and losses	
29 September 2000 – 1 January 2005: 945 Wikipedia: Verifiability–1,010 Israeli total: - 644–773 Israeli civilians killed by Palestinians; - 215–301 Israeli security force personnel killed by Palestinians	29 September 2000 – 1 January 2005: 3,179–3,354 Palestinians total: - 2,739–3,168 Palestinians killed by Israel's security forces;* - 34 Palestinians killed by Israeli civilians; - 152–406 Palestinians killed by Palestinians; Thousands detained
55 foreign citizens total: - 45 foreign citizens killed by Palestinians; - 10 foreign citizens killed by Israeli security forces	
*For the controversial issue of the Palestinian civilian/combatant breakdown, see Casualties.	

The **Second Intifada**, also known as the **Al-Aqsa Intifada** (Arabic: انتفاضة الأقصى *Intifāḍat al-'Aqṣā*; Hebrew: אל-אקצה אינתיפאדה *Intifādat El-Aqtzah*), was a period of intensified Israeli–Palestinian violence, and which the Palestinian describe as an uprising against Israel. The violence started in September 2000, after Ariel Sharon made a visit to the Temple Mount, seen by Palestinians as highly provocative; and Palestinian demonstrators, throwing stones at police, were dispersed by the Israeli army, using tear gas and rubber bullets.

High numbers of casualties were caused among civilians as well as combatants: the Palestinians by numerous suicide bombings and gunfire; the Israelis by tank and gunfire and air attacks, by numerous targeted killings, and by responses to demonstrations. The death toll, including both military and civilian, is estimated to be about 3,000 Palestinians and 1,000 Israelis, as well as 64 foreigners.[1683]

Many consider the Sharm el-Sheikh Summit on 8 February 2005 to be the end of the Second Intifada, when Palestinian President Mahmoud Abbas and Israeli Prime Minister Ariel Sharon agreed that all Palestinians factions would stop all acts of violence against all Israelis everywhere and, in parallel, that Israel would cease all its military activity against all Palestinians everywhere. They also reaffirmed their commitment to the Roadmap for peace process. Sharon also agreed to release 900 Palestinian prisoners of the 7,500 being held at the time, and to withdraw from West Bank towns. However, the violence continued into the following years, though suicide bombings decreased significantly.

Etymology

Second Intifada refers to a second Palestinian uprising, following the first Palestinian uprising, which occurred between December 1987 and 1993. "Intifada" (انتفاضة) translates into English as "uprising." Its root is an Arabic word meaning "the shaking off." It has been used in the meaning of "insurrection" in various Arab countries. The Egyptian riots of 1977 were called the "bread intifada".[1684] The term refers to a revolt against the Israeli occupation of the Palestinian Territories.

Al-Aqsa Intifada refers to the Al-Aqsa Mosque, the place where the intifada started. It is the name of a mosque, constructed in the 8th century CE at Al-Haram Al-Sharif, also known as the Temple Mount in the Old City of Jerusalem, a location considered the holiest site in Judaism and third holiest in Islam.

The Intifada is sometimes called the **Oslo War** (אוסלו (מלחמת by some Israelis who consider it to be the result of concessions made by Israel following the Oslo Accords, and **Arafat's War**, after the late Palestinian leader whom some blamed for starting it. Others have named what they consider disproportionate response to what was initially a popular uprising by unarmed demonstrators as the reason for the escalation of the Intifada into an all out war.

Background

Oslo Accords

Under the Oslo Accords, signed in 1993 and 1995, Israel committed to the phased withdrawal of its forces from parts of the Gaza Strip and West Bank, and affirmed the Palestinian right to self-government within those areas through the creation of a Palestinian Authority. For their part, the Palestine Liberation Organization formally recognised Israel and committed to adopting responsibility for internal security in population centres in the areas evacuated. Palestinian self-rule was to last for a five-year interim period during which a permanent agreement would be negotiated. However, the realities on the ground left both sides deeply disappointed with the Oslo process. Israelis and Palestinians have blamed each other for the failure of the Oslo peace process. In the five years immediately following the signing of the Oslo accords, 405 Palestinians and 256 Israelis were killed, which for the latter represented a casualty count higher than that of the previous fifteen years combined (216, 172 of whom were killed during the First Intifada).

From 1996 Israel made extensive contingency plans and preparations, collectively code-named "Musical Charm," in the eventuality that peace talks might fail. In 1998, after concluding that the 5-year plan stipulated in the Oslo Talks would not be completed, the IDF implemented an Operation Field of Thorns plan to conquer towns in Area C, and some areas of Gaza, and military exercises at regimental level were carried out in April 2000 to that end. Palestinian preparations were defensive, and small scale, more to reassure the local population than to cope with an eventual attack from Israel. The intensity of these operations led one Brigadier General, Zvi Fogel to wonder whether Israel's military preparations would not turn out to be a self-fulfilling prophecy.[1685]

In 1995, Shimon Peres took the place of Yitzhak Rabin, who had been assassinated by Yigal Amir, a Jewish extremist opposed to the Oslo peace agreement. In the 1996 elections, Israelis elected a right-wing coalition led by the Likud candidate, Benjamin Netanyahu who was followed in 1999 by the Labor Party leader Ehud Barak.

Camp David Summit

From 11 to 25 July 2000, the Middle East Peace Summit at Camp David was held between United States President Bill Clinton, Israeli Prime Minister Ehud Barak, and Palestinian Authority Chairman Yasser Arafat. The talks ultimately failed with each side blaming the other. There were four principal obstacles to agreement: territory, Jerusalem and the Temple Mount, refugees and the right of return, and Israeli security concerns. Disappointment at the situation over

the summer led to a significant fracturing of the PLO as many Fatah factions abandoned it to join Hamas and Islamic Jihad.

On 13 September 2000, Yasser Arafat and the Palestinian Legislative Council postponed the planned unilateral declaration of an independent Palestinian state.

Continued settlement

While Peres had limited settlement construction at the request of US Secretary of State, Madeleine Albright, Netanyahu continued construction within existing Israeli settlements and put forward plans for the construction of a new neighbourhood, Har Homa, in East Jerusalem. However, he fell far short of the Shamir government's 1991–92 level and refrained from building new settlements, although the Oslo agreements stipulated no such ban. Construction of Housing Units Before Oslo: 1991–92: 13,960, After Oslo: 1994–95: 3,840, 1996–1997: 3,570.

With the aim of marginalising the settlers' more militant wing, Barak courted moderate settler opinion, securing agreement for the dismantlement of 12 new outposts that had been constructed since the Wye River Agreement of November 1998, but the continued expansion of existing settlements with plans for 3,000 new houses in the West Bank drew strong condemnation from the Palestinian leadership. Though construction within existing settlements was permitted under the Oslo agreements, Palestinian supporters contend that any continued construction was contrary to its spirit, prejudiced the outcome of final status negotiations, and undermined Palestinian confidence in Barak's desire for peace.

Timeline

2000

The Middle East Peace Summit at Camp David from 11 to 25 July 2000, took place between United States President Bill Clinton, Israeli Prime Minister Ehud Barak, and Palestinian Authority Chairman Yasser Arafat. It failed with the latter two blaming each other for the failure of the talks. There were four principal obstacles to agreement: territory, Jerusalem and the Temple Mount, Palestinian refugees and the right of return, and Israeli security concerns.

Sharon visits Temple Mount

On 28 September, Israeli opposition leader Ariel Sharon together with a Likud party delegation surrounded by hundreds of Israeli riot police, visited the Temple Mount. Al-Aqsa Mosque is part of the compound and is widely considered the third holiest site in Islam. Israel asserted its control by incorporating East Jerusalem into Jerusalem in 1980, and the compound is the holiest site in Judaism. Sharon was only permitted to enter the compound after the Israeli Interior Minister had received assurances from the Palestinian Authority's security chief that no problems would arise if he made the visit. Sharon did not actually go into the Al-Aqsa Mosque and went during normal tourist hours. Colin Shindler writes, "Shlomo Ben-Ami, the Minister of Internal security, was told by Israeli intelligence that there was no concerted risk of violence. This was implicitly confirmed by Jibril Rajoub, the Palestinian head of Preventive Security on the West Bank, who told Ben-Shlomo that Sharon could visit the Haram, but not enter a mosque on security grounds."

Shortly after Sharon left the site, angry demonstrations by Palestinian Jerusalemites outside erupted into rioting. The person in charge of the waqf at the time, Abu Qteish, was later indicted by Israel for using a loud-speaker to call on Palestinians to defend Al-Aqsa at the time, which action Israeli authorities claimed was responsible for the subsequent stone-throwing in the direction of the Wailing Wall.[1686] Israeli police responded with tear gas and rubber bullets, while protesters hurled stones and other projectiles, injuring 25 policemen, of whom one was seriously injured and had to be taken to hospital. At least three Palestinians were wounded by rubber bullets.

The stated purpose for Sharon's visit of the compound was to assert the right of all Israelis to visit the Temple Mount; however, according to Likud spokesman Ofir Akunis, the purpose was to "show that under a Likud government [the Temple Mount] will remain under Israeli sovereignty." Ehud Barak in the Camp David negotiations had insisted that East Jerusalem, where the Haram was located, would remain under complete Israeli sovereignty.[1687] In response to accusations by Ariel Sharon of government readiness to concede the site to the Palestinians, the Israeli government gave Sharon permission to visit the area. When alerted of his intentions, senior Palestinian figures, such as Yasser Arafat, Saeb Erekat, and Faisal Husseini all asked Sharon to call off his visit.

The Palestinians, some 10 days earlier, had just observed their annual memorial day for the Sabra and Shatila massacre. The Kahan Commission had concluded that Ariel Sharon, who was Defense Minister during the Sabra and Shatila massacre, was found to bear personal responsibility "for ignoring the danger of bloodshed and revenge" and "not taking appropriate measures to prevent bloodshed." Sharon's negligence in protecting the civilian population of Beirut, which had come under Israeli control amounted to a *non-fulfillment of a duty with which the Defence Minister was charged,* and it was recommended that Sharon be dismissed as Defence Minister. Sharon initially refused to resign, but after the death of an Israeli after a peace march, Sharon did resign as Defense minister, but remained in the Israeli cabinet.

The Palestinians condemned Sharon's visit to the Temple Mount as a provocation and an incursion, as were his armed bodyguards that arrived on the scene with him. Critics claim that Sharon knew that the visit could trigger violence, and that the purpose of his visit was political. According to one observer, Sharon, in walking on the temple Mount, was "skating on the thinnest ice in the Arab-Israeli conflict."[1688] According to Yossef Bodansky,

<templatestyles src="Template:Quote/styles.css"/>

> *Clinton's proposal [...] included explicit guarantees that Jews would have the right to visit and pray in and around the Temple Mount... Once Sharon was convinced that Jews had free access to the Temple Mount, there would be little the Israeli religious and nationalist Right could do to stall the peace process. When Sharon expressed interest in visiting the Temple Mount, Barak ordered GSS chief Ami Ayalon to approach Jibril Rajoub with a special request to facilitate a smooth and friendly visit. [...] Rajoub promised it would be smooth as long as Sharon would refrain from entering any of the mosques or praying publicly. [...] Just to be on the safe side, Barak personally approached Arafat and once again got assurances that Sharon's visit would be smooth as long as he did not attempt to enter the Holy Mosques. [...]*
>
> *A group of Palestinian dignitaries came to protest the visit, as did three Arab Knesset Members. With the dignitaries watching from a safe distance, the Shabab (youth mob) threw rocks and attempted to get past the Israeli security personnel and reach Sharon and his entourage. [...] Still, Sharon's deportment was quiet and dignified. He did not pray, did not make any statement, or do anything else that might be interpreted as offensive to the sensitivities of Muslims. Even after he came back near the Wailing Wall under the hail of rocks, he remained calm. "I came here as one who believes in coexistence between Jews and Arabs," Sharon told the waiting reporters. "I believe that we can build and develop together. This was a peaceful visit. Is it an instigation for Israeli Jews to come to the Jewish people's holiest site?"*[1689]

Shlomo Ben-Ami, the then acting Israeli Foreign Minister, has maintained, however, that he received Palestinian assurances that no violence would occur, provided that Ariel Sharon not enter one of the mosques.

According to *The New York Times*, many in the Arab world, including Egyptians, Palestinians, Lebanese and Jordanians, point to Sharon's visit as the beginning of the Second Intifada and derailment of the peace process. According to Juliana Ochs, Sharon's visit 'symbolically instigated' the second intifada. Marwan Barghouti said that although Sharon's provocative actions were a rallying point for Palestinians, the Second Intifada would have erupted even had he not visited the Temple Mount.[1690]

First days of the Intifada

On 29 September 2000, the day after Sharon's visit, following Friday prayers, large riots broke out around the Old City of Jerusalem. After Palestinians on the Temple Mount threw rocks over the Western Wall at Jewish worshippers, Israeli police fired back. The switch to live ammunition occurred when the chief of Jerusalem's police force was knocked unconscious by a rock.[1691] Police then switched to live ammunition, killing four Palestinian youths. Up to 200 Palestinians and police were injured. Another three Palestinians were killed in the Old City and on the Mount of Olives. By the end of the day, 7 Palestinians had been killed and 300 had been wounded. 70 Israeli policemen were also injured in the clashes.

In the days that followed, demonstrations erupted all over the West Bank and Gaza. Israeli police responded with live fire and rubber-coated bullets. In the first five days, at least 47 Palestinians were killed, and 1,885 were wounded. In Paris, as Jacques Chirac attempted to mediate between the parties, he protested to Barak that the ratio of Palestinian and Israeli killed and wounded on one day were such that he could not convince anyone the Palestinians were the aggressors. He also told Barak that "continu(ing) to fire from helicopters on people throwing rocks" and refusing an international inquiry was tantamount to rejecting Arafat's offer to participate in trilateral negotiations.[1692] On 27 September, an Israeli soldier was killed and another lightly wounded in a bombing by Palestinian militants near the Gaza Strip settlement of Netzarim. Two days later, Palestinian police officer Nail Suleiman opened fire on an Israel Border Police Jeep during a joint patrol in the West Bank city of Qalqiliyah, killing Supt. Yosef Tabeja. During the first few days of riots, the IDF fired approximately 1.3 million bullets.[1693]

According to Amnesty International the early Palestinian casualties were those taking part in demonstrations or bystanders. Amnesty further states that approximately 80% of the Palestinians killed during the first month were in demonstrations where Israeli security services lives were not in danger.

On 30 September 2000, the death of Muhammad al-Durrah, a Palestinian boy shot dead while sheltering behind his father in an alley in the Gaza Strip was caught on video. Initially the boy's death and his father's wounding was attributed to Israeli soldiers. The scene assumed iconic status, as it was shown around the world and repeatedly broadcast on Arab television. The Israeli army initially assumed responsibility for the killing and apologised, and only retracted 2 months later, when an internal investigation cast doubt on the original version, and controversy subsequently raged as to whether indeed the IDF had fired the shots or Palestinian factions were responsible for the fatal gunshots.[1694]

October 2000 events

The "October 2000 events" refers to several days of disturbances and clashes inside Israel, mostly between Arab citizens and the Israel police. The events also saw large-scale rioting by both Arabs and Jews. Twelve Arab citizens of Israel and a Palestinian from the Gaza Strip were killed by Israeli police, while an Israeli Jew was killed when his car was hit by a rock on the Tel-Aviv-Haifa freeway. During the first month of the Intifada, 141 Palestinians were killed and 5,984 were wounded while 12 Israelis were killed and 65 wounded.

A general strike and demonstrations across northern Israel began on 1 October and continued for several days. In some cases, the demonstrations escalated into clashes with the Israeli police involving rock-throwing, firebombing, and live-fire. Policemen used tear-gas and opened fire with rubber-coated bullets and later live ammunition in some instances, many times in contravention of police protocol governing riot-dispersion. This use of live ammunition was directly linked with many of the deaths by the Or Commission.

On 8 October, thousands of Jewish Israelis participated in violent acts in Tel Aviv and elsewhere, some throwing stones at Arabs, destroying Arab property and chanting "Death to the Arabs."

Following the riots, a high degree of tension between Jewish and Arab citizens and distrust between the Arab citizens and police were widespread. An investigation committee, headed by Supreme Court Justice Theodor Or, reviewed the violent riots and found that the police were poorly prepared to handle such riots and charged major officers with bad conduct. The Or Commission reprimanded Prime Minister Ehud Barak and recommended Shlomo Ben-Ami, then the Internal Security Minister, not serve again as Minister of Public Security. The committee also blamed Arab leaders and Knesset members for contributing to inflaming the atmosphere and making the violence more severe.

Ramallah lynching and Israeli response

On 12 October, PA police arrested two Israeli reservists who had accidentally entered Ramallah, where in the preceding weeks a hundred Palestinians had been killed, nearly two dozen of them minors.[1695] Rumours quickly spread that Israeli undercover agents were in the building, and an angry crowd of more than 1,000 Palestinians gathered in front of the station calling for their death. Both soldiers were beaten, stabbed, and disembowelled, and one body was set on fire. An Italian television crew captured the killings on video and then broadcast his tape internationally. A British journalist had his camera destroyed by rioters as he attempted to take a picture. The brutality of the killings shocked the Israeli public, who saw it as proof of a deep-seated Palestinian hatred of Israel and Jews. In response, Israel launched a series of retaliatory air-strikes against Palestinian Authority targets in the West Bank and Gaza Strip. The police station where the lynching had taken place was evacuated and destroyed in these operations. Israel later tracked down and arrested those responsible for killing the soldiers.

November and December

Clashes between Israeli forces and Palestinians increased sharply on 1 November, when three Israeli soldiers and six Palestinians were killed, and four IDF soldiers and 140 Palestinians were wounded. In subsequent days, casualties increased as the IDF attempted to restore order, with clashes occurring every day in November. A total of 122 Palestinians and 22 Israelis were killed. On 27 November, the first day of Ramadan, Israel eased restrictions on the passage of goods and fuel through the Karni crossing. That same day, the Jerusalem settlement of Gilo came under Palestinian heavy machine gun fire from Beit Jala. Israel tightened restrictions a week later, and Palestinians continued to clash with the IDF and Israeli settlers, with a total of 51 Palestinians and 8 Israelis killed in December.

2001

The Taba Summit between Israel and the Palestinian Authority was held from 21 to 27 January 2001, at Taba in the Sinai peninsula. Israeli prime minister Ehud Barak and Palestinian President Yasser Arafat came closer to reaching a final settlement than any previous or subsequent peace talks yet ultimately failed to achieve their goals.

On 17 January 2001, Israeli teenager Ofir Rahum was murdered after being lured into Ramallah by a 24-year-old Palestinian, Mona Jaud Awana, a member of Fatah's Tanzim. She had contacted Ofir on the internet and engaged in an online romance with him for several months. She eventually convinced him to drive to Ramallah to meet her, where he was instead ambushed by three

Palestinian gunmen and shot over fifteen times. Awana was later arrested in a massive military and police operation, and imprisoned for life. Five other Israelis were killed in January, along with eighteen Palestinians.

Ariel Sharon, at the time from the Likud party, ran against Ehud Barak from the Labour party. Sharon was elected Israeli Prime Minister 6 February 2001 in the 2001 special election to the Prime Ministership. Sharon refused to meet in person with Yasser Arafat.

Violence in March resulted in the deaths of 8 Israelis, mostly civilians, and 26 Palestinians. In Hebron, a Palestinian sniper killed ten-month-old Israeli baby Shalhevet Pass. The murder shocked the Israeli public. According to the Israel police investigation the sniper aimed deliberately at the baby.

On 30 April 2001, seven Palestinian militants were killed in an explosion, one of them a participant in Ofir Rahum's murder. The IDF refused to confirm or deny Palestinian accusations that it was responsible.

On 7 May 2001, the IDF naval commandos captured the vessel *Santorini*, which sailed in international waters towards Palestinian Authority-controlled Gaza. The ship was laden with weaponry. The Israeli investigation that followed alleged that the shipment had been purchased by Ahmed Jibril's Popular Front for the Liberation of Palestine - General Command (PFLP-GC). The ship's value and that of its cargo was estimated at $10 million. The crew was reportedly planning to unload the cargo of weapons-filled barrels—carefully sealed and waterproofed along with their contents—at a prearranged location off the Gaza coast, where the Palestinian Authority would recover it.

On 8 May 2001, two Israeli teenagers, Yaakov "Koby" Mandell (13) and Yosef Ishran (14) were kidnapped while hiking near their village. Their bodies were discovered the next morning in a cave near where they lived. *USA Today* reported that, according to the police, both boys had "been bound, stabbed and beaten to death with rocks." The newspaper continued, "The walls of the cave in the Judean Desert were covered with the boys' blood, reportedly smeared there by the killers."

After a suicide bombing struck Netanya on 18 May 2001, Israel for the first time since 1967 used warplanes to attack Palestinian Authority targets in the West Bank and Gaza, killing 12 Palestinians. In the past, airstrikes had been carried out with helicopter gunships.

On 1 June 2001, an Islamic Jihad suicide bomber detonated himself in the Tel Aviv coastline Dolphinarium dancing club. Twenty-one Israeli civilians, most of them high school students, were killed and 132 injured. The attack significantly hampered American attempts to negotiate cease-fire.

Figure 216: *Military equipment confiscated from Karine A*

The 12 June Murder of Georgios Tsibouktzakis by Palestinina snipers was later tied to Marwan Barghouti.

A total of 469 Palestinians and 199 Israelis were killed in 2001. Amnesty International's report on the first year of the Intifada states:

> *The overwhelming majority of cases of unlawful killings and injuries in Israel and the Occupied Territories have been committed by the IDF using excessive force. In particular, the IDF have used US-supplied helicopters in punitive rocket attacks where there was no imminent danger to life. Israel has also used helicopter gunships to carry out extrajudicial executions and to fire at targets that resulted in the killing of civilians, including children. ... Hamas and Islamic Jihad have frequently placed bombs in public places, usually within Israel, in order to kill and maim large numbers of Israeli civilians in a random manner. Both organizations have fostered a cult of martyrdom and frequently use suicide bombers.*

Palestinian terrorists committed a number of suicide attacks later in 2001, among them the Sbarro restaurant massacre with 15 civilian casualties (including 7 children), the Nahariya train station suicide bombing and the Pardes Hanna bus bombing, both with 3 civilian casualties, the Ben Yehuda Street bombing with 11 civilian deaths, many of them children, and the Haifa bus 16 suicide bombing with 15 civilian casualties.[1696]

2002

In January 2002, the IDF Shayetet 13 naval commandos captured the *Karine A*, a freighter carrying weapons from Iran towards Israel, believed to be intended for Palestinian militant use against Israel. It was discovered that top officials in the Palestinian Authority were involved in the smuggling, with the Israelis pointing the finger towards Yasser Arafat as also being involved.

Palestinians launched a spate of suicide bombings and attacks, aimed mostly at civilians, against Israel. On 3 March, a Palestinian sniper killed 10 Israeli soldiers and settlers and wounded 4 at a checkpoint near Ofra, using an M1 Carbine. He was later arrested and sentenced to life imprisonment. The rate of the attacks increased, and was at its highest in March 2002. In addition to numerous shooting and grenade attacks, that month saw 15 suicide bombings carried out in Israel, an average of one bombing every two days. The high rate of attacks caused widespread fear throughout Israel and serious disruption of daily life throughout the country. March 2002 became known in Israel as "Black March." The wave of suicide bombings culminated with the Passover massacre in Netanya on 27 March, in which 30 people were killed at the Park Hotel while celebrating Passover. In total, around 130 Israelis, mostly civilians, were killed in Palestinian attacks during March 2002.

On 12 March United Nations Security Council Resolution 1397 was passed, which reaffirmed a Two-state solution and laid the groundwork for a Road map for peace. Arab leaders, whose constituencies were exposed to detailed television coverage of the violence in the conflict, set out a comprehensive Arab Peace Initiative, which was outlined by Saudi Arabia on 28 March. Arafat endorsed the proposal, while Israel reacted coolly, virtually ignoring it.[1697,1698,1699]

On 29 March, Israel launched Operation Defensive Shield, which lasted until 3 May. The IDF made sweeping incursions throughout the West Bank, and into numerous Palestinian cities. Arafat was put under siege in his Ramallah compound.[1700] The UN estimated that 497 Palestinians were killed and 1,447 wounded by the Israeli response from 1 March to 7 May, although B'Tselem registered 240 killed. Most of the casualties were members of Palestinian security forces and militant groups. Israeli forces also arrested 4,258 Palestinians during the operation. Israeli casualties during the operation totaled 30 dead and 127 wounded. The operation culminated with the recapturing of Palestinian Authority controlled areas.

Jenin

Between 2 and 11 April, a siege and fierce fighting took place in Jenin, a Palestinian refugee camp. The camp was targeted during Operation Defensive Shield after Israel determined that it had "served as a launch site for numerous terrorist attacks against both Israeli civilians and Israeli towns and villages in the area." The Jenin battle became a flashpoint for both sides. Eventually, The

Figure 217: *IDF Caterpillar D9*

battle was won by the IDF, after it operated a dozen of Caterpillar D9 armored bulldozers who cleared Palestinian booby traps, detonated explosive charges, razed buildings and gun-posts and proved impervious to attacks by Palestinian militants.

During the IDF's operations in the camp, Palestinian sources alleged that a massacre of hundreds of people had taken place. A senior Palestinian Authority official alleged in mid-April that some 500 had been killed. During the fighting in Jenin, Israeli officials had also initially estimated hundreds of Palestinian deaths, but later said they expected the Palestinian toll to reach "45 to 55." In the ensuing controversy, Israel blocked the United Nations from conducting the first-hand inquiry unanimously sought by the Security Council, but the UN nonetheless felt able to dismiss claims of a massacre in its report, which said there had been approximately 52 deaths, criticising both sides for placing Palestinian civilians at risk. Based on their own investigations, Amnesty International and Human Rights Watch charged that some IDF personnel in Jenin had committed war crimes but also confirmed that no massacre had been committed by the IDF. Both human rights organizations called for official inquiries; the IDF disputed the charges.

After the battle, most sources, including the IDF and Palestinian Authority, placed the Palestinian death toll at 52–56; HRW said this total consisted of at least 27 militants and 22 civilians, while the IDF said that 48 militants and 5 civilians had been killed.[1701] According to Human Rights Watch, 140 buildings

Figure 218: *The aftermath of a bus bombing in Haifa in 2003.*

had been destroyed. The IDF reported that 23 Israeli soldiers had been killed and 75 wounded.

Bethlehem

From 2 April to 10 May, a stand-off developed at the Church of the Nativity in Bethlehem. IDF soldiers surrounded the church while Palestinian civilians, militants, and priests were inside. During the siege, IDF snipers killed 8 militants inside the church and wounded more than 40 people. The stand-off was resolved by the deportation to Europe of 13 Palestinian militants whom the IDF had identified as terrorists, and the IDF ended its 38-day stand-off with the militants inside the church.

2003

Following an Israeli intelligence report stating that Yasir Arafat had paid $20,000 to al-Aqsa Martyrs' Brigades, the United States demanded democratic reforms in the Palestinian Authority, as well the appointment of a prime minister independent of Arafat. On 13 March 2003, following U.S. pressure, Arafat appointed Mahmoud Abbas as Palestinian prime minister.

Following the appointment of Abbas, the U.S. administration promoted the Road map for peace—the Quartet's plan to end the Israeli–Palestinian conflict by disbanding militant organizations, halting settlement activity and establishing a democratic and peaceful Palestinian state. The first phase of the plan demanded that the Palestinian Authority suppress guerrilla and terrorist attacks and confiscate illegal weapons. Unable or unwilling to confront militant organizations and risk civil war, Abbas tried to reach a temporary cease-fire agreement with the militant factions and asked them to halt attacks on Israeli civilians.

On 20 May, Israeli naval commandos intercepted another vessel, the *Abu Hassan*, on course to the Gaza Strip from Lebanon. It was loaded with rockets, weapons, and ammunition. Eight crew members on board were arrested including a senior Hezbollah member.

On 29 June 2003, a temporary armistice was unilaterally declared by Fatah, Hamas and Islamic Jihad, which declared a ceasefire and halt to all attacks against Israel for a period of three months. Violence decreased somewhat in the following month but suicide bombings against Israeli civilians continued as well as Israeli operations against militants.

Four Palestinians, three of them militants, were killed in gun battles during an IDF raid of Askar near Nablus involving tanks and armoured personnel carriers (APCs); an Israeli soldier was killed by one of the militants. Nearby Palestinians claimed a squad of Israeli police disguised as Palestinian labourers opened fire on Abbedullah Qawasameh as he left a Hebron mosque. YAMAM, the Israeli counter-terrorism police unit that performed the operation stated that Qawasemah opened fire on them as they attempted to arrest him.

On 19 August, Hamas coordinated a suicide attack on a crowded bus in Jerusalem killing 23 Israeli civilians, including 7 children. Hamas claimed it was a retaliation for the killing of five Palestinians (including Hamas leader Abbedullah Qawasameh) earlier in the week. U.S. and Israeli media outlets frequently referred to the bus bombing as shattering the quiet and bringing an end to the ceasefire.

Following the Hamas bus attack, Israeli Defence Forces were ordered to kill or capture all Hamas leaders in Hebron and the Gaza Strip. The plotters of the bus suicide bombing were all captured or killed and Hamas leadership in Hebron was badly damaged by the IDF. Strict curfews were enforced in Nablus, Jenin, and Tulkarem; the Nablus lockdown lasted for over 100 days. In Nazlet 'Issa, over 60 shops were destroyed by Israeli civil administration bulldozers. The Israeli civil administration explained that the shops were demolished because they were built without a permit. Palestinians consider Israeli military curfews and property destruction to constitute collective punishment against innocent Palestinians.

Figure 219: *Early Israeli construction of West Bank barrier, 2003*

Unable to rule effectively under Arafat, Abbas resigned in September 2003. Ahmed Qurei (Abu Ala) was appointed to replace him. The Israeli government gave up hope for negotiated settlement to the conflict and pursued a unilateral policy of physically separating Israel from Palestinian communities by beginning construction on the Israeli West Bank barrier. Israel claims the barrier is necessary to prevent Palestinian attackers from entering Israeli cities. Palestinians claim the barrier separates Palestinian communities from each other and that the construction plan is a de facto annexation of Palestinian territory.

Following a 4 October suicide bombing in Maxim restaurant, Haifa, which claimed the lives of 21 Israelis, Israel claimed that Syria and Iran sponsored the Islamic Jihad and Hezbollah, and were responsible for the terrorist attack. The day after the Maxim massacre, IAF warplanes bombed an alleged former Palestinian training base at Ain Saheb, Syria, which had been mostly abandoned since the 1980s. Munitions being stored on the site were destroyed, and a civilian guard was injured.

2004

In response to a repeated shelling of Israeli communities with Qassam rockets and mortar shells from Gaza, the IDF operated mainly in Rafah – to search and destroy smuggling tunnels used by militants to obtain weapons, ammunition, fugitives, cigarettes, car parts, electrical goods, foreign currency, gold, drugs, and cloth from Egypt. Between September 2000 and May 2004, ninety tunnels connecting Egypt and the Gaza Strip were found and destroyed. Raids in Rafah left many families homeless. Israel's official stance is that their houses were captured by militants and were destroyed during battles with IDF forces. Many of these houses are abandoned due to Israeli incursions and later destroyed. According to Human Rights Watch, over 1,500 houses were destroyed to create a large buffer zone in the city, many "in the absence of military necessity", displacing around sixteen thousand people.

On 2 February 2004, Israeli Prime Minister Ariel Sharon announced his plan to transfer all the Jewish settlers from the Gaza Strip. The Israeli opposition dismissed his announcement as "media spin" but the Israeli Labour Party said it would support such a move. Sharon's right-wing coalition partners National Religious Party and National Union rejected the plan and vowed to quit the government if it were implemented. Yossi Beilin, peace advocate and architect of the Oslo Accords and the Geneva Accord, also rejected the proposed withdrawal plan. He claimed that withdrawing from the Gaza Strip without a peace agreement would reward terror.

Following the declaration of the disengagement plan by Ariel Sharon and as a response to suicide attacks on Erez crossing and Ashdod seaport (10 people were killed), the IDF launched a series of armored raids on the Gaza Strip (mainly Rafah and refugee camps around Gaza), killing about 70 Hamas militants. On 22 March 2004, an Israeli helicopter gunship killed Hamas leader Sheikh Ahmed Yassin, along with his two bodyguards and nine bystanders, and on 17 April, after several failed attempts by Hamas to commit suicide bombings and a successful one that killed an Israeli policeman, Yassin's successor, Abdel Aziz al-Rantissi was killed in an almost identical way, along with a bodyguard and his son Mohammed.

The fighting in Gaza Strip escalated severely in May 2004 after several failed attempts to attack Israeli checkpoints such as Erez crossing and Karni crossing. On 2 May, Palestinian militants attacked and shot dead a pregnant woman and her four young daughters. Amnesty International classified it as a crime against humanity and stated that it "reiterates its call on all Palestinian armed groups to put an immediate end to the deliberate targeting of Israeli civilians, in Israel and in the Occupied Territories". Additionally, on 11 and 12 May, Palestinian militants destroyed two IDF M-113 APCs, killing 13 soldiers and mutilating

Figure 220: *Israeli forces uncover a smuggling tunnel in Gaza, May 2004*

their bodies. The IDF launched two raids to recover the bodies in which about 20–40 Palestinians were killed and great damage was caused to structures in the Zaitoun neighbourhood in Gaza and in south-west Rafah.

Subsequently, on 18 May the IDF launched Operation Rainbow with a stated aim of striking the militant infrastructure of Rafah, destroying smuggling tunnels, and stopping a shipment of SA-7 missiles and improved anti-tank weapons. A total of 41 Palestinian militants and 12 civilians were killed in the operation, and about 45–56 Palestinian structures were demolished. Israeli tanks shelled hundreds of Palestinian protesters approaching their positions, killing 10. The protesters had disregarded Israeli warnings to turn back. This incident led to a worldwide outcry against the operation.

On 29 September, after a Qassam rocket hit the Israeli town of Sderot and killed two Israeli children, the IDF launched Operation Days of Penitence in the north of the Gaza Strip. The operation's stated aim was to remove the threat of Qassam rockets from Sderot and kill the Hamas militants launching them. The operation ended on 16 October, leaving widespread destruction and more than 100 Palestinians dead, at least 20 of whom were under the age of 16. Thirteen-year-old Iman Darweesh Al Hams was killed by the IDF when she strayed into a closed military area: the commander was accused of allegedly firing his automatic weapon at her dead body deliberately to verify the death. The act was investigated by the IDF, but the commander was cleared of all wrongdoing, and more recently, was fully vindicated when a Jerusalem district court found the claim to be libellous, ruled that NIS 300,000 be paid by the journalist and TV company responsible for the report, an additional NIS 80,000 to be paid in legal fees and required the journalist and television company to air a correction. According to Palestinian medics, Israeli forces killed at least 62 militants and 42 other Palestinians believed to be civilians. According to a count performed by *Haaretz*, 87 militants and 42 civilians were killed. Palestinian refugee camps were heavily damaged by the Israeli assault. The IDF announced that at least 12 Qassam launchings had been thwarted and many terrorists hit during the operation.

On 21 October, the Israeli Air Force killed Adnan al-Ghoul, a senior Hamas bomb maker and the inventor of the Qassam rocket.

On 11 November, Yasser Arafat died in Paris.

Escalation in Gaza began amid the visit of Mahmoud Abbas to Syria in order to achieve a Hudna between Palestinian factions and convince Hamas leadership to halt attacks against Israelis. Hamas vowed to continue the armed struggle sending numerous Qassam rockets into open fields near Nahal Oz, and hitting a kindergarten in Kfar Darom with an anti-tank missile.

On 9 December five Palestinians weapon smugglers were killed and two were arrested in the border between Rafah and Egypt. Later that day, Jamal Abu Samhadana and two of his bodyguards were injured by a missile strike. In the first Israeli airstrike against militants in weeks, an unmanned Israeli drone plane launched one missile at Abu Samahdna's car as it travelled between Rafah and Khan Younis in the southern Gaza Strip. It was the fourth attempt on Samhadana's life by Israel. Samhadana is one of two leaders of the Popular Resistance Committees and one of the main forces behind the smuggling tunnels. Samhadana is believed to be responsible for the blast against an American diplomatic convoy in Gaza that killed three Americans.

On 10 December, in response to Hamas firing mortar rounds into the Neveh Dekalim settlement in the Gaza Strip and wounding four Israelis (including an 8-year-old boy), Israeli soldiers fired at the Khan Younis refugee camp (the origin of the mortars) killing a 7-year-old girl. An IDF source confirmed troops opened fire at Khan Younis, but said they aimed at Hamas mortar crews.

The largest attack since the death of Yasser Arafat claimed the lives of five Israeli soldiers on 12 December, wounding ten others. Approximately 1.5 tons of explosives were detonated in a tunnel under an Israeli military-controlled border crossing on the Egyptian border with Gaza near Rafah, collapsing several structures and damaging others. The explosion destroyed part of the outpost and killed three soldiers. Two Palestinian militants then penetrated the outpost and killed two other Israeli soldiers with gunfire. It is believed that Hamas and a new Fatah faction, the "Fatah Hawks", conducted the highly organised and coordinated attack. A spokesman, "Abu Majad", claimed responsibility for the attack in the name of the Fatah Hawks claiming it was in retaliation for "the assassination" of Yasser Arafat, charging he was poisoned by Israel.

2005

Palestinian presidential elections were held on 9 January, and Mahmoud Abbas (Abu Mazen) was elected as the president of the PA. His platform was of a peaceful negotiation with Israel and non-violence to achieve Palestinian objectives. Although Abbas called on militants to halt attacks against Israel, he promised them protection from Israeli incursions and did not advocate disarmament by force.

Violence continued in the Gaza Strip, and Ariel Sharon froze all diplomatic and security contacts with the Palestinian National Authority. Spokesman Assaf Shariv declared that "Israel informed international leaders today that there will be no meetings with Abbas until he makes a real effort to stop the terror." The freezing of contacts came less than one week after Mahmoud Abbas was elected, and the day before his inauguration. Palestinian negotiator Saeb Erekat, confirming the news, declared "You cannot hold Mahmoud Abbas accountable when he hasn't even been inaugurated yet."

Following international pressure and Israeli threat of wide military operation in the Gaza Strip, Abbas ordered Palestinian police to deploy in the northern Gaza Strip to prevent Qassam rocket and mortar shelling over Israeli settlement. Although attacks on Israelis did not stop completely, they decreased sharply. On 8 February 2005, at the Sharm el-Sheikh Summit of 2005, Sharon and Abbas declared a mutual truce between Israel and the Palestinian National Authority. They shook hands at a four-way summit that also included Jordan and Egypt at Sharm al-Sheikh. However, Hamas and Islamic Jihad said the truce is not binding for their members. Israel has not withdrawn its demand to dismantle terrorist infrastructure before moving ahead in the Road map for peace.

Many warned that truce is fragile, and progress must be done slowly while observing that the truce and quiet are kept. On 9–10 February night, a barrage of 25–50 Qassam rockets and mortar shells hit Neve Dekalim settlement, and another barrage hit at noon. Hamas said it was in retaliation for an attack in which one Palestinian was killed near an Israeli settlement. As a response to the mortar attack, Abbas ordered the Palestinian security forces to stop such attacks in the future. He also fired senior commanders in the Palestinian security apparatus. On 10 February, Israeli security forces arrested Maharan Omar

Shucat Abu Hamis, a Palestinian resident of Nablus, who was about to launch a bus suicide attack in the French Hill in Jerusalem.

On 13 February 2005, Abbas entered into talks with the leaders of the Islamic Jihad and the Hamas, for them to rally behind him and respect the truce. Ismail Haniyah, a senior leader of the group Hamas said that "its position regarding calm will continue unchanged and Israel will bear responsibility for any new violation or aggression."

In the middle of June, Palestinian factions intensified bombardment over the city of Sderot with improvised Qassam rockets. Palestinian attacks resulted in 2 Palestinians and 1 Chinese civilian killed by a Qassam, and 2 Israelis were killed. The wave of attacks lessened support for the disengagement plan among the Israeli public. Attacks on Israel by the Islamic Jihad and the al-Aqsa Martyrs' Brigades increased in July, and on 12 July, a suicide bombing hit the coastal city of Netanya, killing 5 civilians. On 14 July, Hamas started to shell Israeli settlements inside and outside the Gaza Strip with dozens of Qassam rockets, killing an Israeli woman. On 15 July, Israel resumed its "targeted killing" policy, killing 7 Hamas militants and bombing about 4 Hamas facilities. The continuation of shelling rockets over Israeli settlements, and street battles between Hamas militants and Palestinian policemen, threatened to shatter the truce agreed in the Sharm el-Sheikh Summit of 2005. The Israeli Defence Force also started to build up armored forces around the Gaza Strip in response to the shelling.

End of the Intifada

The ending date of the Second Intifada is disputed, as there was no definite event that brought it to an end.

- Some commentators such as Sever Plocker consider the intifada to have ended in late 2004. With the sickness and then death of Yasser Arafat in November 2004, the Palestinians lost their internationally recognised leader of the previous three decades, after which the intifada lost momentum and lead to internal fighting between Palestinian factions (most notably the Fatah–Hamas conflict), as well as conflict within Fatah itself.
- Israel's unilateral disengagement from the Gaza Strip, announced in June 2004 completed in August 2005, is also cited, for instance by Ramzy Baroud,[1702] as signalling the end of the intifada.
- Some consider 8 February 2005 to be the official end of the Second Intifada, although sporadic violence still continued outside PA control or condolence. On that day, Palestinian President Mahmoud Abbas and Israeli Prime Minister Ariel Sharon met at the Sharm el-Sheikh Summit where they vowed to end attacks on each other. In addition, Sharon agreeing to release 900 Palestinian prisoners and withdraw from West Bank

towns. Hamas and Palestinian Islamic Jihad (PIJ) refused to be parties to the agreement, arguing the cease-fire was the position of the Palestinian Authority only. Five days later Abbass reached agreement with the two dissenting organisations to commit to the truce with the proviso that Israeli violation would be met with retaliation.

Schachter addressed the difficulties in deciding when this intifada ended. He reasoned that suicide bombing was the best criterion, being arguably the most important element of second intifada-related violence, and that according to this criterion the intifada ended during 2005.

Cause of the Second Intifada

The Second Intifada started on 28 September 2000, after Ariel Sharon, a Likud party candidate for Israeli Prime Minister, made a visit to the Temple Mount, also known as Al-Haram Al-Sharif, an area sacred to both Jews and Muslims, accompanied by over 1,000 security guards. He stated on that day, "the Temple Mount is in our hands and will remain in our hands. It is the holiest site in Judaism and it is the right of every Jew to visit the Temple Mount."

This visit was seen by Palestinians as highly provocative; and Palestinian demonstrators, throwing stones at police, were dispersed by the Israeli Army, using tear gas and rubber bullets.[1703] A riot broke out among Palestinians at the site, resulting in clashes between Israeli forces and the protesting crowd.

Some believe the Intifada started the next day, on Friday, 29 September, a day of prayers, when an Israeli police and military presence was introduced and there were major clashes and deaths.

The Mitchell Report

The Sharm el-Sheikh Fact-Finding Committee (an investigatory committee set up to look into the causes behind the breakdown in the peace process, chaired by George J. Mitchell) published its report in May 2001.[1704] In the Mitchell Report, the government of Israel asserted that:

> *The immediate catalyst for the violence was the breakdown of the Camp David negotiations on July 25, 2000, and the "widespread appreciation in the international community of Palestinian responsibility for the impasse". In this view, Palestinian violence was planned by the PA leadership, and was aimed at "provoking and incurring Palestinian casualties as a means of regaining the diplomatic initiative".*

The Palestine Liberation Organization, according to the same report, denied that the Intifada was planned, and asserted that "Camp David represented nothing less than an attempt by Israel to extend the force it exercises on the ground to negotiations." The report also stated:

> From the perspective of the PLO, Israel responded to the disturbances with excessive and illegal use of deadly force against demonstrators; behavior which, in the PLO's view, reflected Israel's contempt for the lives and safety of Palestinians. For Palestinians, the widely seen images of Muhammad al-Durrah in Gaza on September 30, shot as he huddled behind his father, reinforced that perception.

The Mitchell report concluded:

> The Sharon visit did not cause the "Al-Aqsa Intifada". But it was poorly timed and the provocative effect should have been foreseen; indeed it was foreseen by those who urged that the visit be prohibited.

and also:

> We have no basis on which to conclude that there was a deliberate plan by the PA to initiate a campaign of violence at the first opportunity; or to conclude that there was a deliberate plan by the [Government of Israel] to respond with lethal force.

Views on the Second Intifada

Palestinians have claimed that Sharon's visit was the beginning of the Second Intifada, while others have claimed that Yasser Arafat had pre-planned the uprising.

Some, like Bill Clinton, say that tensions were high due to failed negotiations at the Camp David Summit in July 2000. They note that there were Israeli casualties as early as 27 September; this is the Israeli "conventional wisdom", according to Dr. Jeremy Pressman, and the view expressed by the Israeli Foreign Ministry. Most mainstream media outlets have taken the view that the Sharon visit was the spark that triggered the rioting at the start of the Second Intifada. In the first five days of rioting and clashes after the visit, Israeli police and security forces killed 47 Palestinians and wounded 1885, while Palestinians killed 5 Israelis.

Palestinians view the Second Intifada as part of their ongoing struggle for national liberation and an end to Israeli occupation,[1705] whereas many Israelis consider it to be a wave of Palestinian terrorism instigated and pre-planned by then Palestinian leader Yasser Arafat.

Some have claimed that Yasser Arafat and the Palestinian Authority (PA) had pre-planned the Intifada. They often quote a speech made in December 2000 by Imad Falouji, the PA Communications Minister at the time, where he explains that the Intifada had been planned since Arafat's return from the Camp David Summit in July, far in advance of Sharon's visit. He stated that the Intifada "was carefully planned since the return of (Palestinian President) Yasser Arafat from Camp David negotiations rejecting the U.S. conditions". David Samuels quotes Mamduh Nofal, former military commander of the Democratic Front for the Liberation of Palestine, who supplies more evidence of pre-28 September military preparations. Nofal recounts that Arafat "told us, Now we are going to the fight, so we must be ready". Barak as early as May had drawn up contingency plans to halt any intifada in its tracks by the extensive use of IDF snipers, a tactic that resulted in the high number of casualties among Palestinians during the first days of rioting.

Support for the idea that Arafat planned the Intifadah comes from Hamas leader Mahmoud al-Zahar, who said in September 2010 that when Arafat realized that the Camp David Summit in July 2000 would not result in the meeting of all of his demands, he ordered Hamas as well as Fatah and the Aqsa Martyrs Brigades, to launch "military operations" against Israel. al-Zahar is corroborated by Mosab Hassan Yousef, son of the Hamas founder and leader, Sheikh Hassan Yousef, who claims that the Second Intifada was a political maneuver premeditated by Arafat. Yousef claims that "Arafat had grown extraordinarily wealthy as the international symbol of victimhood. He wasn't about to surrender that status and take on the responsibility of actually building a functioning society."

Arafat's widow Suha Arafat reportedly said on Dubai television in December 2012 that her husband had planned the uprising.

"Immediately after the failure of the Camp David [negotiations], I met him in Paris upon his return.... Camp David had failed, and he said to me, 'You should remain in Paris.' I asked him why, and he said, 'Because I am going to start an intifada. They want me to betray the Palestinian cause. They want me to give up on our principles, and I will not do so,'" the research institute [MEMRI] translated Suha as saying.

Israel began a unilateral pullout from Lebanon in compliance with UN Resolution 425 (1978) in May 2000, which was declared completed on 16 June. The move was widely interpreted by Arabs as an Israeli defeat and was to exercise a profound influence on tactics adopted in the Al Aqsa Uprising.[1706] the PLO official Farouk Kaddoumi told reporters: "We are optimistic. Hezbollah's resistance can be used as an example for other Arabs seeking to regain their rights." Many Palestinian officials have gone on record as saying that the intifada had been planned long in advance to put pressure on Israel. It is disputed however whether Arafat himself gave direct orders for the outbreak, though he did not intervene to put a break on it[1707] A personal advisor to Arafat, Manduh Nufal, claimed in early 2001 that the Palestinian Authority had played a crucial role in the outbreak of the Intifada. Israeli's military response demolished a large part of the infrastructure built by the PA during the years following the Oslo Accords in preparation for a Palestinian state.[1708] This infrastructure included the legitimate arming of Palestinian forces for the first time: some 90 paramilitary camps had been set up to train Palestinian youths in armed conflict. Some 40,000 armed and trained Palestinians existed in the occupied territories.

On 29 September 2001 Marwan Barghouti, the leader of the Fatah Tanzim in an interview to *Al-Hayat*, described his role in the lead up to the intifada.

> *I knew that the end of September was the last period (of time) before the explosion, but when Sharon reached the al-Aqsa Mosque, this was the most appropriate moment for the outbreak of the intifada.... The night prior to Sharon's visit, I participated in a panel on a local television station and I seized the opportunity to call on the public to go to the al-Aqsa Mosque in the morning, for it was not possible that Sharon would reach al-Haram al-Sharif just so, and walk away peacefully. I finished and went to al-Aqsa in the morning.... We tried to create clashes without success because of the differences of opinion that emerged with others in the al-Aqsa compound at the time.... After Sharon left, I remained for two hours in the presence of other people, we discussed the manner of response and how it was possible to react in all the cities (bilad) and not just in Jerusalem. We contacted all (the Palestinian) factions.*

Barghouti also went on record as stating that the example of Hezbollah and Israel's withdrawal from Lebanon was a factor which contributed to the Intifada.

According to Nathan Thrall, from Elliott Abrams's inside accounts of negotiations between 2001 and 2005, it would appear to be an inescapable conclusion that violence played an effective role in shaking Israeli complacency and furthering Palestinian goals: the U.S. endorsed the idea of a Palestinian State, Ariel Sharon became the first Israeli Prime Minister to affirm the same idea, and even spoke of Israel's "occupation", and the bloodshed was such that Sharon also decided to withdraw from Gaza, an area he long imagined Israel keeping.[1709] However, Zakaria Zubeidi, former leader of the Al-Aqsa Martyrs' Brigades, considers the Intifada to be a total failure that achieved nothing for the Palestinians.

Casualties

The casualty data for the Second Intifada has been reported by a variety of sources and though there is general agreement regarding the overall number of dead, the statistical picture is blurred by disparities in how different types of casualties are counted and categorized.

The sources do not vary widely over the data on Israeli casualties. B'Tselem reports that 1,053 Israelis were killed by Palestinian attacks through 30 April 2008.[1710] Wikipedia:Verifiability Israeli journalist Ze'ev Schiff reported similar numbers citing the Shin Bet as his source in an August 2004 *Haaretz* article where he noted:

> The number of Israeli fatalities in the current conflict with the Palestinians exceeded 1,000 last week. Only two of the country's wars – the War of Independence and the Yom Kippur War – have claimed more Israeli lives than this intifada, which began on September 29, 2000. In the Six-Day War, 803 Israelis lost their lives, while the War of Attrition claimed 738 Israeli lives along the borders with Egypt, Syria and Lebanon.

There is little dispute as to the total number of Palestinians killed by Israelis. B'Tselem reports that through 30 April 2008, there were 4,745 Palestinians killed by Israeli security forces, and 44 Palestinians killed by Israeli civilians. B'Tselem also reports 577 Palestinians killed by Palestinians through 30 April 2008.

Between September 2000 and January 2005, 69 percent of Israeli fatalities were male, while over 95 percent of the Palestinian fatalities were male.[1711] "Remember These Children" reports that as of 1 February 2008, 119 Israeli children, age 17 and under, had been killed by Palestinians. Over the same time period, 982 Palestinian children, age 17 and under, were killed by Israelis.[1712]

Combatant versus noncombatant deaths

Regarding the numbers of Israeli civilian versus combatant deaths, B'Tselem reports that through 30 April 2008 there were 719 Israeli civilians killed and 334 Israeli security force personnel killed. In other words, 31.7% of those killed were Israeli security force personnel, while 68.3% were civilians.

B'Tselem reports that through 30 April 2008, out of 4,745 Palestinians killed by Israeli security forces, there were 1,671 "Palestinians who took part in the hostilities and were killed by Israeli security forces", or 35.2%. According to their statistics, 2,204 of those killed by Israeli security forces "did not take part in the hostilities", or 46.4%. There were 870 (18.5%) who B'Tselem defines as "Palestinians who were killed by Israeli security forces and it is not known if they were taking part in the hostilities".

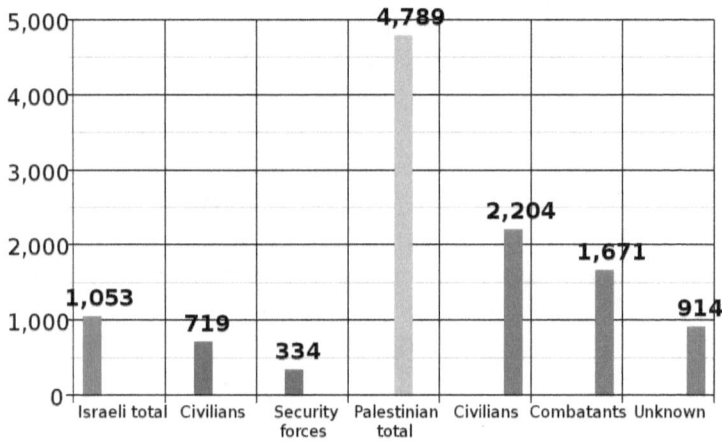

Figure 221:
The chart is based on B'Tselem casualty numbers. It does not include the 577 Palestinians killed by Palestinians.

The B'Tselem casualties breakdown's reliability was questioned and its methodology has been heavily criticized by a variety of institutions and several groups and researchers, most notably Jerusalem Center for Public Affairs's senior researcher, retired IDF lieutenant colonel Jonathan Dahoah-Halevi, who claimed that B'Tselem repeatedly classifies terror operatives and armed combatants as "uninvolved civilians", but also criticized the Israeli government for not collecting and publishing casualty data.[1713] Caroline B. Glick, deputy managing editor of *The Jerusalem Post* and former advisor to Benjamin Netanyahu, pointed to several instances where, she claimed, B'Tselem had misrepresented Palestinian rioters or terrorists as innocent victims, or where B'Tselem failed to report when an Arab allegedly changed his testimony about an attack by settlers. The Committee for Accuracy in Middle East Reporting in America (CAMERA), which said that B'Tselem repeatedly classified Arab combatants and terrorists as civilian casualties.

The Israeli International Policy Institute for Counter-Terrorism (IPICT), on the other hand, in a "Statistical Report Summary" for 27 September 2000, through 1 January 2005, indicates that 56% (1542) of the 2773 Palestinians killed by Israelis were combatants. According to their data, an additional 406 Palestinians were killed by actions of their own side. 22% (215) of the 988

Israelis killed by Palestinians were combatants. An additional 22 Israelis were killed by actions of their own side.

IPICT counts "probable combatants" in its total of combatants. From their full report in September 2002:

> A 'probable combatant' is someone killed at a location and at a time during which an armed confrontation was going on, who appears most likely – but not certain – to have been an active participant in the fighting. For example, in many cases where an incident has resulted in a large number of Palestinian casualties, the only information available is that an individual was killed when Israeli soldiers returned fire in response to shots fired from a particular location. While it is possible that the person killed had not been active in the fighting and just happened to be in the vicinity of people who were, it is reasonable to assume that the number of such coincidental deaths is not particularly high. Where the accounts of an incident appear to support such a coincidence, the individual casualty has been given the benefit of the doubt, and assigned a non-combatant status.

In the same 2002 IPICT full report there is a pie chart (Graph 2.9) that lists the IPICT combatant breakdown for Palestinian deaths through September 2002. Here follow the statistics in that pie chart used to come up with the total combatant percentage through September 2002:

Combatants	Percent of all Palestinian deaths
Full Combatants	44.8%
Probable Combatants	8.3%
Violent Protesters	1.6%
Total Combatants	**54.7%**

On 24 August 2004, *Haaretz* reporter Ze'ev Schiff published casualty figures based on Shin Bet data. The *Haaretz* article reported: "There is a discrepancy of two or three casualties with the figures tabulated by the Israel Defense Forces."

Here is a summary of the figures presented in the article:

- Over 1,000 Israelis were killed by Palestinian attacks in the al-Aqsa Intifada.
- Palestinians sources claim 2,736 Palestinians killed in the Intifada.
- The Shin Bet has the names of 2,124 Palestinian dead.
- Out of the figure of 2,124 dead, Shin Bet assigned them to these organizations:
  - 466 Hamas members
  - 408 Fatah's Tanzim and al-Aqsa Martyrs' Brigades

- 205 Palestinian Islamic Jihad
- 334 of "Palestinian security forces – for example, Force 17, the Palestinian police, General Intelligence, and the counter security apparatus"

The article does not say whether those killed were combatants or not. Here is a quote:

> *The Palestinian security forces – for example, Force 17, the Palestinian police, General Intelligence, and the counter security apparatus – have lost 334 of its members during the current conflict, the Shin Bet figures show.*

As a response to IDF statistics about Palestinian casualties in the West Bank, the Israeli human rights organization B'Tselem reported that two thirds of the Palestinians killed in 2004 did not participate in the fighting.

Prior to 2003, B'Tselem's methodology differentiated between civilians and members of Palestinian military groups, rather than between combatants and non-combatants, leading to criticism from some pro-Israel sources. B'Tselem no longer uses the term "civilian" and instead describes those killed as "participating" or "not participating in fighting at the time of death".

Others argue that Palestinian National Authority has, throughout the Intifada, placed unarmed men, women, children and the elderly in the line of fire, and that announcing the time and place of anti-occupation demonstrations via television, radio, sermons, and calls from mosque loudspeaker systems is done for this purpose.

In 2009, historian Benny Morris stated in his retrospective book *One States, Two States* that about one third of the Palestinian deaths up to 2004 had been civilians.

Palestinians killed by Palestinians

B'Tselem reports that through 30 April 2008, there were 577 Palestinians killed by Palestinians. Of those, 120 were "Palestinians killed by Palestinians for suspected collaboration with Israel". B'Tselem maintains a list of deaths of Palestinians killed by Palestinians with details about the circumstances of the deaths. Some of the many causes of death are crossfire, factional fighting, kidnappings, collaboration, etc.[1714]

Concerning the killing of Palestinians by other Palestinians, a January 2003 *The Humanist* magazine article reports:

<templatestyles src="Template:Quote/styles.css"/>

> *For over a decade the PA has violated Palestinian human rights and civil liberties by routinely killing civilians—including collaborators, demonstrators, journalists, and others—without charge or fair trial. Of the total number of Palestinian civilians killed during this period by both Israeli and Palestinian security forces, 16 percent were the victims of Palestinian security forces.*
>
> *... According to Freedom House's annual survey of political rights and civil liberties, Freedom in the World 2001–2002, the chaotic nature of the Intifada along with strong Israeli reprisals has resulted in a deterioration of living conditions for Palestinians in Israeli-administered areas. The survey states:*
>
> *Civil liberties declined due to: shooting deaths of Palestinian civilians by Palestinian security personnel; the summary trial and executions of alleged collaborators by the Palestinian Authority (PA); extra-judicial killings of suspected collaborators by militias; and the apparent official encouragement of Palestinian youth to confront Israeli soldiers, thus placing them directly in harm's way.*

Internal Palestinian violence has been called an *'Intra'fada* during this Intifada and the previous one.

Aftermath

On 25 January 2006, the Palestinians held general elections for the Palestinian Legislative Council. The Islamist group Hamas won with an unexpected majority of 74 seats, compared to 45 seats for Fatah and 13 for other parties and independents. Hamas is officially declared as a terrorist organization by the United States and the European Union and its gaining control over the Palestinian Authority (such as by forming the government) would jeopardize international funds to the PA, by laws forbidding sponsoring of terrorist group.

On 9 June, seven members of the Ghalia family were killed on a Gaza beach. The cause of the explosion remains uncertain. Nevertheless, in response, Hamas declared an end to its commitment to a ceasefire declared in 2005 and announced the resumption of attacks on Israelis. Palestinians blame an Israeli artillery shelling of nearby locations in the northern Gaza Strip for the deaths, while an Israeli military inquiry cleared itself from the charges.

On 25 June, a military outpost was attacked by Palestinian militants and a gunbattle followed that left 2 Israeli soldiers and 3 Palestinian militants dead. Corporal Gilad Shalit, an Israeli soldier, was captured and Israel warned of an imminent military response if the soldier was not returned unharmed. In the early hours of 28 June Israeli tanks, APCs and troops entered the Gaza

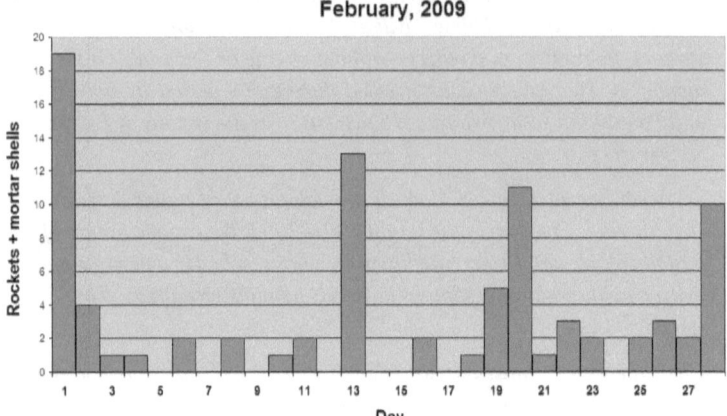

Figure 222: *Rocket and mortar shells from Gaza into Israel, February 2009*

strip just hours after the air force had taken out two main bridges and the only powerstation in the strip, effectively shutting down electricity and water. Operation Summer Rains commenced, the first major phase of the Gaza–Israel conflict, which continues to run independently of the intifada.

On 26 November 2006, a truce was implemented between Israel and the Palestinian Authority. A 10 January 2007, Reuters article reports: "Hamas has largely abided by a November 26 truce which has calmed Israeli-Palestinian violence in Gaza."

An intensification of the Gaza–Israel conflict, the Gaza war, occurred on 27 December 2008 (11:30 a.m. local time; 09:30 UTC) when Israel launched a military campaign codenamed *Operation Cast Lead* (Hebrew: עופרת מבצע (צוקה') targeting the members and infrastructure of Hamas in response to the numerous rocket attacks upon Israel from the Gaza Strip. The operation has been termed the *Gaza massacre* (Arabic: مجزرة غزة) by Hamas leaders and much of the media in the Arab World.[1715,1716]

On Saturday, 17 January 2009, Israel announced a unilateral ceasefire, conditional on elimination of further rocket and mortar attacks from Gaza, and began withdrawing over the next several days. Hamas later announced its own ceasefire, with its own conditions of complete withdrawal and opening of border crossings. A reduced level of mortar fire originating in Gaza continues, though Israel has so far not taken this as a breach of the ceasefire. The frequency of the attacks can be observed in the thumbnailed graph. The data corresponds to the article "Timeline of the 2008–2009 Israel–Gaza conflict", using mainly *Haaretz* news reports from the 1 February up to the 28 February. The usual

IDF responses are airstrikes on weapon smuggling tunnels.Wikipedia:Citation needed

Deaths in 2006

The violence continued on both sides throughout 2006. On 27 December the Israeli Human Rights Organization B'Tselem released its annual report on the Intifada. According to which, 660 Palestinians, a figure more than three times the number of Palestinians killed in 2005, and 23 Israelis, have been killed in 2006. From a 28 December *Haaretz* article: "According to the report, about half of the Palestinians killed, 322, did not take part in the hostilities at the time they were killed. 22 of those killed were targets of assassinations, and 141 were minors." 405 of 660 Palestinians were killed in the 2006 Israel-Gaza conflict, which lasted from 28 June till 26 November.

Tactics

Palestinian tactics ranged from mass protests and general strikes, similar to the First Intifada, to armed attacks on Israeli soldiers, security forces, police, and civilians. Methods of attack include suicide bombings, launching rockets and mortars into Israel, kidnapping of both soldiers and civilians, including children, shootings, assassination, stabbings, stonings, and lynchings.

Israeli tactics included curbing Palestinians' movements through the setting up of checkpoints and the enforcement of strict curfews in certain areas. Infrastructural attacks against Palestinian Authority targets such as police and prisons was another method to force the Palestinian Authority to repress the anti-Israeli protests and attacks on Israeli targets .Wikipedia:Citation needed

Palestinians

Militant groups involved in violence include Hamas, Palestinian Islamic Jihad, Popular Front for the Liberation of Palestine (PFLP) and the al-Aqsa Martyrs' Brigades. They waged a high-intensity campaign of guerrilla warfare against Israeli military and civilian targets inside Israel and in the occupied territory, utilizing tactics such as ambushes, sniper attacks, and suicide bombings. Military equipment was mostly imported, while some light arms, hand grenades and explosive belts, assault rifles, and Qassam rockets were indigenously produced. They also increased use of remote-controlled landmines against Israeli armor, a tactic that was highly popular among the poorly armed groups. Car bombs were often used against "lightly hardened" targets such as Israeli armored jeeps and checkpoints. Also, more than 1,500 Palestinian drive-by shootings killed 75 people in only the first year of the Intifada.

Among the most effective Palestinian tactics was the suicide bombing (*see List*). Conducted as a single or double bombing, suicide bombings were generally conducted against "soft" targets, or "lightly hardened" targets (such as checkpoints) to try to raise the cost of the war to Israelis and demoralize the Israeli society. Most suicide bombing attacks (although not all) targeted civilians, and conducted on crowded places in Israeli cities, such as public transport, restaurants, and markets.

One recent development is the use of suicide bombs carried by children. Unlike most suicide bombings, the use of these not only earned condemnation from the United States and from human rights groups such as Amnesty International, but also from many Palestinians and much of the Middle East press. The youngest Palestinian suicide bomber was 16-year-old Issa Bdeir, a high school student from the village of Al Doha, who shocked his friends and family when he blew himself up in a park in Rishon LeZion, killing a teenage boy and an elderly man. The youngest attempted suicide bombing was by a 14-year-old captured by soldiers at the Huwwara checkpoint before managing to do any harm.

In May 2004, Israel Defense minister Shaul Mofaz claimed that United Nations Relief and Works Agency for Palestine Refugees in the Near East's ambulances were used to take the bodies of dead Israeli soldiers in order to prevent the Israel Defense Forces from recovering their dead. Reuters has provided video of healthy armed men entering ambulance with UN markings for transport. UNRWA initially denied that its ambulances carry militants but later reported that the driver was forced to comply with threats from armed men. UNRWA still denies that their ambulances carried body parts of dead Israeli soldiers.

In August 2004, Israel said that an advanced explosives-detection device employed by the IDF at the Hawara checkpoint near Nablus discovered a Palestinian ambulance had transported explosive material.

Some of the Palestinian reaction to Israeli policy in the West Bank and Gaza Strip has consisted of non-violent protest, primarily in and near the village of Bil'in. Groups such as the Palestinian Centre for Rapprochement, which works out of Beit Sahour, formally encourage and organize non-violent resistance. Other groups, such as the International Solidarity Movement openly advocate non-violent resistance. Some of these activities are done in cooperation with internationals and Israelis, such as the weekly protests against the Israeli West Bank Barrier carried out in villages like Bi'lin, Biddu and Budrus. This model of resistance has spread to other villages like Beit Sira, Hebron, Saffa, and Ni'lein. During the Israeli re-invasion of Jenin and Nablus, "A Call for a Non-violent Resistance Strategy in Palestine" was issued by two Palestinian Christians in May 2002.

Figure 223: *IDF Caterpillar D9 armoured bulldozer. Military experts cited the D9 as a key factor in keeping IDF casualties low.*

Non-violent tactics have sometimes been met with Israeli military force. For example, Amnesty International notes that "10-year-old Naji Abu Qamer, 11-year-old Mubarak Salim al-Hashash and 13-year-old Mahmoud Tariq Mansour were among eight unarmed demonstrators killed in the early afternoon of May 19, 2004 in Rafah, in the Gaza Strip, when the Israeli army open fire on a non-violent demonstration with tank shells and a missile launched from a helicopter gunship. Dozens of other unarmed demonstrators were wounded in the attack." According to Israeli army and government officials, the tanks shelled a nearby empty building and a helicopter fired a missile in a nearby open space in order to deter the demonstrators from proceeding towards Israeli army positions.

Israel

The Israel Defense Forces (IDF) countered Palestinian attacks with incursions against militant targets into the West Bank and Gaza Strip, adopting highly effective urban combat tactics. The IDF stressed the safety of their troops, using such heavily armored equipment as the Merkava heavy tank and armored personnel carriers, and carried out airstrikes with various military aircraft including F-16s, drone aircraft and helicopter gunships to strike militant targets. Much of the ground fighting was conducted house-to-house by well-armed and well-trained infantry. Due to its superior training, equipment, and numbers,

Figure 224: *The Israeli Air Force (IAF) AH-64 Apache were used as platform for shooting guided missiles at Palestinian targets and employed at the targeted killings policy against senior militants and terrorists leaders.*

the IDF had the upper hand during street fighting. Palestinian armed groups suffered heavy losses during combat, but the operations were often criticized internationally due to the civilian casualties often caused. Palestinian metalworking shops and other business facilities suspected by Israel of being used to manufacture weapons are regularly targeted by airstrikes, as well as Gaza Strip smuggling tunnels.

Israeli Caterpillar D9 armored bulldozers were routinely employed to detonate booby traps and IEDs, to demolish houses along the border with Egypt that were used for shooting at Israeli troops, to create "buffer zones", and to support military operations in the West Bank. Until February 2005, Israel had in place a policy to demolish the family homes of suicide bombers after giving them a notice to evacuate. Due to the considerable number of Palestinians living in single homes, the large quantity of homes destroyed, and collateral damage from home demolitions, it became an increasingly controversial tactic. Families began providing timely information to Israeli forces regarding suicide bombing activities in order to prevent the demolition of their homes, although families doing so risked being executed or otherwise punished for collaboration, either by the Palestinian Authority or extrajudicially by Palestinian militants. The IDF committee studying the issue recommended ending the practice because the policy was not effective enough to justify its costs to Israel's image internationally and the backlash it created among Palestinians.[1717]

With complete ground and air superiority, mass arrests were regularly conducted by Israeli military and police forces; at any given time, there were about 6,000 Palestinian prisoners detained in Israeli prisons, about half of them held temporarily without a final indictment, in accordance with Israeli law.

The tactic of military "curfew" – long-term lockdown of civilian areas – was used extensively by Israel throughout the Intifada. The longest curfew was in Nablus, which was kept under curfew for over 100 consecutive days, with generally under two hours per day allowed for people to get food or conduct other business.

Security Checkpoints and roadblocks were erected inside and between Palestinian cities, subjecting all people and vehicles to security inspection for free passage. Israel defended those checkpoints as being necessary to stop militants and limit the ability to move weapons around. However some Palestinian, Israeli and International observers and organizations have criticized the checkpoints as excessive, humiliating, and a major cause of the humanitarian situation in the Occupied Territories. Transit could be delayed by several hours, depending on the security situation in Israel. Sniper towers were used extensively in the Gaza Strip before the Israeli pullout.

The Israeli intelligence services Shin Bet and Mossad penetrated Palestinian militant organizations by relying on moles and sources within armed groups, tapping communication lines, and aerial reconnaissance. within the groups the Israeli Security Forces (IDF, Magav, police YAMAM and Mistaravim SF units) to thwart hundreds of suicide bombings by providing real-time warnings and reliable intelligence reports, and a list of Palestinians marked for targeted killings.

Israel extensively used "targeted killings", the assassinations of Palestinian leaders involved in perpetrating attacks against Israelis, to eliminate imminent threats and to deter others from following suit, relying primarily on airstrikes and covert operations by Shin Bet to carry them out. Israel has been criticized for the use of helicopter gunships in urban assassinations, which often results in civilian casualties. Israel in turn has criticized what it describes as a practice of militant leaders hiding among civilians in densely populated areas, thus turning them into unwitting human shields. In one of the most controversial killings, the Mossad (Israeli foreign intelligence service) allegedly killed Hamas leader Mahmoud al-Mabhouh in Dubai, using forged passports to slip agents into Dubai. Throughout the Intifada, the Palestinian leadership suffered heavy losses through targeted killings.

The practice has been widely condemned as extrajudicial executions by the international community, while the Israeli High Court ruled that it is a legitimate measure of self-defense against terrorism.[1718] ManyWikipedia:Manual of Style/Words to watch#Unsupported attributions criticize the targeted killings for placing civilians at risk, though its supporters believe it reduces civilian casualties on both sides.

In response to repeated rocket attacks from the Gaza Strip, the Israeli Navy imposed a maritime blockade on the area. Israel also sealed the border and closed Gaza's airspace in coordination with Egypt, and subjected all humanitarian supplies entering the Strip to security inspection before transferring them through land crossings. Construction materials were declared banned due to their possible use to build bunkers. The blockade has been internationally criticized as a form of "collective punishment" against Gaza's civilian population.

Although Israel's tactics also have been condemned internationally, Israel insists they are vital for security reasons in order to thwart terrorist attacks. Some cite figures, such as those published in *Haaretz* newspaper, to prove the effectiveness of these methods (Graph 1: Thwarted attacks (yellow) vs successful attacks (red)[1719] – Graph 2: Suicide bombing within the "green line" per quarter[1720]).

International involvement

The international community has long taken an involvement in the Israeli–Palestinian conflict, and this involvement has only increased during the al-Aqsa Intifada. Israel currently receives $3 billion in annual military aid from the United States, excluding loan guarantees. Even though Israel is a developed industrial country, it has remained as the largest annual recipient of US foreign assistance since 1976. It is also the only recipient of US economic aid that does not have to account for how it is spent. The Palestinian Authority receives $100 million annually in military aid from the United States and $2 billion in global financial aid, including "$526 million from Arab League, $651 million from the European Union, $300 million from the US and about $238 million from the World Bank". According to the United Nations, the Palestinian territories are among the leading humanitarian aid recipients.

Additionally, private groups have become increasingly involved in the conflict, such as the International Solidarity Movement on the side of the Palestinians, and the American Israel Public Affairs Committee on the side of the Israelis.

In the 2001 and 2002 Arab League Summits, the Arab states pledged support for the Second Intifada just as they had pledged support for the First Intifada in two consecutive summits in the late 1980s.[1721]

Effects on Oslo Accords

Since the start of the al-Aqsa Intifada and its emphasis on suicide bombers deliberately targeting civilians riding public transportation (buses), the Oslo Accords are viewed with increasing disfavor by the Israeli public.

In May 2000, seven years after the Oslo Accords and five months before the start of the al-Aqsa Intifada, a survey[1722] by the Tami Steinmetz Center for Peace Research at the Tel Aviv University found that 39% of all Israelis support the Accords and that 32% believe that the Accords will result in peace in the next few years. In contrast, the May 2004 survey found that 26% of all Israelis support the Accords and 18% believe that the Accords will result in peace in the next few years; decreases of 13% and 16% respectively. Furthermore, later survey found that 80% of all Israelis believe the Israel Defense Forces have succeeded in dealing with the al-Aqsa Intifada militarily.

Economic costs

Israel

The Israeli commerce experienced a significant negative impact, particularly due to a sharp drop in tourism. A representative of Israel's Chamber of Commerce estimated the cumulative economic damage caused by the crisis at 150 to 200 billion Shekels, or US$35–45 billion – against an annual GDP of $122 billion in 2002. The Israeli economy recovered as suicide bombings sharply decreased after 2005, following IDF's and Shin-Bet's efforts.

Palestinian Authority

The Office of the United Nations Special Coordinator in the Occupied Territories (UNSCO) estimated the damage to the Palestinian economy at over $1.1 billion in the first quarter of 2002, compared to an annual GDP of $4.5 billion.

Bibliography

- Schulz, Helena Lindholm; Hammer, Juliane (2003). *The Palestinian Diaspora: Formation of Identities and Politics of Homeland*. Routledge. ISBN 978-0-415-26820-2.<templatestyles src="Module:Citation/CS1/styles.css"></templatestyles>
- Catignani, Sergio (March 2008). *Israeli Counter-Insurgency and the Intifadas: Dilemmas of a Conventional Army*[1723]. Routledge. ISBN 978-0-203-93069-4. Retrieved 14 February 2012.<templatestyles src="Module:Citation/CS1/styles.css"></templatestyles>

- Yousef, Mosab Hassan (2011). *Son of Hamas: A Gripping Account of Terror, Betrayal, Political Intrigue, and Unthinkable Choices*[1724]. Tyndale House. ISBN 978-1-85078-985-7. Retrieved 4 January 2013.<templatestyles src="Module:Citation/CS1/styles.css"></templatestyles>

Israeli West Bank barrier

<indicator name="pp-default"> 🔒 </indicator> <indicator name="pp-default"> 🔒 </indicator> <indicator name="pp-default"> 🔒 </indicator>

The **Israeli West Bank barrier** or **wall** (for further names see here) is a separation barrier in the West Bank or along the Green Line. Israel considers it a security barrier against terrorism, while Palestinians call it a racial segregation or apartheid wall.[1725,1726,1727] At a total length of 708 kilometres (440 mi) upon completion, the border traced by the barrier is more than double the length of the Green Line, with 15% running along it or in Israel, while the remaining 85% cuts at times 18 kilometres (11 mi) deep into the West Bank, isolating about 9% of it, leaving an estimated 25,000 Palestinians isolated from the bulk of that territory.[1728]

The barrier was built during the Second Intifada that began in September 2000, and was defended by the Israeli government as necessary to stop the wave of violence inside Israel that the uprising had brought with it. The Israeli government says that the barrier has been effective, as the number of suicide bombings carried out from the West Bank fell from 73 (between 2000 and July 2003 – the completion of the "first continuous segment"), to 12 (from August 2003 to the end of 2006). While the barrier was initially presented as a temporary security measure in a time of heightened tensions, it has since been rapidly associated with a future political border between Israel and Palestine.

Barrier opponents claim it seeks to annex Palestinian land under the guise of security and undermines peace negotiations by unilaterally establishing new borders. Opponents object to a route that in some places substantially deviates eastward from the Green Line, severely restricts the travel of many Palestinians and impairs their ability to commute to work within the West Bank or to Israel. The International Court of Justice issued an advisory opinion stating that the barrier is a violation of international law.[1729,1730] In 2003, the United Nations General Assembly adopted a resolution that stated the wall contradicts international law and should be removed; the vote was 144–4 with 12 abstentions.[1731]

Israeli West Bank barrier

Figure 225: *The barrier route as of July 2011: 438 km (272 mi) finished, 58 km (36 mi) under construction, 212 km (132 mi) planned.*

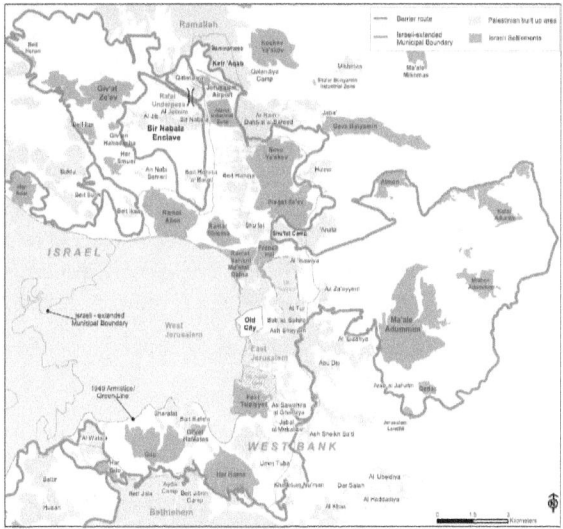

Figure 226: *The barrier in Jerusalem, 2007*

Figure 227: *The barrier between Abu Dis and East Jerusalem, June 2004*

Names

In Hebrew, descriptions include: **separation fence** (🔊 גדר ההפרדה Wikipedia:Media helpFile:He-Gader_Hahafrada.ogg, *Geder HaHafrada*); **separation wall** (Hebrew: חומת ההפרדה, *kHomat HaHafrada*) and **security fence** (גדר הביטחון, *Geder HaBitakhon*).[1732,1733]

In Arabic, it is called **wall of apartheid** 🔊 جدار الفصل العنصري Wikipedia:Media helpFile:ArWestBankBarrier.ogg, *jidar al-fasl al-'unsuri*.

In English, the BBC's style guide uses the terms **barrier** (sometimes **separation barrier** or **West Bank barrier**) as do *The Economist*,[1734] PBS[1735] and the *New York Times*.[1736] The Israeli Ministry of Foreign Affairs uses the phrase **security fence** in English.[1737] The International Court of Justice has used the term **wall** explaining "the other expressions sometimes employed are no more accurate if understood in the physical sense." It is also referred to as the **Apartheid Wall** or **Apartheid Fence** in a derogatory manner.[1738] **Seam zone** (Hebrew: מרחב התפר) refers to the land between the 1949 Armistice Agreement Line and the fence.

Structure

About 90–95% of the barrier will be constructed as a "multi-layered fence system" with the IDF's preferred design having three fences, pyramid-shaped stacks of barbed wire on the two outer fences, a lighter-weight fence with intrusion detection equipment in the middle, an anti-vehicle ditch, patrol roads on both sides, and a smooth strip of sand for "intrusion tracking".

Figure 228: *Graffiti on the road to Bethlehem in the West Bank stating "Ich bin ein Berliner"*

Figure 229: *Route 443 near Giv'at Ze'ev Junction, with pyramid-shaped stacks of barbed wire forming a section of the Israeli West Bank barrier*

Figure 230: *Israeli West Bank barrier – North of Meitar, near the southwest corner of the West Bank, in 2006.*

The barrier contains an on-average 60-metre (200 ft) wide exclusion area. The width of some sections is larger (up to 100 metres (330 ft)) due to topographic conditions.[1739] The width of some sections (about 6% of the barrier) is 3 metres (9.8 ft) where the barrier is constructed as a concrete wall up to 8 metres (26 ft) high. These sections are narrower, require less land, and provide more protection against snipers. Wall construction is more common in urban settings, e.g., Qalqilyah and Jerusalem, and in areas where people have been killed by snipers, e.g., the Trans-Israel Highway.

Route

The barrier runs partly along or near the 1949 Jordanian–Israeli armistice line ("Green Line") and partly through the West Bank diverging eastward from the armistice line by up to 20 km (12 mi) to include on the western side several of the areas with concentrations of highly populated Israeli settlements, such as East Jerusalem, the Ariel Bloc (Ariel, Karnei Shomron, Kedumim, Immanuel etc.),[1740] Gush Etzion, Givat Ze'ev, Oranit, and Maale Adumim.

The barrier nearly encircles some Palestinian towns, about 20% follows the armistice line,[1741] and a projected 77,000 ha (191,000 acres), or about 13.5 percent, of the West Bank area (including East-Jerusalem) is on the west side of the wall. According to a study of the April 2006 route by the Israeli human

Figure 231: *The barrier between northern West Bank and the Gilboa*

rights organization B'Tselem, 8.5% of the West Bank area will after completion be on the Israeli side of the barrier, and 3.4% partly or completely surrounded on the eastern side.[1742] Some 27,520 to 31,000 Palestinians will be captured on the Israeli side.[1743] Another 124,000, on the other hand, will effectively be controlled and isolated. Some 230,000 Palestinians in Jerusalem will be placed on the West Bank side. Most of the barrierWikipedia:Vagueness was built at the northern and western edges of the West Bank, mostly beyond the Green Line and created 9 enclaves, which enclosed 15,783 ha (39,000 acres). An additional barrier, circa 10 km long, run south of Ramallah.[1744]

Israel states that the topography does not permit putting the barrier along the Green Line in some places because hills or tall buildings on the Palestinian side would make the barrier ineffective against terrorism.[1745] The International Court of Justice states that in such cases it is only legal to build the barrier inside Israel.

The barrier route has been challenged in court and changed several times. Argument presented to the court has reiterated that the cease-fire line of 1949 was negotiated "without prejudice to future territorial settlements or boundary lines" (Art. VI.9).[1746]

Timeline

In 1992, the idea of creating a physical barrier separating the Israeli and Palestinian populations was proposed by then-prime minister Yitzhak Rabin. In 1994, a first barrier was constructed along the Green Line between Bat Hefer and Tulkarm.

In 1995, the Shahal commission was established to discuss how to implement a separation barrier. In 2000, Prime Minister Ehud Barak approved financing of a 74 km (46 mi) fence between the Wadi Ara region and Latrun. On 23 June 2002, the Ariel Sharon Government definitely approved the plan in principle[1747] and work at the barrier began.

By 2003, 180 km (112 mi) had been completed and in 2004, Israel started the southern part of the barrier. By 2006, 362 km (224.9 mi) of the barrier had been completed, 88 km (54.7 mi) was under construction and 253 km (157.2 mi) had not yet been started. By 2012, 440 km (273.4 mi) (62%) of the barrier had been completed, 57 km (35.4 mi) (8%) was under construction and 212 km (131.7 mi) (30%) had not yet been started, with little progress made by 2014. In September, 2014, the government voted to not reauthorize the barrier in the Gush Etzion area.[1748]

Effectiveness

- v
- t
- e[1749]

Suicide bombings have decreased since the construction of the barrier. Al-Aqsa Martyrs' Brigades, Hamas, and the Palestinian Islamic Jihad have been less able to conduct attacks in Israel, which have decreased in areas where the barrier has been completed.[1750]

The Israeli Ministry of Foreign Affairs and the Israel Security Agency report that in 2002, there were 452 fatalities from terrorist attacks. Before the completion of the first continuous segment (July 2003) from the beginning of the Second Intifada, 73 Palestinian suicide bombings were carried out from the West Bank, killing 293 Israelis and injuring over 1,900. After the completion of the first continuous segment through the end of 2006, there were only 12 attacks based in the West Bank, killing 64 people and wounding 445. Terrorist attacks declined in 2007 and 2008 to 9 in 2010.

The Ministry of Foreign Affairs predicts that completion of the barrier will continue to prevent terrorist attacks[1751] since "[a]n absolute halt in terrorist activities has been noticed in the West Bank areas where the fence has been constructed."

Israeli officials (including the head of the Shin Bet) quoted in the newspaper *Maariv* have said that in the areas where the barrier was complete, the number of hostile infiltrations has decreased to almost zero. *Maariv* also stated that Palestinian militants, including a senior member of Islamic Jihad, had confirmed that the barrier made it much harder to conduct attacks inside Israel. Since the completion of the fence in the area of Tulkarm and Qalqilyah in June 2003, there have been no successful attacks from those areas. All attacks were intercepted or the suicide bombers detonated prematurely. In a March 23, 2008 interview, Palestinian Islamic Jihad leader Ramadan Shalah complained to the Qatari newspaper *Al-Sharq* that the separation barrier "limits the ability of the resistance to arrive deep within [Israeli territory] to carry out suicide bombing attacks, but the resistance has not surrendered or become helpless, and is looking for other ways to cope with the requirements of every stage" of the intifada.[1752]

Other factors are also cited as causes for the decline. According to *Haaretz*, a 2006 report by the Shin Beit concluded that "[t]he fence does make it harder for them [terrorists]" but that attacks in 2005 decreased due to increased pursuing of Palestinian militants by the Israeli army and intelligence organizations, Hamas's increased political activity, and a truce among Palestinian militant groups in the Palestinian Territories. Haaretz reported, "[t]he security fence is no longer mentioned as the major factor in preventing suicide bombings, mainly because the terrorists have found ways to bypass it." Former Israeli Secretary of Defence Moshe Arens says that the reduction in Palestinian violence is largely due to the IDF's entry into the West Bank in 2002.[1753]

Effects on Palestinians

The barrier has many effects on Palestinians including reduced freedoms, reduction of the number of Israel Defense Forces checkpoints and road closures, loss of land, increased difficulty in accessing medical and educational services in Israel, restricted access to water sources, and economic effects.

Reduced freedoms

In a 2005 report, the United Nations stated that: <templatestyles src="Template:Quote/styles.css"/>

> ... it is difficult to overstate the humanitarian impact of the Barrier. The route inside the West Bank severs communities, people's access to services, livelihoods and religious and cultural amenities. In addition, plans for the Barrier's exact route and crossing points through it are often not fully revealed until days before construction commences. This has led to considerable anxiety amongst Palestinians about how their future lives will be impacted. ... The land between the Barrier and the Green Line constitutes some of the most fertile in the West Bank. It is currently the home for 49,400 West Bank Palestinians living in 38 villages and towns.[1754]

An often-quoted example of the effects of the barrier is the Palestinian town of Qalqilyah, a city of around 45,000, which is surrounded almost on all sides by the barrier. One 8 meter-high concrete section of this wall follows the Green Line between the city and the nearby Trans-Israel Highway. According to the BBC, this section, referred to as an "anti-sniper wall," is intended to prevent gun attacks against Israeli motorists on the Trans-Israel Highway. The city is accessible through a military checkpoint on the main road from the east, and an underground tunnel built in September 2004 on the south side connects Qalqilyah with the adjacent village of Habla. In 2005, the Israeli Supreme Court ordered the government to change the route of the barrier in this area to ease movement of Palestinians between Qalqilyah and five surrounding villages. In the same ruling, the court rejected the arguments that the fence must be built only on the Green Line. The ruling cited the topography of the terrain, security considerations, and sections 43 and 52 of The Hague Regulations 1907 and Article 53 of the Fourth Geneva Convention as reasons for this rejection.

In early October 2003, the IDF OC Central Command declared the area between the separation barrier in the northern section of the West Bank (Stage 1)

Figure 232: *Palestinian children running towards the barrier, August 2004*

and the Green Line a closed military area for an indefinite period. New directives stated that every Palestinian over the age of twelve living in the enclaves created in the closed area have to obtain a "permanent resident permit" from the Civil Administration to enable them to continue to live in their homes, approximately 27,250 people in all. Other residents of the West Bank have to obtain special permits to enter the area.

Fewer checkpoints and roadblocks

In June 2004, *The Washington Times*[1755] reported that the reduced Israeli military incursions in Jenin have prompted efforts to rebuild damaged streets and buildings and a gradual return to a semblance of normality, and in a letter dated October 25, 2004, from the Israeli mission to Kofi Annan, Israel's government pointed out that a number of restrictions east of the barrier have been lifted as a result of it, including a reduction in checkpoints from 71 to 47 and roadblocks from 197 to 111. *The Jerusalem Post* reports that, for some Palestinians who are Israeli citizens living in the Israeli Arab town of Umm el-Fahm (population 42,000) near Jenin, the barrier has "significantly improved their lives" because, on one hand, it prevents would-be thieves or terrorists from coming to their town and, on the other hand, has increased the flow of customers from other parts of Israel who would normally have patronised Palestinian business in the West Bank, resulting in an economic boom. The report states that the downsides are that the barrier has divided families in half and "damaged Israeli Arabs' solidarity with the Palestinians living on the other side of the Green Line".[1756]

A UN report released in August 2005 observed that the existence of the barrier "replaced the need for closures: movement within the northern West Bank, for example, is less restrictive where the Barrier has been constructed. Physical obstacles have also been removed in Ramallah and al-Bireh Governorate and Jerusalem Governorate where the Barrier is under construction." The report says that more freedom of movement in rural areas may ease Palestinian access to hospitals and schools, but also says that restrictions on movement between urban population centers have not significantly changed.

Loss of land

Parts of the barrier are built on land seized from Palestinians, or between Palestinians and their lands In a 2009 report, the UN said that the most recent barrier route allocates more segments to be built on the Green Line itself compared to previous draft routes of the barrier. However, in its current route the barrier is annexing 9.5% of the total area of the West Bank to the Israeli side of the barrier.

In early 2003, 63 shops straddling the Green Line were demolished by the IDF during construction of the wall in the village of Nazlat Issa. In August 2003, an additional 115 shops and stalls (an important source of income for several communities) and five to seven homes there were also demolished.[1757]

According to the United Nations Relief and Works Agency (UNRWA), 15 communities were to be directly affected, numbering about 138,593 Palestinians, including 13,450 refugee families, or 67,250 people. In addition to loss of land, in the city of Qalqilyah one-third of the city's water wells lie on the other side of the barrier. The Israeli Supreme Court says the Israeli government's rejection of accusations of a *de facto* annexation of these wells, stating that "the construction of the fence does not affect the implementation of the water agreements determined in the (interim) agreement".

The United Nations Economic and Social Commission for Western Asia (ESCWA) estimates that in the north of the West Bank about 80 per cent of Palestinians who own land on the other side of the barrier have not received permits from the Israeli authorities, and hence cannot cultivate their fields.

Israel has built a barrier in the Jordan Valley near the Jordanian border. A plan to build another barrier between the West Bank and the Jordan valley was abandoned because of international condemnation after the 2004 International Court ruling, instead instituting a restrictive permit regime for Palestinians.[1758] However, it has changed the route to allow settlements to annex parcels of land.[1759] The existing barrier cuts off access to the Jordan River for Palestinian farmers in the West Bank.[1760] Israeli settlement councils already have de facto control of 86 percent of the Jordan Valley and the Dead Sea[1761] as the settler population steadily grows there.[1762] In 2013, Ehud Barak, Israeli Defense Minister at the time, proposed that Israel should consider unilateral disengagement from the West Bank and the dismantling of settlements beyond the separation barrier, but maintain a military presence in the Jordan Valley along the West Bank-Jordan border.[1763]

Health and medical services

Médecins du Monde, the Palestinian Red Crescent Society and Physicians for Human Rights-Israel have stated that the barrier "harms West Bank health". Upon completion of the construction, the organizations predict, the barrier would prevent over 130,000 Palestinian children from being immunised, and deny more than 100,000 pregnant women (out of which 17,640 are high risk pregnancies) access to healthcare in Israel. In addition, almost a third of West Bank villages will suffer from lack of access to healthcare. After completion, many residents may lose complete access to emergency care at night. In towns near Jerusalem (Abu Dis and al-Eizariya), for example, average time for an ambulance to travel to the nearest hospital has increased from 10 minutes to over 110 minutes. A report from Physicians for Human Rights-Israel states that the barrier imposes "almost-total separation" on the hospitals from the population they are supposed to serve. The report also said that patients from the West Bank visiting Jerusalem's Palestinian clinics declined by half from 2002 to 2003.

Economic changes

In 2013, the World Bank cited estimates of costs to the West Bank economy attributable to "barriers" combined with "checkpoints and movement permits" of USD $185m and $229m.[1764] Foreign Affairs contributor David Makovsky estimated the number of West Bank Palestinians who lived on the Israeli side in 2004 as "fewer than one percent" but noted that a larger number living in enclaves like Qalqiliya adjacent to the fence were also adversely affected.[1765] The Israeli human rights organisation B'Tselem says that "thousands of Palestinians have difficulty going to their fields and marketing their produce in other areas of the West Bank. Farming is a primary source of income in the Palestinian communities situated along the Barrier's route, an area that constitutes one of the most fertile areas in the West Bank. The harm to the farming sector is liable to have drastic economic effects on the residents – whose economic situation is already very difficult – and drive many families into poverty."

Legality

United Nations Security Council

In October 2003, a United Nations resolution to declare the barrier illegal where it deviates from the Green Line and should be torn down was vetoed by the US in the United Nations Security Council.

On May 19, 2004, the United Nations passed Security Council Resolution 1544 reiterating the obligation of Israel, the occupying Power, to abide scrupulously by its legal obligations and responsibilities under the Fourth Geneva Convention, and called on Israel to address its security needs within the boundaries of international law. In a special emergency session of the General Assembly, the United Nations asked the International Court of Justice [ICJ] to evaluate the legal status of the barrier. Israel chose not to accept ICJ jurisdiction nor make oral statements, and instead submitted a 246 page written statement containing the views of the Government of Israel on Jurisdiction and Propriety to the Court.[1766]

International Court of Justice

In a 2004 advisory opinion by the International Court of Justice, "Israel cannot rely on a right of self-defence or on a state of necessity in order to preclude the wrongfulness of the construction of the wall". The Court asserted that "the construction of the wall, and its associated régime, are contrary to international law."

So in the July 9, 2004 advisory opinion the ICJ advised that the barrier is a violation of international law, that it should be removed, that Arab residents should be compensated for any damage done, and that other states take action to obtain Israel's compliance with the Fourth Geneva Convention. The ICJ said that an occupying power cannot claim that the lawful inhabitants of the occupied territory constitute a "foreign" threat for the purposes of Article 51 of the UN Charter. It also explained that necessity may constitute a circumstance precluding wrongfulness under certain very limited circumstances, but that Article 25 of the International Law Commission's Articles on Responsibility of States for Internationally Wrongful Acts (ARSIWA) bars a defense of necessity if the State has contributed to the situation of necessity. The Court cited illegal interference by the government of Israel with the Palestinian's national right to self-determination; and land confiscations, house demolitions, the creation of enclaves, and restrictions on movement and access to water, food, education, health care, work, and an adequate standard of living in violation of Israel's obligations under international law. The Court also said that Israeli settlements had been established and that Palestinians had been displaced in violation of Article 49, paragraph 6, of the Fourth Geneva Convention.[1767] On request of the ICJ, Palestine submitted a copious statement.[1768] The UN Fact Finding Mission and several UN Rapporteurs subsequently said that in the movement and access policy there has been a violation of the right not to be discriminated against on the basis of race or national origin.[1769]

Israeli supporters of the barrier stood in the plaza near the courthouse, holding the portraits of 927 terror victims. The organization Christians for Israel helped bring the No. 19 bus, on which eleven civilians were killed, to the Hague.

Israel

In April 2003, B'Tselem stated that "Israel has made cynical use of security claims to justify grave human rights violations in the Occupied Territories...Among other things the determination of the route of the barrier was based on political considerations, the attempt to leave the settlements to the west of the barrier, and protection of access routes for religious sites - none of which are at all related to military considerations. This situation is likely to render the entire separation barrier project illegal according to international law."[1770]

On June 30, 2004, the Supreme Court of Israel ruled that a portion of the barrier west of Jerusalem violated the rights of Palestinians, and ordered 30 km (19 mi) of existing and planned barrier to be rerouted. However, it did rule that the barrier is legal in principle and accepted the Israeli government's assertion that it is a security measure.

On September 15, 2005, the Supreme Court of Israel ordered the Israeli government to alter the route of the barrier to ensure that negative impacts on Palestinians would be minimized and proportional.[1771]

Opinions of the barrier

United Nations

In December 2003, Resolution ES-10/14 was adopted by the United Nations General Assembly in an emergency special session. 90 states voted for, 8 against, 74 abstained. The resolution included a request to the International Court of Justice to urgently render an advisory opinion on the following question.

> *"What are the legal consequences arising from the construction of the wall being built by Israel, the occupying Power, in the Occupied Palestinian Territory, including in and around East Jerusalem, as described in the report of the Secretary-General, considering the rules and principles of*

international law, including the Fourth Geneva Convention of 1949, and relevant Security Council and General Assembly resolutions?"

The court concluded that the barrier violated international law.[1772] On 20 July 2004, the UN General Assembly accepted Resolution ES-10/15 condemning the barrier with 150 countries voting for the resolution and 10 abstaining. 6 countries voted against: Israel, the US, Australia, the Federated States of Micronesia, the Marshall Islands and Palau. The US and Israel rejected both the verdict and the resolution. All 25 members of the European Union voted in favour of the resolution after it was amended to include calls for Israelis and Palestinians to meet their obligations under the "roadmap" peace plan.

Israeli opinions

According to a survey conducted by the Tami Steinmetz Center for Peace Research, an academic research institution of Tel Aviv University, there was overwhelming support for the barrier among the Jewish population of Israel: 84% in March 2004 and 78% in June 2004.[1773]

Some Israelis oppose the barrier. The Israeli Peace Now movement has stated that while they would support a barrier that follows the 1949 Armistice lines, the "current route of the fence is intended to destroy all chances of a future peace settlement with the Palestinians and to annex as much land as possible from the West Bank" and that the barrier would "only increase the blood to be spilt on both sides and continue the sacrificing of Israeli and Palestinian lives for the settlements."[1774] Some Israeli left wing activists, such as Anarchists Against the Wall and Gush Shalom, are active in protests against the barrier, especially in the West Bank towns of Bil'in and Jayyous.[1775,1776]

Shaul Arieli, a senior member of the Council for Peace and Security and one of the architects of the Geneva Initiative wrote in *Haaretz* in March 2009 of the importance "to complete the fence along a route based on security considerations." Arieli found the fence to be justified due to legitimate concerns of Palestinian terrorism and violence, but was critical of the then-government's alleged negligence of completing the fence due to budgetary and political considerations. He called on the public to "demand that the new government complete the fence quickly and along a logical route."[1777]

Daniel Ayalon, Israel's ambassador to the United States, suggested that reduced ability to conduct attacks would "save the political process" because the barrier would neutralize the ability of militant groups "to hold that process hostage" by conducting these acts.[1778]

Natan Sharansky, Minister of Housing and Construction at the time, viewed the security fence as an option for Israel to defend itself, because the Palestinian

Authority had not become a partner in fighting terror, as it was obliged to do under all the agreements that it signed[1779]

The Anti-Defamation League heavily criticized the ruling of the Court of Justice condemning the West Bank Barrier, asserting that the outcome was stacked against Israel in advance through the biased wording of the submission. It said that Israel was systematically excluded from any say in the Court's makeup and asserted that an anti-Israel environment prevails at the General Assembly, which "regularly demonize[s] Israel". According to the ADL, the politicized nature of the process that produced the opinion threatens to undermine the integrity of the Court and contravene constructive efforts to promote peace in the region.

Palestinian opinions

The Palestinian population and its leadership are essentially unanimous in opposing the barrier. A significant number of Palestinians have been separated from their own farmlands or their places of work or study, and many more will be separated as the barriers near Jerusalem are completed. Furthermore, because of its planned route as published by the Israeli government, the barrier is perceived as a plan to confine the Palestinian population to specific areas.[1780] They state that Palestinian institutions in Abu Dis will be prevented from providing services to residents in the East Jerusalem suburbs, and that a 10-minute walk has become a 3-hour drive in order to reach a gate, to go (if allowed) through a crowded military checkpoint, and drive back to the destination on the other side.[1781]

More broadly, Palestinian spokespersons, supported by many in the Israeli left wing and other organizations, say that the hardships imposed by the barrier will breed further discontent amongst the affected population and add to the security problem rather than solving it.

In his November 2006 interview with Al-Manar TV, Palestinian Islamic Jihad leader Ramadan Salah said that the barrier is an important obstacle, and that "if it weren't there, the situation would be entirely different."[1782]

The Palestinian National Authority has accused the U.S. of rewarding construction of the barrier and replied, "[t]he U.S. assurances are being made at the expense of the Palestinian people and the Arab world without the knowledge of the legitimate Palestinian leadership. They are rewarding illegal occupation, settlement and the apartheid wall."[1783]

For over five years, hundreds of Palestinians and Israeli activists have gathered every week to protest the barrier at the town of Bil'in. A number of Palestinian protesters have been killed by the IDF while protesting. Covert operatives of

Figure 233: *Replica section of the Israeli Barrier, built in London in 2013, as part of the international protest against the Israeli wall*

the Israeli government have posed as protesters and threw stones in the general direction of the IDF to create a pretext for arresting protesters. Protesters posed as members of the fictional "Na'vi" race of the major motion picture "Avatar" during protests following release of the movie, in an effort to compare the Palestinian struggle with that of the fictional Na'vi race, who must defend themselves and their homeland against foreign invaders.

Between 23 December 2013 and 5 January 2014 a major demonstration against the wall was staged in London, in the grounds of St James's Church, Piccadilly. The demonstration was entitled "Bethlehem Unwrapped", and featured a large section of replica wall, reproducing both the fabric of the Israeli wall, and the graffiti to be found on it. Protesters staffed the wall in order to explain the demonstration to visitors and passers-by. Large signs were erected, drawing attention to intentional protest against the wall. Particular reference was made to the International Court of Justice judgement of 9 July 2004 that the security wall contravened international law. The demonstration took place just days after the death of Nelson Mandela, and prominence was therefore given on billboards to Mandella's statement "The UN took a strong stand against apartheid... We know too well that our freedom is incomplete without the freedom of the Palestinians". The replica wall, which was 8 metres tall (the same height as the actual wall) was constructed as an art installation by

Justin Butcher, Geof Thompson, and Dean Willars, who also credited Deborah Burtin of Tipping Point North South. They invited visitors to add additional graffiti, particularly in the forms of prayers for peace.[1784] St James' Church, which allowed the demonstration on its grounds, and permitted its own church building to be almost entirely hidden by the wall, issued a public statement supporting the right of Israel to defend its borders, but condemning the wall, and the suffering which it caused to Palestinian peoples.[1785] The church statement drew attention to the request of the World Council of Churches for all Christians to oppose the wall.

Other International opinions

The Red Cross

The Red Cross has declared the barrier in violation of the Geneva Convention. On February 18, 2004, The International Committee of the Red Cross stated that the Israeli barrier "causes serious humanitarian and legal problems" and goes "far beyond what is permissible for an occupying power".

Human rights organizations

Amnesty International, Human Rights Watch and other Human rights groups have protested both the routing of the wall and the means by which the land to build the wall was obtained.[1786] The Israeli women of Machsom Watch regularly monitor events at checkpoints and report their findings. In a 2004 report Amnesty International wrote that "The fence/wall, in its present configuration, violates Israel's obligations under international humanitarian law."[1787]

They continue:

> *Since the summer of 2002 the Israeli army has been destroying large areas of Palestinian agricultural land, as well as other properties, to make way for a fence/wall which it is building in the West Bank.*
>
> *In addition to the large areas of particularly fertile Palestinian farmland that have been destroyed, other larger areas have been cut off from the rest of the West Bank by the fence/wall.*
>
> *The fence/wall is not being built between Israel and the Occupied Territories but mostly (close to 90%) inside the West Bank, turning Palestinian towns and villages into isolated enclaves, cutting off communities and families from each other, separating farmers from their land and Palestinians from their places of work, education and health care facilities and other essential services. This in order to facilitate passage between Israel and more than 50 illegal Israeli settlements located in the West Bank.*

World Council of Churches

On February 20, 2004 the World Council of Churches demanded that Israel halt and reverse construction on the barrier and strongly condemned "violations of human rights and humanitarian consequences" that resulted from the construction of the barrier. While acknowledging Israel's serious security concerns and asserting that the construction of the barrier on its own territory would not have been a violation of international law, the statement called on "member Churches, Ecumenical Councils of Churches, Christian World Communions and specialized ministries of churches to condemn the wall as an act of unlawful annexation."

United States opinion

In 2003, when the Bush administration was considering reducing loan guarantees to Israel to discourage construction of the fence, then Secretary of State Colin Powell criticized the project. He said, "A nation is within its rights to put up a fence if it sees the need for one. However, in the case of the Israeli fence, we are concerned when the fence crosses over onto the land of others." Response from pro-Israel members of Congress criticized the possible reduction in loan assistance. For example, Senator Joe Lieberman, D-Conn., said, "The administration's threat to cut aid to Israel unless it stops construction of a security fence is a heavy-handed tactic." Lieberman criticized the threat as improper between allies, and continued, "The Israeli people have the right to defend themselves from terrorism, and a security fence may be necessary to achieve this."

On April 14, 2004, President of the United States George W. Bush said "In light of new realities on the ground, including already existing major Israeli population centers, it is unrealistic to expect that the outcome of final status negotiations will be a full and complete return to the armistice lines of 1949, and all previous efforts to negotiate a two-state solution have reached the same conclusion."[1788]

On May 25, 2005, Bush said, "I think the wall is a problem. And I discussed this with Ariel Sharon. It is very difficult to develop confidence between the Palestinians and Israel with a wall snaking through the West Bank." The following year, addressing the issue of the barrier as a future border, he said in a letter to Sharon on April 14, 2004 that it "should be a security rather than political barrier, should be temporary rather than permanent and therefore not prejudice any final status issues including final borders, and its route should take into account, consistent with security needs, its impact on Palestinians not engaged in terrorist activities." President Bush reiterated this position during a May 26, 2005 joint press conference with Palestinian leader Mahmoud Abbas in the Rose Garden.

In 2005, Hillary Clinton, at the time a U.S. Senator from New York, said she supports the separation fence Israel is building along the edges of the West Bank, and that the onus is on the Palestinian Authority to fight terrorism. "This is not against the Palestinian people," she said during a tour of a section of the barrier being built around Jerusalem. "This is against the terrorists. The Palestinian people have to help to prevent terrorism. They have to change the attitudes about terrorism."

In 2007, Senator Charles Schumer said: "As long as the Palestinians send terrorists onto school buses and to nightclubs to blow up people, Israel has no choice but to build the Security Wall."

European Union opinion

According to EU foreign policy chief Catherine Ashton, the EU considers the barrier to be illegal to the extent it is built on Palestinian land.[1789]

Canadian opinion

The Canadian Government recognizes Israel's right to protect its citizens from terrorist attacks, including through the restriction of access to its territory, and by building a barrier on its own territory for security purposes. However, it opposes the barrier's incursion into and the disruption of occupied territories. Considering the West Bank (including East Jerusalem) to be "occupied territory", the Canadian government considers the barrier to be contrary to international law under the Fourth Geneva Convention. It opposes the barrier and the expropriations and the demolition of houses and economic infrastructure preceding its construction.[1790]

Border opinions

Although the Barrier is purported to be a temporary defense against Palestinian attacks, many view it as significant in terms of future negotiations over Israel's final borders. Some speculate that because sections of the barrier are not built along the Green Line but in the West Bank, the real purpose is to acquire territory. Some people describe the barrier as the *de facto* future border of the State of Israel. James Zogby, president of the Arab American Institute, has said that the barrier has "unilaterally helped to demarcate the route for future Israeli control over huge West Bank settlement blocks and large swathes of West Bank land". According to B'Tselem, "the overall features of the separation barrier and the considerations that led to determination of the route give the impression that Israel is relying on security arguments to unilaterally establish facts on the ground ..." Chris McGreal in *The Guardian* writes that the barrier is, "evidently intended to redraw Israel's borders".

Some have speculated that the barrier will prejudice the outcome of border negotiations in favor of the Israelis. Yossi Klein Halevi, Israeli correspondent for *The New Republic*, writes that "[b]uilding over the green line, by contrast, reminds Palestinians that every time they've rejected compromise – whether in 1937, 1947, or 2000 – the potential map of Palestine shrinks... The fence is a warning: If Palestinians don't stop terrorism and forfeit their dream of destroying Israel, Israel may impose its own map on them... and, because Palestine isn't being restored but invented, its borders are negotiable."

The Israeli Deputy Defence Minister in 2000 stated that the barrier did not necessarily delineate the boundaries of a future Palestinian State.

On March 9, 2006, *The New York Times* quoted then-acting Israeli Prime Minister Ehud Olmert as stating that if his Kadima party wins the upcoming national elections, he would seek to set Israel's permanent borders by 2010, and that the boundary would run along or close to the barrier.

In 2012 it was reported that Israel had presented principles for drawing a border, which essentially propose to turn the West Bank separation barrier into the border with a future Palestinian state.[1791]

Apartheid opinions

Ahmad Hajihosseini, Observer for the Organization of the Islamic Conference (OIC), said that building and maintaining the wall is a crime of apartheid, isolating Palestinian communities in the West Bank and consolidating the annexation of Palestinian land by Israeli settlements.

Malcolm Hedding, a South African minister who worked against South African apartheid and Executive Director of the International Christian Embassy in Jerusalem, said that the West Bank barrier has nothing to do with apartheid and everything to do with Israel's self-defense. He said that Israel has proven its desire to reach an accommodation with the Palestinians while granting political rights to its own Arab citizens within a liberal democratic system, but that the Palestinians remain committed to Israel's destruction. By contrast, he says, it was a tiny minority in South Africa that held power and once democracy came, the National Party that had dominated the masses disappeared.

Art, books, film

The wall has been used as a canvas for many paintings and writings. It has been called the "world's largest protest graffiti". Some of these (but not all) have been removed by the Israelis, and sometimes by people on the Palestinian side.

Figure 234: *Graffiti paintings on the wall by British graffiti artist Banksy*

Figure 235: *Section of West Bank barrier located on Route 443, near Jerusalem. Painting was likely done by the official contractor.*[1792]

Graffiti on the Palestinian side of the wall has been one of many forms of protest against its existence, demanding an end to the barrier, or criticizing its builders and its existence ("Welcome to the Ghetto-Abu Dis" and "Blessed are the Peacemakers").

In August 2005, U.K. graffiti artist Banksy painted nine images on the Palestinian side of the barrier. He describes the barrier as "the ultimate activity holiday destination for graffiti writers", and returned in December 2007 with new images for "Santa's ghetto" in Bethlehem.

The exhibition "Santa's Ghetto in Bethlehem 2007" was co-organized by Banksy and a number of other artists with the aim of drawing attention to poverty in the West Bank and boosting tourism. On the wall, it features, among other images, a peace dove dressed in a bulletproof vest that is being aimed at, a young girl frisking a soldier, a donkey that is facing a soldier who is checking his identity papers, as well as a rat, one of Banksy's recurring themes, with a slingshot. One of Italian artist Blu's contributions to the project, featured a walled Christmas tree surrounded by a number of stumps. American contemporary artist Ron English pasted portraits of Mickey Mouse dressed as a Palestinian with the slogan "You are not in Disneyland anymore" on the wall. In an expression of frustration, Palestinian artist "Trash", glued the lower part of a leg on the wall that is appearing to kick through it.

Although many artists received positive attention and reviews, some Palestinian people had negative opinions toward the artists' movement. A street artist from New York, Swoon, put two works on the Sentry towers in Bethlehem. She did not anticipate that some Palestinians would be opposed to her efforts. Swoon states that there was much enthusiasm from the kids of the Aida refugee camp, who were excited about the new artwork going on the wall. While the kids were excited, many elders believed that the children would grow up with the wrong, positive idea of the wall. One elder from the refugee camp claimed that "they don't necessarily want the kids to start viewing that area positively, and so they see the work as a thing of beauty, but in a place where beauty shouldn't be" (Parry, 10). Most international artists felt that they were creating "something for the people trapped behind wall, as well as creating an international symbol that would be broadcast around the world. [The elder man] wasn't speaking about international symbols, but about what it means to live in the shadow of an 80 foot guard tower" (Parry, 10). Although the graffiti artists felt that they were making a statement with their pieces that would help bring attention and help to the Palestinians, many Palestinians feel that it turns the wall into something beautiful. By painting on the wall, some Palestinians feel that the wall turns into a work of art instead "of an aggressive prison Wall" (Parry, 10). Of course, transforming the wall into something positive was not the intention of the artists. They thought that their work would bring out the oppressiveness and the emotion responses of the people affected by the wall.[1793]

On June 21, 2006, when he visited Israel to give a concert, Pink Floyd's Roger Waters wrote "Tear down the wall" on the wall, a phrase from the Pink Floyd album *The Wall*.

In 2007, with their project "Face2Face", French artists JR and "Marco", organized what was then (until at least 2010), considered to be the largest illegal photography exhibition ever made. In monumental formats, portraits of Israelis and Palestinians of similar professions and backgrounds were pasted next to each other on the wall. The idea was to highlight similarities rather than differences between the peoples. The project spanned over eight cities on both sides of the wall such as Bethlehem, Jericho, Ramallah and Jerusalem. The project was subsequently hosted by a number of exhibitions around the world including the Biennale di Venezia in Italy, the Foam-Musée de la Photographie in Amsterdam, the summer photography festival "Recontres d'Arles" in Arles, Southern France, Artitud in Berlin, Germany, Artcurial in Paris, France and the Rath Museum in Geneva, Switzerland. JR's work, including "Face2Face" is currently shown at the Watari-Um Museum in Tokyo, Japan.

As part of a Dutch-Palestinian collaboration, led by Palestinian activist Faris Arouri, Internet users were invited to submit 80-character long messages to be spray-painted on the security barrier in exchange for a donation of 30 Euro. Messages that included or incited racism, hate, violence or pornography were rejected. About two-thirds of the money raised was donated to social, cultural and educational grassroots projects such as the renovation of the Peace and Freedom Youth Forum's open Youth Center in Bir Zeit. When the project was ended, it was claimed to have reached 550,000,000 people worldwide and placed 1,498 messages on the wall. One of the organizers of "Send a message", Justus van Oel, a Dutch theater director, commissioned South African anti-apartheid activist and theologian Farid Esack to compose a letter to be placed on the wall in 2009. The result was a 1,998-word letter in English written in a single line and stretching over 2.6 km (1.6 mi) near the town of Ramallah, comparing the situation in the Palestinian territories to the South African apartheid era.

The British photojournalist William Parry has recently published a book entitled *"Against the Wall"* The wall was the primary focus of British playwright David Hare's dramatic monologue *Wall*, which is being adapted as a live-action/animated feature-length documentary by the National Film Board of Canada, to be completed in 2014.

The barrier is also the subject of the 2011 documentary film, *5 Broken Cameras*, which documents the story of Emad Burnat, a Palestinian farmer of the

Palestinian village of Bil'in, who had intended to use his videocamera to record vignettes of his son's childhood but ended up filming the resistance movement to the Israeli separation wall that was erected through his village. This award-winning film tells the story of the nonviolent protests of the village residents and the international and Israeli activists who join them, and of how in the course of his filming one after another of his cameras is shot or smashed.

Other barriers

Two similar barriers, the Israeli Gaza Strip barrier and the Israeli-built 7–9 meter (23–30 ft) wall separating Gaza from Egypt (temporarily breached on January 23, 2008), which is currently under Egyptian control, are also controversial.

In February 2004 *The Guardian* reported that Yemeni opposition newspapers likened the barrier Saudi Arabia was building to the Israeli West Bank barrier, while *The Independent* headed an article with "Saudi Arabia, one of the most vocal critics in the Arab world of Israel's "security fence" in the West Bank, is quietly emulating the Israeli example by erecting a barrier along its porous border with Yemen".

Head of Saudi Arabia's border guard, Talal Anqawi, dismissed comparisons with Israel's West Bank barrier: "The barrier of pipes and concrete could in no way be called a separation fence. What is being constructed inside our borders with Yemen is a sort of screen ... which aims to prevent infiltration and smuggling," he said. "It does not resemble a wall in any way."

Detailed timeline

In 1992, the idea of creating a physical barrier between the Israeli and Palestinian populations was proposed by then-prime minister Yitzhak Rabin, following the murder of an Israeli teenage girl in Jerusalem. Rabin said that Israel must "take Gaza out of Tel Aviv" in order to minimize friction between the peoples.[1794,1795] Following an outbreak of violent incidents in Gaza in October 1994, Rabin said: "We have to decide on separation as a philosophy. There has to be a clear border. Without demarcating the lines, whoever wants to swallow 1.8 million Arabs will just bring greater support for Hamas." Following an attack on HaSharon Junction, near the city of Netanya, Rabin made his goals more specific: "This path must lead to a separation, though not according to the borders prior to 1967. We want to reach a separation between us and them. We do not want a majority of the Jewish residents of the state of Israel, 98% of whom live within the borders of sovereign Israel, including a united Jerusalem, to be subject to terrorism."[1796]

Figure 236: *Inside the West Bank on the West Bank barrier*

Figure 237: *West Bank Barrier, Palestinian side*

In 1994, the first section of a barrier (slabs of concrete contiguous for miles) was constructed. The section follows the border between Bat Hefer and Tulkarm communities.

In 1995, the Shahal commission was established by Yitzhak Rabin to discuss how to implement a barrier separating Israelis and Palestinians. Israeli Prime Minister Ehud Barak, prior to the Camp David 2000 Summit with Yasser Arafat, vowed to build a separation barrier, stating that it is "essential to the Palestinian nation in order to foster its national identity and independence without being dependent on the State of Israel".

In November 2000, during Israeli-Palestinian peace negotiations in Washington, Prime Minister Ehud Barak approved financing of a 74 km (46 mi) fence between the Wadi Ara region and Latrun. Not until 14 April 2002, the Cabinet of Prime Minister Ariel Sharon decided to implement the plan and establish a permanent barrier in the Seam Area. On 23 June 2002, the government definitely approved the plan in principle. By March 2003, infrastructure and construction work along most of the approved route had begun. At the end of 2002, due to government inaction, several localities who suffered the most from lack of a border barrier had already started to build the barrier using their own funds directly on the green-line.

In 2003, 180 km (112 mi) had been completed. In 2004, Israel started the southern part of the barrier. In February 2004, the Israeli government said it would review the route of the barrier in response to US and Palestinian concerns. In particular, Israeli cabinet members said modifications would be made to reduce the number of checkpoints Palestinians had to cross, and especially to reduce Palestinian hardship in areas such as the city of Qalqilyah which the barrier completely surrounds. On February 20, 2005, the Israeli cabinet approved the barrier's route on the same day it approved the execution of the Gaza disengagement plan.[1797,1798] The length of the route was increased to 670 km (416 mi) (about twice the length of the Green Line) and would leave about 10% of the West Bank, including East Jerusalem and nearly 50,000 Palestinians on the Israeli side.[1799] It also put the large settlement Maale Adumim and the Gush Etzion bloc on the Israeli side of the barrier, effectively annexing them.[1800] The final route, when realized, closes the Wall separating East Jerusalem, including Maale Adumim, from the West Bank. Before, the exact route of the barrier had not been determined, and it had been alleged by opponents that the barrier route would encircle the Samarian highlands of the West Bank, separating them from the Jordan valley. In June 2004, in exchange for Finance Minister Benjamin Netanyahu's support Israel's planned withdrawal from Gaza, Prime Minister Sharon pledged to build an extension of the barrier to the east of the settlement Ariel to be completed before the finish of the withdrawal from the Gaza Strip. Despite the ICJ ruling that the wall beyond the Green Line is illegal, Ariel Sharon reiterated on September 8, 2004, that the large settlement blocs of Ariel, Ma'aleh Adumim and Gush Etzion will be on the Israeli side of the Barrier. He also decided that the Barrier would run east of Ariel, but its connection with the main fence be postponed.[1801] Israel appropriated Palestinian private land to build upon the fence and started preparations for the construction of the wall to the farthest point inside the West Bank ever, 22 km beyond the Green Line, 3.5 kilometers long, and 100 meters wide.[1802]

In 2005, the Israeli Supreme Court made reference to the conditions and history that led to the building of the barrier. The Court described the history of violence against Israeli citizens since the breakout of the Second Intifada and the loss of life that ensued on the Israeli side. The court ruling also cited the attempts Israel had made to defend its citizens, including "military operations" carried out against "terrorist acts", and stated that these actions "did not provide a sufficient answer to the immediate need to stop the severe acts of terrorism. ... Despite all these measures, the terror did not come to an end. The attacks did not cease. Innocent people paid with both life and limb. This is the background behind the decision to construct the separation fence (Id., at p. 815)." As of February 2005, about 209 km (130 mi) of the Barrier had been completed.[1803]

In 2006, 362 km (224.9 mi) of the barrier had been completed, 88 km (54.7 mi) was under construction and 253 km (157.2 mi) had not yet been started. On April 30, 2006, the route was revised by a cabinet decision, following a suicide bombing in Tel Aviv.[1804,1805] In the Ariel area, the new route corrects an anomaly of the previous route that would have left thousands of Palestinians on the Israeli side. The Alfei Menashe settlement bloc was reduced in size, and the new plan leaves three groups of Palestinian houses on the Palestinian side of the fence. The barrier's route in the Jerusalem area will leave Beit Iksa on the Palestinian side; and Jaba on the Israeli side, but with a crossing to the Palestinian side at Tzurif. Further changes were made to the route around Eshkolot and Metzadot Yehuda, and the route from Metzadot to Har Choled was approved.[1806,1807]

In 2012, 440 km (273.4 mi) (62%) of the barrier had been completed, 57 km (35.4 mi) (8%) was under construction and 212 km (131.7 mi) (30%) had not yet been started, with little progress made by 2014.

As of September 2014, eight years after approving the 45 km stretch of barrier enclosing Gush Etzion, no progress has been made on it, and Israel reopened the debate. The fence is scheduled to go through the national park, the Nahal Rafaim valley, and the Palestinian village of Battir. The Israeli land appropriated in Gva'ot would be on the Palestinian side of the barrier.[1808] On 21

September 2014, the government voted to not reauthorize the barrier in the Gush Etzion area.

External links

 Wikimedia Commons has media related to *Israeli West Bank barrier*.

- Palestinian Film Looks at Suicide Bombers[1809]
- Interview Neazh Mashiah – Director of the Israeli separation barrier project[1810] on YouTube

Maps

- *West Bank Barrier Status 2012*[1811] including sections that are under construction, frozen or being dismantled, and specifying which sections are wall. August 2012, Geneva Initiative
- *West Bank access restrictions*[1812] (10.4 MB!). December 2012, OCHAoPt, on *Map Centre*[1813]
- *Humanitarian Atlas 2012*[1814] (49.1 MB!). December 2012, OCHAoPt, on *Map Centre*[1813]
- *Barrier route*[1815]. July 2008, OCHAoPt
- *"Barrier route"*[1816] (PDF).<templatestyles src="Module:Citation/CS1/styles.css"></templatestyles> (2.10 MB). June 2012, B'Tselem
- *The Separation Barrier in the West Bank*[1817]. April 2006, B'Tselem, on MidEastWeb, *Map of Israel Security Barrier ("Wall") – Current Status (2006)*
- Barrier Gates: Northern West Bank[1818] at the Internet Archive PDF (1.21 MB). March 2005, OCHAoPt, on web.archive.org
- *West Bank Closures*[1819] (2.5 MB). December 2003, OCHAoPt
- *Israeli Security Barrier ("Wall") – Current Status (2005) and Evolution*[1820]. February 2005 versus August 2003, MidEastWeb
- *Who's in, Who's out*[1821] (Names in Hebrew). October 2003, Ma'ariv, on MidEastWeb, *"First Disclosure of Historic Document: The Final Route of the Separation Fence"*
- *First plan*[1822]. May 2002, Haaretz, on MidEastWeb

General news resources

- Compilation of articles about the fence[1823] from *Ha'aretz*
- *Q&A: What is the West Bank barrier?*[1824] BBC News special feature
- *Guide to the West Bank barrier*[1825] BBC News
- *Israeli city says barrier is 'working'*[1826] BBC News
- *Bitter Lemons Edition with Israeli and Palestinian views on the Separation Barrier*[1827]
- Israel annexes land from West Bank using the 'Separation Wall'[1817] further impedes peace process.
- *Impact of the Barrier on East Jerusalem*[1828]. OCHAoPt, June 2007 Update No. 7 (8.7 MB). Includes maps.

Israeli government and courts

- Israel Ministry of Foreign Affairs *Anti-Terrorist Fence* Homepage[1829]
- Israel Ministry of Defense *Security Fence* Homepage[1830]
- 2004 Israeli Supreme Court ruling[1831] (RTF format)
- 2005 Israeli Supreme Court ruling[1832]
- "Full text of Israel's document as presented to the ICJ"[1833] (PDF).<templatestyles src="Module:Citation/CS1/styles.css"></templatestyles> (1.6
- Israel Ministry of Foreign Affairs Statement on ICJ Advisory Opinion[1834]
- Unofficial Summary of State of Israel's Response regarding the Security Fence[1835]

United Nations and International Court of Justice rulings

- ICJ Advisory Opinion[1836], as well as separate opinions of some judges.
- Compilation of UN documents relating to the barrier[1837].
- UN OCHA Humanitarian Information Centre in the occupied Palestinian territory[1838] reports, analysis, detailed maps.
- "Commission on Human Rights: Report on 61st session"[1839] (PDF). Archived from the original[1840] (PDF) on 2006-02-09.<templatestyles src="Module:Citation/CS1/styles.css"></templatestyles> (2.25 MB).

Links to articles opposing the barrier

- Gush Shalom site about the Separation Wall[1841]
- B'Tselem (Israeli Information Center for Human Rights in the Occupied Territories) page about the Separation Barrier[1842]
- Machsom Watch daily reports on checkpoints in the barrier[1843]
- Anarchists against the Wall[1844]
- "Beyond the Wall" an Ir Amim Report on the barrier in Jerusalem[1845]

- International Red Cross and Red Crescent Movement statement on the West Bank barrier[1846]
- *A Wall as a Weapon*[1847] OpEd by Noam Chomsky, originally published in *The New York Times*
- Electronic Intifada[1848]
- *Palestinian grassroots Anti-Apartheid Wall Campaign* [1849]
- The separation wall and the village of Ni'lin at IMEU.net[1850]
- *Video of Wall and Fence, and walking through a checkpoint at the Qalandiya Checkpoint November 2004 produced by filmmaker and journalist Ray Hanania*[1851]
- *A Public Service announcement (60 seconds) on the Wall produced by filmmaker and journalists Ray Hanania* [1852]

Links to articles in favor of the barrier

- *Not an "Apartheid Wall"*[1853] on HonestReporting.com
- *Background Info: The Security Fence*[1854] on imra.org.il
- Is Israel's Security Barrier Unique?[1855] article by Ben Thein in *Middle East Quarterly*
- Research articles on the ICJ decision[1856]
- *"Reply to the ICJ Advisory Opinion"*[1857] (PDF).<templatestyles src="Module:Citation/CS1/styles.css"></templatestyles> (2.29 MB), detailed 193 page book supporting a position in favor of the barrier.
- "How I Learned to Love the Wall"[1858] Irshad Manji, *The New York Times* March 18, 2006
- You Are Judging and I Am Burying My Husband[1859] by Fanny Haim (*Yediot Ahronot*), February 23, 2004
- *Israel's Security Fence*[1860] on Jewish Virtual Library
- StandWithUs "In-depth brochure with pictures, polls, reports, stats"[1861] (PDF). Archived from the original[1862] (PDF) on 2006-07-10.<templatestyles src="Module:Citation/CS1/styles.css"></templatestyles> (2.83 MB)
- IsraCast: The Hague Hearing. Legal Advisor Daniel Taub: 'The International Court Is Trying Victims Of Terror And Not Terrorists'[1863]
- Statement by Daniel Taub, Director, General Law Division, Ministry of Foreign Affairs at Press Conference of Israeli Delegation[1864] 23 February 2004, Israeli demonstrators at The Hague carry pictures of victims of Palestinian terror
- The Controversial Fence[1865]
- Zohar Palti, Israel's Security Fence: Effective in Reducing Suicide Attacks from the Northern West Bank[1866], The Washington Institute for Near East Policy, July 7, 2004

Israeli disengagement from Gaza

<indicator name="pp-default"> 🔒 </indicator>

Part of a series on
the Israeli–Palestinian conflict
Israeli–Palestinian peace process

- v
- t
- e[1867]

The **Israeli disengagement from Gaza** (Hebrew: ההתנתקות תוכנית, *Tokhnit HaHitnatkut*; in the Disengagement Plan Implementation Law), also known as "Gaza expulsion" and "Hitnatkut", was the withdrawal of the Israeli army from inside the Gaza Strip, and the dismantling of all Israeli settlements in the Gaza Strip in 2005.[1868]

Despite the disengagement, the Gaza Strip is still considered by the United Nations, international human rights organisations and most legal scholars to be under military occupation by Israel,[1869] though this is disputed by Israel and other legal scholars. Following the withdrawal, Israel has continued to maintain direct external control over Gaza and indirect control over life within Gaza: it controls Gaza's air and maritime space, and six of Gaza's seven land crossings, it maintains a no-go buffer zone within the territory, and controls Gaza's population registry, and Gaza remains dependent on Israel for its water, electricity, telecommunications, and other utilities.

The disengagement was proposed in 2003 by Prime Minister Ariel Sharon, adopted by the government in June 2004, approved by the Knesset in February 2005 and enacted in August 2005. Israeli citizens who refused to accept

Figure 238: *Map of the Gaza Strip in May 2005, a few months prior to the Israeli withdrawal. The major settlement blocs were the blue-shaded regions of this map.*

government compensation packages and voluntarily vacate their homes prior to the August 15, 2005 deadline, were evicted by Israeli security forces over a period of several days. The eviction of all residents, demolition of the residential buildings and evacuation of associated security personnel from the Gaza Strip was completed by September 12, 2005. The eviction and dismantlement of the four settlements in the northern West Bank was completed ten days later. A total of 8,000 Jewish settlers from all 21 settlements in the Gaza Strip were relocated. The average settler received compensation of more than U.S $200,000.

Demographic concerns, retaining a Jewish majority in Israeli-controlled areas, played a significant role in the development of the policy, being partly attributed to the campaign by demographer Arnon Soffer.

Rationale and development of the policy

In his book *Sharon: The Life of a Leader*, Israeli Prime Minister Ariel Sharon's son Gilad wrote that he gave his father the idea of the disengagement. Sharon had originally dubbed his unilateral disengagement plan, the "separation plan" or *Tokhnit HaHafrada* before realizing that, "separation sounded bad, particularly in English, because it evoked apartheid."

In a November 2003 interview, Ehud Olmert, Sharon's deputy leader, who had been "dropping unilateralist hints for two or three months", explained his developing policy as follows:[1870]

> There is no doubt in my mind that very soon the government of Israel is going to have to address the demographic issue with the utmost seriousness and resolve. This issue above all others will dictate the solution that we must adopt. In the absence of a negotiated agreement - and I do not believe in the realistic prospect of an agreement - we need to implement a unilateral alternative... More and more Palestinians are uninterested in a negotiated, two-state solution, because they want to change the essence of the conflict from an Algerian paradigm to a South African one. From a struggle against 'occupation,' in their parlance, to a struggle for one-man-one-vote. That is, of course, a much cleaner struggle, a much more popular struggle - and ultimately a much more powerful one. For us, it would mean the end of the Jewish state... the parameters of a unilateral solution are: To maximize the number of Jews; to minimize the number of Palestinians; not to withdraw to the 1967 border and not to divide Jerusalem... Twenty-three years ago, Moshe Dayan proposed unilateral autonomy. On the same wavelength, we may have to espouse unilateral separation... [it] would inevitably preclude a dialogue with the Palestinians for at least 25 years.[1871]

Sharon suggested his disengagement plan for the first time on December 18, 2003 at the Fourth Herzliya Conference. In his address to the Conference, Sharon stated that "settlements which will be relocated are those which will not be included in the territory of the State of Israel in the framework of any possible future permanent agreement. At the same time, in the framework of the Disengagement Plan, Israel will strengthen its control over those same areas in the Land of Israel which will constitute an inseparable part of the State of Israel in any future agreement."[1872] It was at this time that he began to use the word "occupation". Bernard Avishai states that the Gaza withdrawal was designed to obviate rather than facilitate peace negotiations: Sharon enivisaged at the same time annexing Jerusalem, the Jordan Valley, and the major settlements like Ma'ale Adumim and Ariel which he had in the meantime developed, and thereby isolate Palestinians on the West Bank in territory that constituted less than half of what existed beyond the Green Line.[1873]

Sharon formally announced the plan in his April 14, 2004 letter to U.S. President George W. Bush, stating that "there exists no Palestinian partner with whom to advance peacefully toward a settlement".[1874]

On June 6, 2004, Sharon's government approved an amended disengagement plan, but with the reservation that the dismantling of each settlement should be voted separately. On October 11, at the opening of the Knesset winter session, Sharon outlined his plan to start legislation for the disengagement in the beginning of November and on October 26, the Knesset gave its preliminary approval. On February 16, 2005, the Knesset finalized and approved the plan.

In October 2004, Prime Minister Ariel Sharon's senior adviser, Dov Weissglass, explained the meaning of Sharon's statement further:

> *The significance of the disengagement plan is the freezing of the peace process, and when you freeze that process, you prevent the establishment of a Palestinian state, and you prevent a discussion on the refugees, the borders and Jerusalem. Effectively, this whole package called the Palestinian state, with all that it entails, has been removed indefinitely from our agenda. And all this with authority and permission. All with a presidential blessing and the ratification of both houses of Congress.*
>
> *That is exactly what happened. You know, the term 'peace process' is a bundle of concepts and commitments. The peace process is the establishment of a Palestinian state with all the security risks that entails. The peace process is the evacuation of settlements, it's the return of refugees, it's the partition of Jerusalem. And all that has now been frozen.... what I effectively agreed to with the Americans was that part of the settlements would not be dealt with at all, and the rest will not be dealt with until the Palestinians turn into Finns. That is the significance of what we did.*

Demographic concerns, the maintenance of a Jewish majority in Israeli-controlled areas, played a significant role in the development of the policy.

The rationale for the disengagement has been partly attributed to Arnon Soffer's campaign regarding "the danger the Palestinian womb posed to Israeli democracy."[1875] Sharon mentioned the demographic rationale in a public address on 15 August 2005, the day of the disengagement, as follows: "It is no secret that, like many others, I had believed and hoped we could forever hold onto Netzarim and Kfar Darom. But the changing reality in the country, in the region, and the world, required of me a reassessment and change of positions. We cannot hold on to Gaza forever. More than a million Palestinians live there and double their number with each generation."[1876,1877] At the same time, Shimon Peres, then Vice Prime Minister, stated in an interview that: "We are disengaging from Gaza because of demography".[1877]

Continued control of Gaza was considered to pose an impossible dilemma with respect to Israel's ability to be a Jewish and democratic state in all the territories it controls.[1878]

Political approval process

Failing to gain public support from senior ministers, Sharon agreed that the Likud party would hold a referendum on the plan in advance of a vote by the Israeli Cabinet. The referendum was held on May 2, 2004 and ended with 65% of the voters against the disengagement plan, despite some polls showing approximately 55% of Likud members supporting the plan before the referendum. Commentators and the press described the rejection of the plan as a blow to Sharon. Sharon himself announced that he accepted the Likud referendum results and would take time to consider his steps. He ordered Minister of Defense Shaul Mofaz to create an amended plan which Likud voters could accept.

On June 6, 2004, Sharon's government approved an amended disengagement plan, but with the reservation that the dismantling of each settlement should be voted separately. The plan was approved with a 14–7 majority but only after the National Union ministers and cabinet members Avigdor Liberman and Binyamin Elon were dismissed from the cabinet, and a compromise offer by Likud's cabinet member Tzipi Livni was achieved.

Following the approval of the plan, it was decided to close the Erez industrial zone and move its factories to cities and towns in Israel such as Ashkelon, Dimona, Yeruham, and Sderot. Ehud Olmert, then the Minister of Industry, Trade, and Labor, stated that the closing was part of Israel's plan to withdraw from the Gaza Strip.

As a result of the passing of the plan (in principle), two National Religious Party (NRP) ministers, Effi Eitam and Yitzhak Levi, resigned, leaving the government with a minority in the Knesset. Later, the entire faction quit after their calls to hold a national referendum were ignored.

Sharon's pushing through this plan alienated many of his supporters on the right and garnered him unusual support from the left-wing in Israel. The right believes that Sharon ignored the mandate he had been elected on, and instead adopted the platform of his Labor opponent, Amram Mitzna, who was overwhelmingly defeated when he campaigned on a disengagement plan of far smaller magnitude. At that time, Sharon referred to Gaza communities such as Netzarim as "no different than Tel Aviv", and said that they are of such strategic value that "the fate of Netzarim is the fate of Tel Aviv."

Many on both sides remained skeptical of his will to carry out a withdrawal beyond Gaza and the northern West Bank. Sharon had a majority for the plan in the government but not within his own party. This forced him to seek a National Unity government, which was established in January 2005. Opponents of the plan, and some ministers, such as Benjamin Netanyahu and former minister Natan Sharansky, called on Sharon to hold a national referendum to prove that he had a mandate, which he refused to do.

On September 14, the Israeli cabinet approved, by a 9–1 majority, plans to compensate settlers who left the Gaza Strip, with only the NRP's Zevulun Orlev opposing. The government's plan for compensation used a formula that based actual amounts on location, house size, and number of family members among other factors. Most families were expected to receive between US$200,000 and 300,000.

On October 11, at the opening of the Knesset winter session, Sharon outlined his plan to start legislation for the disengagement in the beginning of November. In a symbolic act, the Knesset voted 53–44 against Sharon's address: Labor voted against, while the National Religious Party and ten members of Likud refused to support Sharon in the vote.Wikipedia:Please clarify

On October 26, the Knesset gave preliminary approval for the plan with 67 for, 45 against, 7 abstentions, and 1 member absent. Netanyahu and three other cabinet ministers from Sharon's ruling Likud government threatened to resign unless Sharon agreed to hold a national referendum on the plan within fourteen days.

On November 9, Netanyahu withdrew his resignation threat, saying "In this new situation [the death of Yasser Arafat], I decided to stay in the government". Following the vote fourteen days earlier, and Sharon's subsequent refusal to budge on the referendum issue, the three other cabinet ministers from the Likud party backed down from their threat within days.

On December 30, Sharon made a deal with the Labor Party to form a coalition, with Shimon Peres becoming Vice Premier, restoring the government's majority in the Knesset.

On February 16, 2005, the Knesset finalized and approved the plan with 59 in favor, 40 opposed, 5 abstaining. A proposed amendment to submit the plan to a referendum was rejected, 29–72.

On March 17, the Southern Command of the Israel Defense Forces issued a military order prohibiting Israeli citizens not living in the Gaza Strip settlements from taking up residence there.

On March 28, the Knesset again rejected a bill to delay the implementation of the disengagement plan by a vote of 72 to 39. The bill was introduced by a group of Likud MKs who wanted to force a referendum on the issue.

On August 7, Netanyahu resigned just prior to the cabinet ratification of the first phase of the disengagement plan by a vote of 17 to 5. Netanyahu blamed the Israeli government for moving "blindly along" with the disengagement by not taking into account the expected upsurge in terrorism.

On August 10, in his first speech before the Knesset following his resignation, Netanyahu spoke of the necessity for Knesset members to oppose the proposed disengagement.

> "Only we in the Knesset are able to stop this evil. Everything that the Knesset has decided, it is also capable of changing. I am calling on all those who grasp the danger: Gather strength and do the right thing. I don't know if the entire move can be stopped, but it still might be stopped in its initial stages. [Don't] give [the Palestinians] guns, don't give them rockets, don't give them a sea port, and don't give them a huge base for terror."Wikipedia:Citation needed

On August 15, Sharon said that, while he had hoped Israel could keep the Gaza settlements forever, reality simply intervened. "It is out of strength and not weakness that we are taking this step", repeating his argument that the disengagement plan has given Israel the diplomatic initiative.

On August 31, the Knesset voted to withdraw from the Gaza-Egypt border and to allow Egyptian deployment of border police along the demilitarized Egyptian side of the border, revising the previously stated intent to maintain Israeli control of the border.

Description of the plan

The Gaza Strip contained 21 civilian Israeli settlements and the area evacuated in the West Bank contained four, as follows:

In the Gaza Strip (21 settlements):

- Bedolah
- Bnei Atzmon (Atzmona)
- Dugit
- Elei Sinai
- Gadid
- Gan Or
- Ganei Tal
- Katif
- Kfar Darom
- Kfar Yam
- Kerem Atzmona
- Morag
- Neve Dekalim
- Netzarim
- Netzer Hazani
- Nisanit
- Pe'at Sadeh
- Rafiah Yam
- Slav
- Shirat Hayam
- Tel Katifa

In the West Bank (4 settlements):

- Kadim
- Ganim
- Homesh
- Sa-Nur

Hermesh and Mevo Dotan in the northwestern West Bank were included in the original disengagement plans,Wikipedia:Citation needed but were dropped from the plans in March.

Sharon said that his plan was designed to improve Israel's security and international status in the absence of political negotiations to end the Israeli–Palestinian conflict. About nine thousand Israeli residents within Gaza

Figure 239: *Israeli–Palestinian coordination effort, 2005*

were instructed to leave the area or face eviction by the night of Tuesday August 16, 2005.Wikipedia:Citation needed

Under the Revised Disengagement Plan adopted on June 6, 2004, the IDF was to have remained on the Gaza-Egypt border and could have engaged in further house demolitions to widen a 'buffer zone' there (Art 6). However, Israel later decided to leave the border area, which is now controlled by Egypt and the Palestinians, through the PNA. Israel will continue to control Gaza's coastline and airspace and reserves the right to undertake military operations when necessary. (Art 3.1). Egypt will control Gaza's Egyptian border. Israel will continue to provide Gaza with water, communication, electricity, and sewage networks.[1879]

The agreements brokered, according to Condoleezza Rice, stipulated that,

- For the first time since 1967, Palestinian authorities would have complete control over exits and entrances to their territory.
- That both parties to the agreement, Israel and Palestinians, would upgrade and expand crossings to facilitate the movement of people and goods between Israel, Gaza and the West Bank.
- Palestinians would be allowed the use of bus and truck convoys to move between Gaza and the West Bank.
- Obstacles to movement in the West bank would be lifted.
- A Palestinian seaport was to be constructed on the Gaza littoral.

Figure 240: *Residents protest during the forced evacuation of the Israeli community Kfar Darom. August 18, 2005.*

- A Palestinian airport was considered important by both sides. and the United States was encouraging Israel to entertain the idea that construction to that end was to be resumed.[1880]

Because the Palestinian Authority in Gaza did not believe it had sufficient control of the area at this time, foreign observers such as the International Committee of the Red Cross, Human Rights Watch and various legal experts[1881] have argued that the disengagement will not end Israel's legal responsibility as an occupying power in Gaza. Israel and Egypt have concluded an agreement under which Egypt can increase the number of police on its side of the border, while the IDF evacuates the Gazan side. The text of the agreement is not yet public.

Execution of the plan

The disengagement began with Operation "Yad l'Achim" (Hebrew: יד מבצע לאחים, "Giving brothers a hand").

The aim of the operation was to give the Gush Katif settlers the option to leave voluntarily. IDF soldiers helped the settlers who chose to do so by packing their belongings and carrying them. During the operation, soldiers went into settlers' homes and presented them with removal decrees. In addition, the IDF arranged crews of social nurses, psychologists, and support to youths.

Figure 241: *Residents protest against the evacuation of the Israeli community Kfar Darom. The sign reads: "Kfar Darom will not fall twice!". August 18, 2005*

Figure 242: *A group of residents refuses to evacuate the Israeli settlement Bedolach. August 17, 2005*

On April 8, 2005, Defense Minister Shaul Mofaz said that Israel should consider not demolishing the evacuated buildings in the Gaza Strip, with the exception of synagogues (due to fears of their potential desecration, which eventually did occur), since it would be more costly and time consuming. This contrasted with the original plan by the Prime Minister to demolish all vacated buildings.

On May 9, the beginning of the evacuation of settlements was officially postponed from July 20 until August 15, so as to not coincide with the Jewish period of The Three Weeks and the fast of Tisha B'Av, traditionally marking grief and destruction.

On July 13, Sharon signed the closure order of Gush Katif, making the area a closed military zone. From that point on, only residents who presented Israeli ID cards with their registered address in Gush Katif were permitted to enter. Permits for 24–48 hours were given to select visitors for a few weeks before the entire area was completely sealed off to non-residents. Despite this ban, opponents of the disengagement managed to sneak in by foot through fields and bare soil. Estimates range from a few hundred to a few thousand people for those there illegally at that time. At one point, Sharon contemplated deploying Israel Border Police (*Magav*) forces to remove non-residents, but decided against it, as the manpower requirement would have been too great.

At midnight between August 14 and 15, the Kissufim crossing was shut down, and the Gaza Strip became officially closed for entrance by Israelis. The evacuation by agreement continued after midnight of the August 17 for settlers who requested a time extension for packing their things. The Gush Katif Municipal Council threatened to unilaterally declare independence, citing the Gaza Strip's internationally disputed status and Halacha as a foundation. Meanwhile, on August 14, Aryeh Yitzhaki proclaimed the independence of Shirat HaYam as "The Independent Jewish Authority in Gaza Beach", and submitted appeals for recognition to the United Nations and Red Cross.

On August 15, the evacuation commenced under the orders of Maj. Gen. Dan Harel of the Southern Command. At 8 a.m., a convoy of security forces entered Neve Dekalim and began evacuating residents. Although many settlers chose to leave peacefully, others were forcibly evicted, while some attempted to block buses and clashed with security forces. The evacuations of six settlements then commenced as 14,000 Israeli soldiers and police officers forcibly evicted settlers and "mistanenim" (infiltrators). They went house to house, ordering settlers to leave and breaking down the doors of those who did not. There were scenes of troops dragging screaming and sobbing families from houses and synagogues, but with less violence than expected. Some of the soldiers were also observed sobbing, and there were instances of soldiers joining settlers in prayer before evicting them. Some settlers lit their homes on fire as they evacuated so as to leave the Palestinians nothing. Settlers blocked roads, lit fires, and pleaded with soldiers to disobey orders. One West Bank settler set herself on fire in front of a Gaza checkpoint, and in Neve Dekalim, a group of fifteen American Orthodox Jews barricaded themselves in a basement and threatened to light themselves on fire.

Kfar Darom was next evacuated. Residents and their supporters strung up barbed wire fences around the area, and security forces cut their way in. Some 300 settlers barricaded themselves in the local synagogue, while another group barricaded themselves on the roof with barbed wire, and pelted security forces with various objects. Police removed them by force after negotiations failed, and there were injuries to both settlers and officers. On August 17, the settlement of Morag was evacuated by 200 police officers.

On August 18, Shirat HaYam was evacuated by military and police forces, after infiltrators had been removed and the settlement's speaker system was disabled after settlers used it to call on troops to disobey orders. Youth placed obstacles made of flammable materials and torched tires and garbage dumpsters. Fires spread to Palestinian areas, and IDF bulldozers were deployed to put them out. A number of people also barricaded themselves in the synagogue and public buildings and on a deserted rooftop. Aryeh Yitzhaki defended his home with an M16 rifle, and dozens of settlers barricaded themselves inside or on the roof of his home, with at least four of those on the rooftop being armed. A brief stand-off with security forces ensued, and snipers were deployed after Yitzhaki threatened to fire at troops. Security forces stormed the rooftop and arrested settlers without any violence. IDF and police forces evacuated the home after Yitzhaki surrendered weapons and ammunition belonging to his group, but were met with bags of paint and whitewash thrown by settlers, and Yitzhaki's wife and another right-wing activist initially refused to evacuate and lay on the ground holding their infants.

Bedouin citizens of Israel from the village of Dahaniya, situated in the no-man's land on the Israel-Gaza Strip border, were evacuated and resettled in Arad. The village had a long history of cooperation with Israel, and the residents, who were viewed in Gaza as traitors, had asked to be evacuated due to security concerns.[1882,1883,1884]

On August 19, *The Guardian* reported that some settlers had their children leave their homes with their hands up, or wearing a Star of David badge, to associate the actions of Israel with Nazi Germany and the Holocaust. On August 22, Netzarim was evacuated by the Israeli military. This officially marked the end of the 38-year-long presence of Israeli settlers in the Gaza Strip, though the official handover was planned for several weeks later.

The evacuation of the settlers was completed by 22 August, after which demolition crews razed 2,800 houses, community buildings and 26 synagogues.[1885]

Two synagogues, whose construction allowed for them to be taken apart and reassembled, were dismantled and rebuilt in Israel. The demolition of the homes was completed on September 1, while the Shirat HaYam hotel was demolished later.

On August 28, the IDF began dismantling Gush Katif's 48-grave cemetery. All of the bodies were removed by special teams of soldiers supervised by the Military Rabbinate and reburied in locations of their families' choosing. In accordance with Jewish law, all soil touching the remains was also transferred, and the dead were given second funerals, with the families observing a one-day mourning period. All coffins were draped in the Israeli flag on the way to reburial. The transfer was completed on September 1.

The IDF also pulled out its forces in the Gaza Strip, and had withdrawn 95% of its military equipment by September 1. On September 7, the IDF announced that it planned to advance its full withdrawal from the Gaza Strip to September 12, pending cabinet approval. It was also announced that in the area evacuated in the West Bank the IDF planned to transfer all control (excluding building permits and anti-terrorism) to the PNA – the area will remain "Area C" (full Israeli control) *de jure*, but "Area A" (full PNA control) *de facto*.

When the disengagement began, Israel had not yet decided on whether or not to withdraw from the Philadelphi Route, a narrow strip of land serving as a buffer zone along the border between the Gaza Strip and Egypt. Although Sharon was initially opposed to withdrawing from the Philadelphi Route, he relented after legal advisers told him that it was impossible to declare Israel had fully withdrawn from the Gaza Strip so long as it controlled the border with Egypt. On August 28, the Israeli government approved the Philadelphi Accord, under which Egypt, which was prohibited from militarizing the Sinai without Israeli approval as per its peace treaty with Israel, was authorized to deploy 750 border guards equipped with heavy weaponry to the Philadelphi Route. The agreement was approved by the Knesset on August 31. On September 12, the IDF withdrew all forces from the Philadelphi Route.

The Israeli Supreme Court, in response to a settlers' petition to block the government's destruction of the synagogues, gave the go-ahead to the Israeli government. Sharon decided not to proceed with their demolition, however. On September 11, the Israeli cabinet revised an earlier decision to destroy the synagogues of the settlements. The Palestinian Authority protested Israel's decision, arguing that it would rather Israel dismantle the synagogues. On September 11, a ceremony was held when the last Israeli flag was lowered in the IDF's Gaza Strip divisional headquarters. All remaining IDF forces left the Gaza Strip in the following hours. The last soldier left the strip, and the Kissufim gate was closed on the early morning of September 12. This completed

Figure 243: *Residents of Elei Sinai camping in Yad Mordechai, just over the border from their former homes.*

the Israeli pullout from the Gaza Strip. However, an official handover ceremony was cancelled after the Palestinian Authority boycotted it in response to Israel's decision not to demolish the synagogues. On September 20, the IDF temporarily entered the northern Gaza Strip, constructing a buffer zone parallel to the border near Beit Hanoun before pulling out. On September 21, Israel officially declared the Gaza Strip to be an extraterritorial jurisdiction and the four border crossings on the Israel-Gaza border to be international border crossings, with a valid passport or other appropriate travel documents now required to cross through them.

All of the greenhouses in the settlements were supposed to be intact after the Economic Cooperation Foundation raised $14 million to buy the greenhouses for the Palestinian Authority, although about half of them were previously demolished by their own owners before being evacuated for lack of the agreed payment.

On September 22, the IDF evacuated the four settlements in the northern West Bank. While the residents of Ganim and Kadim, mostly middle-class seculars, had long since left their homes, several families and about 2,000 outsiders tried to prevent the evacuation of Sa-Nur and Homesh, which had a larger percent of observant population. Following negotiations, the evacuation was

Figure 244: *A protest camp in Tel Aviv by members of Netzer Hazani left without homes*

completed relatively peacefully. The settlements were subsequently razed, with 270 homes being bulldozed. In Sa-Nur, the synagogue was left intact, but was buried under mounds of sand by bulldozers to prevent its destruction by the Palestinians.

During the pullout, hundreds of people were arrested for rioting, and criminal charges were filed against 482 of them. On January 25, 2010, the Knesset passed a bill granting a general amnesty to around 400 of them, mostly teenagers. While most had by then finished serving their sentences, their criminal records were expunged. The people who were not pardoned as part of this amnesty had either been convicted of crimes that involved endangering human life, and involved the use of explosives or serious violence, or had a previous criminal record.

Following Israel's withdrawal, on 12 September Palestinian crowds entered the settlements waving PLO and Hamas flags, firing gunshots into the air and setting off firecrackers, and chanting slogans. Radicals among them desecrated 4 synagogues as the world's cameras rolled, a sight one observer interprets as demonstrating Sharon's understanding of public relations. Destroyed homes were ransacked. Hamas leaders held celebratory prayers in Kfar Darom synagogue as mobs continued to ransack and loot synagogues. Palestinian Authority security forces did not intervene, and announced that the synagogues would be destroyed. Less than 24 hours after the withdrawal, Palestinian Authority bulldozers began to demolish the remaining synagogues.[1886] Hamas took credit for the withdrawal, and one of their banners read: 'Four years of resistance beat ten years of negotiations.'

Greenhouses

A widespread opinion has it that Israel left Gazans with a generous endowment consisting of a rich infrastructure of greenhouses to assist their economic regrowth, and that this was immediately destroyed by the Palestinians.[1887,1888,1889,1890,1891,1892,1893,1894] Two months prior to the withdrawal, half of the 21 settlements' greenhouses, spread over 1,000 acres, had been dismantled by their owners, leaving the remainder on 500 acres, placing its business viability on a weak footing. International bodies, and pressure from James Wolfensohn, Middle East envoy of the Quartet, who gave $500,000 of his own money, offered incentives for the rest to be left to the Palestinians of Gaza. An agreement was reached with Israel under international law to destroy the settlers' houses and shift the rubble to Egypt. The disposal of asbestos presented a particular problem: some 60,000 truckloads of rubble required passage to Egypt.[1895]

The remaining settlements' greenhouses were looted by Palestinians for 2 days after the transfer, for irrigation pipes, water pumps, plastic sheeting and glass, but the greenhouses themselves remained structurally intact, until order was restored. Palestinian Authority security forces attempted to stop them, but did not have enough manpower to be effective. In some places, there was no security, while some Palestinian police officers joined the looters. The Palestine Economic Development Company (PED) invested $20,000,000 and by October the industry was back on its feet. Subsequently, the harvest, intended for export via Israel for Europe, was essentially lost due to Israeli restrictions on the Karni crossing which "was closed more than not", leading to losses in excess of $120,000 per day. Economic consultants estimated that the closures cost the whole agricultural sector in Gaza $450,000 a day in lost revenue. 25 truckloads of produce per diem through that crossing were needed to render the project viable, but only rarely were just 3 truckloads able to obtain transit at the crossing, which however functioned only sporadically, with Israel citing security concerns. It appears that on both sides corruption prevailed, such as instances of Gazans negotiating with Israeli officers at the crossing and offering bribes to get their trucks over the border. By early 2006, farmers, faced with the slowness of transit, were forced to dump most of their produce at the crossing where it was eaten by goats. Ariel Sharon fell ill, a new Israeli administration eventually came to power and Wolfensohn resigned his office, after suffering from obstacles placed in his way by the U.S. administration, which was sceptical of the agreements reached on border terminals. Wolfensohn attributed this policy of hindrance to Elliott Abrams. Further complications arose from Hamas's election victory in January 2006, and the rift that emerged between Hamas and Fatah. He attributed the electoral success of Hamas to the frustration felt by Palestinians over the non-implementation of these agreements, which shattered their brief experience of normality. "Instead of hope, the Palestinians saw that they were put back in prison," he concluded.[1896] The project was shut down in April 2006 when money ran out to pay the agricultural workers.

Aftermath

After Israel's withdrawal, the Palestinians were given control over the Gaza Strip, except for the borders, the airspace and the territorial waters. The area of the dismantled West Bank settlements remained part of Area C, (area under full Israeli civil and military control). On 23 September, hours after rockets were shot into Israel, a Hamas pickup truck in the Jabaliya Refugee camp was struck by a missile, killing 10 militants and injuring 85 people. On 26 September, Israel killed Palestinian Islamic Jihad commander Mohammad Khalil and his bodyguard with a missile strike; on 29 September Israel closed all Hamas charities on the West Bank, and as part of a five-day offensive fired artillery into the Gaza Strip.[1897]

A British Parliamentary commission, summing up the situation eight months later, found that while the Rafah crossing agreement worked efficiently, from January–April 2006, the Karni crossing was closed 45% of the time, and severe limitations were in place on exports from Gaza, with, according to OCHA figures, only 1,500 of 8,500 tons of produce getting through; that they were informed most closures were unrelated to security issues in Gaza but either responses to violence in the West Bank or for no given reason. The promised transit of convoys between Gaza and the West Bank was not honoured; with Israel insisting that such convoys could only pass if they passed through a specially constructed tunnel or ditch, requiring a specific construction project in the future; Israel withdrew from implementation talks in December 2005 after a suicide bombing attack on Israelis in Netanya by a Palestinian from Kafr Rai.[1898]

Compensation and resettlement

Under legislation passed by the Knesset, evacuated settlers were to be compensated for the loss of their homes, lands, and businesses. Originally, the law only allowed anyone age 21 or over who had lived in one of the evacuated settlements for over five consecutive years to be compensated, but the Israeli

Supreme Court ruled that compensation for younger settlers should also be included in compensation payments to evacuated families. Settlers who lived in the area for at least two years were eligible for more money. The Israeli government offered bonuses to settlers who moved to the Galilee or Negev, and implemented a program in which settlers had the option to build their own homes, with the option of a rental grant. The Housing Ministry doubled the number of apartments available in the Negev. Farmers were offered farmland or plots of land on which to build a home, in exchange for reduced compensation. Land was to be compensated at a rate of $50,000 per dunam (approximately $202,000 per acre), with homes being compensated at a rate per square meter. Workers who lost their jobs were eligible for unemployment benefits ranging from minimum wage to twice the average salary, for up to six months. Workers aged 50 to 55 were offered years' worth of unemployment benefits, and those over 55 were eligible for a pension until age 67. A special category was created for communities that moved en masse, with the government funding the replacement of communal buildings. In cases where communities did not stay together and communal property was lost, individuals would receive compensation for donations made to those buildings. Taxes on compensation sums given to business owners were reduced from ten to five percent. The total cost of the compensation package as adopted by the Knesset was 3.8 billion NIS (approximately $870 million). Following an increase in the number of compensation claims after the disengagement, another 1.5 billion NIS (approximately $250 million) was added. In 2007, a further $125 million was added to the compensation budget. Approximately $176 million was to be paid directly to the evacuees, $66 million to private business owners, and the rest was allocated to finance the government's pullout-related expenses. Yitzhak Meron, the lawyer who represented the evacuees, in dealing with the government offices, recently (11.08.2014) described how this came about, as well as his perception of the situation.[1899]

According to an Israeli committee of inquiry, the government failed to properly implement its compensation plans. By April 2006, only minimal compensation (approximately $10,000) had been paid to families to survive until they obtained new jobs, which was difficult for most people, considering that most of the newly unemployed were middle-aged and lost the agricultural resources that were their livelihood. Those seeking compensation also had to negotiate legal and bureaucratic hurdles.

This criticism received further support from State Comptroller Micha Lindenstrauss's, report, which determined that the treatment of the evacuees was a "big failure" and pointed out many shortcomings.

By 2007, 56.8% of evacuees had found jobs, 22.3% were unemployed and seeking work, and 31.2% of evacuees were unemployed and living off government benefits rather than seeking work. The average monthly salary among the evacuees was NIS 5,380 (about $1,281), a slight rise of 2.1 percent from the average salary the year before. This was, however, a sharp drop of 39% from the settlers' average monthly income before the disengagement. The average salary among evacuees was lower than the general average, as compared to above average before the disengagement. In addition to a drop in salary, the evacuees also suffered a drop in their standard of living due to the increased price of goods and services in their places of residence as compared to the settlements. Following the disengagement, settlers were temporarily relocated to hotels, sometimes for as long as half a year, before moving to mobile homes as temporary housing known as 'caravillas', before they could build proper homes. By June 2014, about 60% of evacuees were still living in these caravillas. Only 40% had moved to permanent housing, although construction of permanent settlements for the evacuees continues to progress. By July 2014, eleven towns for the evacuees had been completed with the expellees joining ten additional towns. Many of the permanent settlements under construction were given names reminiscent of the former Gaza settlements. By August 2014, unemployment among evacuees had dropped to 18%. In 2010 a bill was introduced in the Knesset providing a basic pension to business owners whose businesses collapsed.

New Gush Katif Communities

- Bustan HaGalil
- Neve Yam new community
- Avnei Eitan
- Maskiot
- Netzer, new neighborhood in Ariel
- Netzer Hazani new community
- Palmachim
- Yad Binyamin
- Nitzan
- Be'er Ganim new community
- Hertzog new neighborhood in Ashkelon
- Ganei Tal new community
- Karmei Katif new community
- Bnei Dekalim new community
- Neta new community in Tel Katifa
- Shomriya new community
- Teneh Omarim
- Bat Hadar

- Mavki'im
- Talmei Yafeh
- Shavei Darom new community
- Nave new community
- Bnei Netzarim new community

Fatah–Hamas conflict

Following the withdrawal, Hamas was elected as the Palestinian government which started the chain reaction leading to Operation "Summer Rains" later within that year.

In December 2006, news reports indicated that a number of Palestinians were leaving the Gaza Strip, due to political disorder and "economic pressure" there.[1900] In January 2007, fighting continued between Hamas and Fatah, without any progress towards resolution or reconciliation.[1901] Fighting spread to several points in the Gaza Strip with both factions attacking each other. In response to constant attacks by rocket fire from the Gaza Strip, Israel launched an airstrike which destroyed a building used by Hamas.[1902] In June 2007 the Fatah–Hamas conflict reached its height and Hamas took control over the Gaza Strip.[1903]

Museum

In August 2008, a museum of Gush Katif opened in Jerusalem near Machane Yehuda. Yankeleh Klein, the museum director, sees it as an artistic commemoration of the expulsion from the 21 Gaza settlements, and the evacuees' longing to return. The art displayed in the museum is that of Gaza evacuees along with pieces by photographers and artists who were involved in the disengagement or were affected by it.[1904]

In the newly renovated Katif Center, more properly called the "Gush Katif Heritage Center in Nitzan," Israel, they combine modern technology with guided tours by Gush Katif expellees to provide a very emotional experience. Project Coordinator Laurence Beziz notes that. "Our goal is to tell the story of 35 years of pioneering the land of Israel in Gush Katif and to allow an insight as to what life was in Gush Katif."

Criticisms and opinions

The unilateral disengagement plan has been criticized from various viewpoints. In Israel, it has been criticized by the settlers themselves, supported by the Israeli right, who saw Ariel Sharon's action as a betrayal of his previous policies of support of settlement. Conversely, the disengagement has been criticized by parts of the Israeli left, who viewed it as nothing more than a mode of stalling negotiations and increasing Israeli presence in the West Bank.Wikipedia:Citation needed The disengagement also did not address wider issues of occupation. Israel retained control over Gaza's borders, airspace, coastline, infrastructure, power, import-exports, etc.

Anti-withdrawal

Within Israel, disengagement has been criticized heavily, both for its very execution, and for the manner in which it was carried out.

From the very beginning, Sharon was accused of hijacking the mandate he received for a cause for which he had not been elected.Wikipedia:Citation needed In 2003, Sharon was elected over Labor Party chairman, Amram Mitzna. Mitzna ran on a platform that included a separation plan very similar to Sharon's Disengagement Plan. Sharon ran with an opposing platform, rejecting the idea of unilateral separation from the West Bank and the Gaza Strip. At a certain point, Sharon even declared that Netzarim's fate was the same as Tel Aviv's.Wikipedia:Citation needed

In the cabinet's initial June vote over the plan Benjamin Netanyahu, then Finance Minister, announced he would vote in favor of the plan only if Sharon promised to hold a national referendum to decide the fate of the Gaza Strip and the northern West Bank. Such a referendum was never held, in spite of Sharon's commitment.Wikipedia:Citation needed

Druze MK Ayoob Kara (Likud) strongly opposed the plan, saying it will be "terrible for Israeli security." Kara warned that Hamas would take over the Gaza Strip and use it as a base from which to attack Israel.[1905]

Some IsraelisWikipedia:Manual of Style/Words to watch#Unsupported attributions believe that the disengagement's aftermath is a disgrace. This view holds that Sharon was in such a rush to execute his plan that he did not plan accordingly for the residents that were evicted.Wikipedia:Citation needed Most of the former settlers were housed in hotels and guesthouses for the first few months, being threatened with further eviction numerous times. People were still residing in hotel rooms right up until Passover (in April) of 2006, more than eight months after losing their homes.Wikipedia:Citation needed

Pro-withdrawal

The Disengagement Plan was also criticized by both Israelis and other observers from the opposite viewpoint as an attempt to make permanent the different settlements of the West Bank, while the Gaza strip was rendered to the Palestinian National Authority as an economically uninteresting territory with a Muslim population of nearly 1.4 million, seen as a "threat" to the Jewish identity of the Israeli democratic state. As Leila Shahid, speaker of the PNA in Europe declared, the sole fact of carrying out the plan unilaterally already showed that the plan was only thought of according to the objectives of Israel as viewed by SharonWikipedia:Citation needed. Brian Cowen, Irish Foreign Minister and speaker of the European Union (EU), announced the EU's disapproval of the plan's limited scope in that it did not address withdrawal from the entire West Bank. He said that the EU "will not recognize any change to the pre-1967 borders other than those arrived at by agreement between the parties." However, Europe has given tentative backing to the Disengagement plan as part of the road map for peace. CriticsWikipedia:Manual of Style/Words to watch#Unsupported attributions pointed out that, at the same time that Sharon was preparing the withdrawal, he was favoring settlements in the West Bank, among them Ma'ale Adumim, the largest Israeli settlement near Jerusalem. According to Peace Now, the number of settlers increased by 6,100 compared with 2004, to reach 250,000 in the West Bank. In an October 6, 2004, interview with *Haaretz*, Dov Weissglass, Sharon's chief of staff, declared: "The significance of the disengagement plan is the freezing of the peace process.... When you freeze that process, you prevent the establishment of a Palestinian state and you prevent a discussion on the refugees, the borders and Jerusalem. Disengagement supplies the amount of formaldehyde that is necessary so there will not be a political process with the Palestinians."

Positions of foreign governments

United States

President George W. Bush endorsed the plan as a positive step towards the road map for peace. At a joint press conference with Ariel Sharon on April 11, 2005 he said:

> *I strongly support [Prime Minister Sharon's] courageous initiative to disengage from Gaza and part of the West Bank. The Prime Minister is willing to coordinate the implementation of the disengagement plan with the Palestinians. I urge the Palestinian leadership to accept his offer. By working together, Israelis and Palestinians can lay the groundwork for a peaceful transition.*

And in his May 26, 2005, joint press conference welcoming Palestinian leader Mahmoud Abbas to the White House, President George W. Bush elaborated:

> *The imminent Israeli disengagement from Gaza, parts of the West Bank, presents an opportunity to lay the groundwork for a return to the road map.... To help ensure that the Gaza disengagement is a success, the United States will provide to the Palestinian Authority $50 million to be used for new housing and infrastructure projects in the Gaza.*

On April 11, 2005, President George W. Bush stated:

> *As part of a final peace settlement, Israel must have secure and recognized borders, which should emerge from negotiations between the parties in accordance with UNSC Resolutions 242 and 338. In light of new realities on the ground, including already existing major Israeli population centers, it is unrealistic that the outcome of final status negotiations will be a full and complete return to the armistice lines of 1949.*

In his May 26, 2005 joint press conference with Palestinian leader Mahmoud Abbas, in the Rose Garden, President George W. Bush stated his expectations *vis-a-vis* the Roadmap Plan as follows:

> *Any final status agreement must be reached between the two parties, and changes to the 1949 Armistice lines must be mutually agreed to. A viable two-state solution must ensure contiguity of the West Bank, and a state of scattered territories will not work. There must also be meaningful linkages between the West Bank and Gaza. This is the position of the United States today, it will be the position of the United States at the time of final status negotiations.*

European Union

Javier Solana, High Representative for the Common Foreign and Security Policy (CFSP), stated on June 10, 2004:

> *I welcome the Israeli Prime Minister's proposals for disengagement from Gaza. This represents an opportunity to restart the implementation of the Road Map, as endorsed by the UN Security Council.*

The Irish Minister for Foreign Affairs, Brian Cowen (Ireland having Presidency of the EU at the time), announced the European Union's disapproval of the plan's limited scope in that it does not address withdrawal from the entire West Bank. He said that the EU "will not recognize any change to the pre-1967 borders other than those arrived at by agreement between the parties." However, Europe has given tentative backing to the Disengagement Plan as part of the road map for peace.

United Nations

Kofi Annan, United Nations Secretary-General, commended on August 18, 2005 what he called Israeli Prime Minister Sharon's "courageous decision" to carry through with the painful process of disengagement, expressed the hope that "both Palestinians and Israelis will exercise restraint in this challenging period", and "believes that a successful disengagement should be the first step towards a resumption of the peace process, in accordance with the Road Map", referring to the plan sponsored by the diplomatic Quartet – UN, EU, Russia, and the United States – which calls for a series of parallel steps leading to two states living side-by-side in peace by the end of the year.

Ibrahim Gambari, Under-Secretary-General for Political Affairs, told the Security Council on August 24, 2005:

> *Israel has demonstrated that it has the requisite maturity to do what would be required to achieve lasting peace, and the Israeli Defence Forces (IDF) has demonstrated their ability to discharge their mission with carefully calibrated restraint. Prime Minister Sharon should be commended for his determination and courage to carry out the disengagement in the face of forceful and strident internal opposition.*

Public opinion

Palestinian

The PA, in the absence of a final peace settlement, has welcomed any military withdrawal from the territories, but many Palestinian Arabs have objected to the plan, stating that it aims to "bypass" past international agreements, and instead call for a complete withdrawal from the West Bank and Gaza Strip. Their suspicions were further aroused when top Sharon aide Dov Weisglass was quoted in an interview with Israeli newspaper *Haaretz* on October 6, 2004, as saying that the disengagement would prevent a Palestinian state for years to come (see above).

This incident has bolstered the position of critics of the plan that Sharon is intentionally trying to scuttle the peace process. Israeli officials, including Weisglass, denied this accusation, and media critics have asserted that the Weisglass interview was widely distorted and taken out of context.Wikipedia:Citation needed

On August 8, 2005, *Haaretz* quoted a top Palestinian Authority religious cleric, Sheikh Jamal al-Bawatna, the mufti of the Ramallah district, in a fatwa (a religious edict) banning shooting attacks against Israeli security forces and settlements, out of concern they might lead to a postponement of the pullout. According to *Haaretz*, this is the first time that a Muslim cleric has forbidden shooting at Israeli forces. On August 15, 2005, scenes of delight took place across the Arab world, following the long-ingrained suspicion that the disengagement would not take place.

Israeli opinions

A September 15, 2004 survey published in *Maariv* showed that:

- 69% supported a general referendum to decide on the plan; 26% thought that approval in the Knesset would be enough.
- If a referendum were to be held, 58% would vote for the disengagement plan, while 29% would vote against it.

Polls on support for the plan have consistently shown support for the plan in the 50-60% range, and opposition in the 30–40% range. A June 9, 2005, Dahaf Institute/Yedioth Ahronoth poll showed support for the plan at 53%, and opposition at 38%.[1906] A June 17, telephone poll published in *Maariv* showed 54% of Israel's Jews supporting the plan. A poll carried out by the Midgam polling company, on June 29 found support at 48% and opposition at 41%,[1907] but a Dahaf Institute/Yedioth Ahronot poll of the same day found support at 62% and opposition at 31%. A poll conducted the week of July 17 by the Tel Aviv University Institute for Media, Society, and Politics shows that Israeli approval of the disengagement is at 48%; 43% of the respondents believe that Palestinian terrorism will increase following disengagement, versus 25% who believe that terrorism will decline.

On July 25, 2004, the "Human Chain", a rally of tens of thousands of Israelis to protest against the plan and for a national referendum took place. The protestors formed a human chain from Nisanit (later moved to Erez Crossing because of security concerns) in the Gaza Strip to the Western Wall in Jerusalem a distance of 90 km. On October 14, 2004, 100,000 Israelis marched in cities throughout Israel to protest the plan under the slogan "100 cities support Gush Katif and Samaria".

On May 16, 2005, a nonviolent protest was held throughout the country, with the protesters blocking major traffic arteries throughout Israel. The protest was sponsored by "HaBayit HaLeumi", and was hailed by them as a success, with over 400 protestors arrested, half of them juveniles. Over 40 intersections throughout the country were blocked, including:

- The entrance to Jerusalem
- Bar Ilan/Shmuel Hanavi Junction in Jerusalem
- Sultan's Pool Junction outside the Old City of Jerusalem
- Geha Highway
- Golumb St. corner of Begin Blvd in Jerusalem

On June 9, 2005, a poll on Israeli Channel 2 showed that public support for the plan had fallen below 50 percent for the first time.

On July 18, 2005, a nonviolent protest was held. The protest began in Netivot near Gaza. The protest march ended July 21 after police prevented protesters from continuing to Gush Katif. On August 2, 2005, another protest against disengagement began in Sderot, with approximately 50,000 attendees. On August 10, 2005, in response to calls from Jewish religious leaders, including former Chief Rabbis Avraham Shapira, Ovadia Yosef, and Mordechai Eliyahu, between 70,000 (police estimate) and 250,000 (organizers' estimate) Jews gathered for a rally centered at the Western Wall in prayer to ask that the planned disengagement be cancelled. The crowds that showed up for the rally overwhelmed the Western Wall's capacity and extended as far as the rest of the Old City and surrounding Jerusalem neighborhoods. The prayer rally was the largest of its kind for over 15 years, since the opposition to the Madrid Conference of 1991.Wikipedia:Citation needed[1908,1909] On August 11, 2005, between 150,000 (police estimates) and 300,000 (organizers' estimates) people massed in and around Tel Aviv's Rabin Square for an anti-disengagement rally. Organizers called the event "the largest expression of public protest ever held in Israel."Wikipedia:Citation needed According to a police spokesman, it was one of the largest rallies in recent memory.

Those advocating suspension or cancellation of the plan have often quoted one or more of these arguments:

- The religious approach maintains that Eretz Israel was promised to the Jews by God, and that no government has the authority to waive this inalienable right. In their view, inhabiting all of the land of Israel is one of the most important mitzvot.
- The political approach, owing much to existing right-wing ideology, claims that the areas to be evacuated constitute Israeli territory as legitimately as Tel Aviv or Haifa, and that relocating settlers is illegal and violates their human rights. Some have gone as far as labelling it a war crime. In the wake of the Sharm el-Sheikh Summit of February 2005, some have claimed that now that there is a negotiation partner on the Palestinian side, the plan has become redundant.
- The military approach says that the plan is disastrous to Israeli security – not only will prevention of Qassam rockets and other attacks from Gaza become nearly impossible after the withdrawal, but implementation of the plan will be an important moral victory for Hamas and other organizations, and will encourage them to continue executing terrorist attacks against Israel.

Orange ribbons in Israel symbolize opposition to the disengagement; it is the color of the flag of the Gaza coast Regional Council. Blue ribbons (sometimes blue-and-white ribbons) symbolized support for the disengagement and are intended to invoke the Israeli flag.

American opinions

Polls in the U.S. about the question of the Gaza pullout produced varied results. One poll commissioned by the Anti-Defamation League, and conducted by the Marttila Communications Group from June 19–23, 2005 among 2200 American adults, found that 71% of respondents felt that the Disengagement Plan is closer to a "bold step that would advance the Peace Process" than to a "capitulation to terrorist violence", while 12% felt that the plan is more of a "capitulation" than a "bold step".

Another poll commissioned by the Zionist Organization of America, and conducted by McLaughlin & Associates on June 26, 2005 – June 27, 2005, with a sample of 1,000 American adults, showed U.S. opposition to the proposed disengagement. Respondents, by a margin of 4 to 1 (63% to 16%) opposed "Israel's unilateral withdrawal from a section of Gaza and northern Samaria and forcing 10,000 Israeli Jews from their homes and businesses" and by a margin of 2.5 to 1 (53% to 21%), agreed with the statement that "this Gaza Plan sends a message that Arab terrorism is being rewarded."

Morton Klein, President of the Zionist Organization of America, criticized the Anti-Defamation League-commissioned poll, stating that the question in the poll was not whether or not respondents agreed with the Disengagement Plan, but was a subjective characterization of primary motives behind it: whether Israeli politicians are acting more for the sake of capitulating to terrorism or for the sake of continuing the road map. The Anti-Defamation League, in turn, criticized the ZOA-commissioned poll, calling its wording "loaded."

Israeli media coverage

The Israeli media systematically overstated "the threat posed by those opposed to disengagement and emphasiz[ed] extreme scenarios", according to the Israeli media monitoring NGO Keshev ("Awareness").[1910,1911] Keshev's report states that

> throughout the weeks before the disengagement, and during the evacuation itself, the Israeli media repeatedly warned of potential violent confrontation between settlers and security forces. These scenarios, which never materialized, took over the headlines.

Based on Keshev's research, the Israeli print and TV media "relegated to back pages and buried deep in the newscasts, often under misleading headlines" items that "mitigat[ed] the extreme forecasts."[1912] Editors delivered "one dominant, ominous message: The Police Declares High Alert Starting Tomorrow, Almost Like a State of War" Channel 1 (main news headline, August 14, 2005)[1913]

"The discrepancy between the relatively calm reality emerging from most stories and the overall picture reflected in the headlines is evident in every aspect of the disengagement story: in the suppression of information about the voluntary collection of weapons held by the settlers in the Gaza Strip; in reporting exaggerated numbers of right-wing protesters who infiltrated the Strip before the evacuation; in misrepresentation of the purpose of settler protest (which was an exercise in public relations, not a true attempt to thwart the disengagement plan); and in playing down coordinated efforts between the Israeli security forces and the settlers."

The price for this misrepresentation was paid, at least in part, by the settlers, whose public image was radicalized unjustifiably. After the disengagement was completed without violence between Israelis and a sense of unity and pride pervaded society, "the media chose to give Israeli society, and especially its security forces, a pat on the back."

Bibliography

- Rynhold, Jonathan; Waxman, Dov (2008). "Ideological Change and Israel's Disengagement from Gaza". *Political Science Quarterly*. The Academy of Political Science. **123** (1): 11–37. JSTOR 20202970[1914].<templatestyles src="Module:Citation/CS1/styles.css"></templatestyles>has
- Cook, Jonathan (2006). *Blood and Religion: The Unmasking of the Jewish and Democratic State*[1915]. Pluto Press. ISBN 978-0-7453-2555-2.<templatestyles src="Module:Citation/CS1/styles.css"></templatestyles>

External links

Wikimedia Commons has media related to *Israel's unilateral disengagement plan*.

Wikinews has related news: *Israel completes Gaza strip, West Bank pull-outs*

Official documents

- The Cabinet Resolution Regarding the Disengagement Plan[1916], Revised Disengagement Plan – Main Principles. Israel MFA, 6 June 2004
- PM Sharon's Statement on the Day of the Implementation of the Disengagement Plan[1917] from the Prime Minister's Office
- Israel's Disengagement Plan: Renewing the Peace Process[1918] Official website from the Israel Ministry of Foreign affairs.
- Jan 2005.htm Israel's Disengagement Plan: Selected Documents[1919] Official website from the Israel Ministry of Foreign affairs.
- Ariel Sharon's Disengagement Plan and President Bush's letter accepting it[1920] at MidEastWeb for Coexistence[1921]
- Map of disengagement plan showing settlements to be evacuated[1922] at MidEastWeb for Coexistence[1921]
- Map[1923]

News reports

- Pullout[1924] Coverage from Ynetnews
- Pictures of the Mass Prayer Rally against the disengagement plan at the Western Wall in Jerusalem[1925]
- Pictures of the Mass Rally in Tel Aviv against the disengagement plan[1926]
- U.S. Jews Divided on Pullout (FOX News)[1927]
- Gaza withdrawal is a defeat for Israel, says PA foreign minister[1928]Wikipedia:Link rot by Khaled Abu Toameh, published in *The Jerusalem Post* August 21, 2005
- IDF to disinter 48 Gaza graves[1929]Wikipedia:Link rot by Arieh O'Sullivan, published in *The Jerusalem Post* August 25, 2005
- Anti-pullout signs posted at Yad Vashem[1930] by Etgar Lefkovits, published in the Jerusalem Post September 1, 2005
- The settlers' retreat was the theatre of the cynical[1931] There was no 'sensitivity training' when bulldozers went into Rafah by Jonathan Steele (*The Guardian*, August 19, 2005)

- Israel's Gaza pullout might ease relations with Kuwait[1932] by the Associated Press, published in USA Today 10/30/2005
- "Unsettled in Gaza, The Pullout That's Dividing Israelis"[1933] by Warren Bass, *The Washington Post* Sunday, July 17, 2005; Page B02

Commentary

- Ariel Sharon's Disengagement Plan – From Ariel Sharon's Life Story – A biography[1934]
- Gaza and Victory?[1935] commentary by Joey Tartakovsky assistant editor of the Claremont Review of Books published on Victor Davis Hanson's Private Papers blog
- Right Strategy Again; Gaza pullout will turn terror morass to conventional standoff[1936] by Victor Davis Hanson, August 29, 2005.
- Disengagement and ethnic cleansing[1937] Israel's pullout from Gaza is openly justified by demography - in other words, the need to maintain a Jewish majority by Daphna Baram (*The Guardian*, August 16, 2005)
- AIPAC Memo – Israel Carrying Out Historic Withdrawal From Gaza and Parts of the West Bank[1938] PDF Memorandum from the American Israel Public Affairs Committee August 29, 2005
- AIPAC Memo – Israel Implementing Disengagement Despite High Costs[1939] PDF Memorandum from the American Israel Public Affairs Committee August 29, 2005
- The Gaza "Disengagement" Plan from a chabad perspective[1940]
- Blood and Religion: The Unmasking of the Jewish and Democratic State
- In Gaza, a Test Case for Peace[1941] Daniel Ayalon, *Washington Post*, July 20, 2005

2006–2009: Olmert

2006 Gaza cross-border raid

2006 Gaza cross-border raid	
Part of Gaza–Israel conflict	
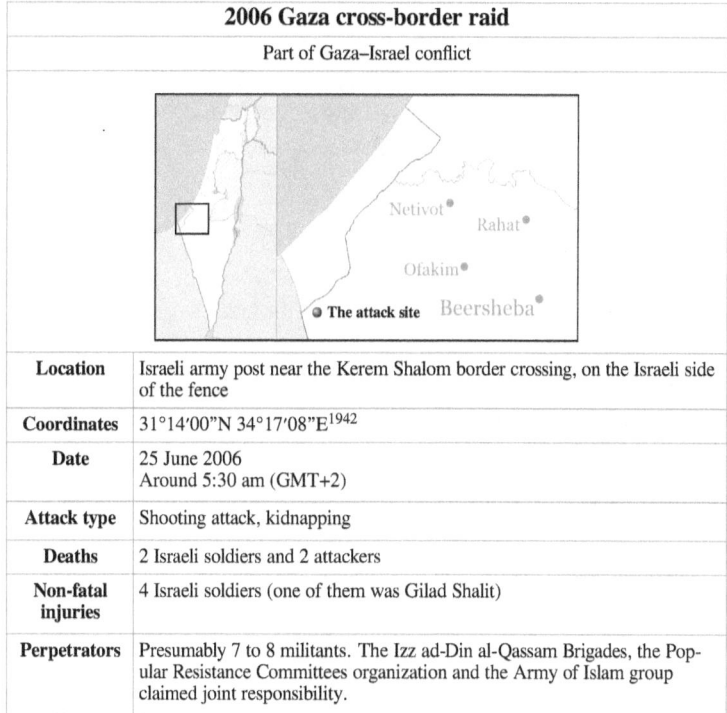	
Location	Israeli army post near the Kerem Shalom border crossing, on the Israeli side of the fence
Coordinates	31°14′00″N 34°17′08″E[1942]
Date	25 June 2006 Around 5:30 am (GMT+2)
Attack type	Shooting attack, kidnapping
Deaths	2 Israeli soldiers and 2 attackers
Non-fatal injuries	4 Israeli soldiers (one of them was Gilad Shalit)
Perpetrators	Presumably 7 to 8 militants. The Izz ad-Din al-Qassam Brigades, the Popular Resistance Committees organization and the Army of Islam group claimed joint responsibility.

The **2006 Gaza cross-border raid** was a cross-border raid which was carried out on 25 June 2006 in which a Palestinian militant squad thought to consist of 7 to 8 militants managed to cross the border through an underground attack tunnel near the Kerem Shalom Crossing and attack Israel Defense Forces (IDF) military positions. In the attack, two IDF soldiers and two Palestinian

Figure 245: *Gilad Shalit on Hamas poster, Nablus 7 May 2007*

militants[1943] were killed, four IDF soldiers were wounded, and one wounded soldier Gilad Shalit was captured and taken to the Gaza Strip.

Hamas' military wing, the Izz ad-Din al-Qassam Brigades, claimed responsibility, together with the Popular Resistance Committees (which includes members of Fatah, Islamic Jihad, and Hamas), and a previously unknown group calling itself the Army of Islam.

This event led to the eruption of the Operation Summer Rains. Shalit was held as a hostage in the Gaza Strip by the Hamas, and was only released as part of a prisoner swap on 18 October 2011.

The capture of Gilad Shalit was the first incident of a capture of an IDF soldier by the Palestinians since the Kidnapping of Nachshon Wachsman in 1994.

Background

In February 2005, the PA President Mahmoud Abbas and Israeli Prime Minister Ariel Sharon announced a ceasefire which effectively ended the Second Intifada. Hamas unilaterally agreed to abide by the ceasefire.Wikipedia:Citation needed Under the direction of Sharon, Israel completed withdrawal from Gaza in September 2005.

To international surprise, Hamas won the Palestinian elections in January 2006, which were declared democratic by observers. The 'Quartet' demanded that Hamas renounce violence, recognize Israel, and accept previous Israeli-Palestinian agreements, which Hamas refused to do, resulting in aid being withheld. Israel imposed a blockade and sanctions on Gaza, and withheld customs revenue. Hamas had announced a ceasefire in 2005 and until 10 June 2006, Hamas did not take responsibility itself for the firing of ordnance into Israel, but the group's leader had said in February that it did not intend to impede other groups from carrying out "armed resistance" against Israel. However, Hamas was implicated in rocket and terror attacks carried out by other groups, as well as engaging in its own attacks, despite the ceasefire.[1944]

On 8 June 2006, Jamal Abu Samhadana, Hamas' Inspector General in the Ministry of the Interior and founder of the Popular Resistance Committees, was killed in an IAF air-strike on the Salah al-Dein Brigades training camp in Gaza. Samhadna's supporters threatened to revenge his death. The Israeli military said Samhadana and the other targeted militants were planning an attack on Israel. The next day rockets were fired at Israel from Fatah-controlled Gaza, and a few hours later a Palestinian family was killed in an explosion attributed to IDF shelling of a reported launch site. Hamas formally withdrew from its 16-month ceasefire, and began openly taking responsibility for the ongoing Qassam rocket attacks.

The attack and the capture

On Sunday morning, 25 June 2006, at about 5:30 am (GMT+2) an armed squad of Palestinian militants from the Gaza Strip crossed the border into Israel via a 300-meter-long underground tunnel they dug near the Kerem Shalom border crossing.[1945] The militants surfaced in Israeli territory shielded by a row of trees, and came up behind IDF border positions facing Gaza. As militants from within the Gaza Strip bombarded Israeli positions with mortar and anti-tank fire, the militant squad split into three cells.

One cell aligned itself behind a Merkava Mark III tank, another behind a concrete watchtower, and another behind an armored personnel carrier. The militants simultaneously opened fire on their targets. The militants that attacked the tank blew open its rear door with an RPG. The tank's gunner, Corporal Gilad Shalit, was wounded by the RPG blast, suffering a broken left hand and a light shoulder wound. Two of the militants then approached the tank. The RPG hit caused the tank to go up in flames, and its fire extinguisher system was activated. However, the engine stopped working and the ventilation system failed to work as a result, creating suffocating conditions inside. The tank's commander and driver climbed out to escape, and were gunned down by the militants. A militant then climbed onto the tank's turret and threw grenades into the tank, wounding another crew member. Shalit climbed out of the tank to escape the suffocating conditions, and as he emerged onto the turret, he saw one of the militants climbing onto the tank, with his AK-47 strapped to his back. Shalit at this point could have easily killed the militant using the .50 caliber machine gun mounted on the turret, but instead surrendered to him. He later told IDF investigators that he was confused and in a state of shock, and thus never thought of shooting him. Shalit was then taken to Gaza with the militants. An Israeli tank soon arrived on the scene and an IDF observation post witnessed their escape, although it was not known at the time that the militants had a captive Israeli soldier with them, and the tank did not open fire in time, as the commander was awaiting permission. When permission was finally granted, the tank opened fire with its machine guns.

The squad's third member was positioned near a road, and fired an RPG at an IDF jeep driven by a captain. After the captain returned fire, the militant fled towards a tunnel dug along the fence, throwing grenades. An IDF armored vehicle fired at him, but missed, and he escaped.

Two militants attacked the watchtower, raking it with RPG and small-arms fire, wounding two soldiers manning the tower. One militant crept towards the tower and placed an explosive charge next to the bottom doors. The ensuing explosion damaged the tower's communication cables. The militant then attempted to climb the stairs, while the second militant remained on the ground as backup. IDF soldiers in the tower spotted the militant climbing the stairs and opened fire, killing him in the upper part of the stairway. The second militant was spotted by an IDF lookout, and soldiers then opened fire and killed him.

The third cell attacked an empty armored personnel carrier placed as a decoy before retreating, firing an RPG which damaged it and caused it to burst into flames.[1946]

Immediately afterwards the Palestinian militant squad made their way back into the Gaza Strip, with Shalit, through the ground after they blew an opening in the security fence and disappeared. As they retreated, the militants left behind explosive charges. Meanwhile, large Israeli military forces arrived at the site and began helping the wounded. The charges left behind by the militants exploded as IDF troops were combing the area, lightly injuring three soldiers. When they reached the tank the soldiers discovered the two bodies and a wounded crewman. When it became clear that the fourth crew member was missing, an abduction alert was declared, and various Israeli forces entered Gaza.

The Palestinian militancy organizations responsible for raid took responsibility for the attack, for the first time, a day after the attack – the Izz ad-Din al-Qassam Brigades (the armed wing of Hamas), the Popular Resistance Committees organization (which includes members of Fatah, Islamic Jihad, and Hamas) and the Army of Islam group issued a joint statement on 26 June 2006, in which they claimed responsibility for the raid and offered information on Shalit only if Israel agreed to release all female Palestinian prisoners and all Palestinian prisoners under the age of 18, who were held without charges and tried without the right of defense.

Shalit became the first Israeli soldier captured by Palestinians since Nachshon Wachsman in 1994.[1947]

Casualties

Israeli soldiers

- Staff Sergeant Pavel Slutzker, 20, of Dimona
- Lieutenant Hanan Barak, 20, of Arad

Palestinian militants

- Muhammed Farawneh, 22, of Khan Yunis, Army of Islam member
- Hamed Rantisi, 22, of Rafah, Popular Resistance Committees member

The perpetrators

A day after the attack, the following organizations claimed responsibility for the operation – the Izz ad-Din al-Qassam Brigades (the armed wing of Hamas), the Popular Resistance Committees (which includes members of Fatah, Islamic Jihad, and Hamas), and a previously unknown group calling itself the Army of Islam.

Israeli retaliation

Following the capture of Corporal Gilad Shalit, the IDF launched Operation Summer Rains. In addition various international bodies conducted diplomatic activity, among them Egypt, in an attempt to release Shalit. Due to the fact that Shalit is a French citizen, France attempted to release him through diplomatic means. However, the captors, who operated under the orders of Khaled Mashal and the Hamas military leadership, refused to release him. According to David Siegel, a spokesman at the Israeli embassy in Washington, D.C., "Israel did everything it could in exhausting all diplomatic options and gave Mahmoud Abbas the opportunity to return the abducted Israeli... This operation can be terminated immediately, conditioned on the release of Gilad Shalit."

On the night of 28–29 June 2006, the IDF arrested dozens of Hamas leaders in the West bank, including 20 Palestinian parliament members and eight Palestinian ministers. This retaliation operation was reportedly planned several weeks in advance. On the same day, four Israeli Air Force aircraft flew over Syrian President Bashar Assad's palace in Latakia, as an IDF spokesperson said that Israel views the Syrian leadership as a sponsor of Hamas.

On 1 July 2006, Shalit's captors issued another demand to the Israelis, demanding that Israel release an additional 1,000 Palestinian prisoners (in addition to all female and young prisoners, as previously demanded) and end Israel's incursions into Gaza. Two days later, the captors issued a 24-hour ultimatum for meeting their demands, threatening unspecified consequences if Israel refused. Hours after the ultimatum was issued, Israel officially rejected the demands, stating that: "there will be no negotiations to release prisoners".

On 3 July 2006 Shalit's captors made an ultimatum according to which they demanded that Israel must fulfill all of its demands by 4 July 2006 at 6:00 am. However, the captors did not specify exactly what would happen if the demands were not met. The Israeli Prime Minister's office formally rejected the ultimatum. After the ultimatum period expired the Army of Islam group announced that no more information would be released about Shalit's fate.

Operation Summer Rains, which failed to achieve its main objective (the release of Shalit), ended on 26 November 2006 when the Israeli prime minister Ehud Olmert and Palestinian Authority President Mahmoud Abbas agreed on a cease-fire, after the Palestinian militancy organizations agreed to stop firing rockets on Sderot and after Israel agreed to cease IDF operations in the Gaza Strip.

Aftermath

Hamas high-ranking commander Abu Jibril Shimali, whom Israel considers responsible for coordinating the abduction of Shalit, was killed during the violent clashes between Hamas and the al-Qaida-affiliated Jund Ansar Allah organization in Gaza in August 2009.[1948]

On 2 October 2009, Israel received a video clip of 2:42 minutes length in which Gilad Shalit was filmed. In exchange, Israel released 20 Palestinian prisoners. During the same day the video clip was broadcast on television channels worldwide. The video, which was published publicly after the Shalit family approval to do so, showed Gilad Shalit in uniform reading a pre-written message, in which he urged the Israeli government to finalize the deal for his release. In addition, during the video clip Shalit stood up for a few seconds and moved towards the camera so that his health condition would be evident in the video,

Figure 246: *After more than five years in Hamas captivity IDF soldier Gilad Shalit was released and returned to Israel, while nearly a thousand Palestinian and Arab-Israeli prisoners are being released in exchange, 18 October 2011*

as much as possible. In addition, during the video clip Shalit was holding an Arab newspaper from 14 September 2009 in order to prove that the video was recorded just before its release.

Shalit was released in a prisoner exchange on 18 October 2011. The Hamas commander who directed the raid, Raed al Atar, was killed in an Israeli airstrike during the 2014 Israel-Gaza conflict.[1949]

Official reactions

Involved parties

- Israel:

- Israeli Prime Minister Ehud Olmert stated that Israel held the Palestinian Authority, the Hamas government and President Mahmoud Abbas "responsible for this event — with all this implies."
- Chief of Staff of the Israel Defense Forces Lt. Gen. Dan Halutz stated that "The Palestinians are responsible for the fate of the kidnapped soldier, and we will do everything in our power to retrieve him."

- Palestinian territories:

- Palestinian Authority President Mahmoud Abbas condemned the attack and stated that "We have always warned against the danger of certain groups or factions leaving the national consensus and carrying out operations for which the Palestinian people will always have to pay the price". In addition Abbas called on the international community "to prevent Israel from exploiting the attack to carry out large-scale aggression in the Gaza Strip".
- Ghazi Hamad, the spokesman of the Hamas government in Gaza, called for Shalit's captors "to protect his life and treat him well" and called on Israel "not to escalate the situation."

International

- USA – The US state department released a statement saying "We urge both sides to exercise restraint and avoid steps which further escalate the situation"[1950]

External links

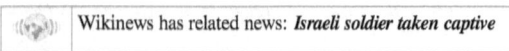 Wikinews has related news: *Israeli soldier taken captive*

- Palestinians launch raid from Gaza[1951] – published on TVNZ on 26 June 2006
- Gunmen use Gaza tunnel for raid / 4 die, 1 kidnapped as Palestinians catch Israeli army by surprise at border crossing[1952] – published on the *San Francisco Chronicle* on 26 June 2006
- Militants' Raid on Israel Raises Gaza Tension[1953] – published on the *New York Times* on 26 June 2006
- Palestinian militants infiltrate Israel, attack Israeli army post[1954] – published on the *New York Times* on 25 June 2006
- Israeli soldier 'seized' in raid[1955] – published on BBC News on 25 June 2006

2009–present: Netanyahu II

2011 Israeli social justice protests

2011 Israeli social justice protests	
Part of the 2011 Israeli middle class protests	
Demonstrators in Tel Aviv on 6 August 2011	
Date	14 July 2011 – 29 October 2011
Location	Israel
Goals	Providing solutions to the various hardships of the middle class and lower class in Israel (such as housing costs, cost of living and the erosion of the middle class and lower class)
Methods	Demonstrations, civil disobedience, civil resistance, sit-ins, movement for recall elections, online activism, protest camps occupations, self-immolations
Status	Ended
Lead figures	
See expanded section	

The **2011 Israeli social justice protests** (Hebrew: חֶבְרָתִי צֶדֶק מֶחָאָת), which are also referred to by various other names in the media, were a series of demonstrations in Israel beginning in July 2011 involving hundreds of thousands of protesters from a variety of socio-economic and religious backgrounds opposing the continuing rise in the cost of living (particularly housing) and the deterioration of public services such as health and education. A common rallying cry at the demonstrations was the chant; "The people demand social justice!".

As the protests expanded during August 2011, the demonstrations began to also focus on other related issues relating to the social order and power structure in Israel.

The housing protests which sparked the first demonstrations began as a result of a Facebook protest group that initially led hundreds of people to establish tents in the Rothschild Boulevard in the center of Tel Aviv, an act which soon gained momentum, media attention and began a public discourse in Israel regarding the high cost of housing and living expenses. Soon afterwards, the protests spread to many other major cities in Israel as thousands of Israeli protesters began establishing tents in the middle of central streets in major cities as a means of protest. As part of the protests, several mass demonstrations have been held across the country, in which hundreds of thousands of people have participated.

A major focus of the protests have been what organizers have termed *social justice*. Part of the movement is about changing the social order, and the economic system. Calls to topple the government were made by some parts of the protests. Criticism of the protests includes accusations of a political agenda rather than a social one with revelations of funding from specific left-wing individuals and organizations like S. Daniel Abraham and the New Israel Fund. Maariv journalist Kalman Libeskind claimed that the spontaneous protests had actually been three months in the planning by Stan Greenberg and orchestrated by left-wing organizations and the National Left. Criticism within the protests accused the 'protest leaders' of not publicizing specific goals, the lack of visibility of their goals, and the damaging impact of media focus being on a few activists.

Following the first large-scale protests in early August, the government announced that a series of measures would be taken to solve the housing shortage, some of which were already under preparation and ratification, and some which were new measures proposed in response to the demands of the protest movement leadership.[1956] In addition, Prime Minister Benjamin Netanyahu appointed a team of ministers and senior staff members from his office, headed by Finance Minister Yuval Steinitz, to negotiate with the protest leadersWikipedia:No original research as well as the Trajtenberg Committee. Since that time, there was significant criticism of the Prime Minister's perceived insensitivity to the public sentiment, prompting speculation that general sympathy for the protest movement may cause one or more members of the governing coalition to leave the government, triggering national elections.

On 22 June 2012, Daphne Leaf and several other activists tried to restart the housing protests by re-erecting a tent encampment on Rothschild Boulevard. The municipality had not given a permit and as a result Leaf, along with eleven other activists, were arrested when they resisted the twenty policemen and municipal inspectors who arrived to dismantle the tents which were confiscated.

Naming

The most common name for the protests in Israel (both during and after the protests) was "**The social protest**" (החברתית המחאה Ham*echaa Hahevratit*) the protests have also been referred to as the **Housing Protest** (מחאת הדיור *Mechaat HaDiyur*),[1957,1958] **Social justice protest** (מחאת צדק חברתי *Mechaat Tzedek Hevrati*),[1959] the **Cost of Living protest** (מחאת יוקר המחייה *Mechaat Yoker HaMekhiya*), the **Real estate protest** (מחאת הנדל"ן *Mechaat HaNadlan*),[1960] the **Tents protest** (מחאת האוהלים *Mechaat HaOhalim*)[1961,1962] and less frequently the **middle class protest** (מחאת מעמד הביניים *Mechaat Maamad HaBeynaim*).[1963]

Background

Motivations

Numerous factors have led to the protests, in particular rising cost of housing and living expenses in Israel, but also various ongoing issues such as government corruption, rising poverty rates which the OECD defined as being twice the average of other developed countries, and a widening gap between rich and poor.[1964]

Demographic structural factors, such as a large percentage of educated but dissatisfied youth within the population, extreme poverty in the haredi Jewish sector, and high unemployment in the Arab-Israeli population have spread the cause of the protests amongst a wide swathe of the Israeli population.[1965] Many have also blamed the erosion of Israel's traditional egalitarian socio-economic model for the rise in public dissatisfaction, claiming that the rise of American-style social structures in Israel is incompatible with Zionist ideology(The word Zion does not exist in the referred article).[1966]

A major catalyst for public anger has been the significant rise in the cost of living, particularly for the lower and middle class. Although average salaries in Israel tend to be lower than those in the Western world, the cost of many consumer goods is relatively high – particularly basic necessities on which long established price controls have gradually been lifted. Since 2007, Israel has also experienced a gradual rise in housing prices. This increase followed a decade-long period of low housing costs, between 1996 and 2005, as well as a long history of significant government involvement in the public housing sector. According to data from the Israel Central Bureau of Statistics, from 2005 to 2011 apartment rental prices rose 34% on average, 49% in the Gush Dan region around Tel Aviv. A survey published by the Housing and Construction Minister of Israel revealed that in 2010, 129 average monthly salaries were required for the purchase of an average priced apartment, an amount significantly higher than countries in the Western world.

Events leading to the protests

In April 2011, about three months before the cost of living protests began, Boaz Gaon, son of prominent Israeli businessman Benny Gaon, presented activists with a ten-point plan by Democratic pollster and political strategist Stan Greenberg to defeat the right-wing. It was recommended that not one organization should coordinate the struggle, rather to divide up the effort with as many initiatives in as many locations as possible. Maariv journalist Kalman Libeskind suggested that the protests were a result of this plan.

During June 2011, a month before the housing protest began, another significant large scale demonstration took place in Israel. Commonly referred to by the media as the cottage cheese boycott, this event saw the Israeli public protest against the high cost of many products in Israel and specifically in this case, the high price of cottage cheese. The protest was successful and led to a drop in the retail price of cottage cheese.[1967,1968] This was the first time in Israel that a public protest organized by means of social networking had such a wide public effect in Israel.

In July 2011, 25-year-old Israeli video editor Daphne Leef had to vacate the central Tel Aviv apartment where she had lived for three years due to major renovations in her building. Leef soon found out that apartment rental prices in the Tel Aviv metropolitan area had skyrocketed. Consequently, she initiated a small-scale public tent protest. Leef opened a Facebook protest page, inviting others to join her protest, and pitched a tent in Habima Square in Tel Aviv. In response, protesters gathered in the streets around Rothschild Boulevard in Tel Aviv, as well as in Zion Square in Jerusalem.

The use of Protest camps have been described by the protest leaders as being inspired by the Hooverville tent cities in the Central Park of New York City and in many other cities throughout the United States in which many Americans were forced to live during the Great Depression in the United States.

The use of social networks for public protests began to increase in the early 2010s, with the most significant one being the large-scale demonstrations in Arab countries in the Middle East that led to a change of government in several

Figure 247: *The protest compound on Rothschild Boulevard in Tel Aviv, 21 July 2011*

countries such as Egypt (see 2011 Egyptian revolution). Some see a connection between the Arab Spring protests and the 2011 Israeli housing protests, as the common denominator is, firstly, the use of social networking to organize public protests,[1969,1970,1971] and secondly the fact that these two waves of protests stem from the increase in the cost of living, that they were organized mostly by young people, and that the protesters claims include not only economic demands but also demands for changes in the policies and practices of the ruling government.[1972]

Protests

Timeline

July

- **14 July 2011:** 25-year-old Daphne Leef pitches a tent in the Habima Square in Tel Aviv and in addition opens a Facebook protest page, where she invites others to join her protest.
- **15 July 2011:** In response to Leef's protest, many protesters gathered in the streets around Rothschild Boulevard in Tel Aviv where about 50 tents were pitched.

Figure 248: *Demonstrators in Beersheba on 30 July 2011*

- **16 July 2011:** the National Union of Israeli Students joined the protests.
- **17 July 2011:** the Hashomer Hatzair movement joined the protests.
- **23 July 2011:** tens of thousands of demonstrators participated in the protest movement's first rally held in the center of Tel Aviv which included a mass march from the tent compound at Habima Square to the Tel Aviv Museum of Art Plaza, where the main rally was held.[1973]
- **24 July 2011:** a protest broke out in Jerusalem, in which 1,000 demonstrators marched towards the Knesset while causing major traffic disruptions.
- **26 July 2011:** Prime Minister Binyamin Netanyahu announced new housing programs aimed at addressing the housing shortage in Israel and at supporting the students.
- **28 July 2011:** the first "strollers march" took place in which thousands of Israeli parents took part, protesting against the high costs of raising children in Israel.
- **30 July 2011:** between 85,000 and 150,000 people took part in mass rallies in major cities across Israel. Demonstrations were held in Jerusalem, Tel Aviv, Haifa, Beersheba, Kfar Saba, Ra'anana, Baqa al-Gharbiya, Ashdod, Nazareth, Kiryat Shmona, Modi'in-Maccabim-Re'ut, Netanya, Ashkelon, Tiberias, the Savion Junction, and the Jordan Valley.

August

- **6 August 2011:** between 200,000 and 350,000 protesters took part in mass rallies in major cities across Israel. Demonstrations took place in Tel Aviv (150,000 – 300,000), Jerusalem (30,000), Kiryat Shmona (3,000), Hod HaSharon (1,000), Modi'in-Maccabim-Re'ut (5,000), Ashkelon (500), Dimona (200), and Eilat (1,000).
- **7 August 2011:** some 1,300 parents staged "strollers marches" in Giv'atayim, Karmiel, and Pardes Hanna-Karkur. In Tel Aviv, some 100 right-wing activists marched in Rothschild Boulevard, protesting what they called the "anarchistic nature of the leftist housing protest".
- **13 August 2011:** at most 75,000 people took part in mass rallies in major cities across Israel. Demonstrations took place in Haifa, Beersheba, Afula, Eilat, Rosh Pinna, Nahariya, Dimona, Petah Tikva, Modi'in-Maccabim-Re'ut, Beit She'an, Netanya, Ramat HaSharon, Hod HaSharon, Rishon LeZion, Beit Shemesh, and Ashkelon.[1974]

<templatestyles src="Multiple_image/styles.css" />

3 September protest in Tel Aviv

- **22 August 2011:** The activists, including Daphne Leef, decided to take over abandoned buildings. Tens of activists, including members of Knesset Dov Khenin (Hadash) and Nitzan Horowitz (New Movement – Meretz) stormed a building on Dov Hoz street in Tel Aviv and waved placards calling for affordable housing.
- **26 August 2011:** Protesters occupied a second abandoned building in Tel Aviv, on Bialik St., and had planned on staying longer but removed soon after and the building sealed by police.
- **27 August 2011:** In Tel Aviv, around 10,000 protesters marched from Habima Square to the intersection of Ibn Gvirol and Shaul Hamelech streets, where a rally was held.

Figure 249: *29 October protest, Tel-aviv*

September

- **3 September:** A protest billed as the "March of the Million" sees an estimated 460,000 people taking to the streets throughout the country, 300,000 of which in Tel Aviv.
- **6–7 September:** The Tel Aviv municipality visits tent sites and posts notices that the area needs to be evacuated. Early next morning, city workers arrive to clear tents and other items and are called "Nazis in city hall uniforms" by activists. There were also violent demonstrations at the Tel Aviv city hall against the evacuation of the tents and over 30 activists were arrested.
- **27 September:** In press conference, protesters warned Prime Minister Netanyahu that he has a month to make "real and serious recommendations" or "on October 29, just before the Knesset returns to session, we will take to the streets in full force. This year we will take the country back into our hands, rock and roll."

October

- **3 October:** The symbol of the protest movement, the tent encampment on Tel Aviv Rothschild Boulevard, was dismantled by police.
- **15 October:** An "occupy Tel Aviv" protest held on Rothschild. Several hundred gathered at Tel Aviv Museum plaza where opinions are voiced in "Hyde Park" speakers corner.

Figure 250: *Signs in the Social Protest camp in Tel-Aviv, [OccupyTLV]. The particular signs, shown here, protest judicial corruption, highlighting the cases of self-immolated social protest activist Moshe Silman, of Roman Zadorov, who is widely believed to be falsely convicted on murder, he never committed, and Tax-Authority whistle-blower Rafi Rotem, at the time criminally prosecuted for harassing public officials.*

- **29 October:** With renewed vigor, tens of thousands of protesters took to the streets of most Israeli cities, except for Beersheva.
- **28 November 2012:** The Occupy-style encampment on Rothschild Avenue, which survived for over a year, was transferred by mutual agreement with the Tel-Aviv Municipality to a new location, near the Tel-Aviv Center/Arlozorov train station. The encampment at the new site survives to this date (July 2015), through a system of monthly extensions. Several attempts by the Municipality to evict the encampment failed, and its existence was also given a stamp of approval through a court process in late 2014- early 2015.

Cities and regions

Tel Aviv

Tel Aviv has been at the epicenter of much of the crisis and has experienced ongoing protests every day from 14 July 2011 onwards. The largest protests were held in downtown Tel Aviv, which has been considered the protest movement's most effective symbol. Hundreds of thousands of people have been estimated to participate in the protests rallies in Tel Aviv. By late 2015, the social protest camp in Tel-Aviv, near the Arlozorov train station, is the only one remaining in Israel

Rishon-Lezion

Some tents were established at Rishon-Lezion's municipal park already in late July 2011.

Jerusalem

Haifa

On 13 August 2011 circa 25,000 people turned out to demonstrate in the Haifa downtown protest with leading local activists, deputy mayor of haifa, Shai Abuhatsira and chairman of the university of Haifa students union, Yossi Shalom.[1975]

Beersheba

On 13 August 2011 more than 20,000 people turned out to demonstrate in Beersheba.

Holon

There were approximately 10 illegally built shacks in Jessie Cohen neighborhood in Holon, built by people from the lower class. On 7 September the shacks were evacuated.

Continuation of the protest into 2012

Even though the protest ebbed in late 2011, it was revived in 2012. From early 2012, plans were made by various groups to revive the protest. This time the municipality of Tel-Aviv made a preemptive move by warning about no tolerance for any tents being placed on Rothschild St., so tents were instead placed near the railway station in Tel-Aviv. This time protesters were divided in two major camps, as some activists criticized Leef for using upper class donors to finance her protest.

On 22 June 2012, Daphni Leef was arrested at a demonstration in Tel Aviv while her arm was broken. On the following day, her supporters held a massive demonstration where 85 protesters were arrested and glass windows of banks were smashed.

As a result of the split within the protest movement, two separate social justice demonstrations were held in Tel-Aviv on 14 July 2012, to commemorate the first anniversary of the social justice protest.[1976]

Government reactions

The Israeli Prime Minister Binyamin Netanyahu initially reacted to the protests by stating that he is aware of the crisis, and that "the government is working to fix the plague that haunts us for many years. We are a small country, there is great demand and not enough apartments. Help me pass the reform in the Israel Lands Administration". Netanyahu also clarified that "It would take between a year to three years until we would begin seeing results."

Government housing plans

On 26 July 2011, Prime Minister Netanyahu announced a new housing plan, including significant incentives for contractors who build smaller apartments, rent-earmarked housing and student housing, and plans to add 50,000 apartments to Israel's housing market over the next two years. The plan would allow contractors to purchase land from the Israel Land Administration up to 50% cheaper if they agree to build small apartments. Contractors bidding on rent-earmarked housing projects would be obligated to rent out 50% of their apartments built for a period of at least ten years, at 30% of their current value, and would be allowed to sell the other 50% of apartments at a price they can set. Contractors would be allowed to raise rent rates annually, in accordance with the consumer price index. Contractors and land developers who build student housing would be given land for free, but would have to agree to government-supervised rent rates for twenty years. Netanyahu's plan also called for six newly appointed national housing boards to authorize housing projects with little bureaucracy. The boards' mandate would be reviewed every eighteen months. Netanyahu also said that the government would promote the construction of 10,000 housing units for students, and would subsidize students' transportation to allow them to seek housing further away from universities.

Trajtenberg Committee

On 8 August 2011, Prime Minister Netanyahu appointed a committee to pinpoint and propose solutions to Israel's socioeconomic problems. The committee's task was to hold discussions with "different groups and sectors within the public", and subsequently make proposals to the government's socioeconomic cabinet, headed by Finance Minister Yuval Steinitz. Professor Manuel Trajtenberg, chairman of the Planning and Budgeting Committee of the Council for Higher Education, former head of the National Economic Council, and the former Chief Economic Adviser to the Prime Minister, was appointed to head the committee. The committee consists of 14 members, 10 of whom are government or public officials.[1977,1978,1979]

Figure 251: *Daphne Leef speaking at a protest rally in Tel Aviv, 23 July 2011*

Protest leadership

The 2011 Israeli housing protests have no formal leadership.Wikipedia:Citation needed

Amongst the most prominent activists in the protests are Daphne Leef,[1980] Stav Shaffir, Yigal Rambam, Jonathan Levy, Orly Weisselberg, Roee Neuman, Jonathan Miller, Regev Kontas, Adam Dovz'insky,Itzik Shmuli, Baroch Oren and Boaz Gaon. Actively contributing and supporting the protests were newspaper columnists Roy Arad and Shlomo Kraus.

Adam Dovz'insky, who took a prominent part at the beginning of the protests with a hunger strike that ended when he collapsed and needed medical attention, would later declare that the Rothschild Blvd leadership does not want solutions but rather to topple the Netanyahu government, that the protests seemed to be the end themselves, not a means toward achieve negotiations. Dovz'insky also said he had information connected the protests with European anarchists.

Demands of the protesters

The initial objective of the leaders of the protest movement focused on reducing the costs of housing in Israel. For the most part, the protest leadership has declared that they would not offer any concrete solutions to the crisis on the grounds that it is not their role, but the government's role. However, the demonstrators in Tel Aviv have promised to work together with the Knesset members and other decision makers to promote legislation aimed at protecting apartment renters against exploitation of their hardships by landlords, in a way that would correspond to similar legislation worldwide. At some of the public events, protesters call revolution, for Netanyahu's resignation, and the downfall of the government.[1981]

Nevertheless, in August 2011, as the protests grew significantly, the demands became more radical as they began to call for a sweeping overhaul of the Israeli economy and society which would change the current Neo liberal approach of the Netanyahu government to a more social approach. The list of demands for broader changes in the Israeli society and governance, articulated by protesters and activists, includes the following:

Demand	Ref
1. A new taxation system would be implemented (which would include lower indirect taxes and higher direct taxes).	1982,1983
2. Free schooling from an early age.	
3. Privatization of state-owned enterprises would end.	
4. More resources would be invested on public housing and public transportation.	

Organizations and individuals who have joined the protest

Many movements and organizations have joined the protest. According to the Israeli newspaper "Israel HaYom", two weeks prior to the protest, the Israeli social movement "the National Left" sought people on Facebook "who have unreasonable rent fees" to start a campaign to lower the cost of housing for young people. On the day on which the protest began, "the National Left" movement called its activists to get to the Rothschild Boulevard, and organized the delivery of 20 tents to the encampment. In an interview with the Israeli morning show "HaOlam HaBoker" the chairman of the movement, Eldad Yaniv, addressed "Israel HaYom"'s report and explained that the movement "organizes many protests like this throughout country and it just happened that

Figure 252: *A group of demonstrators from the HaShomer HaTzair (white laces), HaMahanot HaOlim (buttons) and HaNoar HaOved VeHaLomed (red laces) Israeli Socialist youth movements in the demonstration in Haifa on 30 July 2011*

Figure 253: *Speeches at the demonstration for the residents of southern Tel Aviv, a tent camp in the garden of Lewinsky*

this one became popular".[1984] Several activists posted Daphne Leef's call on the movement's web site and invited their friends to join the encampment.[1985] The movement also initiated the establishment of a website to accompany the protest[1986,1987] and assisted in managing the encampment, in part by the introduction of "popular assemblies" for making decisions on the conduct of the protest.[1988,1989]

The protest also gained support from the National Union of Israeli Students and the local student unions throughout Israel, who helped establish the encampments and organized transportation to the demonstration in Tel Aviv. The Jewish U.S.-based non-profit organization "New Israel Fund" gave guidance and logistical support to the encampments in Kiryat Shmona, Be'er Sheva and elsewhere.[1990] The head of the Shatil activist wing of the New Israel Fund admitted that the group was working behind the scenes and coordinating multiple tent locations and published a report on its activities. Most of the protests were financed by online donations.

The Zionist extra-parliamentaryWikipedia:Citation needed group "Im Tirtzu", which initially supported the protests, later announced that it would stop its involvement due to the participation of the "New Israel Fund". The Bnei Akiva and the "Rannim" movements (both of the religious Zionism) announced that they would also stop their involvement in the protests in Tel Aviv. The "Rannim" movement later announced it would continue its participation in the protest but only in the Jerusalem encampment.[1991]

The protests were also joined by "The Coalition for Affordable Housing" and "The Headquarters for a Liable Housing" who bind the following organizations: Association for Civil Rights in Israel, Bimkom, Women Lawyers for Social Justice, Society for the Protection of Nature in Israel, Movement for Quality Government in Israel, Greenpeace Israel, Mizrahi Democratic Rainbow Coalition and the Israel Union for Environmental Defense. Additional organizations who joined the protests include the Koach La Ovdim General trade union, the Socialist–Zionist youth movements HaNoar HaOved VeHaLomed and Hashomer Hatzair, the non-Zionist left-wing organization Ma'avak Sotzialisti the Israeli human rights organization Rabbis for Human Rights,[1992] Physicians for Human Rights-Israel,[1993] and the political parties Meretz and Hadash.

The protests also gained the support of various Israeli mayors and local councils, including the mayor of Tel Aviv Ron Huldai, the mayor of Jerusalem Nir Barkat[1994] and the chairman of the Union of Local Authorities in Israel, Shlomo Bohbot. Knesset members from both the coalition and the opposition have expressed their support for the struggle; some even visited the various protest encampments. Two weeks after the start of the protest, the chairman of the Histadrut, Ofer Eini, met with protest leaders and announced that the Histadrut would assist them in their contacts with the government.[1995]

Jimmy Wales, a co-founder of Wikipedia, visited the tent cities in Tel Aviv where the protests were taking place. He said, "It's wonderful that in the democracy here, people have the right to go out and express their opinion. I do not know if I agree with the protest or not, because I'm not familiar with the economic and social situation in Israel, but the very fact that freedom of speech and discourse are free in Israel is remarkable."[1996]

The New Israel Fund had originally denied its role[1997] in the development of the protests, but in a January 2012 message, it says that the protestors "organized themselves in new and existing organizations, virtual and community initiatives, local and national groups. Mapping the initiatives, which were initiated by Shatil and the New Israel Fund, outlines the role of this 'big bang'."[1998]

Public opinion

According to a poll by Channel 10 on 2 August 2011, there is broad public support for the protesters, including 98% of Kadima supporters, and 85% of Netanyahu's Likud supporters.

Along with the massive support the housing protest has gained, as the protest kept developing and, various public figures and organizations, mostly affiliated with the political right in Israel, gradually increased their criticism of the protests and their organizers. Most of the criticism has focused on the allegations that the protests were not spontaneous, and that they were scheduled and planned by various left-wing media and political organizations in Israel. It is alleged that these organizations exploited the protests initiated by Daphne Leef as well as the economic distress that exists among large sections of the Israeli public in order to promote a political agenda that they finance, and which is primarily designed to overthrow the current right-wing government headed by Benjamin Netanyahu; it is alleged that finding actual solutions to the housing crises in Israel is only a secondary concern.[1999],[2000] The Tel-Aviv city hall was criticized for indirectly supporting the protests at 40,000ILS per day, price including electricity and clean services. While the protests in general have been peaceful, some incidents of violence have been reported. On 4 August 2011, two activists were arrested following an attempt to burn down the tent of right-wing activists participating at the Rothschild location. At a press conference held on 26 July 2011 Daphne Leef responded to the various allegations made against her and the protest organizers and stated the following:[2001]

<templatestyles src="Template:Quote/styles.css"/>

What hasn't been said about me in the recent days? When we came here with our tents about ten days ago, some said we are spoiled children from Tel Aviv, some said we are leftists, but after more cities from across the country and as more people from across the entire political spectrum in Israel joined the protests – all understood that we represent all the people.

Responses

Political

- The mayor of Jerusalem Nir Barkat stated that "the government must produce affordable housing" and that "I expect the government and the Israel Lands Administration to take responsibility for the matter." Barkat pointed to the model which was pioneered by the Jerusalem Municipality, which allows young people to live in affordable housing in Jerusalem.
- The mayor of Tel Aviv Ron Huldai also declared that "the tent demonstrations are justified and appropriate" and that "the [central] government is abandoning social issues to market forces." Nevertheless, Huldai oversaw the eviction of protest sites in autumn 2011.
- MK Nitzan Horowitz of Meretz showed his support in the protests and referred to the protesters as "the new homeless people of Netanyahu and Finance Minister Yuval Steinitz." Fellow MK Isaac Herzog of the Labour party stated that "all efforts to encourage affordable housing construction in Tel Aviv fail due to the resistance of the Israeli Finance ministry, the Israel Lands Administration, the Israeli ministers and due to the position of the prime minister against government intervention of market prices," and that "it's time to examine an intervention." Herzog also stated that "you deserve not only to eat cottage, but also to build a cottage."
- Protest organizers and opposition MKs such as Shelly Yachimovich of the Labor Party dismissed Prime Minister Netanyahu's proposed reforms as "spin", and accused the Prime Minister of using the housing crisis as a cover to advance his program of land privatization. At the same time, green organizations have warned that Netanyahu's proposals would lead to the destruction of open spaces in the centre of the country by land developers, and the removal of community input into the land development process.
- Knesset Speaker Reuven Rivlin announced that it is necessary to keep a free market in Israel and to be careful that the protest activists won't lead Israel towards the path of destruction and anarchy.[2002]
- Israeli minister Benny Begin also criticized the protests, stating that it is a political struggle "with speech writers", aimed at overthrowing the Prime Minister of Israel, under the guise of protesting housing issues which "did

not develop recently, and which would not be solved any time soon".[2003] Another government minister, Yuli Edelstein stated that among the organizers there are "anarchists associated with the Communist Party, Little foxes whom hang out along the protesters. They call Israel a fascist state, and this just shows how much they do not care for the protests."[2004]
- David Amar, the Mayor of Nesher, attacked the inhabitants of the encampment in Rothschild stating that "You're going through the Rothschild boulevard in at 1:30 am and all you can see is Hookahs and sushi. If they bring Sushi worth 35 NIS to the encampment – it indicates that their situation is not particularly difficult. This is not a protest".
- Knesset member Miri Regev has stated that Daphne Leef "represents the extreme left".[2005] In response, Leef stated that she felt embarrassed about the violent confrontation which occurred during Regev's visit to the encampment; however, Leef emphasized that contrary to Regev's belief, the protests were first and foremost a social struggle and not a political one.[2006]
- On 20 July 2011, "Im Tirtzu" announced that they would not take part in the housing protests any more because they claimed that the New Israel Fund and various radical left-wing groups are directly involved in the housing protests. Officials in the organization stated that "Daphne Leef's struggle, who is perceived in the media as the initiator of the struggle, is actually a video editor working for the NIF and Shatil."[2007]
- In September 2011, Knesset member Aryeh Eldad said that 'there is no doubt that the extreme-left and post-zionists are funding the protests. The thousands who are protesting their plight do not understand that they are marionettes in a game larger than housing costs and baby strollers'.[2008]
- Shimon Sheves, former General Director of the Office of the Prime Minister under Yitzhak Rabin and former Israeli Labor Party activist, confirmed that a new political party was being formed in the aftermath of the summer protests but refused to reveal names other than that it would be people from the National Left organization. Disenchanted with the Labor party, he affirmed that he would stand behind the new party.

Religious figures

- The prominent Israeli modern orthodox rabbi Yuval Sherlo stated that in his opinion the protest movement has become anarchist in nature and therefore he personally finds it difficult to relate with it. He stated that the protest organizers need to change course: "After a big burst of justified pain and anger, without which the troubling issues would not have not been brought up on to the agenda, the protests have been exhausted". Sherlo stated that despite the wide public criticism raised against the Netanyahu government, "this government has done quite a few good things to promote employment, balance payments, and is responsible for the fact that Israel's macro-economic situation is quite good". Later on, Sherlo gave a speech in the movement's protest rally in Jerusalem in which he called on Prime Minister Netanyahu "to embrace these people".

- On 16 August 2011 prominent Israeli orthodox rabbi Israel Meir Lau, who is the former Ashkenazi Chief Rabbi of Israel and current Chief Rabbi of Tel Aviv, held a discussion on the ongoing protests with representatives from the National Union of Israeli Students at the offices of the Rabbinate in Tel Aviv. Lau noted that the protest movement is unprecedented in Israel, and added that "this is the first time I remember ever having seen this many people who didn't know each other before, coming together – outside of a time of war. You have captured my heart." In addition, Lau promised to contact Prime Minister Netanyahu personally and tell him to honor the mandate of the Trachtenberg committee and accept its recommendations.

Media

- Ben-Dror Yemini, an editor at Maariv, used his 26 August 2011 weekend column to report a strong left-wing turn of the protests that would attempt to connect the 'social justice' to the events leading up to anticipated September protests on the West Bank. Yemini revealed an agreement summarized after protest leaders met with left-wing leaders and anarchists including the heads of the National Left and Peace Now to discuss combining activities such as marches to the 'border' and to bring the Palestinians into the protest.
- Shay Golden, the assistant editor in chief of Maariv and former editor at the Haaretz newspaper has said that he has been made an enemy of the protests since he criticized the media coverage. He accused his media colleagues of forgetting their journalistic responsibilities and subsequently becoming spokespeople for the protests, and silencing opposing voices.
- Yair Lapid, a journalist and television personality who would later become Minister of Finance, has supported the protest since its first days. During the second week of the protest, he published an article in his weekly Yedioth Ahronoth column titled "The Slaves Revolt", where he sympathized with the protestors and implicitly blamed the Netanyahu government for its unjust allocation of resources.

External links

 Wikimedia Commons has media related to *Demonstrations and protests against housing prices in Israel in 2011*.

- The official website of the protest organizers[2009] (Hebrew)
- The protests Facebook page[2010]
- Shatil and Israel's New Awakening[2011]

Collected coverage

- Social justice protests[2012] collected coverage at *Jerusalem Post*
- Israeli housing protests[2013] collected coverage at *Haaretz*

2014 Israel–Gaza conflict

<indicator name="pp-default"> 🔒 </indicator>

Operation Protective Edge 2014	
Part of the Gaza–Israel conflict	
  (left) A home in Gaza bombed by Israel (right) Iron Dome missile defense system in operation	
Date	8 July – 26 August 2014 (7 weeks)
Location	Gaza Strip Israel
Result	Victory claimed by both sides • According to Israel and Palestinian president Abbas, Hamas was severely weakened and achieved none of its demands • According to Hamas, Israel was repelled from Gaza
Belligerents	
⬚ Israel	Gaza Strip • Hamas • Islamic Jihad • DFLP[2014] • PFLP • PRC • al-Aqsa Martyrs' Brigades • Abdullah Azzam Brigades
Commanders and leaders	

Benjamin Netanyahu (Prime Minister) Moshe Ya'alon (Defense Minister) Benny Gantz (Chief of General Staff) Amir Eshel (Air Force Commander) Ram Rothberg (Naval Commander) Sami Turgeman (Southern Commander) Mickey Edelstein Gaza Division Yoram Cohen (Chief of Shin Bet)	Khaled Mashal Leader of Hamas Ismail Haniyeh Deputy chief of Hamas Mohammed Deif Head of Izz ad-Din al-Qassam Brigades Ramadan Shalah Leader of PIJ
Units involved	
Israel Defense Forces • Israel Army • Israeli Air Force • Israeli Navy • Shin Bet	Izz ad-Din al-Qassam Brigades al-Aqsa Martyrs' Brigades Abu Ali Mustapha Brigades Al-Nasser Salah al-Deen Brigades Al-Quds Brigades
Strength	
176,500 active personnel 565,000 reservists (2012 figures, of which not all are directly involved)	Al-Qassam Brigades: 20,000–40,000 Al-Quds Brigades: 8,000
Casualties and losses	
67 soldiers and 6 civilians (1 Thai) killed, 469 soldiers and 87 civilians wounded[2015]	**Hamas GHM:** 2,310 killed,[a][2016] 10,626 wounded **UN HRC:** 2,251 killed[2017][b] **Israel MFA:** 2,125 killed[2018][c]
At least 23 Gazans executed by Hamas	

a 70% civilians
b 65% civilians
c 36% civilians, 44% combatants, 20% uncategorized males aged 16-50

The **2014 Israel–Gaza conflict** also known as **Operation Protective Edge** (Hebrew: מִבְצָע צוּק אֵיתָן, *Miv'tza Tzuk Eitan*, lit. "Operation Strong Cliff")[2019] The IDF's official Arabic name for the operation, translated into English, is "Operation Resolute Cliff".</ref> and sometimes referred to as the **2014 Gaza war**, was a military operation launched by Israel on 8 July 2014 in the Hamas-ruled Gaza Strip.[2020] Following the kidnapping and murder of three Israeli teenagers by Hamas members, the IDF conducted *Operation Brother's Keeper* to arrest militant leaders, Hamas fired rockets into Israel and a seven-week conflict broke out. The Israeli airstrikes and ground bombardment, the Palestinian rocket attacks and the ground fighting resulted in the death of thousands of people, the vast majority of them Gazans.

The stated aim of the Israeli operation was to stop rocket fire from Gaza into Israel, which increased after an Israeli crackdown on Hamas in the West Bank was launched following the 12 June kidnapping and murder of three Israeli teenagers by two Hamas members.[2021,2022] Conversely, Hamas's goal was to bring international pressure to bear to lift Israel's blockade of the Gaza Strip, end Israel's offensive, obtain a third party to monitor and guarantee compliance with a ceasefire,[2023] release Palestinian prisoners and overcome its political isolation.[2024] According to the BBC, in response to rocket fire from the Gaza Strip, Israel launched air raids on Gaza.[2025]

On 7 July, after seven Hamas militants died in a tunnel explosion in Khan Yunis which was caused by an Israeli airstrike (per Hamas, Nathan Thrall, BBC and a senior IDF official) or an accidental explosion of their own munitions (per the IDF), Hamas assumed responsibility for rockets fired into Israel and launched 40 rockets towards Israel.[2026] The operation officially began the following day, and on 17 July, the operation was expanded to an Israeli ground invasion of Gaza with the stated aim of destroying Gaza's tunnel system; Israeli ground forces withdrew on 5 August. On 26 August, an open-ended ceasefire was announced. By that date, the IDF reported that Hamas, Islamic Jihad and other militant groups had fired 4,564 rockets and mortars from Gaza into Israel, with over 735 intercepted in flight and shot down by Iron Dome. Most Gazan mortar and rocket fire hit open land. More than 280 fell on areas in Gaza, and 224 struck residential areas. Militant rocketry also killed 13 Gazan civilians, 11 of them children.[2027,2028] The IDF attacked 5,263 targets in Gaza; at least 34 known tunnels were destroyed and two-thirds of Hamas's 10,000-rocket arsenal was used up or destroyed.

Between 2,125 and 2,310 Gazans were killed and between 10,626 and 10,895 were wounded (including 3,374 children, of whom over 1,000 were left permanently disabled[2029]). Gazan civilian casualty rates estimates range between 70% by the Gaza Health Ministry, 65% by United Nations Protection Cluster by OCHA (based in part Gaza Health Ministry reports), and 36% by Israeli officials, The UN estimated that more than 7,000 homes for 10,000 families were razed, together with an additional 89,000 homes damaged, of which roughly 10,000 were severely affected by the bombing.[2030] Rebuilding costs were calculated to run from 4-6 billions dollars, over 20 years.[2031]

67 Israeli soldiers, 5 Israeli civilians (including one child)[2032] and one Thai civilian were killed and 469 IDF soldiers and 261 Israeli civilians were injured. On the Israeli side, the economic impact of the operation is estimated at NIS 8.5 billion (approximately 2.5 billion USD) and GDP loss of 0.4%.

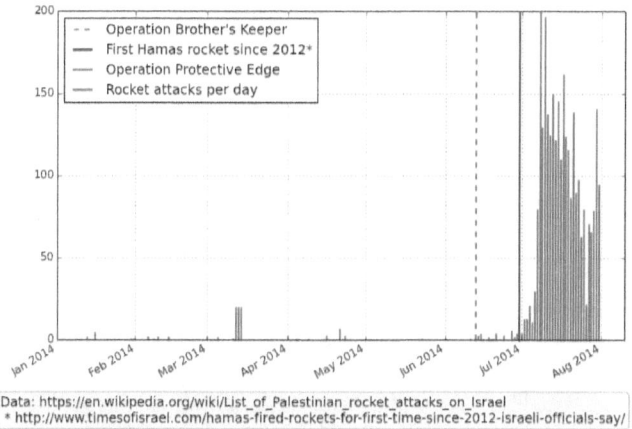

Figure 254: *Histogram of Palestinian rocket attacks on Israel per day and start of the military operation (in red), 2014*

Background

In February 2005 Israel, the Palestinian National Authority, Hamas and Islamic Jihad committed to a ceasefire, which according to some marks end to the Second Intifada. Some place the end-date earlier in October 2004 Others signal the death of Yasser Arafat in November 2004 and the subsequent rise of Hamas as heralding the end of the major period conflict that was the second intifada.[2033] However Palestinian suicide bombings against Israelis continued following the February ceasefire. Schachter, addressing the range of end-date options, pointed to the progressive decrease in suicide bombings starting in 2004 and culminating in an indeterminate end period in 2005. On 17 March 2005 the 13 main Palestinian factions, including Hamas and Islamic Jihad agreed to be bound by the February agreement, conditional on cessation of Israeli military operations.

Concurrent to the Second Intifada, Israeli prime minister Ariel Sharon proposed the Israeli disengagement from Gaza in 2003, which was approved by the Israeli government in June 2004, and the Knesset in February 2005. The unilateral withdrawal plan was executed in August 2005 and completed in September 2005.[2034] Nonetheless, the ICRC, the UN and various human rights organizations consider Israel still to be the *de facto* occupying power due to its control of Gaza's borders, air space and territorial waters.[2035]

The following year (2006) Hamas won a majority of seats in the Palestinian legislative elections. This outcome surprised Israel and the United States who had anticipated the return of the Fatah opposition to power and, together with the Quartet, they demanded Hamas accept all previous agreements, recognize Israel's right to exist, and renounce violence. When Hamas refused, they cut off aid to the Palestinian Authority. In mid-2006 an Israeli soldier was captured by Hamas in a cross-border raid. The United States and Israel, in response to Fatah moves in October 2006 to form a unity government with Hamas, tried to undo the elections by arming and training Fatah to overthrow Hamas in Gaza.[2036] In June 2007 Hamas took complete power of Gaza by force.

Israel then defined Gaza as a "hostile territory" forming no part of a sovereign state and put Gaza under a comprehensive economic and political blockade,[2037] which also denied access to a third of its arable land and 85% of its fishing areas. It has led to considerable economic damage and humanitarian problems in Gaza. The overwhelming consensus of international institutions is that the blockade is a form of collective punishment and illegal.[2038] Israel maintains that the blockade is legal and necessary to limit Palestinian rocket attacks from the Gaza Strip on its cities and to prevent Hamas from obtaining other weapons.[2039] Israel carried out Operation Cast Lead in December 2008 with the stated aim of stopping rocket attacks from Hamas militants. It led to a decrease in Palestinian rocket attacks. The UN Fact Finding Mission on the Gaza Conflict concluded that the operation was "a deliberately disproportionate attack designed to punish, humiliate and terrorize a civilian population, radically diminish its local economic capacity both to work and to provide for itself, and to force upon it an ever increasing sense of dependency and vulnerability".[2040] The Israeli government's analysis concludes that the report perverts international law to serve a political agenda and sends a "legally unfounded message to states everywhere confronting terrorism that international law has no effective response to offer them".[2041]

First Hamas–Fatah reconciliation (2011)

Influenced in the Arab Spring and by demonstrations in Ramallah and Gaza, the gap between Hamas and Fatah was bridged in 2011. After the Palestinian president Mahmoud Abbas declared his willingness to travel to Gaza and sign an agreement, the IDF killed two Hamas activists in Gaza; the IDF stated the killings were in response to the launching of a single Qassam rocket, which hit no one, but *Yedioth Ahronoth*'s Alex Fishman argued they were a "premeditated escalation" by Israel. In an interview with CNN, Israeli prime minister Benjamin Netanyahu declared that the reconciliation talks were calls for Israel's destruction, and strongly opposed the idea of a unity government.

November 2012 ceasefire and its violations

On 14 November 2012, Israel launched Operation Pillar of Defence in the Gaza Strip. The operation was preceded by a period with a number of mutual Israeli–Palestinian responsive attacks.[2042] According to the Israeli government, the operation began in response to the launch of over 100 rockets at Israel during a 24-hour period, an attack by Gaza militants on an Israeli military patrol jeep within Israeli borders, and an explosion caused by IEDs, which occurred near Israeli soldiers, on the Israeli side of a tunnel passing under the Israeli West Bank barrier. The Israeli government stated that the aims of the military operation were to halt rocket attacks against civilian targets originating from the Gaza Strip and to disrupt the capabilities of militant organizations. The Palestinians blamed the Israeli government for the upsurge in violence, accusing the IDF of attacks on Gazan civilians in the days leading up to the operation. They cited the blockade of the Gaza Strip and the occupation of West Bank, including East Jerusalem, as the reason for rocket attacks. A week later, on 21 November, Egypt brokered a ceasefire to the conflict which contained the following agreements:

1. Israel should stop all hostilities in the Gaza Strip land, sea and air, including incursions and targeting of individuals.
2. All Palestinian factions shall stop all hostilities from the Gaza Strip against Israel, including rocket attacks and all attacks along the border.
3. The crossings should be opened, facilitating the movement of people and goods; Israel should refrain from restricting residents' movements and from targeting residents in border areas; procedures of implementation should be dealt with 24 hours after the start of the ceasefire.

Violations

Both Israel and Hamas argue that the other violated the 2012 ceasefire agreement, resulting in 1 Israeli and 8 Gazan deaths and 5 Israeli and 66 Gazan injuries. According to the Israeli Security Agency (Shabak) there was a sharp decrease in attacks from Gaza in 2013. Nevertheless, 63 rockets (average 5 per month) were launched in 36 rocket attacks in addition to various mortar attacks, all prohibited by the November 2012 ceasefire. The Palestinian Centre for Human Rights (PCHR) reported monthly Israeli attacks involving drones, missiles, small arms fire and airstrikes. Six of the deaths in Gaza occurred in the border area's Access Restricted Areas (ARAs, non-demarcated zones within Gazan territory unilaterally defined by Israel as being of restricted access), despite the ceasefire's prohibition on Israeli attacks on these areas. OCHAO, more broadly sourced data, reported 11 deaths in Gaza and 81 injuries for 2013.

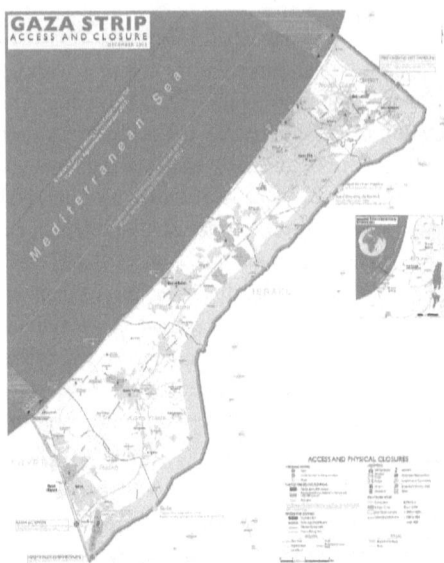

Figure 255: *Gaza Strip: access and closure*

Figure 256: *A sculpture in Sderot made from rocket debris*

Figure 257: *Some of the weapons captured in Khan Yunis.*

In the first three months after the IDF Operation Pillar of Defense, according to Ben White, two mortar shells struck Israeli territory, while four Gazans were shot dead and 91 were wounded by Israeli forces who fired inside Gazan territory on 63 occasions, made 13 incursions into the Strip, and attacked the Gazan fishing fleet 30 times.[2043] Israeli attacks on Gaza steadily increased during the second half of 2013, notwithstanding the decrease in attacks from Gaza.Wikipedia:Verifiability

From December 2012 to late June/early July 2014, Hamas did not fire rockets into Israel, and tried to police other groups doing so. These efforts were largely successful; Netanyahu stated in March 2014 that the rocket fire in the past year was the "lowest in a decade." According to Shabak, in the first half of 2014 there were 181 rocket attacks compared to 55 rocket attacks in whole 2013.

As occasional rocket fire continued, the blockade of Gaza continued in direct violation of the ceasefire agreement. "Crossings were repeatedly shut and buffer zones were reinstated. Imports declined, exports were blocked, and fewer Gazans were given exit permits to Israel and the West Bank."

Israel halted construction material going to Gaza after it stated that it had discovered a tunnel leading into Israel, some 300 m from a kibbutz. The IDF said it was the third tunnel discovered that year and that the previous two were packed with explosives.

According to the Israeli Ministry of Foreign Affairs, there were 85 rocket attacks in the first five months of 2014. Most of the 85 rockets were fired in March, after the IDF killed 3 members of Islamic Jihad. The members of the PIJ say they were firing rockets in response to an incursion by Israeli tanks and bulldozers into Gazan territory east of the Khan Yunis area. The IDF said they were conducting routine military patrols near the Gaza border when they came under fire, and thus responded with airstrikes.[2044,2045]

Second Hamas–Fatah reconciliation

Leading up to the collapse of the 2013–14 Israeli–Palestinian peace talks, in the face of Netanyahu's perceived reluctance to make desired concessions, Mahmoud Abbas decided to forge a deal with Hamas.[2046] With its alliance with Syria and Iran weakened, the loss of power by the Muslim Brotherhood in Egypt after a coup d'ètat in Egypt, and the economic impact of the closure of its Rafah tunnels by Abdel Fattah el-Sisi, on 23 April 2014, ending seven divisive years, Hamas agreed to reconciliation under a unity government with the other main Palestinian faction, Fatah.[2047] The government accepted by Hamas was to be run exclusively by PNA technocrats.

This Palestinian unity government was sworn in by 2 June 2014 and Israel announced it would not negotiate any peace deal with the new government and would push punitive measures. Netanyahu took Palestinian unity as a threat rather than an opportunity.[2048] On the eve of the agreement he stated that the proposed reconciliation would "strengthen terrorism", and called on the international community to avoid embracing it. Most of the outside world, including the European Union, Russia, China, India, Turkey, France and the United Kingdom, proved cautiously optimistic, and subsequently expressed their support for new arrangement. The United States, more skeptical, announced it would continue to work with the PNA-directed unity government.[2049] Israel itself suspended negotiations with the PNA[2050] and, just after[2051] the announcement, launched an airstrike, which missed its target and wounded a family of three bystanders. Netanyahu had warned before the deal that it would be incompatible with Israeli–Palestinian peace and that Abbas had to choose between peace with Hamas and peace with Israel. When a reconciliation deal was signed, opening the way to the appointment of the new government, Netanyahu chaired a security cabinet which voted to authorise Netanyahu to impose unspecified sanctions against the Palestinian Authority.

On 4 June, the day before Naksa Day, the Israeli Housing and Construction Ministry published tenders for 1,500 settlement units in the West Bank and East Jerusalem in a move Minister Uri Ariel said was an "appropriate Zionist response to the Palestinian terror government." Marwan Bishara, senior political analyst at *Al Jazeera*, alleged that Israel had hoped to disrupt the Palestinian national unity government between Fatah and Hamas by its operation.

Figure 258: *Street in Ramallah after an IDF raid during Operation Brother's Keeper, June 2014Wikipedia:Citation needed*

Immediate events

On 12 June 2014, three Israeli teenagers were abducted in the West Bank: Naftali Fraenkel, Gilad Shaer, and Eyal Yifrah. Israel blamed Hamas, with Israeli prime minister Benjamin Netanyahu saying that he had "unequivocal proof" that Hamas was involved and that the abduction was linked to Palestinian reconciliation, and the IDF stated that the two men Israel suspected of having kidnapped the teenagers were known members of Hamas. No evidence of Hamas involvement was offered by Israeli authorities at the time.[2052] High-ranking members of Hamas denied the group had any involvement in the incident, and ex-Shin Bet chief Yuval Diskin doubted Hamas had any involvement. The Palestinian Authority in the West Bank attributed the abductions to the Qawasameh clan, notorious for acting against Hamas's policies and any attempts to reach an entente with Israel.[2053] Hamas political chief Khaled Meshal said he could neither confirm nor deny the kidnapping of the three Israelis, but congratulated the abductors. The kidnappings were condemned by human rights organizations. Documents released by Israel suggest that Hamas member Hussam Qawasmeh organized the kidnappings with $60,000 provided by his brother Mahmoud through a Hamas association in Gaza, after requesting support for a "military operation". On 20 August, Saleh al-Arouri, an exiled Hamas leader based in Turkey, claimed responsibility for the kidnapping of

Figure 259: *Factory bursts in flames after rocket attack in Sderot, Israel, 28 June 2014*

the three Israeli teens: "Our goal was to ignite an intifada in the West Bank and Jerusalem, as well as within the 1948 borders... Your brothers in the Al-Qassam Brigades carried out this operation to support their imprisoned brothers, who were on a hunger strike... The mujahideen captured these settlers in order to have a swap deal." Palestinian security forces said the kidnappings were organized by Saleh al-Arouri. Khalid Meshaal, head in exile of Hamas's political wing since 2004, acknowledged that Hamas members were responsible, but stated that its political leaders had no prior knowledge of the abduction, were not involved in military details and learnt of it through the ensuing Israeli investigations. He also said that while Hamas was opposed to targeting civilians, he understood that Palestinians "frustrated with oppression" were exercising a "legitimate right of resistance" against the occupation by undertaking such operations.[2054,2055] Israel states that the IDF and the Shin Bet have foiled between 54 and 64 kidnapping plots since 2013. The PA said it had foiled 43 of them.

Withholding evidence in its possession suggesting that the teens had been killed immediately until 1 July, Israel launched Operation Brother's Keeper, a large-scale crackdown of what it called Hamas's terrorist infrastructure and personnel in the West Bank, ostensibly aimed at securing the release of the kidnapped teenagers. During the operation, 11 Palestinians were killed and 51 wounded in 369 Israeli incursions into the West Bank through to 2 July,[2056] and between 350 and 600 Palestinians, including nearly all of Hamas's West Bank leaders, were arrested. Among those arrested were many people who had only recently been freed under the terms of the Gilad Shalit prisoner exchange. Israeli military spokesman Lt. Col. Peter Lerner defended the arrests, stating that Hamas members had carried out 60 abduction attempts on Israelis in the West Bank "in the last year and a half", and that "Hamas does not need to give a direct order." The arrests yielded no information about the abduction. Amnesty International and Human Rights Watch stated that certain aspects of the operation amounted to collective punishment, and B'tselem said in a press release that the actions have caused "disproportionate harm to the basic rights of Palestinians". During the course of the operation, Israel said it had uncovered a Hamas plot to launch a massive wave of violence throughout the West Bank, with the goal of overthrowing the Palestinian Authority. The purported coup plotters were arrested and their weapons stockpiles were seized[2057]

On 30 June, search teams found the bodies of the three missing teenagers near Hebron. After their burial, an anti-Arab riot broke out, and a Palestinian teenager was murdered in revenge. His killing sparked Arab rioting. Israel police arrested six suspects belonging to the Beitar Jerusalem F.C. supporters' group La Familia and charged three of them with murder.

As part of its crackdown and concurrent to rocket fire from Gaza, Israel conducted air strikes against Hamas facilities in the Gaza Strip. Hamas apparently refrained from retaliating, though it did not impede other factions from firing rockets towards Israel. From 1 May to 11 June, six rockets and three mortar shells were launched from Gaza towards Israel. From 12 to 30 June 44 rockets and 3 mortar shells were launched from Gaza. On 29 June, an Israeli airstrike on a rocket crew killed a Hamas operative, while at least 18 rockets were launched from Gaza through the next day by Hamas according to both J.J. Goldberg and Assaf Sharon, with Goldberg stating that it was the first time Hamas directly launched rockets since the conflict in 2012. Overnight, on 30 June – 1 July, Israeli airstrikes struck 34 Gaza targets in what officials stated was a response to the Sunday rocketry,[2058] while Stuart Greer reported the strikes were revenge for the deaths of the three youths.[2059] From the day of the abductions on 12 June through 5 July 117 rockets were launched from Gaza and there were approximately 80 Israeli airstrikes on Gaza.

Israel sought a ceasefire but refused to accept Hamas's condition that Palestinians arrested in the West Bank crackdown be released. In a meeting held on 2 July to discuss the crisis, Hamas reportedly tried but failed to persuade armed factions in Gaza to uphold the truce with Israel.[2060] Following escalating rocket fire from Gaza, Israel issued a warning on 4 July that it "would only be able to sustain militant rocket fire for another 24, or maximum 48, hours before undertaking a major military offensive." Hamas declared it was prepared to halt the rocket fire in exchange for an agreement by Israel to stop airstrikes. Netanyahu said Israel would only act against further rocket attacks.[2061] On 5 July, Hamas official Osama Hamdan said rocket fire would continue until Israel lifted its import restrictions on Gaza and the Palestinian Authority transferred money to pay Hamas civil servants. Between 4 and 6 July, a total of 62 rockets were fired from Gaza and the IAF attacked several targets in Gaza.[2062,2063,2064] The following day, Hamas assumed formal responsibility for launching rocket attacks on Israel. Hamas increased rocket attacks on Israel, and by 7 July had fired 100 rockets from Gaza at Israeli territory; at the same time, the Israeli Air Force had bombed several sites in Gaza. Early on 8 July, the IAF bombed 50 targets in the Gaza Strip. Israel's military also stopped a militant infiltration from the sea. Brigadier General Moti Almoz, the chief spokesman of the Israeli military, said: "We have been instructed by the political echelon to hit Hamas hard." Hamas insisted that Israel end all attacks on Gaza, release those re-arrested during the crackdown in the West Bank, lift the blockade on Gaza and return to the cease-fire conditions of 2012 as conditions for a ceasefire.

Operation timeline

Phase 1: Air strikes

As the Israeli operation began, and the IDF bombarded targets in the Gaza Strip with artillery and airstrikes, Hamas continued to fire rockets and mortar shells into Israel in response. A cease-fire proposal was announced by the Egyptian government on 14 July, backed by Palestinian president Mahmoud Abbas; the Israeli government accepted it and temporarily stopped hostilities on the morning of 15 July, but Hamas rejected it in "its current form", citing the fact Hamas has not been consulted in the formation of the ceasefire and it omitted many of their demands. By 16 July, the death toll within Gaza had surpassed 200 people.

Phase 2: Ground invasion

On 16 July, Hamas and Islamic Jihad offered the Israeli government a 10-year truce with ten conditions centred on the lifting of the blockade and the release of prisoners who were released in the Gilad Shalit prisoner swap and were re-arrested; it was not accepted. On 17 July, a five-hour humanitarian ceasefire, proposed by the UN, took place. Approximately five and a half hours prior to the ceasefire's effect, the IDF sighted 13 armed Hamas militants emerging

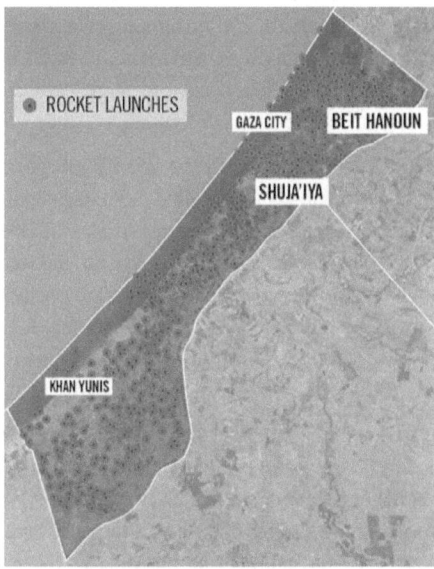

Figure 260: *IDF-released map of rocket launch sites in Gaza*

Figure 261: *Israeli troops and tanks near the Gaza border*

from a Gazan tunnel on the Israeli side of the Gaza border. IDF destroyed the tunnel's exit, ending the incursion. After the ceasefire, IDF began a ground offensive on the Gaza Strip focused on destroying tunnels crossing the Israel border. On 20 July, the Israeli military entered Shuja'iyya, a populous neighborhood of Gaza City, resulting in heavy fighting.

On 24 July, over 10,000 Palestinians in the West Bank protested against the Israeli operation; 2 Palestinian protesters died. 150 Hamas militants who surrendered to the IDF were being questioned about Hamas operations.[2065] On 25 July, an Israeli airstrike killed Salah Abu Hassanein, the leader of Islamic Jihad's military wing. On 26 July, another humanitarian ceasefire took place for twelve hours, followed by a unilateral extension by Israel for another twenty-four hours, which was rejected by Hamas. The Palestinian death toll in the Gaza Strip topped 1,000.

On 1 August, the US and UN announced that Israel and Palestine had agreed to a 72-hour ceasefire starting at 08:00. There was dispute about the terms of the ceasefire: Israel and the US stated that they allowed Israel to "continue to do operations to destroy tunnels that pose a threat to Israeli territory that lead from the Gaza Strip into Israel proper as long as those tunnels exist on the Israel side of their lines"; Hamas said that it would not accept such a condition. The ceasefire broke down almost immediately after it started. Israel blamed Hamas for violating the ceasefire, saying a group of Israeli soldiers were attacked by Palestinian militants emerging from a tunnel. Palestinians said the IDF was the first to breach the ceasefire when at 08:30 it destroyed 19 buildings while undertaking work to demolish tunnels. According to the PLO, the Palestinian Authority and Gazan sources, Hamas attacked an Israeli unit, killing an Israeli officer (Hadar Goldin, who was initially thought to have been captured) while Israeli forces were still engaged in military activities in Rafah on Gaza's territory before the truce came into effect. Tweets reported the battle in Rafah before the deadline for the cease-fire.[2066] Hamas also killed two soldiers in a suicide bombing attack. Senior Hamas leader Moussa Abu Marzouk accused Israel of creating pretexts to undermine the Gaza ceasefire and said that Palestinian fighters abducted the officer and killed the two soldiers before the start of the humanitarian truce, which a Hamas witness has stated began at 7:30 and lasted five minutes,[2067] while Israel said the event took place at 09:20, after the 08:00 start of the ceasefire.[2068,2069,2070]

Phase 3: Withdrawal of Israeli troops

On 3 August, IDF pulled most of its ground forces out of the Gaza Strip after completing the destruction of 32 tunnels built by Hamas and other militants.[2071] On 5 August, Israel announced that it had arrested Hossam Kawasmeh on 11 July, and suspected him of having organized the killing of the three teenagers. According to court documents, Kawasmeh stated that Hamas members in Gaza financed the recruitment and arming of the killers.

On 10 August, another Egyptian proposal for a 72-hour ceasefire was negotiated and agreed upon Israeli and Palestinian officials, and on 13 August it was extended for another 120 hours to allow both sides to continue negotiations for a long-term solution to end the month-long fighting. On 19 August, a 24-hour ceasefire extension renewal was violated just hours after agreement with 29 Hamas rockets fired in 20 minutes, with IAF airstrikes in response, killing 9 Gazans. The Israeli delegation was ordered home from Cairo.

On 21 August, an Israeli airstrike in Rafah killed three of Hamas's top commanders: Mohammed Abu Shammala, Raed al Atar and Mohammed Barhoum. During the period from 22 to 26 August, over 700 rockets and mortar shells fired into Israel, killing 3 Israelis. On 26 August, Israel and Hamas accepted another cease-fire at 19:00.

Result and post-conflict events

On 16 September, Mortar shell fired to Israel for the first time since the ceasefire. Citizens worried that the fighting would resume with the Gaza Strip at the beginning of the new year (Rosh Hashanah). Defense Minister, Moshe Ya'alon estimated that fighting would not resume with the Gaza Strip at the end of this month. Abbas call for UNSC resolution to end Mideast conflict. Hollande, French president show supported in his effort. On Tuesday, 20 September, negotiations between Israel and Gaza will begin in Cairo.

According to Palestinians on 1 October, Israeli forces entered the Gaza Strip and fired upon Palestinian farmers and farms. No injuries were reported.

IDF reported that on 31 October a rocket or a mortar shell was launched from Gaza into southern Israel without causing harm.

On 23 November, a Palestinian farmer was shot dead in Gaza, marking the first time a Palestinian from Gaza had been killed by Israeli fire since a seven-week war between Israel and Hamas militants ended with an Egyptian-brokered ceasefire on 26 August. The Israeli army said two Palestinians had approached the border fence and had ignored calls to halt, prompting troops to fire warning shots in the air. "Once they didn't comply, they fired towards their lower extremities. There was one hit," a spokeswoman said.

Figure 262: *A map showing the location of damage in Gaza*

Impact

On Gaza residents

As of 20 July 2014[2072], hospitals in Gaza were ill-equipped and faced severe shortages of various kinds of medicine, medical supplies, and fuel. Egypt temporarily reopened the Rafah crossing with Gaza to allow medical supplies to enter and injured Palestinians to receive treatment in Egypt. Due to the operation, prices of food, including fish and produce, rose dramatically. A 21 July news report stated that over 83,000 Palestinians had taken shelter in UN facilities. Fatah officials accused Hamas of mishandling humanitarian aid meant for civilians. According to them, Hamas took the aid, which included clothing, mattresses, medicine, water, and food, and distributed it among Hamas members or sold it on the black market for profit.

According to the United Nations Office for the Coordination of Humanitarian Affairs (OCHA), over 273,000 Palestinians in the Gaza Strip had been displaced as of 31 July 2014, of whom 236,375 (over eleven percent of the Gazan population) were taking shelter in 88 UNRWA schools. UNRWA exhausted its capacity to absorb displaced persons, and overcrowding in shelters risked the outbreak of epidemics. 1.8 million people were affected by a halt or reduction of the water supply, 138 schools and 26 health facilities were damaged, 872 homes were totally destroyed or severely damaged, and the homes of

Figure 263: *Ruins of buildings in Beit Hanoun, August 2014*

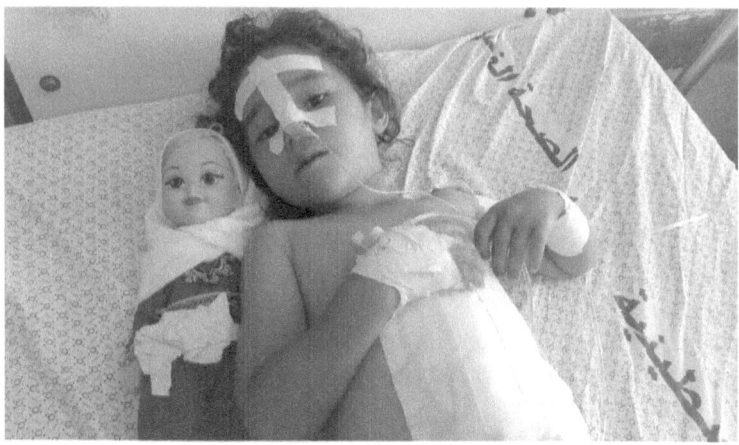

Figure 264: *Five-year-old Shaymaa al-Masri was injured on 9 July 2014.*

5,005 families were damaged but still inhabitable. Throughout the Gaza Strip, people received only 2 hours of electricity per day. Power outage had an immediate effect on the public health situation and reduced water and sanitation services, with hospitals becoming dependent on generators. On 2 September, UNRWA reported that 58,217 people were sheltering in 31 of their school buildings, a fifth of their buildings.

OCHA estimated that at least 373,000 children required psychosocial support. "Intense overcrowding, compounded by the limited access of humanitarian staff to certain areas, is increasingly undermining the living conditions at many shelters and raising protection concerns. Water supply has been particularly challenging..." More than 485,000 internally displaced persons were in need of emergency food assistance.

Gaza City, home to 500,000, suffered damage to 20-25% of its housing. Beit Hanoun, with 70% of its housing stock damaged, is considered uninhabitable, with 30,000 residents there in need of accommodation. The only power station in the Strip was damaged on 29 July, and the infrastructure of power transmission lines and sewage pumps was severely damaged, with a major sewage pipe catering to 500,000 badly damaged. Among the infrastructure targeted and destroyed by Israel's bombing campaign were 220 factories in various industrial zones, including a major carpentry enterprise, construction companies, a major biscuit factory, dairy farms and livestock, a candy manufacturer, the orange groves of Beit Hanoun, Gaza's largest mosques, and several TV stations. Farms, as a consequence of damage or the presence of unexploded ordnance dropped during the conflict, are often inaccessible, and the damage to agriculture was estimated at over $200 million. 10 out of 26 hospitals closed.[2073,2074]

According to the Palestinian Ministry of Endowments and Religious Affairs, 203 mosques were damaged during the war, with 73 being destroyed completely. Two of Gaza's three Christian churches were also damaged, with the third suffering some damage to peripheral buildings owned by the parish. In the light of the damage to mosques, Manuel Musallam informed Muslims they could call their prayers from Christian churches.[2075] In contrast to Operation Pillar of Defensive, which did not damage a single mosque, Israel maintained that Hamas had a routine military use of mosques and that made them legitimate military targets. According to the IDF, 160 rockets were launched from mosques during the war. It also stated that mosques were used for weapon storage, tunnel entrances, training and gathering of militants. In one Associated Press report, residents denied that mosques damaged by Israeli forces had been used for military purposes.

The UN calculated that more than 7,000 homes for 10,000 families were razed, together with an additional 89,000 homes damaged, of which roughly 10,000

Figure 265: *A kindergarten in central Israel during a rocket attack.*

were severely affected by the bombing. Rebuilding costs were calculated to run from 4-6 billions dollars, over 20 years.

On Israeli residents

Hamas and other Islamist groups in Gaza fired rockets and mortars at Israeli towns and villages. Despite Israel's use of the Iron Dome missile defense systems, six civilians were killed, including an Arab Israeli and a Thai civilian worker.[2076] An Israeli teen was seriously injured in a rocket strike in the city of Ashkelon.[2077] Medical health professionals have noted that Israeli teens prone to mental health problems suffer increasingly during both short-term and long-term conflicts. Experts have identified a number of mental health symptoms which rise during conflict, including anxiety, depression, obsessive-compulsive disorder, interpersonal sensitivity, phobias, and paranoia. There is some doubt whether these issues will dissipate after the conflict is resolved.[2078]

Rocket attacks from Gaza caused damage to Israeli civilian infrastructure, including factories, gas stations, and homes.[2079]

At the onset of the operation, the Israeli government canceled all programs within 40 km (25 mi) of Gaza, and requested all people stay at home or near shelter. All summer camps were closed and universities canceled their final exams. Additionally, all gatherings of 300 or more people were banned. Due to

Figure 266: *One of the shelter signs that were placed in the Ben Gurion Airport because of the rocket attacks on Israel.*

the trajectory of rocket fire from Gaza, many flights in and out of Ben-Gurion Airport were delayed or rerouted. and flights to Ben-Gurion airport were interrupted for some days after a Hamas rocket struck an area in its vicinity. Hamas called the FAA flight ban a "great victory". Michael Ross wrote that the decision was driven by anxiety and caused considerably more damage than the potential danger it prevented.

About 4,600 claims for direct damage and 28,000 for indirect damage such as missed work days were submitted to Israel's Tax Authority, which paid ₪133 million for direct damage and ₪1.51 billion for indirect damage.

The Bedouin communities in the Negev, living in many habitations built illegally and unrecognised by the Israeli government, were classified as "open areas" and so their 200,000 residents did not have warning sirens or anti-rocket protection.

In Israel, an estimated 5,000 to 8,000 citizens temporarily fled their homes due to the threat of rocketry from Gaza.[2080] The economic cost of the operation is estimated at NIS 8.5 billion (approximately 2.5 billion USD) and GDP loss of 0.4%. At the conclusion of hostilities 3,000-3,700 claims for damages had been submitted by Israelis, and $41 million paid out for property damage and missed work days. Reconstruction costs were estimated at approximately $11 million.[2081]

Casualties and losses

Palestinian

Reports of casualties in the conflict have been made available by a variety of sources. Most media accounts have used figures provided by the government in Gaza or non-governmental organizations.

Current reports of the proportion of those killed who were civilians/militants are incomplete, and real-time errors, intentional data manipulation, and diverse methodologies produce notable variations in various sides' figures. For example, the Hamas-run Interior Ministry has issued instructions for activists to always refer to casualties as "innocent civilians" or "innocent citizens" in internet posts. However, B'Tselem has stated that after the various groups finish their investigations, their figures are likely to end up about the same. UNICEF and the Gaza Health Ministry reported that from 8 July to 2 August 296–315 Palestinian children died due to Israeli action, and 30% of civilian casualties were children; by 27 August, the total number of children killed had risen to 495–578, according to OCHA and the Gaza Health Ministry. In March 2015, OCHA reported that 2,220 Palestinians had been killed, of whom 1,492 were civilians (551 children and 299 women), 605 militants and 123 of unknown status.[2082] According to ITIC, 48.7% of the identified casualties were militants and in some cases children and women participated in military operations. In December 2014, the ITIC published a list of 50 Gazan militants killed in the war whose names did not appear on the casualty lists released by Hamas. In 2015, it released a list of another 50 militants, including 43 from Hamas, who had been killed in the war and were not listed by Hamas. The ITIC estimated the number of Hamas-affiliated militants killed in the war at 600-650, and claimed that Hamas unofficially reported that it lost 400 fighters, although it estimated that this was lower than the actual figure and excluded those affiliated with Hamas' security apparatus and civilian infrastructure that supported it's military activity.[2083] The Islamic Jihad Movement in Palestine was reported as claiming that 121 or 123 of its fighters were killed in the war. The ITIC estimated that the true figure was several dozen higher, up to 150 or 170.[2084] In a September 2014 meeting with foreign journalists, a senior Israeli intelligence officer said that to date, the IDF had determined that 616 of the dead were militants, including 341 from Hamas, 182 from Islamic Jihad, and 93 from smaller Palestinian factions.[2085] Israel later updated it's estimate to 936 of the dead being confirmed militants and 428 others whose status as civilians or militants could not be ascertained. Of the 936 identified as militants, 631 were from Hamas, 201 from Islamic Jihad, and 104 from smaller factions such as Fatah networks and organizations affiliated with global jihad.

The IDF captured the bodies of 19 Hamas fighters killed during the war. Israel continues to hold the bodies pending a prisoner exchange deal.[2086]

According to the main estimates between 2,125 and 2,310 Gazans were killed and between 10,626 and 10,895 were wounded (including 3,374 children, of whom over 1,000 were left permanently disabled[2087]). The Gaza Health Ministry, UN and some human rights groups reported that 69–75% of the Palestinian casualties were civilians; Israeli officials estimated that around 50% of those killed were civilians. On 5 August, OCHA stated that 520,000 Palestinians in the Gaza Strip (approximately 30% of its population) might have been displaced, of whom 485,000 needed emergency food assistance and 273,000 were taking shelter in 90 UN-run schools.

Human rights groups and the UN use the Gaza Health Ministry's number of Palestinians killed in Gaza as preliminary and add to or subtract from it after conducting their own investigations. For example, human rights groups say that the casualty count provided by the Health Ministry most likely includes victims of Hamas executions, domestic violence, and natural deaths, but they (the human rights groups) remove the accused collaborators (who were shot as close range) from their own counts. Israel contends that the Health Ministry's casualty count also includes deaths caused by rocket or mortar malfunctions.

Source	Total killed	Civilians	Militants	Unidentified	Percent civilians	Last updated	Notes
Hamas GHM	2,310	≈1,617	≈693	—	70%	3 January 2015	Defines as a civilian anyone who is not claimed by an armed group as a member.
UN HRC	2,251	1,462	789	—	65%	22 June 2015	Total killed referenced information from Hamas GHM.[2088] Cross-referenced information from GHM with other sources for civilian percentage
Israel MFA	2,125[2089]	761	936	428	36% of the total 44% combatant 20% unidentified	14 June 2015	Uses its own intelligence reports as well as Palestinian sources and media reports to determine combatant deaths.

According to the OCHA 2015 overview, of the 2,220 Palestinians killed in the conflict, 742 fatalities came from 142 families, who suffered the loss of 3 or more family members in individual bombing incidents on residential buildings. According to data provided by the Palestinian International Middle East Media Center, 79.7% of the Palestinians killed in Gaza were male, with the majority between 16 and 35 (fighting-age). In contrast, a New York Times analysis states that males of ages that are most likely to be militants form 9% of the population but 34% of the casualties, while women and children under 15, who are least likely to be legitimate targets, form 71% of the general population and 33% of the casualties. Israel has pointed to the relatively small numbers of fatalities among women, children and men over 60, and to instances of Hamas fighters being counted as civilians (perhaps due to the broad definition of "civilian" used by the Gaza Health Ministry), to support its view that the number of the dead who were militants is 40–50%. The IDF calculates that 5% of Gaza's military forces were killed in the war. Jana Krause, from the war studies department at King's College London, stated that "a potential explanation other than combatant roles" for the tendency of the dead to be young men "could be that families expect them to be the first ones to leave shelters in order to care for hurt relatives, gather information, look after abandoned family homes or arrange food and water." ITIC reported instances in which children and teenagers served as militants, as well as cases where the ages of casualties reported by GHM were allegedly falsified, with child militants listed as adults and adults listed as children.

Abbas said that "more than 120 youths were killed for violating the curfew and house arrest orders issued against them" by Hamas, referring to reports that Hamas targeted Fatah activists in Gaza during the conflict. Abbas said that Hamas also executed more than 30 suspected collaborators without trial. He said that "over 850 Hamas members and their families" were killed by Israel during the operation.[2090,2091,2092] During the fighting between Israel and Gaza, solidarity protests occurred in the West Bank, during which several Palestinians died; see Reactions.

Israeli

A total of 67 IDF soldiers were killed, including one who died of his injuries after two and a half years in a coma, and two soldiers, Staff Sergeant Oron Shaul and Second Lieutenant Hadar Goldin, whose bodies were taken by Hamas and are currently being held in Gaza.[2093] Another 469 soldiers were injured. The IDF said that 5 soldiers were killed and 23 were wounded by friendly fire. In addition, Palestinian rocket fire killed 5 civilians in Israel (including 1 Thai civilian), while another 2 Israeli civilians died by heart-attacks related to hearing the sirens.[2094] One other person died due to natural causes brought on by the conflict. According to Magen David Adom, 837 civilians were treated for shock (581) or injuries (256): 36 were injured by shrapnel, 33 by debris from shattered glass and building debris, 18 in traffic accidents which occurred when warning sirens sounded, 159 from falling or trauma while on the way to shelters, and 9 in violence in Jerusalem and Maale Adumim.[2095]

The first Israeli civilian death occurred at the Erez border crossing with Gaza when a Chabad rabbi, delivering food and drinks on the front line, was killed by mortar fire. The second Israeli civilian killed was a 32-year-old Bedouin who was hit by a rocket in the Negev Desert.[2096] A Thai migrant worker was also killed by mortar fire while working at a greenhouse in the Ashkelon Coast Regional Council. In addition, an elderly woman in Haifa collapsed and died of heart failure during an air-raid siren.[2097] On 22 August, a 4-year-old Israeli child was killed by a mortar fired from Gaza. A barrage of mortar fire killed two Israeli civilians in the Eshkol region, an hour before a ceasefire went into effect.

Economic impact

Palestinian officials estimated on 4 September that, with 17,000 homes destroyed by Israeli bombing, the reconstruction would cost $7.8 billion, which is about 3 times Gaza's GDP for 2011.[2098] Gaza City suffered damage to 20–25% of its housing and Beit Hanoun with 70% of its housing uninhabitable. *The New York Times* noted that damage in this third war was more severe than in the two preceding wars, where in the aftermath of the earlier Operation Cast Lead the damage inflicted was $4 billion, 3 times the then GDP of Gaza's economy. Strikes on Gaza's few industries will take years to repair. Gaza's main power plant on Salaheddin Road was damaged. Two sewage pumping stations in Zeitoun were damaged. The biggest private company in Gaza, the Alawda biscuit and ice cream factory, employing 400, was destroyed by a shelling barrage on 31 July, a few days after undertaking to supply its Choco Sandwich biscuits to 250,000 refugees in response to a request from the World Food Programme; other strikes targeted a plastics factory, a sponge-making plant, the offices of Gaza's main fruit distribution network, the El Majd Industrial and Trading Corporation's factory for cardboard box, carton and plastic bag production, Gaza's biggest dairy product importer and distributor, Roward International. Trond Husby, chief of the UN's Gaza development programme in Gaza, commented that the level of destruction now is worse than in Somalia, Sierra Leone, South Sudan and Uganda.

A number of tunnels leading into both Israel and Egypt were destroyed throughout the operation. There were reports that the tunnels between Gaza and Egypt were bringing an estimated $700 million into Gaza's economy through goods or services. Several Palestinians argued that the tunnels had

Figure 267: *Quds Day 2014 pro-Palestinian protest in Berlin, 25 July 2014*

been critical to supporting the residents of Gaza, either through the employment they provided or through the goods that they allowed in—goods which were otherwise not available unless shipped through Egypt. However, tunnels along the Israeli border serve a purely military purpose.

During the ground invasion, Israeli forces destroyed livestock in Gaza. In Beit Hanoun, 370 cows were killed by tank shelling and airstrikes. In Beit Lahiya, 20 camels were shot by ground forces. Israel's Minister of Finance estimated that the operation would cost Israel NIS 8.5 billion (approximately 2.5 billion USD), which is similar to Operation Cast Lead in 2009 and higher than Operation Pillar of Defense in 2012. The forecast included military and non-military costs, including military expenditure and property damage. The calculation indicated that if the operation lasted 20 days, the loss in GDP would be 0.4%.

Reactions

International

International reactions to the 2014 Israel–Gaza conflict came from many countries and international organizations around the world.

Canada was supportive of Israel[2099] and critical of Hamas. The BRICS countries called for restraint on both sides and a return to peace talks based on

Figure 268: *Pro-Israel demonstration in Helsinki, Finland*

the Arab Peace Initiative. The European Union condemned the violations of the laws of war by both sides, while stressing the "unsustainable nature of the status quo", and calling for a settlement based on the two-state solution. The Non-Aligned Movement, the Arab League, and most Latin American countries were critical of Israel, with some countries in the latter group withdrawing their ambassadors from Israel in protest. South Africa called for restraint by both sides and an end to "collective punishment of Palestinians". Wikipedia:Citation needed

There were many pro-Israel and pro-Palestine demonstrations worldwide, including inside Israel and the Palestinian territories. According to OCHA, 23 Palestinians were killed and 2,218 were wounded by the IDF (38% of the latter by live fire) during these demonstrations.[2100,2101,2102]

Concerns were raised regarding rising anti-Semitism and related violence Wikipedia:Naming conventions (geographic names) deemed related to the conflict.

United States

U.S. President Obama acknowledged Israel's right to defend itself, but urged restraint by both sides. Meanwhile, the United States Congress expressed vigorous support for Israel. It passed legislation providing Israel with an additional $225 million in military aid for missile defense with a bipartisan 395-8 vote in the House of Representatives and by unanimous consent in the Senate. This was in addition to strong measures supporting Israel's position passed with overwhelming support in both houses. Israel received strong statements of bipartisan support from the leadership and members of both houses of Congress for its actions during the conflict.

During the U.S. Presidential campaigns of 2016, Democratic candidate Bernie Sanders criticized Israel for its treatment of Gaza, and in particular criticized Netanyahu for "overreacting" and causing unnecessary civilian deaths.[2103] In April 2016 the Anti-Defamation League called on Sanders to withdraw remarks he made to the New York Daily News, which the ADL said exaggerated the death toll of the 2014 Israel–Gaza conflict. Sanders said "over 10,000 innocent people were killed", a number far in excess of Palestinian or Israel sources' estimates.[2104] In response, Sanders said that he accepted a corrected number of the death toll as 2,300 during the course of the interview, which was taped, and that he would make every effort to set the record straight. The written transcript of the interview failed to note that Sanders said "Okay" to the corrected number presented by the interviewer during the course of the interview.[2105]

Gaza

On 6 August 2014, thousands of Palestinians rallied in Gaza in support of Hamas, they demanded an end to the blockade of Gaza. After 26 August ceasefire, the Palestinian Center for Policy and Survey Research conducted a poll in the West Bank and the Gaza Strip: 79% of respondents said that Hamas had won the war and 61% said that they would pick Hamas leader Ismail Haniyeh as the Palestinian president, up from 41% before the war.

According to *The Washington Post*, a percentage of Gazans held Hamas accountable for the humanitarian crisis and wanted the militants to stop firing rockets from their neighborhoods to avoid Israeli reaction.[2106] Some of the Gazans have attempted to protest against Hamas, which routinely accuses protesters of being Israeli spies and has killed more than 50 such protesters.Wikipedia:Identifying reliable sources Around 6 August, Palestinian protesters reportedly attacked and beat up Hamas spokesperson Sami Abu Zuhri because they blamed Hamas for inciting Operation Protective Edge.

Figure 269: *A pro-Israeli demonstration supporting Israel and the Israel Defense Forces in Tzuk Eytan*

An unknown number of Palestinians, estimated in the hundreds or thousands, have tried to flee to Europe due to the conflict. The Palestinian rights group Adamir collected the names of 400 missing persons. In what was described by International Organization for Migration as the "worst shipwreck in years", a boat carrying refugees was rammed by smugglers and capsized off the coast of Malta, resulting in the deaths of about 400 people. According to interviews with survivors, they paid smugglers between $2,000-$5,000 or used legal travel permits, to get to Egypt. One refugee who died had considered the boat to be rickety but told his father "I have no life in Gaza anyway".

Israel and the West Bank

A majority of the Israeli public supported Operation Protective Edge. A poll conducted after a temporary ceasefire came into effect during the war in July found that 86.5% of Israelis polled opposed the ceasefire.[2107] Another poll in July found 91% support for the operation among the Jewish public, with 85% opposed to stopping the war and 51% in support of continuing the war until Hamas was removed from power in Gaza, while 4% believed the war to be a mistake.[2108] Two other polls found 90% and 95% support for the war among the Jewish public.[2109] Towards the end of the war, after Israel announced the withdrawal of ground forces from Gaza, a poll found 92% support for the war among the Jewish public, and that 48% believed that the IDF had used the appropriate amount of firepower in the operation, while 45% believed it had used too little and 6% believed it had used too much. The poll also found that 62% of Israeli-Arabs believed the operation was unjustified while 24%

Figure 270: *Banner on a kindergarten in Kiryat Ono saying "Dear soldiers! Take care of yourselves! You are our heroes!"*

Figure 271: *Demonstration against Operation Protective Edge in Tel Aviv, Israel.*

believed it was justified, and that 62% believed too much firepower was used, 10% believed too little firepower was used, and 3% thought the appropriate amount of firepower was used.[2110]

The war saw strained relations between Israeli Jews and Israeli Arabs. Many Arab businesses temporarily closed as part of a general strike in solidarity with Gaza, leading to Israeli Foreign Minister Avigdor Lieberman to call for the boycott of Arab businesses that participated in the strike. Thousands demonstrated against the war, including some who threw stones and blocked streets. About 1,500 Arabs were arrested over involvement in protests against the war. Numerous Arabs were fired or disciplined by their employers over comments against Israel and the war on social media. The most notable case was that of a psychological counselor who worked for the Lod municipality, who was terminated on the orders of the Mayor of Lod after writing a Facebook post expressing joy over the deaths of 13 Israeli soldiers in the Battle of Shuja'iyya. Arabs reported an increase in racism and violence from right-wing Jews. However, some Israeli Jews against the war joined in anti-war protests, and a handful were also arrested.[2111,2112,2113,2114]

There were continuous protests and clashes in the West Bank. The funeral of Mohammed Abu Khdeir on 4 July was joined by thousands of mourners, and was accompanied by clashes across east Jerusalem throughout the weekend.Wikipedia:Manual of Style/Dates and numbers#Chronological items According to OCHA, 23 Palestinians were killed and 2,218 were wounded by the IDF, 38% of the latter by live fire. According to the PLO, 32 Palestinians were killed in the West Bank in the period 13 June – 26 August, nearly 1400 were wounded by Israeli fire and 1,700 were detained in the largest offensive in the West Bank since the Second Intifada. The PLO also stated that 1,472 settlement homes had been approved over the summer.

During the war there were over 360 attacks on Jews from the West Bank, a spate that was thought by the *Jerusalem Post* to have "peaked" on 4 August with a tractor attack in Jerusalem and the shooting of a uniformed soldier in the French Hill neighborhood, leading to an increase in security in the city.

On 1 September, Israel announced a plan to expropriate 1,000 acres of land in the West Bank, reportedly as a "reaction to the deplorable murder in June of three Israeli teenagers", which Amnesty International denounced as the "largest land grab in the Occupied Palestinian Territories since the 1980s". The EU complained about the land expropriation and warned of renewed violence in Gaza; the US called it "counterproductive".

Alleged violations of international humanitarian law

A number of legal and moral issues concerning the conflict arose during course of the fighting. Various human rights groups have argued that both Palestinian rocket attacks and Israeli targeted destruction of homes of Hamas and other militia members violated international humanitarian law and might constitute war crimes, violations of international humanitarian law.[2115] Navi Pillay, the United Nations High Commissioner for Human Rights, accused Hamas militants of violating international humanitarian law by "locating rockets within schools and hospitals, or even launching these rockets from densely populated areas." She also criticized Israel's military operation, stating that there was "a strong possibility that international law has been violated, in a manner that could amount to war crimes", and specifically criticizing Israel's actions in Gaza as disproportionate.

Amnesty International found evidence that "[d]uring the current hostilities, Hamas spokespeople reportedly urged residents in some areas of the Gaza Strip not to leave their homes after the Israeli military dropped leaflets and made phone calls warning people in the area to evacuate", and that international humanitarian law was clear in that "even if officials or fighters from Hamas or Palestinian armed groups associated with other factions did in fact direct civilians to remain in a specific location in order to shield military objectives from attacks, all of Israel's obligations to protect these civilians would still apply." B'tselem found that Hamas had breached provisions of International Humanitarian Law (IHL), both firing from civilian areas and firing at Israeli civilian areas. It also stated that the Israeli policy of bombing homes, formulated by government officials and the senior military command, though claimed to be in conformity with IHL, was 'unlawful', and designed to 'block, a priori, any allegations that Israel breached IHL provisions', in that it relies on an interpretation that leaves 'no restrictions whatsoever on Israeli action' so that 'whatever method it chooses to respond to Hamas operations is legitimate, no matter how horrifying the consequences.'[2116,2117]

Hamas leader Ismail Haniyeh urged the Palestinian Authority to sign the Rome Statute of the International Criminal Court (ICC);[2118] the fact that the PA has not done so yet has prevented the ICC from launching a formal investigation. Wikipedia:Please clarify ICC prosecutor Geoffrey Nice said that a "decision to do nothing clearly emerges from the meeting" with the PA foreign minister Riad Malki. The UNHRC has appointed a panel led by William Schabas to investigate war crimes allegations by both sides. Israel criticized Schabas as biased because he repeatedly made statements against Israel and in support of Hamas, and has announced its own investigations of both military and civilian leadership and the conduct during the war. Schabas denied any bias, but on 2 February 2015 resigned from the position. According to the *New York Times*, "Of 44 cases initially referred to army fact-finding teams for preliminary examination, seven have been closed, including one involving the death of eight members of a family when their home was struck on 8 July, the first day of the Israeli air campaign, and others are pending." Human rights organizations have expressed little confidence in Israel's measures, citing past experience. Moreover, several human rights organizations were denied access to Gaza by Israel, rendering it impossible for them to carry out on-site investigations. B'Tselem has refused to participate in the army investigation.

Alleged violations by Hamas

Killing and shooting of Gazan civilians

Twenty civilians from Shuja'iyya were killed while protesting against Hamas. A few days later, Hamas reportedly killed two Gazans and wounded ten after a scuffle broke out over food handouts.

The IDF stated on 31 July that more than 280 Hamas rockets malfunctioned and fell inside the Gaza strip, hitting sites including Al-Shifa Hospital and the Al-Shati refugee camp, killing at least 11 and wounding dozens. Hamas denied that any of its rockets hit the Gaza Strip., but Palestinian sources said numerous rocket launches ended up falling in Gaza communities and that scores of people have been killed or injured. Israeli Military sources said the failed Hamas launches increased amid heavy Israeli air and artillery strikes throughout the Gaza Strip. They said the failed launches reflected poorly-assembled rockets as well as the rush to load and fire projectiles before they are spotted by Israeli aircraft. While the Al-Shifa Hospital incident is disputed, early news reports have suggested that the strike was from an Israeli drone missile. Amnesty International concluded that the explosion at the Shati refugee camp on 28 July in which 13 civilians were killed was caused by a Palestinian rocket, despite Palestinian claims it was an Israeli missile.[2119]

Killing of suspected collaborators

During the conflict, Hamas executed Gazan civilians it accused of having collaborated with Israel; thirty on 30 July; forty-six on 21/22 August,[2120] including twenty-five as part of a campaign codenamed "Strangling Necks"; four on 23 August;[2121] and eighteen more at other times. Overall, Hamas executed between 30-40 suspected collaborators during Operation Protective Edge alone, according to Abbas. Abbas condemned the executions, calling them murders and a crime.[2122]

Abbas' Secretary-General, Al-Tayyib Abd al-Rahim, condemned the "random executions of those who Hamas called collaborators", adding that some of those killed had been detained for more than three years.[2123] Amnesty International, Human Rights Watch and Palestinian human rights groups condemned the executions. Bodies of the victims were brought to hospitals to be added to the number of civilian casualties of Israeli operation. According to a Shin Bet official, "not even one" of the alleged collaborators executed by Hamas provided any intelligence to Israel, while the Shin Bet officially "confirmed that those executed during Operation Protective Edge had all been held in prison in Gaza in the course of the hostilities."

Senior Hamas official Moussa Abu Marzouk confirmed that some victims were kept under arrest before the conflict began and were executed to satisfy the public without due legal procedure.

Shurat HaDin filed a suit with the ICC charging Khaled Mashaal with war crimes for the executions of 38 civilians. Hamas co-founder Ayman Taha was found dead; *Al-Quds Al-Arabi* reported he had been shot by Hamas for maintaining contact with the intelligence services of several Arab countries; Hamas stated he was targeted by an Israeli airstrike.

On 26 May 2015 Amnesty International released a report saying that Hamas carried out extrajudicial killings, abductions and arrests of Palestinians and used the Al-Shifa Hospital to detain, interrogate and torture suspects. It details the executions of at least 23 Palestinians accused of collaborating with Israel and torture of dozens of others, many victims of torture were members of the rival Palestinian movement, Fatah.

Endangerment of Civilians

Human shields

The European Union condemned Hamas, and in particular condemned "calls on the civilian population of Gaza to provide themselves as human shields."[2124] Confirmation of this practice was produced by correspondents from France24, *The Financial Times*, and RT, who respectively filmed a rocket launch pad which was placed in a civilian area next to a hotel where international journalists were staying, reported on rockets being fired from near Al-Shifa Hospital, and reported on Hamas firing rockets near a hotel.[2125] In September 2014, a Hamas official acknowledged to an Associated Press reporter that the group had fired rockets from civilian areas.

While the Israeli government repeatedly stated that many civilian casualties were the result of Hamas using the Gazan population as human shields[2126] several British media organizations (including *The Guardian*, and *The Independent*) dismissed such claims as "myths" and the BBC's Middle East editor

Jeremy Bowen likewise said he "saw no evidence of Hamas using Palestinians as human shields." Additionally the London-based NGO, Amnesty International, dismissed such claims, stated it was unable to verify them and emphasized that even if they were true the IDF would still have a responsibility to protect civilians.[2127]

The statements fall into two categories: using civilian structures like homes, mosques and hospitals to store munitions in or launch rockets from, and urging or forcing civilian population to stay in their homes, to shield militants. Israeli soldiers have also said Hamas operatives directly employed women and children as involuntary human shields to evade pursuit, while Hamas and others have said such accusations are false. Asa Kasher, who helped to write the Israel Defense Forces's Code of Conduct, argued that "Israel cannot forfeit its ability to protect its citizens against attacks simply because terrorists hide behind non-combatants. If it did so, it would be giving up any right to self-defense."

Use of civilian structures for military purposes

The UN High Commissioner for Human Rights (UNHCHR) Navi Pillay accused Hamas militants of violating international humanitarian law by "locating rockets within schools and hospitals, or even launching these rockets from densely populated areas." But she added that this did not absolve Israel from disregarding the same law. The UNHCHR report recognised that "the obligation to avoid locating military objectives within densely populated areas is not absolute. The small size of Gaza and its population density make it difficult for armed groups to always comply with this requirement."

In a 2015 report, Amnesty International states that "There are credible reports that, in certain cases, Palestinian armed groups launched rockets or mortars from within civilian facilities or compounds, including schools, at least one hospital and a Greek Orthodox church in Gaza City. In at least two cases, accounts indicate that attacks were launched in spite of the fact that displaced Gazan civilians were sheltering in the compounds or in neighbouring buildings.".

Israel has stated that many mosques, schools and hospitals were used to store weapons. The IDF spokesman said that mortar shells were fired from a boys' school that served as a shelter for refugees. There were reports of the use of mosques to store weapons, and having launch sites very close to civilian structures. Gaza's Greek Orthodox archbishop has said that Hamas used the church compound, which sheltered 2000 Muslim civilians, to launch rockets into Israel. France 24 correspondent Gallagher Fenwick reported that a Hamas rocket-launching pad was placed in densely populated neighborhood of Gaza City, about 50 meters from the hotel where the majority of international media

Figure 272: *Explosives were allegedly two steps away from a baby's bed in Gaza during the war.*

were staying and 100 meters from a UN building. Fenwick said that "children can be seen playing on and near the rocket launcher".

Israel released footage of Palestinian militants launching rockets from a school and a cemetery. In at least one case a cemetery was targeted by an Israeli airstrike.

According to Shabak, the Israeli internal security service, some militants, when interrogated, admitted using civilian buildings for military purposes. The admissions included more than ten mosques that were used for gatherings, training, storage of weapons, tunnel activities and military observations. During interrogations, one militant said that he was instructed in case of successful abduction using a tunnel to take the victim to a kindergarten located near its opening.

On 24 August, Israel released part of what it says is a Hamas training manual on urban warfare, which states "the process of hiding ammunition inside buildings is intended for ambushes in residential areas and to move the campaign from open areas into built up and closed areas" and "residents of the area should be used to bring in the equipment...take advantage of this to avoid [Israeli] spy planes and attack drones." The manual also explains how fighting from within civilian population makes IDF operations difficult and what the benefits of civilian deaths are.[2128] Hamas spokesman Sami Abu Zuhri dismissed the document as a "forgery...aimed at justifying the mass killings of Palestinian civilians."

On 12 September, Ghazi Hamad, a senior Hamas official, acknowledged for the first time that Hamas did fire rockets from civilian areas and said "some mistakes were made".[2129]

In Israel

Israeli and Jewish critics of the war, including Uri Avnery and Gideon Levy wrote that in their own war of independence in 1948 (and earlier), Jews hid weapons in synagogues, kindergartens and schools as well.[2130,2131] Other critics have noted that the headquarters of the IDF and Shin Bet, as well as an Israeli military training facility, are also located near civilian centers. Correctness of such comparison is denied by Ross Singer, who notes that "the legacy of both the Irgun and Lehi was and to a large degree still is a matter of public debate", while Zionist paramilitary groups "rarely if ever" fired weapons "from within civilian population centers" and routinely evacuated civilians from areas of conflict.[2132] Commentators brought up the current high population density of Gaza in conjunction with Palestinian military activities and installations being in or near civilian structures.[2133]

Legality

Using civilian structures to store munitions and launch attacks from is unlawful, and the Fourth Geneva Convention states that "The presence of a protected person may not be used to render certain points or areas immune from military operations."[2134] On the other hand, another convention says that "Any violation of these prohibitions shall not release the parties to the conflict from their legal obligations with respect to the civilian population and civilians, including the obligation to take the precautionary measures."[2135]

According to Harriet Sherwood, writer for the Guardian, even if Hamas were violating the law on this matter, it would not legally justify Israel's bombing of areas where civilians are known to be. Amnesty International stated that "Indiscriminate and disproportionate attacks (where the likely number of civilian casualties or damage to civilian property outweighs the anticipated military advantage to be gained) are ... prohibited." It said that "Israel's relentless air assault on Gaza has seen its forces flagrantly disregard civilian life and property". Human Rights Watch has said that in many cases "the Israeli military has presented no information to show that it was attacking lawful military objectives or acted to minimize civilian casualties." An investigation by Human Rights Watch found that "in most of the sites we investigated so far (in this conflict) we found no valid military targets". A high-level group of former diplomats

Figure 273: *Photo taken during the 72-hour ceasefire between Hamas and Israel on 6 August 2014. A destroyed ambulance in Shuja'iyya in the Gaza Strip.*

and military experts concluded that "the IDF acted within the bounds of international law during the war." The Israeli government issued a report saying that its military actions were "lawful and legitimate" and that "Israel made substantial efforts to avoid civilian deaths." The High Level Military Group, composed of military experts from Australia, Colombia, France, Germany, India, Italy, Britain, the United States, and Spain, released an assessment on Operation Protective Edge acknowledging Israel made "unprecedented efforts" to avoid civilian casualties exceeding international standards.[2136]

Medical facilities and personnel

Medical units including hospitals and medical personnel have special protections under international humanitarian law. They lose their protection only if they commit, outside their humanitarian function, "acts harmful to the enemy." More than 25 medical facilities were damaged in the conflict; one attack on Al-Aqsa hospital killed 5 people. In many cases, ambulances and other medical personnel were hit. Amnesty International has condemned the attacks and said that there is "mounting evidence" that Israel deliberately targeted hospitals and medical personnel; Israel said it had not.

A Finnish reporter from *Helsingin Sanomat* reported seeing rockets fired from near the Gaza Al-Shifa hospital.[2137] The IDF said that in several cases Hamas used Wafa hospital as a military base and used ambulances to transport its fighters.[2138] According to the Israeli Shabak, many of the militants it interrogated said that "everyone knew" that Hamas leaders were using hospitals for hiding. Hamas security reportedly wore police uniforms and blocked access to certain parts of the hospitals. One of the interrogated militants reportedly said that civilians seeking medical attention usually were thrown out by the security. The Washington Post described Al-Shifa hospital as a "de facto headquarters for Hamas leaders, who can be seen in the hallways and offices." Amnesty International reported that: "Hamas forces used the abandoned areas of al-Shifa hospital in Gaza City, including the outpatients' clinic area, to detain, interrogate, torture and otherwise ill-treat suspects, even as other parts of the hospital continued to function as a medical centre".

French-Palestinian journalist Radjaa Abu Dagga[2139] reported that Hamas militants interrogated him in Gaza's main hospital (Al-Shifa); his report was later removed from his paper's website at his request.

Mohammed Al Falahi, Secretary General of Red Crescent, UAE said that Hamas militants fired on Israeli planes from Red Crescent's field hospital in order to provoke retaliation, attacked Red Crescent team on their way back and planted land mines on their path.

Urging or forcing civilians to stay in their homes

The IDF has released photographs which it says show civilians on rooftops, and a video of Hamas spokesperson Sami Abu Zuhri saying "the fact that people are willing to sacrifice themselves against Israeli warplanes in order to protect their homes [...] is proving itself".[2140,2141] The EU has strongly condemned "calls on the civilian population of Gaza to provide themselves as human shields" and US Congress-members introduced bills condemning Hamas for using human shields.[2142,2143] Wikipedia:Neutral point of view#Due and undue weight Civilians and activists in Gaza used themselves as 'human shields' in attempts to prevent Israeli attacks.

Hamas officials said human shields were not used.[2144] One Gazan stated that "nobody is safe and nobody can flee anywhere because everywhere is targeted." Many reporters, including from the BBC,[2145] the Independent and the Guardian said that they found no evidence of Hamas forcing Palestinians to stay and become unwilling human shields.

Fatah officials said that Hamas placed over 250 Fatah members under house arrest or in jail, putting them under threat of being killed by Israeli strikes and shooting them in the legs or breaking their limbs if they tried to leave.[2146] According to Abbas, more than 300 Fatah members were placed under house arrest and 120 were executed for fleeing.

Amnesty International reported that it did "not have evidence at this point" that Palestinian civilians were intentionally used by Hamas or Palestinian armed groups during the current hostilities to "shield" specific locations or military personnel or equipment from Israeli attacks". It additionally said that "public statements referring to entire areas are not the same as directing specific civilians to remain in their homes as "human shields" for fighters, munitions, or military equipment" and that "even if officials or fighters from Hamas or Palestinian armed groups ... did in fact direct civilians to remain in a specific location in order to shield military objectives ..., all of Israel's obligations to protect these civilians would still apply." Human Rights Watch said many of the attacks on targets appeared to be "disproportionate" and "indiscriminate".

Human Rights Watch attributed many civilian deaths to the lack of safe places to flee to, and accused Israel of firing at fleeing civilians. It stated that there are many reasons that prevent civilians from abiding by warnings, and that the failure to abide by warnings does not make civilians lawful targets.[2147]

A survey of Gazan residents by the Gatestone Institute addressed the subject of human shields, with respondents issuing statements such as "People received warnings from the Israelis and tried to evacuate... Hamas shot some of those people... The rest were forced to return to their homes and get bombed"; "Hamas imposed a curfew: anyone walking out in the street was shot without being asked any questions. That way Hamas made sure people had to stay in their homes even if they were about to get bombed"; and "My father received a text-message from the Israeli army warning him that our area was going to be bombed, and Hamas prevented us from leaving."

Rocket attacks on Israeli civilians

Human rights organizations, including Amnesty International, pointed to Hamas's rocket attacks on Israeli cities as violations of international law and war crimes. Palestinian ambassador to the UN Human Rights Council, Ibrahim Khraishi stated in a 9 July interview on PA TV that the "missiles that are now being launched against Israel – each and every missile constitutes a crime against humanity, whether it hits or misses, because it is directed at civilian targets".

Hamas political figure Khaled Mashaal has defended the firing of rockets into Israel, saying that "our victims are civilians and theirs are soldiers".[2148] According to one report, "nearly all the 2,500–3,000 rockets and mortars Hamas has fired at Israel since the start of the war seem to have been aimed at towns", including an attack on "a kibbutz collective farm close to the Gaza border", in which an Israeli child was killed. Former Israeli Lt. Col. Jonathan D. Halevi stated that "Hamas has expressed pride in aiming long-range rockets at

Figure 274: *House destroyed by a rocket in Yehud.*

strategic targets in Israel including the nuclear reactor in Dimona, the chemical plants in Haifa, and Ben-Gurion Airport", which "could have caused thousands" of Israeli casualties "if successful".

According to Israel, Hamas continued to fire rockets at the Erez border crossing while sick and wounded Gazans tried to enter Israel for treatment. The Erez border crossing is the only legal border crossing between Gaza and Israel. Other people affected by this included journalists, UN workers, and volunteers.[2149,2150]

Military use of UN facilities

The United Nations Relief and Works Agency for Palestine Refugees in the Near East (UNRWA) has a number of institutions and schools in the Gaza region, and, as of 24 July 23 had been closed. Hamas took advantage of the closures to employ some of these vacant UNRWA buildings as weapon storage sites.[2151] UNRWA officials, on discovering that three[2152,2153] such vacated schools had been employed for storing rockets, condemned Hamas's actions, calling it a "flagrant violation of the neutrality of our premises."[2154]

On 16 July, 22 July, and on 29 July, UNRWA announced that rockets had been found in their schools. Israel's foreign minister Avigdor Lieberman stated that UNRWA had turned over some discovered rockets to Hamas. Israel Democracy Institute Vice President, Mordechai Kremnitzer, accused the UNRWA of war crimes for handing over the rockets, while Hebrew University Professor

Robbie Sabel stated that the UNRWA "had no legal obligation to hand the rockets over to Israel" and had little other choice in the matter.[2155] UNRWA states the armouries had been transferred to local police authorities under the Ramallah national unity government's authority, in accordance with "long-standing UN practice in UN humanitarian operations worldwide".[2156] UN Secretary Ban Ki-moon ordered an investigation.[2157]

On 30 July, the IDF said that they had discovered the entrance to a tunnel concealed inside a UNRWA medical clinic in Khan Yunis. The clinic was rigged with explosives, which then exploded and killed three Israeli soldiers. This report was later corrected by the Coordinator of Government Activities in the Territories, the military unit that implements government policies in the Palestinian areas, who later that day stated that despite its UNRWA sign, the site was not registered as belonging to UNRWA.

Intimidation of journalists

Israeli officials said Hamas intimidates journalists in Gaza. A French reporter said that he was "detained and interrogated by members of Hamas's al-Qassam Brigade" in Gaza's Al-Shifa hospital, and forced to leave Gaza; he later asked the newspaper to remove his article from their site.[2158,2159] Some journalists reported threats on social media against those who tweet about rocket launch sites. John Reed of *The Financial Times* was threatened after he tweeted about rockets being fired from near Al-Shifa Hospital, and RT correspondent Harry Fear was told to leave Gaza after he tweeted that Hamas fired rockets from near his hotel. Isra al-Modallal, head of foreign relations for the Hamas Information Ministry, said Hamas did deport foreign journalists who filmed Hamas rocket launches, stating that by filming the launch sites the journalists were collaborating with Israel.[2160,2161] The Foreign Press Association (FPA) in Israel and the Palestinian territories protested what it called "blatant, incessant, forceful and unorthodox methods employed by the Hamas authorities ... against visiting international journalists in Gaza", saying several had been harassed or questioned over information they reported. It also said that Hamas was trying to "put in place a 'vetting' procedure" that would allow the blacklisting of specific journalists. The *Jerusalem Post* said UNRWA workers were threatened by Hamas at gun-point during the war, but Christopher Gunness, UNRWA spokesman, said "I have checked and double checked with sources in Gaza and there is no evidence of death threats made to UNRWA personnel."

Some FPA members disputed the FPA's comments, including *New York Times* Jerusalem bureau chief Jodi Rudoren, who wrote "every reporter I've met who was in Gaza during [the] war says this Israeli/now FPA narrative of Hamas harassment is nonsense." *Haaretz* interviewed many foreign journalists and found "all but a few of the journalists deny any such pressure". They said

Hamas's intimidation was no worse than what they got from the IDF, and said no armed forces would permit reporters to broadcast militarily sensitive information; and that, furthermore, most reporters seldom saw Hamas fighters, because they fought from concealed locations and in places that were too dangerous to approach.[2162]

Alleged violations by Israel

Israel received some 500 complaints concerning 360 alleged violations. 80 were closed without criminal charges, 6 cases were opened on incidents allegedly involving criminal conduct, and in one case regarding 3 IDF soldiers in the aftermath of the Battle of Shuja'iyya, a charge of looting was laid. Most cases were closed for what the military magistrates considered to be lack of evidence to sustain a charge of misconduct. No mention was made of incidents during the "Black Friday" events at Rafah.[2163,2164]

According to Assaf Sharon of Tel Aviv University, the IDF was pressured by politicians to unleash unnecessary violence whose basic purpose was 'to satisfy a need for vengeance,' which the politicians themselves tried to whip up in Israel's population. Asa Kasher wrote that the IDF was pulled into fighting "that is both strategically and morally asymmetric" and that like any other army it made mistakes, but the charges it faces are "grossly unfair". The Israeli NGO Breaking the Silence, reporting on its analysis of 111 testimonies concerning the war by some 70 IDF soldiers and officers,[2165] cited one veteran's remark that "Anyone found in an IDF area, which the IDF had occupied, was not a civilian," to argue that this was the basic rule of engagement. Soldiers were briefed to regard everything inside the Strip as a threat. The report cites several examples of civilians, including women, being shot dead and defined as "terrorists" in later reports.[2166,2167] Since leaflets were dropped telling civilians to leave areas to be bombed, soldiers could assume any movement in a bombed area entitled them to shoot. In one case that came under investigation, Lt Col Neria Yeshurun ordered a Palestinian medical centre to be shelled to avenge the killing of one of his officers by a sniper.[2168]

Civilian deaths

Many of those killed were civilians, prompting concern from many humanitarian organisations. An investigation by Human Rights Watch concluded that Israel had probably committed war crimes on three specific incidents involving strikes on UNWRA schools.[2169] Amnesty International stated that: "Israeli forces have carried out attacks that have killed hundreds of civilians, including through the use of precision weaponry such as drone-fired missiles, and attacks using munitions such as artillery, which cannot be precisely targeted, on very densely populated residential areas, such as Shuja'iyya. They have also directly attacked civilian objects." B'tselem has compiled an infogram listing families killed at home in 72 incidents of bombing or shelling, comprising 547 people killed, of whom 125 were women under 60, 250 were minors, and 29 were over 60. On 24 August, Palestinian health officials said that 89 families had been killed.

Nine people were killed while watching the World Cup in a cafe, and 8 members of a family died that Israel has said were inadvertently killed. A Golani soldier interviewed about his operations inside Gaza said they often could not distinguish between civilians and Hamas fighters because some Hamas operatives dressed in plainclothes and the night vision goggles made everything look green. An IDF spokesperson said that Hamas "deploys in residential areas, creating rocket launch sites, command and control centers, and other positions deep in the heart of urban areas. By doing so, Hamas chooses the battleground where the IDF is forced to operate."[2170] The highest-ranking U.S. military officer, Army General Martin Dempsey, the chairman of the Joint Chiefs of Staff, said that "Israel went to extraordinary lengths to limit collateral damage and civilian casualties". Later in his speech he said, "the Pentagon three months ago sent a 'lessons-learned team' of senior officers and non-commissioned officers to work with the IDF to see what could be learned from the Gaza operation, to include the measures they took to prevent civilian casualties and what they did with tunneling." Col. Richard Kemp told The Observer "IDF has taken greater steps than any other army in the history of warfare to minimise harm to civilians in a combat zone"

Warnings prior to attacks

In many cases the IDF warned civilians prior to targeting militants in highly populated areas in order to comply with international law. Human rights organizations including Amnesty International, confirmed that in many cases, Palestinians received warnings prior to evacuation, including flyers, phone calls and roof knocking. A report by Jaffa based NGO Physicians for Human Rights, released in January 2015, said that Israel's alert system had failed, and that the roof-knock system was ineffective.[2171] The IDF was criticized for not giving civilians enough time to evacuate. In one case, the warning came less than one minute before the bombing. Hamas has told civilians to return to their homes or stay put following Israeli warnings to leave. In many cases, Palestinians evacuated; in others, they have stayed in their homes. Israel condemned Hamas's encouragement of Palestinians to remain in their homes despite warnings in advance of airstrikes. Hamas stated that the warnings were a form of psychological warfare and that people would be equally or more unsafe in the rest of Gaza.

Amnesty International said that "although the Israeli authorities claim to be warning civilians in Gaza, a consistent pattern has emerged that their actions

Figure 275: *Ruins of a residential area in Beit Hanoun.*

do not constitute an "effective warning" under international humanitarian law." Human Rights Watch concurred. Many Gazans, when asked, told journalists that they remained in their houses simply because they had nowhere else to go. OCHA's spokesman has said "there is literally no safe place for civilians" in Gaza.[2172] Roof knocking has been condemned as unlawful by Amnesty International and Human Rights Watch as well as the United Nations Fact Finding Mission in the 2008 war.

Destruction of homes

Israel targeted many homes in this conflict. UNWRA official Robert Turner estimated that 7,000 homes were demolished and 89,000 were damaged, some 10,000 of them severely.[2173] This has led to many members of the same family being killed. B'Tselem documented 59 incidents of bombing and shelling, in which 458 people were killed. In some cases, Israel has stated that these homes were of suspected militants and were used for military purposes. *The New York Times* noted that the damage in this operation was higher than in the previous two wars and stated that 60,000 people had been left homeless as a result. The destruction of homes has been condemned by B'Tselem, Human Rights Watch and Amnesty International as unlawful, amounting to collective punishment and war crimes.

Israel destroyed the homes of two suspects in the case of the abduction and killing of the three teenagers. The house demolition has been condemned by B'Tselem as unlawful.

Palestinians returning to their homes during the ceasefire reported that IDF soldiers had trashed their homes, destroyed home electronics such as TV sets, spread feces in their homes, and carved slogans such as "Burn Gaza down" and "Good Arab = dead Arab" in walls and furniture. The IDF did not respond to a request by *The Guardian* for comment.

On 5 November 2014, Amnesty International published a report examining eight cases where the IDF targeted homes, resulting in the deaths of 111 people, of whom 104 were civilians. Barred from access to Gaza by Israel since 2012, it conducted its research remotely, supported by two contracted Gaza-based fieldworkers who conducted multiple visits of each site to interview survivors, and consulted with military experts to evaluate photographic and video material. It concludes, in every case, that "there was a failure to take necessary precautions to avoid excessive harm to civilians and civilian property, as required by international humanitarian law" and "no prior warning was given to the civilian residents to allow them to escape." As Israel did not disclose any information regarding the incidents, the report said it was not possible for Amnesty International to be certain of what Israel was targeting; it also said that if there were no valid military objectives, international humanitarian law may have been violated, as attacks directed at civilians and civilian objects, or attacks which are otherwise disproportionate relative to the anticipated military advantage of carrying them out, constitute war crimes.

The report was dismissed by the Israeli Ministry of Foreign Affairs as "narrow", "decontextualized", and disattentive of alleged war crimes perpetrated by Hamas. Amnesty, it asserted, was serving as "a propaganda tool for Hamas and other terror groups." Anne Herzberg, legal adviser for NGO Monitor, questioned the accuracy of the UN numbers used in the report, saying that they "essentially come from Hamas."

Shelling of UNRWA schools

There were seven shellings at UNRWA facilities in the Gaza Strip which took place between 21 July and 3 August 2014. The incidents were the result of artillery, mortar or aerial missile fire which struck on or near the UNRWA facilities being used as shelters for Palestinians, and as a result at least 44 civilians, including 10 UN staff, died. During the 2014 Israel-Gaza conflict, many Palestinians fled their homes after warnings by Israel or due to air strikes or fighting in the area. An estimated 290,000 people (15% of Gaza's population) took shelter in UNRWA schools.

On three separate occasions, on 16 July, 22 July and on 29 July, UNRWA announced that rockets had been found in their schools. UNRWA denounced the groups responsible for "flagrant violations of the neutrality of its premises". All of these schools were vacant at the time when rockets were discovered; no rockets were found in any shelters which were shelled. The Israel Defense Forces (IDF) stated that "Hamas chooses where these battles are conducted and, despite Israel's best efforts to prevent civilian casualties, Hamas is ultimately responsible for the tragic loss of civilian life. Specifically in the case of UN facilities, it is important to note the repeated abuse of UN facilities by Hamas, namely with at least three cases of munitions storage within such facilities."[2174]

The attacks were condemned by members of the UN (UNRWA's parent organization) and other governments, such as the U.S., have expressed "extreme concern" over the safety of Palestinian civilians who "are not safe in UN-designated shelters." The Rafah shelling in particular was widely criticized, with Ban Ki-moon calling it a "moral outrage and a criminal act" and US State Department calling it "appalling" and "disgraceful". UN High Commissioner for Human Rights Navi Pillay said that both Hamas militants and Israel might have committed war crimes. A Human Rights Watch investigation into three of the incidents concluded that Israel committed war crimes because two of the shellings "did not appear to target a military objective or were otherwise indiscriminate", while the third Rafah shelling was "unlawfully disproportionate". On April 27, 2015, the United Nations released an inquiry which concluded that Israel was responsible for the deaths of at least 44 Palestinians who died in the shelling and 227 were injured.

Infrastructure

On 23 July, twelve human rights organizations in Israel released a letter to Israeli government warning that "Gaza Strip's civilian infrastructure is collapsing". They wrote that "due to Israel's ongoing control over significant aspects of life in Gaza, Israel has a legal obligation to ensure that the humanitarian needs of the people of Gaza are met and that they have access to adequate supplies of water and electricity." They note that many water and electricity systems were damaged during the conflict, which has led to a "pending humanitarian and environmental catastrophe". The Sydney Morning Herald reported that "almost every piece of critical infrastructure, from electricity to water to sewage, has been seriously compromised by either direct hits from Israeli air strikes and shelling or collateral damage."

Between five and eight of the 10 power lines that bring electricity from Israel were disabled, at least three by Hamas rocket fire. On 29 July, Israel was reported to bomb Gaza's only power plant, which was estimated to take a year to repair. Amnesty International said the crippling of the power station amounted to "collective punishment of Palestinians". Human Rights Watch has stated that "[d]amaging or destroying a power plant, even if it also served a military purpose, would be an unlawful disproportionate attack under the laws of war". Israel immediately denied damaging the power plant, stating there was "no indication that [IDF] were involved in the strike ... The area surrounding the plant was also not struck in recent days." Contradicting initial reports that it would take a year to repair, the power plant resumed operation on 27 October.

Attacks on journalists

17 journalists were killed in the conflict, of which five were off-duty and two (from Associated Press) were covering a bomb disposal team's efforts to defuse an unexploded Israeli artillery shell when it exploded. In several cases, the journalists were killed while having markings distinguishing them as press on their vehicles or clothing. IDF stated that in one case it had precise information that a vehicle marked "TV" that was hit killing one alleged journalist was in military use. Several media outlets, including the offices of *Al-Jazeera*, were hit. The International Federation of Journalists has condemned the attacks as "appalling murders and attacks". Journalists are considered civilians and should not be targeted under international humanitarian law. The Israeli army said it does not target journalists, and that it contacts news media "in order to advise them which areas to avoid during the conflict". Israel has made foreign journalists sign a waiver stating that it is not responsible for their safety in Gaza, which Reporters Without Borders calls contrary to international law. The Director-General of UNESCO, Irina Bokova, who in August 2014 condemned the killing of Al Aqsa TV journalist Abdullah Murtaja, withdrew her comments after it was revealed that Murtaja was also a combatant in Hamas's Al Qassam Brigade, and said she "deplore[d] attempts to instrumentalize the profession of journalists by combatants"

ITIC published a report analyzing a list of 17 names published by Wafa News Agency based on information originating from Hamas-controlled Gaza office of the ministry of information that supposedly belong to journalists killed in the operation. The report says that 8 of the names belong to Hamas or Islamic Jihad operatives, or employees of the Hamas media.

Israel bombed Hamas's Al-Aqsa radio and TV stations because of their "propaganda dissemination capabilities used to broadcast the messages of (Hamas's) military wing." Reporters Without Borders and Al-Haq condemned the attacks, saying "an expert committee formed by the International Criminal Court's prosecutor for the former Yugoslavia, to assess the NATO bombing campaign of 1999, specified that a journalist or media organization is not a legitimate target merely because it broadcasts or disseminates propaganda." The U.S. government classifies Al-Aqsa TV as being controlled by Hamas, a "Specially Designated Global Terrorist," and states that it "will not distinguish between a business financed and controlled by a terrorist group, such as Al-Aqsa Television, and the terrorist group itself."[2175] Wikipedia:No original research

Human shields

The UN High Commissioner for Human Rights Navi Pillay accused Israel of having "defied international law by attacking civilian areas of Gaza such as schools, hospitals, homes and U.N. facilities. "None of this appears to me to be accidental," Pillay said. "They appear to be defying — deliberate defiance of — obligations that international law imposes on Israel."" The Jaffa based NGO Physicians for Human Rights stated in a report in January 2015 that the IDF had used human shields during the war. IDF criticized the report's conclusions and methodology which "cast a heavy shadow over its content and credibility".[2176] Defense for Children International-Palestine reported that 17-year-old Ahmad Abu Raida was kidnapped by Israeli soldiers who, after beating him up, used him as a human shield for five days, forcing him to walk in front of them with police dogs at gunpoint, search houses and dig in places soldiers suspected there might be tunnels.[2177,2178] Several of the key claims could not be verified because his Hamas-employed father said he forgot to take photographs of the alleged abuse marks and discarded all the clothing IDF soldiers supposedly provided Abu Raida when he was freed.[2179]

The IDF confirmed that the troops suspected Ahmad of being a militant based on the affiliation of his father (a senior official in Gaza's Tourism Ministry) with Hamas and so detained him during the ground operation. The IDF and Israeli authorities challenged the credibility of DCI-P noting their "scant regard for truth". The IDF Military Advocate General opened criminal investigation into the event.

Military operations, weaponry and techniques

Gaza

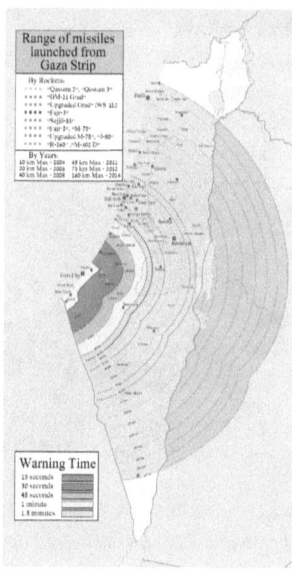

Figure 276: *Range of rockets launched from Gaza Strip*

Rockets

The rockets used by Gazan militias vary in range, size and lethality. They include the Syrian-made (Chinese-designed) M-302[2180] and the locally-made M-75, which have the range to target Tel-Aviv.[2181,2182,2183,2184] Other rockets include the Soviet Katyushas and Qassams.[2185] The Israeli Defense Force reported that at the beginning of the 2014 conflict, Hamas had close to 6,000 rockets in its possession. This included 1,000 self-produced short range rockets (15–20 km range), 2,500 smuggled short range rockets, 200 self-made Grad rockets, and 200 smuggled Grad rockets. In addition, to these short range rockets, Hamas held an assortment of mid and long range rockets, both self-made and smuggled, that totaled over several thousand.[2186]

According to the Fars News Agency, Fajr-5 (long range Iranian) rockets have a warhead of 150–200 kg.[2187] According to Theodore Postol, the vast majority of Gazan artillery rocket warheads contain 10- to 20-pound explosive loads. Postol states that this fact makes bomb shelters more effective for protection. Mark Perry states that the "vast majority of the rockets are unsophisticated Qassams, with a 10-20 kg warhead and no guidance system". He also stated that "Hamas' arsenal is considerably weaker today than it was in 2012". Regarding the Fajr-5, he stated that Iran had not transferred full-fledged rockets to Hamas, it only transferred technology to manufacture them. He also stated that "its guidance system was crude, at best, and its warhead nearly non-existent."

Figure 277: *IDF soldier overlooking an uncovered tunnel in the Gaza Strip*

The UNHRC, quoting Amnesty International, states that armed groups in Gaza have used BM-21 Grad rockets with ranges varying from 20 km to 48 km, in addition to locally produced rockets reaching as far as 80 km, such as the M-75 and J-80. The majority of the rockets have no guidance system. Mortars having a range of up to 8 km, have been actively used along the Green Line. Other weapons include rocket-propelled grenades, home-made drones, SA 7 Grail anti-aircraft missiles, Kornet 9M133 anti-tank guided missiles, and a wide array of small arms, rifles, machine guns and hand grenades.

According to the IDF, of all the 4,564 projectiles fired at Israel, 224 hit built-up areas, 735 were intercepted by the Iron Dome, 875 fell inside Gaza[2188] and the rest fell in open territory or failed to launch.

According to OCHA, Palestinian militants fired 4,844 rockets and 1,734 mortar shells towards Israel.[2189] 25% of Gazan rockets had sufficient effectiveness to threaten to reach populated areas.[2190]

Gazan tunnels

Hamas, the governing authority in the Gaza Strip, has constructed a sophisticated network of military tunnels since it seized control of the Strip in 2007. The tunnel system branches beneath many Gazan towns and cities, such as Khan Yunis, Jabalia and the Shati refugee camp. The internal tunnels, running some dozens of kilometres within the Gaza Strip, have several functions. Hamas uses the tunnels to hide its arsenal of rocketry underground, to facilitate communication, to permit munition stocks to be hidden and to conceal militants, making detection from the air difficult.[2191] Hamas leader Khalid Meshal has said in an interview with Vanity Fair that their tunnel system is a defensive structure designed to place obstacles against Israel's powerful military arsenal, to protect its people, and engage in counter-strikes against the IDF when Gaza is attacked, and that it has never caused the death of civilians, being safer than their system of unguidable missiles which are not intended to threaten civilians but strike indiscriminately.[2192]

The cross-border tunnels were used in the capture of Gilad Shalit in 2006, and multiple times during the 2014 conflict.[2193] Destroying the tunnels was a primary objective of Israeli forces in the 2014 conflict. The IDF reported that it "neutralized" 32 tunnels, fourteen of which crossed into Israel. On at least four occasions during the conflict, Palestinian militants crossing the border through the tunnels engaged in combat with Israeli soldiers. In practice, only Israeli military targets have successfully been attacked through them.[2194] The UNHRC Commission of Inquiry on the Gaza Conflict found "the tunnels were only used to conduct attacks directed at IDF positions in Israel in the vicinity of the Green Line, which are legitimate military targets." Israeli officials condemned the UNHRC report.

The UN Commission of Inquiry found the tunnels "caused great anxiety among Israelis that the tunnels might be used to attack civilians." Ihab al-Ghussein, spokesman for the Hamas-run interior ministry, describes the tunnels as an exercise of Gaza's "right to protect itself."

Israeli officials reported four "incidents in which members of Palestinian armed groups emerged from tunnel exits located between 1.1 and 4.7 km from civilian homes."[2195] The Israeli government refers to cross-border tunnels as "attack tunnels" or "terror tunnels." According to Israel, the tunnels enabled the launch of rockets by remote control,[2196] and were intended to facilitate hostage-taking and mass-casualty attacks.[2197]

Other weaponry

Hamas has also used a "crude, tactical" drone, reported to be Iranian-made and named "Ababil-1".

Palestinian militant groups have also used anti-tank rockets against armoured vehicles, as well as against groups of Israeli soldiers. Some armored personnel carriers were hit by missiles, and the Israeli Trophy system reportedly intercepted at least 15 anti-tank missiles shot at Merkava IV tanks. Anti-tank mines had also been used against armored vehicles.

Figure 278: *IDF Artillery Corps fires a 155 mm M109 howitzer, 24 July 2014*

Israel

Israel used air, land and naval weaponry. The artillery includes Soltam M71 guns and US-manufactured Paladin M109s (155-mm howitzers). The aerial weaponry includes drones and F-16 fighter jets. Drones are used to constantly monitor the Gaza strip.[2198,2199] The IDF fired 14,500 tank shells and 35,000 other artillery shells during the conflict.

The IDF stated that it attacked 5,263 targets in Gaza, including:

- 1,814 rocket and mortar launch or otherwise related sites
- 191 weapon factories and warehouses
- 1,914 command and control centers
- 237 government institutions supporting the militant activity
- hundreds of military outposts inside buildings

According to OCHA figures, Israel fired 5,830 missiles in 4,028 IAF air raids, the IDF's ground forces shot off 16,507 artillery and tank projectiles, and the Israeli navy's off-shore fleet fired 3,494 naval shells, into the Gaza Strip.

Overall, Israel fired 34,000 unguided shells into Gaza. Of these 19,000 were high-explosive artillery shells, marking a 533% rise in the launching of artillery ordnance compared to Operation Cast Lead. Shelling of civilian areas with 155 mm (6.1 in) shells using Doher howitzers, with a kill radius of 150 yards (140 m), also increased.[2200,2201]

According to Palestinian authorities, 8,000 bombs and 70,000 artillery shells, or 20,000 tons of explosives (the equivalent of two low-yield tactical nuclear weapons), had been dropped on Gaza.[2202] The Sydney Morning Herald quoted an anonymous expert who estimated that 10,000 tonnes of explosives were dropped from the air alone, which does not include tank and artillery shells.

Between 32 and 34 known tunnels were destroyed or neutralized, 13 of them destroyed completely.

The performance of the Iron Dome defense system was considered effective, achieving an almost 90% success rate.[2203] Israel's early warning sirens and extensive shelters have been an effective defense against Gazan rocketry.[2204] They are less effective against short-range mortars because the residents have less time to react.

Media coverage

Portrayals of the conflict in different media outlets varied. U.S. news sources were often more sympathetic to Israel while British news sources featured more criticism of Israel. Commentators on both sides claimed that the media was biased either for or against Israel. According to an article by Subrata Ghoshroy published in the Bulletin of the Atomic Scientists, most United States media focused on Hamas rockets, of which only 3% actually strike populated areas (causing little damage), with less attention paid to Palestinian casualties, or to why Gazans back Hamas's rocket campaign.[2205] As the conflict progressed and Palestinian deaths increased, British media became somewhat more critical of Israel. Within Israel, the newspaper *Haaretz* issued an editorial stating that the "soft Gaza sand... could turn into quicksand" for the Israeli military and also warned about the "wholesale killing" of Palestinian civilians; the article declared: "There can be no victory here". The *Sydney Morning Herald* apologised for running an allegedly antisemitic cartoon after Australian Attorney-General George Brandis denounced it as "deplorable."[2206] Israel was accused of waging a propaganda war, and on both sides, sympathetic authors released video games relating to the conflict. In Israel, according to Naomi Chazan, the Gaza war sparked "an equally momentous conflagration at the heart of Israeli society": attempts to question government policy were met with severe verbal and physical harassment, incidents of Arab-bashing occurred daily, and 90% of internet posts on the war were found to be racist or to constitute incitement.[2207]

Figure 279: *U.S. Secretary of State John Kerry and Benjamin Netanyahu, Tel Aviv, 23 July 2014*

Diplomatic efforts

A number of diplomatic efforts were made to resolve the conflict. These attempts included efforts by United States Secretary of State John Kerry to broker a ceasefire between Israel and Hamas, like the meeting in Paris with European G4 foreign ministers and his counterparts of Qatar and Turkey.[2208] Egypt brokered a number of ceasefires between Hamas and Israel.

Efforts to reconstruct Gaza

An international conference took place on 12 October 2014 in Cairo, where donors pledged US$5.4 billion to the Palestinians with half of that sum being "dedicated" to the reconstruction of Gaza, which was more than the US$4 billion Abbas first sought. Japan pledged US$100 million in January 2015. The EU pledged €450 million to rebuilding Gaza.

As of 1 February 2015, only US$125 million of the $2.7 billion for reconstruction had been paid out, leaving tens of thousands of Gazans still homeless. In February 2015, 30 international aid organizations including UNRWA, the World Health Organization as well as NGOs such as Oxfam, ActionAid and Save the Children International released a statement saying that: "we are alarmed by the limited progress in rebuilding the lives of those affected and tackling the root causes of the conflict." They stated that "Israel, as the occupying power, is the main duty bearer and must comply with its obligations under international law. In particular, it must fully lift the blockade within the framework of United Nations Security Council Resolution 1860 (2009)". Catherine Weibel, UNICEF's Communication Chief in Jerusalem said: "Four infants died from complications caused by the bitter cold in Gaza in January... All were from families whose houses were destroyed during the last conflict and were living in extremely dire conditions."

Only one percent of the needed building material had been delivered. The mechanism agreed between Hamas and the Palestinian Authority, meant to allow delivery of such material, have not worked.

Hamas spokesman blamed Israel for causing an electricity crisis. Israel provided 50,000 liters of fuel for generators running during blackouts and repaired three power lines damaged during storms within a week.

On 15 September 2014, a Fatah spokesperson accused Hamas of misappropriating US$700 million of funds intended to rebuild Gaza. On 6 January Hamas spokesperson said that Palestinian national consensus government ministers admitted redirecting rebuilding funds to PNA budget. Israel's military estimated that 20% of cement and steel allowed by Israel to be delivered to Gaza for the reconstruction efforts were taken by Hamas. Arne Gericke, a member of the European Parliament said "It would sicken most [European] taxpayers to know that the EU itself could be directly contributing to the tragic cycle of violence".

External links

Wikimedia Commons has media related to *Operation Protective Edge*.

- Gaza-Israel conflict: Is the fighting over?[2209]. BBC News Online
- Operation Protective Edge[2210]. Israel Defense Forces
- Gaza: Two Years since the 2014 hostilities[2211]. United Nations Office for the Coordination of Humanitarian Affairs
- The 2014 Gaza Conflict: Factual and Legal Aspects[2212]. Israel Ministry of Foreign Affairs
- Gaza truce: Is there a winner?[2213] Al Jazeera English
- Operation Protective Edge[2214]. Jewish Virtual Library
- Protective Edge Stats[2215]. Google Docs, Sheets and Slides

Appendix

References

[1] Oren 2003, p. 5.
[2] Morris, Benny (2008), *1948: The First Arab-Israeli War* https://books.google.com/books?id= CC7381HrLqcC&pg=PA332&lpg=PA332, Yale University Press, p.205, New Haven, .
[3] Anita Shapira, *L'imaginaire d'Israël : histoire d'une culture politique* (2005), *Latroun : la mémoire de la bataille*, Chap. III. 1 l'événement pp. 91–96
[4] Benny Morris (2008), p. 419.
[5] Morris, 2008, p. 332.
[6] This includes the entire military personnel count – both combat units and logistical units.<ref name = "Gelber12">Gelber (2006), p. 12.
[7] Pollack, 2004; Sadeh, 1997
[8] At maximum, not half of the forces of the Israelis but these numbers include only the combat units sent to the former mandate-territory of Palestine, not the entire military strength. UNIQ-ref-0-4ba7306c809995b7-QINU
[9] Morris 2008, pp. 404–06.
[10] David Tal, *War in Palestine, 1948: Israeli and Arab Strategy and Diplomacy*, p. 153.
[11] Benny Morris (2008), p. 401.
[12] Zeev Maoz, *Defending the Holy Land*, University of Michigan Press, 2009 p. 4: 'A combined invasion of a Jordanian and Egyptian army started ... The Syrian and the Lebanese armies engaged in a token effort but did not stage a major attack on the Jewish state.'
[13] Rogan and Shlaim 2007 p. 99.
[14] Cragg 1997 pp. 57, 116.
[15] Benvenisti, Meron (1996), *City of Stone: The Hidden History of Jerusalem*, University of California Press, . p. 27
[16] Morris, 2001, pp. 259–60.
[17] Morris, 2008, pp. 66–69
[18] UNITED NATIONS: General Assembly: A/RES/181(II): 29 November 1947: Resolution 181 (II). Future government of Palestine. http://domino.un.org/unispal.nsf/0/7f0af2bd897689b785256c330061d253
[19] Greg Cashman, Leonard C. Robinson, *An Introduction to the Causes of War: Patterns of Interstate Conflict from World War 1 to Iraq*, https://books.google.com/books?id= x7K2GYnXRngC&pg=PA165 Rowman & Littlefield 2007 p. 165.
[20] Benjamin Grob-Fitzgibbon, *Imperial Endgame: Britain's Dirty Wars and the End of Empire*, https://books.google.com/books?id=NUeYAAAAQBAJ&pg=PT57 Palgrave/Macmillan 2011 p. 57
[21] Ilan Pappé (2000), p. 111
[22] Morris 2008, p. 76
[23] Efraïm Karsh (2002), p. 30
[24] Benny Morris (2003), p. 101
[25] Yoav Gelber (2006), pp. 51–56
[26] Dominique Lapierre et Larry Collins (1971), chap. 7, pp. 131–53
[27] Benny Morris (2003), p. 163
[28] Dominique Lapierre et Larry Collins (1971), p. 163
[29] Benny Morris (2003), p. 67
[30] Henry Laurens (2005), p. 83
[31] David Tal, *War in Palestine, 1948: Israeli and Arab Strategy and Diplomacy,* Routledge 2004 p. 89.
[32] David Tal, pp. 89–90.
[33] Dominique Lapierre et Larry Collins (1971), pp. 369–81
[34] Benny Morris (2003), pp. 242–43
[35] Benny Morris (2003), p. 242

[36] Henry Laurens (2005), pp. 85–86
[37] Benny Morris (2003), pp. 248–52
[38] Benny Morris (2003), pp. 252–54
[39] Martin Van Creveld, *Sword and the Olive: A Critical History of the Israeli Defense Force*, Public Affairs (1998) 2002 p. 78
[40]
[41] Gelber, p. 73; Karsh 2002, p. 25.
[42] W. Khalidi, 'Plan Dalet: Master Plan for the Conquest of Palestine', J. Palestine Studies 18(1), pp. 4–33, 1988 (reprint of a 1961 article)
[43] Joseph, Dov. "The Faithful City – The Siege of Jerusalem, 1948." Simon and Suchuster, 1960. Congress # 60 10976. pp. 23, 38.
[44] Levin, Harry. "Jerusalem Embattled – A Diary of the City under Siege." Cassels, 1997. pp. 32, 117. Pay £P2 per month. c.f. would buy 2lb of meat in Jerusalem, April 1948. p. 91.
[45] Benny Morris (2004), p. 16
[46] Gelber (2006), p. 73
[47] D. Kurzman, "Genesis 1948", 1970, p. 282.
[48] Henry Laurens, *La Question de Palestine*, vol.3, Fayard 2007 p. 70
[49] Morris, 2008, pp. 397–98.
[50] Moshe Naor,*Social Mobilization in the Arab/Israeli War of 1948: On the Israeli Home Front*, Routledge 2013 p. 15.
[51] Pappe, Ilan. *The Ethnic Cleansing of Palestine*.
[52] Pappé, 2006, pp.xii, 86–126
[53] Gelber 2006 p. 306
[54] Morris 2008 p. 119
[55] Gelber (2006), p. 11
[56] Henry Laurens, *La Question de Palestine*, Fayard, 2007 p. 32.
[57] Gelber (2006), p. 11.
[58] Morris 2008 p. 187; quoting p. 24 of Kirkbride's memoirs https://books.google.com/books?id=i8FcAgAAQBAJ&pg=PA24
[59]
[60] Rogan and Shlaim 2007 p. 110.
[61] Morris, 2008, p. 310
[62] Sela, 2002, p. 14.
[63] Morris (2008), pp. 190–92
[64] Tal,*War in Palestine, 1948: Israeli and Arab Strategy and Diplomacy*, p. 154.
[65] Zamir, 2010, p. 34
[66] Tripp, 2001, p. 137.
[67] Morris, 2004 pp. 76, 82, 104, 126, 130, 202, 253
[68] Shlaim, 2001, p. 97.
[69] Shlaim, 2001, p. 99.
[70] Benny Morris (2003), p. 189.
[71] Martin Van Creveld,*Sword and the Olive: A Critical History of the Israeli Defense Force,*, Public Affairs (1998) 2002 p. 75
[72] Morris (2003), pp. 32–33.
[73] Morris (2008), p. 81.
[74] Benny (2008), p. 174.
[75] Martin Van Creveld, *Sword and the Olive: A Critical History of the Israeli Defense Force*, https://books.google.com/books?id=baa0OKb51rIC&pg=PA80, Public Affairs (1998) 2002 p. 78
[76] Morris 2008 p. 185
[77] Morris, 2003, p. 35.
[78] Morris, 2008, p. 401
[79] Collins and LaPierre, 1973 p. 355
[80] Morgan, Michael L.:*The Philosopher as Witness: Fackenheim and Responses to the Holocaust*, p. 182

[81] Ben Gurion, David *War Diaries, 1947–1949*. Arabic edition translated by Samir Jabbour. Institute of Palestine Studies, Beirut, 1994. p. 303.
[82] Later, in the midst of the war, Yitzhak Rabin was succeeded by Joseph Tebenkin who led Operation Ha-Har.
[83] Morris, 2008: pp. 176–77
[84] Laffin, John: *The Israeli Army in the Middle East Wars 1948–73*, p. 8
[85] Laurens, vol. 3 p. 69.
[86] Gelber (2006), p. 50.
[87] Ma'an Abu Nawar, *The Jordanian-Israeli war, 1948–1951: a history of the Hashemite Kingdom of Jordan*, p. 393.
[88] Benny Morris, *Victimes : histoire revisitée du conflit arabo-sioniste*, 2003, pp. 241, 247–55.
[89] Pollack 2004, p. ?.
[90] D. Kurzman, 'Genesis 1948', 1972, p. 382.
[91] I. Pappe, "The ethnic cleansing of Palestine", 2006, p. 129.
[92] Pollack, 2002, pp. 149–55.
[93] Yoav Gelber, 2006, "Sharon's Inheritance" http://www.aisisraelstudies.org/2006papers/Gelber%20Yoav%202006.pdf
[94] Rogan and Shlaim 2001, p. 8.
[95] Pollack, 2002, pp. 15–27.
[96] D. Kurzman, "Genesis 1948", 1972, p. 556.
[97] Pollack, 2002, p. 150.
[98] Gelber, p. 55
[99] Morris, 2008, pp. 322 and 326.
[100] Uthman Hasan Salih. *DAWR AL-MAMLAKA AL-'ARABIYYA AL-SA'UDIYYA FI HARB FI-LASTIN 1367H/1948* (The role of Saudi Arabia in the Palestine war of 1948), Revue d'Histoire Maghrébine [Tunisia] 1986 13(43–44): 201–21.
[101] Morris, 2008, p. 205; cites British diplomatic communications.
[102] Gelber, p. 200
[103] Gelber, p. 203
[104] Gelber, p. 239
[105] Morris, 2008, p. 269.
[106] Yoav Gelber, *Palestine 1948*, 2006 – Chap. 8 "The Arab Regular Armies' Invasion of Palestine".
[107] Sean F. McMahon,*The Discourse of Palestinian-Israeli Relations: Persistent Analytics and Practices,* Routledge 2010 p. 37: "If it wasn't for the Arab invasion there would have been no stop to the expansion of the forces of Haganah who could have, with the same drive, reached the natural borders of western Israel". Walid Khalidi, "Plan Dalet: Master Plan for the Conquest of Palestine," *Journal of Palestine Studies*, Vol. 18, No. 1, Special Issue: Palestine 1948, (Autumn,1988), pp. 4–33, p. 19.
[108] Yoav Gelber (2006), p. 130.
[109] Morris, 2008, p. 263
[110] Wallach et al. (Volume 2, 1978), p. 29
[111] Tal, 2004, p. 179
[112] Morris, 2008, p. 239
[113] tal 2004 p. 182
[114] *War in Palestine, 1948: Israeli and Arab Strategy and Diplomacy. David Tal.*
[115] Morris, 2008, pp. 229–30
[116] (Benny (2008), "1948: The First Arab-Israeli War", Yale University Press, New Haven,).Mordechai Weingarten
[117] *The Palestine Post: State of Israel is Born* (1948)
[118] Pollack 2002, pp. 448–57
[119] Morris, 2008, pp. 253–54
[120] Tal, 2004, pp. 251
[121] Morris (2008), p. 261
[122] Morris, 2008, p. 235
[123] Morris, 2001, pp. 217–18.

[124] Morris, 2008, p. 262.
[125] Aloni, 2001, pp. 7–11.
[126] Gershoni, pp. 46–47
[127] Gelber, 2004, Kinneret, p.220
[128] Morris, 2008, pp. 269–71
[129] Bregman, 2002, p. 24 citing Ben Gurion's diary of the war
[130] Security Council, S/1025, 5 October 1948, REPORT BY THE UNITED NATIONS, MEDIATOR ON THE OBSERVATION OF THE TRUCE IN, PALESTINE DURING THE PERIOD FROM 11 JUNE, TO 9 JULY 1948 https://unispal.un.org/UNISPAL.NSF/0/7D468BBE932AC79C802564C00037B882 , During the period of the truce, three violations occurred ... of such a serious nature... the *Altalena* incident, the Negeb convoys, and the question of the water supply to Jerusalem.... 1. the attempt by ...the Irgun Zvai Leumi to bring war materials and immigrants, including men of military age, into Palestine aboard the ship *Altalena* on 21 June... 2. Another truce violation occurred through the refusal of Egyptian forces to permit the passage of relief convoys to Jewish settlements in the Negeb... 3. The third violation of the truce arose as a result of the failure of the Transjordan and Iraqi forces to permit the flow of water to Jerusalem.
[131] Alfred A. Knopf. *A History of Israel from the Rise of Zionism to Our Time.* New York. 1976. p. 330.
[132] Gelber, 2006, Kinneret, p.226
[133] Gideon Levy and Alex Levac, 'Drafting the blueprint for Palestinian refugees' right of return,' http://www.haaretz.com/weekend/twilight-zone/1.550550 at Haaretz 4 October 2013: 'In all the Arab villages in the south almost nobody fought. The villagers were so poor, so miserable, that they didn't even have weapons ... The flight of these residents began when we started to clean up the routes used by those accompanying the convoys. Then we began to expel them, and in the end they fled on their own.'
[134] David Tal, *War in Palestine, 1948: Israeli and Arab Strategy and Diplomacy*, Routledge 2004 p. 307.
[135] Herzog and Gazit, 2005, p. 86
[136] Lorch, Netanel (1998). *History of the War of Independence*
[137] Kadish, Alon, and Sela, Avraham. (2005) "Myths and historiography of the 1948 Palestine War revisited: the case of Lydda," *The Middle East Journal*, 22 September 2005; and Khalidi, Walid. (1998) Introduction to Munayyer, Spiro. The fall of Lydda https://web.archive.org/web/20110718144237/http://www.palestine-studies.org/enakba/Memoirs/Munayyer,%20The%20Fall%20of%20Lydda.pdf. *Journal of Palestine Studies*, Vol. 27, No. 4, pp. 80–98.
[138] Map of the Attacks http://www.allthatremains.com/Maps/IsraeliMiliteryDuringTheTruce07-08-48-To-07-18-48.jpg.
[139] A. Ilan, *Bernadotte in Palestine*, 1948 (Macmillan, 1989) p. 194
[140] J. Bowyer Bell, Assassination in International Politics, *International Studies Quarterly*, vol. 16, March 1972, pp. 59–82.
[141] Review of Kati Marton's biography.
[142] Shapira, Anita. Yigal Allon; Native Son; A Biography Translated by Evelyn Abel, University of Pennsylvania Press p. 247
[143] Gelber, 2006, p. 33
[144] Shlomo Ben-Ami (Shlomo Ben-Ami (2006), pp. 41–42)
[145] Morris 2008, p. 404
[146] Aloni, 2001, p. 18.
[147] Aloni, 2001, p. 22.
[148] Cohen, Michael Joseph: *Truman and Israel* (1990)
[149] Adrian, p. 7
[150] Adrian, p. 59
[151] L. Carl Brown (2013), p. 126.
[152]
[153] //en.wikipedia.org/w/index.php?title=Template:Nakba&action=edit
[154] General Progress Report and Supplementary Report of the United Nations Conciliation Commission for Palestine, Covering the Period from 11 December 1949 to 23 October 1950

https://unispal.un.org/UNISPAL.NSF/0/93037E3B939746DE8525610200567883 , published by the United Nations Conciliation Commission, 23 October 1950. (U.N. General Assembly Official Records, 5th Session, Supplement No. 18, Document A/1367/Rev. 1)

[155] Government of Palestine, *A Survey of Palestine*, Supplement, p. 10 (1946)

[156] http://www.history.ac.uk/reviews/paper/hughesMatthew.html The War for Palestine. Rewriting the History of 1948 by Eugene L. Rogan and Avi Shlaim . Retrieved 8 August 2009. Archived https://www.webcitation.org/5iwzyIK8U?url=http://www.history.ac.uk/reviews/paper/hughesMatthew.html 11 August 2009.

[157] //en.wikipedia.org/w/index.php?title=Template:Jewish_exodus_from_Arab_and_Muslim_countries&action=edit

[158] Sachar, pp. 395–403.

[159] Devorah Hakohen, *Immigrants in Turmoil: Mass Immigration to Israel and Its Repercussions in the 1950s and after,* https://books.google.com/books?id=fYOiPrm-6PsC&pg=PA292 Syracuse University Press 2003 p.267

[160] Displaced Persons http://www.ushmm.org/wlc/article.php?lang=en&ModuleId=10005462 retrieved on 29 October 2007 from the U.S. Holocaust Museum.

[161] Tom Segev, *1949. The First Israelis*, Owl Books, 1986, p. 96.

[162] Devorah Hakohen, *Immigrants in Turmoil: Mass Immigration to Israel and Its Repercussions in the 1950s and after,* https://books.google.com/books?id=fYOiPrm-6PsC&pg=PA292 Syracuse University Press 2003 pp. 24, 31, 42, 45.

[163] Avi Shlaim, *The Debate about 1948* http://users.ox.ac.uk/~ssfc0005/The%20Debate%20About%201948.html, International Journal of Middle East Studies, 27:3, 1995, pp. 287–304.

[164] Avi Shlaim, "The Debate about 1948", *International Journal of Middle East Studies*, Vol. 27, No. 3 (Aug. 1995), pp. 287–304.

[165] Benny Morris, "Benny Morris on fact, fiction, & propaganda about 1948", *The Irish Times*, 21 February 2008, reported by Jeff Weintraub http://jeffweintraub.blogspot.com/2008/02/benny-morris-on-fact-fiction-propaganda.html

[166] https://www.jewishvirtuallibrary.org/jsource/images/maps/1948war2.jpg

[167] https://books.google.com/books?id=Wn6gAAAAMAAJ

[168] https://books.google.com/books?id=qSpIAAAAMAAJ

[169] https://books.google.com/books?id=CC7381HrLqcC&pg=PA332&lpg=PA332

[170] https://web.archive.org/web/20060629024035/http://www.bartleby.com/67/3770.html

[171] https://web.archive.org/web/20051204222100/http://www.haaretzdaily.com/hasen/pages/ShArt.jhtml?itemNo=101419

[172] http://www.jpost.com/Defense/Article.aspx?id=277511

[173] http://www.israelvets.com/pictorialhist_air_force.html

[174] https://www.youtube.com/watch?v=HHmBiATUono

[175] https://www.youtube.com/watch?v=yUDcL4y0R1I

[176] https://www.knesset.gov.il/holidays/eng/independence_day_war.htm

[177] http://domino.un.org/UNISPAL.NSF/

[178] http://www.historyguy.com/arab_israeli_wars.html

[179] http://www.mideastweb.org/briefhistory.htm

[180] http://webarchive.loc.gov/all/20020913220119/http://www.zmag.org/shalom-meqa.htm

[181] http://news.bbc.co.uk/1/hi/in_depth/middle_east/israel_and_the_palestinians/key_documents/1681322.stm

[182] http://news.bbc.co.uk/1/shared/spl/hi/middle_east/03/v3_ip_timeline/html/1948.stm

[183] http://israeliwarofindependence.blogspot.com/

[184] http://users.ox.ac.uk/~ssfc0005/Israel%20and%20the%20Arab%20Coalition%20in%201948.html

[185] http://www.time.com/time/magazine/article/0,9171,779710,00.html

[186] http://www.time.com/time/magazine/article/0,9171,798381,00.html

[187] Armistice Agreement between Egypt and Israel https://unispal.un.org/UNISPAL.NSF/0/9EC4A332E2FF9A128525643D007702E6 UN Doc S/1264/Corr.1 23 February 1949

[188] Armistice Agreement between Lebanon and Israel https://web.archive.org/web/20110726121052/http://unispal.un.org/UNISPAL.NSF/0/71260B776D62FA6E852564420059C4FE UN Doc S/1296 23 March 1949

[189] General Armistice Agreement between the Hashemite Jordan Kingdom and Israel https://unispal.un.org/UNISPAL.NSF/0/F03D55E48F77AB698525643B00608D34 UN Doc S/1302/Rev.1 3 April 1949

[190] Israel-Syrian General Armistice Agreement https://unispal.un.org/UNISPAL.NSF/0/E845CA0B92BE4E3485256442007901CC UN Doc S/1353 20 July 1949

[191] mfa.gov.il Article IV. 3. "The provisions of this Agreement are dictated exclusively by military considerations and are valid only for the period of the Armistice" http://www.mfa.gov.il/MFA/Foreign+Relations/Israels+Foreign+Relations+since+1947/1947-1974/Israel-Egypt+Armistice+Agreement.htm

[192] 1949 Lebanon / Israeli Armistice Agreement Article V https//books.google.com The case for Palestine: an international law perspective By John B. Quigley Page 89

[193] The Politics of Partition; King Abdullah, The Zionists, and Palestine 1921–1951 Avi Shlaim Oxford University Press Revised Edition 2004 pp. 299, 312

[194] UN Press Release PAL/537 4 November 1949 - UN Press Officer in Jerusalem "when the villagers returned to Wadi Fukin under the supervision of the United Nations observers on September 6, they found most of their houses destroyed and were again compelled by the Israeli Army to return to Arab territory." http://domino.un.org/UNISPAL.NSF/85255a0a0010ae82852555340060479d/7b5942522358001885256a76006377eb

[195] Israel Ministry of Foreign Affairs, Israel-Syria Armistice Agreement http://www.mfa.gov.il/mfa/foreignpolicy/mfadocuments/yearbook1/pages/israel-syria%20armistice%20agreement.aspx

[196] *The Missing Peace - The Inside Story of the Fight for Middle East Peace* (2004), by Dennis Ross. pp 584-585

[197] Avi Shlaim (2000) p. 57

[198] 2 Israel-s position on its frontiers http://www.mfa.gov.il/MFA/Foreign%20Relations/Israels%20Foreign%20Relations%20since%201947/1947-1974/2%20Israel-s%20position%20on%20its%20frontiers

[199] 3 Attitude of the parties on the territorial issue http//www.mfa.gov.il

[200] Authority of the United Nations Truce Supervision Organization and of the Syrian-Israeli Mixed Armistice Commission: United Nations Security Council Resolution, May 18, 1951 http://avalon.law.yale.edu/20th_century/mid006.asp

[201]

[202] Morris, Benny (1993) *Israel's Border Wars, 1949 - 1956. Arab Infiltration, Israeli Retaliation, and the Countdown to the Suez War*. Oxford University Press, . Page 246. "about one-third" of the attackers came from Unit 101 the rest were from the 890th Paratroop Battalion. Gives the number of civilians killed as 50 to 60.

[203] UN Doc S/RES/101(1953) S/3139/Rev.2 24 November 1953 https://unispal.un.org/UNISPAL.NSF/0/CBF7840E8148DF86852560C2006FEAEB Attack on village Qibya - SecCo censures Israel's action, requests Jordan to prevent crossings

[204] E H Hutchison "Violent Truce"

[205] UN Doc S/3196/Add.1 https://unispal.un.org/UNISPAL.NSF/0/892A3A8D9B8F538E0525672100719A67 dated 6 April 1954 from the representative of Israel to the President of the Security Council

[206] Benny Morris, *Israel's Border Wars, 1949-1956: Arab Infiltration, Israeli Retaliation, and the Countdown to the Suez War*.

[207] Israeli Minister's http://domino.un.org/unispal.NSF/9a798adbf322aff38525617b006d88d7/3dd863c66da0823b052564e3004b10ea!OpenDocument Statement to the Knesset, May 28, 1958

[208] UN Doc S/4030 of 17 June 1958 https://unispal.un.org/UNISPAL.NSF/0/B150F4C5505CDA730525650000381049 Report of UN personnel present at the Mount Scopus incident give a different version of events than the Israeli Government position. The route of the patrol was contested (the route was outside the fence of the "Jewish owned property" line)and no firing came from the Hospital a single sniper from the orchard area apparently kept the police patrol under fire and when a Jordanian patrol turned up the Israeli patrol then fired on the Jordanian patrol who returned fire. when the truce was arranged the sniper continued firing and Lt.-Colonel Flint was killed carrying a white flag

[209] http://avalon.law.yale.edu/
[210] http://avalon.law.yale.edu/20th_century/arm01.asp
[211] http://avalon.law.yale.edu/20th_century/arm03.asp
[212] http://avalon.law.yale.edu/20th_century/arm02.asp
[213] http://avalon.law.yale.edu/20th_century/arm04.asp
[214] https://web.archive.org/web/20040604202236/http://domino.un.org/UNISPAL.nsf/Web%20Search%20Simple2%21OpenForm
[215] https://archive.org/details/violenttrucearab006617mbp
[216] Benvenisti, 412–416
[217] Morris, Benny (1993) *Israel's Border Wars, 1949–1956: Arab Infiltration, Israeli Retaliation, and the Countdown to the Suez War*. Oxford University Press, . Page 179.
[218] Allon, Yigal, (1970) *Shield of David. The Story of Israel's Armed Forces*. Weidenfeld & Nicolson. SBN 297 00133 7. Page 235. Allon attributes a identical quote to Moshe Dayan, Israel's Chief of Staff.
[219] Burns, Lieutenant-General E.L.M. (1962) *Between Arab and Israeli*. George G. Harrap. Pages 50, 38.
[220] Benny Morris, *Israel's Border Wars, 1949–1956: Arab Infiltration, Israeli Retaliation and the Countdown to the Suez War*, Oxford University Press, 1993, pp. 258–59.
[221] Morris. Page 393. Teveth. Page 244.
[222] Dayan, Moshe (1965) *Diary of the Sinai Campaign 1956*. Sphere Books edition (1967) page 32. "He was gravely wounded, the bullet striking his windpipe, but his life was saved by the medical officer of the unit, who crawled to him under fire and performed a tracheotomy with his pocket knife."
[223] Ze'ev Derori, *Israel's Reprisal Policy, 1953–1956: The Dynamics of Military Retaliation*, Frank Cass (2005) p. 152
[224] http://cosmos.ucc.ie/cs1064/jabowen/IPSC/php/authors.php?auid=6292
[225] Morris, Benny (1993) *Israel's Border Wars, 1949 – 1956. Arab Infiltration, Israeli Retaliation, and the Countdown to the Suez War*. Oxford University Press, . Pages 215, 216.
[226] e.g. Still used twenty years later.
[227] http://content.cdlib.org/view?docId=ft2290045n&chunk.id=ch4
[228] http://ark.cdlib.org/ark:/13030/ft2290045n/
[229] http://www.stanford.edu/group/SHR/5-1/text/beinin.html
[230] https://web.archive.org/web/20041216171802/http://www.jafi.org.il/education/juice/service/week2.html
[231] http://www.allaboutpalestine.com/The_Lavon_Affair.html
[232] https://web.archive.org/web/20060214143058/http://users.skynet.be/terrorism/html/israel_susannah.htm
[233] Stewart (2013) p 133
[234]
[235] History's worst decisions and the people who made them, pp. 167–172
[236] Casualties in Arab–Israeli Wars https://www.jewishvirtuallibrary.org/jsource/History/casualties.html, *Jewish Virtual Library*
[237] Casualties Of Mideast Wars http://articles.latimes.com/1991-03-08/news/mn-2592_1_civil-war, *Los Angeles Times*
[238] Varble, *Derek The Suez Crisis 1956*, Osprey: London 2003, p. 90
[239] Britain France Israel Egypt War 1956 http://www.onwar.com/aced/nation/ink/israel/fsinai1956.htm
[240] A History of the Israeli Army: 1870 - 1974 - Zeev Schiff - كتب Google https://books.google.com/books?id=SaFtAAAAMAAJ&q=5000#search_anchor
[241] Also named: *Suez Canal Crisis, Suez War, Suez–Sinai war, Suez Campaign, Sinai Campaign, Operation Musketeer* (', "**Suez Crisis**"/ "**the Tripartite Aggression**"; ; ' "Operation Kadesh", or ', "**Sinai War**")
[242] Roger Owen "Suez Crisis" *The Oxford Companion to the Politics of the World*, Second edition. Joel Krieger, ed. Oxford University Press Inc. 2001.
[243] Turner, Barry. *Suez 1956: The First Oil War*. pp. 21–24.
[244] Sachar. *A History of Israel from the Rise of Zionism to Our Time*.

[245] Varble, Derek (2003) p. 11.
[246] Varble, Derek (2003) p. 12.
[247] Yergin, p. 480
[248] State of Business: Middle-East Echoes http://www.time.com/time/magazine/article/0,9171, 824597,00.html, *Time*, 12 November 1956
[249] Donald Watt, "Britain and the Suez Canal", Royal Institute of International Affairs, 1956, p. 8.
[250]
[251] Butler, p. 111.
[252] Darwin, p. 208.
[253] Vakikiotis, P. J. *Nasser and His Generation*, pp. 230–232.
[254] Butler, p. 112.
[255] Darwin, p. 210
[256] See: Michael N. Barnett, *Confronting the Costs of War: Military Power, State, and Society in Egypt and Israel* (Princeton, NJ: Princeton University Press, 1992), 82–83.
[257] Gaddis, John Lewis (1998) p. 168.
[258] Gaddis, John Lewis (1998) p. 167.
[259] Sayed-Ahmed, Muhammad Add al-Wahab "Relations between Egypt and the United States of America in the 1950s", pp. 89–99 from *Contemporary Egypt: through Egyptian eyes* edited by Charles Tripp, Routledge: London, 1993, p. 90.
[260] Burns, William *Economic Aid and American Policy towards Egypt 1955–1981* p. 11.
[261] Gaddis, John Lewis (1998) pp. 167–168.
[262] Neff, Donald *Warriors at Suez*, p. 43.
[263] Neff, Donald *Warriors at Suez*, Simon & Schuster: New York, 1981, pp. 18–19 & 195.
[264] Vakikiotis, P. J. *Nasser and His Generation*, pp. 41–42.
[265] Burns, William *Economic Aid and American Policy Towards Egypt, 1955–1981*, State University of New York: Albany, 1985, p. 11.
[266] Neff, Donald *Warriors at Suez*, p. 177.
[267] Thornhill, Michael "Britain, the United States and the Rise of an Egyptian Leader", pp. 892–921 from *English Historical Review*, Volume CXIV, Issue #483, September 2004, pp. 893–894.
[268] Thornhill, Michael "Britain, the United States and the Rise of an Egyptian Leader", pp. 892–921 from *English Historical Review*, Volume CXIV, Issue #483, September 2004, p. 900.
[269] Burns, William *Economic Aid and American Policy towards Egypt*, p. 11.
[270] Thornhill, Michael "Britain, the United States and the Rise of an Egyptian Leader", p. 899.
[271] Gaddis, John Lewis (1998) p. 169.
[272] Neff, Donald *Warriors at Suez*, pp. 43–44.
[273] Neff, Donald *Warriors at Suez*, pp. 44–45.
[274] Thornhill, Michael "Britain, the United States and the Rise of an Egyptian Leader", pp. 906–907.
[275] Sayed-Ahmed, Muhammad Add al-Wahab "Relations between Egypt and the United States of America in the 1950s", pp. 89–99 from *Contemporary Egypt: through Egyptian eyes* edited by Charles Tripp, Routledge: London, 1993, p. 91.
[276] Burns, William *Economic Aid and American Policy*, p. 24.
[277] Sayed-Ahmed, Muhammad Add al-Wahab "Relations between Egypt and the United States of America in the 1950s", pp. 89–99 from *Contemporary Egypt: through Egyptian eyes* edited by Charles Tripp, Routledge: London, 1993, pp. 91–92.
[278] Sayed-Ahmed, Muhammad Add al-Wahab "Relations between Egypt and the United States of America in the 1950s", pp. 89–99 from *Contemporary Egypt: through Egyptian eyes* edited by Charles Tripp, Routledge: London, 1993, p. 92.
[279] Gaddis, John Lewis (1998) pp. 170–172.
[280] Gaddis, John Lewis (1998) p. 171.
[281] Love, Kenneth *Suez*, McGraw-Hill: New York, 1969, pp. 306–307.
[282] Gaddis, John Lewis (1998) p. 170–71.
[283] Burns, William *Economic Aid and American Policy towards Egypt*, p. 24.
[284] Burns, William *Economic Aid and American Policy towards Egypt*, pp. 16–17 & 18–22.

285 Neff, Donald *Warriors at Suez*, p. 73.
286 Neff, Donald *Warriors at Suez*, pp. 93–94.
287 Goldman, Marshal *Soviet Foreign Aid*, New York: Fredrich Prager, 1968, p. 60.
288 Adamthwaite, Anthony "Suez Revisited" pp. 449–464 from *International Affairs*, Volume 64, Issue #3, Summer 1988 p. 450.
289 Kyle, Keith *Suez*, London: I.B. Tauris, 2011, p. 115.
290 Kyle, Keith *Suez*, London: I.B. Tauris, 2011, pp. 116–117.
291 Kyle, Keith *Suez*, London: I.B. Tauris, 2011, p. 117.
292 Vatikiotis, P. J. *Nasser and his Generation*, pp. 252–253.
293 Vatikiotis, P. J. *Nasser and His Generation*, pp. 250–253.
294 Neff, Donald *Warriors at Suez*, p. 160.
295 Neff, Donald *Warriors at Suez*, pp. 160–161.
296 Neff, Donald *Warriors at Suez*, pp. 162–163.
297 Neff, Donald *Warriors at Suez*, pp. 234–236.
298 Neff, Donald *Warriors at Suez*, p. 235.
299 Burns, William *Economic aid and American Policy towards Egypt*, pp. 24–25 & 26–27.
300 Burns, William *Economic aid and American Policy towards Egypt*, pp. 27–28.
301 Darwin, p. 211
302 Kissinger, p. 529
303 Neff, Donald *Warriors at Suez*, pp. 178–179.
304 Mason, Edward & Asher, Robert *The World Bank Since Bretton Woods*, Washington: Brookings Institution, 1973, p. 638
305 Neff, Donald *Warriors at Suez*, p. 180.
306 Neff, Donald *Warriors at Suez*, pp. 182–183.
307 Isaac Alteras, *Eisenhower and Israel: U.S.-Israeli relations, 1953–1960* (1993) ch 7–8
308 Gaddis, John Lewis (1998) pp. 168–169.
309 Kissinger, p. 528
310 Gaddis, John Lewis (1998) p. 172.
311 Gaddis, John Lewis (1998) pp. 171–172.
312 Neff, Donald *Warriors at Suez*, pp. 130–131.
313 Neff, Donald *Warriors at Suez*, pp. 135–136.
314 Neff, Donald *Warriors at Suez*, p. 136.
315 Neff, Donald *Warriors at Suez*, pp. 168–169.
316 Vatikiotis, P. J. *Nasser and His Generation*, pp. 306–307.
317 Vatikitos, P. J. *Nasser and His Generation*, p. 252.
318 Kissinger, p. 530
319 BBC On This Day, 1956: Egypt seizes Suez Canal http://news.bbc.co.uk/onthisday/hi/dates/stories/july/26/newsid_2701000/2701603.stm
320 Sachar, p. 455
321 What we failed to learn from Suez https://www.telegraph.co.uk/culture/3656288/What-we-failed-to-learn-from-Suez.html. Telegraph (1 November 2006). Retrieved on 8 September 2011.
322 Turner, Barry *Suez 1956*, London: Hodder & Stoughton, 2006, p. 181.
323 Turner, Barry *Suez 1956*, London: Hodder & Stoughton, 2006, pp. 231–232.
324 Turner, Barry *Suez 1956*, London: Hodder & Stoughton, 2006, p. 232.
325 Keith Kyle *Suez: Britain's End of Empire in the Middle East* (I.B. Tauris, 2003), pp. 225–226.
326 Kyle, Keith *Suez*, London: I.B. Tauris, 2011, p. 144.
327 Kyle, Keith *Suez*, London: I.B. Tauris, 2011, p. 145.
328 Kyle, Keith *Suez*, London: I.B. Tauris, 2011, p. 156.
329 Brian Carroll; From Barton to Fraser; Cassell Australia; 1978
330 *Le Canal de Suez et la nationalisation par le Colonel Nasser*, Les Actualité Française – AF, 08.01.1956 http://mp4.ina.fr/ogp/contenu_video.php?id_notice=AFE85006880&random=3614851046
331
332 Charles Williams, *Harold Macmillan* (2009) p. 250-252

[333] Robert Rhodes James, *Anthony Eden: A Biography* (1986), pp 462–5, quote p 472 dated 31 July 1956
[334] C. Philip Skardon, *A Lesson for Our Times: How America Kept the Peace in the Hungary-Suez Crisis of 1956* (2010) pp 194–5
[335] Chaim Herzog and Shlomo Gazit, *The Arab–Israeli Wars: War and Peace in the Middle East from the 1948 War of Independence to the Present* (3rd ed. 2008) pp. 113–117
[336] Zeev Schiff, *A History of the Israeli Army*, pp. 65–66, Simon and Schuster (1974)
[337] Soviets Threaten Israel, Ben-Gurion Responds https://www.jewishvirtuallibrary.org/jsource/History/bulganin.html. Jewishvirtuallibrary.org. Retrieved on 8 September 2011.
[338] Varble, Derek (2003) p. 21.
[339] Varble, Derek (2003) p. 26.
[340] Varble, Derek (2003) p. 22.
[341] Neff, Donald *Warriors at Suez*, p. 295.
[342] Neff, Donald *Warriors at Suez*, pp. 295–296.
[343] Neff, Donald *Warriors at Suez*, p. 309.
[344] Neff, Donald *Warriors at Suez*, p. 310.
[345] Neff, Donald *Warriors at Suez*, pp. 321–322.
[346] Neff, Donald *Warriors at Suez*, pp. 323–324.
[347] Neff, Donald *Warriors at Suez*, p. 324.
[348] Neff, Donald *Warriors at Suez*, pp. 335–336.
[349] The Protocol of Sèvres 1956 Anatomy of a War Plot http://users.ox.ac.uk/~ssfc0005/The%20Protocol%20of%20Sevres%201956%20Anatomy%20of%20a%20War%20Plot.html. Users.ox.ac.uk. Retrieved on 8 September 2011.
[350] Kyle, Keith *Suez Britain's End of Empire*, London: I.B. Tauris 2011, p. 176.
[351] Varble, Derek (2003) p. 24.
[352] Turner, Barry *Suez 1956*, London: Hodder & Stoughton, 2006, p. 201.
[353] Varble, Derek (2003) p. 25.
[354] Varble, Derek (2003) p. 15.
[355] Varble, Derek (2003) p. 16.
[356] Varble, Derek (2003) pp. 16–17.
[357] Varble, Derek (2003) p. 17.
[358] Varble, Derek (2003) p. 18.
[359] Varble, Derek (2003) pp. 18–19.
[360] Varble, Derek (2003) p. 19.
[361] Varble, Derek (2003) p. 20.
[362] Varble, Derek (2003) p. 28.
[363] Benny Morris, *Righteous Victims*, p. 289
[364] Varble, Derek (2003) pp. 28–29.
[365] Herzog (1982) p. 118
[366] Norton, Bill (2004) – *Air War on the Edge – A History of the Israeli Air Force and its Aircraft since 1947*
[367] Varble, Derek (2003) p. 29.
[368] Varble, Derek (2003) p. 31.
[369] Varble, Derek (2003) p. 32.
[370] Varble, Derek (2003) p. 33.
[371] Varble, Derek (2003) pp. 32–33.
[372] Herzog, *The Arab–Israeli Wars*, p. 138 Random House, (1982)
[373] Nordeen, Lon *Fighters Over Israel* London 1991, p. 198
[374] Bishop, Chris ed. *The Aerospace Encyclopedia of Air Warfare Volume Two: 1945 to the present* Aerospace Publishing London 1997, pp. 148–153
[375] Midshipman RJH Griffiths, HMS Newfoundland: *The Night we sank the Domiat*
[376] House of Commons Debates 19 December 1956 vol 562 c180W http://hansard.millbanksystems.com/written_answers/1956/dec/19/hms-crane-aircraft-attack. Hansard.millbanksystems.com (19 December 1956). Retrieved on 8 September 2011.
[377] Carter, Geoffrey – *Crises do Happen: The Royal Navy and Operation Musketeer, Suez, 1956*
[378] Max Wurmbrand, The Valiant of Israel, p. 80, Massada Press Ltd (1967)

379

[380] Pimlott – editor *British Military Operations, 1945–1984* London: Guild Publishing 1984 p. 78
[381] Varble, Derek (2003) p. 35.
[382] Varble, Derek (2003) pp. 32–35.
[383] Varble, Derek (2003) pp. 35–36.
[384] Varble, Derek (2003) p. 36.
[385] Varble, Derek (2003) p. 37.
[386] Varble, Derek (2003) p. 38.
[387] Varble, Derek (2003) pp. 38–39.
[388] Varble, Derek (2003) p. 39.
[389] Varble, Derek (2003) p. 40.
[390] Varble, Derek (2003) p. 41.
[391] Varble, Derek (2003) pp. 41–43.
[392] Varble, Derek (2003) p. 43.
[393] *Special Report of the Director of the United Nations Relief and Works Agency for Palestine Refugees in the Near East* https://unispal.un.org/UNISPAL.NSF/0/6558F61D3DB6BD4505256593006B06BE , Covering the period 1 November 1956 to mid-December 1956, New York, 1957
[394] *Rafah* http://cosmos.ucc.ie/cs1064/jabowen/IPSC/php/place.php?plid=210, Palestine: Information with Provenance (PIWP database)
[395] Varble, Derek (2003) p. 45.
[396] Varble, Derek (2003) p. 46.
[397] Joe Sacco produces comics from the hot zones http://articles.latimes.com/2010/feb/04/entertainment/la-et-joe-sacco4-2010feb04. New York Times.
[398] UNRWA Report to the UN General Assembly November 1 – December 14, 1956 http://domino.un.org/unispal.nsf/0/6558f61d3b6bd4505256593006b06be?OpenDocument
[399] Varble, Derek (2003) p. 86.
[400] Varble, Derek (2003) pp. 86–87.
[401] Morris, Benny (1993) *Israel's Border Wars, 1949–1956. Arab Infiltration, Israeli Retaliation, and the Countdown to the Suez War.* Oxford University Press, . p. 408. "On 3 November, the day Khan Yunis was conquered, IDF troops shot dead hundreds of Palestinian refugees and local inhabitants in the town. One UN report speaks of 'some 135 local resident' and '140 refugees' killed as IDF troops moved through the town and its refugee camp 'searching for people in possession of arms'. In Rafah, which fell to the IDF on 1–2 November, Israeli troops killed between forty-eight and one hundred refugees and several local residents, and wounded another sixty-one during a massive screening operation on 12 November, in which they sought to identify former Egyptian and Palestinian soldiers and Fedayeen hiding among the local population.... Another sixty-six Palestinians, probably Fedayeen, were executed in a number of other incidents during screening operations in the Gaza Strip between 2 and 20 November.... The United Nations estimated that, all told, Israeli troops killed between 447 and 550 Arab civilians in the first three weeks of the occupation of the Strip."
[402] Varble, Derek (2003) p. 48.
[403] Varble, Derek (2003) p. 49.
[404] Kaufman, Bill, Slettedahl Macpherson, Heidi (2005) *Britain and the Americas: culture, politics, and history.* ABC-CLIO, p. 939.
[405] Brown, Neville (2013) *Global Instability and Strategic Crisis.* Routledge, p. 40.
[406] Dunbabin, J.P.D. (1994). *International Relations Since 1945: The post-imperial age : the great powers and the wider world.* Longman, p. 294.
[407] Smith, Peter C. (2007). *Midway: Dauntless Victory: Fresh Perspectives on America's Seminal Naval Victory of World War II.* Pen & Sword, p. 277.
[408] Varble, Derek (2003) p. 50.
[409] Varble, Derek (2003) p. 51.
[410] Varble, Derek (2003) p. 53.
[411] Varble, Derek (2003) p. 54.
[412] Varble, Derek (2003) pp. 54–55.
[413] Varble, Derek (2003) pp. 50–52.

[414] Varble, Derek (2003) p. 52.
[415] Neff, Donald *Warriors at Suez*, p. 399.
[416] Neff, Donald *Warriors at Suez*, p. 400.
[417] Adamthwaite, Anthony "Suez Revisited" pp. 449–464 from *International Affairs*, Volume 64, Issue #3, Summer 1988 pp. 457–458.
[418] Adamthwaite, Anthony "Suez Revisited" pp. 449–464 from *International Affairs*, Volume 64, Issue #3, Summer 1988 p. 458.
[419] Varble, Derek (2003) p. 56.
[420] Varble, Derek (2003) p. 59.
[421] Varble, Derek (2003) p. 60.
[422] Varble, Derek (2003) pp. 60–61.
[423] Varble, Derek (2003) p. 61.
[424] Varble, Derek (2003) p. 55.
[425] Varble, Derek (2003) p. 62.
[426] Varble, Derek (2003) pp. 62–63.
[427] Varble, Derek (2003) p. 63.
[428] Varble, Derek (2003) p. 65.
[429] Varble, Derek (2003) p. 66.
[430] Varble, Derek (2003) p. 87.
[431] Varble, Derek (2003) pp. 87–88.
[432] Varble, Derek (2003) p. 88.
[433] Varble, Derek (2003) p. 88
[434] Varble, Derek (2003) p. 89.
[435] Varble, Derek (2003) pp. 89–90.
[436] Varble, Derek (2003) p. 90.
[437] Varble, Derek (2003) p. 77.
[438] Varble, Derek (2003) pp. 66–68.
[439] Varble, Derek (2003) p. 67.
[440] Varble, Derek (2003) p. 69.
[441] Varble, Derek (2003) pp. 66–70.
[442] Varble, Derek (2003) pp. 70–71.
[443] Varble, Derek (2003) p. 71.
[444] Varble, Derek (2003) p. 72.
[445] Varble, Derek (2003) p. 78.
[446] Varble, Derek (2003) pp. 78–79.
[447] Varble, Derek (2003) p. 79.
[448] Varble, Derek (2003) p. 80.
[449] Varble, Derek (2003) p. 91.
[450]
[451] Donald Neff, *Warriors at Suez*. Amana Books, Vermont. 1988. p. 414. Quotes UN report: "thousands of wounded and dead bodies all over Sanai (sic)". Neff estimates 4000 Egyptians wounded and 6000 captured or missing in Sinai and a further 900 wounded by the Anglo-French.
[452] Varble, 1956, 2003, p. 90
[453] Cole, Robert *A.J.P. Taylor the Traitor Within the Gates*, London: Macmillan 1993, p. 149.
[454] Cole, Robert *A.J.P. Taylor the traitor Within the Gates*, London: Macmillan 1993, p. 149
[455] Turner, Barry *Suez 1956*, London: Hodder & Stoughton, 2006, pp. 230 & 254–255.
[456] Turner, Barry *Suez 1956*, London: Hodder & Stoughton, 2006, p. 254.
[457] Turner, Barry *Suez 1956*, London: Hodder & Stoughton, 2006, p. 210.
[458] Turner, Barry *Suez 1956*, London: Hodder & Stoughton, 2006, pp. 206–210.
[459] Pryce-Jones, David *The Closed Circle: An Interpretation of the Arabs*, Chicago: Ivan Dee, 2002, p. 4.
[460] Neff, Donald *Warriors at Suez*, p. 388.
[461] Turner, Barry *Suez 1956*, London: Hodder & Stoughton, 2006, pp. 230–231.
[462] Neff, Donald *Warriors at Suez*, pp. 388–389.

[463] House of Commons Debate, 1 November 1956, http://hansard.millbanksystems.com/commons/1956/nov/01/egypt-and-israel
[464] Wilson, A. N. *Our Times*, Hutchinson: London 2008, p. 65.
[465] Wilson, A. N. *Our Times*, Hutchinson: London 2008, pp. 65–66.
[466] Wilson, A. N. *Our Times*, Hutchinson: London 2008, p. 66.
[467] Adamthwaite, Anthony "Suez Revisited" pp. 449–464 from *International Affairs*, Volume 64, Issue #3, Summer 1988 p. 463.
[468] Turner, Barry *Suez 1956*, London: Hodder & Stoughton 2006, p. 354.
[469] Adamthwaite, Anthony "Suez Revisited" pp. 449–464 from *International Affairs*, Volume 64, Issue #3, Summer 1988 pp. 455–456.
[470] Adamthwaite, Anthony "Suez Revisited" pp. 449–464 from *International Affairs*, Volume 64, Issue #3, Summer 1988 pp. 456–457.
[471] Adamthwaite, Anthony "Suez Revisited" pp. 449–464 from *International Affairs*, Volume 64, Issue #3, Summer 1988 p. 456.
[472] Kyle, Keith *Suez Britain's End of Empire*, London: I.B. Tauris 2011, p. 441.
[473] Kyle, Keith *Suez Britain's End of Empire*, London: I.B. Tauris 2011, pp. 441–442.
[474] Russell Braddon, *Suez: Splitting of a Nation* (London: Collins, 1973), p. 111, p. 113.
[475] Alan Sked and Chris Cook, *Post-War Britain: A Political History* (London: Penguin, 1984), p. 134.
[476] Dominic Sandbrook, *Never Had It So Good: A History of Britain from Suez to the Beatles* (London: Abacus, 2006), p. 18.
[477] Wilson, A. N. *Our Times*, Hutchinson: London 2008, pp. 66–67.
[478] Sir Anthony Eden, *Full Circle* (London: Cassell, 1960), p. 546.
[479] Sandbrook, p. 19.
[480] Brian Harrison, *Seeking a Role: The United Kingdom, 1951-1970* (Oxford: Oxford University Press, 2009), p. 105, p. 112.
[481] Lawrence Black, 'The Bitterest Enemies of Communism': Labour Revisionists, Atlanticism and the Cold War", *Contemporary British History*, 15:3, Autumn 2001, pp. 50-51.
[482] Lawrence James, *The Rise and Fall of the British Empire* (London: Abacus, 1998), p. 583.
[483] Braddon, p. 111.
[484] Braddon, p. 113.
[485] Barbara Castle, *Fighting All The Way* (London: Pan, 1994), p. 253.
[486] Kenneth O. Morgan, *Britain Since 1945: The People's Peace* (Oxford: Oxford University Press, 2001), p. 156.
[487] James Callaghan, *Time and Chance* (London: Collins, 1987), p. 515.
[488] Sked and Cook, p. 134.
[489] Varble, Derek (2003) p. 88.n
[490] Neff, Donald *Warriors at Suez*, p. 391.
[491] Pike, Francis *Empires at War*, London: I.B. Tauris 2009, p. 303.
[492] Turner, Barry *Suez 1956*, London: Hodder & Stoughton, 2006, p. 328.
[493] Lacey, Robert *The Kingdom*, New York: Avon 1981, p. 315.
[494] Establishment of UNEF, Background https://www.un.org/en/peacekeeping/missions/past/unef1backgr2.html at UN.org
[495] John Allphin Moore and Jerry Pubantz, *Encyclopedia of the United Nations* (2008) 2:399
[496] Hendershot, Robert; *Family Spats: Perception, Illusion, and Sentimentality in the Anglo-American Special Relationship*
[497] UNGA Emergency Special Sessions https://www.un.org/ga/sessions/emergency.shtml. Un.org. Retrieved on 8 September 2011.
[498]
[499] Dietl, Ralph "Suez 1956: A European Intervention?" pp. 259–273 from *Journal of Contemporary History*, Volume 43, Issue #2, April 2008, p. 273.
[500] Schwarz, Hans-Peter *Konrad Adenauer: A German Politician and Statesman in a Period of War, Revolution and Reconstruction, 1952–1967* Oxford: Berghahn Books, 1995 pp. 241–242.
[501] Schwarz, Hans-Peter *Konrad Adenauer: A German Politician and Statesman in a Period of War, Revolution and Reconstruction, 1952–1967* Oxford: Berghahn Books, 1995 p. 242.

[502] Schwarz, Hans-Peter *Konrad Adenauer: A German Politician and Statesman in a Period of War, Revolution and Reconstruction, 1952–1967* Oxford: Berghahn Books, 1995 p. 244.
[503] Eisenhower and Israel: U.S.-Israeli Relations, 1953–1960, Isaac Alteras, University Press of Florida, 1993 https://books.google.com/books?id=ydRHCPWngioC&pg=PA246, , p. 246. Books.google.com. Retrieved on 8 September 2011.
[504] A Restless Mind: Essays in Honor of Amos Perlmutter, Amos Perlmutter, Benjamin Frankel, Routledge, 1996 https://books.google.com/books?id=qkK_j0qz9EgC&pg=PA105, , Michael Brecher Essay, pp. 104–117. Books.google.com. Retrieved on 8 September 2011.
[505] Neff, Donald *Warriors at Suez*, p. 403.
[506] Turner, Barry *Suez 1956*, London: Hodder & Stoughton, 2006, p. 368.
[507] Suez Crisis http://www.globalsecurity.org/military/ops/suez.htm. Globalsecurity.org (26 July 1956). Retrieved on 8 September 2011.
[508] Kyle, Keith *Suez: Britain's End of Empire in the Middle East*, p. 458
[509] Gaddis, John Lewis *We Now Know*, 1998, pp. 237–240.
[510] Gaddis, John Lewis *We Now Know*, 1998, pp. 245–246.
[511] Gaddis, John Lewis *We Now Know*, 1998, p. 240.
[512] Gaddis, John Lewis *We Now Know*, 1998, pp. 239–240.
[513] Gaddis, John Lewis *We Now Know*, 1998, p. 239.
[514] Williams, Charles *Harold Macmillan* (2009) pp. 259–261
[515] Kyle, Keith *Suez: Britain's End of Empire in the Middle East*, p. 464
[516] Kennett Love, *Suez: The Twice-Fought War* (New York: McGraw Hill, 1969), p. 651
[517] The Suez Crisis of 1956 http://www.historylearningsite.co.uk/suez_crisis_1956.htm . Historylearningsite.co.uk (30 March 2007). Retrieved on 8 September 2011.
[518] The effect of Prime Minister Anthony Eden's illness on his decision-making during the Suez crisis http://qjmed.oxfordjournals.org/content/98/6/387.full. Qjmed.oxfordjournals.org (6 May 2005). Retrieved on 8 September 2011.
[519] Alteras, Issac *Eisenhower and Israel: U.S.-Israeli relations, 1953–1960* p. 243
[520] Service Cinématographique des Armées SCA reportage de Paul Corcuff, 22 December 1956 http://www.ecpad.fr/ecpa/PagesDyn/result.asp?reportageid=1012 French Ministry of Defense archives ECPAD MO56141AR14
[521] Kyle, Keith *Suez: Britain's End of Empire in the Middle East*, p. 493
[522] "Suez: The 'betrayal' of Eden" http://news.bbc.co.uk/1/hi/world/middle_east/6085264.stm, BBC News (30 October 2006). Retrieved on 8 September 2011.
[523] Suez Canal Crisis http://novaonline.nvcc.edu/eli/evans/his135/Events/Suez56.htm. Novaonline.nvcc.edu. Retrieved on 8 September 2011.
[524] Delauche, Frederic *Illustrated History of Europe: A Unique Guide to Europe's Common Heritage* (1992) p. 357
[525] Gaddis, John Lewis (1998) p. 173.
[526] Kyle, Keith *Suez*, London: I.B. Tauris, 2011, p. 522.
[527] Gaddis, John Lewis (1998) p. 236.
[528] Gaddis, John Lewis (1998) pp. 236–237.
[529] Gaddis, John Lewis (1998) pp. 236–239.
[530] Gaddis, John Lewis (1998) pp. 173–174.
[531] Gaddis, John Lewis (1998) pp. 174–175.
[532] Varble, Derek (2003) p. 92.
[533] Dietl, Ralph "Suez 1956: A European Intervention?" pp. 259–273 from *Journal of Contemporary History*, Volume 43, Issue #2, April 2008, pp. 273–274.
[534] Dietl, Ralph "Suez 1956: A European Intervention?" pp. 259–273 from *Journal of Contemporary History*, Volume 43, Issue #2, April 2008, p. 274.
[535] Varble, Derek (2003) p. 84.
[536] Vatikiotis, P. J. *Nasser and His Generation*, p. 275.
[537] Vatikiotis, P. J. *Nasser and His Generation*, p. 277.
[538] Vatikiotis, P. J. *Nasser and His Generation*, p. 321.
[539] //en.wikipedia.org/w/index.php?title=Template:Jewish_exodus_from_Arab_and_Muslim_countries&action=edit

[540] Laskier, Michael "Egyptian Jewry under the Nasser Regime, 1956–70" pp. 573–619 from *Middle Eastern Studies*, Volume 31, Issue #3, July 1995, p. 579.
[541] Laskier, Michael "Egyptian Jewry under the Nasser Regime, 1956–70" pp. 573–619 from *Middle Eastern Studies*, Volume 31, Issue #3, July 1995, pp. 579–580.
[542] Laskier, Michael "Egyptian Jewry under the Nasser Regime, 1956–70" pp. 573–619 from *Middle Eastern Studies*, Volume 31, Issue #3, July 1995, p. 581.
[543] Jewish Refugees from Arab Countries https://www.jewishvirtuallibrary.org/jsource/History/jewref.html. Jewishvirtuallibrary.org. Retrieved on 8 September 2011.
[544] WWII Behind Closed Doors: Stalin, the Nazis and the West . Biographies . Anthony Eden https://www.pbs.org/behindcloseddoors/biographies/eden.html. PBS. Retrieved on 8 September 2011.
[545] Adamthwaite, Anthony, "Suez Revisited", *International Affairs*, Volume 64, Issue #3, Summer 1988 page 449.
[546] US-UK Special Relationship 06 | Intelligence Analysis and Reporting http://spyinggame.wordpress.com/2011/07/30/us-uk-special-relationship-06/. Spyinggame.wordpress.com (30 July 2011). Retrieved on 8 September 2011.
[547] Sowerwine, Charles *France Since 1870*, London: Palgrave Macmillan, 2009 p. 278.
[548] *Affaire de Suez, Le Pacte Secret http://www.france5.fr/programmes/articles/histoire/734-affaire-de-suez-le-pacte-secret.php*, Peter Hercombe et Arnaud Hamelin, France 5/Sunset Presse/Transparence, 2006
[549] Keith Kyle reviews *Divided we stand* by W. Scott Lucas and *Blind Loyalty* by W. J. Hudson· LRB 25 February 1993 http://www.lrb.co.uk/v15/n04/keith-kyle/lacking-in-style. Lrb.co.uk. Retrieved on 8 September 2011.
[550] Herzog, p. 141
[551]
[552] MILITARIA • Toon onderwerp – Suez Crisis: Operation Musketeer http://militaria.forum-xl.com/viewtopic.php?f=53&t=599. Militaria.forum-xl.com. Retrieved on 8 September 2011.
[553] //www.amazon.com/dp/B000H47WG4
[554] //doi.org/10.1177%2F0022009408089032
[555] //www.amazon.com/dp/B0040YOVBQ
[556] https://books.google.com/books?id=8IG54d7vzKkC
[557] https://books.google.com/books?id=zLfnAAAAIAAJ&pg=PA120
[558] http://jah.oxfordjournals.org/content/99/1/24.full.pdf
[559] //doi.org/10.1093%2Fjahist%2Fjas073
[560] http://www.sahistory.org.za/sites/default/files/file%20uploads%20/jonathan_pearson_sir_anthony_eden_and_the_suez_cbook4you.org_.pdf
[561] https://web.archive.org/web/20070110234732/http://www.azure.org.il/magazine/magazine.asp?id=355
[562] http://www.weeklystandard.com/Content/Public/Articles/000/000/012/484pbqjx.asp?page=2
[563] https://web.archive.org/web/20061001211346/https://www.jafi.org.il/education/100/maps/sinai.html
[564] http://www.suezcrisis.ca/
[565] http://news.bbc.co.uk/1/hi/world/middle_east/5199392.stm
[566] http://www.isj.org.uk/index.php4?id=249&issue=112
[567] https://web.archive.org/web/20061125122924/http://www.servicehistorique.sga.defense.gouv.fr/04histoire/dossierdushd/suez/suezcarr2.htm
[568] http://www.bodley.ox.ac.uk/dept/scwmss/projects/suez/suez.html
[569] https://web.archive.org/web/20101120140143/http://britains-smallwars.com/suez/suez-index.html
[570] http://www.cvce.eu/obj/speech_by_gamal_abdel_nasser_26_july_1956-en-d0ecf835-9f40-4c43-a2ed-94c186061d2a.html
[571] http://nasser.bibalex.org/Speeches/browser.aspx?SID=495
[572] https://archive.org/details/gov.archives.arc.653946
[573] http://www.britishpathe.com/record.php?id=61875
[574] https://www.nfb.ca/film/blue_vanguard
[575] Oren, p. 237

[576] Krauthammer 2007.
[577] Tucker 2004, p. 176.
[578] Griffin 2006, p. 336.
[579]
[580] Zaloga, Steven (1981). *Armour of the Middle East Wars 1948–78 (Vanguard)*. Osprey Publishing.
[581] *Warfare since the Second World War*, By Klaus Jürgen Gantzel, Torsten Schwinghammer, p. 253
[582] *Wars in the Third World since 1945*, (NY 1991) Guy Arnold
[583] Gerhard, William D.; Millington, Henry W. (1981). "Attack on a SIGINT Collector, the USS Liberty" (PDF). NSA History Report, U.S. Cryptologic History series. National Security Agency. partially declassified 1999, 2003.
[584] Both USA and Israel officially attributed the USS *Liberty* incident as being due to mistaken identification.
[585] Some sources date the agreement to 4 November, others to 7 November. Most sources simply say "November". Gawrych (2000) p. 5
[586] Schiff, Zeev, *History of the Israeli Army*, Straight Arrow Books (1974) p. 145
[587] Churchill & Churchill, *The Six Day War*, Houghton Mifflin Company (1967) p. 21
[588] Pollack, Kenneth, *Arabs at War: Military Effectiveness 1948–1991*, University of Nebraska Press (2002), p. 290
[589] Segev, 2007, pp.149–52.
[590] Hart, 1989 p. 226
[591] Oren 2002/2003, p. 312; Burrowes & Douglas 1972, pp. 224–25
[592] Herzog 1982, p. 148
[593] John Quigley, *The Six-Day War and Israeli Self-Defense: Questioning the Legal Basis for Preventive War* https://books.google.com/books?id=0zEi3qGWLFIC&pg=PA32, Cambridge University Press, 2013, p. 32.
[594] Shlaim (2007) p. 238
[595] Cohen, Raymond. (1988), p. 12
[596] " LBJ Pledges U.S. to Peace Effort https://news.google.com/newspapers?nid=1310&dat=19670619&id=valVAAAAIBAJ&sjid=JeEDAAAAIBAJ&pg=5448,4112160", *Eugene Register-Guard* (19 June 1967). See also Johnson, Lyndon. "Address at the State Department's Foreign Policy Conference for Educators" http://www.presidency.ucsb.edu/ws/?pid=28308 (19 June 1967).
[597] Churchill po. 52 and 77
[598] Quigley, *The Six-Day War and Israeli Self-Defence*, p. 60. (Cambridge University Press)
[599] Stone 2004, p. 217.
[600] Pollack 2004, p. 294
[601] Pollack 2004, p. 59
[602] Ehteshami and Hinnebusch 1997, p. 76.
[603] Mutawi 2002, p. 42.
[604] Pollack 2004, pp. 293–94
[605]
[606] Oren, 176; Benny Morris, *Righteous Victims*, 318.
[607] Pollack 2004, p. 58.
[608] de Mazarrasa, Javier (1994) (in Spanish). Blindados en España 2ª Parte: La Difícil Postguerra 1939–1960. Valladolid, Spain: Quiron Ediciones. p. 50.
[609] Perrett, Bryan (1999). *Panzerkampfwagen IV medium tank: 1936–1945*. Oxford, United Kingdom: Osprey. p. 44.
[610] Oren 2002, p. 172
[611] Bowen 2003, p. 99 (author interview with Moredechai Hod, 7 May 2002).
[612] Oren 2002, electronic edition, Section "The War: Day One, June 5".
[613] Bowen 2003, pp. 114–15 (author interview with General Salahadeen Hadidi who presided over the first court martial of the heads of the air force and the air defense system after the war).
[614] Oren 2002 p. 171
[615] Pollack 2005, p. 474.

[616] Oren, 176, says 282 out of 420. Morris, 318, says 304 out of 419. Mark Tessler, *A History of the Israeli–Palestinian Conflict* (Indiana, 1994), p. 396, says over 350 planes were destroyed.
[617] Long 1984, p. 19, Table 1.
[618] Oren, p. 178
[619] Oren, p. 175
[620] Pollack 2004, p. 59.
[621] Oren, p. 180
[622] Oren, p. 181
[623] Oren, p. 202
[624] Oren, p. 182
[625] Simon Dunstan, *The Six Day War 1967: Sinai* https://books.google.com/books?id=ESv1lwg537AC&pg=PT125, Osprey Publishing, 2012, p. 125
[626] Leslie Stein, *The Making of Modern Israel: 1948–1967* https://books.google.com/books?id=nWkYAAAAQBAJ&pg=PT181, Polity Press, 2013 p. 181.
[627] Oren, p. 201
[628] Hammel 1992, p. 239
[629] Oren, p. 212
[630] Oren, p. 211
[631]
[632] Oren, p. 248
[633] Oren 2002, pp. 184–185.
[634] "On June 5, Israel sent a message to Hussein urging him not to open fire. Despite shelling into West Jerusalem, Netanya, and the outskirts of Tel Aviv, Israel did nothing." The Six Day War and Its Enduring Legacy http://www.washingtoninstitute.org/templateC05.php?CID=2080. Summary of remarks by Michael Oren at the Washington Institute for Near East Policy, 29 May 2002.
[635]
[636] Shlaim, 2001, p. 244.
[637] Oren, pp. 187–88
[638] Oren, p. 187
[639] Shlaim 2001, p. 245.
[640] Oren, p. 188–89
[641] Oren, pp. 191–92
[642] Oren, p. 222
[643] http://www.sixdaywar.org/contest/easternfront.asp
[644] Oren, p. 203
[645] Oren, pp. 222–23
[646] Oren, p. 224
[647] Oren, p. 219
[648] Shlaim 2001, p. 246.
[649] Sachar 1976. p. 642.
[650] Oren 2002, electronic edition, Section "Damascus and Jerusalem".
[651] Oren 2002, electronic edition, Section "The War: Day Five, June 9".
[652] Morris, 2001, p. 325
[653] Hammel 1992, p. 387
[654] Oren, p.280
[655] Oren, pp. 281–82
[656] Oren, p. 283
[657] Oren, p. 295
[658] Oren 2002, electronic edition, Section "Playing for the Brink".
[659] Sachar 1976. p. 660.
[660] Oren 2002, electronic edition, Section "Aftershocks".
[661]
[662]
[663]
[664]

665 Churchill & Churchill 1967, p. 189
666 UN Security Council meeting 1347 https://unispal.un.org/unispal.nsf/
9a798adbf322aff38525617b006d88d7/cd0beba6a1e28eff0525672800567b2c?OpenDocument (5 June 1967)
667 Churchill & Churchill 1967, p. 179.
668 Bron, Gabby 'Egyptian POWs Ordered to Dig Graves, Then Shot By Israeli Army' http://www.umassd.edu/specialprograms/mideastaffairs/witness2.htm , *Yedioth Ahronoth*, 17 August 1995.
669 Bar-Zohar, Michael 'The Reactions of Journalists to the Army's Murders of POWs', *Maariv*, 17 August 1995.
670 Prior 1999, pp. 209–10; Bar-On, Morris and Golani 2002; Fisher, Ronal 'Mass Murder in the 1956 War', *Ma'ariv*, 8 August 1995.
671 Laub, Karin, *Associated Press*, 16 August 1995. Retrieved from the Wayback Machine. 14 October 2005.
672 "Israel Reportedly Killed POWs", 17 August 1995
673 Segev, T., 2007, p. 374
674 Mansour 1994, p. 89
675 Green 1984
676 Smith, 15 September 1967
677 Bowen 2003, p. 89.
678 Phythian 2001, pp. 193–94.
679 Shlaim; Louis (2012) pp. 8, 53, 60, 75, 193, 199, 297
680 Podeh, *Middle East Quarterly*, Winter 2004, pp. 51-62
681 Hattendorf 2000
682 Shlaim; Louis (2012) p. 8
683 Shlaim; Louis (2012) p. 60
684 Shlaim; Louis (2012) p. 75
685 Shlaim; Louis (2012) p. 199
686 Tim Fischer, 'Six days of war, 40 years of secrecy,' http://www.theage.com.au/news/opinion/six-days-of-war-40-years-of-secrecy/2007/05/26/1179601730257.html&rct=j&frm=1&q=&esrc=s *The Age* 27 May 2007.
687 John Quigley, *The Six-Day War and Israeli Self-Defense: Questioning the Legal Basis for Preventive War* https://books.google.com/books?id=0zEi3qGWLFIC&pg=PA93, Cambridge University Press 2013 p. 93. Cf Dean Rusk, *As I Saw it: A Secretary of State's Memoirs*, W.W. Norton, 1990 pp. 386–88.
688 Brams & Togman 1998, p. 243; Youngs 2001, p. 12
689 [[Amos Oz http://www.abc.net.au/rn/features/inbedwithphillip/episodes/151-amos-oz/] interview with Phillip Adams,] 10 September 1991, re-broadcast on ABC Radio National 23 December 2011
690 Oren, p. 309
691 The "Status Quo" on the Temple Mount http://jcpa.org/article/status-quo-on-temple-mount/ November–December 2014
692 Jerusalem in the unholy grip of religious fervor http://www.timesofisrael.com/jerusalem-in-the-unholy-grip-of-religious-fervor/, Times of Israel. 6 November 2014
693 Cave of the Patriarchs http://www.chabad.org/special/israel/points_of_interest_cdo/aid/588225/jewish/Cave-of-the-Patriarchs.htm Chabad.org
694 Oren, p. 332
695 The Rise – and Rise – of French Jewry's Immigration to Israel http://www.haaretz.com/misc/haaretzcomsmartphoneapp/dailybrief/.premium-1.636848 Judy Maltz, 13 January 2015. haaretz.com
696 Tolts, Mark. Post-Soviet Aliyah and Jewish Demographic Transformation http://bjpa.org/Publications/downloadPublication.cfm?PublicationID=11924
697 Oren 2002, pp. 306–07
698 Włodzimierz Rozenbaum, CIAO: Intermarium, *National Convention of the American Association for the Advancement of Slavic Studies*, Atlanta, Ga., 8–11 October 1975.
699 Communiqué: Investigation regarding communist state officers who publicly incited hatred towards people of different nationality. http://www.ipn.gov.pl/portal/en/2/238/Communiqu_

Investigation_regarding_communist_state_officers_who_publicly_incited_.html *Institute of National Remembrance*, Warsaw. Publication on Polish site of IPN: 25 July 2007.

[700] Herzog 1989, p. 253.
[701] Shlaim 2001, p. 254.
[702] Sela 1997, p. 108.
[703] Morris (2001) p. 327
[704] Shay Fogelman, "The disinherited" http://www.haaretz.com/weekend/magazine/the-disinherited-1.304959, *Haaretz*, 30 July 2010
[705] http://www.digitaljournalist.org/issue0003/arm01.htm
[706] http://www.thejc.com/arts/arts-interviews/david-rubinger-picture
[707] https://www.theguardian.com/world/2007/may/06/israelandthepalestinians.features1
[708] https://books.google.com/books?id=ydRHCPWngioC&pg=PA246&dq=&ei=5TIBSaGOBI6UMajtqKcL&client=
[709] https://www.jewishvirtuallibrary.org/jsource/History/67_War.html
[710] http://www.archives.gov.il/archives/#/Archive/0b071706800171a0/File/0b071706807e13c6
[711] http://select.nytimes.com/gst/abstract.html?res=F20615FD3D5B107B93C1A8178ED85F438685F9
[712] http://www.cgsc.edu/carl/resources/csi/content.asp
[713] http://www.sixdaywar.co.uk/nassers_challenge-martin-gilbert.htm
[714] https://web.archive.org/web/20090525133657/http://www.mepc.org/journal_vol6/9902_hajjar.asp
[715] http://www.mfa.gov.il/MFA/MFAArchive/2000_2009/2004/1/Background%20on%20Israeli%20POWs%20and%20MIAs
[716] http://www.mfa.gov.il/MFA/History/Modern+History/Israel+wars/The+Six-Day+War+-+June+1967.htm
[717] https//pqasb.pqarchiver.com
[718] https://web.archive.org/web/20120402101751/http://meria.idc.ac.il/journal/2005/issue2/jv9no2a2.html
[719] https://select.nytimes.com/gst/abstract.html?res=FA0812F9385E137A93CBA9178DD85F438685F9
[720] https//books.google.com
[721] https://www.washingtonpost.com/wp-dyn/content/article/2007/05/17/AR2007051701976.html
[722] //www.worldcat.org/issn/0740-5421
[723] http://www.lbjlib.utexas.edu/johnson/archives.hom/oralhistory.hom/McNamaraR/McNamara-SP1.PDF
[724] https://pqasb.pqarchiver.com/boston/access/663999751.html?FMT=ABS&date=Sep%2016,%201983
[725] http://www.unu.edu/unupress/unupbooks/80858e/80858E00.htm#Contents
[726] https://books.google.com/books?id=g9bBJusRJIMC&pg=PA94
[727] https://fas.org/nuke/guide/russia/agency/mf-med.htm
[728] http://muse.jhu.edu/journals/israel_studies/v010/10.2oren.pdf
[729] http://www.thelibertyincident.com/docs/Parker2.pdf
[730] //doi.org/10.1525%2Fjps.1997.27.1.00p0164l
[731] http://www.meforum.org/587/the-lie-that-wont-die-collusion-1967
[732] https//books.google.com
[733] https://www.cia.gov/library/center-for-the-study-of-intelligence/csi-publications/csi-studies/studies/vol49no1/html_files/arab_israeli_war_1.html
[734] http://www.saeedshafqat.com/articles/islamic_world_and_south_asia.pdf
[735] https://books.google.com/books?id=8YhNPNeBh8IC&pg=PA199
[736] https://select.nytimes.com/gst/abstract.html?res=FB0816FE3B5E137A93C7A8178DD85F438685F9
[737] http://www.salon.com/news/opinion/feature/2007/06/04/six_day_war
[738] https//web.archive.org
[739] https://web.archive.org/web/20090717074012/http://www.parliament.uk/commons/lib/research/rp2001/rp01-008.pdf

[740] https://books.google.com/books?id=vNb5VkyxDlYC&printsec=frontcover&dq=Image+and+reality+of+the+Israel-Palestine+conflict#v=onepage&q&f=false
[741] http://therealnews.com/t2/index.php?option=com_content&task=view&id=31&Itemid=74&jumival=19230
[742] http://www.azure.org.il/article.php?id=456
[743] http://www.sixdaywar.co.uk/news_articles-three-soldiers.htm
[744] http://www.sixdaywar.co.uk/
[745] https://www.youtube.com/watch?v=C4Ooaqtk-Cg
[746] https://www.youtube.com/watch?v=OnsMfKmaizE
[747] http://i-cias.com/e.o/sixdaywr.htm
[748] https://history.state.gov/historicaldocuments/frus1964-68v19
[749] http://www.shapell.org/manuscript.aspx?169472
[750] https://web.archive.org/web/20151018141352/http://unispal.un.org/UNISPAL.NSF/0/7D35E1F729DF491C85256EE700686136
[751] https//web.archive.org
[752] http//www.hcef.org
[753] http://www.sixdaywar.co.uk/6_day_war_aftermath_prof_adler_intro.htm
[754] http://www.isracast.com/narkiss.asx
[755] https://web.archive.org/web/20160201184820/https://www.isracast.com/article.aspx?id=374
[756] http://imra.org.il/story.php3?id=18226
[757] http://jafi.org/NR/exeres/4B21CC9B-BCD1-43FA-82F5-4355BE6EED30
[758] http://mfa.gov.il/MFA/AboutIsrael/History/Pages/The%20War%20of%20Attrition%20-1968-70.aspx
[759] *Russian Aviation and Air Power in the Twentieth Century*, Robin D. S. Higham, John T. Greenwood, Von Hardesty, Routledge, 1998, p.227
[760] Fruchter-Ronen I, (2008), pp. 244–260
[761] Morris (1999), p. 368
[762] Wallach, Jedua; Ayalon, Avraham; Yitzhaki, Aryeh (1980). "Operation Inferno". in Evyatar Nur. *Carta's Atlas of Israel*, Volume 2
[763] Schiff, Zeev, *A History of the Israeli Army (1870–1974)*, Straight Arrow Books (San Francisco, 1974) p. 246,
[764] Benny Morris, *Righteous Victims: A History of the Zionist-Arab Conflict, 1881–2001*, Random House (1999), page 362.
[765] Nicolle and Cooper, 32–33
[766] Saad el-Shazly, *The Crossing of Suez*. p. 195.
[767] Uri Bar, *The Watchman Fell Asleep: The Surprise Of Yom Kippur And Its Sources*. p.15.
[768] Insight Team of the London Sunday Times, *Yom Kippur War*, Double Day & Company (1974) Page 42
[769] Zeev Schiff, History of the Israeli Army 1870–1974, Straight Arrow Books (1974), page 246
[770] A list of known Soviet army losses of manpower during The War of attrition http://www.hubara-rus.ru/heroes.html
[771] Karsh, Efraim: *The Cautious Bear: Soviet Military Engagement in Middle East Wars in the Post-1967 Era*
[772] Herzog (1982), 220
[773] Schiff, Ze'ev, *History of the Israeli Army*, Straight Arrow Books (1974), p. 253
[774] Pollack 2002, p. 95.
[775] Pollack 2002, p. 94.
[776] Pollack 2002, p. 96.
[777] Herzog, Chaim, *The Arab-Israeli Wars*, Random House, (New York, 1982), 196
[778] El Gamasy, *The October War, 1973* p.99
[779] Rothrock, James, Live by the Sword: Israel's Struggle for existence in the Holy Land, WestBow Press (2011) 48–49
[780] Egyptian Air-to-Air Victories since 1948 http://www.acig.info/CMS/index.php?option=com_content&task=view&id=185&Itemid=47
[781] El Gamasy, *The October War, 1973* p.101

[782] Saada, Tass & Merrill, Dean *Once an Arafat Man: The True Story of How a PLO Sniper Found a New Life* Illinois 2008 pp 4–6
[783] Zeev Maoz, Defending the Holy Land, A Critical Analysis of Israel's Security and Foreign Policy, University of Michigan Press, 2006, pages 244–246
[784] Herzog, The Arab-Israeli Wars page 205
[785] Nicolle and Cooper, 31
[786] Chaim Herzog, *The Arab-Israeli Wars*, Random House New York (1982) p.214
[787] Mordechai Naor, *The Twentieth Century In Eretz Israel*, Konemann (1996), 409
[788]^ "The War of Attrition as Reflected in Egyptian Sources" (1995), p. 107, by Mustafa Kabha (Hebrew)
[789] http://www.kuwait-history.net/vb/showthread.php?p=70299#post70299, Kuwait commemorates the return of 16 soldiers from the Yarmouk Brigade
[790] Nicolle and Cooper, 32
[791] Nicolle and Cooper, 33
[792] Sachar, Howard: *Israel and Europe: An Appraisal in History*, p. 171-172
[793] Schiff (1974) p246
[794] Chaim Herzog, *The Arab-Israeli Wars*, Random House New York, (1982) p.220
[795] Morris (1999) p362
[796] Insight Team of the London *Sunday Times* (1974) p42
[797] https://books.google.com/books?id=1BYk_sXT6tsC
[798] http://www.acig.org/artman/publish/article_263.shtml
[799] http://www.us-israel.org/jsource/Society_&_Culture/69iaf.html
[800] https://web.archive.org/web/20060629235830/http://weekly.ahram.org.eg/archives/67-97/sup8.htm
[801] https//web.archive.org
[802] "See Security Council Document S/10070 Para 2." http://domino.un.org/unispal.nsf/9a798adbf322aff38525617b006d88d7/9c1564a379bc943d0525654f005d71cc!OpenDocument&Highlight=2,S%2F10070
[803] Resolution 242: Response from the affected parties http://www.sixdaywar.org/content/242response.asp www.sixdaywar.org
[804] The Jarring Mission- First Phase- Excerpts from Report by Secretary General U Thant- 4 January 1971, Israeli MFA http://www.mfa.gov.il/MFA/Foreign+Relations/Israels+Foreign+Relations/since+1947/1947-1974/3+The+Jarring+Mission-+First+Phase-+Excerpts+from.htm
[805] Aide-memoire presented to Israel and Egypt by Ambassador Gunnar Jarring http://www.ipcri.org/files/jarring.html
[806] The Jarring initiative and the response, Israeli MFA http://www.mfa.gov.il/MFA/Foreign+Relations/Israels+Foreign+Relations/since+1947/1947-1974/28+The+Jarring+initiative+and+the+response-+8+Febr.htm
[807] Policy, Background: The Components of a Secure Peace, 10 March 1971, Embassy of Israel, Washington DC
[808] Reuven Pedatzur, "Seeds of Peace", Haaretz http://www.haaretz.com/weekend/week-s-end/seeds-of-peace-1.315172
[809] http://www.duo.uio.no/publ/IAKH/2007/58588/HuldaxMxrkxxMasteroppgavexixhistorie.pdf
[810] http://www.haaretz.com/weekend/week-s-end/seeds-of-peace-1.315172
[811] //tools.wmflabs.org/geohack/geohack.php?pagename=Munich_massacre&params=48_10_47_N_11_32_57_E_region:DE-BY_scale:50000_type:event
[812] "First official Olympic ceremony held in memory of Munich victims" http://www.jpost.com/Israel-News/Sports/First-official-IOC-ceremony-in-memory-of-Munich-victims-463185, jpost.com; accessed 5 September 2017.
[813] Reeve, Klein and Groussard.
[814] Klein, pp. 35–36.
[815] Cooley.
[816] Reeve, Simon. *One Day in September*, 2001.
[817] Interview with Heinz Hohensinn in One Day in September
[818] Groussard.

[819] Interview with Tröger in *One Day in September*
[820] Interview with Ulrich Wegener in *One Day in September*.
[821] Reeve, pp. 103, 107.
[822] Groussard, p. 349.
[823] Reeve, pp. 115–16.
[824] Reeve, pp. 106–07.
[825] Groussard, pp. 354–55.
[826]
[827] Reeve, pp. 118-20.
[828] Reeve, pp. 121–22.
[829] Reeve, pp. 236–37.
[830] Olympics Massacre: Munich - The real story https://www.independent.co.uk/news/world/europe/olympics-massacre-munich-the-real-story-5336955.html, *The Independent*, 22 January 2006.
[831] Guardian article on the massacre https://www.theguardian.com/fromthearchive/story/0,12269,1298214,00.html, 7 September 1972.
[832] BBC News article on commemoration at 2004 Olympics http://news.bbc.co.uk/2/hi/europe/3581866.stm, 20 August 2004.
[833] "11 Israeli victims of '72 Munich Olympic massacre officially commemorated in Rio" http://www.jewishjournal.com/olympics/article/11_israeli_victims_of_72_munich_olympic_massacre_officially_commemorated_in, *Jewish Journal*, 5 August 2016; accessed 5 September 2017.
[834] Morris.
[835] Melman.
[836] "Munich: Mossad breaks cover" http://film.guardian.co.uk/news/story/0,,1695135,00.html by Ewen MacAskill and Ian Black, *The Guardian*, 26 January 2006.
[837] Shalev, Noam 'The hunt for Black September' http://news.bbc.co.uk/2/hi/programmes/this_world/4627388.stm. BBC. Retrieved 4 March 2012.
[838] Reeve, p. 188.
[839] Neo-Nazi 'aided Munich Olympics massacre' http://www.thelocal.de/national/20120617-43199.html, The Local 17 June 2012
[840] Abu Daoud.
[841] https://fas.org/irp/eprint/calahan.htm
[842] https//web.archive.org
[843] http://www.haaretz.com/hasen/pages/ShArtStEng.jhtml?itemNo=683846&contrassID=1&subContrassID=1&title=%27title%27
[844] https://web.archive.org/web/20110714203422/http://www.nox-mag.com/article/Rings+Of+Fire/
[845] https://web.archive.org/web/20100225132035/http://www.munich11.com/
[846] http://www.time.com/time/magazine/article/0,9171,1137646-1,00.html
[847] https://web.archive.org/web/20120902152411/http://www.archives.gov.il/NR/exeres/73045DBE-484C-419E-BCE1-6C32896F8E16%2Cframeless.htm?NRMODE=Published
[848] See <ref>. Foreword.
[849] Insight Team of the London *Sunday Times*, p. 450.
[850] "Israel's victory came at the cost of heavy casualties, and Israelis criticized the government's lack of preparedness." YOM KIPPUR WAR http://www.history.com/topics/yom-kippur-war#FWNE.fw..yo007800.a at history.com http://www.history.com/
[851] "The 1973 war thus ended in an Israeli victory, but at great cost to the United States." The 1973 Arab-Israeli War https://history.state.gov/milestones/1969-1976/arab-israeli-war-1973 at website https://history.state.gov/ of Office of the Historian
[852] Morris, 2011, Righteous Victims, p. 437
[853] Morris, 2011 p.433, "Bashan ... 500 square kilometers ... which brought it within 20 miles of Damascus"
[854] Perez, Cuba, *Between Reform and Revolution*, pp. 377–379. Gott, Cuba, *A New History*, p. 280.
[855] Insight Team of the London *Sunday Times*, p. 372–373.
[856] The number reflects artillery units of caliber 100 mm and up

[857] Shazly, p. 272.
[858] Haber & Schiff, pp. 30–31.
[859] Bourne, Peter G. (1986). *Fidel: A Biography of Fidel Castro*. New York: Dodd, Mead & Company.
[860] Journal "الأهرام"،"Al Ahram". 14 October 1974
[861] "القوة الثالثة، تاريخ القوات الجوية المصرية." *Third Power: History of Egyptian Air Force* Ali Mohammed Labib. pp. 187
[862] Dunstan, p. 200.
[863] Rabinovich p. 497
[864] Herzog 1975, p. 37.
[865] Insight Team of the London Sunday Times 1974, p. 15.
[866] Herzog 1982, p. 321.
[867] Hammad (2002), pp.237–276
[868] Gawrych (1996), p.60
[869] Herzog, *Heroes of Israel*, p. 253.
[870] Podeh, p.106.
[871] Podeh p.107.
[872] Rabinovich, p. 13.
[873] Morris 2001, p. 390.
[874] Heikal, 22.
[875] Rabinovich, p. 39.
[876] Rabinovich, p. 25.
[877] Herzog 1982, pp. 315, 321.
[878] Herzog 1982, p. 315.
[879] Herzog 1975, p. 26.
[880] Herzog 1982, p. 229.
[881] Shazly, p. 207.
[882] Gawrych 1996, p. 24.
[883] Schiff, p. 12
[884] Rabinovich, p. 51.
[885] Rabinovich, p. 50.
[886] Rabinovich, p. 57.
[887]
[888] Doron Geller, " Israeli Intelligence and the Yom Kippur War of 1973 http://www.jafi.org.il/education/juice/service/week11.html November 27, 2005.
[889] Christopher Andrew and Vasili Mitrokhin, *The World Was Going Our Way: The KGB and the Battle for the Third World*, Basic Books, 2006.
[890] Rabinovich, p. 89.
[891] The national security archive, declassified archival records, The October War and U.S. Policy. http://www.gwu.edu/~nsarchiv/NSAEBB/NSAEBB98/octwar-10.pdf
[892] Sachar, Howard M. *A History of Israel from the Rise of Zionism to Our Time*. Alfred A. Knopf, 2007, p. 755.
[893] William B. Quandt, *Peace Process*, p. 105.
[894] Rabinovich, p. 454.
[895] Gawrych 1996, p. 27.
[896] Rabinovich, prologue.
[897] Rabinovich, p. 62.
[898] Shazly, pp. 224–225.
[899] Shazly, pp. 225–226.
[900] Shazly, p. 189.
[901] Shazly, pp. 55–56.
[902] Garwych, p. 28.
[903] Shazly, p. 232
[904] Hammad, pp.90–92, 108.
[905] , p. 278.
[906] *Arabs at War: Military Effectiveness* (Pollack), p. 108.

[907] Rabinovich, p. 115.
[908] Pollack, p. 125.
[909] Gawrych, p. 81.
[910] *The Yom Kippur War 1973: The Sinai* – Simon Dunstan and Kevin Lyles.
[911] Shazly, p. 228.
[912] Shazly, p. 229.
[913] Cohen, *Israel's Best Defense*, p. 354.
[914] Pollack, p. 11.
[915] Shazly, p. 233.
[916] Haber & Schiff, p. 32.
[917] Schiff, p. 294.
[918] Herzog, *The War of Atonement*, Little, Brown and Company, 1975, p. 156.
[919] Insight Team of the London *Sunday Times*, pp. 169, 170.
[920] Pollack, *Arabs at War: Military Effectiveness 1948–1991*, University of Nebraska Press, p. 110
[921] Pollack, *Arabs at War: Military Effectiveness 1948–1991*, University of Nebraska Press, p. 108.
[922]
[923] Hammad, p. 133.
[924] Nicolle & Cooper p. 40.
[925] Pollack, p. 112.
[926] Hammad, pp. 712–714.
[927] Hammad, pp.717–722.
[928] Gawrych 1996, p. 38. In his memoirs, Adan, commenting on one of the commando operations in the north, noted that "Natke's experience fighting the stubborn Egyptian commandos who tried to cut off the road around Romani showed again that this was not the Egyptian Army we had crushed in four days in 1967. We were now dealing with a well-trained enemy, fighting with skill and dedication."
[929] Insight Team of the London *Sunday Times*, pp. 169–170.
[930] Rabinovich, p. 354.
[931] Gawrych 1996, pp. 41–42.
[932] Dunstan and Lyles, p. 64.
[933] Gawrych, 1996, pp. 43–44.
[934] Rabinovich, p. 234.
[935] Gawrych 1996, pp. 44–52.
[936] Gawrych 2000, pp. 192, 208.
[937] Herzog, 1982, pp. 255–256.
[938] Shazly, p. 241.
[939] Herzog 1982, p. 256.
[940]
[941] Herzog, 1982, p. 258.
[942] Shazly, p. 317.
[943] Schiff, *A History of the Israeli Army*, p. 310.
[944] Rabinovich, p. 353.
[945] Rabinovich, p. 355.
[946] Haber & Schiff, p. 144.
[947] Pollack, p. 117.
[948] Herzog, *The Arab–Israeli Wars*, Random House, p. 260.
[949] Yom Kippur War: Embattled Israeli Bridgehead at Chinese Farm http://www.historynet.com/yom-kippur-war-embattled-israeli-bridgehead-at-chinese-farm.htm
[950] Pollack, Kenneth, *Arabs at War: Military Effectiveness 1948–91*, University of Nebraska Press, pp. 116, 126 & 129.
[951] El-Gamasy, p. 276.
[952] Herzog, 1982, pp. 257–258.
[953] Pollack, p. 118.
[954] Rabinovich, pp. 374–375.
[955] Rabinovich, pp. 389–391.
[956] Pollack, p. 511.

[957] Pollack, pp. 124–25
[958] Rabinovich, pp. 393–393.
[959] Rabinovich, p. 425.
[960] Sharon, Gilad: *Sharon: The Life of A Leader* (2011)
[961] Rabinovich, p. 427.
[962] Pollack, pp. 118–19.
[963] Hammad (2002), pp. 335–408.
[964] Gawrych (1996), pp. 62–64.
[965] Pollack, p. 129
[966] Pollack, p. 119.
[967] Pollack, pp. 119–20.
[968] Boyne, p. 181
[969] Pollack, p. 120.
[970] Rabinovich, p. 401.
[971] Dunstan, p. 107.
[972] Herzog, *The War of Atonement*, Little, Brown and Company (1975), pp. 236–7.
[973] Pollack, p. 122.
[974] Rabinovich, pp. 428–429.
[975] O'Ballance, p. 120.
[976] Rabinovich, p. 445.
[977] O'Ballance, p. 121.
[978] O'Ballance, p. 122.
[979] *The Leader-Post*, October 25, 1973, issue.
[980]
[981] Boyne, p. 183.
[982] Hoyne, p. 205.
[983] Boyne, p. 214
[984] Rabinovich, p. 452.
[985] Rabinovich, p. 458.
[986] Adan, p. 284.
[987] Gawrych, pp. 73–74.
[988] Rabinovich, p. 463.
[989] The October War and U.S. Policy http://www.gwu.edu/~nsarchiv/NSAEBB/NSAEBB98/#VII, *Collapse of the Ceasefire*.
[990] William B. Quandt, *Peace Process*, p. 120.
[991] Gawrych, 1996, p. 73.
[992] Hammad, pp. 483, 487–490.
[993] Nicolle, David & Cooper, Tom: *Arab MiG-19 and MiG-21 units in combat*.
[994] Rabinovich, pp. 466–475.
[995] Rabinovich, p. 465
[996] Rabinovich, p. 487.
[997] Gawrych, p.74
[998] Dupuy, pp. 543–545, 589.
[999] David T. Buckwalter, The 1973 Arab–Israeli War. http://www.au.af.mil/au/awc/awcgate/navy/pmi/1973.pdf
[1000] Herzog, *Arab–Israeli Wars*, p. 283.
[1001] Shazly, p. 293.
[1002] Shazly, p. 323.
[1003] Rabinovich, p. 486
[1004] Rabinovich, p. 493.
[1005] Aloni, Shlomo: *Arab–Israeli Air Wars, 1947–82*.
[1006] Rabinovich, p. 477.
[1007] Rabinovich, p. 467.
[1008] Neff, p. 306.
[1009] Johnson and Tierney, p. 176.
[1010] Shazly, p. 295.

[1011] El-Gamasy, p. 302.
[1012] Morris, 2011, Righteous Victims, p. 436
[1013] Peter Caddick-Adams, "Golan Heights, battles of", *The Oxford Companion to Military History*, ed. Richard Holmes. Oxford University Press, 2001.
[1014] O'Ballance (1978). Chapter 7: "The Syrians attack", pp. 119–146.
[1015] Rabinovich (2017) p 158
[1016] Rabinovich (2017) p 57
[1017] Rabinovich (2017) p 64
[1018] Rabinovich (2017) p 159
[1019] Rabinovich (2017) p 171
[1020] Rabinovich (2017) p 172-173
[1021] Rabinovich (2017) p 282
[1022] Asher & Hammel (1987), p. 88-105
[1023] Asher & Hammel (1987), p. 100
[1024] Asher & Hammel (1987), p. 105
[1025] Asher & Hammel (1987), p. 103
[1026] Rabinovich (2017) p 161
[1027] Rabinovich (2017) p 162
[1028] Asher & Hammel (1987), p. 107
[1029] Asher & Hammel (1987), p. 118
[1030] Rabinovich (2017) p 170
[1031] Insight Team of the London *Sunday Times*, pp. 291–293.
[1032] Rabinovich (2017) p 173-174
[1033] Rabinovich (2017) p 174
[1034] Asher & Hammel (1987), p. 140-144
[1035] Asher & Hammel (1987), p. 193-197
[1036] Asher & Hammel (1987), p. 196
[1037] Asher & Hammel (1987), p. 202
[1038] Asher & Hammel (1987), p. 227
[1039] Asher & Hammel (1987), p. 240
[1040] Rabinovich (2017) p 178-179
[1041] Rabinovich (2017) p 163, 179
[1042] Asher & Hammel (1987), p. 108
[1043] Asher & Hammel (1987), p. 123-124
[1044] Asher & Hammel (1987), p. 125
[1045] Asher & Hammel (1987), p. 127
[1046] Rabinovich (2017) p 177
[1047] Rabinovich (2017) p 178
[1048] Rabinovich (2017) p 179
[1049] Rabinovich (2017) p 182-183
[1050] Asher & Hammel (1987), p. 136
[1051] Rabinovich (2017) p 184-185
[1052] Asher & Hammel (1987), p. 138-139
[1053] Asher & Hammel (1987), p. 158-159
[1054] Rabinovich (2017) p 187
[1055] Rabinovich (2017) p 194
[1056] Rabinovich (2017) p 195
[1057] Rabinovich (2017) p 198
[1058] Rabinovich (2017) p 199
[1059] Bar-Joseph (2012), p. 220
[1060] Rabinovich (2017) p 200
[1061] Asher & Hammel (1987), p. 157
[1062] Rabinovich (2017) p 189
[1063] Rabinovich (2017) p 185
[1064] Asher & Hammel (1987), p. 106
[1065] Asher & Hammel (1987), p. 134-135

[1066] Rabinovich (2017) p 188
[1067] Bar-Joseph (2012), p. 227
[1068] Asher & Hammel (1987), p. 170
[1069] Rabinovich (2017) p 190
[1070] Rabinovich (2017) p 209
[1071] Asher & Hammel (1987), p. 171
[1072] Rabinovich (2017) p 218
[1073] Rabinovich (2017) p 185-186
[1074] Asher & Hammel (1987), p. 155
[1075] Rabinovich (2017) p 193
[1076] Rabinovich (2017) p 206
[1077] Rabinovich (2017) p 233
[1078] Rabinovich (2017) p 207
[1079] Rabinovich (2017) p 218-219
[1080] Asher & Hammel (1987), p. 155
[1081] Rabinovich (2017) p 231-233
[1082] Asher & Hammel (1987), p. 136-137
[1083] Asher & Hammel (1987), p. 178
[1084] Rabinovich (2017) p 246-247
[1085] Richard B. Parker (ed.), 2001, *The October War—A Retrospective* Gainsville: University of Florida Press, p 102–3; p 119
[1086] Asher & Hammel (1987), p. 55
[1087] Asher & Hammel (1987), p. 58
[1088] Asher & Hammel (1987), p. 60
[1089] Asher & Hammel (1987), p. 64
[1090] Asher & Hammel (1987), p. 65
[1091] Asher & Hammel (1987), p. 63
[1092] *The Daily Telegraph*, October 9, 1973 issue, page 2
[1093] Rabinovich, p. 304.
[1094] Rabinovich, p. 433.
[1095]
[1096] Pollack, *Arabs at War*, 2002, p. 167, gives total numbers for the Iraqi force by the end of the conflict as 60,000 men, more than 700 T-55 tanks', 500 APCs, more than 200 artillery pieces, two armored divisions, two infantry brigades, twelve artillery battalions, and a special forces brigade.
[1097] Dunstan, Simon: *The Yom Kippur War: The Arab–Israeli War of 1973*
[1098] Situation Report in the Middle East as of 1200 EDT, October 23, 1973 http://www.gwu.edu/~nsarchiv/NSAEBB/NSAEBB98/octwar-59.pdf, Department of State Operations Center
[1099] Rabinovich, p. 450
[1100] Rabinovich, pp. 450–451.
[1101]
[1102] Jonathan B. A. Bailey. *Field Artillery and Firepower*. Naval Institute Press, 2004, p. 398.
[1103] David Rodman, "Friendly Enemies: Israel and Jordan in the 1973 Yom Kuppur War", *The Israel Journal of Foreign Affairs*, Vol. 6 No. 1 (January 2012), pp. 95–96.
[1104] Hammad, pp. 100–101.
[1105] Almog, "Israel's Navy beat the odds", United States Naval Institute — *Proceedings* (March 1997), Vol. 123, Iss. 3; p. 106.
[1106] Dunstan, *The Yom Kippur War*, p. 114.
[1107] Bolia, *Overreliance on Technology: Yom Kippur Case Study* http://www.army.mil/professionalwriting/volumes/volume2/september_2004/9_04_4.html
[1108] Rabonovich, *The Boats of Cherbourg*, pp. 256–262.
[1109] Dupuy, *Elusive Victory*, pp. 562–563.
[1110] Herzog, *The Arab–Israeli Wars*, p. 312.
[1111] Vego, *Naval Strategy and Operations in Narrow Seas* (Routledge: 1999), at p. 151.
[1112] Almog, Ze'ev (March 1997). "Israel's Navy beat the odds" – *United States Naval Institute – Proceedings* (Annapolis: United States Naval Institute)

[1113] O'Ballance, p. 157.
[1114] Insight Team of the London *Sunday Times*, pp. 212–213.
[1115] Safran, Nadav: *Israel—The Embattled Ally*, p. 312
[1116] El Gammasy, *The October War, 1973* pp. 215–216.
[1117] Shazly, p. 287.
[1118] O'Ballance, p. 160.
[1119] Herzog (1975), pp. 268–269.
[1120] Morris, *Righteous Victims*, p. 432.
[1121] Herzog, *The Arab–Israeli Wars*, p. 314.
[1122] Annati, Anti-ship missiles and countermeasures—part I (ASM), *Naval Forces* (2001), Vol. 22, Iss. 1; p. 20.
[1123] Insight Team of the London *Sunday Times*, pp. 279, 429.
[1124] Insight Team of the London *Sunday Times*, pp. 429, 449.
[1125] Official Gazette of Syria (11 July 1974).
[1126] Schiff, p. 90.
[1127] "War and Lack of Inner Peace" http://info.jpost.com/C003/Supplements/30YK/art.34.html , Michael S. Arnold, *The Jerusalem Post*, September 17, 1999.
[1128] Insight Team of the London *Sunday Times*, p. 429.
[1129] Insight Team of the London *Sunday Times*, pp. 449–450.
[1130] Sarna, Igal (2000), *The Man Who Fell Into a Puddle: Israeli Lives*, Vintage Books/Random House, pp. 144–148.
[1131] Sarna, p. 148.
[1132] Matthew T. Penney, "Intelligence and the 1973 Arab–Israeli War" in President Nixon and the Role of Intelligence in the 1973 Arab–Israeli War, symposium held by CIA, January 30, 2013. https://www.cia.gov/library/publications/historical-collection-publications/arab-israeli-war/nixon-arab-isaeli-war.pdf
[1133] William Burr (ed.), "State Department Intelligence and Research Predicted 1973 Arab–Israeli War", The National Security Archive at George Washington University http://www.gwu.edu/~nsarchiv/NSAEBB/NSAEBB415/.
[1134] October 6 conversation between Henry Kissinger, Brent Scowcroft and Chinese Ambassador to the United States Huan Chen. Transcript http://www.gwu.edu/~nsarchiv/NSAEBB/NSAEBB98/octwar-17.pdf. George Washington University National Security Archive.
[1135] George Lenczowski, *American Presidents and the Middle East* (1990), p. 129.
[1136] William B. Quandt, *Peace Process*, p. 109.
[1137] October 9, 1973, conversation (8:20–8:40 am) between Israeli Ambassador to the United States Simcha Dinitz, military attaché General Mordechai Gur, Henry Kissinger, Brent Scowcroft, and Peter Rodman. Transcript http://www.gwu.edu/~nsarchiv/NSAEBB/NSAEBB98/octwar-21a.pdf George Washington University National Security Archive.
[1138] Cohen, Avner. " The Last Nuclear Moment https://www.nytimes.com/2003/10/06/opinion/the-last-nuclear-moment.html" *The New York Times*, October 6, 2003.
[1139] October 9, 1973, conversation (6:10–6:35 pm) between Israeli Ambassador to the United States Simcha Dinitz, Henry Kissinger, Brent Scowcroft, and Peter Rodman. Transcript http://www.gwu.edu/~nsarchiv/NSAEBB/NSAEBB98/octwar-21b.pdf George Washington University National Security Archive.
[1140]
[1141] Krisinger, Chris J. "Operation Nickel Grass – Airlift in Support of National Policy" http://www.airpower.maxwell.af.mil/airchronicles/apj/apj89/spr89/krisinger.html , *Aerospace Power Journal*, Spring 1989.
[1142] Rabinovich, p. 491.
[1143] Haber & Schiff, p. 382.
[1144] Shazli p.275–276
[1145] Haber & Schiff, p. 282.
[1146] Gawrych 1996, p. 56.
[1147] El Gamasy, *The October War, 1973*, p. 276.
[1148] Shazly, pp. 251–252.
[1149] O'Ballance, p. 182.

[1150] Schiff, 303
[1151] Shazly, p. 275.
[1152] Shazly, pp. 274–275. Shazly states that " ... the Soviet Union mounted a sea-borne resupply operation: no less than 63,000 tons, mainly to Syria, by October 30"
[1153] Quandt, 25–26 (pdf pages 37–38), gives the airlift total as approximately 12,500 tons; Quandt 23 (pdf page 35) gives the sealift total as approximately 63,000 tons.
[1154] Hammad, p. 382.
[1155] https://fas.org/nuke/guide/israel/doctrine/index.html
[1156] Rabinovich, p. 325.
[1157] O'Ballance, pp. 165–166.
[1158] Porter, Bruce D. – *The USSR in Third World Conflicts, Soviet Arms and Diplomacy in Local Wars*, p. 135.
[1159] William B Quandt, *Peace Process*, p. 121.
[1160] Rabinovich, p. 479.
[1161] Rabinovich, p. 480.
[1162] Rabinovich, p. 484.
[1163] Rabinovich, p. 485.
[1164]
[1165] Kuwaraswamy. p.60. "On the Egyptian front, the Libyan (manned by Egyptians), Algerian and Iraqi squadrons took part in bombing Israeli targets and providing air assistance to ground operations. Additional Arab forces operating on the Egyptian front were a Libyan armored brigade and a Kuwaiti infantry battalion which had been deployed in Egypt before the war, and an Algerian armored brigade which arrived on 17 October. Neither of these units took an active part in the war. After the cease-fire went into effect, a Sudanese infantry brigade also arrived in the front."
[1166] Perez, *Cuba: Between Reform and Revolution*, pp. 377–379.
[1167] Bourne, Peter G. (1986), *Fidel: A Biography of Fidel Castro*. New York: Dodd, Mead & Company.
[1168] Shazly, pp. 83–84.
[1169] Israeli F-4s Actually Fought North Korean MiGs During the Yom Kippur War http://www.businessinsider.com/israel-north-korea-dogfight-yom-kippur-war-2013-6?IR=T
[1170] List of Arab contributions by country http://www.almasryalyoum.com/news/details/536573; Kuwait Defense Minister, His Highness Sheikh Saad Al-Salim Al-Sabah visiting Egyptian front in 1972 and issues war operation order 3967 to enact Al-Jahra Force
[1171] Kuwaiti Ministry of Defense http://www.mod.gov.kw/MOD/Arabic_P/index.jsp
[1172]
[1173] Rabinovich, I. *The War for Lebanon, 1970–1985*. p.105. "Lebanon was perceived as Israel's one harmless neighbour, a state that since 1949 had not taken part in the Arab–Israeli wars ..."
[1174]
[1175]
[1176]
[1177]
[1178] Rabinovich, 497.
[1179]
[1180]
[1181] John Pimlott, Michael Orr, *The Middle East Conflicts: From 1945 to the Present*, London: Orbis Publishing (1983), p. 99.
[1182]
[1183] O'Ballance, p. 129
[1184] Military Lessons of the Yom Kippur War: Historical Perspectives http://csel.eng.ohio-state.edu/courses/ise817/papers/creveld_military_lessons.pdf, Martin van Creveld, p. 47
[1185]
[1186]
[1187] Quandt 2005, pp. 123–124.
[1188] Drysdale, A. & Hinnebusch, R.: *Syria and the Middle East Peace Process*. Council on Foreign Relations Press, New York, 1991.

[1189] Tristam, P.: *The Egyptian-Israeli Disengagement Treaties of 1974 and 1975* http://middleeast. about.com/od/arabisraeliconflict/a/me080421.htm . About.com, accessed 2012.
[1190] Rabinovich, pp. 497–498.
[1191] Rabinovich, p. 499.
[1192] Rabinovich, p. 501.
[1193] Rabinovich, p. 503
[1194] Rabinovich, p. 502.
[1195] Findings of the Agranat Commission http://www.jafi.org.il/education/jafi75/timeline6f.html, The Jewish Agency for Israel, see "January 30" on linked page. Retrieved June 9, 2005.
[1196] Rabinovich, p. 237.
[1197] The Middle East: a glossary of terms https://www.theguardian.com/world/2001/may/15/ israel2. *Guardian* Unlimited, May 15, 2001.
[1198] Shazly, p. 331
[1199] Shazly, p. 334.
[1200]
[1201] Rabinovich, p. 356.
[1202] Blum, Howard (2007), *The Untold Story of the Yom Kippur War*, HarperCollins, p. 298.
[1203] Schiff, Zeev (1973), *October Earthquake, Yom Kippur 1973*, University Publishing Projects, pp. 194–195.
[1204] Smith, Charles D. (2006), *Palestine and the Arab–Israeli Conflict*, New York: Bedford, p. 329.
[1205] Israel Ministry of Foreign Affairs: *Interim Agreement with Egypt: 1975* http://www.mfa.gov. il/MFA/Facts+About+Israel/Israel+in+Maps/Sinai+Interim+Agreement-+1975.htm. Israel Ministry of Foreign Affairs, 2008.
[1206] Friedman, George: "Israeli–Palestinian peace talks; again." https://www.stratfor.com/weekly/ 20100823_israeli_and_palestinian_peace_talks_again Stratfor, August 23, 2010.
[1207] Shipler, David: " Israel Completes Pullout, Leaving Sinai to Egypt https://www.nytimes.com/ 1982/04/26/world/israeli-completes-pullout-leaving-sinai-to-egypt.html". *The New York Times*, 25 April 1982: A1.
[1208] Karsh, p. 86.
[1209] Doing Business in Syria: 2010 Country Commercial Guide for U.S. Companies http://www. buyusainfo.net/docs/x_121370.pdf , U.S. Commercial Service, United States of America Department of Commerce, retrieved May 21, 2010.
[1210] https://web.archive.org/web/20070610033855/http://www-cgsc.army.mil/carl/download/ csipubs/gawrych/gawrych_intro.pdf
[1211] http://www-cgsc.army.mil/carl/download/csipubs/gawrych/gawrych_intro.pdf
[1212] https://web.archive.org/web/20110507130100/http://www.cgsc.edu/carl/download/csipubs/ gawrych/gawrych_pt1.pdf
[1213] http://cgsc.leavenworth.army.mil/carl/download/csipubs/gawrych/gawrych_pt1.pdf
[1214] https://web.archive.org/web/20110507130122/http://www.cgsc.edu/carl/download/csipubs/ gawrych/gawrych_pt2.pdf
[1215] http://cgsc.leavenworth.army.mil/carl/download/csipubs/gawrych/gawrych_pt2.pdf
[1216] https://web.archive.org/web/20110507130200/http://www.cgsc.edu/carl/download/csipubs/ gawrych/gawrych_pt3.pdf
[1217] http://cgsc.leavenworth.army.mil/carl/download/csipubs/gawrych/gawrych_pt3.pdf
[1218] https://web.archive.org/web/20110507130226/http://www.cgsc.edu/carl/download/csipubs/ gawrych/gawrych_pt4.pdf
[1219] http://cgsc.leavenworth.army.mil/carl/download/csipubs/gawrych/gawrych_pt4.pdf
[1220] https://web.archive.org/web/20110507130253/http://www.cgsc.edu/carl/download/csipubs/ gawrych/gawrych_pt5.pdf
[1221] http://cgsc.leavenworth.army.mil/carl/download/csipubs/gawrych/gawrych_pt5.pdf
[1222] https://web.archive.org/web/20110507130315/http://www.cgsc.edu/carl/download/csipubs/ gawrych/gawrych_pt6.pdf
[1223] http://cgsc.leavenworth.army.mil/carl/download/csipubs/gawrych/gawrych_pt6.pdf
[1224] https://web.archive.org/web/20110507130346/http://www.cgsc.edu/carl/download/csipubs/ gawrych/gawrych_pt7.pdf
[1225] http://cgsc.leavenworth.army.mil/carl/download/csipubs/gawrych/gawrych_pt7.pdf

[1226] https://web.archive.org/web/20090319143113/http://www-cgsc.army.mil/carl/download/csipubs/gawrych/gawrych_notes.pdf
[1227] http://www-cgsc.army.mil/carl/download/csipubs/gawrych/gawrych_notes.pdf
[1228] //www.worldcat.org/oclc/65842089
[1229] //doi.org/10.2307%2F2539368
[1230] //www.jstor.org/stable/2539368
[1231] //www.worldcat.org/oclc/482431341
[1232] https://web.archive.org/web/20121002131554/http://www.rand.org/pubs/reports/2006/R1864.pdf
[1233] https://www.rand.org/pubs/reports/2006/R1864.pdf
[1234] https://web.archive.org/web/20150526160709/http://www.israelcfr.com/documents/7-3/7-3-6-DavidRodman.pdf
[1235] http://www.israelcfr.com/documents/7-3/7-3-6-DavidRodman.pdf
[1236] https//web.archive.org
[1237] http://www.foia.cia.gov/collection/president-nixon-and-role-intelligence-1973-arab-israeli-war
[1238] https://wikileaks.org/plusd/pressrelease/
[1239] https://www.youtube.com/watch?v=8GnB6vW6L18
[1240] https://www.youtube.com/watch?v=hQZAnt7zIhk
[1241] https://www.youtube.com/watch?v=q5eGgUF9zhk
[1242] 1976: Israelis rescue Entebbe hostages http://news.bbc.co.uk/onthisday/hi/dates/stories/july/4/newsid_2786000/2786967.stm, BBC
[1243] *Entebbe: The Most Daring Raid of Israel's Special Forces*, The Rosen Publishing Group, 2011, by Simon Dunstan, p. 58
[1244] Brzoska, Michael; Pearson, Frederic S. *Arms and Warfare: Escalation, De-escalation, and Negotiation*, Univ. of S. Carolina Press (1994) p. 203
[1245] Ulrich Beyerlin: *Abhandlungen: Die israelische Befreiungsaktion von Entebbe in völkerrechtlicher Sicht.* http://www.zaoerv.de/37_1977/37_1977_2_a_213_243.pdf (PDF-Datei; 2,3 MB) auf: zaoerv.de Max-Planck-Institut für ausländisches öffentliches Recht und Völkerrecht, 1977.
[1246] Sources state varying numbers of passengers, between 228 and 246; the higher figure is taken from *The New York Times*.
[1247] Claims by various authors that the separation was made between Jews and non-Jews<ref>
[1248] – A review of *Hitler's children* by Julian Becker,;
[1249] David Kaplan, " A Historic Hostage-Taking Revisited https://www.jpost.com/Features/A-historic-hostage-taking-revisited," *The Jerusalem Post*, 3 August 2006, Retrieved 4 July 2018.
[1250] "Vindication for the Israelis" http://www.time.com/time/magazine/article/0,9171,914380,00.html. *Time*. 26 July 1976.
[1251] "War of Words over a Tense Border" http://www.time.com/time/magazine/article/0,9171,914382,00.html. *Time*. 26 July 1976.
[1252] Grimes, Paul. "Rescuing the Entebbe Hostages" https://www.nytimes.com/1976/07/30/archives/rescuing-the-entebbe-hostages.html. *The New York Times*. Friday, 30 July 1976. (The Weekend, p. 51).
[1253] Lipkin-Shakhak, Tali. "The Forgotten Hero of Entebbe" http://www.historama.com/online-resources/articles/israel/dan_shomron_on_1976_entebbe_raid.html. Historama. 16 June 2006.
[1254] "Israel marks 30th anniversary of Entebbe" https://www.usatoday.com/news/world/2006-07-04-palestinian-pressure_x.htm. Associated Press in *USA Today*. 5 July 2006.
[1255] http://www.ynetnews.com/articles/0,7340,L-4824146,00.html
[1256] 40 years after Entebbe, Israeli hostages reflect back on a saga of survival http://www.haaretz.com/israel-news/.premium-1.723000 *Haaretz*
[1257] Now confidential cabinet papers released under the Freedom of Information Act show that the British High Commission in Kampala received a report from a Ugandan civilian that Mrs Bloch had been shot and her body dumped in the boot of a car which had Ugandan intelligence services number plates. UNIQ-ref-0-4ba7306c809995b7-QINU

[1258] "Body of Amin Victim Is Flown Back to Israel" https://www.nytimes.com/1979/06/04/archives/body-of-amin-victim-is-flown-back-to-israel.html. The New York Times. 4 June 1979, Monday, p. A3.
[1259]
[1260]
[1261] Security Council. United Kingdom of Great Britain and Northern Ireland and United States of America: draft resolution. Document S/12138, 12 July 1976.
[1262] Security Council, Official Records, 1943th meeting, 14 July 1976, S/PV.1943, p. 18.
[1263] Security Council. Benin, Libyan Arab Republic and United Republic of Tanzania: draft resolution. Document S/12139, 12 July 1976.
[1264] USS *Ranger* Bicentennial Cruise Book http://ussranger.org/home/ranger-history
[1265] "Entebbe Postscript", *Flight International*, 17 July 1976, p. 122. Retrieved from Flightglobal Archive http://www.flightglobal.com/pdfarchive/view/1976/1976%20-%201254.html
[1266] *Air et cosmos*, Issues 618–634, Impr. Reaumur., 1976, p. 48 (in French)
[1267] Sharon Roffe-Ofir "Entebbe's open wound" http://www.ynet.co.il/english/articles/0,7340,L-3270234,00.html Ynet, 7 February 2006
[1268] Josh Hamerman "Battling against 'the falsification of history'" http://www.ynetnews.com/articles/0,7340,L-3384084,00.html Ynetnews, 4 February 2007
[1269] Dershowitz, Alan M. *Preemption: A Knife that Cuts both Ways*, W. W. Norton (2006) p. 91
[1270] Houghton, David Patrick. *U.S. Foreign Policy and the Iran Hostage Crisis*, Cambridge Univ. Press (2001) pp. 86–87
[1271] https://www.youtube.com/watch?v=csab-m6QuZk
[1272] https://www.youtube.com/watch?v=p4Bou72k2fY
[1273] https://www.youtube.com/watch?v=Z1ct-meb6U0
[1274] https://www.youtube.com/watch?v=ffRQ6e29Dw0
[1275] https://www.youtube.com/watch?v=DJU1VsgI_-I
[1276] https://www.youtube.com/watch?v=lemwyO054OI
[1277] https://www.telegraph.co.uk/news/worldnews/middleeast/israel/11701064/Israels-raid-on-Entebbe-was-almost-a-disaster.html
[1278] http://www.strategyandtacticspress.com/library-files/ST232-Web.pdf
[1279] http://www.isayeret.com/
[1280] http://newssearch.bbc.co.uk/onthisday/hi/dates/stories/july/4/newsid_2786000/2786967.stm
[1281] http://news.bbc.co.uk/2/hi/middle_east/5101412.stm
[1282] http://news.bbc.co.uk/1/hi/programmes/age_of_terror/7303356.stm
[1283] http://www.ynetnews.com/articles/0,7340,L-3980051,00.html
[1284] //tools.wmflabs.org/geohack/geohack.php?pagename=Operation_Entebbe&params=0_02_42.8784_N_32_27_13.1616_E_source:itwiki_type:event
[1285] Camp David Accords – Israeli Ministry of Foreign Affairs http://www.mfa.gov.il/MFA/Peace%20Process/Guide%20to%20the%20Peace%20Process/Camp%20David%20Accords
[1286] Stein, Kenneth. *Heroic Diplomacy: Sadat, Kissinger, Carter, Begin, and the Quest for Arab–Israeli Peace*. Taylor & Francis, 1999, pp. 228–229
[1287] "Stein, Kenneth 2000, pp. 229–228"
[1288] George Lenczowski, *American Presidents and the Middle East*, Duke University Press, 1990 p.164. From Zbigniew Brzezinski, *Power and Principle: Memoirs of the National Security Advisor 1977–1981*, (New York: Farrar, Straus and Giroux, 1983), p.88.

> [Carter] outlined to Begin his program, which consisted of five points: (1) achieve a comprehensive peace affecting all of Israel's neighbors: (2) peace to be based on UN Resolution 242: (3) peace would involve open borders and free trade; (4) peace would call for Israeli withdrawal from occupied territories to secure borders; (5) a Palestinian entity (but not an independent nation) should be created. Begin responded that he could accept all of these points except the Palestinian entity.

[1289] The Middle East: ten years after Camp David, William B. Quandt, pg. 9
[1290] Stein 1999, p.7.
[1291] Feron, James. "Menachem Begin, Guerrilla Leader Who Became Peacemaker." https://query.nytimes.com/gst/fullpage.html?res=9E0CE3DC1E30F93AA35750C0A964958260&sec=&spon=&pagewanted=2 *The New York Times*. 9 March 1992. 15 February 2009.

[1292] Foreignpolicyblogs.com http://israel.foreignpolicyblogs.com/category/peace-process/page/2/
[1293] Stein 1999, p.252.
[1294] "The Camp David Accords." http://www.jimmycarterlibrary.org/documents/campdavid/letters.phtml *Jimmy Carter Library and Museum.* 21 July 2001. 28 April 2008.
[1295] Jimmy Carter Library, *The Framework for Peace in the Middle East* http://www.jimmycarterlibrary.gov/documents/campdavid/accords.phtml , 17 September 1978
[1296] Stein, 1999, p.254.
[1297] Gold, 175
[1298] UNGA, 7 December 1978, *Resolution 33/28 A. Question of Palestine* https://unispal.un.org/UNISPAL.NSF/0/45650594884CB837852560DD0051C2AF (doc.nr. A/RES/33/28)
[1299] UNGA, 6 December 1979, *Resolution 34/70. The situation in the Middle East* https://unispal.un.org/UNISPAL.NSF/0/6118CF31EC9EB7FB852560DA006E47F3 (doc.nr. A/RES/34/70)
[1300] UNGA, 12 December 1979, *Resolution 34/65 B. Question of Palestine* https://unispal.un.org/unispal.nsf/0/1CFBE54A74E1AB8B852560DA006DE34D . [doc.nr. A/RES/34/65 (A-D)]
[1301] Jimmy Carter Library, *Framework for the Conclusion of a Peace Treaty between Egypt and Israel* http://www.jimmycarterlibrary.gov/documents/campdavid/frame.phtml
[1302] "Egypt" https://www.state.gov/r/pa/ei/bgn/5309.htm#relations *U.S. Department of State.* March 2008. 28 April 2008.
[1303] Benhorin, Yitzhak. "Israel still top recipient of US foreign aid." http://www.ynetnews.com/articles/0,7340,L-3362402,00.html *Ynetnews.* 2 August 2007. 28 April 2008.
[1304] Sela, "Arab–Israel Conflict", 100
[1305] Sela, "Sinai Peninsula," 774
[1306] Armstrong, 414
[1307] Ronen, Joshua. "Poll: 58% of Israelis back Oslo process." http://www.tau.ac.il/jcss/Hjerus1.html *Tel Aviv University.* 7 June 2001. 28 April 2008.
[1308] http://www.mfa.gov.il/MFA/Peace+Process/Guide+to+the+Peace+Process/Camp+David+Accords.htm
[1309] https://web.archive.org/web/20110216081558/http://www.jimmycarterlibrary.gov/documents/campdavid/index.phtml
[1310] http://knesset.gov.il/process/docs/autonomy1977_eng.htm
[1311] https://web.archive.org/web/20141110091752/https://repository.library.georgetown.edu/handle/10822/552609
[1312] https://web.archive.org/web/20120312181034/http://repository.library.georgetown.edu/handle/10822/552494/browse?type=title
[1313] http://www.nysun.com/article/43906
[1314] http://news.bbc.co.uk/2/hi/middle_east/6107160.stm
[1315] http://www.begincenter.org.il/
[1316] https://web.archive.org/web/20080502195917/http://www.tau.ac.il/jcss/Hjerus1.html
[1317] https://query.nytimes.com/gst/fullpage.html?res=9F00E1DE1F3CF935A15753C1A9649C8B63
[1318] https://web.archive.org/web/20100612011440/http://www.ismi.emory.edu/PrimarySource/Camp_David__25th_Anniversary_Forum.pdf
[1319] Kober, Avi: *Israel's Wars of Attrition: Attrition Challenges to Democratic States*, p. 64
[1320] Israeli Ministry of Foreign Affairs. Statement to the press by Prime Minister Begin on the massacre of Israelis on the Haifa-Tel Aviv Road http//www.mfa.gov.il . Historical Documents Archive: March 12, 1978.
[1321] Cobban, p. 94, Shlaim p. 369
[1322]
[1323] Private Kevin Joyce was kidnapped and is presumed dead. See Guardian article here 20-year hunt for kidnapped Irish soldier almost over | UK news | The Observer http://observer.guardian.co.uk/uk_news/story/0,6903,486689,00.html
[1324] //doi.org/10.1525%2Fjps.1992.21.3.00p01145
[1325] //www.jstor.org/stable/2537518
[1326] http://www.alsminiature.com/als.litani.html
[1327] http://www.liberty05.com/civilwar/civil77.html
[1328] http://www.globalsecurity.org/military/world/war/israel-terror.htm

[1329] http://www.globalsecurity.org/military/world/war/lebanon.htm
[1330] https://web.archive.org/web/20080609231529/http://www.lebanon-israel.info/
[1331] Eligar Sadeh *Militarization and State Power in the Arab-Israeli Conflict: Case Study of Israel, 1948–1982*, https://books.google.com/books?id=TGHcpPPJrswC&pg=PA119 *Universal-Publishers, 1997 p.119.*
[1332] Mira M. Sucharov, *The International Self: Psychoanalysis and the Search for Israeli-Palestinian Peace*, https://books.google.com/books?id=LYBby9M1rBYC&pg=PA95 SUNY Press, 2012 p.95:'Gioven the widely perceived strategic failure of the war'.
[1333] http://mfa.gov.il/MFA/AboutIsrael/History/Pages/The%20Arab-Israeli%20Wars.aspx – "In retaliation, the IDF attacked Lebanon once again and succeeded in its original purpose to wipe out terrorist bases in the south of Lebanon. A series of simultaneous, amphibious operations was remarkably successful. Subsequently, however, the mission was enlarged and the capture of Beirut signalled the transition to a long drawn-out war. It failed to achieve its ultimate purpose. A peace treaty with Lebanon was signed, but not ratified; the Christian government of fragmented Lebanon was too weak to prevail."
[1334] Globalsecurity.org, THE ISRAELI EXPERIENCE IN LEBANON, 1982–1985 http://www.globalsecurity.org/military/library/report/1987/SGC.htm, Major George C. Solley, Marine Corps Command and Staff College, 10 May 1987. Retrieved 7 February 2014.

> The third goal was to remove Syrian presence from Lebanon. The recognition that this goal was obviously unsuccessful must betempered by an awareness of the Lebanese situation since 1982. Even when the first two aims seemed to have been met, Syrian recalcitrance acted as a stumbling blocks the Syrians would by nomeans agree to a withdrawal from Lebanon in conjunction with the Israelis and therefore were able to effectively scuttle the 17 May, Agreement between Israel and Lebanon before it had any chance of fulfillment; Syria offered a haven for PLO fighters in the Bekaa Valley from which they could stage raids on the IDF in Lebanon and from which many have now moved back into Beirut and Sidon; and despite having taken severe losses during the June fighting, Syria was able to quickly replace those losses with better Soviet equipment accompanied by a number of Soviet advisors.

[1335] Morris, p. 559
[1336] Wars, Internal Conflicts, and Political Order: A Jewish Democracy in the Middle East https//books.google.com, Gad Barzilai, pp. 148
[1337] Gabriel, Richard, A, *Operation Peace for Galilee, The Israeli-PLO War in Lebanon*, New York: Hill & Wang. 1984, p. 164, 165,
[1338]
[1339] [Ze'ev Schiff, Ehud Ya'ari, *Israel's Lebanon War*, https://books.google.com/books?id=z99HgBsKp3sC&pg=PA98 Simon and Schuster 1985 pp.98f:'Argov had been shot by an unusual weapon of Polish manufacture known as a WZ 63, . Israeli intelligence knew that this late-model weapon had been supplied to Abu Nidal's organization but not yet to other terrorist groups. .The key point that the intelligence officers wanted to convey to the Cabinet was that Abu Nidal's organization was an exception among the Palestinian terror groups. Once among Yasser Arafat's closest friends, Abu Nidal had over the years turned into the chairman's most vicious enemy . Abu Nidal referred to Arafat contemptuously as "the Jewess's son" and had made repeated attempts on his life. Arafat, in return, had pronounced a death sentence on Abu Nidal.'
[1340] Kai Bird, *The Good Spy: The Life and Death of Robert Ames*, https://books.google.com/books?id=SjctAgAAQBAJ&pg=PT288 Random House 2014 p.288:'When Prime Minister Menachem Begin was told that the assassins were Abu Nidal's men -sworn enemies of Arafat and the PLO- he reportedly scoffed,"They're all PLO, Abu Nidal, Abu Shmidal- we have to strike at the PLO".'
[1341] Kahalani, *A Warriors Way* https//books.google.com, Shapolsky Publishers (1994) pp. 299–301
[1342] Harvey W. Kushner, *Encyclopedia of Terrorism* https//books.google.com Sage Publications (2003), p.13
[1343] Note that scholars describe this variously as a pretext (i.e. an excuse for a pre-planned invasion) or as the actual provocation which sparked an otherwise avoidable conflict
[1344] Friedman, p. 157

[1345] Benny Morris (2004). *The Birth of the Palestinian Refugee Problem Revisited*. Cambridge University Press. pp xiv–xx. (pbk.)

[1346] Kissinger, Henry (1999). *Years of Renewal*, Phoenix Press. p. 1022. "*I think with sadness of these civilized men who in a turbulent part of the world had fashioned a democratic society based on genuine mutual respect of religion. Their achievement did not survive. The passions sweeping the area were too powerful to be contained by subtle constitutional arrangements. As it had attempted in Jordan, the Palestinian movement wrecked the delicate balance of Lebanon's stability. Before the peace process could run its course, Lebanon was torn apart. Over its prostrate body of writing all the factions and forces of the Middle East still chase their eternal dreams and act out their perennial nightmares.*"

[1347] Morris, p. ???

[1348] Morris, p. 503

[1349] Morris, p. 505

[1350] Morris, p. 509

[1351] Schiff & Ya'ari, pp. 35–36

[1352] Morris, p. 507

[1353] Kameel B. Nazr (2007) *Arab and Israeli Terrorism: The Causes and Effects of Political Violence*. McFarland & Company. https://books.google.com/books?id=QRXURzwdXS4C&printsec=frontcover#v=onepage&q&f=false

[1354] Reagan, p. 66

[1355] Fisk, p. 194

[1356] Friedman, Thomas L. "Israeli Jets Raid P.L.O. in Lebanon; Shelling follows". *The New York Times*, 10 May 1982, p. 1.

[1357] Cobban, p. 112

[1358] UN Doc S/PV.2292 http://domino.un.org/unispal.nsf/0/43220e2368a3ddf7052568000052412c?OpenDocument , 17 July 1981.

[1359] Gilad Sharon (2011). *Sharon: The Life of a Leader*. Translated by Mitch Ginsberg. Harper Collins. Chapter 14 https://books.google.com/books?id=jLq-12NxKZkC&printsec=frontcover&source=gbs_ge_summary_r&cad=0#v=onepage&q&f=false

[1360] Colin Shindler (1995)The Land Beyond Promise: Israel, Likud and the Zionist Dream.pp 117. I.B.Tauris & Co Ltd.

[1361] Ball, George W. *Error and Betrayal in Lebanon*, p. 35.

[1362] John Boykin (2002), Cursed Is the Peacemaker (Belmont, CA: Applegate Press: 0971943260). Quoted in PHILIP HABIB AND ARIEL SHARON: FROM THE ARCHIVES (2007)http://delong.typepad.com/sdj/2007/03/philip_habib_an.html

[1363] Reagan, pp. 87–90

[1364] Shlaim 2007, p. 412

[1365] Maoz, p. 181

[1366] Yevgeny Primakov, *Russia and the Arabs: Behind the Scenes in the Middle East from the Cold War to the Present*, https://books.google.com/books?id=qXHKs5WaNgMC&pg=PA201 Basic Books 2009 p.201.

[1367] Shlaim 1999, pp. 396–397

[1368] Schiff & Ya'ari 1984, pp. 97, 99–100.

[1369] Chomsky, p. 197

[1370] Shlaim 1999, p. 404

[1371] Herzog & Gazit, pp. 340–343

[1372] Hogg, Ian V., Israeli War Machine, Hamlyn Publishing Group Ltd, (1983) p. 171-175

[1373] Gerald Cromer, *A War of Words: Political Violence and Public Debate in Israel*, https://books.google.com/books?id=0UCQAgAAQBAJ&pg=PA116 Frank Cass 2004 p.116.

[1374] Davis, H. Thomas: *40 Km Into Lebanon: Israel's 1982 Invasion*

[1375] Mommsen, Klaus: *60 YEARS ISRAEL NAVY: Chel Ha'Yam Ha'Yisraeli*

[1376] הקטנה פלסטין נגד – לבנון מלחמת באר,י גלעד Gil'ad Be'eri, "The Lebanon War" – "Confronting "Little Palestine" in Lebanon"

[1377] ספרים, ידיעות הוצאת השנייה", לבנון מלחמת על האמת בלבנון, "שבויים לימור, ויואב שלח עפר 2007, עמוד 327 (Hebrew)

Ofer Shelah and Yoav Limor, "Captives in Lebanon – The Truth about the Second Lebanon War", 2007 – page 327
[1378] Rabinovich, p. 510
[1379] Herzog & Gazit, pp. 347–348
[1380] Walker, pp. 162–63
[1381] Herzog & Gazit, pp. 349
[1382]
[1383] Rebecca Grant The Bekaa Valley War http://www.airforce-magazine.com/MagazineArchive/Pages/2002/June%202002/0602bekaa.aspx. Air Force Magazine Online 85 (June 2002). Retrieved 22 August 2009
[1384] Seale, pp. 382–83.
[1385] Seale, p. 391
[1386] "Flashback: Sabra and Shatila massacres" http://news.bbc.co.uk/2/hi/middle_east/1779713.stm, *BBC News Online* (London), 24 January 2002.
[1387] *Armies in Lebanon 1982–84*, Samuel Katz and Lee E. Russell, Osprey Men-At-Arms series No. 165, 1985
[1388] lb0161 https://web.archive.org/web/20050228055759/http://lcweb2.loc.gov/cgi-bin/query2/r?frd%2Fcstdy%3A%40field%28DOCID%2Blb0161%29
[1389] lb0163 https://web.archive.org/web/20041029055052/http://lcweb2.loc.gov/cgi-bin/query/r?frd%2Fcstdy%3A%40field%28DOCID%2Blb0163%29
[1390] Israeli Elite Units since 1948, Samuel Katz, Osprey Elite series 18,
[1391]
[1392] Schiff & Ya'ari, pp. 83–84
[1393] Schiff & Ya'ari, pp. 134–135
[1394] Sayigh, p. 524
[1395] Fisk, pp. 255–257
[1396] cited in Waines An Introduction to Islam (2004)
[1397] 657 killed from 1982–1985 (Wars, Internal Conflicts, and Political Order: A Jewish Democracy in the Middle East https//books.google.com, Gad Barzilai, pp. 148), 1,216 killed from 1982–2000 (Imperfect Compromise: A New Consensus Among Israelis and Palestinians https//books.google.com, Michael I. Karpin) = 559 killed 1985–2000
[1398] 1 killed between June 1982 and June 1992 (Israelis See Little Apparent Gain From Invasion http://www.csmonitor.com/1992/0605/05013.html/%28page%29/2, *Csmonitor*, retrieved 4 February 2014), 9 killed from 1985–1999 (Israeli Civilians Killed/Wounded On the Lebanese Border https://www.jewishvirtuallibrary.org/jsource/History/lebciv.html, *Jewish Virtual Library*, retrieved 14 February 2014)
[1399] American Jewish Committee Archives http://www.ajcarchives.org/AJC_DATA/Files/Vol_85__1985.pdf American Jewish Yearbook 1985. p. 126.
[1400] American Jewish Committee Archives http://www.ajcarchives.org/AJC_DATA/Files/Vol_85__1985.pdf American Jewish Yearbook 1985. p. 130.
[1401] American Jewish Committee Archives http://www.ajcarchives.org/AJC_DATA/Files/Vol_85__1985.pdf, American Jewish Yearbook 1985. p. 260.
[1402] Warschawski, Michel (April–May 2006). "Inside the Anti-Occupation Camp" http://www.ameu.org/page.asp?iid=266&aid=576&pg=3 , *The Link* (Americans for Middle East Understanding).
[1403] Israelis at huge rally in Tel Aviv demand Begin and Sharon resign https://www.nytimes.com/1982/09/26/world/israelis-at-huge-rally-in-tel-aviv-demand-begin-and-sharon-resign.html New York Times, 26 September 1982
[1404] Morris, p. 551
[1405] "Security Council Endorses Secretary-General's Conclusion On Israeli Withdrawal From Lebanon as of 16 June" https://www.un.org/News/Press/docs/2000/20000618.sc6878.doc.html, UN Press release SC/6878, 18 June 2000.
[1406] Arak, Joel (29 October 2004). "Osama Bin Laden Warns America: Terror Leader Admits For First Time That He Ordered 9/11 Attacks" http://www.cbsnews.com/stories/2004/10/30/terror/main652425.shtml, CBS News.

[1407] U.N. General Assembly, Resolution 37/123, adopted between 16 and 20 December 1982. http://daccess-dds-ny.un.org/doc/RESOLUTION/GEN/NR0/426/01/IMG/NR042601.pdf? OpenElement Retrieved 4 January 2010. (If link doesn't work, try: U.N. https://www.un.org/→ welcome → documents → General Assembly Resolutions → 1982 → 37/123.)

[1408] Voting Summary U.N. General Assembly Resolution 37/123D. http://unbisnet.un.org:8080/ipac20/ipac.jsp?profile=voting&index=.VM&term=ares37123d#focus Retrieved 4 January 2010,

[1409] Leo Kuper, "Theoretical Issues Relating to Genocide: Uses and Abuses", in George J. Andreopoulos, *Genocide: Conceptual and Historical Dimensions*, University of Pennsylvania Press, 1997, , p. 37.

[1410] http://lcweb2.loc.gov/frd/cs/

[1411] https://books.google.com/books?id=8a9jjx_JO60C&lpg=PP1&pg=PA255#v=onepage&q&f=false

[1412] https://books.google.com/books?id=z99HgBsKp3sC&pg=PA35

[1413] http://www.liberty05.com/civilwar/civi2.html

[1414] https://web.archive.org/web/20070207084106/http://www.ariel-sharon-life-story.com/14-Ariel-Sharon-Biography-1982-The-Lebanon-War.shtml

[1415] http://www.ynetnews.com/articles/0,7340,L-3284684,00.html

[1416] http://www.haaretz.com/hasen/spages/1065945.html

[1417] //doi.org/10.1111%2Fj.1465-7287.2001.tb00049.x

[1418] http://gozansky.co.il/?p=433

[1419] //doi.org/10.1111%2Fj.1465-7287.1998.tb00511.x

[1420] References: • Helmer, Daniel Isaac. Flipside of the Coin: Israel's Lebanese Incursion Between 1982-2000. DIANE Publishing, 2010.

[1421] 657 killed from 1982-1985 (Wars, Internal Conflicts, and Political Order: A Jewish Democracy in the Middle East https//books.google.com, Gad Barzilai, pp. 148), 1,216 killed from 1982-2000 (Imperfect Compromise: A New Consensus Among Israelis and Palestinians https//books.google.com, Michael I. Karpin) = 559 killed 1985-2000

[1422] Luft, Gal. "Israel's Security Zone in Lebanon - A Tragedy? http://www.meforum.org/70/israels-security-zone-in-lebanon-a-tragedy" Middle East Quarterly, September 2000, 13-20.

[1423] A Hezbollah recruiting drive covers its losses and deeper involvement inside Syria http://www.startribune.com/a-hezbollah-recruiting-push-covers-its-deeper-role-in-syria/362954261/

[1424] *Hezbollah makes explosive return: Israel's proxy militia under fire in south Lebanon https://www.independent.co.uk/news/world/hizbollah-makes-explosive-return-israels-proxy-militia-under-fire-in-south-lebanon-1461794.html.* Charles Richards, The Independent. 18 August 1993. Retrieved 15 August 2009.

[1425]

[1426] UN Press Release SC/6878 https://www.un.org/News/Press/docs/2000/20000618.sc6878.doc.html. (18 June 2000). *Security Council Endorses Secretary-General's Conclusion On Israeli Withdrawal From Lebanon As Of 16 June.*

[1427] Naseer H. Aruri, Preface to the 3rd(?) edition, *Israel's Sacred Terrorism*, Livia Rokach, Association of Arab-American University Graduates,

[1428] Livia Rokach, *Israel's Sacred Terrorism*, Association of Arab-American University Graduates,

[1429] Avi Shlaim, The Protocol of Sèvres,1956: Anatomy of a War Plot http://users.ox.ac.uk/~ssfc0005/The%20Protocol%20of%20Sevres%201956%20Anatomy%20of%20a%20War%20Plot.html, *International Affairs*, 73:3 (1997), 509–530

[1430] *Urban Operations: An Historical Casebook.* " Siege of Beirut http://www.globalsecurity.org/military/library/report/2002/MOUTGawrych.htm", by George W. Gawrych. US Army Combat Studies Institute, Fort Leavenworth, KS. 2 October 2002. Available at globalsecurity.org.

[1431] Major George C. Solley, *The Israeli Experience in Lebanon, 1982–1985* http://www.globalsecurity.org/military/library/report/1987/SGC.htm, US Marine Corps Command and Staff College, Marine Corps Development and Education Command, Quantico, Virginia. 10 May 1987. Available from GlobalSecurity.org

[1432] 1982 Lebanon Invasion http://news.bbc.co.uk/2/hi/middle_east/7381364.stm. BBC News.

[1433] Norton, Augustus Richard; *Journal of Palestine*, 2000

[1434] https://www.nytimes.com/1985/08/06/world/2-israeli-soldiers-and-3-guerrillas-killed-in-south-lebanon-shootout.html
[1435] Blanford, Nicholas, *Warriors of God - Inside Hezbollah's Thirty-Year Struggle Against Israel*, Random House, New York, 2011, pp. 85-86
[1436] Journal of Palestine Studies. Volume XVII No 3 (67) Spring 1988. Page 221. Chronology compiled by Katherine M. LaRiviere
[1437] Ross, Michael *The Volunteer: The Incredible True Story of an Israeli Spy on the Trail of International Terrorists* (2006)
[1438] UN Resolution 638 https://www.jewishvirtuallibrary.org/jsource/UN/unres638.html, reprinted by Jewish Virtual Library
[1439] Tension grows in South Lebanon as Israel bombs guerrilla targets. https://www.nytimes.com/1991/11/08/world/tension-grows-in-south-lebanon-as-israel-bombs-guerrilla-targets.html New York Times, 8 November 1991.
[1440] Time Magazine: Vengeance is Mine (2 March 1992)
[1441] https://www.nytimes.com/1992/03/08/world/car-bomb-kills-an-israeli-embassy-aide-in-turkey.html
[1442] http://articles.latimes.com/1993-08-20/news/mn-25732_1_israeli-soldiers
[1443] Haberman, Clyde (3 June 1994). " Dozens Are Killed As Israelis Attack Camp in Lebanon" https://www.nytimes.com/1994/06/03/world/dozens-are-killed-as-israelis-attack-camp-in-lebanon.html. The New York Times.
[1444] http://www.aparchive.com/metadata/youtube/01c0dbdb439c452d0831116acf3d244b
[1445] http://www.aparchive.com/metadata/youtube/c2fcea9abdeb7373dcf286bdd429f344
[1446] http://articles.latimes.com/1997/aug/29/news/mn-27055
[1447] Blanford, p. 190-192
[1448] *Survey of Arab-Israeli Relations*, p. 232
[1449] Blanford, p. 204
[1450] Lebanon Country Assessment http://www.asylumlaw.org/docs/lebanon/ind01b_lebanon_ca.pdf . United Kingdom Home Office, October 2001.
[1451] Blanford, pp. 243-244
[1452] Harb, Zahera, *Channels of Resistance in Lebanon - Liberation Propaganda, Hezbollah and the Media*, I.B. Tauris, London-New York, 2011, pp.214-216
[1453] Country Profile: Lebanon Timeline http://news.bbc.co.uk/2/hi/middle_east/country_profiles/819200.stm, BBC News.
[1454] *Camp David and After: An Exchange* http://www.nybooks.com/articles/15501. (An Interview with Ehud Barak). New York Review of Books, Volume 49, Number 10. 13 June 2002. Retrieved online, 15 August 2009.
[1455] Margaret Hall, *American Myopia* https://web.archive.org/web/20060723035439/http://www.ucis.pitt.edu/ceris/docs/Symp06_HallPaper.pdf: American Policy on Hizbollah. The Muslim World: Questions of Policy and Politics. Cornell University undergraduate research symposium. 8 April 2006.
[1456] "...*Hezbollah enjoys enormous popularity in Lebanon, especially in southern Lebanon...*", Ted Koppel on NPR report: *Lebanon's Hezbollah Ties* https://www.npr.org/templates/story/story.php?storyId=5555771. All Things Considered, 13 July 2006.
[1457] BBC: "On This Day, May 26th" http://news.bbc.co.uk/onthisday/hi/dates/stories/may/26/newsid_2496000/2496423.stm.
[1458] CNN report: *Hezbollah flag raised as Israeli troops withdraw from southern Lebanon* http://archives.cnn.com/2000/WORLD/meast/05/24/israel.lebanon.02/index.html. 24 May 2000.
[1459] Kober, Avi, *Israel's Wars of Attrition: Attrition Challenges to Democratic States*, p. 165
[1460] Kim Murphy. " Israel and PLO, in Historic Bid for Peace, Agree to Mutual Recognition http://articles.latimes.com/1993-09-10/news/mn-33546_1_mutual-recognition," *Los Angeles Times*, 10 September 1993.
[1461] 'Saddam olsaydı İsrail'e dersini verirdi' http://www.zaman.com.tr/dunya_saddam-olsaydi-israile-dersini-verirdi_789991.html , *Zaman*
[1462] "Profile: Marwan Barghouti" https://www.bbc.com/news/world-middle-east-13628771 BBC News. 26 November 2009. Accessed 9 August 2011.

[1463] Kober, Avi. "From Blitzkrieg To Attrition: Israel's Attrition Strategy and Staying Power." *Small Wars & Insurgencies* 16, no. 2 (2005): 216–240.
[1464] Lockman; Beinin (1989), p. 5. https//books.google.com
[1465] Nami Nasrallah, 'The First and Second Palestinian *intifadas*,' in David Newman, Joel Peters (eds.) *Routledge Handbook on the Israeli-Palestinian Conflict* https://books.google.com/books?id=kftqQdNNDWAC&pg=PA61, Routledge, 2013, pp. 56–68, p. 56.
[1466] Berman 2011, p. 41.
[1467] Michail Omer-Man The accident that sparked an Intifada http://www.jpost.com/Features/In-Thespotlight/The-accident-that-sparked-an-Intifada, 12/04/2011
[1468] David McDowall,*Palestine and Israel: The Uprising and Beyond*, University of California Press, 1989 p. 1
[1469] Ruth Margolies Beitler, *The Path to Mass Rebellion: An Analysis of Two Intifadas* https://books.google.com/books?id=FVd5dJGBYMsC&pg=PR11, Lexington Books, 2004 p.xi.
[1470] BBC: A History of Conflict http://news.bbc.co.uk/1/shared/spl/hi/middle_east/03/v3_ip_timeline/html/1987.stm
[1471] Walid Salem, 'Human Security from Below: Palestinian Citizens Protection Strategies, 1988–2005,' in Monica den Boer, Jaap de Wilde (eds.), *The Viability of Human Security*,Amsterdam University Press, 2008 pp. 179–201 p. 190.
1472
1473
[1474] Rami Nasrallah, 'The First and Second Palestinian Intifadas,' in Joel Peters, David Newman (eds.) *The Routledge Handbook on the Israeli-Palestinian Conflict* https://books.google.com/books?id=kftqQdNNDWAC&pg=PA61, Routledge 2013 pp. 56–68 p. 61
[1475] Arthur Neslen, *In Your Eyes a Sandstorm: Ways of Being Palestinian* https://books.google.com/books?id=Xnc7ZyVPt6UC&pg=PA122, University of California Press, 2011 p. 122.
[1476] B'Tselem http://www.btselem.org/english/statistics/first_Intifada_Tables.asp Statistics; Fatalities in the first Intifada.
[1477] Mient Jan Faber, Mary Kaldor, 'The deterioration of human security in Palestine,' in Mary Martin, Mary Kaldor (eds.) *The European Union and Human Security: External Interventions and Missions* https://books.google.com/books?id=sHOMAgAAQBAJ&pg=PA101, Routledge, 2009 pp. 95–111.
[1478] 'Intifada,' in David Seddon, (ed.)*A Political and Economic Dictionary of the Middle East*, Taylor & Francis 2004, p. 284.
[1479] Human Rights Watch, *Israel, the Occupied West Bank and Gaza Strip, and the Palestinian Authority Territories*, November, 2001. Vol. 13, No. 4(E), p. 49
[1480] Amitabh Pal, *"Islam" Means Peace: Understanding the Muslim Principle of Nonviolence Today* https://books.google.com/books?id=UF79Qxid7YkC&pg=PA191, ABC-CLIO, 2011 p. 191.
[1481] Lockman; Beinin (1989), p. https://books.google.com/books?id=KYPVNdzXUJkC&pg=PA37-38.
[1482] Ackerman; DuVall (2000), p 407. https://books.google.com/books?id=OVtKS9DCN0kC&pg=PA403
[1483] Ackerman; DuVall (2000), p 401. https://books.google.com/books?id=OVtKS9DCN0kC&pg=PA401
[1484] Robinson, Glenn E. "The Palestinians." *The Contemporary Middle East*, Third Edition. Boulder, Colorado: Westview Press, 2013. 126–127.
[1485] Helena Cobban, 'The PLO and the Intifada', in Robert Owen Freedman, (ed.) *The Intifada: Its Impact on Israel, the Arab World, and the Superpowers*, University Press of Florida, 1991 pp. 70–106, pp. 94–95.'must be considered as an essential part of the backdrop against which the intifada germinated'.(p. 95)
[1486] Helena Cobban, 'The PLO and the Intifada', p. 94. In the immediate aftermath of the 6 Day War in 1967, some 15,000 Gazans had been deported to Egypt. A further 1,150 were deported between September 1967 and May 1978. This pattern was drastically curtailed by the Likud governments under Menachem Begin between 1978 and 1984.
[1487] Lockman; Beinin (1989), p. 32. https://books.google.com/books?id=KYPVNdzXUJkC&pg=PA32

[1488] M. B. Qumsiyeh *Popular Resistance in Palestine; A History of Hope and Empowerment*, Pluto Press; New York 2011.pp. 135
[1489] Shay (2005), p. 74. https://books.google.com/books?id=4kGIpMI5HC0C&pg=PA74
[1490] Anita Vitullo, 'Uprising in Gaza,' in Lockman and Beinin 1989 pp. 43–55 pp. 43–44.
[1491] Vitullo, p. 44 The first incident involved two unarmed men, one a well-known Gaza businessman, at a roadblock. The second occurred in a residential raid, where subsequently a small cache of weapons were found in the cars of four men. The army them bulldozed their homes. A general strike took place, and in response Israel arrested and ordered the deportation of Shaykh 'Abd al-'Aziz Awad, who was held responsible for the growth of popular support for Islamic Jihad, on 15 November.
[1492] Vitullo, pp45-6. The settlers did not report the killing. An Israeli schoolteacher was arrested for the incident after a ballistics test was undertaken, but an Israel judge released him after a week, in the wake of Israeli settler protests. Settlers said she had been throwing stones.
[1493] Shalev (1991), p. 33.
[1494] Nassar; Heacock (1990), p. 31. https://books.google.com/books?id=_P5W5ErBQRYC&pg=PA31
[1495] Lockman; Beinin (1989), p. 39. https://books.google.com/books?id=KYPVNdzXUJkC&pg=PA39
[1496] MERIP http://www.merip.org/palestine-israel_primer/intifada-87-pal-isr-primer.html Palestine, Israel and the Arab-Israeli Conflict, A Primer
[1497] "What amazed this writer . was the interesting departure from the norms of the past. Palestinians in the Occupied Territories were continuously insisting that they would not resort to arms. Any escalation in the use of violence on their part would be as a last resort, for defensive purposes only", Souad Dajani, cited Pearlman, *Violence, Nonviolence, and the Palestinian National Movement*, p. 106
[1498] 6Pearlman, ibid. p. 107.
[1499] Pearlman, p. 112.
[1500] Walid Salem p. 189
[1501] Mark Tessler, *A History of the Israeli-Palestinian conflict*, Indiana University Press, 1994 p. 677.
[1502] Vitullo p. 46.
[1503] Ruth Margolies Beitler, *The Path to Mass Rebellion: An Analysis of Two Intifadas*, Lexington Books, 2004 p.xiii.
[1504] Vitullo, p. 46:'Although Palestinians rushed to aid the man, no one cooperated with military interrogators, who arrested scores of people and clamped a curfew on the area.'
[1505] Ruth Margolies Beitler,*The Path to Mass Rebellion: An Analysis of Two Intifadas*, p. 116 n.75.
[1506] Tessler, *A History of the Israeli-Palestinian conflict*, pp. 677-8.
[1507] Vitullo, p. 46. writes 20 year old man.
[1508] 'Intifada,' in David Seddon,(ed.) *A Political and Economic Dictionary of the Middle East*, p. 284.
[1509] Vitullo p. 47 challenges this:'To the contrary, the protests showed restraint and rationality. .Demonstrations were not "peaceful" but neither did they turn Palestinians into mindless mobs. Youths stripped one Israeli down to his underwear in front of Shifa hospital, but then let him run back to his fellow soldiers. A young Palestinian took another soldier's rifle away from him, broke it in two, then handed it back'.
[1510] Vitullo, p. 47
[1511] Shlaim (2000), pp. 450–1.
[1512] Audrey Kurth Cronin, 'How fighting ends: asymmetric wars, terrorism and suicide bombing,' inHolger Afflerbach, Hew Strachan (eds.) *How Fighting Ends: A History of Surrender*, Oxford University Press, 2012 pp. 417-433, p. 426
[1513] Pearlman, p. 115.
[1514]
[1515] Juan José López-Ibor, Jr., George Christodoulou, Mario Maj, Norman Sartorius, Ahmed Okasha (eds.), *Disasters and Mental Health*. https://books.google.it/books?id=1aUq67aKpeAC&pg=PA231 John Wiley & Sons, 2005 p. 231.
[1516] WRMEA http://www.washington-report.org/backissues/1297/9712081.html Donald Neff *The Intifada Erupts, Forcing Israel to Recognize Palestinians*

[1517] Sumantra Bose, *Contested Lands: Israel-Palestine, Kashmir, Bosnia, Cyprus, and Sri Lanka*, https://books.google.it/books?id=lFVVyJr_xbwC&pg=PA243 Harvard University Press, 2007 p. 243

[1518] Nami Nasrallah, 'The First and Second Palestinian *intifadas*,' in David Newman, Joel Peters (eds.) *Routledge Handbook on the Israeli-Palestinian Conflict*, https://books.google.com/books?id=kftqQdNNDWAC&pg=PA61 Routledge, 2013, pp. 56–67, p. 56.

[1519] Ruth Margolies Beitler, *The Path to Mass Rebellion: An Analysis of Two Intifadas*, p. 120

[1520] Human Rights Watch (HRW) (1991) *Prison Conditions in Israel and the Occupied Territories. A Middle East Watch Report*. Human Rights Watch. Pages 18, 64.

[1521] McDowall (1989), p. 2. https//books.google.com

[1522] Vitullo pp. 51-2,

[1523] Morris (1999), p. 612.

[1524] Sergio Catignani, *Israeli Counter-Insurgency and the Intifadas: Dilemmas of a Conventional Army*, https://books.google.com/books?id=mfNBodDl0hgC&pg=PA81 Routledge, 2008 pp. 81-84.

[1525] Anita Vitullo, pp. 50-1

[1526] Sela, Avraham. "Arab Summit Conferences." *The Continuum Political Encyclopedia of the Middle East*. Ed. Sela. New York: Continuum, 2002. pp. 158-160

[1527] Sosebee, Stephen J. "The Passing of Yitzhak Rabin, Whose 'Iron Fist' Fueled the Intifada" *The Washington Report on Middle East Affairs*. 31 October 1990. Vol. IX #5, pg. 9

[1528] Aburish, Said K. (1998). *Arafat: From Defender to Dictator*. New York: Bloomsbury Publishing pp. 201-228

[1529] Ruth Margolies Beitler, *The Path to Mass Rebellion: An Analysis of Two Intifadas*, p. 128.

[1530] Nassar; Heacock (1990), p. 115. https://books.google.com/books?id=_P5W5ErBQRYC&pg=PA115

[1531] Resolution 44/2 of 06.10.89; Resolution 45/69 of 06.12.90; Resolution 46/76 of 11.12.91

[1532] *Yearbook of the United Nations 1989* http://unispal.un.org/UNISPAL.NSF/0/DF0BB291D1E55CF4052565B80063E183, Chapter IV, Middle East. 31 December 1989.

[1533] Division for Palestinian Rights (DPR), The question of Palestine 1979–1990 http://unispal.un.org/UNISPAL.NSF/0/50670C9C0FF4C6308025645F005EAAA4 , Chapter II, section E. *The intifadah and the need to ensure the protection of the Palestinians living under Israeli occupation*. 31 July 1991.

[1534] McDowall (1989), p. https://books.google.com/books?id=YWorYnKGZ5YC&pg=PA3

[1535] Nassar; Heacock (1990), p. 1. https://books.google.com/books?id=_P5W5ErBQRYC&pg=PA1

[1536] UNGA, *Resolution "43/21. The uprising (intifadah) of the Palestinian people"* http://unispal.un.org/UNISPAL.NSF/0/3BD6ABF508EFE04E852560D30070EC3B . 3 November 1988 (doc.nr. A/RES/43/21).

[1537] Shlaim (2000), p. 455.

[1538] Shlaim (2000), p. 466.

[1539] Pearlman, p. 113

[1540] Shlaim (2000), pp. 455–7.

[1541] Foreign Policy Research Institute http://www.fpri.org/peacefacts/023.199511.sicherman.rabinappreciation.html Yitzhak Rabin: An Appreciation By Harvey Sicherman

[1542] Roberts; Garton Ash (2009) p. 37. https//books.google.com

[1543] Noga Collins-kreiner, Nurit Kliot, Yoel Mansfeld, Keren Sagi (2006) *Christian Tourism to the Holy Land: Pilgrimage During Security Crisis* Ashgate Publishing, Ltd., and

[1544] https://books.google.com/books?id=OVtKS9DCN0kC

[1545] https://books.google.com/books?id=FRSVtzxH_10C

[1546] https://books.google.co.il/books?id=R7jvDS3OiAUC

[1547] https://books.google.com/books?id=m2fdWT3CuyQC

[1548] https://books.google.com/books?id=KYPVNdzXUJkC

[1549] https://books.google.com/books?id=YWorYnKGZ5YC

[1550] https://books.google.com/books?id=_P5W5ErBQRYC

[1551] http://civilresistance.info/rigby1991

[1552] https://books.google.com/books?id=BxOQKrCe7UUC

[1553] https://books.google.com/books?id=4kGIpMI5HC0C
[1554] https://www.jewishvirtuallibrary.org/jsource/History/intifada.html
[1555] http://www.intifada.com/palestine.html
[1556] http://www.un.org/Docs/scres/1987/scres87.htm
[1557] https://www.theguardian.com/israel/Story/0,2763,1275360,00.html
[1558] http://libcom.org/library/rebellion-palestine-le-brise-glace
[1559] http://repository.library.georgetown.edu/handle/10822/552681
[1560] http://repository.library.georgetown.edu/handle/10822/552494/browse?type=title
[1561] http://repository.library.georgetown.edu/handle/10822/552641
[1562] //en.wikipedia.org/w/index.php?title=Template:Israeli%E2%80%93Palestinian_peace_process&action=edit
[1563] *Declaration of Principles on Interim Self-Government Arrangements* https://web.archive.org/web/20021115183950/http://knesset.gov.il/process/docs/oslo_eng.htm (DOP), 13 September 1993. From the Knesset website
[1564] *Israeli-Palestinian Interim Agreement on the West Bank and the Gaza Strip* https://web.archive.org/web/20021115180646/http://knesset.gov.il/process/docs/heskemb_eng.htm, 28 September 1995. From the Knesset website
[1565] *Mideast accord: the overview; Rabin and Arafat sign accord ending Israel's 27-year hold on Jericho and the Gaza Strip* https://www.nytimes.com/1994/05/05/world/mideast-accord-overview-rabin-arafat-sign-accord-ending-israel-s-27-year-hold.html?pagewanted=all. Chris Hedges, New York Times, 5 May 1994.
Quote of Yitzhak Rabin: "We do not accept the Palestinian goal of an independent Palestinian state between Israel and Jordan. We believe there is a separate Palestinian entity short of a state."
[1566] Just Vision, *Oslo Process* http://www.justvision.org/glossary/oslo-process. Retrieved December 2013
[1567] MEDEA, *Oslo peace process* http://www.medea.be/en/countries/occupied-palestinian-territories/oslo-peace-process/. Retrieved December 2013
[1568] From the Framework for Peace in the Middle East, part of the 1978 Camp David Accords and blueprint for the Oslo Accords: • *Egypt and Israel agree that, ... there should be transitional arrangements for the West Bank and Gaza for a period not exceeding five years. In order to provide full autonomy to the inhabitants, under these arrangements the Israeli military government and its civilian administration will be withdrawn as soon as a self-governing authority has been freely elected by the inhabitants of these areas to replace the existing military government.* • *Egypt, Israel, and Jordan will agree on the modalities for establishing elected self-governing authority in the West Bank and Gaza. The delegations of Egypt and Jordan may include Palestinians from the West Bank and Gaza or other Palestinians as mutually agreed. The parties will negotiate an agreement which will define the powers and responsibilities of the self-governing authority to be exercised in the West Bank and Gaza. A withdrawal of Israeli armed forces will take place and there will be a redeployment of the remaining Israeli forces into specified security locations. The agreement will also include arrangements for assuring internal and external security and public order. A strong local police force will be established, which may include Jordanian citizens. In addition, Israeli and Jordanian forces will participate in joint patrols and in the manning of control posts to assure the security of the borders.* • *When the self-governing authority (administrative council) in the West Bank and Gaza is established and inaugurated, the transitional period of five years will begin. As soon as possible, but not later than the third year after the beginning of the transitional period, negotiations will take place to determine the final status of the West Bank and Gaza and its relationship with its neighbors and to conclude a peace treaty between Israel and Jordan by the end of the transitional period. These negotiations will be conducted among Egypt, Israel, Jordan and the elected representatives of the inhabitants of the West Bank and Gaza.*
(See JimmyCarterLibrary, *The Framework for Peace in the Middle East* http://www.jimmycarterlibrary.gov/documents/campdavid/accords.phtml (1978). Accessed December 2013)
[1569] *By Hook and by Crook—Israeli Settlement Policy in the West Bank* http://www.btselem.org/download/201007_by_hook_and_by_crook_eng.pdf, p. 90. B'Tselem, July 2010

[1570] *Israeli Settlements in Occupied Arab Lands: Conquest to Colony* http//www.palestine-studies. org, p. 29. Journal of Palestine Studies, Vol. 11, No. 2 (Winter, 1982), pp. 16-54. Published by: University of California Press on behalf of the Institute for Palestine Studies

[1571] *Israel-PLO Recognition: Exchange of Letters between PM Rabin and Chairman Arafat* https://unispal.un.org/UNISPAL.NSF/0/36917473237100E285257028006C0BC5 , 9 September 1993

[1572] Tom Lansford, *Political Handbook of the World 2014* https://books.google.co.uk/books?id=iC_VBQAAQBAJ&pg=PA1627, pp. 1627, 1630-1631. CQ Press, March 2014. pp.1629-1630: ", and 18 months after the election of the Palestinian Council, which was designated to succeed the PNA as the primary Palestinian governmental body."

[1573] *Annex I: Protocol Concerning Redeployment and Security Arrangements* https://web.archive.org/web/20021125095250/http://knesset.gov.il/process/docs/heskemb2_eng.htm, Article I *Redeployment of Israeli Military Forces and Transfer of Responsibility*. Annex I to the Interim Agreement on the West Bank and the Gaza Strip (Oslo II)

[1574]

[1575] *What is Area C?* http://www.btselem.org/area_c/what_is_area_c. B'Tselem, 9 October 2013

[1576] *4 May 1999 and Palestinian Statehood: To Declare or Not to Declare?* https://www.jstor.org/stable/2537930?seq=1#page_scan_tab_contents. Azmi Bishara, Journal of Palestine Studies Vol. 28, No. 2 (Winter, 1999), pp. 5-16

[1577] *The Discourse of Palestinian-Israeli Relations: Persistent Analytics and Practices* https://books.google.com/books?id=Xq6MAgAAQBAJ&pg=PA5, p. 5. Sean F. McMahon, Routledge, 2009

[1578] *Will we always have Paris?* http://www.gazagateway.org/2012/09/will-we-always-have-paris . Gaza Gateway, 13 September 2012

[1579] *Text on UNISPAL* https://unispal.un.org/UNISPAL.NSF/0/FD15ECA93FD9AF2785257000005A5810

[1580]

[1581] *Palestinians in the West Bank chafe under 'early empowerment'* http://www.csmonitor.com/1994/0914/14091.html.

[1582] *Text on Israel Ministry of Foreign Affairs website* http://mfa.gov.il/MFA/ForeignPolicy/Peace/Guide/Pages/Further%20Transfer%20of%20Powers%20and%20Responsibilities.aspx

[1583] *Postscript to Oslo: The Mystery of Norway's Missing Files* http://www.palestine-studies.org/jps/fulltext/42078. Hilde Henriksen Waage, Journal of Palestine Studies, Vol. XXXVIII, No. 1 (Autumn 2008), pp. 54–65; ISSN 1533-8614
"Had the missing documents ... been accessible at the time of writing, there seems no doubt that the findings of my report would have shown even more starkly the extent to which the Oslo process was conducted on Israel's premises, with Norway acting as Israel's helpful errand boy .... Given the overwhelming imbalance of power between the Israelis and the Palestinians, Norway probably could not have acted otherwise if it wanted to reach a deal—or even if it wanted to play a role in the process at all. Israel's red lines were the ones that counted, and if the Palestinians wanted a deal, they would have to accept them, too .... The missing documents would almost certainly show why the Oslo process probably never could have resulted in a sustainable peace. To a great extent, full documentation of the back channel would explain the disaster that followed Oslo."

[1584] *Truth and reconciliation* http://israelipalestinian.procon.org/view.background-resource.php?resourceID=000921 Al-Ahram Weekly, 14–20 January 1999, Issue 412

[1585] //tools.wmflabs.org/geohack/geohack.php?pagename=Assassination_of_Yitzhak_Rabin&params=32_04_54.8_N_34_46_51.4_E_region:IL-TA_type:event_scale:50000

[1586] Smith, Charles D. *Palestine and the Arab-Israeli Conflict A History with Documents*, , pp. 464, 466.

[1587] Smith, pp. 458, 468

[1588] *Rabbinic Response: Jewish Law on the Killing of Yitzhak Rabin*, by Rabbi Arthur Waskow, The Shalom Center, 14 November 2005

[1589] Ephron, p. 135

[1590] Ephron, pp. 148-57

[1591] Barak T: Ten years have passed, friend http://tam.co.il/28_10_2005/magazin1.htm. *Tel Aviv Newspaper*
[1592] Perry D: *Israel and the Quest for Permanence*, p. 216.
[1593] 'Soldier for peace' Rabin buried http://www.cnn.com/WORLD/9511/rabin/funeral/wrap/index.html
[1594] " "World Leaders in Attendance at the Funeral of the Late Prime Minister Yitzhak Rabin http://www.mfa.gov.il/MFA/MFAArchive/1990_1999/1995/11/World%20Leaders%20at%20PM%20Rabin-s%20." 6 November 1995. Ministry of Foreign Affairs.
[1595] " Eulogy for the Late Prime Minister and Defense Minister Yitzhak Rabin by U.S. President Bill Clinton http://www.mfa.gov.il/MFA/MFAArchive/1990_1999/1995/11/Rabin%20Eulogy-%20President%20Clinton." 6 November 1995. Ministry of Foreign Affairs.
[1596] " Eulogy for the Late Prime Minister and Defense Minister Yitzhak Rabin by His Majesty King Hussein of Jordan http://www.mfa.gov.il/MFA/MFAArchive/1990_1999/1995/11/Rabin%20Funeral-%20Eulogy%20by%20King%20Hussein." 6 November 1995. Ministry of Foreign Affairs.
[1597] "http://vorige.nrc.nl/redactie/Web/Nieuws/19951106/01.html" NRC Handelsblad, 6 November 1995.
[1598] " Eulogy for the Late Prime Minister and Defense Minister Yitzhak Rabin by Russian Prime Minister Viktor Chernomyrdin http://www.mfa.gov.il/MFA/MFAArchive/1990_1999/1995/11/Rabin%20Funeral-%20Eulogy%20by%20Viktor%20Chernomyrdin." 6 November 1995. Ministry of Foreign Affairs.
[1599] " Eulogy for the Late Prime Minister and Defense Minister Yitzhak Rabin by Felipe Gonzalez, Prime Minister of Spain and Current EU President http://www.mfa.gov.il/MFA/MFAArchive/1990_1999/1995/11/Rabin%20Funeral-%20Eulogy%20by%20Felipe%20Gonzalez." 6 November 1995. Ministry of Foreign Affairs.
[1600] " Eulogy for the Late Prime Minister and Defense Minister Yitzhak Rabin by Acting Prime Minister and Foreign Minister Shimon Peres http://www.mfa.gov.il/MFA/MFAArchive/1990_1999/1995/11/Rabin%20Funeral-%20Eulogy%20by%20PM%20Peres." 6 November 1995. Ministry of Foreign Affairs.
[1601] " Eulogy for the Late Prime Minister and Defense Minister Yitzhak Rabin by Boutros Boutros-Ghali, Secretary-General of the United Nations http://www.mfa.gov.il/MFA/MFAArchive/1990_1999/1995/11/Rabin%20Funeral-%20Boutros-Ghali%20Eulogy." 6 November 1995. Ministry of Foreign Affairs.
[1602] " Eulogy by Noa Ben-Artzi Filosof for Her Grandfather, the Late Prime Minister and Defense Yitzhak Rabin http://www.mfa.gov.il/MFA/MFAArchive/1990_1999/1995/11/Rabin%20Eulogy%20by%20Noa%20Ben-Artzi." 6 November 1995. Ministry of Foreign Affairs.
[1603] " Eulogy for the Late Prime Minister and Defense Minister Yitzhak Rabin by Former Dir-Gen PM's Office Shimon Sheves http://www.mfa.gov.il/MFA/MFAArchive/1990_1999/1995/11/Rabin%20Funeral-%20Eulogy%20by%20Shimon%20Sheves." 6 November 1995. Ministry of Foreign Affairs.
[1604] " Eulogy for the Late Prime Minister and Defense Minister Yitzhak Rabin by Egyptian President Hosni Mubarak http://www.mfa.gov.il/MFA/MFAArchive/1990_1999/1995/11/Rabin%20Funeral-%20Eulogy%20by%20Hosni%20Mubarak." 6 November 1995. Ministry of Foreign Affairs.
[1605] Eulogy for the Late Prime Minister and Defense Minister Yitzhak Rabin by Director of PM's Bureau Eitan Haber http://www.mfa.gov.il/MFA/MFAArchive/1990_1999/1995/11/Rabin%20Funeral-%20Eulogy%20by%20Eitan%20Haber." 6 November 1995. Ministry of Foreign Affairs.
[1606] Eulogy for the Late Prime Minister and Defense Minister Yitzhak Rabin by President Ezer Weizman http://www.mfa.gov.il/MFA/MFAArchive/1990_1999/1995/11/Rabin%20Funeral-%20Eulogy%20by%20President%20Weizman." 6 November 1995. Ministry of Foreign Affairs.
[1607] Ephron, pp. 229–30
[1608] http://news.bbc.co.uk/2/hi/middle_east/4431728.stm
[1609] http://news.bbc.co.uk/2/hi/middle_east/4432332.stm
[1610] https://web.archive.org/web/20090727000353/http://www.professors.org.il/docs/20000204-haa-rabin-doctors.txt
[1611] http://video.google.com/videoplay?docid=-7368409094401324350&q=rabin+murder

[1612] https://web.archive.org/web/20081003055702/http://www.cnn.com/WORLD/9512/israel_rabin/rabin_assasination.mov
[1613] http://koenraadelst.bharatvani.org/articles/fascism/2murders.html
[1614] http://www.thisamericanlife.org/radio-archives/episode/570/the-night-in-question
[1615] //en.wikipedia.org/w/index.php?title=Template:Israeli%E2%80%93Palestinian_peace_process&action=edit
[1616] Y. Yehoshua and B. Chernitsky, *Ahmad Qurei' - Abu 'Alaa: A Brief Political Profile of the Nominated Palestinian Prime Minister* http://www.memri.org/report/en/print953.htm; Middle East Media Research Institute (MEMRI), 18 September 2003
[1617] Akram Hanieh, *The Camp David Papers* http://www.palestine-studies.com/files/pdf/jps/2759.pdf . Articles, published in *al-Ayyam* in seven installments between 29 July and 10 August 2000. Journal of Palestine Studies XXX, no. 2 (Winter 2001), pp. 75-97.
[1618] Amnon Kapeliouk, *A summit clouded by suspicion* http://www.haaretz.com/culture/books/a-summit-clouded-by-suspicion-1.75548; Haaretz, 23 November 2001.
[1619] Jeremy Pressman, *International Security*, vol 28, no. 2, Fall 2003, *"Visions in Collision: What Happened at Camp David and Taba?"* http://belfercenter.ksg.harvard.edu/files/pressman.pdf. On http://belfercenter.ksg.harvard.edu/publication/322/visions_in_collision.html. See pp. 7, 15-19
[1620] Oren Yiftachel, *Ethnocracy: Land and Identity Politics in Israel/Palestine*, https://books.google.com/books?id=VD082HtsKRsC&pg=PA75 University of Pennsylvania Press 1006 p.75.
[1621] Shyovitz, David. "Camp David 2000." https://www.jewishvirtuallibrary.org/jsource/Peace/cd2000art.html *Jewish Virtual Library*.
[1622] Robert Malley and Hussein Agha, *Camp David: The Tragedy of Errors* http://www.nybooks.com/articles/archives/2001/aug/09/camp-david-the-tragedy-of-errors/?page=3 (part 4). New York Review of Books, 9 August 2001.
[1623] Decoding the Conflict Between Israel and the Palestinians, Charles River Editors https://books.google.com/books?id=HVTpUHEcfncC&pg=PA1993-IA4#v=onepage&q&f=false, Chapter 17
[1624] Hassner, Ron E. War on Sacred Grounds. 2009. Ithaca: Cornell University Press. pp. 78–88. www.waronsacredgrounds.org http://www.waronsacredgrounds.org
[1625] Hassner, Ron E. War on Sacred Grounds. 2009. Ithaca: Cornell University Press. p.80 www.waronsacredgrounds.org http://www.waronsacredgrounds.org
[1626] *Abu Mazen's speech at the meeting of the PLO's Palestinian Central Council* https://unispal.un.org/UNISPAL.NSF/0/172D1A3302DC903B85256E37005BD90F , 9 September 2000
[1627] Jewish Virtual Library, July 2000, *The proposed division of Jerusalem* https://www.jewishvirtuallibrary.org/jsource/Peace/jerdivide.html. Accessed 2013-06-21. Archived https://www.webcitation.org/6HpG9ZTN4?url=http://www.jewishvirtuallibrary.org/jsource/Peace/jerdivide.html 2013-07-02.
[1628] Foundation for Middle East Peace (FMEP), *Principles of Camp David's "American Plan"* http://www.fmep.org/reports/archive/vol.-10/no.-5/principles-of-camp-davids-american-plan. Settlement Report, Vol. 10 No. 5, September–October 2000. Accessed 2013-07-06. Archived https://www.webcitation.org/6I2rOuyyd?url=http://www.fmep.org/reports/archive/vol.-10/no.-5/principles-of-camp-davids-american-plan 2013-07-11.
[1629] Gilead Sher (2006), p. 102
[1630] Madeleine Albright (2003), p. 618
[1631] Gilead Sher (2006), p. 101 and pp. 247–249.
[1632] "Actual Proposal Offered At Camp David" https://www.jewishvirtuallibrary.org/jsource/Peace/rossmap2.html. Map from Dennis Ross book, *The Missing Peace: The Inside Story of the Fight for Middle East Peace*. NY: Farrar, Straus and Giroux, 2004.
[1633] Gilead Sher (2006), pp. 110–111
[1634] ProCon, 30 April 2008, *What were the 2000 Clinton parameters, and were they an acceptable solution?* http://israelipalestinian.procon.org/view.answers.php?questionID=000429
[1635] Embassy of the United States, Israel, 3 January 2001, *Excerpts: State Dept. spokesman on Mideast peace prospects (Both sides accept Clinton's parameters with reservations)* http://www.usembassy-israel.org.il/publish/peace/archives/2001/january/me0103b.html . Statement and press conference with discussion.

[1636] Ari Shavit, *Continuation of Eyes wide shut* http://www.haaretz.com/continuation-of-eyes-wide-shut-1.35091 (interview with Ehud Barak). Haaretz, 4 September 2002. (← *Eyes wide shut* http://www.haaretz.com/eyes-wide-shut-1.35090)
[1637] MidEastWeb, *The Taba Proposals and the Refugee Problem* http://www.mideastweb.org/taba.htm. Accessed 2013-07-06. Archived https://www.webcitation.org/6I2rPJxDN?url=http://www.mideastweb.org/taba.htm 2013-07-11.
[1638] Jeremy Pressman, 1 December 2004, *Lost Opportunities* http://www.bostonreview.net/jeremy-pressman-lost-opportunities-israel-palestine; Boston Review: Dennis Ross, *The Missing Peace*
[1639] Eran, Oded. "Arab-Israel Peacemaking." *The Continuum Political Encyclopedia of the Middle East*. Ed. Avraham Sela. New York: Continuum, 2002. p. 145.
[1640] Kenneth Levin (2005), p. 422.
[1641] Segal, Jerome M. "Ha'aretz – 1 October 2001." http://www.peacelobby.org/HaaretzOctober1001.htm *The Jewish Peace Lobby*. 1 October 2001.
[1642] Ross, Michael – *The Volunteer* (2007)
[1643] Alexander, Edward. "Review of The Oslo Syndrome: Delusions of a People Under Siege." http://www.meforum.org/article/962 *Middle East Forum*. Spring 2006.
[1644] Dershowitz, Alan. Interview. "Noam Chomsky v. Alan Dershowitz: A Debate on the Israeli-Palestinian Conflict." http://www.democracynow.org/article.pl?sid=05/12/23/1450216 *Democracy Now!*. 23 December 2005.
[1645] Robert Malley, *Fictions About the Failure At Camp David* https://www.nytimes.com/2001/07/08/opinion/fictions-about-the-failure-at-camp-david.html?pagewanted=all&src=pm. New York Times, 8 July 2001
[1646] Gush Shalom, *Barak's generous offers* http://zope.gush-shalom.org/home/en/channels/downloads/baraks_offers/barak_eng.swf. Accessed 2015-12-19. Archived https://www.webcitation.org/6I2rOSN5A?url=http://zope.gush-shalom.org/home/en/channels/downloads/baraks_offers/barak_eng.swf 2013-07-11.
[1647] 2003 Charles Enderlin book, *Shattered Dreams: The Failure of the Peace Process in the Middle East, 1995–2002* https://books.google.com/books?id=a3XfsUSR0yUC. Use the Google Book Search form at the bottom of the linked page to find the quotes. Shlomo Ben-Ami quoted on page 195.
[1648] Shlomo Ben-Ami vs Norman Finkelstein Debate. "Fmr. Israeli Foreign Minister Shlomo Ben Ami Debates Outspoken Professor Norman Finkelstein on Israel, the Palestinians, and the Peace Process" http://www.democracynow.org/2006/2/14/fmr_israeli_foreign_minister_shlomo_ben *Democracy Now!*. 14 February 2006.
[1649] "The Camp David II Negotiations: How Dennis Ross Proved the Palestinians Aborted the Peace Process" http://www.palestine-studies.org/journals.aspx?id=7317&jid=1&href=fulltext . By Norman G. Finkelstein. *Journal of Palestine Studies*. Winter 2007 issue. Article is excerpted from his longer essay called *Subordinating Palestinian Rights to Israeli "Needs"*
[1650] Klein, Menahem. Shattering a Taboo: The Contacts towards a Permanent Status Agreement in Jerusalem, 1994–2001. 2001. Jerusalem: Jerusalem Institute for Israeli Studies. cited in Hassner, ibid., p.81 http://www.waronsacredgrounds.org
[1651] Israeli Poll 1 27–31 July 2000. Harry S. Truman Institute for the Advancement of Peace, 2000.http://truman.huji.ac.il/upload/truman_site_poll01_July2000.pdf
[1652] http://truman.huji.ac.il/upload/truman_site_poll01_July2000.pdf Truman.huji.ac.il
[1653] http://www.mfa.gov.il/MFA/Government/Speeches%20by%20Israeli%20leaders/2000/Statement%20by%20PM%20Barak%20on%20Conclusion%20of%20the%20Camp%20Da
[1654] https://www.jewishvirtuallibrary.org/jsource/Peace/benamidiary.html
[1655] https://www.webcitation.org/6I2rOuyyd?url=http://www.fmep.org/reports/archive/vol.-10/no.-5/principles-of-camp-davids-american-plan
[1656] http://www.foxnews.com/story/0,2933,50830,00.html
[1657] https://www.motherjones.com/news/qa/2004/10/09_404.html
[1658] https://www.jewishvirtuallibrary.org/jsource/Peace/cd2000toc.html
[1659] https://web.archive.org/web/20120111230312/http://www.passia.org/publications/bookmaps/page2.htm
[1660] http://www.mfa.gov.il/MFA/Peace+Process/Guide+to+the+Peace+Process/The+Middle+East+Peace+Summit+at+Camp+David-+July+2.htm

[1661] http://www.mideastweb.org/campdavid2.htm
[1662] http://www.mideastweb.org/campdavid%20orient.htm
[1663] http://www.fmep.org/maps/redeployment-final-status-options/west-bank-final-status-map-presented-by-israel-jul-2000/west_bank_final_status_map.gif/view
[1664] https://web.archive.org/web/20060222163153/http://www.peres-center.org/media/Upload/61.pdf
[1665] http://www.monde-diplomatique.fr/cartes/taba2001
[1666] http://mondediplo.com/2000/12/12campdavid
[1667] https://web.archive.org/web/20020514192706/http://infopal.org/palnews/mapf2.jpg
[1668] https://web.archive.org/web/20010816073137/http://infopal.org/palnews/mapf1.jpg
[1669] http://zope.gush-shalom.org/home/en/channels/downloads/baraks_offers/barak_eng.swf
[1670] http://www.nybooks.com/articles/14380
[1671] http://www.nybooks.com/articles/14529
[1672] http://www.nybooks.com/articles/15501
[1673] http://www.nybooks.com/articles/15502
[1674] http://www.nybooks.com/articles/15540
[1675] https://web.archive.org/web/20040702123224/http://www.emory.edu/COLLEGE/JewishStudies/stein/Articles/mei91000.html
[1676] http://www.slate.com/?id=2064500
[1677] https://web.archive.org/web/20040422111155/http://www.gush-shalom.org/archives/barak.html
[1678] https://web.archive.org/web/20060928202633/http://gush-shalom.org/archives/benami_eng.html
[1679] https://web.archive.org/web/20060815050733/http://www.gush-shalom.org/archives.html
[1680] https://web.archive.org/web/20040118192757/http://www.peacelobby.org/HaaretzOctober1001.htm
[1681] http://belfercenter.ksg.harvard.edu/publication/322/visions_in_collision.html
[1682] Saddam: 'İsrail'e sınırımız olsa çoktan girmiştik' http://hurarsiv.hurriyet.com.tr/goster/ShowNew.aspx?id=-186926 (Hürriyet)
[1683] B'Tselem – Statistics – Fatalities 29.9.2000-15.1.2005 http://old.btselem.org/statistics/english/Casualties.asp?sD=29&sM=09&sY=2000&eD=15&eM=1&eY=2005&filterby=event&oferet_stat=before, B'Tselem.
[1684] https://libcom.org/history/1977-egypts-bread-intifada
[1685] Hillel Frisch, *The Palestinian Military: Between Militias and Armies*, https://books.google.com/books?id=SLdwp_4BZhMC&pg=PA102 Routledge, 2010 p.102.
[1686] Hillel Cohen, https://books.google.com/books?id=KRKsAgAAQBAJ&pg=PA73 *The Rise and Fall of Arab Jerusalem: Palestinian Politics and the City Since 1967*, Routledge, 2013 p.73
[1687] Rashmi Singh, *Hamas and Suicide Terrorism: Multi-causal and Multi-level Approaches* https://books.google.com/books?id=AQ_TOiLtdtAC&pg=PA38 Routledge, 2013 p.38
[1688] Colin Shindler, *A History of Modern Israel*, https://books.google.com/books?id=oSQgAwAAQBAJ&pg=PA283 Cambridge University Press, 2013 p.283
[1689] Yossef Bodansky, *The High Cost of Peace* (Prima Publishing, 2002) pp. 353–354
[1690] Goldberg, Jeffrey. *Prisoners: A Story of Friendship and Terror*. New York: Vintage Books, 2008. p. 258.
[1691] Colin Shindler, *A History of Modern Israel*, https://books.google.com/books?id=oSQgAwAAQBAJ&pg=PA283 Cambridge University Press, 2013 p.283
[1692] : "Your account of events does not match the impression of any country in the world," he said. "At Camp David, Israel did in fact make a significant step towards peace, but Sharon's visit was the detonator, and everything has exploded. This morning, sixty-four Palestinians are dead, nine Israeli-Arabs were also killed, and you're pressing on. You cannot, Mr Prime Minister, explain this ratio in the number of [killed and] wounded. You cannot make anyone believe that the Palestinians are the aggressors....When I was a company commander in Algeria, I also thought I was right. I fought the guerilas. Later I realized I was wrong. It is the honour of the strong, to reach out and not to shoot. Today you must reach out your hand. If you continue to fire from helicopters on people throwing rocks, and you continue to refuse an international inquiry, you

are turning down a gesture from Arafat. You have no idea how hard I pushed Arafat to agree to a trilateral meeting. ..'

[1693] Earlier estimates gave a million bullets and projectiles shot by Israeli forces in the first few days, 700,000 in the West Bank and 300,000 in the Gaza strip. See Ben Kaspit, "Jewish New Year 2002—the Second Anniversary of the Intifada," *Maariv* 6 September 2002 (Heb), in Cheryl Rubenberg, *The Palestinians: In Search of a Just Peace*, Lynne Rienner Publishers, 2003 p. 324, p. 361 n. 5. The figure was revealed by Amos Malka, then-director of Military Intelligence. Moshe Ya'alon, who later became the Israeli Chief of Staff, denied the 1.3 million figure, claiming that the number reflected the demand of the command units for supplemental ammunition. []

[1694] Nitzan Ben-Shaul, *A Violent World: TV News Images of Middle Eastern Terror and War* https://books.google.com/books?id=QFBiclfUJ04C&pg=PA118 Rowman & Littlefield, 6 March 2007 pp.118–120.

[1695] Eve Spangler, *Understanding Israel/Palestine: Race, Nation, and Human Rights in the Conflict* https://books.google.com/books?id=v2AICgAAQBAJ&pg=PA183 Springer, 2015 p.183

[1696] Statistics | B'Tselem http://old.btselem.org/statistics/english/casualties.asp?sD=29&sM=09&sY=2000&eD=26&eM=12&eY=2008&filterby=event&oferet_stat=before

[1697] Barry Rubin,Judith Colp Rubin, *Yasir Arafat: A Political Biography* https://books.google.com/books?id=KRjiBwAAQBAJ&pg=PT427 Oxford University Press, 2003 p.427 n.14

[1698] Neil Caplan, *The Israel–Palestine Conflict: Contested Histories*, https://books.google.com/books?id=JyAgn_dD43cC&pg=PT167 John Wiley & Sons, 2011 p.167

[1699] Galia Golan, *Israeli Peacemaking Since 1967: Factors Behind the Breakthroughs and Failures* https://books.google.com/books?id=-zqDBAAAQBAJ&pg=PA170 Routledge, 2014 p.170.

[1700] *Arafat Siege Could End Soon* http://www.cbsnews.com/stories/2002/04/29/world/main507467.shtml. CBS, 29 April 2002

[1701] Harel and Issacharoff (2004), pp. 257–258

[1702] Review of

[1703]

[1704] PDF http://eeas.europa.eu/mepp/docs/mitchell_report_2001_en.pdf

[1705] Schulz and Hammer, 2003, pp. 134–136.

[1706]

[1707]

[1708] Nasser Abufarha, *The Making of a Human Bomb: An Ethnography of Palestinian Resistance* https://books.google.com/books?id=WpMi4fsKu0AC&pg=PA77 Duke University Press, 2009 p.77.

[1709] Nathan Thrall, 'What Future for Israel?,' http://www.nybooks.com/articles/archives/2013/aug/15/what-future-israel/ *New York Review of Books* 15 August 2013 pp.64–67.

[1710] B'Tselem – Statistics – Fatalities http://www.btselem.org/English/Statistics/Casualties.asp , B'Tselem.

[1711]

[1712] Comprehensive list of all Israeli and Palestinian child casualties, age 17 and under, listed since September 2000 along with the circumstances of their deaths.

[1713] Includes translation of article in Hebrew in *Haaretz* presenting Dahoah-Halevi's report. Original Haaretz report in Hebrew:

[1714] "B'Tselem – Statistics – Fatalities. Palestinians killed by Palestinians in the Occupied Territories" http://www.btselem.org/english/statistics/Casualties_Data.asp?Category=23&region=TER. Detailed B'Tselem list.

[1715] "Hamas slammed the silent and still Arab position on Gaza massacre" –

[1716] "it's impossible to contain the Arab and Islamic world after the Gaza massacre" –

[1717] Gabi Siboni, Defeating Suicide Terrorism in Judea and Samaria, 2002–2005 http://www.inss.org.il/uploadimages/Import/(FILE)1298360394.pdf, "**Military and Strategic Affairs**", Volume 2, No. 2, October 2010.

[1718] Israeli High Court Backs Military On Its Policy of Targeted Killings https://www.washingtonpost.com/wp-dyn/content/article/2006/12/14/AR2006121400430.html. Scott Wilson, Washington Post, 15 December 2006

[1719] http://www.haaretz.co.il/hasite/images/printed/P080404/zza.jpg

[1720] http://www.haaretz.co.il/hasite/images/printed/P080404/a.0.0804.10.2.9.jpg
[1721] Sela, Avraham. "Arab Summit Conferences". *The Continuum Political Encyclopedia of the Middle East*. Ed. Sela. New York: Continuum, 2002. pp. 158–160
[1722] The Peace Index Project conducted at the Tami Steinmetz Center for Peace http://www.bicohen.tau.ac.il/templ001/manage.asp?siteID=5&lang=2&pageID=199
[1723] https://books.google.com/books?id=2C3NcBIl_60C
[1724] https://books.google.com/books/about/Son_of_Hamas.html?id=6qqwLB05IocC
[1725] http://www.huffingtonpost.com/rick-steves/the-security-fence-the-an_b_4296601.html
[1726] http://www.mfa.gov.il/mfa/foreignpolicy/terrorism/palestinian/pages/saving%20lives-%20israel-s%20anti-terrorist%20fence%20-%20answ.aspx#1
[1727] Dona J. Stewart, *The Middle East Today: Political, Geographical and Cultural Perspectives*, https://books.google.com/books?id=JYE2eOEmwmkC&pg=PA223 Routledge, 2013 p. 223.
[1728] UN OCHA (Office for the Coordination of Humanitarian Affairs), 'Barrier Update: Special Focus', (2011), http://www.ochaopt.org/documents/ocha_opt_barrier_update_july_2011_english.pdf
[1729] " International Court of Justice finds Israeli barrier in Palestinian territory is illegal https://www.un.org/apps/news/story.asp?NewsID=11292". *UN News Centre*. United Nations. 9 July 2004.
[1730] " Legal Consequences of the Construction of a Wall in the Occupied Palestinian Territory https://web.archive.org/web/20040902090629/http://www.icj-cij.org/icjwww/ipresscom/ipress2004/ipresscom2004-28_mwp_20040709.htm". *International Court of Justice*. 9 July 2004. Archived from the original http://www.icj-cij.org/icjwww/ipresscom/ipress2004/ipresscom2004-28_mwp_20040709.htm on 2 September 2004.
[1731] Semple, Kirk (22 October 2003). " U.N. Resolution Condemns Israeli Barrier https://www.nytimes.com/2003/10/22/international/middleeast/un-resolution-condemns-israeli-barrier.html". *The New York Times*.
[1732] Robert Zelnick, *Israel's Unilateralism: Beyond Gaza*, Hoover Press, 2006, p 30-31 https//books.google.com, , 9780817947736
[1733] Fiona de Londras, *Detention in the 'War on Terror': Can Human Rights Fight Back?*, Cambridge University Press, 2011, pp. 177–78 https//books.google.com, " ,
[1734] http://www.economist.com/node/2119356
[1735] https://www.pbs.org/pov/5brokencameras/photo_gallery_background.php#.VD3fNmQf201
[1736] https://www.nytimes.com/2014/07/13/sunday-review/for-israelis-and-palestinians-separation-is-dehumanizing.html?_r=0
[1737] http://www.mfa.gov.il/mfa/foreignpolicy/terrorism/palestinian/pages/saving%20lives-%20israel-s%20security%20fence.aspx
[1738] The Road Map to Nowhere: Israel/Palestine Since 2003, Tanya Reinhart (2006)
[1739] *Behind the barrier: Human Rights Violations as a Result of Israel's Separation Barrier* http://www.btselem.org/download/200304_behind_the_barrier_eng.pdf, pp. 5–8. Yehezkel Lein, B'Tselem, March 2003. Here available http://www.btselem.org/publications/summaries/200304_behind_the_barrier. p. 8: "The average width of the barrier complex is sixty meters. Due to topographic constraints, a narrower barrier will be erected in some areas and will not include all of the elements that support the electronic fence. However, as the state indicated to the High Court of Justice, "in certain cases, the barrier will reach a width of one hundred meters due to the topographic conditions."
[1740] https://www.jewishvirtuallibrary.org/jsource/Peace/arielbloc.html
[1741] *Preliminary Analysis of the Humanitarian Implications of February 2005 Barrier Projections* https://unispal.un.org/UNISPAL.NSF/0/659581cf3863644f85256fbf0068c624 . OCHAoPt, 8 March 2005
[1742] *Separation Barrier – Statistics* http://www.btselem.org/separation_barrier/statistics. B'Tselem, update 16 July 2012
[1743] *Barrier Route Projections – Update 5* http://www.ochaopt.org/documents/OCHABarrierProj_6jul06_web.pdf . OCHAoPt, July 2006
[1744] *Barrier Route Projections – Update 2: Preliminary Analysis* http://www.ochaopt.org/documents/Barrierprojections_Jan04%20_25Feb04_eng.pdf . OCHAoPt, January 2004
[1745] *Map of Israel Security Barrier ("Wall")- Current Status (2006)* http://www.mideastweb.org/thefence.htm MidEastWeb, June 2006

[1746] *Jordanian-Israeli General Armistice Agreement, April 3, 1949* http://www.yale.edu/lawweb/avalon/mideast/arm03.htm . The Avalon Project

[1747] UN Division for Palestinian Rights, *Monthly media monitoring review, December 2000* https://unispal.un.org/UNISPAL.NSF/0/3790975C4E7E4084852569D6006553B3 . See par. 25

[1748] West Bank Battir barrier off the table for now http://www.jpost.com/Israel-News/West-Bank-Battir-barrier-off-the-table-for-now-375973 – Retrieved 21 September 2014

[1749] //en.wikipedia.org/w/index.php?title=Template:Israeli%E2%80%93Palestinian_peace_process&action=edit

[1750] Israel's Security Fence https://www.jewishvirtuallibrary.org/jsource/Peace/fence.html (Jewish Virtual Library)

[1751] Israeli Ministry of Foreign Affairs http://securityfence.mfa.gov.il/mfm/Data/48152.doc

[1752] Intelligence and Terrorism Information Center at the Israel Intelligence Heritage & Commemoration Center (IICC) http://www.terrorism-info.org.il/malam_multimedia/English/eng_n/html/ct_250308e.htm

[1753] Moshe Arens: The fence, revisited http://www.haaretz.com/hasen/spages/1031952.html *Haaretz* October 28, 2008.

[1754] *The Humanitarian Impact of the West Bank Barrier on Palestinian Communities* https://unispal.un.org/UNISPAL.NSF/0/32943465E443DEFE8525700C0066B181 , Update No. 5, March 2005. OCHAoPt. Original PDF http://www.ochaopt.org/documents/OCHABarRprt05_Full.pdf (1.9 MB). See Chap. 1, *Findings and Overview*

[1755] Washington Times – Mideast security barrier working http://www.washingtontimes.com/world/20040624-112922-9037r.htm

[1756] Variables.theArticle:headline | Jerusalem Post http://fr.jpost.com/servlet/Satellite?pagename=JPost/JPArticle/Printer&cid=1087441302553

[1757] MIFTAH-Bad Fences Make Bad Neighbors – Part V: Focus on Zayta http://www.miftah.org/Display.cfm?DocId=2401&CategoryId=4

[1758] Israel has de facto annexed the Jordan Valley http://www.btselem.org/settlements/20060213_annexation_of_the_jordan_valley, B'tselem, February 13, 2006.

[1759] Akiva Eldar, Israel effectively annexes Palestinian land near Jordan Valley http://www.haaretz.com/news/diplomacy-defense/israel-effectively-annexes-palestinian-land-near-jordan-valley-1.396225, *Haaretz*, November 18, 2011.

[1760] Ferry Biedermann, Mideast: Environment Too Encounters a Barrier http://www.ipsnews.net/2004/11/mideast-environment-too-encounters-a-barrier/, Inter Press Service, November 25, 2004.

[1761] Beyond the E-1 Israeli settlement http://www.maannews.net/eng/ViewDetails.aspx?ID=576374, Ma'an News Agency, March 3, 2013.

[1762] EU on verge of abandoning hope for a viable Palestinian state http://www.belfasttelegraph.co.uk/news/world-news/eu-on-verge-of-abandoning-hope-for-a-viable-palestinian-state-28701935.html, *The Belfast Telegraph*, January 12, 2012.

[1763] Barak: consider unilateral separation from West Bank http://www.jewishjournal.com/israel/article/barak_consider_unilateral_separation_from_west_bank *The Jewish Journal of Greater Los Angeles*, March 4, 2013.

[1764] Report No. AUS2922, West Bank and Gaza: Area C and the Future of the Palestinian Economy, October 2, 2013; Page 30; http://documents.worldbank.org/curated/en/2013/10/18836847/west-bank-gaza-area-c-future-palestinian-economy

[1765] Id. How to Build a Fence at the Wayback Machine (archived February 19, 2006), pp. 50–64. David Makovsky, Foreign Affairs, volume 83, issue 2, March/April 2004.

[1766] Written Statement of the Government of Israel on Jurisdiction and Propriety http://www.icj-cij.org/docket/files/131/1579.pdf

[1767] International Court of Justice Advisory Opinion, "Legal Consequences of the Construction of a Wall in the Occupied Palestinian Territory", paragraphs 120–137 and 163 ; English version http://www.unhcr.org/refworld/pdfid/414ad9a719.pdf

[1768] Permanent Observer of Palestine, 30 January 2004, *Written statement submitted by Palestine* http://domino.un.org/pdfs/Palestine.pdf

[1769] See the report of The UN Fact Finding Mission on Gaza, A/HRC/12/48, 25 September 2009, paragraph 1548

[1770] *Behind The Barrier: Human Rights Violations Resulting from Israel's Construction of the Separation Barrier* http://www.btselem.org/press_releases/20030413. B'Tselem, 13 April 2003
[1771] HCJ 2056/04, 30 June 2004 http://elyon1.court.gov.il/files_eng/04/560/020/a28/04020560.a28.pdf; B'Tselem, 16 September 2005 *High Court in precedent-making decision: Dismantle section of the Separation Barrier* http://www.btselem.org/topic-page/high-court-precedent-making-decision-dismantle-section-separation-barrier; HCJ 7957/04, 15 September 2005 http://elyon1.court.gov.il/files_eng/04/570/079/a14/04079570.a14.pdf
[1772]
[1773] Peace Index / Most Israelis support the fence, despite Palestinian suffering http://www.haaretz.com/hasen/pages/ShArt.jhtml?itemNo=402996&contrassID=1. Haaretz. Israel News. Ephraim Yaar, Tamar Hermann. March 10, 2004
[1774] Peace Now : Opinions > Peace Now Positions http://www.peacenow.org.il/site/en/peace.asp?pi=69&docid=1237&pos=2
[1775] AATW – Anarchists against the wall http://www.awalls.org/
[1776] Gush Shalom – Israeli Peace Bloc http://zope.gush-shalom.org/home/en/channels/video/bilin-2006-01-20/
[1777] Remember the separation fence? http://www.haaretz.com/hasen/spages/1074560.html , *Haaretz* By Shaul Arieli
[1778] Israel's ambassador defends security fence http://www.washingtontimes.com/op-ed/20030825-090132-1658r.htm by Daniel Ayalon (*The Washington Times*) August 26, 2003
[1779] Natan Sharansky: *The Case for Democracy* p. 214
[1780] Your Financial News Source http://www.haaretzdaily.com/hasen/pages/ShArt.jhtml?itemNo=248438
[1781] Israel and the Occupied Territories: The place of the fence/wall in international law\n 1 Amnesty International https://www.amnesty.org/en/library/info/MDE15/016/2004/en
[1782] Bulletin on November 11, PIJ leader Abdallah Ramadan Shalah interview to Al-Manar TV http://www.intelligence.org.il/eng/eng_n/html/pij151106e.htm (Intelligence and Terrorism Information Center at the Center for Special Studies (C.S.S)). November 15, 2006
[1783] Bush and Sharon: Much ado about more than nothing – a commented celebrity scrapbook http://www.mideastweb.org/log/archives/00000244.htm
[1784] "The Wall" installation page, on the Bethlehem Unwrapped http://bethlehem-unwrapped.org/?page_id=214 website.
[1785] Statement and commentary at The Guardian https://www.theguardian.com/commentisfree/2014/jan/02/bethlehem-unwrapped-not-taking-sides-israel-security-wall newspaper on-line.
[1786] http://hrw.org/english/docs/2005/03/10/isrlpa10290.htm Human Rights Watch
[1787] Amnesty International
[1788] Bush, George W. (April 14, 2004). "President Bush Commends Israeli Prime Minister Sharon's Plan" https://georgewbush-whitehouse.archives.gov/news/releases/2004/04/20040414-4.html. White House.
[1789] Israel rebukes Ashton for voicing 'concern' on military trial (EUObserver, August 26, 2010) http://euobserver.com/9/30676
[1790] Department of Foreign Affairs and International Trade:
[1791] *Israel proposes West Bank barrier as border* https://news.yahoo.com/israel-proposes-west-bank-barrier-border-204613514.html. Dan Perry and Mohammed Daraghmeh, Associated Press, 27 January 2012
[1792] "... Under painted arches one can glimpse expanses of green lawns and perpetually blue skies, painted by an artist on the gray concrete that hides the Arabs' homes." (Gideon Levy, "What You See and What You Don't on the Maccabim-Reut Highway to Jerussalem," *Ha'aretz*, 20 January 2005, Source: *Journal of Palestine Studies*, Vol. 34, No. 3 (Spring, 2005), pp. 113-15)
[1793] Against The Wall http://site.ebrary.com/lib/nyulibrary/docDetail.action?docID=10491579
[1794]
[1795] *Israeli-Palestinian Conflict: from Balfour Promise to Bush Declaration: The Complications and the Road for a Lasting Peace* https://books.google.com/books?id=AMqLgW_B_BAC&pg=PA325, pp. 325–26. Gabriel G. Tabarani, AuthorHouse, 2008;
[1796] *Routledge Handbook on the Israeli-Palestinian Conflict* https://books.google.com/books?id=kftqQdNNDWAC&pg=PA191, p. 191. Gerald M. Steinberg, Routledge, 2013;

[1797]

[1798] *Move to annex settlements overshadows Israeli cabinet's approval of Gaza pullout* https://www.theguardian.com/world/2005/feb/21/israel1. Chris McGreal, The Guardian, 21 February 2005

[1799]

[1800] *Map of the West Bank Barrier: New Route Comparison* http://www.ochaopt.org/documents/WestBank_Barrier_Feb05.pdf . UN-OCHA, February 2005

[1801] *Sharon: Key settlement blocs to stay inside fence* http://www.haaretz.com/print-edition/news/sharon-key-settlement-blocs-to-stay-inside-fence-1.134226. Aluf Benn, Haaretz, 9 September 2004

[1802] *Despite U.S. deal, Israel starts Ariel fence* http://www.haaretz.com/print-edition/news/despite-u-s-deal-israel-starts-ariel-fence-1.125156 Arnon Regular, Haaretz, 14 June 2004

[1803] *Official map*, February 20, 2005 https://www.jewishvirtuallibrary.org/jsource/images/maps/fence10.jpg

[1804] *Israel cabinet approves changes to security fence route* http://jurist.law.pitt.edu/paperchase/2006/04/israel-cabinet-approves-changes-to.php . Jurist, April 30, 2006

[1805] *Official map* http://www.seamzone.mod.gov.il/Pages/ENG/images/Seamzone_map_eng.jpg

[1806] *Status reports Israeli Ministry of Defense* http://www.seamzone.mod.gov.il/Pages/ENG/news.htm#news45

[1807] Map of the West Bank Barrier Update – Overview of changes to the route http://www.ochaopt.org/documents/WB_Barrier_Overview_Changes_July06.pdf . UN-OCHA, July 2006

[1808]

[1809] https://www.nytimes.com/2005/09/06/movies/06para.html

[1810] https://www.youtube.com/watch?v=IpeoE04Ylmo

[1811] http://www.geneva-accord.org/mainmenu/west-bank-barrier-status-2012

[1812] https://web.archive.org/web/20131111154525/http://www.ochaopt.org/documents/ocha_opt_west_bank_access_restrictions_dec_2012.pdf

[1813] https://web.archive.org/web/20131111130353/http://www.ochaopt.org/generalmaps.aspx?id=96

[1814] https://web.archive.org/web/20131111130332/http://www.ochaopt.org/documents/ocha_opt_humaitarian_atlas_dec_2012_web.pdf

[1815] https://web.archive.org/web/20080910163530/http://www.ochaopt.org/documents/BarrierRouteProjections_July_2008.pdf

[1816] http://www.btselem.org/sites/default/files2/201206_btselem_map_of_wb_eng.pdf

[1817] http://www.mideastweb.org/thefence.htm

[1818] //web.archive.org/web/20090327180832/http://www.humanitarianinfo.org/opt/maps/barrier/BrrWBN_gates0305.pdf

[1819] https://web.archive.org/web/20131111130327/http://www.ochaopt.org/documents/wb_closure1203_300.pdf

[1820] http://www.mideastweb.org/thefence_05.htm

[1821] http://www.mideastweb.org/thefence1.htm

[1822] http://www.mideastweb.org/israelfence.htm

[1823] https://web.archive.org/web/20041028082014/http://www.haaretz.com/hasen/pages/ShArt.jhtml?itemNo=326257

[1824] http://news.bbc.co.uk/1/hi/world/middle_east/3111159.stm

[1825] http://news.bbc.co.uk/2/shared/spl/hi/guides/456900/456944/html/nn1page1.stm

[1826] http://news.bbc.co.uk/1/hi/world/middle_east/3654720.stm

[1827] http://www.bitterlemons.org/previous/bl120307ed10.html

[1828] https://unispal.un.org/pdfs/BR_Update30July2007.pdf

[1829] http://securityfence.mfa.gov.il/

[1830] https://web.archive.org/web/20041010163622/http://www.seamzone.mod.gov.il/Pages/ENG/default.htm

[1831] http://www.haaretz.com/hasite/images/iht_daily/D010704/hcfen0604.rtf

[1832] http://www.zionism-israel.com/hdoc/High_Court_Fence.htm

[1833] http://securityfence.mfa.gov.il/mfm/Data/49486.pdf

[1834] http://www.mfa.gov.il/mfa/about%20the%20ministry/mfa%20spokesman/2004/Statement%20on%20ICJ%20Advisory%20Opinion%209-July-2004

[1835] http://www.mfa.gov.il/MFA/Government/Law/Legal+Issues+and+Rulings/Summary+of+Israels+Response+regarding+the+Security+Fence+28-Feb-2005.htm
[1836] http://www.icj-cij.org/docket/index.php?p1=3&p2=4&k=5a&case=131&code=mwp&p3=4
[1837] https://web.archive.org/web/20130116101454/http://unispal.un.org/unispal.nsf/vSubject?OpenView&Start=1&Count=270&Expand=90#90
[1838] http://www.reliefweb.int/rw/dbc.nsf/doc104?OpenForm&rc=3&cc=pse
[1839] https://web.archive.org/web/20060209124215/http://www.ohchr.org/english/bodies/chr/docs/61chr/reportCHR61.pdf
[1840] http://www.ohchr.org/english/bodies/chr/docs/61chr/reportCHR61.pdf
[1841] https://web.archive.org/web/20040915081717/http://www.gush-shalom.org/thewall/
[1842] http://www.btselem.org/english/Separation_Barrier/index.asp
[1843] https://web.archive.org/web/20051025130126/http://www.machsomwatch.org/eng/homePageEng.asp?link=homePage&lang=eng
[1844] http://www.awalls.org/
[1845] https://web.archive.org/web/20110721144900/http://www.ir-amim.org.il/Eng/_Uploads/dbsAttachedFiles/BeyondTheWalEng(1).doc
[1846] http://www.icrc.org/Web/Eng/siteeng0.nsf/iwpList4/F06BB484D900B227C1256E3E00324D96
[1847] https://web.archive.org/web/20041013161904/http://www.commondreams.org/views04/0223-02.htm
[1848] http://electronicintifada.net/bytopic/apartheidwall.shtml
[1849] http://www.stopthewall.org
[1850] https://web.archive.org/web/20081211061745/http://imeu.net/news/article0013888.shtml
[1851] https://web.archive.org/web/20070226222032/http://video.google.com/videoplay?docid=3981406756866553772&hl=en
[1852] https://web.archive.org/web/20110622113235/http://video.google.com/videoplay?docid=-3322403523120637763&hl=en
[1853] https://web.archive.org/web/20041028042249/http://www.honestreporting.com/articles/critiques/Not_an_-Apartheid_Wall-.asp
[1854] http://www.imra.org.il/story.php3?id=21411
[1855] http://www.meforum.org/article/652
[1856] https://web.archive.org/web/20051210105858/http://www.defenddemocracy.org/research_topics/research_topics_list.htm?topic=8745
[1857] http://www.mythsandfacts.com/media/user/documents/Eli%20Hertz%20Reply%204-21-05D.pdf
[1858] https://www.nytimes.com/2006/03/18/opinion/18manji.html?ex=1300338000&en=5bcee9d86aa4e6c5&ei=5090&partner=rssuserland&emc=rss
[1859] http://securityfence.mfa.gov.il/mfm/web/main/document.asp?DocumentID=49517&MissionID=45187
[1860] http://www.us-israel.org/jsource/Peace/fence.html
[1861] https://web.archive.org/web/20060710060914/http://www.standwithus.com/flyers/IsraelFenceBro.pdf
[1862] http://www.standwithus.com/flyers/IsraelFenceBro.pdf
[1863] http://www.isracast.com/Transcripts/270204a_trans.htm
[1864] http//www.mfa.gov.il
[1865] https://web.archive.org/web/20071013215754/http://www.omedia.org/Show_Article.asp?DynamicContentID=2210&MenuID=726&ThreadID=1014017
[1866] http://www.washingtoninstitute.org/policy-analysis/view/israels-security-fence-effective-in-reducing-suicide-attacks-from-the-north
[1867] //en.wikipedia.org/w/index.php?title=Template:Israeli%E2%80%93Palestinian_peace_process&action=edit
[1868] Note: Four settlements in the northern West Bank were also evacuated at the same time.
[1869]

*
*

[1870] Cook 2006, p. 103.

[1871] Maximum Jews, Minimum Palestinians https://www.haaretz.com/1.4759973: Ehud Olmert speaks out: Israel must espouse unilateral separation - withdrawal to lines of its own choosing. It's the only answer to the demographic danger, says this latter-day realist., 13.11.2003

[1872] FMA, "Address by PM Ariel Sharon at the Fourth Herzliya Conference" Dec 18, 2003 http://www.mfa.gov.il/MFA/PressRoom/2003/Pages/Address%20by%20PM%20Ariel%20Sharon%20at%20the%20Fourth%20Herzliya.aspx: "We wish to speedily advance implementation of the Roadmap towards quiet and a genuine peace. We hope that the Palestinian Authority will carry out its part. However, if in a few months the Palestinians still continue to disregard their part in implementing the Roadmap then Israel will initiate the unilateral security step of disengagement from the Palestinians."

[1873] Bernard Avishai, Sharon's Dark Greatness,' http://www.newyorker.com/news/news-desk/ariel-sharons-dark-greatness' Ariel *The New Yorker* 13 January 2014

[1874] *Exchange of letters between PM Sharon and President Bush* http://www.mfa.gov.il/mfa/foreignpolicy/peace/mfadocuments/pages/exchange%20of%20letters%20sharon-bush%2014-apr-2004.aspx. MFA, 14 April 2004

[1875]

[1876] 15 August 2005, Sharon's speech on Gaza pullout http://news.bbc.co.uk/1/hi/world/middle_east/4154798.stm

[1877] Cook 2006, p. 104.

[1878] Rynhold & Waxman 2008, p. 27"...While this ideological shift did not make unilateral disengagement inevitable, it certainly made it highly probable, because it represented a strategic move toward addressing the threat to Israel's Jewish and democratic character posed by indefinitely continuing the occupation"

[1879] "The Cabinet Resolution Regarding the Disengagement Plan" http://www.mfa.gov.il/mfa/foreignpolicy/peace/mfadocuments/pages/revised%20disengagement%20plan%206-june-2004.aspx . Israel MFA, 6 June 2004

[1880] *Foreign Policy Aspects of the War Against Terrorism: Fourth Report of Session, 2005–2006* https://books.google.com/books?id=p1e2L97W9zwC&pg=PA80, Great Britain: Parliament: House of Commons: Foreign Affairs Committee, The Stationery Office, 2006 pp. 71–84

[1881] IHLresarch.org http://www.ihlresearch.org/opt/feature.php?a=55

[1882] Gushkatif.net http://www.gushkatif.net/sites/kefaryam.htm , Gush Katif, Summer 2005: Kefar Yam

[1883] SFgate.com http://www.sfgate.com/cgi-bin/article.cgi?f=/c/a/2005/07/17/MNG5GDPEJT1.DTL, A quiet fear in a 'village of traitors' Arabs who were informants for Israel to lose Gaza homes – as will town's original residents

[1884] "Villagers reject 'traitor' label but can't shed fear it brings," Martin Patience, *USA Today*, June 12, 2005, USAtoday.com https://www.usatoday.com/news/world/2005-06-12-gaza-traitor_x.htm

[1885] Thomas G. Mitchell, *Israel/Palestine and the Politics of a Two-State Solution*, https://books.google.com/books?id=ogShiGv2eicC&pg=PA78 McFarland 2013 p. 78.

[1886] Jpost.com http://fr.jpost.com/servlet/Satellite?pagename=JPost/JPArticle/ShowFull&cid=1126405205939

[1887] Ezra Levant, 'Israel must defend itself,' http://www.torontosun.com/2014/07/28/israel-must-defend-itself Toronto Sun 28 July 2014. 'In 2005, Israel gave Palestinians at least part of a state – the Gaza Strip. Israel forcibly removed every Jew who lived there, and handed the place over to the Palestinians. Israel even gifted 3,000 greenhouses that were owned by the Jews who used to live there, as a ready-made industry. It is unlikely that Gaza could have become an Arab Hong Kong. But stranger things have happened, as the city of Dubai shows. But instead of setting to work building Gaza as a prosperous, or at least peaceful, mini-state, the Palestinians chose sharia law and a terrorist government that has fired thousands of rockets at Israel from amongst Gaza's houses and schools. Those 3,000 greenhouses? Like the Jews themselves, gifts from the Jews had to be destroyed.'

[1888] Charles Krauthammer 'Moral Clarity in Gaza,' https://www.washingtonpost.com/opinions/charles-krauthammer-moral-clarity-in-gaza/2014/07/17/0adabe0c-0de4-11e4-8c9a-923ecc0c7d23_story.html *Washington Post*, July 17, 2014:'To help the Gaza economy, Israel gave the Palestinians its 3,000 greenhouses that had produced fruit and flowers for export.

It opened border crossings and encouraged commerce. And how did the Gaza Palestinians react to being granted by the Israelis what no previous ruler, neither Egyptian, nor British, nor Turkish, had ever given them – an independent territory? First, they demolished the greenhouses. Then they elected Hamas.'

[1889] Richard Chesnoff, 'Gaza and Palestinian Leadership: The More It Changes, the More it Gets Worse,' http://www.huffingtonpost.com/richard-z-chesnoff/gaza-and-palestinian-leadership_b_5589766.html Huffington Post 22 July 2014. 'Ariel Sharon, finally withdrew Israel's troops from Gaza and evacuated Israeli settlers from the rich fruit and vegetable producing settlements they had established along the strip. The corrupt Palestinian Authority took over full control of Gaza. Even the network of miraculously flourishing greenhouses that Israeli settlers had built became Palestinian, something Israel hoped would help convince the Gaza leadership to keep peaceful borders with the Jewish state. That didn't happen. The chain of greenhouses was soon looted and all but completely destroyed.'

[1890] J. J. Goldberg, 'What, Exactly, Is Hamas Trying to Prove?' https://www.theatlantic.com/international/archive/2014/07/what-exactly-is-hamas-trying-to-prove/374342/ The Atlantic 13 July 2014:' In the days after withdrawal, the Israelis encouraged Gaza's development. A group of American Jewish donors paid $14 million for 3,000 greenhouses left behind by expelled Jewish settlers and donated them to the Palestinian Authority. The greenhouses were soon looted and destroyed, serving, until today, as a perfect metaphor for Gaza's wasted opportunity.'

[1891] Alan Dershowitz, 'The 'occupation of Gaza' canard,' http://www.jpost.com/Opinion/Columnists/The-occupation-of-Gaza-canard-369370 Jerusalem Post 31 July 2014:"The settlers left behind greenhouses, farm equipment and other valuable civilian assets worth millions of dollars. '

[1892] Lee Smith, 'Land for Death,' http://tabletmag.com/jewish-news-and-politics/187071/land-for-death Tablet 19 November 2014: 'If only Ariel Sharon's 2005 disengagement from Gaza had led to the peace and co-existence between Israel and Gazans that the international community's peace advocates promised! If only the greenhouses left by Israeli settlers had become the foundation for Gazan agriculture, producing world famous oranges and tomatoes, prized by Brooklyn's top chefs! But that's not what happened. Palestinians laid waste to the greenhouses.'

[1893] Yair Rosenberg, citing Hillary Clinton 'Watch Hillary Clinton vs. Jon Stewart on Gaza,' http://tabletmag.com/scroll/179536/watch-hillary-clinton-vs-jon-stewart-on-gaza Tablet 17 July 2014. '"You know, when Israel withdrew from Gaza ... they left a lot of their businesses–there was a really very valuable horticultural business that was set up by the Israelis who had lived in Gaza. And the idea was that this would be literally turned over–money was provided, there would be a fund that would train Palestinians in Gaza to do this work. And basically the leadership said 'we don't want anything left from Israel' [and] destroyed it all. That mentality to me is hard to deal with".'

[1894] Justin Schwegel, 'The Greenhouse propaganda – How Gazan history is being rewritten to dehumanize Palestinians,' http://mondoweiss.net/2014/08/propaganda-dehumanize-palestinians Mondoweiss 10 August 2014.

[1895] Steven Erlanger, 'Israeli Settlers Demolish Greenhouses and Gaza Jobs,' https://www.nytimes.com/2005/07/15/international/middleeast/15mideast.html?pagewanted=all&_r=0 New York Times July 15, 2005

[1896]

[1897] P R. Kumaraswamy, *The A to Z of the Arab-Israeli Conflict*, https://books.google.com/books?id=hKXvCSc93zEC&pg=PR40 Scarecrow Press, 2009 p.xl.

[1898] Raanan Ben-Zur, where 5 Israelis were killed '5 killed in Netanya bombing ,' http://www.ynetnews.com/articles/0,7340,L-3179585,00.html Ynet 5 December 2005.

[1899] Hebrew http://www.inn.co.il/News/News.aspx/281873

[1900] SFgate.com http://www.sfgate.com/cgi-bin/article.cgi?f=/n/a/2006/12/09/international/i104249S77.DTL, More Palestinians flee homelands, Sarah El Deeb, Associated Press, December 9, 2006.

[1901] • JPost.com http://fr.jpost.com/servlet/Satellite?cid=1167467655416&pagename=JPost/JPArticle/ShowFull , Hamas, Fatah continue clashes; 8 killed, Jpost.com 1/3/07. • Excite.com http://apnews.excite.com/article/20070131/D8N050P00.html, Palestinian Cease-Fire Holds on

1st Day, Ibrahim Barzak, 1/31/07, Associated Press • Excite.com http://apnews.excite.com/article/20070130/D8MVFSI00.html, Cease-Fire Starts Taking Hold in Gaza, Ibrahim Barzak, 1/30/07, Associated Press. • Yahoo.com https://news.yahoo.com/s/nm/20070201/wl_nm/palestinians_dc, Hamas attacks convoy, Associated Press, 2/1/07. • Yahoo.com https://news.yahoo.com/s/ap/20070515/ap_on_re_mi_ea/israel_palestinians ; Hamas kills 8 in Gaza border clash, By Ibrahim Barzak, Associated Press Writer, 5/15/07. • Yahoo.com https://news.yahoo.com/s/ap/20070515/ap_on_re_mi_ea/israel_palestinians_34;_ylt=AjoLFAN_35SNS_Y9GqjHedwUvioA , Top Palestinian security official quits, by Sarah El Deeb, Associated Press, 5/14/07 • BBC.co.uk http://news.bbc.co.uk/2/hi/middle_east/6653437.stm, Resignation deepens Gaza crisis BBC, 5/14/07.

[1902] Yahoo.com https://news.yahoo.com/s/nm/20070516/ts_nm/palestinians_dc , Israel attacks in Gaza amid factional violence, by Nidal al-Mughrabi, Associated Press, 5/16/07.
[1903] Yahoo.com https://news.yahoo.com/s/afp/20070516/wl_mideast_afp/mideastpalestinian , Gaza bloodshed alarms West's Arab allies by Hala Boncompagni, Associated Press, 5/16/07.
[1904] Jpost.com http://fr.jpost.com/servlet/Satellite?cid=1218710379199&pagename=JPost/JPArticle/ShowFull, Jerusalem Post article on the new Gush Katif museum.
[1905] Gaza withdrawal 'victory for terrorism' http://www.worldnetdaily.com/news/article.asp?ARTICLE_ID=43770. World Net Daily, 13 April 2005.
[1906] Angus-Reid.com http://www.angus-reid.com/polls/index.cfm/fuseaction/viewItem/itemID/7905
[1907] Arutzsheva.com http://www.arutzsheva.com/news.php3?id=84852
[1908] IsraelReporter.com http://israelreporter.com/2005/08/11/inn-largest-prayer-rally-at-kotel-in-years-250000-worshippers/
[1909] Jpost.com http://fr.jpost.com/servlet/Satellite?pagename=JPost/JPArticle/ShowFull&cid=1123640627654
[1910] Keshev.org http://www.keshev.org.il/siteEn/default.asp
[1911] Keshev.org http://www.keshev.org.il/siteEn/FullNews.asp?NewsID=93&CategoryID=9
[1912] Disconnected: The Israeli Media's Coverage of the Gaza Disengagement, Keshev, January 2006 http://www.keshev.org.il/FileUpload/Keshev_Report_January_06_Eng.pdf
[1913] Keshev.org http://www.keshev.org.il/FileUpload/Keshev_Report_January_06_Eng.pdf
[1914] //www.jstor.org/stable/20202970
[1915] https://books.google.com/books?id=joztAAAAMAAJ
[1916] https//web.archive.org
[1917] http://www.pmo.gov.il/PMOEng/Communication/PMSpeaks/speech150805.htm
[1918] http://www.mfa.gov.il/MFA/Peace+Process/Guide+to+the+Peace+Process/Israels+Disengagement+Plan-+Renewing+the+Peace+Process+Apr+2005.htm
[1919] http://www.mfa.gov.il/MFA/Peace+Process/Guide+to+the+Peace+Process/Israeli+Disengagement+Plan+20
[1920] http://www.mideastweb.org/disengagement.htm
[1921] http://www.mideastweb.org/
[1922] http://www.mideastweb.org/israel_disengagement_map_2005.htm
[1923] https://web.archive.org/web/20061231201745/http://strategicassessments.org/library/Disengagement/SAI%20ITAG%20DISENGAGEMENT%20MAP.pdf
[1924] http://www.ynetnews.com/home/0,7340,L-3491,00.html
[1925] http://www.arutzsheva.com/news.php3?id=87555
[1926] http://www.arutzsheva.com/news.php3?id=87581
[1927] http://www.foxnews.com/story/0,2933,165944,00.html
[1928] http://fr.jpost.com/servlet/Satellite?pagename=JPost/JPArticle/ShowFull&cid=1124590916759
[1929] http://fr.jpost.com/servlet/Satellite?pagename=JPost/JPArticle/ShowFull&cid=1124938373005
[1930] https//web.archive.org
[1931] https://www.theguardian.com/comment/story/0,3604,1552190,00.html
[1932] https://www.usatoday.com/news/world/2005-10-30-israel-kuwait_x.htm
[1933] https://www.washingtonpost.com/wp-dyn/content/article/2005/07/15/AR2005071502187.html

[1934] https://web.archive.org/web/20070216051658/http://www.ariel-sharon-life-story.com/18-Ariel-Sharon-Biography-2004-Disengagement-Plan.shtml
[1935] https://web.archive.org/web/20050924145849/http://victorhanson.com/articles/tartakovsky083005.html
[1936] http://victorhanson.com/wordpress/?p=4287
[1937] https://www.theguardian.com/comment/story/0,3604,1549816,00.html
[1938] https://web.archive.org/web/20070614084552/http://www.aipac.org/PDFDocs/AIPAC%20Memo%20-%20Disengagement%20Unprecedented082905.pdf
[1939] https://web.archive.org/web/20070614084553/http://www.aipac.org/PDFDocs/AIPAC%20Memo%20-%20Disengagement%20Risks082905.pdf
[1940] http://www.chabad.org/library/article.asp?AID=319985
[1941] https://www.washingtonpost.com/wp-dyn/content/article/2005/07/19/AR2005071901552.html
[1942] //tools.wmflabs.org/geohack/geohack.php?pagename=2006_Gaza_cross-border_raid&params=31_14_00_N_34_17_08_E_
[1943] Q&A: Israeli soldier held in Gaza http://news.bbc.co.uk/2/hi/middle_east/6238858.stm, BBC News, Monday, 25 June 2007.
[1944] Hamas Must End Attacks Against Civilians https://www.hrw.org/en/news/2005/06/08/hamas-must-end-attacks-against-civilians, Human Rights Watch, 8 June 2005
[1945] Two soldiers killed, one missing in Kerem Shalom terror attack http://www.mfa.gov.il/MFA/Government/Communiques/2006/Two+soldiers+killed+one+missing+in+Kerem+Shalom+terror+attack+25-Jun-2006.htm. Mfa.gov.il. Retrieved on 2011-08-29.
[1946] Shay, Shaul: *Islamic terror abductions in the Middle East*
[1947]
[1948] Hamas: Head of Al-Qaida affiliate killed in Gaza http://haaretz.com/hasen/spages/1107639.html , *Haaretz*, 18 August 2009
[1949] http://nymag.com/daily/intelligencer/2014/08/israeli-strikes-hit-3-top-hamas-leaders.html
[1950] US urges restraint amid tension over kidnapped Israeli soldier – Forbes.com https://www.forbes.com/feeds/afx/2006/06/26/afx2840950.html
[1951] http://tvnz.co.nz/view/page/411366/765968
[1952] http://articles.sfgate.com/2006-06-26/news/17298966_1_israeli-soldiers-popular-resistance-committees-israeli-air-strike
[1953] https://www.nytimes.com/2006/06/26/world/middleeast/26mideast.html?pagewanted=all
[1954] https://www.nytimes.com/2006/06/25/word/africa/25iht-web.0626gaza.2041377.html
[1955] http://news.bbc.co.uk/2/hi/middle_east/5115092.stm
[1956] http://www.nrg.co.il/online/1/ART2/263/592.html. Nrg.co.il. דירות אלף 50 נאשר ...נתניהו: nrg – פוליט/מדיני – חדשות
[1957] http://www.nrg.co.il/online/1/ART2/270/336.html?hp=1&cat=479&loc=7. Nrg.co.il. לצעירים שייבת המחאה – nrg קדם עלי – דעות – חדשות
[1958] http://www.mako.co.il/news-specials/social-protest/Article-212b10ebf91b131017.htm&sCh=3d385dd2dd5d4110&pId=565984153. Mako.co.il. ערים ב-20 ענק הפגנות – בשבת מח"א: יוצאת הדיור מחאת – 2 חדשות
[1959] Israeli social justice protests continue http://www.upi.com/Top_News/World-News/2011/08/14/Israeli-social-justice-protests-continue/UPI-65041313324094/. Upi.com (14 August 2011).
[1960] http://www.globes.co.il/news/article.aspx?did=1000665858. Globes.co.il (24 July 2011). גלובס – ספין על יחשוב שנתניהו לפני יימאס לשכנים הנדל"ן: מחאה
[1961] http://news.walla.co.il/?w=//1850601. News.walla.co.il. חדשות וואלה! – החלשות השכבות בנגדר דעה: l האוהלים מחאה
[1962] http://www.haaretz.co.il/hasite/spages/1235430.html. Haaretz.co.il (20 July 2011). הארץ – וחברה חינוך – בכיף מוחים כאן אביב: בתל רוטשילד בשדרות האוהלים מחאה
[1963] http://www.ynet.co.il/articles/0,7340,L-4108044,00.html. Ynet.co.il (20 June 1995). נפץ חומר רואים אחורה. חושבים קדימה, מסתכלים
[1964] "Mass protests and tent cities shake Israeli government" http://www.irishtimes.com/newspaper/world/2011/0815/1224302449821.html. The Irish Times (8 August 2011).

¹⁹⁶⁵ "10 reasons why summer 2011 was momentous in Israeli history" http://english.themarker.com/11-reasons-why-summer-2011-was-momentous-in-israeli-history-1.387139?localLinksEnabled=false. *The Marker*, 28 September 2011.
¹⁹⁶⁶ "Say no to the American way" http://www.ynetnews.com/articles/0,7340,L-4130150,00.html. *Yediot Ahronot*, 3 October 2011.
¹⁹⁶⁷ Levinson, Charles. (1 July 2011) Israeli Facebook Campaign Keeps Lid on Cheese Prices https://www.wsj.com/articles/SB10001424052702304584004576417543687962906. *The Wall Street Journal*.
¹⁹⁶⁸ A very middle-class protest: Complaints over price of COTTAGE CHEESE spark Israel's biggest demonstration http://www.dailymail.co.uk/news/article-2023688/Complaints-cottage-cheese-prices-spark-protests-Israel.html. *Daily Mail*. (8 August 2011).
¹⁹⁶⁹ "ISRAEL: Is the Arab Spring spreading to the Jewish state?" http://latimesblogs.latimes.com/babylonbeyond/2011/07/israel-protests-spread-demanding-social-justice.html. *Los Angeles Times*. (26 July 2011).
¹⁹⁷⁰ Has the Arab spring spread to Israel? http://www.globalpost.com/dispatches/news/regions/middle-east/israel-and-palestine/has-the-arab-spring-arrived-israel. *Global Post* (26 July 2011).
¹⁹⁷¹ חדשות וואלה! - נתניהו" את רודף הערבי "האביב ערב: בעיתוני מסוקרת האוהלים מחאת http://news.walla.co.il/?w=/0/1846206. News.walla.co.il.
¹⁹⁷² Egypt's Workers Rise Up http://www.thenation.com/article/158680/egypts-workers-rise. *The Nation* (17 February 2011).
¹⁹⁷³ Protesters block streets in Tel Aviv after landmark rally http://972mag.com/breaking-protesters-block-streets-in-central-tel-aviv/. 972mag.com.
¹⁹⁷⁴ Lior, Ilan. (13 August 2011) Tens of thousands take to Israel's streets as social protests move out of Tel Aviv – Haaretz Daily Newspaper | Israel News http://www.haaretz.com/news/national/tens-of-thousands-take-to-israel-s-streets-as-social-protests-move-out-of-tel-aviv-1.378465. *Haaretz*.
¹⁹⁷⁵ Yagna, Yanir. (14 August 2011) Israel's periphery 'proved it is part of the struggle' – Haaretz Daily Newspaper | Israel News http://www.haaretz.com/news/national/israel-s-periphery-proved-it-is-part-of-the-struggle-1.378601. *Haaretz*.
¹⁹⁷⁶ Lior, Ilan. (13 July 2012) "Israeli demonstrators to mark first anniversary of social protest" Ha'aretz, July 13, 2012 http://www.haaretz.com/news/national/israeli-demonstrators-to-mark-first-anniversary-of-social-protest-1.450795. *Haaretz*.
¹⁹⁷⁷ Trajtenberg oversees first meetin... JPost – Diplomacy & Politics http://www.jpost.com/DiplomacyAndPolitics/Article.aspx?id=233085. *The Jerusalem Post*. (3 January 2013).
¹⁹⁷⁸ Keinon, Herb. (3 January 2013) PM appoints team to meet protest ... JPost – Diplomacy & Politics http://www.jpost.com/DiplomacyAndPolitics/Article.aspx?id=232872. *The Jerusalem Post*.
¹⁹⁷⁹ Bassok, Moti. (10 August 2011) Prime Minister's expert panel says no new budget expected for 2012 – Haaretz Daily Newspaper | Israel News http://www.haaretz.com/print-edition/news/pm-s-expert-panel-says-no-new-budget-expected-for-2012-1.377878. *Haaretz*.
¹⁹⁸⁰ Tel Aviv's Tahrir Square – IWPR Institute for War & Peace Reporting – P50643 http://iwpr.net/report-news/tel-aviv's-tahrir-square
¹⁹⁸¹ הארץ - וחברה חינוך - לתושביה" מתנכרת "המדינה הארץ; ברחבי הפגינו אדם בני אלף כ-150 http://www.haaretz.co.il/hasite/spages/1236548.html
¹⁹⁸² AFP: Israeli protesters seek radical change https://www.google.com/hostednews/afp/article/ALeqM5h2FQMmJLEz3KWXEEQ0EvpC0v19Vg?docId=CNG.b297b50cc6bfa351b47c8255989665aa.a61. Google.com (8 August 2011).
¹⁹⁸³ Buck, Tobias. (9 August 2011) Swelling list of demands fuels Israel protests – FT.com https://webcache.googleusercontent.com/search?q=cache:QtNTQadtCkIJ:www.ft.com/cms/s/0/6b9d9c08-c299-11e0-9ede-00144feabdc0.html. Webcache.googleusercontent.com.
¹⁹⁸⁴ האוהלים מחאת את יצר הלאומי השמאל - הבוקר העולם http://reshet.ynet.co.il/Shows/Haolam_Haboker/videomarklist,187816/
¹⁹⁸⁵ בית זה אהל | אקטיביזם http://activism.org.il/node/948#comment-937. Activism.org.il.
¹⁹⁸⁶ יולי 14 | אקטיביזם http://activism.org.il/node/961 . Activism.org.il (18 July 2011).
¹⁹⁸⁷ הכלס | אקטיביזם http://activism.org.il/node/963 . Activism.org.il (19 July 2011).

[1988] אקטיביזם | האוהלים | מאבק תרומות http://activism.org.il/node/962 . Activism.org.il (18 July 2011).
[1989] אקטיביזם | תקציר עממיות אסיפות לניהול מהיר מדריך http://activism.org.il/node/966 . Activism.org.il (19 July 2011).
[1990] מרקר דה – חדשות – המחאה במימון תסייע החדשה הקרן TheMarker http://www.themarker.com/news/1.671269. Themarker.com (20 July 2011).
[1991] נט ירושלים – החומות מול מוקמת הירושלמית האוהלים עיר http://www.jerusalemnet.co.il/article/38429. Jerusalemnet.co.il (21 July 2011).
[1992] האדם זכויות למען רבנים – משפט שומרי http://rhr.org.il/heb/?page_id=4&event_id=13
[1993] בישראל האזרח לזכויות האגודה | המחאה את לרסק מנסות שהרשויות חשש הדיור: מאבק http://www.acri.org.il/he/?p=14471. Acri.org.il.
[1994] השגה" בר דיור לייצר הממשלה "על ירושלים: עיריית ראש 2 – חדשות http://www.mako.co.il/news-israel/local/Article-8f84911717e2131004.htm. Mako.co.il.
[1995] גלובס – פעולה" עמכם "נשתף האוהלים: למפגיני עיני http://www.globes.co.il/news/article.aspx?did=1000667958. Globes.co.il.
[1996] Wikipedia founder visits Tel Aviv's tent city http://www.jpost.com/Headlines/Article.aspx?id=232838. The Jerusalem Post. (3 January 2013).
[1997] New Israel Fund Alone in Funding Israel Protests http://www.forward.com/articles/141891/. Forward.com.
[1998] New Israel Fund Comes Clean on Role in Tent Protests http://www.jewishpress.com/news/breaking-news/new-israel-fund-comes-clean-on-role-in-tent-protests/2012/01/17/. Jewishpress.com.
[1999] עשו של וחידיים יעקב של הקול האוהלים: מחאה News1 – ראשונה מחלקה חדשות http://www.news1.co.il/Archive/003-D-62157-00.html. News1 (25 July 2011).
[2000] מועילים' 'איריוטים – הדיור מפגיני News1 – ראשונה מחלקה חדשות http://www.news1.co.il/Archive/003-D-62225-00.html. News1 (27 July 2011).
[2001] המאהלים למחאת פומבית להצטרף סירב דרעי אריה ראשון: פרסום 2 – חדשות http://www.mako.co.il/news-military/politics/Article-c2bb973cbd66131004.htm&sCh=31750a2610f26110&pId=2082585621. Mako.co.il.
[2002] חדשות וואלה! – אנרכיה" ניצני "מזהה ריבלין: ראובן הכנסת יו"ר | האוהלים מחאת http://news.walla.co.il/?w=/1/1846374. News.walla.co.il.
[2003] חדשות וואלה! – המחאה המקדמים פוליטים יש בגין: בני האוהלים! מחאת http://news.walla.co.il/?w=/22/1846369. News.walla.co.il.
[2004] וקומוניסטים" אנרכיסטים בזויים, "המפגינים תוקף: חליבוד – 2 חדשות http://www.mako.co.il/news-military/politics/Article-1372d95e7698131004.htm. Mako.co.il.
[2005] היום ישראל http://www.israelhayom.co.il/site/newsletter_article.php?id=12053. Israel-hayom.co.il (17 July 2011).
[2006] חדשות – הנגע לתיקון דברים עושה הממשלה הנדלן: מחאת על נתניהו – נענה10 http://news.nana10.co.il/Article/?ArticleID=815348. News.nana10.co.il.
[2007] ערוץ 7 http://www.inn.co.il/News/News.aspx/223078. Inn.co.il.
[2008] החדשים" הישראלים "אנחנו – היום ישראל http://www.israelhayom.co.il/site/newsletter_article.php?id=12727. Israelhayom.co.il.
[2009] http://j14.org.il
[2010] https://www.facebook.com/J14.Israel
[2011] http://www.shatil.org.il/english/shatil-israel-new-awakening/
[2012] http://www.jpost.com/Israel/Home.aspx
[2013] http://www.haaretz.com/meta/Tag/Israel%20housing%20protest
[2014] " Qassam brigades claim rocket, mortar fire at southern Israel http://www.maannews.net/eng/ViewDetails.aspx?ID=715014", Ma'an News Agency, Monday 21 July 2014.
[2015] Cease fire in Operation "Protective Edge" is holding MDA sums up 50 days of saving lives http://www.mdais.com/316/7004.htm, Magen David Adom, 29 August 2014: 'During the 50 days of Operation "Protective Edge", MDA teams treated 842 civilians, including 6 who were killed by shrapnel of rockets, and another 36 who were injured by shrapnel in varying degrees, including: 10 casualties in serious condition, 6 in a moderate condition and 20 who were slightly wounded. In addition, MDA teams also treated during Operation "Protective Edge" 33 people who were

injured by shattered glass and building debris, 18 who were injured in road traffic accidents which occurred when the sirens were heard, including 1 person in a serious condition, and the rest lightly or moderately wounded. 159 people were injured as a result of falling and trauma on the way to the shelters and 581 people suffered anxiety attacks.'

[2016] 'Ministry: Death toll from Gaza offensive topped 2,310,' http://www.maannews.net/eng/ViewDetails.aspx?ID=751290 Ma'an News Agency 3 January 2015.

[2017] Based on figures of the Palestinian Ministry of Health P;149 UNIQ-ref-0-4ba7306c809995b7-QINU

[2018] UNIQ-ref-1-4ba7306c809995b7-QINU p.10, 1;21 "Israel does not presume to be able to produce a definitive account of all fatalities that occurred during the 2014 Gaza Conflict."

[2019] Turkish Anadolu Agency reported that an Israeli military spokesman had explained that the non-literal translation of the operation's name into English was to "give a more 'defensive' connotation".<ref>

[2020] Though Hamas governs the Gaza Strip, the majority of the international community (including the UN General Assembly, the United Nations Security Council, the European Union, the International Criminal Court, and many human rights organizations) consider Israel to be occupying Gaza, as it controls the region's airspace, coastline and most of its borders.

[2021] Jack Khoury, Hamas claims responsibility for three Israeli teens' kidnapping and murder' http://www.haaretz.com/news/diplomacy-defense/1.611676, *Haaretz*, 21 August 2014.

[2022] 'Mashal: Hamas was behind murder of three Israeli teens' http://www.ynetnews.com/articles/0,7340,L-4562328,00.html, Ynet, 22 August 2014.

[2023] Ehab Zahriyeh, 'Citing past failures, Hamas demands an enforceable cease-fire,' http://america.aljazeera.com/articles/2014/7/16/gaza-ceasefire-accountability.html Al-Jazeera,16 July 2014.

[2024] 'Hamas and Israel cling to their war aims,' http://www.dw.de/hamas-and-israel-cling-to-their-war-aims/a-17801137 Deutsche Welle 23 July 2014.

[2025] 'Hamas 'ready for Gaza ceasefire' if Israeli raids stop,' https://www.bbc.com/news/world-middle-east-28156268 BBC News 4 July 2014.

[2026] Christa Case Bryant, 'Ending détente, Hamas takes responsibility for today's spike in rocket fire (+video)' http://www.csmonitor.com/World/Middle-East/2014/0707/Ending-detente-Hamas-takes-responsibility-for-today-s-spike-in-rocket-fire-video, Christian Science Monitor, 7 July 2014: "After days of steadily increasing strikes, Hamas militants in Gaza launched at least 40 rockets tonight alone in what appears to be a decision to escalate the conflict. The dramatic spike in rocket attacks is likely to put significant pressure on Israeli Prime Minister Benjamin Netanyahu to heed calls for an all-out offensive against the Islamist movement, which Israel and the US consider a terrorist organization. While there has been intermittent rocket fire from Gaza since the cease-fire that ended the November 2012 Pillar of Defense conflict, Israel has credited Hamas with largely doing its best to keep the various militant factions in line. Today, however, Hamas took direct responsibility for the fire for the first time, sending a barrage of dozens of rockets into Israel in the worst day of such violence in two years."

[2027] 'Palestinian armed groups killed civilians on both sides in attacks amounting to war crimes,' https://www.amnesty.org/en/articles/news/2015/03/palestinian-armed-groups-killed-civilians-on-both-sides-in-2014-gaza-conflict/ Amnesty International 26 March 2015

[2028] 'Unlawful and deadly Rocket and mortar attacks by Palestinian armed groups during the 2014 Gaza/Israel conflict,' https://www.amnesty.org/download/Documents/MDE2111782015ENGLISH.PDF Amnesty International, 26 March 2015.

[2029] *Operation Protective Edge: A war waged on Gaza's children,* http://www.dci-palestine.org/sites/default/files/operationprotectiveedge.awarwagedonchildren.160415.pdf Defence for Children International-Palestine, Ramallah, 16 April 2015.

[2030] 'UN doubles estimate of destroyed Gaza homes,' http://www.ynetnews.com/articles/0,7340,L-4605408,00.html Ynet 19 December 2015.

[2031] 'Housing group: 20 years to rebuild Gaza after fighting with Israel ,' http://www.haaretz.com/news/diplomacy-defense/1.613194 Haaretz 30 August 2014.

[2032] Israeli child 'killed by rocket fired from Gaza' https://www.bbc.co.uk/news/world-middle-east-28904028, BBC

[2033] Review of

[2034] 'The Guardian view on the causes of the fighting in Gaza' https://www.theguardian.com/commentisfree/2014/jul/25/guardian-view-causes-fighting-gaza, *The Guardian*, 25 July 2014.

[2035] page 16

[2036] Nathan Thrall, 'Our Man in Palestine,' http://www.nybooks.com/articles/archives/2010/oct/14/our-man-palestine/ The New York Review of Books, 14 October 2010: 'Dayton, meanwhile, was overseeing the recruitment, training, and equipping of Abbas's rapidly expanding security forces. Khaled Meshaal, chief of Hamas's politburo, delivered a fiery speech denouncing "the security coup" as a "conspiracy" supported by "the Zionists and the Americans"—charges Fatah denied. In February 2007, on the brink of civil war, Fatah and Hamas leaders traveled to Mecca, where they agreed to form a national unity government, a deal the US opposed because it preferred that Fatah continue to isolate Hamas. Fayyad became finance minister in the new government, despite, he says, American pressure not to join. The Peruvian diplomat Alvaro de Soto, former UN envoy to the Quartet, wrote in a confidential "End of Mission Report" that the violence between Hamas and Fatah could have been avoided had the US not strongly opposed Palestinian reconciliation. "The US", he wrote, "clearly pushed for a confrontation between Fateh and Hamas."'

[2037] Elizabeth Spelman, 'The Legality of the Israeli Naval Blockade of the Gaza Strip' http://webjcli.org/article/view/207/277, *Web Journal of Current Legal Issues*, Vol 19, No 1, 2013

[2038] * " UN independent panel rules Israel blockade of Gaza illegal http://www.haaretz.com/news/diplomacy-defense/un-independent-panel-rules-israel-blockade-of-gaza-illegal-1.384267", *Haaretz* (story by Reuters), 13 September 2011.

[2039] "Position paper on the naval blockade on Gaza." http://www.mag.idf.il/163-4314-en/patzar.aspx 8 September 2010.

[2040] page 408

[2041] Initial Response to Report of the Fact Finding Mission on Gaza http://www.mfa.gov.il/NR/rdonlyres/FC985702-61C4-41C9-8B72-E3876FEF0ACA/0/GoldstoneReportInitialResponse240909.pdf , Israeli Ministry of Foreign Affairs; accessed 22 November 2014.

[2042] *Why the mullet, not the Israel Navy, are to blame for the death of a Gaza fisherman* http://www.haaretz.com/news/features/why-the-mullet-not-the-israel-navy-are-to-blame-for-the-death-of-a-gaza-fisherman.premium-1.472845. Amira Hass, Haaretz, 29 October 2012 (premium article)

[2043] Ben White, "What a 'period of calm' looks like in the Occupied Territories" http://www.aljazeera.com/indepth/opinion/2013/02/2013220152044327694.html, *Al-Jazeera*, 22 February 2013.

[2044] IAF strike kills 3 Gaza terrorists in response to mortar shells fire http://www.ynetnews.com/articles/0,7340,L-4497657,00.html, Yoav Zitun, Elior Levy, 11 March 2014, ynetnews

[2045] Tzvi Ben-Gedalyahu, "IDF Kills Three Terrorists Immediately after Mortar Shell Attack" http://www.jewishpress.com/news/idf-kills-three-terrorists-immediately-after-mortar-shell-attack/2014/03/11, 11 March 2014.

[2046] Assaf Sharon, "Failure in Gaza" http://www.nybooks.com/articles/archives/2014/sep/25/failure-gaza, *New York Review of Books*, 25 September 2014, pp. 20-24.

[2047] Mouin Rabbani, 'Israel mows the lawn' http://www.lrb.co.uk/v36/n15/mouin-rabbani/israel-mows-the-lawn, *London Review of Books*, Vol. 36 No 15, 31 July 2014, p. 8.

[2048] Julia Amalia Heyer, 'Ex-Israeli Security Chief Diskin: All the Conditions Are There for an Explosion' http://www.spiegel.de/international/world/interview-with-former-israeli-security-chief-yuval-diskin-a-982094.html, *Der Spiegel*, 24 July 2014: 'It was a mistake by Netanyahu to attack the unity government between Hamas and Fatah under the leadership of Palestinian President Mahmoud Abbas. Israel should have been more sophisticated in the way it reacted.'

[2049] Mitchell Plitnick, "Palestinian Unity Causing Political Ripples in Washington" http://www.ipsnews.net/2014/06/palestinian-unity-causing-political-ripples-in-washington, Inter Press Service 2 June 2014.

[2050] "Abbas goes big with Hamas deal; the Temple Mount fault line" http://www.al-monitor.com/pulse/originals/2014/04/palestine-hamas-fatah-mahmoud-abbas.html, *Al-Monitor*, 26 April 2014

[2051] "Israeli air strike in Gaza wounds 12: medical officials" https://www.reuters.com/article/2014/04/23/us-palestinian-israelstrike-idUSBREA3M17520140423, Reuters, 23 April 2014.

[2052] Robert Tait. "Hamas kidnapping: Islamist group to blame for youths' 'kidnapping', Benjamin Netanyahu says" https//www.telegraph.co.uk, *The Telegraph*, 15 June 2014.

[2053] Shlomi Eldar "Accused kidnappers are actually rogue Hamas branch" http://www.al-monitor.com/pulse/originals/2014/06/qawasmeh-clan-hebron-hamas-leadership-mahmoud-abbas.html, *Al-Monitor*, 29 June 2014.

[2054] 'Hamas: We wouldn't target civilians if we had better weapons,' http://www.haaretz.com/news/diplomacy-defense/1.612039 Haaretz 23 August 2014.

[2055] "justified the killings as a legitimate action against Israelis on "occupied" lands."

[2056] James Marc Leas, 'Attack First, Kill First and Claim Self-Defense: Palestine Subcommittee Submission to UN Independent Commission of Inquiry on the 2014 Gaza Conflict,' http://www.councilforthenationalinterest.org/new/attack-first-kill-first-and-claim-self-defense/#.VN9NFE05Dcs Council for the National Interest 21 January 2015.

[2057] cf.

[2058] Nick Logan, 'Mourning, military strikes after Israeli teens found dead' http://globalnews.ca/news/1426608/mourning-military-strikes-after-israeli-teens-found-dead/, *Global News*, 1 July 2014.

[2059] Stuart Greer, Tensions arise in Israel following murder of teens https://news.yahoo.com/video/tensions-rise-israel-following-murder-225301495.html , *Yahoo News*, 1 July 2014: 'Prime Minister Binjamin Netanyahu vowed Hamas will pay a heavy price. [...] Their bodies were discovered on Monday, after the biggest Israeli ground operation nearly in a decade. Israel's revenge came swiftly with fighters pounding dozens of Hamas targets overnight in Gaza and the West Bank.'

[2060] Allison Beth Hodgkins, "Why Hamas Escalated, When Before They Didn't," http://politicalviolenceataglance.org/2014/07/15/why-hamas-escalated-when-before-they-didnt/ Political Violence @ a Glance 15 July 2014: 'there was a meeting in Gaza around 2 July in which Hamas apparently tried to convince the various armed factions to uphold the truce. They failed. The other factions in the meeting saw no reason to uphold a truce, especially since the newly formed government of national consensus decided not to pay the salaries of Gazan civil servants as supposedly promised in the unity deal. The street wanted escalation and so they would have it, calls for moderation be damned.

[2061] 'Hamas, ready for Gaza ceasefire' if Israeli raids stop' https://www.bbc.com/news/world-middle-east-28156268, BBC News, 4 July 2014.

[2062] Code red sirens blare in Sderot marking 25th rocket on Friday http://www.ynetnews.com/articles/0,7340,L-4538037,00.html, Ynet News 4 July 2014

[2063] "After a night of silence, IAF attacks three Gaza targets" http://www.ynetnews.com/articles/0,7340,L-4538120,00.html, Ynet News, 5 July 2014.

[2064] "Gaza rockets continue to hit southern Israel" http://www.ynetnews.com/articles/0,7340,L-4538739,00.html, Ynet News; 6 July 2014.

[2065] globes http://www.globes.co.il/en/article-150-hamas-terrorists-surrender-to-idf-1000957726
[2066]

[2067] 'Hamas reveals first image of Shalit in captivity,' http://www.ynetnews.com/articles/0,7340,L-4695315,00.html Ynet 28 August 2015.

[2068] Gaza Fighting Intensifies as Cease-Fire Falls Apart https://www.nytimes.com/2014/08/02/world/middleeast/israel-gaza-conflict.html?_r=0, Jodi Rudoren, and Isabel Kershneraug, 1 August 2014: "Israel said the attack, from under a house near the southern border town of Rafah, took place at 9:20 a.m., soon after the 8 a.m. onset of the temporary truce ..."

[2069] Netanyahu says Israeli military 'will take as much time as necessary' in Gaza https//www.washingtonpost.com, Griff Witte and Sudarsan Raghavan, 2 August 2014, Washington Post.

[2070] Captured, killed or missing? Fate of Israeli soldier remains unknown http://www.cnn.com/2014/08/01/world/meast/mideast-crisis/, by Mariano Castillo, Chelsea J. Carter and Salma Abdelaziz of CNN, 1 August 2014

[2071] Israel withdraws most troops from Gaza http://bigstory.ap.org/article/israeli-begins-redeploying-along-gaza-border *Associated Press*

[2072] //en.wikipedia.org/w/index.php?title=2014_Israel%E2%80%93Gaza_conflict&action=edit

[2073] Martin Lejeune, 'Touring the devastated industrial zones of Gaza' http://www.maannews.net/eng/ViewDetails.aspx?ID=721265, Ma'an News Agency, 18 August 2014.

[2074] Jason Burke, 'Gaza homes 'uninhabitable' as tens of thousands come back to rubble' https://www.theguardian.com/world/2014/aug/11/damage-gaza-homes-israel-hamas-conflict, *The Guardian*, 11 August 2014.

[2075] 'Gaza's Christians and Muslims grow closer in defiance of Israeli attacks,' http://www.middleeasteye.net/news/gazas-christians-and-muslims-grow-closer-defiance-israeli-attacks-372261379 Middle East Eye 30 July 2014:"When they destroy your mosques, call your prayers from our churches".'

[2076] "Israeli Arabs caught in the middle" http://www.dailymail.co.uk/wires/ap/article-2707252/Israeli-Arabs-caught-middle-Gaza-war.html, *Daily Mail*; accessed 23 November 2014.

[2077] "Rocket seriously injures Israeli teen in Ashkelon" http://www.jewishexponent.com/headlines/2014/07/rocket-seriously-injures-israeli-teen-in-ashkelon-dual-citizens-leave-gaza, Jewish-Exponent.com, July 2014; accessed 23 November 2014.

[2078] " Israeli teens' mental health worsens when Arab-Israeli conflict does http://www.timesofisrael.com/long-conflict-wears-on-teen-psyche-14-year-study." *The Times of Israel*, 4 August 2014.

[2079] "Rocket caused massive damage to the gas station, and a fire has broken out" http://www.haaretz.com/news/diplomacy-defense/.premium-1.604437, *Haaretz*, 12 July 2014.

[2080]

[2081] 'The economic cost of the war in Gaza, http://money.cnn.com/2014/08/29/news/economy/gaza-rebuilding-cost/ CNN News 29 August 2014

[2082] *Fragmented Lives: Humanitarian Overview, 2014* http://reliefweb.int/sites/reliefweb.int/files/resources/annual_humanitarian_overview_2014_english_final.pdf OCHA March 2015.

[2083] https://www.terrorism-info.org.il/Data/articles/Art_20841/E_105_15_1379706052.pdf

[2084] https://www.terrorism-info.org.il/en/20711/

[2085] https//www.washingtonpost.com

[2086] https//www.washingtonpost.com

[2087] *Operation Protective Edge: A war waged on Gaza's children,* http://www.dci-palestine.org/sites/default/files/operationprotectiveedge.awarwagedonchildren.160415.pdf Defence for Children International-Palestine, Ramallah, 16 April 2015.

[2088] P.149: Palestinian Ministry of Health, quoted in A/HRC/28/80/Add.1, para. 24.

[2089]

[2090] Fatah, Hamas Preparing Groundwork to Dissolve Palestinian Authority Unity Govt http://www.jewishpress.com/news/breaking-news/fatah-hamas-preparing-groundwork-to-dissolve-palestinian-authority-unity-govt/2014/09/07, Hana Levi Julian, 7 September 2014, Jewish Press

[2091] Abbas threatens to break up unity government http://www.i24news.tv/en/news/international/middle-east/42879-140907-abbas-threatens-to-break-up-unity-government , 7 September 2014, i24news

[2092] Khaled Abu Toameh, Fatah members killed in Gaza during war, Abbas reveals http://www.jpost.com/Arab-Israeli-Conflict/Fatah-members-killed-in-Gaza-during-war-Abbas-reveals-374661, jpost.com, 7 September 2014; accessed 22 November 2014.

[2093] https://www.ynetnews.com/articles/0,7340,L-4814444,00.html

[2094] Netanyahu: Obama Warned Me Against Sending Troops into Gaza http://www.jewishpress.com/news/us-news/netanyahu-obama-warned-me-against-sending-troops-into-gaza/2017/04/20 By David Israel, Jewish Press, 20 April 2017

[2095] Cease fire in Operation "Protective Edge" is holding MDA sums up 50 days of saving lives http://www.mdais.com/316/7004.htm, Magen David Adom, 29 August 2014

[2096] "Bedouin 'defenseless' as man killed, 4 injured by Gaza rocket" http://www.timesofisrael.com/negev-bedouin-defenseless-as-man-killed-4-injured-by-gaza-rocket, *The Times of Israel*; accessed 22 July 2014.

[2097]

[2098] Scale of Gaza destruction unprecedented, rehabilitation will cost $7.8 billion, PA says http://www.jpost.com/Arab-Israeli-Conflict/Scale-of-Gaza-destruction-unprecedented-rehabilitation-will-cost-78-billion-PA-says-374460, jpost.com; retrieved 4 September 2014.

[2099] "Canadian Prime Minister Harper Praised for Statement in Support of Israel's Gaza Campaign" http://www.algemeiner.com/2014/07/13/canadian-prime-minister-harper-praised-for-statement-in-support-of-israels-gaza-campaign, Algemeiner.com; retrieved 25 August 2014.

[2100] (outdated figures)

[2101] Gideon Levy, 'The IDF's real face' http://www.haaretz.com/opinion/.premium-1.613212, *Haaretz*, 30 August 2014

[2102] Protection of Civilians: OCHA Weekly Report 24-30 June 2014, West Bank http://www.ochaopt.org/documents/ocha_opt_protection_of_civilians_weekly_report_2014_7_04_english.pdf : as of 30 June (prior to Operation Protective Edge), 17 Palestinians had been killed by Israeli forces in 2014; Protection of Civilians: OCHA Weekly Report 2-8 September 2014, West Bank http://www.ochaopt.org/documents/ocha_opt_protection_of_civilians_weekly_report_2014_9_13_english.pdf : as of 8 September (after Operation Protective Edge), the number had risen to 40

[2103] Bernie Sanders accuses Netanyahu of overreacting in Gaza war http://www.timesofisrael.com/bernie-sanders-accuses-netanyahu-of-overreacting-in-gaza-war/ The Times of Israel, 19 November 2015

[2104] US Jewish group slams Bernie Sanders for misstatements on 2014 Gaza war http://www.jpost.com/Diaspora/US-Jewish-group-slams-Bernie-Sanders-for-misstatements-on-2014-Gaza-war-450507 The Jerusalem Post, 6 April 2016

[2105] Sanders tells ADL he knows he got his Gaza death toll number wrong http://www.timesofisrael.com/sanders-tells-adl-he-knows-he-got-his-gaza-death-toll-number-wrong/ Times of Israel, 8 April 2016

[2106] "As war with Israel shatters lives, more Gazans question Hamas decisions" https//www.washingtonpost.com, *The Washington Post*, 12 August 2014.

[2107] https://www.newsweek.com/majority-israelis-are-unhappy-ceasefire-poll-argues-261555

[2108] https://www.timesofisrael.com/poll-85-of-israeli-jews-want-to-keep-fighting/

[2109] https://www.vox.com/2014/7/31/5955077/israeli-support-for-the-gaza-war-is-basically-unanimous

[2110] https://en.idi.org.il/press-releases/12789

[2111] https://www.timesofisrael.com/israeli-arabs-caught-in-the-middle-of-gaza-war/

[2112] http://www.timesofisrael.com/liveblog_entry/lod-psychologist-fired-for-joyful-post-on-soldier-deaths/

[2113] https://www.timesofisrael.com/after-gaza-arab-israelis-fear-rising-discrimination/

[2114] https://www.haaretz.com/4-israeli-arabs-disciplined-over-anti-war-facebook-posts-1.5256408

[2115] "52 Palestinians killed in bombings of homes in Gaza Strip, which are unlawful" http://www.btselem.org/gaza_strip/20140713_palestinians_killed_in_illegal_attacks_on_houses, B'tselem, 13 July 2014; accessed 22 July 2014.

[2116] 'Black Flag:The legal and moral implications of the policy of attacking residential buildings in the Gaza Strip, summer 2014,' http://www.btselem.org/download/201501_black_flag_eng.pdf B'tselem 28 January 2015, pp.48-49.

[2117] Gili Cohen, 'IDF broke international law in dozens of Gaza war strikes, Israeli rights group says,' http://www.haaretz.com/news/diplomacy-defense/1.639462 Haaretz 28 January 2015.'The Israel Defense Forces broke international law at least in some of the dozens of strikes it made against homes during the fighting in Gaza last summer, . More than 70 percent of the people killed in 70 incidents examined by B'Tselem were non-combatants, according to the report . In these 70 strikes, 606 Palestinians were killed, B'Tselem says, including 93 children under age 5, 129 children ages 5 to 14, and 42 teens, ages 14 to 18. This figure also included 135 women ages 18 to 60, and 37 men over 60 years old.'

[2118] 'Haniyeh urges Abbas to stop 'stalling' on ICC' http://www.maannews.net/eng/ViewDetails.aspx?ID=727004, Ma'an News Agency, 12 September 2014.

[2119] Isabel Kershner, Amnesty International Sees Evidence of Palestinian War Crimes in '14 Gaza Conflict https//www.nytimes.com, *New York Times* (25 March 2015)

[2120] Hamas executes 18 suspected collaborators with Israel in Gaza http://www.jpost.com/Arab-Israeli-Conflict/Hamas-executes-11-more-Palestinians-suspected-of-collaboration-with-Israel-371952, JPost.com; accessed 22 November 2014.

[2121] Hamas executes four more 'collaborators' http://www.ynetnews.com/articles/0,7340,L-4562519,00.html, Ynetnews; accessed 22 November 2014.

[2122] Abbas slams Hamas for intransigence http://www.ynetnews.com/articles/0,7340,L-4565455,00.html, Ynetnews; accessed 23 November 2014.

[2123] PA slams Hamas executions of alleged collaborators http://www.maannews.net/eng/ViewDetails.aspx?ID=722656, Maan News Agency

[2124] European Union: Hamas, other Gaza terror groups must disarm http://www.haaretz.com/news/diplomacy-defense/.premium-1.606703, Haaretz, 22 July 2014.

[2125] " Hamas threatening journalists in Gaza who expose abuse of civilians http://www.timesofisrael.com/hamas-threatening-journalists-in-gaza-who-expose-abuse-of-civilians/." The Times of Israel. 28 July 2014.

[2126] "Hamas again uses Gazan civilians as human shields to prevent the Israeli Air Force from attacking operatives' houses" http://www.terrorism-info.org.il/en/article/20669 The Meir Amit Intelligence and Terrorism Information Center; retrieved 13 July 2014.

[2127] https//web.archive.orgDocument – Israel and the Occupied Palestinian Territories: Israel/Gaza conflict, July 2014

[2128] Hamas' disturbing 'human shields' manual https://nypost.com/2014/08/05/hamas-manual-details-civilian-death-plan-israel/, Bob Fredericks, NY Post, 5 August 2014

[2129] Hamas acknowledges its forces fired rockets from civilian areas http://www.haaretz.com/news/diplomacy-defense/1.615478, Haaretz (AP story), 12 September 2014; (same AP story:) Hamas admits to rocket fire from residential areas http://www.timesofisrael.com/hamas-admits-to-rocket-fire-from-residential-areas/, *Times of Israel* (AP story), 12 September 2014.

[2130] Uri Avnery, The Meaning of the British Vote on Palestine http://www.counterpunch.org/2014/10/17/the-meaning-of-the-british-vote-on-palestine/ Counterpunch 17–19 October 2014: 'Another assertion is that these buildings were used by Hamas to hide their arms. A person of my age reminded us this week in Haaretz that we did exactly the same during our fight against the British government of Palestine and Arab attackers: our arms were hidden in kindergartens, schools, hospitals and synagogues. In many places there are now proud memorial plaques as a reminder.'

[2131] Gideon Levy, Weapons of mass distraction http://www.haaretz.com/opinion/.premium-1.620260, Haaretz, 12 October 2014: 'There was no Jewish settlement in the country that did not have a "slik" – as these storage sites were known – all in the heart of "civilian population concentrations", of course. At Ein Ganim there was a slik in a synagogue (permitted to bombard); at Nahalal, it was under the cow-urine removal pump (bombard it); the Aldema slik was in the courtyard of a home in the Borochov neighborhood of Givatayim (bomb it); the slik at Café Piltz was in the drinks storage room (demolish it). The Etzel pre-state underground had its own slik under the Torah Ark in the Hurva Synagogue in Jerusalem's Old City. Weapons in a synagogue? That was the cynicism of these organizations. Schools served as training installations, even as weapons production workshops.

[2132] Ross Singer, 'Hamas = Haganah? A response to Gideon Levy,' http://blogs.timesofisrael.com/hamas-haganah-a-response-to-gideon-levy *The Times of Israel*, 15 October 2014

[2133] "FactCheck: Does Hamas use civilians as human shields?" http://blogs.channel4.com/factcheck/factcheck-hamas-civilians-human-shields/18534 , channel4.com/factcheck; accessed 28 July 2014.

[2134] The Fourth Geneva Convention, part III: Status and Treatment of Protected Persons, Art 28 http://www.icrc.org/applic/ihl/ihl.nsf/Article.xsp?action=openDocument&documentId=732D7EA50DF1A5ECC12563CD0051BBF0.

[2135] The Fourth Geneva Convention, Article 51 https://www.icrc.org/ihl/WebART/470-750065

[2136] http://www.high-level-military-group.org/pdf/hlmg-assessment-2014-gaza-conflict.pdf

[2137] VIDEO: Finnish reporter sees rockets fired from Gaza hospital http://www.ynetnews.com/articles/0,7340,L-4553643,00.html, ynet, 2 August 2014.

[2138] "Hamas Uses Hospitals and Ambulances for Military Purposes" http://www.idfblog.com/blog/2014/07/28/hamas-uses-hospitals-ambulances-military-purposes, IDF blog, 28 July 2014.

[2139] Journalists threatened by Hamas for reporting use of human shields //www.jpost.com/Operation-Protective-Edge/Journalists-threatened-by-Hamas-for-reporting-use-of-human-shields-369619

[2140] "Is Hamas using human shields in Gaza?" http://www.cnn.com/2014/07/23/world/meast/human-shields-mideast-controversy, CNN.com, 23 July 2014; accessed 28 July 2014.

[2141] "Is Hamas using human shields in Gaza?" https://www.nytimes.com/2014/07/24/world/middleeast/israel-says-hamas-is-using-civilians-as-shields-in-gaza.html, 24 July 2014; accessed 28 July 2014.

[2142] " Bills condemning Hamas on 'human shields' introduced in Congress http://www.jta.org/2014/07/29/news-opinion/politics/bills-condemning-hamas-on-human-shields-introduced-in-congress." Jewish Telegraphic Agency. 29 July 2014.

[2143] " Ted Cruz, Kirsten Gillibrand team up on Hamas http://www.politico.com/story/2014/07/hamas-israel-ted-cruz-kirsten-gillibrand-109457.html." Politico. 29 July 2014.

[2144] Al Jazeera English report https://www.youtube.com/watch?v=TydoLmhMaDo; accessed 22 July 2014.

[2145] "Jeremy Bowen's Gaza notebook: I saw no evidence of Hamas using Palestinians as human shields" http://www.newstatesman.com/world-affairs/2014/07/jeremy-bowens-gaza-notebook-i-saw-no-evidence-hamas-using-palestinians-human, *New Statesman*; accessed 28 July 2014.

[2146]

[2147] HRW: Israel targets fleeing Palestinian civilians http://rt.com/news/177964-israel-fleeing-civilians-hrw/ RT. 5 August 2014. Accessed 6 August 2014

[2148] "In defiant speech, Mashaal denies ceasefire close" http://www.timesofisrael.com/in-defiant-speech-mashaal-denies-ceasefire-close, *The Times of Israel*; accessed 28 July 2014.

[2149] Hamas 'fires at sick Gazans trying to leave for medical treatment' http://www.ynetnews.com/articles/0%2c7340%2cL-4564025%2c00.html, Ynet News, Assaf Kamar, 1 September 2014

[2150] Waiting to transport sick, drivers at Gaza crossing come under attack http://www.timesofisrael.com/waiting-to-transport-sick-drivers-at-gaza-crossing-come-under-attack/, The Times of Israel, Lazar Berman and Marissa Newman, 24 August 2014

[2151] Colum Lynch, "The U.N. Takes Fire in Gaza" http://thecable.foreignpolicy.com/posts/2014/07/24/un_relief_agency_under_attack_in_gaza_conflict, Foreign Policy, 24 July 2014.

[2152] "UN admits its schools in Gaza were used to store Hamas rockets" http://www.worldtribune.com/2014/07/23/un-acknowledges-facilities-gaza-used-store-hamas-rockets , *The World Tribune*, 23 July 2014.

[2153] Chandler, Adam. "Hamas Rockets Found in Second United Nations School" http://www.thewire.com/global/2014/07/hamas-rockets-found-in-second-united-nations-school/374874, *The Wire*, 22 July 2014.

[2154] France-Presse, Agence. " UNRWA investigating discovery of 20 rockets found in empty Gaza school https://www.theguardian.com/world/2014/jul/17/unrwa-investigating-20-rockets-empty-gaza-school-palestinian." *The Guardian*. Friday, 18 July 2014.

[2155] "Did UNRWA Commit a War Crime by Handing Rockets Over To Hamas" http://www.jpost.com/Operation-Protective-Edge/Did-UNRWA-commit-a-war-crime-by-handing-rockets-over-to-Hamas-368348, *Jerusalem Post*, 22 July 2014.

[2156] "UN agency handed rockets back to Hamas, Israel says" http://www.timesofisrael.com/un-agency-handed-rockets-back-to-hamas-israel-says, timesofisrael.com; accessed 28 July 2014.

[2157] Ban Orders Review Following Allegations That UNRWA Gave Rockets Back To Hamas,' http://www.jta.org/2014/07/24/default/ban-orders-review-following-allegations-unrwa-gave-rockets-back-to-hamas. Jewish Telegraphic Agency, 24 July 2014.

[2158] " Tu dois quitter Gaza au plus vite et arrêter de travailler http://www.liberation.fr/monde/2014/07/24/tu-dois-quitter-gaza-au-plus-vite-et-arreter-de-travailler_1069701." *Liberation*. 24 July 2014.

[2159] Debinski, Gabrielle, Or Avi-Guy and Tzvi Fleischer. " Trapped in Gaza: How Hamas punishes reporters for the truth http://www.theaustralian.com.au/opinion/trapped-in-gaza-how-hamas-punishes-reporters-for-the-truth/story-e6frg6zo-1227007768903." *The Australian*. 31 July 2014.

[2160] "Hamas deported journalists, spokesperson reportedly admits" http://www.haaretz.com/news/middle-east/1.610801, Haaretz.com; accessed 22 November 2014.

[2161] Hamas Spox: We Deported Foreign Journalists for Filming Missile Launches http://www.algemeiner.com/2014/08/15/hamas-spox-we-deported-foreign-journalists-for-filming-missile-launches/, Algemeiner.com

[2162] Anshel Pfeffer, "Foreign press: Hamas didn't censor us in Gaza, they were nowhere to be found" http://www.haaretz.com/news/features/.premium-1.609589, *Haaretz*, 8 August 2014.

[2163] Israeli army exonerates itself in scores of investigations into 2014 Gaza war crimes http://www.maannews.com/Content.aspx?id=772843, Ma'an News Agency 25 August 2016.

[2164] Gili Cohen, Closes Probes of Alleged Crimes, Some Involving Civilian Deaths, in 2014 Gaza War,' http://www.haaretz.com/israel-news/.premium-1.738447' IDF Haaretz 24 August 2016.

[2165] Neve Gordon, 'The Day After,' http://www.lrb.co.uk/2015/05/04/neve-gordon/the-day-after London Review of Books 4 May 2015.

[2166] Peter Beaumont, 'Israeli soldiers cast doubt on legality of Gaza military tactics,' https://www.theguardian.com/world/2015/may/04/israeli-soldiers-cast-doubt-on-legality-of-gaza-military-operation The Guardian 4 May 23015.

[2167] Gili Cohen, 'Report: Army veterans slam IDF policy in Gaza war,' http://www.haaretz.com/news/diplomacy-defense/.premium-1.654823 Haaretz 4 May 2015.

[2168] Peter Beaumont, 'Video contradicts account of Israeli officer who killed Palestinian teenager,' https://www.theguardian.com/world/2015/jul/13/video-raises-doubts-over-account-of-israeli-officer-who-killed-palestinian-teenager The Guardian 13 July 2015.

[2169] "HRW: Israel likely to have committed Gaza war crimes" http://www.maannews.net/eng/ViewDetails.aspx?ID=726796, Ma'an News Agency 10 September 2014.

[2170] Simone Wilson, 'The fury (and boredom) of war: Battlefield stories of courage, fear and frustration from IDF soldiers in Gaza' http://www.jewishjournal.com/articles/item/the_fury_and_boredom_of_war_battlefield_stories_of_courage_fear_and_frustra, *The Jewish Journal*, 20 August 2014.

[2171] Elior Levy, 'One family, three dead, three maimed: 'Black Friday' in Gaza,' http://www.ynetnews.com/articles/0,7340,L-4618203,00.html Ynet 24 January 2015.

[2172] 'No safe place for civilians' in Gaza, U.N. says https://www.reuters.com/article/2014/07/22/us-palestinians-israel-un-aid-idUSKBN0FR14820140722, Reuters.com; accessed 28 July 2014.

[2173] 'Warning on funds, UN doubles estimate of destroyed Gaza homes,' http://www.maannews.net/eng/ViewDetails.aspx?ID=748278 Ma'an News Agency 28 December 2014.

[2174] Gaza crisis: a closer look at Israeli strikes on UNRWA schools https://www.theguardian.com/world/2014/aug/08/-sp-gaza-israeli-strikes-unrwa-schools, Raya Jalabi, Tom McCarthy, Nadja Popovich, 8 August 2014, *The Guardian*

[2175] Gaza bank, TV station see U.S. sanctions http://edition.cnn.com/2010/US/03/19/treasury.hamas/, cnn.com, 19 March 2010.

[2176] Gili Cohen, 'NGO accuses IDF of gross abuses during Gaza war,' http://www.haaretz.com/news/diplomacy-defense/.premium-1.638179 Haaretz 21 January 2015.

[2177] Palestinian teen: I was used as a human shield in Gaza http://972mag.com/palestinian-teen-i-was-used-as-a-human-shield-in-gaza/95800, 972mag.com; retrieved 22 August 2014.

[2178] Israeli forces use Palestinian child as human shield in Gaza http://www.dci-palestine.org/documents/israeli-forces-use-palestinian-child-human-shield-gaza, Defence for Children International Palestine. Retrieved 22 August 2014.

[2179] Fares Akram & Judi Rudoren, "Teenager Cites Ordeal as Captive of Israelis" https://www.nytimes.com/2014/08/25/world/middleeast/gaza-strip-palestinian-teenager-cites-ordeal-as-captive-of-israelis-soldiers.html, nytimes.com; 24 August 2014.

[2180] " Syrian made M302 http://www.jpost.com/Operation-Protective-Edge/Syrian-made-M302-rocket-fired-by-Hamas-at-Hadera-362008." *The Jerusalem Post*. Accessed 12 August 2014.

[2181] " Long range Hamas rockets http://m.ibtimes.com/long-range-hamas-rockets-are-evidence-ties-syria-iran-israelis-say-1624646." *IBTimes*. 10 August 2014.

[2182] " Hamas firing chia designed rockets http://www.nbcnews.com/storyline/middle-east-unrest/hamas-firing-china-designed-syria-made-m-302-rockets-israel-n152461." *NBC News*. Accessed 12 August 2014.

[2183] " M75 strikes Tel Aviv http://www.maannews.net/eng/ViewDetails.aspx?ID=714851." *Maan News* Accessed 12 August 2014.

[2184] " Hamas produces rockets as fighting winds down https://www.theguardian.com/world/video/2014/aug/13/hamas-rockets-cease-fire-israel-video." *The Guardian.* 13 August 2014.

[2185] " Hamas Rocket Arsenal http://www.businessinsider.com.au/hamas-rocket-arsenal-2014-7." *Business Insider.* July 2014.

[2186] https://www.idfblog.com/blog/2014/07/10/6-million-lives-in-danger-the-deadly-rocket-arsenal-of-hamas/. "Israel Defense Forces Blog". 10 July 2014.

[2187] Iran supplied Hamas with Fajr-5 missile technology https://www.theguardian.com/world/2012/nov/21/iran-supplied-hamas-missile-technology, Saeed Kamali Dehghan, The Guardian, 21 November 2012

[2188]

[2189] *Humanitarian Bulletin Monthly Report, June-August 2014,* http://www.ochaopt.org/documents/ocha_opt_the_humanitarian_monitor_2014_10_03_english.pdf OCHA 30 September 2014.

[2190] Alon Ben David, 'Iron Dome Blunts 90% Of Enemy Rockets,' http://aviationweek.com/defense/iron-dome-blunts-90-enemy-rocketAviation Week 1 September 2014.

[2191] Jim Michaels, 'Extent of tunnels under Gaza takes Israel by surprise,' https://www.usatoday.com/story/news/world/2014/07/31/hamas-tunnels-israel-cu-chi/13421873/ USA Today 31 July 2014.

[2192] Adam Ciralsky, 'Hamas's Khalid Mishal on the Gaza War, Tunnels, and ISIS,' http://www.vanityfair.com/news/politics/2014/10/khalid-mishal-hamas-interview Vanity Fair 21 October 2014.

[2193] Gal Perl Finkel, The IDF vs subterranean warfare http://www.jpost.com/Opinion/Analysis-The-IDF-vs-subterranean-warfare-464229, The Jerusalem Post, August 16, 2016.

[2194] : "A senior military official estimated tonight (Thursday) in a conversation with Army Radio that the IDF can complete the task of destroying the tunnels within 48 hours. The military official said: 'all the tunnels were aimed at military targets and not at the Gaza-vicinity communities'..."

[2195] "Official Israeli sources describe 'cross-border tunnel attacks' as one of 'two primary means to target Israeli civilians,' explaining that, 'Hamas placed tunnel openings close to residential communities in Israel'."

[2196]

[2197] , citing

[2198] Israeli Drones Buzz Over Ghost Towns of Gaza http://abcnews.go.com/International/video/israeli-drones-buzz-ghost-towns-gaza-24628058, Alex Marquardt, ABC News, 18 July 2014

[2199] Gaza's Tunnels, Now Used to Attack Israel, Began as Economic Lifelines http://news.nationalgeographic.com/news/2014/07/140721-gaza-strip-tunnels-israel-hamas-palestinians/, James Verini, National Geographic, 21 July 2014

[2200] Charlie Hoyle, 'Israel shelling in Gaza war unprecedented despite inaccuracy,' http://www.maannews.com/eng/ViewDetails.aspx?ID=760268 Ma'an News Agency 4 April 2015.

[2201] Robert Perkins, 'Under Fire:Israel's artillery policies scrutinised,' https://aoav.org.uk/wp-content/uploads/2015/03/AOAV-Under-Fire-Israels-artillery-policies-scrutinised.pdf Action on Armed Violence December 2014.pp.10-14.

[2202] Ma'an News, Police: Israel dropped 'equivalent of 6 nuclear bombs' on Gaza, http://www.maannews.net/eng/ViewDetails.aspx?ID=722484

[2203] Iron Dome Blunts 90% Of Enemy Rockets http://aviationweek.com/defense/iron-dome-blunts-90-enemy-rockets – Aviationweek.com, 1 September 2014

[2204]

[2205] Subrata Ghoshroy, 'Israel's Iron Dome: a misplaced debate' http://thebulletin.org/israel's-iron-dome-misplaced-debate7349, *Bulletin of the Atomic Scientists,* 29 July 2014.

[2206] Dean, Sarah. " The way-too-far side: Sydney newspaper apologises for 'anti-Semitic' cartoon after Attorney-General brands it 'deplorable' http://www.dailymail.co.uk/news/article-2715083/Fairfax-apologises-anti-Semitic-cartoon-Attorney-General-brands-deplorable.html." *The Daily Mail.* 4 August 2014.

[2207] Naomi Chazan, 'Israel's other war: Moral attrition' http://blogs.timesofisrael.com/israels-other-war-moral-attrition-2/#ixzz3BPndDAar, *The Times of Israel*, 25 August 2014.
[2208] *The New York Times*. 5 August 2014.
[2209] https://www.bbc.com/news/world-middle-east-28252155
[2210] https://www.idfblog.com/operationgaza2014/
[2211] https://www.ochaopt.org/content/gaza-two-years-2014-hostilities-august-2016
[2212] http://mfa.gov.il/MFA/ForeignPolicy/IsraelGaza2014/Pages/2014-Gaza-Conflict-Factual-and-Legal-Aspects.aspx
[2213] http://www.aljazeera.com/programmes/insidestory/2014/08/gaza-truce-there-winner-201482714583180993.html
[2214] http://www.jewishvirtuallibrary.org/operation-protective-edge
[2215] https://docs.google.com/spreadsheets/d/1AqLhz84lMCcvopizH52MPKb8gsbLEuBF7U2rk51tFXw

Article Sources and Contributors

The sources listed for each article provide more detailed licensing information including the copyright status, the copyright owner, and the license conditions.

1948 Arab–Israeli War *Source:* https://en.wikipedia.org/w/index.php?oldid=865100424 *License:* Creative Commons Attribution-Share Alike 3.0 *Contributors:* A D Monroe III, A.h. king, Adapad, Aexon79, Airplaneman, Al-Andalusi, AmirSurfLera, Amphicoelias, Anders Feder, Andrwsc, AntanO, Anticitizen 98, Antillarum, Arjayay, Arminden, AsceticRose, Ashurbanippal, Averysoda, Axeman89, BD2412, Banedon, Bender235, BethNaught, Bgwhite, Bolter21, Calthinus, CapLiber, Catriona, Certes, Chewings72, Chipperdude15, Chymicus, Codrinb, CopperSquare, CsikosLo, Cyberbot II, Dan Koehl, Dan100, Daniel1212, Davidbena, Dawnseeker2000, De wafelenbak, Dewritech, Dreddis Rules, E.M.Gregory, Eggishorn, Egsan Bacon, Ekips39, Equinox, Eric Kvaalen, Eudialytos, Expokerer, Faceless Enemy, Fayenatic london, Funnyhat, GabrielF, Gadget850, Gfcan777, Grant65, GregKaye, GünniX, Haakonsson, Hairy Dude, Heavenlyblue, Hertz1888, Hohum, Howcheng, Huldra, IRISZOOM, Icewhiz, Iwant2write, J 1982, Jd22292, Joehedaya1, John of Reading, Johnmcintyre1959, Jon Kolbert, Jonesey95, Jonney2000, Jprg1966, Jweiss11, Kahtar, Kaltenmeyer, Klemen Kocjancic, Kndimov, Kollserp, Kombucha, Kritikos99, Krosshair1, Kumdano9, Lemnaminor, LightandDark2000, Lisa, Lollipoplollipoplollipop, MacAuslan, Makeandtoss, Malayedit, Malik Shabazz, Markunator, Markus1423, MarnetteD, Mikeblas, Mikrobølgeovn, Mogism, Monochrome Monitor, Monopoly31121993, Mortense, Murph9000, Natg 19, NiD.29, Niceguyedc, Nick3069, Nishidani, Novis-M, Octopus1066, Onceinawhile, Otutusaus, Padres Hana, Paine Ellsworth, Paul K., Phantomsnake, Pluto2012, Pppery, QueenCake, R'n'B, Reenem, Rgelb93, Rhododendrites, Rigadoun, Rjwilmsi, Romanm, SUM1, Sct72, Sean.hoyland, Sefarkas, Seraphim System, Sfan00 IMG, Simbagraphix, Srich32977, Steinsplitter, Steverci, TAnthony, Tanbircdq, That's Pretty Good, The PIPE, TheIntrovertedDude, Trahelliven, Trappist the monk, Ulf Heinsohn, Valenciano, Varnent, Vasyaivanov, Wayfarer, Whoop whoop pull up, Wikiliki, Wingedsubmariner, Winterst, Wlglunight93, Xezbeth, Ykantor, Yossimgim, ZScarpia, Zero0000, Zyxw, חורון ינ״ב .... ??

1949 Armistice Agreements *Source:* https://en.wikipedia.org/w/index.php?oldid=856648491 *License:* Creative Commons Attribution-Share Alike 3.0 *Contributors:* 78.26, Againme, Al Ameer son, Alaney2k, Aloha, Amoruso, AnonMoos, Anti Career Wikians, Ary29, Ashley kennedy3, Atrix20, B, BD2412, BOT-Superzerocool, BU Rob13, Bazonka, Bender235, Bgwhite, Byelf2007, CJCurrie, CasualObserver'48, Chesdovi, Chronos Phaenon, Cloj, ClueBot NG, Coemgenus, Curpsbot-unicodify, DLinth, Dan Pelleg, Don Radlauer, Doright, Eequor, Eleland, Emperorbma, Enthusiast01, Epeefleche, Faigl.ladislav, Fayenatic london, Gabbe, Gaius Cornelius, Galatz, Gilabrand, Good Olfactory, Hadal, Herbie keys, Hugo999, Huldra, Humus sapiens, I m dude2002, IRISZOOM, IZAK, Ian Pitchford, Icewhiz, Igorp lj, Ike∼enwiki, Imbris, Jaakobou, JamesAM, Jason Quinn, Jayjg, John Z, Johnkatz1972, Jprg1966, Kendrick7, Lapsed Pacifist, Leifern, Magioladitis, Magnusmarkussen, Marokwitz, Mattflaschen, Mboverload, Mild Bill Hiccup, Mimihitam, Mintguy, Molinari, Mor2, Natg 19, Night w, Nightstallion, No More Mr Nice Guy, Now3d, Number 57, Onceinawhile, Oren neu dag, Oshers2005, OwenBlacker, PBP, Padres Hana, Palestine-info, Paul K., Paul foord, Ptbotgourou, Reenem, Rich Farmbrough, Rjwilmsi, Scott Illini, Sdrawkcab, Seraphim System, Shrike, Slleong, Sm8900, Sol Goldstone, Sophus Bie, Sro23, Steven Crossin, Talknic, Telecineguy, Tewfik, Tide rolls, Uriber, Warrenfish, Wickeynl, Widr, Wik, Wikiliki, Yet Another User 2, Ynhockey, Zeq, Zero0000, חורון, ינ״ב 88 anonymous edits .... ??

Austerity in Israel *Source:* https://en.wikipedia.org/w/index.php?oldid=836964890 *License:* Creative Commons Attribution-Share Alike 3.0 *Contributors:* A&D∼enwiki, AdamProcter, Albany NY, Allens, Amire80, CasualObserver'48, Chefallen, Cogent, DabMachine, DarkKing Rayleigh, Datepalm17, EagleOne, FoCuSandLeArN, Hawkania, Hmains, Hovev∼enwiki, Huddyhuddy, Humus sapiens, IZAK, Itai, Jprg1966, Lairor, Lawrencekhoo, MattShelley, Monochrome Monitor, Morza, Mrmuk, Naamatt2, Number 57, Pearle, PedanticHipster, PiMaster3, Plutonium27, Re2fliopes, Reenem, Remember the dot, Rich Farmbrough, Rjwilmsi, Robofish, Shalom Yechiel, Shyamsunder, Simon Adler, Tim!, Yoninah, Zleitzen, חורון, ינ״ב 21 anonymous edits 87

Reprisal operations *Source:* https://en.wikipedia.org/w/index.php?oldid=860090777 *License:* Creative Commons Attribution-Share Alike 3.0 *Contributors:* 8HGasma, Abou hmed, Al Ameer son, Aliayad1000, All I Want to Do, AndresHerutJaim, Andrwsc, Avaya1, Averysoda, BD2412, Bender235, BobHalford806, CasualObserver'48, Chrismorey, CommonsDelinker, Dalai lama ding dong, DuncanHill, E.w.bullock, Edward, Favonian, Fetchcomms, Firgkas, Gilabrand, Good Olfactory, GrahamHardy, Greyshark09, Hebrides, Hmainsbot1, Huldra, IRISZOOM, Jabotito48, Jesse 8W, Jheald, Jiujitsuguy, Jn045, John of Reading, Jprg1966, Jtgelt, Keramiton, Liftarn, LilHelpa, Makecat, Mcarling, Metarese, Meters, Michael Zeev, Mikrobølgeovn, Nableezy, Neils51, Niceguyedc, Ohconfucius, Orenburg1, Outeraven, P. S. Burton, Padres Hana, Plastikspork, Poliocretes, R'n'B, Reenem, Rich Farmbrough, Sakiv, Sean.hoyland, Simon Adler, Slon02, Sonntagsbraten, Stopgrammartime, Tahran, TheCuriousGnome, Vfrickey, Wlglunight93, Ykantor, Ynhockey, ZScarpia, Zaher.Kadour, חורון, ינ״ב 57 anonymous edits 91

Lavon Affair *Source:* https://en.wikipedia.org/w/index.php?oldid=859639178 *License:* Creative Commons Attribution-Share Alike 3.0 *Contributors:* 'Merikan, 3d-geo, 9080WR7060, Abnn, Aboudaqn, Abu ali, Adoniscik, Ahmad2099, Alf.laylah.wa.laylah, Alfons2, AndresHerutJaim, Anomalocaris, Aquillion, Arado, Ardfern, Arminden, Armon, Ashley Y, Auntof6, Avaya1, Averysoda, Baatarsaikan, Babajobu, Bender235, BillyTFried, Blindjustice, Bobo192, Brewcrewer, CasualObserver'48, Cattus, Cerejota, Chendy, Cliftonian, ClueBot NG, CultureDrone, DICKERSON3870, DagosNavy, Davshul, Dear cobain, DieWeisseRose, Doctor Gary 5, El bot de la dieta, ElComandanteChe, Elmondo21st, Equilibrial, Evad37, EvilZionist, Ezzex, Fefour, Frederico1234, GangofOne, Garion96, Gilabrand, GordonUS, Greyshark09, Groucho1943, Grover cleveland, HKT, Harfarhs, Harizotoh9, Heptor, Hugo999, Huldra, IZAK, Ian Pitchford, Ira Leviton, Itsmejudith, Jayjg, Jeancey, Jim Fitzgerald, Jodamn, JonD93, JoshuaZ, Jpgordon, JzG, Kaaveh Ahangar∼enwiki, KantElope, Khazar2, Kintetsubuffalo, Klemen Kocjancic, Lapsed Pacifist, Laurinavicius, Leifern, Lisagosselin, M2k41, Madler, Magabund, Magioladitis, Matthew Fennell, MeanMotherJr, Moez, Monochrome Monitor, Mox La Push, Mr. Hicks The III, NYCJosh, Nableezy, Nassiriya, Naxal De Rojadio, Nudve, Number 57, Nøkkenbuer, Owain the 1st, Padres Hana, PalestineRemembered, Patar knight, Petri Krohn, Plot Spoiler, Poliocretes, PrestonH, Prunesqualer, Quadell, Queen Geedorah88, QuizzicalBee, Rami R, RayKiddy, Rich Farmbrough, Rjwilmsi, Ruakh, Sajed Mahmud, Santasa99, Severino, Shamir1, Shpoffo, Sreifa, Sremiasc221, Stefanomione, Steven J. Anderson, TAnthony, Tec15, Tegwarrior, TerryAlex, TheEgyptian, Thefixing, Themightyquill, Therecordkeeperkeeper, Thrindel, Uncle.bungle, Valliant1967, WLRoss, Wgfcrafty, Whoop whoop pull up, Wikiacc, Wllmevans, Woohookitty, Wowlookitsjoe, Wwikix, Xezbeth, Yamb, Ynhockey, Zad68, Zeq, Zero0000, Δ, רפאים, מרול 153 anonymous edits 97

Suez Crisis *Source:* https://en.wikipedia.org/w/index.php?oldid=863159587 *License:* Creative Commons Attribution-Share Alike 3.0 *Contributors:* A2soup, Abierma3, Al Ameer son, Alchemic Psycho, Alfie Gandon, Anomalocaris, Arminden, Ashurbanippal, Atotalstranger, AusLondonder, Averysoda, Aviados, BD2412, Bamyers99, Banedon, BarrelProof, Bender235, BeowulfSmith, Bgwhite, BillGarrisonJr, Binksternet, Blaue Max, Blelbach, Blurryman, Boardhead, Brigade Piron, Britannicus, Brozozo, Brycehughes, Buckshot06, Byteflush, CLSwiki, Cannolis, CapnZapp, CentreLeftRight, Chipperdude15, Chris the speller, Chrisahn, Clivemacd, Cloptonson, CommonsDelinker, Concrete Cloverleaf, Coreydragon, Corvus tristis, Crosbiesmith, Cyberbot II, Dan100, Davidbena, DePiep, DeeJaye6, Dgorsline, Dimadick, Dismas, Djakarta97, Dolphin51, Dsavage87, Dutch Ninja, Eastfarthingan, Eddaido, Equinox, Erictheenquirer, Ernestogon, Fnlayson, Fragglet, GeneralBelly, Gmaeir33, GraemeLeggett, GünniX, Haeinous, Hairy Dude, Headbomb, Hmbr, Hoggsbison47, Hohum, I2padams, Iadmc, Ibadibam, Ibrahim.ID, Ineuw, Ira Leviton, Iseult, J 1982, JackDouglag, Jacobdaun, Jameslwoodward, Jandalhandler, Jayjg, Jc86035, Jennica, JimMacAllistair, Jmg38, John of Reading, Jozrael, Jprg1966, Jrt989, Jtgelt, JuanRiley, KTo288, Keith-264, Kevin Murray, Khazar2, Kintetsubuffalo, Knife-in-the-drawer, Krazytea, Last edited by:, Laszlo Panaflex, Laurencebeck, LeverageSerious, LilHelpa, Ll1324, Llammakey, Mandruss, Mar4d, MarSch, Maschen, Masterblooregard, Mattflaschen, Mauls, Medhat moussa, Methestes, Mikrobølgeovn, MosheEmes, Mr. Guye, MrDemeanour, MrEdTheTalkingHorseEditor, MuhannadDarwish, N0n3up, Nngnna, No such user, Noclador, Notreallydavid, ORANSIGLOT, Oceanflynn, OliverBel, Omnipaedista, Omnisome, Onceinawhile, Openlydialectic, Orenburg1, Oshwah, Ossguy, Padres Hana, Paoting, Paulturtle, Pavel Vozenilek, PcPrincipal, Penbat, Pjessen, RGloucester, Ratto33, Reb1981, Reenem, Richard Keatinge, Rjensen, RobbieIanMorrison, Ross Fraser, Rothorpe, Rrburke, Rui Gabriel Correia, SUM1, Sajed Mahmud, Satanic Conspiracy, Silvertone953, Simbagraphix, Slatersteven, Sobreira, Soetermans, SteveStrummer, Stickee, Th4n3r, That man from Nantucket, The-, TheTimesAreAChanging, Thnidu, Thucydides411, Tom.Reding, Trackteur, Tshuva, Twobells, Tyrol5, Unreal7, Valenciano, VeryangryBrit, WatermillockCommon, Wavelength, Wee Curry Monster, Wlglunight93, Xyl 54, Yeterli, Ykantor, Ylee, Épico, חורון ינ״ב 105

Six-Day War *Source:* https://en.wikipedia.org/w/index.php?oldid=865292633 *License:* Creative Commons Attribution-Share Alike 3.0 *Contributors:* 1618033golden, Adapad, Aldux, Amosshapira, Anders Feder, Andy M. Wang, Anotherclown, AntanO, Anythingyouwant, Arado, Arminden, Ashtul, Ashurbanippal, AttilaTotalWar, Averysoda, BD2412, BU Rob13, Bender235, Bgwhite, BiggestSataniaFanboy89, Btphelps, Cannolis, CapLiber, Carlson288, Catsmoke, Cibervicho, Clarityfiend, Cwobeel, Cyberbot II, Czar, DRAGON BOOSTER, Dailycare, Dan100, Davemck, Davidbena, DeCausa, Dewritech, DocWatson42, Dthomsen8, Eat me, I'm an azuki, EtherealGate, Ewen, Gabbe, GabrielF, George Ho, Gfcan777, Gilsrafnorn, Gmaeir33, Gob Lofa, Gog the Mild, Gregzsidisin, Greyshark09, Guy1890, Haeinous, Hammersbach, Harfarhs, Hddty., Here2help, Hibernian, Hmains, Howcheng, Huldra, IRISZOOM, Ibadibam, Icewhiz, Ichesseckleinedeutschenkinde, IjonTichyIjonTichy, J 1982, Jay D. Easy, Jd22292, Jiffles1, JoeSperrazza, Johnmcintyre1959, Jon Kolbert, Jonesey95, Jprg1966, JungerMan Chips Ahoy!, Justinholmes, Kaltenmeyer, Keramiton, LEachenow, Lakryum, LightandDark2000, LilyKitty, Look2See1, LoveFerguson, Makeandtoss, Mandruss, Manxruler, Marloweperel, Mattflaschen, MeanMotherJr, Medende, Mevina2, Monochrome Monitor, Moriori, MuhannadDarwish, Mztourist, Nick.mon, Nikoroman, Nishidani, No More Mr Nice Guy, Noclador, Number 57, OJOM, Onceinawhile, Palindromedairy, Parkwells, Pasaban, Patar knight, Pfeldman, Phatom87, Pluto2012, Poliocretes, Predestiprestidigitation, Quisqualis, Recherchedienst, Reenem, RekishiEJ, Rms125a@hotmail.com, Roshu Bangal, Royalcourtier, Ryan1783, Sa.vakilian, Samuele1709, Sander.v.Ginkel, Sepsis II, SiBr4, Simon Adler, Sliverpool9, SparklingPessimist, Srich32977, Swazzo, Tanbircdq, Tdadamemd sioz, TeriEmbrey, The Banner, Tim bates, Tonygreenstein, Too Many Food Service Professionals, TopGun, Tpbradbury, Tuylrnicracker666, Uglemat, Unbuttered Parsnip, Underneaththesun, Valenciano, Vigilius, WikiTryHardDieHard, Wikievil666, Wikiliki, Wlglunight93, Xiaphias, YSSYguy, Ykantor, ZScarpia, Zero0000, Zumoarirodoka, דוד, ינ״ב ש׳, קודקוד חורון, אנט צחוב, ابجورة 189

War of Attrition *Source:* https://en.wikipedia.org/w/index.php?oldid=857176034 *License:* Creative Commons Attribution-Share Alike 3.0 *Contributors:* 85Hikmat, Ahpook, Aidan Condron, Aliayad1000, AndresHerutJaim, Art LaPella, Ashashyou, BD2412, BU Rob13, Backendgaming, Bart133, Battlecatz, Bender235, Benittop, Bgwhite, Bodida, CambridgeBayWeather, Chris the speller, Citation bot 1, Clarityfiend, ClueBot NG, Colonies Chris, Coltsfan, CommonsDelinker, DIMIESEP, DadaNeem, DagosNavy, DanTD, Dawn Bard, DePiep, Dewritech, DocWatson42, Drmies, EkoGraf, Elockid, Emmette Hernandez Coleman, FeatherPluma, Frietjes, Gadget850, Gatyonrew, Gob Lofa, Graham87, Greyshark09, HJackyboy, Haakonsson, Heroeswithmetaphors, Ifarted79, Igorp lj, Illegitimate Barrister, Inglok, Ironholds, JMCC1, Jabotito48, Jethro B, Jiujitsuguy, Jmj713, Johnthetruth, Jonesey95, Joseon Empire, Joshbrown44, Jprg1966, Jrmx, KingTut1982, Look2See1, Lotje, Magioladitis, Makeandtoss, Marcocapelle, Maurice Carbonaro, Mdnavman, MelissaLond, Mikrobølgeovn, Mild Bill Hiccup, Mimihitam, Mogism, Mortense, Motique, Mztourist, Nableezy, Nick Number, Nightscream, Nihiltres, Nihlus1, OJOM, Ohconfucius, Ohiostandard, Onceinawhile, Onepebble, Ospalh, Paul A, Plastikspork, Pol098, Poliocretes, Popcorn1101, Pssymoneyweed247, Quinton Feldberg, Qwertyytrewqqwerty, RASAM, Reenem, Rich Farmbrough, Samo.head, Sherif9282, ShipFan, Soaproot~enwiki, Sobreira, Tandrum, Uglemat, Vanthesubieu, Vsmith, Wasteland1, Wavelength, Whoop whoop pull up, Wikifan12345, Wilson44691, Woohookitty, YMB29, Ykantor, Zero0000, Δ, Шуфель, 115 anonymous edits 245

Jarring Mission *Source:* https://en.wikipedia.org/w/index.php?oldid=820695448 *License:* Creative Commons Attribution-Share Alike 3.0 *Contributors:* Ashley kennedy3, CConnla77, Enthusiast01, Former user 2, Good Olfactory, GregKaye, Greyshark09, HistoryBuff1983, Hmains, IRISZOOM, Igorp lj, John Z, Johnkatz1972, Lameimpala, Leifern, PMLawrence, Pbr2000, Pronamel, Ykantor, 2 anonymous edits 260

Munich massacre *Source:* https://en.wikipedia.org/w/index.php?oldid=865522804 *License:* Creative Commons Attribution-Share Alike 3.0 *Contributors:* Aabdullayev851, Abductive, Ahecht, Ahmad20012001, Ahmrrrmed terrror, AlanSiegrist, Alaney2k, ApprenticeFan, Arbor to SJ, Aschesiegen, Aschon5841, Ashleyydianee, Averysoda, Axl, BD2412, Baatarsaikan, Baking Soda, BassPlyr23, Baumann15, Becky2618, Bellerophon5685, Bender235, Best facts wiki, Billhpike, BrownHairedGirl, Buchbibliothek, CAPTAIN RAJU, CRussG, CambridgeBayWeather, Checkingfax, Citadel48, Cla68, ClueBot NG, Coltsfan, CommonsDelinker, Crystallizedcarbon, DMacks, DVdm, DadaNeem, DangerouslyWaywardNight, Daniel Case, Debouch, Diannaa, Discospinster, DonQuixote, Doughrash, E.M.Gregory, Egeymi, Elisfkc, Epson Salts, Evans1982, Favonian, Floating drinion, FoxyOrange, Fraggle81, G0mx, GHcool, Galatz, Gbenny, Gil gosseyn, Gilliam, Girlstyle, Gould363, Governor Jerjerrod, Grammarian3.14159265359, Grayfell, GregorB, Greyshark09, Hairy Dude, Harfarhs, Hbdragon88, Hmains, Hohum, IRISZOOM, InedibleHulk, Iwant2write, J 1982, JJBers, JackofOz, Janko, Jarble, Jd22292, Jersey92, Jim Michael, Jim1138, John of Reading, JoshDonaldson20, Jprg1966, Katastasi, Keiiri, Kevin0927, Kevin092772, Kieronoldham, Kind Tennis Fan, Kiyoweap, Klaus iezzi, KylieTastic, Lbelser, Lostprofile, Lotje, LouisAlain, MShabazz, Mandruss, Materialscientist, MeanMotherJr, MlcSATX, Mohsen1248, Munich1158, MusikAnimal, Myxomatosis57, Nableezy, NeilN, Nekko09, Nickst, Nihiltres, Nøkkenbuer, Onceinawhile, PanchoS, Parkwells, Parsley Man, Peter James, Peterkingiron, Philip Cross, Popcornduff, Pppery, Primefac, RekishiEJ, Rivertorch, Rivkid007, Rms125a@hotmail.com, SGGH, SMcCandlish, Santana134, Satani, Sathya dyan, Scoundr3l, Sean.hoyland, Sepguilherme, Sir Joseph, SparklingPessimist, Spintendo, Srich32977, Sroc, Steffens123, Steve03Mills, Stratocaster27, Strikerman, Tbm1998, Teddy.Coughlin, TenTonParasol, TiMike, Tim!, TracyMcClark, Tzowu, Undescribed, User2534, VEO15, Vasyaivanov, Vieque, WhiteChips, Wikimandia, William Avery, Xris0, Yairchaim, Yamaha5, Ykliu, Yojimbo1941, יניב הורון, 135 anonymous edits 263

Yom Kippur War *Source:* https://en.wikipedia.org/w/index.php?oldid=865119291 *License:* Creative Commons Attribution-Share Alike 3.0 *Contributors:* 7uperWkipedan, Aequitas333, Ain92, Aisteco, Albrecht, AlexiusHoratius, Alpinu, Andy M. Wang, AntonioDsouza, Arado, Attack Ramon, AttilaTotalWar, Averysoda, Axeman89, Baking Soda, Bender235, Bgwhite, Blacktiger87, Blue Danube, Bolter21, Buckshot06, CIreland, Capt Jim, Catsmoke, Clarityfiend, Clpo13, Crowsnest, Cyberbot II, Dan100, Dawnseeker2000, Dilidor, DocWatson42, Drdpw, Eggishorn, Erictheenquirer, Fitzcarmalan, Frip the bip!, GeneralizationsAreBad, GizzyCatBella, Gog the Mild, GoldenRainbow, Greenshed, Greyshark09, GünniX, HCPUNXKID, Haakonsson, Hairy Dude, Headhitter, Heptor, Hirsutism, Hmains, Howcheng, Huldra, IRISZOOM, Iadmc, Icewhiz, Illegitimate Barrister, Indy beetle, Infantom, Infor4fun, Ivario, J 1982, Jandalhandler, Jeppiz, JewishPride6, Jmg38, Jo-Jo Eumerus, John, John of Reading, Jprg1966, JuanRiley, Just a guy from the KP, KConWiki, Katangais, Kiteinthewind, LightandDark2000, LilHelpa, MWAK, Mannerheimo, Markunator, Matttoothman, Mccapra, Mikrobølgeovn, Mild Bill Hiccup, Mmeijeri, Mohamed Gmail11, Monochrome Monitor, Mortense, Moxfyre, MusikAnimal, Mztourist, Narky Blert, Nick.mon, Nihiltres, Nishidani, Notreallydavid, Onceinawhile, ParadiseDesertOasis8888, PaulPGwiki, PersianFire, Phantomsnake, Poliocretes, Polmandc, Prinsgezinde, Quondum, Reenem, Rjensen, Rjwilmsi, Rodw, Roger 8 Roger, Rothorpe, Samsoncity, Seraphim System, Smyth, Snake5311, Soap, Sophie means wisdom, Supertom123456, Swazzo, TAnthony, Tarook97, TheNavigatrr, Thucydides411, Tigercompanion25, TypoBoy, WNYY98, WatermillockCommon, Wavelength, Yairchaim, Ykantor, Ylee, Грищук ЮН, יניב הורון 290

Operation Entebbe *Source:* https://en.wikipedia.org/w/index.php?oldid=858469008 *License:* Creative Commons Attribution-Share Alike 3.0 *Contributors:* 23haveblue, 331dot, AEMoreira042281, Abductive, Ahpook, Alexb102072, AlphAlphA, Anomalocaris, Anthony Appleyard, Asd36f, Ashley Pomeroy, Averysoda, Axslayer33, BD2412, BU Rob13, Baatarsaikan, Bender235, BlackBeast, Bluenosepiperflyer, Boomer Vial, Brigade Piron, BrownHairedGirl, CaitlinMMurphy, CambridgeBayWeather, Carbon Caryatid, Carlotm, Carlson288, CentreLeftRight, Charles Essie, Chewings72, Chianti, Citadel48, ClueBot NG, Coltsfan, CommonsDelinker, Continentaleurope, Cumulus, Cyberbot II, DaL33T, Davidbena, Dcirovic, Deeday-UK, Delius, Demiurge1000, Deryck Chan, Diannaa, Dodger67, E-Soter, Eaglestorm, El C, Elisfkc, Ericamick, Esrever, Ferratarisam, Feudonym, Footwiks, Ftxs, Gilabrand, Graham87, Hamish59, HandsomeFella, Harryboyles, Hb2019, Hohum, HolyT, Huggy82, Hummingbird, Hvd69, Ivario, JB82, JCGDIMAIWAT, JDavidQ, JaventheAlderick, Jaywubba1887, Jessicapierce, John, Johnkatz1972, Jon Kolbert, Joseph2302, Jpgordon, Jprg1966, Julesd, Keith D, Kingsindian, Korny O'Near, KrakatoaKatie, Loco70, Lokalkosmopolit, Lopifalko, Lotje, Luckiest0522, M2k41, MRD2014 (public), Mandruss, Mannerheimo, Marcocapelle, MartinKassemJ120, Masssly, Materialscientist, MeanMotherJr, Mgiganteus1, Michael A Bekoff, Michael Hardy, Mickey Featherstone, Mike Mounier, Mikrobølgeovn, MilborneOne, Mogism, Monochrome Monitor, Moonchild101, Mzilikazi1939, N509FZ, NikNaks, Notreallydavid, Nystart!!, Nyttend, Ohconfucius, OnBeyondZebrax, Othondafos, PBS, Pashute, Phinn, Piouche, Poliocretes, Precision123, RHodnett, Redknight055, Reenem, Rgelb93, Rich Farmbrough, Richsummers, Rsquire3, Salociin, ScrapIronIV, Sheila1988, Shrike, Silentbob2001, Silvio1973, Simon Adler, Sn1per, Spintendo, Sportingboi, Srich32977, Stefan2, TAnthony, Tegel, Tetes123, The 6th Floor, The Rambling Man, TheRealSingapore, Tim!, Tucoxn, Underlying lk, Valenciano, Verne Equinox, Vpab15, Westie85, WhisperToMe, Wikiliki, WilliamJE, Wwikix, Xezbeth, Xocoyotzin, YSSYguy, Yaakovaryeh, Ykilstein, Zaclock, Zero0000, Zeroground7, Zozoulia, יניב הורון, 維基小霸王 , 104 anonymous edits 375

Camp David Accords *Source:* https://en.wikipedia.org/w/index.php?oldid=865087909 *License:* Creative Commons Attribution-Share Alike 3.0 *Contributors:* 1exec1, Ace of Raves, Alan Liefting, AsceticRose, Ashurbanippal, Askhal, Atmathm, Barthomew, Bender235, Bhrdkor, Bogger, Botteville, Calabe1992, CanadianLinuxUser, Capedia, Cattus, Charles Essie, Charlesdrakew, Chrisloveswow, Clarificationgiven, ClueBot NG, CommonsDelinker, Counterboint, DaPigNZ, Dailycare, Dbucks155, Denisarona, Dewritech, Dimadick, Dl2000, DocWatson42, Donner60, Eflatmajor7th, Endofskull, Epeefleche, Equilibrial, Excirial, Federalist51, Felicia777, Flix11, GHcool, Gibbs516, Gog the Mild, Good Olfactory, Grandia01, HMSLavender, Hairy Dude, Hertz1888, Howcheng, IRISZOOM, Irfankichloo, J 1982, Jackmcbarn, Jambobambo, JamesMoose, Johnhagen, Josh3580, Jprg1966, KConWiki, Kaltenmeyer, Khazar2, Ks0stm, LJU2ORD, Lexzierose19, Loveless, LuK3, MagicHik, Mannerheimo, Mccapra, MelbourneStar, Metamatica, MusikAnimal, NeilN, Nesij, Noahrollns77, Number 57, Peyre, Philip Trueman, Pigsonthewing, Pkbwcgs, Presidentman, Randy Kryn, Rcmason, Reenem, Robert Brockway, Scottmcmillin, Shadowjams, Snow Blizzard, Sparkie82, Srjalapeno, Strike Eagle, Sven Manguard, T m.plante, TGC55, Thehegemon42, ThirdDolphin, TonyTheTiger, Tonyg23, Underlying lk, WIERDGREENMAN, WQL, Wickey-nl, Widr, Wikiliki, Wikipelli, Xezbeth, Zamaster4536, Zozoulia, מבעת-זרם, 196 anonymous edits 395

1978 South Lebanon conflict *Source:* https://en.wikipedia.org/w/index.php?oldid=861644816 *License:* Creative Commons Attribution-Share Alike 3.0 *Contributors:* A rihani, Abonazzi, Addoula~enwiki, Allstarecho, Altmany, Amorymeltzer, AndresHerutJaim, Andrwsc, Anotherclown, Ardfern, Art LaPella, AsceticRose, Avaya1, Averysoda, BR64, Bender235, BiggestSataniaFanboy89, BlarghHgralb, Bolter21, Bryan Derksen, Buttockhat, Calbaer, Canadian Monkey, Cedrus-Libani, Charlesdrakew, Cloj, Colonies Chris, CommonsDelinker, Cyde, CylonCAG, Davidcannon, Davshul, De Administrando Imperio, Delirium, Dimadick, Doug Danner, Dractrack, Edward, ElUmmah, Eleland, Equitor, Former user 2, Freefry, Frietjes, FunkMonk, Future Perfect at Sunrise, Gaius Cornelius, Gdr, George, Gerrynobody, Greyshark09, Ground Zero, Guy Montag, Hammersoft, HanzoHattori, Headbomb, Hillbillyholiday, HistoryBuff1983, HokieRNB, Howcheng, Humus sapiens, IRISZOOM, IZAK, Ian Pitchford, James Wallace~enwiki, Jaraalbe, Jayjg, Jmg38, John Z, JosHall 93, Jprg1966, Kendrick7, Kirill Lokshin, Kosmopolis, Lightmouse, LittleSmall~enwiki, Lord Hamm, LordAmeth, M. Butterfly, MK8, Mais oui!, MathKnight, Michael Zeev, Michaelk1981, Mikrobølgeovn, Momma's Little Helper, Monupics, Moshe Constantine Hassan Al-Silverburg, Munchkin2013, NSH001, Nielswik, Nimur, Number 57, OOODDD, Ohconfucius, Oren1973, PaulinSaudi, Pearle, Pecher, Plastikspork, Rami R, Reenem, Rich Farmbrough, Rjwilmsi, Robert Brockway, Russ3Z, Rwendland, RyanEberhart, Samsara, Sean.hoyland, Seergenius, Shalom Yechiel, Shrike, Sittmarierose333, Sobreira, Stumink, Style, Surv1v4l1st, TAnthony, Tasc, Tewfik, That Guy, From That Show!, TheCheeseManCan, Thomas Blomberg, Tim!, Toya, Tpb, U109, Wavelength, Widefox, Wikifan12345, Wmahan, Ynhockey, Yuber, Zupez zeta, Żyrafał, Δ, Александър, كاشف عقيل, 104 anonymous edits .... ??

1982 Lebanon War *Source:* https://en.wikipedia.org/w/index.php?oldid=861185117 *License:* Creative Commons Attribution-Share Alike 3.0 *Contributors:* Abonazzi, Absolutelypuremilk, Adavidb, All Rows4, AmirSurfLera, Ashurbanippal, Athomeinkobe, Avaya1, Averysoda, Axeman89, Bassganglia, Bender235, BethNaught, BiggestSataniaFanboy89, Bisswah Inc., CasualObserver'48, CentreLeftRight, Cheerioswithmilk, Chris the speller, Cloj, ClueBot NG, CommonsDelinker, DRAGON BOOSTER, DadaNeem, Dan100, Dawnseeker2000, Degen Earthfast, Dl2000, DocWatson42, DreadfullyDistinct, Eagle4000, Erictheenquirer, EstebanRivera86, Flyer22 Reborn, Frosty, FunkMonk, Gabbe, Gigar44, Gob Lofa, Greyshark09, GünniX, Hftf, Hmains, Howcheng, IRISZOOM, Ifadly, InverseHypercube, Ira Leviton, JDiala, Jandalhandler, John of Reading, Johnuniq, Jprg1966, Just a guy from the KP, JustAGal, Kermanshahi, Kingsindian, Kndimov, L293D, LilHelpa, LoveFerguson, MWAK, Marchjuly, Marcocapelle, Mark Arsten, Markhurd, MarshallBagramyan, Materialscientist, Mattflaschen, Mhhossein, Mikrobølgeovn, Mild Bill Hiccup, Mr.User200, MrDemeanour, Mudwater, Munchkin2013, Nableezy, Narky Blert, Natg 19, Niceguyedc, Nick Number, Nihiltres, Nimur, Nishidani, No More Mr Nice Guy, Ohconfucius, Onceinawhile, Oren1973, PaleoNeonate, Philip Cross, Podiaebba, Powwowpuppies, Qwirkle, Reenem, Rjwilmsi, Roberticus, Rockypedia, Russ3Z, Sean.hoyland, Sfan00 IMG, Shrike, Sinai Horus, St170e, Stamptrader, Stumink, SubirGrewal, TAnthony, Termitesoldier9, The Rambling Man, TheAbleCommunist, TheNavigatrr, TheTimesAreAChanging, Thisissparta12345, Tim!, Tlbail01, ToonLucas22, Trappist the monk, Werieth, Widr, Wlglunight93, Yschilov, ZScarpia, Zero0000, יניב הורון, 99 anonymous edits .... ??

1983 Israel bank stock crisis *Source:* https://en.wikipedia.org/w/index.php?oldid=856376417 *License:* Creative Commons Attribution-Share Alike 3.0 *Contributors:* Alex Shih, Alfons2, Arminden, Binohonam, Bot-Schafter, Cadeburner, Cecody, Chris the speller, Fintor, Flamingoflorida, Former user 16,

Gilabrand, Hmains, Huldra, Ian Pitchford, Jamcib∼enwiki, John of Reading, Kaydern, Lachambre, Linguistical, Marchjuly, Mauls, Melcous, Melonkelon, Number 57, Okedem, Padres Hana, PiMaster3, Rahul Gaitonde, Reenem, Rhadow, Rich Farmbrough, Rjwilmsi, Robofish, Shuki, Shyamsunder, Superzohar, Tim!, Wassermann∼enwiki, Wikiliki, Ynhockey, 18 anonymous edits .... ??

South Lebanon conflict (1985–2000) *Source:* https://en.wikipedia.org/w/index.php?oldid=863349375 *License:* Creative Commons Attribution-Share Alike 3.0 *Contributors:* Abonazzi, Abou hmed, AndresHerutJaim, Ashrf1979, Ashurbanippal, Askhaiz, Averysoda, Baba Mica, Bender235, Benyaminln, Bilal66, CambridgeBayWeather, Catlemur, Chris the speller, ClueBot NG, Coltsfan, CommonsDelinker, Cptnono, DanTD, DePiep, Dewritech, Dl2000, Download, EkoGraf, Elockid, Eugene-elgato, Faigl.ladislav, Faizhaider, Favonian, Flayer, FriedrickMILBarbarossa, George Ho, Gob Lofa, Greyshark09, Guinsberg, HCPUNXKID, HammerKinFan, Hammersoft, Hasschaya, Howcheng, Huldra, IRISZOOM, Iluvwiki1, InverseHypercube, Israelusa123, Iwant2write, Jabotito48, Je.est.un.autre, JellWaffle, John of Reading, Johs12345, Jokkmokks-Goran, Josve05a, Jprg1966, Jurrikarsen, Klemen Kocjancic, Koavf, Kool777456, Ktr101, KylieTastic, Lankiveil, Lapsed Pacifist, Lihaas, LilHelpa, Magioladitis, Marchjuly, MarnetteD, Materialscientist, Matthew Fennell, Maurice Carbonaro, Maximilianklein, Michael Zeev, Mikrobølgeovn, MkativerataCCI, Mogism, Mr.User200, MrPenguin20, Nableezy, Natg 19, Nick Number, Nimur, Nishidani, No More Mr Nice Guy, O Fenian, Ohconfucius, Oren1973, PKT, Parsa1993, Pgallert, Plastikspork, Poyani, Professor keith donald, R'n'B, Reaper Eternal, Reenem, RevelationDirect, Sean.hoyland, ShakespeareFan00, Shrike, Sobreira, Sonntagsbraten, SpidErxD, Spoon!, Stumink, Tabletop, Taeguk, Taurniul, Termitesoldier9, The Madras, Tom.Reding, Toshio Yamaguchi, VernoWhitney, Werieth, Ynhockey, Zero0000, ZxxZxxZ, Δ, 65 anonymous edits 467

First Intifada *Source:* https://en.wikipedia.org/w/index.php?oldid=864817511 *License:* Creative Commons Attribution-Share Alike 3.0 *Contributors:* 625cb, Alexb102072, Andreasmperu, Aoomr, Apeters26, Arminden, Arxiloxos, BD2412, BU Rob13, Behead komi, Bender235, Blocky1OOO, Boldsteps, Bolter21, Brimz, BrokeTheInterweb, Carolmooredc, Charles Essie, ClueBot NG, CommonsDelinker, Corriebertus, Daniel Case, David Fuchs, Delija Do Groba, Dl2000, Dlv999, E.M.Gregory, Egeymi, Eik Corell, Epicgenius, Etan J. Tal, Excirial, Eyesnore, EzA+lSeb Nnakari, EzraShimon, Ezzex, Freefry, FutureTrillionaire, GeneralizationsAreBad, GoShow, Good Olfactory, Greyshark09, Hbdragon88, Hmains, Huldra, Igorp lj, Ijon, IranitGreenberg, Iridescent, Iwant2write, JDiala, JHunterJ, JaCorbett873, Jerals098, Jim1138, John of Reading, Joshbrown44, Jpl09c, Jprg1966, Justttt, Kingsindian, Kwikwag, Labellesanslebete, LawDog92015, Lightlowemon, Lotje, Magioladitis, Malik Shabazz, Marcocapelle, Mark Ironie, Markunator, McSquidwich, MelissaLond, Michael N Haddad, Mikrobølgeovn, Mogism, Moony22, Nableezy, Neil P. Quinn, Nirbochon, Nishidani, Ohconfucius, OlEnglish, Omnipaedista, Oshwah, Pararrei, PasterofMuppets, Patrick.N.L, Peacedance, Plot Spoiler, R'n'B, Reenem, Rubbish computer, Sakiv, SantiLak, Sean.hoyland, Shrike, ShulMaven, Sonntagsbraten, Srednuas Lenoroc, Stefan2, Stevietheman, Stumink, Tbm1998, Trappist the monk, Uglemat, Usaar33, Wavelength, Whoop whoop pull up, WhyDoIKeepForgetting, Wickey-nl, Widgety Function, Widr, Wikitiki89, Yesthenj, Zero0000, 144 anonymous edits 486

Oslo Accords *Source:* https://en.wikipedia.org/w/index.php?oldid=863951135 *License:* Creative Commons Attribution-Share Alike 3.0 *Contributors:* Aconant, AlexEng, Alpha Monarch, Amakuru, Arminden, Bbb23, Bender235, Brewcrewer, Capistranese, Clean Copy, ClueBot NG, Deadbeef, Deborahjay, Debresser, DemocraticLuntz, Djbclark, Dl2000, Donner60, Edeneiniwon, Enthusiast01, Ethically Yours, Favonian, Flyer22 Reborn, FourViolas, Freefry, Fuschia96, J 1982, John of Reading, Jprg1966, Kiwi113x, Loco588, Lornesossin, MShabazz, Mattflaschen, Miraclexix, Nihil novi, Nihiltres, Nomoskedasticity, Onceinawhile, Oshwah, Pauljeffersonks, Place Clichy, PottersWood, Qualitatis, Richard Jay Morris, Robert Brockway, RolandR, Sean.hoyland, Sudopeople, Tdv123, TheTimesAreAChanging, Thomasihkim, Tony999, TracyMcClark, Triggerhippie4, Unchartered, Wickey-nl, Wlglunight93, Yet Another User 2, Ymblanter, Yuvn86, Zero0000, 51 anonymous edits 501

Assassination of Yitzhak Rabin *Source:* https://en.wikipedia.org/w/index.php?oldid=856651861 *License:* Creative Commons Attribution-Share Alike 3.0 *Contributors:* Abebenjoe, AlexKarpman∼enwiki, AllanTom, Alvis, Anomalocaris, Ariel Sokolovsky, Arjayay, Asbl, Austriacus, Avenueceramique, Avi Abu Felafel, BTTNext, Bender235, Benstown, BernXiT, Bgwhite, Billhpike, Biruitorul, Bob.v.R, Brandmeister, Brewcrewer, Calton, CasualObserver'48, Cbdorsett, Clarityfiend, ClueBot NG, Coldtrack, Colonies Chris, Compulsory Purchase Order, Cyanolinguophile, DBigXray, Dale Stern, Davecrosby uk, Davshul, Dawnseeker2000, DemocraticLuntz, Denni, DocWatson42, DragonflySixtyseven, Egeymi, Eggishorn, Eleland, Elite compact, Enoshd, Epbr123, Evenmadderjon, Galatz, Gidonb, Gilabrand, Gothic2, Grahamdubya, GregU, Groyolo, Gus Polly, Haham hanuka, Headbomb, Helgihg, Hibernian, Howcheng, Hugo999, Iamsorandom, Ian Pitchford, Icewhiz, Indefatigable, Jayjg, Jim Fitzgerald, Jim Michael, John, Jonesey95, Joseph Solis in Australia, Jpbowen, Jprg1966, Keilana, Kempler video, Kitch, KnightRider∼enwiki, Kurykh, Lambiam, LaszloWalrus, Laurinavicius, Lightlowemon, Lionessofgd, Madalibi, MagicatthemovieS, Malayedit, Mandarax, MarchOrDie, Marek69, Marokwitz, Marudubshinki, Materialscientist, Mattflaschen, MeanMotherJr, Mr T (Based), Neutrality, Nishidani, Nizzi G, Njmike, Noon, Nudve, Number 57, OCNative, Od Mishehu, Olisamir, Oren neu dag, Outback the koala, Padres Hana, Paragon of Arctic Winter Nights, Pclz, Phil Boswell, PinchasC, Prevan, ProudIrishAspie, Rami R, Reenem, Rentir, Rich Farmbrough, Shemtovca, Shreyas310, Shuki, Sir Joseph, Sol Goldstone, Sonyes, SpockMonkey, Srich32977, Synergy, Tayaravaknin, Technopat, Telaviv1, Telecart, The Anomebot2, The Bushranger, The Rambling Man, The Wordsmith, TheWikipediaPersonGuy2016, Thecurran, Tim!, TommyBoy, Vanamonde93, VoABot II, Volunteer Marek, Wikiliki, Zero0000, Zzyzx11, הורון, יניב, ערן 149 anonymous edits 511

2000 Camp David Summit *Source:* https://en.wikipedia.org/w/index.php?oldid=860726783 *License:* Creative Commons Attribution-Share Alike 3.0 *Contributors:* 101historyfan101, A.Jacobin, AMuseo, Adamdaley, Archwayh, Arjayay, Atrix20, AttilaTotalWar, Averysoda, BD2412, Back to the ol' stomping grounds, Bad Dryer, Bdell555, Bender235, Bgwhite, Bless sins, Cachedio, Charles Essie, Chewings72, ClueBot NG, Cyberbot II, DMY, DRosenbach, Dalai lama ding dong, Darius Dhlomo, Dcljr, Demetrius Phalereus of Wikipedius, Dlv999, Dr. R.R. Pickles, Drsmoo, El C, Endo-Plexor, Equilibrial, Esebi95, Eyalmc, Faigl.ladislav, Felipe P, FergusM1970, Flyer22 Reborn, Funga, GHcool, Galoubet, Gedindigo, Gilabrand, Glane23, Good Olfactory, Graeme Bartlett, GregKaye, Gronk Oz, Gzuckier, Harelx, Haydon43, Hertz1888, Hugo999, Huldra, HupHollandHup, IRISZOOM, Inductiveload, InverseHypercube, J 1982, Jeff5102, Jethro B, Jfc12, John of Reading, Jon72790, Joshdboz, Khazar2, Kosher Fan, Liftarn, Lightsmiles, LilHelpa, Lotje, MZMcBride, MagicatthemovieS, Marcocapelle, Matthewosburn, MelbourneStar, MeteorMaker, Midrashah, Millennium bug, Mimihitam, Mogism, Muhandes, Nishidani, Ohconfucius, Onceinawhile, Peace in holyland 2012, Penguins Are Animals 5327, PersianPBF, Pinetreejungle, Plot Spoiler, Ptbotgourou, RJFJR, Redound, Reenem, Renamed user Sloane, Rhombus, Rich Farmbrough, Rjwilmsi, S. Neuman, Sabri76, Sakiv, Sanguinalis, Sean.hoyland, Secret Saturdays, Sepsis II, SpeckInTheUniverse, Teiresia, Thingg, Thomasnetrpm, Thoredge, Tim!, TreasuryTag, Vanished user lt94ma34le12, Veritnight, Wickey-nl, Wlglunight93, YUL89YYZ, Zero0000, 111 anonymous edits .... ??

Second Intifada *Source:* https://en.wikipedia.org/w/index.php?oldid=860725862 *License:* Creative Commons Attribution-Share Alike 3.0 *Contributors:* Abi.144, Agtx, Alexb102072, Alias1004, Allthefoxes, AmirSurfLera, Andres arg, Anomalocaris, Arjayay, Arminden, Ashurbanippal, Averysoda, Avraham, Bender235, Bgwhite, Blocky1OOO, Brewcrewer, Capistranese, Charles Essie, Chewings72, Chris the speller, Clarinetguy097, ClueBot NG, CommonsDelinker, Conklaven, Crito10, Cyberbot II, Danielabdillah03, Debresser, Diblidabliduu, Donner60, E.M.Gregory, Eik Corell, Elialevine, Enthusiast01, Erictheenquirer, Estevezj, Faceless Enemy, Fexlajahd, FutureTrillionaire, GHcool, Gazkthul, George Ho, GoingBatty, GregKaye, Greyshark09, Haydon43, Hephacrestos, Hmains, Huldra, IRISZOOM, Icewhiz, Illegitimate Barrister, Inkbug, Iridescent, Iwant2write, JDiala, Jamesrl1967, Je.est.un.autre, Jimbov22, John of Reading, Jojojava, Jon Kolbert, Jonosbro, Jprg1966, Jurrikarsen, Keith D, Kingsindian, Kolbasz, KylieTastic, Lancidre, Lbaer84, LilHelpa, Lioness, LoveFerguson, MShabazz, Magioladitis, Marcocapelle, Markhburton, Marloweperel, Materialscientist, MathKnight, Mikrobølgeovn, Moawd, Mogism, Monochrome Monitor, Mumbo-jumbophobe, NSH002, Nableezy, Natg 19, NawlinWiki, Neelix, Niceguyedc, Nishidani, Onel5969, Paolocarouche, PaulinSaudi, Plot Spoiler, Point by point, Progress4all, Reenem, Rjwilmsi, RupJana, Sakiv, SantiLak, Sean.hoyland, Sepsis II, Shrike, ShulMaven, Sirpenguin4211, Solomonfromfinland, SpeckInTheUniverse, Spliff Joint Blunt, Sudopeople, Tassedethe, The Last Arietta, Tomh903, Trappist the monk, Tzadikv, Uishaki, Unreal7, Valenciano, Visite fortuitement prolongée, Vortex2 LA, Wavelength, Whoop whoop pull up, Why should I have a User Name?, Wickey-nl, Ymblanter, Yschilov, Zero0000, ÄDA - DÄP, Στύξ, הורון, יניב 96 anonymous edits 533

Israeli West Bank barrier *Source:* https://en.wikipedia.org/w/index.php?oldid=858504667 *License:* Creative Commons Attribution-Share Alike 3.0 *Contributors:* "I think not!" -Descartes. And then he disappeared., Al-Andalusi, Alaney2k, Arminden, Averysoda, BD2412, Bender235, BethNaught, Bolter21, BoogaLouie, Brewcrewer, Catsmoke, ClueBot NG, CommonsDelinker, Concus Cretus, Continentaleurope, DatGuy, Daviddwd, DePiep, Debresser, Diyamo, FourViolas, FreedomEnergy, French Espresso, GabrielF, Galatz, GentleTunaTestsIt, GeorgeofOrange, GhostOfPhilLeeds, Gilliam, Gilsrafnorn, Giraffedata, Gluten is a tent test, Gob Lofa, GoingBatty, GregKaye, GünniX, HJ Mitchell, Helterskelter80, Humuskedasticity, Intent Latte Guests, Jprg1966, K6ka, Kamel Tebaast, Kane5187, Keith D, Kelisi, Kingsindian, Landingdude13, Leeuwe, Llywelyn2000, MShabazz, Magioladitis, Malik Shabazz, Marcocapelle, Marek69, Marxistfounder, Mayz, Michael Glass, Mifter, Mild Bill Hiccup, Mkkamran, MollificationDesperation, Nableezy, NawlinWiki, Nayefc, Nightscream, Nishidani, Nomoskedasticity, Penwhale, Place Clichy, Pluto2012, Quackslikeaduck, Qualitatis, Quondum, Rich Farmbrough, Ricosenna, Saturnalia0, Sean.hoyland, SeattliteTungsten, Sepsis II, Settleman, SevenOrEleven, Shrike, Silent Statute Gent, SolomonTwo, Srich32977, StrawWoodBrick, Take The Long Road Home, TeapotDame, The Anomebot2, The Vintage Feminist, Tom.Reding, Tritomex, Vortex2 LA, Vsmith, WOSlinker, Wlglunight93, YoMamaSoDumb, Zero0000, ZeroMostelZL, דוד, ש', عماد الدين المقدسي, 35 anonymous edits 572

Israeli disengagement from Gaza *Source:* https://en.wikipedia.org/w/index.php?oldid=864066635 *License:* Creative Commons Attribution-Share Alike 3.0 *Contributors:* (14$H, 205ywmpq, Aaronshavit, Adamreinman, Al-Andalusi, AndresHerutJaim, ArwinJ, Ashurbanippal, BD2412, Bender235, BernardZ, Bgwhite, Bob K31416, BobaFett85, Bolter21, Bongwarrior, Bonissen, Brandmeister, CartoonDiablo, Chris the speller, ChrisGualtieri, ClueBot NG, Cptnono, Crunchysnails, Cuchullain, D Namtar, DadaNeem, Dan Koehl, Davehi1, Davemck, Debresser, DemocraticLuntz, DivineAlpha, Dlv999, Economust, Eli-kh, Emeraldcityserendipity, Emmette Hernandez Coleman, Erictheenquirer, Ezmode, Froy1100, Funandtrvl, Galatz, Gigar44, Grafmatic, Grammaracademy, Greyshark09, Ground Zero, Hebrides, HelpingUlearn, Hertz1888, Honeylemonz, Howcheng, Hugo999, Hut 8.5, Hvn0413, IJA, IRISZOOM, Icewhiz, Ira Leviton, Iwant2write, Jacier8899, Jacklee, Joe407, Johnmcintyre1959, Joseph Solis in Australia, Jprg1966, Keith D, Keleti-p, Khazar, Kordas, Liam987, LilHelpa, LoneWolf1992, Lotje, Magioladitis, Mahmudmasri, Marcocapelle, Marokwitz, Mattflaschen, Me, Myself, and I are Here, MeanMotherJr, Metallurgist, Milkawke91, Mimihitam, Mogism, Motique, Muslim lo Juheu, NPz1, Nableezy, Neutrality, Niceguyedc, Nick Number, Nishidani, Number 57, Okedem, Omnipaedista, Onceinawhile, Ottawakismet, Palobserver, Penguins Are Animals 5327, Philip Cross, PottersWood, Qualitatis, R'n'B, RBK613, Rami R, Red Jay, Reenem, Rich Farmbrough, Roeyb, Roscelese, Saebvn, Sean.hoyland, SebastianHelm, Shuki, Slashme, Smyth, Srich32977, StarryGrandma, Staszek Lem, SwisterTwister, TheCuriousGnome, Tim!, Tom.Reding, Topbanana, Ttrexster, Wc1, WereSpielChequers, Whaleboy123, Wickey-nl, Wingman417, Wlglunight93, Ynhockey, Yosef.Raziel, הורון, יניב אומנות, 76 anonymous edits 603

2006 Gaza cross-border raid *Source:* https://en.wikipedia.org/w/index.php?oldid=862824631 *License:* Creative Commons Attribution-Share Alike 3.0 *Contributors:* $1LENCE D00600D, Ahmad20012001, AndresHerutJaim, Averysoda, Ayytro, BD2412, BDD, Bender235, Boneyard90, Catlemur, CommonsDelinker, Dewritech, Dl2000, DuncanHill, Erictheenquirer, Greyshark09, Hbdragon88, Iwant2write, Jb1944, Jokkmokks-Goran, Jprg1966, Marco 2 en, Marloweperel, Nickst, ProudIrishAspie, Qualitatis, R'n'B, Reenem, ShulMaven, Sonsaru, TheCuriousGnome, Tim!, Tony1, Trappist the monk, Veritnight, Wickey-nl, Yamaguchi先生, Δ, 18 anonymous edits .... ??

2011 Israeli social justice protests *Source:* https://en.wikipedia.org/w/index.php?oldid=864478427 *License:* Creative Commons Attribution-Share Alike 3.0 *Contributors:* Alonsusz, Avivi, BD2412, BabbaQ, Bender235, Bnjsd2016, Brandmeister, Brightgalrs, Cattus, Charles Essie, Chris the speller, Cnilep, CommonsDelinker, Cybercobra, Debresser, Derek R Bullamore, Dewritech, DynamoDegsy, E.F Edits, Ericl, Gaius Cornelius, Gal deren d, Gertiu32, Good Olfactory, HarryBowman, Heart of Destruction, Hmains, Holdoffhunger, ImprovingWiki, Ira Leviton, Iridescent, Jeroen, John of Reading, Johnkatz1972, Joseph Zernik, Ktr101, Kudzu1, Leer5454, Lihaas, MTN～enwiki, Mais oui!, Manuel Santiago, Mnemosientje, Mogism, Motique, Nandt1, Neutrality, Ohconfucius, Omnipaedista, PanchoS, Phiwikiii, Polentarion, Poliocretes, Quebec99, Rami R, Reenem, Rjwilmsi, Sen Penrose, Sfan00 IMG, Shuki, Someone35, Soosim, Stefanomione, Stillmans39, Superzohar, Tamarenda, The Egyptian Liberal, The Rambling Man, TheCuriousGnome, The-JJJunk, Tim!, Trappist the monk, Trivialist, Uheh135, Vanisaac, Wikifan12345, WilliamH, Woohookitty, Xgrui, Yairge, Yamb, Yellowdesk, Ynhockey, Yoninah, Yug, Zvika, אירוס, 69 anonymous edits .... ??

2014 Israel–Gaza conflict *Source:* https://en.wikipedia.org/w/index.php?oldid=864286731 *License:* Creative Commons Attribution-Share Alike 3.0 *Contributors:* 1234567891Oabcdefghijklmnop, Absolutelypuremilk, Ahmad20012001, Andy M. Wang, AntanO, AussieLegend2, Avaya1, Averysoda, Avisnacks, BD2412, Baking Soda, Bender235, Bgwhite, Blocky1OOO, Bruriyah, Cliftonian, ClueBot NG, Coffeeandcrumbs, CommonsDelinker, Dan Koehl, Dcirovic, DemocraticLuntz, Diannaa, Dl2000, Dr Bargouthi, Drsmoo, EdJohnston, EkoGraf, Elaz85, Elysans, Enigmaman, Erictheenquirer, EvergreenFir, FallingGravity, Floatjon, Fremantle99, Garageland66, GeneralizationsAreBad, Gilsrafnorn, Gob Lofa, Greyshark09, Guy1286, GünniX, Hanay, Hertz1888, Hinittic, Hires an editor, Howcheng, Howicus, IRISZOOM, Icewhiz, Iwant2write, JDiala, JJMC89, Jeffreytlew, Jerodlycett, John of Reading, Jon Kolbert, K.e.coffman, Keith D, Khazen48, Kingsindian, Knowledde77345, Kvwiki1234, LilHelpa, Lottolads, LoveFerguson, Lr0^"k, Majora, Malik Shabazz, MarnetteD, MathKnight, MathKnight-at-TAU, Mathieu ottawa, Mhhossein, Mikeblas, Mikrobølgeovn, Mogism, Monopoly31121993, MusikAnimal, Nakon, Narky Blert, Nezi1111, Nishidani, Nur68, Oiyarbepsy, Ost316, PasterofMuppets, Pianoman320, PinkAmpersand, Pkbwcgs, Point by point, Pppery, Quadash1648, Qualitatis, RBK613, Reenem, Rpaster93, Rtedb, Rubbish computer, Rupert loup, Safiel, Saidfont, Saltimbanques, Sepsis II, Shemtovca, Sherpajohn, Shrike, Skynorth, Softlavender, Spliff Joint Blunt, StjJackson, TAnthony, Tdl1060, The Rambling Man, Thenewsmartkid, TracyMcClark, Trappist the monk, Triggerhippie4, Tritomex, Uhooep, Valoem, VanEman, WarKosign, Wavelength, Wickey-nl, Ynhockey, Yschilov, יניב, ארז, יעקב הורון, وسام زقوت, 32 anonymous edits .... ??

Image Sources, Licenses and Contributors

The sources listed for each image provide more detailed licensing information including the copyright status, the copyright owner, and the license conditions.

Image *Source:* https://en.wikipedia.org/w/index.php?title=File:Padlock-blue.svg *Contributors:* User:AzaToth, User:Eleassar 1
Image *Source:* https://en.wikipedia.org/w/index.php?title=File:Raising_the_Ink_Flag_at_Umm_Rashrash_(Eilat).jpg *License:* Creative Commons Attribution-Sharealike 3.0 *Contributors:* AnonMoos, Geagea, Hanay, Jaredzimmerman (WMF), LLs, Matanya, Neukoln, Poliocretes, Ran Ayase, Ranbar, Steinsplitter, Triggerhippie4, Wieralee, Yann, علي المزارف 1
Image *Source:* https://en.wikipedia.org/w/index.php?title=File:Flag_of_Israel.svg *License:* Public Domain *Contributors:* The Provisional Council of State Proclamation of the Flag of the State of Israel of 25 Tishrei 5709 (28 October 1948) 2
Image *Source:* https://en.wikipedia.org/w/index.php?title=File:Badge_of_the_Israel_Defense_Forces.svg *License:* Creative Commons Attribution-Sharealike 3.0 *Contributors:* Flag_of_the_Israel_Defence_Forces.svg: Meronim derivative work: User:Zscout370 (Return fire) 2
Image *Source:* https://en.wikipedia.org/w/index.php?title=File:Flag_of_Druze.svg *License:* Public Domain *Contributors:* Copyright (c) 2005 Verdy p (also fr:User:Verdy_p) (attribution line, when needed) 2
Image *Source:* https://en.wikipedia.org/w/index.php?title=File:Flag_of_Hejaz_1917.svg *License:* Public domain *Contributors:* () 2
Image *Source:* https://en.wikipedia.org/w/index.php?title=File:Arab_Liberation_Army_(bw).svg *License:* Creative Commons Attribution-Sharealike 3.0 *Contributors:* Vallecyofdawn, modified by Zscout370 2
Image *Source:* https://en.wikipedia.org/w/index.php?title=File:Flag_of_the_Muslim_Brotherhood.gif *License:* Public Domain *Contributors:* Cathy Richards, Denniss, Jeff G., Mikrobølgeovn, Ratatosk 2
Image *Source:* https://en.wikipedia.org/w/index.php?title=File:Flag_of_Pakistan.svg *License:* Public Domain *Contributors:* User:Zscout370 2
Image *Source:* https://en.wikipedia.org/w/index.php?title=File:Flag_of_Anglo-Egyptian_Sudan.svg *License:* Creative Commons Attribution-Sharealike 3.0 *Contributors:* User:Abjiklam 2
Image *Source:* https://en.wikipedia.org/w/index.php?title=File:Flag_of_the_Arab_League.svg *License:* Public Domain *Contributors:* Flad 2
Image *Source:* https://en.wikipedia.org/w/index.php?title=File:Flag_of_Egypt_(1922–1958).svg *License:* Public Domain *Contributors:* Alkari, AnonMoos, Billinghurst, BomBom, Burts, Cycn, Dharmadhyaksha, F l a n k e r, Faris knight, FreshCorp619, Herbythyme, JMCC1, Jdx, Kajk, Kookaburra, Mattes, Mysid, Nagy, Oren neu dag, Rotemliss, Sangjinhwa, Sarang, SiBr4, Urmas, Ранко Николић, کورش, 9 anonymous edits 2
Image *Source:* https://en.wikipedia.org/w/index.php?title=File:Flag_of_Jordan.svg *License:* Public Domain *Contributors:* User:SKopp 2
Image *Source:* https://en.wikipedia.org/w/index.php?title=File:Flag_of_Iraq_(1921–1959).svg *License:* Public Domain *Contributors:* Antemister, Ashashyou, Ashrf1979, Burts, FreshCorp619, Illegitimate Barrister, J. Patrick Fischer, Madden, Mathonius, MrPenguin20, R-41∼commonswiki, Sportsguy17, Takabeg, Zscout370, Ранко Николић, 4 anonymous edits 2
Image *Source:* https://en.wikipedia.org/w/index.php?title=File:Flag_of_Syria_(1932-1958;_1961-1963).svg *License:* Public Domain *Contributors:* User:AnonMoos 2
Figure 1 *Source:* https://en.wikipedia.org/w/index.php?title=File:UN_Palestine_Partition_Versions_1947.jpg *License:* UN map *Contributors:* User:Zero0000 4
Figure 2 *Source:* https://en.wikipedia.org/w/index.php?title=File:PikiWiki_Israel_21221_The_Palmach.JPG *License:* Public Domain *Contributors:* Articseahorse, Crazy Ivan, Netanel h, Pikiwikisrael 6
Figure 3 *Source:* https://en.wikipedia.org/w/index.php?title=File:Avia_S-199_in_June_1948_(Israeli_Air_Force).png *License:* Public Domain *Contributors:* Articseahorse, Joshbaumgartner, NeverDoING, Poliocretes, Steinsplitter, Wieralee, Ynhockey, 2 anonymous edits 8
Figure 4 *Source:* https://en.wikipedia.org/w/index.php?title=File:King_Abdullah,_Jerusalem,_29_May_1948.jpg *License:* Public Domain *Contributors:* John Roy Carlson 12
Figure 5 *Source:* https://en.wikipedia.org/w/index.php?title=File:Tanks_of_the_Israeli_8th_Armoured_Brigade_(1948).jpg *License:* Public Domain *Contributors:* Joram Field 16
Figure 6 *Source:* https://en.wikipedia.org/w/index.php?title=File:The_British_Army_in_the_United_Kingdom_1939-45_H37168.jpg *License:* Public Domain *Contributors:* Ain92, Alexpl, Fæ, Labattblueboy, Rcbutcher 17
Figure 7 *Source:* https://en.wikipedia.org/w/index.php?title=File:BrenCarrierShualeiShimshon.png *License:* Public Domain *Contributors:* Ashashyou, Brakeet, Ynhockey, חובבשירה, 1 anonymous edits 18
Figure 8 *Source:* https://en.wikipedia.org/w/index.php?title=File:The_British_Army_in_North_Africa_1940_E443.2.jpg *License:* Public Domain *Contributors:* Ain92, Fæ, Gunbirddriver2, HantsAV, Labattblueboy 20
Figure 9 *Source:* https://en.wikipedia.org/w/index.php?title=File:1948_Arab_Israeli_War_-_May_15-June_10.svg *License:* Public Domain *Contributors:* Mr. Edward C. Krasnoborski and Mr. Frank Martini, Department of History, U.S. Military Academy Honza.havlicek (talk) 21
Figure 10 *Source:* https://en.wikipedia.org/w/index.php?title=File:Butterfly_Armoured-car_Gvar-Am-israel1948.jpg *License:* Creative Commons Attribution-Sharealike 3.0 *Contributors:* Brakeet, Geagea, Hanay, Poliocretes, Ykantor 22
Figure 11 *Source:* https://en.wikipedia.org/w/index.php?title=File:Nirim1948_1.jpg *License:* Public Domain *Contributors:* Geagea, Ynhockey 23
Figure 12 *Source:* https://en.wikipedia.org/w/index.php?title=File:Negba1948Defenses.jpg *License:* Public Domain *Contributors:* Geagea, Ynhockey 24
Image *Source:* https://en.wikipedia.org/w/index.php?title=File:Handasa-burma001.jpg *License:* Public Domain *Contributors:* File Upload Bot (Magnus Manske), Netanel h, OgreBot 2, Wieralee, Yuval Y 26
Image *Source:* https://en.wikipedia.org/w/index.php?title=File:Burma_Road_1948.jpg *License:* Public Domain *Contributors:* Original uploaded by Golf Bravo) 26
Image *Source:* https://en.wikipedia.org/w/index.php?title=File:Latroun_(11_juin).png *License:* Creative Commons Attribution-Sharealike 3.0 *Contributors:* Ceedjee 26
Image *Source:* https://en.wikipedia.org/w/index.php?title=File:1948-Jordanian_artillery_shelling_Jerusalem.jpg *Contributors:* Bobamnertiopsis, File Upload Bot (Magnus Manske), OgreBot 2, חובבשירה 26
Image *Source:* https://en.wikipedia.org/w/index.php?title=File:Arab_Legion_soldier_in_ruins_of_Hurva.jpg *License:* Public Domain *Contributors:* John Roy Carlson 26
Image *Source:* https://en.wikipedia.org/w/index.php?title=File:Jewish_Quarter_Refugees.jpg *Contributors:* Chesdovi, Daniel Baránek, Pessimist2006, Talmoryair, עידוד 26
Figure 13 *Source:* https://en.wikipedia.org/w/index.php?title=File:Prof_Fekete_Rector_Heb_Uni-water-allocation.jpg *License:* Public Domain *Contributors:* Alan, Geagea, Kopiersperre, Mjrmtg, Ramaksoud2000, Yann, Ykantor 27
Figure 14 *Source:* https://en.wikipedia.org/w/index.php?title=File:Afulahagana.jpg *License:* Public Domain *Contributors:* לא יידע לסמל ידוע, אמיר. אברהם 28
Figure 15 *Source:* https://en.wikipedia.org/w/index.php?title=File:Deganiatank1.jpg *License:* GNU Free Documentation License *Contributors:* Almog, Articseahorse, BotAdventures, Bukvoed, Gandvik, MGA73bot2, 1 anonymous edits 29
Figure 16 *Source:* https://en.wikipedia.org/w/index.php?title=File:PikiWiki_Israel_20772_The_Palmach.jpg *License:* Public Domain *Contributors:* Netanel h, Pikiwikisrael 30
Figure 17 *Source:* https://en.wikipedia.org/w/index.php?title=File:Egyptian_Plane_TA_1948.png *License:* Public Domain *Contributors:* Articseahorse, Ashashyou, Cobatfor, Geagea, PeterWD, Poliocretes, YoavR, חובבשירה, 3 anonymous edits 31
Figure 18 *Source:* https://en.wikipedia.org/w/index.php?title=File:Egyptian_bombing_1948.jpg *License:* Public Domain *Contributors:* Ashashyou, Geagea, Poliocretes, Sonntagsbraten, YoavR 32
Figure 19 *Source:* https://en.wikipedia.org/w/index.php?title=File:Avia-S-199-IAF-101Sqn-Tel-Nof-Israel-1948-01.jpg *License:* Public Domain *Contributors:* Articseahorse, Joshbaumgartner, OgreBot 2, Wieralee 33
Figure 20 *Source:* https://en.wikipedia.org/w/index.php?title=File:Spitfire-MkIX-hatzerim-1-2.jpg *License:* Creative Commons Attribution 2.5 *Contributors:* User:Bukvoed 33
Figure 21 *Source:* https://en.wikipedia.org/w/index.php?title=File:Israeli_B-17Gs_01011953.JPG *License:* Public Domain *Contributors:* CyberXRef, Flayer, Geagea, Joshbaumgartner, MK-3B-NBN, Poliocretes 34
Figure 22 *Source:* https://en.wikipedia.org/w/index.php?title=File:Northland_Color_1.jpg *Contributors:* Aschroet, BotMultichill, FSV, KTo288, KudzuVine 35
Figure 23 *Source:* https://en.wikipedia.org/w/index.php?title=File:Palestine_Military_Situation,_June_11,_1948,_Truman_Papers.jpg *License:* Public Domain *Contributors:* Onceinawhile 36
Figure 24 *Source:* https://en.wikipedia.org/w/index.php?title=File:Altalena_off_Tel-Aviv_beach.jpg *License:* Public Domain *Contributors:* Bukk, Christophe cagé, Faigl.ladislav, Geagea, Matanya, Mattes, Netanel h, Stunteltje, רועי א, 1 anonymous edits 38
Figure 25 *Source:* https://en.wikipedia.org/w/index.php?title=File:6pdr-Aibdis.jpg *License:* Public Domain *Contributors:* Ain92, Ashashyou, Matanya, Netanel h, OgreBot 2 40

Figure 26 *Source:* https://en.wikipedia.org/w/index.php?title=File:IDFSoldierInLyddaOrRamla.png *License:* Public Domain *Contributors:* Brakeet, Bukvoed, NatanFlayer, Ynhockey, 1 anonymous edits ... 41
Figure 27 *Source:* https://en.wikipedia.org/w/index.php?title=File:LyddaAirportCapture.png *License:* Public Domain *Contributors:* Brakeet, Bukvoed, Ori~, Ronaldino, Ynhockey, 1 anonymous edits ... 42
Figure 28 *Source:* https://en.wikipedia.org/w/index.php?title=File:Ramla_prisoners_of_war,_July_12-13,_1948.png *License:* Public Domain *Contributors:* Geagea, J 1982, Ori~, Schekinov Alexey Victorovich, Ynhockey ... 43
Figure 29 *Source:* https://en.wikipedia.org/w/index.php?title=File:PikiWiki_Israel_2184_1948_war_תואמצעה_חמחלם.jpg *License:* Creative Commons Attribution 2.5 *Contributors:* Netanel h, Pikiwikisrael, Ynhockey, 2 anonymous edits ... 44
Figure 30 *Source:* https://en.wikipedia.org/w/index.php?title=File:1948_arab_israeli_war_-_Oct.jpg *License:* Public Domain *Contributors:* 1989, Humus sapiens~commonswiki, Talmoryair, Timeshifter ... 46
Figure 31 *Source:* https://en.wikipedia.org/w/index.php?title=File:Zionist_mortar_team_outside_Zafzaf_in_October_1948.png *Contributors:* Palestine Remembered ... 47
Figure 32 *Source:* https://en.wikipedia.org/w/index.php?title=File:Israeli_soldiers_in_battle_with_the_Arab_village_of_Sassa.jpg *License:* Creative Commons Attribution-Sharealike 3.0 *Contributors:* Geagea, Huldra, Marcus Cyron, Matanya, Poliocretes, Steinsplitter ... 47
Figure 33 *Source:* https://en.wikipedia.org/w/index.php?title=File:Israelis_at_Faluja.jpg *License:* Public Domain *Contributors:* Ashashyou, Huldra, Masur, Padres Hana, Ynhockey ... 49
Figure 34 *Source:* https://en.wikipedia.org/w/index.php?title=File:Beersheba_1948.jpg *License:* Public Domain *Contributors:* Alonr, Amirki, Bot-Multichill, Brakeet, Bukvoed, Daniel Baránek, Geagea, Hidro, Hovev, NatanFlayer, Poliocretes, Wieralee, 2 anonymous edits ... 49
Figure 35 *Source:* https://en.wikipedia.org/w/index.php?title=File:Negev_Brigade_soldiers_1948.jpg *License:* Public Domain *Contributors:* Geagea, Poliocretes, Sonntagsbraten ... 50
Figure 36 *Source:* https://en.wikipedia.org/w/index.php?title=File:Beit_Natif_1948.jpg *License:* Public Domain *Contributors:* Israeli GPO photographer ... 50
Figure 37 *Source:* https://en.wikipedia.org/w/index.php?title=File:Operation_Horev.jpg *License:* Public Domain *Contributors:* Israeli GPO photographer ... 52
Figure 38 *Source:* https://en.wikipedia.org/w/index.php?title=File:Ramle_Funeral_1949.jpg *License:* Public Domain *Contributors:* Geagea, Nirvi, יעקב חובבשירה ... 53
Figure 39 *Source:* https://en.wikipedia.org/w/index.php?title=File:1947-UN-Partition-Plan-1949-Armistice-Comparison.svg *License:* Public Domain *Contributors:* AnonMoos ... 57
Image *Source:* https://en.wikipedia.org/w/index.php?title=File:Man_see_school_nakba.jpg *License:* Public Domain *Contributors:* Adnanmuf~commonswiki, BotMultichill, EChastain, SpacemanSpiff, Timeshifter, 1 anonymous edits ... 58
Image *Source:* https://en.wikipedia.org/w/index.php?title=File:Yemenites_go_to_Aden.jpg *License:* Public Domain *Contributors:* Akamol, Alonr, BDaniel, Blackcat, Chenspec, G.dallorto, Geagea, Kippi70, MGA73bot2, Matanya, Mcapdevila, Tomer T, Túrelio, דוד ,ש׳ 1 anonymous edits ... 60
Image *Source:* https://en.wikipedia.org/w/index.php?title=File:Commons-logo.svg *License:* logo *Contributors:* Anomie, Callanecc, CambridgeBayWeather, Jo-Jo Eumerus, RHaworth ... 68
Figure 40 *Source:* https//en.wikipedia.org *License:* UN map *Contributors:* Onceinawhile ... 72
Figure 41 *Source:* https://en.wikipedia.org/w/index.php?title=File:Israeli_delegation_to_the_1949_Armistice_Agreements_talks.jpg *License:* Public Domain *Contributors:* Israeli delegation ... 73
Figure 42 *Source:* https://en.wikipedia.org/w/index.php?title=File:1947-UN-Partition-Plan-1949-Armistice-Comparison.svg *License:* Public Domain *Contributors:* AnonMoos ... 78
Figure 43 *Source:* https://en.wikipedia.org/w/index.php?title=File:Israel_Austerity.jpg *License:* Public Domain *Contributors:* Benzoyl, BotMultichill, Funandtrvl, Gampe, Geagea, Hanay, Hidro, Hovev, Matanya, יעקב חובבשירה, ... 88
Figure 44 *Source:* https://en.wikipedia.org/w/index.php?title=File:Wonder_Pot.jpg *License:* Creative Commons Attribution-Sharealike 3.0 *Contributors:* Yoninah ... 89
Figure 45 *Source:* https://en.wikipedia.org/w/index.php?title=File:1956_Ministry_price_notification_poster_placed_inside_a_local_grocery_store_in_Israel,_Kfar_Saba.jpg *Contributors:* User:Huddyhuddy ... 89
Figure 46 *Source:* https://en.wikipedia.org/w/index.php?title=File:Pinhas_Lavon.jpg *License:* Public Domain *Contributors:* Ashashyou, Geagea, Ingsoc, Talmoryair, 1 anonymous edits ... 98
Figure 47 *Source:* https://en.wikipedia.org/w/index.php?title=File:Meir_Max_Bineth.jpg *License:* Public Domain *Contributors:* Ashashyou, Bot-Multichill, Kippi70, YoavR, דוד ,ש׳ פארוק ... 100
Image *Source:* https://en.wikipedia.org/w/index.php?title=File:Tanks_Destroyed_Sinai.jpg *License:* Public Domain *Contributors:* United States Army Heritage and Education Center ... 105
Image *Source:* https://en.wikipedia.org/w/index.php?title=File:Flag_of_the_United_Kingdom.svg *License:* Public Domain *Contributors:* Anomie, Good Olfactory, Jo-Jo Eumerus, MSGJ, Mifter ... 105
Image *Source:* https://en.wikipedia.org/w/index.php?title=File:Flag_of_France.svg *License:* Public Domain *Contributors:* Anomie, Fastily, Jo-Jo Eumerus ... 105
Figure 48 *Source:* https://en.wikipedia.org/w/index.php?title=File:Canal_de_Suez.jpg *License:* Creative Commons Attribution 2.5 *Contributors:* User:YolanC ... 107
Figure 49 *Source:* https://en.wikipedia.org/w/index.php?title=File:1956-07-30_Suez_Canal_Seized.ogv *Contributors:* Universal Studios ... 122
Figure 50 *Source:* https://en.wikipedia.org/w/index.php?title=File:Suez_Canal,_Port_Said_-_ISS_2.jpg *Contributors:* NASA astronaut ... 122
Figure 51 *Source:* https://en.wikipedia.org/w/index.php?title=File:Suez_nationalization.ogv *License:* Public Domain *Contributors:* National Archives ... 125
Figure 52 *Source:* https://en.wikipedia.org/w/index.php?title=File:Portrait_Menzies_1950s.jpg *Contributors:* National Library of Australia ... 128
Figure 53 *Source:* https://en.wikipedia.org/w/index.php?title=File:Suez_Crisis.ogv *License:* Public Domain *Contributors:* National Archives . 132
Figure 54 *Source:* https://en.wikipedia.org/w/index.php?title=File:1956-08-06_Suez_Crisis.ogv *Contributors:* Universal ... 135
Figure 55 *Source:* https://en.wikipedia.org/w/index.php?title=File:AMX-13_at_Latrun4.JPG *License:* Creative Commons Attribution 2.5 *Contributors:* User:Katangais ... 137
Figure 56 *Source:* https://en.wikipedia.org/w/index.php?title=File:1956_Suez_war_-_conquest_of_Sinai.jpg *License:* Public Domain *Contributors:* 1989, Ain92, Francis Schonken, JHistory, JMCC1, Kaidor, Karlfk, Lipothymia, Mmccalpin, NeverDoING, QWerk, Ruthven, Snek01, Talmoryair, Thuresson, Timeshifter, דוד ש׳ ... 138
Figure 57 *Source:* https://en.wikipedia.org/w/index.php?title=File:M4A4-Sherman-latrun-2.jpg *License:* Creative Commons Attribution 2.5 *Contributors:* User:Bukvoed ... 139
Figure 58 *Source:* https://en.wikipedia.org/w/index.php?title=File:Meteor_IAF_1954.jpg *License:* Public Domain *Contributors:* CyberXRef, DAAyanz, Flayer, Geagea, Hovev, Joshbaumgartner, NatanFlayer, NiD.29, חובבשירה, 1 anonymous edits ... 140
Figure 59 *Source:* https://en.wikipedia.org/w/index.php?title=File:Tzniha-mitle.jpg *License:* Public Domain *Contributors:* Uri Dan ... 141
Figure 60 *Source:* https://en.wikipedia.org/w/index.php?title=File:Flickr_-_Israel_Defense_Forces_-_IDF_Jeep_Waving_at_French_Bomber.jpg *License:* Creative Commons Attribution-Sharealike 3.0 *Contributors:* Brakeet, Geagea, Matanya, OgreBot 2, Rillke, Visite fortuitement prolongée, דוד ,ש׳ רדיומן ... 142
Figure 61 *Source:* https://en.wikipedia.org/w/index.php?title=File:Israeli_troops_in_sinai_war.jpg *License:* Public Domain *Contributors:* Alan, Claritas, Daniel Baránek, Geagea, Matanya, NatanFlayer, Neukoln, NeverDoING, Nudve~commonswiki, Orlovic, Quenhitran, Ramaksoud2000, Stout256, Wieralee, Yann, YehudaTelAviv64, Шуфель, דוד ,ש׳ 1 anonymous edits ... 143
Figure 62 *Source:* https://en.wikipedia.org/w/index.php?title=File:AMX-13-.jpg *License:* GNU Free Documentation License *Contributors:* Bukvoed, Citypeek, MGA73bot2, Matanya (usurped), Netanel h, OgreBot 2, 1 anonymous edits ... 144
Figure 63 *Source:* https://en.wikipedia.org/w/index.php?title=File:1956-11-01_War_in_Egypt.ogv *Contributors:* Universal ... 145
Figure 64 *Source:* https://en.wikipedia.org/w/index.php?title=File:Ibrahim_al-Awwal1956.jpg *License:* Public Domain *Contributors:* Uploader: User Golf Bravo ... 146
Figure 65 *Source:* https://en.wikipedia.org/w/index.php?title=File:Egypt-Israel_Disturbances.ogv *License:* Public Domain *Contributors:* Movietone News/National Archives ... 148
Figure 66 *Source:* https://en.wikipedia.org/w/index.php?title=File:Suez_Sea_Venom.jpg *License:* Public Domain *Contributors:* Royal Navy official photographer ... 151
Figure 67 *Source:* https://en.wikipedia.org/w/index.php?title=File:Sea_Hawk_899_NAS_on_cat_HMS_Eagle_(R05)_Suez_1956.jpg *License:* Public Domain *Contributors:* Royal Navy official photographer ... 152
Figure 68 *Source:* https://en.wikipedia.org/w/index.php?title=File:Port_Said_from_air.jpg *License:* Public Domain *Contributors:* Fleet Air Arm official photographer ... 154
Figure 69 *Source:* https//en.wikipedia.org *License:* Public Domain *Contributors:* Ashashyou, Innotata, Themightyquill ... 156
Figure 70 *Source:* https://en.wikipedia.org/w/index.php?title=File:British_tanks_in_Port_Said.jpg *License:* Public Domain *Contributors:* Ashashyou, Avocato, Avron, Brakeet, Bukvoed, Catsmeat, Cobatfor, Docu, Fæ, High Contrast, NeverDoING ... 158
Figure 71 *Source:* https://en.wikipedia.org/w/index.php?title=File:1956-11-12_Near_East_Crisis.ogv *Contributors:* Universal ... 159
Figure 72 *Source:* https://en.wikipedia.org/w/index.php?title=File:1956-08-09_Press_Parley.ogv *Contributors:* Universal ... 165

Figure 73 *Source:* https://en.wikipedia.org/w/index.php?title=File:Nasser_and_Eisenhower,_1960.jpg *License:* Public Domain *Contributors:* Al Ameer son, Jeff G., OgreBot 2, Rafic.Mufid ... 166
Figure 74 *Source:* https://en.wikipedia.org/w/index.php?title=File:1956-04-12_Full_Scale_War_Looms.ogv *Contributors:* Universal Newsreels 167
Figure 75 *Source:* https://en.wikipedia.org/w/index.php?title=File:1957-02-14_Tel_Aviv_Israel.ogv *Contributors:* Universal Newsreels ... 172
Figure 76 *Source:* https://en.wikipedia.org/w/index.php?title=File:Suez_Crisis_aftermath.ogv *License:* Public Domain *Contributors:* National Archives ... 173
Figure 77 *Source:* https://en.wikipedia.org/w/index.php?title=File:Statue_of_de_Lesseps.jpg *License:* Public Domain *Contributors:* Ashashyou, Avocato, JMCC1 ... 175
Figure 78 *Source:* https://en.wikipedia.org/w/index.php?title=File:Tiran_Guns_IMG_0937.JPG *License:* Public Domain *Contributors:* deror_avi 182
Image *Source:* https://en.wikipedia.org/w/index.php?title=File:Six_Day_War_Territories.svg *License:* Creative Commons Attribution-Sharealike 3.0 *Contributors:* User:Ling.Nut, User:Rafy ... 189
Image *Source:* https://en.wikipedia.org/w/index.php?title=File:Flag_of_the_United_Arab_Republic.svg *License:* GNU Free Documentation License *Contributors:* AnonMoos, Ashashyou, Burts, Coup de crayon 2011, Cycn, Denelson83, FDRMRZUSA, Fry1989, Homo lupus, Illegitimate Barrister, Leyo, Ludger1961, MGA73bot2, Master911∼commonswiki, Permjak, R-41∼commonswiki, Reisio, Roxanna, Sabtoor999999, Sangjinhwa, SiBr4, Sreejithk2000, TFCforever, Thuresson, 7 anonymous edits ... 189
Image *Source:* https://en.wikipedia.org/w/index.php?title=File:Flag_of_Iraq_(1963-1991);_Flag_of_Syria_(1963-1972).svg *Contributors:* - ... 189
Image *Source:* https://en.wikipedia.org/w/index.php?title=File:Flag_of_Iraq_(1963-1991).svg *Contributors:* - ... 189
Image *Source:* https://en.wikipedia.org/w/index.php?title=File:Flag_of_Iraq_(1963–1991);_Flag_of_Syria_(1963–1972).svg *License:* Public Domain *Contributors:* Kookaburra and other uploaders ... 190
Figure 79 *Source:* https://en.wikipedia.org/w/index.php?title=File:Nasser_and_Egyptian_pilots_pre-1967.gif *License:* Public Domain *Contributors:* Al Ameer son, Ashashyou, Greenshed, Poliocretes, Vantey, שי דוד ... 192
Figure 80 *Source:* https://en.wikipedia.org/w/index.php?title=File:6dayswar1.jpg *License:* Creative Commons Attribution-Sharealike 2.0 *Contributors:* רחמים (חזי) יחזקאל ... 197
Figure 81 *Source:* https://en.wikipedia.org/w/index.php?title=File:Hatzerim_Mirage_20100129_1.jpg *License:* Creative Commons Attribution-Sharealike 3.0 *Contributors:* Oren Rozen ... 197
Figure 82 *Source:* https://en.wikipedia.org/w/index.php?title=File:1967_Six_Day_War_-_conquest_of_Sinai_5-6_June.jpg *License:* Public Domain *Contributors:* 1989, Abaniyuwe, JMCC1, Karlfk, Ruthven, Shizhao ... 199
Figure 83 *Source:* https://en.wikipedia.org/w/index.php?title=File:PikiWiki_Israel_16401_Israel_Defense_Forces.jpg *License:* Creative Commons Attribution 2.5 *Contributors:* נוימן יהושע ... 199
Figure 84 *Source:* https://en.wikipedia.org/w/index.php?title=File:6_Day_War-Amos.jpg *License:* Attribution *Contributors:* רוגל רפי (Transfered by מתניה/Original uploaded by ROSENMAN424) ... 201
Figure 85 *Source:* https://en.wikipedia.org/w/index.php?title=File:Sharon_ageila.JPG *License:* Public Domain *Contributors:* Wiki1609 ... 202
Figure 86 *Source:* https://en.wikipedia.org/w/index.php?title=File:AMX-13-latrun-2.jpg *License:* Creative Commons Attribution 2.5 *Contributors:* User:Bukvoed ... 203
Figure 87 *Source:* https://en.wikipedia.org/w/index.php?title=File:1967_Six_Day_War_-_conquest_of_Sinai_7-8_June.jpg *License:* Public Domain *Contributors:* 1989, Francis Schonken, Ilmari Karonen, Karlfk, Lipothymia, Mang o34, Ruthven, Talmoryair, Thuresson, Timeshifter, Милан Јелисавчић 206
Figure 88 *Source:* https://en.wikipedia.org/w/index.php?title=File:1967-06-06_Mid-East.ogv *Contributors:* Universal ... 207
Figure 89 *Source:* https://en.wikipedia.org/w/index.php?title=File:Flickr_-_Government_Press_Office_(GPO)_-_Israeli_Gun_Boat.jpg *License:* Creative Commons Attribution-Sharealike 3.0 *Contributors:* Alan Liefting, Articseahorse, Discasto, Flayer, Fæ, Geagea, Matanya, Poliocretes ... 207
Figure 90 *Source:* https://en.wikipedia.org/w/index.php?title=File:1967_Six_Day_War_-_The_Jordan_salient.jpg *License:* Public Domain *Contributors:* 1989, Humus sapiens∼commonswiki, Mang o34, Talmoryair, Timeshifter ... 209
Figure 91 *Source:* https://en.wikipedia.org/w/index.php?title=File:Ammunition_Hill_Museum_Exhibits_P1010036.JPG *License:* Public Domain *Contributors:* deror_avi ... 212
Figure 92 *Source:* https://en.wikipedia.org/w/index.php?title=File:Ammunition_Hill_Museum_Exhibits_P1010039.JPG *License:* Public Domain *Contributors:* deror_avi ... 212
Figure 93 *Source:* https://en.wikipedia.org/w/index.php?title=File:Ammunition_Hill_Museum_Exhibits_P1010035.JPG *License:* Public Domain *Contributors:* deror_avi ... 215
Figure 94 *Source:* https://en.wikipedia.org/w/index.php?title=File:1967_Six_Day_War_-_Battle_of_Golan_Heights.svg *License:* Public Domain *Contributors:* Honza Havlíček ... 218
Figure 95 *Source:* https://en.wikipedia.org/w/index.php?title=File:PikiWiki_Israel_7250_Kids_in_the_shelter_kibbutz_Dan.JPG *License:* Creative Commons Attribution 2.5 *Contributors:* Chenspec, Frederico1234, FunkMonk, Geagea, Jay8g, Lotje, Netanel h, Pikiwikisrael, עדירל, יעקב, שי' דוד, 1 anonymous edits ... 218
Figure 96 *Source:* https://en.wikipedia.org/w/index.php?title=File:Israeli_tanks_advancing_on_the_Golan_Heights._June_1967._D327-098.jpg *Contributors:* Assaf Kutin ... 221
Figure 97 *Source:* https://en.wikipedia.org/w/index.php?title=File:1967-06-09_Egypt_Accepts_UN_Cease-Fire.ogv *Contributors:* Universal Newsreels ... 222
Figure 98 *Source:* https://en.wikipedia.org/w/index.php?title=File:1967-06-13_Cease-Fire.ogv *Contributors:* Universal ... 224
Image *Source:* https://en.wikipedia.org/w/index.php?title=File:Suez_canal_map.jpg *License:* Public Domain *Contributors:* CIA ... 245
Image *Source:* https://en.wikipedia.org/w/index.php?title=File:Flag_of_the_Soviet_Union_(1955–1980).svg *License:* Creative Commons Attribution-ShareAlike 3.0 Unported *Contributors:* Cmapm ... 245
Image *Source:* https://en.wikipedia.org/w/index.php?title=File:Flag_of_Palestine.svg *License:* Public Domain *Contributors:* Orionist, previous versions by Makaristos, Mysid, etc. ... 245
Image *Source:* https://en.wikipedia.org/w/index.php?title=File:Flag_of_Cuba.svg *License:* Public Domain *Contributors:* Anime Addict AA, Beao, Benzoyl, Cathy Richards, Charlesjsharp, Cycn, Dbenbenn, Denelson83, DerBorg, EclecticArkie, Emijrp, F l a n k e r, FreshCorp619, Fry1989, Homo lupus, Huhsunqu, J.delanoy, Jdx, Klemen Kocjancic, Ludger1961, MAXXX-309, Madden, Mattes, Neq00, NeverDoING, Persiana, Ricordisamoa, SKopp, Sarang, SiBr4, Spacebirdy, TFerenczy, ThomasPusch, Torstein, Túrelio, Zscout370, 10 anonymous edits ... 245
Figure 99 *Source:* https://en.wikipedia.org/w/index.php?title=File:Mastvic.jpg *License:* Creative Commons Attribution-Sharealike 3.0 *Contributors:* User:צהוב קודקוד ... 249
Figure 100 *Source:* https://en.wikipedia.org/w/index.php?title=File:INSEilat.jpg *License:* Creative Commons Attribution-Sharealike 3.0 *Contributors:* User:צהוב קודקוד ... 250
Figure 101 *Source:* https://en.wikipedia.org/w/index.php?title=File:Karama_aftermath_1.jpg *License:* Public Domain *Contributors:* Jordanian Military Photographer ... 251
Figure 102 *Source:* https//en.wikipedia.org *License:* Public Domain *Contributors:* Not credited ... 251
Figure 103 *Source:* https://en.wikipedia.org/w/index.php?title=File:F-4E_Israel_HAPIM0321.jpg *License:* GNU Free Documentation License *Contributors:* Itayba on he.wikipedia.org ... 253
Figure 104 *Source:* https://en.wikipedia.org/w/index.php?title=File:SA-3_system.jpg *License:* Public Domain *Contributors:* Ashashyou, BokicaK, Ellin Beltz, File Upload Bot (Magnus Manske), High Contrast, NoCultureIcons, OgreBot 2 ... 254
Figure 105 *Source:* https://en.wikipedia.org/w/index.php?title=File:PikiWiki_Israel_381_Firdan_Bridge_1969_גשר_פירדאן_1969.jpg *License:* Creative Commons Attribution 2.5 *Contributors:* Ashashyou, Geagea, JMCC1, NatanFlayer, Netanel h, Pikiwikisrael, Poliocretes, Wieralee, חובבשירה, 1 anonymous edits ... 254
Figure 106 *Source:* https://en.wikipedia.org/w/index.php?title=File:HaatashaUSSR.jpg *License:* Public Domain *Contributors:* Soaproot ... 256
Figure 107 *Source:* https://en.wikipedia.org/w/index.php?title=File:Hatasharibon.jpg *License:* Public Domain *Contributors:* Wikipod ... 256
Figure 108 *Source:* https//en.wikipedia.org *License:* Public Domain *Contributors:* Auntof6, Kaiketsu, OgreBot 2, TLSuda ... 261
Figure 109 *Source:* https://en.wikipedia.org/w/index.php?title=File:MunichIsraeliOlympicFront.jpg *License:* GNU Free Documentation License *Contributors:* Apalsola, BotMultichillT, Bricklayer, Gras-Ober, HaileyS, High Contrast, MGA73bot2, OgreBot 2, Robert Weemeyer ... 266
Figure 110 *Source:* https://en.wikipedia.org/w/index.php?title=File:Connollystraße_31_-_Gedenktafel.jpg *License:* Creative Commons Attribution 3.0 Germany *Contributors:* High Contrast ... 284
Figure 111 *Source:* https://en.wikipedia.org/w/index.php?title=File:München_1972_Gedenkstein.jpg *License:* Creative Commons Attribution-ShareAlike 3.0 Unported *Contributors:* Andreas Thum ... 284
Figure 112 *Source:* https://en.wikipedia.org/w/index.php?title=File:FFB_Olympia-Denkmal_Fliegerhorst.jpg *License:* Creative Commons Attribution-Sharealike 3.0 *Contributors:* Cholo Aleman ... 285
Figure 113 *Source:* https://en.wikipedia.org/w/index.php?title=File:Munich_olympics_victim.jpg *License:* Creative Commons Zero *Contributors:* Pesis ... 286
Figure 114 *Source:* https://en.wikipedia.org/w/index.php?title=File:Five_victims_of_the_Munich_massacre.JPG *License:* Creative Commons Attribution-Sharealike 3.0 *Contributors:* שי דוד ... 286

Figure 115 *Source:* https://en.wikipedia.org/w/index.php?title=File:Mark_Podwal_Munich_Massacre_Remembrance_Drawing.jpg *License:* Creative Commons Attribution-Sharealike 3.0 *Contributors:* Mark Podwal ... 287

Image *Source:* https://en.wikipedia.org/w/index.php?title=File:Bridge_Crossing.jpg *License:* Public Domain *Contributors:* Ashashyou, BotMultichill, FSIII, File Upload Bot (Magnus Manske), FutureTrillionaire, Mattes, Mattflaschen, Nabak, Netanel h, OgreBot 2, Poliocretes, Roxanna, Soerfm, 2 anonymous edits ... 290

Image *Source:* https://en.wikipedia.org/w/index.php?title=File:Flag_of_the_United_States.svg *License:* Public Domain *Contributors:* Anomie, Jo-Jo Eumerus, MSGJ, Mr. Stradivarius ... 290

Image *Source:* https://en.wikipedia.org/w/index.php?title=File:Flag_of_Egypt_(1972-1984).svg *License:* Public Domain *Contributors:* Current vector version by Editor at Large ... 290

Image *Source:* https://en.wikipedia.org/w/index.php?title=File:Flag_of_Syria_(1972-1980).svg *License:* Public Domain *Contributors:* Flag_of_Egypt_1972.svg: Current vector version by Editor at Large derivative work: Orange Tuesday (talk) ... 290

Image *Source:* https://en.wikipedia.org/w/index.php?title=File:Flag_of_Saudi_Arabia.svg *License:* Public Domain *Contributors:* Alhadramy Alkendy, Alkari, Ancintosh, Anime Addict AA, AnonMoos, BRPever, Bobika, Brian Ammon, CommonsDelinker, Cycn, Denelson83, Duduziq, Ekabhishek, Er Komandante, FDRMRZUSA, Fabioravanelli, File Upload Bot (Magnus Manske), Fry1989, Gazimagomedov, Herbythyme, Homo lupus, INeverCry, Itsemurhaja, Jeff G., Klemen Kocjancic, Lokal Profil, Love Krittaya, Love monju, Mattes, Menasim, Meno25, Mnmazur, Mohammed alkhater, Nagy, Nard the Bard, Nightstallion, Palosirkka, Pitke, Pmsyyz, Ranveig, Ratatosk, Reisio, Ricordisamoa, Saibo, Sarang, SiBr4, Wouterhagens, Zscout370, Zyido, 18 anonymous edits ... 290

Image *Source:* https://en.wikipedia.org/w/index.php?title=File:Flag_of_Libya_(1972–1977).svg *License:* Creative Commons Attribution-Sharealike 3.0,2.5,2.0,1.0 *Contributors:* TRAJAN 117 ... 290

Image *Source:* https://en.wikipedia.org/w/index.php?title=File:Flag_of_Tunisia.svg *License:* Public Domain *Contributors:* entraîneur: BEN KHALIFA WISSAM ... 290

Image *Source:* https://en.wikipedia.org/w/index.php?title=File:Flag_of_Algeria.svg *License:* Public Domain *Contributors:* This graphic was originaly drawn by User:SKopp. ... 290

Image *Source:* https://en.wikipedia.org/w/index.php?title=File:Flag_of_Morocco.svg *License:* Public Domain *Contributors:* Anime Addict AA, AymanFlad, Barryob, Bgag, Cimoi, Cycn, Denelson83, Denniss, Djampa, Doodledoo, Earth Resident, EugeneZelenko, Fastily, Flad, Foroa, Fred J, Fry1989, Gmaxwell, Herbythyme, J. Patrick Fischer, Klemen Kocjancic, Krinkle, Leyo, Mattes, Meno25, Mindspillage, Myself488, Odder, Offnfopt, Omar-toons, Orrling, OsamaK, Permjak, Ppntori, Reisio, Rodejong, Sangjinhwa, Sarang, SiBr4, Steinsplitter, Str4nd, TFCforever, ThomasPusch, Vispec, Xiquet, Yougarten, Zscout370, ∼riley, 11 anonymous edits ... 290

Image *Source:* https://en.wikipedia.org/w/index.php?title=File:Flag_of_the_Soviet_Union.svg *License:* Public Domain *Contributors:* A1, Ahmadi∼commonswiki, Akihiro Nagai 2, Alex Smotrov, Alvis Jean, Art-top, BagnoHax, Beetsyres34, Benzoyl, Brandmeister∼commonswiki, Cathy Richards, Counny, Cycn, Daphne Lantier, Denniss, Dynamicwork, ELeschev, Endless-tripper, Ericmetro, EugeneZelenko, F l a n k e r, FDRMRZUSA, Fred J, FreshCorp619, Fry1989, G.dallorto, Garynysmon∼commonswiki, Herbythyme, Homo lupus, I am dies, Illegitimate Barrister, Jake Wartenberg, Li-sung, Loic26, MaggotMaster, Michaelversatile, MrAustin390, Ms2ger, Nightstallion, Palosirkka, Patrickpedia, PeaceKeeper97, Pianist, R-41∼commonswiki, RainbowSilver2ndBackup, Rainforest tropicana, S.A. Julio (old), Sammimack, Sangjinhwa, Sarang, Sebyugez, Skeezix1000, Solbris, Storkk, Str4nd, Tabasco∼commonswiki, Thespoondragon, ThomasPusch, Tiven2240, Toben, Twilight Chill, User000name, Xgeorg, Zscout370, Илья Драконов, Полицюнер, Ранко Николић, Серп, Тоны4, יהל'יזיושמר, 65 anonymous edits ... 290

Figure 116 *Source:* https://en.wikipedia.org/w/index.php?title=File:Anwar_Sadat_cropped.jpg *License:* Public Domain *Contributors:* BomBom, J 1982, STB-1, Silesianus, Sir James, Stewi101015, Zhuyifei1999 ... 297

Figure 117 *Source:* https://en.wikipedia.org/w/index.php?title=File:Golda_Meir2.jpg *License:* Public Domain *Contributors:* Marion S. Trikosko 303

Figure 118 *Source:* https://en.wikipedia.org/w/index.php?title=File:Hatzerim_290110_Sukhoi_7.jpg *License:* Creative Commons Attribution-Sharealike 3.0 *Contributors:* Oren Rozen ... 304

Figure 119 *Source:* https://en.wikipedia.org/w/index.php?title=File:1973_sinai_war_maps.jpg *License:* Public Domain *Contributors:* 1989, Francis Schonken, Hohum, Liftarn, Ondrejk, Talmoryair, Thuresson, Timeshifter ... 306

Figure 120 *Source:* https://en.wikipedia.org/w/index.php?title=File:Israeli_A-4_Skyhawk_Wreckage.jpg *License:* Public Domain *Contributors:* LeCaire ... 307

Figure 121 *Source:* https://en.wikipedia.org/w/index.php?title=File:Egyptian_MIG_21s_during_Yom_Kippur_War.jpg *License:* Public Domain *Contributors:* Asclepias, Blacktiger87, Jo-Jo Eumerus, Rathfelder, Rottweiler, ShakespeareFan00 ... 307

Figure 122 *Source:* https://en.wikipedia.org/w/index.php?title=File:MirageIIIShotDownByMiG-21.jpg *License:* Public Domain *Contributors:* Aaron Shpigel, Articseahorse, Ashashyou, Joshbaumgartner, PeterWD ... 308

Figure 123 *Source:* https://en.wikipedia.org/w/index.php?title=File:Destroyed_m60.jpg *License:* Public Domain *Contributors:* User:SreeBot 311

Figure 124 *Source:* https://en.wikipedia.org/w/index.php?title=File:Israeli_Tank_Battles_Egyptian_Forces_in_the_Sinai_Desert_-_Flickr_-_Israel_Defense_Forces.jpg *License:* Creative Commons Attribution-Sharealike 2.0 *Contributors:* Israel Defense Forces ... 312

Figure 125 *Source:* https://en.wikipedia.org/w/index.php?title=File:1973_sinai_war_maps2.jpg *License:* Public Domain *Contributors:* 1989, Abu badali∼commonswiki, Doanri, Finale Lösung, Hohum, Liftarn, Talmoryair, Timeshifter, Wikiliki ... 313

Figure 126 *Source:* https://en.wikipedia.org/w/index.php?title=File:Israeli_Tanks_Cross_the_Suez_Canal_-_Flickr_-_Israel_Defense_Forces.jpg *License:* Creative Commons Attribution-Sharealike 2.0 *Contributors:* Israel Defense Forces ... 315

Figure 127 *Source:* https://en.wikipedia.org/w/index.php?title=File:IDF_Ismailia_Clash.jpg *License:* Public Domain *Contributors:* Haramati 317

Figure 128 *Source:* https://en.wikipedia.org/w/index.php?title=File:M48_tank_wrecks_at_Suez_Canal_1981.jpg *License:* Public Domain *Contributors:* USN ... 318

Figure 129 *Source:* https://en.wikipedia.org/w/index.php?title=File:Yom_Kippur_War_map.svg *License:* Creative Commons Attribution-Sharealike 2.5 *Contributors:* Andrew Hampe, BokicaK, ChrisO, Hohum, Jarekt, Koraiem, Kordas, MaGa, Raul654, Sarang, Slowking4, Szajci, Timeshifter, Wikipeder ... 321

Figure 130 *Source:* https://en.wikipedia.org/w/index.php?title=File:Soldier_Ismailiya.jpg *License:* Creative Commons Attribution 2.5 *Contributors:* עמר נאור ... 322

Figure 131 *Source:* https://en.wikipedia.org/w/index.php?title=File:Assad_Tlass_war_1973.jpg *License:* Public Domain *Contributors:* FunkMonk, Rafic.Mufid, Roxanna, 1 anonymous edits ... 326

Figure 132 *Source:* https://en.wikipedia.org/w/index.php?title=File:1973_Yom_Kippur_War_-_Golan_heights_theater.jpg *License:* Public Domain *Contributors:* Department of History, U.S. Military Academy. See Department Maps page. ... 327

Figure 133 *Source:* https://en.wikipedia.org/w/index.php?title=File:Shot_Kal-.jpg *License:* GNU Free Documentation License *Contributors:* Original uploader was נחמן at he.wikipedia ... 329

Figure 134 *Source:* https://en.wikipedia.org/w/index.php?title=File:Israeli_Tank_on_Golan_Heights_-_Flickr_-_The_Central_Intelligence_Agency.jpg *License:* Public Domain *Contributors:* The Central Intelligence Agency ... 331

Figure 135 *Source:* https://en.wikipedia.org/w/index.php?title=File:PikiWiki_Israel_4223_Israel_Defense_Forces.jpg *License:* Creative Commons Attribution 2.5 *Contributors:* גולדשמידט דני ... 332

Figure 136 *Source:* https://en.wikipedia.org/w/index.php?title=File:Syrian_Tank_Blocked_From_Attacking_an_IDF_Post_-_Flickr_-_Israel_Defense_Forces.jpg *License:* Creative Commons Attribution-Sharealike 2.0 *Contributors:* Israel Defense Forces ... 337

Figure 137 *Source:* https://en.wikipedia.org/w/index.php?title=File:October_9_Damascus_Strike.jpg *License:* Public Domain *Contributors:* Bgag, Infrogmation, Netanel h, Poliocretes ... 338

Figure 138 *Source:* https://en.wikipedia.org/w/index.php?title=File:The_Bloody_Valley_of_Tears_Battle_-_Flickr_-_Israel_Defense_Forces.jpg *License:* Creative Commons Attribution-Sharealike 2.0 *Contributors:* Israel Defense Forces ... 340

Figure 139 *Source:* https://en.wikipedia.org/w/index.php?title=File:Destruction_in_the_al-Qunaytra_village_in_the_Golan_Heights,_after_the_Israeli_withdrawal_in_1974.jpg *License:* Public Domain *Contributors:* Roxanna, 1 anonymous edits ... 340

Figure 140 *Source:* https://en.wikipedia.org/w/index.php?title=File:Battle_Latakia_en.svg *License:* Creative Commons Attribution-Sharealike 2.5 *Contributors:* Lohe & user:lilyu ... 343

Figure 141 *Source:* https://en.wikipedia.org/w/index.php?title=File:Battle_baltim_en.svg *License:* Creative Commons Attribution-Sharealike 3.0 *Contributors:* Nirvi ... 344

Figure 142 *Source:* https://en.wikipedia.org/w/index.php?title=File:Baniasfmkesh.jpg *License:* Creative Commons Zero *Contributors:* צהוב קודקוד 346

Figure 143 *Source:* https://en.wikipedia.org/w/index.php?title=File:Israeli_M48_tank_captured_by_Egypt.jpg *License:* Creative Commons Attribution 3.0 *Contributors:* Wrightbus ... 350

Figure 144 *Source:* https://en.wikipedia.org/w/index.php?title=File:Nickel_Grass_M60_C-5.jpg *License:* Public Domain *Contributors:* USAF (In: "Remember when ... Operation Nickel Grass" by John Lacomia, 60th Air Mobility Wing History Office, posted 31 O ... 351

Figure 145 *Source:* https://en.wikipedia.org/w/index.php?title=File:Damaged_BMP-1.jpg *License:* Public Domain *Contributors:* Ashashyou, Ferbr1, High Contrast, Jakednb, SuperTank17, 1 anonymous edits ... 353

Figure 146 *Source:* https://en.wikipedia.org/w/index.php?title=File:Israeli_and_Egyptian_Generals_Meet_in_Sinai_-_Flickr_-_Israel_Defense_Forces.jpg *License:* Creative Commons Attribution-Sharealike 2.0 *Contributors:* Israel Defense Forces ... 354

Figure 147 *Source:* https://en.wikipedia.org/w/index.php?title=File:JG-8_Schautafel.jpg *Contributors:* Billyhill ... 356

Figure 148 *Source:* https://en.wikipedia.org/w/index.php?title=File:Hatzerim_Mirage_20100129_1.jpg *License:* Creative Commons Attribution-Sharealike 3.0 *Contributors:* Oren Rozen 361
Figure 149 *Source:* https://en.wikipedia.org/w/index.php?title=File:Downed_Mirage.jpg *License:* Public Domain *Contributors:* Articseahorse, Ashashyou, Hohum, Joshbaumgartner, Netanel h, PeterWD, Sherif9282, Sophus Bie 361
Figure 150 *Source:* https://en.wikipedia.org/w/index.php?title=File:1974_in_Golan.ogv *License:* Public Domain *Contributors:* National Archives 362
Figure 151 *Source:* https://en.wikipedia.org/w/index.php?title=File:UN_Kilometer_101.jpg *License:* Public Domain *Contributors:* Ashashyou, Brakeet, DieBuche, File Upload Bot (Magnus Manske), Netanel h, OgreBot 2, Zaccarias, 1 anonymous edits 363
Figure 152 *Source:* https://en.wikipedia.org/w/index.php?title=File:Sadat_and_Begin_clean3.jpg *License:* Public Domain *Contributors:* Leffler, Warren K., photographer. Work for hire made for U.S. News and World Report 368
Figure 153 *Source:* https://en.wikipedia.org/w/index.php?title=File:T62-valley_of_tears.jpg *License:* Creative Commons Attribution-Sharealike 3.0 *Contributors:* Jakednb 370
Image *Source:* https://en.wikipedia.org/w/index.php?title=File:PFLP-GC_Flag.svg *License:* Creative Commons Attribution-Sharealike 3.0 *Contributors:* User:MrPenguin20 375
Image *Source:* https://en.wikipedia.org/w/index.php?title=File:Revolutionäre_Zellen.svg *License:* Creative Commons Attribution-Sharealike 3.0 *Contributors:* Revolutionäre Zellen, vectorized by user:freemesm 375
Image *Source:* https://en.wikipedia.org/w/index.php?title=File:Flag_of_Uganda.svg *License:* Creative Commons Zero *Contributors:* tobias ... 375
Image *Source:* https://en.wikipedia.org/w/index.php?title=File:Airbus_A300B4-203,_Air_France_AN0792167.jpg *Contributors:* Ardfern, Duch, Fæ, N509FZ 377
Figure 154 *Source:* https://en.wikipedia.org/w/index.php?title=File:Entebbe_Airport_DF-ST-99-05538.jpg *License:* Public Domain *Contributors:* SRA Andy Dunaway 384
Figure 155 *Source:* https://en.wikipedia.org/w/index.php?title=File:Flickr_-_Government_Press_Office_(GPO)_-_Rescued_Air_France_Passengers.jpg *License:* Creative Commons Attribution-Sharealike 3.0 *Contributors:* Geagea, Matanya, Poliocretes, Steinsplitter 385
Figure 156 *Source:* https://en.wikipedia.org/w/index.php?title=File:Flickr_-_Government_Press_Office_(GPO)_-_Dora_Bloch's_Family_Pays_Last_Respects.jpg *License:* Creative Commons Attribution-Sharealike 3.0 *Contributors:* Geagea, Matanya, Poliocretes, 1 anonymous edits 386
Figure 157 *Source:* https://en.wikipedia.org/w/index.php?title=File:Entebbe-international-airport-2009-002.jpg *License:* Public Domain *Contributors:* LTC David Konop, United States Army Africa (SETAF), Public Affairs Officer 390
Figure 158 *Source:* https://en.wikipedia.org/w/index.php?title=File:Entebbe-international-airport-2009-003.jpg *License:* Public Domain *Contributors:* LTC David Konop, United States Army Africa (SETAF), Public Affairs Officer 390
Figure 159 *Source:* https://en.wikipedia.org/w/index.php?title=File:Entebbe-international-airport-2009-001.jpg *License:* Public Domain *Contributors:* LTC David Konop, United States Army Africa (SETAF), Public Affairs Officer 391
Figure 160 *Source:* https://en.wikipedia.org/w/index.php?title=File:Entebbe-international-airport-2009-004.jpg *License:* Public Domain *Contributors:* LTC David Konop, United States Army Africa (SETAF), Public Affairs Officer 391
Figure 161 *Source:* https://en.wikipedia.org/w/index.php?title=File:Entebbe-international-airport-2009-005.jpg *License:* Public Domain *Contributors:* LTC David Konop, United States Army Africa (SETAF), Public Affairs Officer 391
Image *Source:* https://en.wikipedia.org/w/index.php?title=File:Begin,_Carter_and_Sadat_at_Camp_David_1978.jpg *License:* Public Domain *Contributors:* Fitz-Patrick, Bill, photographer 395
Figure 162 *Source:* https://en.wikipedia.org/w/index.php?title=File:Six_Day_War_Territories.svg *License:* Creative Commons Attribution-Sharealike 3.0 *Contributors:* User:Ling.Nut, User:Rafy 397
Figure 163 *Source:* https://en.wikipedia.org/w/index.php?title=File:Camp_David,_Menachem_Begin,_Anwar_Sadat,_1978.jpg *License:* Public Domain *Contributors:* Archwayh, Auntof6, Faigl.ladislav, Geagea, Infrogmation, Lipothymia, Makthorpe, Martin H., Monopoly31121993, Neelix, Pikiwikisrael, Shalom, TCY 398
Figure 164 *Source:* https://en.wikipedia.org/w/index.php?title=File:Begin_Brzezinski_Camp_David_Chess.jpg *License:* Public Domain *Contributors:* , for the Executive Office of the President of the United States 400
Figure 165 *Source:* https://en.wikipedia.org/w/index.php?title=File:Sadat_and_Begin_and_their_delegations_at_Camp_David,_September_17,_1978_(10729645586).jpg *License:* Public Domain *Contributors:* Central Intelligence Agency from Washington, D.C. 401
Figure 166 *Source:* https://en.wikipedia.org/w/index.php?title=File:Carter,_Brzezinski_and_Vance_at_Camp_David,_1977.jpg *License:* Public Domain *Contributors:* Official White House Photo Uploader Perceval 402
Figure 167 *Source:* https://en.wikipedia.org/w/index.php?title=File:Sadat_and_Begin_clean3.jpg *License:* Public Domain *Contributors:* Leffler, Warren K., photographer. Work for hire made for U.S. News and World Report 403
Image *Source:* https://en.wikipedia.org/w/index.php?title=File:Gnome-mime-sound-openclipart.svg *Contributors:* User:Eubulides 404
Image *Source:* https//en.wikipedia.org *License:* Public Domain *Contributors:* Miller Center of Public Affairs 404
Figure 168 *Source:* https://en.wikipedia.org/w/index.php?title=File:Carter_and_Sadat_White_House2.jpg *License:* Public Domain *Contributors:* Leffler, Warren K., photographer or Trikosko, Marion S., photographer. Work for hire made for U.S. News and World Repor 408
Image *Source:* https://en.wikipedia.org/w/index.php?title=File:Wikisource-logo.svg *License:* Creative Commons Attribution-Sharealike 3.0 *Contributors:* ChrisiPK, Guillom, INeverCry, Jarekt, JuTa, Leyo, Lokal Profil, MichaelMaggs, NielsF, Rei-artur, Rocket000, Romaine, Steinsplitter 411
Image *Source:* https://en.wikipedia.org/w/index.php?title=File:PikiWiki_Israel_4220_Israel_Defense_Forces.jpg *License:* Creative Commons Attribution 2.5 *Contributors:* גולדשמידט דני 412
Image *Source:* https://en.wikipedia.org/w/index.php?title=File:Flag_of_Lebanon.svg *License:* Public Domain *Contributors:* Traced based on the CIA World Factbook with some modification done to the colours based on information at Vexilla mund 412
Image *Source:* https://en.wikipedia.org/w/index.php?title=File:Flag_of_Palestine_-_short_triangle.svg *License:* Public Domain *Contributors:* Orionist 412
Figure 169 *Source:* https://en.wikipedia.org/w/index.php?title=File:BlueLine.jpg *License:* Creative Commons Attribution-Sharealike 2.5 *Contributors:* 99of9 / * The map is made by Thomas Blomberg using the UNIFIL map, deployment as of July 2006 as source. 415
Figure 170 *Source:* https://en.wikipedia.org/w/index.php?title=File:UNIFIL_in_lebanon_1981.jpg *License:* Creative Commons Attribution-Sharealike 2.0 *Contributors:* Marco K. from Hollanda 417
Image *Source:* https://en.wikipedia.org/w/index.php?title=File:Lebanese_Army,_Beirut,_Lebanon_1982.jpg *License:* Creative Commons Attribution 2.0 *Contributors:* James Case from Philadelphia, Mississippi, U.S.A. 418
Image *Source:* https://en.wikipedia.org/w/index.php?title=File:Forces_Libanaises_Flag.svg *License:* Attribution *Contributors:* Oren neu dag . 418
Image *Source:* https://en.wikipedia.org/w/index.php?title=File:Flag_of_Kataeb_Party.svg *License:* Creative Commons Attribution-Sharealike 3.0 *Contributors:* User:MrPenguin20 418
Image *Source:* https://en.wikipedia.org/w/index.php?title=File:Al-Tanzim_logo.png *License:* Public Domain *Contributors:* Al-Tanzim_logo.jpg: Original uploader was Salimzwein at en.wikipedia derivative work: Kobac (talk) 418
Image *Source:* https://en.wikipedia.org/w/index.php?title=File:Flag_of_Syria.svg *License:* Public Domain *Contributors:* see below 418
Image *Source:* https://en.wikipedia.org/w/index.php?title=File:Flag_of_the_Amal_Movement.svg *License:* Public Domain *Contributors:* Lexicon 418
Figure 171 *Source:* https://en.wikipedia.org/w/index.php?title=File:Israeli_troops_in_south_Lebanon_(1982).jpg *License:* Creative Commons Attribution-ShareAlike 3.0 Unported *Contributors:* BotMultichill, Bukvoed, FunkMonk, Huldra, MGA73bot2, OgreBot 2, Steinsplitter, TheCuriousGnome, חובבשירה, 2 anonymous edits 428
Figure 172 *Source:* https://en.wikipedia.org/w/index.php?title=File:GunfireTarget5-17June1982.png *License:* Creative Commons Attribution-Sharealike 3.0 *Contributors:* Geagea, OgreBot 2, Poliocretes, צהוב קודקוד בריאן, ... 429
Figure 173 *Source:* https://en.wikipedia.org/w/index.php?title=File:Syrian_Tank_burning_in_Tzuk_Track.jpg *License:* GNU Free Documentation License *Contributors:* Avneref 431
Figure 174 *Source:* https://en.wikipedia.org/w/index.php?title=File:Destroyed_MEA_aircraft_1982.jpg *License:* Public Domain *Contributors:* PHAN ROBERT FEARY 433
Figure 175 *Source:* https://en.wikipedia.org/w/index.php?title=File:AntiSAMStrike.png *License:* Creative Commons Attribution-Sharealike 2.5 *Contributors:* user:Nehemia G 435
Figure 176 *Source:* https://en.wikipedia.org/w/index.php?title=File:Romach4.5Leb91982.jpg *License:* Creative Commons Attribution-Sharealike 3.0 *Contributors:* Flayer, Geagea, Poliocretes, צהוב קודקוד 436
Figure 177 *Source:* https://en.wikipedia.org/w/index.php?title=File:Lebanon_PLO_ammunition_stadium_1982.jpg *License:* Public Domain *Contributors:* PHAN ROBERT FEARY 437
Figure 178 *Source:* https://en.wikipedia.org/w/index.php?title=File:Masada_cobra.jpg *Contributors:* Original uploader was אסף.צ at he.wikipedia 439
Figure 179 *Source:* https://en.wikipedia.org/w/index.php?title=File:Merkavah_Tank_of_Tzur_Maor_and_his_Crew.jpg *License:* Creative Commons Attribution-Sharealike 3.0 *Contributors:* User:Avneref 440
Figure 180 *Source:* https://en.wikipedia.org/w/index.php?title=File:Merkava-1-latrun-1.jpg *License:* Creative Commons Attribution 2.5 *Contributors:* User:Bukvoed 442
Figure 181 *Source:* https://en.wikipedia.org/w/index.php?title=File:Syrian_team_with_Milan.jpg *License:* Public Domain *Contributors:* FlickreviewR, L'amateur d'aéroplanes, Marco Plassio, Ominae, SkoraPobeda, 1 anonymous edits 443

Figure 182 *Source:* https://en.wikipedia.org/w/index.php?title=File:Syrian_SAM.jpg *License:* Public Domain *Contributors:* BotMultichill, Brakeet, Bukvoed, High Contrast, Nudve~commonswiki, SuperTank17, 1 anonymous edits 443

Figure 183 *Source:* https://en.wikipedia.org/w/index.php?title=File:Lebanese_Army_APC,_Beirut_1982.jpg *License:* Creative Commons Attribution 2.0 *Contributors:* James Case from Philadelphia, Mississippi, U.S.A. 444

Figure 184 *Source:* https://en.wikipedia.org/w/index.php?title=File:Civil_war_Lebanon_map_1983a.gif *License:* GNU Free Documentation License *Contributors:* uk:User:Oleksii0 451

Figure 185 *Source:* https://en.wikipedia.org/w/index.php?title=File:Ras_biada_south_lebanon.jpg *License:* Creative Commons Attribution-Sharealike 3.0 *Contributors:* User:Oren1973 451

Figure 186 *Source:* https://en.wikipedia.org/w/index.php?title=File:Shakuf_El-Hardun_military_post_in_south_lebanon.jpg *License:* Creative Commons Attribution-Sharealike 3.0 *Contributors:* User:Oren1973 452

Figure 187 *Source:* https://en.wikipedia.org/w/index.php?title=File:Litani_river_lebanon.jpg *License:* Creative Commons Attribution-Sharealike 3.0 *Contributors:* User:Oren1973 452

Figure 188 *Source:* https://en.wikipedia.org/w/index.php?title=File:Beaufortnorthern_military_post_south_lebanon_1995.jpg *License:* Creative Commons Attribution-Sharealike 3.0 *Contributors:* User:Oren1973 453

Figure 189 *Source:* https://en.wikipedia.org/w/index.php?title=File:Aaichiye_to_Rayhan_military_patrol_in_south_lebanon.jpg *License:* Creative Commons Attribution-Sharealike 3.0 *Contributors:* User:Oren1973 453

Image *Source:* https://en.wikipedia.org/w/index.php?title=File:PD-icon.svg *License:* Public Domain *Contributors:* Alex.muller, Anomie, Anonymous Dissident, CBM, Jo-Jo Eumerus, MBisanz, PBS, Quadell, Rocket000, Strangerer, Timotheus Canens, 1 anonymous edits 458

Image *Source:* https://en.wikipedia.org/w/index.php?title=File:Military_post_birkat_hukban_south_lebanon.jpg *License:* Creative Commons Attribution-Sharealike 3.0 *Contributors:* User:Oren1973 467

Image *Source:* https://en.wikipedia.org/w/index.php?title=File:InfoboxHez.PNG *Contributors:* User:Khaerr 467

Image *Source:* https://en.wikipedia.org/w/index.php?title=File:Flag_of_the_Lebanese_Communist_Party.svg *License:* Public Domain *Contributors:* BotMultichill, Cycn, FAEP, File Upload Bot (Magnus Manske), Fry1989, Homo lupus, MichaelFreyTool, Netanel h, OgreBot 2, Sarang, 2 anonymous edits 467

Figure 190 *Source:* https://en.wikipedia.org/w/index.php?title=File:BlueLine.jpg *License:* Creative Commons Attribution-Sharealike 2.5 *Contributors:* 99of9 / * The map is made by Thomas Blomberg using the UNIFIL map, deployment as of July 2006 as source. 468

Figure 191 *Source:* https://en.wikipedia.org/w/index.php?title=File:Civil_war_Lebanon_map_1983a.gif *License:* GNU Free Documentation License *Contributors:* uk:User:Oleksii0 471

Figure 192 *Source:* https://en.wikipedia.org/w/index.php?title=File:Ras_biada_south_lebanon.jpg *License:* Creative Commons Attribution-Sharealike 3.0 *Contributors:* User:Oren1973 472

Figure 193 *Source:* https://en.wikipedia.org/w/index.php?title=File:IDF_military_patrol_near_ayshiyeh_Lebanon.jpg *License:* Creative Commons Attribution-Sharealike 3.0 *Contributors:* User:Oren1973 473

Figure 194 *Source:* https://en.wikipedia.org/w/index.php?title=File:Israeli_tank_position_in_Shamis_al_urqub_near_Aaichiye_sounth_lebanon_1997.jpg *License:* Creative Commons Attribution-Sharealike 3.0 *Contributors:* User:Oren1973 473

Figure 195 *Source:* https://en.wikipedia.org/w/index.php?title=File:Shakuf_El-Hardun_military_post_in_south_lebanon.jpg *License:* Creative Commons Attribution-Sharealike 3.0 *Contributors:* User:Oren1973 474

Figure 196 *Source:* https://en.wikipedia.org/w/index.php?title=File:Military_post_birkat_hukan_south_lebanon.jpg *License:* Creative Commons Attribution-Sharealike 3.0 *Contributors:* User:Oren1973 475

Figure 197 *Source:* https://en.wikipedia.org/w/index.php?title=File:Khardala_Bridge_dec_1988.jpg *License:* Creative Commons Attribution-Sharealike 3.0 *Contributors:* Torw 476

Figure 198 *Source:* https://en.wikipedia.org/w/index.php?title=File:Aaichiye_to_Rayhan_military_patrol_in_south_lebanon.jpg *License:* Creative Commons Attribution-Sharealike 3.0 *Contributors:* User:Oren1973 477

Figure 199 *Source:* https://en.wikipedia.org/w/index.php?title=File:Beaufortnorthern_military_post_south_lebanon_1995.jpg *License:* Creative Commons Attribution-Sharealike 3.0 *Contributors:* User:Oren1973 477

Figure 200 *Source:* https://en.wikipedia.org/w/index.php?title=File:Beaufort_Castle_IDF_Military_post_south_Lebanon.jpg *Contributors:* User:Oren1973 478

Figure 201 *Source:* https://en.wikipedia.org/w/index.php?title=File:Carcom_IDF_military_post_in_Lebanon_1998.jpg *Contributors:* User:Oren1973 478

Figure 202 *Source:* https://en.wikipedia.org/w/index.php?title=File:IDF_tank_near_Shreife_IDF_military_post_in_lebanon.jpg *Contributors:* User:Oren1973 479

Figure 203 *Source:* https://en.wikipedia.org/w/index.php?title=File:Galagalit_IDF_military_patrol_south_lebanon.jpg *License:* Creative Commons Attribution-Sharealike 3.0 *Contributors:* User:Oren1973 479

Figure 204 *Source:* https://en.wikipedia.org/w/index.php?title=File:South_leb_army_hezbo_khomemi.JPG *License:* Public Domain *Contributors:* Articseahorse, Brakeet, Chyah, Faigl.ladislav, File Upload Bot (Magnus Manske), Geagea, Huldra, OgreBot 2, SuperTank17 483

Figure 205 *Source:* https://en.wikipedia.org/w/index.php?title=File:Israel_outpost.JPG *License:* Public domain *Contributors:* File Upload Bot (Magnus Manske), Jwh, OgreBot 2, Rodhullandemu 485

Figure 206 *Source:* https://en.wikipedia.org/w/index.php?title=File:IDF_bedouin_memorial_wall.jpg *License:* Creative Commons Attribution-Sharealike 3.0 *Contributors:* User:Oren1973 486

Image *Source:* https://en.wikipedia.org/w/index.php?title=File:Jabalya1988roadblock.jpg *License:* Creative Commons Attribution-Sharealike 3.0 *Contributors:* יעקב 486

Image *Source:* https://en.wikipedia.org/w/index.php?title=File:Flag_of_Hamas.svg *License:* Public Domain *Contributors:* Guilherme Paula, Oren neu dag 487

Image *Source:* https://en.wikipedia.org/w/index.php?title=File:Flag_of_the_Islamic_Jihad_Movement_in_Palestine.svg *License:* Creative Commons Attribution-Sharealike 3.0 *Contributors:* User:MrPenguin20 487

Image *Source:* https://en.wikipedia.org/w/index.php?title=File:Flag_of_Iraq_(1991-2004).svg *Contributors:* - 487

Figure 207 *Source:* https://en.wikipedia.org/w/index.php?title=File:Intifada_erase_slogan.jpg *License:* Creative Commons Attribution-Sharealike 3.0 *Contributors:* יעקב 491

Figure 208 *Source:* https://en.wikipedia.org/w/index.php?title=File:TireNail1-2.jpg *License:* Creative Commons Attribution-Sharealike 3.0 *Contributors:* Etan J. Tal 492

Image *Source:* https://en.wikipedia.org/w/index.php?title=File:Israel-Palestine_peace.svg *License:* Creative Commons Attribution-Sharealike 3.0 *Contributors:* User:Wickey-nl 501

Image *Source:* https://en.wikipedia.org/w/index.php?title=File:RabinSquare.jpg *License:* GNU Free Documentation License *Contributors:* Cccc3333 at en.wikipedia 511

Figure 209 *Source:* https://en.wikipedia.org/w/index.php?title=File:Flickr_-_Government_Press_Office_(GPO)_-_THE_FAMILY_OF_PM_YITZHAK_RABIN_AT_HIS_FUNERAL.jpg *License:* Creative Commons Attribution-Sharealike 3.0 *Contributors:* DGtal, Geagea, Ijon, Illegitimate Barrister, Matanya, Ranbar, Tomtom, רדיומן 512

Figure 210 *Source:* https://en.wikipedia.org/w/index.php?title=File:Rabin_Grave.jpg *License:* Creative Commons Attribution 2.0 *Contributors:* SqueakyMarmot 513

Figure 211 *Source:* https://en.wikipedia.org/w/index.php?title=File:Kikar_rabin.jpg *License:* Copyrighted free use *Contributors:* Avi1111, Ori~, Poliocretes, Shalom, Wst, Yuval Y, יעל י 514

Figure 212 *Source:* https://en.wikipedia.org/w/index.php?title=File:Rabins'_Grave.JPG *License:* Creative Commons Attribution-ShareAlike 3.0 Unported *Contributors:* User:Pharos 515

Figure 213 *Source:* https://en.wikipedia.org/w/index.php?title=File:ShalomHaver_-_Yitzhak_Rabin's_Funeral.ogv *License:* Public Domain *Contributors:* ערן 516

Image *Source:* https://en.wikipedia.org/w/index.php?title=File:Wikiquote-logo.svg *License:* Public Domain *Contributors:* Rei-artur 517

Figure 214 *Source:* https://en.wikipedia.org/w/index.php?title=File:Video_Recording_of_Photo_Opportunity_at_Camp_David_-_NARA_-_6037428.ogv *License:* Public Domain *Contributors:* ATX-NL, Addy Rozenbaum, Archwayh, Ldorfman, Michael Barera, Reguyla, SecretName101, Senapa, Xgeorg, 1 anonymous edits 521

Figure 215 *Source:* https://en.wikipedia.org/w/index.php?title=File:Arafat&Clinton&Barak.jpg *License:* Public Domain *Contributors:* Sharon Farmer 521

Image *Source:* https://en.wikipedia.org/w/index.php?title=File:Flickr_-_Israel_Defense_Forces_-_Standing_Guard_in_Nablus.jpg *License:* Creative Commons Attribution-Sharealike 2.0 *Contributors:* Israel Defense Forces 533

Figure 216 *Source:* https://en.wikipedia.org/w/index.php?title=File:Karin_A_weapons.jpg *License:* Public Domain *Contributors:* Aschroet, Cecil, DGtal, Illegitimate Barrister, Streamline8988, Talmoryair, 2 anonymous edits 544

Figure 217 *Source:* https://en.wikipedia.org/w/index.php?title=File:IDF-D9L003.jpg *License:* Creative Commons Attribution-Sharealike 3.0 *Contributors:* Lior34 546

Figure 218 *Source:* https://en.wikipedia.org/w/index.php?title=File:Autobus_v_Haifě.jpg *License:* Public Domain *Contributors:* B. Železník 547

Figure 219 *Source:* https://en.wikipedia.org/w/index.php?title=File:Caterpillar1133.jpg *License:* Creative Commons Attribution 2.0 *Contributors:* joeskillet 549

Figure 220 *Source:* https://en.wikipedia.org/w/index.php?title=File:Flickr_-_Israel_Defense_Forces_-_40_Kilogram_Explosive_Found_At_Bottom_of_Tunnel.jpg *License:* Creative Commons Attribution-Sharealike 3.0 *Contributors:* Matanya, Netanel h 551
Figure 221 *Source:* https://en.wikipedia.org/w/index.php?title=File:Intifada_deaths.svg *License:* Public Domain *Contributors:* Timeshifter ..560
Figure 222 *Source:* https://en.wikipedia.org/w/index.php?title=File:Rockets_and_mortar_February_2009.JPG *License:* Public Domain *Contributors:* Thevoyftp 564
Figure 223 *Source:* https://en.wikipedia.org/w/index.php?title=File:IDF-D9-Zachi-Evenor-001.jpg *License:* Creative Commons Attribution 2.0 *Contributors:* Ain92, Closeapple, FAEP, Flayer, FlickreviewR, Matanya, MathKnight, MathKnight-at-TAU, Poliocretes, Triggerhippie4, 1 anonymous edits 567
Figure 224 *Source:* https://en.wikipedia.org/w/index.php?title=File:AH-64Apache004.jpg *License:* Creative Commons Attribution-ShareAlike 3.0 Unported *Contributors:* MathKnight 568
Figure 225 *Source:* https://en.wikipedia.org/w/index.php?title=File:Barrier_route_July_2011.png *License:* Creative Commons Attribution 3.0 *Contributors:* User:Wickey-nl 573
Figure 226 *Source:* https://en.wikipedia.org/w/index.php?title=File:Jerusalem-barrier_June_2007-OCHAoPt.jpeg *License:* UN map *Contributors:* Timeshifter, Wickey-nl 573
Figure 227 *Source:* https://en.wikipedia.org/w/index.php?title=File:AbuDisWall.jpg *License:* GNU Free Documentation License *Contributors:* Zero 574
Figure 228 *Source:* https://en.wikipedia.org/w/index.php?title=File:Bethlehem_Wall_Graffiti_-_Ich_bin_ein_Berliner.jpg *License:* Creative Commons Attribution-Sharealike 3.0,2.5,2.0,1.0 *Contributors:* Marc Venezia 575
Image *Source:* https://en.wikipedia.org/w/index.php?title=File:Loudspeaker.svg *License:* Public Domain *Contributors:* User:Dbenbenn, User:Optimager, User:Tsca, User:Dbenbenn, User:Optimager, User:Tsca, User:Dbenbenn, User:Optimager, User:Tsca 574
Figure 229 *Source:* https://en.wikipedia.org/w/index.php?title=File:BarbedWireFence1.jpg *License:* Creative Commons Attribution 3.0 *Contributors:* Etan J. Tal 575
Figure 230 *Source:* https://en.wikipedia.org/w/index.php?title=File:West_Bank_Fence_South_Hebron.JPG *License:* Public Domain *Contributors:* User:Eman 576
Figure 231 *Source:* https://en.wikipedia.org/w/index.php?title=File:Pesah_213.jpg *License:* GNU Free Documentation License *Contributors:* File Upload Bot (Magnus Manske), MGA73bot2, OgreBot 2, Wouterhagens 577
Figure 232 *Source:* https://en.wikipedia.org/w/index.php?title=File:Palestinian_children_and_Israeli_wall.jpg *License:* Creative Commons Attribution 2.0 *Contributors:* Picture taken by Justin McIntosh, ...581
Figure 233 *Source:* https://en.wikipedia.org/w/index.php?title=File:Israel_Wall_in_London.JPG *License:* Creative Commons Attribution-Sharealike 3.0 *Contributors:* User:Timothy Titus 588
Figure 234 *Source:* https://en.wikipedia.org/w/index.php?title=File:Banksy,_gandhi_graffiti_on_apartheid_wall.jpg *License:* Public Domain *Contributors:* Szater 593
Figure 235 *Source:* https://en.wikipedia.org/w/index.php?title=File:WestBankBarrier443.jpg *License:* Creative Commons Attribution 3.0 *Contributors:* Etan J. Tal 593
Figure 236 *Source:* https://en.wikipedia.org/w/index.php?title=File:Inside_the_West_Bank_on_the_West_Bank_barrier.JPG *License:* Creative Commons Attribution-Sharealike 3.0 *Contributors:* User:Joshua Doubek 597
Figure 237 *Source:* https://en.wikipedia.org/w/index.php?title=File:West_Bank_Barrier_Palestine_side.JPG *License:* Creative Commons Attribution-Sharealike 3.0 *Contributors:* User:Joshua Doubek 597
Figure 238 *Source:* https://en.wikipedia.org/w/index.php?title=File:Gaza_strip_may_2005.jpg *License:* Public Domain *Contributors:* Orrling, Timeshifter 604
Figure 239 *Source:* https://en.wikipedia.org/w/index.php?title=File:Flickr_-_Israel_Defense_Forces_-_Israeli_and_Palestinian_Coordination_Effort.jpg *License:* Creative Commons Attribution-Sharealike 2.0 *Contributors:* Israel Defense Forces 610
Figure 240 *Source:* https://en.wikipedia.org/w/index.php?title=File:Flickr_-_Israel_Defense_Forces_-_The_Evacuation_of_Kfar_Darom_(4).jpg *License:* Creative Commons Attribution-Sharealike 2.0 *Contributors:* Israel Defense Forces 611
Figure 241 *Source:* https://en.wikipedia.org/w/index.php?title=File:Flickr_-_Israel_Defense_Forces_-_The_Evacuation_of_Kfar_Darom_(16).jpg *License:* Creative Commons Attribution-Sharealike 2.0 *Contributors:* Israel Defense Forces 612
Figure 242 *Source:* https://en.wikipedia.org/w/index.php?title=File:Flickr_-_Israel_Defense_Forces_-_The_Evacuation_of_Bedolach_(22).jpg *License:* Creative Commons Attribution-Sharealike 2.0 *Contributors:* Israel Defense Forces 612
Figure 243 *Source:* https://en.wikipedia.org/w/index.php?title=File:Elley-Sinai-refugee-camp01.jpg *License:* Creative Commons Attribution-Sharealike 2.5 *Contributors:* User:MathKnight 616
Figure 244 *Source:* https://en.wikipedia.org/w/index.php?title=File:Nezer_Hazani_protest_in_Tel_Aviv.jpg *License:* Creative Commons Attribution-ShareAlike 3.0 Unported *Contributors:* User:ToastieIL 617
Image *Source:* https://en.wikipedia.org/w/index.php?title=File:Wikinews-logo.svg *License:* Creative Commons Attribution-Sharealike 3.0 *Contributors:* Vectorized by Simon 01:05, 2 August 2006 (UTC) Updated by Time3000 17 April 2007 to use official Wikinews colours and ap 631
Figure 245 *Source:* https://en.wikipedia.org/w/index.php?title=File:Gilad_Shalit_on_Hamas_poster.jpg *License:* Creative Commons Attribution 2.0 *Contributors:* Tom Spender 634
Figure 246 *Source:* https://en.wikipedia.org/w/index.php?title=File:Flickr_-_Israel_Defense_Forces_-_Gilad_Shalit_Salutes_Israel_Prime_Minister_Benjamin_Netanyahu.jpg *License:* Creative Commons Attribution-Sharealike 2.0 *Contributors:* Israel Defense Forces 639
Image *Source:* https://en.wikipedia.org/w/index.php?title=File:Israel_Housing_Protests_Tel_Aviv_August_6_2011b.jpg *License:* Creative Commons Attribution-Sharealike 2.0 *Contributors:* Eman, FlickreviewR, TeleComNasSprVen 641
Figure 247 *Source:* https://en.wikipedia.org/w/index.php?title=File:Real_Estate_Protest_in_Tel_Aviv_25.7.2011_1.jpg *License:* Creative Commons Attribution-Sharealike 3.0 *Contributors:* User:Itzuvit 645
Figure 248 *Source:* https://en.wikipedia.org/w/index.php?title=File:Beer_Sheva_2011_housing_protests812.jpg *License:* Creative Commons Zero *Contributors:* User:Eman 646
Image *Source:* https://en.wikipedia.org/w/index.php?title=File:March_of_the_million_rallies_in_tel_aviv_1.jpg *License:* Creative Commons Attribution-Sharealike 2.0 *Contributors:* Closeapple, Djembayz, FlickreviewR, Lymantria, MGA73bot2, ProfessorX 647
Image *Source:* https://en.wikipedia.org/w/index.php?title=File:March_of_the_million_rallies_in_tel_aviv.jpg *License:* Creative Commons Attribution-Sharealike 2.0 *Contributors:* Djembayz, FlickreviewR, Hic et nunc, Lymantria, MGA73bot2, Mattes, Ynhockey, 1 anonymous edits ...647
Figure 249 *Source:* https://en.wikipedia.org/w/index.php?title=File:Israel_social_justice_protests_Rabin_Square_Tel_aviv_29_october_2011.jpeg *License:* Creative Commons Attribution-Sharealike 2.0 *Contributors:* avivi 648
Figure 250 *Source:* https://en.wikipedia.org/w/index.php?title=File:ALL_GOOG_NIGHT.JPG *Contributors:* User:Joseph Zernik 649
Figure 251 *Source:* https://en.wikipedia.org/w/index.php?title=File:Daphne_Leef_דפני_ליף.jpg *License:* Creative Commons Attribution-Sharealike 3.0 *Contributors:* User:Rafimich 652
Figure 252 *Source:* https://en.wikipedia.org/w/index.php?title=File:Demonstration_against_the_housing_prices_in_Haifa_30.7.2011_–_Horev_Square,_Ahuza_(36).JPG *License:* Creative Commons Attribution-Sharealike 3.0 *Contributors:* Hanay 654
Figure 253 *Source:* https://en.wikipedia.org/w/index.php?title=File:Discours_lors_de_la_manifestation_pour_les_habitants_du_sud_de_Tel-Aviv.jpg *License:* Creative Commons Attribution-Sharealike 3.0 *Contributors:* User:Roi Boshi 654
Image *Source:* https://en.wikipedia.org/w/index.php?title=File:The_home_of_the_Kware'_family,_after_it_was_bombed_by_the_military.jpg *Contributors:* Bobamnertiopsis, Russavia, Sean.hoyland, TheRealHuldra, بدارين 660
Image *Source:* https://en.wikipedia.org/w/index.php?title=File:Iron_Dome_in_Operation_Protective_Edge.jpg *License:* Creative Commons Attribution 2.0 *Contributors:* Israel Defense Forces from Israel 660
Image *Source:* https://en.wikipedia.org/w/index.php?title=File:Flag_of_the_Israel_Defense_Forces.svg *License:* Creative Commons Attribution-Sharealike 3.0 *Contributors:* User:Meronim 661
Image *Source:* https://en.wikipedia.org/w/index.php?title=File:Israel_Air_Force_Flag.svg *Contributors:* - 661
Image *Source:* https://en.wikipedia.org/w/index.php?title=File:Naval_Ensign_of_Israel.svg *License:* Public Domain *Contributors:* User:Denelson83, User:Makaristos 661
Figure 254 *Source:* https://en.wikipedia.org/w/index.php?title=File:Histogram_of_Palestinian_rocket_attacks_on_Israel_per_day,_2014.png *Contributors:* User:Kozrty 663
Figure 255 *Source:* https://en.wikipedia.org/w/index.php?title=File:Gaza_closure_December_2012.jpg *License:* Creative Commons Attribution 3.0 *Contributors:* User:Wickey-nl 666
Figure 256 *Source:* https://en.wikipedia.org/w/index.php?title=File:PikiWiki_Israel_29526_Israel_Defense_Forces.JPG *License:* Creative Commons Attribution 2.5 *Contributors:* udi Steinwell 666
Figure 257 *Source:* https://en.wikipedia.org/w/index.php?title=File:Weapons_Found_in_Khan_Yunis,_Gaza_(14736403021).jpg *License:* Creative Commons Attribution 2.0 *Contributors:* Israel Defense Forces from Israel 667
Figure 258 *Source:* https://en.wikipedia.org/w/index.php?title=File:Street_in_Ramallah_after_IDF_raid_during_Operation_Brother's_Keeper_June_2014_2.jpg *License:* Creative Commons Attribution-Sharealike 3.0 *Contributors:* User:Azzam Talahmi 669
Figure 259 *Source:* https://en.wikipedia.org/w/index.php?title=File:SderotBurningFactory1.JPG *License:* Creative Commons Attribution-Sharealike 3.0 *Contributors:* User:NatanFlayer 670

Figure 260 *Source:* https://en.wikipedia.org/w/index.php?title=File:Map-of-rockets-launches-from-gaza-from-2014-07-08-to-2014-07-31_2.jpg *License:* Creative Commons Attribution-Sharealike 2.0 *Contributors:* User:Neo139 673
Figure 261 *Source:* https://en.wikipedia.org/w/index.php?title=File:Armored_Corps_Operate_Near_the_Gaza_Border_(14754144934).jpg *License:* Creative Commons Attribution 2.0 *Contributors:* Israel Defense Forces 673
Figure 262 *Source:* https://en.wikipedia.org/w/index.php?title=File:Israeli_Strikes_on_North_Gaza.jpg *Contributors:* User:Nrg800 676
Figure 263 *Source:* https://en.wikipedia.org/w/index.php?title=File:20140805_beit_hanun8.jpg *Contributors:* Wickey-nl, بدارين 677
Figure 264 *Source:* https/en.wikipedia.org *Contributors:* Ashashyou, Monopoly31121993, Sean.hoyland, TheRealHuldra, بدارين, 1 anonymous edits 677
Figure 265 *Source:* https://en.wikipedia.org/w/index.php?title=File:Operation_Protective_Edge_(14665449614).jpg *License:* Creative Commons Attribution 2.0 *Contributors:* Israel Defense Forces from Israel 679
Figure 266 *Source:* https://en.wikipedia.org/w/index.php?title=File:Shelter_sign_in_Ben_Gurion_Airport_during_Operation_Protective_Edge.jpg *License:* Creative Commons Attribution-Sharealike 3.0 *Contributors:* OgreBot 2, Triggerhippie4 680
Figure 267 *Source:* https://en.wikipedia.org/w/index.php?title=File:Al-Quds_2014_Berlin_20140725_173841.jpg *Contributors:* Denis Barthel 685
Figure 268 *Source:* https://en.wikipedia.org/w/index.php?title=File:Tzuk-Eytan-Helsinki-protest-1.jpg *Contributors:* Hanay, MathKnight, 1 anonymous edits 686
Figure 269 *Source:* https://en.wikipedia.org/w/index.php?title=File:MyIsraelFacebook--ProTzukEytan001.jpg *License:* Creative Commons Attribution 3.0 *Contributors:* JuTa, MathKnight, בריאן 688
Figure 270 *Source:* https://en.wikipedia.org/w/index.php?title=File:Kindergarten_in_Kiryat_Ono_in_August_2014.jpg *Contributors:* User:Vcohen 689
Figure 271 *Source:* https://en.wikipedia.org/w/index.php?title=File:Peace_demonstration_in_Tel_Aviv.jpg *License:* Creative Commons Attribution-Sharealike 3.0 *Contributors:* User:Guy Butavia 689
Figure 272 *Source:* https://en.wikipedia.org/w/index.php?title=File:Weapons_Found_in_a_Child's_Room_in_Gaza_(14568987517).jpg *License:* Creative Commons Attribution 2.0 *Contributors:* Israel Defense Forces 695
Figure 273 *Source:* https://en.wikipedia.org/w/index.php?title=File:Destroyed_ambulance_in_the_CIty_of_Shijaiyah_in_the_Gaza_Strip.jpg *Contributors:* User:Boris Niehaus 697
Figure 274 *Source:* https://en.wikipedia.org/w/index.php?title=File:House_in_Israel_Destroyed_by_Hamas_Rocket_(14713208821).jpg *License:* Creative Commons Attribution 2.0 *Contributors:* Israel Defense Forces from Israel 700
Figure 275 *Source:* https://en.wikipedia.org/w/index.php?title=File:20140805_beit_hanun7.jpg *Contributors:* Triggerhippie4, Wickey-nl, بدارين 704
Figure 276 *Source:* https://en.wikipedia.org/w/index.php?title=File:Rockets_from_gaza_(en).png *Contributors:* User:Dekel E 709
Figure 277 *Source:* https://en.wikipedia.org/w/index.php?title=File:IDF_Soldiers_Uncover_Tunnels_in_Gaza_(14513059999).jpg *License:* Creative Commons Attribution-Sharealike 2.0 *Contributors:* Israel Defense Forces from Israel 710
Figure 278 *Source:* https://en.wikipedia.org/w/index.php?title=File:Artillery_Corps_in_Gaza_(14550733300)a.jpg *License:* Creative Commons Attribution 2.0 *Contributors:* Caismeat, MathKnight, Sean.hoyland, Tm 712
Figure 279 *Source:* https://en.wikipedia.org/w/index.php?title=File:John_Kerry_and_Benjamin_Netanyahu_July_2014.jpg *License:* Public Domain *Contributors:* FlickreviewR 2, Geagea, MathKnight-at-TAU, Tennisace101, 1 anonymous edits 714

License

Creative Commons Attribution-Share Alike 3.0
//creativecommons.org/licenses/by-sa/3.0/

Index

.380 ACP, 514

A-4 Skyhawk, 257, 307, 310, 351
Aaichiye, 473, 477
Abba Eban, 76, 235
Abbas al-Musawi, 419, 467, 476
ABC Radio National, 734
Abd Al Aziz Awda, 534
Abd al-Karim Qasim, 180
Abd al-Qadir al-Husayni, 5
Abdel Aziz al-Rantissi, 534, 550
Abdel Fattah el-Sisi, 668
Abdel Ghani el-Gamasy, 236, 291, 363
Abdel Hakim Amer, 106, 138, 142, 152, 177, 190, 196, 205, 206
Abdul Karim Obeid, 476
Abdullah Azzam Brigades, 660
Abdullah I of Jordan, 2, 4, 63
Abdul Munim Riad, 190, 246, 252, 259
Abdul Rahman Arif, 190
Abdul Rahman Hassan Azzam, 2, 11
Ablex Publishing, 64
Abraham Rabinovich, 310, 342, 458
Abraham Yoffe, 150
Abu Ageila, 52, 139, 172
Abu-Ageila, 205
Abu Ali Mustafa, 534
Abu Ali Mustapha Brigades, 661
Abu Daoud, 281
Abu Dis, 524, 574, 583, 587
Abu Hasan (boat), 548
Abu Jihad, 494
Abu Nidal, 416, 446
Abu Nidal group, 427
Abu Nidal Organization, 420, 446
Abu Tor, 211, 214
Abu Uwayulah, 139, 143, 147
Abu Zaabal, 256
Academy Award, 287
Academy Award for Best Documentary Feature, 287
AckermanDuVall2000, 755
Acre (city), 7
Acre, Israel, 36

Adam Curtis, 411
Adam Roberts (scholar), 498
Aden, 182
Administrative divisions of the Oslo Accords, 615
Admiral Barjot, 127
Adnan Al-Gashey, 267, 273
Adnan al-Ghoul, 552
Adolf Hitler, 264
Advisory opinion of the ICJ, 584
Aerial refueling, 381
Aero L-29 Delfín, 359
Aéronavale, 155
Aérospatiale SA 321 Super Frelon, 359
Afif Ahmed Hamid, 267, 283
Afula, 28, 210, 647
AGM-45 Shrike, 359
AGM-65 Maverick, 352
Agranat Commission, 301, 365
Agreement on Disengagement between Israel and Syria, 364
Agreement on Movement and Access, 509
AH-1 Cobra, 439, 440
AH-64 Apache, 407, 476, 568
Aharon Barak, 401, 403
Aharon Yariv, 279, 363
Ahmad Ismail Ali, 246, 291, 312
Ahmad Saadat, 534
Ahmed Ali al-Mwawi, 2, 19
Ahmed Bouchiki, 279
Ahmed Jibril, 543
Ahmed Qurei, 503, 549
Ahmed Yasin, 534
Ahmed Yassin, 550
Ahron Bregman, 63, 183, 411, 417, 532, 720
AIM-7 Sparrow, 359
AIM-9 Sidewinder, 359
Ain al-Hilweh, 431
Ain es Saheb airstrike, 549
Airbus A300, 377, 378
Aircraft carrier, 151
Aircraft hijacking, 376, 378
Aircraft registration, 377, 378
Air France, 15, 376, 377

801

Air interdiction, 309
Airlift, 350, 351
Air-raid shelter, 713
Air superiority, 34
Air supremacy, 191, 198
Ajalon, 9
Ajloun, 196, 211, 345
A. J. P. Taylor, 160
AK47, 384
AK-47, 196, 220, 270, 359, 384
AKM, 265, 359
Akram Haniyah, 530
Alan Dershowitz, 34, 527, 771
Al-Aqsa Intifada, 526
Al-Aqsa Martyrs Brigades, 534, 547, 554, 558, 561, 565, 579, 660, 661
Al-Aqsa Mosque, 228, 523, 535, 538
Al Aqsa TV, 707
Al-Ayyam (Ramallah), 530
Albert Mandler, 204, 221, 291
Al-Dawayima, 78
Alea iacta est, 210
Alec Kirkbride, 11
Al-Eizariya, 524, 583
Alexander Haig, 355, 423, 425
Alexandria, 99, 121, 133, 208, 229, 345, 347, 360
Alexandroni Brigade, 15, 28, 30, 53
Alexey Kosygin, 356
Aley District, 455
Al-Faluja, 71
Alfei Menashe, 599
Alfred A. Knopf, 259, 458
Alfred Seidl, 281
Algeria, 117, 277, 281, 290, 352, 357
Algerian War, 60, 178
Al-Hamma Incident, 94
Al-Haq, 707
Al-Hayat, 558
Ali Aslan, 291
Alignment (political party), 365, 462
Ali Hassan Salameh, 279
Al-Issawiya, 84, 214
Alistair Horne, 184
Aliyah, 61, 87, 179, 383
Aliyah Bet, 35
Al Jahra Force, 358
Al Jazeera, 668
Al-Jazeera, 776, 777
Al Jazeera English, 715
Allan Dulles, 170
Allenby Bridge, 231
Allen Dulles, 120, 135
Allies of World War I, 108
All-Palestine Government, 14
All-Palestine Protectorate, 91

All Things Considered, 754
Al-Malkiyya, 30
Al-Manar, 483
Al-Manar TV, 587
Al-Monitor, 777, 778
Al-Mourabitoun, 447
Al-Muzayria, 42
Al-Nasser Salah al-Deen Brigades, 661
Al-Nuqayb, 96
Al-Qaida, 638
Al-Qassam Brigades, 661, 670
Al-Qubab, 42
Al-Quds Al-Arabi, 693
Al-Quds Brigades, 661
Al-Qusaymah, 142
Al Schwimmer, 8
Al-Sharq, 579
Al-Shati (camp), 494, 710
Al-Shifa Hospital, 693
Altalena Affair, 38
Al-Tanzim, 418, 448
Aluf, 365, 380
Amal Movement, 418, 424, 448, 455, 467, 468, 474, 481
Ambush, 565
American Broadcasting Company, 273
American Civil War, 402
American Colony, Jerusalem, 213
American-Israeli Cooperative Enterprise, 234
American Israel Public Affairs Committee, 570, 632
American Jewish Joint Distribution Committee, 61, 179
Aminadav, 95
Amir Eshel, 661
Amitzur Shapira, 267, 283
Amman, 34, 95, 119, 217, 252, 490
Ammunition, 550
Ammunition hill, 213
Amnesty International, 540, 546, 550, 566, 589, 671, 694, 699, 703, 767, 776
Amnon Biran, 380
Amos Malka, 764
Amram Mitzna, 607, 623
AMX 13, 203
AMX-13, 136, 157, 195, 203
Anadolu Agency, 776
Anarchists Against the Wall, 586
Anarchy, 657
Anata, 524
Andreas Baader, 264, 268
André Beaufre, 106, 136, 183
Andre Spitzer, 267, 270, 282, 283
Aneurin Bevan, 162
Anglo-American relations, 296
Anglo-Egyptian Sudan, 2

Anglo-Egyptian Treaty of 1936, 4, 110
Anglo-Egyptian War, 108
Anglo-German Naval Agreement, 165
Anita Shapira, 67
An-Nakhl Fortress, 143, 206
Ansar, Lebanon, 489
Anthony Eden, 105–107, 119, 171, 179
Anthony Hopkins, 389
Anti-aircraft, 447
Anti-aircraft warfare, 196, 359
Anti-Defamation League, 587, 629, 687
Antipatris, 36
Anti-Semitism, 686
Antisemitism in the Arab world, 60, 178
Anti-tank, 551
Anti-tank guided missile, 296, 305
Anti-tank warfare, 305
Antoine Lahad, 412, 467, 483
Anton Fliegerbauer, 283
Antonov An-12, 195, 352, 359
Antonov An-22, 352
Anwar Al-Sadat, 247
Anwar El Sadat, 246, 397, 398, 409
Anwar Sadat, 227, 258, 291, 297, 368, 380, 395, 396, 398, 401, 403, 404, 408, 520
A. N. Wilson, 161, 187
Apartheid, 572, 574
April 2011 Cairo agreement, 664
Aqaba, 20
Aql Hashem, 467, 483
Arab, 277, 399
Arab American Institute, 591
Arab citizens of Israel, 59, 140, 141, 541, 688
Arab Cold War, 110
Arab conspiracy theories, 226
Arab–Israeli conflict, 60, 91, 105, 110, 178, 189, 245, 246, 290, 293, 375, 404, 407
Arabic, 447
Arabic language, 190, 246, 292, 298, 420, 534, 564, 574
Arabic transliteration, 496
Arab-Israeli, 639, 643
Arab Jews, 61, 179
Arab League, 4, 5, 11, 14, 60, 296, 369, 407, 495, 570, 686
Arab League Summit, 570
Arab Legion, 7, 12, 18, 25, 26, 42, 194
Arab Liberation Army, 2, 5, 17, 18, 30, 46
Arab Liberation Front, 446
Arab Peace Initiative, 545, 686
Arabs, 557
Arab Spring, 644, 664
Arab states, 2
Arab world, 62, 106, 293, 369, 564
Arad, Israel, 614, 637
A-Ram, 524

Arcade game, 389
Area C (West Bank), 504
Aref al-Aref, 58, 59
Arieh OSullivan, 631
Ariel (city), 576, 599, 605, 621
Ariel Sharon, 84, 94, 106, 115, 135, 141, 186, 190, 202, 203, 291, 301, 305, 310, 311, 325, 419, 422, 426, 428, 441, 467, 526, 534, 535, 538, 543, 550, 553, 555, 598, 603, 618, 663
Arish, 21, 34, 40, 52, 139, 196, 201, 227, 322
Arkhangelsk, 170
Armed Forces Day (Egypt), 369
Armistice, 56, 71
Armored bulldozer, 546, 568
Armored car (military), 447
Armored Corps (Israel), 17
Armored division, 198
Armored fighting vehicle, 440
Armored fighting vehicles, 439
Armored personnel carrier, 56, 198, 315, 317, 351
Armored personnel carriers, 420
Armored warfare, 305
Armoured bulldozer, 567
Armoured fighting vehicle, 195, 359
Armoured personnel carrier, 195, 341, 359, 384, 467, 548, 550
Arms race, 116
Arms shipments from Czechoslovakia to Israel 1947–1949, 38
Arms shipments from Czechoslovakia to Israel 1947–49, 16
Army of Islam (Gaza Strip), 637
Army of the Holy War, 2, 5
Arnon Soffer, 604, 606
Arnoun, 482
Arthur L. Herman, 176, 187
Artillery, 14, 20, 198, 705
Artillery tanks, 195, 359
Artisan, 62
Aryeh Eldad, 658
Aryeh Shalev, 365
Aryeh Yitzhaki, 613, 614
Asad Ghanma, 190
Asaf Simhoni, 106
Asa Kasher, 694, 702
Asbestos, 618
Ashdod, 25, 51, 54, 347, 428, 550, 646
Ashkelon, 25, 51, 72, 607, 621, 646, 647
Ashkenazi Jews, 659
Ashraf Marwan, 299
Askar (Palestine), 548
Assaf Sharon, 702
As-Saiqa, 444, 446
As-Samu, 96, 192

Assassination, 45
Assassination of Anwar Sadat, 369
Assassination of Yitzhak Rabin, **511**, 517, 536
Assault rifle, 565
Associated Press, 494, 632, 693, 707, 771, 778
Associated University Presses, 64
Association for Civil Rights in Israel, 655
Association for Jewish Theatre, 389
Aswan Dam, 120
Asymmetric warfare, 247
Atef Bseiso, 280
Athens International Airport, 376
Atlanticism, 126
Attack helicopter, 567, 569
At Tiri Incident, 416
Attorney general, 385
At-Tur (Mount of Olives), 524
Augustus Richard Norton, 414
Auschwitz, 76
Austerity, 87
Austerity in Israel, 61, **87**, 179
Autocannons, 447
Avery Brundage, 276
Avia S-199, 8, 16, 25, 32, 56
Aviation Week, 784
Avi Dichter, 534
Avigdor Ben-Gal, 330
Avigdor Kahalani, 330
Avigdor Liberman, 607
Avigdor Lieberman, 690, 700
Avi Shlaim, 59, 66, 67, 417, 426, 459, 498, 721, 753
Avnei Eitan, 621
Avraham Adan, 1, 147, 310, 315
Avraham Dar, 99
Avraham Lanir, 348
Avraham Sela, 59, 67, 230, 411, 459, 757, 762, 765
Avraham Shapira, 628
Avraham Yoffe, 15, 106, 202
Avri Elad, 99
Avro Anson, 31, 56
Awali River, 438, 442, 471
A Wing and a Prayer (film), 63
Ayalon Prison, 101
Ayman Taha, 693
Ayoob Kara, 623
Ayshiyeh, 473
Aziz Sedki, 270
Azores, 350
Azzam Pasha quotation, 11

B-10 recoilless rifle, 196
B-11 recoilless rifle, 196, 359
B-17 Flying Fortress, 56
Baabda, 434

Baalbek, 432, 448
Baal teshuva movement, 229
Baathist Iraq, 290, 487, 534
Bab-el-Mandeb, 346
Baby boom, 228
Bachir Gemayel, 419, 420, 441
Baghdad, 229
Baghdadi Jews, 60, 178
Baghdad Pact, 109, 118
Bahr El-Baqar primary school bombing, 257
Baking, 89
Balance of power (international relations), 296
Balfour Declaration, 3
Ballantine Books, 411
Balqa Governorate, 250
Baltic Sea, 108
Baltim, 345
Bandar bin Sultan, 527
Bandung Conference, 115
Bangalore torpedo, 213
Bangalore torpedoes, 77
Banha, 316
Baniyas, 346
Bank, 87, 461
Bank Hapoalim, 461
Ban Ki-moon, 701, 706
Bank Leumi, 461
Bank Mizrahi-Tfahot, 461
Bank of Israel, 463, 464
Banksy, 593, 594
Bantustan, 523
Baqa al-Gharbiya, 646
Barak Armored Brigade, 331
Barbados, 456
Barbara Castle, 164
Bar-Ilan University, 512
Bar Lev Line, 245, 247, 252, 307
Bar-Lev Line, 319
Barricade, 487
Barry Rubin, 764
Barry Turner (journalist), 163
Bashir Gemayel, 422, 426, 470
Basic Books, 751
Bat Hadar, 621
Bat Hefer, 578, 598
Baton (law enforcement), 494
Battalion, 203
Battir, 599
Battle for Jerusalem (1948), 25
Battle near Majdal, 51
Battle of Abu-Ageila (1967), 202
Battle of Ammunition Hill, 212
Battle of annihilation, 133
Battle of Badr, 298
Battle of Baltim, 344, 345
Battle of Beersheba (1948), 51

Battle of Dien Bien Phu, 180
Battle of Gaza (2007), 664
Battle of Haifa (1948), 59
Battle of Ismailia, 317, 319
Battle of Jerusalem (1948), 15
Battle of Jezzine (1982), 431
Battle of July 12, 40
Battle of Karameh, 250, 251, 259
Battle of Latakia, 343, 344
Battle of Marsa Talamat, 344
Battle of Nirim, 24
Battle of Nitzanim, 25
Battle of Rafah (1948), 52
Battle of Rafah (1949), 21
Battle of Ramat Rachel, 15
Battle of Rumani Coast, 249
Battle of Shujaiyya, 690, 702
Battle of Shujaiyya (2014), 674
Battle of Stalingrad, 177
Battle of Suez, 323
Battle of Sultan Yacoub, 433
Battle of the Beaufort (1982), 430
Battle of the Chinese Farm, 316
Battle of the Sinai (1973), 314
Battle of Yad Mordechai, 24
Battle rifle, 275
Battleship, 151
Battles of Fort Budapest, 309
Battles of Kfar Darom, 24
Battles of Latrun, 15
Battles of Latrun (1948), 34
Battles of the Kinarot Valley, 29
Battles of the Sinai (1948), 52
Bavaria, 274
Baysan, 36
Bayt Nattif, 50
Bazooka, 359
BBC, 187, 517, 574, 693, 754
BBC News, 412, 601, 640, 753, 754, 776, 778
BBC News Online, 715
Beacon Press, 65
Beatrix of the Netherlands, 516
Beaufort Castle, Lebanon, 429, 442
Beaufort (film), 457
Bedolach, 612
Bedolah, 609
Bedouin, 54, 614, 684
Beer Ganim, 621
Beerot Yitzhak, 41
Beersheba, 24, 48, 49, 51, 95, 646, 647, 650
Beer Sheva, 655
Beirut, 182, 279, 281, 345, 420
Beirut-Damascus Highway, 444
Beisan, 7
Beisky Commission, 462
Beitar Jerusalem F.C., 671

Beit Hanoun, 677, 678, 684, 685, 704
Beit Iksa, 599
Beit Jala, 542
Beit Jala raid, 94
Beit Jalla, 94
Beit Lahiya, 685
Beit Sahour, 490
Beit Shean, 647
Beit Shemesh, 647
Beit Susin, 26
Beit Yahoun, 482
Bejski Commission, 465
Bekaa Valley, 429, 443
Bell UH-1, 270
Bell UH-1 Iroquois, 359
Ben-Ami, 720
Ben-Dror Yemini, 659
Benghazi, 376, 378
Ben Gurion, 92, 469
Ben Gurion Airport, 680
Ben-Gurion Airport, 680
Ben Gurion International Airport, 45, 376, 377
Benina International Airport, 376
Benito Mussolini, 119
Benjamin Disraeli, 108
Benjamin Netanyahu, 377, 387, 388, 512, 536, 560, 607, 623, 642, 656, 661, 664
Benjamin Peled, 333, 375
Benjamin Telem, 291
Benny Begin, 657
Benny Gantz, 661
Benny Gaon, 644
Benny Morris, 59, 66, 231, 238, 243, 259, 279, 288, 347, 458, 489, 494, 497, 562, 719, 726, 736
Ben Shemen, 286
Berber Jews, 61, 179
Bereavement in Judaism, 515
Beretta 84F, 511, 514
Beretta M1951, 359
Bergen-Belsen concentration camp, 267
Berlin Crisis of 1961, 175
Bernard Avishai, 605, 770
Bernie Sanders, 687
Beth-Horon, 213
Bethlehem, 3, 95, 211, 216, 490, 523, 547, 575
Bf-109, 33
BGM-71 TOW, 352, 359, 434
Bilin, 566, 586, 587
Bill Bowerman, 267
Bill Clinton, 516, 519–521, 529, 530, 536, 537, 556
Bimkom, 655
Bint Jubayl, 469
Binyamin Elon, 607
Binyamin Gibli, 98

Binyamin Netanyahu, 646, 651
Binyamin Peled, 291
Biopic, 388
Bir Gifgafa Airfield, 192, 306
Birzeit University, 489
Bizerte, 182
Black market, 88
Black Sea, 352
Black September, 245, 276
Black September in Jordan, 296, 413, 468, 470
Black September (Jordan), 421
Black September Organization, 263, 265
Black sheep (term), 344
Black Swan class sloop, 145
Black Swan (imprint), 64
Blockade of the Gaza Strip, 662, 664, 665, 715
Blood and Religion: The Unmasking of the Jewish and Democratic State, 632
Bloomsbury Publishing, 757
Blu (artist), 594
Blue Line (Lebanon), 73, 455
Blue ribbon, 628
BM21, 446
BM-21 Grad, 195, 359
BMP-1, 330, 353, 359
Bnei Akiva, 655
Bnei Atzmon, 609
Bnei Dekalim, 621
Bnei Netzarim, 622
Boaz Gaon, 644
Boeing 707, 383
Boeing 727, 271
Boeing B-17 Flying Fortress, 7, 34
Bofors 40 mm, 196
Bofors 40 mm gun, 359
Booby trap, 546, 568
Border checkpoint, 565
Borders with Palestinian territories, 502
Boresight (firearm), 335
Boston University, 414
Boutros Boutros-Ghali, 516
Boycott, 303, 487
Bra'shit, 475
Breach of the Gaza-Egypt border (2008), 596
Breakdown cranes, 172
Breaking the Silence (non-governmental organization), 702
Bren carrier, 24
Bren Gun, 56
Brian Cowen, 624
BRICS, 685
Bridgehead, 304
Brigade, 198
Brigadier General, 467
Brigadier-General, 365
Bright Rwamirama, 388

Brigitte Kuhlmann, 378
Brinkmanship, 299
Brinksmanship, 175
British Army of the Rhine, 124
British Commonwealth, 123
Brookings Institution, 396
Browning Hi-Power, 359
Bruce Mackenzie (British intelligence operative), 381
BTR-152, 195, 359
BTR-40, 195, 359
BTR-50, 195, 359
BTR-60, 195, 359
BTselem, 493, 545, 559, 562, 577, 583, 585, 591, 600, 681, 691, 692, 703, 763, 764, 766, 780
Bulldozer, 548
Bulletin of the Atomic Scientists, 713, 784
Bundesgrenzschutz, 269
Bundeswehr, 271, 274, 275
Bureau of Intelligence and Research, 349
Bureij, 494
Burma Road (Israel), 26
Burt Lancaster, 389
Bus, 571
Bush, George W, 767
Bustan HaGalil, 621

C-130 Hercules, 351
C-141 Starlifter, 351
C-47, 31
C-47 Dakota, 56
C-47 Skytrain, 19
C-5 Galaxy, 351
Cabinet of Israel, 210, 379, 607
Cairo, 34, 99, 110, 153, 229, 270, 301, 325, 326, 509
Cairo fire, 110
Cambridge University Press, 65–68, 765
Camp David, 369, 396, 398, 401, 519, 521
Camp David 2000 Summit, 60, 410, 557, 592, 598
Camp David Accords, 230, 232, 293, 368, **395**
Camp David Accords (1978), 520
Canada, 228
Canadian Military Pattern truck, 22
Canon de 65 M (montagne) modele 1906, 25
CAR-15, 359
Car bomb, 565
Carden Loyd tankette, 56
Cargo bay, 383
Carmeli Brigade, 15, 28, 29, 48
Caroline B. Glick, 560
Caspar Weinberger, 426
Cast a Giant Shadow, 63
Casualties, 420, 534

Casus belli, 191, 341, 420
Category:Articles contradicting other articles, 271
Catherine Ashton, 591
Causes of the 1948 Palestinian exodus, 58, 59
Cave of the Patriarchs, 228
CBS News, 369
Ceasefire, 39, 224, 245, 672
Cease-fire, 577, 638, 672
Central Intelligence Agency, 113, 353
Central Treaty Organisation, 111
Centurion tank, 136, 157, 195, 203, 312, 329, 359
CH-53 Sea Stallion, 255, 351
Chabad, 229, 684
Chaim Bar-Lev, 314
Chaim Herzog, 229, 248, 258, 309, 317, 324, 360, 386, 458
Chaimite V200, 447
Chancellor of Germany (Federal Republic), 268
Chancellor of the Exchequer, 171
Channel 1 (Israel), 630
Charismatic authority, 409
Charles Bronson, 389
Charles de Gaulle, 181
Charles de Gaulle Airport, 377
Charles Enderlin, 762
Charles Keightley, 106, 136
Charles Krauthammer, 770
Charles R. Brown, 151
Charles R. H. Tripp, 67
Charles Schumer, 591
Chef de mission, 267
Cheryl Rubenberg, 240
Chess, 400
Chief of General Staff (Israel), 487, 639, 661
Chief of Naval Operations, 227
Chief of Staff, 127
Chief of the Imperial General Staff, 130
Chief Rabbi, 659
Chief Rabbinate of Israel, 659
Child suicide bombers in the Israeli–Palestinian conflict, 566
Chouf District, 447, 455
Christian Pineau, 127
Christian Science Monitor, 776
Christopher Gunness, 701
Chronological items, 296, 690
Church of the Holy Sepulchre, 12
Church of the Nativity, 547
C.I.A, 14
CITEREFBerman2011, 755
CITEREFCook2006, 769, 770
CITEREFHerzog1975, 739
CITEREFHerzog1982, 739

CITEREFInsight Team of the London Sunday Times1974, 739
CITEREFPollack2002, 736
CITEREFPollack2004, 719
CITEREFRynholdWaxman2008, 770
CITEREFSchiffYaari1984, 751
Cities in Israel, 642
City Line (Jerusalem), 74
Civil defense siren, 196, 360
Civil disobedience, 487, 641
Civil Guard (Israel), 534
Civil resistance, 641
Claremont Review of Books, 632
Clash of personalities, 153
Close air support, 306
Cluster bomb, 430
Cluster bombs, 414
CNN, 664, 754
CNN News, 779
Coastal Road massacre, 413, 421
Cobra (missile), 196
Code name, 267
Coffee, 90
Cohen on the Bridge, 388
Cold peace, 408
Cold War, 105, 109, 110, 245, 247, 290, 296
Colin Powell, 590
Collaborationism, 488, 568
Collective punishment, 548, 570
Collective security, 192
Colombia, 172
Columbia University Press, 259
Combat engineering, 306
Combat Engineering Corps, 217
Combat Studies Institute, 236, 753
Combat support, 193
Combined Arms Research Library, 236
Commander of the Israeli Air Force, 661
Commando, 247, 444
Committee for Accuracy in Middle East Reporting in America, 560
Commons:Category:1948 Arab-Israeli War, 68
Commons:Category:1967 Arab-Israeli War, 243
Commons:Category:1982 Lebanon War, 460
Commons:Category:Camp David Accords, 411
Commons:Category:Demonstrations and protests against housing prices in Israel in 2011, 660
Commons:Category:First Intifada, 499
Commons:Category:Israeli West Bank barrier, 600
Commons:Category:Israels unilateral disengagement plan, 631
Commons:Category:Munich massacre, 289

Commons:Category:Operation Protective Edge, 715
Commons:Category:Operation Thunderbolt, 393
Commons:Category:Suez Crisis, 187
Commons:Category:War of Attrition, 260
Commons:Category:Yom Kippur War, 374
Commonwealth Prime Ministers Conference, 123
Communist Party, 658
Communists, 97
Condoleezza Rice, 610
Connollystraße, 265
Conscription, 9
Consulate General of France in Jerusalem, 23
Consulate General of the United States, Jerusalem, 27
Consumer price index, 463, 651
Continuum Publishing, 67
Control tower, 384
Controversies relating to the Six-Day War, 191
Convention of Constantinople, 108, 123
Cooking oil, 88
Coordinator of Government Activities in the Territories, 507
Copyright status of work by the U.S. government, 458
Corpus separatum (Jerusalem), 6, 57, 78
Cost of living, 641, 645
Cottbus, 356
Council for Peace and Security, 586
Council for the National Interest, 778
CounterPunch, 781
Counter-terrorist, 376
Country, 685
Covering fire, 156
Covert operation, 97
Covert operations, 99
Credit (finance), 87
Crime against humanity, 550
Crime of apartheid, 592
Criminal negligence, 101
Critical Situation, 388
Cromwell tank, 16, 43, 56
Cuba, 245, 259, 290, 357
Cuban Missile Crisis, 175
Cup Final (film), 457
Curfew, 569
Curfews, 565
Curtiss C-46 Commando, 8
Cyclothymic, 133
Cyprus, 151, 182, 296
Cyprus Emergency, 136
Cyrus Vance, 396, 402
Czech arms deal, 120
Czechoslovakia, 8, 15, 18, 32, 34, 118

Dabur class patrol boat, 344
Dag Hammarskjöld, 168
Dahaf Institute, 627
Dahaniya, 614
Daimler Armoured Car, 56
Dalal Mughrabi, 413
Damascus, 34, 44, 229, 290, 293, 301, 338, 339, 341–343, 354, 366, 436
Damia Bridge, 211
Damietta, 345
Damour, 423, 428, 442
Dan Alon, 267
Dan Halutz, 534, 639
Dan Harel, 613
Daniel Ayalon, 388, 586
Daniel Yergin, 108, 187
Dan, Israel, 217, 218
Daniyal, 42
Danny Matt, 204, 314
Dan Shomron, 375, 380, 382, 487
Daphna Baram, 632
Daphne Leef, 644, 645, 652, 655, 656
Dassault Mirage 5, 359
Dassault Mirage III, 97, 194, 195, 249, 255, 258, 308, 359
Dassault Mystere IV, 144
Dassault Mystère IV, 137
Dassault Ouragan, 137, 146, 195
Dassault Super Mystère, 195, 359
David Ben Gurion, 121, 130
David Ben-Gurion, 2, 5, 7, 29, 55, 87, 91, 93, 101, 106, 132, 181, 215
David Elazar, 190, 219, 291, 302, 358
David Hare (playwright), 595
David Ivri, 440
David Ivry, 419
Davidka, 9, 56
David Makovsky, 583
David Mark Berger, 267, 283
David Pryce-Jones, 160
David Reynolds (English historian), 186
David Rubinger, 232
David Samuels (political scientist), 557
David Shaltiel, 2, 15, 43
David S. Painter, 186
David Tal (historian), 186
Dawah, 448
Day of Revenge, 61, 178
Day to mark the departure and expulsion of Jews from the Arab countries and Iran, 61, 179
Dead Sea, 522
Dean Rusk, 227, 734
Death and ransoming of Oron Shaul, 683
Declaration of Independence (Israel), 87
Decolonization, 173

De facto, 615
DEFCON, 353
Defense Condition, 355
Defense for Children International, 708, 776, 779
Defense in depth, 51
Defense Minister of Israel, 507
Defensive wall, 572
Defile (geography), 141
Degania Alef, 29
De Havilland Mosquito, 54
De Havilland Sea Venom, 151, 153
De Havilland Vampire, 145
Deir al-Balah, 54, 489
Deir Yassin, 43
Deir Yassin massacre, 6, 59
De jure, 615
Demilitarisation, 190
Demilitarized zone, 75
Democracy Now, 528, 762
Democratic Front for the Liberation of Palestine, 446, 487, 490, 534, 557, 660
Democratic Party (United States), 166
Demographics, 60
Demography, 632
Demonstration (people), 511, 641
Denis Sassou Nguesso, 516
Dennis Ross, 527, 530, 722
Department of Foreign Affairs and International Trade, 767
Deputy Leader of Israel, 608
Deputy leaders of Israel, 605, 606
Derek Hopwood, 242
Derek Penslar, 459
Dershowitz, Alan, 762
Der Spiegel, 76, 265, 280, 282, 777
Destroyer, 146
Détente, 298
Deutsche Welle, 776
Devaluation, 463
Development town, 61, 62, 179
Deversoir Air Base, 290
Diane Kunz, 185
Dimona, 607, 637, 647
Diplomatic immunity, 281
Diplomatic recognition, 369
Director of the Central Intelligence Agency, 302, 355
Direct taxes, 653
Disinformation, 299, 454
Displaced persons camps in post-World War II Europe, 61
Disputed statement, 22, 46, 455, 484
Division (military), 198, 326, 342
Djibouti, 383
Dolphinarium massacre, 543

Dome of the Rock, 523
Dominican Republic, 456
Dominion, 109
Dominique Lapierre, 64
Donald Neff, 489
Dore Gold, 64, 411
Dorot, 22
Dortmund, 281
Doubleday & Company, 260
Douglas A-4 Skyhawk, 359
Dov Khenin, 647
Dov Weissglass, 606, 624
Dov Yosef, 64, 87
Dragunov sniper rifle, 359
Drive-by shooting, 565
D. R. Thorpe, 177
Druze, 7, 366, 413, 447, 455, 482, 623
DShK, 196, 359
Dubai, 569
Due and undue weight, 12, 698
Duffel bag, 265
Dugit, 609
Dwight D. Eisenhower, 107

East Africa, 381
East African Rift, 383
Eastern Bloc, 118, 455
East German Air Force, 356
East Germany, 357
East Jerusalem, 57, 74, 189, 191, 230, 493, 509, 522, 537, 574, 576, 587, 665
Economic bubble, 463
Economic Cooperation Foundation, 616
Edgar J. Scherick, 389
Edgar OBallance, 347
Editorializing, 119
Edward Boyle, Baron Boyle of Handsworth, 165
Edward Heath, 180
Effi Eitam, 607
Efraim Karsh, 59, 65, 510
Egoz Reconnaissance Unit, 481
Egypt, 17, 71, 95, 97, 105, 106, 109, 189, 190, 245, 246, 260, 277, 290, 292, 326, 395, 397, 488, 520, 550, 552, 553, 570, 610, 645
Egypt–Gaza barrier, 596
Egypt–Israel Peace Treaty, 76, 248, 368, 369, 396, 404, 406, 410
Egyptian Air Force, 54, 144, 196, 205, 209, 248, 310, 313, 316, 320
Egyptian Armed Forces, 138
Egyptian Army, 246, 247
Egyptian-Czech arms deal, 94
Egyptian Islamic Jihad, 410
Egyptian-Israeli Peace Treaty, 426

Egyptian Jews, 97
Egyptian military, 3
Egyptian nationalism, 98
Egyptian National Railways, 172
Egyptian Navy, 51, 146, 249, 250
Egyptian people, 409
Egyptian President, 106
Egyptian Revolution of 1952, 110
Ehud Barak, 279, 455, 467, 469, 483, 484, 519–521, 526, 529, 530, 534, 536, 537, 541–543, 583, 598, 754
Ehud Olmert, 592, 605, 607, 638, 639
Ehud Yaari, 445, 458, 498
Eid al-Adha, 489
Eilat, 1, 53, 169, 346, 347, 647
Ein Gev, 29
Ein Vered, 28
Eisenhower Doctrine, 174, 175
Eitan Haber, 514, 516
Elad Peled, 194
El Al, 351
El Amir Farouq, 51
El Arish, 32
El Audja el Hafir, history of Palestine, 73, 84
Electronic countermeasures, 344
Electronic warfare, 432
Elei Sinai, 609, 616
El Gamil, 153
Elias Atallah, 419, 467
Elias Sarkis, 426
Eli Berman, 497
Eli Cohen, 220
Elie Hobeika, 419
Eliezer Halfin, 265, 267, 283
ELINT, 227
Elizabeth Taylor, 389
Eli Zeira, 300, 365
Ellinikon International Airport, 376, 378
Elliott Abrams, 558, 619
E.L.M. Burns, 94
El-Qantarah el-Sharqiyya, 200, 310
Emergency special session, 167
Emerging Conflict, 470
En:Amazon Standard Identification Number, 184, 185
Enclave, 522
Enclave and exclave, 577
En:Digital object identifier, 184, 186, 239, 373, 417, 466
Endnote A, 487
Endnote killed, 661
Endnote reference name H1none, 220
Engineering Corps (Israel), 221
English Electric Canberra, 136
English language, 395
En:International Standard Serial Number, 238

En:JSTOR, 373, 417, 630
En:OCLC, 373
Entebbe, 380
Entebbe (film), 389
Entebbe International Airport, 375, 376, 378
Entente cordiale, 108
Eretz Israel, 628
Erez Crossing, 491, 509, 627
Erez Gerstein, 467, 482
Erich Honecker, 357
Erskine Barton Childers, 184
Eshkolot, 599
Esther Roth-Shahamorov, 267
Etzioni Brigade, 15, 43, 44
European Economic Community, 177
European Parliament, 715
European Union, 177, 570, 624, 686, 693, 714
Eviction, 610
Exodus of Irans Jews, 61, 178
Explosive belt, 565
Export, 87
Expulsion of the Palestinians: The Concept of Transfer in Zionist Political Thought, 1882–1948, 68
Ezer Weizman, 54, 190, 401, 403, 516

F-16, 712
F-16 Fighting Falcon, 407, 567
F1 grenade (Russia), 359
F-4 Phantom, 253
F-4 Phantom II, 255, 257, 258, 351
F4 Phantom II, 257
F4U Corsair, 155
F-84F, 155
Facebook, 642
Fadi Frem, 419
Fairmont The Norfolk Hotel, 387
Faisal–Weizmann Agreement, 410
Faisal Husseini, 490, 522, 538
Fait accompli, 129, 160
Fajr-5, 709
Fajr rockets, 474
False flag, 97
Faluja Pocket, 51, 73
Family reactions, riots and funeral, 690
Farhud, 60, 178
Farid Esack, 595
Farouk Kaddoumi, 557
Farouk of Egypt, 13, 110
Far-right politics, 512
Fars News Agency, 709
Fascist, 658
Fasting, 301
Fatah, 279, 413, 487, 490, 534, 548, 561, 563, 619, 622, 634, 637, 664, 668, 682
Fatah–Hamas conflict, 554

Fatah Hawks, 553
Fatwa, 626
Fawzi al-Qawuqji, 2
Fawzi Mahfuz, 419
Fedayeen, 139, 278
Feisal II, 123
Felipe González, 516
Ferdinand de Lesseps, 121, 175
Fiddler on the Roof, 265
Fifth column, 10, 141
Fighter-bomber, 299
File:Africa relief location map.jpg, 376
File:ArWestBankBarrier.ogg, 574
File:He-Gader Hahafrada.ogg, 574
File:President Carters Remarks on Joint Statement at Camp David Summit (September 17, 1978) Jimmy Carter.ogv, 404
Finance Minister of Israel, 623, 657
Finnish people, 697
First emergency special session of the United Nations General Assembly, 167
First International Bank of Israel, 461
First Intifada, **486**, 535, 536, 565, 570
First Sea Lord, 157
First skirmishes and battle of June 2, 24
First World, 455
First World War, 108
Flag of Canada, 182
Flag of Israel, 629
Flanking manoeuvre, 139
FN FAL, 196, 359
FN MAG, 196, 359
Fog of war, 209
Folke Bernadotte, 39, 45
Football at the 1972 Summer Olympics, 277
Footwear, 88
Force 17, 279, 562
Ford, 447
Foreign Affairs Minister of Israel, 388
Foreign and Commonwealth Office, 55
Foreign Ministry in Bonn, 265
Foreign Policy, 782
Foreign relations of South Africa during apartheid, 126
Fouga Magister, 195, 211
Fourth Geneva Convention, 495, 580, 584, 696
Fox, 658
Framework for Peace in the Middle East, 502, 758
France, 15, 16, 71, 106, 211, 228
France24, 693
France 24, 694
Francophile, 168
Frank Shorter, 269
Freedom House, 563
Free education, 653

Free Lebanon Army, 418
Free Lebanon State, 418, 420
Free market, 657
Free Officers Movement (Egypt), 110
French aircraft carrier Arromanches (R95), 151
French aircraft carrier La Fayette (R96), 151
French battleship Jean Bart (1940), 151
French cruiser Georges Leygues, 149
French Fourth Republic, 105
French Hill, 214, 554, 690
French language, 395
French Navy, 136
French Prime Minister, 127
Friendly fire, 25, 157, 204, 481, 683
FROG-7, 338
Frogman, 208
FT-17, 56
Full moon, 298
Furniture, 88
Fürstenfeldbruck, 274–276, 285
Fürstenfeldbruck Air Base, 270

G4 (EU), 714
Gabi Ashkenazi, 534
Gabi Siboni, 764
Gabriel (missile), 345, 359
Gadid, 609
Gad Tsobari, 267
Gad Yaacobi, 489
Galilee, 3, 5, 7, 45, 54, 56, 217, 620
Galilee Squadron, 31
Gal On, 41
Gamal Abdel Nasser, 13, 91, 94, 98, 106, 190–192, 206, 209, 230, 246, 251, 255, 294, 407
Gamal Abdul Nasser, 110
Ganei Tal, 621
Ganei Tal, Hof Aza, 609
Ganim, 609
Gan Or, 609
Gary A. Olson, 234
Gatestone Institute, 699
Gaza beach blast, 563, 635
Gaza City, 14, 34, 35, 51, 94, 149, 205, 674
Gaza coast Regional Council, 628
Gaza Division, 661
Gaza–Israel conflict, 564, 633, 660
Gaza–Jericho Agreement, 505, 506, 508
Gaza Strip, 1, 3, 24, 52, 57, 72, 92, 95, 105, 129, 139, 148, 164, 189, 191, 205, 224, 230, 282, 294, 404, 486–488, 502, 522, 536, 540, 548, 550, 553, 554, 566, 596, 603, 609, 613, 634, 635, 660, 661, 666, 705, 710
Gaza Strip smuggling tunnels, 550

Gaza War (2008–09), 564, 704
Gazit, Shlomo, 458
Gelber, 717
General Secretary of the Communist Party of the Soviet Union, 255
General Staff of the Israel Defense Forces, 487, 661
General strikes, 487, 565
Geneva Accord (2003), 550
Geneva Conference (1973), 363, 399, 410
Geneva Convention, 589
Geneva Conventions, 347
Geneva Initiative, 586, 600
Genocide, 456
Geoffrey Shindler, 763
Geographic coordinate system, 263, 394, 511, 633
George Brandis, 713
George Friedman, 368
George Habash, 376
George Hawi, 419, 467
George J. Mitchell, 555
George Lenczowski, 238, 744, 748
George M. Humphrey, 171
George W. Bush, 590, 605
George Wildman Ball, 425
Gerald Kaufman, 494
Gerald Templer, 106, 130, 153
Gerboise Bleue, 181
Germany, 90
Gesher Bnot Yaacov, 75
Gesher, Israel, 28
Gettysburg National Military Park, 402
Geulim, 28
Gezer (kibbutz), 26
Ghajar, 469
Ghetto, 594
Gideon Levy, 696, 720, 767, 780, 781
Gidi Pass, 206, 299, 312
Gilad Shalit, 563, 633–635, 672, 711
Gilad Shalit prisoner exchange, 639, 671
Gilbert Murray, 163
Gilboa Regional Council, 577
Gilead Sher, 530
Gilo, 542
Givatayim, 647
Givat HaEm, 220, 221
Givati Brigade, 15, 24, 40
Givat Zeev, 524, 575, 576
Glasnost, 440
Global News, 778
Gloster Meteor, 140, 145
Glubb Pasha, 14, 18, 42
GMC (automobile), 447
God, 628

Golan Heights, 84, 95, 189, 191, 217, 225, 231, 250, 290, 292, 299, 310, 326, 456, 468, 469
Golani Brigade, 15, 28, 51, 96, 220, 222, 341, 382, 430, 442, 481, 482, 703
Golda Meir, 5, 7, 13, 76, 102, 247, 261, 268, 278, 291, 301, 303
Gold reserves, 124
Google Book Search, 762
Google Docs, Sheets and Slides, 715
Google Video, 517
Governance of the Gaza Strip, 661, 710
Government budget deficit, 90
Graffiti, 487
Granta Books, 517
Great Bitter Lake, 305, 314
Great Depression, 644
Green belt, 320
Greenhouse, 616, 618
Green Island (Egypt), 252
Greenland, 35
Green Line (Israel), 57, 71, 73, 78, 140, 295, 296, 522, 572, 576, 582, 591, 598, 599, 605
Greenpeace, 655
Greenwich Mean Time, 633, 635
Greenwood Publishing, 64, 67
Gross Domestic Product, 464
Ground forces, 382
Grundgesetz, 274
GSG 9, 272, 274
Guardians of the Cedars, 447
Guards Independent Parachute Company, 154
Gudrun Krämer, 65
Guerrilla, 468
Guerrilla warfare, 421, 565
Guided missile, 568
Gulf of Aqaba, 121, 129, 145
Gulf of Eilat, 346
Gulf of Suez, 312, 321, 344, 346
Gulf War, 487
Gunnar Hägglöf, 165
Gunnar Jarring, 260, 294
Gun-truck, 447
Gush Emunim, 232
Gush Etzion, 216, 524, 576, 598
Gush Katif, 552, 613, 622, 627
Gush Shalom, 527, 532, 586
Guy Arnold, 732
Guy Millard, 123
Guy Mollet, 105, 106, 117, 125, 127, 130
Gvaot, 599

Haaretz, 68, 232, 288, 460, 552, 570, 579, 586, 601, 624, 660, 701, 713, 720, 766, 767, 776–778, 780, 781, 783

HaBayit HaLeumi, 627
Habib Tanious Shartouni, 441
Habima Square, 644, 646
Habis al-Majali, 2
Habla, 580
Hadash, 454, 647, 655
Hadassah Medical Center, 210
Hadera, 46
Hadita, 42
Hafez al-Assad, 91, 281, 291, 295, 326, 342, 397, 419
Hagai Amir, 517
Haganah, 2, 5, 7–9, 14, 16
Haidar Abdel-Shafi, 490
Haifa, 7, 30, 35–37, 45, 54, 146, 334, 413, 549, 628, 646, 647, 650, 684
Haifa bus 16 suicide bombing, 544
Haifa Oil Refinery massacre, 48
Haim Bar-Lev, 106, 148, 246, 291, 354
Haim Cohn, 101
Haj Amin al-Husseini, 2
Hakim Rifle, 359
Halacha, 613
Half-staff, 277
HaMahanot HaOlim, 654
Hamas, 487, 490, 510, 534, 548, 550, 557, 561, 565, 579, 596, 617, 622, 623, 628, 634, 637, 638, 660–663, 669, 682, 687, 706, 710
Hamas rockets failing, 710
Hamat Gader, 94
Hanan Ashrawi, 490
Hand grenade, 384
Hani al-Hassan, 380
HaNoar HaOved VeHaLomed, 654, 655
Hans-Dietrich Genscher, 269
Hans Tabor, 233
Hapoel HaMizrachi, 462
Har Adar, 27, 213
Har Choled, 599
Hardened Aircraft Shelter, 196
Harel Brigade, 15, 26–28, 194, 213
Har Homa, 509, 537
Harold Macmillan, 129, 171, 180
Harold Wilson, 180
Harvard Medical School, 527
Harvard University, 527
Harvard University Press, 65, 757
Hasan Salama, 2, 30
Hasbaya, 442
HaSharon Junction, 596
Hashemite, 111
Hashemites, 4, 118
Hashomer Hatzair, 646, 654, 655
Hassan al-Banna, 72
Hassan Nasrallah, 467, 480, 482

Hassan Yousef, 557
Hatzor, 214
Hatzor Airbase, 54
Hawker Hunter, 97, 194, 195, 217, 252, 356, 359
Hawker Hurricane, 19, 56
Hawker Sea Hawk, 152, 153
Hawker Tempest, 54
Head of state, 516
Health Minister of the Gaza Strip, 682
Health Ministry of the Gaza Strip, 661
Heavy machine guns, 447
Hebrew, 284
Hebrew calendar, 511, 516
Hebrew language, 87, 88, 91, 97, 190, 246, 292, 383, 420, 534, 564, 574, 603, 611, 641, 661
Hebrew University, 27, 75
Hebrew University of Jerusalem, 84, 213
Hebron, 19, 48, 72, 95, 96, 209, 216, 522, 523, 543, 548
Hebron Protocol, 508
Heckler & Koch G3, 271, 275
Helena Cobban, 415, 755
Helicopter, 151, 328
Help:Media, 404
Helsingin Sanomat, 697
Helsinki, Finland, 686
Henry Cabot Lodge Jr., 172
Henry Hershkowitz, 267
Henry Kissinger, 185, 261, 268, 296, 387, 396
Henry Kyemba, 385
Henry Laurens (scholar), 58, 718
Henry Luce, 125
Herbert Hoover Jr., 170
Herbert Morrison, 124
Herman Wouk, 68
Hermesh, 609
Hermonit, 328
Herzog, Chaim, 237
Hesder, 512
Hew Strachan, 756
Hezbollah, 416, 418, 438, 448, 455, 456, 467, 468, 470, 472, 476, 480, 548, 549
HIAS, 61, 179
High Representative for the Common Foreign and Security Policy, 625
Highway 2 (Israel), 541
Highway 6 (Israel), 576
Hijaz, 4
Hilde Henriksen Waage, 510
Hillary Clinton, 591, 771
Hish (Haganah corps), 9
Histadrut, 102, 462, 656
History of the Israeli–Palestinian conflict, 59
History of the Jews in Kenya, 387

813

History of the Jews in the Ottoman Empire, 60, 178
History of the Jews under Muslim rule, 60, 178
HMS Albion (R07), 151
HMS Bulwark (R08), 151
HMS Diana (D126), 146
HMS Eagle (R05), 151
HMS Mendip (L60), 146
HMS Newfoundland, 146
HMS Ocean (R68), 151
HMS Theseus (R64), 151
HMS Zealous (R39), 247, 249, 258
Hodder & Stoughton, 392, 725
Hod HaSharon, 647
Holidays in Egypt, 369
Holiest sites in Islam (Sunni), 538
Holocaust, 10, 90
Holon, 650
Homesh, 609
Hookah, 658
Hoover Press, 765
Hooverville, 644
Horst Buchholz, 389
Hosni Mubarak, 369, 410, 516
Hostage, 376
Hostage-taking, 263
Hotchkiss H35, 8, 56
Houghton Mifflin Company, 67
House demolition, 548
House demolition in the Israeli–Palestinian conflict, 691
House of Saud, 118
Housing and Construction Minister of Israel, 644
Howard Morley Sachar, 67
Hudna, 548, 552
Huffington Post, 771
Hugh Gaitskell, 119, 123
Hugh Stockwell, 106, 127, 136
Hugh Trevor-Roper, 162
Hula, Lebanon, 48, 483
Hula Valley, 219
Huleiqat, 49
Hull-down, 359
Human chain, 627
Human rights groups and the Middle East, 589
Human rights organization, 577
Human Rights Watch, 546, 589, 611, 671, 696, 699, 702, 704, 755, 767
Human shield, 569, 693, 708
Human shields, 698
Humber Armoured Car, 56
Hungarian Revolution of 1956, 164, 173, 174
Hungary national football team, 277
Hunt-class destroyer, 146
Hurghada, 345

Hürriyet, 763
Hurva Synagogue, 26
Husayn Suicide Commandos, 448
Husni al-Zaim, 2
Hussein of Jordan, 91, 190, 192, 209, 210, 251, 268, 294, 341, 343, 516
Huwwara Checkpoint, 566

IAI Nesher, 359
Ian Black (journalist), 63
Ibrahim el Awal, 146
Ibrahim Gambari, 626
Ibrahim Kulaylat, 419
Iceland, 456
Ich bin ein Berliner, 575
ICRC, 663
Iddo Netanyahu, 387, 393
Identification in Nazi camps, 379
Ide Oumarou, 424
IDF Caterpillar D9, 341, 546, 567, 568
IDF Sword Battalion, 2
Idi Amin, 375, 376, 378
Ihab al-Ghussein, 711
IHC M14 Half-track, 56
Ilan Pappé, 10, 59, 66, 68
Ilyushin Il-14, 140, 195, 359
Ilyushin Il-18, 195, 359
Ilyushin Il-28, 130, 138, 195, 198, 359
Imad Mughniyyah, 448
Image and Reality of the Israel–Palestine Conflict, 262
Iman Darweesh Al Hams, 551
Immanuel (town), 576
Immigrant camps (Israel), 61, 62, 179
Imperialism, 173
Import, 87
Improvised explosive device, 481, 552, 568, 665
Im Tirtzu, 655, 658
Inaam Raad, 419
Inari Karsh, 65
Independence, 4
Indian Ocean, 107, 108, 139
Indirect taxes, 653
Infantry fighting vehicle, 56, 195, 359
Inflation, 90
In Islam, 555
Ink Flag, 1, 53
INS Eilat (1955), 146
Insight (Sunday Times), 260
Institute for National Security Studies (Israel), 764
Institute for Palestine Studies, 65, 68
Institute of National Remembrance, 735
Insubordination, 101
INS Yaffo (1955), 146

Intelligence agency, 99
Intelligence and Terrorism Information Center, 681, 707
Internally displaced person, 414, 678
Internal Security Forces, 445
International Affairs (journal), 753
International Christian Embassy in Jerusalem, 592
International Committee of the Red Cross, 348, 589
International community, 246
International Court of Justice, 572, 574, 584, 588
International Criminal Court, 691, 693
International Federation of Journalists, 707
International humanitarian law, 691, 697
International law and the Arab–Israeli conflict, 410
International Olympic Committee, 264, 269, 273
International organization, 685
International Organization for Migration, 688
International Policy Institute for Counter-Terrorism, 560
International recognition of the State of Palestine, 76
International Red Cross, 449
International Red Cross and Red Crescent Movement, 583, 602
International relations, 414
International Solidarity Movement, 566, 570
International Standard Book Number, 63–68, 84, 85, 102, 103, 183–187, 234–243, 259, 260, 262, 287–289, 370–374, 392, 393, 411, 417, 458, 459, 497, 498, 517, 571, 572, 630
Internecine, 446
Internet Archive, 187, 600
Inter Press Service, 766, 777
Involuntary manslaughter, 275
Iqrit, 48, 264
Iran, 346, 468, 470, 544, 549
Iran–Iraq War, 490
Iran–Israel proxy conflict, 467
Iran hostage crisis, 387
Iranian Jews in Israel, 61, 179
Iraq, 74, 109, 111, 182, 281, 341, 398, 407, 437
Iraq (1958–1968), 189
Iraqi Air Force, 19, 211
Iraqi Intelligence Service, 427
Iraqi Jews in Israel, 61, 179
Iraq Suwaydan, 51
Iraq War, 534
Irgun, 2, 6, 9, 23, 43
Irina Bokova, 707

Irish Government, 625
Iron Dome, 660, 662, 710
Iron Triangle (Lebanon), 445
Irshad Manji, 602
Irvin Kershner, 389
IS-3, 138
Isaac Herzog, 657
Islamic calendar, 369
Islamic Jihad Movement in Palestine, 487, 489, 490, 534, 543, 579, 660, 662, 663, 672, 681
Islamic Jihad Organization, 448
Islamic Revolutionary Guard Corps, 448
Ismail Haniyeh, 534, 661, 687, 691
Ismailia, 110, 311, 319, 322
Ismaïlia, 252
Isra al-Modallal, 701
Israel, 1, 2, 17, 21, 22, 61, 71, 87, 91, 105, 106, 179, 189, 190, 230, 245–247, 255, 260, 268, 290, 292, 375, 395, 397, 412, 413, 418, 421, 456, 461, 467, 468, 486, 487, 501, 511, 520, 533, 534, 565, 591, 641, 657, 660, 661, 663
Israel Air Force, 435
Israel Army, 661
Israel Atomic Energy Commission, 336
Israel at the 1972 Summer Olympics, 263
Israel at the Olympics, 263
Israel Border Police, 140, 534, 540, 613
Israel Broadcasting Authority, 374
Israel Central Bureau of Statistics, 644
Israel Council on Foreign Relations, 743
Israel Defense Forces, 2, 15, 18, 23, 91, 92, 101, 137, 191, 264, 292, 299, 376, 409, 413, 420, 468, 486, 489, 534, 544, 550, 566, 567, 571, 587, 608, 633, 639, 661, 662, 683, 688, 706, 712, 715
Israel Defense Forces checkpoint, 550, 569, 580
Israel Democracy Institute, 700
Israel Discount Bank, 461, 462, 464, 465
Israel–Jordan peace treaty, 76, 232, 409, 410, 503
Israel – Palestine Liberation Organization letters of recognition, 503
Israel–Palestine Liberation Organization letters of recognition, 508
Israel HaYom, 653
Israeli agora, 463
Israeli Air Force, 31, 33, 44, 51, 53, 54, 140, 144, 146, 147, 193, 209, 210, 248, 249, 252, 253, 298, 309, 310, 315, 333, 339, 346, 360, 381, 432, 439, 549, 552, 568, 638, 661, 672, 712
Israeli Air Force Museum, 197, 304
Israeli Arab, 581

Israeli Army, 189, 485, 534
Israeli Central Command, 580
Israeli checkpoint, 598
Israeli Civil Administration, 487, 505, 508
Israeli coastal plain, 56
Israeli Declaration of Independence, 2, 3, 21, 59
Israeli Defence Forces, 548
Israeli disengagement from Gaza, 232, **603**, 663
Israeli economy, 653
Israeli Foreign Ministry, 503, 556
Israeli–Lebanese Ceasefire Understanding, 480
Israeli–Lebanese conflict, 412, 467
Israeli–Palestinian conflict, 231, 263, 413, 418, 486, 501, 505, 519, 533, 534, 547, 570, 578, 603, 609
Israeli–Palestinian Joint Water Committee, 507
Israeli–Palestinian peace process, 293, 410, 501, 519, 578, 603
Israeli Gaza Strip barrier, 550, 596
Israeli government, 247, 572
Israeli Intelligence Community, 365
Israeli Labor Party, 368, 488, 657, 658
Israeli League for Human and Civil Rights, 492
Israeli-Lebanese conflict, 418
Israeli legislative election, 1973, 365
Israeli legislative election, 1977, 469
Israeli military, 511
Israeli Military Censor, 102
Israeli military intelligence, 97
Israeli Ministry of Foreign Affairs, 777
Israeli National Security Council, 365
Israeli naval campaign in Operation Yoav, 51
Israeli Navy, 35, 51, 137, 146, 150, 208, 249, 324, 344, 436, 442, 570, 661, 712
Israeli new shekel, 620
Israeli Northern Command, 358
Israeli occupation of southern Lebanon, 418, 450, 455, 484
Israeli occupied territories, 292, 399
Israeli-occupied territories, 232, 488, 511
Israeli-Palestinian peace process, 572
Israeli pound, 88
Israeli Prime Minister, 13
Israelis, 378, 556
Israeli Security Forces, 269, 365, 487, 553, 569
Israeli settlement, 232, 487, 502, 522, 524, 550, 576, 592, 609
Israeli settlements, 520
Israeli settler, 409, 488
Israeli Supreme Court, 101
Israeli Supreme Court opinions on the West Bank Barrier, 585
Israeli targeted killings, 550, 569

Israeli West Bank barrier, 533, 549, 566, **572**, 665
Israel Land Administration, 651
Israel Lands Administration, 657
Israel Meir Lau, 659
Israel Military Industries, 9
Israel Mixed Armistice Commission, 77
Israel police, 534, 541
Israel prime ministerial election, 2001, 543
Israel Railways, 172
Israel Securities Authority, 462
Israels housing bubble, 642
Israels Secret Wars: A History of Israels Intelligence Services, 63
Israel Standard Time, 383
Israels unilateral disengagement plan, 409, 533, 550, 554, 569, 598
Israel Tal, 106, 148, 190, 200, 291, 327
Israel Union for Environmental Defense, 655
Isser Harel, 101
ISU-152, 195, 359
Itzik Shmuli, 652
Ivone Kirkpatrick, 124
Ivory Coast, 456
Izz ad-Din al-Qassam Brigades, 633, 634, 637, 661

Jaba, Jerusalem, 599
Jabalia, 486, 710
Jabalia Camp, 487
Jabaliya Camp, 491
Jabel Mukaber, 211
Jacques Chirac, 540
Jacques Massu, 106, 154
Jacques Rogge, 278
Jaffa, 3, 7, 36, 703, 708
Jaffa Gate, 43
Jaffa riots, 9
Jam, 90
Jamal Abu Samhadana, 534, 552, 635
Jamal al-Bawatna, 626
Jamal Al-Gashey, 267, 273, 281
James Callaghan, 164
James Schlesinger, 355
James Tully (Irish politician), 410
James Wolfensohn, 618
James Woods, 389
James Zogby, 591
Jan Egeland, 503
Jarring Mission, 247, **260**
Javier Solana, 625
Jawaharlal Nehru, 126
Jayyous, 586
J. Bowyer Bell, 63, 720
Jean Chrétien, 516
Jefferson Caffery, 113

Jeffrey T. Richelson, 66
Jenin, 28, 36, 216, 523, 545, 581
Jericho, 214, 217, 523
Jericho (missile), 350
Jerusalem, 3, 26, 27, 36, 42, 45, 57, 75, 78, 194, 399, 488, 515, 520, 523, 548, 554, 576, 587, 593, 596, 627, 628, 646, 647
Jerusalem Brigade, 194, 304
Jerusalem bus 2 massacre, 548
Jerusalem Center for Public Affairs, 560
Jerusalem Corridor, 28, 51
Jerusalem Governorate, 582
Jerusalem in Judaism, 538
Jerusalem Law, 538
Jerusalem Post, 416, 631, 660, 690, 701, 771
Jew, 87, 628
Jewish Agency for Israel, 62
Jewish and democratic state, 606
Jewish Colonial Trust, 462
Jewish diaspora, 228
Jewish exodus from Arab and Muslim countries, 60, 61, 178
Jewish exodus from Arab lands, 3
Jewish insurgency in Palestine, 3
Jewish Migration from Lebanon Post-1948, 61, 178
Jewish Quarter (Jerusalem), 27
Jewish refugees, 90
Jewish state, 12
Jewish Virtual Library, 522, 602, 715, 761, 766
Jews, 378
Jezreel Valley, 56, 194
Jezzine, 429, 431, 442
JIMENA, 61, 179
Jim McKay, 273
Jimmy Carter, 368, 369, 395, 396, 398, 403, 404, 408, 414, 520
Jimmy Carter Library and Museum, 749
Jimmy Wales, 656
Jimzu, 42
J. J. Goldberg, 771
J.J. Goldberg, 671
Joel Beinin, 103, 497
Joe Lieberman, 590
Joey Tartakovsky, 632
Jo Grimond, 124
Johan Jørgen Holst, 504
Johannes Strijdom, 126
John Bagot Glubb, 2, 27, 119
John Foster Dulles, 112, 166, 175
John K. Cooley, 269, 288
John Kerry, 714
John Lewis Gaddis, 174
John Mearsheimer, 494
John Quigley (academic), 732, 734

John Saxon, 389
Joint session of the United States Congress, 404
Jomo Kenyatta, 381
Jomo Kenyatta International Airport, 381, 383
Jonathan Dahoah-Halevi, 560
Jonathan Netanyahu, 393
Jonathan Steele, 631
Jordan, 3, 4, 17, 22, 56, 71, 75, 91, 96, 111, 132, 140, 189, 190, 245–247, 252, 260, 267, 290, 341, 397, 468, 488, 553
Jordanian annexation of the West Bank, 1, 3, 57, 75, 78, 228, 293
Jordanian Armed Forces, 194
Jordanian Army, 194, 210
Jordan River, 216, 219, 349, 583
Jordan Valley (Middle East), 194, 257, 582, 598, 605, 646
José Padilha, 389
Joseph J. Sisco, 295
Joseph Stalin, 5
Josephs Tomb, 228
Jos Hermens, 277
Joshua Landis, 68
Joshua Shani, 380
Josip Broz Tito, 115
Journal of Palestine Studies, 528, 530, 719, 720, 762
JR (artist), 595
Judea, 216
Judith M. Brown, 63
July 26th new government housing plans announcements, 646
Juma Oris, 386
Jundallah (Lebanon), 448
Jund Ansar Allah, 638
Justice for Jews from Arab Countries, 61, 179
Justice ministry, 385

K-13 (missile), 359
Kader Asmal, 457
Kadesh (Israel), 139
Kadim, 609
Kadima, 592
Kafra, Lebanon, 480
Kafr Birim, 264
Kafr Qasim, 140
Kafr Qasim massacre, 140
Kafr Rai, 619
Kahan Commission, 441, 457, 538
Kai Bird, 750
Kalashnikov assault rifle, 272
Kalman Libeskind, 642
Kampala, 385
Karabiner 98k, 56, 359
Karachi, 165
Karameh, 250

Karen Armstrong, 411
Karine A, 544
Karmei Katif, 621
Karmiel, 647
Karnei Shomron, 576
Karni crossing, 542, 550, 618, 619
Karsh, 717
Kataeb Party, 281, 418, 422, 441
Katif (moshav), 609
Katyusha rocket launcher, 358, 446, 474, 480, 709
Kedumim, 576
Kehat Shorr, 267, 270, 283
Keith Feiling, 162
Keith Kyle, 185
Kenneth Keating, 303
Kenneth Levin, 530
Kenneth M. Pollack, 259
Kenneth Pollack, 66, 248, 308, 309, 314, 450
Kenny Moore, 277
Kenya, 377
Kerem Atzmona, 609
Kerem Shalom, 633, 635
Kerem Shalom Crossing, 633
Kfar Darom, 609, 612, 614
Kfar Etzion massacre, 7
Kfar Maimon, 199
Kfar Saba, 89, 210, 646
Kfar Sirkin, 210
Kfar Yam, 609
Kfar Yona, 28
Kfour, Nabatieh, 481
KGB, 302
Khaled Abu Toameh, 631
Khaled Mashaal, 534, 693, 699
Khaled Mashal, 637, 661
Khalid Islambouli, 410
Khalid Jawad, 267, 283
Khalil al-Wazir, 487
Khalil Wazir, 416
Khan Yunis, 95, 149, 200, 489, 637, 662, 701, 710
Khan Yunis killings, 150
Khartoum Resolution, 230, 246, 262, 294
Khiam detention center, 475
Khulda, 42
Kibbutz, 22, 24, 210, 667
Kibutzim, 462
Kidnapping and murder of Mohammed Abu Khdeir, 671
Kidnapping of Nachshon Wachsman, 634
Kiel, 267
Killed in action, 2, 246, 291, 375, 419, 467, 487, 534
Killing and shooting of Gazan civilians, 682
Killing of suspected collaborators, 682, 683

Kindergarten, 552
Kingdom of Egypt, 3, 4, 22, 91
Kingdom of Iraq, 3, 17, 22
King Farouk I, 2
King Hussein, 397
Kings College London, 683
Kinneret Zmora-Bitan Dvir, 64
Kirkuk–Baniyas pipeline, 165
Kiryat Arba, 522
Kiryati Brigade, 15
Kiryat Ono, 689
Kiryat Shaul Cemetery, 286
Kiryat Shmona, 474, 646, 647, 655
Kissufim, 205, 615
Klaus Kinski, 389
Knesset, 76, 169, 210, 354, 365, 368, 399, 400, 454, 465, 515, 603, 607, 608, 615, 617, 619, 646, 663
Knopf Publishing, 67
Kofi Annan, 581, 626
Komar-class missile boat, 249, 345
Konrad Adenauer, 168, 177
Kremlin, 255
KSR-2 (Russian rocket), 308
Ktziot Prison, 493
Kurdish Jews in Israel, 61, 179
Kurdistan Workers Party, 447
Kurt Waldheim, 386, 424
Kuwait, 171, 358
Kuwaiti Armed Forces, 257

Labor Party (Israel), 536, 550, 607, 623
Labor union, 102
Labour (Israel), 454, 543
La Familia (Beitar supporters group), 671
Lahore, 165
Lake Qaraoun, 442
Lake Tiberias, 336
Lake Victoria, 380
Land for peace, 230
Landing craft, 155
Landing Craft Assault, 155
Landing Vehicle Tracked, 155, 158
Land mine, 339, 565
Land of Israel, 21
Land Rover, 383
Land-Rover, 447
Lapierre collins, 717
Larry Collins (writer), 64
Latakia, 344, 355, 638
Late-2000s financial crisis, 466
Late-2000s recession, 466
Latrun, 19, 26, 42, 75, 210, 213, 370, 522, 578, 598
Laurens, 717, 718
Lausanne Conference, 1949, 76

Lavon Affair, **97**
Leader, 125
League of Nations mandate, 4
Leah Rabin, 515
Lebanese Air Force, 445
Lebanese Armed Forces, 30
Lebanese Army, 444, 450
Lebanese Christian, 468
Lebanese Civil War, 280, 412, 413, 418, 421, 422, 468, 470
Lebanese Council for Development and Reconstruction, 456
Lebanese Forces, 455
Lebanese Forces (militia), 448
Lebanese Front, 418, 448
Lebanese Ground Forces, 444
Lebanese National Movement, 447
Lebanese National Resistance Front, 418, 447, 467
Lebanese Navy, 445
Lebanese pound, 456
Lebanese prisoners in Israel, 475
Lebanon, 17, 48, 71, 118, 217, 260, 267, 296, 338, 358, 412, 418, 548
Lebanon (2009 film), 457
Lee-Enfield, 359
Lee–Enfield rifle, 56
Legion of Honour, 387
Lehi (group), 2, 6, 23, 43, 45
Leila Shahid, 624
Le Monde diplomatique, 531
Leo Kuper, 753
Leonid Brezhnev, 255, 298, 367
Lester B. Pearson, 168, 182
Lester Pearson, 107
Levi Eshkol, 91, 102, 190, 210, 219, 224, 246
Lewisham North by-election, 1957, 164
Library of Congress, 69
Library of Congress Country Studies, 458
Libya, 281, 357, 398
Libyan Arab Republic, 290
Libyan–Egyptian War, 369
Lieutenant Colonel, 377
Light cruiser, 146
Light tank, 29
Light Tank Mk VI, 19, 56
Likud, 368, 426, 469, 511, 536, 538, 543, 607, 755
Lillehammer, 279
Lillehammer affair, 279
List of Arab towns and villages depopulated during the 1948 Palestinian exodus, 59
List of attacks against Israeli civilians before 1967, 91, 117
List of Defense Ministers of Israel, 607

List of emergency special sessions of the United Nations General Assembly, 585, 586
List of Israeli strikes and Palestinian casualties in the 2014 Israel–Gaza conflict, 661
List of Middle East peace proposals, 410
List of Palestinian militant groups suicide attacks, 566
List of Palestinian rocket attacks on Israel, 2009, 664
List of Palestinian rocket attacks on Israel, 2014, 661
List of Palestinian suicide attacks, 565, 572, 579
List of rocket and mortar attacks in Israel in 2008, 564
List of terrorist organisations, 563
List of villages depopulated during the Arab–Israeli conflict, 59
Litani River, 48, 412, 414, 429
Little Triangle, 74
Loaded term, 629
Lockheed C-130 Hercules, 381, 384
Lockheed SR-71 Blackbird, 352
LockmanBeinin1989, 755, 756
Lod, 3, 42, 45, 690
Lod Airport, 36, 42
London Review of Books, 777, 783
Lorraine 37L, 56
Los Angeles Times, 754
Louis Mountbatten, 1st Earl Mountbatten of Burma, 153, 157
Lou Lenart, 8
Lower Galilee, 44
Low-intensity warfare, 476
Lufthansa Flight 615, 264, 276
Luftwaffe, 17
Lüshunkou, 108
Luttif Afif, 264, 267, 283
Luxembourg, 456
Lyndon B. Johnson, 166, 180, 227
Lyndon Johnson, 192
Lynne Rienner Publishers, 764

M107 self-propelled gun, 339, 359
M109 howitzer, 359, 712
M110 howitzer, 359
M113, 475
M-113, 331
M113 Armored Personnel Carrier, 194, 359, 550
M14 rifle, 359
M16 rifle, 359, 614
M1937 Howitzer, 195, 359
M1A1 Abrams, 407
M1 Carbine, 545
M22 Locust, 56

819

M26 grenade, 359
M2 Browning machine gun, 196, 359
M2 Half Track Car, 195, 359
M35A2, 447
M3 Half-track, 56, 195, 359
M3 Scout Car, 56
M40 recoilless rifle, 196, 359
M42 Duster, 447
M-47 Patton, 195
M48 Patton, 194, 195, 216, 318, 350, 351, 359
M-4 Sherman, 203
M4 Sherman, 6, 16, 56
M50 Super Sherman, 195, 203, 447
M5 Half-track, 56
M60 Patton, 311, 351, 359, 440
M72 LAW, 345, 359
Maabarot, 61, 62, 179
Maale Adumim, 524, 576, 598, 605, 624, 684
Maale Akrabim massacre, 93
Maan News Agency, 766, 776, 779, 780, 783, 784
Maariv, 530, 579, 627, 659, 764
Maariv (newspaper), 642, 644
Maavak Sotzialisti, 655
Machane Yehuda, 622
Machon Ayalon, 9
Machsom Watch, 589, 601
Madeleine Albright, 509, 525, 529, 530, 537
Madrid Conference, 487
Madrid Conference of 1991, 410, 486, 496, 628
Magen David Adom, 684
Maghrebi Jews, 61, 179
Maginot Line, 220
Mahal (Israel), 2, 33
Mahmoud Abbas, 282, 523, 530, 534, 535, 547, 552, 553, 590, 625, 637–640, 664, 668
Mahmoud al-Mabhouh, 569
Mahmoud al-Zahar, 557
Mahmoud Riad, 208
Mahsum Korkmaz, 419
Main battle tank, 440
Majdal al-Sadiq, 42
Makarov pistol, 359
Malcolm Hedding, 592
Malcolm Muggeridge, 161
Malha, 44
Malta, 151, 688
Manara, Israel, 46
Mandatory Palestine, 1–3, 7, 56, 59, 72, 75, 110
Mandelbaum Gate, 213
Manila Pact, 109
Manley Laurence Power, 106, 155
Manuel Trajtenberg, 651

Manufacture and use, 196, 359
Maoz Haim, 95
Mapai, 102
Marathon (sport), 277
March, 666
Marcheshvan, 511
Margarine, 88
Marie-Pierre Kœnig, 118
Marjayoun, 470
Marjayun, 469
Mark Perry (author), 709
Mark Podwal, 287
Mark Slavin, 267, 283
Mark Spitz, 277
Marmon-Herrington Armoured Car, 56
Maronite, 413, 418, 420, 426
Maronites, 422, 484
Marrakeh, 475
Marseilles, 345
Marshall Islands, 586
Martin Dempsey, 703
Martin Gilbert, 64, 68, 459
Martin Indyk, 528
Martin Van Creveld, 64, 242, 718
Marvin J. Chomsky, 389
Marwan Barghouti, 487, 534, 540, 544, 558
Marwan Bishara, 668
Maryland, 520
MAS 36, 56
Maskiot, 621
Massacre, 263
Mass arrest, 493
Mass murder, 263
Matan Vilnai, 382
Materiel, 297, 407
Matilda II tank, 19, 56
Maurice Bourgès-Maunoury, 130
Maurice Challe, 131
Maurice Orbach, 100
Mauritania-Israel war of 1967, 228
Mavkiim, 622
Max Hastings, 393
Maxim restaurant suicide bombing, 549
Max M. Fisher, 182
May 17 Agreement, 438, 456, 471
Mazin Qumsiyeh, 489
McDonnell Douglas F-4 Phantom II, 308, 350, 359
McDowall 1989, 757
McGraw-Hill, 63
Mechanized infantry, 194, 198
Medal of Valor (Israel), 337
Médecins du Monde, 583
Medevac, 144
Media:ArWestBankBarrier.ogg, 574
Media:He-Gader Hahafrada.ogg, 574

Mediation, 323
Medical evacuation, 416
Mediterranean, 107, 108
Mediterranean Sea, 72, 196
Medium bomber, 195
Mehola Junction bombing, 495
Meir Amit, 130, 381
Meir Har-Zion, 95
Meir Max Bineth, 99, 100
Meir Rosenne, 403
Meir Vilner, 454
Meitar, 576
Members of Hamas called Qawasameh, 548
Menachem Begin, 76, 368, 395, 396, 398, 401, 403, 404, 419, 420, 422, 520, 755
Menachem Mendel Schneerson, 229
Menahem Begin, 210
Menahem Golan, 389
Mercedes-Benz 600, 383
Mercenary, 445
Merchant, 62
Meretz, 655
Merkava, 440, 442, 567
Merkava III, 635
Merkava Mk. IV, 711
Meron Benvenisti, 68
Messerschmitt Bf-109, 8
Metzadot, 599
Metzadot Yehuda, 599
Mevo Dotan, 609
MG 34, 16
MG-34, 56
MI5, 9
Michael B. Oren, 229
Michael Dekel, 489
Michael Fekete, 27
Michael Foot, 160
Michael Oren, 239, 243
Michael Ross (Mossad officer), 680, 762
Micha Lindenstrauss, 620
Michel Bacos, 387
Mickey Edelstein, 661
Mickey Marcus, 2, 25
Middle class, 641
Middle East, 189, 396
Middle East Eye, 779
Middle East Forum, 762
Middle East peace process, 520
Middle East Policy, 236
Middle East Review of International Affairs, 244
MiG, 384
MiG 15, 130
MiG-15, 138, 144, 219
MiG-17, 195, 198
MiG-19, 195, 198

MiG 21, 219
MiG-21, 195, 198, 257, 259, 296
MiG-23, 299
Migration of Moroccan Jews to Israel, 61, 178
Mikoyan, 247
Mikoyan-Gurevich MiG-17, 248, 359, 377, 385
Mikoyan-Gurevich MiG-19, 359
Mikoyan-Gurevich MiG-21, 195, 249, 359, 377, 385
Mikoyan-Gurevich MiG-25, 354
MILAN, 443
Miles Copeland Jr., 113
Military aid, 570
Military campaign, 564
Military Channel, 388
Military Intelligence Directorate (Israel), 98, 299
Military occupation, 603
Military of Egypt, 407
Military Rabbinate, 615
Military reserves, 302
Military tactics, 297
Militia, 468
Mills bomb, 8, 56
Mil Mi-4, 196
Mil Mi-6, 196, 359
Mil Mi-8, 359
MIM-23 Hawk, 196, 198, 255, 306, 351, 359
MIM-72 Chaparral, 351, 359
Minefield, 327
Minesweeper (ship), 208
Minister for Defence (Ireland), 410
Ministry of Agriculture (Kenya), 381
Ministry of Defense (Israel), 487, 488, 661
Ministry of Finance (Israel), 463
Ministry of Foreign Affairs (Israel), 579, 661, 682, 715
Mirage V, 357
Miri Regev, 658
Miscarriage, 378
Misgav Am, 48
Mishmar HaEmek, 7
Mishmar HaYarden, 30, 36
Mishmeret Yesha, 534
Missile boat, 208, 343
Missile gap, 170
Mitchell Report (Arab–Israeli conflict), 555
Mitla Pass, 141, 206, 256, 299, 312
MIT Press, 260
Mitzvah, 628
Mixed Armistice Commissions, 57, 77, 83, 93
Mizrahi Democratic Rainbow Coalition, 655
Mizrahi Jews, 60, 178
Mizrahi Jews in Israel, 61, 179
M.J. Rosenberg, 528

Mobile artillery, 330
Mobile home, 621
Modern orthodox, 658
Modi Alon, 33
Modiin-Maccabim-Reut, 646, 647
Mohamed Abdel Ghani el-Gamasy, 325
Mohamed Hassanein Heikal, 184, 225, 226
Mohammad Daoud Oudeh, 416
Mohammed Abu Khdeir, 690
Mohammed Deif, 534, 661
Mohammed Safady, 267
Molotov cocktail, 29, 56, 487, 541
Mona Juul, 504
Mondoweiss, 771
Monte Melkonian, 419
Morag, Gaza, 609
Morag (moshav), 614
Moral authority, 176
Mordechai Eliyahu, 628
Mordechai Gur, 143, 190, 194, 213, 412
Mordechai Hod, 190, 246
Mordechai Tzipori, 489
Mordechai Weingarten, 719
Moroccan Jews in Israel, 61, 179
Morocco, 290, 358
Morris1999, 757
Morris Beckman (writer), 67
Morris birth, 717, 718
Mortar (weapon), 56, 253, 553, 662, 705
Mosab Hassan Yousef, 557
Moshav, 62
Moshe Arens, 580
Moshe Bejski, 465
Moshe Carmel, 2, 15, 48
Moshe Dayan, 2, 64, 93, 101, 106, 130, 137, 141, 190, 205, 210, 233, 291, 294, 302, 320, 341, 360, 403, 469
Moshe Gidron, 321
Moshe Katsav, 97, 102
Moshe Marzouk, 100
Moshe Sharet, 92
Moshe Sharett, 76, 91, 93, 101, 469
Moshe Weinberg, 266, 282
Moshe Yaalon, 534, 661, 764
Moshe Ya'alon, 675
Mossad, 99, 220, 264, 271, 278, 288, 299, 376, 569
Mossad LeAliyah Bet, 61, 62, 179
Motti Ashkenazi, 364
Mouin Rabbani, 777
Mountain pass, 293
Mountain War (Lebanon), 455
Mount Hermon, 328, 342, 348, 445
Mount Herzl, 515
Mount of Olives, 84, 540
Mount Scopus, 75, 84, 210, 213, 214, 722

Mount Zion, 43
Movement for Quality Government in Israel, 655
Mufti, 626
Muhammad, 298
Muhammad al-Durrah incident, 540
Muhammad Naguib, 2, 40
Muhammad Neguib, 110
Muhsin Ibrahim, 419
Mujahideen, 670
Mukataa, 545
Muki Betser, 381
Mulago Hospital, 385
Multinational Force in Lebanon, 437
Munich, 263, 274, 277
Munich 1972 & Beyond, 287
Munich Agreement, 123
Munich (film), 282, 287
Munich massacre, **263**
Munich: Mossads Revenge, 287
Munich-Riem airport, 270
Munition, 303
Murat Karayılan, 419
Murder of Dora Bloch, 377, 385
Murder of Georgios Tsibouktzakis, 544
Murder of Tali Hatuel and her four daughters, 550
Muslim, 624
Muslim Brotherhood, 2, 37, 72, 97, 100, 110
Mustaarabi Jews, 61, 179
Mustafa Dirani, 480
Mustafa Hafez, 95
Mustafa Tlass, 291, 347, 419
Muzahim al-Pachachi, 2
My Life (Bill Clinton autobiography), 526
Mystere IV, 195

Nabatieh, 429
Nabatiyeh, 442
Nabih Berri, 419, 467
Nabil Amr, 526
Nablus, 18, 28, 216, 523, 548, 554, 569, 634
Nachshon Wachsman, 637
Nadav Safran, 233
Nafah, 332
Nahal, 442
Nahal Oz, 200, 552
Nahariya, 647
Nahariya train station suicide bombing, 544
Nairobi, 381
Nakba Day, 58, 60
Naksa Day, 668
Names, 572
Naming, 641
Naomi Chazan, 713, 785
Napalm, 148, 206

Napoleonchik, 29, 56
Naqoura, 415
NassarHeacock1990, 756, 757
Nasser, 92
Nasserism, 163
Natan Sharansky, 586, 608
Nathan Thrall, 558, 764
National Film Board of Canada, 595
National Geographic Channel, 388
Nationalization, 461
National Liberation Front (Algeria), 117, 125
National Order of Merit (France), 387
National Pact, 421
National Party of South Africa, 592
National Religious Party, 462, 550, 607, 608
National Security Agency, 190
National Service, 160
National Union (Israel), 550, 607
National Union of Israeli Students, 646, 655
National Unity Government, 193
NATO, 172, 174, 181, 247
Naval Infantry (Russia), 208
Nave, 622
Navi Pillay, 691, 694, 708
Nayef Hawatmeh, 534
Nazareth, 44, 646
Nazi, 264
Nazi Germany, 33, 510, 614
Nazism, 99
Nazlat Issa, 582
Nazlet Issa, 548
Negative (photography), 233
Negba, 24, 41
Negev, 3, 5, 20, 22, 24, 45, 56, 97, 142, 493, 522, 620
Negev Brigade, 15, 53
Negev Desert, 684
Negev Nuclear Research Center, 198
Nekhel, 205
Nelson Mandela, 588
Neo liberal, 653
Neo-Nazism in Germany, 264
Nesher, 658
Netanya, 28, 210, 334, 545, 554, 596, 619, 646, 647
Netherlands, 350, 367
Netivot, 628
Netzarim (settlement), 540, 607, 609, 614
Netzer Hazani, 621
Netzer Hazani, Hof Aza, 609, 617
Neve Dekalim, 553, 609, 613, 614
Neve Gordon, 783
Neve Yam, 621
New American Library, 65
New Gate, 43
New Historian, 231

New Historians, 59
New Israel Fund, 642, 655, 656, 658
New Movement – Meretz, 647
Newsweek, 298
New York Review of Books, 764, 777
New York Times, 294, 640, 771
Nicaragua, 16
Niger, 424
Night of the Gliders, 489
Night vision device, 330
Nikita Khrushchev, 115, 174
Nikolai Bulganin, 169, 174
Nikolai Podgorny, 356
Nile crocodile, 380
Nile Delta, 316, 352, 358
Nile River, 252
Nir-Am, 31
Nir Barkat, 655, 657
Nirim, 23, 55, 205
Nisanit, 609
Nitroglycerine, 99
Nitzan, 621
Nitzana, Israel, 52, 95
Nitzan Horowitz, 647, 657
Nitzanim, 25
No. 13 Squadron RAF, 54
No. 208 Squadron RAF, 54
No. 213 Squadron RAF, 54
No. 6 Squadron RAF, 54
Noam Chomsky, 458, 602
Nobel Peace Prize, 107, 182, 396
No-confidence motion, 454
Non Aligned Movement, 168
Non-Aligned Movement, 296, 686
Nord Noratlas, 154, 195, 208
Nord SS.10, 196
Norman Finkelstein, 242, 261, 528
Norman G. Finkelstein, 262, 762
Norman St John-Stevas, Baron St John of Fawsley, 162
North American P-51 Mustang, 141
North Carolina, 389
North Korea, 357
North Yemen, 437
North Yemen Civil War, 194
NPR, 754
Nuclear weapons and Israel, 350
Nureddin al-Atassi, 190
Nur-eldeen Masalha, 59, 68
Nuri as-Said, 13, 118
Nuri es-Said, 123
Nutrition, 88

Obusier de 155 mm Modèle 50, 359
Obusier de 155 mm Modèle 50, 195

Occupation of the Gaza Strip by Egypt, 1, 3, 57, 75, 78
Occupation (protest), 641
OCHA, 619, 681, 682, 779
October 22 Scud missile attack, 321
October 6 – The Crossing, 309
Odd Bull, 210, 211
Oded Brigade, 15, 30, 142
Odessa, 352
OECD, 643
Ofer Eini, 656
Ofer Shelah, 752
Office of the Historian, 738
Office of the Prime Minister (Israel), 658
Ofira Air Battle, 308
Ofir Akunis, 538
Ofir Rahum, 542
Ofra, 545
Ogaden, 383
Oil embargo crisis, 303
Oil tanker, 109
O Jerusalem, 64
Old City (Jerusalem), 26, 210, 524, 535
Old City of Jerusalem, 540
Old Yishuv, 60, 178
Olympiapark, Munich, 265, 285
Olympic Flag, 277
Olympic Village, Munich, 263
Omar Bradley, 112
One Day in September, 264, 276, 281, 287, 737, 738
One-state solution, 510
Oneworld Publications, 66, 68
Online activism, 641
OPEC, 303, 367
Operation Accountability, 480
Operation An-Far, 40
Operation Assaf, 51
Operation Badr (1973), 292, 306
Operation Badr (Yom Kippur War), 298
Operation Balak, 5, 8, 15, 17
Operation Barak, 15
Operation Black Arrow, 92, 94
Operation Boxer, 253
Operation Brothers Keeper, 670
Operation Bulmus 6, 252
Operation Cast Lead, 664, 684, 685
Operation Cricket, 96
Operation Danny, 15, 42
Operation Days of Penitence, 551
Operation Death to the Invader, 40
Operation Defensive Shield, 533, 545
Operation Dekel, 15, 44
Operation Doogman 5, 333
Operation Eagle Claw, 387
Operation Egged, 95

Operation Elkayam, 95
Operation Entebbe, **375**
Operation Escort, 253
Operation Ezra and Nehemiah, 61, 178
Operation Focus, 193, 196
Operation Gazelle, 305
Operation Gown, 341
Operation Grapes of Wrath, 480
Operation Grapple, 180
Operation Gulliver, 95
Operation Ha-Har, 28, 51, 719
Operation Hametz, 15
Operation Helem, 252
Operation Hiram, 15, 48
Operation Horev, 15, 21, 52
Operation Jonathan (1955), 95
Operation Kedem, 43
Operation Kilshon, 7
Operation Law and Order, 475
Operation Litani, 421, 468
Operation Lulav, 95
Operation Magic Carpet (Yemen), 61, 178
Operation Mole Cricket 19, 432
Operation Musketeer (1956), 133, 146, 152
Operation Nachshon, 6, 15
Operation Nickel Grass, 350, 351
Operation Olive Leaves, 95
Operation Opera, 427
Operation Peace for Galilee, 470
Operation Pillar of Defence, 665
Operation Pillar of Defense, 667, 685
Operation Pleshet, 15, 25
Operation Rainbow, 551
Operation Raviv, 253
Operation Rhodes, 255
Operation Rimon 20, 246, 258
Operation Rooster 53, 255
Operation Sair, 95
Operation Samaria, 95
Operation Shfifon, 15
Operation Shmone, 51
Operation Shoshana, 94
Operation Shoter, 45
Operation Summer Rains, 563, 564, 622, 634, 637
Operation Tagar, 310, 333
Operation Tarnegol, 140
Operation Thunderbolt (film), 389
Operation Thunderbolt (video game), 389
Operation Torch, 180
Operation Uvda, 53
Operation Velvetta, 17
Operation Volcano (Israeli raid), 95
Operation Wrath of God, 264
Operation Yachin, 61, 178
Operation Yevusi, 15

Operation Yiftah, 7, 15
Operation Yoav, 15, 21, 48, 49
Orange ribbon, 628
Oranit, 576
Or Commission, 541
Ordnance QF 6 pounder, 19
Organisation of African Unity, 380
Organization of African Unity, 296, 386
Organization of the Islamic Conference, 592
Origins of the Six-Day War, 191
Orthodox Judaism, 659
Osama bin Laden, 456
Oslo, 297, 502
Oslo Accords, 282, 409, 410, 487, 496, **501**, 511, 520, 522, 535, 536, 550, 571, 587
Oslo I Accord, 486, 501, 503, 508
Oslo II Accord, 501, 506, 508
Oslo peace process, 511
Osprey Publishing, 65, 67, 259, 392
Other countries, 290
Ottoman Empire, 108
Ovadia Yosef, 628
Overthrow, 113
Oxford University Press, 63, 66, 67

P-12 radar, 255
P-15 radar, 255
P-15 Termit, 345, 359
P-51 Mustang, 54, 56
Pahlavi Era (1925 to 1979), 388
Pakistan, 2
Pakistan Air Force, 195, 357
Palau, 586
Palestine Communist Party, 490
Palestine grid, 72
Palestine Liberation Army, 444, 446
Palestine Liberation Organisation, 192
Palestine Liberation Organization, 245, 246, 265, 281, 295, 397, 406, 412, 418, 420, 428, 468, 486, 501, 520, 534, 536
Palestine refugee camps, 58, 59
Palestine (region), 10, 11, 59
Palestine War, 19
Palestinian Army of Islam, 633, 634, 637, 638
Palestinian Authority, 282, 486, 502, 504, 506, 508, 519, 526, 533, 536, 537, 542, 546, 565, 640, 674
Palestinian Center for Policy and Survey Research, 687
Palestinian Christians, 264
Palestinian Civil Police Force, 505
Palestinian expulsion from Kuwait, 496
Palestinian fedayeen, 91, 116, 117, 129, 150, 445
Palestinian Fedayeen insurgency, 91
Palestinian general election, 1996, 506, 508

Palestinian general elections in 1996, 505
Palestinian government of 2014, 668
Palestinian groups involved in political violence, 534
Palestinian insurgency in South Lebanon, 412, 413, 418, 468
Palestinian Islamic Jihad, 619
Palestinian Islamic Jihad Movement, 548, 549, 553, 554, 562, 565, 634, 637
Palestinian Legislative Council, 504, 506, 508, 537, 563
Palestinian legislative election, 2006, 563, 619, 663
Palestinian Liberation Organization, 470
Palestinian National Authority, 282, 506, 510, 534, 545, 547, 553, 557, 562, 568, 587, 610, 615, 616, 639, 663, 715
Palestinian National Security Forces, 534
Palestinian people, 263, 358, 378, 407, 413, 416, 487, 524, 565, 639
Palestinian Peoples Party, 487
Palestinian political violence, 91, 572
Palestinian Popular Struggle Front, 446
Palestinian presidential election, 2005, 553
Palestinian prisoners in Israel, 535, 554
Palestinian refugee, 3, 45, 58, 59, 524
Palestinian refugees, 421, 468
Palestinian return to Israel, 58
Palestinian right of return, 58, 60, 406, 502, 520, 536, 537
Palestinian rocket attacks on Israel, 565, 664
Palestinians, 191, 250, 534, 572, 705
Palestinian Security Services, 504
Palestinian state, 522, 592
Palestinian stone throwing, 541
Palestinian stone-throwing, 487, 493, 538
Palestinian territories, 60, 396, 506
Palestinian tunnel warfare in the Gaza Strip, 633, 662, 674, 701
Palmach, 2, 6, 9, 40
Palmachim, 621
Panhard AML, 195, 357
Panoramic painting, 370
Pantheon Books, 68
Panzer IV, 56, 195
Papua New Guinea, 456
Paratroop, 342
Paratrooper, 194, 198
Paratroopers Brigade, 141, 382, 442
Pardes Hanna bus bombing, 544
Pardes Hanna-Karkur, 647
Paris-Charles de Gaulle Airport, 376, 378
Paris Peace Conference, 1919, 410
Paris Stock Exchange, 121
Passover, 545, 623
Passover massacre, 545

Patrick Seale, 324, 459
Paul Schutzer, 205
Peacekeeping, 182
Peace Now, 454, 586, 624, 659
Peace treaty, 502
Peat Sadeh, 609
Pechora, 254, 359
Peel Commission, 592
Pentateuch, 139
Persian Gulf, 281
Persian Gulf War, 496
Persian Jews, 60, 178
Petah Tikva, 647
Peter-Adrian Cohen, 389
Peter Bourne, 739, 745
Peter Finch, 389
Peter N. Stearns, 67
Petroleum, 108, 367
Petroleum Road, 332
Phalangist, 448
Philadelphi Route, 615
Philip Habib, 420, 437
Philip Mattar, 65
Philippines, 277
Phillip Adams, 734
Physical abuse, 270
Physicians for Human Rights, 583
Physicians for Human Rights-Israel, 655, 703, 708
PIAT, 24, 29, 56, 77
Pied-Noir, 61, 178
Pierre Barjot, 106, 130, 134
Pillbox, 446
Pincer movement, 223
Pinhas Lavon, 97
Pink Floyd, 595
Piraeus, 360
P. J. Vatikiotis, 177
PK machine gun, 359
Plain of Sharon, 74
Plan Dalet, 10, 59
PLO, 246, 279, 413, 414, 421, 455, 456, 496, 674
Point-blank range, 272
Political campaign, 396
Political Science Quarterly, 630
Popular Front for the Liberation of Palestine, 376, 413, 446, 487, 490, 534, 565, 660
Popular Front for the Liberation of Palestine – External Operations, 375, 376, 378
Popular Front for the Liberation of Palestine - General Command, 446, 543
Popular Resistance Committees, 534, 552, 633–635, 637, 660
Population statistics for Israeli Gaza Strip settlements, 603

Port Fouad, 157
Port Fuad, 155
Port Louis, 380
Port of Eilat, 256
Port of Haifa, 45
Port Safaga, 347
Port Said, 35, 122, 130, 154, 156, 158, 177, 208, 257, 316, 320, 345, 358
Port Suez, 305
Portugal, 350
Positions on Jerusalem, 405, 536, 537
Post office, 99
Postwar, 61
Post-War, 61
Post-World War II: North African Jewish migration, 61, 179
Pound sterling, 107
Power vacuum, 175
Praeger Publishers, 64, 67
Preemptive war, 92, 191, 302
Present absentee, 58, 59
President of Egypt, 98, 396
President of Lebanon, 420
President of the United States, 396, 590
President of the United States of America, 536, 537
Pretext, 750
Preventive Security Force, 534, 553
Prime minister, 101
Prime Minister of Canada, 182
Prime Minister of Israel, 303, 377, 396, 487, 511, 631, 642, 648, 661
Prime Minister of the United Kingdom, 171
Princeton University Press, 186
Prisoner of war, 106, 363, 534
Privatization, 653
Progressive Socialist Party, 447, 455
Pro-Israel, 686
Projects working for peace among Israelis and Arabs, 410
Proposals for a Palestinian state, 624
Protest camp, 641, 644
Protest leadership, 641
Protocol Concerning the Redeployment in Hebron, 509
Protocol of Sevres, 131
Protocol of Sèvres, 133, 167, 469
Protocol on Economic Relations, 508
Provisional State Council, 45
Provost (education), 27
Proxy war, 468
Psychosocial support, 678
PT-76, 195, 359
Public housing, 653
Public Radio Exchange, 517
Public transportation, 653

Punctured lung, 514
Purple Line (border), 223, 364
Purple Line (ceasefire line), 339
Python (missile), 359

Qadas, 30
Qalqiliyah, 540
Qalqilyah, 576, 579, 598
Qana, 480
Qassam rocket, 550–554, 565, 699, 709
Qassam rockets, 628
Qatar, 171, 579, 714
Qawasameh tribe, 669
QF 25 pounder, 19
QF 4 inch Mk XVI naval gun, 146
Qibya, 94
Qibya massacre, 80, 93, 94
Qlayaa, 470
Quartet on the Middle East, 547, 618, 626, 664
Quneitra, 40, 224, 328, 338, 340
Quraysh (tribe), 298

R-7 Semyorka, 170
Raanana, 646
Rabbi, 658, 659
Rabbis for Human Rights, 655
Rabin Square, 511, 628
Racewalker, 267
Rachaya Al Foukhar, 442
Rachels Tomb, 84, 228
Racial segregation, 572
Radar, 196, 358
Raed al Atar, 639, 675
Rafael Eitan, 141, 205, 334, 419, 426
Rafah, 148, 200, 550, 637, 674
Rafah crossing, 619
Rafah Preparatory A Boys School, 706
RAF Bomber Command, 151
Rafiah Yam, 609
Rafik Hariri, 456
RAF Luqa, 151
Ragheb Harb, 419
Raid on Entebbe (film), 389
Raid on the Suez Canal, 108
Ralph Bunche, 45, 71
Ramadan, 292, 301, 542
Ramadan Abdullah Mohammad Shallah, 587
Ramadan (calendar month), 369
Ramadan Shalah, 534, 579, 661
Ramallah, 18, 42, 213, 523, 542, 595, 626, 664, 669
Ramallah and al-Bireh Governorate, 582
Ramat David Airbase, 32, 54, 210, 216, 338, 354
Ramat HaSharon, 647
Ramatkal, 365

Ramat Rachel, 27, 95, 210
Ramla, 43, 45, 55, 214
Ramle, 3, 42
Ram Rothberg, 661
Random House, 288, 736
Rangefinder, 330
Raphael Recanati, 464
Ras al-Ein, 30
Ras Gharib, 255
Rasheed Carbine, 359
Rashid Khalidi, 65
Ras Sudar, 209, 312, 344
Rationing, 87
Rationing and Supply Minister of Israel, 87
Rayhan, 477
Raymond A. Hare, 112
Reactions, 683
Reading Power Station, 31
Rebellion, 487
Recall elections, 641
Recoilless rifles, 447
Reconnaissance, 219
Recreational drug use, 550
Red Army, 255
Red Army Faction, 264, 268
Red Crescent Society of the United Arab Emirates, 698
Red Cross, 589, 613
Red Sea, 53, 107, 196, 383
Ref A, 496
Refchomsky1983, 751
RefCobban1984, 751
Referendum, 607
Reffisk2001, 751, 752
Reffriedman2006, 750
RefHerzog2005, 751, 752
Refmaoz2006, 751
RefMorris1999, 750–752
RefRabinovich2004, 752
RefReagan2007, 751
Ref reference name Anone, 232
Ref reference name H1none, 233
Ref reference name Hnone, 233
RefSayigh1999, 752
RefSchiff1984, 751, 752
RefSeale1989, 752
Refshlaim1999, 751
Refshlaim2007, 751
Refugee, 520
Refugee camp, 487
RefWalker1983, 752
RefWallach2, 719
Regnery Publishing, 64, 411
Rehovot, 34
Rejectionist Front, 446
Renault R35, 29, 56

827

Renault R40, 56
René Coty, 106
Reparations Agreement between Israel and West Germany, 90
Reporters Without Borders, 707
Reprisal operations, **91**, 117
Republic of China, 120
Republic of China (1912–1949), 22
Republic of Egypt (1953–1958), 105
Republic of Ireland, 624
Research Department (Aman), 299
Resolution 242, 522
Retroactive nomenclature, 377
Reuters, 777, 778
Reuven Rivlin, 657
Revisionist Zionism, 469
Revolutionary Cells (German group), 375, 378
Revolutionary Cells (RZ), 376
Revolutionary Guards, 448
RGD-5, 359
Rhodes, 71, 72
Rhodesia, 276
Richard Crossman, 164
Richard Dreyfuss, 389
Richard Falk, 457
Richard Kemp, 703
Richard Nixon, 164, 247, 261, 268, 298
Right of return, 45, 527
Right-wing politics, 368
Rigid-hull inflatable, 344
Rio 2016 Olympic Village, 278
Riots in Palestine of 1929, 9
Rise and Fall of Idi Amin, 388
Rishon LeZion, 566, 647
River Jordan, 75
RKG-3 anti-tank grenade, 359
RL-83 Blindicide, 196, 359
Road map for peace, 545, 547, 553, 624, 625
Roadmap for Peace, 502, 535
Robert B. Anderson, 120
Robert Boothby, Baron Boothby, 160
Robert Daniel Murphy, 127
Robert Fisk, 417, 458
Robert Gates, 302
Robert Malley, 527
Robert Menzies, 126, 128
Robert Rhodes James, 185
RobertsGartonAsh2009, 757
Robert Speaight, 161
Robert Wright (journalist), 522
Rockefeller Museum, 214
Rocket, 662
Rocket-propelled grenade, 305, 385
Rodef, 512
Rogers Plan, 247
Roger Waters, 595

Ronald Reagan, 423, 426, 438, 458
Ron Arad (pilot), 484
Ron English (artist), 594
Ron Huldai, 655, 657
Ron Pundak, 503
Roof knocking, 703
Roone Arledge, 273
Rose Garden (Jerusalem), 625
Rosh HaNikra Crossing, 442
Rosh Hashanah, 675
Rosh Pinna, 647
Rothschild Boulevard, 642, 645
Route 443 (Israel), 593
Routledge, 63–66, 571, 736
Rowman & Littlefield, 288
Royal Air Force, 53, 54, 136
Royal Canadian Navy, 35
Royal Egyptian Air Force, 31
Royal Institute of International Affairs, 109
Royal Jordanian Air Force, 194, 252
Royal Navy, 35, 55, 136
Royal Ordnance L7, 195, 359
Roy Arad, 652
Roy Harrod, 164
RPD machine gun, 359
RPD (weapon), 196
RPG-43, 305, 359
RPG-7, 296, 305, 317, 359
RPK, 196, 359
RT (TV network), 693, 701
Rubber bullet, 534, 541
Ruhollah Khomeini, 483
Russia and weapons of mass destruction, 352
Russian Compound, 44
Russo-Japanese War, 108
RWD-13, 31

S-75 Dvina, 196, 359
SA-2 Guideline, 248, 296
SA-3 Goa, 296
SA-6, 443
SA-6 Gainful, 296
SA-7 Grail, 296
Saad Al-Salim Al-Sabah, 745
Saad el-Shazly, 352, 736
Saad El Shazly, 246, 259, 291, 309
Saad Haddad, 412, 416, 419, 424, 448, 470
Saar 3-class missile boat, 346
Sabra and Shatila massacre, 420, 441, 457, 538
Saddam Hussein, 407
Saeb Erekat, 538, 553
Safed, 7, 36, 328, 334
Safsaf, 47
Said al-Muragha, 454
Said K. Aburish, 757
Said Shaaban, 419

Saiful Azam, 211
Salah Jadid, 190
Salah Khalaf, 288
Salah Mustafa, 95
Salients, re-entrants and pockets, 209, 339
Samakh, Tiberias, 29, 36
Samaria, 5, 598, 627, 629
Sami Abu Zuhri, 698
Samir Kuntar, 484
Sami Turgeman, 661
Samsons Foxes, 18
Samuel Segev, 240
Samu Incident, 96, 192
San Francisco Chronicle, 640
Santorini affair, 543
Sa-Nur, 609
Sarah Morris, 287
Saree Makdisi, 66
Satchel (bag), 229
Satellite, 321
Saudi Arabia, 4, 17, 118, 171, 290, 357, 367
Saudi-Yemen barrier, 596
Saud of Saudi Arabia, 165
Saul David, 392
Save the Children, 488, 494
Savion, 646
Sawahre, 524
Sayeret, 279, 341
Sayeret Matkal, 252, 341, 376, 377, 382, 387, 388, 481
Sbarro restaurant massacre, 544
S:Cablegram from the Secretary-General of the League of Arab States to the Secretary-General of the United Nations, 11
Scars of War, Wounds of Peace: The Israeli-Arab Tragedy, 67
Schutzstaffel, 99
Scud, 299, 316, 321
S. Daniel Abraham, 642
Sde Dov Airport, 31
Sderot, 551, 554, 607, 628, 638, 670
Sdot Micha Airbase, 350
Seam Area, 598
Seam zone, 574
Seán MacBride, 457
Sea of Galilee, 29, 44, 84, 95, 219, 337
Second Intifada, 60, 488, 502, 507, 508, 510, **533**, 572, 634, 663, 690
Seconds From Disaster, 274, 287
Second World, 455
Second World War, 108
Secretary-General of the United Nations, 260
Security Council, 406, 424
Security Council Resolution 672, 495
Seewoosagur Ramgoolam, 380
Self-defense, 570

Self-government, 536
Self-immolation, 641
Selwyn Lloyd, 127
Semi-automatic pistol, 511, 514
Separation barrier, 572
Sephardi Jews, 60, 178
Serge Groussard, 264
Sèvres, 132
Shaar HaGolan, 29
Shabbat, 44
Shabtai Teveth, 98
Shadwan, 255
Shahid, 492
Shai Abuhatsira, 650
Shalev1991, 756
Shalhevet Freier, 336
Shalhevet Pass, 543
Shamgar Commission, 516
Shapira, 717
Share repurchase, 461
Sharm al-Sheikh, 553
Sharm el-Sheikh, 139, 142, 150, 166, 192, 208, 299, 344, 383
Sharm el-Sheikh Memorandum (1999), 509
Sharm el-Sheikh Summit of 2005, 535, 553, 554, 628
Shatila refugee camp, 427
Shaul Ladany, 267
Shaul Mofaz, 382, 534, 566, 607, 613
Shavei Darom, 622
Shay2005, 756
Shayetet 13, 208, 252, 253, 345, 430, 442, 481, 543, 544
Shear Yashuv, 217, 481
Shebaa Farms, 416, 455, 469, 484
Sheikh, 557
Sheikh Abed, 48
Sheikh Jarrah, 524
Sheikh Zuweid, 200
Shell (projectile), 705
Shelly Yachimovich, 657
Sherman tank, 56, 475
Sherut Avir, 31
Shia Muslim, 468
Shiite, 448
Shimon Agranat, 364
Shimon Avidan, 2, 15
Shimon Peres, 101, 118, 354, 380, 467, 503, 516, 536, 606, 608
Shimon Sheves, 516, 658
Shin Beit, 579
Shin Bet, 438, 471, 495, 513, 534, 559, 561, 569, 579, 661, 665, 667, 669, 695, 698
Shin-Bet, 571
Shirat HaYam, 609, 613
Shir LaShalom, 515

Shlaim2000, 756, 757
Shlomo Argov, 420, 427
Shlomo Ben-Ami, 67, 528, 530, 539, 541, 720, 762
Shlomo Bohbot, 655
Shlomo Erell, 190
Shlomo Shamir, 15
Shmuel Gonen, 200, 291, 301, 310, 339, 365
Shmuel Rodensky, 265
Shomriya, 621
Shouf, 471
Show trial, 100
Shuafat, 214
Shujaiyya, 674, 692
Shukri al-Quwwatli, 29
Shulamit Aloni, 454
Shurat HaDin, 693
Shuttle diplomacy, 364, 396
Sic, 153, 367
Sidney Holland, 126
Sidon, 428, 438, 442, 472, 482
Siege of Beirut, 437, 449
Siege of Jerusalem (1948), 6
Sierra Leone, 684
Sikorsky CH-53 Sea Stallion, 255, 359, 481
Sikorsky S-58, 196
Silwan, 524
Simcha Dinitz, 323
Simha Flapan, 68
Simon Reeve (British TV presenter), 274
Simon Reeve (UK television presenter), 288
Simon & Schuster, 64, 288
Sinai, 105, 139, 196, 245, 246, 261, 292, 299, 304
Sinai Desert, 309
Sinai Peninsula, 1, 3, 106, 189, 225, 245, 247, 397, 401, 406, 409, 488, 542
Sir Anthony Eden, 171
Sit-ins, 641
Six Days of War, 239, 243
Six-Day War, 60, 71, 76, 173, 177, 178, **189**, 246, 247, 259, 260, 267, 292, 293, 299, 360, 396, 397, 421, 469, 488, 522, 624
Slav (settlement), 609
Slick Goodlin, 54
Sniper, 157, 512, 565
Social justice, 642
Social networking, 645
Social networks, 644
Society for the Protection of Nature in Israel, 655
Socio-economic, 641
Solel Boneh, 381
Solomon ibn Gabirol, 514
Soltam M-68, 359
Somalia, 684

Sortie, 144, 193
South Africa, 228
South End Press, 458
Southern Command (Israel), 608, 613, 661
Southern Lebanon, 1, 3, 412, 413, 420, 421, 467
South Lebanese Army, 422
South Lebanon, 416, 468
South Lebanon Army, 412, 414, 416, 418, 424, 439, 446, 450, 467–470, 475, 482
South Lebanon conflict (1982–2000), 416, 445
South Lebanon conflict (1985–2000), 418, 421, 439, **467**
South Lebanon security belt, 418, 421, 450, 468
South Lebanon security belt administration, 467
South Sudan, 684
South Yemen, 437
Soviet, 296
Soviet Empire, 293
Soviet perspective, 107
Soviet Union, 106, 118, 169, 192, 229, 245–247, 253, 255, 262, 290, 292, 338, 345
Special Envoy, 420
Special Relationship, 174, 180
Spitfire, 31
Sports Illustrated, 277
SR-71, 314
SS, 512
SS.11, 359
SSh-68, 447
Stahlhelme, 269
Stalemate, 292
StandWithUs, 602
Stan Greenberg, 642, 644
Stanley Evans, 164
Star of David, 614
State Comptroller of Israel, 465, 620
State of Israel, 2, 3, 7
State of Palestine, 520, 592
State of the art, 352
Status of Jerusalem, 406, 502
Stav Shaffir, 652
Sten, 8, 56
Sten gun, 153
Stephen Pressfield, 243
Stephen Walt, 494
Sterling area, 124
Stern Gang, 9
Steven Spielberg, 282
Steven Ungerleider, 287
St Jamess Church, Piccadilly, 588
Stock, 461
Strafing, 196
Straight Arrow Books, 260, 736

Straits of Tiran, 105, 107, 121, 129, 189, 190, 192, 406
Strategic depth, 198
Stratfor, 746
Strela 2, 551
Strela-2, 255
Strike (attack), 91
SU-100, 138, 154, 158, 195, 203, 359
Su-7, 195, 198, 257, 357
Submachine gun, 220
Submarine chaser, 35
Sudan, 110, 358
Sud Aviation Vautour, 195
Suez, 249, 252, 293, 322
Suez Canal, 4, 97, 98, 105–107, 121, 200, 202, 205, 245, 246, 254, 290, 292, 321, 401
Suez Canal Company, 108
Suez Crisis, 60, 96, **105**, 178, 192, 259, 293
Suez Port, 321
Sugar, 88
Suicide attack, 543, 548, 554, 566, 571
Suicide bombing, 495, 565, 599, 674
Suicide Bombings, 579
Sukhoi Su-7, 249, 255, 304, 307, 359
Sultans Pool, 627
Summit (meeting), 519
Sunday Times, 260
SUNY Press, 66
Super Frelon, 196, 255
Supermarine Spitfire, 17, 19, 31, 54, 56
Super Sherman, 359
Suppression fire, 385
Suppression of Enemy Air Defenses, 305
Supreme Court of Israel, 364, 585, 620
Surface-to-air, 435
Surface to air missile, 420
Surface-to-air missile, 248, 255, 297, 301, 305
Surface-to-surface, 211
Surface-to-surface missile, 338, 344
Surveillance, 321
Surveillance aircraft, 323
Sushi, 658
Sussex Academic Press, 64
Suzerainty, 110
Sweden, 262, 494
Sweet Water Canal, 320
Sword of Gideon, 287
Sybil Danning, 389
Sydney Morning Herald, 713
Syria, 17, 71, 91, 96, 118, 189, 190, 245, 260, 281, 290, 292, 357, 397, 398, 418, 469, 549, 552, 638
Syria Mixed Armistice Commission, 77
Syrian Air Force, 19, 219, 341
Syrian Army, 420, 443
Syrian Navy, 208

Syrian occupation of Lebanon, 416, 418, 421, 456
Syrian Republic (1946–63), 3, 22, 91
Syrian Social Nationalist Party in Lebanon, 441
Syrian Social National Party, 455

T-34, 138, 446
T-34 tank, 203
T-54, 195, 329
T-55, 195, 296, 337, 352
T-62, 296, 317, 330, 332, 352, 359
T-6 Texan, 31, 56
T-72, 440
Taba (Egypt), 542
Taba, Egypt, 502
Taba summit, 526, 542
Tablet (magazine), 771
Tactical nuclear weapon, 350
Taif Accord, 476
Taif Agreement, 476
Talmei Yafeh, 622
Tami Steinmetz Center for Peace Research, 586
Tank, 198
Tank destroyer, 203
Tantura, 30
Tanzim, 542, 558, 561
Targeted killing, 535, 568
Tarmac-shredding penetration bomb, 196
Tartus, 345
Task Force, 172
Tawfik Abu al-Huda, 13
Tawfiq, Syria, 96
Taxation, 653
Tayibe (Lebanon), 423
Tear gas, 493, 534
Ted Koppel, 754
Tefillin, 229
Tegart fort, 29, 51
Tel Aviv, 3, 14, 25, 31, 45, 54, 88, 210, 217, 301, 378, 413, 454, 511, 596, 599, 607, 617, 623, 628, 641, 642, 646, 647, 659, 689
Tel Aviv Central Bus Station, 31
Tel Aviv Museum of Art, 646
Tel Aviv Sourasky Medical Center, 514
Tel Aviv Stock Exchange, 461
Tel Aviv University, 571, 586, 627, 749
Tel Aviv University Institute for Media, Society, and Politics, 627
Tel Dan, 217
Telex, 345
Tel Katifa, 609, 621
Tel Katzir, 96
Tel Nof Airbase, 34, 350
Template:Israeli–Palestinian peace process, 501, 520, 579, 603

Template:Jewish exodus from Arab and Muslim countries, 61, 179
Template:Nakba, 59
Template:Palestinians, 59
Template talk:Israeli–Palestinian peace process, 501, 520, 579, 603
Template talk:Jewish exodus from Arab and Muslim countries, 61, 179
Template talk:Nakba, 59
Temple Mount, 228, 520, 523, 534–538, 540, 555
Teneh Omarim, 621
Tents, 642
Terje Rød-Larsen, 484, 504
Territorial waters, 227, 619
Terrorism, 267, 550, 627
Thailand, 679
Thai people, 661, 683
The Academy of Political Science, 630
The Age, 734
The Atlantic, 771
The Belfast Telegraph, 766
The Case for Democracy, 767
The Clinton Parameters, 526, 598
The Cottage boycott, 657
The cottage cheese boycott, 644
The Daily Telegraph, 743
The Delta Force, 389
The Economist, 162, 574
The Encyclopedia of World History, 67
The Ethnic Cleansing of Palestine, 66, 68
The Fall of the British Empire, 109
The Fateful Triangle: the United States, Israel and the Palestinians, 458
The Federated States of Micronesia, 586
The Financial Times, 693, 701
The Forgotten Refugees, 61, 179
The Guardian, 161, 591, 596, 614, 693, 705, 777, 783
The Holocaust, 58, 379, 614
The Hope (novel), 68
The Independent, 596, 693
The Israeli operation Kadesh in Sinai, 190
The Jerusalem Post, 560, 581, 631, 784
The Jewish Journal of Greater Los Angeles, 766, 783
The Jews of Libya during the Holocaust, 60, 178
The Journal of American History, 186
The Last King of Scotland (film), 389
The Leader-Post, 741
The Missing Peace, 527, 722
The National Left, 642, 653
The New Republic, 592
The New Yorker, 770
The New York Review of Books, 777

The New York Times, 76, 193, 267, 287, 574, 592, 602, 684, 701, 748
The Observer, 161, 354, 703
Theodore Postol, 709
Theodor Or, 541
The Oslo Syndrome, 527
The Palestine Post, 719
The Peace Treaty between Israel and Lebanon, 450
The Pentagon, 426
The Power of Nightmares, 411
The Prize: The Epic Quest for Oil, Money, and Power, 187
The Spectator, 162
The Sunday Times, 360
The Three Weeks, 613
The Times of Israel, 781, 785
The Wall, 595
The Washington Institute for Near East Policy, 602
The Washington Post, 237, 632, 687
The Washington Times, 581
Third Temple, 333
Thirty-first government of Israel, 618
This American Life, 517
Thomas C. Wasson, 27
Thomas Friedman, 458
Thomas Hinman Moorer, 227
Thomas Risse, 186
Thompson submachine gun, 56
Tiberias, 7, 36, 334, 646
Time Life Books, 459
Timeline of the 2008–2009 Israel–Gaza conflict, 564
Time (magazine), 224, 273
Time Magazine, 754
Timothy Garton Ash, 498
Tiran Straits, 139, 182
Tire, 492
Tisha BAv, 613
Tom Clancys Rainbow Six: Rogue Spear, 389
Tom Segev, 59
To Pay the Price, 389
Topography, 577
Toronto Sun, 770
Torpedo boat, 249, 256
Toyota, 447
Toyota Land Cruiser, 447
Trajtenberg Committee, 642
Transaction Publishers, 63
Transfer Committee, 59
Transjordan Frontier Force, 18
Treblinka, 428
Trevor N. Dupuy, 323
Triangle (Israel), 45
Tripartite Declaration of 1950, 71, 116, 118

Tri-point, 469
Tripoli, Libya, 229
Trophy (countermeasure), 711
Truce, 553, 672
Trygve Lie, 22
TT-33, 265
TT pistol, 359
Tu-16, 195, 198
Tulkarm, 28, 578, 579, 598
Tunis, 494
Tunisia, 290, 320, 358
Tunnel warfare, 710
Tupolev Tu-16, 195, 210, 308, 359
Turkey, 480, 714
Turkish Jews in Israel, 61, 179
TVNZ, 640
Two-state solution, 496, 510, 545, 590, 686
Tyndale House, 572
Tyre headquarters bombings, 438, 471
Tyre (Lebanon), 414, 445
Tyre, Lebanon, 424, 428, 438, 442, 474
Tzipi Livni, 607
Tzurif, 599

U-Bank, 461
Uganda, 375, 376, 684
Uganda Human Rights Commission, 385
Uganda Peoples Defence Force, 382
Uganda-Tanzania War, 386
UK Polaris programme, 180
Ulrich Wegener, 272, 738
Ulrike Meinhof, 264, 268
Ultranationalism, 511
Um-Katef, 203
Umm el-Fahm, 581
Umrah, 300
UN, 582, 663, 705
Under-Secretary-General for Political Affairs of the United Nations, 626
Unemployment, 90
UNESCO, 707
UN General Assembly, 406, 495
UNHRC, 711
Unified National Leadership of the Uprising, 487, 488, 490
UNIFIL, 412, 417
Unilateral, 604
Unilateralism, 355
Union Bank of Israel, 461
Unit 101, 94, 115, 722
Unit 131, 99
Unit 669, 481
United Arab Republic, 190
United Kingdom, 71, 88, 105, 106, 228
United Kingdom general election, 1959, 164, 180

United Kingdom Home Office, 754
United Nations, 71, 84, 106, 268, 293, 580, 584, 603, 613, 706
United Nations Conciliation Commission, 55, 721
United Nations Disengagement Observer Force, 449
United Nations Disengagement Observer Force Zone, 364
United Nations Economic and Social Commission for Western Asia, 582
United Nations Emergency Force, 105, 107, 168, 190, 192, 205, 449
United Nations Fact Finding Mission on the Gaza Conflict, 664, 704
United Nations General Assembly, 4, 55, 123, 167, 456, 572, 584, 585
United Nations General Assembly Resolution 194, 55, 59
United Nations General Assembly Resolution 377, 167
United Nations Human Rights Committee, 661, 682
United Nations Interim Force In Lebanon, 413, 415, 421, 422, 448, 470
United Nations Office for the Coordination of Humanitarian Affairs, 676, 715
United Nations Partition Plan for Palestine, 1, 3, 5, 36, 57, 59, 78
United Nations Relief and Works Agency, 150, 582
United Nations Relief and Works Agency for Palestine Refugees in the Near East, 59, 566, 700, 705
United Nations Secretary-General, 424, 626
United Nations Security Council, 123, 230, 296, 321, 386, 416, 424, 584, 625
United Nations Security Council Resolution 119, 167
United Nations Security Council Resolution 1391, 416
United Nations Security Council Resolution 1397, 545
United Nations Security Council Resolution 1496, 416
United Nations Security Council Resolution 1544, 584
United Nations Security Council Resolution 1583, 416
United Nations Security Council Resolution 1860, 715
United Nations Security Council Resolution 242, 230, 294, 396, 404, 407, 502
United Nations Security Council Resolution 338, 321, 400, 502

United Nations Security Council Resolution 339, 362
United Nations Security Council Resolution 340, 363
United Nations Security Council Resolution 425, 416, 421, 448, 484, 557
United Nations Security Council Resolution 426, 415, 448
United Nations Security Council Resolution 607, 495
United Nations Security Council Resolution 608, 495
United Nations Security Council Resolution 638, 476
United Nations Security Council Resolution 673, 495
United Nations Security Council Resolution 95, 117
United Nations Special Coordinator in the Occupied Territories, 571
United Nations Truce Supervision Organization, 57, 77
United States, 7, 71, 106, 228, 290, 395, 396
United States Air Force, 352
United States Coast Guard, 35
United States Congress, 414, 687
United States Department of Defense, 349
United States Department of State, 231, 349
United States House Committee on Foreign Affairs, 426
United States Marine Corps, 190
United States Marine Corps Training and Education Command, 753
United States National Security Council, 349
United States Navy, 190, 227
United States presidential election, 1956, 174
United States presidential election, 2004, 456
United States presidential election, 2016, 687
United States Secretary of State, 227, 303, 714
United States Senate, 166
United States Sixth Fleet, 151
Universal Carrier, 18, 56
Universal Newsreel, 122, 222, 224
University of California Press, 68
University of Haifa, 650
University of Nebraska Press, 66, 259
Unmanned aerial vehicle, 351, 567
U.N. Resolution 242, 400
UNRWA, 60, 714
UN Security Council, 77, 495, 529, 625
UN Security Council Resolution 1559, 416
UN Security Council Resolution 242, 247, 260, 529, 625
UN Security Council Resolution 338, 529, 625
UN Security Council Resolution 425, 415, 456, 469

Unsupported attributions, 181, 268, 303, 570, 623, 624
Upper Galilee, 48
Uprising, 534
Urban warfare, 567
Uri Avnery, 532, 696, 781
Uri Sagi, 382
Uri Savir, 503
Uruguay, 268
U.S. Air Force, 384
USA Today, 632, 770, 784
U.S. Department of State, 749
US Dollar, 463, 464
Use of civilian structures for military purposes, 703, 704
U.S. Information Agency, 99
USS Coral Sea (CV-43), 151
USS Forrestal (CV-59), 151
USS Liberty (AGTR-5), 227
USS Liberty incident, 732
USS Randolph (CV-15), 151
USS Ranger (CV-61), 387
UTC, 263, 564
U Thant, 260
Uzi, 195, 220, 359
Uzi Narkiss, 190, 210, 246
Uzi submachine gun, 196

Valley of Tears, 340
Vanity Fair (magazine), 784
VDM Verlag, 184
Vice-President of Egypt, 410
Vickers, 56
Vickers Valiant, 136
Victor Davis Hanson, 632
Victor Ostrovsky, 103
Victory, 660
Victory at Entebbe, 389
Vidui, 514
Vietnam War, 180
Viktor Chernomyrdin, 516
Vintage Books, 66, 259, 288, 458
Violet Bonham Carter, 161
Visions of Eight, 287
Voice of the Arabs, 119
Vought F4U Corsair, 153
Vyacheslav Molotov, 125
Vz. 24, 16

Wadi, 314
Wadi Ara, 74, 578, 598
Wadie Haddad, 375, 376
Walid Khalidi, 59, 65, 719
Walter Cronkite, 369
Walter Scheel, 280
Walther MP, 269

Waltz with Bashir, 457
Waqf, 228, 538
War crime, 628, 704
War crimes, 546, 700
War of Attrition, **245**, 294
War of the Camps, 421, 454
Warsaw, 282, 735
Warsaw Pact, 118, 119, 172, 247, 440, 455
Warwick and Leamington by-election, 1957, 164
Washington, DC, 395
Washington, D.C., 261
Washington Institute for Near East Policy, 733
Washington Post, 770
Watergate scandal, 355
Wayback Machine, 531
WBEZ, 517
Weapon, 550
Weidenfeld & Nicolson, 64, 68
West Bank, 1, 3, 57, 93, 94, 140, 189, 191, 194, 209, 225, 230, 293, 295, 397, 401, 404, 486–488, 492, 502, 522, 533, 536, 537, 540, 566, 572, 576, 577, 592, 665, 769
West Bank Areas in the Oslo II Accord, 504, 505, 507, 508, 619
Western Wall, 228, 495, 524, 540, 627, 628
Western world, 106
West Germany, 263
West Germany national football team, 277
West Jerusalem, 27, 56
Westland Wyvern, 154
White House, 282, 396, 408, 521, 625, 767
White House Chief of Staff, 355
White House Rose Garden, 590
Wikinews: Israel completes Gaza strip, West Bank pull-outs, 631
Wikinews: Israeli soldier taken captive, 640
Wikipedia, 656
Wikipedia:Avoid weasel words, 455
Wikipedia:Citation needed, 2, 9, 17, 19, 28, 52, 53, 72, 76, 84, 88, 101, 102, 112, 117, 169, 173, 176, 216, 256, 267, 268, 270, 271, 274, 275, 277, 279, 296, 352, 358, 387, 401, 402, 409, 427, 455, 461, 463, 464, 480, 482, 515, 516, 565, 609, 610, 623, 624, 626, 628, 634, 652, 655, 669, 686
Wikipedia:Citing sources, 131
Wikipedia:Identifying reliable sources, 312, 345, 527, 687
Wikipedia:Link rot, 238, 262, 631
Wikipedia:Media help, 574
Wikipedia:Naming conventions (geographic names), 686
Wikipedia:Neutral point of view, 462

Wikipedia:No original research, 3, 642, 708
Wikipedia:Please clarify, 11, 93, 270, 274, 608, 691
Wikipedia:Vagueness, 97, 577
Wikipedia:Verifiability, 366, 385, 534, 559, 667
Wikisource, 411, 530
Wikisource:Camp David Accords, 411
Wikisource:Camp David Summit Announcement by US President Clinton, 530
Wikisource:Camp David Summit Conclusion by Israeli Prime Minister Ehud Barak, 530
Wikisource:Camp David Summit Conclusion by US President Clinton, 530
Wikt:autonomy, 404
Wikt:entente, 669
Wikt:horny-handed, 164
Wikt:intifada, 496, 535, 670
Wikt:أهلا وسهلا, 192
Wikt:uprising, 496
Wilfried Böse, 375, 378, 379, 383
William B. Quandt, 322, 363, 373
William Colby, 355
William Knowland, 166
William Parry (photojournalist), 595
William P. Rogers, 247, 268
William Quandt, 350
William Roger Louis, 63
William Schabas, 691
William Stevenson (Canadian writer), 393
Willi Pohl, 281
Willy Brandt, 269, 277
Winston Churchill, 100, 172, 180
Withdrawal from the security belt, 557
With Egypt, 21, 168
With Jordan, 228, 576
Wolfgang Kraushaar, 289
Women Lawyers for Social Justice, 655
Wonder Pot, 89
Working class, 641
World Bank, 570
World Council of Churches, 589, 590
World Food Programme, 684
World Health Organization, 714
World Jewish Congress, 100
World Net Daily, 772
World Organization of Jews from Arab Countries, 61, 179
World War II, 33, 88
World War III, 356
WP:NOTRS, 358
W. W. Norton & Company, 517
Wye River Agreement, 537
Wye River Memorandum, 508, 509

Yaakov Dori, 2, 101
Yad Binyamin, 621
Yad La-Shiryon, 370
Yad Mordechai, 616
Yahoo News, 778
Yair Hirschfeld, 503
Yair Lapid, 659
Yakov Springer, 267, 283
Yale University Press, 66, 717
YAMAM, 548, 569
Yamit, 409
Yaphet Kotto, 389
Yasir Arafat, 547
Yasser Arafat, 250, 296, 380, 412, 419, 420, 496, 503, 519–521, 526, 529, 534–538, 542, 545, 556, 557, 598, 608
Yater, 480
Yavne, 36
Yavneel, 31
Yedioth Ahronoth, 454, 627, 659, 664
Yehoram Gaon, 389
Yehoshafat Harkabi, 73, 95
Yehud, 700
Yehuda Avner, 392, 411
Yehuda Lapidot, 43
Yehuda Weisenstein, 267
Yekutiel Adam, 204, 375, 380
Yemen, 4, 17
Yemenite Jews in Israel, 61, 179
Yeruham, 607
Yeshayahu Gavish, 190
Yet a red link, 509
Yevgeny Primakov, 751
Yezid Sayigh, 67
Yibna, 36
Yiftach Brigade, 15, 43
Yigael Yadin, 2, 6, 73
Yigal Allon, 2, 15, 22, 51, 210, 246, 723
Yigal Amir, 511, 536
Yishuv, 3, 5, 10
Yisrael Galili, 2
Yisrael Medad, 411
Yitzhak Hofi, 291, 329, 358
Yitzhak Levi, 607
Yitzhak Olshan, 101
Yitzhak Rabin, 2, 15, 38, 73, 190, 205, 210, 225, 295, 365, 380, 396, 397, 487, 488, 495, 503, 511, 515, 520, 536, 578, 596, 658
Yitzhak Sadeh, 2, 15
Yitzhak Shamir, 487
Ynet, 771, 776, 778, 781, 783
Ynetnews, 394, 460, 631, 749
Yoav Gelber, 12, 59, 64, 719
Yom Kippur, 292

Yom Kippur War, 180, 191, 225, 227, 248, **290**, 396
Yom Yerushalayim, 228
Yonatan Netanyahu, 375, 377, 382, 385
Yoni Netanyahu, 388
Yoram Aridor, 463
Yoram Cohen, 661
Yoram Kaniuk, 64
Yosef Shapira, 489
Yossef Bodansky, 539, 763
Yossef Gutfreund, 266, 283
Yossef Romano, 265, 267, 282
Yossi Beilin, 503, 550
Yossi Klein Halevi, 592
Yossi Melman, 288
Yossi Peled, 202
Yossi Sarid, 454
Yossi Shalom, 650
YouTube, 68, 243, 393, 600
Yugoslavia, 17, 355
Yuli Edelstein, 658
Yuri Andropov, 356
Yusuf Nazzal, 267, 283
Yuval Diskin, 669
Yuval Sherlo, 658
Yuval Steinitz, 642, 651, 657

Zaid ibn Shaker, 190
Zakaria Zubeidi, 558
Zalman Shazar, 246
Zalman Shoval, 512
Zaman (newspaper), 754
Zameen (2003 film), 389
Zbigniew Brzezinski, 402, 748
Zeev Almog, 347, 419
Zeev Friedman, 267, 273, 283
Zeev Maoz, 248, 426, 458
Zeev Schiff, 248, 258, 259, 352, 366, 445, 458, 498, 559
Zelig Shtroch, 267
Zevulun Orlev, 608
Zhou Enlai, 115
Zionism, 5, 60, 178
Zionist Organization of America, 629
Zohar Palti, 602
Zrariyah, 438, 472
ZSU-23-4, 359
ZSU-57-2, 196
Zvi Harry Hurwitz, 411
Zvika Greengold, 332
Zvi Zamir, 271, 278, 288

www.ingramcontent.com/pod-product-compliance
Lightning Source LLC
Chambersburg PA
CBHW021411300426
44114CB00010B/457